Discrimination Law Handbook

Camilla Palmer is a solicitor and partner at Palmer Wade, solicitors specialising in employment discrimination law, she is also a part-time employment tribunal chair. She is the co-author of *Maternity and Parental Rights: A guide to parents' legal rights at work* (Palmer and Wade, 2nd edn, LAG, 2001) and the author of *Legal Rights to Child-friendly Working Hours* (Maternity Alliance, 1998).

Tess Gill is a barrister at Old Square Chambers in London. She specialises in employment and human rights law, with a particular emphasis on discrimination and equal pay. She is a part-time employment tribunal chair and is on the advisory panel of the Equal Opportunities Review and a management committee member of Discrimination Law Association. She is co-author of YourRights.org.uk, Liberty's online guide to human rights launched in May 2002. She is a Centre for Dispute Resolution (CEDR) trained mediator.

Karon Monaghan is a barrister at Matrix Chambers in London. She specialises in discrimination law.

Gay Moon was formerly a solicitor specialising in employment and discrimination law in a Community Law Centre for twenty years. She is currently the Head of the Equalities Project at JUSTICE, Chair of the Discrimination Law Association and Editor of the Discrimination Law Association's Briefings.

Mary Stacey is a solicitor and consultant to Thompsons solicitors, she is a part-time employment tribunal chair. She is the co-author of *Challenging Disability Discrimination at Work* (Stacey and Short, Institute of Employment Rights, 2000).

The Legal Action Group is a national, independent charity which campaigns for equal access to justice for all members of society. Legal Action Group:

- provides support to the practice of lawyers and advisers
- inspires developments in that practice
- campaigns for improvements in the law and the administration of justice
- stimulates debate on how services should be delivered.

Discrimination Law Handbook

Camilla Palmer, Tess Gill, Karon Monaghan, Gay Moon and Mary Stacey

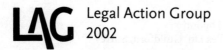

LAG Legal Action Group
2002

This edition published in Great Britain 2002
by LAG Education and Service Trust Ltd
242 Pentonville Road
London N1 9UN

The employment sections of this book were first published in 1987 as *Sex and Race Discrimination in Employment* by Camilla Palmer and Kate Poulton

Second edition published in 1992 as *Discrimination at Work: The law on sex and race discrimination* by Camilla Palmer

Third edition published in 1997 as *Discrimination at Work: The law on sex, race and disability discrimination* by Camilla Palmer, Gay Moon with Susan Cox

British Library Cataloguing in Publication Data
A CIP catalogue record for this book is available from the British Library

ISBN 1 903307 13 9

Typeset by Regent Typesetting, London
Printed in Great Britain by Biddles Ltd, Guildford, Surrey

Foreword

by the Rt Hon Lord Justice Sedley

Tom Lehrer used to assert that the United States Army had taken the democratic ideal to its logical conclusion by abolishing discrimination on every ground including ability. All decision-making involves choice, and all choice involves discrimination. What matters both to individuals and to society, as Lehrer was sarcastically pointing out, is the basis on which choices affecting people's interests and dignity are made.

Although the Westminster Parliament in 1833 legislated to forbid racial and religious discrimination in the Indian Civil Service (to no useful effect, it must be said), it is astonishing to reflect that in this country until barely more than a quarter of a century ago, those who had the power to make choices were still pretty much free to discriminate on grounds of race, disability, gender or anything else that ignited their prejudices. In the society I grew up in it was perfectly legal to put 'No blacks' in advertisements to let accommodation, and nothing happened to employers who simply refused to take on women. I am glad that my children, now with children of their own, cannot believe that such things were possible.

In 1965 a start was made with institutional intervention in the field of race relations, but it was in 1975 that the Sex Discrimination Act was passed and, simultaneously, the Equal Pay Act 1970 came into force. A year later, in 1976, a new Race Relations Act gave individuals the right to sue for race discrimination. This legislation, and that which has now followed in relation to disability, has been an exemplar of what legislation ought to be. It does not simply forbid: it teaches. Every bit as important as the rights it creates and the costs it imposes on discriminators is the cultural change it has helped to bring about. Today even the worst bigot knows that racially and sexually discriminatory behaviour and language are socially unacceptable. Calling the shift political correctness does nothing to diminish it.

To the domestic imperatives to procure more equal treatment of individuals there have been added the European Union's legal requirements and the sometimes radical jurisprudence of the European Court of Justice. Together these now make a massive and complex body of law and practice, which may yet be added to. Discrimination on religious grounds, long forbidden in Northern Ireland, may soon be forbidden in Great Britain, and state-funded denominational schools which turn children away on religious grounds may sooner or later require the United Kingdom to account for itself before the European Court of Human Rights.

Meanwhile, and for the indefinite future, courts and tribunals have to understand and apply an increasingly demanding body of law, and those who conduct cases before them have to be, if anything, ahead of them. A lucidly organised and meticulously researched practice book is as necessary for everybody practising or adjudicating in this field as a map is to a traveller or a score to an orchestra. The Legal Action Group's practice books have furnished a criterion of clarity and accuracy which this, a much revised and expanded edition of an already standard work, not only maintains but enhances. The authors and publishers yet again have the thanks of all of us who see the containment of unacceptable discrimination as one of the benchmarks of a civilised society.

Stephen Sedley
Royal Courts of Justice
August 2002

Acknowledgements

The authors would like to thank, in no particular order, Aileen McColgan, Joanna Wade, Akua Reindorf, Vivienne Gay, Sue Ward, Pip Heskith, Catherine Casserley, Ijeoma Omambala, Joe Korner, Andrew Short, Stuart Bell, Laura Cox, Robin Allen, Petra Sheils, Jacqui McKee, Razia Karim and the staff at Legal Action Group.

Contents

Table of cases

Table of statutes

Table of statutory instruments

Table of European legislation

Directives

Abbreviations

AIA 1996	Asylum and Immigration Act 1996
AML	additional maternity leave
AVC	additional voluntary contribution
BP Regs 2001	Sex Discrimination (Indirect Discrimination and Burden of Proof) Regulations 2001
CCA 1984	County Courts Act 1984
CPR	Civil Procedure Rules
CRE	Commission for Racial Equality
DD Regs 1996	Disability Discrimination Regulations 1996
DDA 1995	Disability Discrimination Act 1995
DD(E) Regs 1996	Disability Discrimination (Employment) Regulations 1996
DfEE	Department for Education and Employment
DL	dependants leave
DRC	Disability Rights Commission
DRCA 1999	Disability Rights Commission Act 1999
DSM-IV	Diagnosis and Statistical Manual of Mental Disorders (4th edn)
DTI	Department of Trade and Industry
EA 2002	Employment Act 2002
EAT	Employment Appeal Tribunal
ECHR	European Convention on Human Rights
ECJ	European Court of Justice
ECtHR	European Court of Human Rights
ED 2000	Employment Directive 2000
EdA 1996	Education Act 1996
EEA	European Economic Area
EOC	Equal Opportunities Commission
EPD 1975	Equal Pay Directive 1975
EqPA 1970	Equal Pay Act 1970
ERA 1996	Employment Rights Act 1996
ET	employment tribunal
ET (Interest) Regs 1996	Employment Tribunals (Interest on Awards in Discrimination Cases) Regulations 1996
ETD 1976	Equal Treatment Directive 1976
EWC	expected week of childbirth
FETO 1998	Fair Employment and Treatment Order 1998

GMF	genuine material factor
GOQ	genuine occupational qualification
GR Regs 1999	Gender Reassignment Regulations 1999
HRA 1998	Human Rights Act 1998
HSE	Health and Safety Executive
HSWA 1974	Health and Safety at Work Act 1974
ICCPR	International Covenant on Civil and Political Rights
ICD	Classification of Impairment, Disability and Handicap
IE	independent expert
JES	job evaluation scheme
LEA	local education authority
LIFO	last in first out
LSC	Legal Services Commission
MHSW Regs 1999	Management of Health and Safety at Work Regulations 1999
MPL Regs 1999	Maternity and Parental Leave etc Regulations 1999
NICA	Northern Ireland Court of Appeal
NRA	normal retirement age
OML	ordinary maternity leave
OPS Regs 1995	Occupational Pension Schemes (Equal Treatment) Regulations 1995
OPS(EAM) Regs 1976	Occupational Pension Schemes (Equal Access to Membership) Regulations 1976
OSSD 1986	Occupational Social Security Directive 1986
PA 1995	Pensions Act 1995
PHA 1997	Protection from Harassment Act 1997
PL	parental leave
PLD 1996	Parental Leave Directive 1996
PSA 1993	Pension Schemes Act 1993
PtWD 1998	Part-time Workers Directive 1998
PTW Regs 2000	Part-time Workers (Prevention of Less Favourable Treatment) Regulations 2000
PWD 1992	Pregnant Workers Directive 1992
RD 2000	Race Directive 2000
RRA 1976	Race Relations Act 1976
RRAA 2000	Race Relations (Amendment) Act 2000
RR(NI)O 1997	Race Relations (Northern Ireland) Order 1997
SDA 1975	Sex Discrimination Act 1975
SENDA 2001	Special Educational Needs and Disability Act 2001
SMP	statutory maternity pay
SSD	Sex Discrimination (Social Security) Directive
TULRCA 1992	Trade Union and Labour Relations (Consolidation) Act 1992
TUPE Regs 1981	Transfer of Undertakings (Protection of Employment) Regulations 1981

CHAPTER 1

Legal structure

continued

The main discrimination provisions

1.1 There is no general prohibition on discrimination in UK law. The Sex Discrimination Act (SDA) 1975, the Race Relations Act (RRA) 1976 and the Disability Discrimination Act (DDA) 1995 define discrimination for the purposes of each of the Acts,[1] and make discrimination unlawful in certain circumstances. The Acts prohibit discrimination in the employment field, in education and in the provision of goods, facilities, services and premises. In addition, the RRA 1976 prohibits discrimination by public and planning authorities, and other domestic statutes and regulations and European law make specific provision for discrimination in various areas. The DDA 1995 extends to Northern Ireland but the SDA 1975 and the RRA 1976 do not, although the Sex Discrimination (Northern Ireland) Order 1976[2] and the Race Relations (Northern Ireland) Order 1997 are materially identical to the Acts.[3]

1.2 The SDA 1975 and the RRA 1976 prohibit direct and indirect discrimination on grounds of sex and race and discrimination by way of victimisation.[4] The SDA 1975 also prohibits direct and indirect discrimination against married people[5] and direct discrimination on the grounds of gender reassignment[6] in the employment-related field.[6a] Neither the SDA 1975 nor the RRA 1976 permits the justification of direct discrimination and the two Acts are otherwise very similar, but the concept of indirect discrimination in RRA 1976 is narrower than that applied by the SDA 1975 in relation to employment

1 SDA 1975 Pt I, RRA 1976 Pt I, DDA 1995 ss5, 14, 20 and 24 (and, when the provisions of the SENDA 2001 come into force, DDA 1995 s28B – see paras 1.32 and 30.134).

2 SI No 1042, NI 15 as amended by Sex Discrimination (Northern Ireland) Order 1988 SI No 1303, NI 13.

3 Except that the Race Relations (Northern Ireland) Order 1997 SI No 869, NI 6, expressly recognises Irish travellers as a racial group for the purposes of the Order. In Great Britain the courts have held that Irish travellers are in any case a racial group as defined by ethnicity for the purposes of the RRA 1976: *O'Leary v Allied Domecq Inns Ltd*, CL950275, July 2000, Central London County Court (unreported).

4 SDA 1975 ss1 and 4; RRA 1976 ss1 and 2.

5 Though not against unmarried people: SDA 1975 s3.

6 Though not indirect discrimination: SDA 1975 s2A.

6a Discrimination against married persons is made unlawful only under SDA 1975 Pt II. Discrimination on the grounds of gender reassignment is made unlawful under SDA 1975 Pt II, ss35A and 35B (barristers and advocates) and SDA 1975 Pt III in relation to vocational training.

and vocational training. There are also differences in the burden of proof provisions.[7]

1.3 The scheme of the DDA 1995 differs considerably from that of the SDA 1975 and the RRA 1976. If less favourable treatment against a disabled person, for a reason which relates to their disability, can be justified it is not unlawful.[8] Further, the DDA 1995 does not prohibit indirect discrimination in the same terms as the SDA 1975 and RRA 1976, but the wider definition of discrimination has the effect of covering many forms of indirect discrimination. In addition, the DDA 1995 imposes obligations on employers and service providers to make reasonable adjustments to their arrangements, practices and premises in order to accommodate disabled people.[9] The DDA 1995 also prohibits discrimination by way of victimisation.[10]

1.4 Article 14 of the European Convention on Human Rights (ECHR) prohibits unjustified discrimination on any ground in the enjoyment of the other rights and freedoms set out in the ECHR. The Human Rights Act (HRA) 1998 makes it unlawful for a public authority to act in a way which is incompatible with a convention right,[11] and courts and tribunals must interpret legislation compatibly with the convention rights in so far as it is possible to do so.[12] 'Public authorities' include public sector employers and service providers, as well as bodies with mixed private and public functions.[13] Importantly, courts and tribunals are also public authorities and are therefore bound to act compatibly with the convention rights.[14] The main provisions of the ECHR, including article 14, are scheduled to the HRA 1998 and incorporated into domestic law by the Act.[15]

1.5 There is also a substantial amount of EC law in the field of sex discrimination. All directly effective European law has primacy over domestic law. Thus, courts and tribunals must ensure that their interpretation of domestic legislation is consistent with the Community

7 As a result of the Sex Discrimination (Indirect Discrimination and Burden of Proof) Regulations 2001 SI No 2660, which implement the EC Directive on the burden of proof in cases of discrimination based on sex (Council Directive 98/52/EC).

8 DDA 1995 ss5(1)(b), 14(2), 20(1) and 24(1).

9 Ibid ss6(1), 15(1), 21(1) and (2).

10 Ibid s55.

11 HRA 1998 s6.

12 Ibid s3.

13 Ibid s6(3)(b).

14 Ibid s6(3)(a).

15 Ibid s1 and Sch 1.

provisions. If they are unable to read domestic legislation in this way they must disapply the offending provision of domestic law.[15a]

Discrimination in employment

Sex discrimination

1.6 Under the SDA 1975 it is unlawful for an employer to discriminate against employees, applicants or contract workers on the ground of sex or gender reassignment, or because they are married.[16] Employees must not be dismissed or subjected to any detriment on these grounds.[17] In addition, they must not be subjected to discrimination in the way in which they are afforded access to opportunities.[18] Employers must not discriminate against applicants or against contract workers in deciding who should be offered work or in the terms on which work is offered.[19] There are certain exceptions where sex is a genuine occupational qualification.[20]

1.7 It is also unlawful for other bodies in the employment field who are not employers, such as partnerships and qualifying bodies, to discriminate.[21] The SDA 1986 contains provisions relating to sexually discriminatory provisions in collective agreements and rules of undertakings.[22]

1.8 The SDA 1975 was passed in order to implement the Equal Treatment Directive (ETD),[23] which provides that men and women should be treated equally as regards access to employment, vocational training and promotion, and working conditions. The ETD is a directly effective provision of Community law. It may be directly relied upon by individuals in certain circumstances, but only against the state and emanations of the state.[23a]

15a See chapter 10 below.

16 Though, as mentioned above, it is only unlawful to discriminate *directly* or to victimise in relation to gender reassignment: SDA 1975 ss2A and 4.

17 SDA 1975 s6(2)(b).

18 Ibid s6(2).

19 Ibid ss6(1) and 9(2).

20 Ibid ss7 and 9(3B).

21 Ibid ss11–16.

22 As amended by the Trade Union and Labour Relations (Consolidation) Act 1992 and the Trade Union Reform and Employment Rights Act 1993.

23 Council Directive 76/207/EEC.

23a See chapter 10 below.

1.9 The Equal Opportunities Commission (EOC) has published a code of practice for the elimination of discrimination on grounds of sex and marriage and the promotion of equality of opportunity in employment. The code, published under the SDA 1975,[24] provides guidance for employers about practices which should be adopted to promote equality. It does not have the same standing as either legislation or case-law. Failure by an employer to observe any provision of a code of practice is not itself unlawful, but may be taken into account by a tribunal or court.[25] The European Commission has also issued a code of practice on the protection of the dignity of men and women at work.[26] This should be taken into account by employment tribunals (ETs) in determining complaints of sex discrimination, and sexual harassment in particular, in the employment field.

Equal pay

1.10 The SDA 1975 does not deal with discrimination in pay and other contractual terms or pensions. These are covered by the Equal Pay Act (EqPA) 1970 and the Pensions Act (PA) 1995.

1.11 The EqPA 1970 provides that a man and woman working for the same employer should receive the same pay and be subject to the same contract terms if:

- they are doing similar work;[27] or
- a job evaluation scheme has rated the man's and the woman's work as equivalent;[28] or
- they are doing work of equal value.[29]

The EqPA 1970 operates by implying an equality clause into the contract of employment. The entitlement to equal pay does not arise if the 'material factor' defence applies.[30]

1.12 The EqPA 1970, as amended by the SDA 1986, further provides that discriminatory provisions in collective agreements and rules of employers, trade unions, employers' associations, professional organisations and qualifying bodies are void or unenforceable.[31]

24 SDA 1975 s56A.
25 Ibid s56A(10).
26 Annexed to Council Recommendation 92/131/EEC of 27 November 1991.
27 EqPA 1970 s1(2)(a).
28 Ibid s1(2)(b).
29 Ibid s1(2)(c).
30 Ibid s1(3).
31 SDA 1986 s6.

1.13 The EqPA 1970 is the domestic implementation of article 141 of the EC Treaty (formerly article 119) and the Equal Pay Directive (EPD).[32] These provisions of Community law require member states to ensure that men and women receive equal pay for equal work. Article 141 can be directly relied upon by individuals, either against the state or against other bodies.[33] However, ETs currently do not have jurisdiction to hear 'stand-alone' EC law claims, so an applicant who wishes to rely on article 141 in an ET must bring his or her case under some provision of domestic law (usually the EqPA 1970).[34] Other courts can hear 'stand-alone' EC law claims, but cannot hear EqPA 1970 claims.

1.14 In 1997 the EOC produced the EOC Code of Practice on equal pay. The status of the code, which was issued under the EqPA 1970, is the same as that of the codes of practice issued under the SDA 1975[34a] and RRA 1976.

Pensions

1.15 The Pensions Act (PA) 1995 provides for equal treatment for men and women in occupational pension schemes. It covers terms on which people become members of a scheme and the way members are treated. An occupational pension scheme is treated as containing an equal treatment rule where a woman is employed on like work, work rated as equivalent or work of equal value to a man.[35] This is enforced in the same way as an equal pay claim.

1.16 There are two EC directives which enshrine in European law the principle of equal treatment in occupational pension schemes.[36]

32 Council Directive 75/117/EEC.

33 *Van Gend en Loos* [1963] ECR 1, ECJ; Case 43-75 *Defrenne v SABENA (No 2)* [1976] ECR 0455, [1976] ICR 547, ECJ; *Pickstone v Freemans plc* [1989] AC 66, [1988] IRLR 357, HL; Case 262/88 *Barber v Guardian Royal Exchange Assurance Group* [1990] ECR I-1889, [1990] IRLR 240, ECJ.

34 *Biggs v Somerset CC* [1996] 2 All ER 734, [1996] IRLR 203; *Staffordshire CC v Barber* [1996] 2 All ER 748, [1996] IRLR 209. This principle is currently under challenge to the Court of Appeal in *Alabaster v Woolwich plc and Social Security Secretary of State for* [2002] EWCA Civ 211.

34a See para 1.9 above.

35 PA 1995 s62(3).

36 Respectively, Council Directives 86/378/EEC and 96/97/EC.

Race discrimination

1.17 The scheme of the RRA 1976 is similar to that of the SDA 1975 as regards discrimination in the employment field. However the RRA also covers matters relating to pay, contractual terms and pensions; there are no separate provisions relating to discrimination on grounds of race in these areas. Further, the Race Relations (Amendment) Act (RRAA) 2000 extends the scope of vicarious liability under the RRA 1976 to cover chief constables of police, who were not previously liable for the discriminatory acts of their officers in the employment field or otherwise.[37]

1.18 The Commission for Racial Equality (CRE) has produced a code of practice for the elimination of discrimination and the promotion of equality of opportunity in employment.[38] Unlike the code of practice issued by the EOC under the SDA 1975, the CRE code provides guidance for trade unions and employment agencies. Its status is the same as the EOC codes of practice issued under the SDA 1975 and the EqPA 1970.

1.19 The Race Directive (RD)[39] is an EC legislative measure which gives effect to the principle of equal treatment between persons irrespective of racial or ethnic origin (but not nationality). It prohibits direct and unjustifiable indirect discrimination on grounds of race. The RD's definition of indirect discrimination is broader than that of the RRA 1976, and differs also from that contained in the SDA 1975. The RD also introduces a victimisation provision which is likely to have wider impact than the victimisation provisions in RRA 1976.[40] The RD, unlike the RRA 1976, expressly includes harassment as a form of race discrimination. The directive must be implemented by the UK by 19 July 2003.

37 *Farah v Metropolitan Police Commissioner* [1998] QB 65; *Liversidge v Chief Constable of Bedfordshire Police* [2002] IRLR 15. The amendments do not extend to sex discrimination so that, on the face of the SDA 1975 a chief officer of police is not liable for the sexually discriminatory acts of his or her police officers under the SDA 1975.

38 RRA 1976 s47.

39 Council Directive 2000/43/EC.

40 RD art 9. See by comparison the impact of the ETD: Case 185/97 *Coote v Granada Hospitality Ltd* [1998] ECR I-5199, [1998] IRLR 656.

Disability discrimination

1.20 The DDA 1995 prohibits discrimination against employees and applicants by employers who have 15 or more employees.[41] It is supplemented by the Disability Discrimination (Meaning of Discrimination) Regulations 1996 and the Disability Discrimination (Employment) Regulations 1996.[42] The circumstances in which employers are prohibited from discriminating are similar to those set out in the SDA 1975 and RRA 1976. However, the meanings given to 'discrimination' in the DDA 1995 are very different to that contained in the SDA 1975 and the RRA 1976. Discrimination (other than victimisation) under the DDA 1995 may be justified[43] (unlike direct discrimination under the SDA 1975 and RRA 1976). Further, unjustified failures by employers to make reasonable adjustments to any arrangements made by them or on their behalf, and to any physical feature of their premises if those arrangements or physical features place a disabled person at a substantial disadvantage, will amount to unlawful discrimination under the DDA 1995.[44]

1.21 The Secretary of State for Education and Employment has issued a code of practice for the elimination of discrimination in the field of employment against disabled people or people who have had a disability. The status in tribunal proceedings of the code, which was issued under the DDA 1995,[45] is the same as that of the codes issued under the SDA 1975, EqPA 1970 and RRA 1976.[46] The DDA 1995 also provides that the Secretary of State may issue guidance as to the matters which might be taken into account in determining whether a particular impairment constitutes a disability for the purposes of the DDA 1995.[47] Guidance has been issued and, with the code of practice, is regarded by tribunals as a useful aid for interpretation of the DDA 1995 and as important authority in marginal cases.[48]

41 DDA 1995 s7(1), amended by Disability Discrimination (Exception for Small Employers) Order 1998 SI No 2618. 'Discrimination' is defined by DDA 1995 s5.

42 Respectively, SI No 1455 and SI No 1456.

43 DDA 1995 s5(1)(b).

44 Ibid s6.

45 Ibid s53.

46 Ibid.

47 Ibid s3: guidance on matters to be taken into account in determining questions relating to the definition of disability, SI 1996 No 1996.

48 See *Goodwin v Patent Office* [1999] IRLR 4, EAT; *Greenwood v British Airways plc* [1999] IRLR 600, EAT and *Vicary v British Telecommunications plc* [1999] IRLR 680, EAT.

1.22 The Employment Directive[49] (the ED) is an EC legislative measure which prohibits, among other things, discrimination in employment and occupation on the ground of disability. It imposes a duty on employers to take proportionate and appropriate measures to enable disabled people to have access to, participate or advance in employment and to undergo training. On implementation, the ED will apply to all employers except the armed forces. The parts of the ED which apply to disability must be implemented in domestic law by 2 December 2006.

Other employment legislation

1.23 The Employment Rights Act (ERA) 1996 gives employees some protection against unfair dismissal, redundancy and dismissal on the ground of pregnancy. There are, however, some qualifying conditions. The most important of these is that, in order to claim protection from unfair dismissal (apart from on certain automatically unfair grounds such as those related to pregnancy) an employee must have worked for the employer for one year.[50] The ERA 1996 also gives women the right to maternity leave and to their job back on return from maternity leave.[51] These provisions are supplemented by a large number of regulations, including the Maternity and Parental Leave, etc, Regulations 1999.[52]

1.24 The Part-time Workers (Prevention of Less Favourable Treatment) Regulations 2000 came into force on 1 July 2000.[53] They protect employees and other workers against any less favourable treatment on the ground of their part-time status. Such discrimination is not unlawful if it is objectively justified.

1.25 The ED requires member states to ensure that citizens receive equal treatment in employment and occupation. The grounds on which discrimination is prohibited are religion and belief, disability,

49 Council Directive 2000/78/EC.

50 ERA 1996 s108.

51 Ibid Pt VIII.

52 SI No 3312. Further, the Employment Act 2002 and draft Regulations (the Maternity and Parental Leave (Amendment) Regulations 2002 and the Paternity and Adoption Leave Regulations 2002) make new provision where expected week of childbirth (or birth in some cases) or adoption is on or after 6 April 2003. In addition the Employment Act 2002 and further Regulations will introduce a new right for employees to request a new working pattern in order to care for children under 6 years old (or disabled children under the age of 18) for whom they have responsibility. See chapters 18–21 below.

age and sexual orientation. The provisions relating to religion and belief and to sexual orientation must be implemented in the UK by 2 December 2003 and those relating to age and disability by 2 December 2006.

Human rights

1.26 Article 14 ECHR, which sets out the non-discrimination principle, applies to employment disputes only in limited circumstances. This is because it is necessary for the treatment complained of to fall within the scope of one of the substantive convention rights for article 14 to apply, and no convention right deals expressly with employment. In addition, only public authority employers are subject to a direct duty under the HRA 1998, although courts and tribunals are required to interpret all legislation compatibly with the convention rights so far as it is possible to do so. Nevertheless ECHR art 14 and certain other of the convention rights, in particular ECHR art 8 (the right to respect for private and family life), may be relevant in discrimination cases (see further chapter 9).

Discrimination in education

Sex and race discrimination

1.27 The SDA 1975 and the RRA 1976 outlaw discrimination on grounds of sex or race in the provision of education. Most educational establishments are covered by the SDA 1975 and RRA 1976, including state and independent schools, special schools, universities and other bodies designated by the Home Secretary. Single sex establishments, and establishments which are effectively single sex, are exempted from most of the provisions in the SDA 1975.[54] So, too, are some physical training courses.[55]

1.28 All educational establishments covered by the SDA 1975 and RRA 1976 are subject to specific provisions. They must not discriminate against pupils or applicants in relation to admissions, and they must not discriminate against pupils in relation to access to benefits, services or facilities.[56] Pupils must not be excluded or subjected to any

53 SI No 1551.
54 SDA 1975 s26.
55 Ibid s28.
56 SDA 1975 s22(a)–(b); RRA 1976 s17(a)–(b).

detriment on grounds of sex or race.[57] Local education authorities (LEAs) and certain other educational establishments are also subject to a general duty to ensure that:

- facilities for education provided by it and ancillary benefits and services are provided without sex discrimination;[58] and
- in carrying out their functions they have due regard to the need to eliminate unlawful racial discrimination and to promote equality of opportunity and good relations between people of different racial groups.[59]

LEAs must not to do any act which constitutes sex or race discrimination in carrying out their functions under the Education Acts.[60]

1.29 The RD, described above (see para 1.19), prohibits discrimination in relation to education.[61]

1.30 The CRE has issued non-statutory codes of practice for the elimination of racial discrimination in education for England and Wales and also for Scotland.[62] It is likely that a court would pay close attention to the contents of these codes.

Disability discrimination

1.31 The DDA 1995 applies in part to the provision of educational services from September 2002.[63] It does already introduce requirements on educational establishments to publish annual disability statements setting out information about the facilities they provide to disabled people. The relevant provisions are no longer contained in the DDA 1995, but are to be found in the Education Act (EdA) 1996.[64] In addition, in relation to their non-educational activities, educational establishments are subject to the duty placed upon providers of goods,

57 SDA 1975 s22(c); RRA 1976 s17(c).

58 SDA 1975 s25(1).

59 RRA 1976 s71. Governing bodies of LEA maintained schools and other institutions are also obliged to prepare a written statement of their policies for promoting race equality before 31 May 2002 and to undertake an impact assessment and monitoring exercise of their policies: see RRA 1976 (Statutory Duties) Order 2001 SI No 3458.

60 SDA 1975 s23; RRA 1976 s18. See also *R v Birmingham City Council ex p EOC* [1989] AC 1155, [1989] IRLR 173.

61 RD art 3.

62 The codes, which were published in 1998, predate the RRAA 2000.

63 DDA 1995 s19(5).

64 Ibid ss29(1)–(2) and 30(7)–(9) were repealed before they came into force, and are now in EdA 1996 s317(6)–(7).

services, facilities and premises not to discriminate against disabled people. These activities include leisure services such as school trips, governing body meetings, fund-raising events, and the use of school sports facilities by the local community.[65]

1.32 The Special Educational Needs and Disability Act (SENDA) 2001 amends the DDA 1995 and the EdA 1996 by introducing further provision in relation to discrimination, on grounds of disability in educational establishments. Some of these amending provisions come into force in September 2002. Once they are in force, discrimination in the provision of education will be outlawed under the DDA 1995.[66] The scope of this prohibition will be similar to that of the SDA 1975 and the RRA 1976,[67] though the meanings given to discrimination under the education provisions of the DDA 1995[68] will be different to those in the SDA 1975 and RRA 1976. The SENDA 2001 amendments will also subject LEAs to a duty to prepare, review and implement accessibility strategies,[69] and introduce a statutory presumption that children with special educational needs will be educated in mainstream schools.[70] The Secretary of State has issued Codes of Practice in relation to both schools and providers of post-16 education related services.

Human rights

1.33 Article 2 of the first protocol to the ECHR imposes an obligation on the state to ensure that nobody is denied the right to education. The provision, which is incorporated into domestic law by the HRA 1998, also requires the state to respect the right of parents to secure education in conformity with their own religious and philosophical convictions. Other convention rights which are relevant in the education field are article 6 (the right to a fair hearing); article 8 (the right to respect for private and family life); and article 10 (the right to freedom of expression). A person who is discriminated against in circumstances which fall within the scope of any of these articles may also invoke the protection afforded by article 14 ECHR.

65 See DfEE Circular 12/97, *Guidance on Disability Statements for LEAs*, September 1997.

66 DDA 1995 s28A.

67 Ibid ss28A, 28F and 28R.

68 Ibid s28B.

69 Ibid s28D.

70 Ibid s1, substituting EdA 1996 s316, in force from 1 January 2002 (SI 2001 No 2217, as amended by SI 2001 No 2614).

1.34 LEAs and public sector educational establishments are 'public authorities' under the HRA 1998, and so are subject to a duty to act compatibly with the convention rights. Private schools, in relation to some of their functions, may also be subject to the duty because of their mixed public and private functions.

Discrimination by planning authorities

Race discrimination

1.35 The RRA 1976 makes it unlawful for a planning authority to discriminate on grounds of race. Neither the SDA 1975 nor the DDA 1995 contain any such prohibition. The CRE has issued non-statutory guidance directed at the elimination of racial discrimination by planning authorities.[71] It is likely that a court would pay close attention to the contents of the guidance.

Discrimination by public authorities

Sex, race and disability discrimination

1.36 The provisions of the SDA 1975, RRA 1976 and DDA 1995 cover public authorities in respect of certain of their functions, for example, in relation to employment by public authorities, in relation to services and facilities provided by them, and in relation to housing provided or managed by them.

Race discrimination

1.37 The RRAA 2000 has introduced a new and broad provision into the RRA 1976 outlawing discrimination by public authorities in the carrying out of any of their functions.[72] A 'public authority' includes a body whose functions are mixed private and public, but only in respect of those of its functions which are of a public nature.[73] The main intention behind this new provision was to bring within the scope of the

71 *Planning for a Multi Racial Britain* (CRE, 1993).

72 RRA 1976 s19B(1).

73 Ibid s19B(2). Certain bodies and certain acts are excluded by RRA 1976 ss19(B)(3), 19C, 19D and 19F.

RRA 1976 all of the functions of the police. This followed the recommendation of the Stephen Lawrence inquiry report.[74] In addition the RRAA 2000 amended the RRA 1976 so as to make the chief constable of police vicariously liable for the discriminatory acts of his or her police officers, both within and outside the employment sphere.[75]

1.38 The RRAA 2000 also amended the RRA 1976 to introduce new and broad statutory duties upon specified bodies.[76] By order introduced under the RRA 1976 as amended by the RRAA 2000, obligations are imposed upon specified bodies variously to produce race equality schemes; to prepare written statements of policies for promoting race equality; and to undertake impact assessments and ethnic monitoring.[77]

Discrimination in the provision of goods, facilities, and services and clubs

Sex and race discrimination

1.39 People who provide services or facilities to the public or a section of the public must not discriminate on grounds of sex or race in refusing or deliberately omitting to provide services or facilities to others.[78] People who provide goods, facilities or services to the public or a section of it must not discriminate in refusing or deliberately omitting to provide goods of like quality or in like manner and on like terms as are normal in the provider's case to others.[79] These provisions apply to people who normally provide goods, facilities or services, and not to those who do so only occasionally.

74 Sir William Macpherson of Cluny, *The Stephen Lawrence Inquiry*, Cm 4262-I (TSO, 1999). See further chapter 29 below.

75 RRA 1976 s76A.

76 Ibid s71 and Sch 1A as amended by RRA 1976 (General Statutory Duty) Order 2001 SI No 3457. The Commission for Racial Equality (CRE) has issued a statutory Code of Practice and four non-statutory guides directed at public authorities to assist them in meeting the new statutory duty: 'Code of Practice on the Duty to Promote Race Equality (2002), in force on 30 May 2002 (SI No 1435 of 2002); 'A Guide for Public Authorities' (2002) CRE; 'A Guide for Schools' (2002) CRE; 'A Guide for Institutions of Further and Higher Education' (2002) CRE; and 'Ethnic Monitoring: A Guide for Public Authorities', (2002) CRE.

77 RRA 1976 (Statutory Duties) Order 2001 SI No 3458.

78 SDA 1975 s29(1)(a); RRA 1976 s20(1)(a).

79 SDA 1975 s29(1)(b); RRA 1976 s20(1)(b).

1.40 The RRA 1976 prohibits discrimination in relation to the membership of political and social clubs with a membership of more than 25,[80] although the SDA 1975 does not. Sex discrimination by private clubs is not outlawed under the facilities and services provision of the SDA 1975, since private membership clubs cannot be said to provide services or facilities to the public or a section of it.[81]

1.41 The RD described above (see para 1.19) prohibits discrimination in relation to social protection, including social security and healthcare; social advantages and access to the supply of goods and services.[82]

Disability discrimination

1.42 Discrimination against disabled people by service providers is prohibited by the DDA 1995. Services include facilities and goods. Service providers must not treat disabled customers less favourably in refusing or deliberately omitting to provide them with services, or in the standard of service they provide to disabled customers, or in the terms on which services are offered.[83] Service providers are also obliged to make reasonable adjustments to their practices in order to accommodate disabled people if it is impossible or unreasonably difficult for a disabled person to access their services.[84] The DDA 1995 applies to any provider who deals directly with the public, irrespective of its size, but discrimination on grounds of disability in the provision of services is not unlawful if it can be justified (see further chapter 30).[85]

1.43 From 2004, service providers will be subject to a duty to make modifications to their premises in order to accommodate disabled customers in certain circumstances.[85a] The Secretary of State has published a code of practice in relation to rights of access to facilities, services and premises, which provides guidance on the prevention of discrimination against disabled people in this context. The code may be used as evidence in court or tribunal proceedings. Failure by a

80 RRA 1976 s25.
81 The position is different in relation to pubs or clubs open to the public: see chapter 29.
82 RD art 3.
83 DDA 1995 s19(1).
84 Ibid s21.
85 Ibid s20(3).
85a Ibid s21(2) and Disability Discrimination Act 1995 (Commencement No 9) Order 2001 SI No 2030.

service provider to observe any provision of a code of practice is not itself unlawful, but it may be taken into account by a tribunal or court.[86]

Human rights

1.44 The HRA 1998 may be relevant in a range of situations relating to the provision of goods, services and provisions by public authorities or bodies with mixed public and private functions. Of particular relevance may be article 1 of the first protocol to the ECHR, which protects certain property rights and is incorporated into UK law by the HRA 1998.[86a]

Discrimination in relation to premises

Sex and race discrimination

1.45 People who have the power to dispose of premises, including land and residential and business premises, are prohibited from discriminating on grounds of sex or race in selling, renting or otherwise allocating their premises. They may not discriminate in the terms on which the premises are offered or by refusing an application for the premises, or in the treatment of any person in relation to a list of people in need of premises of the same description.[87] People who manage premises must not discriminate on grounds of sex or race in relation to benefits and services or by evicting occupiers or subjecting them to any detriment.[88]

1.46 Both the SDA 1975 and the RRA 1976 contain exceptions for small premises and owner-occupiers.[89] The SDA 1975 also provides exceptions in relation to premises, such as hospitals, on which particular services are provided,[90] and in cases where 'serious embarrassment' is likely if men and women share facilities on the premises.[91] Local authorities and other public bodies concerned with the disposal of premises are subject to a general duty to eliminate unlawful race

86 DDA 1995 s53A.
86a HRA 1998 s1 and Sch 1.
87 SDA 1975 s30(1); RRA 1976 s21(1).
88 SDA 1975 s30(2); RRA 1976 s21(2).
89 SDA 1975 ss30 and 32; RRA 1976 ss21 and 22.
90 SDA 1975 ss33–35.
91 Ibid s35

discrimination and to promote equality of opportunity between persons of different racial groups, as described above.[92]

1.47 The CRE has issued a code of practice in non-rented (owner occupied) housing and a code of practice in rented housing.[93] Both codes provide examples of good practice. Failure by a person to observe any provision of the codes is not itself unlawful but it may be taken into account by a tribunal or court.[94]

1.48 The RD, described above (see para 1.19), prohibits discrimination in relation to access to housing.[95]

Disability discrimination

1.49 Discrimination against disabled people in relation to the selling, renting, allocation or management of premises is regulated by the DDA 1995.[96] So, too, is discrimination against disabled occupiers in relation to the use of facilities or benefits. Further, occupiers must not be unjustifiably evicted or subjected to any detriment on the grounds of their disability.[97] Disability-related discrimination is not unlawful if it can be justified.[98] The DDA 1995 currently imposes no duty to make adjustments to the physical features of premises in order to make them accessible to disabled people, although a duty of that kind will be introduced in 2004.[98a] There are exceptions to the discrimination prohibitions in relation to owner-occupiers and small dwellings.[99]

Human rights

1.50 The ECHR is of considerable relevance to housing. Article 8 guarantees respect for privacy and family life and the home. A person's home is not restricted to a place in which he or she has a proprietary

92 RRA 1976 s71.

93 The codes are issued under RRA 1976 s47 and brought into effect by Race Relations Code of Practice (Non Rented Housing) Order 1992 SI No 619 and Race Relations Code of Practice (Rented Housing) Order 1991 SI No 227 respectively.

94 RRA 1976 s47(10).

95 RD art 3.

96 DDA 1995 s22(1).

97 Ibid s22(3).

98 Ibid s24.

98a DDA 1995 s27 and Disability Discrimination Act 1995 (Commencement No 9) Order 2001SI No 2030.

99 DDA 1995 ss22(2) and 23(1).

interest, and it can even include business premises.[100] In addition, article 1 of the first protocol to the ECHR guarantees certain property rights. In conjunction with article 14, either article 8 or article 1 of the first protocol may allow a person to complain that he or she has been discriminated against on one ground or another in relation to housing or the use of premises. Only public authorities and bodies with mixed public and private functions are directly liable to individuals under the HRA 1998, although courts and tribunals must interpret legislation in accordance with it.

Adjudication structure

1.51 Employment cases under the SDA 1975, EqPA 1970, RRA 1976, DDA 1995 and ERA 1996 can only be brought in ETs.[101] The Employment Tribunals Act 1996[102] consolidates statutes relating to employment tribunals and the Employment Appeal Tribunal (EAT). Regulations cover all procedural aspects of employment cases.[103]

1.52 The county courts hear cases under the SDA 1975, RRA 1976 and DDA 1995 in areas other than employment. Cases under the HRA 1998 are dealt with in the most appropriate tribunal or court, depending on the nature of the complaint.[104] The Civil Procedure Rules deal with procedure in the civil courts.

1.53 Once the education-related amendments to the DDA 1995 made by SENDA 2001 are in force, they will extend the jurisdiction of the Special Educational Needs Tribunal and change its name to the Special Educational Needs and Disability Tribunal. This extended jurisdiction will permit the tribunal to hear certain complaints brought under the DDA 1995. The structure of tribunals and courts and the relevant procedures are fully explained in chapter 32.

100 *Niemitz v Germany* (1997) 23 EHRR 513.
101 Formerly industrial tribunals.
102 Formerly the Industrial Tribunals Act 1996.
103 Employment Tribunals (Constitution and Rules of Procedure) Regulations 2001 SI No 1171.
104 HRA 1998 s7.

Interpretation of discrimination law

1.54 The complexity of discrimination and equal pay law has been the subject of much judicial comment. It is always worth bearing in mind the purpose of the legislation. In *Jones v Tower Boot Co Ltd*[105] the Court of Appeal had no hesitation in holding that a purposive interpretation should be adopted. According to Waite LJ:

> The legislation now represented by the Race and Sex Discrimination Acts currently in force broke new ground in seeking to work upon the minds of men and women and thus affect their attitude to the social consequences of differences between the sexes and of skin colour. Its general thrust was educative, persuasive, and (where necessary) coercive. The relief accorded to the victims (or potential victims) of discrimination went beyond the ordinary remedies of damages and injunction – introducing, through declaratory powers in the court or tribunal and recommendatory powers in the relevant Commission, provisions with a pro-active function, designed as much to eliminate the occasions for discrimination as to compensate its victims or punish its perpetrators ... Consistently with the broad front on which it operates, the legislation has traditionally been given a wide interpretation.[106]

Waite LJ then quoted approvingly from *Savjani v IRC*:[107]

> ... the Act was brought in to remedy a very great evil. It is expressed in very wide terms, and I should be slow to find that the effect of something which is humiliatingly discriminatory in racial matters falls outside the ambit of the Act.

The same principles apply to sex discrimination.

1.55 In *London Underground v Edwards (No 2)*[108] (a case about the impact of anti-social hours on a female lone parent), the EAT echoed the view expressed by the Court of Appeal in *R v Employment Secretary ex p Seymour Smith*[109] that the purpose of the ETD was to eliminate all sex discrimination in the employment field: 'Equality of treatment is the paramount consideration'. In *Edwards,* Morison J declared for the EAT that:

> ... the more clear it is that the employers unreasonably failed to show

105 [1995] IRLR 464.
106 Ibid para 31.
107 [1981] 1 QB 458 at 466.
108 [1997] IRLR 157, para 22. The EAT's decision in the case was upheld by the CA at [1998] IRLR 364.
109 [1995] IRLR 464.

flexibility in their employment practices, the more willing the Tribunal should be to make a finding of unlawful discrimination.[110]

1.56 The principles applying to equal treatment were aptly summarised by the Advocate General in *P v S and Cornwall County Council*,[111] in which he expressed his 'profound conviction' that:

> ... what is at stake is a universal fundamental value, indelibly etched in modern legal traditions and in the constitutions of the more advanced countries: *the irrelevance of a person's sex with regard to the rules regulating relations in society* [his emphasis].

1.57 In the context of disability, the EAT, in overturning an ET decision that a person with paranoid schizophrenia was not disabled, expressed the approach in this way:

> A tribunal should bear in mind that with social legislation of this kind, a purposive approach to construction should be adopted. The language should be construed in a way which gives effect to the stated or natural meaning of the words.[112]

Thus a broad and purposive interpretation should be given to the SDA 1975, the RRA 1976 and the DDA 1995. In addition, as the SDA 1975, RRA 1976 and DDA 1995 form part of a 'trio of Acts ... which contain similar statutory provisions although directed at different forms of discrimination, it is legitimate if necessary to consider [all of] those Acts on resolving any issue of interpretation which may arise [under either one of those Acts]'.[113a] Furthermore, as stated above, a court is bound to interpret legislation consistently with EC law and to disapply any provision inconsistent with directly effective EC law.[113] A court or tribunal is also under a statutory obligation to interpret all legislation consistently with the convention rights incorporated by the HRA 1998, so far as it is possible to do so.[114]

110 [1997] IRLR 157, para 32. An appeal to the Court of Appeal was dismissed at [1998] IRLR 364.

111 Case 13/94 [1996] ECR I-2143, [1996] IRLR 347, para 24.

112 *Goodwin v Patent Office* [1999] IRLR 4.

113 *Litster v Forth Dry Dock and Engineering Co Ltd* [1989] 2 WLR 634, [1989] IRLR 161; Case 271/91 *Marshall v Southampton and South-West Hampshire Area Health Authority (No 2)* [1993] ECR I-4367, [1993] IRLR 445.

113a *Anyanwu and another v South Bank Students' Union and others* [2001] IRLR 305, HL; per Lord Bingham at para 2.

114 HRA 1998 s3.

CHAPTER 2

Grounds of discrimination

continued

Key points

2.1
- Discrimination on grounds of sex, married status, gender reassignment, race (widely defined) and disability is regulated by express domestic legislative provisions.
- The protection afforded in relation to the various grounds of discrimination varies. For example, direct and indirect discrimination on grounds of sex, married status and race are regulated (though, in the case of married status, only in the employment field). Only direct discrimination on grounds of gender reassignment is regulated (again, only in connection with employment and vocational training). Disability discrimination is defined very differently and includes less favourable treatment and some (but not all) cases of indirect discrimination (see chapter 6), and the duty on employers to make reasonable adjustments to prevent a disabled person from being at a substantial disadvantage in the work place.
- Definitions of indirect discrimination also differ between, on the one hand, employment-related discrimination on grounds of sex and marriage and, on the other hand, race discrimination and discrimination on grounds of sex and married status outside the employment context.
- UK domestic provisions must be read in the light of the European Convention on Human Rights (ECHR) , incorporated into domestic law by the Human Rights Act (HRA) 1998.
- Domestic sex discrimination employment-related provisions (including those concerning married status and gender reassignment) must also be read in the light of EC provisions. This will not be the case for race and disability discrimination until 2003 and 2006 respectively, when the Race Directive (RD) and the Employment Directive (ED) come into force.

Background and statutory provisions

2.2 This chapter considers the different grounds of discrimination regulated by domestic and EC law. Domestic provisions provide relatively comprehensive protection against discrimination on grounds of race, sex and disability (and, in Northern Ireland, religious belief or opinion and political belief),[1] and provide some protection against employment and vocational training-related discrimination on grounds of married status and gender reassignment. The statutory regulation of discrimination covers workers (not just employees) and does not depend on the number of hours worked or length of service (see paras 11.28–11.44 below).

2.3 Race, sex and disability as prohibited grounds of discrimination are explored in this chapter. They cannot, however, be considered in isolation from other grounds of discrimination such as age, and sexual orientation. The Employment Directive (ED),[2] which must be implemented in the UK by 2003–06,[3] regulates discrimination on grounds of sexual orientation, religion and belief, age and disability. The last of these grounds is already the subject of UK-wide domestic legislation, and is considered at paras 2.49–2.105 below. The others, however, will require the adoption of new legislative provisions. They will be considered in chapters 8 and 9.

2.4 The ED applies only to employment-related discrimination (broadly defined – see further chapter 10). But article 14 ECHR regulates discrimination 'on any ground such as sex, race, colour, language, religion, political or other opinion, national or social origin, association with a national minority, property, birth or other status'. Article 14 has been incorporated into domestic law by the HRA 1998. The reach of this article is limited by its application only to the 'enjoyment of the rights and freedoms set forth in this Convention'. But, as will be seen below and in chapter 9, it is not without significance for domestic discrimination law.

2.5 The 'discrimination' regulated by domestic provisions varies between the grounds covered. So, for example, while direct and indirect discrimination on grounds of sex, married status and race are regulated, only direct discrimination on grounds of gender reassignment is prohibited by the Sex Discrimination Act (SDA) 1975. The Disability Discrimination Act (DDA) 1995 does not employ the terminology of 'direct' and 'indirect' discrimination. Instead, it prohibits less favourable treatment 'for a reason which relates to' a disabled person's disability, and defines as discrimination a failure to make reasonable accommodation of a disabled person's needs. And whereas

1 In particular of race: see paras 1.37–1.38, 2.32–2.46 and 5.26 for example.

2 Council Directive 2000/78/EC.

3 December 2003 in respect of discrimination on grounds of sexual orientation and religion and belief, 2006 in respect of discrimination on grounds of age and disability.

no general justification of direct discrimination is permitted under the Race Relations Act (RRA) 1976 or the SDA 1975, the DDA 1995 does permit the justification of all disability discrimination. The definitions of indirect discrimination applicable to sex and married status in the employment context, furthermore, differ from those which apply elsewhere.[4]

2.6 The range of protection accorded in respect of the various grounds of discrimination also differs. Discrimination in connection with gender reassignment or married status is regulated only in the employment and vocational training context (and then only, in the former case, if the discrimination is 'direct'[5]). Race discrimination, on the other hand, is regulated also in relation to housing, education, and the pro-vision of goods and services both by private suppliers and by public authorities.[6]

2.7 EC law, the ECHR and HRA 1998 have been mentioned above. The UK statutory provisions regulating discrimination must be read in the context of both. At present, and until 2003, EC law regulates only employment-related discrimination on grounds of sex and gender reassignment. The RD,[7] which must be implemented in the UK by July 2003, extends the reach of EC law to race discrimination both within and outside the employment sphere. And the ED further extends the scope of EC law to employment-related discrimination on grounds of sexual orientation, disability, age and religion or belief. The implications of these directives for race and disability discrimination will be explored briefly in this chapter as well as elsewhere in the book (chapters 10, 11 and 13), and the implications for discrimination on currently unregulated grounds in chapter 8.

Discrimination and the Human Rights Act 1998

2.8 The HRA 1998 has been mentioned above, as has article 14 ECHR. Its implications for discrimination on currently unregulated grounds are considered in chapters 8 and 10. But the HRA 1998 may also impact

4 This as a result of Council Directive 97/80/EC, implemented in the UK by the Sex Discrimination (Indirect Discrimination and Burden of Proof) Regulations 2001 SI No 2660.

5 See para 2.25.

6 The coverage of the RRA 1976 has been extended to cover public authorities by the Race Relations (Amendment) Act 2000 – see further paras 1.37–1.38.

7 Council Directive 2000/43/EC.

on the interpretation of those statutory provisions which regulate race, sex and disability discrimination.

2.9 The HRA 1998 provides (s6) that it is unlawful for a public authority to act incompatibly with a convention right unless required by legislation so to do. Section 3 requires that the courts interpret legislative provisions, where possible, so as to accord with the convention provisions. To the extent, therefore, that domestic legislation leaves unregulated a ground of discrimination[8] which is actionable under the ECHR, the HRA 1998 would provide a means to challenge it. This could be done directly (by suing the public authority under HRA 1998 s7 for breach of HRA 1998 s6). Alternatively, where the discrimination at issue could be regulated by means of creative interpretation of an existing statutory provision, the courts' interpretive obligations under s3 could be relied upon. These issues are considered further in chapter 9.

2.10 The HRA 1998 provides a remedy only in respect of discrimination which is contrary to the ECHR. Article 14, which regulates discrimination, does so only where the discrimination concerns 'the enjoyment of any of the rights and freedoms' guaranteed by the convention. Whereas, as shall be seen below, this restriction is relatively unproblematic where sexual orientation or religious discrimination is at issue (these being within the scope of articles 8 and 9 ECHR respectively), the position is more complex when it comes to discrimination connected with disability or age. Whether such discrimination contravenes the convention depends on the circumstances in which it takes place.[9] Further, the application of the convention rights in the context of employment appears to be heavily circumscribed by the European Court of Human Rights' recognition of the balancing interests of employers. These issues are considered as relevant below and in chapter 9.

'Sex' and related grounds of discrimination

Sex discrimination

2.11 The SDA 1975 regulates direct and indirect discrimination on grounds of sex (s1) and married (but not unmarried) status (s3), but in connection

8 Or see discussion of *Amin v Entry Clearance Officer, Bombay* [1983] 2 AC 818 (paras 2.15–2.16 below), a type of discrimination (such as certain types of sex discrimination by the Crown).

9 See eg *Botta v Italy* (1998) 4 BHRC 81 and *Nelson v UK* (1986) 49 DR 170.

with gender reassignment only regulates direct discrimination (s2A). Both women and men are protected (s2), with the effect that 'positive' discrimination in favour of women (ie, discrimination against men) is unlawful except where it falls within the very limited 'positive action' provisions (see further chapter 5). 'Woman' includes a female of any age and 'man' a male of any age.

2.12 The Equal Pay Act (EqPA) 1970 provides that a woman (or man) is entitled to the same contractual terms (including pay) as those employed by a suitable comparator of the opposite sex, unless the employer can show that any difference is genuinely due to a material factor other than sex. A suitable 'comparator', as we see in chapter 22 is one who is employed, broadly, by the same employer in the same workplace, on 'like work', 'work rated as equivalent' or work of equal value to that done by the equal pay applicant.

2.13 Any less favourable treatment of a woman because she is pregnant or on maternity leave is automatically sex discrimination (see para 16.13). However, during maternity leave it is not clear whether a woman can bring an EqPA 1970 claim comparing herself with a man not on leave (see further para 18.33).

2.14 The EC provisions dealing with sex discrimination are article 141 EC and the Equal Pay Directive (EPD),[10] which regulate discrimination in relation to 'pay' very broadly defined, and the Equal Treatment Directive (ETD),[11] which regulates other employment-related discrimination. Article 141 is directly effective both vertically and horizontally, and so takes precedence over any inconsistent domestic provisions (see chapter 10). The ETD has vertical direct effect but, where the employer is in the private sector, imposes only interpretive obligations in respect of domestic provisions (see further chapter 10).

2.15 The HRA 1998 may provide protection where there is a gap in UK or EC law. The likely area for litigation in the sex discrimination context is the application of the prohibition on discrimination in the provision of goods and services in SDA 1975. The House of Lords decided, in *Amin v Entry Clearance Officer, Bombay*,[12] that this provision applied only to those activities of the Crown which resembled those carried out by private actors. The decision placed activities such as immigration control and aspects of tax control and policing, among other things, beyond the scope of the anti-discrimination legislation. Its impact was largely removed, in the race discrimination

10 Council Directive 75/117/EEC.

11 Council Directive 76/207/EEC.

12 [1983] 2 AC 818.

field, by the Race Relations (Amendment) Act 2000, further considered in chapter 29. No amendments have, as yet, been made to the SDA 1975 or the DDA 1995.

2.16 The possible application of the HRA 1998 has been mentioned above. Taking the facts in *Amin* itself, sex discrimination in immigration rules *might* amount to a breach of article 8 (the right to family life) read with article 14. Assuming a breach were established, it would contravene HRA 1998 s6 unless required (broadly speaking) by primary legislation. Alternatively, the courts might regard themselves as constrained by HRA 1998 s3 to interpret the SDA 1975 so as to apply, contra *Amin*, to immigration.

Married status

2.17 The prohibition on marital discrimination only applies to employment. It is worth reiterating that SDA 1975 s2 regulates only discrimination against married people. The ETD refers to *sex* discrimination on grounds of marital or family status. In *Murray v Navy Army Air Force Institute*[13] an employment tribunal (ET) held that the ETD went no further than the SDA 1975 in this respect. The prohibition by SDA 1975 on this form of discrimination does not apply to engaged but unmarried people, nor to other single people whether or not they cohabit or have children. A comparator for the purposes of SDA 1975 s3, whether real or hypothetical, must be an unmarried person of the same sex as the married applicant. Discrimination as between a married woman and an unmarried man may, on the other hand, amount to direct or indirect sex discrimination (see further para 2.11 and chapter 7).

2.18 Any discrimination against 'lone parents' (understood as referring to those with primary care of children) may be unlawful indirect discrimination (see further chapter 7) because of the disproportionately female composition of this group. The Employment Act 1989 and accompanying regulations, however, permit some discrimination in favour of lone parents (and, therefore, against married persons) in relation to training.

13 (1998) DCLD 36.

Gender reassignment

2.19 There are an estimated 5,000 people in the UK who have undergone gender reassignment.[14] EC law treats discrimination connected with gender reassignment as discrimination on the ground of sex and so, it would appear, prohibits both direct and unjustified indirect discrimination on this ground, although only in the employment and vocational training context. In *P v S and Cornwall CC*[15] the European Court of Justice (ECJ) ruled that discrimination connected with gender reassignment breached the ETD. The case involved the dismissal of the applicant who had been employed as a man, in connection with her decision to undergo gender reassignment treatment.[16] The ECJ ruled that discrimination on grounds of gender reassignment was discrimination on grounds sex of contrary to the ETD. The court reasoned that such discrimination was based 'essentially if not exclusively, on the sex of the person concerned'.

2.20 The decision in *P v S and Cornwall CC* had the effect that the SDA 1975, as it applied to public authorities (emanations of the state), had to be interpreted to prohibit discrimination connected with gender reassignment. In 1997, in *Chessington World of Adventures Ltd v Reed*, the Employment Appeal Tribunal (EAT) held that it was possible to interpret the SDA 1975 so as to prohibit discrimination in connection with gender reassignment, with the effect that the judgment in *P v S and Cornwall CC* applied to those working in the private as well as the public sector.[17] The Sex Discrimination (Gender Reassignment) Regulations (GR Regulations) 1999[18] amended the SDA 1975 to prohibit direct discrimination, in the employment context,[19] on the ground that a person intends to undergo, is undergoing, or has undergone gender reassignment.

14 *A Guide to the Sex Discrimination (Gender Reassignment) Regulations 1999 SI 1999 No 1102*, available free from Prolog Ltd, PO Box 5050, Sudbury, Suffolk CO10 6QZ, tel 0845 6022260.

15 Case 13/94 [1996] ECR I-2143; [1996] IRLR 347.

16 In all cases concerning transsexuals it is good practice to use language that recognises the desired gender of the person in question. This chapter follows that practice, which should always be adopted in litigation.

17 [1998] IRLR 56. See chapter 10.

18 SI No1102. The Sex Discrimination (Northern Ireland) Order 1976 was amended by the Sex Discrimination (Gender Reassignment) Regulations (Northern Ireland) 1999 SI No 311 to cover transsexuals from 1 August 1999.

19 The ETD does not extend beyond the employment context. The coverage of the GR Regulations 1999 is to SDA 1975 Pts II and III. See chapter 11.

Statutory protection

2.21 The SDA 1975 (s2A) now prohibits direct discrimination against a person on the grounds that he or she intends to undergo, is undergoing or has undergone gender reassignment.[20] 'Gender reassignment' is defined for the purposes of the SDA 1975 as 'a process which is undertaken under medical supervision for the purpose of reassigning a person's sex by changing physiological or other characteristics of sex, and includes any part of such a process'. Protection starts from the time that the person *intends* to undergo such treatment, rather than when he or she actually starts it.

2.22 The SDA 1975, rather than the EqPA 1970, regulates discrimination in pay and other contractual terms in connection with gender reassignment.[21] 'Discrimination' includes less favourable treatment in the application of arrangements for any absence due to the need to undergo gender reassignment treatment.[22] But SDA 1975 s2A(3) states that the comparison in such a case is with a person who is absent as a result of sickness or injury or someone whose absence is due to some other cause. The amended SDA 1975 provides for genuine occupational qualification exceptions to the prohibition on this form of discrimination. These are considered in chapter 11.

2.23 One of the very earliest gender reassignment cases taken under the SDA 1975 after its amendment by the GR Regulations 1999 was *O'Keefe v National School of Hypnosis and Advanced Psychotherapy*,[23] which involved discrimination against a woman clinical hypnotherapist and psychotherapist in connection with her employer's discovery that she had been born a man. Dr O'Keefe won her sex discrimination case.

Possible gaps in domestic protection

2.24 Rather more complex is the situation in which a worker is discriminated against because of the relationship between his/her sex and that of his/her partner. This issue is considered in the context of sexual orientation discrimination at paras 8.5–8.26. It also arose, in connection with gender reassignment, in *KB v NHS Pensions Agency and Secretary of State for Health*.[24] The case, which pre-dated the GR Regula-

20 SDA 1975 s2A as amended by the GR Regs.
21 Ibid s6(8).
22 Ibid s2A(3).
23 Case 6000264/99 (unreported).
24 14 December 2000, unreported, although the EAT's decision is reported at [1999] ICR 1192.

tions 1999, concerned the position of an NHS worker whose partner had been born female but had undergone gender reassignment. The NHS pension scheme only made provision for a surviving 'spouse'. Under UK law, the applicant's partner was considered a woman and so marriage between them was not possible. This will change following the ECtHR ruling in *Goodwin v UK*.[24a] The lower courts, having ruled that the situation was akin rather to *Grant v South West Trains* (see chapter 8)[25] than to *P v S and Cornwall CC*, had rejected the applicant's claim under article 141 and the ETD. The Court of Appeal has referred to the ECJ the question whether such discrimination is contrary to EC law. The judgment is awaited.

Indirect discrimination connected with gender reassignment – domestic and EC approaches

2.25 The SDA 1975, as amended, does not regulate *indirect* discrimination on grounds of gender reassignment. It is likely, however, that such discrimination contravenes EC law. The ETD, under which the decision in *P v S and Cornwall CC* was reached, requires the UK government to prohibit 'any discrimination whatsoever on grounds of sex' as regards working conditions. The directive specifically refers to direct and indirect discrimination.[26] Accordingly, the 1999 amendments to the SDA 1975 are almost certainly inadequate to implement the ETD.

Protecting gender-reassigned litigants

2.26 Many of those discriminated against in connection with their gender reassignment will be unwilling to take legal action if it entails their public identification. The ET Rules[27] have no specific provision for protecting the identity of applicants in this context. But article 6 ETD requires that those wronged by a failure to comply with the directive must be provided with an effective remedy. The EAT ruled as a preliminary issue in *Chief Constable of West Yorkshire Police v A*[28] that this provision entitled the court to make a permanent restricted reporting

24a Application 28957/95; 11 July 2002. See para 2.29 below.

25 Case 249/96 [1998] ECR I-621; [1998] IRLR 206.

26 ETD art 4.

27 ET Rules of Procedure, scheduled to the ET (Constitution and Rules of Procedure) Regulations 2001 SI No 1171. These supersede the ET (Constitution and Procedure) Regulations 1993.

28 [2000] IRLR 465.

order in a gender reassignment case. The High Court has jurisdiction to make a similar order.[28a]

Good practice guidance

2.27 The UK Parliamentary Forum on Transsexualism has produced a code of practice regarding discrimination on grounds of transsexualism.[29] This makes a number of recommendations about how employers should develop their equal opportunities procedures and adapt their harassment policies to cover transsexuals. It also provides examples of good employment practice in this context. In particular, the code recommends that consideration should be given to 'strategies which minimise personal exposure'. This can include updating personnel records to reflect workers' current names, titles and sex and agreeing in advance the process and procedures to be adopted during a worker's gender reassignment.

Gender reassignment and the Human Rights Act 1998

2.28 The SDA 1975 does not regulate discrimination in connection with gender reassignment outside the field of employment and vocational training. Given the application of the relevant provisions of EC law to employment alone, the only source for challenge to other manifestations of discrimination consists of the ECHR as implemented in the UK by the HRA 1998.

2.29 It is likely that article 8 ECHR, when read with article 14 ECHR, will be used to protect against discrimination on the ground of gender reassignment. For a long period the European Court of Human Rights (ECtHR) ruled in a series of cases that the UK government's refusal to permit the amendment of birth certificates to acknowledge the true sex of gender reassigned transsexuals was within the government's 'margin of appreciation'.[30] However, in the case of *Goodwin v UK*[31] that have now ruled that this continuing refusal is in breach of articles 8 and 12 ECHR. They observed:

> In short, the unsatisfactory situation in which post-operative transsexuals live in an intermediate zone as not quite on gender or another is no longer sustainable.[32]

28a CPR Pt 39.2

29 Published by Press for Change, 1998.

30 See para 9.18 below.

31 Application No 28957/95, judgment 11 July 2002.

32 Ibid para 90.

This means that the government will have to legislate to permit gender reassigned transsexuals to alter their birth certificates and to permit them to marry in their new gender. The appropriate means for implementing this change is within the government's 'margin of appreciation'. However, it will have far reaching effects for gender reassigned transsexual who have been prevented from receiving their rights by their inability to change their birth certificates. It is disappointing that once again the ECtHR has failed to make a separate finding under article 14 ECHR saying that no separate issue arises under article 14.

2.30 This means that none of the old cases of *Corbett v Corbett,*[33] *Rees v UK*[34] and *Sheffield and Horsham v UK*[35] which did not recognise the right of transsexuals to alter their birth certificates are likely to be followed.

Future developments

2.31 Transsexuals continue to suffer serious prejudice which has no place in a society based on equality. Following the decision in *Goodwin v UK*, this will have to change. There can be little doubt that, over time, the need for thorough-going protection against discrimination on grounds of gender reassignment will be recognised. Since article 13 EC enables the EU to legislate to prevent sex discrimination (which, according to the ECJ in *P v S and Cornwall CC*, includes discrimination in connection with gender reassignment), action from Europe may pave the way. Alternatively, the implementation of the proposed Single Equality Act in Northern Ireland could establish a model for modern equality legislation.[36] Finally, there remains a hope that the government will accept the freestanding protection in protocol 12 to the ECHR (see para 9.56). If the protocol was adopted and incorporated into domestic law it would provide a stronger legal basis for protection in connection with gender reassignment by removing the requirement that article 14 be read in connection with another convention article.

33 [1970] 2 All ER 33.

34 (1986) 9 EHRR 56.

35 (1999) 27 EHRR 163.

36 See *Programme for Government: Making a Difference 2001–2004*, Northern Ireland Executive, 2001 and *Position Paper: The Single Equality Bill*, Equality Commission for Northern Ireland, 2001.

Race discrimination

2.32 The RRA 1976, which regulates discrimination in employment, education, the provision of goods and services, prohibits discrimination on 'racial grounds'. These are, in turn, defined by s3 of the Act as being on grounds of colour, race, nationality, or ethnic or national origins.

2.33 Both direct and indirect discrimination are regulated by RRA 1976.[37] A 'racial group' is a group of people defined by reference to colour, race, nationality, ethnic or national origins; RRA 1976 s3(1) provides that a person can be a member of more than one racial group and that references to a person's racial group include any racial group into which they fall. Thus in *Orphanos v Queen Mary College*[38] the House of Lords concluded that a Cypriot could claim to belong to three racial groups: Cypriot, non-British or non-EC. A racial group may, further, be made up of two or more distinct racial groups for the purposes of the RRA 1976.[39]

Colour

2.34 Different treatment of members of the same racial group on the grounds of colour, for example, less favourable treatment of darker-skinned than lighter-skinned African-Caribbeans, would fall within the RRA 1976. In *Lambeth LBC v Commission for Racial Equality (CRE)*,[40] for example, the less favourable treatment of white applicants than that of a group comprising African-Caribbeans and Asians was discrimination on grounds of colour.

Nationality

2.35 The definition of nationality used in the RRA 1976 includes citizenship.[41] With the exception of some stateless people, nationality is acquired by everybody at birth. It can be altered by choice as well as being unilaterally removed.

37 For instance, indirect discrimination occurs when an unjustifiable requirement or condition applied to the applicant is one which is to his or her detriment because he or she cannot comply with it, and is also one with which a considerably smaller proportion of the applicant's 'racial group' than of others can comply – see further para 7.8.

38 [1985] AC 761; [1985] IRLR 349.

39 See RRA 1976 s3(2).

40 [1990] IRLR 230.

41 RRA 1976 s78(1).

2.36 In *Northern Joint Police Board v Power*,[42] the EAT held that 'nationality' and 'national origins' have different meanings for the purposes of the RRA 1976. Within the context of England, Scotland, Northern Ireland and Wales, the proper approach to 'nationality' is to categorise all as falling under the 'British' umbrella, and to regard the population as citizens of the UK. Thus, less favourable treatment of, say, Scottish people is not discrimination on grounds of *nationality*. However, England and Scotland were once separate nations and an allegation of discrimination on the basis of *national origins* (paras 2.37–2.42 below) could be made in relation to the different treatment of English and Scottish people. The same reasoning ought to apply to discrimination against a Welsh or Irish person.

National origins

2.37 In *Northern Joint Police Board v Power*,[43] the EAT accepted that English and Scottish people were of different 'national origins', with the effect that discrimination against an English police officer (because he was not Scottish) was race discrimination for the purposes of the RRA 1976.[43a]

2.38 In *Tejani v Superintendent Registrar*[44] the Court of Appeal concluded that 'national origins' refers to a particular place or country of origin. So, where an applicant was treated less favourably on the grounds that he was born abroad, without reference to any particular place or country, the court found that there was no discrimination on grounds of national origin. This was so even where a person born in the UK would not have been treated in the same way.

2.39 This judgment has been strongly criticised. It would appear to permit discrimination against those from 'abroad' provided that no particular country is mentioned. The narrow approach taken to the meaning of 'national origins' is arguably inconsistent with a purposive approach to the construction of the RRA 1976. The judgment in *Tejani* arguably also fails to take into account the definition of racial grounds in RRA 1976 s3(2) which makes it clear that the fact that a racial group is made up of two or more distinct racial groups does not prevent it from constituting a particular racial group for the purposes of the Act.

42 [1997] IRLR 610.

43 Ibid.

43a The same approach was followed in *BBC Scotland v Souster* [2001] IRLR 150, see also para 2.47 below.

44 [1986] IRLR 502.

2.40 In *Orphanos v Queen Mary College*[45] (which was not cited to the court in *Tejani*) the House of Lords was asked to determine a claim of indirect discrimination on grounds of nationality. Mr Orphanos alleged that a policy of charging 'overseas' students higher fees than 'home' students,[46] amounted to indirect discrimination on grounds of nationality. Their Lordships accepted that a complainant could be a member of a number of racial groups and that racial groups could be defined negatively as, for example, non-British or non-EU. The observations of the House of Lords on this point are obiter but they are likely to be of persuasive value in seeking to challenge the analysis adopted in *Tejani*.

2.41 In *Gwynedd CC v Jones*[47] the EAT rejected the argument that the 'Welsh' nation and ethnic group could be sub-divided into Welsh-speaking and non-Welsh-speaking nations and ethnic groups. The case concerned discrimination against Welsh people on grounds they were not Welsh-speaking.

2.42 Someone who has two national origins (for example, an English mother and an Irish father) can belong to both racial groups.

Ethnic origins

2.43 The term 'ethnic origins' is wider than the term 'racial origins'. The term 'ethnic origins' is to be construed in a broad cultural and historical sense. In *Mandla v Dowell Lee*,[48] which remains the leading case, the House of Lords ruled that an 'ethnic group' must regard itself, and be regarded by others, as a distinct community. Their Lordships identified at least two characteristics as essential to this end. First, the group must have a long, shared history whose memory it keeps alive and which consciously distinguishes it from other groups. Second, the group must have a cultural tradition of its own, including family and social customs and manners, often, but not necessarily, associated with religious observance. The House of Lords identified a number of other relevant characteristics, one or more of which will be commonly found in an ethnic minority group and will help to distinguish that group from the wider community. These are:

- either a common geographical origin or descent from a small number of common ancestors;

45 [1985] IRLR 349.

46 Home students being defined as those ordinarily resident in the UK or other EC country for at least three years before 1982.

47 [1986] ICR 833.

48 [1983] 2 AC 548; [1983] IRLR 209.

- a common language, not necessarily peculiar to the group;
- a common literature peculiar to the group;
- a common religion different from that of the neighbouring groups or from the general community surrounding it; and
- a sense of being a minority or being an oppressed or dominant group within a larger community.

Applying these tests, the House of Lords concluded that Sikhs were a distinct racial group within the meaning of RRA 1976. Their Lordships also agreed that a person could fall into a particular racial group either by birth or by adopting and following the customs of the group; provided a person feels a member and is accepted as such, that is sufficient.[49]

Ethnicity and religion

2.44 Where a religious group is also a group linked by ethnic origin, its members will be protected by the RRA 1976 from discrimination connected with their membership of the group. So, for example, Jewish people have been recognised as a racial group for the purposes of the RRA 1976[50] while Muslims and Christians, who come from many ethnic groups, are not so protected.

2.45 Neither Rastafarians nor Muslims have been accepted as distinct ethnic groups for the purposes of the RRA 1976. In *Dawkins v Department of the Environment*[51] the Court of Appeal decided that, although Rastafarians were a separate group with identifiable characteristics, they did not meet the definition of an ethnic group, in part at least, because their shared history (then 60 years) was not sufficiently long. And tribunals have refused to accept Muslims as a distinct ethnic group because of the religion's geographical spread.[52] Having said this, discrimination against Muslims (direct or indirect) may amount to indirect race discrimination given that, in the UK, the largest constituent ethnic group of Muslims derives from the Indian subcontinent.[53] This issue is further considered at chapter 7 and para 8.29 below.

49 Per Lord Fraser with whom Lords Edmund-Davies, Roskill and Brandon expressly agreed and Lord Templeman appeared to concur.

50 *Seide v Gillette Industries* [1980] IRLR 427.

51 [1993] IRLR 284.

52 See also *Nyazi* v *Rymans Ltd*, EAT/6/8 (unreported, available on LEXIS).

53 See, eg, the facts in *Walker* v *Hussain* [1996] IRLR 11.

2.46 The Court of Appeal has ruled that 'Gypsies' constitute an ethnic group within *Mandla* if defined in the narrow sense of 'Romanies'.[54] This was so because of the group's shared history, geographical origin, distinct customs and language. The court also ruled that a racial group remained a racial group even if a substantial proportion of its membership assimilated to the dominant group, as long as there remained a discernible minority of the group which adhered to its culture and customs. The Race Relations (Northern Ireland) Order 1997,[55] which implements the RRA 1976 in Northern Ireland, expressly recognises the 'Irish Traveller Community' as a racial group. In any case Irish Travellers have been held to be a 'racial group' defined by reference to ethnicity for the purposes of RRA 1976.[56]

2.47 In *BBC Scotland v Souster* the Court of Sessions held that the English and Scots are racial groups on the basis of their *national* origins but not by reference to their *ethnic* origins.[57] The court held that the concept of nationality is not restricted to citizenship but can cover cases where nationality has been acquired by marriage or adoption or where the individual claims to have been discriminated against because he or she is perceived to have become a member of a racial group.

Discrimination on grounds of another's race

2.48 The courts have held that the words 'racial grounds' are capable of covering any reason or action based on race, including the race of another. In *Showboat Entertainment Centre Ltd v Owens*[58] the EAT upheld a complaint of race discrimination brought by a white employee who was sacked for refusing to follow an instruction to exclude black people from the place that he worked. And in *Weathersfield (trading as Van & Truck Rentals) v Sargent*[59] the Court of Appeal upheld a complaint brought under the RRA 1976 by a receptionist sacked for failing to carry out instructions to discriminate against black customers. There the court stated that upholding her complaint involved giving a broad meaning to the expression 'racial grounds', but that this was a justifiable and appropriate approach to the legislation.

54 *CRE* v *Dutton* [1989] IRLR 8.

55 Race Relations (Northern Ireland) Order 1997 SI No 869, NI 6.

56 *O'Leary v Allied Domecq Inns Ltd*, CL950275, July 2000 (unreported).

57 [2001] IRLR 150.

58 [1984] IRLR 7.

59 [1999] IRLR 94.

Discrimination in connection with disability

2.49 The DDA 1995 regulates discrimination in employment, in the provision of goods, facilities and services, (to a limited extent) in education, and in public transport. The DDA 1995 prohibits discrimination 'for a reason which *relates to the disabled person's disability*', unless it can be shown to be justified. 'Disability' is defined in accordance with the Act (see below). By contrast with the SDA 1975 and the RRA 1976, the DDA 1995 adopts an asymmetrical approach to discrimination: whereas the SDA 1975 and RRA 1976 prohibit discrimination against men as well as women, white as well as black, the DDA 1995 prohibits discrimination only against 'disabled persons'[60] (defined to include those who have had a disability in the past[61]). Only the victimisation provisions may be used by those who are not disabled. The aim of the DDA 1995 is to level the playing field for disabled people and the Act does not regulate positive discrimination in favour of the disabled.

Definition of 'disability'

2.50 A statutory definition of disability is contained in DDA 1995 ss1 and 2 supplemented by Schs 1 and 2; the Disability Discrimination (Meaning of Disability) Regulations (DD Regulations) 1996,[62] and statutory guidance issued by the Secretary of State for Education and Employment under DDA 1995 s3[63] (the Guidance). The Guidance states that, in the vast majority of cases, there is unlikely to be any doubt whether or not a person has or has had a disability. The Guidance is intended to provide assistance in marginal cases and cannot be used in clear cases as an extra hurdle for an applicant to jump.[64]

2.51 The Guidance is not intended to be an authoritative definition of disability. It is not legally binding. But a court or ET that has to decide issues related to the definition of disability must take into account any aspects of the Guidance which appear to it to be relevant.

2.52 The burden of proof is on the applicant to prove that he or she is

60 A 'disabled person' is a person who has a disability for the purposes of the DDA 1995: DDA 1995 s1(2)

61 Ibid s2(1).

62 SI No 1455.

63 Guidance On Matters to be Taken Into Account in Determining Questions Relating to the Definition of Disability (HMSO, 1996).

64 *Vicary v British Telecommunications plc* [1999] IRLR 680; *Goodwin v Patent Office* [1999] IRLR 4.

disabled. In order to be regarded as 'disabled' for the purposes of the DDA 1995:

- a person must have an impairment;
- the impairment must have an adverse effect;
- the adverse effect must be substantial;
- the substantial adverse effect must be long term; and
- the long term substantial effect must affect normal day to day activities.

Impairment

2.53 Although it is the starting point of the definition of disability under the DDA 1995, the term 'impairment' is not defined either in the DDA 1995 or in the Guidance. It means some damage, defect, disorder or disease, compared with a person having a full set of physical and mental equipment in normal condition. A reference to a person having a 'physical or mental impairment' means simply that the person has something wrong with them physically or mentally.[65]

2.54 The World Health Organisation's International 'Classification of Impairment, Disability and Handicap' (ICD) is a useful guide which defines 'impairment' as any loss or abnormality of psychological, physiological or anatomical structure or function. The Guidance makes it clear that sensory impairments such as those that affect vision or hearing are included within the definitions of physical or mental impairment.[66]

Physical impairment

2.55 Although 'physical impairment' is not defined or explained in the DDA 1995, many common and recognised conditions such as arthritis, epilepsy, cancer, diabetes, will qualify as physical impairments. If someone claims to be suffering from physical injury but the medical evidence is that the symptoms are the manifestation of the person's psychological state, rather than of any organic physical pathology, this 'functional or physical overlay' does not amount to a physical impairment for the purposes of the DDA 1995.

2.56 In *Rugamer v Sony Music Entertainment UK Ltd, McNicol v Balfour*

65 *Rugamer v Sony Music Entertainment UK Ltd, McNicol v Balfour Beatty Rail Maintenance Ltd* [2001] IRLR 644; *College of Ripon and York St John v Hobbs* [2002] IRLR 185.

66 Guidance, Pt I, para 12.

Beatty Rail Maintenance Ltd[67] the EAT ruled that the dividing line between a physical and mental impairment depended not on whether a physical or mental function or activity was affected, but rather on whether the nature of the impairment itself was physical or mental. This analysis sits uneasily with the assertion in the Guidance that it is not necessary to consider how an impairment was caused,[68] and with the more recent decision in *College of Ripon and York St John v Hobbs.*[69] There, a jointly instructed expert testified that symptoms of muscle cramps, twitching and muscle weakness were not attributable to an organic disease. The ET's decision that Dr Hobbs had a physical impairment was upheld by the EAT which ruled that it was unnecessary to distinguish between an underlying fault, shortcoming or defect of, or in, the body, on the one hand; and evidence of the manifestations or effects to the body, on the other. The question is whether there is evidence – either direct or by inference – that there was something physically wrong with the applicant.

2.57 The DD Regulations 1996 provide that addictions to, or dependency on, non-medically prescribed drugs or treatment do not amount to 'impairments' for the purposes of the Act. This means that dependency on alcohol, cigarettes or 'street-traded' drugs would not be a qualifying impairment. However, a disease which results from such a dependency or substance abuse, such as liver or lung disease, will amount to an impairment for the purposes of the DDA 1995.

Mental impairment

2.58 The term 'mental impairment' is defined in DDA 1995 Sch 1 as including an impairment resulting from or consisting of a mental illness only if it is a 'clinically well recognised illness'.[70]

2.59 A 'clinically well recognised illness' is one which is recognised by a respected body of medical opinion.[71] Mental impairment may be established by proof of a mental illness specifically mentioned as such in the ICD[72] or in some other classification of very wide professional acceptance, or proof by some other means of a medical illness

67 [2001] IRLR 644.

68 Guidance, Pt I, para 11.

69 [2002] IRLR 185.

70 DDA 1995 Sch 1(1). DDA 1995 s68 provides that the definition of 'mental impairment' used in the DDA 1995 is not the same as the special meaning of 'mental impairment' used in the Mental Health Act 1993.

71 Guidance, Pt I, para 14.

72 Guidance, Pt I, para 14; *Morgan v Staffordshire University* [2002] IRLR 190.

recognised by a respected body of medical opinion. The fourth possible route to establishing the existence of a mental impairment under the DDA 1995 would be proof by substantial and specific medical evidence of a mental impairment which neither results from nor consists of a mental illness. Loose descriptions such as 'anxiety', 'stress' or 'depression' are not used in the ICD, nor are they generally accepted terms. Of themselves, they are insufficient to establish a mental impairment. It is necessary – if mental impairment is disputed by a respondent – for an applicant to obtain a medical report identifying the mental illness by reference to the ICD or other classification system relied on. The report should also set out the symptoms of the applicant by reference to the diagnostic guidelines. A medical report from a GP may be sufficient – the EAT has stressed that a consultant psychiatrist's report will not be necessary in every case.[73] (See further paras 2.101–2.105 below.)

2.60 If a condition comes within the diagnostic guidelines of the ICD a mental impairment will have been identified, even if it does not warrant a diagnosis under another classification system such as the fourth edition of the *Diagnosis and Statistical Manual of Mental Disorders* (DSM-IV).[74] A mental illness identified in, for example, the DSM-IV, but not the ICD, would also be likely to be accepted as clinically well-recognised.

2.61 Conditions like schizophrenia,[75] clinical depression or anxiety that comes within the generalised anxiety disorder ICD classification,[76] agoraphobia, post-traumatic stress disorder,[77] bulimia nervosa,[78] gender identity dysphoria[79] and bi-polar affective disorder (formerly known as manic depression) are within the definition of mental impairment. But 'mental impairments' recognised for the purposes of the DDA 1955 are not limited to mental illnesses. The Guidance makes it clear that 'mental impairment' includes a wide range of

73 *Morgan v Staffordshire University* [2002] IRLR 190.

74 *Blackledge v London General Transport Services Ltd*, EAT 1073/00, 3 August 2001 (unreported, available on LEXIS).

75 *Goodwin v Patent Office* [1999] IRLR 4.

76 *Leonard v South Derbyshire Chamber of Commerce* [2001] IRLR 19; *Kapadia v Lambeth LBC* [2000] IRLR 14; *Morgan v Staffordshire University* [2002] IRLR 190.

77 *Abadeh v British Telecommunications* [2001] IRLR 23.

78 *Gittins v Oxford Radcliffe NHS Trust*, EAT 193/99, 4 May 2000 (unreported, available on LEXIS).

79 *Ashton v Chief Constable of West Mercia Constabulary*, EAT 1381/99, 27 July 2000, (unreported, available on LEXIS).

impairments, including learning difficulties, which relate to mental functioning.[80]

2.62 The diagnosis of a clinically well-recognised illness does not automatically lead to a finding that the employee will qualify as disabled. All parts of the DDA 1995 definition of disability must be met. In *Gittins v Oxford Radcliffe NHS Trust*,[81] for example, the EAT accepted that although a nurse with bulimia had a clinically well-recognised condition, she was not disabled within the terms of the DDA 1995 because the condition did not have a substantial effect on her day to day activities.

2.63 Specific behaviours which might otherwise fall within the definition of 'mental impairment' have been excluded by the DD Regulations 1996.[82] These are:

- a tendency to set fires;
- a tendency to steal;
- a tendency to physical or sexual abuse of other persons;
- exhibitionism;
- voyeurism;
- seasonal allergic rhinitis (ie, hayfever), except where it aggravates the effect of another condition;[83]
- addiction to or dependency on alcohol, nicotine, or any other substance (other than in consequence of the substance being medically prescribed).[84]

But an impairment caused by the addiction or substance – such as cirrhosis, cancer or delirium tremens – will be covered by the DDA 1995.

'Normal day to day activities'

2.64 An applicant's impairment – whether physical or mental – must have a *substantial adverse effect* on his or her ability to carry out *normal day to day activities* in order to bring the applicant within the definition of disability in DDA 1995. The model of disability in DDA 1995 is *functional*, being concerned with how a person's functions are actually affected, as opposed to how either the individual or society perceives

80 Guidance, Pt I, para 13.

81 EAT 193/99, 4 May 2000 (unreported, available on LEXIS).

82 DD Regs 1996 reg 4(1).

83 Ibid reg 4(2) and (3).

84 Ibid reg 3.

the person to be affected. People are not, therefore, protected by the DDA 1995 from prejudice based on groundless assumptions about the extent to which people with particular conditions or appearances are affected.[85]

2.65 The DDA 1995 provides that an impairment is to be treated as affecting a person's ability to carry out normal day to day activities if and only if it affects one or more of the following exhaustive list of capacities, abilities or capabilities:

- mobility;
- manual dexterity;
- physical co-ordination;
- continence;
- the ability to lift, carry or otherwise move everyday objects;
- speech, hearing or eyesight;
- memory or ability to concentrate, learn or understand;
- the perception of the risk of physical danger.[86]

Although the EAT has confidently stated that what is a 'normal day to day activity' is 'best left unspecified: easily recognised, but defined with difficulty',[87] the volume of case-law tells a different story. A number of principles have now been established.

2.66 In *Goodwin v Patent Office*[88] the EAT observed that people with disabilities are likely habitually to 'play down' the effect of their disabilities on their daily lives and develop coping mechanisms so that they can perform certain normal day to day activities. Consequently, the fact that a person can carry out certain normal day to day activities does not mean that his or her ability to carry out such activities is not impaired if, for example, he or she can only do them with difficulty. A disabled person might find certain activities harder, may take longer to perform then or be able to do them only in a particular way, or may find them painful or difficult to undertake.[89]

2.67 The focus of the DDA 1995 is on what a person cannot do, rather than what he or she can still do. Determining whether a person is disabled under the Act is not a question of balancing individual losses

85 An exception to this is made for people with severe disfigurements: DDA 1995 Sch 1, para 3(1) and Pt II; Guidance, paras A16 and 17. See paras 2.92–2.93 below.

86 DDA 1995 Sch 1, para 4.

87 *Goodwin v Patent Office* [1999] IRLR 4.

88 Ibid.

89 For example, in *Ekpe v Metropolitan Police Commissioner* [2001] IRLR 605, Mrs Ekpe could only scrub pans by holding them in the crook of her elbow because of a wasting of the intrinsic muscles of her right hand.

of function directly against retained ability. So, for example, a tribunal erred in contrasting an applicant's ability to eat, drink and catch a ball with her inability to negotiate pavement edges in order to conclude that her normal day to day activities were not substantially adversely affected.[90]

2.68 The importance of a tribunal looking at matters in the round has been reiterated and expressed in a variety of ways in the case-law and the Guidance.[91] The evidence must be taken as a whole in determining whether the impairment has had an adverse and substantial effect on any of the listed capacities. The tribunal must make an overall assessment and take a proper account of the overarching effect of the impairment.

2.69 In many cases it will be obvious that an impairment adversely affects a person's ability to carry out a range of normal day to day activities, and it will be obvious that the adverse effect is substantial. Where this is the case, a detailed consideration of precisely how a person is affected in relation to the matters listed above will be unnecessary.[92] The Guidance makes it clear that the purpose of the list is to provide help in cases where there may be doubt as to whether the effects on a person's normal day to day activities are substantial.[93] An unwavering following of the Guidance is discouraged. But where there is uncertainty about whether or not a person falls within the definition of a disabled person it will be important that specific reference is made to it.

2.70 In deciding whether an activity is a 'normal day to day activity' an ET or court should take account of how far it is normal for most people and carried out by most people on a daily or frequent and fairly regular basis.[94] An activity does not have to be done by both sexes to be 'normal'.[95] What is 'normal' has been defined as anything which is not abnormal or unusual.[96] Whether an activity is normal must be

90 *Leonard v South Derbyshire Chamber of Commerce* [2001] IRLR 19.

91 See, eg, *Ekpe v Metropolitan Police Commissioner* [2001] IRLR 605, *Leonard v South Derbyshire Chamber of Commerce* [2001] IRLR 19 and *Goodwin v Patent Office* [1999] IRLR 4.

92 Guidance, Pt II, para C5.

93 Ibid Pt II, para C12.

94 Ibid Pt II, para C2.

95 In *Ekpe v Metropolitan Police Commissioner* [2001] IRLR 605, the ET had wrongly concluded that since applying make-up and using hair rollers were activities only done by women (and not even all of them) they could not be said to be normal for most people as women account for only half the population.

96 *Ekpe*, ibid.

determined without regard to whether it is normal for the particular applicant. In *Abadeh v British Telecommunications plc*,[97] for example, the fact that travelling by underground and flying were not normal day to day activities for the applicant was not relevant. In addition, the question whether such travelling activities were 'normal day to day' activities should not be answered by reference to individual forms of transport, but by looking at transport as a whole.

2.71 A normal day to day activity is not necessarily a work activity.[98] But if an applicant's work includes normal day to day activities, evidence of that work and the way she or he performs it can be relevant.[99] Examples of activities that have been held to be 'normal day-to-day activities' include making beds, doing housework and minor DIY tasks, sewing,[100] travelling by underground or plane,[101] putting in hair rollers and applying make-up.[102] Account can be taken of symptoms which arise at work when there is an overlap between normal day to day activities and work activities.[103]

2.72 In *Cruikshank v Vaw Motorcast Ltd*[104] the EAT ruled that a person whose asthma was triggered by the work environment was entitled to judge the effect on his day to day activities by reference to his condition at work, even though his asthma was much worse while he was in the workplace and quickly improved when he was away from the fumes there.

2.73 Where the impairment is a mental illness (such as depression amounting to a generalised anxiety disorder) an adviser should always consider whether, because of the illness, the applicant is unable to sustain a physical activity over a reasonable period even if he or she has the physical ability to perform the task.[105]

2.74 The DDA 1995 contains special provisions relating to children.[106] If a child under six has an impairment which does not yet have an effect on his/her ability to carry out the 'normal day to day activities' listed in the Act (see para 2.65 above), the impairment is deemed to

97 [2001] IRLR 23.
98 Guidance, Pt II, para C3.
99 *Law Hospital NHS Trust v Rush* [2001] IRLR 611.
100 *Vicary v British Telecommunications plc* [1999] IRLR 680.
101 *Abadeh v British Telecommunications plc* [2001] IRLR 23.
102 *Ekpe v Metropolitan Police Commissioner* [2001] IRLR 605.
103 *Law Hospital NHS Trust v Rush* [2001] IRLR 611.
104 [2002] IRLR 24.
105 Guidance, Pt II, para C7.
106 DD Regs 1996 reg 6.

have a substantial and long term adverse effect on the child's ability to carry out those tasks if the impairment would normally have that effect on a person over six.

2.75 The effect of the impairment is to be judged at the time of the alleged discrimination.[107]

'Substantial adverse effect'

2.76 The effect on a person's normal day to day activities must be adverse and substantial. Although 'substantial' is not defined in the DDA 1995 itself the Guidance states that a 'substantial' effect is one which is more than 'minor' or 'trivial',[108] while a 'substantial' effect is one which has been described by the EAT as anything which is more than insubstantial.[109]

2.77 The time taken by a person with an impairment to carry out a normal day to day activity should be taken into account when assessing whether or not the effect of an impairment is substantial. The comparison is with the time that the activity might be expected to take if the person did not have the impairment.[110] The way an activity is carried out is another factor to be considered. The proper comparison is with the way that a person might be expected to carry out the activity if he or she did not have the impairment.[111]

2.78 Environmental factors like temperature, humidity, time of day or night, how tired or stressed the person is, may have an effect on the severity of the impairment. The impact of environmental factors should always be considered when assessing whether adverse effects are substantial.[112]

2.79 Whether the effect of an impairment is substantial is not a medical issue but a question of fact and the evidence of the applicant and possibly family and colleagues will be necessary to establish, or question, the severity of effect.[113]

107 *Cruikshank v Vaw Motorcast Ltd* [2002] IRLR 24.

108 Guidance, Pt II, para A1.

109 *Ekpe v Metropolitan Police Commissioner* [2001] IRLR 605.

110 Guidance, Pt II, para A2.

111 Ibid Pt II, para A3.

112 Ibid Pt II, para A10.

113 *Vicary v British Telecommunications plc* [1999] IRLR 680; *Abadeh v British Telecommunications plc* [2001] IRLR 23.

Cumulative effects

2.80 The Guidance makes it clear that an impairment which has an adverse effect on more than one of the eight activities listed at para 2.65 above, but which does not have a *substantial* adverse effect on any one of them could, when all those effects are added up and taken together, be said to have a substantial adverse effect on the person's ability to carry out normal day to day activities.[114] The Guidance uses the example of a person with mild cerebral palsy who might experience minor effects in a number of the eight areas which, taken together, could create substantial adverse effects on a range of normal day to day activities: tiredness may make walking more difficult for example; visual perception may be poor; and the person may experience problems with co-ordination and balance. In *Gardener v Lifespan Healthcare NHS Trust*[115] an ET ruled that the accumulation of difficulties caused by chronic fatigue syndrome (ME) had a substantial adverse effect on the applicant.

Cumulative impairments

2.81 Where a person has more than one impairment and the impairments, considered separately, do not have a substantial adverse effect, it is important to consider whether if, taken together, the impairments have a substantial adverse effect on the person's ability to carry out normal day to day activities.[116]

Coping strategies

2.82 If a person can reasonably be expected to modify behaviour to prevent or reduce the effects of an impairment on normal day to day activities so that it ceases to have a substantial adverse effect on the person's ability to carry out normal day to day activities, that person would not meet the definition of a disabled person.[117] But in *Vicary v British Telecommunications plc*[118] the EAT cautioned ETs and others about unrealistic expectations of how disabled persons could or should modify their behaviour to prevent or reduce the effects of an impairment on normal day to day activities. The court warned of the dangers of ETs (and others) having stereotypical images of disabled people in their

114 Guidance, Pt II, para A4.

115 Case 1500507/98, 17 November 1998 (unreported).

116 Guidance, Pt II, para A6.

117 Ibid Pt II, para A7.

118 [1999] IRLR 680.

minds when approaching the question of whether or not someone suffers from a disability. The EAT accepted that a person fitting the stereotyped image of a disabled person (wheelchair-user or moving with difficulty) might suffer from a physical impairment for the purposes of the DDA 1995. But it did not follow that those who did not fulfil this stereotype were inherently less likely to have a physical or mental impairment falling within the DDA 1995.

2.83 It is important that individuals who have developed 'coping strategies' are not unduly penalised as a result. The Guidance therefore requires that the possibility of a person's 'coping strategies' (ability to manage the effects of an impairment) breaking down in certain circumstances must be taken into account when assessing the effect of the impairment.[119] If, for example, a person whose speech impediment is ordinarily well controlled is placed under pressure or stress (as in an interview situation), his or her coping mechanisms may break down causing the impediment to re-emerge.

2.84 Similarly, advice from a medical practitioner to a disabled person to behave in a particular way to reduce the impact of the impairment may be counted as treatment and disregarded (see immediately below).[120]

Effects of treatment

2.85 The DDA 1995 provides that, where a person's impairment is being treated or corrected, the treatment or corrective measures are to be disregarded for the purposes of deciding whether he or she is 'disabled' for the purposes of the Act. The impairment is to be assessed as having the effect it would have without the treatment or corrective measures in question.[121]

2.86 Medical treatment is not defined in the DDA 1995. In *Kapadia v Lambeth LBC*[122] the Court of Appeal confirmed the EAT's view that counselling with a consultant clinical psychologist fell within the definition of medical treatment. The DDA 1995 provides that the use of a prosthesis or other aid is a measure to be disregarded for these purposes.[123] And in *Vicary*, the EAT offered the obiter view that the reference to 'aids' in the Guidance refers to zimmer frames, sticks or

119 Guidance, Pt II, para A8 Guidance.

120 Ibid Pt II, para A9.

121 DDA 1995 Sch 1, para 6(1).

122 [2000] IRLR 14.

123 DDA 1995 Sch 1, para 6(2).

wheelchairs rather than to household objects such as electric tin openers. The effect of treatment must be disregarded even where the measures adopted for treatment result in the effects of the impairment being completely under control.[124] So, for example, a person who suffers from severe epilepsy which is well controlled by medication must be assessed on the basis of the impact of his condition on his ability to carry out normal day to day activities without the medication. And a person with a hearing impairment who always uses a hearing aid must be assessed with reference to the effect of the hearing impairment, without the aid, on her ability to carry out normal day to day activities.

2.87 The one exception to this rule involves sight corrections. The DDA 1995 provides that the correction, by spectacles or contact lenses, of visual impairments is to be taken into account for the purposes of the Act, and the only effects which are to be considered in the case of a person with a sight impairment are those which remain when glasses or contact lenses are used.[125] So, for example, in *Kirker v British Sugar plc*[126] an ET ruled that a visually impaired chemist was disabled for the purpose of the DDA 1995 because even with glasses he could not see well enough to drive.

2.88 DDA 1995 Sch 1 para 6 applies only to *continuing* medical treatment, that is, to measures which 'are being taken', rather than to *concluded* treatment the effects of which may be more readily ascertained. A distinction must be drawn, accordingly, between continuing and concluded medical treatment. Where treatment has ceased, its effects should be taken into account in assessing the degree of the applicant's disability. Continuing treatment may mask or ameliorate the effects of a disability to the extent that it appears not to have a substantial adverse effect. If the final outcome of such treatment cannot be determined, or if it is known that its termination would result in a relapse or worsening of the applicant's medical condition, the treatment must be disregarded under DDA 1995 Sch 1 para 6(1). But where the medical evidence satisfies a tribunal that the effect of the continuing medical treatment is to create a permanent improvement, the effects of that treatment should be taken into account in order to assess the disability as measures are no longer needed to treat or correct it once the permanent improvement has been established.[127]

124 Guidance, Pt II, para A12.

125 DDA 1995 Sch 1 para 6(3).

126 Case 2601249/97, 5 December 1997 (unreported).

127 *Abedeh v British Telecommunications plc* [2001] IRLR 23.

Progressive conditions

2.89 The DDA 1995 makes special provision for progressive conditions – conditions which are likely to change and develop over time.[128] The Act gives examples of such conditions: cancer, HIV infection, muscular dystrophy, and multiple sclerosis.[129] This list is not exhaustive.

2.90 A person who has a progressive condition will be treated as having an impairment with a substantial adverse effect from the moment any impairment resulting from that condition first has some effect on his or her ability to carry out normal day to day activities. The adverse effect need not be continuous and it need not be substantial, but it has to be shown that it is a condition which is likely to result in a substantial effect on normal day to day activities at some stage in the future. People with (currently) asymptomatic or latent conditions, or with a predisposition to develop disabling conditions in the future, will not be covered by the DDA 1995 unless the condition has begun to have some effect. The government is committed to legislating to provide that HIV infection and cancer will be treated as a disability from the date of diagnosis.

2.91 In *University of Surrey v Mowat-Brown*[130] the applicant, who had MS, had few symptoms. The medical evidence, three or four years after diagnosis, was that the condition was 'quiescent'. His DDA 1995 claim failed as he could not show the likelihood of substantial future adverse effect.

Severe disfigurements

2.92 The DDA 1995 deviates from the functional test in its treatment of severe disfigurements. An impairment which consists of a severe disfigurement is to be treated as having a substantial adverse effect on the ability of a person to carry out normal day to day activities regardless of its actual effects.[131] Examples of disfigurements given in the Guidance include scars, birthmarks, limb or postural deformation and diseases of the skin.[132] Assessment of the severity of a disfigurement is mainly a matter of degree, and the location of the disfigurement may be taken into account.[133] There is an underlying

128 Guidance, Pt II, para A15.
129 DDA 1995 Sch 1, para 8(1)(a).
130 [2002] IRLR 235.
131 DDA 1995 Sch 1 para 3.
132 Guidance, Pt II, para A17.
133 Ibid.

assumption that the more visible the disfigurement, the more likely it is to be severe, thus taking account of the prejudices and perceptions of others.

2.93 The DD Regulations 1996 provide that any disfigurement which consists of a tattoo (which has not been removed), non-medical body piercing, or something attached through such piercing, is to be treated as not having a substantial adverse effect on the person's ability to carry out normal day to day activities. Although the DD Regulations 1996 can be amended over time, there is at present no general exclusion of deliberately acquired and/or self-inflicted disfigurements.

'Long term' impairments

2.94 The substantial and adverse effects of a person's physical or mental impairment must also be 'long term' to afford that person protection under the DDA 1995. The Act provides that the effect of an impairment is long term if:

- it has lasted for at least 12 months;
- it is likely to last for at least 12 months; or
- it is likely to last for the rest of the affected person's life.[134]

2.95 In *Greenwood v British Airways plc*[135] it was held that the applicant's condition could be considered up to and including the date of the tribunal hearing in deciding whether the effect was likely to last 12 months. The approach to assessing the likely duration of the effects is therefore different to the assessment of whether the impairment has a substantial and adverse effect, which is to be judged at the time of the alleged discrimination.

2.96 The Guidance and the DDA 1995 itself recognise that the effect of the impairment may not be the same throughout the relevant period. The main adverse effect might disappear while other adverse effects continue or develop. Provided that the impairment continues to have or is likely to have a substantial adverse effect on the ability to carry out normal day to day activities throughout the period, there is a long term effect.[136]

2.97 The Guidance also provides that, if an impairment has had a substantial adverse effect which has ceased, but is likely to recur, then that substantial effect is to be treated as continuing.[137] The Guidance

134 DDA 1995 Sch 1 para 2(1).
135 [1999] IRLR 600.
136 Guidance, Pt II, para B2.
137 Guidance, Pt II, para B3; DDA 1995 Sch 1 para 2(2).

gives the example of a person suffering with rheumatoid arthritis who may experience effects for a number of weeks and then have a period of remission. If the effects are likely to recur, they are to be treated as if they were continuing. If the effects are likely to recur beyond 12 months after their first occurrence, the effects are to be treated as long term.[138] Conditions which recur sporadically or for short periods can still qualify.

2.98 The Guidance suggests that the likelihood of recurrence should be considered, taking all the circumstances of the case into account. This should include consideration of what steps, if any, the person might reasonably be expected to take to prevent the recurrence – taking medication, for example, or carrying out certain exercises. Where there is a possibility that a person's coping strategies might break down so that there is a greater likelihood of a recurrence, this possibility should be taken into account when assessing the likelihood of a recurrence.[139]

Past disabilities

2.99 The employment provisions of the DDA 1995 apply equally to a person who had, but no longer has, a disability within the meaning of the Act.[140] This important but often forgotten provision is particularly useful if a sickness or medical record is held against an employee after he or she has fully recovered. The provision is particularly important in the area of mental health. Those who have been disabled by reason of significant mental impairments will be entitled to the protection of the DDA 1995 on the grounds that they *have had* a disability even where no recurrence of the impairment has taken place or is expected to take place at the time of the acts of discrimination (such as was the case in *Greenwood v British Airways plc*).[141] All those who were registered disabled under Disabled Persons (Employment) Act 1944 s6 on both 12 January 1995 and on 2 December 1996 are regarded as having had a disability until 2 December 1999. After that, they will be deemed to be people who have had a disability in the past.[142]

2.100 Where a person complains about an act of discrimination based on a past disability which had a substantial adverse effect on his or her

138 Guidance, Pt II, para B4.
139 Guidance, Pt II, para B5.
140 DDA 1995 s2 and Sch 2.
141 [1999] IRLR 600.
142 DDA 1995 Sch 1 para 7(2)(b).

ability to carry out normal day to day activities, it does not matter whether the DDA 1995 was in force at the time of the past disability.

Medical evidence in disability discrimination cases

2.101 An applicant must establish the fact of an impairment. When there is any doubt or dispute about a person's physical or mental impairment, or the effect of it, a medical report should be obtained. In the case of mental impairments where there is an additional hurdle for applicants to establish their condition as a clinically well recognised illness, see paras 2.58–2.63 above and the detailed guidance in *Morgan v Staffordshire University*.[143] The report should set out the nature of the condition or impairment (with evidence of it being clinically well-recognised in mental impairment cases) and the symptoms experienced by the applicant.

2.102 It is important to identify any medical treatment the applicant has received; whether such treatment is on-going or concluded; and the effect of the condition or impairment if it was not treated (or if the effect of the treatment was to be ignored). Where the length of time the effects of the impairment might last is in issue, a medical opinion would be useful. In cases of a progressive condition, especially one not listed as an example in the DDA 1995 or Guidance[144] a medical report or reference may be needed to establish that the condition is progressive – ie, that it is likely to change and develop over time in the applicant's case.

2.103 When a claim includes an alleged failure by an employer to make reasonable adjustments (see chapter 6, particularly paras 6.15–6.37) and the employer's knowledge of the disability and its effects are relevant, a medical report should also cover how and over what period the impairment is likely to have manifested itself.

2.104 While ETs and courts are expected to have only a rudimentary lay person's knowledge and understanding of medical matters it is not for a doctor to offer an opinion about what is or is not a normal day to day activity. Nor should a doctor offer any judgment as to whether the effect of a condition is or is not substantial. These are matters for the ET to decide.[145]

2.105 The ET may make an order for medical reports to be obtained and

143 [2002] IRLR 190.

144 DDA 1995 Sch 1 para 8(1)(a).

145 *Vicary v British Telecommunications plc* [1999] IRLR 680.

exchanged at a directions hearing if the clinical aspects of disability are in dispute. Ideally, a joint medical report can be ordered but this is not always possible or appropriate. In *De Keyser Ltd v Wilson*[146] the EAT emphasised that those instructing an expert should be careful not to be partisan or in any way to attempt to influence the expert's opinion. The court also laid down a detailed series of guidelines on how expert evidence should be collected in ET cases. A precedent letter of instruction to a doctor appears at appendix B.

146 [2001] IRLR 324.

CHAPTER 3

Direct discrimination

continued

Key points

3.1
- Direct discrimination is less favourable treatment of a person on one of the protected grounds (see chapter 2).
- The complainant must identify the act(s) which constitute the less favourable treatment alleged.
- 'Less favourable treatment' may include a denial of choice and acts of discouragement. Generally, any unwelcome difference in treatment will be 'less favourable treatment'.
- The 'less favourable treatment' must be treatment different to that which has been – or would have been – afforded a person from a different relevant group (whether sex or race-based or connected with married status or gender reassignment) in the same or comparable circumstances.
- The protected ground must be an important factor or effective cause of the treatment but need not be the only cause. Motive and intention are irrelevant. The question is, 'but for' the complainant's race, sex, etc, would he or she have been treated in the way alleged?
- The following principles apply when proving discrimination:
  - very little direct discrimination today is overt or even deliberate;
  - tribunals should look for indicators from a time before or after the act complained of, which may show that a decision was or was not affected by race or sex;
  - where there is a difference of race or sex, the alleged discriminator should be asked for an explanation for the difference in treatment;
  - where there is evidence of bias or failure to follow equal opportunities or other proper procedures this may point to conscious or unconscious racial or sexual bias having entered into the process;
  - credibility is not necessarily conclusive as a witness may be credible, honest and mistaken;
  - an employer which argues that it behaves equally badly to all employees (in order to refute an allegation of unlawful discrimination) must provide evidence to prove this;
  - a tribunal may infer discrimination from findings of primary fact. It must record its conclusions and any inferences made by it.
- In employment-related sex discrimination cases not concluded at

tribunal by 12 October 2001, the burden of proof shifts to the employer to show that there is a non-discriminatory reason for its actions once the applicant has shown facts (less favourable treatment and a difference of sex) from which it may be presumed that direct discrimination has occurred.

Background and statutory provisions

3.2 The Race Relations Act (RRA) 1976 and Sex Discrimination Act (SDA) 1975 have been in place for more than a quarter of a century, but substantial inequalities persist between men and women, white and ethnic minority workers. Generally, because of the increased awareness of the laws making discrimination unlawful, discrimination is less overt than it might have been in the past and proving it is often very difficult. This has been acknowledged by tribunals and courts which have accepted that it is necessary to look at all the surrounding circumstances and to probe employers (and others) about the reasons for their actions, in order to determine whether race, sex or other prohibited grounds have played a part.

3.3 As stated in chapter 1, it is only unlawful to discriminate in prescribed circumstances, such as recruitment, promotion, harassment and dismissal in the employment context, and these are set out in detail in chapter 11 (see also chapters 14 and 15). The principles relating to the definition of direct discrimination generally apply in the same way to discrimination in employment and in other areas such as housing, education and the provision of services. Questions of proof differ between employment-related sex discrimination, in respect of which the Burden of Proof Regulations (BP Regulations) 2001[1] apply, and other unlawful direct discrimination. Furthermore, whereas direct discrimination on grounds of race and sex is prohibited (subject to express exceptions) in employment, education, the provision of goods and services, etc, direct discrimination against married people is only prohibited in employment (SDA 1975 Pt II) and gender reassignment discrimination is only prohibited in employment in relation to SDA 1975 Pt II so far as it applies to vocational training.[2]

1 Sex Discrimination (Indirect Discrimination and Burden of Proof) Regulations 2001 SI No 2660 reg 3.

2 SDA 1975 s2A in relation to gender reassignment, 'employment-related' discrimination is broadly defined to include discrimination in relation to barristers (SDA 1975 ss35A and 35B). Unlike discrimination connected with

3.4 A substantial body of case-law (UK and EC) needs to be taken into account in relation to direct discrimination. It is summarised in this chapter. EC law applies directly only to employment-related sex discrimination. The principles developed in relation to sex discrimination are generally applied also to race discrimination cases. In *Anyanwu and another v South Bank Students' Union and others*[2a] Lord Bingham said:

> Since the 1976 Act is one of a trio of Acts [with the Sex Discrimination Act 1975 and the Disability Discrimination Act 1995] which contain similar statutory provisions although directed to different forms of discrimination, it is legitimate if necessary to consider those Acts in resolving any issue of interpretation which may arise on this Act.[2b]

This chapter covers direct discrimination on grounds of race, sex, gender reassignment and married status. Direct discrimination relating to pregnancy or maternity leave, which is also unlawful direct sex discrimination, is discussed in detail in chapter 16 and 18.

Definition of direct discrimination

3.5 The definition of direct discrimination is set out in RRA 1976 s1(1)(a) and SDA 1975 ss1(1)(a) and 3. RRA 1976 s1 provides that:

> (1) A person discriminates against another in any circumstances relevant for the purpose of any provision of this Act if –
> (a) on racial grounds he treats that other less favourably than he treats or would treat other persons ...[3]

SDA 1975 s1 is in similar terms, except that the 'less favourable treatment' must be 'on the ground of' the complainant's sex. The new Directives define direct discrimination as occurring when one person is treated less favourably than another person has been or would be treated in a comparable situation. This reflects the definition under RRA 1976 but not the SDA 1975, which will have to be amended. SDA 1975 s2 provides that the definition of direct discrimination applies

married status, however, only direct discrimination connected with gender reassignment is covered by the SDA 1975 (though for the possible conflict with Equal Treatment Directive 76/207/EEC see further chapter 10).

2a [2001] IRLR 305, HL.

2b Ibid at para 2.

3 Racial grounds are defined and explained at paras 2.32–2.48.

equally to discrimination against men, with the exception of special treatment given to women in connection with pregnancy or childbirth.[4] Thus, it is unlawful to discriminate against (and, therefore, in favour of) both women and men unless one of the exceptions applies (see chapter 11), or the discrimination falls within the narrow positive action provisions (see chapter 5).

3.6 SDA 1975 s3 provides that a person discriminates against a married person of either sex if, on the ground of his or her marital status, he treats that person less favourably than he treats or would treat an unmarried person of the same sex. SDA 1975 s2A provides that person A discriminates against another person B if he treats B less favourably than he treats or would treat other people, and does so on the ground that B intends to undergo, is undergoing or has undergone gender reassignment.[5]

'Less favourable treatment'

3.7 The first step in establishing direct discrimination is to show that the act complained of by the complainant amounts to 'less favourable treatment'. 'Less favourable treatment', even when coupled with a difference of race, sex, etc, is not itself sufficient to establish unlawful direct discrimination. But it is a necessary ingredient.

3.8 The fact that a complainant feels that he or she has been unfavourably treated does not of itself establish unfavourable treatment.[6] This is a question for the tribunal to determine. In most situations, the fact that the complainant was subjected to 'less favourable treatment' than others will be clear. This treatment may consist, for example, of the denial of an opportunity, failure to shortlist for a job, dismissal, harassment, exclusion from school, refusal to provide a service, and so on.

3.9 A mere denial of choice may amount to 'less favourable treatment'.

4 SDA 1975 s2(2).

5 Ibid s2A(2), (3) and (4) provide that where A makes arrangements (including terms, conditions or arrangements on which employment, a pupillage, or tenancy or vocational training is offered) in relation to a person's absence from work or vocational training, it will be less favourable treatment if the arrangements are less favourable for B because he or she is undergoing gender reassignment than if the absence was due to sickness or injury (see para 2.22). Where the absence is for a reason other than sickness or injury the question then is whether it is reasonable for B to be treated no less favourably.

6 *Burrett v West Birmingham Health Authority* [1994] IRLR 7, EAT.

In *R v Birmingham City Council ex p Equal Opportunities Commission (EOC)*[7] the House of Lords ruled, in a case in which the allocation of more grammar school places to boys than to girls was at issue, that a successful claim under the SDA 1975 did not require proof that selective education was 'better' than non-selective education. It was enough that, by denying the girls the same opportunity as the boys, the council was depriving them of a choice which was valued by them (or at least by their parents) and which was obviously valued, on reasonable grounds, by many others. The House of Lords approved the Court of Appeal decision in *Gill v El Vino Co Ltd*[8] in which it was held that a refusal to serve women at a bar (even though they would be served when sitting at tables) was unlawful because it deprived them of the option of standing at the bar. There the Court of Appeal had held that:

> ... if a man wishes to take a drink in El Vinos he can drink, if he wishes, by joining a throng which crowds round the bar and where he can join his friends and pick up, no doubt, many an interesting piece of gossip, particularly if he is a journalist ... But if a woman wishes to go to El Vinos, she is not allowed to join the throng before the bar ... Is she being less favourably treated than men; I think that permits of only one answer: of course she is. She is not being permitted to drink where she may want to drink.[8a]

The deprivation of choice itself is sufficient to amount to less favourable treatment.

3.10 Words or acts of discouragement can amount to less favourable treatment of the person discouraged.[9] So, for example, discouraging a woman from applying for a job because she is or might become pregnant would amount to 'less favourable treatment' for the purposes of the SDA 1975.

Motivation

3.11 The intention or motive of the respondent is not a necessary condition of liability.[10] The test is whether, *but for* the person's race, sex or married status, he or she would have been subjected to the treatment complained of. In *James v Eastleigh BC*,[11] the House of Lords held that

7 [1989] AC 1155; [1989] IRLR 173.
8 [1983] 1 All ER 398; [1983] IRLR 206.
8a *Gill v El Vino Co Ltd* [1983] 1 All ER 398, per Griffiths LJ at 402.
9 *Simon v Brimham Associations* [1987] IRLR 307.
10 *R v Birmingham City Council ex p EOC* [1989] AC 1155; [1989] IRLR 173.
11 [1990] 2 AC 751; [1990] IRLR 288.

this 'but for' test avoids complicated questions relating to concepts such as intention, motive, reason or purpose. It is not relevant whether the discriminator acted for what he or she considered to be a 'good' motive, such as to avoid industrial unrest[12] or to protect the complainant from discrimination by colleagues. Proof of motive will be helpful evidence from which discrimination might be proved.

Segregation

3.12 RRA 1976 s1(2) provides that segregating a person or people from others on racial grounds constitutes less favourable treatment. To date no race discrimination complaint has succeeded on this ground. This is, in large part, because of the way the courts have interpreted the provision. In *FTATU v Modgill; PEL v Modgill*[13] a particular paint shop in a factory had a workforce comprised entirely of Asian employees. White workers had been employed in the past but, as vacancies had arisen, they had been filled entirely by Asians largely because employment was by 'word of mouth' and vacancies were filled by existing (Asian) workers alerting others to them. A complaint of segregation contrary to the RRA 1976 was made by some of the Asian paint shop workers but dismissed by the Employment Appeal Tribunal (EAT). According to Slynn J, as he then was:

> ... had there been evidence of a policy to segregate, and of the fact of segregation arising as a result of the company's acts, that might well have constituted a breach of the legislation; but it does not seem to us that there was evidence to support that position. We do not consider that the failure of the company to intervene and to insist on white or non-Asian worker going into the shop, contrary to the wishes of the men to introduce their friends, itself constituted the act of segregating persons on racial grounds within the meaning of section 1(2).[13a]

It seems that a claim of direct discrimination based on segregation will succeed only where it is the result of a deliberate policy.

3.13 Sex segregation is not expressly prohibited by the SDA 1975, which contains no provision comparable to RRA 1976 s1(2). Segregating people by sex or married status is not unlawful, accordingly, unless it *also* amounts to 'less favourable treatment'.[14]

12 *Din v Carrington Viyella Ltd* [1982] IRLR 281, EAT.

13 [1980] IRLR 142.

13a Ibid at 146.

14 Which of course it may be if it entails a denial of choice (see para 3.9 above) .

Comparators

3.14 Except where the discrimination is race or sex-specific (such as in racial abuse and pregnancy cases[15]), a finding of direct discrimination requires a comparison between the treatment received by the complainant and that which was or would have been received by an actual or hypothetical comparator of a different sex, race, etc. When making a comparison between the complainant and another, the 'relevant circumstances' must 'be the same or not materially different'. RRA 1976 s3(4) and SDA 1975 s5(3) provide that:

> A comparison of the case of a person of a particular racial group with that of a person not of that group under s1(1) [RRA 1976] must be such that the relevant circumstances in the one case are the same, or not materially different, in the other.[16]
>
> A comparison of the cases of persons of different sex or marital status under s1(1) or 3(1) [SDA 1975] must be such that the relevant circumstances in the one case are the same, or not materially different, in the other.[17]

3.15 The test under the SDA 1975 and the RRA 1976 is the same. The question to be asked in each case is whether a person of a different sex or racial group than the complainant, in the same or similar circumstances as him or her, would have been treated in the same way.[18]

Nature of the comparison and relevant comparators

3.16 It is a common misunderstanding that, in order to prove discrimination, it is always necessary for the complainant to show that he or she was treated less favourably than another actual person. It is certainly helpful, in proving unlawful discrimination, to have a particular person of a different racial group or sex, whose treatment can be compared with the complainant's. Neither the SDA 1975 nor the RRA 1976 require an actual comparator. RRA 1976 s1(1)(a) and SDA 1975 s1(1)(a) look to how another was treated *or would have been treated* and, accordingly, comparisons with hypothetical comparators are acceptable and common.

3.17 In *Chief Constable of West Yorkshire v Vento*[19] the complainant

15 See, eg, *Webb v EMO Air Cargo Ltd (No 2)* [1995] 4 All ER 577; [1995] IRLR 645, HL.

16 RRA 1976 s3(4).

17 SDA 1975 s5(3).

18 For gender reassignment see para 2.21.

19 [2001] IRLR 124.

complained that her dismissal at the end of her probationary period was unlawful sex discrimination. The employment tribunal (ET) found there was no actual male comparator in the same position as the complainant, but that a hypothetical male probationer would have been offered a permanent post. The ET looked at how four other police constables had been treated in various circumstances which were not the same as those of the complainant and held that 'there are elements in the treatment of all the comparators that lead us to conclude that the applicant was less favourably treated than a hypothetical male officer would have been in the same circumstances'. The EAT upheld the ET's decision, stating that tribunals could and should look at how the employers treated actual non-identical, but not wholly dissimilar, cases:

> We would readily accept that the treatment of an actual male comparator whose position was wholly akin to Mrs Vento's in relation to the ... incident was not in evidence. It followed that the Tribunal had to construct a picture of how a hypothetical male comparator would have been treated in comparable surrounding circumstances. One permissible way of judging a question such as that is to see how unidentical but not wholly dissimilar cases had been treated in relation to other individual cases ... As for constructing the hypothetical case from actual but dissimilar cases, the Tribunal refer in some detail to four actual comparators ... But the Tribunal did not treat any of the four cases, as we see it, as being a relevant actual comparator. That is why the Tribunal turned, as it had to, to a *hypothetical* male officer in the same circumstances. The Tribunal used the four actual cases as if building blocks in the construction of the neighbourhood in which the hypothetical male officer was to be found. For the Tribunal to have relied on the four actual comparator cases in that way was not only not an error of law, it was, as it seems to us, the only proper way for it to proceed on the evidence put before it.[20]

3.18 In a case in which an actual comparator is relied upon, the question whether the relevant circumstances are the same as between the complainant and the comparator for the purposes of RRA 1976 s3(4) or SDA 1975 s5(3) is one of fact for the ET and courts to decide. The danger with relying on an actual comparator is that the ET and courts will decide that the 'relevant' circumstances (whatever these may be taken to be) of the applicant and his or her comparator are not the same. If there is any significant danger that this might happen it is better to

20 *Chief Constable of West Yorkshire v Vento* [2001] IRLR 124 at 125. See also *Leeds Private Hospital Ltd v Parkin*, EAT 519/89 (unreported).

argue, in the alternative, one or more actual or hypothetical comparators.

3.19 In *Wakeman v Quick Corporation*,[21] three London-based managers employed by a Japanese company challenged the fact that they were paid less than Japanese managers who were temporarily seconded to work in London. The respondents argued that the higher pay was attributable to the secondees' status as ex-pat workers (ie, to compensate them for the extra expense of living abroad and to encourage them to move temporarily to the UK), rather than to their Japanese race or nationality.[22] The Court of Appeal accepted that the circumstances of the comparators (the Japanese managers) were materially different (by reason of their status as secondees) to those of the British managers, so that no comparison could properly be made under RRA 1976 s3(4). Because there was a material difference in their circumstances, it was impossible to conclude that the applicants were being treated less favourably, on racial grounds, than their chosen comparators.

3.20 The Court of Appeal did not consider whether the difference in pay was appropriate to compensate the Japanese managers for being away from home, but relied on the fact that managers in Japan (whether Japanese or British) were paid equally to support the conclusion that no discrimination had occurred. This points to the shortcomings in the model of equality adopted by the SDA 1975 and the RRA 1976. In *Wakeman*, Chadwick LJ did accept that the RRA 1976 permitted comparisons to be made with hypothetical comparators. Once the decision was reached that the comparators chosen by the applicants were not in the same relevant circumstances as them, the question whether the difference in pay (which was very substantial) was justifiable (or, if it was not, whether its disproportionate nature justified an inference of race discrimination), faded from view. The ET did not ask this question and the Court of Appeal held that it did not need to do so.

3.21 More recently, however, the Court of Appeal adopted a different approach in *Balamoody v UK Central Council for Nursing, Midwifery and Health Visiting*.[23] There the court held that an ET would err if it

21 [1999] IRLR 424.

22 Note that if the comparison was between a woman and a man the claim would have to be under the Equal Pay Act 1970, not the SDA 1975. The RRA 1976, unlike the SDA, covers contractual and non-contractual terms.

23 [2002] IRLR 288, but see *Williams v HM Prison Service* EAT, 7 February 2002 (1236/01) IDS Brief 713 where *Balamoody* was distinguished because there was no other comparator in *Balamoody*.

failed to direct itself to the need for a control group against which to test the alleged discriminatory treatment if a hypothetical comparator is required. In such a case the ET must construct a hypothetical comparator and test the case against that benchmark (see also para 3.17 above). This applies even if the applicant relies only on an actual comparator.

3.22 Another problematic application of the comparator requirement occurred in *Shamoon v Chief Constable of the Royal Ulster Constabulary*.[24] The applicant, a chief inspector in the RUC, had been told she could not conduct appraisals because of complaints outstanding against her. She claimed a breach of the SDA 1975 and sought to compare herself with two male chief inspectors who, not being the subject of complaints, were allowed to conduct appraisals. The Northern Ireland Court of Appeal (NICA) held that her 'relevant circumstances' were not the same as those of her comparators. NICA ruled that, 'in the absence of evidence of a regular way in which persons in the same circumstances are treated, a complainant has to prove that at least one other person in comparable circumstances has been treated differently, which may tend to show how others would be treated if they and not the complainant had been concerned'.

3.23 NICA's approach was flawed. The legislation makes it clear that there is no need for an actual comparator. The question, under RRA 1976 s3(4) and SDA 1975 s5(4), is whether the respondent has treated a woman less favourably than he treats *or would treat* a man in similar circumstances. Like has to be compared with like. If the relevant circumstances of the applicant and her comparator are different, the respondent may be able to show that the difference in treatment is due to those different circumstances, rather than to sex or race. Even prior to the implementation of the BP Regulations 2001,[25] such different circumstances ought not entirely to exclude a finding of direct discrimination based on a hypothetical comparator. The question in *Shamoon* ought perhaps to have been whether a male chief inspector, with the same complaints against him, would have been treated in the same way as the applicant. Certainly, now that the BP Regulations are in force, it ought to be for the employer to prove that the disputed difference in treatment was caused by the explanation relied upon (see further para 3.85 below).

24 [2001] IRLR 520.

25 Sex Discrimination (Indirect Discrimination and Burden of Proof) Regulations 2001 SI No 2660, and see para 3.85 below.

3.24 In *Martins v Marks & Spencer plc*[26] the Court of Appeal held that a comparison had to be made between the treatment of the 27-year-old African-Caribbean applicant and that of an applicant of the same age and a different racial group with similar experience and qualifications applying for the job. Again, to the extent that this suggests that an *actual*, rather than a *hypothetical*, comparator is required, the judgment is flawed. If, for example, the sole applicant for a job is not appointed because he or she is black, unlawful direct discrimination will have occurred notwithstanding the absence of a hypothetical comparator (unless an exception applies – see chapter 11). No actual comparator existed in *Martins*, so the comparison should have been with a hypothetical comparator. The main point made by the Court of Appeal was that it could not be inferred from the fact that the interviewers acted in a biased way towards Ms Martins that they would not have acted in the same way in dealing with another applicant of a different racial group. This aspect of the case is considered at para 3.64 below

3.25 The *Balamoody* decision now makes it clear that, in the absence of an actual comparator, the ET and court must construct a hypothetical comparator to show how a person of the other racial group (or sex or marital status) would have been treated. This is a matter of law, not discretion, and is obligatory.

Hypothetical circumstances

3.26 In comparing relevant circumstances the facts of the particular case, rather than hypothetical possibilities, must be taken into account. In *Grieg v Community Industry & Ahern*,[27] for example, the applicant had been refused a job on a painting and decorating team because she would have been the only woman on the team. The employer argued that, if a man had applied for a job with an all-woman team, he would equally have been refused. The EAT ruled that the relevant question was whether a man would have got the job the applicant applied for, rather than what would have happened had a man applied for a job in an all-female team.

3.27 Similarly, in the Northern Irish case of *Smyth v Croft Inns Ltd*,[28] a Catholic barman was told that he could stay or go after his manager had been told by an anonymous threat that the barman should not be

26 [1998] IRLR 326.

27 [1979] IRLR 158.

28 [1996] IRLR 84.

in the bar the following week, as Protestant customers objected to his presence. He resigned and claimed direct discrimination on the ground of his religion and constructive dismissal. NICA ruled that the comparison was between the Catholic barman and a hypothetical Protestant barman working in the same bar who was not dismissed because of his religious belief, rather than a hypothetical Protestant barman working in a Catholic bar in a 'nationalist' area, who would have been treated in the same way if he had been threatened.

3.28 In both *Grieg* and *Smyth* the discriminators sought to rely on 'relevant circumstances' which were themselves discriminatory. As will be seen below, this is not acceptable.

3.29 In *Bain v Bowles*[29] a male applicant living in Italy complained that he was not allowed to put an advertisement in *The Lady* magazine for a housekeeper. *The Lady* refused to publish advertisements for female employees outside the UK when the employer was male, because of concerns about the sexual harassment of girls who accepted positions with male employers outside the UK. The Court of Appeal rejected *The Lady's* argument that the relevant circumstances were different and upheld the complaint. The magazine's motive (concern about harassment) did not affect the 'relevant circumstances'.

The 'relevant circumstances' must not be discriminatory

3.30 In *James v Eastleigh BC*,[30] female pensioners were permitted free access to a council swimming pool at age 60 (women's state pensionable age at the time), men not until 65 (men's state pensionable age at the time). The House of Lords held that, as the state pensionable age was itself discriminatory, it could not be treated as a relevant circumstance in making the comparison under SDA 1975 s5(3). Any comparison which took a discriminatory base line was wrong in the House of Lords' view. Their Lordships stated that the question was: 'would the complainant have received the same treatment from the defendant but for his or her sex?' This applies where the differential treatment resulted from the application of a gender-based criterion (such as, here, state pensionable age) as well as where it was directly based on sex.

3.31 In *Dhatt v McDonalds Hamburgers Ltd*,[31] on the other hand, the Court of Appeal held that a factor which itself discriminates on racial

29 [1991] IRLR 356.

30 [1990] 2 AC 751; [1990] IRLR 288.

31 [1991] IRLR 130.

grounds can qualify as a relevant circumstance. The applicant, who had been born in India, had indefinite leave to remain in the UK, a status which meant that his right to work was unrestricted. His immigration status was marked on his passport but his employers, who demanded that all non-EC citizens produce a work permit, did not recognise his passport as demonstrating his entitlement to work in the UK. He argued that the requirement to produce a work permit, which was not imposed by law, discriminated directly on grounds of nationality, his employers not applying it to British and other EC citizens. The Court of Appeal held that Mr Dhatt could not compare himself with UK and EC nationals whose circumstances were different because they were not required to have permission to work. This approach, which incorporates discrimination into the comparison, appears to conflict with the decision of the House of Lords in *James v Eastleigh BC*. *James* was distinguished by the Court of Appeal on the basis that there the council had adopted the discriminatory criterion, whereas in *Dhatt* the discrimination was sanctioned by statute. This distinction is unsustainable (contrary to the holding of the Court of Appeal in *Dhatt*, the discrimination was not sanctioned by statute), the two decisions are inconsistent and the House of Lords' decision in *James* should prevail.[32]

3.32 All race and sex considerations should be excluded when considering the comparison between the treatment of the complainant and the treatment of a person in a similar situation except his or her attitude to race (or sex). In *Showboat Entertainment Centre Ltd v Owens*[33] an employee was dismissed for refusing to carry out an unlawful discriminatory instruction – namely, to exclude black people. The EAT upheld the finding of race discrimination and held that the correct comparison was as between the dismissed employee and another employee who did not refuse to carry out the unlawful instruction, rather than between the dismissed employee and others refusing to carry out instructions.[34]

32 Note that *Dhatt* was followed in *Ice Hockey Super League Ltd v Henry*, EAT 1167/99, 2 March 2001 (unreported). Arguably, this decision is wrong for the same reasons that *Dhatt* is wrong (see also *IDS Brief* 686).

33 [1984] IRLR 7.

34 And see *Weathersfield (t/a Van & Truck Rentals) v Sargent* [1999] IRLR 94, in which the Court of Appeal approved *Showboat*.

Dress codes and 'less favourable treatment'

3.33 Different dress codes for men and women have frequently been upheld by the courts. In *Schmidt v Austicks Bookshops Ltd*[35] the EAT held a rule that women not wear trousers did not amount to less favourable treatment on grounds of sex. This was, the EAT held, because no restriction could be applied to the men which was equivalent to that applied to the women. The EAT also held that, in so far as a comparison was possible, the employers had treated both female and male staff alike by imposing a clothing and appearance code upon them, although the codes differed between men and women. This aspect of the decision, however, rested on the fact that men were not permitted to wear T-shirts – a restriction which, incidentally, applied also to women employees. The EAT did not comment on this fact.

3.34 The reasoning in *Schmidt* must be wrong. The proper question is simply whether, 'but for' her sex, the complainant would have been allowed to wear trousers in a situation where men could wear trousers. The answer is 'yes'. It is irrelevant that men would not be asked to wear skirts – that is an entirely hypothetical question. If men have the choice of wearing trousers, then women should also be able to do so if they wish. What is seen as an 'appropriate' dress code for women and men is likely to reinforce stereotypes and thus to be inherently discriminatory.

3.35 The Court of Appeal nevertheless approved *Schmidt* in *Smith v Safeway plc*,[36] in which a man challenged a rule which prohibited him, but permitted women, to have long hair. The EAT had found that Safeway's dress and appearance code did not make identical provision for men and women, but that the rules for men and women were equally rigorously applied. The Court of Appeal ruled that, in order to win a sex discrimination claim, it was necessary for a complainant to show not merely that the sexes were treated differently, but that the treatment of one sex was less favourable than the treatment given to the other. A code providing for a conventional standard of appearance for both sexes was likely to operate equally favourably between the sexes. The EAT concluded that 'looking at the code as a whole, neither case was to be treated less favourably as a result of its application'.

3.36 Again, the approach taken by the Court of Appeal in *Safeway* can be challenged. A deprivation of choice *is* less favourable treatment. In

35 [1977] IRLR 360.
36 [1996] IRLR 456.

R v Birmingham City Council ex p EOC[37] the House of Lords ruled that, in order to show less favourable treatment, it was enough to show that girls were deprived of a choice that was valued by them. Clearly, in the *Safeway* case, Mr Smith considered that he had been deprived of such a choice and been treated less favourably. The decision in *Safeway* is also inconsistent with the decision of the House of Lords in *James v Eastleigh BC*[38] where the 'but for' test of less favourable treatment was approved. Clearly, but for the fact that Mr Smith was a man, the male 'dress code' would not have applied to him. Safeway's requirement of conformity with the male dress code is plainly a sex-based requirement. Furthermore, the denial of choice is based on assumptions about the proper appearance of men and women that are both sex-based and also likely to disadvantage ethnic minorities. The decision in *Smith v Safeway* is almost certainly wrong and, bearing as it did on the applicant's appearance outside work as well as at work, may well be inconsistent with article 8 of the European Convention on Human Rights (ECHR) which protects the right to private life (the ECHR and the Human Rights Act 1998, by which it is implemented in domestic law, are further discussed in chapter 9).

Establishing 'less favourable treatment' without a comparator

3.37 Where the treatment is sex or race-specific there is no need for a comparator. Thus, discrimination on the ground of a woman's pregnancy or her capacity to bear children is sex discrimination without the need to compare her situation to that of any man. The European Court of Justice (ECJ) has now clearly established that discrimination against a woman because she is pregnant is a breach of the ETD, and the SDA 1975 must be interpreted in line with this. There is no need, according to the ECJ in *Webb v EMO Air Cargo Ltd*,[39] to show that a man in similar circumstances would have been treated more favourably.

3.38 In *Sidhu v Aerospace Composite Technology Ltd*[40] the Court of Appeal held that, in cases where the very action complained of was less favourable treatment on sexual or racial grounds, a comparison with a person of another racial group was unnecessary. Thus, in cases of racist abuse or sexual or racial harassment, where it is clear that the

37 [1989] AC 1155; [1989] IRLR 173.

38 [1990] 2 AC 751; [1990] IRLR 288.

39 Case 32/193 [1994] ECR I-3567; [1994] IRLR 482.

40 [2000] IRLR 456.

treatment is on the ground of race and/or sex, it is not necessary to compare the treatment of the complainant with that of someone else (see further chapter 28).[41]

3.39 In *Sidhu* the EAT held that the employers' decision not to discipline the applicant for retaliatory action when the assault was racial was a race-specific decision so there was no need for a comparator. The Court of Appeal ruled in the same case that the equal application of a race-neutral policy of disregarding provocation and other mitigating factors was not treatment which could be described as race-specific. Accordingly, it was necessary to show more favourable treatment of a comparator (real or hypothetical) in the application of that policy if direct discrimination were to be made out. The Court of Appeal also declared, however, that in certain cases a comparison would be unnecessary, because the very action complained of would itself be less favourable treatment on sexual or racial grounds. On the facts of *Sidhu*, the initial racial attack did not occur in the course of the perpetrators' employment (see para 31.10 below) and, accordingly, fell outside the RRA 1976. Because the employers did not treat the complainant less favourably in the application of its policy on fighting, his complaint of race discrimination had to be dismissed.

3.40 There is no need for a comparator where the claimant has been treated less favourably by being stereotyped. In *Ealing LBC v Garry*[42] the EAT held that, in cases where racial stereotyping has been found, it is not necessary to compare the treatment the claimant received with that of a comparator (see further para 3.50 below).

'On the ground of race or sex' – discrimination and causation

3.41 Once the complainant has shown that he or she has been treated less favourably, he or she must then show that the reason for the less favourable treatment was race or sex.[43] The House of Lords ruled, in

41 The position appears to be different where the discrimination is on grounds of sexual orientation – see *Pearce v Governing Body of Mayfield Secondary School* [2001] IRLR 448, CS, discussed at para 8.20. Leave to appeal has been granted in *Ministry of Defence v MacDonald* [2001] IRLR 669, CA, discussed at para 8.17, which also concerned in part an allegation of harassment connected with sexual orientation.

42 *IDS Brief* 675.

43 *Nagarajan v London Regional Transport* [1999] 4 All ER 65; [1999] IRLR 572.

R v Birmingham City Council ex p EOC,[44] that direct sex discrimination occurs if a female would have received the same treatment as a male 'but for' her sex. *James v Eastleigh BC*[45] reaffirmed the importance of the 'but for' test in identifying sex or race-based criteria.

3.42 In *O'Neill v Governors of St Thomas More Upper School*,[46] an unmarried teacher of 'religious education and personal relationships' was dismissed when it became clear that she was pregnant as a result of a relationship with a local Catholic priest. The ET rejected her complaint of sex discrimination, stating that 'an important motive for the dismissal was not the Applicant's pregnancy *per se* but the fact that the pregnancy was by a Roman Catholic priest' and that, as a result, her position as a teacher was untenable. The ET found that the respondents had mixed motives. The EAT ruled that these mixed motives were inextricably linked to her pregnancy and hence it was not possible to say that the ground for dismissal was anything other than pregnancy.

3.43 In *O'Neill*, the EAT set out the relevant guidelines relating to causation:

- The test is not one of subjective mental processes of the respondents, ie as to their intentions, motives, beliefs or subjective purposes. Those considerations may be relevant to remedies for discrimination, but they are not relevant to liability ... The relevant question is: 'Would the applicant have received the same treatment but for her sex?'
- In answering the question whether the applicant would have received the same treatment 'but for' her sex, three principles apply:
  - First, the tribunal's approach to the question of causation should be 'simple, pragmatic and commonsensical'.
  - Second: '[t]he basic question is: what, out of the whole complex of facts before the tribunal, is the "effective and predominant cause" or the "real and efficient cause" of the act complained of? As a matter of common sense not all the factors present in a situation are equally entitled to be treated as a cause of the crucial event for the purpose of attributing legal liability for the consequences.'[47]

44 [1989] AC 1155; [1989] IRLR 173.

45 [1990] 2 AC 751; [1990] IRLR 288.

46 [1996] IRLR 372.

47 In *Nagarajan v London Regional Transport* [1999] 4 All ER 65; [1999] IRLR 572, the House of Lords asked variously whether 'racial grounds were a cause, the activating cause, a substantial and effective cause, a substantial reason, an important factor'.

– Third, 'the event or factor alleged to be causative of the matter complained of need not be the only or even the main cause of the result complained of (though it must provide more than just the occasion for the result complained of). It is enough if it is an effective cause.'

3.44 The approach in *O'Neill* was given support by the House of Lords in *Nagarajan v London Regional Transport*[48] in which their Lordships held that the reason *why* the discriminator acted on racial grounds is irrelevant when deciding whether an act of racial discrimination occurred. As had been established in *R v Birmingham City Council ex p EOC*,[49] and *James v Eastleigh BC*,[50] conscious motivation is not required for direct discrimination.[51]

3.45 It is not a good defence for a discriminator to show that he or she discriminated against a woman or a person of a particular racial group not because he or she wanted to but, for example, because of pressure from others, customer preference, to save money, or to avoid controversy. In *Din v Carrington Viyella Ltd (Jersey Kapwood Ltd)*,[52] for example, the applicant (a Pakistani) was involved in a row with his foreman which ended in the foreman pushing him. The manager refused to make the foreman apologise, which angered Mr Din's workmates (who were also Pakistani). When Mr Din returned from an extended period of leave the firm refused to re-employ him in order to avoid further industrial unrest. The ET accepted that the employer's motives were industrial, rather than racial. On appeal the EAT ruled that motive, while relevant, was not the decisive factor, and that the respondents' refusal to re-employ Mr Din had been discriminatory. If an act of racial discrimination had given rise to industrial unrest, to seek to banish the unrest by removing the person discriminated against was unlawful. Similarly in *R v Commission for Racial Equality (CRE) ex p Westminster City Council*,[53] the withdrawal of an offer of employment to a black road sweeper by a manager who feared a racially motivated strike was held by the High Court to be racial discrimination.

3.46 The applicant in *Fire Brigades Union v Fraser*[54] brought proceed-

48 [1999] 4 All ER 65; [1999] IRLR 572, HL.

49 [1989] AC 1155; [1989] IRLR 173.

50 [1990] 2 AC 751; [1990] IRLR 288

51 See also *Chief Constable of Greater Manchester Police v Hope* [1999] ICR 338, EAT.

52 [1982] IRLR 281, EAT.

53 [1984] IRLR 230.

54 [1998] IRLR 697.

ings against the union on the ground that it had discriminated against him contrary to SDA 1975 s12(3) by refusing to afford him access to representation or legal assistance (see further para 12.19). The union had, instead, supported a woman who had made allegations of harassment against him. The Court of Sessions ruled that no facts had been established which justified an inference that the union's refusal of representation to a man accused of sexual harassment (when the victim was given support) was on the basis of sex, as opposed to conduct. The court held that the inferences drawn by the ET were based not on any facts but on speculation, and that the tribunal had not been entitled to find that a woman accused of sexual harassment would have been treated differently. This highlights the importance of tribunals making findings of fact. Thus:

- motive and intention to discriminate are not necessary but, if apparent, will be good evidence of unlawful discrimination;
- the test is an objective, not a subjective one;
- race or sex must be at least a substantial or important factor behind the disputed treatment;
- the tribunal's approach must be simple, pragmatic and commonsensical, but where an inference is drawn it must be based on findings of fact, not assumptions.

Discrimination on the ground of another's race or sex

3.47 The definition of direct discrimination is worded slightly differently in the RRA 1976 and the SDA 1975. Under the RRA 1976, discrimination 'on racial grounds' is unlawful. Under the SDA 1975, discrimination against a woman 'on the ground of her sex' is unlawful. This means that, under the RRA 1976, someone can complain that he or she has been discriminated against on the ground of someone else's race. This will change when the Equal Treatment Directive is revised. This defines direct discrimination in the same way as the Race Directive and the RRA 1976 and SDA 1975 will therefore have to be amended in due course.

3.48 In *Zarcynska v Levy*,[55] the EAT ruled that a barmaid dismissed for refusing to comply with an instruction not to serve black customers had been discriminated against on racial grounds. This decision was

55 [1978] IRLR 532.

followed in *Showboat Entertainment Centre Ltd v Owens*[56] in which the white manager of an amusement centre was dismissed for refusing to comply with an instruction to exclude young blacks from the centre.

Stereotyping

3.49 Preconceptions that people of a particular race, sex or marital status possess or lack certain characteristics may be discriminatory. The Court of Appeal so held in *Coleman v Skyrail Oceanic Ltd*,[57] in which the employer had dismissed the applicant on the assumption that men were more likely to be the primary supporters of a family than women. In *Horsey v Dyfed CC*,[58] in which the employer had assumed that most women (and therefore the applicant) would follow their husbands if they moved jobs, the EAT relied on the Court of Appeal decision in *Coleman* in ruling that direct sex discrimination had occurred.

3.50 In *Hurley v Mustoe*[59] the EAT held that a policy not to employ women with children breached the SDA 1975. The EAT held that the policy directly discriminated against women and also that, if it was in fact a policy against employing persons of either sex with small children and applied to men and women alike, it amounted to unlawful indirect discrimination on the grounds of marital status contrary to SDA 1975 s3(1)(b). Furthermore, the EAT held that women with children are to be treated as individuals. No employer is bound to employ unreliable employees, men or women. Employers must investigate each case and not simply apply a rule of convenience, or a prejudice, to exclude a whole class of women or married people because some members of that class may not be suitable employees.[60] In *Cockroft v Restus Ltd*,[61] an ET ruled that it was unlawful discrimination to assume that the work (as a warehouse assistant) was for a 'big strong lad' and was unsuitable for a 'young lady'.

56 [1984] IRLR 7 and see *Weathersfield (t/a Van & Truck Rentals) v Sargent* [1999] IRLR 94.
57 [1981] IRLR 398.
58 [1982] IRLR 395.
59 [1981] ICR 490.
60 [1981] IRLR 208.
61 ET 12420/89 (unreported).

Justifying direct discrimination?

3.51 Although a respondent may rely on the specifically permitted genuine occupational qualifications for a job (see para 11.70) and there are certain statutory exceptions set out at para 11.94, neither the SDA 1975 nor the RRA 1976 makes any general provision for the justification of direct discrimination equivalent to the provision made for indirect discrimination and of discrimination under the DDA 1995. Some argue that, under EC law, direct discrimination may be justified.[62] However, this view appears to be based on a misinterpretation of case-law such as *Roberts v Birds Eye Walls Ltd*.[63] In any event, domestic law should prevail to the extent that it is more favourable than the EC provisions.

3.52 *Roberts* (also discussed at para 27.66) is an equal pay case concerned with a bridging pension provision (whereby the employer gave employees top-up payments so that they received the same pension benefits as if they had worked until the state pension age). The employer reduced the amount payable to women between the age of 60 and 65 because it was assumed that they would receive an old age pension from the state. The Advocate General considered this was direct discrimination, but that it was justifiable because the employer was trying to achieve substantive equality. The ECJ held that there was no discrimination because men and women were in a different position. According to the court:

> Article [141] cannot be interpreted in a way as to create unequal treatment, whereby some women gain a two-fold benefit.

This must be correct. The important point is that the same calculation was carried out for men and women; the state pension was deducted from the top-up payments. Men and women received the same total amount (from the employer and the state), so there was substantive equality. As the ECJ recognised, this was not a question of justifying direct discrimination.

3.53 The House of Lords has stated unequivocally, in *Ratcliffe* v *North Yorkshire CC*,[64] that there can be no question of justifying direct discrimination (see para 25.34). This contrasts with the position under the DDA 1995. In *Clark v TDG Ltd (t/a Novacold)*[65] Mummery LJ

62 See, eg, the remarks of Lord Browne-Wilkinson in *Strathclyde Regional Council v Wallace* [1998] 1 All ER 394; [1998] IRLR 146.

63 Case 132/92 [1993] ECR I-5579; [1994] IRLR 29.

64 [1995] 3 All ER 597; [1995] IRLR 439.

65 [1999] IRLR 318, para31.

pointed out that the defence of justification permitted in respect of less favourable treatment provision under that Act is not reflected in either the SDA 1975 or the RRA 1976.

Proving discrimination

The main principles

3.54 Direct discrimination requires evidence of less favourable treatment on the ground of a person's race, sex, etc. Proving direct discrimination is often difficult, as direct evidence of discrimination is often not available. In *Glasgow City Council v Zafar*[66] the House of Lords accepted that:

> ... claims of [race and sex discrimination] present special problems of proof for complainants since those who discriminate on grounds of race or gender do not in general advertise their prejudices.

3.55 In *Wallace v South Eastern Education and Library Board*[67] Lord Lowry stated that:

> Only rarely would direct evidence be available of discrimination on the ground of sex; one is more often left to infer discrimination from the circumstances. If this could not be done, the object of the legislation would be largely defeated, so long as the authority alleged to be guilty of discrimination made no expressly discriminatory statements and did not attempt to justify its actions by evidence.

In *Nagarajan*[68] the House of Lords recognised that '[d]irect evidence of a decision to discriminate on racial grounds will seldom be forthcoming. Usually the grounds of the decision will have to be deduced, or inferred, from the surrounding circumstances.' Lord Nicholls went on to remark, for their Lordships, that:

> ... all human beings have preconceptions, beliefs, attitudes and prejudices on many subjects. It is part of our make-up ... Many people are unable, or unwilling, to admit even to themselves that actions of theirs may be racially motivated. An employer may genuinely believe that the reason why he rejected an applicant had nothing to do with the applicant's race. After careful and thorough investigation of a claim members of an employment tribunal may decide that the proper inference to be drawn from the evidence is

66 [1998] 2 All ER 953; [1998] IRLR 36.

67 [1980] IRLR 193.

68 *Nagarajan v London Regional Transport* [1999] 4 All ER 65; [1999] IRLR 572.

> that, whether the employer realised it at the time or not, race was the reason why he acted as he did. It goes without saying that in order to justify such an inference the tribunal must first make findings of primary fact form which the inference may properly be drawn ... Members of racial groups need protection from conduct driven by unrecognised prejudice as much as from conscious and deliberate discrimination.[69]

3.56 The classic guidance on the proof of discrimination was set out by the Court of Appeal in *King v Great Britain China Centre.*[70] It should be noted that this approach applies now only in respect of discrimination other than employment-related sex discrimination, proof of which is considered at para 5.85 below. In *King*, Neil LJ ruled that:

- 'It is for the applicant who complains of racial discrimination to make out his or her case. Thus, if the applicant does not prove the case on the balance of probabilities he or she will fail.'
- 'It is important to bear in mind that it is unusual to find direct evidence of racial discrimination. Few employers will be prepared to admit such discrimination even to themselves. In some cases the discrimination will not be ill-intentioned but merely based on an assumption that "he or she would not have fitted in".'
- 'The outcome of the case will therefore usually depend on what inferences it is proper to draw from the primary facts found by the tribunal. These inferences can include, in appropriate cases, any inferences that it is just and equitable to draw in accordance with section 65(2)(b) of the [RRA 1976] from an evasive or equivocal reply to a questionnaire.'
- 'Though there will be some cases where, for example, the non-selection of the applicant for a post or for promotion is clearly not on racial grounds, a finding of discrimination and a finding of a difference in race will often point to the possibility of racial discrimination. In such circumstances the tribunal will look to the employer for an explanation. If no explanation is then put forward or if the tribunal considers the explanation to be inadequate or unsatisfactory it will be legitimate for the tribunal to infer that the discrimination was on racial grounds. This is not a matter of law but, as May LJ put it in *Noone v North West Thames Regional Health Authority*[71] "almost common sense".' At this stage, in sex

69 *Nagarajan v London Regional Transport* [1999] IRLR 572 at para 17, per Lord Nicholls.

70 [1991] IRLR 513.

71 [1988] IRLR 195, CA.

discrimination employment cases, under the BP Regulations, the burden would move to the employer to show that there was a non-discriminatory reason – see further para 3.85 below.

- 'It is unnecessary and unhelpful to introduce the concept of a shifting evidential burden of proof. [As stated above, in sex discrimination employment cases, the burden does move to the employer.] At the conclusion of all the evidence the tribunal should make findings as to the primary facts and draw such inferences as they consider proper from those facts. They should then reach a conclusion on the balance of probabilities, bearing in mind both the difficulties which face a person who complains of unlawful discrimination and the fact that it is for the complainant to prove his or her case.'

3.57 *King* was referred to in *Qureshi v Victoria University of Manchester*,[72] in which the EAT set out the main issues for decision in discrimination claims. These were approved by the Court of Appeal in *Anya* (see para 3.59) and are summarised at para 3.61.

3.58 Without any direct evidence of discrimination the court or tribunal must look at the surrounding circumstances, before and after the act of discrimination as well as the act itself, to see if there is any evidence of discrimination. Such evidence may give rise to an inference that the act or decision complained of was tainted by discrimination.

Anya v University of Oxford

3.59 The most important decision of recent years, and one which is essential reading for anyone involved in a claim of discrimination, is *Anya v University of Oxford.*[73] In it, the Court of Appeal acknowledged the difficulties of proving direct discrimination and set out the way in which a tribunal should deal with such complaints. The court approved the principles set out in *King v Great Britain China Centre*,[74] *Qureshi v Victoria University of Manchester* and *Glasgow City Council v Zafar*,[75] but applied them so as to make proof of discrimination easier than had previously been the case. The decision, which was reached under the RRA 1976, applies equally to the SDA 1975,

72 [2001] ICR 863, EAT. In *Anya* the Court of Appeal commented on the fact that this decision was 'mystifyingly unreported'.

73 [2001] IRLR 377.

74 [1991] IRLR 513.

75 [1998] 2 All ER 953; [1998] IRLR 36.

although it has been superseded in employment-related sex discrimination cases by the BP Regulations, discussed below at para 3.85.

3.60 Dr Anya, a black Nigerian, applied for a post as a post-doctoral research assistant. He was rejected in favour of a white candidate, Dr Lawrence. The interview panel included Dr Anya's supervisor (Dr Roberts), who had formed a view that Dr Anya was not suitable for the position. He informed another panel member, prior to the interview, about his opinion. Dr Anya did not get the job.

3.61 The ET at first instance found shortcomings in the university's equal opportunities and recruitment procedures and inconsistencies in Dr Roberts' evidence, but it accepted that the reasons for rejecting Dr Anya had to do entirely with a genuine assessment of his scientific strengths and weaknesses, rather than his race. The EAT upheld this decision but the Court of Appeal, pointing out that very little discrimination is overt or even deliberate, allowed Dr Anya's appeal and made the following points:

> It is not unduly onerous to proceed from a process of selection, if it is accompanied by a difference in race, to a request for an explanation.[75a]

Thus, if there is less favourable treatment (such as failure to appoint or promote) and a difference of race (or sex) the employer should be asked to provide an explanation.[76] The Court of Appeal stated:

> In the allocation of jobs by any sensibly-run institution, the explanation will be straightforward: the candidates were interviewed by an unbiased panel on an equal footing, using common criteria which contained no obvious or latent elements capable of favouring one racial group over another; and the best one was chosen. By parity of reasoning, evidence that one or more members of the panel were not unbiased, or that equal opportunities procedures were not used when they should have been, may point to the possibility of conscious or unconscious racial bias having entered into the process. It will always be a matter for the tribunal's conscientious judgment.[77]
>
> The tribunal must consider the direct oral and documentary evidence available, including the answers to the statutory questionnaire. It must also consider what inferences may be drawn from all the primary facts. Those primary facts may include not only the acts which form the subject-matter of the complaint, but also other acts

75a *Anya v University of Oxford* [2001] IRLR 377 at 377.

76 In a sex discrimination employment case, at this stage, the burden would move to the employer to prove a non-discriminatory reason (see para 3.85).

77 *Anya v University of Oxford* [2001] IRLR 377, para 8.

> alleged by the applicant to constitute evidence pointing to a racial ground for the alleged discriminatory act or decision.[78]

> What *King* and *Qureshi* tell tribunals and courts to look for, in order to give effect to the legislation, are indicator from a time before or after the particular decision which may demonstrate that an ostensibly fair-minded decision was, or equally was not, affected by racial bias.[79]

> ... hostility *may* justify an inference of racial bias if there is nothing else to explain it: whether there is such an explanation as the industrial tribunal posit here will depend not on a theoretical possibility that the employer behaves equally badly to employees of all races, but on evidence that he does.[80]

> It is precisely because a witness who by himself comes across as essentially truthful may be shown by documentary evidence or by inconsistency to be less reliable than he seems that the totality of the evidence in a case like this has to be evaluated ...[81]

Anya *and the 'bad management defence'*

3.62 Poor management can often disguise discrimination. Employers may argue that all employees were treated equally badly, and that no one was discriminated against. In *Qureshi v Newham LBC*,[82] the Court of Appeal stressed that incompetence does not become discrimination merely because the person affected is from an ethnic minority. Mr Qureshi was unsuccessful in his job application and alleged that the employer's failure to comply with its equal opportunities policy was discriminatory, there being an assumption that the policy had been applied to other applicants. The Court of Appeal refused to accept that inference, saying that it was likely that the policy had not been applied to other applicants either, and this was due to incompetence not discrimination. Similarly, in *Glasgow City Council v Zafar*[83] the House of Lords found that the fact that the employer had not acted reasonably did not mean that it had treated the employee less favourably than other employees on the ground of his race.

3.63 In *Anya* the Court of Appeal held that an employer who wishes to rely on the fact that he or she treated everyone badly or unreasonably

78 *Anya v University of Oxford* [2001] IRLR 377, para 9.
79 Ibid, para 11.
80 Ibid, para 14.
81 Ibid, para 23.
82 [1991] IRLR 264.
83 [1998] 2 All ER 953; [1998] IRLR 36.

(because, for example, he or she never applied the equal opportunities policy or did not follow procedure) must provide evidence that he or she behaved unreasonably regardless of race or sex. It was not, the court ruled, for the applicant to show that the employer did not behave equally badly to all. As the June 2001 IRLR editorial pointed out, this represents a major constraint on the deployment of the so-called 'bastard' defence. It means that an employer arguing that he or she is just a 'bastard' employer, rather than a 'discriminator', will have to show that he or she is a 'bastard' to all employees irrespective of race or sex. It will not be sufficient to state this baldly to establish a defence to discrimination. This applies equally to complaints outside the employment field. This removes one more burden to complainants who have previously had to disprove the employer's assertion that the reason for the treatment was just general bad management. It should be remembered that, in employment-related sex discrimination cases (see further para 3.85 below), the employer will have to prove a non-discriminatory reason for treatment establishing a prima facie case of discrimination.[84]

3.64 In *Martins v Marks & Spencer*[85] we saw (para 3.24 above) that *biased* treatment does not itself establish *discriminatory* treatment. Nevertheless, after *Anya*, it is for the employer to show positively that it would have acted in a similarly biased way to all applicants. The right question, in these circumstances, was whether Ms Martins would have been refused the job 'but for' her race. As recognised in *Anya*, evidence that one or more members of the panel were not unbiased, or that equal opportunities procedures were not used when they should have been, could point to the possibility of conscious or unconscious racial bias having entered into the process.

3.65 The RRA 1976 and SDA 1975 were designed to encourage employers, schools and other institutions to take steps to increase equal opportunities, eliminate discrimination and to establish procedures with this in mind. Applied to recruitment, selection, exclusion, etc, their aim is to encourage employers, schools and other institutions to adopt more rational, systematic and justifiable procedures, and to record them, so as to eliminate the possibility of unconscious discrimination. *Anya*, the principles of which are not limited to recruitment, is a welcome step which gives effect to the Acts' design.

84 BP Regs 2001, see para 3.85.

85 [1998] IRLR 326

Challenge to Anya

3.66 Since the decision in *Anya,* there has been a further Court of Appeal decision relating to similar facts, in which the applicants complained (pre-BP Regulations) that the failure to appoint them amounted to sex discrimination. In *Wheeler v Durham CC*[86] the Court of Appeal refused to accept that 'in all the circumstances where deviations from ordinary practice occur or where there are differences of treatment which emerge in the selection process, the employer must invariably give an explanation and the tribunal must find it a satisfactory explanation if it is to fail to infer that the decision was reached in breach of the Act. Some conduct of employers will require specific explanation, other conduct or events can be dealt with by way of the general finding which the tribunal made.' The Court of Appeal further held that a selection process inevitably involves a comparison between candidates and matters of impression and judgment on which views may honestly and legitimately differ.

3.67 The Court of Appeal in *Wheeler* stated that it did not follow from *Anya* that an ET had to explore the circumstances of every event in the evidence placed before it. It only has to reach conclusions on the essential issues. The questions, therefore, for the ET in that case were:

- What are the relevant differences of treatment between the complainant and his or her comparator?
- Which specific findings must be made from which an inference of discrimination may or may not be drawn? It is unlikely that a five-minute difference in the interview time will be relevant but a 30-minute difference may be.

What is relevant will, following *Wheeler*, be a question for the ET.

Step-by-step approach necessary to prove direct discrimination

3.68 It is important to be systematic about identifying the steps to be taken in arguing direct discrimination. These steps were identified in *Qureshi v Victoria University of Manchester* and approved in *Anya* in the employment context. However they apply to direct discrimination in any field covered by the SDA 1975 and RRA 1976 other than employment-related sex discrimination, in which the more favourable regime established by the BP Regulations 2001 applies (see para 3.85 below).

- First, it is necessary to identify the act(s) complained of which are

86 [2001] EWCA Civ 844.

said to be discriminatory (such as failure to select, promote or transfer, dismissal, exclusion, harassment or other less favourable treatment). Where there is a dispute about it, it will be necessary for the complainant to prove that the acts complained of actually occurred. There may be a number of different acts of discrimination and, unless there is continuing discrimination (see para 32.53), each act will generally be subject to the three-month time limit (see para 32.42);

- Second, it is necessary to show that the complainant has been treated less favourably than the discriminator treated or would have treated other persons of a different racial group or sex (or, where the claim is on the ground of marital status, a married or unmarried person of the same sex)[87] in the same, or not materi-ally different, relevant circumstances. The comparison is between either:
  - another person in the same or not materially different circumstances; or
  - a hypothetical person in such circumstances.

  This comparative exercise and the meaning of relevant circumstances are explained at para 3.18.
- If there is a difference in treatment involving persons of a different race, sex or marital status, the next question is whether that treatment was on racial grounds or on the ground of sex or marital status. At this stage in sex discrimination employment cases, it is for the employer to show a non-discriminatory reason for the treatment. If he or she fails to do so, the tribunal must uphold the complaint.[88]

3.69 The questions for the court or tribunal are:

- Was race, sex or marital status an *effective* cause? (Apart from employment-related sex discrimination cases, this is for the complainant to show.) Race, sex or marital status need not be the *sole* cause for the act complained of to be on those grounds, so long as it is one of the causes.[89]
- Is there direct evidence that the treatment complained of was done on racial grounds or on the ground of sex or marital status? (For example, an employer who informs a job applicant that she is not wanted because she has children and is thus likely to be unreliable; or that the customers would prefer someone of a different racial group.)

87 SDA 1975 s3(1)(a).

88 Ibid s63A.

89 See *Nagarajan v London Regional Transport* [1999] 4 All ER 65; [1999] IRLR 572, at note 47 above.

- If there is no direct evidence, what is the discriminator's explanation for the less favourable treatment? Unless there is a non-discriminatory reason for the treatment complained of then a court or tribunal may infer that the treatment was meted out on racial grounds, or on the ground of sex or marital status. In employment-related sex discrimination cases, the tribunal *must*, in the absence of an explanation, find that there has been sex discrimination.
- In deciding whether there has been less favourable treatment on the grounds of race, sex or marital status a court or tribunal may look at the surrounding circumstances (both before and after the discrimination) from which an inference may be drawn. (See para 3.61.)

In relation to each of these questions the tribunal must make findings of primary fact, either on the basis of direct (or positive) evidence or by inference from circumstantial evidence.

The evidence

3.70 In *Qureshi v Victoria University of Manchester*[90] the EAT pointed out that the applicant is often faced with the difficulty of discharging the burden of proof in the absence of direct evidence on the issue of racial grounds for the alleged discriminatory actions and decisions. There are special difficulties in a case of inadvertent and unintentional discrimination. The tribunal must consider:

- direct oral and documentary evidence (for rules regulating entitlement to see documents in the hands of the respondent, see para 32.119);
- replies to the questionnaire (see para 32.23);
- what inferences may be drawn from all the primary facts, which include not only the acts complained of but incidents both previous to and subsequent to the acts complained of, (they need not be proven discriminatory acts – see *Anya* and *Qureshi*).

3.71 In addition, statistical evidence of the number of ethnic minorities and women affected by particular decisions may be used to infer discrimination (see para 3.56). The alleged discriminator should be asked (through the questionnaire procedure, written questions[91] or in the court or ET) for an explanation as to why the complainant has been treated differently and for statistical information about the breakdown of men and women and racial groups.

90 21 June 1996, EAT (unreported).

3.72 Relevant information includes whether:

- other people were treated differently in any way, either before, after or at the time of the discriminatory act (and details of their racial group and/or sex);
- the proper procedure has been adopted;
- the equal opportunities policy has been followed.

3.73 In asking an ET to infer discrimination from the facts, there is wide latitude as to what evidence can be put before it. In *Chattopadhyay v Headmaster of Holloway School*[92] the applicant complained that he had been discriminated against in being passed over for promotion. He presented evidence relating to acts that occurred after the decision not to promote him had been taken by the school governors. The EAT held that evidence of events that occurred both before *and* after the act complained of were admissible. Evidence of hostility before or after the event was admitted with a view to showing that the person involved was treating the complainant differently from others, whether he was motivated by racial motives or not. In either case, an explanation was required.

3.74 In *Eke v Customs and Excise Commissioners*[93] the complainant claimed that he had been passed over for promotion. His employers tried to argue that evidence relating to events which took place outside the three-month time limit for an ET complaint could not be used as evidence. The EAT disagreed ruling that, although no award of compensation could be based on incidents prior to the three-month cut-off period,[94] they were admissible as evidence of the discrimination. The Court of Appeal in *Anya* confirmed this.

3.75 Complainants should therefore point to all less favourable treatment when building up a picture of discrimination – they do not have to limit themselves to acts that are overtly racist or sexist, or discrimination which is the subject of the proceedings. However, care should be taken to ensure that such evidence is relevant to the complaints before the tribunal or court.

3.76 Evidence of a discriminatory motive, while not necessary to prove discrimination, will be crucial evidence. As the EAT stated in *Elahi v Bristol and Weston Health Authority*:[95]

> The existence of racial prejudice ... is highly relevant to an issue as to

91 For rules regarding the same, see para 32.118.

92 [1981] IRLR 487.

93 [1981] IRLR 334.

94 Leave not having been given to extend time.

95 EAT 138/89 (unreported).

whether there was discriminatory conduct. It is self-evident that if there is such prejudice, discriminatory conduct is much more likely to have occurred.

In *Saunders v Richmond upon Thames BC*[96] the applicant complained about discriminatory questions put to her at an interview. Although the EAT ruled that the questions were not in themselves discriminatory and unlawful, the fact that they had been asked was evidence in determining whether she had been discriminated against in not being appointed.

Statistics

3.77 Statistical evidence of the numbers of women and black people in a workforce or in a particular part of the workforce may be used as evidence from which discrimination may be inferred. Account should be taken of the codes of practice produced by the CRE and EOC (see further chapters 14 and 15). For example, the CRE's code of practice for the elimination of discrimination and the promotion of equality of opportunity in employment recommends that employers should regularly monitor the effects of selection decisions and personnel practices and procedures, and suggests that this is best done by providing records that show the ethnic origins of existing employees and job applicants.[97] The absence of such records can be used to infer discrimination.

3.78 There is a general statutory duty (under RRA 1976 s71) on specified public bodies, when carrying out their functions:

- to eliminate unlawful racial discrimination; and
- to promote equality of opportunity and good relations between people of different racial groups.

The CRE has issued a Code of Practice which give public authorities practical guidance on steps they should take to tackle race discrimination and promote equal opportunities and good race relations. The Race Relations Act 1976 (Statutory Duties) Order 2001[98] require a wide range of specified public bodies (such as local authorities) to have monitoring arrangements by reference to racial groups. These relate to the numbers of staff in post and applicants for employment, training and promotion broken down by racial group. Where a public body has 150 or more full-time staff, there must be monitoring, by

96 [1977] IRLR 362: see para 14.110.

97 Code, para 1.34.

98 SI No 3458.

racial group, of numbers of staff who receive training; benefit or suffer detriment as a result of its performance assessment procedures; are involved in grievance procedures; are the subject of disciplinary procedures; or cease employment with that person. The monitoring must be published annually. The CRE has published 'Ethnic monitoring: a guide for public authorities.

3.79 In *Marshall v F Woolworth & Co Ltd*[99] the applicant suspected that the reason that she was not offered a job was because she was black. An ET inferred discrimination from the fact that there was no black person working in the store, even though there was a sizeable black population in the locality and about half the job applicants were black.

3.80 In *West Midlands Passenger Transport Executive v Singh*[100] the applicant complained of race discrimination after applying unsuccessfully for promotion to senior inspector. The employer denied this, referring to its equal opportunities policy and a system it had of ethnic monitoring of applications and appointments. While the employer voluntarily produced details of the ethnic origins, qualifications and experience of all applicants for the job of senior inspector, it refused to give details of the ethnic origins of applicants for, and appointees to, posts within a band of grades broadly comparable to senior inspector covering the period since the equal opportunities policy was adopted. The Court of Appeal ruled that the applicant was entitled to information about the number of white and non-white people who applied for similar jobs, categorised as to whether or not they had been appointed, covering the two-year period prior to his own unsuccessful application for promotion. The court held that the statistical material ordered was relevant as it was logically probative of whether the employers discriminated against him.

3.81 In *Singh* the Court of Appeal made the following general points:

- Statistical evidence may establish a discernible pattern in the treatment of a particular group; if that pattern demonstrates a regular failure of members of that group to obtain promotion in particular jobs and under-representation in such jobs, it may give rise to an inference of discrimination. That is why the CRE's code of practice recommends ethnic monitoring.
- Statistics obtained through monitoring are not conclusive in themselves, but if they show racial or ethnic imbalance or disparities, they may indicate areas of racial discrimination.

99 COIT 1404/80, ET.
100 [1988] IRLR 186.

- Any suggestion that it is unreasonable to expect employers to maintain records of the colour or ethnic origins of their employees is inconsistent with the code of practice.
- If a practice is being operated against a group, then, in the absence of a satisfactory explanation in a particular case, it is reasonable to infer that the complainant as a member of the group has been treated less favourably on the ground of race.
- Since the suitability of candidates can rarely be measured objectively and often requires subjective judgment, if there is evidence of a high percentage rate of failure to achieve promotion at particular levels by a certain group, this may indicate that the real reason for refusal is a conscious or unconscious racial attitude that involves stereotyped assumptions about members of that group.
- If evidence of an employer's non-discriminatory attitude is accepted as having probative force, so is evidence of a discriminatory attitude on its part.
- A tribunal may refuse a request for disclosure of documents if it requires the provision of material not readily to hand or if it means the employer embarking on a course which would add unreasonably to the length and cost of the hearing.

3.82 Access to information is not always easy if, for example, large numbers of personnel records are involved. Sometimes it is possible to build a case by pointing to less favourable treatment of other black or female employees, and they may be willing to be witnesses. Applicants should use the SDA 1975 and RRA 1976 questionnaires and tribunal discovery and written answers procedures to obtain such information (see chapter 25). In *Carrington v Helix Lighting*[101] the EAT ruled that the applicant could apply on notice to an ET for a second questionnaire to be served if necessary. The written answers procedure can also be used to ask additional questions (see para 32.118).

EC law: the importance of 'transparency'

3.83 Tribunals should be prepared to draw inferences from primary facts and evidentiary facts (see *Qureshi v Victoria University of Manchester*[102] above). The burden of proof still remains with the applicant, except in employment-related sex discrimination cases in which the applicant has shown less favourable treatment and a difference of sex. The

101 [1990] IRLR 6.
102 21 June 1996, EAT (unreported).

position under EC law may, as a result of the ECJ's decision in *Danfoss*,[103] be different. The facts of that case are set out at para 10.62. In brief, the ECJ there held that:

> Where an undertaking applies a pay system which is characterised by a total lack of transparency, the burden of proof is on the employer to show that his pay practice is not discriminatory where a female worker establishes, by comparison with a relatively large number of employees, that the average pay of female workers is lower than that of male workers.[104]

3.84 The concept of 'transparency' is an important one, as it requires the employer to give a rational explanation for decisions, practices and procedures that appear to be discriminatory. A similar approach is taken in the BP Regulations. Although *Danfoss* concerned equal pay, there appears to be no reason why the principle there established ought not to be applied to other discrimination cases. So, for example, where a disproportionate number of men or white people are appointed or promoted where there are equally qualified female and black applicants, the employer may be required to provide an explanation. Failure to do so may then lead to a finding of sex or race discrimination.

Burden of Proof Regulations 2001

3.85 The BP Regulations 2001 came into force on 12 October 2001 and are intended to implement the Burden of Proof Directive.[105] The amendment takes effect in relation to proceedings not determined in the court or ET by 12 October 2001. This should have been implemented by 22 July 2001 so it is arguable that the government is in breach of the directive in respect of cases heard between that date and 12 October 2001.

3.86 The Regulations amend the SDA 1975, by inserting new ss63A and 66A. Section 63A provides that:

> Where, on the hearing of the complaint, the complainant proves facts from which the tribunal could, apart from this section, conclude in the absence of an adequate explanation that the respondent –
> (a) has committed an act of discrimination against the complainant which is unlawful under Part 2 [the employment field], or

103 Case 109/88 *Handels-og Kontorfunktionaerernes Forbund I Danmark v Dansk Arbejdsgiverforening (acting for Danfoss)* [1989] ECR 3199; [1989] IRLR 532.

104 Ibid, at 533.

105 Council Directive 97/80/EC, as amended by Directive 98/52/EC.

(b) is by virtue of section 41 or section 42 [of the SDA 1975 – liability of employers and aiding unlawful acts, see para 31.30] to be treated as having committed such an act of discrimination against the complainant,

the tribunal shall uphold the complaint unless the respondent proves that he did not commit, or, as the case may be, is not to be treated as having committed, that act.

It follows that an ET must uphold a complaint of sex discrimination where:

- the complainant proves facts from which the ET could, in the absence of an adequate explanation, conclude there had been discrimination; and
- the employer fails to prove that he or she did not discriminate.

Similar provisions apply in relation to discrimination by, or in relation to, barristers and advocates (see SDA 1975 ss35A and 35B) and vocational training under SDA 1975 Pt III which covers discrimination in fields other than employment (see SDA 1975 s66A). In all cases, other than employment-related sex discrimination claims and SDA 1975 claims by barristers and advocates in relation to vocational training under SDA 1975 Pt III, the burden remains on the direct discrimination complainant throughout. The new Directive will change the burden of proof in race discrimination claims so that it is similar to that for sex discrimination claims.

3.87 In an employment case where the complaints prove facts from which the tribunal could conclude 'in the absence of an adequate explanation' that the respondent has committed an unlawful act of discrimination, the burden will shift to the employer to prove a non-discriminatory reason. It is not clear what a complainant will have to show before the burden will shift. It may be that if an applicant applies for a job and is refused and a person of a different sex is appointed, then the burden will shift to the employer to provide an explanation. However, it may be that, provided the employer can show that the appointee was clearly a better candidate, this would be sufficient to show that no 'less favourable treatment' had occurred (this because the relevant circumstances of the applicant and comparators were different – see the discussion at paras 3.18–3.20 above), and to block any shift in the burden of proof would not change. We consider that the former approach is the correct approach, because otherwise the BP Regulations would be unnecessary and would effect no change at all.

CHAPTER 4

Victimisation

Key points

4.1
- 'Victimisation' is regulated as a form of discrimination by the Sex Discrimination Act (SDA) 1975, the Race Relations Act (RRA) 1976 and the Disability Discrimination Act (DDA) 1995.
- The victimisation provisions protect from less favourable treatment those who have done a 'protected act' under the relevant legislation, that is:
  - people who have brought proceedings under the SDA 1975, the RRA 1976 or the DDA 1995; made complaints of unlawful discrimination or have otherwise done anything under or by reference to the relevant Act or (in the case of the SDA 1975), the Equal Pay Act (EqPA) 1970 or Pensions Act (PA) 1995;
  - people who have provided assistance to those who have made such complaints including those who have acted as witnesses.
- The victimisation provisions of the various Acts protect people whatever their sex or racial group, and whether they are disabled or not.
- People who have made complaints of unlawful discrimination are protected only where their complaint:
  - is made in good faith, and
  - is such that, if proved, it would amount to unlawful treatment under the relevant Act.
- Victimisation is not unlawful unless it occurs in circumstances made unlawful by the SDA 1975, the RRA 1976 or the DDA 1995 (ie, in relation to employment, goods and services, etc).
- Victimisation may occur without any conscious motivation on the part of the victimiser.
- A court or tribunal may infer that less favourable treatment was by reason that the complainant had done one of the 'protected acts' in the absence of an adequate explanation otherwise from the victimiser.

Background and statutory provisions

4.2 Victimisation is one form of discrimination made unlawful by the SDA 1975, the RRA 1976 and the DDA 1995.[1] It protects those seeking to enforce the SDA 1975, the EqPA 1970, the RRA 1976 and the

1 SDA 1975 s5(1)(a), RRA 1976 s3(1)(a) and DDA 1995 s55(1).

DDA 1995, either as complainants or witnesses, and those assisting them. Thus, this form of discrimination is not concerned with the sex or racial origins of the complainant or whether or not they are disabled.

4.3 SDA 1975 s4 provides that:

(1) A person ('the discriminator') discriminates another person ('the person victimised') in any circumstances relevant for the purposes of any provision of this Act if he treats the person victimised less favourably than in those circumstances he treats or would treat other persons, and does so by reason that the person victimised has –
(a) brought proceedings against the discriminator or any other person under this Act or the Equal Pay Act 1970 [or Pensions Act (PA) 1995 ss62–65], or
(b) given evidence or information in connection with proceedings brought by any person against the discriminator or any other person under this Act or the Equal Pay Act 1970 [or PA 1995 ss62–65], or
(c) otherwise done anything under or by reference to this Act or the Equal Pay Act 1970 [or PA 1995 ss62–65] in relation to the discriminator or any other person, or
(d) alleged that the discriminator or any other person has committed an act which (whether or not the allegation so states) would amount to a contravention of this Act or give rise to a claim under the Equal Pay Act 1970 [or PA 1995 ss62–65],
or by reason that the discriminator knows the person victimised intends to do any of those things, or suspects the person victimised has done, or intends to do, any of them.
(2) Sub-section (1) does not apply to treatment of a person by reason of any allegation made by him if the allegation was false and not made in good faith.[2]

RRA 1976 s2 is in materially identical terms.[3]

4.4 DDA 1995 s55 deals with victimisation for the purposes of the DDA 1995. It is drafted in somewhat different terms than the victimisation provisions in the SDA 1975 and the RRA 1976, though its meaning and effect is substantially the same. Section 55 provides that:

(1) For the purposes of Part II[4] or Part III,[5] a person ('A') discriminates against another person ('B') if –
(a) he treats B less favourably than he treats or would treat other persons whose circumstances are the same as B's; and
(b) he does so for a reason mentioned in subsection (2).

2 Words in square brackets inserted by PA 1995 s66(2).

3 Except that reference is made to the RRA 1976 rather than the SDA 1975, EqPA 1970 and PA 1995.

4 Discrimination in the employment field.

5 Discrimination outside the employment field.

(2) The reasons are that –
(a) B has –
(i) brought proceedings under against A or any other person under the Act; or
(ii) given evidence or information in connection with such proceedings brought by any person; or
(iii) otherwise done anything under this Act in relation to A or any other person; or
(b) A believes or suspects that B has done or intends to do any of these things.
(3) Where B is a disabled person, or a person who has had a disability, the disability in question shall be disregarded in comparing his circumstances with those of any other person for the purposes of subsection (1)(a).
(4) Subsection (1) does not apply to treatment of a person because of an allegation made by him if the allegation was false and not made in good faith.

The acts set out in SDA 1975 s4(1)(a)–(d), RRA 1976 s2(1)(a)–(d) and DDA 1995 s55(2) (above) are commonly referred to as 'protected acts'.

4.5 The victimisation provisions do not make any act unlawful by themselves. The victimisation provisions merely *define* one form of discrimination for the purposes of the other parts of the Acts.[6] In order to breach the relevant legislation there must also be a 'prohibited act' such as a failure to recruit or promote or other detriment.[7] This is plain from the terms of the legislation itself, and has been confirmed by the EAT in the case of *Nagarajan v Agnew*.[8]

4.6 There are significant differences in the law as it applies to complaints under the SDA 1975, on the one hand, and to the RRA 1976 and the DDA 1995, on the other. These differences, which relate to the scope of the protection afforded complainants in victimisation cases and to the burden of proof, are due to the effect of EC law[9] (which, at present, applies only in employment-related sex discrimination cases). The differences are dealt with as they arise under the headings below.

4.7 In summary, to succeed in a victimisation complaint an applicant must show that:

- he or she did or intended to do (or the discriminator believed or

6 SDA 1975 s5(1)(a), RRA 1976 s3(1)(a) and DDA 1995 s55(1).
7 Under SDA 1975 s6, RRA 1976 s4 and DDA 1995 s4, for example.
8 [1994] IRLR 61.
9 Most recently, the implementation of Council Directive 98/52/EC (Burden of Proof Directive – BPD).

suspected that he or she had done or intended to do) a protected act;

- he or she was treated less favourably;
- the less favourable treatment was 'by reason that' he or she had or intended to do (or the discriminator believed or suspected that he or she had done or intended to do) a protected act; and
- the protected act was not an allegation which was false and not made in good faith.[10]

'Less favourable treatment'

4.8 'Less favourable treatment' has the same meaning as in direct discrimination. Thus 'any disadvantage'[11] or deprivation of choice[12] might constitute less favourable treatment (see chapter 3).

4.9 As with direct discrimination, a victimised person need not show financial or material disadvantage to show less favourable treatment. It is enough to show there has been some disadvantage. Indeed a favourable financial outcome might conceal unlawful discrimination – one cannot 'buy a right to discriminate'.[13]

Need for a comparator (real or hypothetical)

4.10 To establish 'less favourable treatment' it must be shown that the person victimised has been treated less favourably by the discriminator than the discriminator treats or would treat another. In order to show that a person has been less favourably treated, a comparison must be made between the person who has done one of the protected acts set out at paras 4.3–4.4 above and another real or hypothetical comparator.

10 It should be noted that direct and indirect discrimination in the employment field is excluded from the employment provisions of the RRA 1976 where the employment concerned is in a private household and is not otherwise made unlawful: RRA 1976 s4(3). The exclusion does not apply to complaints of victimisation: RRA 1976 s4(3). Likewise the small employer exemption under DDA 1995 s7 (which exempts an employer who has fewer than 15 employees from liability under the employment provisions) does not apply to complaints of victimisation.

11 *Ministry of Defence v Jeremiah* [1980] QB 87; [1979] IRLR 436, para. 27, in which the question of *less* favourable treatment and detriment were subsumed into one question by Lord Brandon.

12 *Gill v El Vinos* [1983] QB 425; [1983] 1 All ER 398.

13 *Ministry of Defence v Jeremiah* [1980] QB 87; [1979] IRLR 436.

Who is the proper comparator?

4.11 The sex, racial group or disability status of the person victimised is irrelevant to any comparison which must be undertaken. Thus, a white woman who is dismissed for complaining about race discrimination against a black employee can claim victimisation under the RRA 1976. Her racial group is irrelevant. This is implied in the wording of the victimisation provisions in the SDA 1975 and the RRA 1976 and is made explicit by the DDA 1995.[14]

4.12 The proper comparison is between a person who has not done one of the protected acts and a person who has done one of the protected acts. The circumstances must otherwise be the same (see para 4.16 below).

4.13 There has been considerable controversy about the relevant circumstances for the purposes of the comparison, but the issue has now been settled by the decision of the House of Lords in *Chief Constable of West Yorkshire v Khan.*[15] Sergeant Khan complained of race discrimination when he was refused promotion over a number of years because of assessments made by his managers. The promotion assessments identified weaknesses in Sergeant Khan that were regarded as making him unsuitable for promotion to a more senior post.

4.14 While Sergeant Khan was awaiting an employment tribunal (ET) hearing of his race discrimination complaint, he applied to a different police force for a promoted post. The second police force requested a reference from Sergeant Khan's employer, the Chief Constable of West Yorkshire. Any reference would have been based on the promotion assessments about which Sergeant Khan complained in his race discrimination case. The Chief Constable took advice and refused to provide a reference because of the outstanding proceedings. He responded to the reference request to the effect that there was an outstanding claim in respect of his failure to support Sergeant Khan's application for promotion, and that he would make no further comment for fear of prejudicing his own case.

4.15 Sergeant Khan commenced proceedings for victimisation arising out of the refusal to provide him with a reference. The question was then whether he should be compared with a person who had brought proceedings against the Chief Constable other than under the RRA

14 DDA 1995 ss4(5), 12(4), 13(3), 19(4) and 22(7), which state that the unlawful acts concerned apply to non-disabled people where the complaint is of victimisation, and s55(3), which states that where a person victimised has any present or past disability this is to be disregarded in undertaking any comparison for the purposes of the victimisation provisions.

15 [2001] 1 WLR 1947; [2001] IRLR 830.

1976, or whether he should be compared to a person who had not brought proceedings at all. The evidence before the ET was that the Chief Constable would have refused a reference to any person who had brought proceedings against him where the accuracy of the reference was going to be the subject matter of dispute in the proceedings, whether or not the proceedings were brought under the RRA 1976. Identifying the proper comparator was therefore very important.

4.16 The House of Lords held that the proper comparator was a person who had not brought proceedings against the Chief Constable at all:

> The statute is to be regarded as calling for a simple comparison between the treatment afforded to the complainant who has done a protected act and the treatment which was or would be afforded to other employees who have not done the protected act. Applying this approach, Sergeant Khan was treated less favourably than other employees. Ordinarily West Yorkshire provides references for members of the force who are seeking new employment.[16]

Thus the proper comparator in a victimisation complaint is a person who has not done the act which gave rise to the less favourable treatment. It is not someone who has done the same act in circumstances unconnected with the SDA 1975, EqPA 1970, RRA 1976 or DDA 1995.[17]

4.17 The treatment of the complainant must have been less favourable than that which the respondent afforded a real comparator, or would have afforded a *hypothetical* comparator, in *those* circumstances.[18]

4.18 A complainant who relies on a real comparator should therefore ensure that their circumstances are the same. It is usually wise in such cases to rely on a hypothetical comparator in the alternative in case the tribunal does not accept that the situation of the real comparator is the same or similar.[18a]

4.19 As with direct discrimination a court or tribunal is entitled, in constructing a 'picture of how a hypothetical ... comparator would have

16 *Chief Constable of West Yorkshire v Khan* [2001] 1 WLR 1947; [2001] IRLR 830, paras 27–28, per Lord Nicholls.

17 Indeed, any other construction, in the context of the SDA 1975, is likely to be inconsistent with arts 5 and 6 of the Equal Treatment Directive (Council Directive 76/207 – ETD); the BPD and, in due course, the Race Directive (Council Directive 2000/43 – RD) and Council Directive 2000/78/EC establishing a general framework for equal treatment in employment and occupation (Employment Directive – ED) – see paras 4.39–4.46 below.

18 The DDA 1995 uses the word 'same' circumstances, but there is no difference in the meaning.

18a *Balamoody v UKCC for Nursing, Midwifery and Health Visiting* [2002] IRLR 288, CA.

been treated, to take account of how the respondent has treated other persons, who have not done protected acts, in different but not dissimilar circumstances'.[19]

'By reason that the person has done a protected act'

4.20 SDA 1975 s4, RRA 1976 s2 and DDA 1995 s55 require, in order to establish victimisation contrary to the discrimination Acts, that the less favourable treatment complained of must be 'by reason' that the person victimised has done a protected act.[20]

4.21 In *Nagarajan v London Regional Transport*[21] the House of Lords held that, in determining whether or not a person has been less favourably treated 'by reason'[22] that he or she has done one of the protected acts, a court or tribunal is not required to determine whether the discriminator was *consciously* motivated or influenced by the fact that the person victimised had done the protected act. Furthermore, the fact that the complainant had done a protected act need not be the *sole* cause of the less favourable treatment – it need only have had a 'significant influence'[23] or been the 'principal' or 'important' cause.[24]

4.22 According to the House of Lords in *Nagarajan v London Regional Transport*: 'although victimisation has a ring of conscious targeting, this is an insufficient basis for excluding cases of unrecognised prejudice'[25] from the victimisation provisions. And in *Khan* their Lordships stated that the relevant question was:

> ... why did the alleged discriminator act as he did? What consciously or unconsciously, was his reason.[26]

4.23 A court or ET is entitled to *infer* that the less favourable treatment of a person who has done one of the protected acts was *by reason of* his or

19 *Chief Constable of West Yorkshire v Vento* [2001] IRLR 124 and *Balamoody v UKCC for Nursing, Midwifery and Health Visiting* [2002] IRLR 288, CA; and see chapter 3.

20 Or intends to do, or is suspected of intending to do, a protected act.

21 [2000] AC 501; [1999] IRLR 572.

22 Mentioned in SDA 1975 s2 and RRA 1976 s4(a)–(d) (see para 4.4 above) or in the case of the DDA 1995 'for [such] a reason' (s55(1)(b)). There is no difference in the meaning between the two.

23 *Nagarajan v London Regional Transport* [2000] AC 501; [1999] IRLR 572, para 19 per Lord Nicholls.

24 Ibid para 35, per Lord Steyn.

25 Ibid para 18, per Lord Nicholls.

26 *Chief Constable of West Yorkshire v Khan* [2001] 1 WLR 1947; [2001] IRLR 830, para 29, per Lord Nicholls.

her having done the protected act, without proof of intent, motive or otherwise, where there is an otherwise inadequate explanation by the discriminator.

4.24 Having said this, the test for victimisation is not a simple 'but for' one. A subjective analysis of why the discriminator treated the complainant less favourably is required. Where the protected act has caused the less favourable treatment it will usually mean that the less favourable treatment was 'by reason' of it. But this will not always be the case, particularly where proceedings are pending. This is an important distinction, because the fact that an applicant has done a protected act will frequently cause another person to act in a particular way, although the latter may have a reason unconnected with the SDA 1975, RRA 1976 or DDA 1995 for so acting.

4.25 In *Khan* the House of Lords held that, although the fact that Sergeant Khan had brought proceedings caused the Chief Constable to refuse a reference, this did not establish that the refusal was 'by reason' of the fact that he had brought proceedings (per Lord Nicholls):

> Employers, acting honestly and reasonably, ought to be able to take steps to preserve their position in pending discrimination proceedings without laying themselves open to a charge of victimisation. This accords with the spirit and purpose of the Act. Moreover, the statute accommodates this approach without any straining of the language. An employer who conducts himself in this way is not doing so because of the fact that the complainant has brought discrimination proceedings. He is doing so because, currently and temporarily, he needs to take steps to preserve his position in the outstanding proceedings. Protected act (a) ('by reason that the person victimised has – (a) brought proceedings against the discriminator ... under this Act') cannot have been intended to prejudice an employer's proper conduct of his defence, so long as he acts honestly and reasonably. Acting within this limit, he cannot be regarded as discriminating by way of victimisation against the employee who brought the proceedings.[27]

4.26 Importantly, the House of Lords in *Khan* was influenced by the fact that Sergeant Khan's complaint of race discrimination was outstanding. Their Lordships held that the pending proceedings had the effect of changing the relationship between Sergeant Khan and the Chief Constable. Once proceedings had been commenced they were not just employer and employee, but also adversaries in litigation. The Chief Constable was entitled to protect himself in respect of that litigation. He could have been roundly criticised and ordered to pay

27 Ibid para 31.

more compensation if he provided a reference based on the promotion assessments when Sergeant Khan was complaining that they were racially discriminatory, and that issue had not been decided. Lord Hoffman gave the following guidance:

> A test which is likely in most cases to give the right answer is to ask whether the employer would have refused the request if the litigation had been concluded, whatever the outcome. If the answer is no, it will usually follow that the reason for refusal was the existence of the proceedings and not the fact that the employee had commenced them. On the other hand, if the fact that the employee had commenced proceedings under the Act was a real reason why he received less favourable treatment, it is no answer that the employer would have behaved in the same way to an employee who had done some non-protected act, such as commencing proceedings otherwise than under the Act.[28]

4.27 On the facts of *Khan* the House of Lords' decision is understandable. It may be, in many cases where legal proceedings are outstanding, that employers have to take steps in connection with those proceedings that are 'less favourable' to the person who brought the proceedings, than to others (by, for example, collecting evidence against an employee; making statements which are adverse to an employee, etc). But an employer will need to show, as in *Khan*, that there was reason apart from the fact that proceedings were commenced that caused the less favourable treatment. A court or tribunal is likely to be satisfied that the less favourable treatment was caused by the bringing of the proceedings where the conduct of an employer or other discriminator is unreasonable, unconnected with the proceedings or dishonest.

Burden of proof

4.28 In employment-related[29] victimisation cases brought under the SDA 1975 (but not the RRA 1976 or DDA 1995),[30] the burden of proof shifts to the respondent once a complainant shows that he or she has done a 'protected act' and has suffered less favourable treatment. This is because of the impact of the Burden of Proof Directive and the

28 *Khan* para 60.

29 SDA 1975 Pt II (cases heard in the ETs) and ss35A and 35B and Pt III cases (heard in the county court) in as far as they relate to vocational training: see Sex Discrimination (Indirect Discrimination and Burden of Proof) Regulations (BP Regs) 2001 SI No 2660, regs 5 and 6.

30 And not sex-related victimisation other than in the employment context.

Burden of Proof Regulations (BP Regulations) 2001 which give it domestic force. The BP Regulations 2001 came into force on 12 October 2001 but apply to any cases instituted before that date (as well as those instituted on or after it) where proceedings are not determined by that date.[31] They insert new sections 63A and 66A into the SDA 1975. SDA 1975 s63A provides as follows:

> (1) This section applies to any complaint presented under section 63 to an employment tribunal.
> (2) Where, on the hearing of the complaint, the complainant proves facts from which the tribunal could, apart from this section, conclude in the absence of an adequate explanation that the respondent –
> (a) has committed an act of discrimination[32] against the complainant which is unlawful by virtue of Part 2, or
> (b) is by virtue of section 41 or 42 to be treated as having committed such an act of discrimination against the complainant,
> the tribunal shall uphold the complaint unless the respondent proves that he did not commit, or, as the case may be, is not to be treated a having committed, that act.

SDA 1975 s66A is in similar terms, but relates to proceedings in the county court under SDA 1975 ss35A and 35B (discrimination in relation to barristers and advocates), and proceedings relating to vocational training.[33] Thus, in any case not determined by 12 October 2001, if a complainant proves (a) less favourable treatment and (b) that he or she has done a protected act, the burden of proof shifts to a respondent to explain the reason for the less favourable treatment in complaints falling within the scope of ss63A and 66A. If the respondent fails to provide a non-discriminatory explanation, the ET or county court will be bound to uphold the complainant's claim.

The protected acts

4.29 The protected acts are those set out in the statutes,[34] and the complainant will need to identify which section they come within. If there is any doubt they can be argued in the alternative.

4.30 These acts are 'protected' whether or not the respondent knew they were done in connection with the anti-discrimination legislation (see *Nagarajan*, and discussion above). However there are limitations,

31 BP Regs 2001 reg 2.

32 Which term includes victimisation: SDA 1975 s(1)(a).

33 See para 12.41.

34 SDA 1975 s4(1)(a)–(d), RRA 1976 s2(1)(a)–(d) and DDA 1995 s55(2)(a)–(b).

largely imposed by case law, on the reach of the protection afforded by these provisions.

'Brought proceedings against the discriminator'

4.31 As can be seen from *Khan* and the discussion above, where the 'protected act' is the bringing of proceedings, a complainant will need to show that the reason for the less favourable treatment was something other than an honest and reasonable step in the proceedings.

'Done anything under or by reference to this Act in relation to the discriminator or any other person'

4.32 In *Kirby v Manpower Services Commission*[35] the EAT held that the complainant had not done something 'under' the RRA 1976 when he reported client employees to the Community Relations Council for discriminatory acts. According to the EAT, 'under' required something to be done under a *specific* provision of the RRA 1976. This would appear to be wrong, as Mr Kirby had plainly done something 'by reference' to the RRA 1976 (this is covered by (c)). But the decision remains important because the DDA 1995 is somewhat narrower in wording than the equivalent provisions in the SDA 1975 and RRA 1976. The DDA 1995 protects a complainant who has:

> ... otherwise done anything *under* this Act in relation to [the discriminator] or any other person.[36]

Where proceedings are brought under the DDA 1995 it will be particularly important for a complainant to identify clearly the precise act and which part of the DDA 1995 it falls under (for example, by serving a questionnaire), and to claim in the alternative.

Alleged that the discriminator or any other person has committed an act which would be a breach of the Acts

4.33 Where the protected act relates to the making of an allegation of discrimination the allegation must be one which, if made out, constitutes a contravention of one of the Acts.[37] In *Waters v Metropolitan*

35 [1980] IRLR 229. This case was overruled by the House of Lords in *Khan* in respect of the approach it took to comparators.

36 Emphasis added.

37 SDA 1975 s4(1)(d), RRA 1976 s2(1)(d) and DDA 1995 s55(2)(a)(iv).

Police Commissioner[38] the Court of Appeal held that an ET correctly dismissed WPC Waters' complaints of victimisation by her employer, when the 'protected act' she relied on was a complaint made to her employer of sexual harassment by a male colleague. This was because the ET found that the sexual harassment took place outside the course of her male colleague's employment.

4.34 The Court of Appeal held that the allegation relied on – though it need not include in terms a statement that an act of discrimination contrary to one of the Acts had occurred – must be such that the asserted facts relied upon are capable of amounting in law to an unlawful act of discrimination. In this case, because the serious acts of sexual harassment[39] relied upon were found by the ET to be outside the course of employment, liability for them could not arise under the employment provisions of the SDA 1975.[40] They could not, therefore, constitute unlawful acts for the purposes of the SDA 1975.

4.35 It appears from the decision in *Waters* that the SDA 1975, RRA 1976 and DDA 1995 require the person victimised to show that he or she has made an allegation that a person has committed an act which, *if proved*, would amount to a contravention of the relevant Act. This amounts to a very narrow interpretation of the victimisation provisions. An allegation of unlawful discrimination by a person would amount to a contravention of one of the Acts only if all the necessary ingredients of unlawful discrimination are made out. A person victimised cannot know that, and ought not to be denied protection because at the time of making the complaint he or she cannot say with certainty that all the ingredients of the legal wrong can be proved. In relation to the DDA 1995 and small employers the impact is particularly harsh. An employee in an organisation employing fewer than 15 people who is victimised as a consequence of making an employment-related complaint of disability discrimination would appear to have no redress under the DDA 1995 victimisation provisions since small employers are exempt from the employment provisions of the DDA 1995. This is in spite of the fact that small employers are not excluded from the victimisation provisions. In respect of certain complaints of victimisation brought under the SDA 1975 a broader interpretation is necessary because of the impact of EC law (see paras 4.39–4.44 below).

4.36 *Kirby* and *Waters* demonstrate that it is very important to identify

38 [1997] IRLR 589.

39 Including vaginal and anal rape.

40 See para 31.4.

carefully the 'protected act' relied upon in any victimisation complaint. It is advisable to argue in the alternative if there are a number of ways in which the complaint may be put. It is also advisable that any complainant when making a complaint of discrimination should make it clear in that complaint that it is a complaint of discrimination under the SDA 1975, the RRA 1976 or the DDA 1995 as the case may be. A generalised complaint that there has been some unspecified discrimination is arguably insufficient.[41]

Bad faith

4.37 A statutory defence is available to employers in respect of a complaint of victimisation. Under SDA 1975 s4(2), RRA 1976 s2(2) and DDA 1995 s55(4), the victimisation provisions do not apply to treatment of a person by reason, or because, of 'any allegation made by him if the allegation was false and not made in good faith'.

4.38 The provisions on victimisation will not protect an employee who has made an allegation which was false *and* which was made in bad faith. Both elements must be satisfied, so that an employee who makes an allegation in good faith that turns out to be false will not lose protection under the victimisation provisions. Similarly, an employee who makes an allegation of discrimination that is true, but which is made for some improper motive, will not lose protection. In practice this defence is very rarely relied upon.

Unlawful acts and EC law

Equal Treatment Directive

4.39 In sex discrimination cases regard must be had to the Equal Treatment Directive (ETD).[42] Article 5(1) ETD states that the '[a]pplication of the principle of equal treatment with regard to working conditions, including the conditions governing dismissal, means that men and women shall be guaranteed the same conditions without discrimin-

41 In *Benn v Hackney LBC* (1994) DCLD 19, the ET held that allegations of a racist or sexist 'culture' did not amount to an allegation that the Acts had been contravened.

42 Council Directive 76/207/EC. In due course, regard will have to be had to the ED and RD in respect of the grounds of discrimination protected by them.

ation on grounds of sex'.[43] Article 6 ETD requires member states to 'introduce into their national legal systems such measures as are necessary to enable all persons who consider themselves wronged by failure to apply to them the principle of equal treatment within the meaning of Article ... 5 to pursue their claims by judicial process'.

4.40 In *Coote v Granada Hospitality Limited*[44] the European Court of Justice (ECJ) considered a claim by a woman who had settled a sex discrimination claim against her former employers, only to find that she had difficulties in finding employment. She alleged that the respondents had failed to provide her with a reference, and claimed that this amounted to victimisation under the SDA 1975.[45] An ET concluded that it did not have jurisdiction to hear the complaints because any failure to provide the reference occurred after the employment relationship had terminated.[46] The EAT, on appeal, referred the case to the ECJ.

4.41 The ECJ held that, particularly having regard to the objective of the ETD (which was 'to arrive at real equality of opportunity for men and women'), article 6 required member states to introduce into their national legal systems 'such measures as are necessary to ensure judicial protection for workers whose employer, after the employment relationship has ended, refuses to provide references as a reaction to legal proceedings brought to enforce compliance with the principle of equal treatment within the meaning of the Directive'.

4.42 The ruling by the ECJ was given domestic effect by the EAT when the case was remitted back to it. In *Coote v Granada Hospitality Limited (No 2)*[47] the EAT took the view that the ECJ's ruling required it, if at all possible, to interpret the SDA 1975 in a way which provided Ms Coote with protection against the victimisation about which she complained where that victimisation was in retaliation for proceedings brought during the course of employment. The EAT concluded that it

43 Art 1(1) ETD provides that its purpose is 'to put into effect in the Member States the principle of equal treatment for men and women as regards access to employment, including promotion, and to vocational training and as regards working conditions and, on the conditions referred to in paragraph 2, social security. This principle is hereinafter referred to as 'the principle of equal treatment'.

44 Case 185/97 [1998] ECR I-5199; [1998] IRLR 656.

45 See para 4.3 above and also para 11.45.

46 In this regard, the ET relied on the Court of Appeal's decision in *Adekeye v Post Office (No 2)* [1997] IRLR 105, see para 11.44.

47 [1999] IRLR 452. This is consistent with the general principles applicable to the application of Community law: *Litster v Forth Dry Dock and Engineering Co Limited* [1990] 1 AC 546; [1989] IRLR 161.

was obliged so to do notwithstanding the Court of Appeal's decision, in *Adekeye v Post Office (No 2)*,[48] that RRA 1976 s4(2) (which is materially identical to SDA 1975 s6(2)) did not apply to acts occurring after the employment relationship had terminated.

4.43 In *Coote (No 2)* the EAT concluded that, having regard to the language of the SDA 1975 and to ensure conformity with the ETD, it was possible to construe SDA 1975 s6 such that Ms Coote's complaint fell within its scope. Accordingly, and in conformity with the principles of EC law, the EAT concluded that the ET had jurisdiction to hear Ms Coote's complaint notwithstanding that it related to an act occurring after the employment relationship had terminated.

4.44 Since the decision in *Coote* the Court of Appeal has indicated that the impact of the ECJ's ruling is very narrow indeed. In *D'Souza v Lambeth LBC*[49] the court confirmed that *Coote* does not affect the court's judgment in *Adekeye (No 2)* in so far as it applies to discrimination under the RRA 1976 (whether that is direct or indirect discrimination or victimisation). The EAT has reached the same conclusion in disability cases – the DDA 1995 does not protect employees against discrimination or victimisation when the events complained of take place after the employment relationship has ended.[50] Even more narrowly, the Court of Appeal decided in *Rhys-Harper v Relaxion Group plc*[51] that the decision in *Coote* does not apply to sex discrimination claims other than those involving victimisation.

Race Discrimination and Employment Directives

4.45 By contrast with the ETD[51a] the new directives – the Race Directive (RD) and the Directive establishing a general framework for equal treatment in employment and occupation (the Employment Directive or ED) – deal expressly with victimisation and provide that member states must introduce 'such measures as are necessary to protect individuals from any adverse treatment or adverse consequence as a reaction to a complaint or to proceedings aimed at enforcing compliance with the principle of equal treatment'.[52] Further, they both provide that member states must ensure that there are mechanisms in place

48 [1997] IRLR 105.

49 [2001] EWCA Civ 794.

50 *Jones v 3M Healthcare Ltd and others* [2002] EWCA Civ 304.

51 [2001] IRLR 460.

51a Though this may change when the revised Equal Treatment Directive is enacted, see chapter 10.

52 Art 9 RD and art 11 ED.

for the enforcement of the obligations arising under them (including those relating to victimisation), even after the relationship in which the discrimination is alleged to have occurred has ended.[53]

4.46 Once the time limits for implementing the RD and ED have expired, and to ensure compliance with them, courts and tribunals should construe the SDA 1975, RRA 1976 and DDA 1995 so as to protect workers against victimisation that occurs after the termination of the employment relationship, as a consequence of acts done to enforce compliance with the obligations arising under the directives. This will mean that the decision in *Adekeye (No 2)* will require reconsideration in the context of victimisation at least, and is likely to be overruled in due course, if not by legislation then by case-law.

Examples of victimisation

4.47 Examples of cases in which victimisation has been found proved include:

- An employee who was refused a secondment because he had spent time in proceedings in race discrimination in the ET and in representing other employees on internal disciplinary matters concerned with allegations of race discrimination.[54]
- A black employee who was unlawfully victimised when he was barred from his company's bonus scheme after he accused his managing director of being a racist.[55]
- A social worker who was not informed as to why his application for promotion had been unsuccessful in accordance with the normal practice after he had made a complaint of race discrimination.[56]
- A university lecturer who had his application for promotion unfairly considered and who was placed last on a list of people entitled to performance-related pay so that he stood little or no

53 Art 7 RD and art 9 ED.

54 *Grant v City of Bradford Metropolitan Council* (1990) DCLD 4.

55 *Leacock v Zeller & Sons plc* (1995) DCLD 23

56 *Shah v Rochdale MBC* (1995) DCLD 25. This case is also interesting because it is a rare case where the respondents relied upon the 'bad faith' defence, arguing that the applicant's original complaint of race discrimination was 'false and not made in good faith'. The tribunal found that his original complaint was not well-founded but concluded that it was made in good faith and it was only where the complaint was both false *and* not made in good faith that the defence might be made out. The tribunal concluded that the complaint was made in good faith and thus rejected the respondent's defence.

chance of receiving such pay after he had brought proceedings in race discrimination against his employer.[57]

- An employee who was made redundant two weeks earlier than she otherwise would have been after she had complained that her manager had sexually harassed her.[58]
- A trade union official who was dismissed because he alleged that his immediate superior had committed acts of racial discrimination.[59]
- A woman who was not shortlisted for a position as a lecturer after she brought a grievance alleging sex discrimination against the university during a period when she was previously employed by them.[60]
- A secretary in a solicitors' firm who was dismissed after she had indicated that she would not support the senior partner as a witness in a sex discrimination claim brought against him by a dismissed pregnant employee.[61]
- An Asian worker who received a written warning after complaining that the way in which the company selected its employees for lay-off was potentially racially discriminatory.[62]
- A barrister who was refused a promotion because she had previously brought proceedings against her employer.[63]
- A woman who was given an unfair reference by her line manager because she had earlier brought sex discrimination proceedings.[64]
- A prison officer who was abused and humiliated by a prison governor after he had previously brought proceedings in race discrimination in the ET.[65]
- A trade union branch official of the GMB who was dismissed and expelled from the union after giving evidence in support of a sex discrimination claim brought by one of the union's female regional industrial officers.[66]
- A senior development officer who was required to relocate after taking race discrimination proceedings against his employer.[67]

57 *Majid v London Guildhall University* (1995) DCLD 25.
58 *Turner v Whitehouse Group Limited* (1996) DCLD 27.
59 *McFadden v Union of Shop, Distributive and Allied Workers* (1996) DCLD 28.
60 *Humberstone v MacFadyen and University of Southampton* (1996) DCLD 30.
61 *Bell v Tocher Neal & Co* (1997) DCLD 32.
62 *Sarai v Calhoun & Kennaugh and Calhoun Holdings Limited* (1997) DCLD 33.
63 *Naidoo v Commission for Racial Equality* (1998) DCLD 35.
64 *Capeling v Environment and Transport Secretary* (2000) DCLD 43.
65 *Johnson v Prison Service* (2000) DCLD 45.
66 *Ball v GMB* (2000) DCLD 45.
67 *Butt v Home Office* (2000) DCLD 46.

CHAPTER 5

Positive action

Key points

5.1
- 'Positive discrimination' (understood as discrimination in favour of a disadvantaged group) is generally prohibited by both the Sex Discrimination Act (SDA) 1975 and the Race Relations Act (RRA) 1976. By contrast, the Disability Discrimination Act (DDA) 1995 prohibits discrimination against, but not discrimination in favour of, disabled people.
- 'Positive discrimination' (discrimination in favour of those of a disadvantaged group) is permitted by the SDA 1975 and the RRA 1976 in very limited circumstances – namely, access to training for work in which that group is very under-represented. Employers are also permitted to encourage those of under-represented groups to apply for work, but not to discriminate at the appointment stage unless race or sex is a genuine occupational qualification for the job. Under the DDA 1995 a duty can arise to make reasonable adjustments to prevent arrangements or physical features from placing disabled people at a substantial disadvantage.
- In Northern Ireland, in which the Fair Employment and Treatment Order 1998 regulates discrimination on grounds of religion and political opinion, duties are imposed on employers to take positive action to prevent discrimination on these grounds.
- Public authorities in Great Britain are under a duty to 'have due regard to the need to eliminate unlawful [race] discrimination and promote equality of opportunity and good race relations in the carrying out of their functions'. In Northern Ireland public authorities are under a duty to have regard to the need to promote equality of opportunity between men and women, people with and without disabilities, people of different religious belief, political opinion, racial group, age, marital status or sexual orientation, and people with and without dependants.
- The Equal Treatment Directive and Article 141 of the EC Treaty permit member states to make limited provision for positive action between equally qualified candidates in circumstances when one sex is under-represented.
- The Race Directive and the Employment Directive provide that member states may make provision for specific measures to prevent or compensate for past disadvantage.

- International human rights law recognises that positive or affirmative action may be necessary in order to overcome past discrimination.

Background and statutory provisions

5.2 This chapter explores the narrowly defined areas in which positive action is permitted by the SDA 1975[1] and the RRA 1976.[2] The DDA 1995, which prohibits only discrimination against (as distinct from discrimination in favour of) those recognised as 'disabled' by the Act is considered only very briefly at para 5.3 below, as are the positive action provisions of Northern Ireland's Fair Employment and Treatment Order (FETO) 1998.[3] The Northern Irish provisions dealing with discrimination on grounds of religious belief and political opinion deal much more extensively with positive action than those which apply, both in Northern Ireland and elsewhere in the UK, to discrimination on grounds of race and sex. They indicate further steps that the law could take to remedy discrimination. Finally, this chapter considers in brief the extent to which EC law permits positive discrimination and the approach to this issue of international human rights provisions.

'Positive action' defined

5.3 The idea of 'equality' embraces concepts both of equality of opportunity and of equality of outcome, the latter more often described as substantive equality. International human rights instruments recognise the importance of substantive equality, a concept which has been only been partially recognised in domestic discrimination laws. The DDA 1995 requires that 'reasonable accommodation' be made in respect of the needs of disabled people (see generally chapters 6 and 30, and see para 6.15), thus permitting (and, indeed, requiring)

1 In Northern Ireland, the Sex Discrimination (Northern Ireland) Order 1976 SI No 1042, NI 15, as amended by the Sex Discrimination (Northern Ireland) Order 1988 SI No 1303, NI 13.

2 In Northern Ireland, the Race Relations (Northern Ireland) Order 1997 SI No 869, NI 6.

3 SI No 3162, NI 21.

positive action in favour of a person in a particular situation of disadvantage. And the prohibition of unjustified indirect discrimination by both the SDA 1975 and the RRA 1976 also serves to demand a measure of positive action to remove obstacles disproportionately disadvantaging particular groups (defined, respectively, by sex or race). Employers should review their employment practices in order to remove any barriers to employment for any significant minority. The introduction of less rigid work patterns, job-sharing or part-time working, for example, will benefit women by enabling those with childcare responsibilities to work. And failure to take these steps may itself render an employer vulnerable to claims of unlawful indirect discrimination. But neither the SDA 1975 nor the RRA 1976 permits, save in the narrowest of circumstances, the targeting of special measures towards people disadvantaged by their sex or racial group.

5.4 The prohibition of unjustified indirect discrimination goes some way towards achieving substantive, rather than merely formal, equality. But recognition is growing among many of the need for increased statutory measures designed to advance substantive equality. Such measures may be described by a number of different names – 'special measures', 'positive action', 'affirmative action', for example. These phrases recognise the need for remedial or other action, often time-limited, that takes into account the specific disadvantage suffered by a person or a group of people.

5.5 The main aim of the UK sex and race legislation is to remove discrimination, rather than positively to favour previously disadvantaged groups. The SDA 1975 and RRA 1976 do permit employers and other bodies to provide training for under-represented racial groups and sexes, and allow employers to 'encourage' those from under-represented groups to apply for jobs. But discrimination at the point of recruitment on the basis of sex or race is unlawful unless it can be justified on one of a very limited number of grounds (see further para 11.90). By contrast, there is no prohibition on positive action in favour of people with disabilities to overcome the disadvantages that they may suffer.

5.6 The government has increasingly recognised the importance of complementing the prohibition of discrimination with an emphasis on the promotion of equal opportunities. New duties have been introduced on public authorities in Northern Ireland to promote equal opportunities across a wide range of grounds,[4] and on public authorities elsewhere in the UK to promote race equality. The impact of

4 See Northern Ireland Act 1998 s75, discussed at para 5.30.

these duties has yet to be tested in the courts. Very limited steps have also been taken to embrace 'positive discrimination' – notably in the recruitment of Catholics to Northern Ireland's overwhelmingly Protestant police force[5] – and in proposals to permit discrimination in favour of women in the selection of parliamentary candidates.[6]

Positive action permitted by domestic law

Race Relations Act 1976

Positive action by employers

5.7 The RRA 1976 permits an employer to take limited positive action in favour of those of a particular racial group (see para 2.33) where, 'in relation to particular work in his employment at a particular establishment in Great Britain' (s38(2)):

(a) there are no persons of that racial group doing that work at that establishment; or
(b) the proportion of persons of that group doing that work at that establishment is small in comparison with the proportion of persons of that group:
 (i) among all those employed by that employer there; or
 (ii) among the population of the area from which that employer normally recruits persons for work in its employment at that establishment.

5.8 Employers are not permitted by RRA 1976 s38(2) to discriminate in favour of people from the under-represented racial group at the point of recruitment. Rather, where one of the conditions set out in s38(2) has been satisfied at any time during the previous 12 months, employers may (and may only) (s38(1)):

- provide training for employees of that particular racial group 'which would help fit them for that work', and/or

5 The FETO 1998 expressly permits what would otherwise be unlawful discrimination on grounds of religion – see further para 5.19 below.

6 Previous Labour Party 'women only' shortlists designed to combat the overwhelmingly disproportionate selection by local constituency parties of male candidates having been ruled unlawful, as in breach of the SDA 1975, by a tribunal in *Jepson & Dyas-Elliott v Labour Party* [1996] IRLR 116, which decision was approved by the Employment Appeal Tribunal (EAT) in *Sawyer v Ahsan* [2000] ICR 1, a case brought under the RRA 1976. More recently, however, see *McDonagh & Treisman v Ali* [2002] EWCA Civ 93, discussed in chapter 12. In any event express provision is made for some positive discrimination by the Sex Discrimination (Election Candidates) Act 2002.

- encourage members of that racial group (whether employees or job applicants) 'to take advantage of opportunities for doing that work at that establishment'.

5.9 The Commission for Racial Equality (CRE) code of practice for the elimination of racial discrimination and the promotion of equality of opportunity in employment recommends that employers should monitor their workforce regularly to see if employees of a particular racial group are concentrated in particular areas of work, with a view to providing training for members of particular racial groups in any work in which they are under-represented. The code further recommends that, where under-representation is found, employers should adopt the following measures:

- job advertisements designed to reach members of the under-represented group(s) and to encourage their applications – the use of publications directed at the relevant racial group is recommended;
- the use of employment agencies and careers offices in areas in which any under-represented group is concentrated;
- recruitment and training schemes for school-leavers designed to reach members of under-represented groups;
- the encouragement of employees from under-represented groups to apply for promotion and/or transfer opportunities;
- the provision of training for members of under-represented groups who lack particular expertise but who show potential.[7]

Positive action by training bodies

5.10 RRA 1976 s37 provides that 'any person' (this includes local authorities and other training providers) may discriminate in the manner set out in s38(1) (ie, by providing training to those of a particular racial group, or encouraging them 'to take advantage of' particular work opportunities) where (s37(1)):

> it reasonably appears to that person that at any time within the [preceding] twelve months:
> (i) there were no persons of that group among those doing that work in Great Britain; or
> (ii) the proportion of persons of that group among those doing that work in Great Britain was small in comparison with the

7 CRE code of practice, para 1.45.

proportion of persons of that group among the population of Great Britain.[8]

5.11 RRA 1976 s37(2) provides that preferential training or encouragement may be afforded in particular geographical areas of Great Britain where those of the particular racial group are under-represented in that area.

Other lawful positive action

5.12 The other forms of 'positive action' permitted by the RRA 1976 consist of:

- 'any act done in affording persons of a particular racial group access to facilities or services to meet the special needs of persons of that group in regard to their education, training or welfare, or any ancillary benefits' (s35);
- 'training by trade unions, employers' organizations and professional bodies to help members of under-represented racial groups to take up posts in the organization, and the encouragement of these people to apply for positions within the organization and [section 38(5)] to become members of it' (s38(3) and (4)).

5.13 The positive action permitted by RRA 1976 s35 could include language training facilities, health or welfare training or training to assist with the setting up or running of a business, though the emphasis on 'access to facilities and services' means that it would be unlikely to extend to the provision of funds to enable someone from a particular racial group to set up in business.

5.14 In *Hughes v Hackney LBC*[9] an employment tribunal (ET) ruled that 'access to facilities and services' was not wide enough to encompass the provision of job opportunities as the provision of a job was neither a 'facility' nor a 'service' unless the job was itself a training post. Discrimination at the point of selection for work is not permissible.[10] Hackney had advertised for gardeners, stating that it warmly welcomed applications from ethnic minorities. The advertisement was lawful under RRA 1976 s38(1)(b) but three white applicants were informed that the posts were open *only* to ethnic minority applicants. The employer argued that the discrimination in recruitment fell within RRA 1976 ss35 and 38.

8 Race Relations (Northern Ireland) Order 1997 art 37 is in similar terms save that the under-representation must be within all or part of Northern Ireland.
9 6 February 1986 (unreported).
10 See the CRE code of practice (para 5.9 above).

5.15 Having dismissed Hackney's argument relating to s35 the ET went on to rule that s38(1)(b)'s 'encouraging' did not extend to providing job opportunities. In addition, Hackney had failed to prove that the proportion of ethnic minority workers doing relevant work at the establishment was small in comparison with the proportion of people of that group among the population from which the council normally recruited. There was a smaller proportion of black gardeners than of black residents of Hackney. But the ET pointed out that only 58 per cent of the council's recruits came from within the borough and that, accordingly, the 'area' by reference to which under-representation was to be judged should not be restricted to Hackney. There was no evidence of where outside Hackney the remaining recruits came from or what proportion of ethnic minority members were within that population.

Sex Discrimination Act 1975

Positive action by employers

5.16 Employers can discriminate in favour of men or women under the same circumstances as outlined at para 5.7 above, ie, where that sex has been under-represented in particular work in the employer's establishment at any time in the preceding 12 months (SDA 1975 s48). The positive action permitted is limited to training and the encouragement of applications as is the case under RRA 1976 s38, and discrimination is unlawful at the point of recruitment unless a genuine occupational qualification or other defence applies (see further para 11.68).

5.17 The Equal Opportunities Commission (EOC) code of practice for the elimination of discrimination on the grounds of sex and marriage and the promotion of equality of opportunity in employment suggests that employers should train their employees for work that is traditionally the preserve of the other sex – by, for example, training women in skilled manual or technical work. It also suggests that employers might need positively to encourage women to apply for management posts and, perhaps, to provide special courses for them. The code also provides that, where one sex is under-represented, employers may wish to consider measures such as advertisements that encourage applications from people of that sex, although it must be made clear that selection will be on merit. Employers could, it is suggested, notify job agencies that they wish to encourage members of one sex to apply, and ask agencies to inform members of that sex that applications from them are particularly welcome. They might also include such statements in job advertisements.

Special training connected with family responsibilities

5.18 SDA 1975 s47(3) provides that special training, but not 'employment', may be provided to people who have been out of work on account of their family responsibilities (whether in connection with young children or otherwise). This provision applies to men as well as women but in practice is likely to be to the benefit primarily of women. Section 47(3) does not permit discrimination in training which amounts to 'employment' under that Act (such as apprenticeships). [11]

Fair Employment and Treatment (Northern Ireland) Order 1998

5.19 The FETO 1998 permits employers to take 'affirmative action' defined as (article 4):

> action designed to secure fair participation [undefined] in employment by members of the Protestant, or members of the Roman Catholic, community in Northern Ireland by means including –
> (a) the adoption of practices encouraging such participation; and
> (b) the modification or abandonment of practices that have or may have the effect of restricting or discouraging such participation.[12]

Northern Irish employers may engage in 'affirmative action' at will, and are not constrained by the under-representation requirements imposed by the RRA 1976 and SDA 1975. They may also (see further below) be required to take such action in response to a religious imbalance in their workforce.

5.20 As is the case under the SDA 1975 and the RRA 1976, the form which positive action may take is limited under the FETO 1998. Employers may (article 76) discriminate on grounds of religious belief in providing training. But they may do so only in relation to *non-employees*, and then only when the under-representation in their

11 See generally chapter 7 and, on the issue of justifying indirect discrimination by reference to societal good, see *Greater Manchester Police Authority v Lea* [1990] IRLR 372.

12 See also the Fair Employment Commission's code of practice, *Fair Employment in Northern Ireland*, s6, 'Duties on Employers'.

workplace of people of the faith targeted has been certified by the Equality Commission (the body now charged in Northern Ireland with overseeing all equality legislation).

5.21 In addition to the discrimination permitted by article 76 the FETO 1998 permits employers (article 72) 'in pursuit of affirmative action' to target training in a particular area or at a particular class of person, that class 'not being a class framed by reference to religious belief or political opinion'. Article 73 permits employers to adopt redundancy procedures designed to secure or maintain fair participation, and which result in the selection for redundancy of a greater proportion of Catholics than Protestants (or vice versa), as long as the procedure 'does not involve the application of any condition or requirement framed by reference to religious belief or political opinion'. Thus, for example, if the pursuit of affirmative action has resulted in a marked increase in the recruitment of Catholics to a previously Protestant workplace, and the traditional 'last-in, first-out' redundancy selection procedure would involve an increase in the degree of under-representation of Catholics in the workplace, an employer may adopt an alternative redundancy procedure to avoid this result without breaching the FETO 1998. And article 75 permits employers to limit recruitment to those who have been unemployed for a particular period. Such is the disproportionate impact of unemployment on Northern Irish Catholics that this would otherwise amount, at least potentially,[13] to unlawful indirect discrimination under the FETO 1998.

5.22 Articles 72, 75 and 76 of the FETO 1998 permit only 'indirect' positive discrimination. Article 76, discussed above, permits direct discrimination in pursuit of affirmative action, though only in very limited circumstances (more limited, indeed, than is the case under the RRA 1976 and the SDA 1975). Article 74 also permits a limited form of direct discrimination in the form of the encouragement by employers, employment agencies and others, in pursuit of affirmative action, of applications for employment or training. Again, as is the case with the equivalent provisions of the SDA 1975 and RRA 1976, Article 74 does not permit discrimination at the point of recruitment.

5.23 The FETO 1998 requires public sector employers, and those private sector employers having at least 10 employees, to register with and submit annual monitoring returns to the Equality Commission.[14]

13 Subject to the possibility of justification.

14 FETO 1998 arts 47–54.

These employers are under a duty to review their employment composition and practices at least every three years, in order to facilitate fair participation in employment. If workforce monitoring discloses an actual or anticipated lack of 'fair participation' on the part of either Catholics or Protestants, employers must (article 55) 'determine the affirmative action (if any) which would be reasonable and appropriate'. Such action may include the establishment of goals and timetables to set out the 'progress towards fair participation in employment in the concern that can reasonably be expected to be made by members of a particular community'. Finally, the Equality Commission is required (article 56):

> ... where a review discloses that members of a particular community are not enjoying, or are not likely to continue to enjoy, fair participation in employment in the concern, [to] make such recommendations as it thinks fit as to the affirmative action to be taken and, assuming the action is taken, as to the progress towards fair participation in employment in the concern, by reference to any period or periods, that can reasonably be expected to be made by members of the community.

5.24 The Commission may seek an undertaking from an employer that affirmative action will be undertaken and, if such an undertaking is refused, or is given and not complied with, may issue a legally enforceable order. This approach is widely considered to have been effective, as the religious imbalance in employment has been significantly reduced since the implementation of fair employment legislation.[15] Additionally, it has been found that the approach of self-assessment, rather than the more adversarial approach of complaints and investigations, has been preferred by employers.[16]

5.25 The Police (Northern Ireland) Act 2000 was passed in response to problem of under-representation of Catholics in the Royal Ulster Constabulary recently highlighted by the Patten report.[17] Section 46 of the Act specifically requires the appointment of equal numbers of Catholics and others to the police force. This is a temporary provision to meet a specific identified need that is 'reviewed on a triennial basis

15 See Equality Commission for Northern Ireland, 'Position paper on the Single Equality Bill' (2001), s9.5. The paper is available from the Equality Commission for Northern Ireland, Equality House, 7–9 Shaftsbury Square, Belfast, BT2 7DP or at www.equalityni.org.

16 Ibid s9.6.

17 *The Report of the Independent Commission on Policing for Northern Ireland* (1999), available at www.belfast.org.uk/report.htm.

and in consultation with the Policing Board'. This will be permitted under EC law when the Employment Directive (ED) comes into force, its lawfulness being expressly recognised by article 18(1) of the directive.

Duties to promote equal opportunities

Race Relations (Amendment) Act 2000

5.26 Section 2 of the Race Relations (Amendment) Act (RRAA) 2000 amended RRA 1976 s71 to impose a new positive 'general' duty on all public authorities in Great Britain to 'have due regard to the need to eliminate unlawful discrimination and promote equality of opportunity and good race relations in the carrying out of their functions'. The public authorities affected by this provision are listed in Schedule 1A to the RRAA 2000, which may be added to by statutory instrument. It includes most public authorities including education authorities, health authorities, central and local government and police authorities.

5.27 The Home Secretary has imposed certain 'specific' duties on specified public authorities to ensure their 'better performance' of their general duties.[18] Such authorities have a duty to prepare and publish racial equality schemes setting out how they intend to meet their general and specific duties. Drawing up such a scheme will involve public authorities in:

- assessing and consulting on the likely impact of their proposed policies on the promotion of race equality;
- monitoring their policies in order to assess any adverse impact on the promotion of race equality;
- publishing the results of such assessment or consultation;
- ensuring public access to the information and services which they provide; and
- training staff in the application of these duties.

5.28 Public authorities which are required to draw up race equality schemes must review their schemes every three years.[19] Additionally, all public authorities who are subject to the 'general' duty (see above) must ethnically monitor their existing staff as well as all applicants for

18 See RRA 1976 s71(2) and RRA 1976 (Statutory Duty) Order 2001 SI No 3458. The public authorities are those specified in Sch 1 to the Order.

19 RRA 1976 (Statutory Duty) Order 2001 reg 2.

jobs, training or promotion and must publish the results annually. Codes of practice with sector-specific guidance for the areas of health, local authorities, police and education has been issued.[20]

Duties on devolved powers

5.29 Greater London Authority Act 1999 s33 provides that, in the exercise of the GLA's powers, it shall have 'due regard to the principle that there should be equality of opportunities for all people'. The Act also requires the authority to make an annual statement about the action that it has taken to give effect to this provision. Government of Wales Act 1998 s43 imposes on the Welsh Assembly a duty 'to make appropriate arrangements with a view to securing that its functions are exercised with due regard to the principle that there should be equality of opportunity for all people', although it is not under a duty to report to any body.

Northern Ireland Act 1998

5.30 Northern Ireland Act 1998 s75 imposes a duty on all public authorities in Northern Ireland to have regard to the need to promote equality of opportunity – not just between men and women, or people with and without a disability, but also between people of different religious belief, political opinion, racial group, age, marital status or sexual orientation, and between people with and without dependants.[21] This duty is potentially enormously significant, not least because of the obligation imposed on public authorities to draw up equality schemes in consultation with those affected.

EC law

Sex equality

5.31 Article 2(4) of the Equal Treatment Directive[22] (ETD) provides that the principle of equal treatment shall be 'without prejudice to measures to promote equal opportunity for men and women'. The meaning of this has been explored by the European Court of Justice (ECJ) in a

20 Available from the CRE at www.cre.gov.uk.
21 Northern Ireland Act 1998 s75.
22 Council Directive 76/207/EEC.

series of four cases,[23] from which it is clear that permitted positive action does not include the selection of a less qualified woman in preference to a better qualified man simply because she belongs to the under represented sex.[24] The circumstances under which a woman may be preferred over an equally qualified man in the event of female under-representation are less clear, not least because of a change of heart by the ECJ in the earlier cases.[25] But it is unlawful discrimination for automatic and unconditional priority to be given to the candidate of the under-represented sex. In order for a national 'positive action' measure to be compatible with the ETD it should apply in conditions of equality between candidates and it must not absolutely and unconditionally prefer the under-represented sex.

5.32 The ECJ has ruled[26] that the ETD does not prevent:

> ... a rule of national case law under which a candidate belonging to the under-represented sex may be granted preference over a competitor of the opposite sex, provided that the candidates possess equivalent or substantially equivalent merits, where the candidatures are subject to an objective assessment which takes account of the specific personal situations of all the candidates.

5.33 Article 119 of the Treaty of Rome was silent on the matter of positive discrimination. But the backlash resulting from the ECJ's first, very narrow ruling on positive action (in *Kalanke*, 1997[27]) resulted in the inclusion in the amended article 141 EC of the following provision:

> (4) With a view to ensuring full equality in practice between men and women in working life, the principle of equal treatment shall not prevent any Member State from maintaining or adopting measures providing for specific advantages in order to make it easier for the under-represented sex to pursue a vocational activity or to prevent or compensate for disadvantages in professional careers.

23 Case 450/93 *Kalanke v Freie Hansestadt Bremen* [1995] ECR I-3051; [1995] IRLR 660. See also Case 409/95 *Marschall v Land Nordrhein-Westfalen* [1997] ECR I-6363, [1998] IRLR 39; Case 158/97 *Badeck v Landesanwalt beim Staatgerichtshof des Landes Hessen* [2000] ECR I-1875, [2000] IRLR 432 and Case 407/98 *Abrahamsson & Anderson v Fogelqvist* [2000] ECR I-5539, [2000] IRLR 732.

24 *Abrahamsson*, ibid.

25 Between Case 450/93 *Kalanke v Freie Hansestadt Bremen* [1995] ECR I-3051; [1995] IRLR 660 and Case 409/95 *Marschall v Land Nordrhein-Westfalen* [1997] ECR I-6363, [1998] IRLR 39.

26 Case 407/98 *Abrahamsson & Anderson v Fogelqvist* [2000] ECR I-5539, [2000] IRLR 732 at 738.

27 [1995] ECR I-3051; [1995] IRLR 660.

In *Abrahamsson & Anderson v Fogelqvist* the ECJ took a relatively narrow approach to this provision, ruling that preferential treatment accorded to a less qualified candidate of the under-represented sex was disproportionate to the legitimate aim recognised by article 141(4) and thus in breach of article 2(4) ETD. The ECJ case-law on positive action is considered further in chapter 9.

Other grounds

5.34 The Race Directive[28] (RD) makes specific provision that, in order to ensure full equality in practice, member states *may* adopt specific measures to prevent or compensate for disadvantages linked to racial or ethnic origin (article 4). The Employment Directive[29] (ED) makes a similar provision in respect of employment-related discrimination on grounds of sexual orientation, religion and belief, disability, and age (article 7). These provisions, like those of the ETD and article 141 EC, merely permit and do not require positive action to ameliorate discrimination. They will not, therefore, require any changes to domestic law.

Other human rights obligations

5.35 Human rights law also recognises that affirmative action may be necessary in order to overcome past discrimination. The implementation of the Human Rights Act (HRA) 1998 makes these provisions of increasing relevance. The HRA 1998, which gives domestic effect to a number of the provisions of the European Convention on Human Rights, is considered in chapter 9. Of those provisions of international law which do not have domestic effect perhaps the most significant is article 26 of the International Covenant on Civil and Political Rights (ICCPR), which provides that:

> All persons are equal before the law and are entitled without any discrimination to the equal protection of the law. In this respect the law shall prohibit and discrimination and guarantee to all persons equal and effective protection against discrimination on any ground such as race, colour, sex, language, religion, political, or other opinion, national or social origin, property, birth or other status.

28 Council Directive 2000/43/EC.

29 Council Directive 2000/78/EC.

5.36 According to the UN Human Rights Committee states may take positive measures (including affirmative action measures) to ensure equal enjoyment of rights without breaching article 26 ICCPR.[30] Additionally, article 2(2) of the International Covenant on the Elimination of All Forms of Racial Discrimination specifically provides for the adoption of 'positive measures' to promote racial equality, and article 4 of the Convention on the Elimination of Discrimination against Women provides for 'temporary special measures' in order to accelerate de facto equality between men and women.

5.37 Although the UK has signed these treaties they have not been directly incorporated into UK law nor has the UK government agreed to the right of individual petition for UK citizens. There is, however, a system of periodic reviews when the UK reports to the relevant UN committee on the progress that the UK government has made on the implementation of their convention obligations. The last report of the UN Committee on the Elimination of Racial Discrimination in August 2000 criticised the UK government for, among other things:

- failing to incorporate the terms of the convention directly into UK legislation;
- failing to allow UK citizens the right of direct petition to the Committee when breaches of the convention are alleged; and
- limiting the use of positive action measures that could be used to remedy racial inequalities.[31]

30 General Comment 18, CCPR/C/SR 901.

31 See www.unhchr.ch/tbs/doc.nsf/(Symbol)/CERD.C.304.Add.102.En?Opendocument.

CHAPTER 6

Disability discrimination

Key points

6.1
- Disability discrimination is different in concept to sex and race discrimination and provides rights for disabled people, rather than a right to equal treatment regardless of disability.
- The Disability Discrimination Act (DDA) 1995 introduced:
  - a right not to be treated less favourably without justification for a reason relating to a person's disability;
  - a duty on employers and others to make reasonable adjustments in certain circumstances;
  - protection from victimisation in connection with the Act.

  The first two issues are considered here, the third in chapter 4.
- The DDA 1995, unlike the Sex Discrimination Act (SDA) 1975 and the Race Relations Act (RRA) 1976, does not categorise discrimination as either 'direct' or 'indirect'. The Act permits the justification of all discrimination except victimisation. The SDA 1975 and the RRA 1976, by contrast, provide a general justification defence only in relation to the indirect discrimination.
- This chapter examines the meaning of disability discrimination in the employment context. The meaning of discrimination in relation to goods and services, education, housing, and transport provisions is somewhat different, and is considered in chapter 30.
- An employer need not know of an employee or job applicant's disability to discriminate against him or her.
- A duty of reasonable adjustment will arise if the employer's work arrangements or the workplace substantially disadvantage a disabled person unless the employer does not, and could not be expected to know of the disability or disadvantage.
- At present, EC law does not deal with disability discrimination, but the disability provisions of the Employment Directive (ED) must be implemented by July 2006. The government proposes to amend the DDA 1995 by October 2004 to comply with the directive.

Background and statutory provisions

6.2 8.5 million people in the UK (one in seven of the adult population) are disabled.[1] Nearly one fifth of the working age population is disabled.

1 Disability Rights Commission (DRC) *Annual Report*, 2000–01.

Only one in ten disabled people is in employment.[2] Individual, legally enforceable protection from discrimination was first introduced in the UK on 2 December 1996, when the employment and some of the goods and services provisions of the DDA 1995 came into force. Prior to this date, the Disabled Persons (Employment) Act 1944 provided a quota system for the employment of disabled people. The entire Act, which created no individual rights, was enforceable only through criminal sanctions and was little used, ineffective, and long-since discredited. Despite its widespread non-observance, no prosecutions were ever brought under it.

6.3 Prior to the adoption of the DDA 1995 there had been 16 unsuccessful attempts to introduce statutory legal rights for people with disabilities. The DDA 1995 was initially seen as a watered-down version of the sex and race discrimination legislation, and was introduced somewhat reluctantly by a Conservative government. Controversially the Act exempted small employers from the employment provisions (see further chapter 13) and provided a general justification defence.[3] No similar exemption or general justification defence was provided by either the SDA 1975 or the RRA 1976, which permits only *indirect* discrimination to be justified other than in particular, narrowly defined circumstances.

6.4 The DDA 1995 is certainly closer in structure and framework to the SDA 1975 and RRA 1976 than it is to the Disabled Persons (Employment) Act 1944, but it is crucially different in its definition of discrimination which this chapter will explore. The two principal forms of 'discrimination' are set out in DDA 1995 ss5 and 6 which prohibit:

- unjustified less favourable treatment for a reason relating to disability, and
- unjustified failure to make reasonable adjustments.

6.5 This chapter will consider the meaning of disability discrimination in the employment context. The definition of discrimination differs slightly in the other fields of activity (such as transport, education, and the provision of goods and services) covered by the DDA 1995. This is considered in chapter 30. The employment definition of discrimination is largely used in relation to discrimination by trade organisations which, relating to the employment field as it is widely defined

2 National Disability Council (predecessor to the DRC) *Annual Report*, 1998–99.

3 The justification defence does not apply to discrimination by way of victimisation.

and is considered in chapter 12 below. The DDA 1995 also differs from the SDA 1975 and RRA 1976 in regulating only discrimination against the disabled (see further chapter 2), rather than (as in the case of the SDA 1975 and RRA 1976) adopting a 'symmetrical' approach'.[4]

6.6 The law on employment-related disability discrimination is found principally in the DDA 1995 and the Disability Discrimination (Employment) Regulations (DD(E) Regulations) 1996.[5] A statutory code of practice for the elimination of discrimination in the field of employment against disabled persons or persons who have a disability was issued in 1996 by the Secretary of State for Education and Employment. This code of practice, like those issued by the Equal Opportunities Commission (EOC) and the Commission for Racial Equality (CRE) (see paras 1.9, 1.14 and 1.18), is admissible in evidence in courts and tribunals. Although it is not intended to be an authoritative statement of the law, its provisions must be taken into account to the extent that they appear to the court or tribunal to be relevant to any question arising in proceedings under the DDA 1995.[6] The code of practice is a particularly useful reference point and provides practical examples and illustrations. It is more expansive than the statutory codes of practice issued under the SDA 1975 and RRA 1976. Tribunals have been criticised for failing to take account of its provisions, and the Employment Appeal Tribunal (EAT) has ruled that employment tribunal (ET) decisions should make express reference to any of its relevant provisions.[7] A significant body of case law has also built up in the five years since the DDA 1995 came into force on the meaning of discrimination under the DDA 1995.

Discrimination by less favourable treatment

6.7 The definition of discrimination by less favourable treatment is set out in DDA 1995 s5(1) which provides that:

(1) an employer discriminates against a disabled person if –
 (a) for a reason which relates to the disabled person's disability, he

4 For instance, protecting the advantaged as well as the disadvantaged. The exception to this is the victimisation provisions which protect both disabled and non-disabled people who are treated less favourably for performing a protected act (see chapter 9).

5 SI No 1456.

6 DDA 1995 s53A.

7 *Goodwin v Patent Office* [1999] IRLR 4.

treats him less favourably than he treats or would treat others to whom that reason does not or would not apply; and
(b) he cannot show that the treatment is justified.

This definition of discrimination can be broken down into three parts. First, the disabled person must show that the treatment complained of was for a reason relating to his or her disability. Second, the disabled person must show that he or she was treated less favourably than others to whom that reason does not (or would not) apply. Third, the employer may escape a finding of unlawful discrimination by justifying the less favourable treatment. Justification is dealt with at para 6.38 below.

'For a reason which relates to his or her disability'

6.8 The DDA 1995 form of words 'for a reason which relates to his or her disability' is a much wider definition of discrimination than the definition of direct discrimination adopted by the SDA 1975 and the RRA 1976 (less favourable treatment *on grounds of* sex or race). It encompasses some acts which would amount to '*indirect* discrimination' under those Acts, as well as those which would amount to *direct* discrimination, or which might not amount to actionable discrimination at all.[8]

6.9 A comparison must be made between the treatment of the disabled employee and that of 'others to whom that reason does not or would not apply'. Again, this model differs significantly from that of the SDA 1975 and RRA 1976 which require a like-for-like comparison of the treatment of the applicant and of others in similar circumstances apart from their race or sex.[9] The narrow statutory focus of the DDA 1995 – looking solely at the reason for the treatment – results in a wider scope for comparison. It does not matter whether in respects other than the fact of disability the comparator is the same as or different from the applicant.[10]

6.10 The definition of discrimination in the DDA 1995 covers less favourable treatment based on straightforward prejudice, such as a decision not to employ someone because he or she has a history of mental health problems. But it also covers many cases which are less

8 *Clark v TDG Ltd t/a Novacold* [1999] IRLR 318, CA.

9 SDA 1975 s5(3) requires that '[a] comparison of the cases of persons of different sex or marital status ... must be such that the relevant circumstances in the one case are the same, or not materially different, in the other'. RRA 1976 s3(4) is materially identical.

10 *Clark v TDG Ltd t/a Novacold* [1999] IRLR 318, CA.

obvious, in which the less favourable treatment is for reasons which appear at first glance to be disability-neutral. In the leading case of *Clark v TDG Ltd t/a Novacold*[11] a disabled employee was dismissed following a period of sickness absence in circumstances when any other employee absent for a similar length of time, for whatever reason, would also have been dismissed. The EAT ruled that Mr Clark had been treated less favourably contrary to DDA 1995 s5(1) because his dismissal was for a reason (his absence) which was related to his disability. It was not necessary for Mr Clark to establish that his employer would not have dismissed a person who was not disabled and who was also absent from work for a comparable period.

6.11 In *Cosgrove v Caesar and Howie*,[12] a case concerning a legal secretary who was dismissed after a year's absence due to depression, the President of the EAT stated that ETs should ask the following questions in order to determine whether discrimination had occurred for the purposes of DDA 1995 s5:

- What was the 'material reason' (the reason the applicant was treated as he or she was)? In *Cosgrove* it was because she had been absent from work for a long period on medical grounds, and her employers were unable to predict when, and if, she would be able to return.
- Was the material reason one that related to the applicant's disability? In *Cosgrove*, it was. The applicant's depression amounted to a disability and it was because of this disability that she was absent from work with an uncertain prognosis.
- Would the employer have dismissed another person to whom that reason did not apply? The answer in *Cosgrove* was 'No'. There would have been no reason to do so unless some other grounds for dismissal applied to that other person.

As with sex and race discrimination, a DDA 1995 comparison may be made with an actual or hypothetical comparator.

Knowledge of disability

6.12 It is now clear that an employer need not know of a person's disability to discriminate against him or her contrary to DDA 1995 s5(1). The early EAT decisions to the contrary must be regarded as wrong in light of the *Clark v Novacold* test (above).[13]

11 [1999] IRLR 318, CA.
12 [2001] IRLR 653.
13 See, eg, *O'Neill v Symm & Co Ltd* [1998] IRLR 233.

6.13 The leading case in this area is *Heinz v Kenrick*,[14] which concerns undiagnosed chronic fatigue syndrome (ME). In it the EAT held that an employer's knowledge of a person's disability is not relevant to the objective question whether that person had suffered less favourable treatment 'for a reason which relate[d] to' his or her disability. The EAT gave an example of a messenger who concealed the fact that he had an artificial leg and could walk only for short distances at a time, and was dismissed without his employers having become aware of his disability because he was unacceptably slow in making his rounds. In such a case the dismissal was for a reason related to the messenger's disability (his slowness), although the employers believed his slowness to be caused by idleness or absenteeism. The messenger would likely be able to show that he was treated less favourably than others to whom that reason does not apply (other employees who did their rounds at an acceptable pace), this whether or not his employers ever knew that the reason for his slowness was that the employee was disabled. The EAT pointed out in *Heinz v Kenrick* that neither the DDA 1995, the code of practice, nor the DD(E) Regulations 1996 require knowledge in DDA 1995 s5(1) cases (this by contrast with the provisions on reasonable adjustment – see para 6.27),[15] and there was no reason to add one to the legislation.

'Less favourable treatment'

6.14 The concept of 'less favourable treatment' not only involves a comparison with an individual or group who has not, or would not, suffer the same treatment. It also requires the alleged victim of discrimination to establish that the treatment he or she has experienced was 'less favourable' than that which another did or would have received. Here, unusually, comparisons with the SDA 1975 and RRA 1976 are apt and reference should be made to paras 3.7–3.10 above for examples of acts and omissions which have constituted 'less favourable treatment' under the SDA 1975 and RRA 1976. The most frequent treatment complained of under the DDA 1995 is of dismissal.[16]

14 [2000] IRLR 144, EAT.

15 See DDA 1955 s6(6).

16 Of the cases issued and/or decided in the UK between 2 December 1996 and 1 September 2000 68.5% concerned dismissal and 8.9% concerned recruitment. (S. Leverton, *Monitoring the DDA 1995 (Phase 2)*, In-house Report 91, Dept for Work and Pensions, 2002).

Duty of reasonable adjustment

Overview

6.15 DDA 1995 s5(2) provides that, in the employment context:

> an employer ... discriminates against a disabled person if –
> (a) he fails to comply with a section 6 duty imposed on him in relation to the disabled person; and
> (b) he cannot show that his failure to comply with that duty is justified.

DDA 1995 s6(1) and (2) provides that:

> (1) Where –
> (a) any arrangements made by or on behalf of an employer, or
> (b) any physical feature of premises occupied by the employer,
> place the disabled person concerned at a substantial disadvantage in comparison with persons who are not disabled, it is the duty of the employer to take such steps as it is reasonable, in all the circumstances of the case, for him to have to take in order to prevent the arrangements or feature having that effect.
> (2) Subsection (1)(a) applies only in relation to –
> (a) arrangements for determining to whom employment should be offered;
> (b) any term, condition or arrangements on which employment, promotion, a transfer, training or any other benefit is offered or afforded.

6.16 The introduction by the DDA 1995 of a positive duty on employers to make reasonable adjustments to assist disabled people in certain circumstances was a new concept in discrimination law. Its purpose was to create genuine equality of opportunity for disabled people and to promote fair treatment at, and equal access to, work. True equality of opportunity in the field of disability cannot be achieved by treating like cases alike. The way in which work and workplaces are structured creates barriers for disabled people, and the aim of the DDA 1995 was to remove some of those barriers. It follows from this that the model of discrimination in the DDA 1995 is not symmetrical. A non-disabled person cannot complain under the Act that he or she is being treated less favourably than disabled colleagues.[17] But it would be a mistake to view the making of an adjustment that is appropriate to a disabled person's needs as a form of special treatment or positive discrimination – a person who is not disabled and does not require, for

17 Although he or she may complain of victimisation under the DDA 1995.

example, a certain type of chair to sit at a workstation without discomfort, does not lose out by not having such a chair.

6.17 The duty of reasonable adjustments is owed to employees and job applicants as a separate and free-standing matter, and is not dependent upon the DDA 1995's prohibition on the less favourable treatment of those with disabilities. A claim that an employer has failed to make reasonable adjustments may be made in isolation or in combination with a claim of less favourable treatment, but does not depend on the latter. Where more than one claim is made under the DDA 1995, tribunals must deal separately and explicitly with each.[18]

6.18 The duty to make reasonable adjustments is contained principally in DDA 1995 s6, hence the shorthand term 'section 6 duty'. Where any arrangement made by or on behalf of an employer, or any physical feature of premises occupied by the employer, places a disabled person at a substantial disadvantage in comparison with those who are not disabled, it is the duty of the employer to take such steps as it is reasonable, in all the circumstances of the case, for him or her to have to take, in order to prevent the arrangements or features from having that effect. The code of practice (particularly paras 4.12 to 4.34 and 6.21) provides amplification, practical guidance and examples.

6.19 By DDA 1995 s5(2) a failure to make a reasonable adjustment, where the duty arises, becomes discrimination if it cannot be justified.[19] The discrimination will be unlawful if the discrimination comes within DDA 1995 s4, which sets out the application of the DDA 1995 to employment (see particularly chapter 13 and generally chapters 14 and 15).

When the duty arises

6.20 In order for the duty to make reasonable adjustments to arise, a disabled person must be placed at a substantial disadvantage, by comparison with persons who are not disabled, by the arrangements made by or on behalf of an employer or any physical feature of premises occupied by the employer (see DDA 1995 s6(1) above). It is for the applicant to show that, and for the ET to decide whether, a s6 duty arises, and unless there is evidence before the ET to establish the duty the claim will fail. The existence or otherwise of a duty is a question of fact for the tribunal.

18 *Butterfield v Rapidmark t/a 3MV*, 9 September 1998, EAT (unreported but available on LEXIS).

19 The justification provision will be repealed by October 2004 – see paras 6.40 and 6.60 below.

6.21 A body of case-law is now becoming established which determines when a duty to adjust arises. A 'substantial' disadvantage has been held by the Court of Appeal to be 'something more than minor and more than trivial', rather than something 'major'.[20] This approach is in line with the code of practice's definition of 'substantial' in other contexts. A comparison must be made to determine whether the disabled person is *substantially* disadvantaged in comparison with people who are not disabled. The code of practice makes it clear (para 4.13) that the comparison can be made with how a hypothetical non-disabled employee would be affected. The DD(E) Regulations (reg 3(2)) provide that a performance-related pay scheme is not to be regarded as placing a disabled person at a substantial disadvantage. This provision will have to be modified to comply with the ED,[21] and the government has pledged that the necessary changes will be made by October 2004.[22] The Government is also committed, by that date, to the introduction of a duty on the public sector to promote equality of opportunity for disabled people.

6.22 The DDA 1995 s6 duty arises only where (s6(1)(a)) 'any arrangements made by or on behalf of an employer', or (s6(1)(b)) 'any physical feature of premises occupied by the employer', substantially disadvantage the disabled person. 'Physical features' are widely defined, and include:[23]

- permanent and temporary features arising from the design or construction of a building;
- any feature on the premises including any approach to, exit from or access to a building;
- fixtures, fittings, furnishings, furniture, equipment or materials in or on the premises; and
- any other physical element or quality of any land comprised in the premises.

6.23 In establishing whether the duty arises it is irrelevant whether the employer occupies the premises under a lease or as freeholder.[24] In *Ridout v TC Group*,[25] in which the lighting in the interview room was

20 *Cave v Goodwin* [2001] EWCA Civ 391, CA.

21 Council Directive 2000/78/EC.

22 *Towards Equality and Diversity* (Consultation document on the implementation of the Race and Employment Directives), available at www.dti.gov.uk/er/equality.

23 DD(E) Regs 1996 reg 9.

24 It may be relevant in considering if the occupier has failed to comply with the s6 duty; see para 6.37 below.

25 [1998] IRLR 628.

in issue, the EAT remarked that it came within the definition of physical feature rather than arrangements. It will usually be best for an applicant to cite both in the originating application.

6.24 DDA 1995 s6(2) provides (above) that an 'arrangement' for the purposes of s6 applies only to arrangements for determining to whom employment should be offered and to any term, condition or arrangement on which employment, promotion, a transfer, training or any other benefit is offered or afforded. In *Kenny v Hampshire CC*[26] the EAT ruled that 'arrangements' referred only to job-related matters – to the way in which a job is structured and organised so as to accommodate those who cannot fit into existing arrangements. The term did not extend to the provision of a helper to carry out personal care functions, but would include facilitating and enabling a disabled worker's personal helper (provided by him or herself) to carry out such services. However, providing an assistant to assist with a disabled person's *work* is an arrangement.[27] The payment – or non-payment – of sick pay can be an 'arrangement'.[28] But an administrative breakdown in the payment of sick pay has, controversially, been held not to constitute an 'arrangement' for the purposes of DDA 1995 s6.[29]

6.25 Dismissal is not of itself an 'arrangement' under DDA 1995 s6(1), the Court of Appeal in *Clark v Novacold* having overturned a previous EAT decision to the effect that DDA 1995 s6(2)'s 'arrangements on which employment ... is afforded' was wide enough to cover arrangements in relation to whether employment continues or is terminated.[30] The Court of Appeal in *Clark* distinguished between pre-dismissal breaches of DDA 1995 s6 duties, and dismissal itself. The actual dismissal cannot be a failure to make a reasonable adjustment, but the circumstances leading up to a dismissal can often breach DDA 1995 s6. In practice, the way to ensure the point is covered is for an applicant to state in an originating application to an ET that the

26 *Kenny v Hampshire CC* [1999] IRLR 76.

27 *Edwards v Mid Suffolk DC* [2001] IRLR 191. In *Mills v Hillingdon LBC*, 18 October 2001, EAT (unreported) however, the respondent's refusal to create a permanent post in a different department to accommodate the applicant's difficulties with stress connected to a depressive illness was said to fall outside the definition of arrangement. It is considered that *Mills* was wrongly decided. Although the creation of a new permanent post may not be a *reasonable* adjustment to be made, it is within the definition of an arrangement on which employment is afforded.

28 *London Clubs Management Ltd v Hood* [2001] IRLR 719.

29 *Mills v Hillingdon LBC*, 18 October 2001, EAT (unreported).

30 [1999] IRLR 318. The EAT decision distinguished was that in *Morse v Wiltshire CC* [1998] IRLR 352.

employer has failed to make reasonable adjustments to the arrangements and/or physical features of premises so as to avoid dismissal. In this way a tribunal will consider the case both as a reasonable adjustment case and as less favourable treatment.

6.26 The statute expressly provides (DDA 1995 s6(11)) that there is no duty to adjust in relation to any benefit under an occupational pension scheme or any scheme to provide a benefit in respect of termination of service; retirement, old age or death; or accident, injury, sickness or invalidity. The disability provisions of the ED will require the government to modify these provisions (see further para 6.59).

Knowledge of disability

6.27 We have seen that the employer's (lack of) knowledge about a disability is not relevant in considering whether disability discrimination by way of less favourable treatment has occurred. The position is different in relation to the duty of reasonable adjustment. There is no s6 duty on an employer in relation to a disabled person (DDA 1995 s6(6)) 'if the employer does not know and could not reasonably be expected to know' that the person is disabled and is likely to be at a substantial disadvantage in the workplace or with the working practices or might be a job applicant. What it is reasonable to expect an employer to know involves an employer doing all he could reasonably be expected to do to actually find out.[31] The code of practice suggests this could be done by giving an employee or job applicant an opportunity to explain in confidence about any disability – for example, on a job application form.

6.28 Employers may argue lack of knowledge at two levels – ignorance of the disability itself, and ignorance of the disadvantage caused by it to the employee or job applicant. The problem is most acute for job applicants – unless they refer to their disability and the adjustments necessary to overcome the difficulty in the application form, an employer may not know nor reasonably be expected to know of it. For example if a job candidate asks for the application form to be given to him on tape or in Braille, an employer will be treated as knowing that the applicant is disabled and at a substantial disadvantage by having to complete a written application form. But if the effect of a disability is particularly obscure or unusual, an employer may not be required to appreciate the steps required to minimise the effect unless they have been spelt out.[32]

31 Code, para 4.57.

32 *Ridout v T.C. Group* [1998] IRLR 628.

6.29 Employees may often give information about a disability to an employer in confidence. The person who they tell may respect that confidence and not pass the information on to the decision-maker. A situation might arise, for example, in which an office worker has told a staff counsellor, but not his supervisor, that he is suffering from cancer. The supervisor might deny the employee permission to take time off for treatment. The code of practice states that if an employer, or an agent of the employer such as an occupational health officer, knows of the disability or the substantial disadvantage in their official capacity – even if the information has been given in confidence – then an employer cannot claim not to know of it.[33] The information gained by the officer on the employer's behalf is imputed to the employer and the duty to make reasonable adjustments will arise. However, if the information is given to a person providing services to employees who is independent of the employer, knowledge will not be imputed to the employer.

What the duty to adjust consists of

6.30 The duty imposed upon an employer by DDA 1995 s6 is a duty to take steps that are reasonable in the circumstances of the particular case so as to prevent the working practices or the workplace from placing the disabled person at a substantial disadvantage. Examples of the type of steps an employer might have to take are set out in DDA 1995 s6(3). These are:

(a) making adjustments to premises;
(b) allocating some of the disabled person's duties to another person;
(c) transferring him or her to an existing vacancy;
(d) altering his or her working hours;
(e) assigning him or her to a different place of work;
(f) allowing him or her to be absent during working hours for rehabilitation, assessment or treatment;
(g) giving, or arranging for him or her to be given training;
(h) acquiring or modifying equipment;
(i) modifying instructions or reference manuals;
(j) modifying procedures for testing or assessment;
(k) providing a reader or interpreter;
(l) providing supervision.

The examples are not exhaustive. Other steps will sometimes have to be taken, but the steps listed have been used to provide an indication

33 Code, para 4.62.

of the scope, and therefore limits, of the DDA 1995.[34] Of the reasonable adjustment cases between 2 December 1996 and 1 September 2000, 35 per cent concerned a transfer to an existing vacancy, 25 per cent the reallocation of duties and 20 per cent the acquisition or modification of equipment.[35]

6.31 DDA 1995 s6(4) lists the matters that must be taken into account in determining the reasonableness of an employer making a particular adjustment:

(a) the extent to which taking the step would prevent the effect in question;
(b) the extent to which it is practicable for the employer to take the step;
(c) the financial and other costs of taking the step and the extent of any disruption;
(d) the extent of the employer's financial and other resources;
(e) the availability of financial or other assistance.

Again the list is not exhaustive and there may be other circumstances that are relevant. But the five specified matters must be taken into account by a tribunal. Some others are suggested in the code of practice – these include the effect on other employees of the adjustment and the extent to which the disabled person is willing to co-operate with the adjustment. The effectiveness and practicability of the adjustment is considered first, then the financial aspect as a whole – the cost and resources available for funding it.

6.32 Determining whether any particular adjustment would be reasonable for the purposes of DDA 1995 s6(1) is a two-fold process. First the tribunal will decide what steps the employer could take to prevent the substantial disadvantage to the disabled applicant in the particular. Second, the tribunal will decide whether it was reasonable for an employer to have to take that particular step, again by reference to the particular case. The tribunal must make a real inquiry into the steps an employer might take and reach its own decision – the question is not whether a reasonable employer, acting reasonably, might have done what the employer did. An objective test must be applied and the tribunal conduct the inquiry afresh.[36]

6.33 How does a tribunal know what steps could be taken and whether they would be reasonable in any given case? The burden of proof probably lies with the employer in establishing that its duty has been

34 *Kenny v Hampshire CC* [1999] IRLR 76.
35 S Leverton, *Monitoring the DDA 1995 (Phase 2)*, op cit.
36 *Morse v Wiltshire CC* [1998] IRLR 352; *Fu v Camden LBC* [2001] IRLR 186, EAT.

met, but the authorities are a little unclear.[37] Often the applicant will identify what adjustments he or she considers should have been made, and it is always preferable to do so. But it is not necessary for these to have been identified at the time of the alleged discrimination. Further, a failure to propose particular adjustments during the tribunal hearing is not necessarily fatal to the claim. In *Cosgrove v Caesar and Howie*[38] neither the applicant nor her GP (who appeared as her medical witness), were able to state what adjustments could have been made, and the employer did not consider the matter at all. The EAT held that it was an error of law to regard the inability of the applicant to suggest any steps as decisive of the employer having satisfied its duty. But there is a real risk that, if an applicant fails to mention a possible adjustment, a tribunal will find that there were no reasonable steps that could be taken, and it will be too late to identify them for the first time on appeal.[39]

6.34 It will not always be the case that an employer which has not addressed its mind to reasonable adjustments will have failed in its duty. The EAT has recognised that there will be cases where the applicant's evidence alone will establish a total unavailability of reasonable and effective adjustments. Since the s6 test is an objective one – whether it was reasonable for an employer to have to take a particular step – it does not relate to what the employer considered, but to what it did and did not do. An employer may have taken no steps because it did not consider any. But if, on an objective assessment by the tribunal, no steps could reasonably have been taken, the employer's duty will not have been breached.[40]

6.35 A tribunal will need to consider whether adjustments proposed by an applicant, which were ignored by the employer and its occupational health advisers, would have amounted to reasonable adjustments.[41] Where the adjustment sought has consisted of redeployment, the EAT has held that, as the potential for alternative employment in effect lay exclusively within the knowledge of the employer, it is for the employer to satisfy the tribunal that there was no alternative employment available either at the time or in the reasonably acceptable future.[42]

37 *Conoco Ltd v Booth*, 30 January 2001, EAT (unreported but available on LEXIS).

38 [2001] IRLR 653.

39 *Allen v Hargrave & Co*, 12 October 1999, EAT (unreported but available on LEXIS).

40 *British Gas Services Ltd v McCaull* [2001] IRLR 60, EAT.

41 *Fu v Camden LBC* [2001] IRLR 186, EAT.

42 *Conoco Ltd v Booth*, 30 January 2001, EAT (unreported but available on LEXIS).

6.36 Examples of adjustments held to have been reasonable include transfer to a vacant post which would not aggravate an applicant's disabling irritable bowel syndrome,[43] allowing a disabled person to be redeployed into a vacant and suitable position without open competition,[44] and making adjustments to take account of the needs of a deaf candidate in interviewing arrangements such as by providing written questions.[45] In *Mulligan v Inland Revenue*,[46] however, that EAT held the 'assessment of performance is a wholly separate issue from the duty to make reasonable adjustments which does not extend necessarily to lowering the quantity of work or volume of work being demanded'. The Inland Revenue had introduced a performance management scheme which assessed performance in terms of output. Mr Mulligan, who was disabled by having no use of his right arm, did not meet accepted targets. The employer had made a number of adjustments to the method and structure of his job by changing his equipment and workstation. Mr Mulligan's argument that a reasonable adjustment would also have been to reduce the minimum requirements for the job was rejected both by the tribunal and the EAT. This does not prevent a duty to adjust from arising, however, if, for example, the provision of an aid or additional training would result in an improvement in the performance of the disabled employee so that he or she would reach the accepted targets.

6.37 Where the issue is whether premises should have been altered, an employer cannot rely on a restriction in the lease as showing the adjustment was not reasonable unless the employer had applied to the lessor in writing for consent to the making of the alteration.[47] If the landlord has unreasonably refused to consent to the alteration, the lessor can be joined to the proceedings.[48] The code of practice provides useful guidance on building regulations, listed buildings and leases.[49]

43 *Tiquin v Abbey National plc*, ET 2202759/98, 31 March 1999 (unreported).

44 *Jewell v Stoke Mandeville Hospital NHS Trust*, ET 2700986/98, 25 May 1999 (unreported).

45 *Hughes v Hillingdon LBC*, ET 6001328/98, 27 July 1999 (unreported).

46 2 December 1999, EAT (unreported but available on LEXIS).

47 DDA 1995 Sch 4, Pt I.

48 See chapter 32.

49 Code, paras 4.35–4.48.

Justification

6.38 The issue of justification is central to the concept of disability discrimination. If an employer proves that the less favourable treatment of a disabled person, or a failure to make a reasonable adjustment, was justified, the DDA 1995 claim will fail. The availability of a justification plea in a case in which the employer has failed to make a reasonable adjustment is to be removed when the disability-related provisions of the ED are implemented in October 2004.[50] This consideration of justification is separate and distinct from the test of whether adjustments are reasonable.

Justification and failure to make reasonable adjustments

6.39 The wording of the justification provisions in a failure to make a reasonable adjustment case is identical to that for the less favourable treatment provisions.[51] There is judicial confusion as to whether the justification test for a reasonable adjustment claim is the same or different to the test for a less favourable treatment case. In some cases justification is discussed as if there is no distinction in its meaning between the two forms of discrimination,[52] while in others the justification in a claim for reasonable adjustments has been treated as an objective test (by contrast with the subjective test – see para 6.47 – which applies in relation to less favourable treatment).[53]

6.40 The difficulty is that, while the wording of the justification defence is the same in both types of case, the claims are quite different, relating as they do to 'treatment' on the one hand, and a failure to comply with a duty on the other. In practice the issue rarely arises in a reasonable adjustment (DDA 1995 s5(2)) claim. If an ET considers that the s6 duty has been breached, it is unlikely to find the breach justified. In this context, then, the justification defence is little used and is considered otiose. It would be unattractive to consider that a failure to make an adjustment which is no more than is reasonable in the

50 This amendment was also urged by the Disability Rights Task Force whose recommendations for reform (*From Exclusion to Inclusion – A Report of the Disability Rights Task Force on Civil Rights for Disabled People*, 1999, available at 194.202.202.185/drtf/full_report/index.htm) described the availability of a justification defence in this context as 'unacceptable'.

51 DDA 1995 s5(1)(b) and (3) for less favourable treatment discrimination and DDA 1995 s5(2)(b) and (4) for the reasonable adjustment duty. See para 6.7 above.

52 See, eg, *Quinn v Schwarzkopf Ltd* [2001] IRLR 67; *Cosgrove v Caesar and Howie* [2001] IRLR 653.

53 *Fu v Camden LBC* [2001] IRLR 186, EAT.

circumstances, was nevertheless justified. The application of the justification test in this context could, however, become more common if the approach taken by the Court of Appeal in *Jones v Post Office*[54] (see para 6.47) is imported wholesale into reasonable adjustment claims. This is further considered below (para 6.49).

The standard of justification required

6.41 The effectiveness of the DDA 1995 depends partly upon the stringency of justification standard – the higher it is, the greater the burden on employers. The threshold for justification under the DDA 1995 has been described by the President of the EAT, however, as 'very low'.[55]

6.42 Early comparisons with sex and race discrimination legislation proved misleading. The DDA 1995 does not use the same words as the SDA 1975 and RRA 1976, which require indirect discrimination to be *objectively* justified if it is not to be unlawful. Early case law which imported the more stringent test in indirect sex and race discrimination cases is no longer reliable authority, following the judgments of the EAT in *H J Heinz Co Ltd v Kenrick*[56] and of the Court of Appeal in *Jones v Post Office*.[57]

6.43 DDA 1995 s5(3) provides that:

> ... treatment is justified if, but only if, the reason for it is both material to the circumstances of the particular case and substantial.

The definition has been said to be 'both necessary and sufficient',[58] meaning that if the reason is material and substantial a tribunal must find the less favourable treatment justified. ETs have no discretion to adopt a broad approach to justification based on their experience as industrial juries.

'Material'

6.44 It is explained in the code of practice (para 4.6) that 'material' means that the reason for the less favourable treatment, or for a failure to make a reasonable adjustment, must relate to the individual circumstances

54 [2001] IRLR 384.

55 *Heinz v Kenrick* [2000] IRLR 144, EAT.

56 Ibid.

57 [2001] IRLR 384.

58 *Heinz v Kenrick* [2000] IRLR 144, EAT.

in question. Of central importance is how close the relationship must be for the reason to be material. In *Jones v Post Office*, Arden LJ held that there must be a reasonably strong factual connection between the employer's reason and the circumstances of the individual case – that the reason must be more than merely relevant or applicable. She also approved an earlier EAT decision that the circumstances of the particular case may include those of both the employee and employer.[59] A mistaken, but genuinely held belief could be 'material'.

'Substantial'

6.45 The reason for the less favourable treatment, or for a failure to make a reasonable adjustment, will only justify the treatment or failure if it is 'substantial' as well as 'material'. How significant the reason must be to be 'substantial' is surprisingly tricky to state. The code of practice states (para 4.6) that the reason must be 'not just minor or trivial'. This is consistent with the meaning of 'substantial' for the purposes of determining whether a person's impairment is sufficient to amount to a 'disability' for the purposes of the DDA 1995 (see chapter 2). But the Court of Appeal has provided a different and higher threshold in the justification context, ruling that 'the reason which the employer adopted as his ground for discrimination must carry real weight and thus be of substance'.[60] We suggest that the Court of Appeal's definition is to be preferred on grounds of principle, and that it takes precedence over the code of practice which does not itself impose legal obligations, is illustrative only, and is not an authoritative statement of the law.

6.46 The code of practice gives examples in paras 4.6 and 4.7 of matters that are or are not likely to be substantial and to justify less favourable treatment. They include the following:

- A factory worker with a mental illness is sometimes away from work due to his disability. Because of that he is dismissed. However the amount of time off is very little more than the employer accepts as sick leave for other employees and so is very unlikely to be a substantial reason.
- Someone who has psoriasis (a skin condition) is rejected for a job involving modelling cosmetics on a part of the body which in his case is severely disfigured by the condition. That would be lawful if his appearance would be incompatible with the purpose of the work.

59 *Baynton v Saurus General Engineers Ltd* [1999] IRLR 604.

60 *Jones v Post Office* [2001] IRLR 384, para 39, per Arden LJ.

This is a substantial reason which is clearly related – material – to the individual circumstances.

The application of the justification test

6.47 In *Jones v Post Office* the Court of Appeal ruled, controversially, that the role of a tribunal in considering justification is limited to assessing whether the employer's decision was irrational or beyond the range of responses open to a reasonable decision-maker. The court there ruled that a tribunal may not conduct the inquiry afresh and base its conclusion on new evidence not before the employer at the time. Nor may it substitute its own view for that of the employer, or assess whether the employer's decision was the best possible decision. A tribunal cannot disagree with a risk assessment which is properly conducted, based on the properly formed opinion of suitably qualified doctors, and produces an answer that is not irrational.

6.48 Mr Jones had had his driving duties restricted to two hours a day on the basis of his employer's medical advice given his insulin-dependent diabetes. The Post Office's doctor advised that longer periods of driving risked a hypoglycaemic attack. At the ET hearing, Mr Jones' medical expert contradicted the employer's doctor's advice and the ET found in Mr Jones' favour. The Court of Appeal overturned the ET decision because the ET had erred in having regard to the post-decision medical evidence and also in judging the issue for itself. The *Jones* case concerned health and safety issues, and the investigative and fact-finding role of the ET in cases which do not concern risk assessments and health and safety issues may be greater. But at least for risk assessment type cases, ETs must operate a band of reasonable responses test similar to that which applies in unfair dismissal cases.[61]

6.49 The application of *Jones* in reasonable adjustment (DDA 1995 s5(2)) cases is particularly problematic. Until the DDA 1995 is amended to exclude the possibility of an employer justifying a failure to comply with a s6 duty, *Jones* has the effect that an employer could justify, *by reference to a band of reasonable responses*, a failure to take what is an *objectively* reasonable step to accommodate a disabled worker's needs. This, in particular, demonstrates why the justification provisions need to be removed in DDA 1995 s5(2) claims.

61 See, eg, *Post Office v Foley* [2000] IRLR 827, CA.

Knowledge and justification and less favourable treatment

6.50 Another aspect of justification in less favourable treatment cases which has generated considerable judicial activity is the effect of knowledge on an employer's ability to justify otherwise discriminatory treatment.[62] Early EAT judgments considered that justification could never be made out if the employer was ignorant of the fact of disability at the relevant time.[63] This is now considered bad law because of the principles laid down in *Jones* and because, in *Callaghan v Glasgow City Council*,[64] the EAT relied on *Jones* to alter its earlier stance. The fact an employer did not know that the disability existed might affect the question of justification, but does not preclude it from successfully arguing that its less favourable treatment was justified. The tribunal must analyse the treatment meted out to see if the reason for it is material and substantial and a decision open to a reasonable decision-maker on the basis of sufficient and suitably expert information available at the time the decision was taken.

Justification of less favourable treatment and the duty to make reasonable adjustments

6.51 Discrimination by less favourable treatment cannot be justified where the employer is under a duty to make a reasonable adjustment but fails (without justification) to make the adjustment, unless the less favourable treatment would have been justified even after that adjustment.[65] The code of practice provides the following illustrative example (para 4.7):

> An employee who uses a wheelchair is not promoted, solely because the workstation for the more senior post is inaccessible to wheelchairs – though it could readily be made accessible by rearrangement of the furniture. If the furniture had been rearranged, the reason for refusing promotion would not have applied. The refusal of promotion would therefore not be justified.

6.52 The code gives another example of an applicant for a typing job who is not the best applicant because her typing speed is too slow due to

62 In reasonable adjustment cases the position is quite different as knowledge is central to the duty itself arising – see para 6.27 above.

63 *Quinn v Schwarzkopf Ltd* [2001] IRLR 67.

64 [2001] IRLR 726.

65 DDA 1995 s5(5).

arthritis in her hands. It may be that a reasonable adjustment, such as an adapted keyboard, would overcome this problem, in which case the employer would be under a duty to make that adjustment. If the adjustment was made the applicant's typing speed would no longer be a 'substantial' reason for refusing to employ her and the reason relied upon (her typing speed) would not justify the less favourable treatment. If, on the other hand, the applicant's typing speed would have remained significantly less than that of the successful candidate even with an adapted keyboard, the reason for her less favourable treatment would amount to a justification if speed was a substantial and material factor (ie, was of practical importance) in relation to the job. In such a case, even if the employer failed without justification to provide the keyboard, the less favourable treatment would still be justified.

6.53 It follows that, even if an applicant has not raised a reasonable adjustment claim, a tribunal may still have to consider whether a s6 duty arises, and whether it has been breached, in order to consider a justification argument on less favourable treatment.[66]

6.54 In practice, the success or failure of cases often turns on the question of justification whose low threshold has been considered. Since the Court of Appeal's decision in *Jones v Post Office*, attention is focused on the employer's investigation at the time of the alleged discriminatory treatment, and tribunals' power to interfere with a reasoned and well-informed decision to treat a disabled worker less favourably is limited.

Performance-related pay

6.55 The DD(E) Regulations 1996 reg 3 provides that less favourable treatment in performance-related pay schemes is justified if it results from the application to the disabled person of a performance-related pay scheme which applies either to all the employer's employees or to a class of employees which include the disabled person, but is not defined by reference to any disability. 'Pay' is defined by reg 2 to mean remuneration of any kind including any benefit, and 'performance' to include performance as assessed by reference to any measure of output, efficiency or effectiveness. The disability provisions of the ED will require the government to modify these provisions (see further para 6.59 below).

66 *Heinz v Kenrick* [2000] IRLR 144, EAT.

Occupational pension schemes

6.56 Occupational pension schemes are deemed to include a non-discrimination rule which relates to the terms upon which disabled people become members of the scheme, and the way in which they are treated as members.[67] The DD(E) Regulations 1996 reg 4, however, deems less favourable treatment resulting from the application of eligibility conditions set for receiving a benefit to be justified in specified circumstances. The benefits covered are those provided under an occupational pension scheme for termination of service, retirement, old age or death, or accident, injury, sickness or invalidity. They do not include sick pay.[68] The circumstances under which the less favourable treatment of a disabled person is deemed to be justified are where the cost of providing the benefit is, by reason of the person's disability, likely to be substantially greater than it would be for a comparable person without a disability. There is no duty to make adjustments in relation to benefits under an occupational pension scheme.[69]

6.57 The DD(E) Regulations 1996 reg 5 also provides that an employer is deemed to be justified in requiring a disabled person to make occupational pension contributions at the same rate as other employees, even though the disabled employee is not eligible to receive benefits at the same rate as other employees, for a reason related to his disability.[70]

6.58 The disability provisions of the ED will require the government to modify these provisions of the DDA 1995 (see paras 6.59 onwards).

Disability and the Employment Directive

6.59 A number of references have been made throughout the chapter to changes which will have to be made to the DDA 1995 to achieve compliance with the disability-related provisions of the ED, and to the government's commitment to introduce these changes by October 2004. The ED prohibits both direct and indirect discrimination, but allows member states to deal with indirect discrimination *either* by adopting the directive's general definition of indirect discrimination,

67 DDA 1995 s17(1)(a) and see chapter 13.
68 *London Clubs Management Ltd v Hood* [2001] IRLR 719.
69 DDA 1995 s6(11).
70 DD(E) Regs 1996 reg 5.

or by dealing with it via what are, in the UK, the existing provisions on reasonable adjustments. The directive uses the term 'reasonable accommodation' which is set out in article 5. The UK government has signalled its intention to continue with the reasonable adjustment provisions.

6.60 The government will, as mentioned above (para 6.38), remove the provision which currently allows employers to justify the failure to make a reasonable adjustment. Direct discrimination will also be expressly excluded from the justification provisions. Less favourable treatment which amounts to *direct* discrimination under the definition adopted by the SDA 1975 and RRA 1976 (ie, discrimination *on grounds of* a person's disability[71]) is most unlikely to be justified under the existing test – groundless prejudice is neither material nor substantial to the particular circumstances of a case. But it will be welcome clarification for the law to state expressly that direct disability discrimination cannot be justified.

6.61 The DDA 1995 provisions which deem certain forms of discrimination justified in performance pay and occupational pension schemes, as well as group insurance (see further para 6.55) will also have to be modified. It is likely that the government will cover performance pay, occupational pensions and group insurance either by fully including them within the reasonable adjustment provisions or by requiring indirect discrimination in these fields to be objectively justified.

6.62 The ED will also require the current exclusions from the scope of the DDA 1995 in the employment context to be significantly reduced in a number of respects, such as by the abolition of the small employer exclusion. These are dealt with in chapter 13.

71 See further chapter 3. Note the contrast between this and discrimination 'for a reason which relates to' a disabled person's disability – particularly under the wide approach adopted by the Court of Appeal in *Clark v TDG Ltd t/a Novacold* [1999] IRLR 318, CA.

CHAPTER 7

Indirect discrimination

continued

Key points

7.1

- The definition of indirect discrimination differs as between employment-related cases taken under the Sex Discrimination Act (SDA) 1975, on the one hand, and those brought under the Race Relations Act (RRA) 1976 and the non-employment-related provisions of the SDA 1975, on the other hand.
- The reason for the different definitions of indirect discrimination lies in the Burden of Proof Directive (BPD) which, as its name suggests, also alters the burden of proof applicable to discrimination. The directive applies only to employment-related discrimination on grounds of sex and married status.
- Although the SDA 1975 governs discrimination in connection with gender reassignment (as well as on grounds of sex and married status), its provisions apply only to direct, rather than indirect, discrimination.
- The DDA 1995 does not regulate indirect discrimination as such, although its definition of (direct) discrimination, coupled with its duty of reasonable accommodation (see further chapter 6) serves to cover most instances of what would otherwise be regarded as 'indirect' discrimination.
- The RRA 1976's definition of indirect discrimination will have to be amended by July 2003, the Race Directive's (RD) definition being similar to that adopted by the BPD. A further, but similar, definition is adopted by the Employment Directive (ED) which will apply to discrimination on grounds of sexual orientation, age, disability and 'religion and belief'.
- It is perhaps not necessary to state that the law regulating indirect discrimination is complex in the extreme. It is to be hoped that coherence will be achieved when the implementation of the new directives is completed.
- The most significant difference between direct and indirect discrimination under the SDA 1975 and the RRA 1976 is that indirect discrimination is subject to a general justification defence. Direct discrimination can be justified only by specific exceptions provided for by the Acts.
- Under the original approach, proof of indirect discrimination requires applicants to establish that there have been applied to them (a) a requirement or condition with which (b) a considerably smaller proportion of their relevant 'group' than of others

can comply and (c) which is to the applicants' detriment because they cannot comply with them. At this point the employer can avoid a finding of unlawful indirect discrimination by proving that the application of the requirement or condition was objectively justified.

- Under the new approach, unlawful indirect discrimination occurs where (a) a provision, criterion or practice is applied to a woman which (b) is such that it would be to the detriment of a considerably larger proportion of women than of men, and (c) is to the applicant's detriment and (d) the employer cannot show to be justifiable irrespective of the sex of the person to whom it is applied.

Background and statutory provisions

7.2 Indirect discrimination is concerned with practices that have the effect, though not the intention, of discriminating against a 'protected group' (ie, a group defined by race, sex or married status). The concept of indirect discrimination is complex, has been little understood by (employment tribunals) ETs and courts, and has too often been wrongly applied.

7.3 The concept of indirect discrimination in UK statute law came from the US, in particular from the decision of the US Supreme Court in *Griggs v Duke Power Co*,[1] a race discrimination claim. But even at the time when *Griggs* was decided the European Court of Justice (ECJ) had already begun to develop a concept of indirect discrimination in relation to the free movement of goods.[2]

7.4 In *Griggs*, job applicants and employees seeking promotion were required either to have attended high school or to pass intelligence tests. It was shown that the standard required was not significantly related to successful job performance, but that it disqualified black workers at a much higher rate than whites. The US Supreme Court ruled that it was unlawful as a form of indirect discrimination. According to Chief Justice Berger, for the court:

> The objective of Congress in the enactment of [anti-discrimination legislation] is plain from the language of the statute. It was to achieve equality of employment opportunities and remove barriers that have

1 401 US 424, (1971) 3 FED 75.

2 See Case 2/56 *Ruhr v ECSC* [1957] ECR 011.

operated in the past to favor an identifiable group of white employees over other employees. Under the Act, practices, procedures, or tests neutral on their face, and even neutral in terms of intent, cannot be maintained if they operate to 'freeze' the status quo of prior discriminatory employment practices.

The CA's opinion, and the partial dissent, agreed that, on the record in the present case, 'whites register far better on the Company's alternative requirements' than Negroes ... This consequence would appear to be directly traceable to race. Basic intelligence must have the means of articulation to manifest itself fairly in a testing process. Because they are Negroes, petitioners have long received inferior education in segregated schools ... Congress did not intend by Title VII, however, to guarantee a job to every person regardless of qualifications. In short, the Act does not command that any person be hired simply because he was formerly the subject of discrimination, or because he is a member of a minority group. Discriminatory preference for any group, minority or majority, is precisely and only what Congress has proscribed. What is required by Congress is the removal of artificial, arbitrary, and unnecessary barriers to employment when the barriers operate invidiously to discriminate on the basis of racial or other impermissible classification.

Congress has now provided that tests or criteria for employment or promotion may not provide equality of opportunity merely in the sense of the fabled offer of milk to the stork and the fox. On the contrary, Congress has now required that the posture and condition of the job-seeker be taken into account. It has – to resort again to the fable – provided that the vessel in which the milk is proffered be one all seekers can use. The Act proscribes not only overt discrimination but also practices that are fair in form, but discriminatory in operation. The touchstone is business necessity. If an employment practice which operates to exclude Negroes cannot be shown to be related to job performance, the practice is prohibited.

7.5 The US and EC definitions of indirect discrimination are general and broad and so can be interpreted to suit individual circumstances of the situation under review. By contrast, the definition of indirect discrimination adopted by the RRA 1976 and (originally) the SDA 1975 is more technical.[3] This will change as a result of the impact of EC law. But the changes are patchy, as explained below, and it is essential therefore to keep in mind whether an indirect discrimination claim concerns sex or race, and whether it relates to employment or some other activity. The different definitions and standards of proof which

3 Though changes have already been made to the SDA 1975, and are to be made to the RRA 1976, as a result of EC law – see para 7.12.

apply to different instances of indirect discrimination are likely to lead to considerable confusion both among lawyers and the general public.

Defining indirect discrimination

7.6 The RRA 1976 uses the definition of indirect discrimination original to that Act and to the SDA 1975. The SDA 1975 uses this original definition in relation to sex discrimination outside the employment field. But it has been amended, in so far as it relates to discrimination in employment on grounds of sex or married status, by the Burden of Proof Regulations (BP Regulations) 2001,[4] which were passed to implement the BPD.[5] The RRA 1976's definition of indirect discrimination will be amended by July 2003 to reflect the definition embraced by the RD,[6] which must be implemented in the UK by that date.

Sex Discrimination Act 1975 – the original approach

7.7 SDA 1975 s1(1) provides that:

> A person discriminates against another in any circumstances relevant for the purposes of any provision of the SDA 1975 if ... (b) he applies to her a requirement or condition which he applies or would apply equally to a man but –
> (i) which is such that the proportion women who can comply with it is considerably smaller than the proportion of men who can comply with it; and
> (ii) which he cannot show to be justifiable irrespective of the sex of the person to whom it is applied; and
> (iii) which is to her detriment because she cannot comply with it.

Race Relations Act 1976

7.8 RRA 1976 s1(1) is materially identical to the same section of the SDA 1975, providing that:

> A person discriminates against another in any circumstances relevant for the purposes of any provision of the RRA 1976 if ... he

4 Sex Discrimination (Indirect Discrimination and Burden of Proof) Regulations 2001 SI No 2660.

5 Council Directive 98/52/EC.

6 Council Directive 2000/43/EC.

applies to that other a requirement or condition which he applies or would apply equally to persons not of the same racial group as that other but –

(i) which is such that the proportion of persons of the same racial group as that other who can comply with it is considerably smaller than the proportion of persons not of that racial group who can comply with it; and

(ii) which he cannot show to be justifiable irrespective of the colour, race, nationality or ethnic or national origins of the person to whom it is applied; and

(iii) which is to the detriment of that other because he cannot comply with it.

7.9 This definition of indirect discrimination set out above (and by SDA 1975 s1(1)(b)) is concerned with 'requirements' or 'conditions' and so appears to exclude 'practices' or 'preferences' (see para 7.31). Otherwise, the approach of UK law accords generally with European and US law in that it has three stages:

- proof by the applicant that a requirement or condition has a disproportionate adverse impact on persons of one sex, or racial group;
- proof by the applicant that the requirement or condition is to his/her detriment because he or she cannot comply with it;
- proof by the respondent that the requirement or condition is justified irrespective of the 'protected ground'.

Whatever the similarities in the EC and domestic provisions, the interpretation of UK law has not always corresponded with the EC approach, which is more concerned with the overall effect of disputed practices than with technicalities. This is further discussed below (see para 7.35).

Sex Discrimination Act 1975 – the new approach

7.10 The BPD resulted in the implementation of the BP Regulations 2001, which have amended the definition of indirect discrimination in so far as it applies to employment-related discrimination on grounds of sex or married status.[7] The BP Regulations have inserted into SDA 1975 s1 a new subsection (2) which provides as follows:

In any circumstances relevant for the purposes of a provision to which this subsection applies [employment-related discrimination on

7 SDA 1975 s1(3) as amended.

> grounds of sex or married status[8]], a person discriminates against a woman if ...
> (b) he applies to her a provision, criterion or practice which he applies or would apply equally to a man, but –
> (i) which is such that it would be to the detriment of a considerably larger proportion of women than of men, and
> (ii) which he cannot show to be justifiable irrespective of the sex of the person to whom it is applied, and
> (iii) which is to her detriment.

7.11 SDA 1975 s3(1)(b) as amended provides a materially identical test for indirect discrimination on grounds of married status (which is regulated only in relation to employment). The EU has just agreed amendments to the ETD to bring the definition for indirect discrimination into line with that for the RD. The UK government will have to implement these changes by 2005.

Race Directive

7.12 Article 2 RD provides that:

> ... indirect discrimination shall be taken to occur where an apparently neutral provision, criterion or practice would put persons of a racial or ethnic origin at a particular disadvantage compared with other persons, unless that provision, criterion or practice is objectively justified by a legitimate aim and the means of achieving that aim are appropriate and necessary.

The UK must adopt a no less favourable definition by 19 July 2003 in relation, at least, to discrimination on grounds of 'racial or ethnic origin'. The RD excludes from its provisions discrimination on grounds of nationality, though such discrimination is caught by article 39 of the EC Treaty (discussed at para 10.24) where it affects nationals of EEA states. *Towards Equality and Diversity*,[9] the government's consultation document on implementing the RD and the ED, does not make clear whether the proposal is to apply the new provisions only to discrimination on grounds of 'racial or ethnic origin'. It does state, however, (para 3.2) the intention 'to use regulations under Section 2(2) of the European Communities Act 1972 to implement the Directives, where practicable'. Further, the proposed timetable (para 3.4) refers only to regulations, rather than to primary legislation. This suggests an inclination to adopt a minimalist approach

8 Including discrimination against barristers and in relation to vocational training: SDA 1975 s1(3)(b) and (c).

9 Available at www.dti.gov.uk/er/equality/index.htm.

which, if adopted in this context, will generate huge confusion and uncertainty and render the race discrimination legislation utterly inaccessible to the non-specialist, never mind the non-lawyer. For further details of the substance of the RD see para 10.84.

The role of intention

7.13 Neither UK nor EC law requires, in order that indirect discrimination be established, that any intention to discriminate be proved. Indeed, the deliberate adoption of a disparately impacting practice in order to exclude people of one sex or a particular racial group (or groups) actually amounts to *direct* rather than *indirect* discrimination. This might occur, for example, if a firm imposed a 'no beard' rule as a prerequisite for employment in order to exclude Sikhs.

7.14 RRA 1976 s57(3) provides that no compensation may be awarded in respect of indirect race discrimination if the discriminator proves that he or she did not intend to discriminate. The SDA 1975 originally included a similar provision which was repealed under threat of *Francovich* claims[10] (see para 10.72).[11] In *Walker v Hussain*[12] the EAT held that, if the respondent is aware of the discriminatory effect of a requirement or condition, he or she will be liable to pay damages.

Establishing indirect discrimination: the *Raval* questions

7.15 A number of specific questions must be answered in order to prove indirect discrimination (whether on the ground of sex or race). In *Raval v DHSS and Civil Service Commission*[13] (a race discrimination case) the EAT suggested that the following ten questions be asked in order to establish whether indirect discrimination had been established:

1. Does the applicant belong to the racial group or groups to which he/she claims to belong?
2. Has the requirement applied to the applicant any and if so what

10 Joined Cases 6/90 and 9/90 [1991] ECR I-5357; [1995] ICR 722, see discussion at para 10.72.

11 Amendment made by Sex Discrimination and Equal Pay (Miscellaneous Amendments) Regulations 1996 SI No 428.

12 [1996] IRLR 11.

13 [1985] IRLR 370.

requirement or condition in the arrangements made by him for the purposes of determining who should be offered the relevant employment? If so,

3. When was such requirement or condition applied to the applicant? (The answer to such question being hereinafter referred to as 'the material time'.)
4. Did such requirement or condition apply to other persons not of the same racial group as the applicant? If so,
5. What are the relevant circumstances necessary to ensure that the proportionate comparison to be made under s1(1)(b)(i) complies with the 'like with like' requirement in s3(4) [RRA]?
6. Within what section of the community does the proportionate comparison fall to be made?
7. Does the application of the proportionate comparison within such community section result in a finding that the proportion of persons in the same racial group as the applicant who could comply with the condition or requirement at the material time is considerably smaller than the proportion of persons not of that racial group who could comply with it?
8. Can the requirement or condition be shown by the respondent to be justifiable, irrespective of any racial factor? If not,
9. Could the applicant at the material time comply with the requirement or condition? If not,
10. Was it to his/her detriment that he/she could not do so?

7.16 The approach taken by the EAT in *Raval* has been followed in other cases, and the questions are dealt with in detail below, some having been subdivided to deal with issues which did not arise in Ms Raval's case. Further, a different order is adopted in order that the question of justification is considered after the establishment by the claimant of a prima facie case of discrimination. Some of the EAT's answers to the questions posed in *Raval* were wrong or confused. Further, the EAT did not have to take into account EC law which did not then (and does not now) have much application to race discrimination cases.[14] Nevertheless, the *Raval* questions still provide a useful framework for the consideration of indirect discrimination.

Question 1: Does the applicant belong to the racial group(s) or gender that he or she claims?

7.17 The purpose of this question is to define the groups to be compared to assess whether there is disparate impact. In sex discrimination cases the comparison is relatively straightforward: it is between men and

14 But see para 10.84.

women (or between married and unmarried people) in the 'relevant pool'.[15] In race discrimination cases the comparison is more difficult. 'Racial group' is defined by colour, race, nationality or ethnic or national origins (see para 2.33).[16] It will be for the applicant to choose the racial group(s) to which he or she claims to belong, since he or she is likely to fall within more than one.

7.18 Although there are similarities between the types of discrimination experienced by ethnic minorities, there are also many important differences between racial groups. The characteristics and economic and social circumstances of different racial groups vary enormously. A minimum height requirement may, for example, disqualify many Asians but very few African-Caribbeans. A requirement to wear skirts may have an adverse impact on Asian Muslim women but not on African-Caribbean women. In some cases a comparison between whites and those of ethnic minorities might reveal little disparity whereas if the comparison was between, for example, Asians and non-Asians, the difference might be very obvious.

7.19 RRA 1976 s3(2) provides that the fact that a racial group comprises two or more racial groups does not prevent it from constituting a particular racial group. So, for instance, in a particular case, all those of ethnic minority groups, all Asians, or all Indians could be described as being of a single racial group. Sub-groups of these groups (such as Sikhs) could also comprise racial groups. A requirement or condition which has a disparate impact on any identifiable racial group(s) may be challenged under the RRA 1976.

7.20 It is important to define the racial group carefully in an RRA 1976 claim. Choosing the wrong group, even if the applicant belongs to it, may be fatal to the case, since disparate impact *on that group* must be proved (see questions 5 to 7 below). It is advisable to consider arguing a claim on the basis of a number of racial groups to which the applicant may belong, bearing in mind the need to show disparate impact. Which of these groups should be chosen (if, indeed, only one is) may best, if possible, be dealt with by agreement before the main hearing.

7.21 In *Orphanos v Queen Mary College*[17] a Cypriot citizen of Greek nationality alleged that the college's policy of charging higher fees to overseas students (defined as those who had not been resident in the UK or another EU country for the previous three years) was indirectly

15 SDA 1975 does not prohibit indirect (as distinct from direct) discrimination on grounds of gender reassignment – see paras 2.20 and 2.25.

16 See RRA 1976 s3.

17 [1985] AC 761;[1985] IRLR 349.

discriminatory on the ground of race. It was agreed by the parties that Mr Orphanos belonged to three racial groups – Cypriot, non-British and non-EU. It was also agreed that the proportion of such groups which could comply with a UK residence requirement was considerably smaller than the proportion of persons not of those racial groups who could so comply.

7.22 The House of Lords ruled that, although it could proceed simply on the basis of the agreed position, and without considering whether the college's concessions had been correctly made, it should attempt to clarify the position. What follows is, accordingly, obiter, though no doubt of persuasive value.

7.23 Their Lordships agreed that Mr Orphanos belonged to three racial groups and that racial groups could be defined negatively – as, for instance, non-British and non-EU. They also accepted that fewer non-British than British people, and fewer non-EU than EU people, could comply with the residence requirement. They did not accept, however, that fewer Cypriots than non-Cypriots could comply. For the purposes of the RRA 1976, the House of Lords ruled, the comparison must be between the case of a person of the same racial group as Mr Orphanos and the case of a person not of that racial group. The comparison must, further, be such that 'the relevant circumstances in the one case are the same, or not materially different, in the other' (see paras 7.47–7.55). The relevant circumstance in *Orphanos* was that the applicant wished to be admitted as a student at the college, so the comparison was between people of his racial group, and those not of his group, who wished to be admitted to the college. Their Lordships thought that no sensible comparison could be made between a group consisting of those of Cypriot nationality and those not of Cypriot nationality, as it would be impracticable to ascertain the numbers of such persons wishing to be admitted to the college.

7.24 There is nothing in the decision to indicate whether their Lordships even considered comparing Cypriots with British people (rather than with 'non-Cypriots'). If they had, disparate impact could have been proved. Nor was it clear from the judgment whether the comparison was between Cypriots and non-Cypriots in the UK, or Cypriots and non-Cypriots in the world. It would not have been difficult to assess the relative numbers of Cypriots and non-Cypriots in the UK, as the majority of non-Cypriots would be British and it would, accordingly, be possible to show that fewer Cypriots than non-Cypriots could comply with the residence requirement. If their Lordships, as it appears, were not restricting the comparison to the UK, then it does indeed become impossible to establish disparate impact. Not only were the comments in relation to Cypriots and non-Cypriots obiter, but they are so fraught with uncertainties that they cannot and should not be followed in subsequent cases.

7.25 The lesson which can be extracted from *Orphanos* is that it is important for applicants who fall into a number of racial groups to argue these in the alternative, taking account of questions 5, 6 and 7 below.

Question 2: Has the respondent applied any 'requirement or condition' to the applicant?

7.26 This question no longer has to be asked in relation to employment-related claims of discrimination on grounds of sex or married status. Nor will it have to be asked, from a date no later than July 2003, in relation to most (if not all) race discrimination claims.[18] The question which replaces it in the sex discrimination context is considered at para 7.43, that which will apply in race discrimination claims at para 7.12.

7.27 There is a substantial overlap between a 'requirement' and a 'condition'. In *Clarke v Eley Kynoch Ltd*[19] the EAT stated that the purpose of the draftsmen in using both words must have been to extend the ambit of what was covered by 'indirect discrimination', so as to include anything which fairly fell within the ordinary meaning of either word. For this reason, the EAT ruled that the phrase should not be given a narrow construction. The employer had argued that selecting part-time workers for redundancy before their full-time counterparts did not amount to applying a 'requirement or condition' to them for the purposes of the SDA 1975 – this on the basis that the former should involve a demand for action by the person to whom it is applied and that the latter should include a qualification for holding a position, but not a qualification for immunity from a disadvantage. Both the ET and the EAT disagreed with the employer's argument, the latter holding (as above) that 'requirement' and 'condition' overlapped and that there was 'no logical or semantic reason' to distinguish qualifications to hold positions from disqualifications from continuing to hold them.

7.28 In *Home Office v Holmes*[20] a woman challenged as indirectly discriminatory on grounds of sex the offer of a job on a full-time basis alone. The employer argued that the 'full-time' proviso was not a

18 With the implementation of the RD.

19 [1982] IRLR 482.

20 [1984] IRLR 299 at 301.

'requirement' for the purposes of SDA 1975 s1(1)(a) but was, rather, an essential part of the job. The EAT rejected the argument, ruling that:

> Requirement or condition are plain words of wide import fully capable (for example) of including an obligation of full–time work and there was no basis for giving them a restrictive interpretation in the light of the policy underlying the Act or in the light of public policy.[21]

7.29 The courts and tribunals initially agreed that a wide interpretation should be given to 'requirement' and 'condition' under the SDA 1975. This, they have said, is in line with the US cases and with the purpose of the legislation, which is to eliminate practices that have a disproportionate impact on women.[22] It has been held, for example, that obligations to work extra hours, and to change shift patterns, were requirements or conditions under that Act[23] (see also para 7.36). But in some cases the courts have taken a less generous approach. In *Brook v Haringey LBC*,[24] for example, the EAT ruled that the adoption of a redundancy selection procedure that favoured predominantly male jobs (such jobs not being included in the pool for redundancy selection) could not amount to indirect sex discrimination. According to the EAT, the employers could not be said to have applied a requirement or condition that, unless someone was a member of one of the trades whose members were not included in the compulsory pool, he or she was at risk of redundancy:

> Those trades were open to women, in due course they might have included a preponderance of women. There are no biological or social elements concerned ... If this submission is well founded, namely that the mere holding of a job or position can constitute a requirement or condition, and is prima facie discriminatory requiring justification, it could be applied to whole factories.

7.30 The approach taken by the EAT in *Brook* was overruled by the Court of Appeal in *Allonby v Accrington and Rossendale College*[25] in which Sedley LJ (with whom Ward LJ and Gage J agreed) stated that *Brook* 'must be regarded as wrongly decided' (1) because the EAT's approach

21 [1984] IRLR 299 at 301.

22 See *Watches of Switzerland v Savell* [1983] IRLR 141.

23 See, respectively, *Robinson v Oddbins Ltd*, ET 4225/95 (unreported); *London Underground Ltd v Edwards* [1995] IRLR 355 and *Headley v Copygraphic Ltd* (1996) DCLD 30.

24 [1992] IRLR 478.

25 [2001] IRLR 364.

in it to 'requirement or condition' was inconsistent with the ECJ's decision in *Enderby v Frenchay Health Authority*,[26] and (2) because the decision was:

> ... based on an erroneous understanding of the Sex Discrimination Act's concept of indirect discrimination, an understanding which conflates it with direct discrimination ... [i]f the requirement or condition is objectively justified notwithstanding its differential impact on men and women, then it can fairly be said that those disadvantaged simply happen to be women. But it is a conclusion, not a premise.

7.31 The other problem that arises in establishing that a 'requirement or condition' has been applied to a discrimination claimant results from the decision of the Court of Appeal in *Perera v Civil Service Commission (No 2)*.[27] The applicant complained of indirect race discrimination when he was refused an appointment because of the employer's reliance on a number of factors including applicants' experience in the UK, command of English, and age, all of which worked to his disadvantage. The Court of Appeal ruled that none of the factors upon which the employer relied could be regarded as a 'requirement or condition', in the sense that failure to comply with any single factor would not have been an 'absolute bar' to getting the job. The court pointed out that a 'brilliant man' [sic] who lacked one of the relevant factors might have been appointed. The difficulty with this approach is that it legitimises a situation in which higher standards are imposed on those who, because of their race or sex, suffer a particular disadvantage. The employer in *Perera* was able to get away with imposing disparately impacting policies or practices without being required to put forward any justification (see below).

7.32 In *Meer v Tower Hamlets LBC*[28] the Court of Appeal followed *Perera* and held that Tower Hamlets' 'preference' for employees with local knowledge was not a 'requirement or condition' under the RRA 1976. This approach has been much criticised. Such a preference certainly disadvantaged some racial groups. It seems clear that the failure to treat it as an act of indirect discrimination is not consistent with the approach taken by the US Supreme Court in *Griggs*. It was recognised in *Meer* itself that EC law may not require proof that a requirement or condition was an absolute bar.

26 Case 127/92 [1993] ECR I-5535; [1993] IRLR 591.

27 [1983] IRLR 166. Compare the approach taken by the EAT in *Watches of Switzerland v Savell* [1983] IRLR 141.

28 [1988] IRLR 399.

7.33 In *Brook* the *Perera* approach was applied to indirect discrimination under the SDA 1975.[29] There, the EAT refused to accept that a rule that, in order to avoid redundancy, potentially redundant employees had to obtain a preset number of points by reference to multiple factors, was a 'condition' under SDA 1975 s1(1)(b). According to Wood J:

> A person who is rejected because he is not the best candidate on an amalgam of factors has not been subjected to any requirement or condition but he has simply failed to defeat his competitors. It is the position of the individual on the list which is the determining factor, not the amount of points scored. The cut-off is unknown until after the event.

7.34 There is nothing in article 141 EC or in the ETD which ties indirect discrimination to a rigid 'requirement or condition' (see *Enderby v Frenchay Health Authority*[30]). The difference between the EC and UK approaches was emphasised in the EAT's decision in *Bhudi v IMI Refiners Ltd*.[31] An ET had ruled that Mrs Bhudi's employers had not indirectly discriminated against her when they dismissed evening cleaners (who were all female) in preference to daytime cleaners (who were all male). The ET held that no requirement or condition had been imposed, since the employers explained that the reason for the dismissal was that the evening cleaners required disproportionate administration. The EAT refused to interpret the SDA 1975 in accordance with *Enderby* (in which the ECJ held that there was no need to identify a requirement or condition in indirect discrimination cases), and held that a 'requirement or condition' must be established. But it allowed the appeal and remitted the case on alternative grounds holding that in effect there may have been a requirement or condition not to work outside normal hours.

7.35 The incompatibility between EC and UK approaches to indirect discrimination was recognised by the EAT in *Falkirk Council* v *Whyte*,[32] when it relied on EC law to uphold a tribunal finding that a woman had been subject to unlawful indirect discrimination when she was denied a managerial post in respect of which management training and supervisory experience were stated to be 'desirable'.

29 [1992] IRLR 478. See also *Jones* v *University of Manchester* [1992] ICR 52, and *Hall v Shorts Missile Systems* (1997) 72 EOR 39, in which the NICA applied the *Brook* approach to Northern Ireland's fair employment legislation.

30 Case 127/92 [1993] ECR I-5535; [1993] IRLR 591.

31 [1994] IRLR 204.

32 [1997] IRLR 560.

According to Lord Johnstone, for the EAT:

> It was [the plaintiffs'] essential submission that one should not interpret the words 'requirement or condition' on any narrow or restricted basis, having regard to the fact that the legislation was based upon [the ETD] ... Since the employers here were part of the emanation of the State, this tribunal ... could apply the Directive without reference to the legislation; but, in any event, if the legislation required it to be interpreted on any particular basis it should be consistent with the purpose of the Directive – the so-called 'purposive approach' which can be found supported by the House of Lords in *Litster v Forth Dry Dock Engineering Co Ltd*[33] ...
>
> [T]he tribunal were ... liberally interpreting what is meant by 'a requirement or condition' within the meaning of the legislation. We consider this approach was open to the tribunal and, being based upon the evidence, not one with which we feel able to interfere as an appellate tribunal. We would observe in passing that if the case turned upon whether or not the relevant factors to become a requirement or condition had to be an absolute bar to qualification for the post in question, we would not be inclined to follow the race discrimination cases and, in particular, that of *Perera*. We consider that each case has to be determined on its own merits, and the status of the factors in question relevant to the application for the post in question very much depends upon the circumstances of a particular case. Some may be too trivial to be regarded as a condition or requirement; but, equally, if material, and it is shown otherwise that qualifying for the particular factor is more difficult for women than for men in the appropriate workplace, we do not see why that should not be a condition or requirement in terms of the legislation in relation to applications for the post, particularly when the relevant factor or factors turn out to be decisive.

7.36 Requirements and conditions are often hidden, and may be difficult to define under the SDA 1975 and RRA 1976. The way in which the requirement or condition is defined is crucial, as a failure correctly to identify a requirement or condition could result in the defeat of what would otherwise be a good claim. A requirement or condition could be found, for example, in:

- a job description;
- a contract of employment;
- a collective agreement;
- a notice, letter or memo;
- union rules or procedures;
- employment practices.

33 [1990] 1 AC 546; [1989] IRLR 161.

7.37 In *Thorndyke v Bell Fruit (North Central) Ltd*[34] an ET ruled that, although a requirement not to have young children was 'not made explicit', it was in the employer's mind and this was sufficient to establish indirect discrimination. Similarly, a requirement to work full-time may not be stated but is often implicit. This will not prevent it being a job 'requirement'.

7.38 In *Allonby v Accrington and Rossendale College*[35] the Court of Appeal held that it is for the applicant to identify the requirement or condition that he or she wishes to challenge. According to Sedley LJ:

> If the applicant can realistically identify a requirement or condition capable of supporting her case ... it is nothing to the point that her employer can with equal cogency derive from the facts a different and unobjectionable requirement or condition.

It is important to look very carefully at what is required, to extract from practices and procedures those requirements that discriminate on the ground of sex or race, and to consider which requirements might best support a finding of adverse impact. The questionnaire procedure may be very useful in teasing out what requirements or conditions have been applied if they are not explicit (see para 32.23).

Contractual requirements or conditions with future consequences

7.39 A contract can include a requirement or condition which does not have immediate effect. Such a requirement or condition may be challenged before it is invoked by virtue of SDA 1975 s77 which provides that:

> (1) A term of a contract is void where –
> (a) its inclusion renders the making of the contract unlawful by virtue of this Act; or
> (b) it is included in furtherance of an act rendered unlawful by this Act; or
> (c) it provides for the doing of an act which would be rendered unlawful by this Act.

7.40 The applicant in *Meade-Hill v British Council*[36] challenged a general mobility clause which required management employees to work in any part of the UK. She argued that the clause breached SDA 1975 ss6 and 77 because, as a married woman earning less than her husband, she would have found it difficult to move her place of work. Even

34 [1979] IRLR 1.
35 [2001] IRLR 364.
36 [1995] IRLR 478.

though the applicant had not yet been required to move, the Court of Appeal held that the clause was indirectly discriminatory, because a greater proportion of women than men were secondary earners and therefore less able or willing to move, and because the clause in the contract was to her detriment.

Direct or indirect discrimination?

7.41 It is important to note that some conditions or requirements are so linked to gender or race that their application amounts, in reality, to direct rather than indirect discrimination. If it is impossible for any member of a racial group to comply with a requirement or condition, the requirement is directly, rather than indirectly, discriminatory. In *Wong v Greater London Council*[37] the EAT ruled that:

> ... a 'condition' has to be one which is such that the proportion of persons of the same racial group as Mr Wong who can comply with it is considerably smaller than the proportion of persons not of that racial group who can comply with it. It is obvious that somebody who is brown cannot comply at all with the condition that the candidate has to be white. Therefore it is really quite impossible to look for a smaller proportion of people who are unable to satisfy the condition.

7.42 The challenge in *James v Eastleigh BC*[38] was to the Council's practice of providing free access to a swimming pool to those of state pensionable age (60 in the case of women, 65 in the case of men). The House of Lords reversed the decision of the Court of Appeal that this amounted to indirect discrimination, ruling that, because the challenged criterion was 'sex-based', it discriminated directly, rather than indirectly, against men. The position would be different if it just so happened that no members of the applicant's sex or racial group who were within the relevant pool for comparison (see below) at a particular time were able to comply with a disputed requirement or condition.

Alternative question 2 where the new approach to indirect discrimination applies

7.43 The test for employment-related indirect discrimination on grounds of sex or married status under the SDA 1975 as amended by the BP Regulations 2001 is whether the respondent has applied any provision, criterion or practice to the applicant.

37 EAT 524/79, 1980 (unreported but available on LEXIS).

38 [1990] 2 AC 751; [1990] IRLR 288.

7.44 The significant change wrought by the BP Regulations 2001 lies in the addition of the words 'criterion' and 'practice'. The word 'provision' is likely to apply to a written term of a contract or collective agreement or rule of an undertaking, while 'criterion or practice' will cover a more informal practice perhaps not found in a written document. These mean that there is no need to show an absolute bar before protection from indirect discrimination provisions can be relied upon. Consequently the *Perera* case and its progeny will no longer be binding where it can be shown that a criterion or preference has an adverse impact upon women.

7.45 The new definition of indirect discrimination will also be significant in a case in which a series of requirements (or preferences), taken together, may have a discriminatory effect. 'Desirable' attributes are now open to examination as potentially discriminatory in their effect. This will expose many more internal procedures than before to scrutiny, and will permit them to continue only to the extent that they may be justified (see paras 7.116–7.131). This should, in the long run, help to eliminate unnecessary and therefore unjustifiable criteria that are discriminatory in effect.

Question 4: Did such requirement or condition apply to other persons not of the same racial group as the applicant?

7.46 *Raval's* question 3 is considered with questions 8 and 9 below, given its close relationship with them. Question 4 is specific in its terms to the original definition of sex discrimination, given its reference to a 'requirement or condition'. It may, however, also be applied to the new definition of indirect discrimination if it is couched as follows:

> Did or would such provision, criterion or practice apply equally to persons of the opposite gender or persons who are not married?

Questions 5 and 6: The 'relevant circumstances' and the pool for comparison

7.47 These questions are so closely connected that it makes more sense to look at them together. Indirect discrimination involves looking at the relative effect of requirements and conditions on men and women, or on different racial groups, to ascertain whether they have a disproportionately adverse effect on one sex or a racial group.

Compare like with like

7.48 Both the SDA 1975 and the RRA 1976 provide that the 'relevant circumstances' for the comparison of the impact of the requirement or condition must be the same or not materially different as between the comparators.[39]

7.49 *Price v Civil Service Commission*[40] involved a challenge to a civil service requirement that job applicants were under the age of 28. The EAT ruled that the comparison was not between all men and all women, but between men and women who might wish to apply for the job and who were otherwise qualified for it (having two A levels). The question was, then, whether a significantly smaller proportion of the women than the men in that 'pool for comparison' were *also* able to comply with the age-related requirement under challenge.

7.50 The appropriate 'pool for comparison' in a case such as *Price* consists of people who qualify for the benefit sought or would do so if the challenged requirement did not apply. Alternatively, if the indirect discrimination alleged relates to selection for a detriment, such as redundancy, the pool is of those from whom the selection is to be made or would be made if the disputed selection criteria was not applied. In either case the question for the tribunal is whether a significantly smaller proportion of women than of men (or of one racial group than of others) in the pool can comply with the disputed requirement or condition (or, in a detriment case, can avoid selection for it).

7.51 It has been suggested that, if the challenge is to the only job requirement (for example, one 'A' level), the comparison should be between women and men generally, as everyone would be qualified apart from those who cannot comply with the challenged requirement. If the challenge is to one of two or more requirements, the comparison should be between men and women qualified in other ways, apart from the requirement in dispute. The major problem with looking only at otherwise qualified applicants (as pointed out by the applicant in *Pearse v City of Bradford*[41]) is that it is often difficult to obtain the actual information about the numbers of potentially qualified applicants. If such information is not immediately available, there is a limit to the lengths to which a tribunal will go to order an employer to discover or create documents necessary to compile the evidence (though see para 32.119).

39 SDA 1975 s5(3); RRA 1976 s3(4).

40 [1977] IRLR 291.

41 [1988] IRLR 379.

What are the relevant circumstances?

7.52 The 'relevant circumstances' will vary from case to case according to who is affected by a 'requirement or condition'. It may be the whole population of the UK, the workers in a particular workplace, or those who have a particular qualification (within a particular workforce or generally).

The relevant circumstances must not themselves be tainted

7.53 Care must be taken to ensure that the 'relevant circumstances' are not themselves tainted by sex, race, etc. In *Kidd v DRG (UK) Ltd*[42] the applicant challenged, as discriminatory on grounds of married status, a redundancy procedure under which part-time workers were dismissed first. The EAT ruled that the pool was the section of the population living in households which needed to provide child care to an extent that would normally be incompatible with acceptance of full-time employment by the person providing it. By defining the relevant circumstances as the need to provide care for children, the EAT restricted the pool to those who largely could not comply with the requirement to be a full-time worker, and omitted all those who could comply with it. This had the effect of making it very difficult for the applicant to establish disparate impact.

7.54 As a matter of law it must be wrong to limit the pool by the very factors (such as child care responsibilities) which gave rise to the applicant's inability to comply with the requirement. Indeed the EAT emphasised in *R v Secretary of State for Education ex p Schaffter*[43] that a tribunal's choice of pool would be open to challenge if it was itself tainted by discrimination. There the applicant challenged, as indirectly discriminatory on grounds of sex, a statutory education scheme which restricted hardship grants for lone parents to those parents who had been married. The scheme fell outside the SDA 1975 and the applicant accordingly relied on the ETD. The evidence was that 80 per cent of lone parents are female, although equal proportions of male and female lone parents had previously been married. The High Court held that to limit the pool to only unmarried lone parents would build discrimination into the comparison, because women were more likely to be unmarried and to have parental responsibility. The court held that the correct pool was that of all lone parents, thereby avoiding the discriminatory effect of selecting the smaller pool.

42 [1985] IRLR 190.
43 [1987] IRLR 53.

7.55 It is unlikely that the pool approved of by the EAT in *Kidd* would be acceptable today, given *Schaffter* and the host of ECJ decisions in which that court has recognised the adverse impact on women of discrimination against part-time workers. Many tribunals now accept that discrimination against part-time workers in most workplaces will be prima facie sex discrimination. What has survived until very recently indeed, however, was the EAT's insistence that the choice of pool is one of fact for the ET.

The pool: a question of fact or law?

7.56 The choice of pool is crucial. The same claim of discrimination (say, against part-time workers) could succeed in one workforce but fail in another, just because of the composition of the workforce. Although in the past this has been characterised as an issue of fact for the ET to decide, the Court of Appeal (per Sedley LJ) held in *Allonby v Accrington and Rossendale College*[44] that:

> ... once the impugned requirement or condition has been defined there is likely to be only one pool which serves to test its effect. I would prefer to characterize the identification of the pool as a matter neither of discretion nor of fact finding but of logic ... Logic may on occasion be capable of producing more than one outcome, especially if two or more conditions or requirements are in issue. But the choice of pool is not at large.

7.57 Where the pool is too small, and is therefore statistically unreliable, it is appropriate for the court to take account of national statistics or patterns. In *London Underground Ltd v Edwards (No 2)*,[45] in which all 2,000 men could comply with the requirement and only one of the 21 women could not comply, the EAT held that:

> ... in assessing the extent of the disproportionate effect, the tribunal is entitled to take account of a wider perspective. It is for this reason that statistics showing the percentage of women in employment who have primary care responsibility for a child, in contrast to the percentage of men in that position are relevant.

How to identify the pool

7.58 In *Barry v Midland Bank plc*[46] the House of Lords considered the question of the relevant pool by which disparate impact could be assessed.

44 [1998] IRLR 364 at 368. See also *Harvest Town Circle v Rutherford* [2001] IRLR 599.
45 [1999] IRLR 364.
46 [1999] 1 WLR 1465; [1999] IRLR 581.

The case concerned a bank clerk who had worked full-time for 11 years before working part-time for three years after maternity leave. She subsequently took voluntary redundancy and was given a severance package based on the years that she had worked and the amount of her final weekly pay at the time that her employment terminated.

7.59 Ms Barry complained that her employers' method of calculating her severance payment did not reflect the fact that she had worked full-time for 11 years. She argued that this aspect of the scheme disadvantaged part-time workers who had previously been full-time, and that these were mainly women. She claimed, accordingly, that the scheme discriminated indirectly against women contrary to the Equal Pay Act (EqPA) 1970 and article 141 EC. She showed that, in the relevant department, 92 per cent of the women worked full-time compared with 99 per cent of the men. She also showed that women formed 95 per cent of the part-time workers. The ET and the EAT decided that she had not been discriminated against. The Court of Appeal and the House of Lords held that it was not right to compare full-time workers with part-time workers, full-time men with full-time women, or part-time men with part-time women workers. Their Lordships concluded that the disadvantaged group was those part-time workers whose hours of work at termination were less than the average of their hours of work throughout their service. The court should then compare what proportion of men fell into this category and what proportion of women did. As these statistics were not available, indirect discrimination was not established. This case highlights the importance of identifying both the disadvantaged and the advantaged groups at an early stage, possible as part of the pre-trial proceedings, so that the appropriate statistics can be obtained.

7.60 The EAT has held that a pool for comparison does not have to be shown to be a statistically perfect match of the people who would be capable of and interested in filling the post offered. In *Greater Manchester Police Authority v Lea*,[47] the EAT held that the ET was entitled to decide that the economically active population was an appropriate pool of persons for the purpose of determining the proportion of men and women who could comply with a condition of not being in receipt of an occupational pension, notwithstanding that the statistical base was wider than perfection would have dictated.

7.61 The limits of tribunal discretion relating to the choice of the pool are illustrated by the decision of the Court of Appeal in *University of*

47 [1990] IRLR 372.

Manchester v Jones.[48] The applicant was a 46-year-old woman who, having graduated as a mature student, applied for a job as a careers adviser. She challenged the age requirement (27–35) imposed by the employer. The court held that the appropriate pool for comparison was all those who had the required qualifications excluding the requirement that was the subject of the complaint. The requirement cannot be subdivided so as to fit an individual case. In this case the court held that the correct pool was that of graduates and not merely mature graduates, since the potentially successful job applicants consisted of graduates, rather than mature graduates.

Defining the pool by area

7.62 The pool for comparison might be limited to a local area or extend across the UK. In cases where the essential issue concerns the requirements or conditions for application for a particular job, and there is no geographical restriction on the area from which people may apply, the pool may be the 'travel to work' area for the job. But if the job is a mobile one or a fairly senior one, a wider area would be more appropriate. In many cases jobs are advertised nationally, in which case the national pool of potential applicants for the job will be relevant. Where the challenge is to a practice (such as a redundancy procedure or promotion) which only affects a particular workforce, the pool may be existing employees (but see *Edwards (No 2)* at para 7.70 below).

Size matters

7.63 The result of the comparison may differ according to the size (and identity) of the groups chosen. If, in a case concerning discrimination against part-time workers, the pool chosen consisted of all workers in the UK, disparate impact by sex would be established as women account for over 80 per cent of part-time workers nationally. Within a particular workforce, however, the picture may be very different.

7.64 In some cases, local factors may produce a geographical distortion. Although this may happen in sex discrimination cases (there could be a particular workforce where the vast majority of part-timers are men) it is fairly rare, as men and women are distributed evenly all over the country. In race discrimination cases, however, the number of ethnic minority workers in the labour market is relatively small, and the number of workers of a particular ethnic minority group

48 [1993] IRLR 218.

may be very small. Further, particular categories of ethnic minority workers are often concentrated in certain parts of the country, particularly in inner city areas.

7.65 A person complaining of a discriminatory requirement in an area in which he or she is the only person in his or her racial group may find it hard to prove reliable statistical disparity, given that he or she will be the only person of his or her racial group in the pool for comparison. Although, strictly speaking, he or she may be able to show that 0 per cent of people in his/her racial group (ie, himself or herself) could comply with the disputed requirement, the courts may be unwilling to accept such statistical data as being representative. If this is the case, the pool must be increased to comprise a representative sample.[49]

7.66 If the practice relates to job applicants, the pool should include at least all those who may have wished to apply for the job. If it does not do so, all those who were deterred from applying because of the impugned requirement will be excluded (see *Orphanos* at para 7.20). It may be impossible to get these statistics, in which case applicants should try to produce the relevant national statistics to support their point.

Selecting the pool

7.67 Ideally, the parties should agree on the relevant pool. If this is not possible, the safest way of proceeding is to put forward alternative pools and provide statistical evidence in relation to each one. The questionnaire procedure can be used (see para 32.23).

7.68 If there is doubt about the identity of the pool, it can be decided by the ET as a preliminary point. If this is not done, the statistical evidence adduced (sometimes at some cost) may prove to be irrelevant.

Question 7: Disparate impact

7.69 *Raval's* question 7 is concerned with disparate impact which must be established in all cases in which indirect discrimination is alleged. The disparate impact test addresses two related issues: first, whether a disputed practice, etc, does actually put one sex or racial group at a disadvantage; second, whether the disadvantage is sufficient to reverse the burden of proof so as to require the other party to provide a justification for the practice.

49 See also *London Underground v Edwards (No 2)* [1998] IRLR 364.

7.70 These points were explored in *London Underground v Edwards (No 2)*, in which Potter LJ explained the purpose of the disparate impact test under the SDA 1975:

> In my view there is a dual statutory purpose underlying the provisions of section 1(1)(b) of the [SDA] and in particular the necessity under sub-paragraph (i) to show that the proportion of women who can comply with a given requirement or condition is 'considerably smaller' than the proportion of men who can comply with it. The first is to prescribe as the threshold for intervention a situation in which there exists a substantial and not merely marginal discriminatory effect (disparate impact) as between men and women, so that it can be clearly demonstrated that a prima facie case of (indirect) discrimination exists, sufficient to require the employer to justify the application of the condition or requirement in question: see sub-paragraph (ii). The second is to ensure that a tribunal charged with deciding whether or not the requirement is discriminatory may be confident that its disparate impact is inherent in the application of the requirement or condition and is not simply the product of unreliable statistics or fortuitous circumstance. Since the disparate impact question will require to be resolved in an infinite number of different employment situations ... an area of flexibility (or margin of appreciation), is necessarily applicable to the question of whether a particular percentage is to be regarded as 'substantially smaller' in any given case.[50]

Potter LJ was considering the definition of indirect discrimination in the SDA 1975 prior to its amendment by the BP Regulations 2001. But the amended definition is not materially different in this respect and it is likely that the courts and tribunals will continue to be guided by the decision in *London Underground.* It is too early as yet to speculate about the judicial approach to the RRA 1976 once it has been amended (as it must be by July 2003) to reflect the approach of the RD which defines indirect discrimination rather differently than in terms of 'an apparently neutral provision, criterion or practice [which] *would put* persons of a racial or ethnic origin *at a particular disadvantage* compared with other persons ...' (emphasis added).

7.71 The original domestic approach to indirect discrimination entails asking whether the proportion of the relevant group which can comply with the disputed requirement or condition is considerably smaller than the proportion of others who can comply. Under the SDA 1975 as amended to comply with the BPD the question is whether the requirement, criterion or practice was to the detriment of a 'considerably

50 [1998] IRLR 364 para 23.

larger' proportion of women than of men. The original test compares the proportions of who *can* comply. The new test compares the proportions of those who *cannot*. It remains to be seen whether this difference of approach will be significant in practice, particularly as it had already been argued that it is necessary even under the original approach to consider the proportions of those who cannot as well as those who can comply.[51]

Establishing disparate impact mathematically

7.72 Proof of disparate impact can be by detailed statistical evidence where it is available. An example of the use of such evidence is included below, in relation to a hypothetical challenge by a Bengali to a minimum height requirement (1.75 metres).

Bengalis	**Non-Bengalis**
1. Find the number of Bengalis in the 'relevant pool' (B in pool)	4. Find the number of non-Bengalis in the 'relevant pool' (NB in pool)
2. Ascertain the number of Bengalis in the pool who are *over* 1.75m tall (B can comply)	5. Ascertain the number of non-Bengalis in the pool who are *over* 1.75m tall (NB can comply)
3. Divide the number of Bengalis who are over 1.75m tall by the number of Bengalis in the pool	6. Divide the number of non-Bengalis who are over 1.75m tall by the total number of non-Bengalis

The proportions found at steps 3 and 6 above can then be compared by asking whether the proportion of Bengalis who *can* comply with the height requirement is considerably smaller than that of the non-Bengalis.

7.73 It can be seen that the key question in a race discrimination case can be stated as:

Is the fraction $\frac{\text{B can comply}}{\text{B in pool}}$ considerably *smaller* than the fraction $\frac{\text{NB can comply}}{\text{NB in pool}}$?

51 See *R v Employment Secretary ex p Seymour Smith (No 2)* [2000] 1 WLR 435; [1999] IRLR 253, para 59, HL; *Barry* v *Midland Bank* [1989] IRLR 581, per Lord Nicholls.

7.74 A minimum height requirement of 1.75 metres would also have an adverse effect on women. In the case of a woman in an employment-related sex discrimination case the steps would be:

Women	**Men**
1. Find the number of women in the 'relevant pool' (W in pool)	4. Find the number of men in the 'relevant pool' (M in pool)
2. Ascertain the number of women in the pool who are under 1.75m tall (W can't comply)	5. Ascertain the number of men in the pool who are under 1.75m tall (M can't comply)
3. Divide the number of women who are under 1.75m tall by the number of women in the pool	6. Divide the number of men who are under 1.75m tall by the total number of men

Again, the proportions found at steps 3 and 6 above can be compared by asking whether the proportion of women who *cannot* comply with the height requirement is considerably larger than that of the men.

7.75 The key question in an employment-related sex discrimination case can be stated as:

Is the fraction $\frac{\text{W can't comply}}{\text{W in pool}}$ considerably *smaller* than the fraction $\frac{\text{M can't comply}}{\text{M in pool}}$?

7.76 The mathematical approach to indirect discrimination is useful in a case in which detailed statistics relating to ability to comply are available. But it is increasingly being accepted that the use of statistics is not always necessary, and that it may not even be appropriate. There may be no relevant statistics, or the statistics which are available may be unreliable because they relate to too small a group. Courts and tribunals are increasingly prepared to take judicial notice of 'ordinary' behaviour.[52] Some, however, are still reluctant to do so, so it is not safe to rely on this approach.

52 See, eg, Millett J in *Meade-Hill v British Council* [1995] ICR 847 at 859, and *London Underground Ltd v Edwards (No 2)* [1998] IRLR 364.

The Jones *prediction test*

7.77 In *Jones v Chief Adjudication Officer*[53] the Court of Appeal formulated a test for indirect discrimination which started by considering what the outcome would be if there was equal treatment as between the different groups, and then considering what the difference was between that predicted and the actual outcome. This approach starts with the assumption that the same proportion of men and women should be able to comply with the disputed requirement or condition as the proportion of men and women in the relevant workforce. In *Jones* the Court of Appeal ruled that:

> What we must consider is whether, if one looks not at individuals but at the population of claimants as a whole, it can be seen that there is indirect discrimination. The parties agree that for this purpose it is the effect, not the intent, of the legislation which counts. They also agree that what was called the 'demographic' argument represents one way in which indirect discrimination can be established. As I understand it, the process for establishing discrimination on this basis takes the following shape. (For ease of illustration, I will assume that the complaint stems from the failure of a woman to satisfy a relevant positive qualification for selection, and that only one such qualification is in issue.)
>
> [Step] 1. Identify the criterion for selection;
> [Step] 2. Identify the relevant population, comprising all those who satisfy all the other criteria for selection . . .
> [Step] 3. Divide the relevant population into groups representing those who satisfy the criterion and those who do not;
> [Step] 4. Predict statistically what proportion of each group should consist of women;
> [Step] 5. Ascertain what are the actual male/female balances in the two groups;
> [Step] 6. Compare the actual with the predicted balances;
> [Step] 7. If women are found to be under-represented in the first group and over-represented in the second, it is proved that the criterion is discriminatory.[54]

This tests whether the indirect discrimination alleged is regulated by the original test (applicable to non-employment-related sex discrimination and to race discrimination) or the amended one (which applies to employment-related sex discrimination). It considers what the position would be if a requirement, condition, etc, had no adverse

53 [1990] IRLR 533.
54 Ibid para 36.

effect, and then how closely the statistics meet that prediction. Following the *Jones* test helps produce the clearest picture of whether and to what extent discrimination is operating.

7.78 It is useful to consider the application of the *Jones* test in practice. Suppose that a local authority employs 6,750 people of whom 3,500 are male and 3,250 are female. The authority decides to grant an additional day's annual holiday to the 160 staff who have over 20 years' service. Of these staff 100 are male and 60 female. A woman complains that this service requirement discriminates indirectly on grounds of sex. Applying the *Jones* approach:

Step 1: The criterion for selection is service for over 20 years.

Step 2: The relevant pool is 6,750 people, ie, 3,500 men and 3,250 women.

Step 3: The relevant pool who satisfy the criteria is 160 people, the remaining 6,590 people do not satisfy the criteria.

Step 4: The assumption is that, if the requirement is non-discriminatory, it will impact equally on women and men. On this assumption, the proportion of women able to comply should be the same as the proportion of men able to comply. It is possible to predict how many men and women respectively should meet the requirement by using the following formula.

Women: $\frac{160 \times 3{,}250}{6{,}750} = 77$ Men: $\frac{160 \times 3{,}500}{6{,}750} = 83$

[Alternatively:

a. Calculate the percentage of men and women in the workforce:

$\frac{3{,}500}{6{,}750} \times 100\% = 51.85\%$ men; $\frac{3{,}250}{6{,}750} \times 100\% = 48.15\%$ women

b. Assuming that the number who can comply (160) is divided as between males and females on the same basis as the whole workforce, calculate what that number should be.

160 x 51.85% = 83 men; 160 x 48.15% = 77 women.]

Step 5: The actual numbers who can comply are 100 men and 60 women,

Step 6: The predicted numbers who can comply are 83 males and 77 females. This means that there are 17 too many men and 17 too few women in the complying group.

Step 7: The calculations show that women are under-represented in the group of people who can comply with the requirement and over-represented in the group who cannot comply with it. Disparate impact is proved.

Using the current example it can be seen that the difference in impact can be expressed in three different ways.

	Women	Men
Proportions Proportions who can comply using the formula	$\frac{\text{W can comply}}{\text{W in pool}}$ $\frac{60}{3,250}$	$\frac{\text{M can comply}}{\text{M in pool}}$ $\frac{100}{3,500}$
Percentages If the proportions above are converted to percentages who can comply the result is:	$\frac{\text{W can comply}}{\text{W in pool}} \times 100\%$ $\frac{60}{3,250} \times 100\% = 1.86\%$	$\frac{\text{M can comply}}{\text{M in pool}} \times 100\%$ $\frac{100}{3,500} \times 100\% = 2.86\%$
The *Jones* test Numbers who can comply compared with the predicted number (see above) if there were equal treatment, ie, *Jones* test.	60 – 77 = 17 too few	100 – 83 = 17 too many

This comparison helps to show up the advantages and disadvantages of each approach. The proportions approach shows that there is a large number of people in each part of the pool. But it is very difficult to make sense of how $^{60}/_{3,250}$ (or even $^{6}/_{325}$) compares with $^{10}/_{3,500}$ (or $^{6}/_{325}$). It therefore makes sense to translate the proportion into a percentage.

7.79 The percentages show the relative size of the two proportions. Although it appears that a one percentage point difference between the two percentages (2.86 per cent men as against 1.85 per cent women) is insignificant, 2.86 per cent is more than one-and-a-half times as large as 1.85 per cent. Once the figures are expressed as percentages the actual numbers are obscured. So a large percentage difference where there is a small pool can appear more significant than it is; correspondingly a small percentage difference in a large pool can appear much less significant than it is. The larger the pool of people the less likely is it that the percentages are fortuitous: one or two people joining the workforce will not eradicate the difference.

7.80 The *Jones* test highlights the difference between the expected outcome and the actual outcome. It most clearly describes the actual discriminatory effect of the requirement or condition and the significance of the disparate impact, although the figures it produces (here 17 too many men, 17 too few women) are significant only when they are contextualised in relation to the total number in the pool (here 6,750).

'Considerably' smaller (or greater) proportions

7.81 In the US, in the past, a 'four-fifths' rule has been used in some situations to establish disparate impact. The American Equal Employment Opportunities Commission took the view that, if the proportion of the relevant group that could comply with a disputed requirement or condition was at least 80 per cent of the proportion of the other group that could comply, any adverse impact would be unlikely to be sufficient to found a discrimination claim. This approach gives rise to many statistical problems, particularly where the figures are very large or very small. It has been rejected by the Northern Ireland Court of Appeal in *McCausland v Dungannon DC*.[55] Different tribunals have taken different views as to what constitutes a 'considerably smaller' proportion. What is 'considerably smaller' is ultimately a question of fact for the ET and, subject to what is said below, the EAT may be reluctant to intervene.

7.82 In *R v Employment Secretary ex p Seymour Smith*[56] two women challenged the two-year qualification period then applied to protection from unfair dismissal, arguing that it discriminated indirectly on grounds of sex. They were able to show that, between 1985 and 1991, the percentage of the female working population disadvantaged by the requirement was 8 per cent larger than the percentage of the male population who were so disadvantaged. Women tend to have shorter periods of continuous employment than men for reasons connected with maternity and childcare.

7.83 The *Seymour-Smith* challenge posed an important question about how great the disparate impact of a disputed requirement or condition had to be before it could be said that the proportion of a group (here women) which could comply with it was 'considerably smaller' than that of others (here men) who could comply. The question was referred to the ECJ which ruled:

> ... the best approach to the comparison of statistics is to consider, on the one hand, the respective proportions of men and in the workforce able to satisfy the requirement of two years' employment under the disputed rule and of those unable to do so, and, on the other, to

55 [1993] IRLR 583.

56 [2000] 1 WLR 435; [1999] IRLR 253, HL. The decision of the CA is at [1995] IRLR 464.

> compare those proportions as regards women in the workforce. It is not sufficient to consider the number of persons affected.[57]

The ECJ's approach, which was rooted in Community law, looked both at those who could and those who could not comply with the requirement or condition. It was supported by the House of Lords. The question remained, however, how great the disparity had to be.

7.84 The SDA 1975 in its original form and the RRA 1976 pose the question whether a *considerably smaller* proportion of the relevant group can comply with the disputed requirement or condition. Since the SDA 1975 had to be construed in a way which was consistent with the ETD, it was inevitable that consideration would be given to the wording of the ETD itself. Article 2 ETD provides that:

> ... the application of the principle of equal treatment means that there shall be no discrimination whatsoever on grounds of sex either directly or indirectly ... [emphasis added]

The ETD makes no mention of 'considerably smaller' or of 'proportions'. Nor does it limit its consideration to those who 'can comply'.

7.85 There is little doubt that the ETD has influenced the interpretation of the SDA 1975 and indeed the RRA 1976. In *Seymour Smith*, for example, Lord Nicholls declared for the majority of the House of Lords that:

> ... given the context of equality of pay or treatment, the latitude afforded by the word 'considerably' should not be exaggerated.

So though the difference has to be considerable, it does not have to be huge. Similarly it must be assumed that, under the SDA 1975 as amended, the difference required for a considerably larger adverse impact is also not to be exaggerated. What is being considered is whether a requirement, condition, practice or criterion affords equal treatment, that is, whether it entails no discrimination whatsoever. If the pool is large enough then a small difference in the two percentages may be important, because it may show that a large *number* of people are disadvantaged by it.

7.86 In *Seymour-Smith* the Court of Appeal found that, in 1985, 370,000 more women than men were disadvantaged by the two-year qualifying period.[58] The court went on to point out that this represented 5 per cent of the total female working population, and concluded that this was sufficient to raise a presumption of indirect discrimination. But

57 Case 167/97 [1999] ECR I-0623; [1999] IRLR 253, para 59.

58 [1995] IRLR 464.

the court was particularly influenced by the persistence of the discriminatory effect over a series of years. The ECJ expressed doubt as to whether the disparate impact of the two-year rule was sufficient to establish a prima facie case of indirect discrimination:

> [I]t appears from the order for reference that in 1985, the year in which the requirement of two years' employment was introduced, 77.4% of men and 68.9% of women fulfilled that condition.
>
> Such statistics do not appear, on the face of it, to show that a considerably smaller percentage of women than men is able to fulfil the requirement imposed by the disputed rule.[59]

The House of Lords, however, concluded by a majority, that such:

> ... persistent and consistent disparity ... in the entire male and female labour forces of the country over a period of seven years cannot be brushed aside and dismissed as insignificant or inconsiderable.[60]

Are the figures fortuitous or do they really show an unequal impact?

7.87 The disparate impact uncovered by proportions, percentages or the *Jones* test could be the result of purely fortuitous or random events. The court or tribunal must determine whether it is 'considerable' (see paras 7.69–7.70 and 7.81). This is a particular problem when percentages alone are compared, because in a small workforce a single person can make a significant difference to the percentages able or unable to comply. The following example shows how the consideration of percentages alone and not the actual numbers could be misleading.

7.88 Suppose a firm has 20 shop floor employees of whom half are male and half female. In order to be promoted to supervisor, a worker must have at least five years' service with the firm. Sixty per cent of the men but only forty per cent of the women comply with this condition. This difference looks 'considerable', but when the percentages are converted back into proportions they do not look so considerably different: six out of the ten men and four of the ten women have worked there for more than five years. If one qualifying man left and was replaced by a new man, and one more woman passed her fifth anniversary in the workplace, the percentage difference would disappear. If, by contrast, the firm had 200,000 workers, the same percentage disparity would be eliminated by 10,000 men leaving and the same number of women passing the five-year mark. Forty per cent of

59 Case 167/97 [1999] ECR I-0623; [1999] IRLR 253, paras 63 and 64.
60 [2000] 1 WLR 435; [1999] IRLR 253.

100,000 is a 'considerably smaller' proportion than sixty per cent. Without careful consideration of the figures behind percentages a court or tribunal could very easily go wrong in deciding whether a disparity is 'considerable'.

7.89 Where there is a small workforce it will help to show that any disparities within the workplace are consistent with a national pattern. The existence of a long-term pattern can also be useful in establishing 'considerable' disparate impact. In *Seymour Smith*, for example, the Court of Appeal was impressed by the 'persistency and consistency' of the figures over a period of seven years. The House of Lords held by a majority in the same case that:

> ... a persistent and constant disparity of the order just mentioned [9/10 over a period of six years] in respect of the entire male and female labour forces of the country over a period of seven years cannot be brushed aside and dismissed as insignificant or inconsiderable.[61]

The relevance of the total proportion of people excluded by the requirement or condition

7.90 The proportion of men and women or of one racial group who can meet a particular requirement may be large in one case and tiny in another. A requirement to have a PhD would clearly be met only by a very small number of people. A requirement to have an English GCSE would be met by a large number. Even though there may be only small numbers involved, the difference between the proportions able to comply may be substantial. Thus if only 2 per cent of men and only 0.5 per cent of women have a PhD the difference is obviously substantial. On these figures four times as many men as women can meet the requirement.

7.91 Normally neither the ease nor difficulty of compliance with a particular requirement or condition will affect its relevance as a tool with which to test adverse impact. Neither Act sets any such limit. However, this has been held not to apply where the numbers of people who can comply are so small as to exclude almost the entirety of the pool. In *Coker and Osamor v Lord Chancellor*,[62] two women challenged as indirectly discriminatory the Lord Chancellor's appointment of his special adviser. The post was never advertised, and it was accepted that the Lord Chancellor did not look outside his circle of acquain-

61 [2000] 1 WLR 435; [1999] IRLR 253.
62 [2002] IRLR 80.

tances when making the appointment. It was also accepted that this circle included more men than women, and that those of African, Caribbean or African-Caribbean origin comprised a very small minority of it. The ET found that the requirement was that the successful applicant must be personally known to the Lord Chancellor. Because this excluded almost the entirety of the pool, the Court of Appeal concluded that it could not amount to indirect discrimination (see further para 7.115).

The disadvantaged group is important

7.92 Even if the original test of indirect discrimination (which focuses on the relative proportions of those which can comply) is applicable, the disadvantaged group remains important. There is of course a straightforward mathematical relationship between the proportion advantaged and the proportion disadvantaged (if 98 per cent of men and 96 per cent of women can comply, then 2 per cent of men and 4 per cent of women cannot comply). 96 per cent and 98 per cent are relatively similar percentages. But 4 per cent is twice as big a proportion as 2 per cent. It must be remembered that the purpose of the test is to see whether the requirement or condition needs to be justified in relation to the person disadvantaged. In *Seymour Smith* the ECJ made it clear that comparison should occur of both compliers and non-compliers.[63] When the case returned to the House of Lords Lord Nicholls found that it was 'unnecessary to reach a firm conclusion on this point'.[64]

7.93 In *Harvest Town Circle v Rutherford*,[65] in which the upper age limits for unfair dismissal compensation were challenged as indirectly discriminatory on grounds of sex, the EAT drew up a useful series of guidelines on how to look at statistics. The court pointed out that, in some cases, the numbers or proportions alone will be sufficient and no sophisticated analysis will be required. But in less obvious cases 'it will be proper for the employment tribunal to look not merely at proportions (as proportions alone can be misleading) but also at numbers, and to look at both disadvantaged and non-disadvantaged groups and even to the respective proportions in the disadvantaged groups expressed as a ratio of each other'.

63 Case 167/97 [1999] ECR I-0623; [1999] IRLR 253.
64 [2000] 1 WLR 435; [1999] IRLR 253, para 61.
65 [2001] IRLR 599.

Relevance of national statistics and evidence of social customs

7.94 Elaborate statistics will not always be available. But the court or ET may take into account its own experience, or commonly known facts (see *Edwards (No 2)*[66]). In *Home Office v Holmes*[67] the ET stated, in finding that fewer women than men could work full-time, that 'it is still a fact that the raising of children tends to place a greater burden on women than it does on men'. In *Kidd v DRG*,[68] by contrast, the ET expressed the rather surprising view that there was no evidence that more women than men, or married women than unmarried women, gave up full-time work to look after children. The EAT upheld the ET's decision, ruling that it was for the ET to decide what could be taken for granted and what needed proper statistical evidence.

7.95 It seems unlikely that an ET would today follow the same approach as that in *Kidd*. In the first place, the ET there took into account the wrong 'relevant circumstances' (see paras 7.47 and 7.53). Second, it apparently received no evidence that women carry the burden of child care. The EAT stressed this point, stating that in future cases it would be essential to produce such evidence. Third, *Kidd* was decided before the decision in *Bilka-Kaufhaus GmbH v Weber von Hartz* (see para 7.117).[69] The view taken by the EAT in Ms Kidd's case was startling – it is simply not true that men take an equal role in child care, and there is ample evidence to support this.

7.96 In *Perera v Civil Service Commission*[69a] the applicant showed that, out of the 47 executive officers in his workplace, 22 (not one of whom was black) were under the age of 32. The proportion of the 13 black workers who could comply with the age requirement was 0 per cent. It may have been coincidence that many of the white workers, but none of the black workers, was less than 32 years of age. The ET relied on the fact that a substantial number of black workers in the UK were adult immigrants, and also that the Civil Service had not put in any evidence to rebut Mr Perera's. The EAT stated that it was most undesirable that in all cases elaborate statistical evidence should be required.

7.97 Statistical evidence of the proportion of men and women or of racial groups nationally who cannot comply with a disputed requirement will always provide an important insight into the causes why a particular requirement is disadvantageous. Evidence of the reasons

66 [1998] IRLR 364.
67 [1984] IRLR 299.
68 [1985] IRLR 190.
69 Case 170/84 [1986] ECR 1607; [1986] IRLR 317.
69a [1977] IRLR 291.

why a particular group or sex has difficulty complying with the requirement will also be relevant. In *CRE v Dutton*[70] (see para 7.108), the Court of Appeal stated clearly that the proportion of gypsies who would satisfy a 'no travellers' condition is considerably smaller than the proportion of non-gypsies who would. Although between one-half and one-third live in houses, it was apparent that a far higher proportion of gypsies led a nomadic way of life than the rest of the population (or, more narrowly, than the rest of the population who might wish to resort to the pub which had banned travellers). The pool for comparison could either have been all gypsies, or those living close to the pub. If these figures are unavailable it may be necessary to refer to national statistics to establish the claim.

7.98 In *London Underground Ltd v Edwards (No 2)*,[71] the applicant was the only woman tube driver who could not comply with a requirement to work a particular shift pattern. Having calculated that 95.2 per cent of women, and 100 per cent of men, could comply with the condition, the ET continued:

> Equality of treatment is the paramount consideration ... The [tribunal] is entitled to have regard to the possibility that, where the number of women as against the number of men is, in percentage terms, very slight, some kind of generalised assumption may exist at the workplace that the particular type of work concerned is 'men's' and not 'women's' work ... in assessing the extent of the disproportionate effect, the tribunal is entitled to take account of a wider perspective. It is for this reason that statistics showing the percentage of women in employment who have primary care responsibility for a child, in contrast to the percentage of men in that position, are relevant.

The Court of Appeal confirmed that the ET had been right to take account of the wider picture:

> It seems to me that the comparatively small size of the female component indicated, again without the need for specific evidence, both that it was either difficult or unattractive for women to work as train operators in any event and that the figure of 95.2 per cent of women unable to comply was likely to be a minimum rather than a maximum figure.

70 [1989] IRLR 8.

71 [1998] IRLR 364.

Relationship between justification and adverse impact

7.99 It has been argued that an applicant does not have to show as much adverse impact if the employers can show no justification for the disputed requirement. In *London Underground v Edwards (No 2)* the EAT ruled that:

> Although there is no direct correlation between the two we would anticipate that in accordance with the purpose of the ETD of eliminating discrimination between the sexes in the employment field, the less justification London Underground had for the way they treated Ms Edwards, the less likely it is that a tribunal will conclude that she has failed to show that the disproportionate effect of the condition was considerable.

7.100 In *Chief Constable of Avon and Somerset Constabulary v Chew*,[72] a differently constituted EAT ruled that:

> ... the obligation to avoid discrimination does not consist of applying requirements having precisely the same impact on men and women employees. The obligation is to avoid applying unjustifiable requirements having considerable disparity of impact.

Question 3: When was such requirement or condition applied to the applicant?

7.101 This question considers whether the applicant could comply with the requirement or condition *at the time when it was applied* to him or her. It will not be relevant that at a different time he or she might have been able to comply with it.

7.102 In *CRE v Dutton*,[73] in which a pub refused to serve 'travellers', the Court of Appeal held that the date at which ability to comply with a requirement falls to be judged is the date at which the requirement has to be fulfilled. The requirement at issue in *Dutton* was that the prospective drinker not be a traveller, and it was alleged that fewer gypsies than non-gypsies could comply with it. The ability to comply had to be judged at the time the gypsy was outside the pub wishing to enter it, rather than at some other date when the gypsy could have acquired housing accommodation and therefore become able to meet the condition for entrance.

7.103 In *Clarke v Eley Kynoch Ltd*,[74] the EAT followed *Dutton* in ruling that the time at which the ability of women workers to comply with a

72 EAT/503/00 (unreported), para 53.

73 [1989] IRLR 8.

74 [1982] IRLR 482.

requirement that, in order to avoid redundancy, they had to work full-time (part-timers being selected first) had to be judged was the time at which it was applied. The employers had argued that one of the part-time workers could, in the past, have transferred to full-time work, though she could not have done so at the time that the redundancies were being negotiated.

7.104 It is often difficult to ascertain when the relevant act was done. In *Cast v Croydon College*[75] the applicant informed her employers of her pregnancy and, before she took maternity leave, asked to return either on a part-time basis or to a job share. Her request was refused as, on her return to work, were her requests to transfer from full-time to part-time work. She eventually handed in her notice, stating that this was 'a direct result of your continuing refusal to allow me to job-share'. The Court of Appeal found that the requests were a continuing act of discrimination which extended up to the date that her employment ended. The court distinguished between situations in which a decision-maker has simply reiterated a refusal, and that in which he or she has reconsidered the matter in question. Where there has been some reconsideration of a decision, time starts to run again. But where a decision is simply repeated and the complainant is referred back to the previous decision, no new complaint arises and no new period of limitation starts. Where successive acts indicate a *policy*, however, the date from which time begins to run is the date on which that policy ceased to apply to the applicant (when, for example, she ceased to be employed). This is further discussed at para 32.53.

7.105 When the ECJ considered the question of time limits in *R v Secretary of State for Employment ex p Seymour Smith*,[76] it concluded that the answer depended on the nature of the action and the provision that is alleged to have been breached. Importantly, the court pointed out that the requirements of EC law should be complied with *at all relevant times*.[77] In particular, where an authority's action is challenged, the legality of the action should be tested at the time it was adopted. Where a national measure impacts on an individual it can be tested at the time of the impact. And if statistics are used it may be appropriate to look at the statistics not only at the time of the adoption of that act, but also subsequently to see if there is a pattern emerging. These are just guidelines, the ECJ considering that the final decision on these matters should be decided by the national courts.

75 [1998] IRLR 318.

76 [2000] 1 WLR 435; [1999] IRLR 253.

77 Ibid para 45.

Question 9: Could the applicant, at the material time, comply with the requirement?

7.106 This question must be asked *only* where the old test for indirect discrimination applies (ie, in cases other than those concerning employment-related discrimination on grounds of sex or married status). The new test for indirect discrimination asks whether a provision, criterion or practice is to the applicant's detriment, without specifying that this must be because of her inability to comply. It remains to be seen how different will be this test in practice.

7.107 Question 9 asks whether the applicant is capable *in practice* of complying, theoretical but impractical possibilities being disregarded. Thus, maximum age limits may discriminate against women who, because of child bearing, enter or re-enter the job market at an older age. In *Price v Civil Service Commission*[78] (para 7.49 above) the EAT stated that:

> ... it is relevant in determining whether women can comply with the condition to take into account the current usual behaviour of women in this respect as observed in practice, putting aside behaviour and responses which are unusual.

7.108 In *Mandla v Lee,*[79] the headmaster of a private school refused to accept a Sikh boy unless he removed his turban and cut his hair. The House of Lords ruled that 'can' means 'can in practice' or 'can consistently with the customs and cultural conditions of the racial group' rather than 'can physically'. *Mandla* was followed by the Court of Appeal in *CRE v Dutton,*[80] in which that court held that the expression 'can comply' means 'can comply without giving up the distinctive customs and cultural rules of gypsies' and that it could not be said that gypsies could comply with the 'no travellers' condition without giving up their customs and culture.

7.109 In *Raval* itself, a requirement to have an English language 'O' level was challenged as being discriminatory on the ground of race. Ms Raval was denied a job with the civil service because she could not comply with this condition. The ET found that the same proportion of Asian and English people could take and pass 'O' level English language. The EAT disagreed, stating that 'can comply' denoted an ability to produce proof that the relevant qualification had been

78 [1977] IRLR 291.
79 [1983] IRLR 209.
80 [1989] IRLR 8.

obtained. It was not correct to suggest that Ms Raval should go and take an 'O' level. Furthermore, the EAT took the view that fewer Asians could pass an English 'O' level as they were bound to be at a disadvantage if English were their second language. (The EAT went on to hold, however, that the requirement was justified and Ms Raval had not suffered a detriment.)

7.110 In *Meade-Hill v British Council*[81] (see para 7.40) the mobility requirement at issue had not yet been enforced by the employers. The Court of Appeal took the view that, for the purposes of SDA 1975 s77, the impact of a requirement must be judged at the moment when the term in question becomes incorporated into a contract, not when it is reasonably foreseeable that the applicant will be unable to comply with it nor when the employer seeks to enforce it.

7.111 In *Clymo v Wandsworth LBC*[82] an ET took the view that there was 'no firm evidence' that the proportion of qualified women librarians who could work full-time was considerably smaller than the proportion of qualified male librarians. The ET ruled that:

> ... at this level of income, and most particularly in the London area, with child minding facilities readily available, people of these qualifications and this combined income and with a professional career both behind and ahead of them could certainly conduct their family arrangements on less old-fashioned bases than the less qualified and more lowly paid.

The EAT did not criticise this finding. But it ignores all the factors that make it difficult for women to combine full-time work and child care, it takes no account of the fact that parents may choose to spend some of their time with their children, and it is contrary to the decision of the House of Lords in *Mandla* and that of the Court of Appeal in *Dutton*. It is not for the courts to engage in reconstructing applicants' domestic arrangements, ignoring current usual behaviour as observed in practice. This was accepted in *London Underground Ltd v Edwards (No 2)*,[83] above, in which Ms Edwards was unable to comply with the new rotas because of her child care needs.

81 [1995] IRLR 478
82 [1989] IRLR 241.
83 [1998] IRLR 364.

Question 10: Was it to the applicant's detriment that he or she could not comply with the requirement or condition?

7.112 As with question 9, this question *does not* apply to allegations of employment-related discrimination on grounds of sex or married status. In such cases the question is simply: 'is the provision, criterion or practice to the applicant's detriment?'

7.113 Where the original test of indirect discrimination applies (ie, other than in allegations of employment-related discrimination on grounds of sex or married status), a woman cannot complain of a requirement being indirectly discriminatory unless she cannot comply with it at the time it is imposed. In *Clymo v Wandsworth LBC*[84] the EAT refused to accept that a requirement to work full-time was to the applicant's detriment because she could not comply with it. The EAT continued by saying that:

> ... in trying to fit society into the framework of the statute and the statute into our society, in every employment ladder there will come a stage at which a woman who has family responsibilities must make a choice.

This is an extraordinary comment, given that the purpose of the discrimination legislation is to enable people other than white men to combine work with customary and cultural practices (which in the case of women include having primary responsibility for child care). It is very difficult to reconcile *Clymo* with the decisions of the House of Lords and Court of Appeal respectively in *Mandla* and *Dutton*, and the decision was doubted by the Northern Ireland Court of Appeal in *Briggs v North Eastern Education and Library Board*.[85] *Clymo* should not be followed on this point.[86]

7.114 It should not be necessary for the applicant to prove that the reason she could not comply with a requirement was because she suffered a disadvantage associated with her sex. Thus, there would not appear to be anything preventing a woman worker complaining of being denied access to a benefit (such as access to training) because she worked part-time even if there was no reason, such as child care responsibilities, for her working part-time. Such a woman apparently

84 [1989] IRLR 241.

85 [1990] IRLR 181.

86 In *Raval*, the EAT concluded that the applicant suffered no detriment because she could have in the past, and could in the future, obtain the qualification. This must be wrong and is inconsistent with *Dutton*.

passes the statutory test. A requirement (to be working full-time in order to qualify for training) has been imposed. She cannot comply with it at the material time (assuming that she is not offered the opportunity at this point to work full-time). The requirement is to her detriment because she cannot comply with it. And the requirement is probably not justifiable. Yet if the same woman complained of a requirement to work full-time in order to get a job she would fail as she could, in practice, comply with it.

7.115 There is nothing in the SDA 1975 that prevents *all* women taking advantage of provisions aimed at removing requirements that discriminate against *some* women. It is irrelevant that, for example, more women than men are appointed to the job in question. And it does not have to be shown that a woman, but for the requirement, would have been successful. What is relevant is whether the specific requirement is more disadvantageous to women than men (see *Price v Civil Service Commission*[87]). Having said this, if it can be shown that the applicant would *not* have been successful even without the challenged requirement or condition, he or she is unlikely to be able to establish that the application of that requirement or condition has amounted to a *detriment*. In *Coker and Osamor v Lord Chancellor*,[88] an ET rejected the second applicant's claim that she had been indirectly discriminated against by the appointment of the Lord Chancellor's special adviser because she was 'not appointable' for reasons unrelated to the requirement that prospective appointees be personally known to the Lord Chancellor. Thus, although the ET (unlike the EAT and the Court of Appeal) accepted that the requirement of personal acquaintanceship indirectly discriminated against the first applicant, it did not accept that it indirectly discriminated against the second.

Question 8: Can the requirement or condition be shown by the respondent to be justifiable, irrespective of any sex, marital or race factors?

7.116 Once the claimant has proved that a requirement or condition (provision, criterion or practice) impacts disparately on him or her as a woman/man or member of a particular racial group, and that it is to his or her detriment because he or she cannot comply with it, the burden of proof shifts to the respondent to prove that its imposition

87 [1977] IRLR 291.
88 [2002] IRLR 80.

was nevertheless justifiable irrespective of the sex or racial group, etc, of those to whom it was applied.

Meaning of 'justifiable'

7.117 The accepted interpretation of 'justifiable' was set out by the ECJ in *Bilka-Kaufhaus GmbH v Weber von Hartz.*[89] It has been adopted generally in discrimination cases (ie, under the SDA 1975, the RRA 1976 and the EqPA 1970). The questions for the court are:

- Is the requirement or condition, etc, imposed other than in order to discriminate on 'protected grounds'?
- Do the means selected to achieve the chosen aim correspond to a real need?
- Are they appropriate to achieve that aim?
- Are they necessary in order to achieve that end?

7.118 In *Hampson v DES*[90] the Court of Appeal applied the *Bilka-Kaufhaus* test to indirect discrimination under the RRA 1976 and stated that it was desirable that the same test of justifiability applied under that Act, the SDA 1975 and the EqPA 1970. The House of Lords agreed with this approach in *Webb v EMO Air Cargo (No 2).*[91] And in *Rainey v Greater Glasgow Health Board,*[92] an EqPA 1970 case, the House of Lords stated (per Lord Keith) that:

> ... there would not appear to be any material distinction in principle between the need to demonstrate objectively justified grounds of difference for purposes of s1(3) material factor defence in equal pay cases and the need to justify a requirement or condition under s1(1)(b)(ii) of the [SDA 1975].

Evidence required to support a defence of justification

7.119 In cases of indirect discrimination it is not sufficient to assert that there is a non-discriminatory justification for the action complained of. Respondents must provide evidence to support this. In *Nimz v Freie und Hansestadt Hamburg,*[93] part-time workers were required to have more years of service than full-timers before being moved to a higher grade. The ECJ held that, in order to justify such a practice, the

89 Case 170/84 [1986] ECR 1607; [1986] IRLR 317.

90 [1990] IRLR 302.

91 [1995] 4 All ER 577; [1995] IRLR 645. See also the decision of the NICA in *Briggs v North Eastern Education and Library Board* [1990] IRLR 181.

92 [1987] AC 224; [1987] IRLR 26.

93 Case 184/89 [1991] ECR I-297; [1991] IRLR 222.

employer had to show that there was a relationship between the nature of the duties performed and the experience afforded by the performance of those duties after a certain number of hours had been worked. The argument that full-time workers acquire necessary skills more quickly and have greater experience, in so far as they were generalisations, could not amount to objective criteria capable of justifying a disparately impacting practice.

7.120 In *Greater Manchester Police Authority v Lea*,[94] the EAT ruled that there had to be 'a nexus established between the function of the employer ... and the imposition of the condition, otherwise it is impossible to carry out the objective balance'. The police had tried to justify a policy of not employing those in receipt of an occupational pension by arguing (1) that people with a pension were likely to be less distressed by unemployment than those who did not have one; (2) that the burden on the state of maintaining the people who had no employment was reduced by their policy of employing those who had no other means of income; and (3) that the policy created additional but undefined employment opportunities for the unemployed.

7.121 The applicants pointed out that the police did not exclude people who had jobs elsewhere. The ET said that there was no need to impose this condition, which was extraneous to the police authority's function. Furthermore, the condition was not appropriate in relation to attaining the object in question, as it did not single out the unemployed to be offered positions, merely those without occupational pensions.

Proportionality

7.122 *Bilka-Kaufhaus* was also considered in detail by the EAT in *Cobb v Employment Secretary*[95] in which it held that tribunals must carry out a balancing exercise, taking into account all the surrounding circumstances and giving due emphasis to the degree of discrimination caused, against the object or aim to be achieved. This is known as a 'proportionality' approach. Employers are entitled to take a broad and rational view as to the appropriate balance, provided that it is based on logic, and is a tenable view. It has been argued that employers are under no obligation to prove that there was no other way of achieving their object, But if an alternative is proposed, and the employer ought reasonably to have considered and adopted it, the ET is very unlikely to find that the discriminatory requirement was justifiable.

94 [1990] IRLR 372.
95 [1989] IRLR 464.

7.123 In *Allonby v Accrington and Rossendale College*[96] the Court of Appeal made it clear that, once an ET has concluded that a condition has a disparate impact on a protected group, it must carry out a critical evaluation of whether the employer's reasons demonstrate a real need to take the action in question. This should include consideration of whether there was another way to achieve the aim in question. If the employers can demonstrate a real need, the ET will then have to consider the seriousness of the disparate impact on the applicant and weigh it against the employer's need to take the action in question. If the employer's aim is itself discriminatory, it cannot be justified. *Allonby* concerned sex discrimination but, as we saw at para 7.8 above, the same test should be applied to cases under the RRA 1976.

Examples of factors pleaded in justification

7.124 The following are some examples of factors that have been taken into account when determining whether a condition is justifiable.

- **Economic considerations.** In *Home Office v Holmes*[97] the employers, in attempting to justify refusing a woman part-time work, said that accommodation and National Insurance costs would rise. The EAT preferred Ms Holmes' evidence that the civil service was losing valuable trained personnel when they left to start families; that, in some departments, efficiency increased when part-time working was introduced; and that, in at least one Civil Service section, part-time workers were regarded as more efficient, better time-keepers and requiring less supervision than their full-time colleagues.

  In *London Underground Ltd v Edwards*[98] the employer tried to justify its new shift patterns for train drivers on the grounds that they were being introduced to cut running costs. The EAT concluded that:

  > London Underground could and, we would add, should, have accommodated Ms Edward's personal requirements ... (they) could have made arrangements which would not have been damaging to their business plans but which would have accommodated the reasonable demands of their employees.

  It is clear that the courts expect employers to consider alternative, non-discriminatory methods to achieve economies. In *Orphanos*,[99]

96 [2001] IRLR 364.

97 [1984] IRLR 299.

98 [1999] IRLR 364.

99 [1985] AC 761; [1985] IRLR 349.

(see para 7.21), the House of Lords pointed out that the government could curtail student-related expenditure by alternative means such as cutting all student grants, increasing all fees or restricting grants by other means.

The existence of separate, non-discriminatory pay bargaining systems for female-dominated and male-dominated professions does not itself justify resulting pay differences between them. In *Enderby*[100] (para 7.34) the ECJ considered the effect of separate Whitley Council agreements for the rates of pay for speech therapists, clinical psychologists and senior pharmacists. The health authority claimed that the pay differentials were due to market forces, namely, that the male-dominated professions had to increase the rates of pay in order to attract candidates. The ECJ concluded that market forces could amount to an objective justification, but that this was a matter for the national courts to resolve. It should, however, be remembered that the market itself is often tainted by sex and race discrimination, as can be seen from the sexual and racial breakdown of the national average weekly wage. Market-related discrimination was recognised by the House of Lords in *Ratcliffe*[101] (see para 25.34).

- **Trade union practices**. The fact that a practice is long-established and supported by trade unionists should not be taken into account. In *Clarke v Eley Kynoch*,[102] (see para 7.27) for example, the EAT held that a union-agreed policy of making part-timers redundant before full-timers was 'grossly discriminatory' and unjustifiable.
- **Health and safety requirements**. In *Panesar v Nestlé Co Ltd*,[103] a rule prohibiting beards in a chocolate factory was accepted by the EAT and the Court of Appeal as justifiable in the interests of hygiene. But this case predated the Court of Appeal's acceptance, in *Hampson*,[104] of the test set out in *Bilka-Kaufhaus*. Now, in order to justify such a rule, an employer ought to have to prove a real threat to hygiene caused by beards (as distinct – see para 7.120 – from other facial hair). If there were other means of achieving the object, such as covering up beards, this less intrusive measure should be adopted instead. So, for example, in *Blakerd v Elizabeth*

100 Case 127/92 [1993] ECR I-5535; [1993] IRLR 591.
101 *Ratcliffe v North Yorkshire CC* [1995] IRLR 439, HL.
102 [1982] IRLR 482.
103 [1980] IRLR 64.
104 [1990] IRLR 302.

Shaw Ltd[105] an ET ruled that the employer's requirement that all employees wear a head covering supplied by the employer discriminated indirectly against a Sikh. (The case was settled with an order that the employer obtain and maintain a supply of white turbans for the use of Sikh employees.)

In *Singh v British Rail Engineering Ltd*,[106] the EAT held that a requirement for railway repair workers to wear protective headgear was justifiable, notwithstanding that Sikhs were obliged by their religion to wear turbans and so could not wear the headgear. The EAT took account of the fact that the majority of workers would resent an exception being made, although it said that this alone would not be sufficient justification for the rule. It also took account of the fact that the employer could be liable for damages if it had knowingly exposed an employee, whom it believed to be inadequately protected, to a real risk. The Employment Act 1989 now exempts Sikhs from wearing safety helmets on construction sites. It is discriminatory to require Sikhs to do so and the employer will not be liable for any injury sustained as a direct result of a failure to wear a helmet. (Note, however, that the exemption applies only to construction sites.)

A question of fact and law

7.125 Justification is a question of mixed fact and law because the correct legal test must be applied to the facts found by the ET. The facts should be interpreted according to the *Bilka-Kaufhaus* test. The appeal courts will only overturn ET decisions if the wrong test was applied, if the ET failed to give an adequate statement of its reasons, or if the decision was perverse.

Government justification on grounds of social policy

7.126 In *Rinner-Kühn v FWW Spezial-Gebäudereinigung GmbH*,[107] the German government argued that it was justified in excluding part-time workers from a sick pay scheme because part-timers working fewer than 10 hours a week are not integrated in and connected with the undertaking in a way comparable to that of other workers. The ECJ ruled that this was a generalised statement that could not be regarded as an objective criterion unrelated to any sex discrimination.

105 [1980] IRLR 64.
106 [1986] ICR 22.
107 Case 171/88 [1989] ECR 2743; [1989] IRLR 493.

The court held that, in order to establish justification for a discriminatory legislative provision the government must show:

- that the measures reflected a necessary aim of its social policy;
- that it was appropriate to the achievement of that aim; and
- that it was necessary for the attainment of that aim.

7.127 In *Nolte*[108] and in *Megner*[109] the ECJ ruled that, in legislating in the field of social policy, governments have a wide discretion. The cases concerned the social security entitlements of employees in 'minor employment' (less than 15 hours a week). The ECJ found that the exclusion of such employees from social security benefits was a 'structural principle' of the German social security scheme, and that it fulfilled a legitimate social policy aim that was appropriate to achieve that aim and necessary in order to do so.

7.128 The real problem in these cases was that there was a demand for such minor employment but that, if employees working these short hours were brought within the social security system, it would encourage employers to employ people outside the system and within the black economy. The rulings in *Nolte* and in *Megner* run contrary to the principles set out in *Rinner-Kühn* (although that case was cited in the ECJ). Since both these cases concern contributory social security benefits, they can be distinguished from statutory employment provisions. The ECJ has subsequently interpreted justification in *Lewark*,[110] an employment case concerned with legislative provisions, in a way which is consistent with the *Rinner-Kühn* criteria, rather than the approach taken in *Nolte* and *Megner*.

7.129 In *R v Employment Secretary ex p EOC*[111] the Employment Secretary claimed that longer qualification periods for part-time workers were justified as they would increase the availability of part-time work. The House of Lords found that an increase in part-time work was a beneficial social policy aim, but it did not accept that these qualification periods were necessary in order to achieve this aim. The Employment Secretary had been unable to produce any evidence that the length of the qualification period for redundancy payments had any effect on job creation. A similar decision was reached in the Court of Appeal in

108 Case 317/93 *Nolte v Landesversicherungsanstalt Hanover* [1995] ECR I-4625; [1996] IRLR 225.

109 Case 444/93 *Megner v Innungskrankenkasse Rheinland-Pfalz* [1995] ECR I-4741; [1996] IRLR 236.

110 Case 457/93 *Kuratorium fur Dialyse und Nierentransplantation e.V. v Lewark* [1996] ECR I-243, ECJ.

111 [1995] 1 AC 1; [1994] IRLR 176.

the case of *R v Employment Secretary ex p Seymour Smith*,[112] in which the Employment Secretary argued that he was justified in imposing a two-year qualification period for unfair dismissal protection because it would promote job creation.

7.130 In both cases a number of research studies on influences on labour-market behaviour covering the last 20 years were studied by the courts. The question of the criteria for justification was referred by the House of Lords to the ECJ which ruled that, in the field of social policy, governments had a 'broad margin of discretion' (which should not, however, be used to frustrate a fundamental principle of EC law such as that of equal pay between men and women[113]). The ECJ was clear that 'mere generalisations' concerning the capacity of a specific measure to encourage recruitment were insufficient to meet the tests for justification. A government must show that the rule reflects a legitimate aim of social policy, that it is unrelated to any discrimination based on sex and that it was reasonable to consider that the means chosen were suitable for attaining this objective.

7.131 The ECJ ruled that 'mere generalisations' were insufficient to provide justification, and the Court of Appeal in *Seymour-Smith* had concluded that:

> We have found nothing in the evidence, either factual or opinion, which obliges or enables us to draw the inference that the increase in the threshold period has led to an increase in employment opportunities.

But the House of Lords ruled, in *Seymour-Smith (No 2)* that:

> The burden placed in the government in this type of case is not as heavy as previously thought. Governments must be able to govern ... If their aim is legitimate, governments have a discretion when choosing the method to achieve their aim. National courts, acting with hindsight, are not to impose an impracticable burden on governments which are proceeding in good faith. Generalised assumptions, lacking any factual foundation, are not good enough. But governments are to be afforded a broad measure of discretion.[114]

112 [2000] 1 WLR 435; [1999] IRLR 253.
113 Case 167/97 [1999] ECR I-0623; [1999] IRLR 253.
114 [2000] 1 WLR 435; [1999] IRLR 253.

CHAPTER 8

'Other' grounds of discrimination

Key points

8.1
- In addition to those grounds of discrimination that are currently the subject of relatively comprehensive express statutory provisions (ie, sex, married status, gender reassignment, race and disability), the Employment Directive (ED) will require the regulation by domestic law of employment-related discrimination on grounds of sexual orientation, age and 'religion or belief'.
- The UK must implement those provisions of the ED which deal with discrimination on grounds of sexual orientation and 'religion or belief' by December 2003, those dealing age-related discrimination by December 2006.
- Discrimination on grounds of sexual orientation is not at present regulated in the UK; attempts which have been made to have it 'read into' the Sex Discrimination Act (SDA) 1975 having failed.
- Discrimination on grounds of 'religion or belief' is unregulated outside Northern Ireland save to the extent that religion is sufficiently closely related to ethnicity so as to fall within the scope of the Race Relations Act (RRA) 1976 (see chapter 2).
- The ED, in particular, permits the protection of collective as well as individual religious freedoms – this has significant implications for competing individual freedoms.
- Discrimination on grounds of age is not yet regulated, and is entrenched in law (see, for example, retirement ages). It may, however, be open to challenge where it operates as indirect sex or race discrimination.
- The provisions of the ED, particularly as regards age, permit a significant amount of discrimination to continue.
- Not only the ED, but also article 14 of the European Convention on Human Rights (ECHR) (incorporated into domestic law by the Human Rights Act (HRA) 1998) is of significance to grounds of discrimination including those not yet regulated by domestic law.
- Article 14 prohibits unjustified discrimination 'on any ground such as sex, race, colour, language, religion, political or other opinion, national or social origin, association with a national minority, property, birth or other status'. Its 'parasitic status', however, means that its usefulness as a tool to combat discrimination is restricted. This is further considered in chapter 9.

Background and statutory provisions

8.2 Chapter 2 dealt with those grounds of discrimination which are currently the subject of express domestic regulation. But these are not the only grounds in connection with which discrimination often occurs. Article 14 ECHR provides that:

> The enjoyment of the rights and freedoms set forth in this Convention shall be secured without discrimination on any ground such as sex, race, colour, language, religion, political or other opinion, national or social origin, association with a national minority, property, birth or other status.

Article 14 has been incorporated into domestic law by the HRA 1998.[1] The reach of this article is limited by its application only to the 'enjoyment of the rights and freedoms set forth in this Convention'. But sexual orientation and religious discrimination fall within the scope of articles 8 and 9 respectively of the ECHR, and some instances of discrimination on other grounds will breach article 14 read with another convention right (see chapter 9).

8.3 Such are the limitations of the convention rights in the employment context and, more particularly, of article 14 itself (see further paras 9.36–9.48), that developments on the EC front may well prove far more significant. The ED[2] regulates discrimination in employment on grounds of sexual orientation, age and religion or belief, as well as disability. Only the last of these grounds is already regulated in domestic law. The ED, which was adopted under the new (post-Amsterdam) article 13 of the EC Treaty, must be implemented in the UK by December 2003 (in relation to sexual orientation and 'religion or belief') and by December 2006 in relation to disability and age.

8.4 The ED requires the elimination of discrimination on any of the prohibited grounds, save where one or other exceptions applies, in relation to access to employment, self-employment, promotion, training, working conditions and dismissal. It also covers pay discrimination and discrimination by professional bodies. The implications for disability discrimination of the ED have been considered at para 6.59. More radical is the obligation imposed by the ED on the UK to introduce legislation to regulate employment-related discrimination connected with sexual orientation, 'religion or belief' and age for the first time. Each of these 'new' grounds of discrimination is considered in turn below.

1 HRA 1998 Sch 1.

2 Council Directive 2000/78/EC.

Discrimination on grounds of sexual orientation

8.5 There is, as yet, no explicit statutory protection against discrimination on the ground of sexual orientation. But such discrimination is widespread and occurs in many different ways.[3] Employers may, for example, display overt prejudice to people they believe to be gay, lesbian or bisexual, or may discriminate in more subtle ways such as in relation to pension provision or other employment-related benefits.

8.6 In some cases, the discrimination is rooted in the way in which the employer believes the public will perceive the business. Discrimination may be directed at the way a person dresses, his or her choice of friends or opinions. Problems may arise from harassment by co-workers, clients or customers of the employer. And it is not uncommon for employers (particularly religious establishments) to have policies in relation to what they describe as 'practicing homosexuals'. This phrase is used to make differentiations by implied reference to the sex life of an individual.

8.7 There is at present no UK legislation that specifically protects gays, lesbians and bisexuals from discrimination. However, in the field of housing the House of Lords decided in 1999 that a long-term homosexual relationship could constitute a 'family' for certain purposes,[4] and fostering and adoption by gay couples has now been sanctioned by British courts.[5] In the field of immigration, same sex partners of UK residents who are not EC nationals have been permitted to immigrate since October 1997.[6] And the government has passed legislation to equalise the age of consent for heterosexual and homosexual sex after an adverse finding by the European Commission on Human Rights.[7] Discrimination both within and outside the employment field remains rife, however, and the need for legal protection against it is widely recognised.

8.8 Attempts have been made in a series of cases to argue that

3 See, eg, 'Equality for Lesbians and Gay Men in the Workplace' (1997) 74 EOR 20 and 'Straight up! Why the law should protect lesbian and gay workers', TUC (2000).

4 *Fitzpatrick v Sterling Housing Association Ltd* [1999] 4 All ER 705.

5 See *T, Petitioner* [1997] SIT 724, *Re W (a minor) (adoption: homosexual adopter)* [1997] 3 All ER 620 and *Re E (adoption: freeing order)* [1995] FLR 382.

6 *Concession Outside the Immigration Rules for Unmarried Partners,* from 10 October 1997. From 2 October 2000, see Immigration Rules paras 295A–295O.

7 *Sutherland v UK* [1998] EHRLR 117 which led to the Sexual Offences (Amendment) Act 2000.

discrimination on grounds of sexual orientation is in fact a type of sex discrimination, and thus prohibited by the SDA 1975 and EC equality laws. These avenues were closed in the case of *Grant v South Western Trains Ltd*[8] in which the European Court of Justice (ECJ) ruled that the Equal Treatment Directive[9] (ETD) did not require same sex partners to be granted the same benefits at work as heterosexual partners.

8.9 The applicant was employed as a clerical worker and was entitled to travel concessions for herself and her 'spouse and dependants'. This expression included 'one common law spouse (of the opposite sex) subject to a statutory declaration being made that a meaningful relationship has existed for a period of two or more years'. Ms Grant's request for a travel pass for her partner was turned down because they were of the same sex. Ms Grant compared her position to that of her male predecessor in the job. He, like her, had had a female partner. He was granted travel concessions for his partner. On this basis, Ms Grant claimed that she too should be entitled to this benefit. The ECJ ruled that the appropriate comparator for the purposes of ascertaining whether Ms Grant had received equal treatment was not a male heterosexual but, rather, a male homosexual. Since a male homosexual would also have been refused a travel pass for his same sex partner, there had been no unlawful sex discrimination.

8.10 These arguments were further explored by the domestic courts in *Smith v Gardner Merchant.*[10] Mr Smith was dismissed after a disagreement with a female colleague who alleged that he had treated her in a 'threatening and aggressive manner'. He responded by claiming that he was being sexually harassed by her because of his sexual orientation. He argued that his treatment was contrary to the SDA 1975. He also claimed to have been discriminated against because his employers chose to dismiss him rather than his female colleague.

8.11 The employment tribunal (ET) accepted that Mr Smith had been discriminated against on grounds of his sexual orientation, but ruled that this did not fall within the ambit of the SDA 1975. The Court of Appeal, in considering both the SDA 1975 and the ETD, ruled that the appropriate comparator was a homosexual woman and that the question that had to be addressed was whether the treatment that he received was less favourable than that to which a homosexual woman in the same situation would have been subject.

8 Case 249/96 [1998] ECR I-0621; [1998] IRLR 206.

9 Council Directive 76/207/EEC.

10 [1998] IRLR 510.

Sexual orientation and the European Convention on Human Rights

8.12 In a number of cases the European Court of Human Rights (ECtHR) has made it clear that unjustified discrimination on grounds of sexual orientation can be contrary to both articles 8 and 14.[11] Article 8(1) provides that '[e]verybody has the right to respect for his private and family life', while article 8 (2) prohibits public authorities from interfering with this right except where:

- the grounds for the interference are 'in accordance with law';
- the interference pursues a pressing social need; and
- is necessary and proportionate to that aim.

8.13 A person's sex life and sexual orientation are aspects of his or her private life that are protected by article 8.[12] There have been no cases, yet, that have recognised a stable relationship between homosexuals as constituting 'family life' within the meaning of article 8. But as the ECHR is a 'living instrument' it must be interpreted in the light of present day conditions, such an interpretation is quite possible in an appropriate case.

8.14 In *Smith and Grady v UK*[13] four members of the Armed Forces who had admitted their homosexuality were subjected to intrusive investigations prior to their dismissal. They complained to the ECtHR that the investigations into their sexual orientation and subsequent discharges were in breach of both article 8 and article 14. The court found that the UK government had breached article 8. It concluded that the detailed interviews about the applicants' sexual behaviour, followed by an immediate discharge which took no account of their previous good service records, was a clear breach of their right to a private life. The court did not make a decision about whether there had been a breach of article 14, considering this unnecessary in the light of its decision on article 8.

8.15 This decision in *Smith and Grady* establishes that intrusive and unjustifiable inquiries by employers into the lives of their employees will violate article 8. Discrimination on grounds of sexual orientation in the application of any convention right may also breach article 14.

11 On art 8 see *Smith and Grady v UK* (1999) 29 EHRR 493; [1999] IRLR 734 and *Lustig-Prean and Beckett v UK* (1999) 29 EHRR 548. On art 14 see *Sutherland v UK* [1998] EHRLR 117, and *Salgueiro da Silva Mouta v Portugal* (2001) 31 EHRR 1055.

12 See *Dudgeon v UK* (1981) 5 EHRR 573 and *Sutherland v UK* [1998] EHRLR 117.

13 (1999) 29 EHRR 493; [1999] IRLR 734.

In *Salguero da Silva Mouta v Portugal*,[14] the refusal of custody to a homosexual parent was held to be discrimination on grounds of sexual orientation in breach of article 14 taken together with article 8. Further, discrimination connected with sexual orientation (dress; friends; opinions, etc) may also violate articles 8 and 14. Adverse decisions based on a supposed knowledge of a person's sex life will almost invariably violate article 8 alone or in conjunction with article 14. Sometimes being clear about the nature of these rights from the outset can assist an employer or other decision-taker to overcome prejudice.

Sexual orientation and the Human Rights Act 1998

8.16 The incorporation by the HRA 1998 of the ECHR into domestic law was mentioned above. Section 6 makes it unlawful for any public authority to act inconsistently with a convention right unless required to do so by legislation.[15] Any unjustified discrimination on the ground of sexual orientation by a public authority will give rise to a claim for damages under HRA 1998 s6 (see further chapter 9). Further, HRA 1998 s3 requires that all legislation be read and given effect to in a way which is compatible with the convention rights, in so far as it is possible to do so. Having regard to this interpretative obligation and the ECHR case-law it is arguable that the SDA 1975 should now be interpreted, as far as possible, to prohibit discrimination on grounds of sexual orientation.

Pre-Human Rights Act 1998 cases

8.17 In the pre-HRA 1998 case of *Secretary of State for Defence v MacDonald*[16] the Scottish EAT concluded that, having regard to the impact of the HRA 1998, sexual orientation discrimination could be properly regarded as sex discrimination. The actual decision rested on a misunderstanding of the convention case-law. However in our view it was certainly open to the EAT to conclude on a (correct) application of the HRA 1998 that sexual orientation discrimination fell within the scope of the SDA 1975. This judgment was overturned on appeal despite a sympathetic minority judgment from Lord Prosser.[17]

14 (2001) 31 EHRR 1055.
15 For further discussion of this see chapter 9.
16 [2000] IRLR 748.
17 [2001] IRLR 431.

8.18 The *MacDonald* case involved blatant discrimination against a gay man who worked for the Royal Air Force. When he arranged for a transfer to the Scottish Air Traffic Control Centre (Military), he became subject to positive vetting procedures during the course of which he declared that he was gay. This led to his compulsory resignation. He complained that the termination of his employment as a result of his admitted homosexuality was unlawful discrimination on grounds of sex and that the questioning about his sexuality during the vetting procedures amounted to sexual harassment. A majority of the Court of Sessions held that the protection in the SDA 1975 against discrimination on grounds of sex did not include a protection against discrimination on grounds of sexual orientation, and that the applicant's treatment should be compared to that of a lesbian employee in the same circumstances. Since it was common ground that a lesbian woman would have been treated in the same way as the applicant, the court ruled that the applicant had not been discriminated against on grounds of his gender. The court was aware that the Air Force's decision would likely be held in due course by the ECtHR to involve a breach of the ECHR, given the earlier decision of that court in *Smith and Grady v UK*.[18] This realisation did not, however, persuade the Court of Sessions to provide a domestic remedy.

8.19 A confusion over the proper comparator in a sexual orientation discrimination case appears to be at the heart of the courts' reluctance to interpret the SDA 1975 as covering such discrimination. Lord Prosser, the minority judge in *MacDonald*, pointed out that it was not appropriate to compare the situation of a lesbian and the situation of a male homosexual, whose situations were analogous but not the same. He pointed out that it was the sex of the complainant's *partner* that was material, not the sexual orientation of the complainant:

> In deciding how to treat any individual, those who applied the policy were concerned with the gender of any individual and any partner.

Thus the proper comparator, according to Lord Prosser, was a person of the opposite sex with a partner of the same sex as the complainant's partner or preferred partner. A woman with a preferred or actual male partner would not have been treated in the same was as Mr McDonald, with his actual or preferred male sexual partner. Thus there was sex discrimination in the treatment of Mr MacDonald. However, this analysis did not prevail.

8.20 The Court of Appeal reached a similar conclusion in *Pearce v*

18 (1999) 29 EHRR 493; [1999] IRLR 734.

Governing Body of Mayfield Secondary School.[19] Ms Pearce, a lesbian, was employed by Mayfield school as a science teacher. From 1992 onwards she received regular homophobic taunts and abuse from her pupils. She was called 'dyke', 'lesbian shit', 'lemon' and 'lezzie'. She reported these incidents to the deputy head teacher, but the school took no action to help or support her. The abuse continued and in 1994 she took sick leave for stress-related illness. The school told her that she should grit her teeth and if necessary 'run away again'. She returned to work and the harassment resumed within a few days. Ms Pearce went off sick again and subsequently took early retirement on health grounds. She brought a complaint on grounds of unlawful sex discrimination against the school.

8.21 The HRA 1998 was not in force at the time of the discrimination complained of by Ms Pearce and therefore all three judges in the Court of Appeal concluded that the decision of the ET could not be upset on the ground that the tribunal had failed to interpret the SDA 1975 consistent with the ECHR.[20] The Court of Appeal therefore ruled, in line with earlier authorities, that Ms Pearce's comparator for the purposes of the SDA 1975 was a male homosexual teacher who would have suffered the same treatment as she did.[21] Hale LJ agreed with the rest of the court that, on the old authorities, sexual orientation discrimination was not sex discrimination. But she delivered a powerfully reasoned judgment to the effect that, had the discrimination occurred after the coming into force of the HRA 1998, she would have concluded otherwise. This was because it was plainly possible to give the SDA 1975 a meaning which was compatible with Ms Pearce's convention rights (and hold that sexual orientation discrimination was covered) by adopting the same approach as that taken by Lord Prosser in *MacDonald*.

Post-Human Rights Act 1998 cases

8.22 No post-HRA 1998 cases on sexual orientation discrimination have yet reached the appeal courts. It is to be hoped that, when such cases do come before them, the courts will follow the reasoning of Lord Prosser and Hale LJ.

19 [2001] IRLR 669.

20 See *R v Lambert* [2001] 3 WLR 514 in which the House of Lords decided that the HRA 1998 had no retrospective effect.

21 See para 28.42 for gender-specific abuse in different contexts.

Employment Directive

8.23 The ED regulates direct and indirect discrimination on grounds of sexual orientation in the sphere of employment only. It obliges the UK to introduce legislation by December 2003. But the protection of the ED is not unlimited. It recognises that sexual orientation discrimination may be lawful where sexuality constitutes a 'genuine occupational qualification' defence such that:

> ... by reason of the nature of the particular occupational activities concerned or of the context in which they are carried out ... such a characteristic constitutes a genuine and determining occupational requirement, provided that the objective is legitimate and the requirement is proportionate.[22]

8.24 Article 4(2) goes on to permit discrimination on grounds of religion or belief by providing that:

> Member States may maintain national legislation in force at the date of adoption of this Directive or provide for future legislation incorporating national practices existing at the date of adoption of this Directive pursuant to which, in the case of occupational activities within churches and other public or private organisations the ethos of which is based on religion or belief ... where, by reason of the nature of these activities or of the context in which they are carried out, a person's religion or belief constitute a genuine, legitimate and justified occupational requirement, having regard to the organisation's ethos ... This difference of treatment shall be implemented taking account of Member States' constitutional provisions and principles, as well as the general principles of Community law, and should not justify discrimination on another ground.
>
> Provided that its provisions are otherwise complied with, this Directive shall thus not prejudice the right of churches and other public or private organisations, the ethos of which is based on religion or belief, acting in conformity with national constitutions and laws, to require individuals working for them to act in good faith and with loyalty to the organisation's ethos.

Article 4(2) is intended to protect the freedom of religious organisations collectively to enjoy their religious rights and freedoms. This is considered further at para 8.43 below. But it should be noted that this provision, particularly the last paragraph of article 4(2), is likely to have significant implications for the rights of gay men, lesbian women and bisexuals. This would seem to permit discrimination by

22 ED Art 4(1).

religious organisations on any ground where the individual concerned was not acting with 'loyalty to the organisation's ethos'. If this is what the ED means then this is very worrying indeed and has obvious implications for the way in which the established churches might treat openly gay men and lesbian women and bisexuals.

8.25 Further, the ED states (para 22 of the preamble) that it 'is without prejudice to national laws on marital status and the benefits dependent thereon'; and (para 13) that it 'does not apply to social security and social protection schemes whose benefits are not treated as income within the meaning given to that term for the purpose of applying Article 141 of the EC Treaty, nor to any kind of payment by the State aimed at providing access to employment or maintaining employment'.

8.26 The ED will cause a great improvement in the protection afforded to gays, lesbians and bisexuals. But its limitations, together with the limitation of its application to the employment sphere, are such that the HRA 1998 will remain relevant even after December 2003.

Discrimination on grounds of 'religion or belief'

8.27 The vast majority of the UK population is nominally Christian.[23] But there are an estimated 1.2–1.5 million Muslims in the UK; about 500,000 Sikhs and Hindus, and about 300,000 Jews.[24] Many of those belonging to minority religions (and, indeed, to various Christian denominations) experience discrimination including (but not only) in relation to employment, education and the media.[25]

8.28 Discrimination on grounds of 'religion or belief' is not confined to the direct form (which would include the refusal of employment because the applicant is a Muslim, or a devout Christian), but also includes indirect discrimination (where, for example, a religious Jew is refused promotion on the grounds that she will not work on a Saturday, or a Muslim on the basis that he attends mosque on a Friday afternoon).

8.29 The RRA 1976 extends protection to religious groups which are

23 About 26 million are nominally Anglican and 5.7 million Catholic. The other Christian denominations account for about 5.5 million according to the Parekh Report, *The Future of Multi-Ethnic Britain* (Runnymede Trust and Profile Books Ltd, 2000), p236.

24 Ibid.

25 See P Weller, A Feldman and K Purdam, *Religious Discrimination in England and Wales* (Home Office, 2001) Home Office Research Study 220 and see also the 1997 report of the Runnymede Trust, *Islamaphobia: a Challenge For Us All*.

regarded as sufficiently racially distinct to amount to an 'ethnic group' (see para 2.41). But this form of protection is denied to those with religious beliefs not closely identified with ethnicity. Only in Northern Ireland, in which the provisions of the Fair Employment and Treatment Order (FETO) 1998[26] apply, is discrimination on grounds of religion (and, incidentally, also 'political belief') comprehensively regulated. The FETO 1998 employs the same concepts of discrimination as those in the RRA 1976 (and, prior to its amendment by the Burden of Proof Regulations 2001[27]), the SDA 1975. Both direct and indirect discrimination are outlawed, although the protection from religious discrimination is specifically disapplied to discrimination in relation to teachers.

8.30 The exclusion of Muslims and others from the religious groups recognised as 'ethnic groups' and protected under the RRA 1976 was mentioned above (para 8.29). But even where religious groups are not recognised as 'ethnic groups' under the RRA 1976, the connection between religion and ethnicity may be sufficient, in particular cases, to provide some protection from indirect discrimination under the RRA 1976. We saw, in chapter 7, that indirect discrimination occurs when a particular racial group (for these purposes, a group defined by colour, national origins, etc) is disproportionately disadvantaged by a practice that is not justifiable.[28] In some contexts, religious or cultural characteristics may coincide disproportionately with racial characteristics with the effect that a requirement or condition[29] that disproportionately disadvantages those of a particular religious group (for example, Muslims) will also have an adverse impact on a racial group (for example, those from the Indian subcontinent).[30] So, for example, a prohibition on the wearing of trousers by women workers will disproportionately disadvantage Muslim women and, in a specific context, may also indirectly discriminate against Bangladeshis. Likewise a rule that no one may have time off on Fridays will disproportionately disadvantage Muslims[31] and may indirectly discriminate against a specific racial group that is predominantly Muslim.

26 SI No 3162, NI 21.

27 Sex Discrimination (Indirect Discrimination and Burden of Proof) Regulations 2001 SI No 2660.

28 The precise definition is more complex and differs according to the context and the ground of discrimination alleged – see paras 7.6–7.12.

29 This being the terminology employed by the RRA 1976.

30 The emphasis is on 'may' because this will depend, in any particular case, on the pool for comparison – see further the discussion below and chapter 7.

31 As well as religious Jews.

8.31 In *Walker v Hussain*[32] an ET concluded that direct discrimination against Muslims amounted, on the facts of the particular case, to indirect race discrimination against Asians. Seventeen Muslim employees had been disciplined for taking time off to observe Eid in the face of a ban on workers taking holidays during the summer months (during which Eid fell that year). The workers had requested leave and had offered to make up the hours missed, but their request had been refused. The ET considered the pool of workers in the work force affected by the ban on leave being taken during the summer months (and, accordingly, during Eid). It concluded that the number of Asian workers in the particular workplace who could comply with a requirement to work during Eid was considerably smaller than the proportion of others who could comply with this requirement. The applicants had, therefore, been indirectly discriminated against on grounds of their racial group.

8.32 *Walker v Hussain* went to the EAT on an appeal against the compensation awarded by the ET, the EAT not being asked to consider the finding on liability. It is worth noting that the ET would not have been in a position to find indirect race discrimination had there not been a very significant overlap between those workers in the particular workplace who were Asian and those who were Muslims.[33]

Employment Directive

8.33 The ED has been mentioned above (para 8.3). Its prohibition on direct and indirect discrimination on grounds of 'religion or belief' must be implemented in the UK by December 2003. The ED does not define what is meant by 'religion'. But the inclusion within the prohibited discrimination of 'belief' as well as 'religion' suggests that it is intended to be broadly interpreted.

8.34 Whatever legislation the government introduces to give effect to the ED, it will have to be certified as compliant with the ECHR, (in particular, article 9).[34] It follows (see below) that it would be unwise for such legislation to define precisely what constitutes a religion or belief.[35]

8.35 The ED's prohibition on religious discrimination is not absolute. Article 4 ED has been reproduced at para 8.23. Article 4(1) would

32 [1996] IRLR 11.

33 Or had the ET taken a wider pool for comparison.

34 See HRA 1998 s19.

35 Because of the width of beliefs protected by the ECHR – see para 8.39 below.

permit, for example, that potential priests or other ministers of religion be required to share the religious beliefs of the church into which they seek ordination. And article 4(2) would permit some discrimination on grounds of religion or belief in access, for example, to teaching jobs in religious schools and, possibly, to a wide range of jobs in 'faith' organisations (it could be argued, for example, that a general maintenance job in a faith-based sheltered housing project should be held by a person of the relevant faith). It is worth bearing in mind, however, that article 4(1) permits only 'legitimate' and 'proportionate' genuine occupational qualifications, and that article 4(2) is subject to 'the general principles of Community law', which include the principle of proportionality. It is also worth noting that article 4(2) does not permit discrimination on grounds other than 'religion or belief'.

Human Rights Act 1998

8.36 The application of the ED only in the employment context has been mentioned above. In relation to religious discrimination, therefore,[36] the ECHR, incorporated in the UK by the HRA 1998, may prove of immense significance over time. Article 9 ECHR provides that:

> 1. Everyone has the right to freedom of thought, conscience and religion; this right includes freedom to change his religion or belief and freedom, either alone or in community with others and in public or private, to manifest his religion or belief, in worship, teaching, practice and observance.
> 2. Freedom to manifest one's religion or beliefs shall be subject only to such limitations as are prescribed by law and are necessary in a democratic society in the interests of public safety, for the protection of public order, health or morals, or for the protection of the rights and freedoms of others.

The impact of article 9 will be felt not only in the employment context but by virtue of its application across the whole range of activities by public authorities (and quite possibly, in the fullness of time, to private bodies through the development of statutory interpretation and the common law[37]). The provision will apply to situations in which decisions are taken, on grounds connected with an individual's or collective entity's[38] religion or belief, in relation to, for example:

36 As in relation to discrimination on grounds of sexual orientation.

37 See further chapter 9.

38 See further para 8.43.

- custody;[39]
- planning;[40]
- housing allocation;
- education;
- taxation;[41] and
- prisoners' rights.[42]

8.37 We saw, above (at para 8.36), that the HRA 1998 can provide a remedy to those whose human rights are violated contrary to the ECHR. The first question which arises for consideration, in this context, is whether the protection of article 9 applies.[43]

8.38 The right to freedom of thought, conscience and religion is unqualified, although the right to manifest religion or belief may be restricted in accordance with article 9(2). The absolute nature of the right to freedom of thought, conscience and religion reflects the importance that the ECHR ascribes to freedom of thought and it has been widely interpreted by the ECtHR. The right to manifest religion or belief may be restricted (article 9(2)) in accordance with those limitations prescribed by law that are necessary in a democratic society in the interests of one of the prescribed grounds. This aspect of article 9 recognises that the right to manifest religion or belief has to be balanced against other needs of society. It has been more narrowly interpreted by the ECHR organs. Thus, for example, in rejecting the application in *C v UK*,[44] which concerned a Quaker's refusal to pay the proportion of his taxes that would be used to pay for armament research, the European Commission ruled that:

> Article 9 primarily protects the sphere of personal beliefs and

39 See *Hoffman v Austria* (1994) 17 EHRR 293.

40 See *Iskcon v UK* (1994) 76A DR 90 and *Manoussakis v Greece* (1997) 23 EHRR 387.

41 See *C v UK* (1983) 37 DR 142.

42 See *X v UK* (1974) 1 DR 199.

43 Also of potential significance in the context of religious discrimination are art 10 (freedom of expression), art 14 (freedom from discrimination in the application of any convention right), art 4(3)(b) (limited recognition of a right of conscientious objection to military service), and art 2 of protocol 1 (which provides a right to education) – the UK government has put a reservation on this provision saying that it accepts it 'only in so far as it is compatible with the provision of efficient instruction and training, and the avoidance of unreasonable public expenditure'.

44 (1983) 37 DR 142, re-affirmed in *X v UK* (1984) 6 EHRR 558. See also *Arrowsmith v UK* (1978) 19 DR 5 in which the Commission, having found that pacifism was a belief within art 9(1), went on to hold that the distribution of leaflets to soldiers in Northern Ireland encouraging them to go absent or refuse to serve was not a 'manifestation' of this belief.

> religious creeds, ie, the area that is sometimes called the *forum internum*. In addition, it protects acts which are intimately linked to these attitudes, such as acts of worship or devotion which are aspects of the practice of a religion or belief in a generally recognised form.

This approach is open to criticism on the grounds that it would have been open to the Commission in *C* to rule that the refusal constituted a 'manifestation' of belief, and then proceed to consider whether the state's interference with it was nevertheless justified within article 9(2). This has not prevented the ECtHR adopting a similar approach in subsequent decisions.[45]

'Religion' under the European Convention on Human Rights

8.39 The ECHR does not define 'religion', nor does it limit its protection to 'religion'. The protection provided by article 9 is in respect of 'thought, conscience and religion', and 'religion and belief'. These concepts have been held to apply to all the main world religions, to the Krishna Consciousness movement, the Divine Light Centrum, the Church of Scientology, Druids, the Moon Sect, pacifism and veganism.[46]

8.40 The right protected under article 9 is not only the right to belong to a defined, traditional, recognised and established religion but also the right not to believe or the right to hold unconventional beliefs that are not subscribed to by others. The ECtHR held in *Kokkinakis v Greece* that:

> As enshrined in article 9, freedom of thought conscience and religion is one of the foundations of a 'democratic society' within the meaning of the Convention. It is, in its religious dimension, one of the most vital elements that go to make up the identity of believers and their conception of life, but it is also a precious asset for atheists, sceptics and the unconcerned.[47]

45 See also *Valsamis v Greece* (1997) 24 EHRR 294 and *Efstratiou v Greece* (App No 24095/94), Rep 1996, in which students who, as Jehovah's Witnesses, were pacifists refused to take part in a parade to commemorate the Greek National day. The ECtHR concluded that taking part in the parade did not have a particular ideological connotation and therefore was not contrary to the pacifist beliefs of the students. This decision clearly involved substituting a judgment of the court for the students' own judgments of conscience.

46 Respectively, *Iskcon v UK* (1994) 76A DR 90; *Omkarananda and the Divine Light Zentrum v Switzerland* (1981) 25 DR 105; *X and Church of Scientology v Sweden* (1979) 16 DR 68; *A.R.M. Chappell v UK* (1987) 53 DR 241; *X v Austria* (App No 8652/79) (1981) 26 DR 89; *Arrowsmith v UK* (1978) 19 DR 5, and *X v UK* (App No 18187/91) 10 February 1993 (unreported).

47 (1994) 17 EHRR 397, para 31.

8.41 But article 9 rights must be capable of being subject to determination and control by law. Thus any test as to the meaning of 'religion' or 'belief' cannot be wholly subjective. The limits to the concepts can be found in the need for a serious ideology, having some cogency and cohesion, although it is clear that it need not be approved by the state nor of a traditional character. In *Campbell and Cosans v UK*[48] the ECtHR stated that: '[t]he term "beliefs" ... denotes a certain level of cogency, seriousness, cohesion and importance'. Thus, article 9 does not provide protection in respect of political views such as those of a prisoner's support group,[49] or to IRA prisoners claiming 'special category status',[50] although it does appear to operate to prevent sanctions against membership of a national political party such as membership of the Communist party.[51]

Application of article 9

8.42 The next question that arises under article 9 relates to the extent of the positive obligations it imposes in respect of the accommodation of religious needs. We saw, above, that indirect discrimination occurs (broadly speaking) when the same rule disproportionately disadvantages particular groups. That disparately impacting practices constitute 'discrimination' is relatively uncontroversial as a matter of law, the SDA 1975 and RRA 1976 both expressly regulating this form of discrimination, and the Disability Discrimination Act (DDA) 1995 doing so in practice, if not in form (see further chapters 3, 6 and 7).[52] We saw at para 8.29 above, however, that domestic law does not, as such, regulate discrimination on grounds of religion. And the application of the ECHR to 'indirect' forms of discrimination on grounds of religion – situations in which religious needs and practices require a measure of accommodation by employers and others – is much less clear.

8.43 In *Ahmad v UK*, for example, the applicant (a Muslim teacher) complained that his employers (a state school) refused to permit him to attend his mosque during school hours on a Friday afternoon. The European Commission rejected his claims under articles 9 and 14 as

48 (1982) 4 EHRR 293, para 36.

49 *Vereniging Rechtswinkels Utrecht v Netherlands* (1986) 46 DR 200.

50 *McFeeley v UK* (1980) 20 DR 44.

51 *Hazar v Turkey* 72 DR 200 at 213, and 73 DR 111 at 115.

52 The DDA 1995 does not expressly regulate indirect discrimination but its very wide formulation of direct discrimination coupled with its imposition of a duty of reasonable accommodation amounts to much the same.

manifestly unfounded, ruling that the employer's refusal to waive his contractual terms of employment amounted not even to an interference with (much less a violation of – see further below), his convention rights. By contrast, Scarman LJ had recognised (dissenting, in the Court of Appeal[53]) that Mr Ahmad should not have been prohibited from taking full-time employment in a state school by reason of his religious convictions.[54] Dealing with the proper construction of Education Act 1944 s30 (which provided that no one should be prohibited from being a teacher in a state school by reason of his or her religious convictions), Scarman LJ stated that a narrow construction of the provision:

> ... would mean that a Muslim, who took his religious duty seriously, could never accept employment as a full-time teacher, but must be content with the lesser emoluments of part-time service. In modern British society, with its elaborate statutory protection of the individual from discrimination arising from race, colour, religion or sex, and against the background of the European Convention, this is unacceptable, inconsistent with the policy of modern statute law, and almost certainly a breach of our international obligations.

Scarman LJ pointed out that it was the authority which was responsible for organising staff timetables; that it could have done so consistent with Mr Ahmad's teaching obligations; and that it ought to have done so in view of the obligations imposed by Education Act 1944 s30.

> It may mean employing a few more teachers either part-time or full-time: but, when that cost is compared with the heavy expenditure already committed to the cause of non-discrimination in our society, expense would not in this context appear to be a sound reason for requiring a narrow meaning to be given to the words of the statute ... Once the full implications of the section in its contractual context are properly understood, I find it impossible to say that [Mr Ahmad's] 45 minutes' absence from class every Friday to go to the mosque constitutes a breach of this contract. In my judgment the industrial tribunal and the appeal tribunal misconstrued the statute and misunderstood the contract.

Scarman LJ's progressive approach did not, however, convince the rest of the Court of Appeal. And even as recently as 1997 the European Commission again rejected the argument that article 9 imposed

53 [1977] ICR 490.

54 See now School Standards and Framework Act 1998 s59(2).

any duty of accommodation on employers in relation to their workers' religious needs. In *Stedman v UK*,[55] the Commission rejected a claim from a religious Christian whose employer had unilaterally varied her contract of employment in order to require her to work on a Sunday. According to the Commission, Ms Stedman had been dismissed for 'failing to agree to work certain hours rather than her religious belief as such and was free to resign and did in effect resign from her employment'. There was no interference with her article 9 rights.

Justification for interference with article 9

8.44 Even if an interference with an article 9 right is established, that interference may be justified (assuming it is with the manifestation of religion or belief, rather than with the religion or belief itself), where it is:

- prescribed by law;
- necessary in a democratic society, in the interests of public safety, the protection of public order, health or morals or the protection of the rights and freedoms of others; and
- proportionate to the aim being pursued.

The application of these tests is further considered in chapter 9.

'Collective' religious rights and the interaction between religion and other protected grounds

8.45 The religious diversity of the UK's population was mentioned at para 8.24 above. This diversity is reflected not only in individuals' beliefs and practices but also in many religious institutions that include, but are not limited to, churches and other places of worship. It is well-known that there are state-funded religious schools. Less well-known is the existence of religious housing organisations and charitable organisations, and firms such as kosher or halal butchers and Christian publishing houses that are run on explicitly religious terms.

8.46 Meaningful religious freedom requires that religious 'collectives', as well as individuals, are respected. Article 4(2) ED represents the EC's attempts to accommodate 'collective' religious freedom by ensuring that religious organisations are free to exercise their 'negative' freedom of association by excluding those who are not similarly minded. The exact boundaries of this freedom are controversial, given its impact on the religious and other freedoms of those found

55 [1997] EHRLR 545.

wanting by such organisations. But it is difficult to dispute that religious freedom requires some accommodation of collective religious needs.

8.47 Article 9 ECHR recognises the collective aspects of religious freedom by protecting the right to manifest religion in public or private including a right to do so in community with others.[56] It may prove very important in relation to organisations, especially schools and housing associations, that are founded on religious or other belief grounds. Such organisations will be able to assert their 'collective' rights under article 9 in defence of claims against them. The scope for this is strengthened by HRA 1998 s13 which provides that, if a court is determining a question that might affect the exercise by a religious organisation of its right to freedom of thought, conscience and religion, it must have particular regard to the importance of this right. It is still unclear what the significance of this provision is, as it appears only to re-affirm the existing position under the ECHR. The section was put in at the insistence of religious leaders. But it would be wrong to conclude that it creates a 'hierarchy of rights' (for example, the right of the religious organisation over the right of an individual not to be discriminated against on grounds of religion, sexual orientation, etc). The ECtHR has been consistent in holding that no such hierarchy exists. The better construction of s13 may, accordingly, be that it is intended to ensure that adequate respect for collective rights is afforded by the domestic courts.

8.48 An example of the possible effect of article 9 on other aspects of existing discrimination law can be seen in a successful sex discrimination case. In *O'Neill v Governors of St Thomas More School*[57] an unmarried woman teacher challenged her dismissal after she became pregnant by a priest. The school considered that her position, as a teacher of religious education, was untenable. The school was found to have breached the SDA 1975 and had to pay compensation.

8.49 The case was heard and determined before the HRA 1998 had come into force and so the school was unable to rely on article 9 ECHR. The implementation of the ED might not make any difference in this context, as article 4(2) permits only that discrimination already permitted at the date the directive was adopted and, further, does not legitimise discrimination on grounds other than religion or belief.

56 For a fuller discussion of this see J Rivers, 'From Toleration to Pluralism: Religious Liberty and Religious Establishment under the United Kingdom's Human Rights Act' in Rex Ahdar (ed), *Law and Religion* (Ashgate, 2000).

57 [1997] ICR 33.

But this kind of conflict between the collective rights of people manifesting a religion or belief, and others seeking to assert individual employment rights, will be a real problem for ETs in the future.[58] It is possible that the decision in *O'Neill* might not be sustainable post-incorporation of article 9. Having said this, the interpretative obligations imposed, on the one hand, by the HRA 1998 will be balanced by the apparently conflicting obligations imposed by EC law, which rigorously prohibits pregnancy-related discrimination.[59] The ECJ may play an important role in determining how such apparent conflicts might be reconciled.[60]

Conclusion

8.50 The government has recognised that it is now necessary to legislate on religious discrimination. A recent Home Office research study discusses the ways in which religious discrimination may be tackled.[61] It is important to ensure that a unified system is put in place so that the courts are not left trying to interpret and balance three different and separate sources of law (EC, ECHR and domestic). Particularly significant is the issue, discussed above, of conflicts between religious and other rights and freedoms

Age discrimination

8.51 Awareness of age discrimination has increased substantially in recent years, and there is pressure on employers and service providers not to impose unnecessary age limitations. Discrimination on grounds of age can occur at both extremes of the age range and indeed even in the middle of the range of working ages. Older workers still have less

58 As public authorities, ETs will be bound by HRA 1998 s6 to act compatibly with convention rights save where prohibited from primary legislation from so doing.

59 See the discussion at para 8.3. Note also the prohibition of sex discrimination by art14 ECHR – see further para 9.36.

60 Conflicts can also be expected to arise between art 9 and art 10 (right to freedom of expression) and the courts will have to balance these: '[t]hose who choose to exercise the freedom to manifest their religion, irrespective of whether they do so as members of a religious majority or minority, cannot reasonably expect to be exempt from all criticism. They must tolerate and accept the denial by others of ... doctrines hostile to their faith.' (*Otto Preminger Institute v Austria* (1995) 19 EHRR 1).

61 B Hepple and T Choudhury, *Tackling Religious Discrimination: Practical Implications for Policy Makers and Legislators*, Home Office Research Study 221.

access to training and promotion and find it difficult to get employment.

8.52 In 1999, the government published a voluntary code of practice on age diversity in employment, which aims to encourage employers to remove unnecessary age limitations.[62] The code of practice recommends that employers review and identify the age profiles of their workforces in order to clarify what action is needed to tackle age discrimination. It then deals with recruitment, selection, promotion, training and development, redundancy and retirement. It recommends in each field that criteria are carefully analysed to ensure that unnecessary references to age or age ranges are omitted; that selection is on merit and in line with the needs of the business and objective job-related requirements, rather than on the basis of preconceptions or stereotypes.

8.53 Research published by the Employers' Forum on Age indicated that the code of practice was having little effect on the way employers were running their businesses.[63] And even the government's own research has shown that, although knowledge of the code is widespread, only one in four employers has adopted its guidelines.[64] The government has now set up an age advisory group to start the process of consulting about new forms of legislation to outlaw age discrimination.[65]

8.54 The Employers Forum on Age has estimated that the adoption of flexible retirement plans could boost the economically active population by 3 million or more, which could in turn raise the gross domestic product by £50 billion or more a year.[66] This is particularly significant given the demographic changes expected during the next 25 years. Over this period the proportion of the population aged over 50 is due to rise from 33 per cent to 41 per cent of the UK total (an increase of 6 million), while at the same time the number aged between 16 and 50 will fall by 1.5 million.[67] A similar pattern is predicted across

62 Available from the 'age positive' website at www.agepositive.gov.uk.

63 Employers Forum on Age, 'Report on a survey of senior decision makers in small and medium enterprises' (1999) and IRS/EFA, 'Employing Older Workers', *IRS Management Review*, Issue 21, April 2001.

64 House of Commons Select Committee on Education and Employment, 7th Report, 2000–01 session, *Age Diversity: Summary of Research Findings* (March 2001), available at www.publications.parliament.uk/pa/cm/cmeduemp.htm.

65 Eurolink Age has also published a code of practice for Europe called *Ageing in Employment: A Euro Code of Good Practice.*

66 Employers Forum on Age, *Ageism: Too Costly to Ignore* (2001).

67 Ibid.

Europe.[68] Groups working with the elderly point to significant discrimination against older people in the provision of healthcare, with resources being prioritised towards younger people, and the under-resourcing of social care for the elderly. The phenomenon of 'elder abuse' (violence towards old people in private or residential homes) is now increasingly recognised, and there have been calls for legislation to provide protection for this vulnerable group.

8.55 No explicit domestic provisions regulate age-related discrimination. Indeed, age-related distinctions underpin access to retirement (voluntary or compulsory), access to pensions and many aspects of education. Employment Rights Act (ERA) 1996 ss109 and 156 also provide an upper age limit in respect of unfair dismissal and redundancy claims. At present, no domestic legislation regulates age-related discrimination on grounds of age. But some such discrimination may amount to indirect sex or race discrimination, where it has an indirect adverse impact on one or other sex or on a particular racial group (see chapter 7). There are five significant cases that deal with age and indirect discrimination.

Age discrimination as sex or race discrimination

8.56 *Price v Civil Service Commission*[69] involved a challenge brought under the SDA 1975 by a 35-year-old woman to a Civil Service maximum age limit of 28 for applicants to executive officer posts. Ms Price successfully argued that, as a considerable number of women aged between 25 and 35 were occupied rearing children, the proportion of women who could comply with this upper age limit was considerably smaller than the number of men who could do so. The EAT commented that 'it should not be said that a person "can" do something merely because it is theoretically possible for him to do so'. The correct test is whether it is in practice harder for women to comply than men.

8.57 In *Perera v Civil Service Commission,*[70] another challenge was made to Civil Service upper age limits. Mr Perera, who was born in Sri Lanka, applied to become an administrative trainee for which the upper age limit was 32. He was 39. He argued that, because of the number of (ethnic minority) adult immigrants into the UK, the

68 'Towards a Society for all ages: Employment, Health, Pensions and Intergenerational Solidarity', conference paper, EC Employment and Social Affairs European Symposium.

69 [1977] IRLR 291.

70 [1982] IRLR 147.

proportion of ethnic minority executive officers who could comply with the age bar was considerably smaller than the proportion of white executive officers who could comply. Mr Perera was able to demonstrate that, in the VAT office in which he worked, 22 of the 34 white executive officers but none of the 13 ethnic minority executive officers, were under the age of 32. The employers produced evidence from two other local VAT offices that followed a similar pattern. The EAT found that Mr Perera had been subject to indirect race discrimination.[71]

8.58 In *Jones v University of Manchester*[72] a 46-year-old job applicant challenged a requirement that the successful appointee be between 27 and 35 years old. Ms Jones argued that this was indirectly discriminatory against women who were mature students. The statistics she produced related only to the impact of the requirement on men and women who had graduated as *mature* students, and the Court of Appeal ruled that she had not established sex discrimination. Had she been able to demonstrate an adverse impact on women in general, she would have proved her case subject to the employer's opportunity to plead justification (see further para 7.61).

8.59 The applicant in *Nash v Mash/Roe Group Ltd*[73] was a warehouse manager between 1972 and his dismissal, aged 69, in 1997. His attempt to claim unfair dismissal and a redundancy payment was blocked on the basis that he had reached the upper age limit imposed by ERA 1996 s109. He challenged the upper age limit as being indirectly discriminatory against men, because there were more economically active men than women between the ages of 65 and 74 than women. He succeeded in the ET but died before the case could be heard on appeal.

8.60 The issues raised in *Nash v Mash/Roe Group Ltd* were taken up in *Harvest Town Circle Ltd v Rutherford*,[74] in which it was alleged that the upper age limits imposed by the ERA 1996 indirectly discriminated on grounds of sex and were contrary to article 141 EC. Mr Rutherford was dismissed on grounds of redundancy at the age of 67. He produced statistics to show that 8 per cent of men over 65 were economically active, compared with 3 per cent of women. The ET concluded that ERA 1996 ss109 and 156 were indirectly discriminatory on

71 Compare the Court of Appeal's decision in *Perera v Civil Service Commission (No 2)* [1983] IRLR 166, discussed at para 7.96.

72 [1993] IRLR 218.

73 [1998] IRLR 168.

74 [2001] IRLR 600.

grounds of sex unless they could be justified. The EAT overruled this decision on the basis that the statistics that had been produced did not establish that more men than women are susceptible to unfair dismissal because those who were economically active could be self-employed or on fixed term contracts and therefore or for other reasons excluded from unfair dismissal and redundancy protection under the ERA 1996. The case was remitted to the ET for a fresh hearing. Clearly further and more persuasive statistics will need to be produced in order to succeed in this argument. The Home Secretary has now intervened in the case.

Employment Directive

8.61 The ED provides that the UK government must put in place domestic legislation to counter age discrimination by 2 December 2006 (see para 10.91). Both direct and indirect discrimination are to be regulated. But article 6 ED provides that age discrimination can be objectively and reasonably justified by a legitimate aim that could include 'legitimate employment policy, labour market and vocational training objectives' if 'the means of achieving that aim are appropriate and necessary'.[75] This could permit a very wide range of exemptions, and it is to be hoped that the UK government will not extend them so broadly as to emasculate the protection provided by the ED.

Human Rights Act 1998

8.62 The HRA 1998 may provide some protection as a result of its incorporation of article 14. Although not expressly mentioned, age would constitute a protected ground under the provision.[76] But article 14 applies only where the discrimination concerns the scope of another convention right. The limitations of that Act in the employment context have been mentioned above (para 8.2) and are considered further in chapter 9.

75 Art 6 ED.

76 *Nelson v UK* 49 DR 170.

CHAPTER 9

Human rights and discrimination

Key points

9.1

- The Human Rights Act (HRA) 1998 permits individuals to enforce most of the rights guaranteed by the European Convention on Human Rights (ECHR) in the domestic courts.
- The rights guaranteed by the HRA 1998 include the right to life (article 2), to freedom from torture, inhuman and degrading treatment (article 3) and from slavery or servitude and forced or compulsory labour (article 4). Those rights are without qualification. All the other rights are qualified where any limitation is prescribed by law, pursues legitimate objectives, and is necessary in a democratic society.
- 'Qualified' rights include the right to freedom of thought, conscience and religion (article 9), expression (article 10) and peaceful assembly and association (article 11); the right to fair trial (article 6) and to respect for private and family life (article 8).
- The right to freedom from discrimination on grounds such as sex, race colour, language, religion, political or other opinion, national or social origin, association with a national minority, property, birth or other status is guaranteed by article 14 but may only be relied upon in connection with the exercise of another convention right.
- Protocol 12 to the ECHR, which provides a free-standing right to be free from discrimination on the same grounds as article 14, has not been ratified by the UK.
- The HRA 1998 requires all legislation, past and present, to be read and given effect, so far as possible, in a way which is compatible with the incorporated convention rights.
- If a piece of legislation is not compatible with the incorporated convention rights the higher courts may make a declaration of incompatibility. The legislation still remains in force, though there is fast track procedure enabling the government to amend it.
- All new legislation must be accompanied by a statement from the responsible minister that it is compatible with the ECHR or, if it is not compatible, that the government wishes to proceed with it.
- Public authorities are required to act compatibly with the ECHR unless they are prevented from doing so by legislation. A body

whose functions are partly public and partly private is a public body in relation to its functions of a public nature.
- An individual may bring an action before a court complaining that a public authority has acted in a way that is incompatible with the ECHR provided he or she is a victim.
- The HRA 1998 does not make ECHR rights directly enforceable against a private body or a public body with some private functions which is acting in a private capacity.

Background and statutory provisions

9.2 The ECHR was implemented in the UK by the HRA 1998. This chapter provides an outline of those of its provisions most relevant to discrimination.

9.3 The ECHR, adopted in 1950, was drafted by the Council of Europe which was formed after the Second World War in an attempt to unify Europe and as a response to the large scale violations of human rights that had occurred during the war.[1] The convention institutions are based in Strasbourg, where the Council of Europe has its headquarters. The ECHR entered into force in 1953 and has been supplemented by various protocols including, most recently, Protocol 12, discussed below.

9.4 Prior to the implementation of the HRA 1998 the rights guaranteed by the ECHR could not be relied upon directly before the UK courts. It was possible to use the ECHR's provisions indirectly as an aid to the construction of legislation in cases of ambiguity.[2] But, prior to October 2000, an individual who wanted to assert a convention right had to petition the European Commission (from November 1999, the European Court of Human Rights – ECtHR). The Commission (now a committee of judges) would determine whether or not the complaint was admissible, in which case it would proceed to a full hearing in front of the court. By 1994 more than 25,000 cases had been registered. Of these, 2,027 were declared admissible.[3] Cases may be found inadmissible for a range of reasons such as the applicant's

1 For a fuller discussion see DJ Harris, M O'Boyle, C Warbrick, *Law of the European Convention on Human Rights* (Butterworths, 1995).

2 *R v Home Secretary ex p Brind* [1999] 1 AC 696 at 760.

3 *Survey of Activities and Statistics: European Commission of Human Rights* (Council of Europe, 1994). Cases declared admissible by the Commission were, unless settled, considered by the ECtHR.

failure to exhaust domestic remedies, the expiry of the six-month time limit for bringing claims, the fact that the applicant is not a 'victim' for the purposes of the convention or that the application is manifestly ill-founded. Legal aid may be available from the ECtHR (which may also award costs), though only once the issue of admissibility has been examined.

9.5 The HRA 1998 was passed in order to permit individuals in the UK to enforce most of the rights guaranteed by the ECHR in the domestic courts, thus removing the necessity to bring claims to the ECtHR in Strasbourg.[4] The rights thus 'domesticated' are set out in Sch 1 to the Act. They include the right to life (article 2) which incorporates (by virtue of article 2 of Protocol 6 to the ECHR) the right not to be subjected to the death penalty; and the right to freedom from torture (article 3) and from slavery (article 4).

9.6 The right to free elections is guaranteed (by article 3 of Protocol 1 to the ECHR), as are the rights to freedom of thought, conscience and religion (article 9); of expression (article 10); and of peaceful assembly and association (article 11). The right to a fair trial in civil and criminal matters is guaranteed by article 6, the right not to be punished retrospectively by article 7, and the right to respect for private and family life by article 8. The right to private property is guaranteed by article 1 of Protocol 1 to the Convention, the right to marry and to education by article 12 and article 2 of Protocol 1 respectively and, most directly relevant for the purposes of this book, the right to freedom from discrimination in the exercise of these various rights is guaranteed by article 14. All these provisions are incorporated into domestic law by the HRA 1998. Protocol 12 to the ECHR, which prohibits discrimination, was adopted by the Committee of Ministers of the Council of Europe on 26 June 2000 and opened for signature on 1 November of the same year. It has not yet been ratified by the UK, much less adopted into domestic law.

9.7 The ECHR's prohibitions on 'torture, inhuman or degrading treatment or punishment' (article 3) and 'slavery or servitude' and 'forced or compulsory labour' (article 4) are without qualification. All the other rights protected by the ECHR are subject to limitation and qualification. The rights may be limited in themselves. So, for example, the 'discrimination' prohibited by article 14 in relation to the enjoyment of convention rights on grounds such as 'sex, race, colour, language, religion, political or other opinion, national or social origin,

4 For a fuller discussion of the application of the HRA 1998 in the UK see K Starmer, *European Human Rights Law* (Legal Action Group, 1999).

association with a national minority, property, birth or other status' is *unjustified* differential treatment of persons in analogous circumstances[5] (see further para 9.30 below). Whether discrimination has occurred will therefore depend on an assessment of whether the applicant is in the same or analogous circumstances as the person alleged to have been treated more favourably and, if so, whether any differential treatment was justifiable. Also article 6's protection of the right to a 'fair trial' applies only in relation to the determination of criminal charges and civil rights and obligations (as distinct, for example, from purely public law matters).

9.8 Other articles provide the right in the first sub-paragraph, the qualifications to it in the second. So, for example, article 8(1) states that 'everyone has the right to respect for his private and family life, his home and his correspondence'. Article 8(2) goes on to provide that:

> There should be no interference by a public authority of the exercise of this right except such as in accordance with the law and is necessary in a democratic society in the interests of national security, public safety or the economic well-being of the country, for the prevention of disorder or crime, for the protection of health or morals, or for the protection of the rights and freedom of others.

The precise terms of the limitations attached to various articles differ. A fundamental reason for qualifying rights is that they raise conflicts with the rights of others, or the interests of society as a whole. For example, the right to freedom of expression guaranteed by article 10 ECHR is likely to conflict with the right to respect for private and family life recognised by article 8. And the right of demonstrators to peaceful assembly guaranteed by article 11 may clash with the same right to peaceful assembly of counter-demonstrators, at least where the authorities reasonably fear that permitting both assemblies may lead to violence.

9.9 Unless a right guaranteed by the ECHR is absolute, the convention permits the state to restrict it where any limitations are prescribed by law; pursue legitimate objectives (generally set out in the relevant article); and are necessary in a democratic society (this requires an assessment of the proportionality of restriction to objective pursued).

9.10 This chapter describes the structure of the HRA 1998 and then considers those convention rights most relevant to discrimination.

5 Or (*Thlimmenos v Greece* (2000) 9 BHRC 12) an unjustified failure to treat different cases differently.

Human Rights Act 1998

9.11 The HRA 1998 creates a statutory requirement that all legislation (past and future) is to be read and given effect, as far as possible, in a way which is compatible with the ECHR.[6] The Act also requires that the minister responsible for introducing legislation must, on its second reading, make a statement either to the effect that the legislation is compatible with the ECHR or that, although it is not so compatible, the government still wishes to proceed with it.[7]

9.12 Turning to the HRA 1998's interpretive provision, s3 provides that: '(1) So far as it is possible to do so, primary legislation and subordinate legislation must be read and given effect in a way which is compatible with the Convention rights'. Section 2 requires that any court or tribunal determining a question that has arisen in connection with a convention right must take into account the ECHR jurisprudence in so far as it is relevant to the proceedings in which that question has arisen. HRA 1998 s3(2) provides that the interpretative obligation imposed by s3(1):

> (b) does not affect the validity, continuing operation or enforcement of any incompatible primary legislation; and
> (c) does not affect the validity, continuing operation or enforcement of any incompatible subordinate legislation if (disregarding any possibility of revocation) primary legislation prevents removal of the incompatibility.[8]

The higher courts may make a declaration of incompatibility in respect of incompatible legislation the validity of which is preserved by s3(2) (the Employment Appeal Tribunal (EAT) does not have the power to rule on compatibility[9]). A fast-track procedure is provided to enable the executive to amend legislation in order to remove incompatibility with the ECHR after a declaration of incompatibility has been made.[10]

9.13 HRA 1998 s6 requires public authorities (including the courts[11]) to act compatibly with the ECHR, unless they are prevented from doing

6 HRA 1998 s3.

7 Ibid s19.

8 It follows that other subordinate legislation can be struck down under the HRA 1998, as it could be even prior to the Act according to the ordinary principles of judicial review.

9 *Whittaker v P & D Watson (t/a P & M Watson Haulage)* (2002) *Times* 26 March, EAT.

10 HRA 1998 s10 and Sch 2.

11 Ibid s6(3).

so by primary legislation or by subordinate legislation whose incompatibility is preserved by HRA 1998 s3(2) (above). The courts therefore have a duty to give effect to the ECHR unless positively prevented from so doing by statute. 'Public authority' does not include the Houses of Parliament, and 'act' does not include a failure to legislate. A body whose functions are partly public and partly private is a 'public authority' in relation to its functions 'of a public nature', but not in relation to acts which are private in nature.[12]

9.14 HRA 1998 s7 provides that an individual may bring an action before the court complaining that a public authority has acted in a way that is incompatible with the ECHR, so long as he or she would be regarded as a 'victim' under the ECHR. A person who has suffered a detriment as a result of the act complained of would be a victim for the purposes of the ECHR and, accordingly, the HRA 1998. Proceedings under HRA 1998 s7 must be brought within a period of one year beginning with the date on which the act complained of took place or such longer period as the court or a tribunal considers equitable having regard to all the circumstances.[13] That time limit is subject to any rule imposing a stricter time limit in relation to the procedure in question[14] (where, for example, a HRA 1998 claim is taken by way of judicial review, proceedings must be brought 'promptly, and in any event not later than three months after the grounds to make the claim first arose'[15]). The fact that a public authority has acted in a way which is incompatible with convention rights may be used as a defence to an action whenever that unlawful act has taken place.[16] But proceedings may only be brought against a public authority under HRA 1998 s7 in respect of actions of the authority which post-date the implementation of the HRA 1998 on 2 October 2000.[17]

9.15 The appropriate court or tribunal in which proceedings should be brought under HRA 1998 s7, and the remedies which such courts or tribunals may provide, have been set out in the Civil Procedure Rules. These provide that a claim that a public authority has acted unlawfully under the Act in respect of a judicial act may only be brought in the High Court. Any other claim may be brought in any court. A court has a wide power to grant such relief, remedies or orders as it considers

12 Ibid s6(3)(b) and (5).
13 Ibid s7(5).
14 Ibid.
15 CPR r54.5(1).
16 HRA 1998 s22(4).
17 Ibid s22(4).

just and appropriate, provided they are within its existing powers.[18] Damages may be awarded in civil proceedings but only by a court which has power to order the payment of damages or compensation in civil proceedings.[19] Damages may only be awarded if necessary to afford 'just satisfaction' and, in determining whether to award damages and the amount to award, the court must take into account the principles applied by the ECtHR when awarding compensation under the convention.[20]

9.16 The HRA 1998 will not make convention rights directly enforceable against a private body, or against a public body with some public functions if it is acting in a private capacity. But even in such cases the court will be under a duty to interpret legislation in conformity with the ECHR wherever possible, and to exercise any judicial discretion compatibly with the ECHR. This is so whether it is applying statute, common law or equitable rules.[21]

9.17 Breaches of convention rights may thus be raised before the courts (a) by claims brought under HRA 1998 s7, claiming breach of s6 of the Act; or (b) by judicial review actions challenging the new ground of illegality created by the HRA 1998 – breach of an ECHR provision. In either case the authority will have a defence under HRA 1998 s6(2) if, as a result of primary legislation, the authority could not have acted differently.[22] The third way in which convention rights may be raised under the HRA 1998 is that they may be available as a defence in both criminal and civil cases brought by public bodies against private individuals. Finally, whether or not a public authority is involved in litigation, a litigant may rely on the court's interpretive obligations under HRA 1998 s3.

Margin of appreciation

9.18 The ECtHR will allow a state a 'margin of appreciation' when ruling on whether a breach of the ECHR has occurred or in relation to articles 8 to 14 in considering whether the treatment is necessary and proportionate in a democratic society. One element in assessing

18 HRA 1998 s8(1).

19 Ibid s8(2).

20 Ibid s8(2), (3) and (4). Such awards are rarely more than £5,000.

21 Ibid s6.

22 Or (HRA 1998 s6(2)(b)), the authority was 'so as to give effect to or enforce one or more provisions of, or made under, primary legislation which cannot be read or given effect in a way which is compatible with the Convention rights'.

whether the state has acted within a margin of appreciation is whether its treatment falls within or departs from a common standard adopted by the states signatory to the ECHR. If the applicants are able to point to a common standard, whether by way of practice or international agreement, that should be a powerful argument against the state's action being regarded as proportionate.[23] The concept of the margin of appreciation is not appropriate when it comes to the application of the HRA 1998 by domestic courts and tribunals,[24] although they can permit some discretion (a substitute margin) to the legislature and executive.

The effect of the Human Rights Act 1998 on discrimination law

9.19 The ECHR provisions having most impact on discrimination law are article 3 (which prohibits torture and inhuman and degrading treatment); article 6 (which protects the right to a fair trial); article 8 (which protects the right to privacy and family life); article 9 (which protects the right to religion and belief); article 10 (which protects the right to freedom of expression); and article 14 (which deals with discrimination in the enjoyment of convention rights). Also important is Protocol 12 to the ECHR, which deals with discrimination and is discussed below (para 9.54). The discussion which follows is brief, largely because, at this early stage post-implementation of the HRA 1998, much of what could be said about the significance of the convention rights to discrimination law is highly speculative.

Article 3 – prohibition of torture and inhuman and degrading treatment and race discrimination

9.20 Article 3 ECHR provides that no one shall be subjected to torture or to inhuman or degrading treatment or punishment. Serious cases of race discrimination may fall under article 3. In *Assenov v Bulgaria*,[25] for example, allegations of police ill-treatment followed the arrest of a

23 See *Rasmussen v Denmark* (1984) 7 EHRR 371, in which a time limit applicable to paternity proceedings which distinguished between husbands and wives was found to exist in other member states and therefore did fall within the state's margin of appreciation.

24 See *R v DPP ex p Kebilene* [2000] 2 AC 326.

25 (1999) 28 EHRR 652.

14-year-old Romani boy. The state failed to investigate despite complaints by Assenov and his parents. The ECtHR found violations of article 3 by reason of the state's failure. The court's ruling referred specifically to ill-treatment by the police or other such agents of the state. Whether ill-treatment within the employment context gives rise to such a duty is likely to depend both in its degree of seriousness and on whether the employer is a public body.

9.21 In *Price v UK*[25a] a disabled person who was four limb deficient and suffered from kidney problems, was detained following her committal for contempt of court. Her cell was not adapted for a disabled person so she had to sleep in her wheelchair. The toilet was inaccessible and she complained of the cold which she felt more acutely as a disabled person. Despite her complaints she was not moved to a suitable cell. Throughout her stay male officers had to lift on to the toilet. She claimed that her detention constituted humiliating and degrading treatment contrary to article 3 ECHR. The ECtHR ruled that her treatment was humiliating treatment. Although the respondent had not shown an intention to humiliate, that did not necessarily preclude a complainant from establishing a breach of article 3. Her detention in circumstances where she was likely to suffer cold, develop sores, and was unable to use the toilet and keep clean, constituted degrading treatment in contravention of article 3.

9.22 The Commission has attached a special importance to discrimination on grounds of race. In *East African Asians v UK*[26] the applicants, who were citizens of the UK and colonies, challenged British immigration legislation that denied admission to the UK to UK passport holders of Asian origin who were resident in East Africa. The Commission found that the legislation discriminated against the applicants on 'grounds of their colour or race' and that article 3 had been violated. The Commission found that 'a special importance should be attached to discrimination based on race' and that such discrimination could, in certain circumstances, itself amount to degrading treatment within the meaning of article 3 ECHR. 'Differential treatment of a group of persons on the basis of race might therefore be capable of constituting degrading treatment when differential treatment on some other ground would raise no such question.'

9.23 It should be noted that 'interference' with the rights protected by article 3, unlike those protected by articles 8, 9, 10 and 14 ECHR, may not be justified by the state.

25a (2002) 34 EHRR 53; [2001] Crim LR 916, (2002) 5 CCLR 306.
26 (1973) 3 EHRR 76.

Article 6 – right to a fair hearing

9.24 Article 6(1) ECHR provides that:

> In the determination of his civil rights and obligations....everyone is entitled to a fair and public hearing within a reasonable time by an independent and impartial tribunal established by law.

This provision was relied on to challenge the Disability Discrimination Act (DDA) 1995's small employer exemption (see chapter 13) in *Whittaker v P & D Watson (t/a P & M Watson Haulage)*.[27] There the EAT ruled that it was not a competent court to make a declaration that the small employer exemption from liability under the DDA 1995 was incompatible with articles 6 and 14 ECHR (see further para 9.54 below), and so had no choice but to dismiss the case and grant leave to appeal to the Court of Appeal which has the power to make a declaration of incompatibility. It is being argued that protection from disability discrimination is a civil right, and the exemption for employers of less than 15 people represents a limitation on access by disabled people to their civil rights. It is further argued that the immunity for small employers is disproportionate as sufficient safeguards are built into the DDA 1995 with the justification provisions and the limit on adjustments to only those which are reasonable. The government is in any event committed to the repeal of the exemption which will be required by the Employment Directive by July 2006. Article 6 may also permit challenge to the non-availability of legal aid in tribunal cases, particularly in complex matters such as equal pay.[28]

Article 8 – respect for private and family life, home and correspondence

9.25 Article 8 provides that:

> (1) Everyone has the right to respect for his private and family life, his home and his correspondence.
> (2) There shall be no interference by public authority if the exercise of this right accepts that such as it is in accordance with the law and is necessary in a democratic society in the interests of national security, public safety or the economic well-being of the country, for the prevention of disorder or crime, for the protection of health or morals, or for the protection of the rights and freedoms of others.

27 (2002) *Times* 26 March. The small employer exemption is provided by DDA 1995 s7.

28 See, in particular, *Airey v Ireland* (1979) 2 EHRR 305.

9.26 Prior to the implementation of the HRA 1998, a wide range of article 8 claims were brought before the ECtHR. Cases deal with the use of medical records in court, phone tapping, dress codes, the rights of children whose parents are deported and the rights of homosexuals and those who have undergone gender reassignment. The ECtHR has ruled that the concept of private life covers an individual's right to develop his or her own personality, and to create relationships with others. In *Niemietz v Germany*,[29] for example, the court held that, in defining private life:

> It would be too restrictive to limit the notion to an 'inner circle' in which the individual may live his own personal life as he chooses and to exclude therefrom entirely the outside world not encompassed within that circle.

Respect for private life must, according to the ECtHR, also include to a certain degree the right to establish and develop relationships with other individuals.[30] Private life may include sexual activities. So, for example, in *Dudgeon v UK*[31] the court expressed the view that a person's sexual life was 'a most intimate aspect' of his or her private life. The court there found that Northern Irish legislation criminalising all homosexual behaviour violated article 8 because it was too far reaching, and therefore not proportionate to any legitimate governmental aim.

9.27 'Private life' can extend to life in the workplace. The case of *Niemietz v Germany*[32] concerned a challenge to the search of a lawyer's office. The court ruled that:

> To interpret the words 'private life' and the 'home' as including certain professional business activities or premises would be consonant with the essential object and purpose of article 8 namely to protect the individual against arbitrary interference by public authorities.

It was accepted by the court in *Niemietz* that some business and pro-

29 (1992) 16 EHRR 97.

30 Though cf *Halford v UK* (1997) 24 EHRR 523 (further discussed below), in which the ECtHR suggested that the breach of art 8 rested on the violation of the applicant's 'reasonable expectation' of privacy. This carried the implication, at least, that the applicant's right under art 8 not to have her telephone tapped could have been removed by a warning about the possibility that she would be recorded, even by the lack of an express assurance as to its suitability for sensitive communications.

31 (1981) 4 EHRR 149.

32 (1992) 16 EHRR 97.

fessional activities may be conducted from a private residence, and that private activities may be conducted from an office. It is possible that activities conducted on business premises might be held to be protected by article 8 only when they might just as well be carried on at home as at the office.

9.28 The right to privacy in respect of 'correspondence' has been extended to protect tapping of telephones, e-mail messages and other forms of sending messages. In *Halford v UK*[33] the applicant, a former Assistant Chief Constable, complained that calls she had made from her office telephone were intercepted by the police in order to gather information for use against her in sex discrimination proceedings. She had been supplied with a telephone designated for her private use in her office, and given an assurance that she could use that phone in connection with her litigation against her employers. The court found that article 8 was engaged, and rejected the UK government's argument that an employer was free to monitor calls made by an employee on telephones which the employer had provided. On the facts, the ECtHR considered that Ms Halford would have had a reasonable expectation of privacy in relation to calls made on her 'private' line. At the time there was no regulatory control of the interception of phone calls on a private network and the government conceded the infringement was not 'in accordance with the law' for the purpose of article 8(2).

9.29 In *Smith and Grady v UK*[34] the ECtHR held that investigations conducted by the Ministry of Defence into the sexual orientation of members of the armed forces, and the subsequent discharge of those service personnel from the armed forces, was an especially grave interference with their private lives. The court rejected the UK government's argument that its ban on gays in the military was justified by the need to preserve the morale of the fighting forces, pointing out the widespread and developing views in other Council of Europe states in favour of the admission of homosexuals into the armed forces. The court noted that 'particularly serious reasons' were required to justify such interferences which concerned 'a most intimate part of an individual's private life'. It rejected an argument that the Ministry of Defence was entitled to rely on the negative attitudes of heterosexual personnel towards gays and lesbians:

> To the extent (the attitudes) represent a predisposed bias on the part of the heterosexual majority against a homosexual minority, these

33 (1997) 24 EHRR 523.
34 (2000) 29 EHRR 493.

> negative attitudes cannot, of themselves, be considered by the Court to amount to sufficient justification for the interferences with the applicant's rights ... anymore than similar negative attitudes towards those of a different race, origin or colour.

9.30 In *Pearce v Governing Body of Mayfield Secondary School*[35] the Court of Appeal found that a lesbian teacher who regularly experienced homophobic taunts and abuse by pupils using words such as 'lesbian', 'dyke' and 'lesbian shit' had no complaint under the Sex Discrimination Act (SDA) 1975. According to the court, discrimination would be established under that Act only if a male homosexual teacher would have been treated more favourably than the applicant had been. The events in this case took place prior to the coming into effect of the HRA 1998. Hale LJ took the view that, had the events occurred after the implementation of the HRA 1998, the applicant might have succeeded:

> For a public authority to subject a person to a sustained campaign of homophobic abuse would be to act in a way which is incompatible with the Convention right to respect for private life under article 8, when read with the prohibition of discrimination and enjoyment of Convention rights under article 14. Sexual behaviour is an important aspect of private life, and the obligation to ensure effective respect for private life goes further than simply refraining from interference with what goes on in the privacy of their home. Discrimination based on sexuality is covered by the prohibition in article 14 because sexuality is in the same category as the characteristics which are listed in article 14.

Hale LJ took the view it would be possible to read and give effect to the SDA 1975 compatibly with those convention rights (see further para 8.20). The other judges did not give an obiter opinion on the point.

9.31 In two cases, *I v UK* and *Goodwin v UK*[35a] the applicants were post-operative male to female transsexuals. I complained about the lack of legal recognition of her post-operative sex, and treatment in relation to employment, social security and pensions and her ability to marry. She was unable to obtain admission on a nursing course as she refused to present her birth certificate showing her as a man. Goodwin complained that she had problems and faced sexual harassment at work during and following her gender reassigment and difficulties with national insurance contributions as she was required to continue to pay them until she was 65 and the basis that she was legally a

35 [2001] IRLR 669.

35a Application numbers 25680/94 and 28957/95 (judgment 11 July 2002).

man. The ECtHR ruled that a serious interference with private life arose from the conflict between social reality in which the applicants were women and the law which treated them as men. This led to feelings of vulnerability, humiliation and anxiety. It took note of the clear and uncontested evidence of an international trend in favour of legal recognition of the new sexual identity of post-operative transsexuals. The essence of the Convention was respect for human dignity and human freedom. Article 8 guaranteed protection to the personal sphere of each individual, including their right to establish their identity as individual human beings. The UK government could no longer claim that the matter fell within the margin of appreciation, save as regards the appropriate means to achieving the right protected under the Convention. There was therefore a breach of article 8 and a breach of article 12 which, although it referred to the right of a man and woman to marry, did not restrict those criteria to biological origins. There was no separate issue under article 14.

Article 9 – freedom of thought, conscience and religion

9.32 Article 9 ECHR provides that:

> (1) Everyone has the right to freedom of thought, conscience and religion: this right includes freedom to change his original belief and freedom, either alone or in community with others and in public or private, to manifest his religion or belief in worship, teaching, practice and observance.
>
> (2) Freedom to manifest one's religion or belief shall be subject only to such limitations as are prescribed by law and are necessary in a democratic society in the interests of public safety, for the protection of public order, health or morals, or for the protection of the rights and freedoms of others.

There is no limitation on the right to hold religious beliefs although, as is evident from the above, the right to manifest religious beliefs may be limited under article 9(2).

9.33 In cases brought under the ECHR the limitations in article 9(2) have been given a wide interpretation, and the right to manifest religion has in practice been extremely limited. So, for example, in *Ahmad v UK*[36] the Commission ruled inadmissible a challenge brought under article 9 to an employer's refusal to allow a Muslim school teacher to attend mosque on Friday afternoon. The Commission

36 (1982) 4 EHRR 126. See also *Ahmad v Inner London Education Authority* [1978] QB 36; [1977] ICR 490 from which the application came.

pointed out the applicant's failure to disclose his need for time off at interview, or during the first six years of employment (when he was employed at such a distance from any mosque as to be excused the religious obligation to attend prayer there on Friday afternoon). The Commission took the view that he had suffered no interference with his rights under article 9 ECHR. Similarly, in *Stedman v UK*,[37] the Commission dismissed a complaint from a Christian that a requirement that she should work on Sundays breached article 9. Although the employer was a private company the Commission agreed that the UK could be required to protect Ms Stedman from its actions. But it ruled her application manifestly ill-founded on the basis that she was dismissed for failing to agree to work certain hours, rather than for her religious beliefs as such, and that she was free to resign.[38] Ms Stedman, like Mr Ahmad, had in the view of the Commission suffered no interference with her right to private life.

9.34 The wide discretion given to the government under article 9(2) ECHR is further illustrated by *X v UK*, in which a prisoner complained that he had been refused permission to keep a religious book in his cell.[39] The book contained an illustrated section on martial arts which the prison authorities considered to be dangerous to the general population. Although the Commission held that there had been an interference with the applicant's article 9 rights, it went on to find that the interference was justified in accordance with article 9(2) ECHR. By contrast, in *Kokinakis v Greece*[40] the ECtHR accepted a complaint made under article 9. The applicants, Jehovah's witnesses, had been convicted of and fined for 'proselytism' (an offence under Greek law) in connection with their engagement in door-to-door evangelism. The ECtHR accepted that there had been an interference, prescribed by law, with their right to manifest their belief. It also accepted that the law had a legitimate aim, namely the protection of the rights and freedoms of others. But it ruled that there had been a violation of article 9, because there the authorities had not demonstrated any pressing need to prosecute and had not considered whether the applicants had used any improper means.

9.35 HRA 1998 s13 provides that, if a court's determination of any question arising under the Act might affect the exercise by a religious

37 (1997) EHRR 545; (1997) 23 EHRR CD.

38 The requirement to work Sundays was imposed after the start of her employment and in breach of her contract of employment.

39 [1976] 5 DR 100.

40 (1993) 17 EHRR 397.

organisation (itself or its members collectively) of the rights protected by article 9, particular regard must be had to the importance of that right. The inclusion of this provision was intended to allay the concerns of members of certain churches that the effect of article 9 would be to prevent them from selecting employees in a manner consistent with the ethos and belief of their organisation. Its effect remains to be seen. In *O'Neill v Governors of St Thomas More Roman Catholic Voluntarily Aided Upper School*,[41] the EAT ruled that a woman dismissed on account of her pregnancy was discriminated against contrary to the SDA 1975. The respondents claimed that the reason for the applicant's dismissal was not the pregnancy as such, but her unmarried status and the fact that the child's father was a local Catholic priest which offended the religious character of the school. It would be of concern if a case such as this was decided differently in the future.

Article 10 – freedom of expression

9.36 Article 10 ECHR provides that:

> (1) Everyone has the right to freedom of expression. This right shall include freedom to hold opinions and to receive and impart information and ideas without interference by public authority and regardless of frontiers. This article shall not prevent States from requiring or licensing a broadcasting, television or cinema enterprises.
>
> (2) The exercise of these freedoms, since it carries with it duties and responsibilities, may be subject to such formalities, conditions, restrictions or penalties as are prescribed by law and are necessary in a democratic society, in the interest of national security, territorial integrity or public safety, for the prevention of disorder or crime, for the protection of health or morals, for the prevention of the reputation or rights of others, for preventing the disclosure of information received in confidence, or for maintaining the authority and impartiality of the judiciary.

9.37 Article 10 may be relevant for complaints of discrimination in respect of dress codes, neither the SDA 1975 nor the RRA 1976 having proven effective to permit challenge to these rules (see para 3.33). It is possible that article 10, read with articles 8 and/or 14 in the case of sex-specific dress codes, article 9 in the case of codes impacting on those of minority religious groups, might remedy this position. In *Kara v*

41 [1996] IRLR 372.

UK,[42] however, a male training administrator employed by Hackney Borough Council was told he could not wear female clothing at work. He complained that his rights under articles 8, 10 and 14 had been breached. The Commission accepted that an individual's mode of dress was an aspect of his or her private life. But it found that the interference with the applicant's rights was justified under article 8(2). First, the interference was 'in accordance with the law' because the employer had a written dress policy. Second, the dress policy protected the 'rights of others', ie, the right of his employers to enhance its public image and facilitate its external contacts. Finally, the interference was not disproportionate, the requirement that employees dress appropriately to their gender being reasonably regarded by the employer as necessary to safeguard their public image.[43]

Article 14 – prohibition of discrimination

9.38 Article 14 ECHR provides that:

> The enjoyment of the rights and freedoms set forth in this Convention shall be secured without discrimination on any ground such as sex, race, colour, language, religion, political or other opinion, national or social origin, association with a national minority, property, birth or other status.

The protection afforded by article 14 is very limited in that it applies only to discrimination in connection with other convention rights. Provided a convention right is engaged, article 14 forbids discrimination on a wide range of grounds. Further, although no claim can succeed under article 14 unless another convention right is engaged, such a claim can succeed even if the substantive article has not been breached.[44]

9.39 Article 14's protection may apply to a right that a state chooses to guarantee although it is not required by the ECHR to do so. So, for

42 (1996) 24 EHRR 205.

43 The Commission further stated that the facts disclosed 'no appearance of a violation of Article 10' and that, although men and women were subject to different ('sex appropriate') dress rules, 'the applicant's complaints [under art 14] disclose no appearance of discrimination on the ground of sex. They must therefore be rejected as manifestly ill-founded ...'

44 *Inze v Austria* (1987) 10 EHRR 394. No infringement of art 1 of Protocol 1 considered alone was found but, because Austrian law gave priority to legitimate over illegitimate heirs, there was a violation of art 14 in combination with art 1 of Protocol 1.

example, in the *Belgian Linguistics (No 2)* case,[45] French-speaking parents complained that the Belgian educational system did not enable their children to be educated in French-speaking schools except if they travelled a considerable distance. The applicants relied upon article 2 of Protocol 1 to the ECHR (which provides a right to education), together with articles 8 and 14. Their claim succeeded only under article 14, the court holding that a rule barring access to certain schools in six communes was discriminatory and disproportionate when there was no equivalent rule for Flemish-speaking children. The ECHR does not require a state to provide any system of education but, in so far as a state does so (and each signatory state in fact provided a general educational system), there is a right not to be discriminated against in its provision which encompassed the right to be educated in one of the national languages.

9.40 In *Abdulaziz Cabales and Balkandali v UK*,[46] too, the ECtHR ruled that there was no obligation on the UK to allow resident alien husbands, who had a right to remain in the UK, to be joined by their wives. But because the UK did allow wives to join their husbands, the question of whether the failure to allow wives in similar circumstances to be joined by their husbands fell within the ambit of the right to respect for family life, and article 14 could be engaged in so far as it could be shown there was differential treatment.

'Discrimination' under article 14

9.41 There are two stages in establishing discrimination for the purposes of article 14. First, the applicant has to show that he or she has been treated differently from others in the same or an analogous situation. The reason for the different treatment may be one of the grounds identified in article 14. Some other grounds, although not listed in the article, have already been accepted as falling within 'other status'. Among these have been illegitimacy, sexual orientation, age, disability, and trade union membership[47] (see further para 9.45).

9.42 Even if the applicant succeeds in establishing different treatment in a comparable situation, a respondent may escape a finding that article 14 has been violated by establishing that the different treatment

45 (1968) 1 EHRR 252.

46 (1985) 7 EHRR 471.

47 Respectively, *Inze v Austria* (1987) 10 EHRR 394; *Salgueiro da Silva Mouta v Portugal* (2001) 31 EHRR 1055 and *Sutherland v UK* [1998] EHRLR 117; *Nelson v UK* 49 DR 170 and *Bouamar v Belgium* (1987) 11 EHRR 1; *Botta v Italy* (1998) 26 EHRR 241 and *National Union of Belgium Police v Belgium* (1975) 1 EHRR 578.

had an objective and reasonable justification. Justification is permitted although the terms of article 14 are expressed absolutely and without qualification, unlike many of the substantive articles. In the *Belgian Linguistics* case the court held that to construe article 14 as forbidding every difference in treatment would produce absurd results.[48]

9.43 In defining the criteria to determine whether a difference in treatment in the exercise of a convention right violated the principle of equal treatment, the court in the *Belgian Linguistics* case extracted principles from the legal practice of many democratic states, and held that there would be violation if the distinction had 'no objective and reasonable justification'. The existence of such a justification must be assessed in relation to the aims and effects of the measures under consideration, regard being had to the principles which normally prevail in democratic society. There must be a legitimate aim and a reasonable relationship with the means employed and the aim sought to be realised.

9.44 Since the decision in the *Belgian Linguistics* case a hierarchy of protected grounds has emerged under article 14 ECHR. Thus, for example, where the differential treatment is on grounds such as membership of one trade union or another, or status as a small or a large landowner, it will breach article 14 only if it has no objective and reasonable justification.[49] Where, on the other hands, differential treatment is on grounds such as sex, race, religion, illegitimacy or nationality, on the other hand, 'very weighty reasons would have to be put forward before the Court could regard a difference of treatment based exclusively [such a] ground ... as compatible with the Convention'.[50] But whatever the ground of discrimination challenged under article 14, justification is possible whether the discrimination is direct or indirect.

9.45 The first stage of justification therefore requires the state to satisfy the court that the differential treatment complained of has a rational aim. There may be a dispute of fact as to what is the aim as in the *Abdulaziz* case,[51] for example, in which the UK asserted that the aim of the disputed legislation was to protect the labour market and to

48 (1968) 1 EHRR 252 at 284.

49 See *National Union of Belgium Police v Belgium* (1975) 1 EHRR 578 and *Swedish Engine Drivers* case (1975) EHRR 617, and *Chassagnou v France* (1999) 7 BHRC 151.

50 See, respectively, *Abdulaziz Cabales and Balkandali v UK* (1985) 7 EHRR 471; *Hoffman v Austria* (1993) 17 EHRR 293; *Markx v Belgium* (1979) 2 EHRR 330 and *Gaygusuz v Austria* (1997) 23 EHRR 365,

51 (1985) 7 EHRR 471.

protect public order. The applicants' claim that the immigration laws were racially motivated was rejected by the court in 1985. But the ECHR is a 'living instrument' which has to be interpreted 'in the light of present day conditions'.[52] It is possible, accordingly, that the court might make a different decision if a case similar to *Abdulaziz* reached it today.

9.46 Aims accepted by the ECtHR as 'legitimate' for the purposes of article 14 have included the protection of the labour market and public order (*Abdulaziz*), the development of linguistic unity (*Belgian Linguistics*), and the support and encouragement of the traditional family (*McMichael v UK*).[53] An attempt to justify differential treatment by generalisations unsupported by evidence may well fail. In *Markx v Belgium*,[54] for example, the ECtHR rejected the respondent's claim, unsupported by any evidence, that the differential treatment of the mothers of legitimate and illegitimate children was justified on the basis that the latter were more likely to abandon their offspring.

9.47 Once a legitimate aim has been established, the next stage is to consider whether the means employed to achieve that aim are proportional to the aim and objective. The state must satisfy the court that there is a fair balance between the protection of the interests of the community and respect of rights and freedom safeguarded by the ECHR.[55] In *National Union of Belgian Police v Belgium*,[56] for example, the ECtHR accepted that denial of consultation rights to a trade union because of its small size in comparison with other unions which were given consultation rights was justified. According to the court, the differential treatment did strike a reasonable balance between the rights of the union and the interests of the employers in ensuring a coherent balanced staff policy. It will assist the applicant in showing that the means adopted are not proportionate to the ends if an alternative means for achieving the same ends which has a less discriminatory impact is identified.

Indirect discrimination

9.48 It was not clear until relatively recently whether article 14 regulated indirect discrimination. The closest to a statement of principle on the

52 *Tyrer v UK* (1979–80) 2 EHRR 1.

53 (1995) 20 EHRR 205.

54 (1979) 2 EHRR 330.

55 *Belgian Linguistics* (1968) 1 EHRR 252.

56 (1975) 1 EHRR 578.

issue was found in the *Belgian Linguistics* case in which, in the context of justification, the ECtHR stated that:

> The existence of such a justification must be assessed in relation to the aims and effects of the measure under consideration regard being had to the principles which normally prevail in democratic societies.

9.49 In *Marks v Belgium*[57] the court stated that article 14 prohibited rules which had the object of prejudicing a particular section of the population, and rules which had that result. But in other cases such as *Abdulaziz* the court declined to make a finding of indirect discrimination. More recently, however, in *Thlimmenos v Greece*,[58] the ECtHR made a clear statement of principle. The applicant, a Jehovah's Witness, was convicted of a felony offence in 1983 for having refused to enlist in the army at a time of general mobilisation. There was no alternative service for conscientious objectors. He was later refused appointment as an accountant on the grounds that he had been convicted of a felony. The court found that the set of facts complained of by the applicant fell within the ambit of article 9, the right to freedom of religion, but made no finding that there had been a violation of that right taken on its own. However, the court found that there had been a breach of article 14 in conjunction with article 9 because:

> The Court has so far considered that the right under article 14 not to be discriminated against in the enjoyment of the rights guaranteed under the Convention is violated when States treat differently persons in analogous situations without providing objective and reasonable justification ... However, the Court considers that this is not the only facet of the prohibition of discrimination in article 14. The right not to be discriminated against in the enjoyment of the rights guaranteed under the Convention is also violated when States without objective and reasonable justification fail to treat differently persons whose situations are significantly different.[59]

9.50 The approach taken by the ECtHR in *Thlimmenos* recognises as 'discrimination' under article 14 that which has long been defined as indirect discrimination by the European Court of Justice in cases such as *Schumacher v HZA Frankfurt-am-Main*.[60] The ECtHR in *Thlimmenos* found that article 14 had been violated because, unlike

57 (1979) 2 EHRR 330.

58 (2000) 9 BHRC 12.

59 Ibid, para 44.

60 [1989] ECR 638; [1990] 2 CMLR 465.

other convictions for serious criminal offences, a conviction for refusing on religious or philosophical grounds to wear the military uniform could not imply any dishonesty likely to undermine the applicant's ability to exercise the profession of accountancy. Consequently, excluding the applicant on the ground that he was an unfit person was unjustified. Further it did not pursue a legitimate aim as it was a further sanction against his refusal to wear military uniform and was disproportionate to the offence.[61]

Positive discrimination and the European Convention

9.51 Article 14 ECHR requires that 'the enjoyment of the rights and freedoms set forth in this Convention shall be secured without discrimination'. The state therefore has a positive obligation to the citizen which goes beyond the negative prohibition on less favourable treatment on particular grounds. There are indications that the positive obligation to enable the citizen to enjoy the rights provided extends to a duty to give effective access to such rights. It was held, for example, in the *Belgian Linguistics* case that not all instances of differential treatment are unacceptable and that 'certain legal inequalities tend only to correct factual inequalities'.

9.52 In *Airey v Ireland*[62] the applicant claimed under articles 6 and 14 that, as a person of limited means she was entitled to positive discrimination in the form of funding for a barrister so that she could enjoy effective equal rights of access to the courts. It was her case that judicial separation was more easily available to those who could afford to pay than those without financial resources. Having found the existence of a positive obligation under article 6(1) the court found it was not necessary to consider the article 14 claim. But in *DG & DW Lindsey v UK*,[63] in the context of a tax advantage for married women, the court ruled that such advantage had 'an objection and reasonable justification in the aim of providing positive discrimination' to encourage married women back to work. There are no criteria for determining whether or not any particular action of reverse discrimination is permissible. Each case is decided according to whether or not the court finds objective justification.

61 (2000) 9 BHRC 12, para 47.
62 (1979) 2 EHRR 305.
63 (1986) 49 DR 181.

The impact of article 14

9.53 As article 14 is not a free-standing right its impact has been limited by the court's reluctance to determine an article 14 claim if it can dispose of a claim under the substantive article heading alone. In *Smith & Grady v UK*,[64] for example, the ECtHR ruled for the first time that the ban on homosexuals in the armed forces was a violation of article 8 (which protects the right to private and family life) and article 13 (which provides the right to an effective remedy). The complaints were brought under article 8 in conjunction with article 14 but, the court having upheld the article 8 complaint, made no finding on the article 14 complaint as it considered that it did not give rise to any separate issues. However, in *Salgueiro da Silva Mouta v Portugal*[65] the court found a violation of article 14 when a gay father's sexual orientation was treated as a negative factor in respect of custody of his daughter. The court held that the Lisbon Court of Appeal had made a distinction dictated by considerations relating to the sexual orientation of the father which could not be tolerated under the ECHR.

9.54 The importance of article 14 under the HRA 1998 may lie in the broad range of circumstances in which complaints of discrimination can be made. In so far as domestic law regulates particular grounds of discrimination such as sex, race and disability (these grounds to be extended by 2003 to include sexual orientation and religion, and by 2006 to include age); the protection afforded by EC and domestic law is likely to be stronger than that available under the HRA 1998. But as the grounds of discrimination regulated by article 14 are not closed, any particular set of circumstances falling within a convention right (such as article 6 – the right to a fair trial, article 8 – the right to private and family life, or article 11 – freedom of assembly and association, for example), may be strengthened by adding an article 14 claim if the applicant has been discriminated against by comparison with a person with a different status. In *Whittaker v P & D Watson*,[66] for example, the claim that the DDA 1995's small employer exemption denied the applicant's right to a hearing relies in part on article 14.

9.55 It must be remembered that, even if the substantive claim fails, the article 14 claim may succeed. Circumstances in which convention rights may be of assistance in combating discrimination will be

64 (2000) 29 EHRR 493.

65 (2001) 31 EHRR 1055.

66 (2002) *Times* 26 March.

substantially enhanced if Protocol 12 to the ECHR is ratified, providing as it does a freestanding right against discrimination (para 9.54 below).

Protocol 12 to the Convention

9.56 On 26 June 2000 the Committee of Ministers of the Council of Europe adopted the text of Protocol 12 and published an explanatory report.[67] So far, the UK has not become a signatory to Protocol 12 and the HRA 1998 does not, therefore, incorporate it. The government has said it has no plans to sign the Protocol as it has objections to it in its current form.[67a]

9.57 The preamble to Protocol 12 refers to 'the fundamental principles according to which all persons are equal before the law and are entitled to equal protection of the law'. It declares that the member states are 'resolved to take further steps to promote the equality of all persons through the collective enforcement of a general prohibition of discrimination' by means of the ECHR. Article 1 provides as follows:

> (1) The enjoyment of any right set forth by law shall be secured without discrimination on any ground such as sex, race, colour, religion, political or other opinion, national or social origin, association with a national minority, property, birth or other status.
> (2) No-one shall be discriminated against by a public authority on any ground such as those mentioned in paragraph (1).

The protection from discrimination in the Protocol extends beyond article 14 in that the first paragraph of article 1 requires that any right set forth by law shall be secured without discrimination. By contrast, the guarantee in article 14 is restricted to the rights and freedoms set forth in the ECHR. Article 14 has no equivalent to article 1(2) of Protocol 12, which provides a general prohibition on discrimination by any public authority on any ground listed in article 1(1).

9.58 The range of protected classes is identical to that in article 14. It is open-ended and it will provide protection in a wide range of situations. The phrase 'any other status' clearly replicates article 14 and must be taken to include sexual orientation, disability, age, birth

67 Available at conventions.coe.int/Treaty/EN/CadreListeTraites.htm.

67a See EOR Number 105, May 2002, for an article by Sandra Fredman on this subject and Written Answer 37, Lord Bassam of Brighton, 11 October 2001, Parliamentary question, 27 September 2001.

inside or outside marriage, marital status, trade union status[68] and poverty. The Council of Europe chose not to include all these grounds specifically but to adopt a non-exhaustive list in order not to be exclusive and to permit expansion to reflect changing needs.[69] Some grounds for discrimination are seen as being particularly serious, having a 'specially protected status', and therefore can only be justified by particularly weighty reasons. These include differential treatment on the basis of gender, race, illegitimacy and sexual orientation.

9.59 The purpose of Protocol 12 is amplified in the accompanying explanatory report, which sets out the history of the Protocol and a commentary on its provisions. The terms 'affirmative action' or 'positive discrimination' are not used in the Protocol, but its preamble states that measures taken to promote full and effective equality will not be prohibited by the principle of non-discrimination, provided that there is an objective and reasonable justification for them. The fact that there are disadvantaged groups or categories of persons, or that inequalities exist, may constitute justifications for adopting measures providing for specific advantages in order to promote equality, provided that the proportionality principle is respected. Such positive measures are not obligatory. The explanatory report also states that the increased protection afforded by Protocol 12 over and above that provided by article 14 ECHR concerns, in particular, cases where a person is discriminated against:

a. In the enjoyment of any rights specifically granted to an individual under national law;
b. In the enjoyment of a right which may be inferred from a clear obligation of a public authority under national law, as where a public authority is obliged by national law to behave in a particular manner;
c. By a public authority in the exercise of a discretionary power (such as granting certain subsidies);
d. By any other act or omission by a public authority (such as the behaviour of law enforcement officers when controlling a riot).

9.60 The explanatory report is guarded as to when article 1 of Protocol 12 might regulate discrimination in relations between private people

68 Respectively, *Salgueiro da Silva Mouta v Portugal* (2001) 31 EHRR 1055; *Sutherland v UK* [1998] EHRLR 117; *Botta v Italy* (1998) 26 EHRR 241; *Nelson v UK* 49 DR 170; *Bouamar v Belgium* (1987) 11 EHRR 1; *Inze v Austria* (1987) 10 EHRR 394; *Rasmussen v Denmark* (1985) 7 EHRR 352; and *National Union of Belgium Police v Belgium* (1975) 1 EHRR 578.

69 Explanatory report, para 20.

(that is to say, as to its horizontal effect). The report concludes that this would be exceptional, and gives two examples of when it might arise. First, if there is a clear lacuna in the domestic law protection; second where in respect of relations between private people the failure to provide protection might be so clear-cut and grave that it might engage clearly the responsibility of the state. It would concern relations in the public sphere which are normally regulated by law and for which the state has a certain responsibility – such as employment contracts or unfair denial of access to restaurants or other services. Purely private matters would not be affected.

CHAPTER 10

Introduction to EC law

continued

Key points

10.1

- There are three main types of EC legislation: treaty articles; regulations and directives:
- A question as to the proper interpretation of EC law may be made by an employment tribunal (ET) or court to the European Court of Justice (ECJ). Legal aid may be available.
- Article 12 of the EC Treaty prohibits discrimination on grounds of nationality and may be relied upon before UK courts. Article 39 EC provides for freedom of movement for workers who are EC nationals.
- Article 141 EC establishes the principle of equal pay for work of equal value. 'Pay' is very broadly defined to include all immediate or future pay that is received directly or indirectly in respect of a worker's employment. Article 141 does not require that a claimant relies on a comparator in the same employment. It is sufficient if they are in the same service.
- Also of significance in the discrimination context are the Equal Pay Directive (EPD), the Equal Treatment Directive (ETD), the Burden of Proof Directive (BPD), the Parental Leave Directive (PLD) and the Part-time Workers Directive (PtWD). The Race Directive (RD) and Employment Directive (ED) prohibit race discrimination and, in the employment context, discrimination on grounds of sexual orientation, religion and belief, disability and age. The RD must be implemented by member states by July 2003; the ED by December 2003 in so far as it deals with discrimination on grounds of sexual orientation and religion or belief, December 2006 in so far as it deals with discrimination on grounds of age and disability.
- Some Treaty provisions, including article 141, have direct vertical and horizontal effect in the UK courts.
- Although directives are addressed to member states, certain of their provisions also have direct vertical effect and are binding on state bodies and public bodies even in the absence of domestic implementation. Directives also have indirect effect through interpretive obligations imposed on national courts in connection with their application of domestic law.
- An individual may request the European Commission to take proceedings against the government for failing to implement domestic legislation.

- Tribunal claims must be brought under domestic statutes whose provisions must be interpreted in accordance with, and may be overridden by, the relevant EC provisions. Until the RD and ED are in force, EC legislation underpins UK anti-discrimination laws only in the case of discrimination on grounds of sex (including married status and gender reassignment) and nationality.

Background and statutory provisions

10.2 The Treaty of Rome had the objective of creating a common market with free movement of goods and services, labour and capital. The view was that economic integration would lead to an optimum rate of economic growth which in turn would lead, according to the preamble to the treaty, to the 'constant improvement of the living and working conditions of their peoples'. Initially, issues of discrimination arose in relation to the free movement of goods and services and there was little intervention by the community in the social field, although article 119 of the Treaty of Rome (now article 141 EC) established the principle that men and women should receive equal pay for equal work.

10.3 In 1973 the heads of government meeting in Paris issued a communiqué in which member states emphasised that vigorous action in the social sphere was just as important as achieving economic and monetary union. The Commission drew up an action programme[1] which led to the adoption of directives on equal pay as between men and women[2] and on equal treatment (on grounds of sex) in employment and social security.[3]

10.4 In 1976, in its landmark judgment in *Defrenne*,[4] the ECJ observed that:

> Article 119 [now 141] pursues a double aim. First ... the aim of article 119 is to avoid a situation in which undertakings established in States

1 [1974] OJ C13/1. The programme had three objectives: the attainment of full and better employment in the community, the improvement of living and working conditions, and increased involvement of management and labour in the economic and social decisions of the community and of workers in the light of the undertaking.

2 Council Directive 75/117/EEC.

3 Respectively, Council Directives 76/07/EEC and 79/7/EC.

4 Case 43/75 *Defrenne v SABENA (No 2)* [1976] ECR 455.

> which have actually implemented the principle of equal pay suffer a competitive disadvantage in intra community competition as compared with undertakings established in States which have not yet eliminated discrimination against women workers as regards pay. Second, this provision forms part of the social objectives of the community, which is not merely an economic union, but is at the same time intended by common action to ensure social progress and seek the constant improvement of living and working conditions of their peoples ... This double aim, which is at once economic and social, shows that the principle of equal pay forms part of the foundations of the community.

Two years later, in *Defrenne (No 3)*,[5] the ECJ recognised equality as a 'fundamental right'. The court ruled that 'respect for fundamental personal human rights is one of the general principles of community law ... There can be no doubt that the elimination of discrimination based on sex forms part of those fundamental rights.'[6] This does not mean that the EC's economic objectives have been forgotten, or that business interests do not provide justification for discrimination. These issues are further discussed below.

10.5 The legislative initiatives of the 1970s have been followed by more action programmes in relation to equal opportunities for men and women. The Community has also developed protection against discrimination in relation to nationality – more particularly, in relation to free movement of workers – and has engaged in action programmes against racism and xenophobia and disability.

Treaty on European Union (Maastricht Treaty)

10.6 The Treaty on European Union, entered into at Maastricht in 1992, embraced the principle of subsidiarity. This requires that the EC should only take action if the objectives could not be sufficiently achieved by the member states acting at national level, and that any action by the Community should not go beyond what is necessary to achieve the objectives of the treaty.

10.7 The social policy agreement, which was removed from the main body of the treaty in order to secure the UK's agreement to it by

5 Case 149/77 *Defrenne v SABENA (No 3)* [1978] ECR 1365.

6 This approach has also been adopted in Case 152/84 *Marshall v Southampton and South West Hampshire Area Health Authority (Teaching)* [1986] ECR 723, [1986] IRLR 140; Case 151/84 *Roberts v Tate & Lyle Industries Limited* [1986] ECR 703; and Case C-167/97 *R v Employment Secretary ex p Seymour-Smith and Perez* [1999] ECR I-623, [1999] IRLR 253.

permitting it to opt out of what became known as the 'social chapter', led to the PLD (see para 10.15).[7] This directive was the first that allowed the social partners to negotiate a framework agreement forming the basis of the directive. It was followed by the BPD (see para 10.64).[8] A change of government in the UK in 1997 resulted in these directives being re-adopted under article 94 EC (formerly article 100) and applied to the UK.

Treaty of Amsterdam

10.8 The Treaty of Amsterdam introduced the promotion of equality between men and women as one of the tasks (article 2) and activities (article 3) of the EC. In addition, it introduced a new article – now article 13 of the re-named Treaty establishing the European Community (EC Treaty). This permits the Council of Ministers, acting unanimously on a proposal from the Commission, to take action to combat discrimination based on sex, racial or ethnic origin, religion and belief, disability, age or sexual orientation. The Treaty of Amsterdam also resulted in significant amendments to article 119 (now article 141 EC) which, *inter alia*, made explicit its requirement of equal pay for work of equal value.

Charter of Fundamental Rights of the European Union

10.9 Chapter III of the Charter of Fundamental Rights of the European Union, which was adopted in 2000,[9] deals with equality rights. It makes provision for:

- equality before the law;[10]
- prohibition of all discrimination on any ground such as sex, race, colour, ethnic or social origin, genetic features, language, religion or belief, political or other opinion, membership of a national minority, property, birth, disability, age or sexual orientation, and, within the scope of the EC and EU Treaties, any discrimination on grounds of nationality;[11]
- respect for cultural, religious and linguistic diversity;[12]

7 Council Directive 96/34/EEC, as amended by Directive 97/75/EEC.
8 Council Directive 97/80/EEC, as amended by Directive 98/52/EEC.
9 [2000] OJ C364/1.
10 Charter, art 20.
11 Ibid art 21.
12 Ibid art 22.

- equality between men and women;[13]
- rights of the child;[14]
- rights of the elderly;[15] and
- integration of people with disabilities.[16]

10.10 The effect of the Charter is still not clear. The UK government has stated that it is not intended to be legally binding on member states.[17] But the European Commission takes a more robust approach:

> The institutions that will have proclaimed the Charter will have committed themselves to respecting it and the Court of Justice of the European Communities will refer to it in its case law. Considering the added value of the Charter, one can safely reckon that sooner or later, the Charter will be integrated into the Treaties.[18]

The Charter has been referred to in the Court of First Instance and in several Advocate Generals' opinions. It is likely to be used increasingly as an aid to interpretation in the future.

The varieties of EC legislation

10.11 There are three main types of EC legislation relevant in the discrimination context. These consist of treaty articles, regulations and directives. In addition, the Treaty of Amsterdam introduced a new decision-making procedure to implement the Employment Title under which the Council of Ministers, having received the views of the Employment Committee,[19] may (acting by qualified majority on a recommendation from the Commission) 'make recommendations to Member States'.[20] There is no sanction for breach of a recommendation. In respect of sexual harassment, for example, the Council passed a non-legally binding resolution on the protection of the dignity of men and women at work.[21] This was followed by a

13 Charter art 23.
14 Ibid art 24.
15 Ibid art 25.
16 Ibid art 26.
17 HC Debates col 354, 11 December 2000.
18 Commission Communication, COM (2000) 644, 11 October 2000.
19 This comprises two nominees from each member state and two from the Commission.
20 Art 128(4) EC.
21 Resolution of 29 May 1990 [1990] OJ C157/3.

Commission recommendation including a code of practice on sexual harassment,[22] which was approved by a Council declaration.[23] Neither recommendations nor codes of practice are legally binding, but they must be taken into account by national courts in certain circumstances – see para 10.53.

Treaty articles

10.12 The provisions of the EC Treaty do not all have the same legal effect. Some, such as article 13, provide a jurisdictional basis for legislative action. Others are intended to set out general principles as an aid to interpretation, and some articles (such as articles 141, 12 and 39) are directly effective. Directly effective treaty provisions have both vertical and horizontal direct effect, and so can be relied upon by an individual against both the state and private bodies – see para 10.14.

Directives

10.13 Directives, which are addressed to the member states, require them to introduce into their national legal systems, within a certain time limit, measures to implement the directives' aims. The way in which directives are implemented is a matter for the member states.

10.14 When the date for implementation has passed but a directive has not been implemented (either fully or at all) by the member state, an employee of a state body can rely directly on its provisions if they are sufficiently clear and precise (see para 10.70). A private sector employee cannot rely directly on a directive, but the ECJ has held that a failure by the state to implement a directive that was intended to confer rights on individuals may give rise to a right to damages against the state – see para 10.72.

10.15 Directives have been preferred by the EC over the more rigid regulations because they permit a degree of flexibility to member states as to how they implement EC law. More recently, that flexibility has been increased by the use of framework directives (such as the Council Directive implementing the framework agreement on

22 Commission Recommendation 92/131/EEC of 27 November 1991, on the protection of dignity of men and women at work.

23 Council Declaration of December 1991, on the implementation of the Commission Recommendation on the protection of dignity of men and women at work including a Code of Practice to combat sexual harassment [1992] C27/01.

parental leave – the PLD) which lay down certain core standards but leave the detail of the operation to the member states and/or their social partners. Further, the use of 'soft law measures' in preference to directives, etc, is in accordance with the principle of subsidiarity, with recourse to binding measures being a last resort.

EC institutions and procedures

10.16 The Council of Ministers is the main decision-making body of the EC. Directives, recommendations and codes may be made by the Council of Ministers. Under the Social chapter, which was negotiated at Maastricht and subsequently integrated into the EC Treaty, a new role was given to the European-level social partners. The social partners (unions and employers' organisations) must be consulted on community proposals, and may negotiate community level agreements. Following consultation with the Commission on a proposal, the social partners may deliver an opinion or a recommendation to the Commission which may then propose legislation on any matter falling within article 137 EC (formerly article 118). This provision facilitates the adoption of directives in certain fields including health and safety at work and sex equality.

References to the European Court of Justice

10.17 Article 234 EC (formerly article 177) enables the ECJ to give preliminary rulings on the proper interpretation of EC law. If a question as to the proper interpretation of the EC law is raised before any court or tribunal of a member state that body may, if it considers that a decision on the question is necessary to enable it to give judgment, request the ECJ to give a ruling. A reference may be made in the UK by an ET, the Employment Appeal Tribunal (EAT), or the Court of Appeal. If such question is raised before a court from which there is no appeal – generally the House of Lords, that court must make a reference to the ECJ unless the correct answer to the question of EC law raised is clear.[24]

24 Where there is no doubt on an issue it is described as 'acte clair' – see *R v Defence Secretary ex p Perkins* [1997] IRLR 297, paras 17–18, and *R v Stock Exchange ex p Else Limited* [1993] QB 545 .

Procedure on referral to the European Court of Justice

10.18 Where the question of a reference to the ECJ arises:

- Both parties can submit to the national court or tribunal draft questions for reference, the court or tribunal making the final decision on the form of the question or questions.
- The national court or tribunal sends its order of reference to the ECJ. This is likely to contain an interim judgment setting out the facts, identifying the issues of law which arise and explaining why a reference is appropriate. Attached to this will be the questions to which the national court seeks an answer from the ECJ.
- These questions are then translated and notified to the parties, the community institutions and all the member states. Other documents in the case may also be sent to the ECJ and will be held by the court, but not translated.
- The parties, the community institutions and the member states have two months from the time that the ECJ notifies them of the registration of the case in which to supply their written submissions to the court.
- There is then an oral hearing at which the parties, the Commission, and each interested member state can have 30 minutes to make oral submissions.
- The Advocate General gives his or her opinion and suggests answers to the questions raised by the national court. Although the Advocate General's opinion is not binding, it is influential and is often followed by the ECJ and referred to by UK courts.
- The ECJ then produces its judgment. The court is not bound to follow its previous decisions, but it usually does so.

10.19 Once the ECJ has handed down its judgment the national court or tribunal must, so far as it is possible to do so, apply the decision to the case. In *Webb v EMO Air Cargo (UK) Ltd*,[25] for example, the ECJ ruled that the dismissal of a pregnant worker was contrary to the ETD.[26] The House of Lords then ruled that the Sex Discrimination Act (SDA) 1975 had to be interpreted in accordance with that ruling.

25 Case 32/93 [1994] ECR I-3657; [1994] IRLR 482 and *(No 2)* [1995] 1 WLR 1454; [1995] IRLR 645 (see para 16.13).

26 Council Directive 76/207/EEC.

Costs and legal aid

10.20 Legal aid can be extended to cover a reference to the ECJ for a preliminary ruling. This will not usually be available if the reference is by an ET, legal aid generally being unavailable in the tribunals (although an applicant may request exceptional funding from the Lord Chancellor). It may, therefore, be advantageous if any reference is made by the EAT or a higher court, although this will result in further delay. Legal aid may also be available from the ECJ, which decides whether to grant legal aid on an application which should be made to the Registrar. There is no form for such an application; the applicant should write direct setting out his or her financial circumstances. The amount of legal aid granted will rarely exceed the costs of travel and hotels.

10.21 The ECJ can make an order for costs, but normally leaves this to the referring court. If the referral has come from an ET, the normal tribunal practice as to costs applies.

Substantive EC legislative provisions

Article 12 EC

10.22 Article 12 EC (formerly article 6) prohibits discrimination on grounds of nationality between citizens of member states:

> Within the scope to of the application of this Treaty, and without prejudice to any special provisions contained therein, any discrimination on grounds of nationality shall be prohibited.

10.23 Article 12 is directly effective.[27] Its application is illustrated by *Grzelczyk v Centre Public d'Aide Sociale d'Ottignies-Louvain-la-Neuve,*[28] in which the ECJ considered the situation of a national of another member state who was resident and studying in Belgium. The applicant applied for a Belgian social security benefit (a minimum subsistence allowance for students) to which he would have been eligible if he had been a Belgian national. He was refused the benefit because he did not have Belgian nationality. The ECJ ruled that entitlement to a non-contributory social security benefit could not be made conditional on nationality of the host member state.

27 Case 36/74 *Walrave and Koch v Association Union Cycliste Internationale* [1974] ECR 1405.

28 Case C-184/99 [2001] ECR I-06193; [2002] 1 CMLR 19.

Article 39 EC

10.24 Article 39 EC (formerly article 48) provides for freedom of movement for workers who are community nationals. It states that:

1. Freedom of movement for workers shall be secured within the Community.
2. Such freedom of movement shall entail the abolition of any discrimination based on nationality between workers of Member States as regards employment, remuneration and other conditions of work and employment.
3. It shall entail the right, subject to limitations justified on grounds of public policy, public security or public health:
   (a) to accept offers of employment actually made,
   (b) to move freely within the territory of member States for this purpose,
   (c) to stay in a Member State for the purpose of employment in accordance with the provisions governing the employment of nationals of that State laid down by law, regulation or administrative action,
   (d) to remain in the territory of a Member State after having been employed in that State, subject to conditions which shall be embodied in implementing regulations to be drawn up by the commission.
4. The provisions of this article shall not apply to employment in the public service.

In *Van Duyn v Home Office*[29] the ECJ ruled that 'article 48 of the Treaty has a direct effect in the legal orders of the Member States and confers on individuals rights which the national courts must protect'.

10.25 As most cases of discrimination against EC nationals are covered by the Race Relations Act (RRA) 1976, article 39 is rarely relied on in the UK. But it may be relied upon where nationality discrimination is not covered by the RRA 1976 – where, for example, there are limitations on the jurisdictional scope of that Act. This might be relevant to workers employed in the travel industry, in shipping, in sport or in transportation. In *Bossa v Nordstress Ltd*,[30] for example, the EAT applied article 39 to protect an Italian national who had a EU passport and was living in the UK. Mr Bossa had been refused a job working for Alitalia as an aircraft cabin crew member based in Italy because, 'as a foreign company providing a leasing service to Alitalia [his prospective employers] cannot employ Italian nationals'. An ET decided that it did

29 Case 41/74 [1974] ECR 1337; [1975] Ch 358.

30 [1998] IRLR 284.

not have jurisdiction to hear his complaint, RRA 1976 s8 excluding employment 'wholly or mainly outside Great Britain'. The EAT held that article 39 EC had direct effect and that it overrode RRA 1976 s8, enabling the ET to hear Mr Bossa's complaint.

10.26 Council Regulation 1612/68 enlarges on the scope of the protection offered by article 39 EC. This regulation prohibits discrimination against nationals of member states in recruitment as well as treatment at work. It also makes provision to enable EC nationals to bring their families to live with them.[31]

Article 141 EC

10.27 Article 141(1) EC (formerly article 119) establishes the principle of equal pay:

> 1. Each Member State shall ensure that the principle of equal pay for male and female workers for equal work or work of equal value[32] is applied.
> 2. For the purpose of this Article, 'pay' means the ordinary basic or minimum wage or salary or any other consideration, whether in cash or in kind, which the worker receives directly or indirectly, in respect of his employment, from his employer.
> 3. Equal pay without discrimination based on sex means:
>   (a) That pay for the same work at piece rate should be calculated on the basis of the same unit of measurement;
>   (b) That pay for work at time rate shall be the same for the same job.

Definition of 'pay'

10.28 Article 141(1) defines 'pay' broadly (see above). The ECJ has further broadened the definitions, holding that pay includes the following:

- immediate or future pay provided it is received directly or indirectly in respect of the worker's employment;[33]
- concessionary travel facilities granted provided by employers to workers;[34]
- payments made by virtue of a collective agreement;[35]

31 Art 10 EC; Reg 1612/68/EEC.

32 Added by the Treaty of Amsterdam.

33 Case 149/77 *Defrenne v SABENA (No 3)* [1978] ECR 1365.

34 Case 12/81 *Garland v British Railways Board* [1982] ECR 359, [1982] IRLR 111; Case 249/96 *Grant v South West Trains Limited* [1998] ECR I-0621, [1998] IRLR 206.

35 Case 33/89 *Kowalska v Freie und Handestadt Hamburg* [1990] ECR I-2591; [1990] IRLR 447.

- payments made under statutory obligation;[36]
- sick pay;[37]
- redundancy payments resulting from voluntary or compulsory redundancy;[38]
- unfair dismissal compensation;[39]
- occupational pensions, survivor's benefits and bridging pensions;[40]
- bonus payments made by employers;[41]
- inconvenient hours supplements;[42]
- ex gratia compensation in the form of paid leave or overtime pay for participation in training courses given by an employer to staff committee members.[43]

Equal pay for work of equal value

10.29 The principle of equal pay for work of equal value was originally found in article 1 EPD.[44] It is intended to redress the undervaluing of jobs done by women which are as demanding as other jobs done by men.[45] Article 141 EC now expressly recognises the concept of equal pay for work of equal value.

36 See, eg, Case 171/81 *Rinner-Kühn v FWW Spezial-Gebäudereinigung GmbH & Co KG* [1989] ECR 2743; [1989] IRLR 493.

37 *Rinner-Kühn*, ibid.

38 Case 262/88 *Barber v Guardian Royal Exchange Assurance Group* [1990] ECR I-1889; [1990] IRLR 240, ECJ, concerned compulsory redundancy. Case 19/81 *Burton v British Railways* [1982] ECR 555; [1982] IRLR 116, ECJ, concerned voluntary redundancy.

39 Case 167/97 *R v Employment Secretary ex p Seymour-Smith and Perez* [1999] ECR I-623, [1999] IRLR 253.

40 Case 170/84 *Bilka-Kaufhaus GmbH v Weber von Hartz* [1986] ECR 1607, [1986] IRLR 317 (supplementary pensions); Case 262/88 *Barber v Guardian Royal Exchange Assurance Group* [1990] ECR I-1889; [1990] IRLR 240 (contracted-out pensions); Case C-109/91 *Ten Oever v Stichting Bedrijfspensioenfonds voor het Glazenwassers-en Schoonmaakbedrijf* [1993] ECR I-4879, [1993] IRLR 601, ECJ (survivor's benefits); Case C-132/92 *Birds Eye Walls Ltd v Roberts* [1993] ECR I-5579, [1991] IRLR 29, ECJ (bridging pensions).

41 Case 33/97 *Lewen v Denda* [1999] ECR I-7243; [2000] IRLR 67.

42 Case 326/98 *Jämställdhetsombudsmannen v Orebro läns landsting* [2000] ECR I-2189; [2000] IRLR 421.

43 Case 360/90 *Arbeiterwohlfahrt der Stadt Berlin v Monika Bötel* [1992] ECR I-3589.

44 Council Directive 75/117/EEC, and is now in the amended art 141(1) EU.

45 See chapter 24.

Directives

10.30 The following directives are relevant to sex discrimination:

- Equal Pay Directive (EPD);
- Equal Treatment Directive (ETD);
- Social Security Directive (SSD);[46]
- Pregnant Workers Directive (PWD);[47]
- Occupational Social Security Directive (OSSD);[48]
- Parental Leave Directive (PLD);
- Burden of Proof Directive (BPD);
- Part-time Workers Directive (PtWD).[49]

10.31 The SSD is referred to at para 27.28. There are further directives on fixed term work[50] and race discrimination[51] and a general framework directive on equal treatment in employment (ED).[52] The last two of these herald an important new stage of development in EC law and are dealt with throughout the book.

Equal Pay Directive

10.32 It is important to note that the EPD contains provisions for the practical application of article 141. The ECJ held in *Jenkins v Kingsgate*[53] that the EPD does not alter the content or scope of the principle of equal pay as defined by article 141. So, for example, the EPD's reference to 'employees' cannot have the effect of narrowing the scope of article 141 (which applies to 'workers') to those employed under a contract of employment.

10.33 The EPD requires member states to:

- introduce into their national legal systems measures to enable all employees to pursue claims for equal pay by judicial process (article 2);

46 Council Directive 79/7/EEC.
47 Council Directive 92/85/EEC.
48 Council Directive 86/378/EEC.
49 Council Directive 97/81/EC as amended by Council Directive 98/23/EC, which extended it to the UK.
50 Council Directive 99/70/EC.
51 Council Directive 2000/43/EC.
52 Council Directive 2000/78/EC.
53 Case 96/80 [1981] ECR 911; [1981] IRLR 228.

- abolish all discrimination arising from laws, regulations or administrative provisions which are contrary to the principle of equal pay (article 3);[54]
- ensure that discriminatory provisions in collective agreements, wage scales, wage agreements or individual contracts of employment are declared null and void or amended (article 4).[55]

In addition, article 6 EPD requires that those who complain of pay-related sex discrimination are protected from victimisation and that member states ensure that effective means are available to ensure that the principle of equal pay is applied.

Equal Treatment Directive

10.34 The ETD prohibits any discrimination whatsoever on the ground of sex, either directly or indirectly, by reference in particular to marital or family status. It prohibits discrimination in:

- access to employment;
- access to training or vocational guidance;
- working conditions;
- promotion; and
- dismissal.

10.35 The ETD applies to collective agreements, individual contracts of employment and internal rules or rules governing independent occupations and professions. Member states are required to introduce into their legal systems measures to enable victims of discrimination to pursue their claims by judicial process.[56] Member states are also

54 See, eg, Case 171/81 *Rinner-Kühn v FWW Spezial-Gebäudereinigung GmbH & Co KG* [1989] ECR 2743; [1989] IRLR 493 (discriminatory law excluding part-time workers from sick pay) and Case 167/97 *R v Employment Secretary ex p Seymour-Smith and Perez* [1999] ECR I-623, [1999] IRLR 253 (complaint that service requirements in national legislation indirectly discriminated against women).

55 See, eg, Case 33/89 *Kowalska v Freie und Handestadt Hamburg* [1990] ECR I-2591; [1990] IRLR 447, in which the ECJ found that the exclusion of part-time workers from the payment of a severance grant on termination of their employment infringed art 141 unless it could be objectively justified, and Case 184/89 *Nimz v Freie und Handestadt Hamburg* [1991] ECR I-0297; [1991] IRLR 222 – see para 7.119. See para 26.11 for domestic implementation of this requirement.

56 Art 6 ETD – this provision could possibly be used to support an argument for legal aid in the ET in cases in which this is necessary to enable a victim to pursue his or her equal treatment claim.

required to introduce measures to protect employees against dismissal by their employer as a reaction to a complaint.[57]

Exceptions and exclusions

10.36 Social security is excluded from the scope of the ETD's equal treatment principle by article 1(2).[58] The directive also provides three further exceptions:

- where the sex of a worker constitutes a determining factor (article 2(2));
- in relation to provisions concerning the protection of women, particularly as regards pregnancy and maternity (article 2(3)); and
- in relation to 'positive action' programmes to promote equal opportunity for men and women, in particular by removing existing inequalities which affect women's opportunities (article 2(4)).

These exceptions and derogations must be interpreted strictly, and are subject to the principle of proportionality.[59] Any exception must also be regularly reviewed. Article 3(2)(c) ETD requires that provisions contrary to the principle of equal treatment concerning protection of women (whether in laws, regulations, administrative provisions or collective agreements) shall be revised when they are no longer required. See also article 5(2)(c) and article 9 which place the member states under a duty periodically to assess any exceptions under article 2(2).

The sex of the worker as a 'determining factor'

10.37 This exception has been implemented in the UK by the provision of an exception to the general prohibition on discrimination in the SDA 1975 where sex is a 'genuine occupational qualification' (see SDA 1975 s7 discussed at para 11.70). The SDA 1975 also provides for particular exceptions to the principle of sex equality, further discussed in

57 See Case 185/97 *Coote v Granada Hospitality Ltd* [1998] ECR I-5199; [1998] IRLR 656, discussed at para 11.44, in which the ECJ ruled that this provision enabled a complaint to be made post-employment when the former employee was victimised for bringing a complaint of discrimination against her former employer in that she was denied a reference.

58 The ECJ has consistently held that, as art 2(2) is a derogation from a fundamental right, it must be narrowly construed. See, eg, Case 116/94 *Meyers v Adjudication Officer* [1995] ECR I-2131; [1995] IRLR 498.

59 Case 22/84 *Johnston v Chief Constable of the RUC* [1986] ECR 1651; [1986] IRLR 263. See also Case 450/93 *Kalanke v Freie und Hansetadt Bremen* [1995] ECR I-3051; [1995] IRLR 660.

chapter 11. In *Commission v UK*[60] the ECJ accepted that certain kinds of employment in private households might fall within article 2(2) ETD, but ruled that a general exception relating to employment in a private household or in undertakings of more than five employees breached the ETD. The SDA 1975 was amended as a result. The ECJ has upheld exceptions limiting access by men to midwifery posts in view of the 'personal sensitivities' which may play 'an important role in relations between midwife and patient',[61] and has permitted the reservation of male positions in male prisons and female positions in female prisons.[62]

10.38 In *Johnston v Chief Constable of the RUC*[63] the ECJ held that certain policing activities in Northern Ireland might be such that the sex of the police officers constituted a 'determining factor' for the purposes of article 2(2) ETD. The court accepted that the policy which led to the non-renewal of the contracts of Ms Johnston and other women, and to the denial to them of firearms training, could be justified in light of the serious internal disturbances in Northern Ireland and the additional risk of assassination and dangers to public safety which could be created by the carrying of firearms by policewomen. Similarly, in *Sirdar v Secretary of State for Defence*[64] the ECJ upheld the exclusion of the applicant from a job as a chef in the Royal Marines as a result of a rule to the effect that every marine, irrespective of his specialisation, had to be capable of fighting in a commando unit (women being banned from combat posts in the UK army). The ECJ accepted that the ban on women in combat roles did not abuse the principle of proportionality and was capable of justification. In *Kreil* v *Germany*,[65] by contrast, the court ruled that German provisions excluding women from all military posts breached the ETD's requirement of equal treatment regardless of sex.

'The protection of women, particularly as regards pregnancy and maternity'

10.39 The scope of this exception to the ETD is discussed in chapter 5. The ECJ made it clear in *Hofmann v Barmer Ersatz Kasse*[66] that the purpose

60 Case 165/82 [1983] ECR 3431; [1982] IRLR 333.
61 Case 318/86 *Commission v France* [1988] ECR 3559.
62 Ibid.
63 Case 165/82 [1983] ECR 3431; [1982] IRLR 333.
64 Case 273/97 [1999] ECR I-7403; [2000] IRLR 4.
65 Case 285/98 *Kreil v Bundes Republik Deutscheland* [2000] ECR I-0069.
66 Case 184/83 [1984] ECR 3047.

of the exception is to protect both 'a woman's biological condition during pregnancy and thereafter until such time as her physiological and mental functions have returned to normal after childbirth' and 'to protect the special relationship between a woman and her child over the period which follows between pregnancy and childbirth, by preventing that relationship being disturbed by the multiple burdens which would result from the simultaneous pursuit of employment'. The ECJ ruled in *Hofmann* that the ETD did not require member states to grant leave to fathers, even in circumstances in which they took unpaid paternity leave to look after their newborn children whose mothers, having completed their initial obligatory period of maternity leave, returned to work. In *Habermann-Beltermann v Arbiterwohlfahrt*[67] the ECJ ruled that a German legislative provision banning the employment of pregnant women at night did not permit an employer to discriminate against a pregnant woman who applied for a job requiring night work. The court took into account the fact that the job in question was for an indefinite period while the prohibition took effect only for a limited period in relation to the total length of the contract.

10.40 In *Jiminez Melgar v Ayuntamiento De Los Barrios*,[67a] Mrs Jiminez Melgar was dismissed from her fixed term part-time contract 9 days after informing her employers that she was pregnant. She brought a claim complaining of a breach of the article 10 of the PWD which prohibits dismissal of a woman from the beginning of her pregnancy to the end of her maternity leave save in exceptional circumstances not connected with their pregnancy and permitted under national legislation. The ECJ held that article 10 had direct effect and the prohibition on dismissal applies to both fixed-term employment contracts and contracts for an indefinite period. If a fixed term contract was not renewed that would not be treated as dismissal and so would not be a breach of article 10, but if based on the workers pregnancy would be direct discrimination contrary to the ETD.

'Positive action'

10.41 Article 2(4) ETD provides that the directive's prohibition on discrimination shall be 'without prejudice to measures which promote equal opportunity for men and women, in particular by removing existing inequalities which affect women's opportunities'. A distinction has been drawn by the ECJ in this context between 'positive action' on the

67 Case 421/92 [1994] ECR I-1657; [1994] IRLR 364.

67a Case 438/99 [2001] IRLR 848.

one hand, and 'positive discrimination' on the other. 'Positive action' falls short of contravening the principle of equal treatment at the point of selection for posts or promotion. It is action taken to identify and remedy practices which allow inequalities to continue in the workplace. Measures such as opening up opportunities for part-time workers, arranging working hours so as to be attractive to women workers, the provision of career breaks, etc, will qualify as 'positive action'. Reviewing criteria for selection to posts to exclude unnecessary qualifications which might exclude women and ensuring women have equal access to training opportunities would also be part of a positive action programme. Chapter 5 deals with this issue in greater detail. 'Positive discrimination' goes further by setting quotas for recruitment or promotion and may discriminate in favour of women at the point of selection or to meet these targets.

10.42 The EC has favoured positive action in the Council's Recommendation on the promotion of positive action for women, which suggests that member states adopt a positive action policy 'designed to eliminate existing inequalities affecting women and working life and to promote a better balance between the sexes in employment'.[68] The recommendation lists steps that member states might take including encouraging women to participate in vocational and continuous training, encouraging women candidates in making applications, adapting working conditions and adjusting working time. In 1998, the Commission published a guide to positive action,[69] but it appears that little further action has been taken.

10.43 There have been a number of decisions by the ECJ as to the circumstances in which discrimination is permitted by article 2(4) ETD. In *Kalanke v Freie und Hansetadt Bremen*[70] the (male) applicant complained about a law which provided that, 'in a case of an assignment to a position in a higher pay, remuneration and salary bracket, women who have the same qualifications as men applying for the same post are to be given priority if they are under represented'. Under-representation was defined as existing where women 'do not make up at least half of the staff in the individual pay, remuneration and salary bracket in the relevant personnel group within the department. This also applies to the function levels provided for in the organisation chart.'

68 Recommendation A4/635/EEC [1984] OJ L331/34.

69 *Positive Action and Equal Opportunities in Employment. A Guide* (European Commission 1988) CB-48-87-525-EN-C.

70 Case 450/93 [1995] ECR I-3051; [1995] IRLR 660.

10.44 When Mr Kalanke applied for the post of section manager, his employers found him equally well qualified as a female candidate but gave her preference as required by the Bremen laws. The ECJ held that national measures relating to access which gave a specific advantage to women to improve their ability to compete on the labour market and pursue a career on equal footing to men were permitted by article 2(4). However, rules which guaranteed women absolute and unconditional priority for appointment or promotion went beyond the limits of the exception in article 2(4). As the law at issue did not have an individual hardship rule which limited positive discrimination if the result was 'unbearable hardship' to the male competitor, it did not fall within article 2(4) ETD.

10.45 In *Marschall v Land Nordrheinwestfalen*[71] a promotion procedure similar to that in *Kalanke* had a saving clause which had the effect that, where there were qualified candidates for a position in which fewer women than men were employed, a woman would not be given preference if reasons specific to the male candidate tilted the balance in his favour. The ECJ ruled that such selection criteria did not breach the ETD provided that, in each individual case, the rule provided for an objective assessment of the candidates which took account of all the criteria specific to the candidate and which permitted the priority accorded to female candidates to be overridden where one or more of those criteria (not themselves discriminatory) tilted the balance in favour of a male candidate.

10.46 In *Badeck v Hessischer Ministerprasident*[72] the ECJ accepted very wide-ranging positive action schemes as consistent with article 2(4) ETD. These included:

- a provision very similar to that upheld in *Marschall*;
- binding targets for appointment to certain academic positions of a proportion of women equal to that of women graduates in the discipline;
- the reservation to women of at least 50 per cent of public training places in trained occupations in which women were under-represented, unless the state had a monopoly of training or insufficient applications were received from women; and
- a guarantee that, in sectors in which women were under-represented, all those who satisfied the requirements set down for a public sector position would be called to interview.

71 Case 409/95 [1997] ECR I-6363; [1988] IRLR 39.

72 Case 158/97 [2000] ECR I-1875; [2000] IRLR 432.

10.47 In *Abrahamsson v Fogelqvist*,[73] by contrast, the ECJ ruled that a Swedish rule which provided that a person of the under-represented sex who possessed sufficient qualifications for a post must be appointed in preference to a better qualified person of the other sex, 'unless the difference between the applicants' qualifications was so great that positive discrimination would be contrary to the requirement of objectivity in the recruitment process', breached article 2(4) ETD. The ECJ ruled that the 'scope and effect' of the savings clause:

> ... cannot be precisely determined, with the result that the selection of a candidate from among those who are sufficiently qualified is ultimately based on the mere fact of belonging to the under-represented sex, and that this is so even if the merits of the candidate so selected are inferior to those of a candidate of the opposite sex. Moreover, candidatures are not subjected to an objective assessment taking account of the specific personal situations of all the candidates.

The court also went on to consider whether the rule was justified under article 141(4) EC, which permits member states to maintain or adopt measures providing for specific advantages which are intended to prevent or compensate for disadvantages in professional careers with the object of ensuring full equality between men and women in professional lives. The court held that that exception did not permit this selection method as it was disproportionate to the aim pursued.

10.48 In *Lommers v Minister van Landbouw, Natuurbeheer en* Visserij,[73a] a male civil servant complained that nursery places were made available only to female employees except in cases of emergencies. He applied for a place but his request was rejected. The ECJ held that provision of a limited number of nursery places for female staff was permissible in principle under article 2(4) ETD where the scheme has been set up to tackle extensive under representation of women and where there was insufficiency of proper affordable childcare facilities, so long as male employees who take care of children themselves were allowed access to the scheme on the same conditions as female staff.

73 Case 407/98 [2000] ECR I-5539; [2000] IRLR 732.
73a Case 476/99 [2002] IRLR 430.

The concept of 'discrimination' under EC law

Direct discrimination

10.49 Establishing direct discrimination on grounds of sex normally requires proof that the treatment complained of is less favourable than that afforded to someone of the opposite sex. The comparison may be with an actual comparator or, in the absence of an identified comparator, proof of how a person of the opposite sex would be treated in similar circumstances may suffice to establish direct discrimination. Such proof may be easy if the discrimination concerned arises from legislation or a rule or regulation that directly discriminates – in such circumstances an actual comparator is unlikely to be necessary.[74] But the ECJ has refused to accept that pay discrimination against an individual woman may be proven by reference to a hypothetical comparator.[75] The question whether and in what circumstances pay-related sex discrimination may be established without reference to an actual comparator has been referred to the ECJ by the Court of Appeal in *Allonby v Accrington & Rossendale College*,[76] and is further considered at para 22.41 below.

10.50 In pregnancy claims, by contrast, the ECJ has held that the ETD requires no male comparator.[77] According to the court:

> Whether a refusal to employ results in direct discrimination on grounds of sex depends on whether the most important reason for the refusal is a reason which applies without distinction to employees of both sexes or whether it applies exclusively to one sex. As employment can only be refused because of pregnancy to women, such a refusal is direct discrimination on grounds of sex.

10.51 Difficulties arise in relation to equal pay claims made during maternity leave, in which the need for a comparator has been fatal to establishing a breach of article 141. In *Gillespie v Northern Health & Social Services Board*,[78] for example, the ECJ held that the applicants were not entitled to equal pay to those not on maternity leave because:

> Although the benefit paid by an employer to a woman on maternity leave constitutes 'pay' within the meaning of article [141 EC and the

74 See, eg, Case 271/91 *Marshall v Southampton and South-West Hampshire Area Health Authority (No 2)* [1993] ECR 1-4367; [1993] IRLR 445.

75 Case 129/79 *Macarthys v Smith* [1980] ECR 1275; [1980] IRLR 210.

76 [2001] IRLR 364.

77 Case 177/88 *Dekker v Stichting Vormingscentrum Voor Jonge Volwassen (VJV-Centrum) Plus* [1990] ECR I-3941; [1991] IRLR 27.

78 Case 342/93 [1996] ECR I-492; [1996] IRLR 214.

> EPD], discrimination involves the application of different rules to comparable situations or the application of the same rule to different situations.[79] Therefore, neither [141 EC nor the EPD] required that women should continue to receive full pay during maternity leave.

According to the ECJ in *Gillespie*, the applicants were entitled to the benefit of an increase in pay awarded in respect of a period prior to their maternity leave that affected their maternity pay, since to deny them the increase discriminated against them as 'workers'. This issue is further explored at para 18.36.

Sexual harassment

10.52 In 1987 a European Commission report on sexual harassment found that most member states provided no effective legal remedy against it.[80] Although it was proposed that a directive should be passed to remedy this situation, the Council of Ministers instead passed a non-legally binding resolution on the protection of dignity of men and women at work.[81] This was followed by a Commission recommendation and a code of conduct[82] which was approved by a Council declaration.

10.53 Neither the recommendation nor the code are legally binding. But in *Grimaldi v Fonds des Maladies Professionnelles*[83] the ECJ held that national courts are bound to take recommendations into account in order to decide disputes before them – in particular where they clarify the interpretation of national rules adopted in order to implement them or when they are designed to supplement binding community measures, such as the ETD. The code and recommendation were taken into account by the EAT in *Wadman v Carpenter Farrer Partnership*.[84]

79 The ECJ set out its reasoning on discrimination as follows: 'it is well-settled that discrimination involves the application of different rules to comparable situations or the application of the same rule to different situations ... The present case is concerned with women taking maternity leave provided for by national legislation. They are in a special position which requires them to be afforded special protection, but which is not comparable either with that of a man or with that of a woman actually at work.'

80 M. Rubenstein, *The Dignity of Women at Work: A report on the problems of sexual harassment in the Member States of the European Communities* (OPEC, Luxembourg, October 1997).

81 Resolution of 29 May 1990 [1990] OJ C157/3.

82 Commission Recommendation 92/131/EEC of 27 November 1991, on the protection of dignity of men and women at work..

83 Case 32/88 [1989] ECR 4407; [1990] IRLR 400.

84 [1993] IRLR 374.

10.54 The definition of sexual harassment contained in the Council resolution is:

> Conduct of a sexual nature, or other conduct based on sex affecting the dignity of women and men at work, including conduct of superiors and colleagues.

Such conduct is deemed to constitute an:

> intolerable violation of dignity of workers or trainees and is unacceptable if:
> – It is unwanted, unreasonable and offensive to the recipient;
> – The person's rejection of or submission to such is used as a basis for a decision which affects access to vocational training, access to employment, promotion, salary or any other employment decision; and/or
> – It creates an intimidating, hostile, or humiliating working environment for the recipient.

10.55 The Commission's code of conduct suggests that conduct constituting sexual harassment may take the form of physical conduct of a sexual nature, ranging from unnecessary touching to assault, verbal conduct of a sexual nature and including unwelcome sexual advances, suggestive remarks and innuendos and non-verbal conduct of a sexual nature, including the display of pornographic or sexually explicit pictures, leering, whistling, or making a sexually suggestive gesture, sex based conduct, such as sex-based comments about appearance or dress.

10.56 Conduct becomes sexual harassment if it is unwanted by the recipient. Both the Council resolution and Commission recommendation make it clear that sexual harassment 'may be, in certain circumstances, contrary to the principle of equal treatment within the meanings of Articles 3, 4 and 5' of the ETD. The code recommends that employers, in both the public and private sectors, should issue policy statements, preferably linked to broader policies of promoting equal opportunities, which expressly state that all employees have a right to be treated with dignity, that sexual harassment will not be permitted and that all employees have a right to complain about any sexual harassment. The policy statement should make clear that:

- employees' complaints will be taken seriously;
- employees' complaints will be dealt with expeditiously; and
- employees will not suffer victimisation of retaliation as a result of making a complaint.

The code further suggests that employers' policy statements should define inappropriate behaviour and should state that appropriate disciplinary measures will be taken against harassers. It emphasises the role of trade unions in encouraging employers to develop policies on sexual harassment, advising their members of their rights not to be sexually harassed, and supporting members when complaints arise.

Indirect discrimination

10.57 The ETD expressly covers indirect discrimination, article 2(1) providing that 'the principle of equal treatment' means 'there shall be no discrimination whatsoever on grounds of sex either directly or indirectly by reference in particular to marital or family status'. Article 141 EC does not expressly cover indirect discrimination, but the ECJ has frequently stated that the principle of equal pay prohibits unjustified indirect discrimination.[85]

10.58 Indirect discrimination was defined by EC legislation for the first time by the BPD (see further para 10.64).[86] The BPD defined indirect discrimination more widely than the SDA 1975 until it was amended in 2001,[87] article 2(2) providing that:

> Indirect discrimination shall still exist where an apparently neutral provision, criterion or practice disadvantages a substantially higher proportion of the members of one sex unless that provision, criterion or practice is appropriate and necessary and can be justified by objective factors unrelated to sex.

10.59 The definition of indirect discrimination adopted by the BPD was broadly in accordance with decisions of the ECJ in cases such as *Bilka-Kaufhaus*[88] in which the court held that:

> A policy which applies independently of a worker's sex but in fact affects more women than men will not constitute an infringement of

85 See Case 170/84 *Bilka-Kaufhaus GmbH v Weber von Hartz* [1986] ECR 1607, [1986] IRLR 317; Case 33/89 *Kowalska v Freie und Handestadt Hamburg* [1990] ECR I-2591; [1990] IRLR 447. In respect of legislation, see Case 171/81 *Rinner-Kühn v FWW Spezial-Gebäudereinigung GmbH & Co KG* [1989] ECR 2743; [1989] IRLR 493 and Case 167/97 *R v Employment Secretary ex p Seymour-Smith and Perez* [1999] ECR I-623, [1999] IRLR 253.

86 Council Directive 97/80/EEC as amended.

87 SDA 1975 s1(1)(b) only referred to the application of 'a requirement or condition'. The wider definition in the BPD has now been added by the implementing regulations (Sex Discrimination (Indirect Discrimination and Burden of Proof) Regulations 2001 SI No 2660).

88 Case 170/84 *Bilka-Kaufhaus GmbH v Weber von Hartz* [1986] ECR 1607, [1986] IRLR 317.

> article [141] if the employer shows that the policy is objectively justified on economic grounds. This requires that the findings by the national Court that the measures chosen by the employer correspond to a real need on the part of the undertaking, are appropriate with a view to achieving the objectives pursued and are necessary to that end.

10.60 In the context of an equal pay claim under article 141 the ECJ has held that a prima facie case of sex discrimination arises where valid statistics disclose an appreciable difference in pay between two jobs or equal value, one of which is carried out almost exclusively by women and the other predominantly by men.[89] It is for the national court to assess whether these statistics appear to be significant and they cover enough individuals and do not illustrate purely fortuitous or short-term phenomena. Further, it appears from later decisions that the reference in *Enderby v Frenchay Health Authority and Secretary of State for Health*[90] to the disadvantaged group being comprised *almost exclusively* of women, and the advantaged group *predominantly* of men, was referring to the facts of the case rather than proposing a test of disparate impact. In *Jämställdhetsombudsmannen v Orebro läns landsting*[91] the ECJ stated that the national courts must verify whether there is a substantially higher proportion of women than men in the disadvantaged group. If so, a breach of article 141 will be established unless the employer can justify the pay difference by showing that there are objective reasons for the difference in pay that are unrelated to any discrimination on the grounds of sex.

10.61 The difference between the two tests is significant. Under the test set by *Enderby*, disparate impact is not established without a very high degree of sex segregation between the disadvantaged group and the advantaged group. Under the *Jämställdhetsombudsmannen* approach, by contrast, disparate impact could be established as between two groups each predominantly of the same gender, provided that the relatively disadvantaged group has a substantially higher proportion of women than the advantaged group.

10.62 The test for establishing disparate impact has been made even less demanding in *R v Employment Secretary ex p Seymour-Smith and Perez*.[92] There the issue for the ECJ was whether the qualification

89 Case 127/92 *Enderby v Frenchay Health Authority and Secretary of State for Health* [1993] ECR I-5535; [1993] IRLR 591.

90 Ibid.

91 Case 326/98 [2000] ECR I-2189; [2000] IRLR 421.

92 Case 167/97 [1999] ECR I-623; [1999] IRLR 253; see also para 7.83 above.

period required to bring an unfair dismissal complaint (which was at the time two years) had a disparate adverse impact on women so as to amount to indirect discrimination contrary to article 141. The court held that, in order to determine if disparate impact had been established, the national court had to verify whether the statistics indicated that a considerably smaller percentage of women than men was able to satisfy the disputed requirement or condition. That would be evidence of apparent sex discrimination. That could also be the case if the statistical evidence revealed a lesser but persistent and relatively constant disparity, over a long period of time, between the proportions of men and women satisfying the requirement. As was pointed out when the case returned to the House of Lords, the approach adopted by the ECJ in *Seymour-Smith* was similar to that provided for by SDA 1975 s1(1)(b).

10.63 A further refinement was added in the case of *Jørgensen v Foreningen Af Speciallæger & Sygesikringens Forhandlingsudvalg*,[93] which concerned a complaint that a collective agreement indirectly discriminated on grounds of sex in respect of various pay-related criteria. The ECJ held that the ETD required a separate assessment to be made of each of the key conditions laid down in the contested provisions, in so far as they amounted to specific measures based on their own criteria of application and affected a significant number of persons belonging to a defined category. The court ruled that, if all that was required was an overall assessment of all the elements that might be involved in the scheme or a set of provisions, it would not allow an effective review of the application of equal treatment and might not comply with the rules governing the burden of proof in matters relating to indirect discrimination on grounds of sex.

Burden of Proof Directive

10.64 The BPD provides, by article 4, that member states shall take such measures as are necessary:

> To ensure that, when persons who consider themselves wrong because the principle of equal treatment has not been applied to them establish, before a Court or other competent authority, facts from which it may be presumed that there has been direct or indirect

93 Case 226/98 [2000] ECR I-2447; [2000] IRLR 726.

94 Case 109/88 *Handels Og Kontorfunktionacrernes Forbund I Danmark v Dansk Arbejdsgiverforening (acting for Danfoss)* [1989] ECR I-3199; [1989] IRLR 532.

discrimination, it shall be for the Respondent to prove that there has been no breach of principle of equal treatment.

The BPD permits member states to introduce rules of evidence that are more favourable to applicants. At para 7.10 we consider how the directive has been implemented in domestic law. Even prior to the adoption of the BPD, the ECJ had held that the burden of proof may shift to the employer in certain circumstances to ensure the effective implementation of the principle of equality. In *Danfoss*,[94] for example, the employer's pay structure provided the same basic wage to all employees but paid additional individual supplements on the basis of mobility, training and seniority. The average wage paid to men was 6.86 per cent higher than that paid to women. The system lacked transparency in that individual employees were not able to identify which elements of their pay related to the various criteria. The ECJ ruled that:

> Where an undertaking applies a pay system which is characterised by a total lack of transparency, the burden of proof is on the employer to show that his pay practice is not discriminatory where a female worker establishes, by comparison with a relatively large number of employees, that the average pay of female workers is lower than that of male workers.

10.65 In *Enderby*[95] the ECJ held that there was a prima facie case of sex discrimination where valid statistics disclosed an appreciable difference in pay between two jobs of equal value, one of which was carried out almost exclusively by women (in this case speech therapists) and the other predominantly by men (in this case pharmacists). In those circumstances it was for the national court to assess whether the statistics appeared to be significant in that they cover enough individuals and do not illustrate purely fortuitous or short term phenomena.

The effect of EC law in the UK

10.66 European Communities Act 1972 s2 provides for general implementation of treaties so that any provision of the EC Treaty which has direct effect is, without any further enactment within the UK, to be given legal effect by the courts. While the contents of directives are addressed to

95 Case 127/92 *Enderby v Frenchay Health Authority and Secretary of State for Health* [1993] ECR I-5535; [1993] IRLR 591.

96 Case 14/83 *Von Colson and Kamann v Land Nordrhein-Westfalen* [1984] ECR 1891.

member states, and require states to provide for domestic implementation to give effect to their provisions, certain parts of directives have direct vertical effect so that they also are binding on the state and public bodies without any domestic implementation.

Interpretative obligations

10.67 In the *Von Colson*[96] and *Marleasing*[97] cases the ECJ ruled that the national courts must interpret national law, as far as is possible, in conformity with the requirements of community law – this subject to the general principles of law, especially the principles of legal certainty and non-retroactivity. In *Webb v EMO*[98] the House of Lords was faced with the question as to whether the SDA 1975 could be interpreted to be consistent with the ETD following a ruling of the ECJ that it was a breach of the ETD to refuse to employ a woman on grounds of pregnancy, and that proof of such sex discrimination did not require a male comparator. The difficulty lay with SDA 1975 s5(3) (see also para 3.14), which required a male comparator in the same or similar relevant circumstances. The House of Lords ruled, per Lord Keith, that:

> ... in a case where a woman is engaged for an indefinite period, the fact that the reason why she will be temporarily unavailable for work at a time when to her knowledge her services will be particularly required is pregnancy is a circumstance relevant to her case, being a circumstance which could not be present in the case of the hypothetical man.

Direct effect

10.68 The ECJ ruled, in *Defrenne (No 2)*,[99] that article 141 was 'directly applicable' and could thus give rise to individual rights that the court must protect. The court further held that the prohibition of discrimination applies 'not only to the actions of public authorities, but also extends to all agreements which are intended to regulate paid labour collectively as well as contracts between individuals'. As a result of this ruling it is clear that article 141 has both vertical and horizontal direct effect.

10.69 In *Defrenne (No 2)* the ECJ ruled that article 141 was not directly

97 *Marleasing SA v LA Comercial Internacional de Alimentacion* [1990] ECR I-4135.

98 Case 32/93 [1994] ECR I-3657; [1994] IRLR 482.

99 Case 43/75 [1976] ECR 455.

effective in the context of 'indirect or disguised discrimination' which required the elaboration by community and national legislative bodies of criteria of assessment. But in *Bilka-Kaufhaus*[100] the court ruled that individuals could rely on article 141 to secure the elimination of indirect discrimination. In practice, the court has found article 141 to be directly effective in a wide range of cases including occupational pensions and survivor's benefits.[101] How far the provision is directly effective to permit women claiming equal pay with men employed by different employers is an issue awaiting clarification when the court rules on two references from the UK.[102]

10.70 The ECJ has ruled that provisions of directives (including the ETD and article 10 PWD) which are unconditional and sufficiently precise, but which have not been fully implemented by the member state, may have vertical direct effect.[103] In such circumstances an individual may rely on the provisions directly against a member state or an 'emanation of the state' in the national courts. Directives have no direct effect as against private individuals. The justification for direct vertical effect is that member states should not be able to take advantage of their own failure to comply with community law to deny rights to individuals. So when Helen Marshall was dismissed as a result of a discriminatory retirement age, she was able to rely on the principle of equal treatment in article 2(1) ETD which provided for equal treatment in respect of dismissal. As her employer was a health authority (a state body), the directive had direct effect.[104] No such argument applies to permit the enforcement of directives against private individuals.

Emanations of the state

10.71 The ECJ has held that state bodies against which directives may be directly enforced include not only central government but also other public authorities, and organisations and bodies that are subject to

100 Case 170/84 *Bilka-Kaufhaus GmbH v Weber von Hartz* [1986] ECR 1607, [1986] IRLR 317

101 See Case 262/88 *Barber v Guardian Royal Exchange Assurance Group* [1990] ECR I-1889; [1990] IRLR 240.

102 See *Allonby v Accrington & Rossendale College* [2001] IRLR 364; *Lawrence v Regent Office Care Ltd* [2000] IRLR 608; and *South Ayrshire Council v Morton* [2002] IRLR 265.

103 Case 152/84 *Marshall v Southampton and South West Hampshire Area Health Authority (Teaching)* [1986] ECR 723; [1986] IRLR 140 and *Jiminez Melgar v Ayuntamiento De Los Barrios* Case 438/99 [2001] IRLR 848, see para 10.40 above.

104 Ibid.

the authority and control of the state or have special powers beyond those which result to the normal rules applicable in relations between individuals.[105] This ruling (in *Foster v British Gas plc*[106]) permitted a British employee of British Gas (pre-privatisation) to rely directly on article 5(1) ETD to claim damages for a discriminatory dismissal. The ECJ ruled that:

> The sole questions under the test laid down by the European Court are whether the employer, pursuant to a measures adopted by the State provides a public service under the control of the State and exercises special powers. That the employer engages in commercial activities, does not perform any of the traditional functions of the State and is not the agent of the State is not relevant to this test.

10.72 Those who work for private employers cannot rely on the direct effect of a directive against their employers in the national courts. They may, nevertheless, have a remedy for breach of EC law. Such a remedy does not depend only upon the interpretive obligations discussed at para 10.67. In *Francovich & Bonifaci v Italy*[107] the ECJ held that community law requires member states to make good any damage caused to individuals by the states' failure adequately to transpose a directive. This ruling has been held to apply only to provisions of a directive which have direct effect.· The necessary conditions for a *Francovich* claim are that:

- the legal provision infringed was intended to confer rights on individuals;
- the breach was sufficiently serious; and
- there was a direct causal link between the breach of the obligation resting on the state and the damage suffered by the injured parties.[108]

Challenging UK law through the European Commission

10.73 The European Commission may, by virtue of article 226 EC, take action against a member state if it considers that the state has not fulfilled its obligations under the treaty. Even if a directive or part of it has no direct effect in UK courts, an individual can request the European Commission to take proceedings against the government for failing

105 See Case 188/89 *Foster v British Gas plc* [1990] ECR I-3313; [1990] IRLR 353.
106 Ibid.
107 Cases 6 and 9/90 [1991] ECR I-5357; [1995] ICR 722.

to implement it in domestic legislation. Such complaints can be started by letter to the Commissioner for Social Affairs. If the Commission considers the complaint to be valid it will ask the member state to submit its observations. Initially the Commission will attempt to reach a settlement. If this is not possible the Commission may deliver a reasoned opinion to the state setting out what measures the state should take. If the infringement does not cease the Commission may bring an action in the ECJ.

10.74 Commission action under article 226 has led to some very important changes to UK legislation. These changes have included the amendment of the Equal Pay Act (EqPA) 1970 to allow claims in respect of equal pay for equal value claims following the decision in *Commission v UK*.[109]

Procedural aspects of EC law

Judicial remedies

10.75 It is an established principle of community law that member states must ensure the legal protection which individuals are entitled to from the direct effect of community law. Unless EC law covers the matter, it is for the domestic legal system of each member state to designate the courts having jurisdiction and to lay down detailed procedural rules governing actions for safeguarding rights of the individual. This is sometimes known as the principle of procedural autonomy. Those rules must not be less favourable than those governing similar domestic actions nor make it virtually impossible or excessively difficult to exercise the rights conferred by community law. This latter condition is called the principle of effective judicial protection.[110]

Time limits

10.76 Normally the relevant domestic time limits will apply to claims based on EC law. In *Emmott v Minister for Social Welfare*[111] the ECJ held that,

108 Case 46/93 *Brasserie du Pecheur SA v Germany (No 3)* [1996] ECR I-1029; [1996] 2 WLR 506 and Case C-92/93 *R v HM Treasury ex p British Telecommunications* [1996] ECR I-1631; [1996] QB 615.

109 Case 61/81 [1982] ECR 2601; [1982] ICR 578.

110 See Case 33/76 *Rewe v Landwirtschaftskammer Saarland* [1976] ECR 1989.

111 Case 208/90 [1991] ECR I-4269; [1991] IRLR 387.

if a directive has not been properly implemented by a member state, time does not start to run. However, in subsequent cases the principle in *Emmott* was restricted to national procedural rules which fixed time limits for bringing cases and not rules as to the period of damages.[112]

10.77 Because article 141 EC is directly effective and directly enforceable in the UK, relevant domestic time limits apply. The non-application of the *Emmott* principle to article 141 claims is demonstrated by the decision of the Court of Appeal in *Biggs v Somerset CC.*[113] The applicant, a part-time teacher, had worked for 14 hours a week prior to her dismissal in 1976. She was unable to bring a claim for unfair dismissal under UK legislation at the time of her dismissal, because she had not worked for sufficient hours per week to qualify for unfair dismissal protection. After the decision in *R v Employment Secretary ex p Equal Opportunities Commission (EOC)*,[114] in which the House of Lords held that hours qualifications for the accrual of continuous service discriminated indirectly against women, Ms Biggs tried to bring an unfair dismissal claim against her former employers under article 141. Her claim was rejected as being out of time. The Court of Appeal held that it was 'reasonably practicable' for her in 1976 to have brought a case similar to that taken by the EOC 14 years later. Applying the statutory provisions for extending time applicable to unfair dismissal claims, the Court of Appeal held that her complaint was not presented within a reasonable period after the expiry of the time limit.[115]

10.78 The approach of the Court of Appeal in *Biggs* may be contrasted with that of the EAT in *BCC v Keeble*[116] in which that court upheld the decision of an ET that it was just and equitable to extend time for a sex discrimination claim related to discriminatory retirement ages where the delay was caused because it was not understood that domestic legislation could be challenged as being contrary to article 141 (then 119) until the decision of the ECJ in *Barber.*[117] *Biggs* was distinguished in that, *Keeble* being a sex discrimination claim, the provisions governing the extension of time were more generous (the test being whether it was just and equitable to extend time, rather than whether

112 Case 338/91 *Steenhorst-Neerings* [1993] ECR I-5475 and Case 410/92 *Johnson (No 2) v Chief Adjudication Officer* [1994] ECR I-5483; [1995] IRLR 157.

113 [1996] IRLR 203.

114 [1995] 1 AC 1.

115 Now found in Employment Rights Act 1996 s111.

116 [1997] IRLR 337.

117 Case 262/88 *Barber v Guardian Royal Exchange Assurance Group* [1990] ECR I-1889; [1990] IRLR 240.

it had been reasonably practicable for the applicant to bring her claim in time).[118] The more generous test enabled the ET to take into account the fact that Ms Keeble's union representative had not been aware that she had a claim until he learnt of the *Barber* case in 1990.

Limits on back-dating of awards

10.79 A further issue has arisen in respect of the claims brought after the expiry of national time limits, for arrears of pay which pre-date national limits on backdating of claims. The applicants in the *Magorrian* case began employment as full-time workers and then moved to part-time work when they had children.[119] When they retired they were not entitled to the more favourable pension benefits available to full-time workers. They brought proceedings under article 141 in 1992. The ECJ ruled that the domestic provisions limiting awards of arrears of pay to a period no earlier than two years before the date on which the proceedings were instituted rendered any action by individuals relying on community law impossible in practice in the context of a claim for recognition of entitlement to full membership and occupational pension schemes (see also *Preston v Wolverhampton Healthcare NHS Trust*[120]).

10.80 In *Levez v T H Jennings (Harlow Pools)*,[121] too, the ECJ ruled that the EqPA 1970's two-year backstop on equal pay awards could not be relied upon if the delay in bringing the claim was attributable to the fact that the employer deliberately misrepresented to the employee the level of remuneration received by the male comparators. When this case was remitted to the UK, the EAT ruled that the prohibition on the two-year limit was of general application.[122] The EAT there held that the six-year limit in the Limitation Act 1980 applied to all claims under the EqPA 1970.

10.81 It is primarily a matter for the member states whether the enforcement of EC law is by way of criminal or civil proceedings, and what form the sanctions or remedies take. But the ECJ has insisted that any sanction provided for by the national system must be such as

118 SDA 1975 s76(5). See further chapter 32.

119 Case 246/96 *Magorrian and Cunningham v Eastern Health and Social Services Board and Department of Health and Social Services* [1997] ECR I-7153; [1998] IRLR 86.

120 Case 78/98 [2000] ECR I-3201; [2000] IRLR 506.

121 Case 326/96 [1998] ECR 1-7835; [1999] IRLR 36.

122 [1999] IRLR 764.

to guarantee effective judicial protection of EC rights. It must also have a real deterrent effect on the employer.[123] It follows that, if a member state chooses to provide an award of compensation as remedy for discrimination, that compensation must be adequate in relation to the damage sustained.

10.82 *Von Colson* involved a challenge to the limitation of compensation in respect of discrimination to a purely nominal amount, namely the reimbursement of travelling expenses.[124] The ECJ held that this would not satisfy article 6 EPD, which requires member states to ensure that the principle of equal pay is applied so that effective means are available to ensure that the principle is observed. In *Marshall v Southampton and South West Hampshire Area Health Authority (Teaching) (No 2)*,[125] the imposition of an upper limit on the amount of compensation received and the exclusion of an award of interest was found to be contrary to article 6 ETD. This position led to the lifting of the limit on compensation in domestic law and regulations providing for payment of interest.

10.83 In *Coote v Granada Hospitality Ltd*[126] the ECJ held that article 6 ETD required member states to ensure judicial protection for workers whose employer, after the employment relationship has ended, refused to provide references as a reaction to legal proceedings brought to enforce compliance with the principle of equal treatment. In consequence, when the case was remitted to the EAT, that court held it was possible to construe the SDA 1975 so as to enable Miss Coote to make a victimisation complaint in relation to events that had occurred after the employment relationship had terminated.

Recent EC developments

Race Directive

10.84 The RD regulates discrimination on grounds of racial or ethnic origin in a wide number of areas from employment to social protection and access to goods and services. The directive operates as an instruction

123 Case 14/83 *Von Colson and Kamann v Land Nordrhein-Westfalen* [1984] ECR 1891.

124 Ibid.

125 Case 271/91 [1993] ECR 1-4367; [1993] IRLR 445.

126 Case 185/97 *Coote v Granada Hospitality Ltd* [1998] ECR I-5199; [1998] IRLR 656. For the restrictive application of this decision by the domestic courts see para 11.47.

from the EU to each member state to put in place directly enforceable legal measures to the minimum standard set out in the directive. Member states have until19 July 2003 to do this.[127]

Scope

10.85 The RD regulates both direct and indirect discrimination on grounds of ethnic or racial origin.[128] It also recognises harassment and instructions to discriminate as forms of discrimination.[129] Direct discrimination is defined in accordance with normal practice (see chapter 3) as occurring when, on 'prohibited grounds', one person is treated less favourably than another person is, has been or would be treated in a comparable situation on grounds of his/her racial or ethnic origin.[130] Indirect discrimination occurs when an apparently neutral provision, criterion or practice is applied or followed that would put people of a racial or ethnic origin at a particular disadvantage.[131] This definition will encompass discriminatory practices that do not constitute a 'must' which have previously been excluded in cases such as *Perera v Civil Service Commission*[132] (see para 7.31). This definition does not depend on statistical evidence about the proportions affected by any disputed provision, criterion or practice. This is important as statistical evidence about different proportions of racial groups is not always available; clearly if it is available it can be very helpful.

10.86 As it refers to a provision, criterion or practice that 'would put' persons at a disadvantage, the definition of indirect discrimination adopted by the RD does not depend on proof that the disadvantage has already occurred. Consequently, this test could be satisfied when a particular disadvantage is anticipated. It ought to be possible to call evidence from sociologists or economists to establish the anticipated discriminatory effect of a disputed provision.

10.87 Indirect discrimination can be permissible if the provision, criterion or practice is objectively justified by a legitimate aim, provided that the means of the achieving that aim are appropriate and necessary.[133]

127 RD art 16.
128 Ibid art 2.
129 Ibid art 2(3) and (4).
130 Ibid art 2(2)(a).
131 Ibid art 2(2)(b).
132 [1983] IRLR 166.
133 RD art 2(2)(b).

10.88 The RD applies to both the public and private sector[134] in relation to:

- conditions for access to employment, including selection criteria and recruitment conditions;
- access to all levels of vocational training and retraining;
- employment and working conditions;
- membership of an organisation of workers or employers, including professional organisations;
- social protection including social security and healthcare;
- social advantages;
- education, and
- access to and supply of goods and services which are available to the public, including housing.

Exceptions

10.89 Differences of treatment based on nationality are expressly excluded from the scope of the RD, although they are covered by the RRA 1976 and articles 12 and 39 EC (in so far as the discrimination is between nationals of EU or EEA member states). Additionally, provisions relating to the entry and residence of third country nationals and stateless people or treatment that arises from this legal status are excluded.[135] Member states may provide that a difference of treatment based on a characteristic related to racial or ethnic origin will not be unlawful discrimination when that characteristic can be shown to be a genuine and determining occupational requirement, that the object is legitimate and the requirement is proportionate.[136]

10.90 The RD does not prevent member states from maintaining or adopting positive action measures to compensate for past disadvantage related to racial or ethnic origin.[137] Neither, however, does the directive require any such action.

Additional provisions

10.91 The RD requires that member states should introduce provisions to protect individuals from any adverse treatment or adverse consequences as a reaction to a complaint being made or proceedings being taken to enforce the principle of equal treatment.[138] The directive

134 RD art 3.
135 Ibid art 3(2).
136 Ibid art 4.
137 Ibid art 5.
138 Ibid art 9.

gives each member state the duty to provide for a right to redress for all victims of such discrimination.[139] Once an applicant establishes before a court or tribunal facts that indicate that there has been discrimination it will be for the respondent (as in cases of sex discrimination after the implementation of the BPD) to prove that no discrimination has occurred.[140]

10.92 The RD requires that member states must allocate an independent organisation to:

- provide independent assistance to victims of such discrimination in pursuing their complaints;
- conduct independent surveys about discrimination, and
- publish reports and make recommendations about such discrimination.[141]

In Great Britain the CRE, and in Northern Ireland the Equality Commission for Northern Ireland, will fulfil these functions.

Employment Directive

10.93 Article 13 EC, which provided the basis on which the RD was adopted, also founded the new ED which regulates direct and indirect discrimination in relation to religion and belief, sexual orientation, age, and disability. The grounds on which the ED regulates discrimination are wide but its scope is narrow – it applies only in the field of employment and occupation. The provisions on religion and belief and sexual orientation must be implemented by 2 December 2003, those on age and disability by 2 December 2006.

10.94 In relation to each of the four grounds of discrimination regulated by the ED, an act that would otherwise be unlawful will be permitted where the nature of the work or occupation or the context in which it is to be carried out creates a genuine and determining occupational need for the job. There must be a legitimate objective and the requirement must be proportionate.

Scope

10.95 The ED prohibits both direct and indirect discrimination on grounds of religion and belief, sexual orientation, disability or age.[142] Like the

139 RD art 15.
140 Ibid art 8.
141 Ibid art 13.
142 ED art 2.

RD, it recognises that harassment and instructions to discriminate are forms of discrimination.[143] Direct and indirect discrimination are defined as by the RD, article 2(2)(b)(ii) ED specifically providing for a duty of reasonable accommodation in relation to disability.

Exceptions

10.96 The equality requirements imposed by the ED are stated to be without prejudice to national laws which, in a democratic society, are necessary for:

- public security;
- the maintenance of public order and prevention of criminal offences;
- the protection of public health and
- the protection of the rights and freedoms of others.[144]

10.97 The ED applies to both public and private sectors in relation to:

- conditions for access to employment or self-employment including selection criteria, recruitment and promotion;
- access to vocational guidance, vocational training or retraining, including work experience;
- employment and working conditions including dismissals and pay; and
- membership of and involvement in an organisation of workers, employers or other professionals.[145]

10.98 The ED specifically excludes differences of treatment on grounds of nationality and treatment which relates to the legal status of third country nationals or stateless persons.[146] It also specifically excludes state social security and social protection schemes from its operation.[147] Further, member states are permitted to exempt the armed forces from the directive's prohibitions on age and disability discrimination.[148]

143 ED art 2(3) and (4).
144 Ibid art 2(5).
145 Ibid art 3.
146 Ibid art 3(2).
147 Ibid art 3(3).
148 Ibid art 3(4). Special provision is made to permit extensive positive discrimination in relation to the police force in Northern Ireland (art 15(1)) and to permit discrimination on grounds of religion in recruitment of teachers there (art 15(2)).

10.99 National legislation can provide for exceptions to the requirement of non-discrimination where the occupational activity or the context in which it is carried out means that a particular characteristic is a genuine and determining occupational requirement. This can be permitted providing that the objective is legitimate and the requirement is proportionate.[149] There is also a specific exception in the case of employment by an organisation with a particular ethos based on religion or belief (discussed at paras 8.24 and 8.33). It will not, in any event, permit organisations with a particular ethos based on religion or belief to discriminate on grounds of age, disability or sexual orientation. The ED requires that member states introduce provisions to protect individuals from any adverse treatment or adverse consequences as a reaction to a complaint being made or proceedings being taken to enforce the principle of equal treatment. Member states must put in place a system of sanctions that must be 'effective, proportionate and dissuasive'.[150]

10.100 Member states must make provision for a reasonable accommodation to be made for people with disabilities in order to ensure that they will receive equal treatment. This obliges employers to take appropriate measures to enable a person with a disability 'to have access to, participate in, or advance in employment, or to undergo training unless such measures would impose a disproportionate burden on the employer'.[151]

10.101 The ED permits the justification under national law of differential treatment on grounds of age, providing that it is objectively and reasonably justified by a legitimate aim such as legitimate employment policy, labour market and vocational training objectives, *and* if the means of achieving that aim are appropriate and necessary. It specifies that such differences of treatment may include:

- the setting of special conditions on access to employment and vocational training, employment and occupation, including dismissal and remuneration conditions, for young people, older workers and people with caring responsibilities in order to promote their vocational integration or ensure their protection;
- the fixing of minimum conditions of age, professional experience or seniority in service for access to employment or to certain advantages linked to employment;
- the fixing of a maximum age for recruitment which is based on the

149 Ibid art 4(1).
150 Ibid art 17.
151 Ibid art 5.

training requirements of the post in question or the need for a reasonable period of employment before retirement.[152]

10.102 Another exception permitted by the ED relates to occupational social security or pension schemes. National legislation can allow such schemes to continue to have age rules relating to admission or entitlement to retirement benefit; the use of age criteria in actuarial calculations will not constitute discrimination on grounds of age provided that it does not result in sex discrimination.[153] Nor does the directive prevent a member state from maintaining or adopting positive action measures to compensate for past disadvantage related to one of the grounds covered by the ED (though, as under the RD, there is no obligation to engage in positive action).[154]

10.103 Once an applicant establishes before a court or tribunal facts that indicate that there has been discrimination, it will be for the respondent to prove that no discrimination has occurred.[155]

New Equal Treatment Directive

10.104 Agreement has just been reached on an amended Equal Treatment Directive (ETD) which will make the provisions in relation to sex discrimination consistent with the new provisions of the RD and ED. Like the ED its scope is narrow, it applies only in the field of employment and occupation, but within this area member states must take into account the objective of equality between men and women when formulating and implementing laws, regulations, administrative provisions, policies and activities.[156] They have until 2005 implement it.

10.105 The ETD applies to both the public and private sector[157] in relation to:

- conditions for access to employment or self-employment including selection criteria, recruitment and promotion;
- access to vocational guidance, vocational training or re-training, including work experience;

152 ED art 6(1).
153 Ibid art 6(2).
154 Ibid art 7.
155 Ibid art 10.
156 ETD art 1.
157 Ibid art 3.

- employment and working conditions including dismissals and pay; and
- membership of and involvement in an organisation of workers, employers or other professionals.[158]

It will put in place a new definition of direct and indirect discrimination in line with the new definitions in the RD and ED.[159] Direct discrimination is defined in accordance with normal practice (see chapter 3) as occurring when, on grounds of sex, one person is treated less favourably than another person is, has been or would be treated in a comparable situation.[160] Indirect discrimination occurs when an apparently neutral provision, criterion or practice is applied or followed would put persons of one sex at a particular disadvantage compared with persons of the other sex.[161] As with the RD and ED this definition will encompass discriminatory practices which do not constitute a 'must', this definition of indirect discrimination does not depend on proof that the disadvantage has already occurred. Indirect discrimination can be permissible if the provision, criterion or practice is objectively justified by a legitimate aim provided that the means of the achieving that aim are appropriate and necessary.[162] Instructions to discriminate are recognised as a form of discrimination.[163]

10.106 It makes specific provision for harassment and sexual harassment as forms of discrimination.[164] Harassment is defined as 'unwanted conduct related to the sex of a person that occurs with the purpose or effect of violating the dignity of a person, and of creating an intimidating, hostile, degrading, humiliating or offensive environment'. Sexual harassment is defined as 'where any form of unwanted verbal, non-verbal or physical conduct of a sexual nature occurs, with the purpose or effect of violating the dignity of a person in particular when creating an intimidating, hostile, degrading, humiliating or offensive environment'.[165] A person's rejection of, or submission to, such forms of harassment may not be used as the basis for any decision affecting that person.[166]

158 ETD art 3.
159 Ibid art 2.
160 Ibid art 2(2)(a).
161 Ibid art 2(2)(b).
162 Ibid art 2(2)(a).
163 Ibid art 2(4).
164 Ibid arts 2(3) and 2(4).
165 Ibid art 2(2).
166 Ibid art 2(3).

10.107 Member states must encourage employers and those responsible for vocational training to take preventative measures to prevent all forms of sex discrimination including harassment. Member states should also:

- encourage social partners to promote equality;
- encourage employers to promote equal treatment in a planned and systematic way; and
- encourage employers to provide to their employees or their representatives appropriate information on the position of men and women within their business and take appropriate measures to improve the situation.[167]

Member states must take measures to abolish any laws, regulations and administrative provisions which are contrary to the principle of equal treatment and ensure that provisions contrary to the principle of equal treatment which are included in contracts or collective agreements or rules governing professional, workers, or employers organisations can be declared null and void or are amended.[168]

10.108 The Directive is expressed to be without prejudice to provisions concerning the protection of women particularly in respect of pregnancy and maternity. It provides that a woman on maternity leave shall be entitled, at the end of her period of maternity leave to return to her job or to an equivalent post on terms that are no less favourable to her. Additionally she may benefit from any improvement in working conditions to which she would be entitled during her absence. Any less favourable treatment of a woman in relation to pregnancy or maternity leave shall constitute discrimination.[169] It is also without prejudice to the rights to recognise paternity and/or adoption leave and those member states that recognise such leave must protect working men and women from dismissal consequent on taking such leave and enable them to return to work on terms that are not less favourable than those that they would have enjoyed but for the taking of leave.[170]

10.109 Member states shall put in place such measures as are necessary to ensure real and effective compensation or reparation for the loss and damage suffered by a person injured by discrimination. These must be dissuasive and proportionate to the damage suffered and

167 ETD art 8b.
168 Ibid art 3(2).
169 Ibid art 2(7).
170 Ibid art 2(7).

may not be restricted by any upper limit.[171] It requires sanctions to deal with infringements of these rights to be 'effective, proportionate and dissuasive'.[172] The duty to apply the principle of equal treatment is now clearly stated to apply even after the relationship in which the discrimination occurred has ended.[173] The Directive gives each member state the duty to provide for a right to redress for all victims of such discrimination.[174]

10.110 As with the RD the ETD requires member states to allocate an independent organisation to:

- provide independent assistance to victims of such discrimination in pursuing their complaints;
- conduct independent surveys about discrimination; and
- publish reports and make recommendations about such discrimination.[175]

In Great Britain the Equal Opportunities Commission, and in Northern Ireland the Equality Commission for Northern Ireland, will fulfil these functions.

10.111 Nor does the Directive prevent a member state from maintaining or adopting positive action measures to compensate for past disadvantage related to one of the grounds covered by the Directive (though, as under the RD, there is no obligation to engage in positive action).[176]

171 Ibid art 6.
172 Ibid art 8d.
173 Ibid art 6.
174 Ibid art 15.
175 Ibid art 8a.
176 Ibid art 7.

CHAPTER 11

Sex and race discrimination in employment

continued

Key points

11.1

- The Sex Discrimination Act (SDA) 1975 and the Race Relations Act (RRA) 1976 prohibit both direct and indirect discrimination in the employment context on grounds of sex, married status and 'race' (including colour, nationality, and ethnic or national origins).
- Both men and women are protected by the prohibition on 'sex' discrimination in the SDA 1975. Married people are protected from discrimination on the grounds of their married status, but single people are not protected from discrimination on grounds either of their unmarried status or their intention to be married.
- EC law provides very broad protection against sex discrimination, and must be taken into account in interpreting the SDA 1975 (and, in some cases, the RRA 1976).
- Employment-related direct discrimination connected with gender reassignment (ie, discrimination against transsexuals) is unlawful under the SDA 1975and EC law. Indirect discrimination connected with gender reassignment is not regulated by the SDA 1975 but may, if related to employment, breach the Equal Treatment Directive (ETD) or article 141 of the EC Treaty.
- Discrimination on grounds of sexual orientation (generally, discrimination against gay men, lesbians, or bisexuals) is not expressly regulated under domestic law, although it may in some cases breach the Human Rights Act (HRA) 1998.
- Northern Ireland's 'fair employment' legislation prohibits discrimination on grounds of religious belief and political opinion. In Great Britain, discrimination on grounds of religion is not regulated as such, though it may in some cases amount to discrimination on grounds of race and may breach the HRA 1998.
- Domestic legislation does not as such regulate discrimination on grounds of age, though such discrimination may in some cases amount to sex, race (or disability) discrimination.
- The SDA 1975 and RRA 1976 protect 'workers' including:
  - job applicants;
  - employees;
  - the self–employed;
  - apprentices;
  - independent contractors;
  - trainees;
  - barristers, trainee barristers, and advocates.

- Neither the SDA 1975 nor the RRA 1976 imposes minimum or maximum age limits in respect of their protection. Most Crown employees are protected by them.
- The SDA 1975 and the RRA 1976 regulate employment-related discrimination (broadly defined) by:
  - employers,
  - partners,
  - trade unions,
  - employers' organisations, and
  - people concerned with the provision of vocational training.
- The SDA 1975 and the RRA 1976 prohibit discrimination:
  - in the arrangements made for deciding who should be offered employment;
  - in the terms and conditions on which a person is offered a job;
  - by refusing or omitting to offer a person a job;
  - by not giving a worker the same opportunities for transfer, training or promotion;
  - by giving a worker fewer benefits, facilities or services;
  - by dismissing a worker; or
  - by subjecting a worker to any other detriment.
- The RRA 1976 also regulates discrimination by affording a worker less favourable terms of employment. Sex discrimination of this type is regulated by the Equal Pay Act (EqPA) 1970, though discrimination on grounds of gender reassignment in contractual terms of employment is regulated by the SDA 1975.
- The SDA 1975 and the RRA 1976 permit a number of exceptions to their prohibitions on discrimination. These are different under the SDA 1975 and RRA 1976, but common to both are positive action and cases in which there is a 'genuine occupational qualification'.
- At present the EC provisions on discrimination relate primarily to discrimination on grounds of sex. These also permit exceptions to the prohibition on sex discrimination including:
  - occupational activities where sex is a determining factor;
  - provisions relating to the protection of women, particularly as regards pregnancy and maternity; and
  - measures to promote equal opportunity for men and women and to remove existing inequalities.
- Some of the exclusions contained in the SDA 1975 may be in breach of EC law.

- The EqPA 1970 regulates discrimination (direct and indirect) in pay and other contractual terms between men and women doing like work, work rated as equivalent under a job evaluation scheme or work of equal value.
- The SDA 1975 and EqPA 1970 are mutually exclusive, though they should be construed as a 'harmonious whole'. If in doubt, it is wise to plead both Acts and also to plead the relevant EC provisions.

Background and statutory framework

11.2 The main statutory provisions discussed in this chapter are the SDA 1975 and the RRA 1976.[1] The Disability Discrimination Act (DDA) 1995 is dealt with in chapters 2, 6 and 13–15.

11.3 The SDA 1975 regulates direct and indirect discrimination on grounds of sex and married status.[2] Since 1 May 1999 the Act has also prohibited direct discrimination on the grounds of gender reassignment. It does not regulate indirect discrimination on this ground. Nor does it regulate direct or indirect discrimination related to gender-reassignment except in relation to employment (broadly defined) and any provision of SDA 1975 Pt III insofar as it applies to vocational training.

11.4 The RRA 1976 prohibits direct and indirect discrimination on grounds of colour, race, nationality, and ethnic or national origins (see para 2.33).[3] Less favourable treatment on grounds of religion is not, as such, regulated in Great Britain (although it is in Northern Ireland). But less favourable treatment of a person on grounds of religion, or failure to take into account a person's religious needs, may amount to direct or indirect race discrimination and/or a breach of the HRA 1998 (see further paras 8.29 and 9.30).

11.5 The SDA 1975 and RRA 1976 only prohibit discrimination in prescribed circumstances. These are set out at para 11.28 below. Briefly, certain acts of discrimination are prohibited in relation to job applicants, employees, the self-employed, contract workers, apprentices,

1 In Northern Ireland, the Race Relations (Northern Ireland) Order 1997 SI No 869, NI 6, whose provisions are materially identical (save that the definition of 'racial group' in art 5 specifically includes Irish travellers as a 'racial group').

2 SDA 1975 ss2 and 3.

3 RRA 1976 s1.

trainees and barristers. The same categories of workers are protected under the RRA 1976 as under the SDA 1975.[4] No maximum age limits or minimum lengths of service requirements apply under the SDA 1975 or the RRA 1976 – protection starts from the first day of employment or, if the discrimination occurs prior to employment, from the date of the discrimination.

11.6 This chapter explains which workers are protected and excluded from protection and the circumstances in which discrimination will be unlawful, and summarises the difference between the SDA 1975 and the EqPA 1970. EC law has been crucial to the development of sex discrimination law in the UK. It will be similarly important to the interpretation and development of discrimination on other grounds. The provisions of EC law are considered in this chapter but the effect of EC law and how to enforce it are covered in chapter 10. The European Convention on Human Rights (ECHR), given effect to in the UK by the HRA 1998, is likely to become increasingly important – particularly in relation to discrimination on grounds of sexual orientation, religion and age. This is further considered in chapter 9.

The impact of EC law

11.7 The detailed provisions of EC law are set out in chapter 10. In brief, article 141 of the EC Treaty can be relied on directly by all workers, whether they work for emanations of the state (generally public sector bodies) or private bodies. Only those who work for emanations of the state can rely directly on directives. In all cases, tribunals and courts must take account of EC law.

11.8 Article 39 EC (formerly article 48) provides that freedom of movement of workers entails 'the abolition of any employment-related discrimination based on nationality'. This provision only applies as between citizens of EEA Member States, and does not apply to third country nationals. It is subject to limitations justified on grounds of public policy, public security or public health, though such limitations may not be applied in a discriminatory manner.[5]

4 The Sex Discrimination (Northern Ireland) Order 1976 SI No 1042 has the same definition of employment – see *Percival-Price v Department of Economic Development* [2000] IRLR 380, in which Northern Ireland's Court of Appeal held that tribunal chairmen were 'workers' who are in 'employment' within EC law (see para 11.56).

5 *Re Colgan* [1997] 1 CMLR 53.

Types of prohibited discrimination

11.9 Unlawful direct discrimination occurs when a person is treated less favourably than a real or hypothetical other on a 'prohibited ground' (ie, on the ground of sex; married status; gender reassignment; race – including colour, nationality, national or ethnic origin or, in Northern Ireland alone, religious belief or political opinion).

11.10 Indirect discrimination (only prohibited on grounds of race, sex and marital status) is concerned with practices that have the effect, though not the intention, of discriminating on one of the prohibited grounds because, for example, of past direct discrimination or existing social conditions or cultural practices (see chapter 7).

11.11 Victimisation occurs when a person is treated less favourably because he or she has made a complaint of discrimination or done a specified protected act under the SDA 1975 or the RRA 1976 (see further chapter 4).

Discrimination on grounds of sex, married status or race

11.12 The RRA 1976 is modelled on the SDA 1975 and the Acts' definitions of direct and indirect discrimination and victimisation are very similar, except that:

- The burden of proof in employment-related sex discrimination cases differs from that imposed by the RRA 1976 and by the SDA 1975 in cases not related to employment. Once the applicant has proved facts from which the tribunal could conclude, in the absence of an adequate explanation, that the respondent has discriminated on grounds of sex, the respondent must show a non-discriminatory reason in order to avoid an adverse finding (see further paras 3.47 and 10.64).
- The RRA 1976 prohibits discrimination against someone because of another person's race – where, for example, a white person is dismissed for refusing to follow instructions from an employer to discriminate against a black person (see further para 2.46). The SDA 1975 contains no such provision.
- Segregation on racial grounds is automatically treated as less favourable treatment by the RRA 1976 (s1(2)). Thus, an employer cannot, for example, provide black and white workers with 'separate but equal' facilities. The SDA 1975 contains no equivalent provision.

Discrimination on grounds of gender reassignment

11.13 SDA 1975 s2A, as amended by the Sex Discrimination (Gender Reassignment) Regulations 1999,[6] prohibits employment-related (and certain vocational training) direct discrimination against a person on the grounds that he or she intends to undergo, is undergoing or has undergone gender reassignment. 'Gender reassignment' is defined for the purposes of the SDA 1975 as 'a process which is undertaken under medical supervision for the purpose of reassigning a person's sex by changing physiological or other characteristics of sex, and includes any part of such a process'.[7]

11.14 As with sex discrimination, the applicant must show not only that he or she has been less favourably treated than another was or would have been, but also that the less favourable treatment related to recruitment, transfer, training, promotion, access to benefits at work, dismissal or other detriment (see para 11.28). The SDA 1975, rather than the EqPA 1970, regulates discrimination connected with gender reassignment in relation to pay and other contractual terms and conditions.[8] Indirect discrimination connected with gender reassignment does not breach the SDA 1975, though it may be contrary to the HRA 1998 and EC law (see para 2.25).

Discrimination on grounds of sexual orientation

11.15 Discrimination on grounds of sexual orientation is not yet specifically prohibited in the UK, but there have been a number of cases in which it has been argued that discrimination against gays and lesbians amounts to sex discrimination contrary to the SDA 1975 and EC law. These have not been successful. Discrimination on grounds of sexual orientation may, however, breach articles 8 and 14 ECHR which, respectively, protect the right to a private life and provide a right not to be discriminated against in the application of any convention right. For the circumstances under which breach of a convention right will be directly challengeable as a breach of the HRA, see chapter 9.[9]

6 SI No 102.

7 SDA 1975 s82 as amended.

8 Ibid s6(8) as amended.

9 *Smith and Grady v UK* (2001) 31 EHRR 620; [1999] IRLR 734 and *Salgueiro da Silva Mouta v Portugal* (2001) 31 EHRR 1055.

Discrimination on grounds of religious and political belief

11.16 Discrimination on grounds of religion or belief is expressly prohibited only in Northern Ireland and not in Great Britain. However, a religious group which has shared 'ethnic origins', as in the case of Sikhs and Jewish people, may be regarded also as a 'racial group' and protected from discrimination (direct and indirect) under the RRA 1976 (see para 8.29). In addition, where a practice, provision or criteria has a disproportionate adverse impact on a religious group which does not itself qualify as a 'racial group' for the purposes of the RRA 1976, but which is sufficiently associated with race that the practice, provision or criteria *also* has a disproportionate adverse impact on a racial group, it may amount to unlawful indirect discrimination under the RRA 1976. The less favourable treatment of a religious group, for example by a refusal to allow Muslims to take holiday for Eid, may be indirect race discrimination against a racial group (for example Asians) where a very significant proportion of Asians in a workplace are Muslim (see further para 8.31).[10]

11.17 The HRA 1998 now provides some protection in respect of religion and belief. Article 9 ECHR establishes an absolute right to freedom of thought, conscience and religion, and the right to manifest a religion or belief subject to such limitations as are prescribed by law and necessary in a democratic society.

11.18 The Fair Employment and Treatment (Northern Ireland) (FETO) Order 1998[11] prohibits discrimination on grounds of religious belief or political opinion. It applies only to Northern Ireland, whose equality legislation is otherwise very similar to that applicable in Great Britain.[12] The FETO 1998 will not be the subject of detailed consideration in this book.

Discrimination on grounds of age

11.19 No statutory provisions prohibit age discrimination, though such discrimination may amount to indirect sex or race discrimination (see further para 8.54).[13] There is a voluntary Code of Practice on Age

10 It would not be direct discrimination against Muslims who comprise a religious group rather than an 'ethnic' one for the purposes of the RRA 1976.

11 SI No 3162.

12 See appendix B.The Northern Ireland government is currently consulting on a Single Equality Act.

13 See, eg, *Harvest Town Circle Ltd v Rutherford* [2001] IRLR 599.

Diversity in Employment, the stated purpose of which is to 'help employers, employees and applicants alike by setting a standard'. The code, which covers recruitment, selection, promotion, training, redundancy, and retirement, is further considered at para 8.50.

Territorial scope of the Sex Discrimination Act 1975 and the Race Relations Act 1976

11.20 The SDA 1975 and RRA 1976 only regulate employment at establishments in Great Britain (England, Scotland and Wales),[14] the almost identical provisions of Northern Irish legislation applying in relation to establishments there. Employment is regarded as being at an establishment in Great Britain unless the employee works wholly outside Great Britain.[15] The Employment Rights Act (ERA) 1996 no longer provides an exception for workers ordinarily working outside Great Britain so an employee working in Great Britain at the time of, for example, a discriminatory dismissal, is likely to be protected by the ERA 1996 as well as the SDA 1975 and/or the RRA 1976.[16]

11.21 Work which is not done *at* an establishment is treated as done at the establishment *from* which it is done or, if not done from any establishment (because, for example, the worker is based at home or travels from place to place), at the establishment to which the worker is most closely connected.[17] Special provisions which apply to employment on ships, aircraft and hovercraft differ slightly between the SDA 1975 and RRA 1976.

11.22 Under the SDA 1975, employment 'in Great Britain' includes:

(a) employment on board a ship registered in Great Britain in which case the place of work is the ship, unless the worker works wholly outside Great Britain, and
(b) employment on an aircraft or hovercraft registered in the UK and operated by a person who has his principal place of business, or is

14 RRA 1976 s4 and SDA 1975 s6, and Interpretation Act 1978 Sch 2, para 5(a). 'Great Britain' includes territorial waters adjacent thereto (RRA 1976 s78(1) and SDA 1975 s82(1)).

15 SDA 1975 s10 and RRA 1976 s8 respectively. Prior to December 1999, workers mainly working outside Great Britain were excluded. This was amended by the Equal Opportunities (Employment Legislation) (Territorial Limits) Regulations 1999 SI No 3163 as from 16 December 1999 to remove 'mainly'.

16 ERA 1996 s196 was repealed by ERA 1999. Whether a worker is protected will depend on the circumstances and the details are outside the scope of this book.

17 SDA 1975 s10(4) and RRA 1976 s8(2).

ordinarily resident, in Great Britain unless the worker works wholly outside Great Britain.[18]

11.23 Under the RRA 1976 the provisions relating to ships (see (a) above) are similar but the Act no longer makes any special provision for employment on aircraft or hovercraft.[19] It would appear that a person employed to work on an aircraft or hovercraft will be treated as working at the establishment with which he or she has the closest connection (see above).

11.24 In *Deria v General Council of British Shipping*[20] a recruitment agency refused to recruit Somali seamen for a ship which was registered in Great Britain but formed part of the Falklands task force. The employer argued that the employment was to be wholly outside Great Britain and that the RRA 1976 did not apply to the recruitment at issue. The Court of Appeal held that the relevant question in a recruitment case related to what was within the contemplation of the parties at the time of the recruitment. The words 'unless the employee does his work wholly outside Great Britain' should read 'unless the employee does *or is to do* his work wholly outside Great Britain' (emphasis added). Although the crew did in fact spend a short time in Great Britain, this was not anticipated at the time of recruitment. The Court of Appeal held, accordingly, that the seamen worked wholly outside Great Britain and fell outside the protection of the RRA 1976.[21]

11.25 It is not unlawful (under RRA 1976 s4) for an employer to discriminate on racial grounds against a seaman who applies abroad for a job on a ship, unless the employment is related to the exploration or exploitation of the seabed or subsoil of the continental shelf.[22] Thus, discriminatory recruitment carried out outside Great Britain is not unlawful unless, of course, the relevant jurisdiction prohibits such

18 SDA 1975 s10(2) and (3).

19 Equal Opportunities (Employment Legislation) (Territorial Limits) Regulations 1999 SI No 3163.

20 [1986] IRLR 108.

21 See also *Ferry Casinos Ltd v Fewster*, EAT 408/91 (unreported, available on LEXIS).

22 RRA 1976 s9. Special provisions relate to the exploration of the sea-bed and subsoil, and the exploitation of their natural resources in the continental shelf (see Employment (Continental Shelf) Act 1978 s1; Sex Discrimination and Equal Pay (Offshore Employment) Order 1987 SI No 930, and Race Relations (Offshore Employment) Order 1987 SI No 929). An order in council may designate certain areas as being within the scope of the SDA 1975, EqPA 1970 and RRA 1976. This has been done in relation to some areas of the continental shelf and oil fields.

discrimination. This exception also applies where a person is brought to Great Britain with a view to employment on any ship.[23] There is no parallel exception under the SDA 1975.

The impact of EC law

11.26 A worker based in an EU country will be protected from sex discrimination under article 141 EC and the Equal Treatment Directive. In addition, article 39 EC provides that freedom of movement entails the abolition of discrimination based on nationality between workers of members states as regards employment. It appears from the ECJ ruling in *Walrave v Koch*[23a] (a case involving article 39), that article 141 may apply in relation to any legal employment relationship entered into within the EC, even if the work is done outside the EC.[24] In *Percival-Price and others v Department of Economic Development and others*,[24a] the Northern Ireland Court of Appeal ruled that the broad meaning of 'worker' adopted by the ECJ in relation to article 39 (*Lawrie-Blum v Land Baden Württenberg*[25]) was to be applied by the domestic courts in relation to 'workers' under article 141 and the ETD.

11.27 In *Bossa v Nordstress Ltd*[25a] the applicant, an Italian national living in Britain, applied for a job as aircraft cabin crew based in Italy. The job required an EC passport. Mr Bossa was refused an interview because the Italian authorities did not allow the company to take employees of Italian nationality back to Italy. An employment tribunal (ET) held that article 39 EC protected Mr Bossa's right to work anywhere within the EC. The Employment Appeal Tribunal (EAT) held that, article 39 having direct effect (see further chapter 10), RRA 1976 s8, which provides that the Act does not apply to employment entirely outside Great Britain, had to be disapplied.

23 RRA 1976 s9(4).

23a [1974] ECR 1405.

24 The ECJ held that art 141 applies where the legal employment relationship was entered into within the EU, even if the work is done outside the EU.

24a [2000] IRLR 380.

25 [1986] ECR 2121, ECJ.

25a [1998] IRLR 284.

Discrimination in 'employment'

Discrimination against job applicants

11.28 It is unlawful under RRA 1976 s4(1) and SDA 1975 s6(1) for an employer to discriminate against a job applicant in relation to employment:

- in the arrangements he or she makes for the purpose of determining who should be offered that employment (for example, selection procedures, advertising);[26]
- in the terms and conditions on which he or she offers that employment (for example, if a woman is offered shorter holidays, fewer perks, lower pay); [27]
- by refusing or deliberately omitting to offer that employment.[28]

The discrimination prohibited by RRA 1976 s4(1) and SDA 1975 s6(1) includes direct and indirect discrimination, and the sections apply to discrimination against men as well as women, and discrimination against white workers as well as black (see chapter 14 for further discussion of discrimination in recruitment).

Relationship between the Sex Discrimination Act 1975 and the Equal Pay Act 1970

11.29 The general position is that the SDA 1975 and the EqPA 1970 are mutually exclusive and in any situation only one will apply. We shall see, below, that the EqPA 1970 rather than the SDA 1975 regulates discrimination in the contractual terms of employment. But the SDA 1975 applies to discrimination in the *offer* of employment, as well as (see para 11.31 below) to non-contractual discrimination during employment. The rules for deciding whether the SDA 1975 applies become complex when considering an offer of employment which discriminates in respect of contractual terms. If it is not clear which applies, any claim should be made under both. It is also wise to add article 141 EC and the ETD.

11.30 In considering whether the EqPA 1970 or the SDA 1975 is the appropriate means to challenge discrimination the rules are as follows:

a) Is the complaint that the terms offered are discriminatory? If so any equality clause that might be implied under the EqPA 1970 if

26 SDA 1975 s6(1)(a) and RRA 1976 s4(1)(a).

27 SDA 1975 s6(1)(b) and RRA 1976 s4(1)(b).

28 SDA 1975 s6(1)(c) and RRA 1976 s4(1)(c).

the woman was employed under those terms must be ignored (SDA 1975 s8(2)).

b) If it is the case that the contractual terms offered would breach the EqPA 1970 if the woman were to accept the offer, the offer will amount to an unlawful act of discrimination (SDA 1975 s8(3)). This is not the case if the employer could show that the reason for the different terms offered was a genuine material factor (other than sex) between her case and that of the man with whom she compares herself such that EqPA 1970 s1(3) would block the woman's equal pay claim. In such a case the offer of employment will not be an unlawful act of discrimination (SDA 1975 s8(4)).
c) The same approach is taken to offers of employment in respect of terms relating to access to or benefits from occupational pension schemes. If the offer would be unlawful under the Pensions Act 1995 if the woman were to accept it (no material factor defence applying) the offer will breach the SDA 1975 (s6(4)).
d) If the EqPA 1970 would not apply (if, for example, there was no man in the same employment), the offer may still be unlawful discrimination contrary to SDA 1975 s6(1)(b). The SDA 1975 does not, however, apply to offers of contractual terms as to the payment of money (SDA 1975 s6(5)), unless such an offer is caught under (b) above.

Discrimination against workers

11.31 Discrimination against workers in the following circumstances is prohibited:

a) refusing or not giving a worker the same opportunities for transfer, training or promotion;[29]
b) giving fewer or less favourable benefits, facilities or services – this includes benefits, facilities or services provided by another person (other than the employer), provided the employer facilitates access to them;[30]
c) dismissing a worker;[31]
d) subjecting a worker to any other detriment (ie, by treating a woman less favourably in any other way – provided such treatment is not excluded by the Act.[32]

29 SDA 1975 s6(2)(a) and RRA 1976 s4(2)(b).

30 Ibid.

31 SDA 1975 s6(2)(b) and RRA 1976 s4(2)(c).

32 Ibid.

Dismissal under (c) includes the expiry of a fixed-term contract that is not renewed and constructive dismissal.[33] The only difference between the SDA 1975 and RRA 1976 is that the RRA 1976, but not the SDA 1975, prohibits discrimination (s4(2)(a)) in the contractual terms of employment. RRA 1976 s4 and SDA 1975 s6 are considered in detail in chapters 14 and 15.

Relationship between the Sex Discrimination Act 1975 and the Equal Pay Act 1970

11.32 The EqPA 1970, in effect, prohibits sex discrimination against workers in contractual terms whether they relate to money or not. A claim might be made under the EqPA 1970 for equal holidays or sick leave, for example. The EqPA 1970 does not, as we have seen at para 11.29 above, apply in relation to *offers* of employment, though offers that discriminate in respect of contractual terms may breach the SDA 1975.

11.33 In order to succeed in an equal pay claim a woman must identify a male comparator doing the same or broadly similar work, work rated as equivalent under a job evaluation study or work otherwise shown to be of equal value. The man must either be in the same employment or in associated employment (for example working for a holding or subsidiary company). In certain circumstances a comparison may be made with men working for other employers in the same service, see chapter 22. If an equal pay claim succeeds, an equality clause is implied into the woman's contract of employment providing her with contractual terms that are no less favourable than those of her comparator.

Workers/employees protected by the Acts

11.34 'Employment', for the purposes of the SDA 1975 and the RRA 1976,[34] is defined as 'employment under a contract of service or of apprenticeship or a contract personally to execute any work or labour'.[35] The definition in the DDA 1995 is materially the same and, like that in the

33 Under the SDA 1975, dismissal specifically includes constructive dismissal and expiry and non-renewal of a fixed term contract (s82(1A)). There is no equivalent section in the RRA 1976, but the EAT has held that dismissal under the RRA 1976 does include constructive dismissal, see para 5.133.

34 Northern Ireland's provisions are in identical terms.

35 SDA 1975 s82(1) and RRA 1976 s78(1). The DDA 1995's definition is at s68(1).

RRA 1976 and SDA 1975, is a much wider definition than that applicable under the ERA 1996, which protects only those working under a contract of employment (employees). The following paragraphs apply to claims of disability discrimination as well as sex and race.

11.35 In *Quinnen v Hovells*[36] the EAT ruled that:

> ... the concept of a contract for the engagement of personal work or labour lying outside the scope of a master-servant relationship is a wide and flexible one, intended by Parliament to be interpreted as such ... Those who engage, even cursorily, the talents, skill or labour of the self-employed are wise to ensure that the terms are equal as between men and women.

However, the coverage of the RRA 1976 and SDA 1975 is not completely comprehensive.

The requirement for a contract

11.36 In order to qualify as 'employment' for the purposes of the RRA 1976, the DDA 1995 and the SDA 1975, the relationship must be governed by a contract, though this need not be in writing. There have been a number of cases in which the absence of a contract defeated a claim under one or other of these statutes.[37] The relevant contract is that between the person doing the work and the person for whom the work is done. In *BP Chemicals Ltd v Gillick*[38] the EAT rejected an agency worker's claim to be employed by the company (BP) for which she carried out the work, there being no contractual relationship between them. Where, as in *Gillick*, the worker's contractual relationship is with the agency rather than with the principal, he or she will be protected by SDA 1975 s9, RRA 1976 s7 and DDA 1995 s12 respectively, rather than under ss6 and 4 of the Acts.

11.37 *Gillick* may be open to doubt in view of the EAT's subsequent decision in *Motorola Ltd v Davidson*[39] in which, in an unfair dismissal claim, the EAT ruled that an agency worker was an employee of the

36 [1984] IRLR 227 and see also *Tanna v Post Office* [1981] ICR 374.

37 See *Wadi v Cornwall and Isles of Scilly Family Practitioners Committee and Medical Practices* [1985] ICR 492 and *Roy v Kensington and Chelsea and Westminster Practitioner Committee* [1992] 2 WLR 239, HL, which concerned doctors. Arguably, these cases, where there was held to be no contract, would now be subject to the interpretation given to 'worker' under the ETD, at least in a sex discrimination claim (see *Percival-Price v Department of Economic Development* [2000] IRLR 380). See also *Hewlett Packard Ltd v O'Murphy* [2002] IRLR 4 in relation to a claim for ordinary unfair dismissal under the ERA 1996.

38 [1995] IRLR 128.

39 [2001] IRLR 4 but see also *Hewlett Packard Ltd v O'Murphy* [2002] IRLR 4.

principal for whom he worked. The applicant in *Motorola* was bound by a contract with the agency, to comply with all reasonable instructions and requests made by the principal. In these circumstances, the EAT ruled that the principal had sufficient day-to-day control of the applicant for the latter to be an employee of the principal. The EAT ruled in *Motorola* that there was no good reason to ignore practical aspects of control that fall short of direct legal rights. Whether there is sufficient day-to-day control will be for the tribunal to decide on the basis of the circumstances of the case. If there is any doubt about the correct respondent it is advisable to claim under both sections of the relevant Act (ie, SDA 1975 ss6 and 9, RRA 1976 ss4 and 7, and DDA 1995 ss4 and 12), naming both the agency and principal as respondents.[40]

11.38 If a contract relates primarily to training and the individual is not also in employment with the provider of the training, the trainee is protected under SDA 1975 s14 and RRA 1976 s13 which make it unlawful, in certain circumstances, for those providing vocational training to discriminate against trainees. The position is slightly different under the DDA 1995 (see further chapter 12). If the worker is receiving training from his or her employer the employment-related provisions of the Act will apply and unjustified discrimination in relation to the training will breach the DDA 1995.

'Personal service'

11.39 In order to qualify as 'employment' under the SDA 1975, RRA 1976 and DDA 1995, the worker must be required personally to undertake the work involved. In *Mirror Group Newspapers Ltd v Gunning*[41] the applicant challenged the respondents' rejection of her application to take over her father's agency contract for the distribution of newspapers. The Court of Appeal held that a contract personally to execute any work or labour means a contract where the dominant purpose is an obligation by one contracting party personally to execute any work or labour. In this case, the dominant purpose was found to be the regular and efficient distribution of newspapers, rather than that the distributor should himself personally carry out the work. It does not appear that EC law was argued. Had it been, it might have provided the protection lacking under the SDA 1975.[42]

40 See also *Montgomery v Johnson Underwood Ltd* [2001] IRLR 269.

41 [1986] IRLR 27.

42 See also *Tanna v Post Office* [1981] ICR 374.

11.40 In *Mankoo v British School of Motoring Ltd*[43] the EAT ruled that a self-employed driving instructor who operated under a franchise agreement was protected by the RRA 1976, as an obligation to carry out the work personally could be implied. In *Hugh-Jones v St John's College, Cambridge*[44] the EAT accepted that a research fellow who had a contract to study and do research was protected under the SDA 1975's definition of employment. In *Byrne Brothers (Formwork) Ltd v Baird*,[45] the EAT considered the impact of a clause in a contract, which enabled the sub-contractor to provide an alternative worker with the prior approval of the contractor, on the personal service obligation required under the definition of worker under the Working Time Regulations 1998.[46] (Regulation 20 defines as a 'worker' protected by the Regulations a person who 'undertakes to do or perform personally any work or services for another party to the contract ...'.) The EAT held that a limited power to appoint substitutes was not inconsistent with an obligation of personal service, and that each case should be looked at on its facts. In this case the power to appoint a substitute was qualified and exceptional.

11.41 There may be circumstances where individuals applying for work under the name of the firm for which they work can be regarded as seeking 'employment' for the purposes of the SDA 1975, RRA 1976 and/or DDA 1995. In *Loughran and Kelly v Northern Ireland Housing Executive*[47] a two-partner firm of solicitors and a sole practitioner applied to join the litigation panel of the Northern Ireland Housing Executive. Membership of the panel would have resulted in their being allocated work by it. In order to join the panel, firms of solicitors had to designate a partner or principal to take overall responsibility for the work, and a solicitor to carry it out. Neither applicant was short listed by the Executive, and both argued that this was because they were Catholics. The House of Lords, by a majority, interpreted 'employment' broadly so as to allow both applicants to claim discrimination under the Fair Employment Act 1989 (now the FETO 1998 – the material provisions of which were and are in identical terms to those of the SDA 1975, RRA 1976 and DDA 1995). Their Lordships reasoned that the applicants who were to be responsible for and carry

43 EAT 657/82 (unreported, available on LEXIS).

44 [1979] ICR 848, though in fact the discrimination was exempt under SDA 1975 s43(2). See also *Parceline v Darien*, EAT 107/95 (unreported).

45 [2002] IRLR 96.

46 SI No 1833.

47 [1998] IRLR 593.

out the Executive's work, were in one case a sole practitioner and in the other a partner, rather than an employee, of his or her firm. A firm could contract to do work personally where 'one or more of the partners is intended to and does execute the work'.

11.42 The decision in *Loughran and Kelly* is limited to its facts, and does not mean that a firm or company will usually be treated as in employment with their client under the RRA 1976, SDA 1975 or DDA 1995.[48] A separate consideration is the rights of the individual *as a partner* of the firm, where the situation is markedly different between the DDA 1995 on the one hand and the SDA 1975 and RRA 1976 on the other. See para 12.11 for the position under the DDA 1995, and para 12.14 for that under the RRA 1976 and SDA 1975.

Volunteers

11.43 In *Armitage v Relate*[49] an ET held that a volunteer counsellor with Relate was in 'employment' for the purposes of the RRA 1976. The ET accepted that there was a legally binding contract whereby the applicant would receive training and, in return, had to carry out at least a minimum amount of work.

Ex-employees

11.44 The application to former employees of the RRA 1976 and the SDA 1975 differs. In *Adekeye v Post Office (No 2)*[50] (a race discrimination claim) the Court of Appeal ruled that 'employment', even under the RRA 1976's extended definition, was brought to an end by dismissal with the effect that no claim could be brought in relation to alleged dismissal in a post-termination appeal procedure. In that case the applicant had been summarily dismissed on 8 June 1991 and was informed on 17 August 1991 that her appeal against dismissal had been unsuccessful. She complained of race discrimination in the conduct of the appeal. The Court of Appeal ruled that she was not a 'person employed' at the date of her appeal hearing. Nor did the Court of Appeal accept that she could argue that she was an 'applicant' seeking reinstatement on appeal (this would have brought her claim within RRA 1976 s4(1)(a) or (c)). The applicant therefore had no remedy in

48 Note, also, that the Race Directive (RD) and Employment Directive (ED) – see further paras 10.84 and 10.93 – protect legal 'persons'.

49 (1994) DCLD 26.

50 [1997] IRLR 105. See also *Nagarajan v Agnew* [1994] IRLR 61, EAT.

respect of the discrimination alleged. This decision was confirmed by the Court of Appeal in *D'Souza v Lambeth LBC*,[51] which is now on appeal to the House of Lords.

11.45 The application of the SDA 1975 to ex-employees was raised in *Coote v Granada Hospitality Ltd*.[52] The complainant had settled a sex discrimination claim against the respondents who subsequently (after her employment with them terminated) refused to provide her with a reference because of her claim against them. She claimed to have been subject to unlawful victimisation under SDA 1975 s4 (see further chapter 4). The EAT took the view that the SDA 1975 did not apply to ex-employees, but made a reference to the ECJ to determine what the ETD required. The ECJ ruled that the directive required member states to ensure protection for workers whose employer, after the employment relationship has ended, takes action against them for bringing a discrimination claim. The ECJ held that the fear of such measures, where no legal remedy is available against them, might deter workers from pursuing a discrimination claim, and that this would jeopardise the principle of equal treatment.

11.46 On the case's return to the EAT, that court ruled in *Coote v Granada Hospitality Ltd (No 2)* that the words 'a woman employed by him' in SDA 1975 s6 were capable of meaning 'who is employed' or 'who has been employed' or both.[53] It was therefore possible to construe the SDA 1975 in conformity with the ETD, and the court was obliged to do so.

11.47 In *Rhys-Harper v Relaxion Group plc*[54] the Court of Appeal held that the applicant could not make a claim under SDA 1975 s6(2) that her employers had failed to investigate adequately a complaint of sexual harassment that she brought after her dismissal. Following the decision in *Adekeye (No 2)* the Court of Appeal held that a tribunal had no jurisdiction to consider a complaint in respect of acts or events which occurred after the termination of employment, save in a case of victimisation within *Coote*. This limitation of the ECJ decision in *Coote* to post-employment victimisation is arguably wrong, there being no indication from that decision that it was intended to be so

51 [2001] EWCA Civ 634. The government is committed, however, to putting into place post-employment protection under the RD (by July 2003) and the ED (by between December 2003 and December 2006 depending on the ground of discrimination at issue) – see further paras 10.84 and 10.93.

52 [1998] IRLR 656.

53 [1999] IRLR 452.

54 [2001] IRLR 460.

limited. The Advocate General in *Coote* referred to the decision of *Kowalska v Freie und Hunsestadt Hamburg*[55] (see para 26.16) in which the ECJ held that article 141 EC applied to benefits paid after the termination of the employment relationship. The ECJ there held that there could be no justification for taking a different course with the ETD.

11.48 The RRA 1976 (and the DDA 1995) will require amendment to cover post-employment victimisation in line with the SDA 1975 following *Coote* in order to comply with the Race Directive (RD)[56] and the Employment Directive (ED)[57] in 2003. In its consultation document the government proposes an amendment 'so as to allow individuals seeking redress in certain situations falling within the scope of the Directives after the relationship between complainant and respondent has ended, for example where an employer refuses to provide a reference for an employee who has brought a discrimination claim based on either Directive. Similar provision will be made in the new legislation on sexual orientation, religion and belief, and age.'[58]

Illegal contracts

11.49 Claims for unfair dismissal and redundancy payments cannot usually be made where the employee's contract of employment has been tainted by illegality (where, for example, the employee is implicated in tax evasion). The position differs in relation to discrimination claims, which are not based on the contract of employment.

11.50 The applicant in *Hall v Woolston Hall Leisure Ltd*,[59] whose dismissal was on the alleged ground of redundancy, won her sex discrimination claim on the basis that the real reason for dismissal was her pregnancy. The employee was aware that her wages were being paid without deduction of PAYE and National Insurance, although she obtained no benefit from this. Her employer argued that she could not recover compensation under the SDA 1975 because her contract of employment was illegal. The Court of Appeal held that, where the performance by the employer of a contract of employment involves illegality of which the employee is aware, public policy does not bar an

55 Case 33/89 [1990] ECR I-2591; [1990] IRLR 447.

56 Council Directive 2000/43/EC

57 Council Directive 2000/78/EC.

58 *Towards Equality*, the Government consultation on implementing the ED and RD, available at www.dti.gov.uk/er/equality.

59 [2000] IRLR 578. See also *Leighton v Michael* [1996] IRLR 67, EAT, which was approved by the Court of Appeal in *Hall*.

employee who is discriminated against on grounds of her sex by being dismissed from recovering compensation. The core of the complaint in *Hall* was sex discrimination, a statutory tort. But the Court of Appeal also ruled that the correct approach to 'illegal' contracts was for the tribunal to consider whether the claim was so inextricably bound up with the illegal conduct that it could not award compensation without appearing to condone the conduct. Thus, if the worker actively participates in the illegal performance of the contract, he or she may not be able to claim discrimination.

11.51 The Court of Appeal also commented in *Hall* that, where the contract of employment is neither entered into for an illegal purpose nor prohibited by statute, its illegal performance will not render it unenforceable unless, in addition to knowledge of the facts that make the performance illegal, the employee actively participates in the illegal performance. The employee in *Hall* was not involved in the employers' unlawful scheme in any way that would have prevented her from enforcing her contract. Nor, pointed out the Court of Appeal, were the character or incidents of the illegality related to the discrimination she suffered or her resulting claim. This may mean that in these circumstances a claim for unfair dismissal and a redundancy payment may also be made (see further paras 15.94 and 15.135).

Special categories of workers

Contract workers

11.52 The SDA 1975 and RRA 1976 prohibit discrimination against contract workers by 'principals', ie, those for whom work is done 'by individuals ("contract workers") who are employed not by the principal himself but by another person, who supplies them under a contract made with the principal'.[60] This prohibition, in respect of which various exceptions are provided, is discussed in detail in chapter 12.

Crown employees

11.53 The SDA 1975 and RRA 1976 apply to House of Commons and House of Lords staff, though they are not treated as employees under contracts of employment or as Crown servants.[61] They apply also to

60 RRA 1976 s7 and SDA 1975 s9 respectively.

61 SDA 1975 ss85A and 85B and RRA 1976 ss75A and 75B provide that Part II applies.

Crown employees in the same way as they apply to other employees.[62] The only exceptions are ministers of the Crown[63] and holders of statutory posts (for example, Commission for Racial Equality and Equal Opportunities Commission commissioners, magistrates, rent officers).[64] The latter exception is not consistent with EC law (see para 11.56). In addition, SDA 1975 s86 and RRA 1976 s76 provide that the Crown and government departments must not discriminate in making appointments or in making arrangements for determining who should be offered a statutory post. The remedy for breach of these provisions is by way of judicial review.

11.54 The RRA 1976 permits certain prescribed public bodies (such as the Bank of England and the British Council) to restrict employment on grounds of birth, nationality, descent or residence, but not race or colour.[65]

Public appointees

11.55 Race Relations (Amendment) Act (RRAA) 2000 s3 extends the scope of the RRA 1976 to government appointments. It also prohibits discrimination by ministers and by government departments in recommending or approving public appointments and in conferring honours, including peerages. This prohibition covers appointments and conferrals of honours by the Queen, which are made on the recommendation of a minister, and applies also to the appointment of members of the House of Lords.[66] The remedy for breach of these provisions is, again, by way of judicial review.

Members of the judiciary

11.56 Although both the SDA 1975 and the RRA 1976 exclude the holders of statutory office (including members of the judiciary) from their protection, no such exception applies under the ETD (or under article 141 EC or the Equal Pay Directive). In *Percival-Price v Department of*

62 SDA 1975 s85; RRA 1976 s75.

63 SDA 1975 s85(2)(a) and (b); RRA 1976 s75(10)(c).

64 See *Department of the Environment v Fox* [1979] ICR 736, EAT; *Knight v Attorney-General* [1979] ICR 194, EAT; *Arthur v Attorney-General* [1999] ICR 631 – see chapter 12.

65 RRA 1976 s75(5). The regulations prescribing these bodies are the Race Relations (Prescribed Public Bodies) (No 2) Regulations 1994 SI No 109.

66 RRA 1976 s76(3)–(11).

Economic Development,[67] a number of full-time tribunal chairmen brought claims under the Northern Ireland equivalent of the SDA 1975 in relation to the judicial pension scheme. Northern Ireland's Court of Appeal held that Community legislation required the inclusion within the definition of workers entitled to challenge sex discrimination under EC law of 'all persons who are engaged in a relationship which is broadly that of employment'. This being the case, the tribunal chairmen were protected under the ETD which took precedence over the domestic provisions.

11.57 The reasoning in the *Percival-Price* case appears to apply equally to judges and others in a comparable position. The significance of the case is not limited to pension cases but applies also to other areas of sex discrimination such as recruitment, promotion, dismissal and detriment. The ETD does not prohibit race discrimination, although the RD will do so after July 2003 (see para 10.84). Applicants to statutory judicial offices cannot bring a claim in the ET under the RRA 1976 and DDA 1995. Any challenge must be by way of judicial review.[67a]

The police

11.58 Under the RRA 1976 after its amendment by the RRAA 2000, applicants to and members of the police force are protected in the same way as other workers.[68] Special provisions still apply under the SDA 1975 which provides that the office of constable shall be treated as employment by the chief constable or police authority, and that an individual officer may be liable for discrimination (see para 31.34).[69] Special constables are also protected by the RRA 1976.

11.59 SDA 1975 s17 provides that regulations under the Police Act 1964 shall not treat men and women differently except as to:

- requirements relating to height, uniform or equipment or allowances in lieu of uniform or equipment – this is likely to be contrary to EC law (see para 10.37);

67 [2000] IRLR 380.

67a *Photis and others v Department of Trade and Industry*, 6 December 2001, EAT.

68 RRA 1976 s16, which provided that a police officer or cadet, or a job applicant was protected in the same way as other employees (and applicants) and the employer was deemed to be the chief officer of police or the police officer, was repealed by RRAA 2000 Sch 3 as from 2 April 2000.

69 *AM v WC and SPV* [1999] IRLR 410, EAT, in which a police sergeant was held liable for harassment of a woman police constable.

- special treatment afforded to women in connection with pregnancy or childbirth; and
- pensions for special constables or police cadets.

11.60 Proceedings should be brought against the chief constable and/or the police authority and, if appropriate, individual employees who have discriminated. The chief constable is liable for acts of discrimination by his or her officers[70] and compensation is paid out of the police fund.[71] Under the SDA 1975 the position is complicated by the EAT's decision in *Chief Constable of Bedfordshire Police v Liversidge*,[72] in which the EAT held that a chief constable could not be liable for acts of race discrimination by one police officer against another. This ruling will apply in relation to cases brought under the RRA 1976 before the implementation of the RRAA 2000, and to all SDA 1975 cases. *Liversidge* has been upheld by the Court of Appeal but leave to appeal to the House of Lords has been sought.

Prison officers

11.61 The SDA 1975 applies to prison officers except that discrimination in relation to height is lawful. This is likely to be contrary to EC law (see para 10.37). A man may become governor of a women's prison. There are no special provisions under the RRA 1976 for prison officers who are treated as any other workers.

The armed forces

11.62 Members of the armed forces are expressly protected by the RRA 1976 and SDA 1975.[73] The only exception is under the SDA 1975 which permits discrimination to ensure 'the combat effectiveness of the naval, military or air forces of the Crown'.[74] This is an inadequately defined and potentially broad exception. It may breach the ETD. However, given that the EC has adopted the same phrase in relation to age and disability,[75] the ECJ may be reluctant to question it.

11.63 In *Sirdar v Army Board and Secretary of State for Defence*[76] the ECJ

70 RRA 1976 s76A as amended by RRAA 2000 s4.
71 SDA 1975 s17(4); RRA 1976 s76A(4).
72 [2002] IRLR 15.
73 SDA 1975 s85(1)(c); RRA 1976 s75(2)(c).
74 SDA 1975 s85(4).
75 ED, para 19 of preamble.
76 Case 273/97 [1999] ECR I-7403; [2000] IRLR 47.

held that employment in the armed forces is subject to the principle of equal treatment and there was no general exception for measures taken for reasons of public security. The court accepted, however, that the exclusion of women from special combat units such as the Royal Marines may be justified under article 2(2) ETD's exception relating to occupational activities for which the sex of the worker is a determining factor (see para 10.37).

11.64 Under both the RRA 1976 and SDA 1975, serving members of the armed forces (but not applicants to the forces) must make their discrimination claims first through the internal procedures provided before going to an ET.[77] In such cases the time limit for bringing a claim is extended from three to six months. The internal procedure requirement does not apply where an internal complaint has been made and has not been withdrawn.[78] In *R v Army Board of Defence Council ex p Anderson*,[79] a case decided before armed forces personnel had a right to apply to the ET, the High Court held that the board must achieve a high standard of fairness, so that there should be a proper hearing, the complainant should have access to all material seen by the board, and the board should meet to consider the evidence.

Barristers and advocates

11.65 It is unlawful for a barrister or barrister's clerk to discriminate on the ground of sex or race in:

- recruiting pupils or tenants;
- the terms offered or given to them;
- training;
- access to benefits, facilities and services;
- in relation to dismissal or any other detriment.[80]

It is also unlawful for a person, such as a solicitor, to discriminate on grounds of race or sex in relation to the giving, withholding or acceptance of instructions to a barrister.

11.66 The provisions relating to barristers and their clerks are slightly

77 RRA 1976 s75 and Race Relations (Complaints to Employment Tribunals) (Armed Forces) Regulations 1997 SI No 2161; SDA 1975 s85(9A–E); Sex Discrimination (Complaints to Employment Tribunals) (Armed Forces) Regulations 1997 SI No 2163.

78 Race Relations (Complaints to Employment Tribunals) (Armed Forces) Regulations 1997 and Sex Discrimination (Complaints to Employment Tribunals) (Armed Forces) Regulations 1997.

79 [1991] IRLR 425, DC.

80 SDA 1975 s35A; RRA 1976 ss26 and 26B.

different from those for other employed and self-employed persons, and claims can only be brought in the county court. Contractual terms, including pay, are covered by the SDA 1975 rather than the EqPA 1970. Similar provisions apply to advocates in Scotland.

Discrimination other than by employers

11.67 In addition to their regulation of discrimination by employers and in relation to barristers and advocates, the SDA 1975 and RRA 1976 prohibit discrimination by:

- 'principals' in relation to contract workers (SDA 1975 s9, RRA 1976 s7);
- partners (SDA 1975 s11, RRA 1976 s10) – though, under the RRA 1976, only where there are six or more partners;[81]
- trade unions and organisations of employers (SDA 1975 s12, RRA 1976 s11);[82]
- qualifying bodies (SDA 1975 s13, RRA 1976 s12);[83]
- people concerned with provision of vocational training (SDA 1975 s14, RRA 1976 s13);
- employment agencies (SDA 1975 s15, RRA 1976 s14).

Different provisions apply to each and they are set out in chapter 12.

Exceptions to the prohibition on discrimination – an introduction

11.68 There are many situations where workers and applicants for employment have no, or only limited, protection against discrimination on grounds of race or sex. The SDA 1975 and RRA 1976 do not prohibit all aspects of discrimination.[84] Further, exceptions are provided even in respect of those areas of discrimination otherwise covered by the

81 This restriction does not apply in relation to the employment by partners of workers (who are not partners).

82 See further para 12.12.

83 See further para 12.25. The Sex Discrimination (Election Candidates) Act 2002 will enable a political party to adopt measures for the selection of candidates for elections (including women-only shortlists) that reduce the present inequality in the numbers of men and women.

84 See *Amin v Entry Clearance Officer, Bombay* [1983] 2 AC 818, also discussed at para 2.15.

various Acts. In this chapter we consider only those exceptions that relate to employment, widely defined.

11.69 It is worth noting that, even where a particular type of discrimination is permitted by the SDA 1975, it may not be permitted by EC law (the ETD or article 141 EC). The ETD, for example, permits of far fewer exceptions than the SDA 1975 in its prohibition of discrimination in access to employment, training, working conditions, promotion and dismissal. Note, however, that only those who work for emanations of the state (see para 10.71) can rely directly on the ETD in UK courts and tribunals. The SDA 1975 ought, where possible, to be interpreted consistently with the ETD and other directives. Private and public sector employees may rely directly on article 141. The application of EC law in various situations is considered further in chapter 10.

Genuine occupational qualifications

11.70 SDA 1975 s7 and RRA 1976 s5 permit employers to discriminate on grounds of sex and race, in cases in which being a man or a woman or a member of a particular racial group is a 'genuine occupational qualification' for the job. The genuine occupational qualification (GOQ) defence does not apply to claims of victimisation. It does, however, apply in relation to:

- the arrangements made for the purposes of determining who should be offered employment;
- refusals or deliberate failures to offer employment; and
- the way that access is afforded to opportunities for promotion or transfer to, or training for, employment.

11.71 The GOQ exceptions apply to 'employment' in the broad sense, as well as to contract work and to partnerships. They apply where some or all of the job duties fall within the GOQs set out below. The GOQ defence does not apply where:

- an employer already has employees of the other sex or of a different race who are capable of performing the relevant duties (see below); and
- it is reasonable to employ them to do these duties; and
- there are enough of them to carry out the duties without undue inconvenience.[85]

85 SDA 1975 s7(4); RRA 1976 s5(4).

11.72 In considering the validity of a GOQ defence, it is necessary to examine the possibility of re-allocating relevant duties. So, for example, in *Wylie v Dee & Co*[86] the applicant was refused a job as sales assistant in a men's clothing store because the job involved taking men's inside leg measurements. The ET rejected the employer's SDA 1975 s2(b) GOQ (see para 11.76), ruling that the measurements did not have to be performed very often and the shop employed seven other male assistants who could be called upon if necessary. For the limits of this approach see the discussion of *Chief Constable of West Yorkshire Police v A*,[87] below.

11.73 Neither the SDA 1975 nor the RRA 1976 states who bears the formal burden of proof in establishing a GOQ. In practice, it is usual for the party (the employer) who seeks to rely on the GOQ to prove that it applies.

GOQs under the Sex Discrimination Act 1975

11.74 The GOQ defence is not available in complaints of discrimination against married persons. It applies only to complaints of sex discrimination and/or discrimination relating to gender reassignment. GOQs will apply under the SDA 1975 in the following situations (s7(2)):

Physiology and authenticity

11.75 Where the essential nature of the job calls for a person of a particular sex for reasons of physiology (excluding physical strength or stamina) or, in dramatic performances or other entertainment, for reasons of authenticity, so that the essential nature of the job would be materially different if carried out by a person of the other sex – an example might be a job as a male model. Mere artistic or aesthetic preferences for one sex over another will not be sufficient. It must be established that the *essential nature* of the job would be materially different if it were carried out by a person of the other sex (s7(2)(a)).

Preservation of decency or privacy

11.76 Where the job needs to be held by a person of a particular sex to preserve decency or privacy because:

- it is likely to involve physical contact with people of the opposite

86 [1978] IRLR 103, see also *Etam plc v Rowan* [1989] IRLR 150.
87 [2002] IRLR 103.

sex in circumstances where they might reasonably object to its being carried out by a person of the other sex; or

- the holder of the job is likely to do his or her work in circumstances where persons of that particular sex might reasonably object to the presence of a person of the other sex because they are in a state of undress or are using sanitary facilities (s7(2)(b)).

This exception is not limited to the job duties that are necessary. It can also apply to matters that are reasonably incidental to the job. In *Sisley v Britannia Security Systems Ltd*,[88] for example, women worked on rotating shifts and were supplied with a bed for rest periods between shifts. The applicant, a man, applied for employment with the company. His application was refused. The employer sought to resist his sex discrimination complaint by raising a GOQ defence. It was held that women workers often removed their uniforms to sleep. It was not possible to provide separate rest room facilities for the applicant. The GOQ defence, therefore, applied.

Work in a private home

11.77 The job is likely to involve the holder of the job doing his/her work, or living, in a private home and needs to be held by a person of a particular sex because objection might reasonably be taken to allowing a person of the other sex the degree of physical or social contact with a person living in the home, or the knowledge of intimate details of such a person's life that is likely, because of the nature or circumstances of the job or of the home, to be allowed to, or available to, the holder of the job (s7(2)(ba)).

11.78 This provision covers employment in private households, jobs involving nursing care, companionship and personal attendance. Generally, tribunals have tended to accept GOQs in relation to single-sex old people's homes, but not in relation to qualified medical staff.

Single sex accommodation

11.79 Where the nature or location of the establishment makes it impracticable for the holder of the job to live elsewhere than in premises provided by the employer, and:

- the only such premises that are available for people holding that kind of job are lived in or normally lived in, by people of a particular sex and are not equipped with separate sleeping accommodation for

88 [1983] IRLR 404.

people of the other sex and sanitary facilities that could be used by the latter in privacy from the former; and
- it is not reasonable to expect the employer either to equip those premises with such accommodation and facilities or to provide other premises for people of the other sex than those who live or normally live on the premises (s7(2)(c)).

This GOQ is intended to apply to jobs in remote or inaccessible places such as lighthouses, oil rigs and ships, where there is a degree of residence. It does not matter whether that residence is temporary or permanent, although the GOQ does not apply to cases in which an employee is obliged to remain on premises for a limited period of time, eating and taking a period of rest.[89] In order to make out this GOQ an employer must establish not only that he has only single sex facilities available, but also that it is reasonable for him not to provide separate facilities for the other sex.

Hospitals, prisons, children's and old people's homes

11.80 Where the nature of the establishment, or of the part of it within which the work is done, requires the job to be held by a person of a particular sex because:
- it is, or is part of, a hospital, prison or other establishment for people requiring special care, supervision or attention; and
- those people are all of that particular sex (disregarding any people of the opposite sex whose presence is exceptional); and
- it is reasonable, having regard to the essential character of the establishment or that part of it, that the job should not be held by a person of the other sex (s7(2)(d)).

In order to make out this GOQ, an employer must satisfy a court or tribunal that it is reasonable to restrict the particular post to a person of a particular sex in the first place. In *Secretary of State for Scotland v Henley*[90] it was accepted that the refusal to employ a woman governor at a male prison would have come within this section. But two women already held similar posts as an 'experiment'. The ET rejected the GOQ defence because there were women in similar jobs. This decision was upheld by the EAT.

89 Ibid.
90 EAT 95/83 (unreported).

Personal services

11.81 Where the holder of the job provides individuals with personal services promoting their welfare or education, or similar personal services, and those services can most effectively be provided by a person of a particular sex (s7(2)(e)). This provision is of potentially wide-ranging application. It might cover social work, probation officers, housing officers and other welfare worker posts. The employer must show that the services in question could most effectively be provided by a person of a particular sex. The application of the equivalent provision of the RRA 1976, which has given rise to substantial litigation, is considered at para 11.91 below. That case-law will apply as appropriate to the SDA 1975.

Employment outside the UK

11.82 Where the job needs to be held by a person of a particular sex because it is likely to involve the performance of duties outside the UK in a country whose laws or customs are such that the duties could not, or could not effectively, be performed by a person of the other sex (s7(2)(g)).

Married couples

11.83 Where the job is one of two to be held by a married couple (s7(2)(h)).

Gender reassignment and GOQs

11.84 SDA 1975 s7A provides that employers may apply the sex-related GOQs to those intending to undergo, undergoing or having undergone gender reassignment where it is shown that the treatment is reasonable in the circumstances. In the context of gender reassignment the GOQs apply not only to recruitment decisions but also to decisions to dismiss. This means that if a postholder originally complied with a GOQ, but ceased to do so by reason of gender reassignment, the employer will be able to dismiss him or her if it is reasonable in all the circumstances to do so.

11.85 The 'normal' SDA 1975 GOQs apply to transsexuals in their original sex or sex of preference. Consequently, where an employer can show that it is a genuine occupational requirement for a post holder to be a man or a woman and that the treatment is reasonable in the circumstances a GOQ will be permitted. In *Chief Constable of West Yorkshire Police v A*[93] the EAT accepted that SDA 1975 s7(2)(b)(i) justified the

93 [2002] IRLR 103.

refusal of a job as a police constable to a woman who had undergone gender reassignment. She was refused employment on the ground that, because she remained legally male despite her gender reassignment, she could not search women suspects without a misrepresentation by the police service as to her sex. The EAT accepted that such searches were part of a constable's duties and that, if the applicant were excused from having to conduct them, questions would be raised by her colleagues. Further, the EAT did not accept that s7(4) (see para 11.71) applied in this particular case since, on the ET's findings, the respondent employers had been forced on occasion to call women officers from other divisions of the police force to conduct searches on women.

11.86 The decision in *Chief Constable of West Yorkshire Police v A* highlights the importance to transsexuals of a right to alter their birth certificates to register their chosen sex. The ECtHR decision in *Goodwin v UK*[94] will therefore be very important to people in A's position. The UK law will have to be amended.

11.87 In addition to the normal GOQs, SDA 1975 s7B provides four supplementary GOQs connected with gender reassignment. The first and second are referred to as permanent exceptions because they continue after the gender reassignment has taken effect, the third and fourth have been called temporary because they are only effective while the job holder is intending to undergo or is actually undergoing gender reassignment. Once the process is complete exceptions (c) and (d) will no longer be applicable. The exceptions apply where:

a) 'The job involves the holder of the job being liable to be called upon to perform *intimate physical searches* pursuant to statutory powers' (s7B(2)(a)); and
b) 'The job is likely to involve the holder of the job doing his work, or living, in a *private home* and needs to be held otherwise than by a person who is undergoing or has undergone gender reassignment, because objection might reasonably be taken to allowing to such a person –
   (i) the degree of *physical or social contact* with a person living in the home, or
   (ii) the *knowledge of intimate details* of such a person's life,
   which is likely, because of the nature or circumstances of the job or of the home, to be allowed to, or available to, the holder of the job' (s7B(2)(b));

94 Application No 28957/95, judgment 11 July 2002. See also para 2.29 above.

c) 'The nature or location of the establishment makes it impracticable for the holder of the job to live elsewhere than in *premises provided by the employer*, and –
   (i) the only such premises which are available for persons holding that kind of job are such that reasonable objection could be taken, for the purpose of preserving decency and privacy, to the holder of the job sharing accommodation and facilities with either sex whilst undergoing gender reassignment, and
   (ii) it is not reasonable to expect the employer either to equip those premises with suitable accommodation or to make alternative arrangements' (s7B(2)(c));

d) 'The holder of the job provides vulnerable individuals with personal services promoting their welfare, or similar personal services, and in the reasonable view of the employer those services cannot be effectively provided by a person whilst that person is undergoing gender reassignment' (s7B(2)(d)).

The particular difficulty posed by s7B(2)(c) and (d) is that it is not always entirely clear when the process of gender reassignment is completed. For some people it can take many years and a series of operations.

11.88 The operation of s7B(2)(a) was considered by the EAT in *Chief Constable of West Yorkshire Police v A* (above). In addition to the GOQ claimed under s7(2)(b)(ii) the chief constable argued that s7B(2)(a) applied to the position of police constable because, under the Police and Criminal Evidence Act 1984, intimate searches may be carried out only by and in the presence of people of the same sex as the person searched.[95] Having ruled in favour of the police service under s7(2)(b)(ii) above, the EAT concluded that 'intimate physical searches pursuant to statutory powers' are carried out only rarely by the police, generally being conducted instead by a nurse or doctor. On this basis the EAT ruled that the likelihood of being called on to perform *intimate* physical searches was too insignificant to impose an absolute bar on the appointment of a transsexual as a police constable by virtue of s7B(2)(a).

11.89 The application of the GOQ defence to transsexuals may be incompatible with the ETD particularly if, as suggested by the decision

95 PACE 1984 s65 defines an 'intimate search' as one which consists of the physical examination of a person's body orifices other than the mouth. There are other statutory powers to perform such searches and they are all similarly defined.

in *Chief Constable of West Yorkshire Police v A*,[96] it effectively bans from the police service those who have undergone gender reassignment.

GOQs under the Race Relations Act 1976

11.90 It is open to an employer to argue that being a member of a particular racial group is a GOQ in the following situations:

- **authenticity** – where (under s5(2)(a)) the job involves acting or other entertainment and authenticity is required; or (s5(2)(b)) being an artist's or photographer's model in the production of a work of art, visual image or sequence of visual images for which a person of that racial group is required for reasons of authenticity; or (s5(2)(c)) working in a place where food or drink is (for payment or not) provided to and consumed by members of the public or a section of the public in a particular setting for which, in that job, a person of that racial group is required for reasons of authenticity; or
- **personal services** – where the holder of the job provides people of that racial group with personal services promoting their welfare, and those services can most effectively be provided by a person of that racial group (s5(2)(d)).

11.91 The courts have recognised that it is a delicate balancing exercise between the need to guard against discrimination and the meeting of genuine and legitimate cultural needs. In *Tottenham Green Under Five's Centre v Marshall*[97] a play-group catering for a wide variety of ethnic groups was held to be entitled to advertise specifically for an African-Caribbean worker to fill a vacancy created when an African-Caribbean worker left. The play group identified the 'personal services' provided by the worker as:

- maintaining the cultural links of the children,
- dealing with their parents,
- reading and talking in patois, and
- skin and hair care.

The EAT emphasised that it would be wrong to erect too high a fence in the way of a responsible employer seeking to rely on this provision, stating that 'where genuine attempts are being made to integrate

96 [2002] IRLR 103.
97 [1989] IRLR 147.

groups into society, too narrow a construction might stifle such initiatives'. The EAT held:

a) the racial group will need to be clearly and, if necessary, narrowly defined because it must be the holder of the post and recipient of the personal services;
b) the holder of the post must be directly involved in the provision of services, though not necessarily on a one-to-one basis;
c) if the post-holder provides several personal services to the recipient, then provided one of those genuinely falls within the section, the defence is established;
d) promoting their welfare is a very wide expression and it would be undesirable to narrow the width of the words;
e) those services can most effectively be provided by a person of that racial group. The words are not 'must be provided' or 'can only be provided'. The question is whether they can be more effectively provided by a member of the relevant racial group.

11.92 In *Tottenham Green Under Fives' Centre v Marshall (No 2)*[98] the ET's decision was again overturned. The EAT held that once (as here) it was established that a relevant duty to provide personal services did exist as part of the job in question, it was not for the ET to disregard that aspect of the job because, in its opinion, the duty was relatively unimportant compared to other aspects of the job. Once a relevant personal service had been established the exception defined in RRA 1976 s5(2)(d) necessarily came into play.

11.93 In *Lambeth LBC v Commission for Racial Equality (CRE)*[99] the respondent advertised to fill managerial vacancies in its housing department, and sought to justify restricting the positions to Asians and African-Caribbeans on the ground that the s5(2)(d) exception applied. The CRE brought proceedings under RRA 1976 s29, alleging that the advertisement was discriminatory. An ET held that the Council had failed to establish a genuine occupational qualification. The EAT upheld this decision, stating as a matter of principle that RRA 1976 s5 should be narrowly construed. The phrase 'personal services' envisages circumstances where direct contact is likely, mainly face-to-face, and where language or a knowledge and understanding of cultural and religious background are of material importance. It was too wide to read 'personal services' as covering any services which ultimately affect an individual. The Court of Appeal

98 [1991] IRLR 162.
99 [1990] IRLR 231.

endorsed this interpretation of the section. Balcombe LJ stated that the use of the word 'personal ... indicated that the identity of the giver and the recipient of the services is important'. The Court of Appeal did not interpret s5(2)(d) as embracing what it regarded as 'positive action'.

Other exceptions common to the Sex Discrimination Act 1975 and the Race Relations Act 1976

11.94 Both the SDA 1975 and the RRA 1976 provide exceptions relating to acts done to safeguard national security, acts done under statutory authority, acts of trade unions and similar bodies and acts of qualifying bodies in relation to which there is a statutory right of appeal. The first three of these exceptions is considered here, the third in chapter 12.

11.95 The exceptions relating to national security and acts done under statutory authority differ significantly between the SDA 1975 and the RRA 1976 as a result of amendments to the former which were required by EC law. The RRA 1976 is, as yet, relatively untouched by EC law but, more recently, has been amended by the RRAA 2000 to comply (in relation to the national security exception) with the jurisprudence of the European Court of Human Rights.[100] No similar amendment has, as yet, been made to the SDA 1975.

National security

11.96 Both the RRA 1976[101] and the SDA 1975[102] originally provided that acts done for the purpose of safeguarding national security were exempt from the provisions of the Acts and, further, that the issue of a certificate by the Home Secretary to the effect that a challenged act of discrimination was done for the purpose of national security or protecting public safety or public order was conclusive evidence of that fact, and excluded scrutiny by a tribunal. The, SDA 1975 s52 now says:

(1) Nothing in Parts II to IV shall render unlawful an act done for the purpose of safeguarding national security.

100 *Tinnelly & Sons Ltd v UK* (1998) 27 EHRR 249.
101 RRA 1976 s42.
102 SDA 1975 s52.

11.97 In *Johnston v Chief Constable of the RUC*[103] the ECJ ruled that Northern Ireland's equivalent of SDA 1975 s52 (as originally enacted) was inconsistent with the ETD, article 6 of which requires member states to introduce into their national legal systems such measures as are necessary to enable everyone who considers that they have been discriminated against under the directive to pursue their claims by judicial process.[104] The Northern Ireland Order and the SDA 1975 were amended accordingly, the Sex Discrimination (Amendment) Order 1988[105] providing that:

> Subsections (2) and (3) of section 52 of the Sex Discrimination Act 1975 ... shall cease to have effect in relation to the determination of the question whether any act is rendered unlawful by Part II of that Act, by Part III of that Act, so far as it applies to vocational training, or by Part IV of that Act taken with Part II or with Part III so far as it so applies.[106]

11.98 National security remains a defence under the SDA 1975, but the Secretary of State no longer has the power to issue a certificate stating that an act was done for the purpose of safeguarding national security. It ought to be noted also that the amendment applies only in relation to employment, broadly defined, and vocational training.[107]

11.99 In 2000, however, there was a much more radical amendment made by the RRAA to RRA 1976 s42. This now provides that:

> Nothing in Parts II to IV shall render unlawful an act done for the purpose of safeguarding national security *if the doing of the act was justified by that purpose* [emphasis added].

11.100 RRA 1976 s69(2) provides that a national security certificate shall be regarded as conclusive evidence of the matters specified in it. A new procedure has been introduced to enable a court hearing proceedings to exclude the applicant, the applicant's representatives or the assessors from all or part of the proceedings if the court considers this step expedient in the interests of national security (where, for example, it intends to consider whether a discriminatory act was justified by national security).[108] In such circumstances the Attorney-General (or in

103 Case 222/84 [1986] ECR 1651; [1986] IRLR 263. See also para 10.38.

104 Sex Discrimination (Northern Ireland) Order 1976 SI No 1042.

105 SI No 249.

106 A materially identical provision amended the Sex Discrimination (Northern Ireland) Order 1976.

107 RRA 1976 s52(2) and (3) continue to apply to SDA 1975 Pt III except in relation to vocational training.

108 New RRA 1976 s67A.

Scotland the Advocate General) may appoint a person to represent the interests of the applicant in the parts of the proceedings from which the applicant or his or her representatives has been excluded.

Acts done under statutory authority

11.101 RRA 1976 s41 exempts from that Act's prohibitions on race discrimination any act of discrimination done:

(a) in pursuance of any enactment or Order in Council; or
(b) in pursuance of any instrument made under any enactment by a Minister of the Crown; or
(c) in order to comply with any condition or requirement imposed by a Minister of the Crown (whether before or after the passing of this Act) by virtue of any enactment.[109]

11.102 In *Hampson v Department of Education and Science*[110] the House of Lords adopted a narrow construction of the words 'in pursuance of any instrument'. A Hong Kong Chinese trained teacher was refused qualified teacher status in England because the Home Secretary determined that her training (three years with a break between the second and third) was not comparable to the three consecutive years required in Britain. The relevant regulations required only that teachers trained abroad had 'comparable' training. The Home Secretary had exercised his discretion to decide that Ms Hampson's training was not comparable to the British qualification. The House of Lords held that the words 'in pursuance of any instrument' were confined to 'acts done in necessary performance of an express obligation contained in the instrument and do not also include acts done in exercise of a power or discretion conferred by the instrument.'

11.103 As the House of Lords pointed out in *Hampson*, almost every discretionary decision taken by a statutory body is taken against a statutory background. A wider construction of the words of the RRA 1976 would lead to an unacceptably wide exemption and defeat the purposes of the legislation.

11.104 RRA 1976 s41(2) also exempts discrimination on the basis of nationality, place of ordinary residence, and length of residence in any particular place where that discrimination is:

(a) in pursuance of any arrangements made (whether before or after the passing of this Act) by or with the approval of, or for the time being approved by, a Minister of the Crown; or

109 This is an interesting reversal of the normal implied repeal convention.
110 [1991] 1 AC 171; [1990] IRLR 302.

(b) in order to comply with any condition imposed (whether before or after the passing of this Act) by a Minister of the Crown.

A ministerial certificate that the arrangements or conditions in question were approved or imposed by a minister is conclusive evidence of the facts stated and a document claiming to be such a certificate is to be deemed to be one unless and until the contrary is proved.

11.105 SDA 1975 s51 originally contained the same blanket exemption from liability under the Act in respects of acts done under 'statutory authority' as that provided by RRA 1976 s52, set out above. This blanket provision was removed by the Employment Act (EA) 1989, which amended s51 and added a new SDA 1975 s51A. The application of SDA 1975 s51 is now limited, in the employment context, to those acts that are:

- necessary to comply with a statutory provision that pre-dated the SDA 1975[111] and which was concerned with the protection of women in relation to:
  - pregnancy or maternity, or
  - other circumstances giving rise to risks specifically affecting women,[112] or
- necessary to comply with a relevant statutory provision for the purposes of the Health and Safety at Work Act 1974 and was done for the purposes of protecting the woman in question.[113]

Trade unions and other professional bodies

11.106 The application of the SDA 1975 and RRA 1976 to trade unions, other organisations of workers, organisations of employers and other trade or professional associations is considered in chapter 12. Here we deal with the discrimination which the SDA 1975 and RRA 1976 permits such bodies to engage in. The SDA 1975 provides that these bodies may give women (or men) access to training to help them take up positions in the organisation or to encourage them to apply where

111 Or was an instrument made by or under an Act predating the SDA 1975.

112 Whether the provision protected only women or other classes of person as well. See further EA 1989 ss1–8 and Sch 1. Sch 1 lists a number of statutory provisions concerned with the protection of women including the prohibition on women working in a factory within four weeks of childbirth, or at sea or on aircraft during pregnancy. Women will be entitled to suitable alternative available work or to be suspended on full pay where, because of pregnancy or childbirth, they cannot work because of such a statutory prohibition (see para 17.55).

113 Or of any class including that woman.

there are no or few women (or men) in those positions. They may encourage women (or men), if they are under-represented, to become members.[114] These provisions are further considered in chapter 5. SDA 1975 s49 also permits unions to reserve seats in the organisation or make extra seats available for such under represented women (or men). The RRA 1976 contains no equivalent provision to s49. Thus it is unlawful for a trade union to reserve a minimum number of places on an organisation's elected or membership body for black or other ethnic minority candidates. Trade unions can, however, provide members of under-represented groups with training in order to help them to take up positions within the organisation (see above) and may encourage people from under-represented racial groups to become members (again, see further chapter 5).[115]

Exceptions unique to the Sex Discrimination Act 1975

11.107 Many of the exceptions unique to the SDA 1975 concern discrimination other than in the employment context and are dealt with in chapter 29. Here we consider only those exceptions concerned with employment. These relate to:

- sex discrimination claims concerned with contractual payments that, aside from falling outside the scope of SDA 1975 s6(2) in any event, are also expressly excluded from challenge under that Act by s6(6) (though they may proceed under the EqPA 1970[116]); and
- employment for the purposes of religion. Sex discrimination is lawful in relation to employment for the purposes of an organised religion where employment is limited to one sex so as to comply with 'the doctrines of the religion or to avoid offending the religious susceptibilities of a significant number of its followers'.[117] A similar provision applies where the discrimination is on grounds relating to gender reassignment.[118]

114 SDA 1975 s48(2) and (3).

115 RRA 1976 s48(3)–(5).

116 Further, where the alleged discrimination relates to gender reassignment such claims are to be brought under the SDA 1975 – see para 2.22.

117 SDA 1975 s19.

118 Ibid s19(3). Also to the conferring of authorisations or qualifications for purposes of an organised religion – see para 12.35.

Exceptions unique to the Race Relations Act 1976

11.108 The RRA 1976, like the SDA 1975, contains exceptions that relate to the employment and non-employment context. Provisions relating to positive action are set out in chapter 5, genuine occupational qualifications are covered at paras 11.70–11.82. Only the former are dealt with here, the latter being considered in chapter 29. They relate to:

- Employment in a private household. RRA 1976 s4(3) provides that the prohibition on direct and indirect race discrimination does not apply 'to employment for the purposes of a private household'. The victimisation provisions (see chapter 4) do apply however. This exception will have to be removed in the implementation of the RD.
- Employment 'in the service of the Crown or by any public body prescribed ... by regulations made by the Minister for the Civil Service' – such regulations may restrict this employment 'to persons of particular birth, nationality, descent or residence (RRA 1976 s75(5)(a)).
- Seamen recruited abroad. The RRA 1976 permits race discrimination when seamen are recruited onto British ships at overseas ports.[119] This exception is due to be removed in the implementation of the RD.
- Training for those not ordinarily resident in the UK. The RRA 1976 provides that race discrimination is permitted for the benefit of a person not ordinarily resident in Great Britain when their employment, education or training is intended to provide training in skills to be exercised outside Great Britain.[120] Again, this exception is likely to be removed by July 2003.
- Partnerships of fewer than six people. RRA 1976 s10 provides that partnerships of less than six are exempt from the RRA 1976 in relation to the arrangements that they make to offer partnerships, the terms of partnerships, the way they afford access to benefits, facilities or services or terminate partnerships. Once again, this exception should be removed by July 2003.
- Sikhs working on construction sites. EA 1989 s11 exempts such workers from statutory requirements to wear safety helmets. Only a Sikh who works or seeks to work on a construction site benefits from this concession. Work elsewhere is not covered. Special

119 RRA 1976 s9.
120 Ibid s6.

provision is made for the consequences in tort if personal injury or loss result. Other minority groups whose religions impose particular dress requirements do not benefit from this or any similar concession. EA 1989 s12(1) deems an employer in the construction industry who requires all workers to wear safety helmets to be indirectly and unlawfully discriminating against any Sikh who is refused employment or suffers some other detriment. The employer cannot justify the requirement or practice. This presumption of unlawful discrimination operates unless the employer has reasonable grounds for believing that the Sikh worker would not wear a turban at all times on the construction site.

Asylum and Immigration Acts 1996 and 1999

11.109 The Asylum and Immigration Act (AIA) 1996 was introduced as part of a range of measures directed at stopping immigrants from working illegally. AIA 1996 s8 aims to ensure that employment is offered only to those entitled to live and work in the UK. AIA 1996 s8 is considered here but it is not, strictly speaking, an exception to the prohibition against race discrimination. It does raise challenges to non-discriminatory employment practices. But far from acting as a defence to a claim under the RRA 1976, it is now clear that s8 must be applied in a manner that does not discriminate on grounds of race.

11.110 Employers who employ people over the age of 16 who have not been granted leave to enter or remain in the UK, or who are not entitled to work in the UK, are liable to criminal prosecution. An employer found to be in breach of the Act may be fined. An employer in breach of the Act could be prosecuted and fined in respect of each employee who is working illegally.[121]

11.111 These provisions do not apply to those who were employed prior to 27 January 1997; nor do they apply to the self-employed. An employer who can establish that he or she was shown, prior to the start of employment, one of the following documents that appeared to relate to the employee will have a defence:

- a document issued by a previous employer, the Inland Revenue, the Benefits Agency, the Contributions Agency, the Employment Service, the Training and Employment Agency (Northern Ireland) or the Northern Ireland Social Security Agency that contains the national insurance number of the person named on the document;

121 AIA 1996 s8.

- a passport that describes the holder as a British citizen or as having the right of abode in, or entitlement to readmission to the UK;
- a passport that contains a certificate of entitlement issued by or on behalf of the UK government certifying that the holder has the right of abode in the UK;
- a certificate of registration or naturalisation as a British citizen;
- a birth certificate issued in the UK, the Republic of Ireland, the Channel Islands or the Isle of Man;
- a passport or national identity card issued by a state which is party to the European Economic Area Agreement, describing the holder as a national of a state which is party to that agreement;
- a passport or other travel document that is endorsed to show that the holder is exempt from immigration control, has indefinite leave to enter or remain in the UK or has no time limit on his/her stay, or a letter issued by the Home Office containing that information;
- a passport or other travel document that is endorsed to show that the holder has current leave to enter, remain in the UK and is not precluded from taking the employment in question, or a letter issued by the Home Office containing that information;
- a UK residence permit issued by a national of a state which is part of the European Economic Area (EEA);
- a passport or other travel document that is endorsed to show that the holder has a current right of residence in the UK as a family member of a named national of a state which is part of the EEA who is resident in the UK;
- a letter from the Home Office that indicates that the person named in it is a British citizen or has permission to take employment;
- a work permit or other approval to take employment issued by the Department for Education and Employment or the Training and Employment Agency (Northern Ireland);
- a passport that describes the holder as a British Dependent Territories citizen and which indicates that that status derives from a connection with Gibraltar.[122]

The documents listed are of equal status under the AIA 1996. So, for example, a person who is unable to produce a document showing his/her National Insurance number should not be treated less favourably if she or he is able to produce any other document listed.

122 Immigration (Restrictions on Employment) Order 1996 SI No 3325.

An employer need only see one of the specified documents. Rejecting a candidate who does not have a particular document even though he or she has one of the others may be unlawful discrimination.[123]

11.112 An employer is not expected to investigate the authenticity of the document produced. It is enough that he or she believed it to be a document of the type specified.[124] In order to make out this defence the employer must take and keep a copy of the document or some other record of it.[125]

Codes of practice

11.113 In 1996 the Home Office issued detailed guidance about what employers must do to avoid a criminal conviction under AIA 1996 s8. The 1996 guidance reminds employers of their obligations under the RRA 1976. This guidance applies also in Northern Ireland where employers have similar obligations under the Race Relations (Northern Ireland) Order (RR(NI)O) 1997.[126]

11.114 Evidence emerged that some employers may be unlawfully discriminating in their efforts to avoid a conviction under s8. So a new code of practice was introduced under an amendment to the AIA 1996 by the Immigration and Asylum Act 1999 s22.[127] The code, which was published on 2 May 2001, aims to provide all employers with guidance on complying with AIA 1996 s8 in a way that does not result in unlawful race discrimination.

11.115 The new code is designed to strengthen the safeguards against race discrimination by re-emphasising employers' statutory duty to avoid race discrimination in their recruitment practices. The code does not impose any legal obligations itself, and it is not an authoritative statement of the law. Failure to observe the code is not a breach of the law. But such a failure is admissible in evidence in any proceedings under the RRA 1976. ETs must take the code into account, if it is relevant.

123 AIA 1999 s22 (see below) and para 26 of the code of practice for all employers on the avoidance of race discrimination in recruitment practice while seeking to prevent illegal working.

124 AIA 1996 s8(2)(a).

125 Ibid s8(2).

126 SI No 869, NI 6.

127 Code of practice for all employers on the avoidance of race discrimination in recruitment practice while seeking to prevent illegal working (published in Immigration (Restrictions on Employment) (Code of Practice) Order 2001 SI No 1436).

11.116 The new code of practice, which came into effect on 6 May 2001, outlines an employer's legal obligations under the RRA 1976, the RR(NI)O 1997 and the AIA 1996, and provides some guidance on best practice in employment procedures to help employers meet these obligations. It is not comprehensive and it is for employers to operate transparent recruitment practices that are consistent with the law and which ensure fair treatment to all applicants.

11.117 The new code repeats the suggestion contained in the earlier code that checks should be built into an employer's recruitment procedure in order to ensure that the employer does not commit an offence under the AIA 1996. The code also warns that checks on potential employees must be carried out in a non-discriminatory way, and that all applicants for employment should be treated in the same way at each stage of the recruitment process. The guidance makes it clear that most people from ethnic minorities are British citizens. It also states that carrying out checks on potential employees on the basis of their appearance or accent is likely to breach the RRA 1976.

11.118 The new code draws heavily on the 1983 CRE Code of Practice for the Elimination of Racial Discrimination and the Promotion of Equality of Opportunity in Employment (see para 1.18). It advises that, as a matter of good practice:

- employers should have clear written procedures for recruitment and selection based on equal and fair treatment for all applicants and should make these known to all relevant staff;
- all job selections should be on the basis of suitability for the post;
- employers should ensure that no prospective job applicants are discouraged or excluded either directly or indirectly because of their appearance or accent;
- employers should not make assumptions about a person's right to work, or immigration status, on the basis of their colour, race, nationality or ethnic or national origins or the length of time they have been in the UK.

11.119 The code emphasises that, to avoid prosecution under the AIA 1996, an employer need only see and either keep or make a copy of one of the documents listed above before the employment begins. There is no need for an employer to ask about an applicant's immigration status, apart from asking if he or she needs permission to work. The code makes the point that such inquiries could mislead an employer into taking decisions that might amount to unlawful racial discrimination. It reminds employers that the best way to ensure that they do not discriminate is to treat all applicants in the same way at each stage of the recruitment process, and suggests that an employer who provides information to prospective applicants or supplies an application form might also include a reminder that the successful applicant will be asked to produce one of the documents listed above.

11.120 An employer may choose to ask for one of the listed documents only from the person actually chosen to fill a vacancy, but must not ask for a document from one applicant without making the same request to all those who are at the same stage of the application process. The code suggests that, if a person is not able to produce one of the listed documents, an employer should not assume that he or she is living or working in the UK illegally, but should refer the person to a Citizens Advice Bureau or other agency for advice. It urges that the employer should try to keep the job open for as long as possible, but adds that he or she is not obliged to do so if there is a need to recruit someone urgently. Finally the code suggests that, as a matter of good practice, employers should monitor the outcomes of recruitment and selection by the ethnicity of job applicants.

11.121 An employer may still be liable under the AIA 1996 even if it uses the services of a recruitment agency to select new staff. This is because the contract of employment is between the employer and employee rather than between the agency and the employee.

CHAPTER 12

Employment-related discrimination by other bodies

Key points

12.1
- The Sex Discrimination Act (SDA) 1975, Race Relations Act (RRA) 1976 and Disability Discrimination Act (DDA) 1995 regulate discrimination other than by employers in the wider employment-related context which includes, for example, the provision of vocational training and decision-making about partners and by qualifying bodies.
- To the extent that bodies such as partnerships, and those concerned with vocational training, act as employers, they are bound by the provisions of the SDA 1975, the RRA 1976 and the DDA 1995 considered in chapters 11, 13, 14 and 15.
- The models adopted differ as between the SDA 1975 and RRA 1976 on the one hand and the DDA 1995 on the other. Some of the provisions made by the former in this context are absent from the latter.
- The implementation of the Employment Directive (ED) will have significant implications for the DDA 1995 in this area.
- The SDA 1975 and RRA 1976 apply to discrimination against partners in very similar terms as those which apply to workers. The DDA 1995 does not, as yet, protect 'partners' properly so-called.
- The SDA 1975, RRA 1976 and DDA 1995 regulate discrimination by trade unions and other trade and professional organisations. The SDA 1975 and RRA 1976 permit some 'positive action' in this area (see further chapter 5) while the DDA 1995 protects only the 'disabled' except in relation to victimisation (see further chapters 2 and 6). Positive action in favour of disabled people is not unlawful and where there is a reasonable adjustment duty it may be unlawful not to make accommodation for disabled people.
- The SDA 1975 and RRA 1976 prohibit discrimination by 'qualifying bodies', the definition of which has given rise to significant litigation in recent years. The DDA 1995 as yet contains no equivalent provisions.
- Neither the SDA 1975 nor the RRA 1976 applies to decisions by qualifying bodies from which a statutory appeal is available.
- The SDA 1975, RRA 1976 and DDA 1995 all regulate discrimination by vocational training bodies. The SDA 1975 and RRA 1976 permit some 'positive action' in this area (see further chapter 5).

- The SDA 1975, RRA 1976 and DDA 1995 prohibit discrimination by employment agencies and by 'principals' against contract workers. The provisions dealing with contract workers are broadly construed to apply even where a number of contractual relationships separate the worker and the alleged discriminator.

Background and statutory provisions

12.2 This chapter considers broadly employment-related discrimination by bodies acting other than as employers. In any case in which a body considered here (such as a trade union, for example, or a partnership) acts as an employer, the employment provisions of the relevant Act apply. An employee claiming discrimination against a trade association employer, for example, will claim under the employment provisions considered in chapters 11 and 13–15, while a member or applicant to the association who claims to have been discriminated against by the association will rely on the provisions discussed here.

12.3 In this chapter we consider the liability of bodies such as trade organisations for discrimination on grounds of disability as well as sex and race. The provisions considered here are SDA 1975 ss9 and 10–16, RRA 1976 ss7 and 10–15, and DDA 1995 ss12–15. They cover discrimination by trade unions, partnerships, qualifying bodies, vocational training bodies, employment agencies and 'principals' (the latter in relation to contract workers – see further para 12.50 below). The provisions of the SDA 1975 and RRA 1976 are very similar while those of the DDA 1995 are, for now, considerably less comprehensive. The DDA 1995, for example, does not regulate discrimination by partners against each other or against prospective partners (contrast para 12.4 below). Nor does it regulate discrimination by qualifying bodies. These gaps will have to be addressed by the government when it implements the ED,[1] whose disability-related provisions it is committed to transposing into domestic legislation by October 2004 (see further chapter 6).

1 Council Directive 2000/78/EC.

Partnerships

Liability for discrimination on grounds of sex and race

12.4 SDA 1975 s11 and RRA 1976 s10 apply similar provisions to partnerships and would-be partnerships to those which govern employment relationships (see para 12.28). Thus, for example, partnerships are prohibited from direct and indirect sex and race discrimination in connection with selection for partnerships. Partnerships and would-be partnerships are able to rely in this context on the genuine occupational qualification (GOQ) defences provided in relation to employment discrimination (see para 11.70). In limited circumstances a partner may also be a worker and be covered in that capacity by the employment-related provisions of the relevant Act.[2]

12.5 RRA 1976 s10(1) and SDA 1975 s11(1) make it unlawful for a firm of partners (which includes a limited partnership[3]) to discriminate 'in relation to a position as partner in the firm':

(a) in the arrangements they make for the purpose of determining who should be offered that position, or
(b) in the terms on which they offer [a person] that position, or
(c) by refusing or deliberately omitting to offer [a person] that position, or
(d) in a case where [a person] already holds that position—
  (i) in the way they afford [him or] her access to any benefits, facilities or services, or by refusing or deliberately omitting to afford [him or] her access to them, or
  (ii) by expelling [him or] her from that position, or subjecting [him or] her to any other detriment.

12.6 SDA 1975 s82(1A) provides that expulsion, for the purposes of SDA 1975 s11(1)(d)(ii), includes constructive dismissal and the expiry without renewal of a fixed term contract. The RRA 1976 contains no equivalent provision.[4]

2 See *Loughran and Kelly v Northern Ireland Health Executive* [1999] AC 428; [1998] IRLR 593, HL, in which it was accepted that the partner of a firm could also be 'employed' for the purposes of the anti-discrimination legislation by a body to which the firm had contracted his or her (named) services. In addition, the term 'partner' properly refers to a self-employed person in business who is remunerated by taking a share of the firm's profits. It is, however, often used loosely and a 'salaried partner' for example, is not a partner in the legal sense and, as an employee, benefits from the protection afforded by the RRA 1976, SDA 1975 and DDA 1995 in relation to workers (see chapters 11, 13, 14 and 15).

3 SDA 1975 s11(5).

4 See para 5.113 for the recognition of 'constructive dismissals' under the RRA 1976 generally.

12.7 RRA 1976 s10 and SDA 1975 s11 apply to 'persons proposing to form themselves into a partnership' as they do to existing partnerships, though the prohibition in RRA 1976 on discrimination in relation to partnership only applies, at present, to firms (and proposed firms) having at least six partners.[5] The SDA 1975 prohibits discrimination 'on grounds of' a person's sex (ie, discrimination against women, men and married people, discrimination on grounds of gender reassignment, and discrimination by way of victimisation), the RRA 1976 prohibits discrimination 'on racial grounds' (see further para 2.33).

12.8 Partners are not generally 'employed' even under the broad definition of the SDA 1975 and RRA 1976,[6] and so it is arguable that those who work wholly or partly outside Great Britain are entitled to bring their complaints of unlawful discrimination to an ET notwithstanding the provisions of SDA 1975 s6(1) and RRA 1976 s4(1), which restrict those Acts' prohibitions on employment-related discrimination to those working in Great Britain (see further para 11.20).

Exceptions and qualifications

12.9 Discrimination in the arrangements made to decide who should be offered a partnership, or in the terms on which a partnership is offered, is not unlawful if being a man or a woman would be a GOQ in an employment situation (see further para 11.70).[7] Equally, discrimination in connection with gender reassignment will be lawful in relation to partnership decisions where it would be lawful in an employment context.[8] The GOQs and supplementary GOQs applicable in the context of gender reassignment are considered at para 11.84.

12.10 SDA 1975 s11(4) provides a further exception to the prohibition on discrimination in relation to provisions made in relation to death or retirement in the following circumstances:

(a) In the terms on which a partnership is offered except insofar as those terms relate to expulsion from partnership;
(b) In the terms on which access to benefits, facilities or services are provided;
(c) By subjecting [a partner] to any other detriment except in so far as the detriment results in her expulsion.

5 RRA 1976 s10(2). This will change with the implementation in the UK of the Race Directive (see para 10.83).
6 See chapter 11 but see also note 2 above.
7 SDA 1975 s11(3).
8 Ibid s11(3B) and (3C).

These exceptions may be inconsistent with the provisions of the Equal Treatment Directive[9] (ETD) (see para 10.34).

Disability discrimination

12.11 In contrast with the SDA 1975 and RRA 1976, the DDA 1995 does not protect partners or prospective partners from discrimination. 'Salaried partners' are protected, however, by the employment-related provisions of the DDA 1995 (see chapter 13).[10] The DDA 1995 will be amended to include partners within the scope of Pt II in order to comply with the ED. The changes, which are expected to be made by October 2004, are likely to mirror the existing RRA 1976 and SDA 1975 provisions.

Trade unions and other professional organisations

12.12 Discrimination by trade unions, other organisations of workers, organisations of employers and other trade or professional associations is prohibited by SDA 1975 s12 and RRA 1976 s11 and also by DDA 1995 ss13–15, which refer collectively to such organisations as 'trade organisations'.[11] The employment provisions of the SDA 1975, RRA 1976 and DDA 1995 cover such organisations' treatment of their own workers,[12] while the provisions discussed below concern the treatment by these organisations of their members and applicants for membership. Trade organisations may also be service providers and be subject to anti-discrimination provisions in this regard as well.

12.13 Under the DDA 1995 there is a separate statutory code of practice on the duties of trade organisations to their disabled members and applicants.[13] Issued in 1999, this code of practice revises paras 7.9 to 13 of the Code of practice for the elimination of discrimination in the field of employment against disabled persons or persons who have had a disability (see further para 1.21).

9 Council Directive 76/207/EEC.

10 And see also *Loughran and Kelly v Northern Ireland Health Executive* [1999] AC 428; [1998] IRLR 593, HL and note 2 above.

11 'Trade' includes any business, 'profession' includes any vocation or occupation – SDA s81(2), RRA 1976 s78(1) and DDA 1995 s68(1).

12 See further chapters 11, 13, 14 and 15.

13 Brought into force on 1 October 1999 by the Disability Discrimination Code of Practice (Trade Organisations) Order 1999 SI No 2638.

12.14 An organisation does not have to have a membership comprised exclusively of employers or workers in order to fall within SDA 1975 s12, RRA 1976 s11 or DDA 1995 s13(4). In *National Federation of Self-Employed and Small Businesses Ltd v Philpott*[14] the Employment Appeal Tribunal (EAT) ruled that a federation whose membership includes the self-employed as well as employers came within these provisions. The same principle is likely to apply to an organisation of workers, so long as it has the objective of protecting and furthering the interests of its members. The size of the organisation's membership is irrelevant – there is no small organisation exemption under the DDA 1995, unlike the exemption for small employers. So a trade organisation with fewer than 15 employees is liable towards its members under the DDA 1995, but not its staff.[15]

12.15 Trade unions and similar organisations may engage in positive action in relation to their members in the limited circumstances discussed at para 10.59 in the context of race and sex. The DDA 1995 does not prohibit positive discrimination in relation to disabled members and the duty of reasonable adjustment may require accommodation to be made for disabled members at a substantial disadvantage. Such an organisation may not otherwise discriminate on the grounds of race or sex (SDA 1975 s12(2) and RRA 1976 s11(2)), and may not discriminate against a disabled person (DDA 1995 s13(1)):

(a) in the terms on which it is prepared to admit a person to membership; or
(b) by refusing, or deliberately omitting to accept, a person's application for membership.[16]

12.16 When a person is already a member of an organisation, that organisation may not discriminate (SDA 1975 s12(3), RRA 1976 s11(3) and DDA 1995 s13(2)):

(a) in the way it affords that member access to any benefits, facilities or services, or by refusing or deliberately omitting to afford that member access to them; or
(b) by depriving that person of membership, or varying the terms on which he or she is a member; or
(c) by subjecting that member to any another detriment.

12.17 A member who complains that an organisation has subjected him or

14 [1997] IRLR 341.

15 The small employer exemption is scheduled for repeal by October 2004 to comply with the ED (see further chapter 6).

16 The DDA 1995 provisions refer to 'refusing to accept, or deliberately not accepting'.

her to a detriment must have been a member of the organisation at the time of the alleged detriment.[17] The prohibition on discrimination in relation to members and would-be members of trade organisations is not restricted to those working wholly or mainly in Great Britain.

12.18 Under the SDA 1975 a trade union or other relevant organisation may discriminate in provisions made in relation to the death or retirement from work of a member.[18] In appropriate circumstances a woman may, however, be able to rely on the provisions of the ETD (see para 10.34).

12.19 In order to succeed with a claim under SDA 1975 s12 or RRA 1976 s11 an applicant must show that the discrimination complained of (whether direct, indirect or by way of victimisation) was on grounds of sex or race respectively. Poor representation (or a refusal to provide representation, support or advice) by a trade union or other organisation will not, of itself, breach the relevant section.[19] The applicant must also show that the less favourable treatment is on grounds of sex or race. So, for example, in *Fire Brigades Union* v *Fraser*[20] the Court of Sessions rejected a complaint under SDA 1975 s12 made by a man who had been refused representation on a charge of sexual harassment. The court held that the applicant was refused representation, not because of his sex, but because he was the alleged perpetrator rather than the victim of the harassment and there was no evidence that a woman accused of harassment would have been treated differently.

12.20 Under the DDA 1995, discrimination in relation to trade organisations covers less favourable treatment (see para 6.7), a failure to make reasonable adjustments where the duty arises (see para 6.15), and victimisation (see chapter 4).[21] chapter 6 sets out a detailed analysis of disability discrimination by less favourable treatment and the reasonable adjustment duty in the employment context. The definition of disability discrimination is materially identical as it applies to trade organisations, and is set out in DDA 1995 ss13–15. In this context, however, the reasonable adjustment provisions are only partially implemented at present. While the duty to make reasonable adjustments to *arrangements* came into force on 1 October 1999, the duty to make reasonable adjustments in respect of the *physical features* of premises will not be introduced until 2004.

17 *Diakou v Islington Unison 'A' Branch* [1997] ICR 121, EAT.
18 SDA 1975 s12(4).
19 *FTATU v Modgill* [1980] IRLR 142, EAT.
20 [1998] IRLR 142.
21 DDA 1995 ss13(3), 14 and 15.

12.21 The code of practice for trade organisations also sets out some helpful examples of potentially unlawful behaviour. One example of less favourable treatment of a disabled person by a trade organisation might be where transport to an annual conference is arranged by a professional association for its members as a membership benefit. A refusal by the association to provide a member with a ticket for the coach on the grounds that she has cerebral palsy and has difficulty controlling and co-ordinating her movements would be less favourable treatment for a reason relating to her disability and, unless the association could justify its actions, would amount to discrimination contrary to the DDA 1995.[22]

12.22 Trade organisations are, as was mentioned above, bound to make reasonable adjustments to accommodate the needs of their disabled members, as well as to refrain from treating them less favourably (subject in either case to a justification defence). What is 'reasonable' will depend on the circumstances. A trade union might have a small number of blind members who are substantially disadvantaged by the fact that all literature about the union and its activities is inaccessible to them. The union might reasonably decide that the provision of special equipment and training of an operator to produce Braille literature in-house would not be reasonable. It is likely, however, that an appropriate step for the union to take would be to have the literature produced in Braille by outside specialist printers at a reasonable cost.[23]

12.23 In a couple of respects the reasonable adjustment provisions differ as between trade organisations and employers. In the first place, there are no special rules relating to insurance services provided to members of trade organisations.[24] Nor does the DDA 1995 provide any list of examples of the type of adjustment that might be made by a trade organisation (contrast DDA 1995 s6(3) at para 6.30 above).

12.24 In addition to their liability in respect of their own discrimination against members, trade unions may also be liable for pressure to discriminate and/or for aiding unlawful acts if they include discriminatory terms in collective agreements. Trade unions may be liable for the discriminatory acts or failures to act of their lay officials as well as for those of their appointed officers. A union will be liable if the acts

22 Disability Discrimination (Trade Organisation) Code of Practice, para 5.1.

23 Ibid para 6.17.

24 Compare DDA 1995 s18, which provides special rules concerning insurance services provided to employees and arrangements between insurers and employers.

complained of were done with the express or implied authority of the union. That authority may have been given or may be implied in advance of the acts complained of; or afterwards.[25] An individual officer or lay official of a union may also be held personally liable for aiding his or her trade union's acts of unlawful discrimination. This will be the case unless that officer can establish that he or she relied on a statement, made to him or her by the union, that the act in question would not be unlawful. Such reliance will only provide a defence if, furthermore, it was reasonable.[26] Knowingly or recklessly making a false statement that an act is not unlawful is an offence punishable by a fine.[27] It appears that an organisation facing a claim under this section cannot rely on the statutory defence that it took such steps as were reasonably practicable to prevent discrimination (see further para 31.14) because the statutory defence applies only to the discriminatory acts or omissions of employees.[28]

Qualifying bodies – race and sex discrimination

12.25 SDA 1975 s13 and RRA 1976 s12 make it unlawful for an authority or body which can confer an authorisation or qualification which is needed for, or facilitates, engagement in a particular profession or trade to discriminate on grounds of sex or race:

(a) in the terms on which it is prepared to confer authorisation or qualification, or
(b) by refusing or deliberately omitting to grant the candidates application for it; or
(c) by withdrawing the authorisation or qualification, or by varying the terms on which it is or may be held.

The DDA 1995 contains no equivalent provision.

12.26 It may be unlawful, for example, for a qualifying body to impose extra training requirements on overseas students,[29] or to refuse to recognise qualifications obtained overseas that are similar to acceptable UK qualifications.[30] The Commission for Racial Equality (CRE)

25 SDA 1975 s41(2); RRA 1976 s32(2); DDA 1995 s58(2).
26 SDA 1975 s42(3); RRA 1976 s33(3).
27 SDA 1975 s42(4); RRA 1976 s33(4).
28 SDA 1975 s41(3); RRA 1976 s32(3).
29 *Bohon-Mitchell v Common Professional Examination Board and the Council of Legal Education* [1978] IRLR 525, ET.
30 *Hampson v Department of Education and Science* [1989] IRLR 69, CA. Rules that are unlawful under the SDA 1975 are also void by virtue of SDA 1975 s77(2).

code of practice provides that overseas degrees and other qualifications should be accepted where comparable with UK qualifications.

12.27 The SDA 1975 includes an additional provision (s13(2)). This requires that, where a qualifying body has a legal duty to satisfy itself of the good character of a candidate before conferring a qualification or authorisation, it must have regard to any evidence that tends to show that the candidate or his or her employees or agents unlawfully discriminate, or have in the past unlawfully discriminated, in the carrying on of any profession or trade.

'Qualifying body'

12.28 A 'qualifying body' is one that can confer an authorisation or qualification which is needed for, or facilitates, engagement in a particular trade or profession. Bodies such as the Law Society and British Medical Association are examples. An organisation can fall within both SDA 1975 ss13 and 12, and RRA 1976 ss12 and 11 (ie, can be both, for example, a professional organisation and also a 'qualifying body').

12.29 In *Tattari v Private Patients Plan Ltd*[31] the Court of Appeal ruled that a commercial provider of medical and health insurance, which stipulated in its commercial agreements that particular qualifications were necessary in order for doctors to be included on its list of specialist practitioners, was not a 'qualifying body' for the purposes of RRA 1976 s12. Taking a rather narrow view of the section, the court held that the insurance company did not confer any authorisation or qualification itself, but merely stated what qualifications it required in order to include practitioners on its list. And in *Arthur v Attorney-General*[32] the EAT ruled that RRA 1976 s12 did not apply to the respondent in his role as appointer of magistrates. According to the EAT, RRA 1976 s12:

> ... is directed to circumstances in which A confers on B a qualification which will enable B to render services for C. Where A and C are the same entity, the section would appear to be inapplicable, otherwise it would apply to every selection panel.

31 [1997] IRLR 586.

32 [1999] ICR 631. See also *Malik v Post Office Counters Ltd* [1993] ICR 93, in which the EAT ruled that the respondents were not a 'qualifying body' in relation to the appointment of sub-postmasters.

12.30 This narrow approach was upheld by the Court of Appeal in *McDonagh and Treisman v Ali,*[33] a case concerning alleged race discrimination by the Labour party arising out of a failure, respectively, to select and reselect the applicants as candidates for election as councillors. The EAT had accepted, in *Sawyer v Ahsan,*[34] that the Labour party acted as a 'qualifying body' under RRA 1976 s12 in selecting candidates to contest local elections. There Lindsay J had relied in part on the oft-cited dicta of Templeman LJ (as he then was) in *Savjani v IRC*[35] that the RRA 1976:

> ... was brought in to remedy very great evil. It is expressed in very wide terms, and I should be very slow to find that the effect of something which is humiliatingly discriminating in racial matters falls outside the ambit of the Act.

12.31 A similar approach had been taken by an employment tribunal (ET), in *Jepson and Dyas-Elliot v Labour Party*[36] to the materially identical SDA 1975 s13 (indeed it was this latter case that resulted in the scrapping by the Labour party of women-only shortlists for parliamentary elections). The ET in the *McDonagh* case rejected the Labour party's claim that the alleged discrimination (which was denied) fell outside RRA 1976 s12. According to the ET:

> We do not hesitate to express the view that we are happy that our deliberations have led us to such a conclusion. On the basis of [the Labour Party's] submissions, a political party could (theoretically) perpetrate deliberate and malicious racial discrimination against one of its members seeking nomination for selection as a political candidate leaving that member with no recourse under the [RRA]. Adopting the dictum of Lord Templeman [in *Savjani*] and the section of the judgment of Lindsay J. [in *Sawyer* applying Templeman LJ's dictum] to which we have referred, such a conclusion would not only be morally repugnant but also something which Parliament could not possibly have intended.

The Labour party's appeal was rejected by the EAT (two of whose three members had heard the *Sawyer* case). But the argument which was rejected there – that any discrimination was challengeable under RRA 1976 Pt III (in particular, s25 which regulates discrimination by

33 [2002] EWCA Civ 93.

34 [1999] IRLR 609.

35 [1981] QB 458 at 466–467.

36 [1996] IRLR 116. Legislation now expressly permits some positive action in this area – see Sex Discrimination (Election Candidates) Act 2002.

'associations' other than those covered by s11[37]), rather than under s12 – was accepted by the Court of Appeal. This aspect of the decision is further considered in chapter 29, our attention here being confined to the court's conclusions in relation to RRA 1976 s12. The Court of Appeal ruled, per Ralph Gibson LJ, that *Sawyer* had been wrongly decided and that the proper application of s12 was in relation to the:

> employment field ... in a wide or loose sense. The obvious application of the section is to cases where a body has among its functions that of granting some qualification on, or authorising, a person who has satisfied appropriate standards of competence, to practice a profession, calling or trade.

12.32 In the court's view, a construction of RRA 1976 s12 that caught within it alleged discrimination in relation to the selection of local election candidates 'runs counter to the approach laid down by this court in *Tattari*' in which it restricted the scope of s12 to 'an authority or body which confers recognition or approval, refers to a body which has the power or authority to confer on a person a professional qualification or other approval needed to enable him to practise a profession, exercise a calling or take part in some other activity', rather than to one 'which is not authorised to or empowered to confer such qualification or permission but which stipulates that for the purpose of its commercial agreements a particular qualification is required'. The Court of Appeal in *McDonagh* further expressed doubt as to whether being a councillor amounted to engagement in a 'profession or occupation' for the purposes of s12.[38]

'Authorisation or qualification'

12.33 An 'authorisation or qualification' includes recognition, registration, enrolment, approval and certification.[39] To 'confer' includes to renew

37 See further chapter 29. Note, however, that RRA 1976 s25 has no counterpart in the SDA 1975. It would appear, accordingly, that sex discrimination in this context is unregulated save to the extent that it is expressly permitted by the 2002 Act.

38 This is partly on the basis that such a position is not remunerated – compare the EAT's decision in *British Judo Association v Petty* [1981] IRLR 484. The Court of Appeal in *McDonagh v Ali* relied on the decisions of the Northern Ireland Court of Appeal in *McLoughlin v Queen's University* [1995] NI 82 and of the House of Lords in *Loughran and Kelly v Northern Ireland Health Executive* [1999] AC 428; [1998] IRLR 593.

39 SDA 1975 s13(3)(a); RRA 1976 s12(3)(a).

or to extend a qualification or authorisation, as well as to confer it for the first time.[40]

12.34 SDA 1975 s13 and RRA 1976 s12 apply to situations where the authorisation or qualification is essential to the trade or profession in question, but also where it merely facilitates entry into or engagement in the particular trade or profession, irrespective of whether the qualifying body intended it to do so.[41] In *Loughran and Kelly v Northern Ireland Housing Executive*[42] the House of Lords held that the word 'qualification' implied some status conferred on a person in relation to his or her work which was either necessary or advantageous to the lawful carrying on of that work.

Exceptions to the prohibitions on discrimination – statutory appeals and religious organisations

12.35 Many of the cases brought under RRA 1976 s12 and SDA 1975 s13 relate to proceedings of the General Medical Council which licenses doctors in the UK. In *Rovenska v GMC*,[43] for example, a Czechoslovakian-qualified doctor challenged, as indirectly discriminatory under RRA 1976 ss1(1)(b) and 12, the Council's language-related qualifying criteria for full registration in the UK. A complicating feature of such claims is found in RRA 1976 s54(2) and SDA 1975 s63(2) which provide that no claims can be brought in the ET under RRA 1976 s13 and SDA 1975 s12 in relation to 'an act in respect of which an appeal, or proceedings in the nature of an appeal, may be brought under any enactment'.

12.36 The impact of RRA 1976 s54 was felt in *Khan v General Medical Council*[44] in which the applicant, an overseas-qualified doctor who had twice been refused full registration by the GMC challenged, as indirectly discriminatory, the Council's conditions for registration. His application to the Review Board for Overseas Qualified Practitioners for review of the Council's decision, made under the Medical Act 1983, had been unsuccessful. The issue for the Court of Appeal was whether the Review Board procedure was 'in the nature of an appeal' under s54(2) despite the fact that the Board's role was restricted to providing an opinion to the President of the GMC, and that it had no power to reverse the GMC's decision. The Court of Appeal ruled that

40 SDA 1975 s13(3)(b); RRA 1976 s12(3)(b).

41 *British Judo Association v Petty* [1981] IRLR 484.

42 [1999] AC 428; [1998] IRLR 593.

43 [1997] IRLR 367.

44 [1993] IRLR 378.

it was, and that the provision by the Medical Act 1983 of the appeal to the Review Board ousted the jurisdiction of the ET.

12.37 RRA 1976 s54(2) and SDA 1975 s63(2) operate so as to prevent challenge to alleged discrimination. This is the case even, according to the Court of Appeal in *Khan*, in a case in which the appeal procedure itself is alleged to be tainted by discrimination. It was argued in the *Khan* case that RRA 1976 s54(2) ought to be given the same construction as SDA 1975 s63(2), which would have to be interpreted so as to provide an 'effective remedy' under the ETD. But according to Hoffman LJ:

> I do not see why it should not be regarded as an effective remedy against sex or race discrimination in the kind of case with which s12(1) of the [RRA] deals. That concerns qualifications for professions and trades. Parliament appears to have thought that, although the industrial tribunal is often called a specialist tribunal and has undoubted expertise in matters of sex and racial discrimination, its advantages in providing an effective remedy were outweighed by the even greater specialisation in a particular field or trade or professional qualification of statutory tribunals such as the Review Board, since the Review Board undoubtedly has a duty to give effect to the provisions of s12 [this having been established by the Divisional Court in *R v Department of Health ex p Gandhi*, below] ... This seems to me a perfectly legitimate view for parliament to have taken. Furthermore, s54(2) makes it clear that decisions of the Review Board would themselves be open to judicial review on the ground that it failed to have proper regard to the provisions of the [RRA 1976]. In my view, it cannot be said that the Medical Act 1983 does not provide the effective remedy required by European law.[45]

12.38 In *R v Department of Health ex p Gandhi*[46] the Divisional Court had ruled that the Health Secretary, in exercising an appellate function in respect of the Medical Practices Committee of the NHS,[47] was bound to consider the allegation of race discrimination upon which the appeal rested (the Health Secretary had resisted this conclusion). The Health Secretary was not required, however, to make a specific finding in relation to the allegation in dismissing the appeal. Further, the appeal being 'nearer the administrative end of the spectrum than the judicial end', the requirements of natural justice were not onerous. In that case Dr Gandhi had not received an oral hearing.[47a]

45 Concurring with Neill LJ with both of whose speeches Waite LJ agreed.

46 [1991] ICR 805.

47 Under the National Health Service Act 1977 and the National Health Service (General Medical and Pharmaceutical Services) Regulations 1974 SI No 160.

47a This case was heard before the HRA 1998 came into force.

12.39 The other significant exclusion from the prohibition on discrimination by qualifying bodies is unique to the SDA 1975, s19(2) of which provides that:

> Nothing in section 13 [SDA 1975] applies to an authorisation or qualification (as defined in that section) for purposes of an organised religion where the authorisation or qualification is limited to one sex so as to comply with the doctrines of that religion or avoid offending the religious susceptibilities of a significant number of its followers.

SDA 1975 s19(4) makes similar provision where the authorisation or qualification is limited to people who are not undergoing and have not undergone gender reassignment.

Disability discrimination

12.40 The DDA 1995 contains no provision equivalent to RRA 1976 s12 and SDA 1975 s13. Qualifying bodies are not, therefore, prohibited from discriminating against disabled people in their capacity as qualifying bodies.[48] In *General Medical Council v Cox*[48a] the EAT reveresed an ET decision and held that the GMC was a qualifying body and not a trade association and therefore outside the scope of the employment provisions in the DDA 1995. The government is, however, committed to ensuring that all qualifying bodies are covered by the DDA 1995 employment provisions by October 2004.[49] The government proposes to allow qualifying bodies to maintain academic and other particular standards if they can objectively justify them, while requiring them to adjust other matters – such as their means of course delivery and assessment, their provision of course materials and the arrangements they make for examinations – if it is reasonable to do so.

Vocational training bodies

12.41 The SDA 1975, RRA 1976 and DDA 1995 contain provisions which prohibit discrimination in relation to vocational training, although these provisions are contained in that part of the DDA 1995 dealing

48 There is limited coverage by the education and goods and services provisions of the DDA 1995 – see chapter 30.

48a EAT 10076/01, 22 March 2002 (unreported), available from EAT website.

49 Except to the extent they are already covered by provisions relating to further and higher education institutions – government consultation document on the implementation of the ED.

50 DDA 1995 Pts III and IX.

with discrimination in the provision of goods and services and education, considered in chapter 30 below.[50] In order to comply with the ED these provisions will need to be strengthened to adopt the same approach as the employment and trade organisation provisions. Race and sex discrimination in relation to education other than that consisting of vocational training (which is undefined by the RRA 1976 and SDA 1975[51]) are dealt with in chapter 29.

12.42 SDA 1975 s14 and RRA 1976 s13, which are materially identical, make it unlawful for any person who provides, makes arrangements for, or facilitates the provision of vocational training to discriminate in the following ways:

(a) In the terms on which a person is afforded access to any training course or other facilities concerned with vocational training; or
(b) by refusing or deliberately omitting to afford such access; or
(c) by terminating a person's training; or
(d) by subjecting a person to any detriment during the course of their training.

Discrimination in relation to arrangements made for the purpose of deciding who should be offered training is not prohibited under the SDA 1975 or the RRA 1976, so that interviewing arrangements are not covered unless the discrimination results in differential access to the training.[52] A claimant bringing a complaint of sex discrimination may, in addition, be able to rely on the ETD which covers vocational training. Chapter 5 considers the positive action which training bodies are permitted to take under the SDA 1975 and RRA 1976.

12.43 One of the relatively few cases decided under the vocational training sections of the RRA 1976 and SDA 1975 is *Lana v Positive Action Training in Housing (London) Ltd.*[53] The applicant had been placed with a firm (WM) as a trainee quantity surveyor, a position she expected to last from 1 October 1998 until 30 September 1999. The applicant had a contract with Positive Action Training by which the respondents agreed to provide her with a work experience placement, and the respondents had a contract with WM whereby the latter paid the respondents £10,000 towards Ms Lana's allowance. When the applicant informed WM, in February 1999, that she was pregnant the company terminated her training contract immediately, telling her that her performance had been unsatisfactory. The respondents then

51 Save for the provision (SDA 1975 s82(1) and RRA 1976 s78(1)) that '"training" includes any form of education or instruction'.

52 Compare SDA 1975 s6(1)(a) and RRA 1976 s4(1)(a).

53 [2001] IRLR 501.

terminated their contract with the applicant on the grounds that they had no funding for continuing her contract and no alternative placement for her.

12.44 An ET rejected the applicant's complaint under SDA 1975 s14, ruling that Ms Lana's contract had not been terminated on grounds of sex. The EAT allowed her appeal, remitting the case for rehearing by a differently constituted ET. The decision is considered in detail in chapter 29. Briefly, the EAT ruled that the respondents could be made responsible for the conduct of WM which was acting as their agent in relation to the applicant's training by virtue of SDA 1975 s41(2) (see further para 31.41). According to the court (per Mr Recorder Langstaff QC), if WM did an act which it had the authority of the respondents to do, but did it in a discriminatory manner, it did so as an agent for the respondent. Since WM had the authority to terminate Ms Lana's training, the respondents were responsible for its having done so in a discriminatory manner.

Exceptions to the prohibitions on discrimination – lone parents and positive action

12.45 Employment Act 1989 s8 provides the Secretary of State with the power to provide for discrimination in favour of lone parents in connection with payment in respect of certain types of training. Such discrimination could otherwise contravene SDA 1975 s3 (which prohibits discrimination against married people). The SDA 1975 (Exemption of Special Treatment for Lone Parents) Order 1989[54] and the SDA 1975 (Exemption of Special Treatment for Lone Parents) Order 1991[55] make provision for the special treatment of lone parents in relation to training.

Employment agencies

12.46 SDA 1975 s15 and RRA 1976 s14 respectively make it unlawful for an employment agency to discriminate on grounds of sex or race. An employment agency is a body which, whether for profit or not, provides services for the purpose of finding employment for workers or supplying employers with workers.[56] State employment services,

54 SI No 2140
55 SI No 2813.
56 SDA 1975 s82(1); RRA 1976 s78(1).

university careers services, private businesses and school careers services are covered by the Acts.[57] Services provided by an employment agency include guidance on careers and any other services related to employment.[58] The provisions in the DDA 1995 relating to employment agencies are in Pt III of that Act and are considered in chapter 30 below.

12.47 It is unlawful for an employment agency to discriminate against any person (RRA 1976 s14 and SDA 1975 s15):

(a) in the terms on which the agency offers to provide any of its services, or
(b) by refusing or deliberately omitting to provide any of its services, or
(c) in the way it provides any of its services.

It is also unlawful for a local education authority or an education authority acting as a careers adviser and employment agency under the Employment and Training Act 1973 to discriminate in the ways set out above.

12.48 The employment agency or local education authority may discriminate in circumstances in which the employer could lawfully refuse to offer employment to the person in question.[59] And if an employment agency or local education authority acts in reliance on a statement made to it by an employer that the employer could lawfully refuse to offer employment, in circumstances such that it was reasonable to rely on the statement, its actions will not be unlawful. It is for the agency or education authority to prove both that it acted in reliance on a statement and that it was reasonable to do so.[60] A person who knowingly or recklessly makes a false or misleading statement that an agency acted in reliance on an employer's statement commits an offence which is punishable by a fine.[61]

12.49 Agencies which accept unlawful discriminatory instructions from employers may be liable for knowingly aiding another person to do an unlawful act.[62] This would cover, for example, agreeing not to send any black candidates for an interview (see also chapter 14).

57 *CRE v Imperial Society of Teachers of Dancing* [1983] ICR 473, EAT.
58 SDA 1975 s15(3); RRA 1976 s14(3).
59 SDA 1975 s15(4); RRA 1976 s14(4).
60 SDA 1975 s15(5); RRA 1976 s14(5).
61 SDA 1975 s15(6); RRA 1976 s14(6).

Principals and contract workers

12.50 We have seen at para 12.46 above that workers are protected from discrimination by employment agencies on grounds of sex and race. They are also protected from discrimination by 'principals' who are, in addition, prohibited from discriminating against disabled people. SDA 1975 s9, RRA 1976 s7 and DDA 1995 s12 apply the Acts' prohibition on discrimination in respect of those doing 'any work for a person ("the principal") which is available for doing by individuals ("contract workers") who are employed not by the principal himself but by another person, who supplies them under a contract made with the principal'.

12.51 The SDA 1975, RRA 1976 and DDA 1995 make it unlawful for the principal to discriminate against a contract worker:

(a) in the terms on which he allows her to do that work, or
(b) by not allowing her to do or continue to do it, or
(c) in the way it affords her access to any benefits, facilities or services or by refusing or deliberately omitting to afford her access to them, or
(d) by subjecting her to any other detriment.[63]

The exceptions to the prohibitions on discrimination imposed by the RRA 1976, SDA 1975 and DDA 1995 in relation to contract workers are the same as those which apply to those in 'employment' (see chapter 11 for sex and race and chapter 13 for disability discrimination). Thus, for example, the GOQ defence[64] applies (see para 11.70), and the prohibition at (c) above does not apply to benefits, facilities or services if the principal provides the same to the public.[65] Likewise under the DDA 1995, the small employer provision exempts principals who employ fewer than 15 employees from liability under that Act.[66]

12.52 The applicant in *CJ O'Shea Construction Ltd v Bassi*[67] was employed by P to make deliveries to O'Shea (the principal). During a delivery he was racially abused by one of O'Shea's employees. The EAT upheld the ET's decision that Mr Bassi did contract work for O'Shea, as the contract between his employer and O'Shea included a term that

62 SDA 1975 s42; RRA 1976 s33.
63 SDA 1975 s9(2); RRA 1976 s7(2).
64 SDA 1975 s9(4); RRA 1976 s7(4).
65 SDA 1975 s9(5); RRA 1976 s7(5).
66 Until the small employer exemption is deleted – by October 2004.
67 [1998] ICR 1130.

deliveries should be made in accordance with O'Shea's instructions. Thus, O'Shea was a principal against whom a claim could be made.

12.53 The DDA 1995's definition of discrimination to include both less favourable treatment and a failure to make reasonable adjustments – in either case subject to a justification defence (see chapter 6) – applies to disabled contract workers under the DDA 1995 s12 as it would do to job applicants and employees by virtue of s4 of the Act. Contract workers are also protected by the DDA 1995 from victimisation whether they are disabled or not. The employment code of practice provides helpful guidance on the provisions (paras 7.1 to 7.8), particularly on the reasonable adjustment provisions.

12.54 It is important to remember that both the 'sending employer' and the principal may be liable to make reasonable adjustments. If the sending employer's own premises place the contract worker at a substantial disadvantage he or she may be liable under the employment provisions (DDA 1995 ss4–6, see chapter 13). In addition, the sending employer has a duty to make reasonable adjustments where a contract worker's disability is likely to place him or her at a similar, substantial disadvantage with all or most of the principals to whom he or she might be supplied – whether in respect of the arrangements or the physical features. The sending employer would have to take such steps as are within his or her power that would overcome the disadvantage wherever it might arise.[68] The principal would not have to make adjustments that the sending employer should make, but would be responsible for any additional reasonable adjustments which are necessary solely because of the principal's own arrangements or premises.

12.55 A bank might, for example, hire a blind word processor operator as a contract worker from an employment business. The employment business is likely to be under a duty to make a reasonable adjustment such as to provide the worker with a specially adapted portable computer because she would otherwise be at a substantial disadvantage in doing the work wherever she did it. In such circumstances the bank would not have to provide a specially adapted computer if the employment business did not.[69] The principal is not liable for the sending employer's breach of the reasonable adjustment duty, but the worker could enforce her claim against the sending employer. If there is any doubt as to which of the sending employer and principal is

68 Disability Discrimination (Employment) Regulations 1996 SI No 1456, reg 7; Employment Code of Practice, para 7.6.

69 Ibid reg 7(3).

responsible for an adjustment, an applicant should bring the claim against both.

12.56 The bank in the example above would be under a duty to co-operate by letting the contract worker use her computer while working for the bank. In addition, if (for example) the worker's keyboard was not compatible with the bank's systems, the bank might be required to make the computer compatible, and the employment business to allow that change to be made. What would be a reasonable adjustment for the hirer or principal – the bank in this example – or indeed the sending employer, to have to make, will depend on the individual circumstances and a particularly relevant factor is likely to be the length of the engagement.

'Contract workers'

12.57 RRA 1976 s7, SDA 1975 s9 and DDA 1995 s9 cover not only contract workers who are actually working, but also the selection of contract workers by the principal from workers supplied by the agency. In *BP Chemicals Ltd v Gillick*[70] an employment agency had a contract to provide personnel for consideration by BP. Staff were paid by the agency which then invoiced BP. The applicant worked under this arrangement from 1988 to 1991, when she stopped work due to pregnancy. She then approached BP with a view to returning to work. She was not given her old job, but was offered a less favourable job. She claimed discrimination against the principal, BP. The EAT held that she could bring a complaint against BP, stating that the company had a duty not to discriminate when selecting contract workers.

12.58 Similarly, in *Patefield v Belfast City Council*[71] Northern Ireland's Court of Appeal held that the council discriminated against the applicant contract worker on grounds of sex when it replaced her with a permanent employee while she was on maternity leave, though it could have lawfully replaced her with a permanent employee at any time while she was actually in post. The court found that, had the applicant not gone on maternity leave, the council would have kept her in her post indefinitely.

12.59 A significant limitation on the protection afforded to contract workers became apparent in *Lloyd* v *IBM (UK) Ltd*[72] in which the EAT

70 [1995] IRLR 128.

71 [2000] IRLR 664.

72 EAT/642/94, 3 February 1995 (unreported). A similar decision was reached in *Rice* v *Fon-a-Car* [1980] ICR 133, in which that which was lacking was a contractual obligation on the part of the supplier.

ruled that the fact that the applicant supplied her services to an employment agency through a company established by her (as is common in the IT sector) excluded her from the protection of the SDA 1975. In *Abbey Life Assurance Company Ltd* v *Tansell*,[73] however, the Court of Appeal took a different view. The court accepted that DDA 1995 s12 'clearly cover[ed] the standard case in which, for example, a person makes office work available for doing by individuals employed by a temping agency'. In such a case the temporary staff would be protected by that provision from discrimination by the principal. But, according to Mummery LJ for the court: 'the language of the section is also reasonably capable of applying to the less common case in which an extra contract is inserted, so that there is no direct contract between the person making the work available and the employer of the individual who is supplied to do that work'.

12.60 Mr Tansell offered his computer skills and services through a company of which he was the sole shareholder, and placed his name with several employment agencies. One of the agencies, MHC Consulting Services, found work for him at Abbey Life. The contractual arrangement was that Mr Tansell's company formed a contract with MHC to supply Mr Tansell's services to Abbey Life. Mr Tansell was put under the control of Abbey Life. Abbey Life paid MHC, which paid Mr Tansell's company, and Mr Tansell received a salary from his company. There was no contract between Abbey Life and either Mr Tansell or his company.

12.61 Mr Tansell failed to convince the ET that he was a contract worker of Abbey Life. The ET ruled that DDA 1995 s12 applied only if there was a direct contractual relationship between the principal and the employer and that, accordingly (although Mr Tansell was a contract worker for MHC, and was employed by his company), Abbey Life was neither principal nor employer. The EAT and the Court of Appeal disagreed. According to the court, s12 does require that there is a contract with the principal, but does not demand that the contract is between the principal and the applicant's employer. So where an employee is supplied through his own company to a principal through an employment agency, the employee still has protection under the DDA 1995 from discrimination by the principal as he is a contract worker for them.

73 [2000] IRLR 387. Mummery LJ went on to suggest that *Lloyd* had been wrongly decided.

Wide interpretation to be given to provisions

12.62 The applicants in *Harrods Ltd v Remick*[74] were three women who worked for concessionaires operating in Harrods. The concessionaires had a contract with Harrods to have a sales counter in the store. One of the conditions was that employees of concessionaires were required to have 'store approval' from Harrods, such approval requiring adherence to a Harrods dress code. The penalty for breaching Harrod's dress code was the store's withdrawal of approval for the worker involved, who would be banned from working there. The applicants, who were refused store approval because they failed to comply with the dress code (one, for example, wore a nose stud), brought race discrimination claims against Harrods.

12.63 The Court of Appeal rejected Harrods' argument that RRA 1976 s7 was limited to cases where the workers were under the managerial power or control of the 'principal'. It was clear to the court that the work done by the applicants was 'work for [Harrods]' even though it was also work done for the concessionaires. As the court pointed out, to require that the 'work' to which s7 applies had to be work in respect of which managerial powers are exercised by the principal would leave people such as the complainants without a personal remedy in the event of discrimination by the principal.[75]

12.64 Harrods also argued that the main purpose of the contract between the principal (Harrods) and the employer (the concessionaires) must be the supply of workers for s7 to apply. The court could see no justification for reading such restrictive words into the provision. It is sufficient that there is a contractual obligation to supply individuals to do work that is 'work for' the principal. The only question under s7 was whether there was a contractual arrangement for the employer to supply individuals to do work which was 'work for' the principal.

12.65 It follows from the decision in *Harrods* that RRA 1976 s7 (and the equivalent SDA 1975 s9) should be interpreted very widely. As the Vice-Chancellor, Sir Richard Scott, stated for the court:

> ... the Act was brought in to remedy a very great evil. It is expressed in very wide terms, and I would be slow to find that the effect of something which is humiliatingly discriminatory in racial matters falls outside the ambit of the Act.[76]

74 [1997] IRLR 583.

75 Although the discrimination would be an unlawful instruction or pressure to discriminate under RRA 1976 ss30 and 31 (SDA 1975 ss39 & 40) – these provisions can only be enforced by the commissions.

76 [1997] IRLR 583, citing Lord Templeman in *Savjani v IRC* [1981] QB 458 at 466–467.

CHAPTER 13

Employment-related disability discrimination

continued

Key points

13.1
- The Disability Discrimination Act (DDA) 1995 prohibits discrimination against people with a disability. 'Discrimination' is defined, in the employment context, to include both less favourable treatment and a failure to make reasonable adjustment, in either case if the treatment or failure was unjustified. The DDA 1995 also prohibits victimisation of both disabled and non-disabled workers.
- The DDA 1995 protects workers (broadly defined), job applicants, apprentices, independent contractors and trainees. However, its coverage is narrower than that of the Sex Discrimination Act (SDA) 1975 or the Race Relations Act (RRA) 1976 in that, for example, it specifically excludes from its provisions police officers and fire fighters, and does not apply to trainee barristers.
- The DDA 1995 applies to disabled workers regardless of their age and length of service.
- The DDA 1995 regulates employment-related discrimination (broadly defined) by employers, trade unions, and employers' organisations. Its application, which is in this respect narrower than that of the SDA 1975 and the RRA 1976, will be widened by July 2006 to conform with the Employment Directive (ED).
- At present, employers with fewer than 15 employees are exempt from the DDA 1995. The 'small employer exemption' will be removed by October 2004.
- The DDA 1995 prohibits discrimination against disabled people:
  - in the arrangements made for deciding who should be offered employment;
  - in the terms and conditions on which a person is offered a job;
  - in the refusal or omission to offer a person a job;
  - by the provision to a worker of less favourable terms of employment;
  - by not giving a worker the same opportunities for transfer, training or promotion;
  - by giving a worker fewer benefits, facilities or services;
  - by dismissing a worker; or
  - by subjecting a worker to any other detriment.
- The DDA 1995 permits a number of exceptions to its prohibitions on discrimination. These exemptions include certain provisions relating to national security and statutory authority.

- A number of amendments will have to be made to the DDA 1995 to achieve compatibility between it and the ED which must be implemented by July 2006. The government is committed to bringing the Act into conformity with the ED by October 2004.

Background and statutory framework

13.2 The main statutory provisions discussed in this chapter are the DDA 1995 and the Disability Discrimination (Employment) Regulations (DD(E) Regulations) 1996. The Code of Practice for the elimination of discrimination in the field of employment against disabled persons or persons who have had a disability is also relevant.

13.3 The types of discrimination prohibited by the DDA 1995 are set out briefly at para 13.6 below and in detail in chapter 6. This chapter considers the scope of the protection from disability discrimination in the field of employment.

13.4 The DDA 1995 only prohibits employment discrimination in prescribed circumstances which are set out fully in this chapter. Generally speaking, the limitations relate to the type of act of discrimination (where and when it takes place), the type of worker discriminated against, and – unlike the RRA 1976 and the SDA 1975 – the type of employer involved. Certain acts of discrimination are prohibited in relation to certain categories of worker, such as job applicants, employees, the self-employed, contract workers, apprentices, and trainees. No maximum age limits or minimum lengths of service requirements apply under the DDA 1995; protection starts from the first day of employment or, if the discrimination occurs prior to employment, from the date of the discrimination. But the categories of worker protected is by no means comprehensive. The DDA 1995 is markedly more restrictive in this respect than the SDA 1975 and RRA 1976, which are dealt with in chapter 11.

13.5 This chapter explains which workers are protected and which are excluded from protection under the DDA 1995, and the circumstances in which disability-related discrimination will be unlawful. It also details the exemptions for certain types of employer and other matters such as the territorial limitations. The changes which will be required by the ED,[1] which must be transposed into domestic law by July 2006, are also set out below.

1 Council Directive 2000/78/EC. See further para 10.93 above.

Types of prohibited discrimination

13.6 The DDA 1995 prohibits three types of disability discrimination. One – victimisation – is materially identical to that prohibited by the SDA 1975 and the RRA 1976 and is considered in chapter 4. Non-disabled as well as disabled people are protected by the DDA 1995 against this form of discrimination. The other prohibited types of discrimination are unique to the DDA 1995. Whereas the SDA 1975 and RRA 1976 prohibit direct and unjustified indirect discrimination (see further Chapters 3 and 7), the DDA 1995 prohibits the unjustified less favourable treatment of a disabled person for a reason related to his or her disability (see further para 6.7), and the unjustified failure to make a reasonable adjustment where a disabled person is substantially disadvantaged by the working arrangements or workplace (see further para 6.15).

Territorial scope of the Disability Discrimination Act 1995

13.7 The DDA 1995 only applies in relation to employment at an establishment in Great Britain[2] or Northern Ireland.[3] Employment is regarded as being at an establishment in Great Britain unless the employee does his or her work wholly outside Great Britain.[4] Work not done *at* an establishment (for example, on-site or home work) is treated as being done at the establishment *from* which it is done. If it is not done from any establishment it is treated as being done at the establishment with which the work has the closest connection.[5]

13.8 Employment on a ship, aircraft or hovercraft is regarded as not being at an establishment in Great Britain and falls outside the DDA 1995's protection.[6] There are regulation-making powers to make exceptions to this rule in certain cases, but they have not yet been used. Neither the SDA 1975 nor the RRA 1976 provide such a blanket exclusion from their prohibitions on discrimination – see further chapter 11. The government will need to implement changes in order to comply with the ED by bringing the provisions for employees on

2 DDA 1995 s6(4).
3 Ibid Sch 8.
4 Ibid s68(2).
5 Ibid s68(5).
6 Ibid s68(3).

board ships, aeroplanes and hovercrafts in line with the existing provisions under the SDA 1975 (see para 11.20).

Small employers

13.9 Quite unlike any provision in either the SDA 1975 or RRA 1976, the employment provisions of the DDA 1995 do not apply to employers with fewer than 15 employees.[7] The small employer exclusion, which was reduced from an original threshold of 20 with effect from 1 December 1998,[8] has always been controversial. Its repeal has been recommended by (amongst others) the Disability Rights Task Force, the Better Regulation Task Force and the Independent Review of the Enforcement of UK Anti-Discrimination Legislation conducted by the University of Cambridge Centre for Public Law and Judge Institute of Management Studies.[9] Although the lowering of the threshold was believed to bring an additional 45,000 employers within the scope of the DDA 1995,[10] the current limit denies around 310,000 disabled people civil rights in relation to employment.[11]

13.10 In calculating the size of the employer account will not be taken of employees of an 'associated company' – one of a group of companies under common control or under the control of one by another.[12] This contrasts with other areas of employment law, where account may be taken of the whole group of companies.[13] The exception to this rule would be if an employment tribunal was prepared to 'lift the corporate veil' and look behind a limited company to the share ownership structure. This would only happen in rare circumstances if it could be

7 DDA 1995 s7.

8 Disability Discrimination (Exemption for Small Employers) Order 1998 SI No 2618 art 2 (which amended DDA 1995 s7 by substituting the figure of 20 with the lower figure of 15).

9 See, respectively, 'From Exclusion to Inclusion, a Report of the Disability Rights Task Force on Civil Rights for Disabled People' (DfEE, 1999); 'Anti-discrimination Legislation', available at www.cabinet-office.gov.uk/regulation/TaskForce/1999/anti-discrimination.pdf; and B Hepple, M Coussey and T Choudhury, *Equality: A New Framework* (Hart, 2000).

10 'The Disability Discrimination Act 1995: The Employment Provisions and Small Employers; A Review' (DfEE, 1998).

11 'From Exclusion to Inclusion', note 9 above, Ch 5, para 21.

12 *Hardie v CD Northern Ltd* [2000] IRLR 87.

13 See, eg, the calculation of the number of employees in order for a trade union to bring a claim for statutory recognition by an employer in Trade Union and Labour Relations (Consolidation) Act 1992 Sch 1 para 7.

shown that the separate legal entity of a company was a cloak for the truth which could be seen by lifting the veil.

13.11 The definition of what is 'employment' and, therefore, of the number of staff who are included for the purposes of calculating the head count for the threshold, includes employment under a contract of service or of apprenticeship and a contract personally to do any work.[14] This corresponds to the broad approach to 'employment' used elsewhere in the DDA 1995 and in the SDA 1975 and RRA 1976 (see further below), and is considerably wider than the definition of employment as an 'employee' used, for example, for unfair dismissal purposes.[15] Accordingly, casual as well as temporary and part-time workers are included in determining the threshold for the application of the DDA 1995 as are contract workers for whom the employer is liable under DDA 1995 s12 (see further para 3.18).[16]

13.12 The government is required by the ED to scrap the small employer exemption and is committed to doing so by October 2004.[17] In the meantime, the exemption for small employers will be challenged under the Human Rights Act (HRA) 1998 in the Court of Appeal in *Whittaker v P & D Watson (t/a P & M Watson Haulage)*.[18] The applicant in this case will seek a declaration that the provision infringes the right to a fair hearing under article 6 of the European Convention on Human Rights (ECHR) – see further chapter 9.

Discrimination in 'employment'

Discrimination against job applicants

13.13 It is unlawful under DDA 1995 s4(1) for an employer to discriminate against a disabled job applicant in relation to employment:

- in the arrangements that the employer makes for the purpose of determining who should be offered that employment (s4(1)(a)); or
- in the terms on which the employer offers that person that employment (s4(1)(b)); or

14 DDA 1995 s68(1).

15 ERA 1996 s230.

16 *Taylor v Lifesign Ltd*, EAT/1437/98, 2000 (unreported, available on LEXIS).

17 'Towards Equality and Diversity: Implementing the Employment and Race Directives', available at www.dti.gov.uk/er/equality/index.htm.

18 (2002) *Times* 26 March.

- by refusing to offer or by deliberately not offering the disabled person employment (s4(1)(c)).

13.14 'Arrangements' has a wide meaning and will cover everything from job advertisements to the final selection procedure. DDA 1995 s4(1)(c) does not require an express refusal of employment, a deliberate failure or omission to offer employment also amounting to actionable discrimination under the provision. What constitutes 'employment' is considered at para 13.18 below.

13.15 The discrimination prohibited by DDA 1995 s4(1) includes discrimination against disabled people by unjustified less favourable treatment, discrimination against disabled people by an unjustified breach of the DDA 1995 s6 duty to make reasonable adjustments, and victimisation of a disabled or non-disabled person in connection with the Act.[19] (See chapter 14 for further discussion of discrimination in recruitment).

Discrimination against workers

13.16 Discrimination against workers – those already employed by an employer – is prohibited in the following circumstances:

- in terms of employment on which the employer affords employment (s4(2)(a));
- in the opportunities afforded, or by the denial or deliberate failure to afford opportunities, for promotion, a transfer, training or the receipt of any other benefit (s4(2)(b));
- by dismissing a worker (s4(2)(c)); or
- by subjecting him or her to any other detriment (s4(2)(c)).

13.17 Again the net is cast wide and DDA 1995 s4(2) covers discrimination in contractual terms and non-contractual matters. Chapters 14 and 15 consider the scope in practice of the prohibitions in the DDA 1995.

Workers falling outside the protection of the Acts

13.18 'Employment' is defined for the purposes of the DDA 1995, as for those of the SDA 1975 and the RRA 1976, as 'employment under a contract of service or of apprenticeship or a contract personally to do

19 By the operation of DDA 1995 s55.

any work'.[20] As mentioned at para 3.11, this definition is much wider than that which applies under the unfair dismissal-related provisions of the Employment Rights Act (ERA) 1996, which protect only those working under contracts of service or apprenticeship. Since the definition of employment is the same in the DDA 1995 as in the RRA 1976 and SDA 1975, the analysis of the law set out at para 11.34 applies equally in relation to the DDA 1995 as it does to the SDA 1975 and the RRA 1976 and readers should refer to these sections for a detailed analysis.

13.19 The DDA 1995 requires that there be a contract between 'employer' and 'employee', though this need not be in writing and may be implied. The worker must be required personally to undertake the work required, although limited powers to substitute another worker will not necessarily be fatal to establishing worker status.[21] There is no requirement for continuity of service, and classification as 'self-employed' either by the contract or for tax purposes does not preclude an individual from being in 'employment' under the DDA 1995. A volunteer has been held to come within the scope of employment in the identically worded RRA 1976.[22]

13.20 There are a number of categories of worker who, although falling within the definition of employment, are either specifically excluded from the DDA 1995 or have the Act's effect modified in relation to them. These categories are dealt with at para 13.23 below.

Ex-employees

13.21 A live issue is the position of ex-employees who complain of discrimination by their former employer after they have ceased to be employed. A frequent complaint is of a failure to provide a reference, or of an inaccurate, adverse reference being given, either for a reason related to the individual's disability or as an act of victimisation connected with the DDA 1995. The Court of Appeal ruled, in *Kirker v British Sugar plc*,[23] that ex-employees who suffer acts of discrimination or victimisation after the employment relationship has ended

20 Ibid s68(1). The Northern Irish provision is almost identical save that the word 'any' before 'work' is omitted (s70(6) and Sch 8 para 47, modifying DDA 1995 s68(1)).

21 In particular the discussion of *Byrne Brothers (Framework) Ltd v Baird* [2002] IRLR 96.

22 *Armitage v Relate* (1994) DCLD 26 – see further para 11.43.

23 [2002] EWCA Civ 304.

are not protected by the DDA 1995. The court there held that the protection of workers 'whom [the employer] employs' in s4(2) was inconsistent with an interpretation covering events which took place after the employment relationship had ended. The use of the present tense, in the court's view, made the meaning plain and unambiguous and only a job applicant or someone employed at the time of the alleged discrimination could challenge it under the DDA 1995. The law will need to be amended to cover post-employment discrimination in order to comply with the ED (see further para 11.48).

Illegal contracts

13.22 Under the DDA 1995, as under the SDA 1975 and RRA 1976, a more relaxed approach is taken to employment relationships tainted by illegality than is the case in unfair dismissal cases or at common law (see further para 15.97). The judgment in *Hall v Woolston Leisure Ltd*[24] discussed there will apply in the context of disability discrimination cases as it does to claims of sex and race discrimination. Where the performance by the employer of a contract of employment involves illegality, and the worker is aware of the illegality (such as where the worker receives some cash in hand and the employer declares a lower salary than the worker is actually paid), public policy does not bar an applicant from receiving compensation for disability discrimination. If, however, a claim is so inextricably bound up with the illegal conduct, a tribunal cannot award compensation if it would appear to be condoning the conduct.

Special categories of workers

13.23 We have seen above the wide definition given to employment under the DDA 1995. However, there are special provisions in relation to some types of employment and the DDA 1995 does not apply at all to several categories of worker.

Contract workers

13.24 A 'contract worker' is protected from disability discrimination by his or her 'principal' (the person who makes work available to the

24 [2000] IRLR 578.

contract worker), even if the principal is not the contract worker's employer.[25] This is discussed in detail at para 12.57.

Crown employees

13.25 The employment provisions of the DDA 1995 apply generally to service in government departments and to service for the Crown and statutory bodies in the same way as to any other employer, but people holding statutory office are not protected by the Act.[26] So, for example, a civil servant is treated as an employee under the DDA 1995 but a lay magistrate is not. While the DDA 1995 employment provisions do not cover statutory office-holders, the staff in the office-holder's office are treated as employees.[27] But although a statutory office-holder is outside the employment provisions in the DDA 1995, the minister or government department making the appointment must not act in a way that would contravene the DDA 1995 employment provisions. The remedy for such behaviour would lie in judicial review proceedings in the Administrative Court.[28]

13.26 The DDA 1995 employment provisions also apply to the staff at both the House of Commons and the House of Lords.[29]

Members of the judiciary

13.27 The position under the DDA 1995 is as for the SDA 1975 and RRA 1976 and readers are referred to para 11.56 above.

Police and fire service

13.28 The employment provisions of the DDA 1995 do not apply to police officers (as statutory office holders) nor to British Transport Police officers, Ministry of Defence Police officers, Royal Parks Constabulary officers or special constables of the UK Atomic Energy Authority.[30] Fire-fighters (in a fire brigade or government department) are also

25 DDA 1995 s12.

26 Ibid s64(2)(a). Also excluded (ibid s64(8)) is service in an office listed in House of Commons Disqualification Act 1975 Sch 2 (Ministerial Offices).

27 DDA 1995 s64(2)(b).

28 Ibid s66.

29 Ibid s65, which also sets out who is deemed to be the employer of staff in the Houses of Parliament.

30 Ibid s64(5)(a).

outside the employment provisions of the Act.[31] Civilian employees of a fire brigade or police force are not excluded from the DDA 1995 as long as, respectively, they may not be required to fight fires and are not police officers or constables.

13.29 The government proposes removing the exclusion of police officers and fire-fighters under the DDA 1995 by October 2004 to comply with the ED.

Prison officers

13.30 Prison officers, with the exception of custody officers, are also excluded from protection under the employment provisions in the DDA 1995.[32] A prison officer is defined in Criminal Justice and Public Order Act 1994 s127, and staff employed in the prison service who do not come within this definition have the protection of the DDA 1995. The government must remove the exemption for prison officers to comply with the ED and is committed to doing so by October 2004.

Armed forces

13.31 Service in any of the naval, military or air forces of the Crown is excluded from the employment provisions in the DDA 1995.[33]

Barristers and advocates

13.32 Unlike the SDA 1975 and RRA 1976, the DDA 1995 does not apply to the recruitment and treatment of trainee barristers and tenants by barristers and barristers' clerks. The government is committed to including barristers and their trainees within the scope of the employment provisions of the DDA 1995 by October 2004 to comply with the ED.

Partners

13.33 Partners in business are also not covered currently by the DDA 1995 – see further para 12.3.

31 DDA 1995 ss64(5)(c) and 64(6).
32 Ibid ss64(5)(b) and 68(8).
33 Ibid s64(7).

Charities and supported employment

13.34 Special provisions apply to charities.[34] Although, as we have seen, the DDA 1995 does not prohibit discrimination in favour of disabled people, it can have the effect of prohibiting discrimination in favour of disabled people with a particular disability by comparison with other disabled people with a different impairment.

13.35 DDA 1995 s10 provides that the DDA's employment provisions do not affect any charitable instrument that confers benefits on one or more categories of person determined by reference to any physical or mental capacity.[35] Nor is it unlawful for a charity to discriminate in the employment context, in pursuing its charitable purposes, so far as those purposes are connected with people determined by reference to any physical or mental capacity.

13.36 Supported employment is also specially provided for by the DDA 1995 with the effect that a person who provides supported employment is not prohibited from treating members of a particular group of disabled people more favourably than others in providing supported employment.[36]

Discrimination other than by employers

13.37 In addition to regulating discrimination by employers, the DDA 1995 prohibits discrimination by those who engage contract workers (s12) and by trade organisations – broadly trade unions and employers' associations (ss13–15). These provisions are considered in detail in chapter 12. The DDA 1995 applies much less widely to employment-related discrimination by people other than employers than the SDA 1975 or the RRA 1976 such as qualifying bodies as explained in chapter 12. This position will be improved when the government introduces changes to comply with the ED.

34 DDA 1995 s10. A 'charity' is defined by the Charities Act 1993 as a body with 'charitable purposes'. In England and Wales, 'charitable purposes' are purposes which are exclusively charitable.

35 A 'charitable instrument' is an enactment or other instrument so far as it relates to charitable purposes (DDA 1995 s10(3)).

36 'Supported employment' means facilities provided, or in respect of which payments are made, under Disabled Persons (Employment) Act 1944 s15 and the Disabled Persons (Employment) Act (Northern Ireland) 1945.

Insurance services

13.38 The DDA 1995 makes specific provision in relation to certain types of insurance-related benefit provided to employees by third parties. If the employer provides insurance benefits such as private health insurance, the employment-related provisions of the DDA 1995 apply to prohibit discrimination against disabled workers in the provision of and in access to such benefits.

13.39 DDA 1995 s18 applies where a provider of insurance services who is not the worker's employer arranges with the employer for his or her workforce (or part of it) to receive or have the opportunity to receive 'insurance services'. Insurance services are defined as the provision of benefits in respect of termination of service (such as enhanced redundancy insurance schemes), retirement, old age or death, accident, injury, sickness or invalidity. If the treatment of a relevant worker by the insurer is such that it would amount to disability discrimination under the goods and services provisions (Pt III) of the DDA 1995 if the insurer were providing services to members of the public, and the relevant worker was a member of the public, it is treated as disability discrimination under Pt II (the employment provisions) of the DDA 1995 and the affected worker may bring his or her claim against the insurer in the employment tribunal. Where the arrangements apply to an employer's entire workforce, all workers are 'relevant workers'. But where the arrangement applies only to a class of workers, a worker must be within that class to gain the protection from the provisions. Discrimination under DDA 1995 Pt III is dealt with in chapter 30.

Exceptions to the prohibition on discrimination

13.40 The DDA 1995 is unlike both the SDA 1975 and the RRA 1976 in its approach to exceptions to the prohibition on discrimination, because justification is intrinsic to the concept of disability discrimination. The DDA 1995 therefore contains no comparable provision to the genuine occupational qualification applicable in race and sex discrimination, as the protection from disability discrimination is itself qualified by the ability of employers and others to justify discrimination. The DDA 1995 does, however, provide a number of specific exceptions even to its qualified prohibitions on discrimination.

National security

13.41 The DDA 1995, by contrast with the SDA 1975 and RRA 1976, provides a blanket exclusion relating to national security.[37] Nothing in the DDA 1995 makes unlawful any act done for the purpose of safeguarding national security. This reflects the position under the original SDA 1975 and RRA 1976 (see para 11.76). DDA 1995 Sch 3 paras 4(1)(b) and 8(1)(b) further state that a certificate signed by or on behalf of a minister of the Crown,[38] which certifies that an act specified in the certificate was done for the purpose of safeguarding national security, is conclusive evidence of the matter certified. A document purporting to be such a certificate shall be received in evidence and, unless the contrary is proved, is deemed to be such a certificate.[39] The certificate is valid in both employment tribunals and courts. Both the SDA 1975 and the RRA 1976 have been significantly amended, having originally dealt with national security issues in a similar way to that still applicable under the DDA 1995 – see further para 11.96.

Statutory authority

13.42 DDA 1995 s59, which is similarly worded to RRA 1976 s41 (see para 11.101), provides that no act or omission is unlawful when it is done:

- in pursuance of any enactment (s59(1)(a));
- in pursuance of any instrument made by a minister of the Crown under any enactment (s59(1)(b)); or
- to comply with any condition or requirement imposed by a minister of the Crown (whether before or after the passing of the DDA 1995) by virtue of any enactment (s59(1)(c)).[40]

'Enactment' includes an Act of Parliament, subordinate legislation such as a regulation passed by statutory instrument, and any Order in Council.[41] An 'instrument' is a piece of subordinate legislation made by a minister under statutory delegated authority.[42] Section 59 applies to enactments and instruments made both before and after the coming into force of the DDA 1995.[43]

37 DDA 1995 s59(3).

38 Or – in Northern Ireland – the Secretary of State (DDA 1995 Sch 8 para 50(2)).

39 DDA 1995 Sch 3 paras 4(2) and 8(2).

40 Ibid s59(1). In Northern Ireland it is the relevant department, rather than the minister of the Crown (DDA 1995 Sch 8 para 39).

41 Ibid s68(1).

42 Ibid s59(2).

43 Ibid s59(2).

13.43 Section 59 is construed narrowly and the case-law under the comparable provisions in the RRA 1976 (see para 11.102) is applicable also to the DDA 1995. Only actions reasonably necessary to comply with a statutory obligation are exempt by virtue of this provision of the DDA 1995, rather than acts done in exercise of a power or discretion conferred by the enactment or instrument.

13.44 The DDA 1995 code of practice (para 4.56) provides an example of the application of s59. If a particular adjustment would breach health and safety or fire legislation then an employer would not have to make it. However, the employer would still have to consider whether he or she was required to make any other adjustment that would not breach any legislation. If, for example, a wheelchair user could not use emergency evacuation arrangements (such as a fire escape) on a particular floor, it might be reasonable to relocate that person's job to a different office in which the problem did not arise.

Other exceptions

13.45 Exceptions and special circumstances which relate to the provision of particular benefits or contractual terms – such as occupational pension schemes and performance-related pay and agricultural wages – are dealt with at paras 6.53, 6.54 and 11.51.

CHAPTER 14

Discrimination in recruitment

continued

Key points

14.1
- The Sex Discrimination Act (SDA) 1975, the Race Relations Act (RRA) 1976 and the Disability Discrimination Act (DDA) 1995 all regulate discrimination in relation to recruitment, transfer, training, promotion, access to benefits at work, dismissal and detriment.
- When the relevant provisions of the Employment Directive (ED) come into force, discrimination on grounds of sexual orientation, religion or belief, and age will be regulated to the extent that it is not already regulated, albeit tangentially, by the SDA 1975 or the RRA 1976.
- Commission for Racial Equality (CRE), Equal Opportunities Commission (EOC) and DDA 1995 codes of practice offer guidance on how to avoid discrimination. Failure to follow them may be taken into account by an employment tribunal (ET) or court.
- It is unlawful to publish an advertisement that indicates that the employer intends to engage in unlawful discrimination (direct or indirect). In sex and race cases the CRE or EOC alone can bring complaints, unless the advertisement is part of the arrangements made for determining who should be offered employment; there are no parallel provisions under the DDA 1995.
- It is unlawful for an employment agency to discriminate against a person under the employment-related provisions of the SDA 1975 and RRA 1976 and the goods and services provisions of the DDA 1995.
- Examples of discriminatory recruitment procedures may include:
  - informal procedures, such as 'word of mouth' recruitment, recruitment by unsolicited letters of application (though see discussion at para 14.45 below);
  - selective recruitment, whereby employers confine their searches to places (such as public schools) that are dominated by white males;
  - head-hunting (again, subject to discussion at para 14.47 below);
  - recruitment through unions whose membership is largely white and/or male;
  - internal recruitment from a workforce that is largely white and/or male.

- A requirement to have UK qualifications or qualifications or experience over and above those necessary for the job may discriminate on grounds of race and/or sex.
- Language and literacy tests and application forms may discriminate on the ground of race.
- Maximum age limits for recruitment may discriminate on grounds of sex and/or race.
- Confining recruitment of staff to particular geographical areas may discriminate on the ground of race.
- A requirement to be mobile may discriminate against women.
- A requirement to hold a driving licence may amount to disability discrimination, as may a stipulation that employees must be 'energetic'.
- An employer may be under a duty to make reasonable adjustments to all stages of the recruitment procedure to prevent a particular disabled person from being at a substantial disadvantage in the selection process.
- Discriminatory attitudes are often revealed in interviews and may be useful evidence for a discrimination complainant.

Background and statutory provisions

14.2 Black and Asian people suffer an unemployment rate of 12 per cent by comparison with the white rate of 5 per cent.[1] This position has declined since 1990 when the black and Asian rate was 11 per cent by comparison with the white 6 per cent.[2] A third of black and Asian people report having encountered race discrimination at work.[3]

14.3 Although an increasing number of women are entering and staying in the workforce after childbirth, full-time female employees still earn only 82 per cent of the average hourly wage of full-time male employees.[4] Women are still not breaking through the glass ceiling, and pregnant women and those returning from maternity leave experience high levels of discrimination.

1 'Black workers deserve better', available from the TUC website: www.tuc.org.uk/equality.

2 Ibid and see 98 *Equal Opportunities Review* 8, July/August 2001.

3 'Race Equality in the North of England', available free from CRE North: tel 0161 835 5515.

4 'Employers and equal pay: survey report, March 2001' Chartered Institute of Personnel and Development, available from www.cipd.co.uk.

14.4 Disabled people are only half as likely as non-disabled people to be in employment and disabled people are over six times as likely as non-disabled people to be out of work and claiming benefits.[5]

14.5 Discrimination is still very common despite over 25 years of anti-discrimination legislation. It often occurs at the recruitment and promotion stage when employers are most likely to show prejudice against ethnic minority, disabled and female applicants. This chapter considers, for the most part, discrimination in recruitment in connection with race, sex, marital status,[6] gender reassignment and disability (as defined by the RRA 1976, the SDA 1975 and the DDA 1995). Maternity and parental rights, discrimination against pregnant women and women on maternity leave, access to child-friendly working hours and less favourable treatment of part-timers are considered in chapters 16 to 21.

14.6 The SDA 1975 and RRA 1976 prohibit direct and indirect discrimination on grounds of sex, race, etc. (The DDA 1995 does not distinguish between direct and indirect discrimination in the same manner as the SDA 1975 and RRA 1976.) All the cases here considered that deal with indirect discrimination were reached prior to the implementation of the Burden of Proof Regulations[7] which amend the definition of indirect discrimination and the burden of proof applicable to *employment-related* sex discrimination (see further paras 3.85–3.87 and 7.10). The provisions on the burden of proof apply to all sex discrimination employment claims not concluded by a tribunal prior to 12 October 2001. In the case of indirect race discrimination complaints the original definition of indirect discrimination still applies and the applicant will have to demonstrate that he or she has been subjected to a 'requirement or condition' with which he or she was unable to comply. In employment-related sex discrimination claims the 'requirement or condition' has been replaced by a 'provision, criterion or practice' and it is no longer necessary to show that the applicant 'cannot comply' with the requirement (see paras 7.10 and 7.106).

5 DfEE, 'Disability Briefing', November 1999.

6 Though most discrimination against married people is indirect and occurs because married couples are more likely to have children than single people (see chapter 7). In *Chief Constable of the Bedfordshire Constabulary v Graham* [2002] IRLR 239, however, the EAT upheld a tribunal's decision that a policy which restricted officers who were married to or in relationships with each other from working together amounted to unjustifiable indirect discrimination against women, a higher proportion of female officers than of male officers being affected by it.

7 Sex Discrimination (Indirect Discrimination and Burden of Proof) Regulations 2001 SI No 2660.

The 'prohibited acts'

14.7 In order to win a discrimination case under the SDA 1975, the RRA 1976 or the DDA 1995 the applicant will have to establish that he or she has been discriminated against on one of the prohibited grounds.[8] The discrimination may be direct or indirect in the case of the SDA 1975 and RRA 1976 (see further Chapters 4 and 7) or, in the case of the DDA 1995, may consist of unjustified less favourable treatment or a failure to make a reasonable adjustment (see chapter 6). In addition, the SDA 1975, RRA 1976 and DDA 1995 all prohibit 'victimisation' in connection with the Acts – see further chapter 4. Also, the discrimination claimant will have to show that the discrimination or victimisation was in the form of a 'prohibited act' under the relevant legislation. Such acts come within four broad categories:

- recruitment;
- transfer, training and promotion;
- access to work-related benefits;[9]
- dismissal and detriment.[10]

14.8 In chapter 15 we deal with SDA 1975 s6(2), RRA 1976 s4(2) and DDA 1995 s4(2), which regulate discrimination in relation to transfer, training and promotion, access to work-related benefits, dismissal and detriment. Here we consider SDA 1975 s6(1), RRA 1976 s4(1) and DDA 1995 s4(1).

14.9 RRA 1976 s4(1), to which SDA 1975 s6(1) and DDA 1995 s4(1) are materially identical, provides that:

> It is unlawful for a person, in relation to employment by him at an establishment in Great Britain, to discriminate against another—
> (a) in the arrangements he makes for the purpose of determining who should be offered that employment; or
> (b) in the terms on which he offers him that employment; or
> (c) by refusing or deliberately omitting to offer him that employment.

There is an overlap between subsections (a) and (c) set out above in

8 'Race', broadly defined, for the purposes of the RRA 1976; sex, married or gender reassignment under the SDA 1975 (though the last of these is covered only in relation to direct discrimination) or disability under the DDA 1995.

9 Sex discrimination in pay and contractual benefits is covered by the Equal Pay Act 1970 – see chapters 22.

10 See chapter 15 for a general discussion of 'detriment', chapter 28 for harassment in particular.

that discrimination in the 'arrangements' for determining who should be offered employment may also lead to a discriminatory refusal or failure to recruit. In order to establish a breach of (c), the complainant must have applied for the job and been refused. Under (a), there is no need for the complainant to have applied for a job. It is sufficient that the arrangements discriminate either directly or indirectly against the complainant.

Codes of practice

14.10 Account must be taken of the EOC, CRE and DDA 1995 codes of practice[11] (see chapter 1 for the effect of these). Where employers follow these codes they are less likely to be found to have discriminated unlawfully. The codes recommend training for those involved in the recruitment process. The EOC code of practice recommends that employers should ensure that personnel staff, line managers and all other employees who may come into contact with job applicants, should be trained in the provisions of the SDA 1975, including the fact that it is unlawful to instruct or put pressure on others to discriminate (see para 14.99 for comparable provisions under the CRE code). The DDA 1995 code of practice is much more comprehensive and provides useful examples (see especially paras 5.1–5.29). It is not possible to refer to all of them in this book.

14.11 The government has produced a voluntary Code of Practice for Age Diversity in Employment[12] which recommends the elimination of unnecessary age limits. A code of practice regarding discrimination on grounds of transsexualism also makes a number of recommendations on good practice for employers.[13] Neither of these codes has statutory force, the former not being accompanied, as yet, by legislative prohibition on age discrimination and the latter not being produced by or on behalf of government.

11 Respectively, the EOC Code of Practice for the elimination of discrimination on grounds of sex and marriage and the promotion of equality of opportunity in employment; the CRE Code of Practice for the elimination of discrimination and the promotion of equality of opportunity in employment and the DDA 1995 Code of Practice for the elimination of discrimination in the field of employment against disabled persons or persons who have had a disability.

12 Issued by the DfEE in July 1999 to promote good employment practice and available from the 'age positive' website at www.agepositive.gov.uk.

13 Published by Press for Change, BM Network, London WC1N 3XX, December 1998.

EC law

14.12 The Equal Treatment Directive[14] (ETD) provides (article 3) that:

> ... there shall be no discrimination whatsoever on grounds of sex in the conditions, including selection criteria, for access to all jobs or posts, whatever the sector or branch of activity, and to all levels of the occupational hierarchy.

The principle of equal treatment under EC law also applies to vocational guidance and training. The ETD should always be taken into account and it is binding where the employer is an emanation of the state (see para 10.73). Note that only sex discrimination is, as yet, covered in any significant degree by EC law. For the impending changes to this see chapter 10

Discriminatory job advertisements

14.13 Under SDA 1975 s38 and RRA 1976 s29 it is unlawful to publish or cause to be published an advertisement which indicates, or might reasonably be understood as indicating, that the employer intends to discriminate, either directly or indirectly on grounds of race, sex or against married people.[15] These sections can only be enforced by the EOC or CRE. The DDA 1995 contains no parallel provisions. In all jurisdictions advertisements may be part of the arrangements made for determining who to recruit, and so discriminatory advertising may be capable of challenge under SDA 1975 s6(1)(a) or RRA 1976 s4(1)(a) or DDA 1995 s4(1)(a) (though see paras 4.9 and 14.24).

'Advertisements'

14.14 The definition of advertisement is very wide. It includes every form of advertisement or notice, whether to the public or not, and whether in a newspaper or other publication, by television or radio, by display of notices, signs, labels, showcards or goods, by distribution of samples, circulars, catalogues, price lists or other material, by exhibition of pictures, models or films, or in any other way.[16] This would cover, for example, advertisements in employment agencies, schools and shops, as well as circulars to existing employees. It is likely that an

14 Council Directive 76/207/EEC.

15 SDA 1975 s38(1) and RRA 1976 s29(1), which apply to Pts II and III of the Acts.

16 SDA 1975 s82(1) and RRA 1976 s78(1).

advertisement sent by email or placed on a website would also come within this definition.

'Discriminatory' advertisements

14.15 The question is whether a reasonable person would consider the advertisement discriminatory. In *Race Relations Board v Associated Newspapers Group Ltd*[17] the Court of Appeal held that the question was 'what is the natural and ordinary meaning of the words ... what would an ordinary reasonable man or woman understand by the words'. The intention of the person placing the advertisement is not conclusive. The use of a gendered job description (such as 'waiter', 'salesgirl', 'postman' or 'stewardess') will be taken to indicate an intention to discriminate contrary to the SDA 1975, unless the advertisement contains an indication to the contrary.[18] Any suggestion that a woman or man or person of a particular racial group will be preferred will amount to unlawful race discrimination unless it comes within one of the exceptions discussed at paras 11.70–11.108.

14.16 Both direct and indirect discrimination in advertisements are prohibited. An advertisement specifying that candidates should be over six feet tall would be unlawful (unless the height requirement could be justified), as would an advertisement stating that candidates should be male, unless a genuine occupational qualification or other defence applied.

14.17 The EOC code of practice suggests that all advertising material and attached literature should be reviewed to ensure that it avoids presenting men and women in stereotyped roles as this tends to perpetuate sex segregation in jobs and may also lead people of the sex not generally associated with a particular job to believe that they would be unsuccessful in applying for it (para 19(a)). In *EOC v Rodney Day Associates Ltd*,[19] for example, an ET held that an advertisement headed 'Genuine career opportunities for rugby players', which was published with a picture of a male rugby player, could indicate an intention to discriminate.

14.18 The CRE code of practice recommends avoiding requirements such as length of residence or experience in the UK and states that, where a particular qualification is required, it should be made clear

17 [1978] 3 All ER 419, CA.

18 SDA 1975 s38(3). See also *EOC v Robertson* [1980] IRLR 44, in which a tribunal considered the question of discriminatory job titles.

19 (1989) 379 IRLIB 11.

that a comparable qualification obtained overseas is as acceptable as one obtained in the UK (para 1.6(b)).

Placing of advertisements

14.19 Placing advertisements in publications read mainly by people of one sex or a particular racial group may be indirectly discriminatory if it cannot be justified. Advertising in trade journals which are available to or only read by existing members of that trade will discriminate indirectly against non-members and those out of work, thus excluding more women and ethnic minority applicants amongst whom there is a higher unemployment rate. An applicant who knows about the advertisement will suffer no disadvantage and is unlikely to be able to establish less favourable treatment for the purposes of an individual complaint (as opposed to enforcement action by the relevant commission). Information relating to where the job advertisement was placed may, however, be used as evidence from which a tribunal or court could be invited to draw an inference of discrimination on the basis that it might indicate that the employer was more inclined to appoint a worker of a particular race or sex.

14.20 The CRE code of practice recommends that employers should try not to confine advertisements to publications which might exclude or disproportionately reduce the numbers of applicants of a particular racial group (para 1.6(a)).[20] The EOC code recommends that job advertising should be carried out in such a way as to encourage applications from suitable candidates of both sexes. This can be achieved both by the wording of the advertisements and, for example, by placing advertisements in publications likely to reach both sexes (para 19(a)). Employers who want to encourage applicants from under-represented groups often use the ethnic minority press and magazines read mainly by women to attract more black and female candidates.

Lawful discrimination

14.21 Some discrimination is permitted by the SDA 1975 and RRA 1976 (see further chapter 11). The DDA 1995 does not prohibit positive discrimination in favour of disabled people. In these circumstances it is not unlawful to publish an advertisement which indicates that

20 Para 1.7 recommends that, where employers send information to applicants, they should include a statement that they are equal opportunity employers.

21 SDA 1975 s38(2).

discrimination will occur.[21] There is one exception to this under the RRA 1976. Where the private household exception applies and an employer can lawfully discriminate on racial grounds, it will still be unlawful to express any racial preference in a job advertisement.[22]

14.22 An advertisement may state a preference for one sex or race in the following situations:

- when a genuine occupational qualification applies (see para 11.70);
- when positive action is allowed (see chapter 5);
- when, under the RRA 1976, employment may be restricted to those of a particular birth place, nationality, descent or place of ordinary residence and/or length of residence for employment by or with the approval of the Crown and certain prescribed bodies (see para 11.108);[23]
- when, under the RRA 1976, applicants of a particular nationality (as distinct from a particular colour or race, or particular ethnic or national origin) are sought for a job outside Great Britain.[24]

Who can complain?

14.23 Only the CRE or EOC can directly challenge a discriminatory advertisement,[25] unless a potential applicant for the job in question can show that the advertisement constituted part of 'the arrangements made' for determining who should be offered employment (see para 14.9).

14.24 If an applicant has unsuccessfully applied for a job, a discriminatory advertisement will be strong (but not conclusive) evidence that he or she failed to get the job as a result of his or her race or sex. The applicant in *Cardiff Women's Aid v Hartup*[26] complained about an advertisement specifying that the successful candidate would be a black or Asian woman. The EAT overturned a ruling that she had been discriminated against contrary to the SDA 1975 and held that the employer had not committed any actionable act of discrimination in placing the advertisement. Causing an advertisement to be published which indicated 'an intention' by a person to do an act of discrimination was unlawful under RRA 1976 s29(1), but only the CRE could take action in respect of this provision. The EAT did not accept

22 This does not come within the exceptions set out in RRA 1976 s29(2).

23 Ibid s75(5).

24 Ibid s29(3).

25 SDA 1975 s72 and RRA 1976 s63.

26 [1994] IRLR 390, EAT. The employers claimed that a genuine occupational qualification applied – see further chapter 11.

that the discriminatory advertisement was also part of the 'arrangements' made by the employer for the purposes of determining who should be offered the job

14.25 The decision in *Hartup* may well be wrong, although the result may have been different if the applicant had been interested in or applied for the job.[27] Advertisements are part of the arrangements for determining who should be offered the job. Many potential candidates will not apply for a job from which they are either specifically excluded or for which they are not apparently qualified. In *Hartup* the exclusion of white women was less favourable treatment on grounds of race (subject to the genuine occupational qualification exception), direct discrimination not requiring any proof of detriment to the complainant.[28]

Liability

14.26 Both the publisher and employer may be liable for a discriminatory advertisement unless the publisher reasonably relied on a statement by the advertiser that the advertisement was lawful.[29]

Job advertisements under the Disability Discrimination Act 1995

14.27 The provisions in the DDA 1995 governing job advertisements differ from those of the SDA 1975 and RRA 1976. The DDA 1995 defines an 'advertisement' as 'every form of advertisement or notice, whether to the public or not',[30] and makes it unlawful for an advertisement to suggest that employers will discriminate against disabled people. If such an advertisement has been placed the tribunal must assume, unless the contrary is shown, that the employer's reason for refusing to offer, or deliberately not offering, the employment to the complainant was related to the complainant's disability. This applies where:

- a disabled person has applied for employment with an employer;
- the employer has refused to offer, or has deliberately not offered, him or her the employment;

27 See *Brindley v Tayside Health Board* [1976] IRLR 364.

28 The position is different with indirect discrimination where detriment must be proved (see *Coker* below). Also where the claim is expressly for 'any other detriment' (see chapter 15).

29 SDA 1975 s38(4) and RRA 1976 s29(4); see also *Bains v Bowles* [1991] IRLR 356.

30 DDA 1995 s11(3).

- the disabled person has lodged a complaint of disability discrimination against the employer;
- the employer has advertised the employment (whether before or after the disabled person applied for it); and
- the advertisement indicated, or might reasonably be understood to have indicated, that any application for the advertised employment would, or might, be determined to any extent by reference to:
  - the successful applicant not having a disability; or
  - the employer's reluctance to make reasonable adjustments.

14.28 The DDA 1995 code of practice gives the example of an advertisement for an office worker which states that gaining access to the workplace building can be difficult. An applicant who can only walk with crutches, but can do office work, is turned down. Because of the wording of the advertisement the ET would have to assume that she did not get the job for a reason relating to her disability unless the employer could prove otherwise.

14.29 There are no special provisions under the DDA 1995 which enable the Disability Rights Commission to take action in respect of discriminatory advertisements.[31]

14.30 As the DDA 1995 provides rights for disabled people, and so goes beyond the right for disabled and non-disabled people to be treated equally, an employer can state that applications from disabled people are welcome and the DDA 1995 code of practice (para 5.10) describes this as a positive and public statement of the employer's policy. Furthermore, the DDA 1995 does not prevent posts being advertised as open only to disabled people except for local authorities which are required to appoint on merit.[32]

Discrimination in other methods of recruitment

14.31 Many employers recruit staff not directly but through other third parties – employment agencies, job centres, careers offices, and schools.

31 This is likely to change with the implementation in the UK of the ED.

32 Local Government and Housing Act 1989 s7.

Recruitment through employment agencies: Race Relations Act 1976 and Sex Discrimination Act 1975

14.32 The SDA 1975 and the RRA 1976 make it unlawful for an employment agency to discriminate against a person on the ground of race, sex or being married (see chapter 12). It is also unlawful for an employer to instruct, procure or induce an employment agency to do an unlawful act, though these provisions are enforceable only by the CRE and EOC.[33]

14.33 In order to avoid indirect discrimination the CRE code of practice recommends that employers should not confine themselves to agencies, schools, etc, in which candidates from racial minorities are not represented, and suggests that employers should use employment agencies and careers offices in areas in which any ethnic minority group(s) currently under-represented in their workplaces are concentrated (para 1.45, and see *Hussein v Saints Complete House Furnishers*[34]).

14.34 The EOC code of practice (para 20) states that, when notifying vacancies to the careers service, employers should specify that these are open to both boys and girls. If dealing with single-sex schools they should ensure, where possible, that both boys' and girls' schools are approached. Mixed schools should be reminded that jobs are open to both boys and girls.

14.35 The DDA 1995's employment provisions do not prohibit discrimination by employment agencies, save in relation to their own workers. But employment agencies are covered by the goods and services provisions discussed in chapter 30.[35] Furthermore, employers who act through agents will also be liable for any actions of their agents done with the employer's express or implied authority.[36] The DDA 1995 code of practice gives the example of an employer who makes it clear to a recruitment agency that he or she will not take kindly to recruits with learning disabilities being put forward by the agency. If the agency complies by not putting such candidates forward the employer will be liable under the DDA 1995 unless the treatment can be justified in an individual case. The agency will also be liable under the goods and services provisions in the DDA 1995.

33 RRA 1976 ss30 and 31; SDA 1975 ss39 and 40.

34 [1979] IRLR 337, ET.

35 DDA 1995 s19(3) explicitly refers to facilities provided by employment agencies as an example of services covered by the legislation.

36 Ibid s58.

Informal recruitment methods

14.36 Many employers do not advertise or use employment agencies but recruit informally, through friends or employees' contacts, or limit recruitment to places (such as particular schools, colleges and universities) in which ethnic minorities and women may be underrepresented. The existence of a divided labour market and a society in which white men are overwhelmingly in positions of power means that informal recruitment methods (such as by word of mouth), or targeted recruitment (where the targeted group is largely white and male), will perpetuate the make up of the workforce and are likely to have an adverse affect on ethnic minorities and women. Such practices may be indirectly discriminatory under the SDA 1975 or RRA 1976.

14.37 The DDA 1995 does not prohibit indirect discrimination as such. But targeted recruitment from, for example, particular schools and colleges that do not have disabled students and are not accessible to disabled students, could in a particular case amount to less favourable treatment for a reason related to the disabled person's disability, unless justified by the prospective employer.

14.38 Informal recruitment may mean that potential candidates may never hear about available jobs, or may do so only when it is too late to apply for them. A potential applicant who finds out about the job when it is too late to apply may be able to claim discrimination on the basis that the recruitment method was a discriminatory arrangement (see *Lord Chancellor v Coker and Osamor*[37] below). Someone who actually applies for a vacancy will only be able to claim discrimination if he or she can show that the selection process to which he or she was subjected was also discriminatory.

14.39 The CRE code of practice states that recruitment should not be through the recommendation of existing employees where the workforce is mainly white and the labour market is predominantly multiracial (para 1.10(a)). Similarly, the EOC code recommends that 'word of mouth' recruitment should be avoided in a workforce predominantly of one sex if, in practice, it prevents members of the other sex from applying (para 19(c)).

14.40 In 1978 the CRE conducted a formal investigation into a company called F Broomfield Ltd. The company, through its transport manager, recruited most of its drivers on the recommendations of existing drivers. All 45 drivers were white and only one non-white driver (the

37 [2001] IRLR 116, EAT and [2002] IRLR 80, CA.

brother-in-law of another driver) had ever been recruited. The CRE concluded that Broomfield applied a condition or requirement that, in order to be considered for recruitment, an applicant had to be recommended by a driver already employed by the company. The employers tried to argue that the practice was justifiable because it produced more reliable staff, but failed to produce any evidence that this was so. The CRE decided that these recruitment procedures constituted unlawful racial discrimination.

14.41 In *Coker* the Lord Chancellor appointed as his special adviser a solicitor (Garry Hart), who was well known to him (and was godfather to the Prime Minister's son). The post was not advertised and no overt selection process was carried out. The Lord Chancellor did not look outside his circle of acquaintances for a special adviser. Two women claimed that this was indirect discrimination, Ms Coker on the ground of sex and Ms Osamor on grounds of race and sex. The ET rejected Ms Osamor's complaint on the basis that, because she was not qualified for the post, she had suffered no detriment in being denied the chance to apply for it. The ET upheld Ms Coker's complaint however, ruling that the Lord Chancellor had imposed a requirement to the effect that the successful candidate must be personally known to him. The ET further found that the requirement had a disproportionate impact on women, and that its imposition on Ms Coker had been to her detriment.

14.42 The Employment Appeal Tribunal (EAT) upheld the Lord Chancellor's appeal and the Court of Appeal rejected the applicants' appeal from the EAT's decision.[38] The Court of Appeal's judgment was mainly concerned with the question of disproportionate impact. The court proceeded on the basis that the Lord Chancellor applied a requirement that 'only those personally known to the Lord Chancellor would be considered' for the position. It then held that, in order to decide whether the requirement had a disproportionate impact, it was first necessary to identify the pool (or group) of people on whom the requirement impacted. This consisted of those who would, but for the challenged requirement, be qualified for appointment. The question then was whether, within the pool, the proportion of women who were known to the Lord Chancellor was 'considerably smaller' than the proportion of men known to him. The pool chosen by the ET was those otherwise eligible for appointment in accordance with a letter written by the Lord Chancellor setting out those qualities which had, in his view, made Garry Hart a suitable special adviser.

38 [2002] IRLR 80 (CA). The ET's decision is at [1999] IRLR 396.

14.43 The Court of Appeal held that a requirement could only have a discriminatory effect if a significant proportion of the pool was able to satisfy that requirement. Because the requirement here – that the appointee be known to the Lord Chancellor – excluded almost the entire pool of those otherwise qualified, its application to the applicants could not constitute indirect discrimination against them. The requirement excluded everyone except Garry Hart. Thus, according to the Court of Appeal, it could have no disproportionate effect on the different groupings within the pool. The court made no comment on the EAT's finding that the applicants suffered no detriment (see para 7.115).

14.44 As a postscript to its decision in *Coker*, the Court of Appeal made two further apparently inconsistent points. First the court stated that, although the applicants' challenge to the practice of making appointments from a circle of family, friends and acquaintances had failed, this practice was nevertheless open to objection because it might not produce the best candidate, it might be likely to result in the appointee being a particular gender or racial group, and it might infringe the principle of equal opportunities. Second, the court stated that its judgment was not concerned with the practice of recruiting by word of mouth or personal recommendation. This could, the court stated (referring to the EOC and CRE codes, which recommend that word of mouth recruitment be avoided) have a disproportionate adverse impact by sex and/or race.

Unsolicited letters of application

14.45 If information about jobs has been obtained from existing workers who are predominantly white men, it is possible that unsolicited letters from their friends will also be from white men. Recruiting from a pool of those who have sent unsolicited application letters may be unlawful indirect discrimination unless justified.

Selective recruitment

14.46 Employers commonly recruit professional staff from places where they will find a disproportionate number of white, male candidates – public schools, for example, or Oxford and Cambridge universities. Such practices may amount to unlawful indirect discrimination unless they can be justified. In 1995 the Policy Studies Institute discovered that many law firms discriminated against ethnic minority applicants by recruiting trainee solicitors from disproportionately white higher education institutes.[39] The chance of an average or below-average ethnic minority candidate achieving a training post was 40 per cent less than that of a comparable white candidate. More recently, some of the larger law firms have started to pre-screen potential applicants to weed out those who have not achieved particular A level grades. Given the disproportionate concentration of many ethnic minority students in relatively disadvantaged educational establishments, this too could amount to unlawful indirect discrimination unless it can be justified

14.47 The practice of 'head-hunting' for top managerial and professional jobs is also common. Firms which use this approach – targeting individuals for the firm's top jobs – are confining their search to those already in such jobs, usually overwhelmingly white men. The CRE code of practice states that job vacancies should be made known to all eligible employees and, in particular, that employers should not confine recruitment unjustifiably to those agencies, job centres, careers offices and schools which, because of their particular source of applicants, provide only or mainly applicants of a particular racial group (para 1.9).

Recruitment through unions

14.48 Sometimes applicants are supplied wholly or mainly through unions. This practice is likely to reproduce the character of the existing workforce and may be discriminatory. The trade union will be treated as an employment agency and may be liable for discrimination (see chapter 12).

14.49 In *Turnbull v Record Production Chapel*[40] the applicant complained that direct and indirect sex discrimination had prevented her from obtaining a job in the production department of the newspaper for which she worked. The 'chapel' (union branch) was found to have directly discriminated against her, as there was evidence that union members and officers had acted in a sexually discriminatory way. The ET also held that indirect discrimination had occurred. The condition for transfer to the job Ms Turnbull wanted (membership of the production chapel) was one with which a considerably smaller

39 Entry into the legal professions: the law student cohort study (year 3, PSI, 1995).
40 EAT 955/83 (unreported, available on LEXIS).

proportion of women than men could comply. SOGAT appealed to the EAT which upheld the findings of discrimination.[41]

14.50 The CRE code of practice recommends that recruitment should not be through procedures whereby applicants are mainly supplied through trade unions, where this means that only members of a particular racial group come forward (para 1.10(b)). The EOC recommends that, where applicants are supplied through trade unions and members of one sex only come forward, this should be discussed with the unions and an alternative approach adopted (para 19(d)).

Recruitment from particular geographical areas

14.51 The recruitment of staff only from particular geographical areas may have an adverse impact on certain racial groups. Residence patterns and discrimination in the housing market mean that some areas, particularly inner-city areas, have a high proportion of black residents, while other areas are mainly white.

14.52 In *Hussein v Saints Complete House Furnishers*[42] the applicant, who had been recommended by a local employment agency for a job at a shop in Liverpool city centre, complained of race discrimination when he was refused employment. His application was rejected by the company because he lived in the city centre area and the employer said it was likely, in view of the high unemployment in the area, that his unemployed friends would start hanging around the shop. Mr Hussein argued that this was indirect race discrimination. Over 50 per cent of the population of Liverpool's city centre was black, compared with 2 per cent in the rest of Merseyside. The requirement not to live in the city centre was therefore one with which fewer black people could comply. The ET held that he had been unlawfully discriminated against.[43] Similarly, in Northern Ireland a requirement that applicants come from a particular geographical area is likely to disproportionately disadvantage either Catholics or Protestants.

41 The EOC took preliminary action under SDA 1975 s73 with a view to seeking an injunction to stop the discrimination. The ET made an order that arrangements for filling vacancies should be reorganised within the same three-month period so that all cleaners would have transfer rights.

42 [1979] IRLR 337.

43 A recommendation was made under RRA 1976 s56 that the company refrain from imposing such residential requirements in future.

Internal recruitment

14.53 Some employers limit recruitment for certain posts to internal candidates alone, either on the ground that this is a cheaper method of recruitment, or to give their own employees a career structure within their workplace. This may have a discriminatory effect if the composition of the existing workforce is racially or sexually skewed, as internal recruitment reinforces the status quo.[44] On the other hand, internal recruitment can offer opportunities for black and female workers who are in low-paid, low-status jobs, who may well find it easier to get promotion within an organisation than outside it. Employers can use the positive action provisions to train under-represented workers to apply for higher grade jobs (see further chapter 15).

14.54 The EOC code of practice states that, if jobs are not advertised externally, employers should ensure that they are published to all eligible employees in a way that avoids restricting applications from either sex (para 19(b)).

Job 'requirements'

14.55 The imposition of different application requirements depending on an applicant's race, sex, marital status or disability will be direct discrimination. The imposition of different application requirements for disabled people will also amount to less favourable treatment and unless justified, may be unlawful and the prospective employer may also be under a duty to make reasonable adjustments to assist a disabled applicant in applying for a job and competing on a level playing field in the selection process. Both the EOC and CRE codes of practice recommend that, when recruiting, employers should treat each individual according to his or her ability to carry out the job, and avoid making generalised assumptions about them on the basis of their sex or racial group (paras 13 and 14 respectively). The reasonable adjustment duty has tremendous potential to assist disabled job applicants gain access to the labour market. It not only includes modifying procedures for testing and assessment, for example, thereby enabling disabled candidates at a substantial disadvantage in the recruitment process, but could also include, in any particular case, making adjustments to enable the successful disabled candidate to take up the post. For example, by making adjustments to the premises, the provision

44 See also *Watches of Switzerland v Savell* [1983] IRLR 141.

of a reader or interpreter, or modifying equipment. However, in *Kenny v Hampshire Constabulary*,[44a] a recruitment case concerning the non-appointment of the best candidate who was a wheelchair user because of the lack of volunteers from within the department to assist the applicant with personal care and toilet functions, the EAT held that the duty of reasonable adjustments stopped short of the employer providing personal care functions, and referred to job-related adjustments. The section 6 duty of reasonable adjustment is discussed fully in chapter 6.

14.56 Direct sex and race discrimination in recruitment does occur. However, much of the discrimination associated with job requirements is indirect. The existence of discrimination in society (including education and the labour market); the fact that men and women and different racial groups have different cultural and social needs (such as women's primary responsibility for childcare); and the fact that some ethnic minority applicants may not have gained their qualifications and/or work experience in the UK, mean that some job requirements have the effect of disproportionately excluding women or ethnic minority candidates. Unless reliance on these requirements is justifiable it is likely to be unlawful.

14.57 Both the EOC and the CRE codes of practice recommend that employers ensure that any job requirements with a disparate impact are justifiable. The CRE code suggests that employers should avoid prescribing requirements like length of residence or experience in the UK and should make clear that a comparable qualification obtained overseas is as acceptable as a UK qualification.

14.58 Job 'requirements' can also breach the DDA 1995. It may be a reasonable adjustment to modify or remove a job requirement that substantially disadvantages a disabled person – for example the requirement for a driving licence when the successful candidate would rarely be required to drive.[45] A job requirement may also entail unjustified less favourable treatment of a disabled job applicant. If, for example, an employer stipulates that employees must be 'energetic', a disabled person whose disabilities result in his or her becoming easily tired may find himself discriminated against for a reason relating to his or her disability. If the job is, in fact, largely sedentary in nature, the employer is unlikely to be able to justify the less favourable treatment and the discrimination will be unlawful.[46]

44a [1999] IRLR 76.

45 See further chapter 6.

46 Ibid.

14.59 The DDA 1995 code of practice points out (paras 5.3–5.6) that:

- the inclusion of unnecessary or marginal requirements in a job specification can lead to discrimination;
- blanket exclusions that do not take account of individual circumstances may lead to discrimination (such as excluding people with epilepsy from all driving jobs);
- stipulating essential health requirements may be discriminatory if not justified;
- stating a preference for certain personal, medical or health-related characteristics may be discriminatory if not necessary for the performance of the job. An example given is of a woman with a learning disability who may not have a preferred qualification (because her learning disability has prevented her from obtaining it) but, if the qualification is not necessary, and she is otherwise the best candidate the employer will have discriminated against her.

Qualifications

14.60 Where a requirement that candidates have any particular qualification disproportionately disadvantages women, men, or those of a particular racial group,[47] an employer will not be able to justify reliance on it on the basis that it is simply a 'useful' tool in the selection procedure. In order to be objectively justified, reliance on a disproportionately impacting requirement or condition must be a *necessary and appropriate* means of achieving a *legitimate objective* (see para 7.116). The CRE code of practice states that care should be taken to ensure that a higher standard of educational qualifications than strictly necessary should not be required (para 1.13(a)).

14.61 A requirement that a candidate has a UK qualification may indirectly discriminate against ethnic minority applicants who have not always lived in the UK and who may have comparable overseas qualifications. In 1978, for example, the Council of Legal Education was held to have unlawfully discriminated by requiring graduates from overseas to complete a two-year course of study before becoming barristers, whereas graduates with a UK degree had to do only one year's study.[48]

14.62 The applicant in *Sunderalingam v Ealing Health Authority*[49] applied

47 Which may – see RRA 1976 s3(2) – consist of more than one racial group.

48 *Bohon-Mitchel v Common Professional Examination Board and Council of Legal Education* [1978] IRLR 525.

49 ET 34674/83 (unreported).

for a state registered nurse secondment scheme but was told he had to take a special test because he did not meet the minimum entry requirement of five O levels. In fact, he had eight O levels, but these were not recognised because they had been taken in Sri Lanka. A white nurse with equivalent qualifications was admitted to the course without taking a test. The health authority admitted that Mr Sunderalingam's qualifications were sufficient for the purposes of the job, and the ET made a finding of discrimination.

14.63 The CRE code recommends that overseas degrees, diplomas and other qualifications that are comparable with UK qualifications should be accepted as equivalents (para 1.13(c)). The Department of Education and Science, the National Equivalents Unit of the British Council or the education department of the appropriate foreign embassy should be able to give advice on whether an overseas qualification is comparable.

14.64 EC Directive 89/48/EEC requires member states to recognize EC professional qualifications and training which are of at least three years duration. Member states are obliged to recognise community professional qualifications and there is an adaptation procedure where the qualifications are lower than those in the host state. The details are outside the scope of this book.

14.65 The DDA 1995 code of practice states (para 5.22) that an employer is entitled to specify that applicants for a job must have certain qualifications. However, if a disabled person is rejected for the job because he lacks a qualification, and the lack of that qualification is related to the disabled person's disability, the employer will have to justify demanding the qualification. Justification under the DDA 1995 requires a showing that the qualification is relevant and significant in terms of the particular job and the particular applicant, and that no reasonable adjustment would change this. An employer specifies that two GCSEs are required for a certain post. This is to show that a candidate has the general level of ability required. No particular subjects are specified. An applicant whose dyslexia prevented her from passing written examinations cannot meet this requirement, but the employer would be unable to justify rejecting her on this account alone if she could show that she nevertheless had the skill and intelligence called for in the post. If the qualification relates to a particular aspect of the job it may be a reasonable adjustment to reassign that part of the job or, if a particular applicant has alternative evidence of the necessary level of competence, to waive the requirement in his or her case.

14.66 An employer is not under a duty to make reasonable adjustments (a s6 duty) if he or she did not know, and could not reasonably have been expected to know, that the disabled person was (or might have been) an applicant for employment, or that the disabled person had a disability and was likely to be put at a substantial disadvantage by comparison with people who were not disabled.[50] The DDA 1995 does not impose a general duty to make adjustments, though the duty may arise in relation to particular job applicants. The code of practice explains (para 4.57) that an employer must do all he or she could reasonably be expected to do to find out if a potential applicant is disabled for the purposes of the DDA 1995. If an employer does not include questions on application forms which enable a job applicant to state whether he or she is disabled and whether adjustments are required, an employer will not have done all he or she could reasonably be expected to have done and will not escape the s6 duty. For job applicants there is something of a dilemma. If they complete the relevant question, there is a fear that they will be discriminated against because of their disabilities. If they do not inform the employer, the s6 duty may not arise.

Experience

14.67 Experience is a common job requirement. Industrial and occupational job segregation in the labour market mean that the majority of women and black workers in the workforce are confined to a relatively small range of occupations, many of which are in low-paid, unskilled industries, particularly the service industries. Some jobs, such as clerical, secretarial, catering and cleaning jobs, are nearly always 'women's jobs'. Others – mainly skilled manual jobs – are done almost exclusively by men. Because of the restricted opportunities for women and black workers in the labour market they may be denied the experience necessary to get many jobs, particularly at higher levels.

14.68 In *Falkirk Council v Whyte*[51] the EAT upheld a tribunal's finding that a woman had suffered unlawful indirect sex discrimination when she was denied a managerial post because she did not have the management training and supervisory experience which were stated to be 'desirable'. The EAT stated that it was a classic situation of indirect sex discrimination, with mostly women in basic grade posts, and mostly men in promoted management posts.

50 DDA 1995 s6(6).
51 [1997] IRLR 560.

14.69 Similar claims have been made under the RRA 1976.[52] In *Azhashemi v Engineering ITB*[53] an Iranian was refused a place on an engineering course because he lacked experience in the UK, although he had experience abroad. This was held to amount to indirect discrimination contrary to the RRA 1976. In *Pratt v Walsall Health Authority*[54] a requirement that candidates evidenced a rapid and vigorous promotion through the ranks was held to be unjustifiable race discrimination because black applicants had greater difficulties achieving such progress due to the effects of discrimination.

14.70 Northern Ireland's Fair Employment and Treatment Order 1998 prohibits discrimination on grounds of religious belief.[55] In *McCausland v Dungannon DC*[56] the respondents decided to fill a manager's post by trawling for applicants already in local government in Northern Ireland. Of those in the relevant pool (those with appropriate qualifications for the vacant post – the tribunal accepted that this was those in Standard Occupational Classifications 1, 2 and 3) 2.1 per cent of Protestants were in local government service compared with 1.5 per cent of the Catholics. Northern Ireland's Court of Appeal declined to decide whether this was a considerably smaller proportion. It sent the case back to the ET which found that the proportion of Catholics who could comply with the requirement to be in local government service was considerably smaller than the proportion of Protestants who could so comply.

14.71 If a disabled person has been hampered in gaining experience for a reason relating to his or her disability an employer would need to justify the imposition of an experience requirement on that person to avoid a finding that he or she was in breach of the DDA 1995. Similarly, if a lack of experience places the disabled person at a substantial disadvantage in comparison to applicants who are not disabled, the s6 duty may arise if the employer knew or could reasonably be expected to know of the particular (potential) applicant, his or her disability, and the effects thereof (see paras 14.58 and 14.59).

52 In *Meer v Tower Hamlets LBC* [1988] IRLR 399 the applicant complained of the criteria used for shortlisting. They included experience of local government, of senior management, of Tower Hamlets and length in present post. This was dismissed because no one factor was essential, so there was no requirement – see now para 7.10.

53 ET 27486/83 (unreported).

54 ET 36145/86 (unreported).

55 SI No 3162. Formerly the Fair Employment Acts 1976 and 1989.

56 [1993] IRLR 583.

Tests and application forms

14.72 Tests have the potential to discriminate directly or indirectly on grounds of sex or race. Tests may also discriminate against disabled candidates and may require adjustment or modification for particular disabled candidates.

14.73 The most obvious type of discrimination is the direct form – if only some candidates are required to take tests, and the decision as to who should do so is made on the basis of race, sex or disability. In *Mallidi v Post Office*,[57] for example, the complainant took an aptitude test to decide whether she could continue in employment. She failed the test and her employment was terminated. An ET upheld her race discrimination claim, finding that three white comparators were given contracts without the need to pass the aptitude test and no satisfactory explanation was given.

14.74 Tests that are required of candidates should not discriminate between them on the prohibited grounds. So, for example, tests of physical strength should not vary between men and women.[58] At the same time tests of strength (as distinct from skill, stamina, dexterity etc) will generally disadvantage women and will be indirectly discriminatory unless justified by the real needs of the job (see para 7.116). Employers should explain and substantiate the relationship between the job and the tests, and tests which are justifiable in relation to some jobs will not be so in relation to others. Psychometric testing of staff is becoming increasingly common. Such tests should be used with caution, however, as they may incorporate direct discrimination and/or result in indirect discrimination.[59]

14.75 Tests must address employers' real needs for staff. In 1989, eight Asian applicants brought a case against British Rail alleging that aptitude and safety tests for train drivers indirectly discriminated against them.[60] British Rail agreed to introduce an improved driver selection procedure, to review its equal opportunities policy and to consider positive action training. The CRE consultants who examined the tests and their results found that the Asians had worked more slowly and accurately than their white counterparts. This put them at a disadvantage as higher scores were available for attempting as many questions as possible. The consultants found that the Asians were inadequately

57 (2001) DCLC 47.

58 See, eg, *Allcock v Chief Constable, Hampshire Constabulary*, ET 3101524/97 (unreported).

59 See 'Psychometrics should make assessment fairer' (1996) 67 EOR 27.

60 'A fair test: Selecting train drivers at British Rail' (CRE).

prepared for these 'test strategies' and that the tests did not relate to the applicants' ability to drive a train.

14.76 The standard of English that may justifiably be required of an applicant will depend on the type of job. An employer will be able to justify a higher standard of English for more technical jobs. For many unskilled jobs, fluency in English, literacy and familiarity with the prevailing culture are irrelevant and should not, therefore, be required. British Leyland used to require applicants for unskilled manual jobs to complete application forms unassisted in their own handwriting. Two Pakistani applicants, who could not read or write English, were refused employment and complained that this was indirectly discriminatory. British Leyland conceded that fewer Pakistani applicants could comply with the requirement and agreed it was not necessary for employees to be able to complete the forms in order to be able to do the work.[61]

14.77 The CRE code of practice states that the ability to complete a form personally should only be used as a means of assessment if this is a valid test of the standard of English necessary for the safe and effective performance of the job (para 1.13(a), (b), (d) and (e)).

14.78 A disabled applicant may be able to claim both less favourable treatment and a failure to make a reasonable adjustment in some circumstances. If, for example, a visually impaired candidate has a job application rejected because she has incorrectly completed a written application form, and the reason for this related to her disability, she will have been less favourably treated for a reason related to the DDA 1995 which the employer will have to justify. If the employer knew, or ought reasonably to have known, of the disability, and that having to complete a written application would place the disabled person at a substantial disadvantage, the s6 duty to adjust will also arise.

14.79 A wide range of possible adjustments might need to be considered in a particular case. A dyslexic candidate may need longer to read questions as may a visually impaired candidate who uses Braille or a magnification aid. Stress and tension can aggravate a disability and affect the results – an adjustment could be considered that will minimise the stress of formal test or exam conditions. Relevant specialist guidance on pre-employment testing may be available depending on the disability concerned. The RNIB, for example, has produced a guidance booklet on psychometric testing for the visually impaired.

61 *Isa and Rashid v BL Cars Ltd*, ET 27083/80 & 32273/79 (unreported); see also *Laparta v Henry Telfer Ltd* and *Ullah v British Steel Corporation*, cited in CRE *Annual Report* 1982.

Codes of practice

14.80 The DDA 1995 code of practice states (para 5.21) that routine testing of all candidates may discriminate against particular individuals. Employers should take account of the needs of a disabled candidate and revise the tests except where the nature and form of the test are necessary to assess a matter relevant to the particular job.

14.81 The CRE code of practice recommends that selection tests should not use irrelevant questions that may be unfamiliar to racial minority applicants (para 1.13), and both the CRE and EOC recommend that selection tests should be reviewed to ensure that they are relevant to the job requirements.

14.82 The EOC code (para 21) states that tests should be reviewed regularly to ensure that they remain relevant and free from unjustifiable bias.

Age limits

14.83 Many employers specify that applicants for a job should be under a certain age, and almost all trade apprenticeships are offered exclusively to those under 25. These maximum age limits may well discriminate against female and black applicants.

14.84 Age bars have been successfully challenged on the basis that they discriminate indirectly on grounds of sex or race (see *Price v Civil Service Commission*,[62] *Perera v Civil Service Commission (No 2)*,[63] discussed in chapter 8). The EOC code (para 13) recommends that employers should only retain age limits if they are necessary and justifiable because otherwise they could constitute indirect discrimination.

14.85 The non-statutory code of practice on age diversity in employment covers good practice in six aspects of the employment cycle: recruitment, selection, promotion, training, redundancy, and retirement.[64] The code states that action to eradicate age discrimination should be taken as part of a wider personnel and equal opportunities strategy to create a flexible and motivated workforce. In brief, the code recommends that:

- advertisements should avoid age limits or language indicating a preferred age;
- selection should be on merit and should focus on skills, abilities and the potential of the candidate;

62 [1978] IRLR 3, EAT.
63 [1983] IRLR 166, CA.
64 DfEE, July 1999.

- employers ought to ensure that interviewers are trained to avoid basing decisions on prejudices and stereotypes.

In cases involving age discrimination, reference should be made to this non-statutory code, though a tribunal cannot make a finding of unlawful discrimination on the basis of age alone. It may, however, take the code into account when considering an indirect sex or race discrimination or an unfair dismissal claim.

Children

14.86 A refusal to employ a woman because she has children might be direct or indirect sex and/or marital discrimination. Lone parents, most of whom are women, are particularly vulnerable. In *Hurley v Mustoe*[65] the applicant was dismissed because she had small children. An ET ruled that this constituted direct sex discrimination, as there was no evidence to support the employer's contention that he applied this policy equally to men and women. It was also held to be indirect marital discrimination, as the employer's policy had an adverse impact on married people who were more likely than their unmarried counterparts to have children. The employer had claimed that his policy was justified because women with children were inherently unreliable. On appeal the EAT ruled that the employer had put forward no evidence to justify the indirect discrimination and pointed out that, if the employer was concerned about a particular employee's reliability, this could be tested by other means such as taking up references.

Hours of work

14.87 Any requirement to work specified hours, such as full-time, overtime, or anti-social hours may be indirect sex or marital discrimination against women. This is covered in chapter 7.

14.88 The DDA 1995 code of practice points out that an employer may need to alter a disabled person's working hours to accommodate his or her needs. This could include allowing the disabled person to work flexible hours to enable additional breaks to overcome fatigue arising from the disability, or changing the disabled person's hours to fit with the availability of a carer.[66]

65 [1981] IRLR 208.
66 Para 4.20 above.

14.89 Rigid working hours will generally discriminate against women but may also discriminate indirectly on the ground of race because of prayer times and religious holidays. In *Walker v Hussain*[67] disciplinary action taken against 17 Asian Muslims for taking time off to celebrate Eid was found to have discriminated indirectly against Asians (see para 8.31). The protection extended to workers in this context may have increased as a result of the incorporation into domestic law of the European Convention on Human Rights, though see chapters 8 and 9 for the shortcomings of the convention in the employment sphere.[68]

14.90 The CRE code of practice recommends that, if cultural and religious needs conflict with existing work requirements, employers should consider whether they can adapt the requirements to fit in with such needs (para 1.24). For example, observant Jews find it harder to comply with the requirement for weekend and evening work because of their Friday evening/Saturday Sabbath. At the moment, discrimination connected with religion is prohibited only where it amounts to race discrimination (see Chapters 2 and 8). But domestic legislation will have to provide protection from discrimination on grounds of religious discrimination by July 2003.

Mobility requirements

14.91 Many jobs require workers to be mobile; they may have to travel in the course of the job, or be prepared to move as and when the company specifies. Such a mobility requirement may discriminate indirectly on grounds of sex. In *Meade Hill v British Council*[69] the applicant challenged a contractual term to the effect that members of middle management had to 'serve in such parts of the UK ... as the Council may in its discretion require'. The Court of Appeal held that such a clause had a disproportionate impact on women. Judicial notice could be taken of the fact that a higher proportion of women than men are secondary earners so would find it impossible in practice to comply with a mobility clause.

14.92 The EOC conducted a formal investigation into the Leeds Permanent Building Society, studying the recruitment of management trainees in 1978/79. It found that the mobility requirement in the contractual form applied by the Society was not justifiable and amounted to unlawful discrimination.

67 [1996] IRLR 11.

68 In particular, the discussions of *Ahmad v UK* (1982) 4 EHRR 293 and *Stedman v UK* (1997) 23 EHRR CD 168.

69 [1995] IRLR 478.

Health requirements and the Disability Discrimination Act 1995

14.93 Medical tests and individual requirements impact especially harshly on disabled people. In particular cases they may breach the DDA 1995. The DDA 1995 code of practice states (at para 5.5) that, although an employer can stipulate essential health requirements, he or she may need to justify doing so, and to show that it would not be reasonable to waive them in an individual case. A requirement that a disabled person undergo a medical test may also breach the DDA 1995 if those who are not disabled are not required to undergo such a test and it cannot be justified by the employer.

14.94 In health cases, as elsewhere, disability discrimination may consist of the less favourable treatment of a disabled person for a reason related to his or her disability, and/or of a failure to make a reasonable adjustment – in each case subject to justification. The applicant in *Hammersmith and Fulham LBC v Farnsworth*[70] was offered a job as a residential social worker subject to a medical report from the local authority's occupational health doctors. The medical report prepared for the Council stated that there was evidence of ill health over a number of years which at times had been severe and had necessitated hospital admission. The report went on to say that Ms Farnsworth's health had been good over the past year, but that, in view of her medical history, the occupational health doctor was concerned that she might be liable to further recurrences in the future and that, if such recurrences occurred, her performance and attendance at work could be affected. The offer of employment was withdrawn.

14.95 The EAT upheld a tribunal decision that Ms Farnsworth had been treated less favourably for a reason related to her health. This treatment was not justified as the Council had failed to inquire further into her medical history, having adopted a practice of denying itself information about the medical history upon which the occupational health doctor had based her report.

14.96 The less favourable treatment of a disabled person may, of course, be justified (see further chapter 6). The applicant in *A v Hounslow LBC*[71] suffered from schizophrenia. His appointment to a post as a laboratory assistant at a school was subject to a routine medical. He disclosed his condition and advice was sought from occupational health and Mr A's psychiatrist. Although he had not had an acute

70 [2000] IRLR 691.

71 EAT/1155/98 (unreported, available on LEXIS).

episode for four years, Mr A had fantasies of mass murder. Occupational health reported that there was a risk of relapse and breakdown which was greater for Mr A than it would be for someone without the condition. If he were to break down, there was a risk of harm to himself and a small risk to staff and pupils. The school decided not to employ him and the ET, upheld by the EAT, found the decision to be justified.

Shortlisting, interviewing and selecting staff

14.97 Shortlisting, interviewing and final selection are all part of the arrangements made for determining who should be employed. In *Nagarajan v London Regional Transport*[72] the House of Lords ruled that interviewing and assessing candidates for a post could amount to making 'arrangements' within s4(1)(a) for the purpose of determining who should be offered that employment. Their Lordships held that, even if there was no discrimination in the setting up of the interview arrangements, the discriminatory operation of the arrangements would be sufficient to breach the relevant Act (there the RRA 1976). Those who set up the arrangements (such as the interview process) may be different from those who carry them out (for example, by doing the interviews).

14.98 In *Brennan v Dewhurst Ltd*[73] the EAT held that, at all stages of applying for and obtaining employment, a woman should be on an equal footing with a man in her ability to obtain the job. The applicant claimed that the shop manager who interviewed her for a job made it obvious by his manner that he did not want a woman. The EAT agreed with the tribunal and held that, even though there was no intention to discriminate or any discrimination in the making of the arrangements, their effect was to discriminate and so they were unlawful. In order to establish liability in relation to the arrangements made for recruitment it was necessary only to show that they *operated* in a discriminatory way.[74]

72 [2000] AC 501; [1999] IRLR 572 in which their Lordships upheld the decision in *Brennan v Dewhurst Ltd* [1983] IRLR 357.

73 [1983] IRLR 357.

74 In *Brennan* the EAT said '[i]f s6(1)(a) does not cover arrangements for the purpose of determining who should be offered employment which are operated in a discriminatory way, to that extent the plain policy of the Act would not be carried out' – see also *Nagarajan v London Regional Transport* [2000] AC 501.

14.99 In order to avoid discrimination in the selection arrangements the CRE code of practice recommends that:

- Gate, reception and personnel staff should be instructed not to treat casual or formal applicants from particular racial groups less favourably than others. These instructions should be confirmed in writing.
- Staff responsible for shortlisting, interviewing and selecting candidates should be:
  - clearly informed of selection criteria and of the need for their consistent application;
  - given guidance or training on the effects that generalised assumptions and prejudices about race can have on selection decisions; and
  - made aware of the possible misunderstandings that can occur in interviews between people of different cultural backgrounds (para 1.14).
- Wherever possible, shortlisting and interviewing should not be done by one person alone but should at least be checked at a more senior level (para 1.14(a)(b)(c)).

14.100 The EOC code (para 23) recommends that applications from men and women should be processed in exactly the same way. There should not be separate lists of male and female or married and single applicants. All those handling applications and conducting interviews should be trained in the avoidance of unlawful discrimination and records of interviews kept, where practicable, showing why applicants were or were not appointed.[75]

14.101 The DDA 1995 code of practice emphasises, in particular, the possible adjustments that might be required at every stage of the recruitment process if an employer knows or ought reasonably to know of an applicant's disability. For example, if a person has difficulty attending at a particular time because of a disability, the code states that it will very likely be reasonable for the employer to have to rearrange the time.

75 For an example of gender-reassignment discrimination in recruitment see *Sheffield v Air Foyle Charter Airlines Ltd* (1998) DCLD 37 in which an ET accepted that the applicant was refused an interview for a position as a pilot in connection with her gender reassignment. She was awarded approximately £70,000 compensation plus interest.

Shortlisting

14.102 Criteria for shortlisting should be decided by all those shortlisting in advance and should be linked to the job description and person specification. Subjectivity is more likely to lead to 'gut' feelings that can be discriminatory. Factors that may be indirectly discriminatory (see above) should be avoided.

14.103 The DDA 1995 code of practice states that 'if an employer knows that an applicant has a disability and is likely to be at a substantial disadvantage because of the employer's arrangements or premises, the employer should consider whether there is any reasonable adjustment which would bring the disabled person within the field of applicants to be considered even though he would not otherwise be within that field because of that disadvantage'.

Interviews

14.104 Many interviewers are not trained to interview candidates in an unbiased, unprejudiced way. The EOC and CRE codes recommend that all members of an interview panel should attend appropriate training.

14.105 In *Staffordshire CC v Bennett*[76] an unqualified white woman was appointed in preference to a well-qualified African-Caribbean woman who was felt by the employers not to have the right personality for the job. One of the interviewers considered that the failure of the African-Caribbean woman to make eye contact was a factor. The unsuccessful candidate was also told that she did not get the job because she would not 'get on' with other staff. The ET concluded that her 'face did not fit' because she was from a different racial background than the interviewers. The EAT upheld the ET's finding of discrimination, noting that Judicial Studies Board training indicated that people of African-Caribbean origin would often avoid eye contact with those in authority as it was regarded as impolite.

14.106 The DDA 1995 code of practice states that the employer should consider if any reasonable adjustments need to be made, such as (paras 5.14–5.20):

- rearranging the time of interview, if difficult for the applicant;
- adjusting the interview arrangements;
- making changes to the way the interview is carried out.

76 EAT 67/94 (unreported, available on LEXIS).

14.107 In *Ridout v TC Group*[77] the applicant had a type of epilepsy which made it difficult for her to remain in a room with bright fluorescent lighting. The EAT upheld the ET's decision that the employer could not be expected to make adjustments because they were unaware of the effect of the lighting on the applicant's rare form of epilepsy. Arguably, once the employers were aware of the epilepsy they should have made inquiries as to what adjustments were needed.[78]

Discriminatory questions

14.108 The questioning in interviews may provide evidence of discrimination if the complainant does not get the job. Words of discouragement at an interview may amount to 'arrangements'. In *Simon v Brimham Associates*[79] the Court of Appeal ruled that words or acts of discouragement can amount to less favourable treatment of the person discouraged. Direct discrimination may occur if a person of a different race or sex would not have been asked the same questions as the applicant. For example, in *Karimjee v University of Newcastle-upon-Tyne*[80] the applicant was asked by the employer to provide documentary evidence of her right to work in the UK. The question was held to be evidence of discrimination because not every applicant was asked the question. Particularly detailed, intrusive and unnecessary questioning of a disabled applicant, where non-disabled candidates are not so treated, is also likely to amount to unjustified less favourable treatment under the DDA 1995. But sensitive questioning as to, for example, adjustments that could be made to assist a disabled person in the workplace, would not be.

14.109 If the same questions are asked of all candidates, but affect the complainant's ability to perform well and as a result he or she is not appointed, this may amount to indirect discrimination. If particular questions are asked only of female or ethnic minority candidates, and affect their ability to perform well in interview, direct discrimination may be made out on the basis that, 'but for' the sex/race of the candidate, he or she would not have been asked such questions and his or her performance would not have been affected. As the Court of

77 [1998] IRLR 628..

78 See also *Hughes v Hillingdon LBC*, ET 6001328/98 (unreported), in which the employer's failure to ensure that recruitment interviewers understood the extent of a deaf applicant's disability, breached its duty to make reasonable adjustments.

79 [1987] IRLR 307. See also *Tower Hamlets LBC v Rabin* [1989] ICR 693, EAT.

80 EAT 545/84 (unreported, available on LEXIS).

Appeal pointed out in *Simon v Brimham Associates*: '[d]iscouragement can amount to less favourable treatment of the person discouraged'.

14.110 The EAT has, however, been remarkably reluctant to find that sex biased questions are in themselves discriminatory, although the questioning in interviews will provide evidence of discrimination if the complainant does not get the job. The applicant in *Saunders v Richmond upon Thames BC*[81] claimed that the council had discriminated against her when it did not appoint her to the job of golf professional. During the course of her interview she had been asked questions such as, 'do you think men respond as well to a woman golf professional as a man?' and 'are there any women golf professionals in clubs?'. Ms Saunders argued that these questions were in themselves discriminatory. The EAT held that the questions were not unlawful, though it did accept that they could be relevant evidence in determining whether there had been discrimination in making the appointment.

14.111 In *Woodhead v Chief Constable of West Yorkshire Police*,[82] too, the EAT accepted that questioning a female applicant on the details of her childcare and domestic arrangements was simply intended to find out how the children were to be cared for and did not breach the SDA 1975. The complainant was asked about the age of her children, whether she had a reliable babysitter, whether her husband was in danger of becoming a househusband, and about his feelings about her becoming a police constable. It is extraordinary that such blatantly discriminatory questioning was not held to be a breach of the SDA 1975.

14.112 The decisions in *Saunders* and *Woodhead* are arguably wrong. *Saunders* was decided before the EOC code of practice was published. The ET did not overtly refer to the code in *Woodhead* and the EAT held that it was not essential that every tribunal should on every occasion recite it as if it were a rubric. Subsequent cases have made it clear that only 'in the rarest' cases should the code be ignored.

14.113 The EOC code of practice states that any interview questions should relate to the requirements of the job. Where it is necessary to assess whether personal circumstances will affect performance of the job (for example, where it involves unsocial hours or extensive travel), this should be discussed objectively, without detailed questions based on assumptions about marital status, children and domestic obligations. Questions about marriage plans or family intentions should not be asked, as they could be construed as showing bias against

81 [1977] IRLR 362.

82 EAT/285/89 (unreported, available on LEXIS).

women. Information necessary for personal records can be collected after a job offer has been made (para 23(a)(b)(c)).[83]

14.114 In *Virdee v ECC Quarries*[84] a Sikh candidate who was asked at interview if he had worked with white technicians before, and whether he had any trouble supervising them, successfully complained of race discrimination. The ET found that the question showed that his race was considered and that this, taken together with the employer's failure to complete a RRA 1976 s65 questionnaire (see para 32.23), founded an inference that there had been unlawful discrimination.

14.115 In an extraordinary decision, the Court of Appeal in *Simon v Brimham Associates*[85] ruled that asking a Jewish applicant about his religion, with the explanation that if he were Jewish he might be precluded from getting the job, was not directly discriminatory – this because the same question was asked of all candidates. This decision should be regarded as wrong, since the question suggests an intention to discriminate depending upon the answer received.

14.116 The DDA 1995 code of practice states (para 5.20) that the DDA 1995 does not prohibit an employer from seeking information about a disability, but that an employer must not use such information to discriminate against a disabled person. An employer should ask only about a disability if it is, or may be, relevant to the person's ability to do the job – if necessary, after reasonable adjustments have been made.

14.117 Indirect discrimination may occur if it appears from the questioning that the employer operates a practice or procedure that has a disproportionate adverse impact on women (or men) or on a racial group, such as questions about childcare responsibilities or religion.

The selection process

14.118 Most tribunal complaints are of direct discrimination.[86] Black and/or female job candidates may suspect that an employer is making discriminatory assumptions and that they are likely to be rejected on the

83 Some tribunals have been more willing to accept that discriminatory questions are a breach of the SDA 1975 or RRA 1976. In *Brice v J Sainsbury plc* (1985) COIT 1709/180, all single applicants for the post of management trainee were asked the question, 'do you plan to get married?', but only single women were asked the question, 'do you plan to have a family?'. A tribunal found that the employer had discriminated in the arrangements made for the purposes of determining who should be offered employment.

84 [1978] IRLR 295.

85 [1987] IRLR 307.

86 Though in some cases it transpires, after the interview, that the employer took account of a factor that is indirectly discriminatory.

ground of sex or race. However, if the employer or his or her agent does not make any overtly sexist or racist remark, and there is no evidence of discrimination in the recruitment material, the applicant may have no more than a hunch that this is why he or she has been rejected.[87]

14.119 A black applicant may be told that the vacancy no longer exists, as the post has been filled. Proof that this is not true may be obtained by telephoning the employer later to find out that the vacancy is still open. Some applicants have got white friends to go and inquire about a job which they themselves have been told is no longer vacant. In *Matan v Famous Names Ltd*[88] a black complainant who was twice rejected for the job of packer won his race discrimination claim after he established that all white people were appointed on their first application, and that the firm still had vacancies.

14.120 In view of the difficulty of getting evidence on employers' attitudes, rejected candidates may have to rely on the drawing of inferences from the facts surrounding the appointment, including a comparison of the qualifications and experience of different candidates and the interviewing and decision-making process (see chapter 3 on proving direct discrimination). This was recognized by the Court of Appeal in *North West Thames Regional Health Authority v Noone*[89] in which the applicant, a Sri Lankan doctor, failed to get a job despite having superior qualifications and experience to other candidates. An ET held that the final selection interview was a sham covering up a wholly subjective decision made on grounds of race. This decision was upheld by the Court of Appeal which pointed out that, while the suitability of candidates was difficult to measure objectively, it was important to have clear selection criteria to avoid discrimination. The employer did not use an objective assessment of qualities such as

87 In some cases such evidence comes out during the proceedings. In *Clarke v Crown Prosecution Service* (2001) DCLD 47 an ET held that the CPS's refusal to appoint a female solicitor was discriminatory. She had been told she was suitable for appointment but then informed that the pre-employment checks were not satisfactory. All 13 other successful candidates were simply appointed. The ET held that had she been male 'she would simply have been regarded as "one of the lads" and would have been given the opportunity to prove her suitability'. As it was, she was referred to as 'Mad Mary' which the ET regarded as '*per se* discriminatory'.

88 (1983) COIT 1399/1450. See also *Hussein v (1) Harrison and (2) CD Bramall (Bradford) Ltd* (1998) DCLD 35, in which the applicant was refused an interview when he applied in his name but was given one when he applied with the name of a white woman.

89 [1988] ICR 813.

leadership, motivation, aptitude and other personal attributes and circumstances.

14.121 In *Baker v Cornwall CC*[90] the Court of Appeal acknowledged that 'discrimination can often result from a wish to preserve an existing pattern of employment ... An excuse such as "we wanted someone who would fit in" is often a danger signal that the choice was influenced not by the qualifications of the successful candidate but by the sex or race of that candidate'.

14.122 In a CRE inquiry into the National Bus Company it emerged that while the company employed many Asian bus conductors, they were not promoted and did not get the more popular jobs of drivers and inspectors. The CRE found evidence that Asian applicants were being stereotyped as too 'weak' or 'passive' for inspector jobs.

14.123 The questionnaire and discovery procedures are considered in chapter 32. They can be crucial in eliciting information in order to prove discrimination. In cases involving alleged discrimination in recruitment it is very important to get access to candidates' application forms, internal memos, the interviewers' notes and all documents relating to the recruitment process. These may reveal the prejudices of the interviewers and discrepancies in the treatment of different candidates from which an inference of discrimination may be drawn.

14.124 It sometimes transpires that the interviewing panel took into account a factor that was indirectly discriminatory. This may only become apparent if the complainant asks why he or she was not appointed or receives replies to a questionnaire. In *Mercer v London School of Economics*,[91] for example, there was no person specification or written criteria for appointment to the post of senior lecturer and no discussion between the interviewers prior to the interview. The applicant subsequently discovered she had not been appointed because the LSE believed the successful candidate would contribute better to a five-star rating in the Research Assessment Exercise.[92] This only became apparent when the LSE gave Ms Mercer reasons for the

90 In *Nwoke v Government Legal Service and Civil Service Commissioners* (1996) DCLD 28 the ET inferred direct discrimination from the fact (among others) that every white candidate with local government experience was marked 'C' or above, whereas no ethnic minority candidate with local government experience was graded 'C' or above. The interviewers had included comments like 'will fit in' on their assessment sheets. The ET held that subjectivity played a large part in the assessments and that the applicant had been discriminated against both on grounds of race and sex.

91 ET 2201988/98 (unreported).

92 The RAE determines the research status of the university and the level of grant.

decision not to appoint her. The ET held that there was a requirement that 'the candidate must demonstrate that they can be submitted to the next RAE whenever that may be'. The ET held that the pool consisted of academics at the LSE and that fewer women than men could comply with this condition which was not justifiable.

14.125 The DDA 1995 code of practice states (paras 5.25–5.26) that 'an employer will have to assess an applicant's merits as they would be if any reasonable adjustments required under the Act had been made. If, after allowing for those adjustments, a disabled person would not be the best person for the job the employer would not have to recruit that person.'

14.126 In *Hammersmith and Fulham LBC v Farnsworth*[93] the applicant was given a provisional job offer which was withdrawn when the Council's health physician consulted her doctor and found she had a history of mental illness. The EAT upheld the ET's decision that this was unlawful discrimination. The ET held that the Council should have inquired about the applicant's illness and why it was considered that it would affect her attendance at work. The ET concluded there was no reason to assume her attendance would be poor.

The importance of transparency in the decision-making process

14.127 Unsuccessful job applicants are given many different reasons for their rejection, some of which are untrue (such as that the post has already been filled when a subsequent inquiry shows that it has not); some ambiguous (such as 'the successful candidate would fit in better' or 'he was more suitable'); and some more specific but still not strictly related to the job specification (for example, where attributes are taken into account that were not mentioned in the job description). In the *Danfoss* case[94] the ECJ stressed the importance of transparency, particularly where there is evidence of a system apparently working to the disadvantage of women.

14.128 Although *Danfoss* was a decision about pay (see para 10.64), it is relevant to other areas such as recruitment, training and promotion. If the workforce is largely white and male, and the rationale for decisions about appointments is not clear, the burden ought perhaps to shift to the employer to justify the racial and sexual imbalance, in the

93 [2000] IRLR 691.

94 Case 109/88 *Handels-og Kontorfunktionaerernes Forbund I Danmark v Dansk Arbejdsgiverforening (acting for Danfoss)* [1989] ECR 3199; [1989] IRLR 532.

same way that the ECJ ruled in *Danfoss* that it should shift where a pay system results in the average pay of female workers being lower than that of male workers. This is in line with the amendments made to the SDA 1975 by the Burden of Proof Regulations. The RRA 1976 will be amended by October 2004 to comply with the Race Directive, which adopts the same approach to proof as the SDA 1975.

Terms on which employment offered must not be less favourable

14.129 It is unlawful, under the SDA 1975, RRA 1976 and DDA 1995, to discriminate in the terms on which employment is offered.[95] This only covers offers of employment, and so will come into play only where an offer has actually been made.[96] Once the person is in employment, the claim under the RRA 1976 and DDA 1995 will be under those sections of the Acts that cover terms of employment.[97] Under the sex discrimination legislation, once the terms become part of the contract, any claim must be made under Equal Pay Act 1970 Pt IV.

95 SDA 1975 s6(1)(b), RRA 1976 s4(1)(b) and DDA 1995 s4(1)(b).

96 See *Ogilvie v (1) Harehills Conservative Club Ltd (2) Parry*, EAT 449/92 (unreported, available on LEXIS).

97 RRA 1976 s4(2)(a) and DDA 1995 s4(2)(a).

CHAPTER 15

Discrimination in employment: promotion, training, transfer, detriment and dismissal

continued

Key points

15.1

- The Sex Discrimination Act (SDA) 1975, the Race Relations Act (RRA) 1976 and the Disability Discrimination Act (DDA) 1995 all regulate discrimination in relation to transfer, training, promotion, access to benefits at work, dismissal and detriment.
- When the relevant provisions of the Employment Directive (ED) come into force, discrimination on grounds of sexual orientation, religion or belief and age will be regulated to the extent that it is not already regulated, albeit tangentially, by the SDA 1975 or the RRA 1976.
- Commission for Racial Equality (CRE), Equal Opportunities Commission (EOC) and DDA 1995 codes of practice offer guidance on how to avoid discrimination. Failure to follow them may be taken into account by an employment tribunal (ET) or court.
- It is unlawful for an employment agency to discriminate against a person on the ground of race or sex or disability (under the DDA 1995 the claim is made under the goods and services provisions unlike sex and race discrimination complaints which are brought under the employment provisions).
- Maximum age limits may discriminate on grounds of sex and/or race.
- A mobility requirement may discriminate against women.
- An employer maybe under a duty to make reasonable adjustments to prevent a disabled person being at a substantial disadvantage in relation to transfer, training, promotion, access to benefits at work, dismissal and detriment.
- It is unlawful to discriminate in the provision of benefits, facilities and services to workers, whether provided by the employer or a third party on behalf of the employer.
- Where the benefits, facilities and services (excluding training) are non-contractual and provided on the same terms to members of the public, the claim is under the non-employment provisions (see chapters 29 and 30).
- Sex discrimination in contractual benefits is covered by the Equal Pay Act (EqPA) 1970 rather than the SDA 1975, except where the discrimination is on grounds of gender reassignment.
- Both the RRA 1976 and DDA 1995 cover discriminatory provisions relating to contractual and non-contractual benefits, facilities and services. The provisions, however, differ between the Acts.

- Examples of benefits, facilities and services are extensive and include loans, subsidies, membership of clubs, company cars, holiday, sick pay, overtime, grievances.
- It is unlawful to discriminate against a worker on grounds of sex, sexual orientation, race or disability by subjecting him or her to 'any other detriment'.
- 'Detriment' is to be interpreted widely and includes any disadvantage not already covered by the Acts; it means no more than putting at a disadvantage.
- 'Detriment' includes, for example, harassment (see chapter 28), subjection to disciplinary action and failure to deal with a grievance.
- A discriminatory dismissal will breach the SDA 1975, RRA 1976 or DDA 1995 and (provided that the qualifying conditions are satisfied) the Employment Rights Act (ERA) 1996.
- Unfair dismissal may be claimed only by employees who are under the normal retiring age, working in Great Britain and (save in the case of automatically unfair dismissals) employed for a continuous period of a year with the same employer.
- To obtain maximum compensation in respect of discriminatory dismissals, claims should be made under both the ERA 1996 and the relevant discrimination provisions.
- Redundancy selection criteria (such as last-in, first-out, based on sickness absence or part-timers first) may be indirectly discriminatory and may also make the resulting dismissals unfair.
- Redundancies and other dismissals linked with retirement or where the retirement age differs for men and women breach the SDA 1975 and, almost certainly, the ERA 1996.
- Redundancy pay should be equal for men and women.

Background and statutory provisions

15.2 Much of the introductory material is at paras 14.2–14.6. The statutory provisions there considered were SDA 1975 s6(1), RRA 1976 s4(1) and DDA 1995 s4(1), which regulate access to employment. Here we consider the application of SDA 1975 s6(2), RRA 1976 s4(2) and DDA 1995 s4(2), which concern discrimination during and in connection with the termination of employment (broadly defined). These provisions are set out at various points below, the chapter considering, in turn, discrimination in access to promotion, transfers and training; in access to opportunities for benefits, facilities and services; and in relation to 'any other detriment'; and, finally, dismissal.

Access to promotion, transfer and training

15.3 It is unlawful to discriminate on grounds of sex, married status, gender-reassignment, race or disability in relation to access to promotion, transfer and training. Discrimination against pregnant women and women on maternity leave is covered in Part III of the book.

Sex Discrimination Act 1975 and Race Relations Act 1976

15.4 SDA 1975 s6(2)(a) provides that:

> It is unlawful for a person, in the case of a woman employed by him at an establishment in Great Britain, to discriminate against her in the way he affords her access to opportunities for promotion, transfer or training, or any other benefits, facilities or serices, or by refusing or deliberately omitting to afford her access to them.

RRA 1976 s4(2)(b) is in materially the same terms. It is also unlawful for those providing vocational training to discriminate on grounds of sex or race.[1] These provisions (and those of the DDA 1995, below) apply only to acts of discrimination in relation to current workers and do not provide protection from discrimination by former employers (such as in a post-dismissal appeal).[2] Former workers may, however, be able to claim the protection of EC law, though as yet only in sex discrimination cases (see chapter 10).

EOC and CRE codes of practice

15.5 The EOC Code of Practice for the elimination of discrimination on grounds of sex and marriage and the promotion of equality of opportunity in employment recommends (at para 25), in relation to promotion, transfer and training, that:

- Where an appraisal system is in operation, the assessment criteria should be examined to ensure that they are not unlawfully

1 SDA 1975 s14 and RRA 1976 s13. See *Lana v Positive Action Training in Housing (London) Ltd* [2001] IRLR 501, discussed in chapter 12.

2 *Rhys-Harper v Relaxion Group plc* [2001] IRLR 460, CA; *D'Souza v Lambeth LBC*, 25 May 2001, CA (unreported, available on LEXIS); and *Kirker v British Sugar plc* [2002] EWCA Civ 304, CA.

discriminatory and the scheme monitored to assess how it is working in practice.

- When a group of workers predominantly of one sex is excluded from an appraisal scheme or from access to promotion, transfer or training, the policy should be reviewed to ensure that there is no unlawful indirect discrimination.
- Promotion and career development patterns should be reviewed to ensure that the traditional qualifications are justifiable requirements for the job to be done. In some circumstances, for example, promotion on the basis of length of service could amount to unlawful indirect discrimination, as it may unjustifiably affect more women than men.
- When general ability and personal qualities are the main requirements for promotion to a post, care should be taken to consider favourably candidates of both sexes with differing career patterns and general experience.
- Rules that restrict or preclude transfers between certain jobs should be questioned and changed if they are unlawfully discriminatory. Employees of one sex may be concentrated in sections from which transfers are traditionally restricted without real justification.
- Policies and practices regarding selection for training, day release and personal development should be examined for unlawful direct and indirect discrimination. Where there is found to be an imbalance in training as between sexes, the cause should be identified to ensure that it is not discriminatory.[3]
- Age limits for access to training and promotion should be questioned.

15.6 The CRE Code of Practice for the elimination of discrimination and the promotion of equality of opportunity in employment[4] makes similar recommendations in relation to recruitment, promotion, transfer, training and dismissal (para 1.16). In relation to transfers and training, the CRE code recommends also that:

- Staff responsible for selecting employees for transfer to other jobs should be instructed to apply selection criteria without unlawful discrimination.

3 This guidance was reinforced by the ECJ in Case 109/88 *Handels-og Kontorfunktionaerernes Forbund I Danmark v Dansk Arbejdsgiverforening (acting for Danfoss)* [1989] ECR 3199; [1989] IRLR 532.

4 RRA 1976 s47.

- Industry or company agreements and arrangements of custom and practice on job transfers should be examined and amended if they are found to contain requirements or conditions that appear to be indirectly discriminatory. For example, if employees of a particular racial group are concentrated in particular sections, the transfer arrangements should be examined to see if they are unjustifiably and unlawfully restrictive and amended if necessary.
- Staff responsible for selecting employees for training (whether induction, promotion or skills training) should be instructed not to discriminate on racial grounds.
- Selection criteria for training opportunities should be examined to ensure that they are not indirectly discriminatory.
- Code of Practice on Age Diversity in Employment

15.7 The Code of Practice on Age Diversity in Employment recommends the encouragement of all employees to take advantage of the relevant training opportunities, emphasising that 'skilled and motivated people are more productive'. It recommends that employers should:

- ensure the training and development needs of all staff are regularly reviewed and that age is not a barrier to training;
- make sure that all employees are aware of the training and development opportunities that are available and are encouraged to use them;
- focus on the individual's and the organisation's needs when providing training and development opportunities;
- look at how training is delivered and ensure different learning styles and needs are addressed.

Disability Discrimination Act 1995

15.8 DDA 1995 s4(2)(b) and (c) is very similar to SDA 1975 s6(2)(a) above, s4(2) providing that:

> It is unlawful for an employer to discriminate against a disabled person whom he employs:
> ...
> (b) in the opportunities which he affords him for promotion, a transfer, training or receiving any other benefit;
> (c) by refusing to afford him, or deliberately not affording him, any such opportunity ...

Disability discrimination has two forms – unjustified less favourable treatment for a reason related to the disabled person's disability and the failure to make reasonable adjustments where the duty arises.

Disability Discrimination Act 1995 code of practice

15.9 The DDA 1995 code of practice stresses that an employer must not discriminate in selection for training, promotion or transfer and must make any necessary reasonable adjustments. It gives an example of an employer who wrongly assumed that a disabled person would be unwilling or unable to undertake demanding training or attend a residential training course, instead of taking an informed decision, and says that he or she may well not be able to justify a decision based on that assumption.

15.10 The DDA 1995 code of practice further states (para 6.4) that employers must not discriminate in assessing a disabled person's suitability for promotion or transfer, in the practical arrangements necessary to enable the promotion or transfer to take place, in the operation of the appraisal, selection and promotion or transfer process or in the new job itself and may have to make a reasonable adjustment. Examples of reasonable adjustments are given in the code.

15.11 The code also states (para 6.5) that the employer should review the arrangements to check that qualifications required are justified for the job. He or she should check that other arrangements, for example systems that determine other criteria for a particular job, do not exclude disabled people who may have been unable to met those criteria because of their disability but would be capable of performing well in the job.

Training

15.12 Few jobs offer training. Where training opportunities exist employers often wish to train those who they think will 'fit in' and are likely to be a good 'investment'. Preference may be given to employees who work long hours, those whom employers consider are likely to stay long-term, and those with long service. These selection criteria may discriminate indirectly against women who often interrupt their working lives to have children. They may also, if coupled with assumptions about women's likely future work patterns, be directly discriminatory.

15.13 The same rules for proving direct and indirect discrimination apply to training as to other areas such as recruitment and promotion, though the complainant does not have to have applied for the training in order to bring a discrimination claim. It is sufficient that an employer has failed to consider a potential trainee on discriminatory grounds.

15.14 Assumptions made on the basis of a person's sex, race or disability are likely to be discriminatory. In *Horsey v Dyfed CC*,[5] for example,

5 [1982] IRLR 395.

the applicant was refused secondment to a two-year training course close to where her husband, who worked some distance away from her job, was based. The council took the view that the applicant would not return to her original job after completing the period of secondment. The EAT ruled that this amounted to unlawful direct discrimination, as it was based on the assumption that married women follow their husbands.

15.15 The CRE code of practice states that, although there is no legal requirement to provide language training, difficulties in communication can endanger equal opportunity in the workforce. The code recommends that:

> Where the workforce includes current employees whose English is limited it is recommended that steps are taken to ensure that communications are as effective as possible. These should include, where reasonably practicable:
> a) provision of interpretation and translation facilities, for example in the communication of grievance and other procedures, and of terms of employment;
> b) training in English language and in communication skills;
> c) training for managers and supervisors in the background and culture of racial minority groups;
> d) the use of alternative or additional methods of communication, where employees find it difficult to understand health and safety requirements, for example
>   – safety signs; translation of safety notices;
>   – instructions through interpreters;
>   – instruction combined with industrial language training.

For provisions relating to positive action in training under the SDA 1975 and RRA 1976 see chapter 5.

15.16 In addition, the provision of training could well be a reasonable adjustment for a disabled employee or job applicant to assist with overcoming any substantial disadvantage in the workplace or the working arrangements. If a disabled person is receiving training as a reasonable adjustment, other staff will not be able to bring a claim for parity of treatment unless there is also sex or race discrimination involved.

Service requirements

15.17 A long-service requirement may discriminate indirectly on grounds of sex or race unless it can be justified by an employer (see *R v Employment Secretary ex p Seymour Smith*,[6] discussed at para 7.82).

6 Case 167/97 [1999] ECR I- 0623; [1999] IRLR 253, ECJ; *(No 2)* [2000] IRLR 363, HL.

'Reasonable adjustments' under the Disability Discrimination Act 1995

15.18 The DDA 1995 code of practice states (para 6.6) that an employer may need to alter the time or location of training for someone with a mobility problem; to make training manuals, slides or other visual media accessible to a visually impaired employee (perhaps by providing Braille versions or having them read out); or to ensure that an induction loop is available for someone with a hearing impairment.

Promotion and transfers

15.19 For those in manual and unskilled jobs, promotion is often out of the question. In jobs with promotion prospects, white workers and men are more likely to benefit. The legal principles that apply to discrimination in promotion and transfers are very similar to those relating to recruitment.

15.20 'Transfer' in this context is, like promotion, viewed as a benefit. If a transfer is unwanted or operates to the worker's disadvantage it will be a detriment (see para 15.70 below).

15.21 The DDA 1995 code of practice gives an example. A garage owner does not consider for promotion to assistant manager a clerk who has lost the use of her right arm, because he wrongly and unreasonably believes that her disability might prevent her performing competently in a managerial post. The employer's failure to consider promoting the disabled employee may breach the DDA 1995.

15.22 The DDA 1995 s6 duty to adjust applies as much to promotion and transfers as in other employment-related discrimination. Several examples are provided in the DDA 1995 code. One of these involves someone disabled with a back injury who is seeking promotion to supervisor. A minor duty involves assisting with the unloading of the weekly delivery van, which the person's back injury would prevent. In assessing her suitability for promotion, the employer should consider whether reallocating this duty to another person would be a reasonable adjustment.

Direct discrimination

15.23 Discrimination in relation to promotion may be direct: 'I don't think we could have a woman as the boss', 'I don't think the white workers would take orders from a black supervisor'. More often, covert discriminatory assumptions are made which maintain the glass ceiling beyond which women and ethnic minority workers are less often found.

15.24 In order to prove direct discrimination in relation to a promotion decision it will generally be necessary to draw inferences from facts (see para 3.54). In deciding whether to draw an inference of discrimination a tribunal might have regard to:

- a lack of advertising, such as in 'word of mouth' promotions;
- a lack of any formal procedures;
- failure to follow existing procedures;
- the use of subjective criteria;
- expectations which are biased in favour of white and male workers – these could be demonstrated by behaviour at an interview;
- suggestions that the person would not 'fit in';
- assumptions that men are often considered to be more aggressive, competitive and ambitious than women, and such characteristics are considered necessary qualities for management;
- racist stereotypes, for example, of Asians as 'passive';
- the fact that promotion often depends to an extent on friendship networks. Because of the social segregation between races in British society this may discriminate against black employees.

15.25 In *Silva v British Airways plc*[7] the applicant, an Asian woman, applied for promotion along with nine other employees. The procedures required all applicants to submit a CV or application form and for managers to draw up a shortlist for interview. Instead of following this procedure, the employers appointed a white woman on the basis that she was 'suitable' for the job. An ET found that the managers deliberately decided to bypass the procedures to enable them to select the white woman and that this was race discrimination.

15.26 In *Deb-Gupta v Board of Governors Beech Hill Infant School and Bedfordshire CC*[8] an Asian teacher failed to get promotion, despite having greater experience than the successful white candidate. Apart from 'grave defects' in the procedure and the dangers of subjectivity, the ET said that great store was placed on the manner in which the answers to questions were given by the interviewees. This might put a person with an 'ethnic minority background' at a 'subjective disadvantage' as 'he or she might not react to a question the same way a white person would'.

7 ET 66783/94, 1996 (unreported).

8 (1994) DCLD 22.

15.27 In *Marrington v University of Sunderland*[9] a female lecturer who was refused promotion because it was believed she would not fit into the male-dominated culture of the university won her sex discrimination claim. The ET took account of the male climate and culture of the university, the statistical evidence of a glass ceiling (beyond which women were not appointed) and the failure to follow a proper objective set of principles when interviewing and marking.

15.28 In *Bourne v Roberts*[10] an ET held that refusal of promotion to an acting manager because of the employer's assumption that he would be under stress connected with gender reassignment breached the SDA 1975.

15.29 Success in a claim under the RRA 1976 or the SDA 1975 requires evidence of discrimination on the ground of race or sex. An unsatisfactory system for promotion or failure to follow procedure might lead to an inference of discrimination (and is often treated suspiciously by an ET) (see paras 3.54–3.76). Tribunals must now uphold employment-related sex discrimination claims once the applicant has proved facts from which it could be concluded that the employer has discriminated, unless the employer can show that it did not discriminate. Proof of race and disability discrimination, however, rests with the applicant (see further chapters 2 and 6).

Indirect discrimination

15.30 Structural barriers exist which may prevent women and black workers from moving up organisational hierarchies. Most of these barriers also prevent women and black workers from getting jobs, and some of these have been identified in chapter 7. Promotion may also depend on factors such as qualifications, experience, length of service, full-time working[11] and age, all of which may discriminate on grounds of sex and/or race. Career structures should be examined to identify these kinds of barriers. Discrimination at the recruitment stage may have a long-term effect, as higher-level jobs are often offered to existing employees. Thus access to the appropriate job at an early stage may be crucial to career prospects.

15.31 In most workplaces there are various points of entry which often differ as between men and women, ethnic minority and white

9 (1994) DCLD 25.

10 (1999) DCLD 42.

11 See, eg, Case 1/95 *Gerster v Freistaat Bayern* [1997] ECR I-5253; [1997] IRLR 699 and see further Chapters 7 and 21.

employees. In *Bath v British Airways Engineering Overhaul Ltd*[12] the applicant, an aircraft component worker in grade 6, was refused a job as a production assistant (a grade 3 job) on the ground that such jobs were open only to certain workers in grades 1, 2 and 4. Ms Bath argued that the requirement for promotion – to be in one of these grades – indirectly discriminated against women who were not represented in them. An ET accepted this, and decided that the restriction was not justifiable. Tribunals in other cases have held that lack of promotion opportunities in the lower grades could form the basis for a claim, the requirement being that to be considered for promotion one had to be in one of the higher grades. In *Bilka-Kaufhaus v Weber von Hartz*[13] the European Court of Justice (ECJ) accepted that restricting benefits and opportunities to higher grades may discriminate on grounds of sex.

15.32 In *Watches of Switzerland v Savell*, too, the EAT ruled that an employer's promotion procedures indirectly discriminated on grounds of sex.[14] Ms Savell argued that the vagueness of her employer's promotion procedures was discriminatory, and complained that:

- impending appointments were not advertised to staff, and women (because they lacked confidence) were less likely than men to ask to be considered for promotion;
- people under consideration for promotion were not interviewed;
- there were no clear guidelines to branch managers about the criteria to be applied in the regular assessments and appraisals and some appraisals, including those of Ms Savell, were out of date;
- the criteria for promotion were not written; they were subjective and were not made known to people in line for promotion;
- the individual managers made a point of promoting their own staff and paid particular attention to training when searching for potential managers, but Ms Savell was unaware of the importance attached to training for which she could have volunteered;
- the failure to consult candidates' branch managers resulted in higher management being unaware that Ms Savell no longer required to stay at the branch where she then worked and was willing to undertake Saturday work.

12 *Bath v British Airways Engineering Overhaul Ltd*, ET 33607/79, 1981 (unreported).

13 Case 170/84 [1986] ECR 1607; [1986] IRLR 317.

14 [1983] IRLR 141.

15.33 Managers often want to see evidence from candidates for promotion that they are ambitious, and frequently assume that women are not. For example, in *Bridge v Tayside Regional Council*[15] the applicant, who had taught music for seven years, failed in her application to become head of department. She was acting head already when the selection board passed her over in choosing a less experienced man for the post. The Board told her that it preferred someone who wanted to move higher up the ladder, and that two of the interviewers thought that men were more ambitious than women, as evidenced by the fact that many more men than women were in senior posts. The ET held that this was indirectly discriminatory as fewer women wanted to be in the grades above head of department and a requirement to do another job of a different nature could not be justified. Since 1983 women's position in the market has changed and an assumption that women are not 'ambitious' may be direct discrimination.

Past discrimination

15.34 Indirect discrimination may occur as a result of past practices that were directly discriminatory and the effects of which are long-lasting. *Steel v Post Office (No 2)*[16] concerned the relative positions of three types of postmen and women: temporary part-time, temporary full-time and permanent full-time. Prior to 1975 women could not attain permanent status. This changed in 1975 but women's seniority which, like men's, was based on length of service as permanent employees, dated only from 1975. In 1977 Ms Steel applied to be transferred to a more popular walk but was refused because the most senior postmen were given the first choice and, although Ms Steel had worked for the Post Office for 16 years, she had only two years' seniority. The EAT ruled that, although the SDA 1975 did not operate retrospectively, some acts of discrimination were of a continuing nature and should, as far as possible, be removed. It was a condition that the successful applicant must be the most senior, fewer women could comply with this condition and, the EAT held, this was not justifiable.

15 S/1789/83.

16 [1978] IRLR 198.

Access to opportunities for benefits, facilities or services

15.35 Under the SDA 1975, RRA 1976, and DDA 1995 it is unlawful for an employer to discriminate against an employee in providing access to any other benefits, facilities or services.[17] However, a non-disabled employee has no right to claim because a disabled person has been provided with access to benefits, facilities or services. The DDA 1995 does not create a right of equal treatment regardless of disability but creates opportunities for disabled people, and an employer may have a legal obligation under its duty of reasonable adjustment to make benefits, facilities and services available to individual disabled people, that are not generally available. In this context, 'benefit' means no more than an advantage.[18] RRA 1976 s4(2)(a) and DDA 1995 s4(2)(a) prohibit discrimination in connection with the *contractual* terms of employment, such discrimination being expressly excluded by the SDA 1975 but being challengeable instead under the EqPA 1970. (An exception to this relates to discrimination on grounds of gender re-assignment in relation to contractual terms including pay which is regulated by SDA 1975 s6(8).)

15.36 The SDA 1975 and RRA 1976 regulate discrimination in access to benefits, facilities or services whether the benefits, facilities or services are provided directly by the employer, or are provided indirectly by some third party.[19] The third party may also be liable (see chapter 31). Although the DDA 1995 contains no identical provision, the employer will be liable if the third party is acting as agent for him or her[20] and the service provider may be liable to the employee under the DDA 1995's goods and services provisions (see chapter 30). The DDA 1995 also contains special provisions making trustees and managers of occupational pension schemes and providers of employee insurance type benefits liable for disability discrimination.[21]

17 SDA 1975 s6(2)(b), RRA 1976 s4(2)(b) and DDA 1995 s4(2) & (4). The wording is slightly different under the DDA 1995 but the meaning is the same. Note that SDA 1975 s6(7), RRA 1976 s4(4) and DDA 1995 s4(3) provide exceptions where non-contractual benefits (apart from training) are provided to employees in the same way as they are to the public.

18 *Peake v Automotive Products Ltd* [1977] IRLR 365, CA, though note that in this case the court held (possibly wrongly) that the advantage was too trivial to be unlawful.

19 SDA 1975 s50(1) and RRA 1976 s40(1).

20 DDA 1995 s58.

21 DDA 1995 ss17 and 18; see chapter 6 and para 15.45 below

15.37 The provisions only apply to current employees, not former employees, unless the claim is one of victimisation under the SDA 1975.[22] The benefits, facilities or services may be contractual or non-contractual. Different provisions apply under the SDA 1975 and EqPA 1970, the RRA 1976 and the DDA 1995:

- discrimination on grounds of sex in relation to non-contractual benefits facilities and services falls within SDA 1975;
- discrimination on grounds of sex in relation to contractual benefits is covered by the EqPA 1970 (see further paras 11.29 and 11.32);
- discrimination on grounds of gender reassignment, whether in relation to contractual or non-contractual benefits, comes within the SDA 1975;
- neither the RRA 1976 nor the DDA 1995 distinguish between contractual and non-contractual benefits. Less favourable treatment relating to the provision of benefits, facilities and services (including pay), whether contractual or non-contractual, is prohibited by the RRA 1976 and DDA 1995.

15.38 If the benefit, facility or service is a discretionary one, a complaint of discrimination may still succeed if it is established that the employer exercised his or her discretion in a discriminatory way. Evidence of a discriminatory pattern in the grant of particular benefits, facilities or services within an organisation may be a useful indicator of past discriminatory treatment.[23] For example, if maximum bonus payments are disproportionately awarded to male employees in a department and rarely or never to women, or if white employees are always granted the most generous car user allowances compared to ethnic minority colleagues, this may be relevant evidence of the discriminatory exercise of a manager's discretion (see *Anya v University of Oxford*[24]).

22 See *Adekeye v Post Office (No 2)* [1997] IRLR 105, CA; *Rhys-Harper v Relaxion Group plc* [2001] IRLR 460; *Coote v Granada Hospitality Ltd (No 2)* [1999] IRLR 452, EAT. See also *Jones v 3M Healthcare Ltd* [2002] EWCA Civ 304, in which the Court of Appeal held that an ex-employee could not complain of disability discrimination or victimisation under the DDA 1995 based on events that occurred after the termination of his employment. This is on appeal to the House of Lords.

23 See *Anya v University of Oxford* [2001] IRLR 377, CA.

24 Ibid.

Pay discrimination and the Race Relations Act 1976

15.39 Pay discrimination is frequently regarded as a problem related to sex, but it may also occur on grounds of race. A worker claiming that he or she is paid less, or has less favourable contractual terms and conditions, than a worker of a different race will have to establish direct or indirect discrimination in order to succeed in an RRA 1976 claim. In other words, he or she will have to prove either that:

- 'but for' his or her race he or she would have been treated more favourably; or
- he or she has suffered a detriment because of his or her inability to comply with a requirement or condition imposed by the employer which, although it applied or would have applied equally to people of a different racial group, was such that people of the applicant's racial group were less likely to be able to comply with it than were others and which the employer has not objectively justified.[25]

15.40 The definition of indirect discrimination under the RRA 1976 has not been affected by the Burden of Proof Regulations (BP Regulations) 2001[26] (see para 7.10), and continues to suffer the shortcomings identified in chapter 7. Direct discrimination remains difficult to prove, not least because of the non-application of the BP Regulations to race discrimination. By contrast with the position under the EqPA 1970, a worker who wishes to claim race discrimination in pay does not have to identify an actual comparator, much less one engaged in like work, work rated as equivalent or work of equal value. It will be sufficient if it can be proved that the worker would have received higher pay had he or she been of a different racial group.

15.41 There have been a number of challenges to racially discriminatory pay practices. In *Campbell v Datum Engineering Co Ltd*,[27] for example, the African-Caribbean applicant (the only ethnic minority employee in a staff of 60) brought a claim under the RRA 1976 when he discovered that he was paid a lower hourly rate than at least one other person who was doing the same work. In the absence of a satisfactory explanation from the employer an ET found that the discrimination was on racial grounds, and he was awarded compensation including an amount for injury to feelings.

25 See para 7.116.

26 Sex Discrimination (Indirect Discrimination and Burden of Proof) Regulations 2001 SI No 2660.

27 (1995) DCLD 24.

15.42 *Sougrin v Haringey Health Authority*[28] arose out of a challenge by three nurses against grading decisions made by their employer. Two of the nurses (Ms Sougrin and Mrs Macdonald) were black, the other white. The employer allowed the white nurse's appeal on the basis that she was acting up into a higher grade for more than 15 per cent of her time. The appeals by the black nurses failed. An ET upheld Mrs Macdonald's claim of race discrimination, finding that the grading system (which provided for automatic regrading if a nurse were 'acting up' to the next grade for at least 15 per cent of the time), indirectly discriminated against her. Mrs Macdonald secured a financial settlement of her claim.[29]

15.43 The difficulties with bringing such pay-related challenges under the RRA 1976 lie in getting evidence of other employees' pay, and in proving that the differences challenged are due to race discrimination. In *Wakeman v Quick Corporation*[29a] a Japanese company paid Japanese managers more than London-based managers, justifying this by the extra cost of living abroad. The position would be improved if the principles of transparency set out in the *Danfoss* case[30] (see para 10.64) were applied in race discrimination cases. This would ensure that, where similar and/or equally valuable jobs are performed by groups of workers in which different racial groups predominate and are paid differently, the employer would be required to explain the pay system and why the difference in pay is not due to race. *Danfoss* does not currently apply outside the sex discrimination sphere. See para 10.83 for discussion of the Race Directive,[31] to be implemented into domestic legislation in 2003, which will improve the situation.

Pay discrimination in relation to transsexuals

15.44 In *B v NHS Trust Pensions Agency and Secretary of State for Health*[32] the EAT held that the denial of survivors' pension benefits to the transsexual partner of a member of the NHS pension scheme on the grounds that the couple were not married did not amount to unlawful

28 [1991] IRLR 447, EAT.

29 Ms Sougrin's claim failed because it was out of time (see para 32.42) – this decision was upheld by the Court of Appeal at [1992] IRLR 416. See also *Wakeman v Quick Corporation* [1999] IRLR 424.

29a [1999] IRLR 424 and see para 3.19 above.

30 Case 109/88 *Handels-og Kontorfunktionaerernes Forbund I Danmark v Dansk Arbejdsgiverforening (acting for Danfoss)* [1989] ECR 3199; [1989] IRLR 532.

31 Council Directive 2000/43/EC.

32 EAT/1211/98, 19 August 1999 (unreported, available on LEXIS).

sex discrimination. The case has been referred by the Court of Appeal to the ECJ.

Pay discrimination and the Disability Discrimination Act 1995

15.45 Pay discrimination is prohibited under the DDA 1995 both when it consists of unjustified less favourable treatment for a reason related to the individual's disability and when it arises out of a failure to make a DDA 1995 s6 adjustment.

15.46 One issue which frequently arises concerns the provision of sick pay to disabled employees who are on sick leave for a reason related to their disability. In *London Clubs Management Ltd v Hood*[33] sick pay was at the manager's discretion. Mr Hood, who was disabled, had received 39.5 days' sick pay in 1998, but in 1999 the manager chose to deny sick pay both to Mr Hood and to other staff absent through ill health because of generally high sickness absence levels in the workplace. Mr Hood successfully argued at an ET that the non-payment of sick pay to him was both unjustified less favourable treatment and a failure to make a reasonable adjustment. But the decision of the ET was overturned on appeal. The ET should not, the EAT ruled, have based its decision on the premise that the treatment complained of was the failure to pay ordinary wages – rather the issue was non-payment of sick pay. Since the manager had exercised her discretion across the board and declined to pay sick pay to any of the staff on sick leave, Mr Hood could not establish that the failure to pay him sick pay was for a reason related to his disability. The EAT considered that the ET's reasons were inadequate in dealing with both the justification point and the application of the DDA 1995 s6 duty and referred the case back for reconsideration.

15.47 The *Hood* case demonstrates that the less favourable treatment of a disabled employee in relation to sick and other forms of pay is likely to amount to less favourable treatment requiring justification by an employer. (Justification under the DDA 1995 is considered in chapter 6.) Under the definition of less favourable treatment in the DDA 1995, a disabled person who is absent for a reason related to their disability and receives either sick pay which is less than normal pay or no pay is being treated less favourably to others to whom that reason does not or would not apply, for instance, those who are not absent

33 *London Clubs Management Ltd v Hood* [2001] IRLR 719.

from work. *Hood* also confirmed that sick pay is pay for the purposes of the DDA 1995 and that payment of sick pay can be a reasonable adjustment that an employer is under a duty to make. It had been argued by the employers in *Hood* that sick pay fell within the exclusion of payments for occupational pensions and insurance type benefits for sickness (see para 15.62 below). This argument was convincingly rejected by the EAT. Whether the payment of sick pay would be a reasonable adjustment in any particular case will depend on the factors set out in DDA 1995 s6(4) (see para 6.31). The DDA 1995 code of practice makes clear that the DDA 1995 does not create a right to disability leave as such. But in certain circumstances the extension of sickness leave – perhaps delaying a decision about terminating employment pending further medical or other advice – may be a reasonable adjustment. The refusal to extend sickness in such circumstances is also likely to amount to less favourable treatment requiring justification. Whether the extended leave is paid would be a factor in determining the reasonableness of such an adjustment and whether non-payment during extended sickness is unlawful less favourable treatment will depend on whether the employers can show that it was material to the particular circumstances of the case (see chapter 6).

15.48 In *Mills v Hillingdon LBC*[34] the EAT took the view that a breakdown in the payment of sick pay was not an arrangement. A distinction was drawn between an administrative error, and a sick pay policy, the latter being an arrangement under the DDA 1995.

15.49 The DDA 1995 provides a number of exceptions to the prohibition on pay-related discrimination. An employer cannot be required to counter a disadvantage caused by premises or by arrangements by increasing the disabled person's pay.[35] There are also special provisions concerning performance related pay (see para 6.55).[36] If a performance-related pay scheme applies to all the workers, or to a class of workers including the disabled employee, the term or practice of assessing pay by performance is taken to be justified. Furthermore, this practice is deemed not to constitute an arrangement and therefore falls outside the DDA 1995 s6 duty of reasonable adjustment. There remains a s6 duty to make reasonable adjustments to improve a disabled employee's performance and enable him or her to achieve the performance targets set. The government will need to include performance-related

34 EAT/0954/00 (unreported).

35 See DDA 1995 code of practice, para 4.18

36 DDA 1995 s5(6); Disability Discrimination (Employment) Regulations (DD(E) Regs) 1996 SI No 1466, reg 3.

pay within the scope of the DDA 1995 in order to comply with the ED[37] by July 2006, and is committed to doing so by October 2004.

15.50 The applicant in *Mulligan v Inland Revenue Commissioner*[38] did not have the use of his right arm. He argued that his performance targets should be lowered to enable him to meet the minimum requirements which he was prevented by his disability from reaching. The Inland Revenue had already made a number of adjustments to prevent Mr Mulligan's disability from reducing his performance. The EAT rejected the claim and stated that the assessment of performance was a wholly separate issue to the making of reasonable adjustments which did not necessarily extend to lowering the quantity or volume of work being demanded of an employee.

15.51 Special provisions operate which allow the Agricultural Wages Board to issue a permit to a disabled worker incapable of earning the minimum wage set by the Board.[39] The permit may set a lower rate of pay and alter other minimum terms and conditions set by the Board, and treatment which complies with the terms of the permit is taken to be justified.[40] A failure to make an adjustment which would improve the agricultural worker's terms and condition beyond the provisions of the permit is also taken to be justified.[41] In other words, to the extent (only) that it is covered by the permit issued by the Agricultural Wages Board in respect of a particular individual, disability-related pay discrimination and discrimination in terms and conditions are not unlawful, and no DDA 1995 s6 duty arises which would involve improving on the derogations from minimum terms authorised by the permit. Holiday entitlement however may not be varied by the permit.

15.52 The DDA 1995 makes special provision for pensions and insurance type benefits. These are set out at para 15.62 below.

Discrimination in access to other benefits, facilities and services

15.53 The list of benefits, facilities and services, discrimination in access to which is prohibited, is extensive. It includes matters such as

37 Council Directive 2000/78/EC.

38 EAT/691/99 (unreported, available on LEXIS).

39 DD(E) Regs 1996 reg 6.

40 Ibid reg 6(a); Agricultural Wages Act 1948; Agricultural Wages (Scotland) Act 1949.

41 DD(E) Regs 1996 reg 6(b).

preferential loans, mortgage subsidies,[42] membership of health clubs, travel allowances, car parking, holiday and sick pay. Examples of less favourable treatment include offering opportunities to do overtime work to men but not women;[43] excluding women from meetings where pay and conditions are discussed;[44] restricting time off to perform public duties,[45] refusing to provide references.[46]

Annual leave

15.54 Provisions relating to annual leave will usually be included in the worker's contract. In addition, the Working Time Regulations 1998[47] provide that all workers are entitled to annual leave of four weeks.[48] Discrimination on grounds of sex, race or disability in relation to annual leave will be unlawful (though, in the case of sex discrimination, properly challenged under the EqPA 1970 rather than the SDA 1975). The holiday entitlement of part-time workers should be pro-rated to that of full-timers (see para 21.73), and women on maternity leave accrue annual leave (see paras 18.25 and 18.30).

15.55 Employers should take into account the special religious needs of workers in determining holiday leave. In *J H Walker Ltd v Hussain*,[49] for example, the employer refused to allow employees to take holidays during May to July when the business was very busy. No exception was made for the celebration of Eid when it fell within this period, and Muslim employees were refused time off despite their offer to work extra hours to make up the time. A large number of Asian employees stayed away over Eid and were given final written warnings for doing so. The EAT upheld the tribunal's decision that this amounted to unjustified indirect discrimination against the Asian workers (see also para 8.31).

15.56 The CRE code of practice points out that workers may want extended leave to visit relatives in their country of origin. This may

42 See *Calder v James Finlay Corporation Ltd* [1989] IRLR 55, EAT.

43 *Baxter v Glostal Architectural Anodising Ltd*, ET 1168/76 (unreported).

44 *Burnett and Tyler v Electric Actuator Co Ltd*, COET 810/99 (unreported).

45 *Bharath v British Airways*, ET 13264/87 (unreported).

46 Case 185/97 *Coote v Granada Hospitality* [1998] ECR I-5199; [1998] IRLR 656, ECJ and *(No 2)* [1999] IRLR 452, EAT.

47 SI No 1833.

48 The details of these provisions are outside the scope of this book but note that holiday entitlement under the Working Time Regulations accrues during sick leave – *Kigass Aero Components Ltd v Brown* [2002] IRLR 312.

49 [1996] IRLR 11.

involve taking their holiday in one period, or taking extra unpaid leave to make a long journey worthwhile. Unjustified refusal to allow a worker to accumulate annual leave, or to allow some extra unpaid leave, may be unjustified indirect race discrimination.

15.57 Time off during working hours for assessment, treatment or rehabilitation might be required in relation to a disabled worker as a DDA 1995 s6 adjustment.[50]

Sick leave and pay

15.58 Issues relating to pregnancy and maternity leave are covered in chapters 17–21. As with other benefits, the entitlement of part-time workers to sick leave and pay should be pro-rated to that of full-timers.

15.59 There are some illnesses which are exclusive to or much more common in certain racial groups. Indirect race discrimination might occur, for example, if an employer treated workers with skin cancer more favourably than those with sickle cell anaemia.

15.60 Sick pay and the DDA 1995 is considered at para 15.45 above. Access to sick leave (whether paid or not) might also be a reasonable s6 adjustment for a disabled worker but the code of practice stresses that the DDA 1995 does not create a right to disability leave.

Failure to investigate a grievance

15.61 Where there is a grievance or other complaints procedure, the failure to investigate an employee's complaint or properly to pursue an individual's grievance may amount to a refusal of access to benefits, facilities or services.[51] The worker will have to show that the failure is on grounds of sex, race or disability in order to succeed in a claim under the relevant Act (see provisions in CRE and EOC codes below).[52] Failure to investigate an employee's complaint or properly to pursue an individual's grievance may also amount to a 'detriment' within the relevant Act – see further below – and this should be argued in the alternative. The Employment Act 2002 will introduce a statutory grievance procedure which will oblige employees to submit a written grievance to the employer, and leave 28 days for a reply, prior to lodging a claim with the ET (see para 32.15).

50 DDA 1995 s6(3). See chapter 6 for a detailed analysis.

51 *Eke v Customs and Excise Commissioners* [1981] IRLR 334, EAT.

52 Note that the burden of proof is different in sex discrimination cases.

Disability discrimination in pensions.

15.62 Pensions are part of pay and usually form part of a worker's contract of employment. Pension schemes, including provision for enhanced redundancy or invalidity benefits, fall within the DDA 1995. But special provisions modify the application of the Act to pension schemes.

15.63 Occupational pension schemes are deemed to include a non-discrimination rule which relates to the terms under which disabled people become members, and are treated as members, of the scheme.[53] This has the effect of implying into the occupational pension scheme rules an overriding rule of non-discrimination against disabled people.[54] The rule applies to the trustees or managers of the pension scheme as it does to employers, but a claim against the pension scheme trustees must be taken through the pension scheme dispute resolution procedure rather than the ET.

15.64 The Disability Discrimination (Employment) Regulations 1996[55] reg 4 deems less favourable treatment resulting from applying eligibility conditions set for receiving a benefit to be justified in specified circumstances. The benefits covered are those provided under an occupational pension scheme for termination of service, retirement, old age or death, accident, injury, sickness or invalidity. They do not include sick pay.[56] Such less favourable treatment is deemed justified if the cost of providing the benefit is, by reason of the disability, likely to be substantially greater than it would be for a comparable person without a disability. An employer is also deemed to be justified in requiring a disabled person to make occupational pension contributions at the same rate as other employees, even though the disabled employee is not eligible, for a reason related to his disability, to receive benefits at the same rate as other employees.[57]

15.65 The duty to make reasonable adjustments is also disapplied in relation to any benefit under an occupational pension scheme, including benefits in respect of termination of service, retirement death or old age, accident, injury, sickness or invalidity.[58] In order to comply with the ED the government must remove the restrictions relating to occupational pensions. It is committed to doing so by October 2004.

53 DDA 1995 s17.
54 Ibid s17(1).
55 SI No 1456.
56 *London Clubs Management Ltd v Hood* [2001] IRLR 719.
57 DD(E) Regs 1996 reg 5.
58 DDA 1995 s6(11).

Codes of practice

EOC code

15.66 The EOC code of practice recommends that employers should regularly review their benefits, etc, to ensure that they are not discriminating unlawfully on grounds of sex or marriage. The code states, for example, (paras 28–29) that part-time work, domestic leave, company cars and benefits for dependants should be available to both male and female employees in the same or not materially different circumstances. Denial of pro rata benefits to part-time employees may be indirect sex discrimination (where the part-timers are women – see chapter 7) and/or a breach of the Part-time Workers Regulations[59] (where they are men and women – see para 21.37). The EOC code also recommends (para 31(c)) that particular care is taken to deal effectively with all complaints of discrimination, victimisation or harassment. It should not be assumed that they are made by those who are over-sensitive.

CRE code

15.67 The CRE code of practice states (para 1.18) that it is unlawful to discriminate on racial grounds in appraisals of employee performance, and recommends that staff should be instructed not to discriminate and that assessment criteria should be examined to ensure that they are not unlawfully discriminatory. The code also recommends that criteria governing eligibility for benefits, facilities and services should be examined to ensure that they are not unlawfully discriminatory. The code points out that employees may request extended leave from time to time in order to visit relations in their countries of origin or who have emigrated to other countries. Many employers have policies that allow annual leave entitlement to be accumulated, or extra unpaid leave to be taken to meet these circumstances. Employers should take care (para 1.21) to apply such policies consistently and without unlawful discrimination.

15.68 The CRE code recommends that, in relation to grievance disputes, employers should not ignore or treat lightly grievances from members of particular racial groups on the assumption that they are oversensitive about discrimination. It also recommends that, where employees have particular cultural and religious needs that conflict with

59 Part-time Workers (Prevention of Less Favourable Treatment) Regulations 2000 SI No 1557.

existing work requirements, employers should consider whether it is reasonably practicable to vary or adapt these requirements to enable such needs to be met. It is recommended, for example, that employers should not refuse employment to a turbanned Sikh who could not comply with unjustifiable uniform requirements. Other examples of needs that employers might attempt to accommodate relate to:

- the observance of prayer times and religious holidays; and
- the wearing of dress such as saris and trousers by Asian women.[60]

DDA 1995 code

15.69 The DDA 1995 code of practice is much more comprehensive that the CRE and EOC codes and should be referred to in every case. In particular, an employer should consider whether reasonable adjustments can be made in order to avoid a disabled person being at a disadvantage. In brief, the main points are:

- It might be a reasonable adjustment to change the hours of work of a worker whose disability means that he or she has difficulty using public transport during rush hours (para 5.27).
- An induction procedure may need to be individually tailored to ensure that a disabled person is introduced into a new working environment in a clearly structured and supported way (para 6.3).
- An employer may need to alter the time or the location of training for someone with a mobility problem, or to make training manuals, slides or other visual media accessible to a visually impaired employee (para 6.6).
- If there are dedicated car parking spaces near to the workplace, it is likely to be reasonable for the employer to allocate one of these spaces to a disabled employee (para 6.7).
- If, as a result of his or her disability, an employer's arrangements or a physical feature of the employer's premises place a disabled employee at a substantial disadvantage in doing his or her existing job, the employer must consider any reasonable adjustment that would resolve the difficulty (para 6.19).
- It may be possible to modify the changed needs of an employee who becomes disabled, or has a disability that worsens. This might be done by rearranging working methods or giving another employee certain minor tasks that the disabled person can no longer do, by providing practical aids or adaptations to premises or

60 CRE code of practice para 1.24.

equipment, or by allowing the disabled person to work at different times or places. It may be a reasonable adjustment for an employer to move a newly disabled person to a different post within the organisation if a suitable vacancy exists or is expected to arise shortly. Additional job coaching may be necessary to enable a disabled person to take on a new job (para 6.20).

'Any other detriment'

15.70 SDA 1975 s6(2)(b) makes is unlawful for an employer to discriminate, in relation to a worker: 'by dismissing her, or subjecting her to any other detriment'. In addition, the Equal Treatment Directive[61] (ETD) provides that men and women shall be guaranteed the same working conditions without discrimination on grounds of sex (see chapter 10).

15.71 RRA 1976 s4(2)(c) and DDA 1995 s4(2)(c) are in materially the same terms to SDA 1975 s6(2)(b). 'Detriment' is a broad catch-all provision intended to cover any disadvantage not already covered by the Acts. In *Home Office v Holmes*[62] the EAT held that 'detriment' under SDA 1975 s6(2)(b) does not have to be a detriment of a different kind to that under SDA 1975 s1(1)(b)(iii) and RRA 1976 s1(1)(b)(iii) (see para 7.112). In order to succeed in challenging such detriment the worker must show, in addition, that he or she has been subjected to direct or indirect discrimination on grounds of sex, married status, gender reassignment, race or disability. Often the discriminatory treatment will be a detriment in itself, so there is substantial overlap between SDA 1975 s1(1)(b)(iii), RRA 1976 s1(1)(b)(iii) and DDA 1995 s5, and RRA 1976 s4(2)(c), SDA 1975 s6(2)(b) and DDA 1995 s4(2)(c).

15.72 'Subjecting' a worker to a detriment includes causing or allowing the discrimination in a case in which the discriminator can control whether it happens.[63] The question is whether the employer has control of the situation and could have prevented the discrimination (see para 31.23).

61 Council Directive 76/207/EEC.

62 [1984] IRLR 299.

63 *Burton v De Vere Hotels Ltd* [1996] IRLR 596 (see para 31.23); see also *Go Kidz Go Ltd v Bourdouane*, EAT 1110/95 (unreported, available on LEXIS), in which an employer was held to have subjected an employee to a detriment by allowing her to return to a situation in which, to the employer's knowledge, she had been harassed.

Proper approach to 'detriment'

15.73 The term 'detriment' is not defined in the SDA 1975, RRA 1976 or DDA 1995, but the courts have interpreted it very widely. In *Barclays Bank plc v Kapur*[64] the Court of Appeal stated that the term should be given its broad and ordinary meaning and 'it is plain that almost any discriminatory conduct by an employer in relation to an employee's employment will be rendered unlawful by [RRA 1976] s4(2)'.

15.74 In *Ministry of Defence v Jeremiah*[65] Brandon LJ took a suitably wide view of the expression, stating that 'subjecting to a detriment' meant no more than putting at a disadvantage. The detriment in that case was that men working overtime were given 'dirty and obnoxious work' while women were not. The fact that an additional payment was made to the men did not make any difference because 'an employer cannot buy a right to discriminate'.

15.75 In *Chief Constable of West Yorkshire v Khan*[66] the applicant complained that he had been victimised when his employers refused to provide a reference because of outstanding proceedings against them (see para 4.25). The House of Lords, following *Jeremiah*, ruled that:

> ... the courts have given the term 'detriment' a wide meaning.[67] In *Ministry of Defence v Jeremiah* Brightman LJ said that 'a detriment exists if a reasonable worker would or might take the view that the [treatment] was in all the circumstances to his detriment'. Mr Khan plainly did take the view ... that not having his assessment forwarded was to his detriment and I do not think that, in his state of knowledge at the time, he can be said to have been unreasonable.

15.76 In *De Souza v Automobile Association* the Court of Appeal held that, if the discrimination was such that a reasonable employee could justifiably complain about his or her working conditions or working environment, even if the employee was prepared to work on in that environment, then it amounted to a detriment.[68] In *Garry v Ealing LBC*[69] the Court of Appeal held that there was a detriment even though the applicant was unaware of it (see below). As Pill LJ stated, for the court:

> The fact that the [applicant] was unaware at the time of what was going on (if that be the case) does not provide the respondents with

64 [1989] IRLR 387.
65 [1980] ICR 13.
66 [2002] 1 WLR 1947; [2001] IRLR 830.
67 Per Lord Hoffman, para 53.
68 [1986] IRLR 103. See also *Strathclyde Regional Council v Porcelli* [1986] IRLR 134.

> a defence if, on analysis, their treatment was to her detriment. In the circumstances, it was no less a detriment in that for a time she was unaware of it. The adage relied on by the EAT that ... 'ignorance is bliss' is misplaced.

15.77 The crux of the test is whether, as a result of any discriminatory remark or action, the claimant was disadvantaged in his or her workplace. That disadvantage may be direct or indirect. In *Shamoon v Chief Constable of the RUC*,[70] Northern Ireland's Court of Appeal ruled that there has to be some physical or economic consequence as a result of discrimination to constitute a detriment. The court held that the applicant in that case had suffered no detriment when she was prevented from carrying out appraisals, since she had no 'right' to conduct them. There was no loss of rank and no financial consequence when the function was removed from her.

15.78 The decision in *Shamoon* is arguably wrong and is inconsistent with *Khan* and the other cases cited above. Carrying out appraisals may well be relevant experience for promotion or for a management position outside the organisation. Removing such a task against the will of the worker is surely a detriment. The court followed the EAT's decision in *Lord Chancellor v Coker and Osamor*,[71] on which in respect of that point some doubt was cast by the Court of Appeal on appeal. *Shamoon* and the EAT's decision in *Coker* should be regarded as wrong on this point.

The subjective and objective test

15.79 The test for 'detriment' is not wholly subjective – the discriminatory treatment complained of must be objectively capable of being a detriment for it to be unlawful. In *Smith v Vodafone UK Ltd*,[72] for example, the applicant complained of sex discrimination when a male co-worker, noticing a punnet of melon slices in front of her, commented '[y]ou've got some lovely melons there'. The ET found that the remark was made because the co-worker thought the melons looked fresh and appetising but that, realising the innuendo, he immediately

69 [2001] IRLR 681 para 29.

70 [2001] IRLR 520.

71 [2001] IRLR 116, EAT. The Court of Appeal's decision is at [2002] IRLR 87. Lord Phillips MR stated that the court had 'more difficulty' with the conclusion that the applicants could not establish detriment than with other aspects of the EAT's decision.

72 EAT 0054/01 (unreported, available on LEXIS).

became embarrassed and apologised to Ms Smith who, with her colleagues, laughed.[73] The ET found that the remark did not amount to sexual harassment. The EAT, dismissing Ms Smith's appeal concluded that the facts disclosed 'hypersensitivity' on her part and that the double meaning of the expression 'melons' did not affect her dignity at work when it was used to refer to the actual melons and was not directed at her breasts. This was distinguishable from *Insitu Cleaning Co Ltd v Heads*[74] because 'big tits' was obviously offensive and demeaning and incapable of bearing any innocent explanation (see chapter 28).

'De minimis' detriment

15.80 In *Peake v Automotive Products Ltd*[75] the Court of Appeal held that a trivial disadvantage in treatment, such as allowing women to leave five minutes early to avoid the crush, was, if a detriment at all, so minor that it was outside the SDA 1975. This must now be regarded as wrong. In *Gill v El Vino Co Ltd*[76] the Court of Appeal held that the refusal to serve women at the bar (even though they would be served when sitting at tables) was unlawful as it deprived the women of the option of standing at the bar. The court in *Gill* ruled that it was 'very difficult to invoke the [de minimis principle] in a situation where that which has been denied to the plaintiff is the very thing that Parliament seeks to provide, namely facilities and services on an equal basis'.

Examples of detriment

15.81 Harassment, which is covered in detail in chapter 28, is perhaps the most commonly litigated example of 'any other detriment' under the discrimination Acts. The following are other examples of what may constitute a detriment. There may, as was noted above, be an overlap with access to benefits, facilities and services.

Discriminatory instructions

15.82 The issuing of a discriminatory instruction is capable of amounting to a 'detriment' under SDA 1975 s6(2)(b), RRA 1976 s4(2)(c) and DDA

73 The possible allusion to breasts.
74 [1995] IRLR 4.
75 [1977] IRLR 365, CA.
76 [1983] IRLR 206.

1995 s4(2)(c) respectively. In *BL Cars Ltd v Brown*[77] the EAT upheld an ET decision that instructions given to gate staff to check the identity of all black employees who entered the premises, after a black employee had been arrested for theft from the company, was discriminatory and a detriment. The EAT later reached a different decision in *Staffordshire CC v Black*,[78] ruling that it was not a detriment to carry out a check on all black workers because of theft by one black worker. But the earlier decision is to be preferred – it is clearly a disadvantage to be subjected to a discriminatory inspection.

Unwanted transfers

15.83 If a worker is moved in order to separate him or her from a racist (or other worker who has discriminated), this will be a detriment. In *Deson v BL Cars*[79] the EAT held that a worker who was moved to less interesting and attractive work had suffered a detriment even though no loss of pay or status was involved.

Subjection to disciplinary action

15.84 Subjection to disciplinary action amounts to a detriment. It will be unlawful discrimination to subject an individual to disciplinary proceedings on grounds of race, sex, married status or disability. The question is whether the person has been treated differently than others have or would have been treated in the same or similar circumstances. Evidence such as the following will help to found an inference of discrimination:

- particular racial groups being escalated through the disciplinary procedures while other colleagues are dealt with more leniently or at a lower level in the procedure;
- inconsistent penalties or sanctions being applied to people of different races;
- particular groups being disproportionately represented in the disciplinary procedure statistics.

15.85 In *Garry v Ealing LBC*[80] an ET concluded that the decision to appoint a special investigator (into allegations of housing benefit fraud) was made because the council assumed that, because Mrs Garry 'was Nigerian this was likely to be a much bigger scale inquiry'. The

77 [1983] IRLR 193.
78 [1995] IRLR 234.
79 EAT 173/80 (unreported, available on LEXIS).
80 [2001] IRLR 681.

assumption was based on racist stereotyping. The applicant had suffered a detriment as a result of the investigation being allowed to drift on without her being aware of what was happening. The Court of Appeal held that there was clearly a 'detriment' when for reasons connected with the applicant's ethnic origin, an investigation by the employers into her activities was continued longer than an ordinary investigation would have been, even though she was unaware that the investigation was continuing.

15.86 The CRE code of practice states that, in applying disciplinary procedures, consideration should be given to the possible effect on an employee's behaviour of:

- racial abuse or other racial provocation;
- communication and comprehension difficulties;
- differences in cultural background or behaviour.[81]

Failure to deal with a grievance or complaint

15.87 Failure to deal with a grievance or complaint may amount to a detriment, or to less favourable treatment in relation to benefits, facilities and services. The failure to deal itself constitutes the detriment, and a successful discrimination complaint will not require that the applicant go on to prove that he or she has suffered some further disadvantage. In such cases a complaint will succeed if the worker can show that the failure to deal properly with his or her grievance or complaint was on racial grounds or on grounds of sex or disability.[82] In *Sandhu v Leicester Foundry Co Ltd*[83] an ET held that an employer's habit of ignoring two Asian workers' justified complaints about racial abuse and unfair allocation of holidays was a detriment on the grounds of race.

15.88 In *Home Office v Coyne*[84] the Court of Appeal held that the employer's failure properly to investigate a complaint of sexual harassment was a detriment, but that there was no evidence that the employee had been treated less favourably. The dissenting judge (Sedley LJ) said that, but for the fact that the applicant was a woman, she would not have found her complaint being neglected on the explicit assumption that she had only herself to blame for her difficulties. This interpretation is to be preferred (see also chapter 28).

81 Paras 1.22–1.23.

82 *Eke v Customs and Excise Commissioners* [1981] IRLR 334, EAT.

83 ET 32180/83 & 5324/84 (unreported).

84 [2000] IRLR 838.

Dress codes

15.89 Employers commonly have dress rules that differ for men and women. The courts have been surprisingly reluctant to find that these are discriminatory and have ruled, instead, that if such codes are different but 'equal', no 'less favourable treatment' is established (see further chapter 3).

15.90 Dress codes may be indirectly discrimination on grounds of race, where a requirement conflicts with a worker's religious or cultural needs.

Access to time off for public duties

15.91 In *Bharath v British Airways*[85] an ET accepted that the refusal to allow an Indian to take time off for public duties as a magistrate amounted to unlawful race discrimination, since non-Indian employees were allowed such time off.

References

15.92 Refusal to provide a reference, or the provision of an unfavourable reason, may amount to a 'detriment'. A significant difficulty that arises in this context concerns the non-application of the discrimination legislation to ex-employees (see para 11.44). The exception to this, however, applies in the context of the SDA 1975 and at least in cases in which the discrimination at issue is 'victimisation' under s4 of that Act. See further paras 11.45–11.46.

Demotion and transfers

15.93 Employees who are demoted or transferred against their will can claim that they have suffered a 'detriment'. In sexual, racial and disability harassment cases the victims rather than the perpetrators are frequently moved. If this happens it is likely to be discrimination (see chapter 28) and to constitute a detriment. There is no need to prove that an enforced transfer involves loss of status or pay – being moved to a less attractive and less interesting job has been held by the EAT to constitute a detriment.

85 ET 13264/87 (unreported). In addition the ETD provides that men and women shall be guaranteed the same conditions without discrimination on grounds of sex (see chapter 10).

Dismissal

15.94 SDA 1975 s6(2)(b) makes it unlawful for an employer to discriminate, in relation to a worker 'by dismissing her', and the ETD applies to conditions governing dismissal.[86] RRA 1976 s4(2)(c) and DDA 1995 s4(2)(c) are in materially the same terms to SDA 1975 s6(2)(b). A worker who has been discriminatorily dismissed may also claim unfair dismissal under the ERA 1996. The right under that Act not to be unfairly dismissed is better known and in some ways broader in scope than the protection afforded in respect of discrimination. However, for disabled workers the s6 duty to make reasonable adjustments may provide greater protection from dismissal than the ERA 1996's unfair dismissal provisions. The detailed provisions relating to unfair dismissal are outside the scope of this book, being only briefly summarised here. Maternity-related dismissals are considered in chapter 16.

15.95 It is important where appropriate that discriminatory dismissals are challenged under both the ERA 1996 and the appropriate discrimination legislation:

- If the discrimination claim is successful, the amount of compensation that can be awarded is unlimited and will normally include a sum for injury to the complainant's feelings.
- A questionnaire can be served under the SDA 1975, RRA 1976 and DDA 1995 but not under the ERA 1996.
- Compensation for unfair dismissal includes a basic award that is the equivalent of the statutory payment for redundancy. This payment is not available under the discrimination provisions.
- If there is a finding of unfair dismissal the employee can claim reinstatement or re-engagement in order to return to his or her job. Again, these rights are not available under the discrimination legislation (see chapter 33).

Claiming unfair dismissal – an introduction

Entitlement to claim

15.96 In order to make a claim for unfair dismissal the applicant must:

- be an employee under a contract of service. (The self-employed and most casual workers are not protected by the ERA. Agency

86 See para 16.48. Pregnancy-related dismissals will also be unlawful under the Pregnant Workers' Directive – see further para 16.7.

workers may be employed by the agency but are unlikely to be employed by any employer for whom they are working.);[87]

- be under the normal retirement age for his or her place of work or, if there is no normal retirement age, be under 65;[88]
- not be working under an illegal contract.[89]

Unfair dismissal protection does not extend to certain groups of workers including the police and share fishermen.

15.97 Employment contracts may be tainted by illegality because, for example, they involve a fraud on the Inland Revenue because wages are paid in cash without deducting tax at source. An employer may not be able to defend a claim of unfair dismissal by an employee on the ground that the contract is illegal if the employer's conduct has been far more blameworthy than that of the employee.[90] Similarly, if one party alone is guilty of some illegal purposes the innocent party will be able to enforce the contract despite an element of illegality.[91]

15.98 The most significant legal exclusions in respect of unfair dismissal are the following:

- people with insufficient qualifying periods of service (less than one year);
- people beyond the relevant retiring age;
- in some cases, people dismissed in connection with a strike or lock-out.

15.99 The Employment Act 2002 introduces a statutory grievance procedure that will become an implied term of all contracts of employment, binding on employers and employees in all work places. The new procedures, which are only likely to have effect in cases of constructive dismissal and not other dismissals, are considered in chapter 32. A new section in the ERA 1996 will provide that, if the employer fails to comply with the requirements of the procedure, the employee will be treated as having been unfairly dismissed.[92] Essentially this will create a new category of automatically unfair dismissal which will arise when an employer has failed to comply with the statutory procedures.

87 See *Hewlett Packard Limited v O'Murphy* [2002] IRLR 4, *Carmichael v National Power plc* [1999] 1 WLR 2042; [2000] IRLR 43, HL, *Ready Mixed Concrete (South East) Limited v Minister of Pensions and National Insurance* [1968] 2 QB 497.

88 ERA 1996 s109; see further para 15.147.

89 Though see para 11.49.

90 *Hewcastle Catering Limited v Ahmed and Elkamah* [1991] IRLR 437.

91 *Newlands v Simmonds and Willer (Hairdressers) Limited* [1981] IRLR 359.

92 ERA 1996 s98A.

So, for example, if an employee is not invited to a disciplinary meeting, any subsequent dismissal will be unfair. Any procedures to which an employee is already contractually entitled will still stand to the extent that they are additional to the statutory procedures and are not inconsistent with them. Any agreement to oust the operation of statutory procedures will have no effect.

'Dismissal' under the Employment Rights Act 1996

15.100 The ERA 1996 defines a dismissal as either:

- termination of the contract by the employer;[93]
- failure to renew a fixed-term contract under the same contract;
- constructive dismissal, where the employee resigns after a serious breach of an important term of the contract by the employer;
- a refusal to allow a woman to return after maternity absence.[94]

If a contract is guaranteed to run for a minimum time, for example, a fixed term of two years terminable thereafter on notice, it will not be regarded as a fixed-term contract.

15.101 In order to establish constructive dismissal the employer's conduct must amount to a breach of contract of employment, which includes a breach of the implied term of trust and confidence.[95] The breach must be sufficiently important to justify the employee resigning, or must be the last in a series of incidents which justify the employee leaving. It is not sufficient that an employee leaves because the employer has acted unreasonably. The employee must leave in response to the breach of contract and not for some other, unconnected reason. The employee must not delay too long in terminating the contract in response to the employer's breach, or he or she may be deemed to have waived the breach and agreed to vary the contract.[96]

15.102 A constructive dismissal may arise in the discrimination context where, for example, sexual or racial harassment has occurred; where an employer refuses to permit a woman to return part-time or on reduced hours after the birth of a child, or unilaterally alters an employee's hours of work so that he or she can no longer continue working;[97] or where a discriminatory promotion procedure is operated.

93 Ibid s95.

94 ERA 1996 s74 and Maternity and Parental Leave, etc, Regulations 1999 SI No 3312, reg 20 – see further para 18.40.

95 *Woods v WM Car Services (Peterborough) Ltd* [1981] IRLR 347, EAT; *Malik v BCCI* [1998] AC 20; [1997] IRLR 462. HL.

96 *Western Excavating v Sharpe* [1978] IRLR 27; *Woods v WM Car Services*, ibid.

97 See *London Underground Limited v Edwards (No 2)* [1998] IRLR 364, CA.

Employees who have been constructively dismissed, or fear they might be, should write to the employer immediately, notifying him or her of the situation and that the employee considers that a substantial breach of his or her employment contract has occurred or is occurring. It is, however, very difficult to predict whether any particular resignation will result in a successful constructive dismissal claim, and very careful consideration should be given to the likelihood of success before resignation.

Ordinary unfair dismissals

15.103 There are two stages in determining whether or not a dismissal is fair under the ERA 1996. First, the employer must establish the principal reason for the dismissal and show that it falls within the category of reasons which the law specifies as being potentially fair reasons. These are outlined below. Second, it is necessary for the tribunal to be satisfied that in all the circumstances the employer acted reasonably in treating the reason as a sufficient ground for dismissing the employee.[98] ACAS has issued a Code of Practice on disciplinary and grievance procedures (2000). By virtue of Trade Union and Labour Relations Act 1992 s207, a failure to observe any provision of the code does not make the employer liable in the proceedings. But the ACAS code is admissible in evidence and any of its provisions which appears to a tribunal or court to be relevant to any question arising in the proceedings shall be taken into account. It is of particular relevance to conduct dismissals (see para 15.107 below).

Capability or qualifications

15.104 To be potentially fair as a 'capability or qualification' reason for dismissal the reason must relate to the capability or qualification of the employee to perform work of the kind that he or she was employed by the employer to do.[99] Capability, in relation to an employee, means capability assessed by reference to skill, aptitude, health or any other physical or mental quality, and 'qualifications' means any degree,

98 ERA 1996 s98(4) which provides: '[t]he determination of the question whether the dismissal was fair or unfair, having regard to the reason shown by the employer (a) depends on whether in the circumstances (including the size and administrative resources of the employer's undertaking) the employer acted reasonable or unreasonably in treating it as a sufficient reason for dismissal of the employee, and (b) shall be determined in accordance with equity and the substantial merits of the case'.

99 Ibid s98(2)(a).

diploma or other academic, technical or professional qualification relevant to the position held.[100]

15.105 The most usual reasons for dismissal by reason of capability are where the employee is unable to do the job because of ill health including ill health absences, or where the employee is considered to be incompetent by the employers. Dismissals for capability which involve disabled employees have to be considered in the context of the DDA 1995 which expressly applies to dismissals (s4(2)(d)). Dismissal for failure to pass an aptitude test may be a potentially fair dismissal on the grounds of lack of qualification.[101] However, an aptitude test would be discriminatory and therefore unfair if it had a disparate impact on one sex or race and was not justifiable because, for instance, it did not relate directly to the ability of the applicant to do the job in question (see chapter 7). It is not for the tribunal to decide whether or not the employee is actually incapable or incompetent. It is sufficient that the employer honestly believes on reasonable grounds that the employee is incapable and incompetent.[102]

15.106 For a dismissal on grounds of capability or qualifications to be fair, the employer has to carry out a fair procedure. This would include a careful appraisal of the employee's performance and a discussion with the employee as to any criticisms. There should be specific warning to the employee of the consequences of there being no improvement and a reasonable opportunity to improve.

Conduct

15.107 Another potentially fair reason for dismissal is one which relates to the conduct of the employee. Common examples of dismissal for misconduct involve contraventions of disciplinary rules, absenteeism, criminal offences and bad time-keeping. Unless the act of misconduct is very grave the employer should give a warning before dismissing the employee. Sometimes women with primary responsibility for young children have problems over time-keeping and absenteeism when, for example, their children are ill. It may be possible in some jobs to argue for the right to flexible working or to job share (see further chapter 21). Alternatively, if a woman is dismissed because she has had to take time off to care for her child, it may be possible to argue that her dismissal is indirectly discriminatory (see Chapters 7 and 21). It is quite common for employees to be dismissed

100 ERA 1996 s98(3).

101 *Blackman v Post Office* [1974] IRLR 46.

102 *Taylor v Alidair Limited* [1978] IRLR 82.

for taking extended leave to visit relatives abroad, or for being late back from these holidays. This may amount to indirect race discrimination, see below.

Redundancy

15.108 It is a potentially fair reason for dismissal that the employee was redundant.[103] However, selection for redundancy may be discriminatory (see below).

Statutory requirements

15.109 It is a potentially fair reason that the employee could not continue to work in the position that he or she held without contravention (either on the employee's part or on that of the employer) of a duty or restriction imposed by or under an enactment.[104] Even if this condition is satisfied a dismissal is unlikely to be fair if some reasonable modification could have been made to the employee's job that would have accommodated the prohibition. In order to satisfy the reasonableness test the employer may have to consider offering the employee any alternative employment that is available, particularly if a long-serving employee is involved. Furthermore, consideration should be given to alternative methods of doing the work that would not be unlawful.

Some other substantial reason justifying dismissal

15.110 If the reason for dismissal does not fall under the above categories it may still be fair if it is 'some other substantial reason of a kind such as to justify the dismissal of an employee holding the position which the employee held'.[105] Although the circumstances which may fall under this heading are not defined, most of the fair dismissals under this heading arise where employers are taking action to protect their business interests, usually by reorganising their workforces or, possibly, by preventing employees from providing confidential information to a competitor. An employee may be asked to accept a change in terms and conditions of employment and the employee's refusal to accept the change may result in dismissal. An employer may reorganise its business to improve efficiency or for sound business reasons.[106]

103 ERA 1996 s98.
104 Ibid s98(2)(d).
105 Ibid s98(1)(b).
106 *Hollister v National Farmers Union* [1979] IRLR 238.

Automatically unfair dismissals

15.111 A dismissal will be automatically unfair when it is wholly or mainly:

- in connection with pregnancy (see chapter 16);
- for reasons related to parental leave or time off for family reasons;[107]
- in connection with the carrying out of his or her duties by a designated health and safety representative;[108]
- in connection with the refusal by a protected shop worker or betting worker to work on a Sunday;[109]
- in connection with a refusal to comply with a requirement of the employer in contravention of the Working Time Regulations 1998 or to forego a right conferred by those Regulations;[110]
- in connection with acting as a trustee of an occupational pension scheme;[111]
- in connection with the carrying out of his or her duties by an employee representative;[112]
- because the employee has made a 'protected disclosure' under the Public Interest Disclosure Act 1998;[113]
- because the employee has asserted a statutory right, such as the right to antenatal care;[114]
- because of the transfer of an undertaking, unless this is for an economic, technical or organisational reason entailing changes to the workplace;[115]
- in connection with trade union membership or activities;[116]
- because the employee has taken part in protected industrial action in certain circumstances;[117] or
- in connection with the statutory recognition of a trade union.[118]

107 ERA 1996 s99 (including adoption and paternity leave).
108 Ibid s100.
109 Ibid s101.
110 Ibid s101A.
111 Ibid s102.
112 Ibid s103.
113 Ibid s103A.
114 Ibid s104.
115 Transfer of Undertakings (Protection of Employment) Regulations 1981 SI No 1794, reg 8.
116 Trade Union and Labour Relations (Consolidation) Act (TULRCA) 1992 s152.
117 Ibid s238A.
118 Ibid s161.

An employee alleging an automatically unfair dismissal bears the burden of establishing that the dismissal was for one of the reasons set out above.

Discriminatory dismissals

15.112 A dismissal which is discriminatory under the SDA 1975 or RRA 1976 will almost certainly be unfair, as in those circumstances it cannot be said that the employer acted reasonably in treating the reason as a sufficient reason for dismissing the employee under ERA 1996 s98(4) (see para 15.103).[119] The position under the DDA 1995 is not the same. In *HJ Heinz Co Ltd v Kenrick*[120] the EAT stated that a finding of disability discrimination will not necessarily mean that a dismissal was unfair under the ERA 1996. In this case the ET had found that the employer had succeeded in showing the potentially fair reason of capability as the reason for dismissal but went on to find that, in the light of its finding of discrimination, the dismissal was unfair. The EAT overturned the ET's finding: in the absence of a category of automatically unfair dismissal for disability discrimination a tribunal must consider each claim separately and assess whether a dismissal is unfair by reference to the ERA 1996, which is a different claim from that of disability discrimination.

15.113 Although technically possible to have a disability-related dismissal which is not unfair, this would be an unattractive outcome and the circumstances in which it may arise in practice are likely to be limited.

15.114 No claim will be possible if the alleged discriminatory act takes place after the dismissal. The applicant in *Rhys-Harper v Relaxion Group plc*[121] was dismissed with one week's notice by letter of 15 October 1998. She brought an internal appeal against the decision, during the course of which she made an allegation that her manager had sexually harassed her during her employment. On 13 November 1998 both her appeal and her complaint were rejected. On 19 February 1999 she brought a sex discrimination claim, alleging that the employers had failed to investigate her complaint properly. Although she succeeded before the ET, the EAT found that, as her employment had

119 In *Clarke v Eley (IMI) Kynock Ltd* [1982] IRLR 482, however, the EAT accepted that an indirectly discriminatory dismissal would not *invariably* be unfair as a matter of law, though it accepted that it would need very special circumstances to render such a dismissal fair.

120 [2000] IRLR 144.

121 [2001] IRLR 460.

terminated on 13 November, she could not bring a claim under the SDA 1975 since the alleged act of discrimination took place after she ceased to be employed.

15.115 Before the Court of Appeal Ms Rhys-Harper relied upon *Coote v Granada Hospitality Limited*,[122] in which the ECJ had ruled that the ETD required that an applicant be able to challenge post-employment victimisation. The court refused her appeal, however, ruling that SDA 1975 s6(2) (which provides that 'it is unlawful for a person, in the case of a woman employed by him ... to discriminate against her') permits only claims brought during the course of employment. An appeal to the House of Lords is pending.[123] The position is the same under the DDA 1995.[124]

15.116 A dismissal may be either directly or indirectly discriminatory. On the general principles applying to determine whether or not dismissal is direct discrimination on racial grounds see *Zafar v Glasgow City Council*.[125] The test under the amended SDA 1975 is set out at paras 3.85 and 7.10. Some examples of direct discrimination are as follows.

Directly discriminatory dismissals

15.117 In *Mallidi v Post Office*[126] an Indian casual worker who was dismissed because she failed an aptitude test was found to have been unlawfully discriminated against on grounds of race. She had taken the test to determine whether she could continue her employment on a permanent contract basis. The Post Office maintained that there was a national mandatory requirement for all staff to pass an aptitude test before being transferred from casual to permanent status, but there was evidence that three white comparators were given contracts without the need to pass the aptitude test. No satisfactory explanation was given as to why the test was applied in certain cases but not in others. The ET inferred that the only explanation for Mrs Mallidi's dismissal was her race.

15.118 In *Chadwick v Eurodis HB Electronics Limited*[127] the dismissal of a dyslexic employee after he refused to take the minutes of a meeting was held to be less favourable treatment related to his disability. It was accepted that Mr Chadwick was a disabled person for the purposes of

122 [1998] IRLR 656, ECJ (see para 11.45).
123 [1997] IRLR 105, CA. See also *Adekeye v Post Office (No 2)* [1997] IRLR 105.
124 *Kirker v British Sugar* [2002] EWCA Civ 304, CA.
125 [1997] 1 WLR 1659, [1998] IRLR 36, HL.
126 (2001) DCLD 47.
127 (2001) DCLD 50.

the DDA 1995 (see further chapter 2). When asked to take the minutes of a day-long meeting he had refused, stating he would find it difficult. His manager had insisted, asking him why he had got a problem with her request. Eventually, she asked someone else to prepare the minutes. Mr Chadwick raised a complaint which resulted in his manager being reprimanded. Two weeks later he was himself dismissed. At the ET the respondent argued that the reason for his dismissal was his 'unacceptable attitude'. The ET found that the real reason for Mr Chadwick's dismissal was his refusal to take the minutes, which was a reason that related to his disability.

15.119 One particularly harsh decision rejecting a complaint of discriminatory dismissal is found in *Sidhu v Aerospace Composite Technology Limited.*[128] Mr Sidhu, a Sikh employed for many years by the respondents, was involved in an argument with a new employee at a family day out at a park organised by the employers. He and his wife were subjected to violence and racial insults by a white employee, Kevin Smith. Mr Sidhu received a cut head and broken glasses. Although he was not the initial aggressor, Mr Sidhu picked up a plastic chair during the incident. He claimed that he did so in self-defence, but some witnesses said that he had wielded it in an aggressive manner although he did not make contact with anyone. Following an investigation by the employers in which Mr Sidhu made it clear that he considered he had been racially abused, he was dismissed for gross misconduct (fighting was specified as such by the disciplinary rules). The ET upheld a complaint of unfair dismissal but dismissed the complaint of racial discrimination, holding that the employers were not vicariously liable for what happened in the park as it was outside the scope of his employment (see para 31.4). The ET's decision was upheld by the Court of Appeal and an appeal is pending in the House of Lords.

15.120 In *North East Midlands Co-operative Society Limited v Allen*[129] the applicant was dismissed following her marriage. The employer operated a rule whereby female employees who got married were deemed to have terminated their original contract and a fresh contract would be negotiated. When they offered the newly-married Ms Allen alternative employment she declined, and was subsequently dismissed on the ground of redundancy. The EAT held that the applicant had been discriminated against on grounds of her sex and married status. Dismissal on the ground of married status will often be unfair.

128 [2000] IRLR 602.
129 [1977] IRLR 212.

15.121 Complaints of discrimination on the grounds of marital status can be made only by people who are married. Women intending to marry are not protected. The applicant in *Bick v Royal West of England School for the Deaf*[130] was dismissed after she told her employer that she was going to get married but before her wedding day. She lost her discrimination claim because she was not actually married at the date of dismissal. The ETD may protect women in Ms Bick's position. It is broader in scope, stating there shall be no discrimination by reference to marital or family status (see further para 2.17). If the employer is a public body, protection may also be afforded by the Human Rights Act 1998 (see chapter 9).

15.122 A dismissal may be on racial grounds if it arises from an unlawful instruction. *Weathersfield Limited v Sargent*[131] concerned a challenge to the constructive dismissal of a white woman who refused to discriminate against black clients. The applicant, a receptionist, was instructed at her induction course to tell ethnic minority potential customers of the car hire business that no vehicles were available for hire. She was so upset by the policy that she resigned and brought a complaint of race discrimination and constructive dismissal. Both complaints were upheld by the Court of Appeal which found that an employee is unfavourably treated on racial grounds if they are required to carry out a racially discriminatory trading policy and, furthermore, that the applicant was constructively dismissed when she resigned after having been given an instruction to discriminate on racial grounds, notwithstanding that she did not tell the employer at the time she left the employment that she did so because of the instruction she had received. The ET was entitled to find that the employee's conduct was consistent with her having left because of the unlawful instruction.

Indirectly discriminatory dismissals

15.123 A dismissal may be unlawful because it is indirectly discriminatory under the RRA 1976 or SDA 1975 (the DDA 1995 does not prohibit indirect discrimination as such but see para 6.8). A contractual mobility clause may, for example, discriminate indirectly against women because a higher proportion of women than men are secondary earners.[132] Thus a dismissal for a refusal to move could be indirectly

130 [1976] IRLR 326.

131 [1999] IRLR 94.

132 *Meade-Hill v British Council* [1995] IRLR 478.

sexually discriminatory. The general provisions in respect of indirect discrimination apply in this context (see chapter 7).

15.124 *Allonby v Accrington and Rossendale College*[133] involved a claim by a part-time hourly paid lecturer who had been employed on a succession of one-year contracts and who was made redundant and told she could only continue working at the college as an agency worker. The Court of Appeal accepted that she had been indirectly discriminated against on the grounds of sex, remitting the question of justification to the ET to consider further. The college had made all its hourly paid part-time lecturers redundant on the same terms. That decision was indirectly discriminatory as two-thirds were women and one-third men. Among those full-time salaried lecturers not made redundant there were slightly more men than women. The decision in *Allonby* is important in a number of respects and is further considered at para 7.30 above.

15.125 The applicant in *Whiffen v Milham Ford Girls School*[134] had been employed as a part-time teacher at the school for five and half years under a series of fixed-term contracts from year to year. When a redundancy situation arose she was not placed in the redundancy selection pool with other teachers, a decision having been taken to dismiss all staff on fixed-term contracts (however long they had been employed) before an objective selection process was embarked upon in respect of the rest of the staff. An ET found that the policy had an adverse impact on women, but held that it was objectively justified as the redundancy policy was gender-neutral. The Court of Appeal found that the reasoning was flawed as in cases of indirect discrimination the policy is always gender-neutral on its face. As there had been no attempt by the employers to show why it was necessary that only permanent employees were permitted to take part in the selection procedure to avoid redundancy, the employers had failed to discharge the burden on them.[135]

15.126 The applicant in *London Underground v Edwards (No 2)*,[136] a single parent with a young child, was employed as a train operator. She complained of changes in the rostering arrangements that required her to

133 [2001] IRLR 364.

134 [2001] IRLR 468.

135 Note the Fixed Term (Prevention of Less Favourable Treatment) Regulations 2002 which from 1 October 2002 allows employees on fixed-term contracts to complain that they have been discriminated against in comparison with comparable permanent employees without the need to show an adverse impact on one sex.

136 [1999] ICR 494.

begin work at 4.45 am and to work some Sundays. When negotiations between management and the unions about special arrangements for single parents did not reach agreement she resigned and claimed unlawful sex discrimination. Her claim was therefore one of constructive dismissal, see below. The Court of Appeal upheld the ET finding that the proportion of female train operators who could comply with the new rostering arrangements was 'considerably smaller' than the proportion of male train operators (see further para 7.70). The court held that, even though only one woman was affected by the rostering arrangement, it would be wrong to ignore the striking fact that not a single man was disadvantaged by the requirement, despite the vast preponderance of men within the group. The ET was also entitled to use its general knowledge and expertise to look outside the pool for comparison and to take into account the national figure that ten times as many female as male single parents have care of a child. It was also entitled to infer from the small number of women employed compared to men that it was either difficult or unattractive for women to work as train operators in any event.

15.127 Dismissal following an employee's extended leave may be indirect race discrimination as it is mainly ethnic minority workers who have extended leave. The key question would be whether such a requirement would be justifiable. Many employers ask employees taking extended leave to sign a contract stating they will return on a given date, and that if they do not return they will be deemed to have terminated their employment. In *Igbo v Johnson Matthey Chemicals Limited*[137] the Court of Appeal ruled that contractual terms which provide for automatic termination of employment if the employee fails to return on the specified date are void because they limit the operation of a statutory right not to be unfairly dismissed.

Disability related dismissals and reasonable adjustments

15.128 An employee who becomes disabled during the course of his or her employment, or whose condition deteriorates during the period of employment, might be dismissed for reasons of capability – particularly because of sickness absence or performance levels. It was clearly established in *Clark v TDG t/a Novocold*[138] that such a dismissal is for

137 [1986] IRLR 215.
138 [1999] IRLR 318

a reason related to disability, even though other staff members absent for a similar length of time for a reason not related to disability would also be dismissed. The issue which must then be determined is whether the less favourable treatment is justified under the DDA 1995 (see chapter 6).

15.129 Although the Court of Appeal held in *Clark* that dismissal itself is not an 'arrangement' capable of triggering the duty of adjustment, a s6 duty is very likely to arise before dismissal and a failure to comply with it will, if unjustified, amount to disability discrimination.[139] A number of cases illustrate the type of adjustment required in the context of dismissal.

15.130 In *Kent CC v Mingo*[140] it was successfully argued that the council's redeployment policy placed the applicant at a substantial disadvantage since it gave preference to redundant or potentially redundant employees while staff unable to do their jobs for capability reasons, including the disabled, were given lower priority under the procedure.

15.131 In *Jewell v Stoke Mandeville Hospital NHS Trust*[141] an ET found that, when the applicant could not do her job because of her disability, the personnel department should have identified a suitable post and redeployed her into it. It was not enough for the department to coach her for interviews and provide internal vacancy details when the posts were to be filled by open competition. However, redeployment obligations stop short of creating a post and extend only to transferring a disabled member of staff to an existing vacancy, possibly with modifications.[142] Such disabled employees are protected from open competition and are probably entitled by the DDA 1995 to priority over other employees (such as redundant employees) seeking redeployment. It may also be necessary for an employer to modify disciplinary and appeal procedures as a reasonable adjustment and as a matter of fairness in ordinary unfair dismissal cases. For example, a disabled employee with learning difficulties may need more time to prepare for a disciplinary hearing or a visually impaired employee may need documents in tape of braille format to enable him or her to participate effectively in the internal hearing.

139 Overturning *Morse v Wiltshire CC* [1998] IRLR 352, EAT.

140 [2000] IRLR 90.

141 ET 2700986/98 (unreported).

142 *Campbell v DSS*, ET 2301393/98 (unreported).

Discriminatory constructive dismissals

15.132 The SDA 1975 expressly includes constructive dismissals within those prohibited by s6(2)(b), s82(1A) of the Act defining 'dismissal' to include the termination of a person's employment or partnership by any act of the employee's (including the giving of notice) in circumstances such that he or she is entitled to terminate it without notice by reason of the conduct of the employer or, as the case may be, the conduct of the other partners.

15.133 Although there is no such statutory definition in the RRA 1976, it has been held that constructive dismissal is covered. In *Derby Specialist Fabrication Limited v Burton*[143] the applicant, who was black, was employed as a welder in the tube shop in which racial abuse was widespread and no action was taken by the employers to check it. Mr Burton resigned when a redundancy situation arose as he believed that the foreman who had made a racist remark when Mr Burton had failed a test would participate in the redundancy selection process. A complaint of constructive dismissal was upheld, the EAT holding that constructive dismissal comes within the term 'dismissal' as used in RRA 1976 s4(2)(c), notwithstanding that the SDA 1975 had been amended expressly to include constructive dismissal, while the RRA 1976 had not. In contrast, in *Metropolitan Police Commissioner v Harley*[144] the EAT held that the phrase 'by dismissing him' in DDA 1995 s4(2)(d) did not include a constructive dismissal. The EAT on this occasion did not consider *Derby* and it seems likely that, in due course, it will be found that the DDA 1995 also covers constructive dismissal.

15.134 In *Bower v Schroder Securities Limited*[145] an ET found that an equities analyst was discriminated against on the grounds of sex when she was paid a bonus that was much less than that given to male colleagues, and that she was also discriminated against in respect of her constructive dismissal. Ms Bower resigned after a series of incidents including receiving a bonus of £50,000 compared to bonuses of £650,000 and £440,000 received by her comparators. The ET also found that sex discrimination was a factor both directly and indirectly contributing to Ms Bower's resignation.

143 [2001] IRLR 69.
144 [2001] IRLR 263.
145 (2001) DCLD 48.

Redundancy dismissals

15.135 An employee may be fairly dismissed under the ERA 1996 on the ground of redundancy. The employer must show that a redundancy situation exists (for example, that the business is closing down or the workforce is being reduced because there is less or no need for such workers) and that the selection procedure was fair.[146] Whether a redundancy situation really exists can be challenged. But employees may claim unfair dismissal on the basis that their selection for redundancy was unfair, and/or that the procedure followed by the employer was flawed. Employees may also challenge redundancy dismissals both under the ERA 1996 and the relevant discrimination provisions if their selection for redundancy was tainted by sex, race or disability discrimination. Whereas only those with one year's service can claim under the ERA 1996 (in relation to which the restrictions discussed at para 15.96 above also apply), employees can claim unlawful discrimination under the SDA 1975, RRA 1976 or DDA 1995 irrespective of their length of service. The special rules which apply during a woman's maternity leave are considered at para 16.49.

Selection for redundancy

15.136 In order to avert a finding of unfair dismissal arising from redundancy the employer must show the basis on which the employee was selected, and must show that it acted reasonably. Certain selection criteria may be indirectly discriminatory, such as one in which part-time workers are made redundant before full-timers. In *Clarke v Eley (IMI) Kynock Ltd*[147] the EAT held that to select part-timers first for redundancy was unlawful discrimination on grounds of sex. The EAT there took into account the fact that the employers were not completely ignorant of the possibility they might be infringing the SDA 1975. It is therefore important that employers are made aware of the discriminatory nature of redundancy practices before employees are made redundant.

15.137 A common custom is to select on the basis of 'last in first out' (LIFO) which may also be indirectly discriminatory on the grounds of sex (because women tend to have shorter service than men) or on grounds of sex or race (or, in Northern Ireland, religion) in cases where recent efforts have been made to diversify a previously homogenous

146 ERA 1996 s105.
147 [1982] IRLR 482.

workforce. Claims of indirect discrimination connected with the application of LIFO have yet to be adequately dealt with by the courts. In *Clarke v Eley* the EAT suggested, obiter, that LIFO was probably not discriminatory, because it had for many years been the most commonly agreed selection criterion for redundancy.

15.138 LIFO was not directly challenged in *Clarke v Eley* but it was in *Brook v Haringey LBC,*[148] in which it was applied as one of a number of criteria in a situation in which significant strides had been made in recent years to diversify a predominantly male workforce. There, as we saw at para 7.29, the EAT applied *Perera v Civil Service Commission (No 2)*[149] and ruled that no absolute requirement or condition had been applied. This aspect of the decision is no longer sustainable in an SDA 1975 case given the amendments made to that Act by the BP Regulations (see further para 7.10). Nor will it be acceptable in an RRA 1976 case once the RD is transposed.

15.139 *Hall v Short Missile Systems Limited,*[150] a Northern Irish case, arose out of a situation in which the LIFO principle had been abandoned in order to avoid indirect discrimination against Catholics in a traditionally Protestant workplace. There the Northern Ireland Court of Appeal held, on very dubious reasoning (and in partial reliance on *Brook*) that the application of LIFO would not have amounted even to prima facie indirect discrimination despite its recognition of the disparate impact such a selection criterion would have had on the Catholic workforce.

15.140 It is likely that cases such as *Brook* and *Hall* would, if they were to arise today, be accepted at least as imposing a burden on the employer to justify prima facie cases of indirect discrimination. In *Brook* the EAT ruled that, even had a case of indirect discrimination been made out, the employer's use of LIFO would have been justified:

> Employers, trade unions, ACAS and commonsense all recognise that length of service is an essential ingredient in any redundancy selection, save in the most exceptional circumstances. Therefore, justification of length of service as a criterion will be a fairly simple burden for an employer to undertake.

As we saw above, length of service was only one of several selection criteria in *Brook* and it was found that the 'waiting given was a product of detailed consultation and the employer's options were limited'. It

148 [1992] IRLR 478.

149 [1983] IRLR 166.

150 [1997] 72 ELR 39; [1996] NI 214. See also *R v Hammersmith and Fulham LBC ex p NALGO* [1991] IRLR 249.

may therefore be possible to distinguish the case. In any event, the decision in *Brook* was reached before *Allonby* (see further para 7.30) in which the Court of Appeal ruled that the question of whether indirect discrimination is justified requires consideration of whether the employer's reasons demonstrate a real need for the action in question and, if they do, whether the disparate impact on the applicant was disproportionate to the employer's need to take the action in question. This is a significantly more difficult test to satisfy than that which formed the basis of the decision in *Brook*.

15.141 Redundancy selection criteria may fall foul of the DDA 1995. The DDA 1995 code of practice provides guidance. An employer who needs to reduce the workforce would have to ensure that any scheme that was introduced for choosing candidates for redundancy did not discriminate against disabled people. If redundancy criteria would apply to a disabled person for a reason relating to the disability, those criteria would have to be 'material' and 'substantial' and the employer would have to consider whether a reasonable adjustment would prevent them applying to the disabled person. Examples of criteria that might relate to disability include sickness absence and performance. What is justified will depend on the circumstances of the particular case. If an employer has failed in its duty to adjust in circumstances in which, had the duty been complied with, the employee would have satisfied the redundancy selection criteria, the employer will not be able to justify the discriminatory dismissal.

15.142 If, for example, output and productivity are the selection criteria for redundancy and a disabled employee is selected for redundancy because his output is lower for a reason related to his disability, in a case in which an employer has failed to comply with a s6 duty (compliance with which would have improved the employee's performance and productivity so that he would not have been selected for redundancy), the employer will be unable to justify selecting the disabled employee for redundancy.

Redundancy consultation

15.143 An employer is legally obliged to consult with recognised trade unions within specified time limits.[151] This consultation process should provide the opportunity to consider if the redundancy procedure is discriminatory. However, the under-representation of women, black workers and disabled workers among union representatives and

151 TULRCA 1992 Pt 4, Ch II.

full-time officials may result in insufficient attention being given to this aspect of the arrangements.

15.144 For a disabled employee, a reasonable adjustment may be required to ensure effective consultation.

Offer of alternative employment

15.145 An employer should offer, where it exists, suitable alternative employment and allow the employee a trial period in the new job of at least four weeks. Unreasonable refusal to accept such employment will result in a loss of redundancy pay.[152]

15.146 The interplay between the s6 duty and the provision of alternative employment is important. Transferring a worker to an existing vacancy is listed as an example of an adjustment in the reasonable adjustment provisions.[153] The duty stops short of creating a vacancy for a disabled redundant employee, but it is considered that disabled redundant employees should be offered suitable alternative employment before other redundant members of staff.[154]

Retirement

15.147 SDA 1975 s6(2)(b) renders unlawful the dismissal of a woman on the ground of her age if a man of the same age in comparable circumstances would not be dismissed.[155] The enforcement of different retirement ages for women and men – and the taking into account of such retirement ages in selecting for redundancy – is therefore unlawful under the SDA 1975.

15.148 Legal support for compulsory retirement comes in the form of ERA 1996 s109 which provides that an employee who has reached the 'normal retirement age' (NRA) for his or her job cannot claim unfair dismissal under that Act. (The upper age limit does not apply to most automatically unfair dismissals – see above. Nor does it apply to claims brought under the SDA 1975, RRA 1976 or DDA 1995.)

15.149 The NRA is the retirement age that 'would be the reasonable expectation or understanding of the employees', rather than, necessarily,

152 ERA 1996 s141.

153 DDA 1995 s6(3)(c).

154 *Mingo v Kent CC* [2000] IRLR 90; *Jewell v Stoke Mandeville Hospital NHS Trust*, ET 2700986/98 (unreported).

155 SDA 1975 s6(2)(b).

the contractual retirement age.[156] The ERA 1996 provides that, where an employer operates different NRAs according to sex, the NRA for the purposes of claiming unfair dismissal is 65. Any employee dismissed before reaching this age will be able to claim unfair dismissal.

15.150 The prohibition on different retirement ages for men and women does not prevent employers from maintaining different retirement ages for different groups of workers, even in cases in which the effect of this is to impose different retirement ages on predominantly male and predominantly female workers. The applicant in *Bullock v Alice Ottley School*[157] launched a sex discrimination claim because she was required to retire at 60 as a member of the school's (predominantly female) domestic staff, whereas (predominantly male) gardeners and maintenance staff were permitted to work until they were 65. The Court of Appeal ruled that there was no evidence in the case to suggest that the retirement ages were directly discriminatory (the school had equalised retirement ages at 60 when required to do so by law but had subsequently increased the retirement age applicable to some posts that were difficult to fill). The court further ruled that any indirect discrimination involved was justified by the employer's 'real and genuine need' for the later retirement age applied to the comparator posts. *Bullock* was decided prior to *Allonby* and a different outcome might be obtained if similar facts were to be litigated today.

15.151 An employer may operate an NRA with limited exceptions. In *Barclays Bank plc v O'Brien*,[158] for example, the employer had equalised previously discriminatory retirement ages to 60 for all employees. After pressure from staff an exception was made for a relatively small category of employees within particular age limits for a limited period of time. The Court of Appeal held that there was no reason to doubt the employer's policy of having an NRA of 60, and that the limited exception did not destroy that. The limited exception is less likely to apply now there has been a common retiring age for over ten years.

Redundancy pay

15.152 An employee dismissed because of redundancy will lose entitlement to redundancy pay if he or she unreasonably refuses an offer of suitable alternative work.[159] An employee is not entitled to redundancy

156 *Brooks v British Telecommunications Limited* [1992] IRLR 66, CA.
157 [1992] IRLR 564.
158 [1994] IRLR 580, CA.
159 ERA 1996 s141.

pay if he or she has been summarily dismissed for gross misconduct.[160] If the dismissal is unfair the employee will be entitled, in addition, to compensation for unfair dismissal (see para 11.95). In discrimination cases compensation is unlimited (see para 33.7).

15.153 Both contractual redundancy payments and statutory redundancy payments are 'pay' within article 141 of the EC Treaty[161] (see further para 10.28) and any payments made in addition to job-seeker's allowance to men who are made redundant between 60 and 65 also constitute 'pay' within article 141, rather than a social security benefit. In *European Commission v Belgium*[162] the ECJ held that, as such a payment was the responsibility of the employer and was due to the employment relationship, it was 'pay'. A redundancy or severance scheme that is indirectly discriminatory will breach article 141 and the EqPA 1970.[163]

15.154 Entitlement to contractual and statutory redundancy payments, like the right to claim unfair dismissal, continues until the NRA or, if this is discriminatory, until 65.[164] The ERA 1996 provides that those approaching retirement age have their redundancy pay reduced by one-twelfth every month after the birthday prior to that date.

15.155 The House of Lords held in *Barry v Midland Bank plc*[165] that a security of employment agreement which provided that severance pay was calculated on the basis of the employee's current pay at the date of termination did not discriminate indirectly against women contrary to article 141 EC, even though the scheme made no allowance for employees whose hours of work fluctuated (thereby disadvantaging predominantly female part-time workers by not taking into account any full-time service they may have had). It was held that the scheme did not have a discriminatory effect as the same rules applied to women and men and to both full-time and part-time workers. The primary objective of the scheme was to provide support for lost income during the period immediately following redundancy, rather than to remunerate for past service. Since the amount lost was the salary being paid at the end of employment, it was not a relevant

160 Ibid s140.

161 *Hammersmith and Queen Charlotte's Special Health Authority v Cato* [1987] IRLR 483, EAT and Case 262/88 *Barber v GRE Assurance Group* [19890] ECR 1889; [1990] IRLR 240, ECJ.

162 Case 173/91 [1993] ECR I-00673; [1993] IRLR 404.

163 See Case 33/89 *Kowalska v Freie und Hansestadt Hamburg* [1990] ECR I-2591; [1990] IRLR 447 and see para 26.16.

164 ERA 1996 s156.

165 [1999] 1 WLR 1465; [1999] IRLR 581.

difference in treatment to base all employees' severance payments on their final salaries.

15.156 One reason why Mrs Barry was unsuccessful in her claim was because she offered no statistics as to the composition of the advantaged and disadvantaged groups in the pool. On appeal it was held that the appropriate pool of men and women for comparison was all those to whom the relevant provisions of the agreement applied at the time of the termination of her employment. It was necessary to look at all part-time workers at that time and the average of their hours throughout their service and to compare the men and women in the advantaged and disadvantaged groups. The disadvantaged group in that pool were those part-time workers whose hours of work at termination were less than the average of their hours of work throughout their service. As no statistics were available, Mrs Barry had failed to prove her case.

Codes of practice relating to redundancy

15.157 The EOC code recommends that:

- redundancy procedures affecting a group of employees predominantly of one sex should be reviewed, so to remove any effects that could be disproportionate and unjustifiable;
- conditions of access to voluntary redundancy benefit should be made available on equal terms to male and female employees in the same or not materially different circumstances;
- where there is downgrading or short-time working (for example, owing to a change in the nature of volume of an employer's business) the arrangement should not unlawfully discriminate on the grounds of sex.

15.158 The CRE code recommends that:

- staff responsible for selecting employees for dismissal, including redundancy, should be instructed not to discriminate on racial grounds;
- selection criteria for redundancies should be examined to ensure that they are not indirectly discriminatory.

15.159 The DDA 1995 code points out that, if a redundancy selection criterion would apply to a disabled person for a reason relating to his or her disability, that criterion would have to be 'material' and 'substantial' and the employer would have to consider whether a reasonable adjustment would prevent the criterion applying to the disabled person after all (see further chapter 6).

CHAPTER 16

Overview of maternity and parental rights in employment

continued

Key points

16.1

- Maternity and parental rights were extended and simplified in 1999/2000 when:
  - ordinary maternity leave was extended from 14 to 18 weeks;
  - additional maternity leave was extended to women with one year's service;
  - unpaid parental leave and 'dependants leave' for workers with dependants was introduced;
  - protection from detriment connected with pregnancy, maternity and parental leave was introduced;
  - notice provisions for maternity leave were simplified.
- A woman has protected status – automatic protection from discrimination on grounds of her pregnancy – from the beginning of her pregnancy until the end of her maternity leave. This covers less favourable treatment in relation to, for example:
  - recruitment;
  - promotion;
  - transfer;
  - training;
  - access to an appraisal;
  - access to other benefits (except pay and certain contractual benefits during maternity leave).
- The dismissal of an employee for a reason related to her pregnancy, absence on maternity, parental or dependants leave will usually be automatically unfair and is likely also to amount to 'ordinary' unfair dismissal and unlawful discrimination.
- Employees who assert or take their maternity and parental rights are also protected from being subjected to a detriment.
- Limited rights to equal treatment for part-timers came into force in July 2000.
- There will be significant improvements in maternity and related rights where the employee's expected week of childbirth is on 6 April 2003 or later.

Background and statutory framework

16.2 This part of the book summarises maternity and parental rights including the right to ante-natal care and health and safety rights (chapter 17); maternity, parental and dependants leave (chapters

18–20) and the right to work part-time and protection of part-timers (chapter 21).

16.3 Many women experience discrimination and/or are dismissed at some stage during their pregnancy and/or maternity leave so it is important, at every stage, to consider maternity and parental rights together with protection from discrimination, dismissal and detriment. This chapter briefly sets out the statutory framework of maternity and parental rights (the detail being covered in subsequent chapters) and then considers discrimination and dismissal law as it affects pregnant woman and those on leave. For a detailed explanation of the law see *Maternity and Parental Rights.*[1]

Main changes to UK law since 1999

16.4 In 1999 and 2000 major changes were introduced to comply with EU law.[1a] In particular:

- maternity law was simplified and ordinary maternity leave was extended to 18 weeks;
- the right to additional maternity leave was extended to women with one year's service at the eleventh week before the expected week of childbirth;
- parental leave was introduced for parents of children under five;
- a right to dependants leave was introduced for workers with dependants;
- new protection from detriment as a result of exercising maternity and parental rights was introduced;
- part-time workers were given limited protection from less favourable treatment than full-timers.

16.5 Further changes are proposed for employees where the expected week of childbirth is on or after 6 April 2003. These include the extension of maternity leave to one year, streamlined notice provisions, the introduction of adoption leave and of two weeks' paternity leave (paid at a flat rate) and significant increases to statutory maternity pay (which, with maternity allowance, is outside the scope of this book).[2] From 2003, employers will be under a duty to consider requests for flexible working arrangements from employees who have worked for

1 Palmer and Wade, 2nd edn, LAG, 2001.

1a As a result of Council Directives 96/34/EC (Parental Leave Directive) and 97/81/EC (Part-time Workers Directive).

2 Regulations implementing the details of these proposals had not been published at the date of writing.

their employer for six months and who have children under six or disabled children up to the age of 18.

16.6 Although the main maternity and parental rights are set out in the Employment Rights Act (ERA) 1996 and the Maternity and Parental Leave Regulations (MPL Regulations) 1999, it is always important also to consider the discrimination legislation (the Sex Discrimination Act (SDA) 1975 and the Equal Pay Act (EqPA) 1970[3]) which sometimes provides greater protection than the specific statutory provisions dealing with pregnancy and maternity and parental leave (see further below). Taking this into account, the main statutory provisions relevant to pregnancy and maternity and parental leave are:

- ERA 1996 (as amended by Employment Relations Act 1999);
- MPL Regulations 1999;[4]
- Management of Health and Safety at Work Regulations (MHSW Regulations) 1999;[5]
- Part-time Employees (Prevention of Less Favourable Treatment) Regulations (PTW Regulations) 2000;[6]
- SDA 1975;
- EqPA 1970; and
- Social Security Act (SSA) 1989 Sch 5.

European Community law

16.7 UK law is either subject to, or must be interpreted in accordance with, EC law,[7] for instance:

- Article 141 of the EC Treaty and the Equal Pay Directive (EPD),[8] which governs equal pay in contractual and non-contractual terms (see paras 10.27 and 10.32);
- Equal Treatment Directive (ETD),[9] which governs access to employment, working conditions and dismissal (see para 10.34);
- Pregnant Workers Directive (PWD);[10]

3 The parallel provisions for Northern Ireland are the Equal Pay Act (Northern Ireland) 1970 and the Sex Discrimination (Northern Ireland) Order 1976 SI No 1042.
4 SI No 3312.
5 SI No 3242.
6 SI No 1551, in force 1 July 2000.
7 The applicability of EC law is set out in chapter 10.
8 Council Directive 75/117/EEC.
9 Council Directive 76/207/EEC.
10 Council Directive 92/85/EEC.

- Parental Leave Directive (PLD) – see chapter 19 and 20; and
- Part-time Workers Directive (PTWD) – see chapter 21.

Coverage of maternity and parental leave

16.8 Only 'employees' (ie, those with a contract of employment) are entitled to full maternity and parental rights under UK statutes. However, the PWD applies to 'workers' which includes casual workers and those who may be classified as self-employed (see chapter 11). The wider category of 'workers' is protected under the SDA 1975 (see chapter 11), rather than the 'employees' covered by the ERA 1996.

16.9 Parents who ordinarily work outside Great Britain are now protected by the ERA 1996,[11] but the Act's protection does not extend to:

- **Members of the armed forces**: ERA 1996 s192 has yet to be implemented. When it is, a complainant will be obliged to go through an internal complaints procedure before bringing proceedings in an ET.[12]
- **Police officers** employed in the police service, although they have similar protection under the Police Regulations 1995.[13] Prison officers, however, are protected.[14]
- **Share fishermen and women** who are either the master or crew of a fishing vessel and are paid by a share in the profits or gross earnings of the vessel.[15]

Meaning of 'childbirth'

16.10 Women are entitled to maternity rights if they give birth to a living child (however premature) or to a child, living or dead, after 24 weeks of pregnancy.[16]

11 The Employment Relations Act 1999 repealed ERA 1996 s196, which had previously excluded this category of workers from maternity rights.

12 ERA 1996 Sch 2 para 16; EC law may, however assist. A member of the armed forces can rely directly on the ETD and PWD: see para 10.71.

13 ERA 1996 s200.

14 Criminal Justice and Public Order Act 1994 s26.

15 ERA 1996 s199(2), but under s199(7) other mariners who are GB residents, who work on board GB-registered ships and who do not work wholly outside GB are not excluded.

16 ERA 1996 s235.

Rights available when the expected week of childbirth is 6 April 2003 or after

The rights	Length of service with same employer	Employment status	Notice requirements	Medical and otherevidence
Paid time off for antenatal care during working hours.	No qualifying period.	Employee (as above).	After 1st appointment, employer may require written proof of appointments.	If requested by employer, medical certificate showing woman is pregnant.
Health and safety protection. Employer has a duty to carry out a risk assesment.	None.	Workers have basic protection, employees have rights to alternative work and paid suspension.	Must notify employer in writing of pregnancy, birth or that she is breastfeeding.	A doctor's letter may help the employer with the risk assessment.
26 weeks of ordinary maternity leave; can start from 11th week before expected week of childbirth (EWC). Will start on date notified unless triggered by pregnancy-related absence in four weeks prior to EWC.	None. All women irrespective of length of service are entitled to OML.	Employee including those on fixed term contracts.	Notice of pregnancy, EWC and start of leave to be given during 15th week before EWC. Start date may be varied by giving 28 days' notice.	If requested by employer, doctor's or midwife's certificate giving EWC.
Additional maternity leave of 26 weeks following ordinary maternity leave (OML).	26 weeks' service at 15th week before EWC.	Employee.	As for OML.	As for OML.

continued

The rights	Length of service with same employer	Employment status	Notice requirements	Medical and other evidence
Rights during maternity leave (contractual rights maintained except pay).	None (rights during OML are more extensive than rights during AML).	Employee (as above).	Only entitled if she has given the correct notice for maternity leave.	None.
Right to return to same job after OML (26 weeks).	None.	Employee (as above).	No notice is required for return at end of 26 weeks. 28 days' notice required if return earlier.	N/A
Right to return to same or similar job after AML (52 weeks).	26 weeks' service at 15th week before EWC.	Employee (as above).	No notice required for return at end of AML. 28 days' notice required if return earlier.	N/A
Unpaid parental leave of 13 weeks for child under 5 years old or disabled child up to the age of 18.	1 year's service by start of parental leave.	Employee, as above, taking leave to care for a child.	Default scheme provides that 21 days may be increased to 28 days' notice of leave.	N/A
Adoption Leave. 52 weeks (26 ordinary and 26 additional) 1st 26 weeks paid at £100 per week (maximum).	26 weeks' service by week notified of matching for adoption.	Employee.	Within 7 days of notification of matching, date of placement, length and start of leave.	N/A

Paternity Leave (birth and adoption). 2 weeks paid at £100 per week.	26 weeks' service by mother's notification week or week in which adopter is notified of matching.	Employee (father, spouse or partner of mother – birth) (spouse or partner of adopter – adoption).	In or before 15th week before EWC (birth); within 7 days' after notification of matching (adoption).	N/A
Dependants leave: unpaid.	No qualifying period.	Employee with responsibility for a dependant .	No minimum notice, but notice of reason must be given as soon as reasonably practicable.	Employer may ask for certificate for child.
Protection from automatically unfair dismissal connected with pregnancy, childbirth, maternity, parental, adoption or paternity leave.	No qualifying period.	Employees ***except***, after AML, those working in firms employing less than six staff where it is not feasible to keep her job open or offer alternative work.	N/A	N/A
Protection from unfair dismissal.	1 year's continuous employment.	Employee.	N/A	N/A
Protection from discrimination (including rights to child-friendly working hours).	No qualifying period.	Worker, including employee, self-employed, contract workers, trainees.	N/A	N/A
Pro rata rights for part-time workers.	No qualifying period.	Worker.	N/A	N/A
Right to request new working patterns.	6 months.	Employee.	Procedure prescribed by regulations.	N/A

Protection from discrimination under the Sex Discrimination Act 1975

16.11 In addition to the specific statutory provisions dealing with pregnancy and with maternity and parental leave, workers are entitled to protection under the SDA 1975 from discrimination 'on the grounds of' sex. Such is the connection between pregnancy, maternity and parental leave and sex, that the SDA 1975 affords valuable additional protection in this context.

16.12 The main differences between the ERA 1996 and the discrimination legislation are:

- There is no qualifying period for protection under the SDA 1975 such as that (one year's continuous employment) which applies in relation to ordinary unfair dismissal.
- Job applicants and workers not qualifying as 'employees' under the ERA 1996 are protected by the SDA 1975. In *Patefield v Belfast City Council*,[18] for example, Northern Ireland's Court of Appeal held that the council discriminated unlawfully against a contract worker (who did not qualify for statutory maternity leave under the ERA) when it replaced her with a permanent employee when she went on maternity leave.
- A questionnaire can be served under the SDA 1975, but not under the ERA 1996.
- There is no cap on the compensation that may be awarded under the SDA 1975, and injury to feelings can be awarded.

The SDA 1975 is further discussed in chapters 11 and 18.

Pregnancy and direct discrimination – 'protected status'

16.13 After many years of uncertainty, the House of Lords accepted in *Webb v EMO Air Cargo (UK) Ltd (No 2)*[19] that discrimination on grounds of pregnancy amounts, automatically, to discrimination on the ground of sex contrary to the SDA 1975. The main principles relating to direct discrimination on the grounds of sex are set out in chapter 3. The Burden of Proof Regulations (BP Regulations) 2001[20] will apply to

18 [2000] IRLR 664, see also *BP Chemicals v Gillick and Roevin Management Services Ltd* [1995] IRLR 128, EAT.

19 [1994] QB 718; [1994] IRLR 482. Their Lordships left open the application of this principle to workers on fixed-term contracts, but see para 16.44.

20 Sex Discrimination (Indirect Discrimination and Burden of Proof) Regulations 2001 SI No 2660 which amended the SDA 1975, see SDA 1975 ss63A and 66A.

pregnancy-related discrimination as to other types of sex discrimination. Once the complainant has raised a presumption of discrimination by, for example, showing that she was treated less favourably and that she is pregnant or on maternity leave, the burden will shift to the employer to show that there was a non-discriminatory reason for the treatment (see para 3.85).

16.14 In most sex discrimination claims the woman must show that she has been treated less favourably than an actual man has been or a hypothetical man would have been treated. Thus, some sort of comparative exercise with the treatment of men is essential (see para 3.14). This is not the case for pregnancy-related discrimination where there is no possible male comparator, as men cannot be pregnant or take maternity leave. No comparator is required where the discrimination, during a woman's pregnancy and maternity leave, is related to pregnancy or maternity leave *and the discriminator is aware that the woman is pregnant.*[21] Direct discrimination occurs when a woman is refused appointment, promotion, training, transfer or appraisal, or when she is dismissed, or subjected to some other detriment for a reason related to her pregnancy or absence on maternity leave. This is the case irrespective of whether a man who was ill or absent would have been treated in the same way.[22] Such direct sex discrimination cannot be justified. This 'automatic' protection given to pregnant women and women on maternity leave (ordinary and additional – see further para 18.6) is often referred to as 'protected status'. It lasts from the beginning of pregnancy until the end of maternity leave. After a woman's return from maternity leave she loses this protected status and her treatment has to be compared to that of a man in a similar situation (see para 16.22).[23]

16.15 Many of the pregnancy discrimination cases concern dismissals (see paras 6.16 and 16.30). But the same principles, set out below, apply to other areas of less favourable treatment, such as failure to appoint.

16.16 In *Dekker*[24] the European Court of Justice (ECJ) held that it was a breach of the ETD for an employer to refuse to appoint a suitable

21 See *Day v T Pickles Farms Ltd* [1999] IRLR 217, EAT; however, see also disability decision *Heinz v Kenrick* [2000] IRLR 144.

22 The position in relation to contractual benefits during maternity leave, where the claim would be under the EqPA 1970, is set out at para 18.32.

23 See Case 179/88 *Handels-og Kontorfunktionaerer-nes Forbund i Danmark (acting for Hertz) v Dansk Arbejdsgiverforening (acting for Aldi Marked K/S)* [1990] ECR I-3979; [1991] IRLR 31, ECJ.

24 Case 177/88 *Dekker v Stichting Vormingscentrum voor Jonge Volwassenen (VJV-Centrum) Plus* [1990] ECR I-3941; [1991] IRLR 27, ECJ.

female applicant because of the cost to the employer. The court ruled that:

> As employment can only be refused because of pregnancy to women, such a refusal is direct discrimination on grounds of sex. A refusal to employ because of the financial consequences of absence connected with pregnancy must be deemed to be based principally on the fact that of the pregnancy. Such discrimination cannot be justified by the financial detriment ... suffered by the employer ... (para 12)

16.17 In *Hertz* the ECJ held that:

> The dismissal of a female worker because of her pregnancy constitutes direct discrimination on grounds of sex, as does also the refusal to recruit a pregnant woman ... [D]uring the maternity leave from which she benefits under national law, a woman is protected from dismissal because of her absence.[25]

16.18 In *Habermann-Beltermann*[26] the ECJ held that:

> ... the termination of an employment contract on account of the employee's pregnancy ... concerns women alone and constitutes, therefore, direct discrimination on grounds of sex.[27]

16.19 Following *Dekker*, *Hertz* and *Habermann-Beltermann*, came *Webb*,[28] which was referred to the ECJ by the House of Lords. Mrs Webb was employed on an indefinite contract to provide cover for a pregnant employee. She became pregnant and was dismissed. The ECJ held that:

- the dismissal of a pregnant woman recruited for an indefinite period cannot be justified because she is unable to work for a temporary period because of her pregnancy;
- there can be no question of comparing the situation of a woman who is unable to work because of her pregnancy with that of a man similarly incapable for medical or other reasons;
- the protection of a woman during pregnancy and childbirth could not depend on whether her presence at work was essential to the proper functioning of the undertaking;
- any less favourable treatment of a woman because she is pregnant

25 Case 179/88 *Handels-og Kontorfunktionaerer-nes Forbund i Danmark (acting for Hertz) v Dansk Arbejdsgiverforening (acting for Aldi Marked K/S)* [1990] ECR I-3979; [1991] IRLR 31, ECJ (paras 12 and 15).

26 Case 421/92 *Habermann-Beltermann v Arbeiterwohlfahrt, Bezirksvetbank Ndb/Opf eV* [1994] ECR I-1657; [1994] IRLR 364.

27 See also Case 207/98 *Mahlburg v Land Mecklenburg-Vorpommern* [2000] ECR I-00549; [2000] IRLR 276.

28 Case 32/93 [1994] ECR I-3657.

or because of the consequences of pregnancy is direct sex discrimination.

16.20 On the return of *Webb* to the House of Lords their Lordships held (in *Webb (No 2)*[29]) that it was unlawful to dismiss a woman who had been employed for an indefinite period when she was temporarily unavailable for work as a result of her pregnancy. It is not clear whether the result would have been the same if Mrs Webb had been employed on a short-term contract and had been unavailable for the whole contract.[30] But in *Tele Danmark A/S v Handels-og Kontorfunktionærernes Forbund i Danmark*[31] the ECJ ruled that the prohibition on pregnancy dismissal applied to fixed-term contracts as it applied to indefinite employment. This case is considered further at para 16.37 below.

16.21 During the protected period a woman must not be treated less favourably 'as a worker' because she is pregnant, about to take maternity leave, is on maternity leave or has taken maternity leave. In *Brown v Rentokil*[32] the ECJ held that the ETD affords a woman protection against dismissal on grounds of her absence throughout the period of pregnancy and during the maternity leave accorded to her under national law. This does not, however, mean that she is entitled to pay and benefits for the period of her maternity leave (see para 18.25).

Protection after maternity leave

16.22 Less favourable treatment after maternity leave is treated differently. In *Hertz* the ECJ held that the protected period, during which any less favourable treatment is direct sex discrimination, lasted until the end of maternity leave. Where an illness arose afterwards, there was no *automatic* discrimination if dismissal was related to the illness, even if the illness was due to pregnancy or childbirth (see para 16.43).

29 [1994] QB 718; [1994] IRLR 482.

30 In *Caruana v Manchester Airport plc* [1996] IRLR 378 the EAT ruled that it might be lawful to refuse to appoint a pregnant woman to a fixed-term contract in respect of which she would be unavailable during the whole of the contract. See, however, Case 109/00 *Tele Danmark A/S v Handels-og Kontorfunktionærernes Forbund i Danmark* [2001] ECR I-06913; [2001] IRLR 853, and Case 438/99 *Jimenez Melgar v Ayuntamiento de Los Barrios* [2001] ECR I-06915; [2001] IRLR 848, ECJ.

31 Ibid.

32 Case 394/96 [1998] ECR I-4185; [1998] IRLR 445 and Case 136/95 *Caisse Nationale d'Assurance Vieillesse des Travailleurs Salaries (CNAVTS) v Thibault* [1998] ECR I-2011; [1998] IRLR 399, ECJ.

Establishing a pregnancy-related reason for discrimination: the 'but for' test

16.23 It is unlikely that an employer will admit to treating a woman less favourably because she is pregnant or on maternity leave. Usually allegations will be made of poor performance, or the woman's treatment attributed to a reorganisation or redundancy situation. It is for the woman to prove facts from which the ET could conclude, in the absence of an adequate explanation, that the less favourable treatment was related to pregnancy, childbirth or maternity leave. The burden then shifts to the employer to show that the treatment was for a non-discriminatory reason (see para 3.85). Important tools in establishing discrimination include the questionnaire procedure and discovery (see paras 32.23 and 32.119).

16.24 The question for the tribunal is: 'would the woman have been treated in the same way *but for* the fact that she was pregnant, had given birth or was on maternity leave?'.[33] In *Lana v Positive Action Training in Housing (London) Ltd*[34] the applicant was dismissed from a training contract when she informed the firm with which she was placed that she was pregnant. The respondent argued that she was dismissed because she was not acquiring the relevant experience and that her performance was not satisfactory. The EAT pointed out that:

> One could well understand anyone, let alone an employment tribunal well used to specious reasons as a cover for discrimination, to conclude that the real reason was something different (para 10).

16.25 Pregnancy need not be the only reason for the less favourable treatment complained of. In *O'Neill v Governors of St Thomas More RCVA Upper School*,[35] the EAT held that the crucial question was whether the dismissal was on the ground of pregnancy, motive being irrelevant. The EAT stated that the event or fact which is said to have caused the discrimination 'need not be the only or even the main cause of the result complained of ... it is enough if it is an effective cause'. Thus,

33 This test was established in the House of Lords in *R v Birmingham City Council ex p Equal Opportunities Commission* [1989] AC 1155; [1989] IRLR 173 and *James v Eastleigh BC* [1990] 2 AC 751; [1990] IRLR 288. It was followed by the EAT in *O'Neill v Governors of St Thomas More RCVA Upper School* [1996] IRLR 372.

34 [2001] IRLR 502; see futher para 16.47.

35 [1996] IRLR 372. Once it has been shown that the less favourable treatment was related to the woman's pregnancy, it is irrelevant that the employer may have a 'good' motive, such as a desire to protect the woman.

where pregnancy is a factor without which the less favourable treatment would not have happened, as in *O'Neill*, this is enough to establish discrimination.

16.26 Stereotyping is likely to be discriminatory (see para 3.49). An assumption that, for example, a woman's job will become less important to her after childbirth, so that she can be given less responsible work, will be discriminatory if acted upon.[36]

16.27 The proof of direct discrimination, including questions of what evidence is relevant, is covered in chapter 3.

Pregnancy and indirect discrimination

16.28 Indirect sex discrimination occurs where a provision, criterion or practice applies equally to women and men, has an adverse impact on one sex and cannot be justified by the employer (see chapter 7).[37] The most common forms of indirect sex discrimination involve the less favourable treatment of part-time workers, and the refusal to allow women to work child-friendly hours.

16.29 The dismissal of a woman because she is working part-time may be an unfair and discriminatory dismissal (see chapters 7 and 21). The less favourable treatment of those taking parental leave or time off for dependants may amount to unlawful indirect discrimination. Both male and female employees can take such leave, so the less favourable treatment of those who do take it would not be direct discrimination (unless a woman taking leave would be treated less favourably in similar circumstances than a man, or vice versa). But more women are likely to take such leave and so women will be disproportionately disadvantaged by less favourable treatment associated with it. The main principles relating to indirect discrimination are covered in chapter 7. Indirect discrimination as it relates to part-time workers is set out in chapter 21.

36 See *Hurley v Mustoe* [1981] IRLR 208, EAT, discussed at para 3.50.

37 The definition of indirect discrimination under the SDA 1975 was amended (in the context of employment-related discrimination alone) by the BP Regs 2001, which came into effect on 12 October 2001. Indirect discrimination is covered in chapter 7.

Dismissal (including redundancy)

16.30 It is still common for women to experience pregnancy-related dismissal and other forms of detrimental treatment associated with their pregnancy and/or absence on maternity leave.[38] This is despite the fact that a dismissal on such grounds is likely to amount to unlawful sex discrimination, as well as both 'automatic' and 'ordinary' unfair dismissal. Dismissal will also be automatically unfair if related to taking other family leave (parental or dependants leave and as from 6 April 2003 adoption and paternity leave) (see chapters 20 and 21).

Definitions of dismissal

16.31 An employee may be 'dismissed', for the purposes of claiming unfair dismissal under the ERA 1996 (or a discriminatory dismissal under the SDA 1975), in any of the following circumstances:

- an express dismissal by the employer;[39]
- the non-renewal of a fixed-term contract by the employer;[40]
- constructive dismissal, where the employee terminates the contract (with or without notice) in circumstances where:
  - she is entitled to terminate it without notice because the employer has committed a fundamental breach of contract which has affected the heart of the employment relationship (this could be a breach of an express term or of an implied term such as the right to mutual trust and confidence between employer and employee[41]), and
  - she resigned as a result of the breach, and
  - she did not delay unduly in accepting the employer's breach as an action terminating the contract. If she does delay she might be taken to have affirmed the contract.

Constructive dismissal is further discussed at para 15.101.

38 The NACAB report 'Birth rights' (March 2001, available from the NACAB website at www.nacab.org.uk), found that there was widespread incidence of unlawful pregnancy-related dismissal or detrimental treatment (see chapter 3 of the report).

39 ERA 1996 s95(1)(a).

40 Ibid s95(1)(b); see *Nelson v Western Health and Social Service Board*, ET 8871935D, 1994 (unreported), in which a woman who had been employed on a series of short-term contracts did not have her contract renewed after she had an ectopic pregnancy.

41 ERA 1996 s95(1)(c) and SDA 1975 s82(1A). See, eg, *Western Excavating v Sharp* [1978] ICR 221 and *Cantor Fitzgerald International v Callaghan* [1999] IRLR 234.

Return to a different job

16.32 Where the employer does not allow an employee to return to the same job after maternity leave but offers her another job, this may be a dismissal (see para 15.42).

Written reasons for dismissal

16.33 If an employee is dismissed while she is pregnant or when her maternity leave is terminated by dismissal, the employer must give written reasons for the dismissal.[42] In other cases, provided the employee has been employed for a year, an employer must provide written reasons on request.

Dismissal during maternity leave

16.34 If an employee's maternity leave is ended by dismissal, her maternity leave ends at the same time. She will continue to be entitled to any statutory maternity pay but not to other benefits – see MPL Regs 1999 reg 7(5).

Possible claims arising during and after pregnancy and maternity leave

16.35 Dismissing a woman because she is pregnant, has had a child, is on maternity leave or has taken maternity leave is likely to be:

- discrimination on grounds of sex;
- an 'automatic' unfair dismissal under ERA 1996 s99 (see para 15.111);[43]
- an 'ordinary' unfair dismissal provided she is an employee with one year's service (see para 15.103).

16.36 Where the dismissal occurs during ordinary maternity leave, additional maternity leave or parental leave, the employee may be entitled to notice pay (see para 18.31).

42 ERA 1996 s92(4) and MPL Regs 1999 reg 20.
43 Read with MPL Regs 1999 reg 20.

Discriminatory dismissals

16.37 Unlawful direct discrimination occurs when a woman is dismissed during the period from the beginning of her pregnancy to the end of her maternity leave, for reasons related to her pregnancy or maternity leave. In the *Tele Danmark A/S* case,[44] the ECJ summarised the important principles relating to pregnancy-related dismissals. The decision is essential reading. The court held that:

> It was also in view of the risk that a possible dismissal may pose for the physical and mental state of pregnant workers, workers who have recently given birth or those who are breastfeeding, including the particularly serious risk that they may be encouraged to have abortions, that the Community legislature, in Article 10 of Directive 92/85 [the PWD], laid down special protection for those workers by prohibiting dismissal during the period from the start of pregnancy to the end of maternity leave (para 26).

16.38 The ECJ further stated that, during that period, there is no exception to or derogation 'from the prohibition on dismissing pregnant workers, save in exceptional cases not connected with their conditions where the employer justifies the dismissal in writing'. The ECJ made the following important points:

- the protection afforded by community law of a woman during pregnancy and after childbirth cannot be dependent on whether her presence at work during the period corresponding to maternity leave is essential to the proper functioning of the undertaking in which she is employed;
- the nature and extent of the economic loss incurred by the employer as a result of the woman's absence because of pregnancy has no bearing on the discriminatory character of the dismissal;
- these same principles apply to fixed-term contracts. It made no difference that the employee did not tell her employer of her pregnancy when she was employed. Nor did it matter whether the employer was a large or small one. Neither the ETD nor the PWD makes any distinction according to the duration of the employment relationship.

16.39 The dismissal of a woman because she is working part-time, or for reasons relating to her taking parental or dependants leave (and in the future, adoption or paternity leave), may be unlawful indirect discrimination (see chapter 21). SDA 1975 s82(1)(A) confirms that

44 Case 109/00 [2001] ECR I-06913; [2001] IRLR 853.

'dismissal' under that Act includes constructive dismissal. So, for example, if a woman resigns because she is not allowed to work reduced hours (and the refusal is not justifiable), she may claim sex discrimination and unfair and discriminatory constructive dismissal (see para 16.31 above) Similarly, if she resigns because she is not allowed to take dependants leave, and can prove indirect sex discrimination (because it is mainly women who take such leave), she may claim unfair and discriminatory constructive dismissal.

16.40 A summary of pregnancy dismissal cases is at paras 16.17–16.21. The two main UK decisions are *Webb* and *Brown v Rentokil*. In *Webb v EMO Air Cargo (UK) Ltd (No 2)*[45] the House of Lords followed the ECJ decision in the same case and held that dismissal of a woman because she was pregnant was discrimination in itself, without the need for a comparison with a man in a similar situation (see para 16.13).

16.41 In *Brown v Rentokil*[46] the ECJ held that dismissal for a reason resulting from pregnancy is automatically sex discrimination and that it does not matter whether the employer's decision is based on pregnancy or on the consequences of pregnancy. It does not matter how a man would be treated in similar circumstances. So the dismissal of a woman for a reason relating to her absence on account of a pregnancy-related illness (which lasted from the beginning of her pregnancy until the start of her maternity leave) was direct sex discrimination.

16.42 Also significant is the decision of the EAT in *Rees v Apollo Watch Repairs plc.*[47] The applicant was dismissed while on maternity leave because the employers found that her replacement was more efficient. The EAT held that she would not have been dismissed had she not been on maternity leave. 'But for' the fact of her maternity leave, no replacement would have been appointed and no comparison would have been made between her performance and that of her replacement. Following *Webb*, this meant that the dismissal was discriminatory. The EAT took the view that the protection afforded to women on maternity leave would be drastically curtailed if an employer was able to defeat a complaint of direct discrimination by saying that he or she preferred the replacement worker, a state of affairs which had arisen solely as a result of the dismissed worker's pregnancy and therefore because of her sex.

16.43 'Protected status' is lost on return from maternity leave (see *Hertz*,

45 [1995] IRLR 645.

46 Case 394/96 [1998] ECR I-4185; [1998] IRLR 445.

47 [1996] ICR 466, EAT.

paras 16.17 and 16.22 above, in which the ECJ held that a pregnancy-related illness that appears after maternity leave should be treated in the same way as any other illness). After maternity leave, the question is whether the woman has been treated less favourably than a man, ignoring any pregnancy-related absence. A woman may, however, have greater protection under the ERA 1996 (see para 16.48 below).

Women on fixed-term contracts

16.44 In the *Tele Danmark* case[48] the ECJ ruled that the dismissal of a woman who was recruited on a six-month contract and who was, because of her pregnancy, unable to work for a substantial part of that period, was unlawful discrimination under the ETD. Two months after the applicant's appointment she told her employer that she was pregnant, and that her estimated week of confinement was about two months later. She was dismissed on the ground that she had not told her employer that she was pregnant when she was recruited. The ECJ held that the same principles apply to women on fixed-term contracts as to women with permanent contracts (see above). The size of the employer's undertaking and financial loss suffered was not relevant (see para 16.38).

16.45 In *Jimenez Melgar v Ayuntamiento de Los Barrios*[49] the ECJ held that the non-renewal of a fixed-term contract which was motivated by the worker's pregnancy was unlawful direct discrimination contrary to the ETD. This is the same as the position under the SDA 1975.

Liability for discrimination

16.46 An employer will generally be liable for discrimination by an employee (see chapter 31).[50] Anything done by a person as agent for another person, with the authority of that other person, will be treated as done by both.[51]

16.47 The applicant in *Lana v Positive Action Training in Housing (London) Ltd*[52] had a training contract with the respondents who placed her with a firm (WM). Her placement was cancelled by the firm in connection with her pregnancy, and the respondents then terminated her

48 Case 109/00 [2001] ECR I-06913; [2001] IRLR 853.

49 Case 438/99 [2001] ECR I-06915; [2001] IRLR 848, although the ECJ held that the dismissal was not a breach of the PWD.

50 SDA 1975 s41(1).

51 Ibid s41(2).

52 [2001] IRLR 502.

training contract on the grounds that circumstances beyond their control had prevented their continuing with the contract. The EAT held that the firm was acting as the agent of the respondents for the purpose of fulfilling the training obligations which the respondents had entered into with Ms Lana. The respondents were, therefore, liable for any discrimination by their agent, provided that the discrimination was done with the respondents' authority.[53] 'Authority' means authority to do an act which is capable of being done in a discriminatory way. The question, therefore, was why the agent terminated Ms Lana's contract. If it was for a reason related to her pregnancy, the termination was discriminatory and Ms Lana would also have had a claim against the agent firm under SDA 1975 s14 (see para 31.41). The case was remitted to a different tribunal.

Automatically unfair dismissal

16.48 ERA 1996 s99 and MPL Regulations 1999 reg 20 provide that it is automatically unfair to dismiss a woman where the reason or principal reason for the dismissal is connected with:

a) The pregnancy of the employee[54] (for example, pregnancy-related sickness, miscarriage, abortion – see para 16.13). Note that the employer must know or believe that the woman is pregnant. This provision is not specifically limited in time and may apply, for example, to dismissal for a pregnancy-related illness which occurs after the end of maternity leave provided it is 'connected' with her pregnancy – see paras 16.43 and 16.51.
b) The fact that the employee has given birth to a child.[55] This only applies where the dismissal takes place during the employee's ordinary or additional maternity leave and brings the leave to an end, so is narrower in time than (a) above.[56] If a woman is dismissed in connection with the continuation of the illness after her return to work she may be able to establish direct or indirect sex discrimination (though not automatic sex discrimination because of *Hertz*).

53 This is the effect of SDA 1975 s41(2) which provides that 'anything done by a person as agent for another person with the authority (whether express or implied, and whether precedent or subsequent) of that other person shall be treated ... as done by that other person as well as by him' – see further para 31.41.

54 MPL Regs 1999 reg 20(3)(a).

55 Ibid reg 20(3)(b).

56 Ibid reg 20(4).

c) The application of a health and safety requirement or recommendation (as defined by ERA 1996 s66(2) (see para 16.58).[57]
d) The fact that the woman took or tried to take the benefit of ordinary maternity leave.[58] This applies, for example, where a woman takes the benefit of or asserts her rights to her contractual terms and conditions during ordinary maternity leave.[59]
e) The fact that a woman:
   (i) took or sought to take additional maternity leave,
   (ii) took or sought to take parental leave, or
   (iii) took or sought to take time off to look after a dependant.[60]
f) The fact that the employee declined to sign a workforce agreement (see para 19.16).[61]
g) The fact that the employee, being either a representative of the workforce or a candidate in an election, carried out any activities in this capacity (see para 19.16).[62]

16.49 The dismissal of a woman on maternity leave will also be automatically unfair where it is wholly or mainly by reason of redundancy, and the employer has failed to offer her an available suitable vacancy (see below).[63] Finally, the selection of a woman for redundancy for a reason related to (a)–(g) above will also result in an automatically unfair dismissal.[64]

16.50 In *Brown v Stockton-on-Tees BC*[65] the House of Lords held that an employer faced with deciding which of several employees to make redundant must disregard the inconvenience that inevitably will result from the fact that one of them is pregnant and will require maternity leave. If he does not do so and makes that absence the factor that determines the pregnant woman's dismissal, that dismissal will be deemed unfair [now ERA 1996 s99].

> I have not doubt that section 60 must be seen as a part of social legislation passed for the specific protection of women and to put them on an equal footing with men. Although it is often a

57 Ibid reg 20(3)(c).
58 Ibid reg 20(3)(d).
59 Ibid reg 19(3).
60 Ibid reg 20(3)(e) From April 2003 this protection will be extended to employees who take adoption and paternity leave.
61 Ibid reg 20(3)(f).
62 MPL Regs 1999 reg 20(3)(g).
63 Ibid reg 20(1)(b).
64 Ibid reg 20(2).
65 [1989] AC 20; [1988] IRLR 263, emphasis added.

considerable inconvenience to an employer to have to make the necessary arrangements to keep a woman's job open for her whilst she is absent from work in order to have a baby, *that is a price that has to be paid as a part of the social and legal recognition of the equal status of women in the work place.*

16.51 A number of important points should be noted:

- The question for the court in deciding whether an automatically unfair dismissal has occurred concerns the reason or principal reason for the dismissal. This differs from the test for discrimination, in which the reason need not even be the principal reason provided it is the effective reason or a substantial reason.
- Where a woman on maternity leave is made redundant she is entitled to be offered any suitable alternative employment that exists. She has priority over other employees and failure to offer her such employment will make the dismissal automatically unfair.[66]
- A woman dismissed after the end of her maternity leave may be able to claim automatically unfair dismissal under MPL Regulations 1999 reg 20(3)(a) even though, because of the decisions in *Hertz* and *Larsson*, she could not make a successful claim of automatic sex discrimination under the SDA 1975.[67] She could, of course, claim sex discrimination by reference to an appropriate male comparator. Regulation 20(3)(a) may apply if she is dismissed for pregnancy-related sickness, in which case she may argue that the dismissal was due to her pregnancy.[68] In *Caledonia Bureau Investment and Property v Caffrey*[69] the EAT held that the dismissal of a woman when she failed to return to work after the expiration of her maternity leave due to post-natal depression was for a reason related to her pregnancy within ERA 1996 s99(1)(a) and was therefore automatically unfair. Thus, if a pregnancy-related illness which arose during maternity leave was the direct cause of dismissal, s99(1)(a) applied to make the dismissal automatically

66 MPL Regs 1999 reg 10. Note, however, there that may be a conflict between the rights of women on maternity leave and, eg, the duty to make reasonable adjustments for disabled employees (see chapter 6).

67 Automatic protection from discrimination ceases at the end of maternity leave, after which the ordinary rules apply and a woman must show that she has been treated less favourably than a man in a similar situation.

68 Note that such a claim cannot be made where the dismissal occurs after return from maternity leave and the reason for the dismissal is that the employee has given birth to a child or she has been made redundant and has not been offered suitable alternative work.

69 [1998] IRLR 110.

unfair. This decision was reached despite the EAT's recognition that the approach left employers exposed for a considerable period of time to the consequences of having to keep such an employee on the books.[70]

- Protection from automatically unfair dismissal starts from day one of employment, as is the case with protection against sex discrimination.

Exceptions to protection from 'automatic' unfair dismissal on grounds of pregnancy

16.52 In three cases, outlined below, a woman may find that her dismissal in connection with pregnancy does not qualify as automatically unfair. These are:

a) In the case of woman returning from additional maternity leave (or from April 2003 additional adoption leave), where:
   (i) the number of employees (including those employed by an associated employer) is five or less, and
   (ii) it is not reasonably practicable for the employer (or a successor) either to allow the woman to return to the same job or to offer her a suitable job that is appropriate for her to do in the circumstances.[71]
b) In the case of a woman returning from additional maternity leave or a person returning from parental leave in excess of four weeks (see para 19.1), where:
   (i) it is not reasonably practicable for a reason other than redundancy for the employer (or successor) to allow the woman either to return to the same job or to a suitable job which is appropriate in the circumstances, and
   (ii) an associated employer offers her a suitable appropriate job, and
   (ii) she accepts or unreasonably refuses that offer.[72]
c) In the case of a woman seeking to return from additional maternity leave, where she failed to notify her employer, when properly required to do so, of the date of childbirth and her intention to return at the end of her additional maternity leave (see para

70 It is not clear whether this interpretation will be followed as it is different from the automatic protection from discrimination that ceases at the end of maternity leave (see para 16.13).
71 MPL Regs 1999 reg 20(6).
72 Ibid reg 20(7).

18.20).[73] The woman will still be entitled to return but the employer can take disciplinary action against her for failing to provide the appropriate notice. It is proposed that this provision will be repealed where the EWC is on or after 6 April 2003.

16.53 The onus is on the employer to show that the exceptions discussed at (a) and (b) above apply.[74] There have been very few cases in which they have been used. Even if a dismissal is prevented from being automatically unfair by virtue of (a), (b) or (c), it may still amount to discrimination contrary to the SDA 1975 and/or to an 'ordinary' unfair dismissal.

16.54 In any case in which a woman can show that, 'but for' her pregnancy or absence on maternity leave (ordinary or additional), she would have been able to return to the same (or even similar) job, she will have a discrimination claim. Where, for example, a small employer decides permanently to replace a woman absent on maternity leave, she is likely to succeed in claiming direct discrimination under the SDA 1975 (see para 16.42). Such a woman may also have an ordinary unfair dismissal claim, given that such claims are not precluded by ERA 1996 s98.

'Ordinary' unfair dismissal

16.55 A discriminatory dismissal is also likely to be an unfair dismissal. However, an employee can only bring a claim if he or she has been employed for one year (see also para 15.98).

16.56 In *Clarke v Eley (IMI) Kynock Ltd*[75] the EAT ruled that it did not follow, as a matter of law, that an indirectly discriminatory dismissal was an unfair one, but that it would need very special circumstances to find such a dismissal fair. Fair grounds for dismissal are:

- capability or qualifications;
- conduct;
- redundancy;
- statutory requirements;
- some other substantial reason justifying dismissal (see chapters 12 and 15).

16.57 The employer must show that the reason for the dismissal is a potentially fair one and the ET must then decide whether the employer

73 Ibid reg 12(2).
74 Ibid reg 20(8).
75 [1982] IRLR 482.

acted reasonably or unreasonably in treating it as a sufficient reason for dismissing the employee. Account will be taken of the merits of the case and procedural fairness. The employer must carry out reasonable investigations in accordance with the *Burchell* test.[76] Ordinary unfair dismissal is considered in more detail at para 15.103.

Dismissal in health and safety cases

16.58 Where the reason or principal reason for an employee's dismissal is that he or she has asserted health and safety rights in a manner covered by the ERA 1996, the dismissal may also be automatically unfair under ERA 1996 s100.[77] This provision would apply where an employee is dismissed because she leaves or proposes to leave her place of work because she believes that she is in serious and imminent danger which cannot otherwise be avoided. So, for example, if a pregnant woman walks out of a workplace situation in which she perceives a serious danger to herself or the foetus, any resulting dismissal would be automatically unfair. Note that a woman cannot succeed with claims for automatically unfair dismissal under both s99 (see para 16.48) and s100 of the 1996 Act, given that there cannot be two 'principal' reasons for dismissal.

Dismissal for assertion of statutory right

16.59 It is automatically unfair to dismiss an employee where the reason or principal reason is that he or she has brought proceedings to enforce a statutory right, such as the right to time off for ante-natal care or sick dependants or other maternity or parental rights.[78]

Dismissal of maternity replacement

16.60 A maternity locum, employed to cover an employee's maternity leave, will have no protection from dismissal until he or she has been employed for a year except where the dismissal is related to pregnancy or is otherwise unlawfully discriminatory. Even if he or she has been employed for a year, the dismissal will be fair if:

- the employer has informed the employee in writing that his or her

76 ERA 1996 s98(4) and *British Home Stores v Burchell* [1978] IRLR 379, EAT.
77 Ibid s100.
78 ERA 1996 s104. As with ERA 1996 s100 there can only be one 'principal' reason.

employment will end when the woman returns from maternity leave; and
- the employer dismisses the locum to give the work back to the returning woman.[79]

Protection from detriment

16.61 An employee must not be subjected to any detriment (ie, treated less favourably) by any act or deliberate failure to act, by her employer for any of the following reasons:
- she is pregnant;
- she has given birth;
- she is the subject of a health and safety requirement or recommendation;
- she took or sought to take the benefits of ordinary maternity leave, additional maternity leave, parental leave or dependants leave (and from 6 April 2003 adoption and paternity leave);
- she declined to sign a workforce agreement or, as a representative of members of the workforce or a candidate in an election, she performed the functions of a representative or candidate.

16.62 To suffer 'detriment' is to be put at a disadvantage. There is no apparent difference between 'detriment' under the MPL Regulations 1999 and 'detriment' under ERA 1996 s6(2)(b). In *McGuigan v TG Baynes*[80] the EAT held that marking a woman down in a redundancy exercise because she had criticised her employer's attitude to women was a detriment even though it made no difference to the decision to select her for redundancy. The EAT ruled that 'subjecting to any other detriment' under the SDA 1975 is to be given its 'broad, ordinary meaning and it is plain that almost any discriminatory conduct by an employer against an employee in relation to his or her employment will be rendered unlawful by s6(2)(b)' (see also para 15.70).

16.63 A dismissal cannot also be a detriment under SDA 1975 s6(2)(b), although 'dismissal' and 'detriment' may be argued in the alternative where it is not clear if there has been a dismissal (where, for example, a claim rests on an alleged constructive dismissal).

79 Ibid s106.

80 EAT 1114/97 (unreported, available on LEXIS).

Claims round-up

16.64 It is important to bear in mind the multitude of claims available to a worker dismissed or subject to other detriment in connection with pregnancy, maternity and/or parental leave. By way of summary, they include:

- sex discrimination;
- 'automatic' unfair dismissal;
- 'ordinary' unfair dismissal;
- wrongful dismissal;
- dismissal on health and safety grounds;
- dismissal for asserting a statutory right;
- unlawful 'detriment' contrary to ERA 1996 s47A and MPL Regulations reg 19.[81]

81 Remedies are dealt with in detail in C Palmer and J Wade, *Maternity and Parental Rights* (LAG, 2001).

CHAPTER 17

Health matters: ante-natal care, sickness and health and safety

continued

Key points

17.1
- All pregnant women are entitled to paid time off for ante-natal care.
- Any less favourable treatment of a woman because of pregnancy-related absence will be unlawful discrimination.
- Employers have specific duties towards pregnant employees and new and breastfeeding mothers which include a duty to carry out a risk assessment to assess any work-related risks to the health and safety of a new or expectant mother or of her baby. If the assessment reveals a risk the employer must:
  - consider whether preventive or protective action can be taken, and, if this would not avoid the risk;
  - vary the woman's working conditions to avoid the risk or, if that is not possible;
  - offer the woman suitable alternative work or, if this is not possible;
  - suspend the woman on full pay for as long as necessary to avoid the risk.

Background and statutory framework

17.2 This chapter covers the right to paid time off for ante-natal care, employers' health and safety obligations and the position of women who have pregnancy-related sickness absence. Dismissal on pregnancy-related grounds is covered in chapter 16.

17.3 The Pregnant Workers Directive (PWD), which prompted many improvements in the protection of pregnant women and new mothers, places great emphasis on health and safety protection. It is of crucial importance to pregnant women and new mothers that employers have strict responsibilities to assess whether there are any health and safety risks associated with their employment and, if there are, to remove the risks.

17.4 The main statutory provisions relevant in this context are:

- Employment Rights Act (ERA) 1996 ss55–57, which set out the right to paid time off for ante-natal care;
- Management of Health and Safety at Work Regulations (MHSW

Regulations) 1999[1] regs 3, 4, 10, 16–18 and Sch 1, which provide for a risk assessment in respect of new or expectant mothers and set out information and notification requirements;
- ERA 1996 ss66–70, which set out the provisions relating to the right to alternative work on health and safety grounds and suspension on full pay;
- Health and Safety at Work Act (HSWA) 1974, which sets out employers' general health and safety obligations.

In addition to the specific legal rights, account must be taken of employers' duties:
- under the Sex Discrimination Act (SDA) 1975 – not to discriminate (see para 16.11);
- under the Equal Pay Act (EqPA) 1970 – not to deprive a woman of benefits (such as sick pay) because she is pregnant;
- under the ERA 1996 – not to subject women to detriment in connection with pregnancy and maternity leave (see paras 16.48 and 16.61);
- under the ERA 1996 – not to dismiss a woman for a reason relating to pregnancy or maternity leave;
- under ERA 1996 ss13–23, not to make an unlawful deduction from wages.

Right to reasonable paid time off for ante-natal care

17.5 The right is available to employees (not other workers) irrespective of length of service and hours of work. Excluded is employment as master, or crew member of a fishing vessel where the employee is paid only by a share in the profits, and employment in the police service (although police have similar protection under the Police Regulations 1995) (see para 16.9).[2]

What is ante-natal care?

17.6 Ante-natal care is care of a pregnant employee who 'has, on the advice of a registered medical practitioner, registered midwife or registered health visitor, made an appointment to attend at any place for the purpose of receiving ante-natal care'.[3] The legislation is no more

1 SI No 3242.
2 ERA 1996 ss199(2) and 200.
3 Ibid s55.

specific than this. The Under-Secretary of State for Employment stated in the parliamentary debates on the Trade Union Reform and Employment Rights Bill that ante-natal care would include relaxation classes.[4]

Requirement for appointment for ante-natal care and certificate

17.7 There is no obligation for the employee to provide proof of the appointment in relation to the first ante-natal visit, though she should obtain the employer's permission to attend. For subsequent appointments, however, if the employer so requires, the employee must provide:

- written proof of the appointment (such as an appointment card); and
- a certificate or note from a registered medical practitioner, midwife or health visitor stating that she is pregnant.[5]

Can the employer refuse time off for ante-natal care?

17.8 An employer can refuse paid time off if the employee fails to comply with the requirements set out in the preceding paragraph. Provided the documents set out there are provided on request, time off cannot otherwise be unreasonably refused. The amount of time off needed for ante-natal care is fairly standard for most women who have uncomplicated pregnancies. There are unlikely to be many situations when an employer could justify refusing time off, although it would not be reasonable for a woman to take part of every day off in order to attend relaxation classes, or to take off more than a few hours at a time. Time off should be allowed for waiting and travelling to and from the appointment.

17.9 A decision about what is reasonable will depend on the particular facts of the case. There is no obligation on the woman to arrange ante-natal care outside working hours or to make up the time she spends

4 House of Commons Standing Committee F, cols 291–292, 12 January 1993; HL Debates, cols 531–532, 25 March 1993. See also the government booklet, *Maternity Rights: A Guide for Employers and Employees* (URN99/1191).

5 ERA 1996 s55(2) and (3).

away from work.[6] Women are frequently not able to choose the time of their appointment.

17.10 A casual worker who is an employee is also entitled to time off to attend an ante-natal appointment at a time when she would normally work. The employer cannot avoid paying her by saying she was not obliged to attend work on the day of the appointment, if it is usually a day when she would attend work.[7]

The right to be paid for time off

17.11 An employee who takes time off for ante-natal care is entitled to be paid as though she was at work.[8] Once the employer has allowed time off, she must be paid at the normal hourly rate which will normally be clear from the agreed terms and conditions or contract of employment. If the employee's hours vary from week to week, these will be averaged over 12 weeks.[9]

Breach of ante-natal provisions

17.12 An employee can complain to an employment tribunal (ET) on the following grounds:

- That she has been unreasonably refused time off.
- That her employer has refused to pay her, in whole or in part, for the time she has taken off work in connection with ante-natal care.[10]
- That she has been dismissed (this includes having been selected for redundancy) because she has taken time off, in which case the reason for the dismissal will be connected to her pregnancy and will be automatically unfair.[11] In *Mains v MD Homes*,[12] for example, an ET accepted that a woman who was dismissed at the end of a

6 *Edgar v Giorgione Inns*, ET 20961/86 (unreported); *Bland v Laws (Confectioners) Ltd*, ET 31081/84 (unreported) and *Sajil v Carraro t/a Foubert's Bar*, COIT 1890/34 (unreported). See also *Holmwood v Smith & Gardener Ltd*, ET 6001899/98 (unreported), in which the ET held that the employer could not insist that the woman take her weekly day off on the days when she had an ante-natal appointment.

7 *Pollard v Greater Manchester Passenger Transport Executive*, ET 2402582/96 (unreported).

8 ERA 1996 s56.

9 Ibid s56(2) and (3).

10 Ibid s57. For time limits see para 17.13.

11 Ibid s99 and MPL Regs 1999 reg 20(3)(a).

12 ET 11642/96 (unreported).

probationary period because of poor attendance connected with her ante-natal appointments was dismissed for a reason connected with pregnancy, and that the dismissal was automatically unfair. Such a dismissal is also likely to be an ordinary unfair dismissal and to be unlawful discrimination contrary to the SDA 1975 (see para 16.13).

- That she has been dismissed and the reason or principal reason for dismissal is that she has alleged that she has been denied the right to paid time off, or complained to a tribunal. Such a dismissal will also be automatically unfair as victimisation connected with the assertion of a statutory right (see para 16.59).[13]
- That she has been subjected to a detriment contrary to Maternity and Parental Leave etc Regulations 1999[14] reg 19. Any less favourable treatment (falling short of dismissal) of a woman because she has either taken or tried to take paid time off for ante-natal care may amount to 'subjecting her to a detriment' contrary to reg 19. Although the regulation makes no express mention of the right to time off for ante-natal care, it can be argued that ante-natal care is so inextricably linked to pregnancy that the real reason for such detriment would be connected with the employee's pregnancy.
- That the action of the employer in withholding wages to which she is entitled in respect of time she has taken off work in connection with ante-natal care amounts to an unlawful deduction of wages.[15]
- That she has been subject to unlawful sex discrimination by reason of anything in the points listed above (see para 16.13).

Remedies

17.13 Where an employer refuses to give time off for ante-natal care or refuses to pay her (in full or in part), a woman can complain to an ET within three months from the date of the appointment (subject to the ET's power to extend time, see para 32.44). If the tribunal upholds the woman's complaint, it must make a declaration to that effect and award compensation equal to the amount the woman should have received had she been given the time off.[16]

17.14 Where a woman is dismissed (or resigns and successfully claims

13 ERA 1996 s104.

14 SI No 3312.

15 ERA 1996 Pt II.

16 Ibid s57(3), (4) and (5).

constructive dismissal) she may receive the basic award for unfair dismissal if she has a year's service or more. She may also, if eligible to claim unfair dismissal or if she is successful in a discrimination claim, recover loss of past and future earnings and injury to feelings (see chapter 33). If she has been subjected to detriment short of dismissal the tribunal can award such compensation as is just and equitable (see para 33.12). For time limits see chapter 32.

Sickness during pregnancy

17.15 It is now clear that any less favourable treatment of a woman because of pregnancy-related sickness is sex discrimination. In *Brown v Rentokil*[17] the applicant was absent for 26 weeks, from almost the beginning of her pregnancy until she went on maternity leave. She was dismissed, in accordance with her contract, after 26 weeks' sickness absence. The European Court of Justice (ECJ) held that the contractual rule was discriminatory (see para 16.41), referring to *Webb*[17a] where the ECJ held that the PWD was introduced precisely because of:

> ... the harmful effects which the risk of dismissal may have on the physical and mental state of women who are pregnant, have recently given birth or breastfeeding, including the particularly serious risk that pregnant women may be prompted voluntarily to terminate their pregnancy (para 21).

Examples of less favourable treatment on grounds of pregnancy-related sickness

17.16 The decision in *Brown* means that it will be discriminatory, for example:

- To dismiss a woman for any absence related to her pregnancy. In *Stephenson v FA Wellworth & Co Ltd*[18] the Northern Ireland Court of Appeal held that 'an illness arising out of and occurring during pregnancy is to be treated in the same way as the pregnancy itself'.
- Not to give a woman her appraisal (and as a result a pay rise) because she is absent as a result of her pregnancy or maternity leave (see *Thibault*,[19] para 16.36).

17 Case 394/96 [1998] ECR I-4185; [1998] IRLR 445.

17a Case 32/93 [1994] ECR I-3657. See para 16.19 above.

18 DCLD 32.

19 Case C-136/95 *Caisse Nationale d'Assurance Vieillesse des Travailleurs Salariés (CNAVTS) v Thibault* [1998] ECR I-2011; [1998] IRLR 399, ECJ.

- Not to consider a woman for promotion because she is absent as a result of her pregnancy.
- To refuse to give a woman a bonus because of pregnancy-related absence. In *GUS Home Shopping Ltd v Green and McLaughlin*,[20] for example, the employer did not pay a 'loyalty bonus' (in respect of co-operation and goodwill while work was transferred from their location to another place of work) to two women who were either off work with pregnancy-related illness or on maternity leave throughout the whole of the period covered by the loyalty bonus. The EAT upheld the ET's decision that this was due to pregnancy or absence on maternity leave and so was discrimination (see para 18.26).
- To treat a woman less favourably at any time (ie, during or after her pregnancy or maternity leave) as a result of pregnancy-related absence. Thus, any period when a woman has a pregnancy-related absence should be ignored by the employer. For example, even if sickness is a factor in a redundancy selection exercise, pregnancy-related absence must not be taken into account irrespective of when the redundancy takes place.[21]
- To dismiss a woman following a disciplinary hearing which she was incapable of attending because of a pregnancy-related condition. Direct sex discrimination occurs when employee is prevented from defending herself at a disciplinary hearing due to her absence for a pregnancy-related reason.[22]

What is pregnancy-related sickness?

17.17 Pregnancy-related sickness includes morning sickness, fatigue, threatened or actual miscarriage or any other illness connected with the pregnancy. Proof that the illness is pregnancy-related may need to be obtained from the woman's doctor.

'Ordinary' sickness followed by pregnancy-related sickness

17.18 If pregnancy has exacerbated an existing medical condition, this should be sufficient to establish that the resulting illness is 'related to

20 [2001] IRLR 75.

21 See Case C-394/96 *Brown v Rentokil* [1998] ECR I-4185; [1998] IRLR 445.

22 *Abbey National plc v Formoso* [1999] IRLR 222.

pregnancy'. If the employee would not have been dismissed 'but for' the pregnancy-related sickness absence, the dismissal will be discriminatory and probably also unfair (see para 16.41).[23]

Sick pay during absence and its effect on statutory maternity pay

17.19 EC law is breached by a contractual sick pay scheme which provides that sick pay is generally payable to sick employees, while excluding those with pregnancy-related sickness. In the *Pedersen* case,[24] employees absent from work due to illness were entitled to full pay unless they were pregnant. The ECJ held that it was a breach of article 141 to deny a pregnant woman the same sick pay as other workers because she was unfit for work because of her pregnancy. This decision will apply to similar cases in the UK.

17.20 An employee's statutory right to sick pay and incapacity benefit will not be affected by her pregnancy. However, if she is on reduced pay during the period when her SMP is calculated (the 8 week/2 month period prior to the 15th week before EWC) it will affect her entitlement to earnings-related statutory maternity pay (see para 17.50).

Sickness on return from maternity leave

17.21 If sickness prevents a woman from returning to work at the end of her maternity leave, she should be treated in the same way as any other sick employee. The employer should not assume that the woman will not return or that she has given up her right to return. Her sickness should be investigated in the normal way. If the sickness is related to her pregnancy it may be automatically unfair to dismiss her (see para 16.48).[25]

23 See *O'Neill v Governors of St Thomas More RCVA Upper School* [1986] IRLR 372, EAT.

24 Case C-66/96 *Handels-og Kontorfunktionaerernes Forbund i Danmark, acting on behalf of Berit Hoj Pedersen v Faellesforeningen for Danmarks Brugsforeninger and Dansk Tandlaegeforening and Kristelig Funktionaer-Organisation* [1998] ECR I-7327; [1999] IRLR 55.

25 But see MPL Regs 1999 reg 20(4).

Health and safety[26]

17.22 EC law puts health and safety at the forefront of maternity rights, imposing a duty on employers to carry out a risk assessment and to avoid or control any risks. It is accepted that any risk is liable to damage not only the mother but also the child. The European Commission Guidance also recognises that conditions that may be considered acceptable in a normal situation may no longer be so during pregnancy.[27] The Health and Safety Executive (HSE) has issued guidance for employers.[28]

17.23 Apart from the specific duties to women of childbearing age, account must also be taken of:

- employers' general duty of care (both in tort and through an implied term in employees' contracts) to take reasonable care of the health and safety of their workers;
- employers' statutory duty under the HSWA 1974 to 'ensure so far as is reasonably practicable' the health, safety and welfare at work of their workers (which includes contract workers). The duty is to take reasonable care to lay down safe systems of work, to provide a safe place of work, to provide safe plant and equipment and a safe working environment.[29]

Main duties towards women who are pregnant or have recently given birth or are breastfeeding

17.24 Under the MHSW Regulations 1999 employers are required to:

- Step 1: carry out risk assessments in relation to these workers;
- Step 2: take any necessary steps to avoid any risk identified in a risk assessment;
- Step 3: inform the employees of any risks identified and steps taken to deal with them;
- Step 4: if necessary, alter working conditions or hours of work to eliminate any identified risk;

26 For more detailed analysis see C Palmer and J Wade, *Maternity and Parental Rights* (Legal Action Group, 2001).

27 EC guidelines on the assessment of chemical, physical and biological agents and industrial processes considered hazardous for the safety or health of pregnant workers who have recently given birth or who are breastfeeding October 2000 – see the HSE website at www.hse.gov.uk.

28 *New and Expectant Mothers at Work – A Guide for Employers*, £6.25 from the HSE. A revised version taking the EC guidelines into account is due out in late 2002.

29 The detail is outside the scope of this book.

- Step 5: if a risk cannot be avoided by the above steps, offer suitable alternative work;
- Step 6: if there is no available alternative work, suspend on full pay.

17.25 Steps 1–3 apply to workers as well as employees but there is an exception for the master or crew of a sea-going ship.[30] Each of these obligations will be considered in turn.

Step 1: Duty to carry out risk assessment

17.26 Employers have a general duty to safeguard the health and safety of their workers.[31] The aim of the risk assessments mentioned above is to identify the protective or preventive measures necessary to ensure health and safety.

17.27 Employers are obliged to carry out a risk assessment wherever there are women of childbearing age in the workplace and the work is of a kind which could involve risk, by reason of her condition, to a new or expectant mother or her baby.[32] The risk may come 'from any processes or working conditions, or physical, biological or chemical agents'.[33] In *Day v T Pickles Farms Ltd*,[34] the Employment Appeal Tribunal (EAT) confirmed that the duty to carry out a risk assessment applies irrespective of whether there actually is a new or expectant mother working in the establishment if there are women of a child-bearing age. The EAT also held that a failure to carry out a risk assessment can amount to a detriment under the SDA 1975 (see para 15.70). A 'new or expectant mother' is an employee who is pregnant; who has given birth (or experienced a stillbirth[35]) within the previous six months; or who is breastfeeding (even if breastfeeding lasts for longer than six months).

17.28 In *Taylor v Thomas Bee Ltd*[36] an ET found that there were very

30 MHSW Regs 1999 reg 2(1).

31 MHSW Regs 1999 reg 3(1).

32 Ibid reg 16(1).

33 Ibid reg 16(1)(b).

34 [1999] IRLR 217. MHSW Regs 1999 reg 16 appears to have improved upon the protection offered by the PWD which only covers women who are pregnant, who have recently given birth or who are breastfeeding. In *Hardman v Miss M Mallon t/a Orchard Lodge Nursing Home* EAT/360/01, 25 March 2002, the EAT held that there 'is a duty on all employers to carry out a risk assessment but in respect of a pregnant worker a failure to carry out such a risk assessment in our judgment *is* discrimination'.

35 MHSW Regs 1999 reg 1.

36 (1996) DCLD 28.

serious shortcomings in the way the risk assessment had been carried out. An instruction to a pregnant woman to continue working with cleaning materials that made her unwell was unreasonable, and her dismissal for refusing to comply with the order was unfair. In addition, the dismissal was for a reason connected with the pregnancy and so was automatically unfair and discriminatory (see paras 16.37 and 16.48).[37]

Scope of risk assessment

17.29 The risk to the new or expectant mother or to her baby can come 'from any processes or working conditions, or physical, biological or chemical agents' including those set out in Annexes I and II to the PDW. Such risks include (but are not limited to):

- extremes of heat or cold;
- movements and postures, travelling, mental and physical fatigue and other physical burdens connected with the activity of the worker, such as heavy lifting;
- exposure to lead or lead derivatives;
- exposure to chemical agents.[38]

17.30 The European Commission's guide refers to working with VDUs, stress (including post-natal depression), passive smoking, work at heights, facilities (including rest rooms).[39] The HSE guide also lists aspects of pregnancy that may affect work, including:

- morning sickness (which may be exacerbated by nauseating smells);
- backache (affected by standing/manual handling/posture);
- varicose veins (affected by standing/sitting);
- frequent visits to toilet;
- increase in size;
- tiredness (affected by overtime and evening work).

These should be taken into account when carrying out a risk assessment.

37 In *Tapp v Chief Constable of Suffolk*, DCLD 33, a pregnant trainee police constable was taken off an important training course because of her pregnancy and suspended from work. An ET upheld her sex discrimination claim, finding that a risk assessment would have shown that this was not necessary for her to be suspended as with minor adjustments she could have carried on with the training course and successfully completed it.

38 MHSW Regs 1999 reg 16(1)(b).

39 November 2000; this is also set out in the HSE guide.

17.31 The risk at work from any infectious or contagious disease (such as German measles) will give rise to obligations on the part of the employer under the MHSW Regulations 1999 only where it is greater than a new or expectant mother may be exposed to outside the workplace.[40]

17.32 The employer must take account of the following:

- current knowledge about hazards including the guidelines drawn up by the European Commission;
- the HSE booklet, *New and Expectant Mothers at Work – A Guide for Employers*;[41]
- the extent of the risk, so that the more serious the risk the more precautions should be taken;
- the need to review the assessment if there are any changes or it is no longer valid.[42]

An employer with five or more employees must record the findings of the risk assessment.[43]

Step 2: Duty to take steps to prevent or avoid any risks

17.33 The employer must make appropriate arrangements for the effective planning, organisation, control, monitoring and review of the required preventive and protective measures which include:

- adapting the workplace and equipment;
- developing a prevention policy in relation to technology, organisation of work, working conditions and social relationships;
- appropriate instructions to employees.[44]

There must be suitable rest facilities for pregnant women and nursing mothers.[45]

Step 3: Provision of information to workers

17.34 The employer must provide employees with comprehensible and relevant information on the risks to their health and safety which

40 MHSW Regs 1999 reg 16(4).

41 See note 28 above.

42 MHSW Regs 1999 reg 3(3).

43 Ibid reg 3(6).

44 This would cover, for example, redistribution of work (such as heavy lifting) to avoid risks to pregnant women.

45 Workplace (Health, Safety and Welfare) Regulations 1992 SI No 2051, as amended.

have been identified by the assessment together with any preventative and protective measures taken.[46]

17.35 The following duties (steps 4, 5 and 6) only apply if the employee has notified the employer in writing of her pregnancy and/or birth and/or that she is breastfeeding.[47] Although it is preferable to give written notice of pregnancy, a sick certificate making it clear that the sickness is pregnancy-related may be sufficient.[48] However, if the employer makes a written request that the employee provide a doctor's or midwife's certificate confirming the pregnancy, the employee must produce this within a reasonable time.[49] Failure to do so means that the employer is under no obligation to take the action set out below.

Step 4: Alteration of working conditions

17.36 Once an assessment has revealed a risk which cannot be otherwise prevented or avoided, the employer must, 'if it is reasonable to do so, and would avoid such risks, alter [the] working conditions or hours of work' of the pregnant, post-partum or breastfeeding woman.[50] The question is whether it is reasonable for the employer to alter working conditions or hours of work. The adjustment should also be reasonable for the employee. A change of hours which may make the work easier in the view of the employer, may in fact prevent the woman taking her child to school, so would not be reasonable for her. If the woman's working conditions or hours are altered, she should continue to receive the same pay and benefits (see para 17.41 below).

Step 5: Offer of suitable alternative work

17.37 If it is not reasonable to alter an employee's working conditions or hours of work, or if any such alteration would not avoid the risk, the employer must offer the woman any suitable alternative work which is available.[51] In order to qualify as 'suitable' such work must be:

- of a kind which is both suitable in relation to her and appropriate for her to do in the circumstances; and

46 MHSW Regs 1999 reg 10.

47 This applies to employees only.

48 *Day v T Pickles Farms Ltd* [1999] IRLR 217.

49 MHSW Regs 1999 reg 18(2) (a).

50 Ibid reg 16(2) and PWD art 5(1).

51 ERA 1996 s67(1).

- such that the terms and conditions are not substantially less favourable to her than her existing terms and conditions.[52]

Account should also be taken of the following factors:

- the status or grade of the worker's current job and the alternative work offered;
- the pay and other remuneration or payments in kind involved;
- the working conditions, hours of work and location of the work; and
- the travelling time to work.

17.38 The employee's condition should be taken into account – it may be unreasonable to expect her to travel further to work than usual, or to work antisocial hours, even though the job offered is in every other respect 'suitable'. To this extent at least the test may be different from the test applied in redundancy situations (see para 15.145).

17.39 In *British Airways v Moore and Botterill*[53] the EAT upheld an ET decision that ground work given to pregnant cabin crew was not suitable because they received only basic pay and not their flying allowances. The ET ruled that the difference in pay meant that the ground-based job was substantially less favourable than the women's normal jobs and so could not be said to be suitable. The ET treated the employees as suspended because, although they were working, they were neither performing the work they normally performed nor doing suitable alternative work.[54] Thus they were entitled to both their basic pay and allowances. If ground work had entitled staff to the same pay, such work would have been suitable.

17.40 An employee who unreasonably refuses suitable alternative work may be suspended and will forfeit her right to be paid while she is suspended.[55]

Step 6: Suspension on full pay

17.41 Where there is a risk from any processes or working conditions or physical, biological or chemical agents and it is not reasonable to alter the working conditions or hours of work and there is no suitable alternative work, then the employer must suspend the employee from

52 Ibid s67(2).
53 [2000] IRLR 296.
54 ERA 1996 s66(3)(b).
55 Ibid s68(2).

work for so long as is necessary to avoid the risk identified by the risk assessment.[56]

17.42 An employee is only entitled to be paid if, as a result of a requirement or recommendation which is 'relevant' for the purposes of the ERA 1996, she is suspended because she is pregnant, has recently given birth or is breastfeeding.[57] The Secretary of State has specified a suspension under the MHWS Regulations 1999 as a suspension under a 'relevant' requirement.[58]

17.43 Not all suspensions from work are as a result of the MHWS Regulations 1999 and therefore not all are as a result of a 'relevant' requirement or recommendation. For example the Secretary of State has recently specified a suspension under the Merchant Shipping and Fishing Vessels (Health and Safety at Work) Regulations 1997[59] as a 'relevant' requirement,[60] thus closing a loophole which excluded pregnant seafarers from full health and safety protection.[61]

17.44 An employee is to be treated as suspended only as long as she continues to be employed by her employer but is not provided with work or (disregarding alternative work for the purposes of step 5 above) does not perform the work she normally performed before her suspension.[62] In other words, if she is performing suitable alternative work she will not be treated as suspended but if she is, for example, working odd days or working in a lower paid job which clearly does not constitute a suitable alternative, she must be treated as suspended.

17.45 An employee who is suspended is entitled to be paid as though she

56 MHSW Regs 1999 reg 16(3). The PWD has similar provisions: art 5 states that, if the risk cannot be avoided by preventive measures, the employer must temporarily adjust the woman's working conditions or working hours. If this is not 'technically and/or objectively feasible or cannot reasonably be required on duly substantiated grounds', the employer must take the necessary measures to move the worker concerned to another job. Failing this, she must be granted leave for the whole of the period necessary to protect her safety or health.

57 ERA 1996 s66(1) and (2).

58 Suspension from Work (on Maternity Grounds) Order 1994 SI No 2930, specified suspensions under MHWS Regs 1999 regs 16(3) and 17 as suspensions under a relevant requirement.

59 SI No 2962.

60 Suspension from Work on Maternity Grounds (Merchant Shipping and Fishing Vessels) Order 1998 SI No 587. The master and crew of a sea-going ship are not protected by the MHSW Regs. See para 17.5 above.

61 The loophole was closed as a result of the decision of the EAT in *Iske v P&O Ferries (Dover) Ltd* [1997] IRLR 401.

62 ERA 1996 s66(3).

63 Ibid s68.

was working unless she has unreasonably refused suitable alternative work.[63]

Effect of suspension on commencement of maternity leave

17.46 A woman who is suspended in the last six weeks of her pregnancy is likely to be treated as absent on account of her pregnancy. She will therefore have to start her maternity leave at the beginning of the six weeks before the expected week of childbirth (see para 18.11). Her maternity pay period would start at the same time. Where the employee's EWC is on or after 6 April 2003, the six weeks will be reduced to four.

Calculation of pay during suspension

17.47 An employee who is entitled to be paid will be entitled to full pay at the normal rate[64] until her maternity leave period begins (see para 18.21). In the absence of any contractual provision, this is calculated in accordance with ERA 1996 ss200–229 which define a 'week's pay'. The calculation date depends on when the suspension occurs.[65] If an employee has a contractual right to be paid while suspended, she must not receive less than she would receive using the statutory calculation. She is not entitled to claim both her contractual and her statutory entitlement.[66]

Rights during suspension

17.48 While she is suspended an employee's contractual and statutory rights as an employee continue.[67] A woman who suffers a detriment as a result of a suspension by, for example, being denied access to promotion or being refused a bonus or commission that is due can make a complaint to an ET.[68] She can also make a complaint of sex discrimination.[69]

64 ERA 1996 s69.

65 Ibid s225(5)(b).

66 Ibid s69(3).

67 A government spokesman stated, during the Trades Union Reform and Employment Rights Bill debates, that 'the employee's contract continues while she is suspended ... Her contractual rights are maintained. No special provision for that is required.' House of Commons Standing Committee F, cols 430–431, 14 January 1993.

68 ERA 1996 s47C; MPL Regs 1999 reg 19(2)(c)

69 Case 333/97 *Lewen v Denda* [1999] ECR I-7243; [2000] IRLR 67.

17.49 A woman who is dismissed because she is suspended will have a claim for automatically unfair dismissal[70] and sex discrimination (see paras 16.37 and 16.48).

Sickness or health and safety suspension?

17.50 A woman who is experiencing a health and safety problem may not be aware of her right to health and safety protection, or her employer may have refused to suspend her. If she is off sick, rather than on a health and safety suspension, she may suffer the following consequences:

- she may receive occupational sick pay, but this may run out before she recovers;
- if she is receiving statutory sick pay during the calculation period for statutory maternity pay (SMP) she may not satisfy the earnings condition for SMP and so may not qualify for SMP, or may qualify only for a far lower rate than that expected;[71]
- if her sick note does not state that her illness is pregnancy-related, her sickness record will be affected and her employer may regard her attendance record as unsatisfactory;
- if her sick note does state that her illness is pregnancy-related her employer may still wrongly take it into account.

17.51 The MHSW Regulations 1999 provide that, if it is not reasonable to alter a woman's working conditions or hours of work, or if such actions would not avoid the risk at issue, the employer must suspend her for so long as is necessary to avoid such risk.

17.52 Under the ERA 1996, an employee can complain about failure to pay her while suspended and a failure to offer any suitable available alternative work, but there is no provision that allows her to enforce the right to be suspended. If she is off sick for health and safety reasons, she will have to argue that her absence should be regarded as a suspension on pregnancy grounds and that she has not been provided with appropriate work or is not doing the work she normally performed before the suspension.

70 ERA 1996 s99; MPL Regs 1999 reg 20(3)(c). She may also have a claim for ordinary unfair dismissal provided she has been employed for at least one year.

71 SMP is calculated according to the woman's earnings in the eight-week or two-month calculation period ending with the fifteenth week before the expected week of childbirth. If the woman is ill during this time and only receiving statutory sick pay, she may not be earning sufficient to qualify for SMP. SMP is outside the scope of this book. See C Palmer and J Wade, *Maternity and Parental Rights* (LAG, 2001).

17.53 In *Hickey v Lucas Service UK Ltd*[72] an ET found that a woman who had been absent during her pregnancy on sick leave certified by her doctor had in fact been suspended from work due to a health and safety risk. She was therefore entitled to be paid her normal pay rather than statutory sick pay during that period. Mrs Hickey's employer had failed to carry out a risk assessment on her job as a stores person although the work involved heavy lifting, and despite the fact that she and her representative had raised her concerns very clearly. She had no alternative but to go off sick for reasons that were clearly pregnancy-related. The ET decided that her absence fell within the meaning of 'suspension on maternity grounds' set out in ERA 1996 s66 (see para 17.41).[73]

Special provisions relating to nightwork

17.54 If a pregnant woman or new mother doing nightwork obtains a certificate from her doctor or midwife stating that it is necessary for her health and safety that she should not be at work, the employer must follow steps five and six above. If no suitable work is available, she must be suspended on full pay for so long as is necessary for her health and safety.[74] So if a woman who is unfit to continue night work is unable to switch to day work offered to her, she is entitled to be suspended. Many women cannot work during the day because of their childcare responsibilities. 'Suitable' work would, further, be work at the same level of pay as nightwork, even if other daytime workers were paid less than nightworkers.[75]

Compulsory leave after childbirth

17.55 It is a criminal offence for an employer to permit an employee to work within two weeks of the birth. It is also a breach of the ERA 1996.[76]

72 ET 1400979/6 (unreported).

73 This is only an ET decision and so is not binding on other tribunals. Arguably, the failure to make provision for a woman to enforce her right to be suspended is a breach of the PWD. The PWD provides that a woman must, if necessary to avoid a health and safety risk, be granted leave if her working conditions cannot be adjusted or she cannot be moved to another job. The directive also states that Member States must introduce measures necessary to enable workers to enforce their rights (art 12) (see chapter 10 for effect of PWD).

74 MHSW Regs 1999 reg 17 and PWD art 7.

75 See *British Airways v Moore and Botterill* [2000] IRLR 296.

76 ERA 1996 s72 and MHSW Regs 1999 reg 8.

The prohibition is for four weeks if the woman works in a factory or workshop.[77] The HSE has responsibility for enforcing this.

Breastfeeding

17.56 A woman cannot postpone her return to work because she is breastfeeding. Neither can an employer delay a woman's return to work because she is breastfeeding unless she is suspended on full pay under the above health and safety duties. There is, apparently, no limit to the length of time a woman may continue breastfeeding and retain health and safety protection. The MHSW Regulations 1999 define a 'new or expectant mother' as an employee who is pregnant; who has given birth within the previous six months; or who is breastfeeding. An employer must ensure there is no risk to her for as long as she is breastfeeding. The EC guidelines, referred to at para 17.22, provide that an absence of facilities for breastfeeding such as a clean room and a fridge could constitute a health and safety risk.

77 Public Health Act 1936 s205, as amended.

Remedies

17.57

Health and safety duty to a pregnant woman or new mother	Who is protected	Relevant section or regulation
Common law duty of care	All workers	
Implied duty of care in contract of employment	Employees	
Congenital Disabilities (Civil Liability) Act 1976	The child	s1
HSWA 1974	Employees;[78] Persons other than employees, eg agency workers and self-employed contractors	s2 s3
MHSW Regs 1999	For risk assessment: all new or expectant mothers *and their babies*, eg agency workers and self-employed contractors	reg 16(1)
	For all subsequent health and safety measures: employees[79] only	reg 16(2) and (3)
	The master and crew of a sea-going ship are not protected in respect of shipboard activities[80]	reg 2
ERA 1996	Employees only (see para 11.34 above for definition and exclusions)	ss66–70

78 Defined by s53 as 'an individual who works under a contract of employment'. This includes police officers who are treated as being an employee by reason of s51A.

79 See para 11.34 for who is an employee.

80 Other health and safety regulations apply to women working on merchant shipping and fishing vessels, see para 17.43.

The following protection is thus available to the following classes of worker:

Who?	Protection	Legislation
All new and expectant mothers and their babies, eg, employees, agency workers	• Common law duty of care • Right to risk assessment and general steps to protect health and safety	HSWA 1974 and MHSW Regs 1999
'Employees' only (ERA definition)	All the above, plus: • implied term in contract • right to be offered suitable alternative work • right to be suspended from work on full pay	 ERA 1996 s67 ERA 1996 s68
A child of the worker or employee	• Right to sue in respect of a disability • Right to risk assessment and general steps to protect health and safety	Congenital Disabilities (Civil Liability) Act 1976 MHSW Regs 1999
Master and crew of a sea-going ship	• Common law duty of care • No protection in respect of shipboard activities from MHSW Regs 1999 but protection under merchant shipping legislation	

Less favourable treatment on health and safety grounds

17.58 SDA 1975 s51 allows an employer to discriminate against a woman in order to comply with a statutory provision concerning the protection of women in connection with pregnancy, childbirth, or health risks specifically affecting women. This is subject, however, to the positive health and safety duties set out above and it does not allow an employer to refuse to appoint (or promote) a woman or to dismiss her because her employment in a particular job would contravene health and safety requirements. She should instead be moved to alternative work or suspended on full pay. The employer could, however, insist on a woman working in a safe environment, provided she does not suffer financially, even if she objects.

17.59 It is unlawful discrimination to refuse to appoint a woman, to dismiss her or to treat her less favourably because of health and safety requirements. In *Habermann-Beltermann*[82] the applicant was employed as a night worker. German law prohibited pregnant women working at night. As a result, when she became pregnant the applicant was dismissed. The ECJ held that the termination of an indefinite contract by reason of pregnancy could not be justified on the ground that a statutory prohibition temporarily prevented the employee from performing night work. The court held that to allow an employer to dismiss a woman because of her temporary inability, during pregnancy, to perform night-time work would be contrary to the objective of protecting women.

17.60 Similarly, in *Mahlburg*[83] a pregnant employee was refused a job on the grounds that, because of the German statutory prohibition on night work by pregnant woman, she would not be able to start work until after her maternity leave. The employer claimed that its refusal to employ her was not directly because of her pregnancy (which would have been sex discrimination), but because health and safety law prohibited a pregnant woman from doing that job. The ECJ, pointing out that the job was of indefinite duration while the pregnancy was not, ruled that the protection due to a pregnant woman was paramount. The employer had discriminated against her on grounds of sex. The ECJ also pointed out that an employer could not justify direct sex discrimination on the grounds that it would be too expensive to wait for a woman to finish her maternity leave.

17.61 In addition to protection from discrimination and dismissal, it is unlawful to subject a woman to a detriment (ie, to treat her less favourably) where she has been suspended on health and safety grounds.[84] The meaning of 'detriment' is further considered at para 16.62.

82 Case 421/92 *Habermann-Beltermann v Arbeiterwohlfahrt, Bezirksvetbank Ndb/Opf eV* [1994] ECR I-1657; [1994] IRLR 364.

83 Case 207/98 *Mahlburg v Land Mecklenburg-Vorpommern* [2000] ECR I-00549; [2000] IRLR 276.

84 ERA 1996 s66(2) and MHSW Regs reg 19(2)(c).

CHAPTER 18

Maternity leave

continued

Key points

18.1 • All women employees are entitled to 18 weeks' ordinary maternity leave (OML) irrespective of their length of service or hours of work; this will increase to 26 weeks where the expected week of childbirth is on or after 6 April 2003.

- Women employed by the same employer for one year (at the beginning of the eleventh week before the expected week of childbirth (EWC)) are entitled to additional maternity leave (AML) which begins at the end of OML and ends 29 weeks after the Sunday before the birth. From April 2003 the qualifying period will be 26 weeks from the notification week and AML will be 26 weeks which will follow immediately after the 26 weeks OML.
- The earliest maternity leave can start is the beginning of the eleventh week before the EWC, unless the baby is born before this date.
- Entitlement to maternity leave turns on the provision of notice by the employee to the employer of the EWC and the date she intends to take leave.
- The assumption is that a woman entitled only to OML will return to work at the end of the 18 weeks (26 weeks where the EWC is on or after 6 April 2003) and that a woman entitled to AML will return at the end of the 29 weeks (52 weeks where the EWC is on or after 6 April 2003). These return dates require no notice from her.
- If a woman intends to return from maternity leave before the end of the maximum period to which she is entitled, she must give 21 days' notice to the employer of her intended date of return. This is to increase to 28 days where the EWC is on or after 6 April 2003.
- With the exception of pay (narrowly defined), all contractual rights continue during OML.
- While the contract continues during AML, the Employment Rights Act (ERA) 1996 requires the continuation of only limited contractual rights during this extended period of leave.
- Statutory holiday accrues throughout OML and AML.

Background and statutory framework

18.2 ERA 1996 (as amended by the Employment Relations Act 1999 and with effect from 6 April 2003 further amended by the Employment Act 2002), together with the Maternity and Parental Leave etc. Regulations (MPL Regulations) 1999[1] provide the statutory framework for maternity leave.[2] A summary of the changes for employees with an EWC of 6 April 2003 or later is included at para 16.55 onwards, but the regulations were in draft at the time of writing so may be subject to change.

18.3 This chapter gives a brief summary of maternity leave rights. It does not cover maternity pay or maternity allowance. Rights during OML and AML are complex and the area is dealt with only in brief in this book.[3]

18.4 There are two types of maternity leave:

- OML of 18 weeks for all women employees irrespective of length of service to be increased to 26 weeks where the EWC is on or after 6 April 2003;
- AML for women employees with one year's service (at the beginning of the eleventh week before the EWC). AML follows on from OML and ends 29 weeks from the Sunday preceding the actual birth. The qualifying period for AML will change from 6 April 2003 and AML will be 26 weeks following 26 weeks OML.

18.5 A woman may be entitled to more favourable rights under her contract or by an agreement (verbal or written) with her employer. Where there is a statutory and contractual right, the employee may take advantage of whichever right is, in any respect, more favourable.[4]

Entitlement to ordinary and additional maternity leave

18.6 Only employees, as distinct from the broader category of 'workers', are entitled to maternity leave. Also excluded from the right to maternity leave are:

1 SI 1999 3312. Where the EWC is on or after 6 April 2003 these will be amended by the Maternity and Parental Leave (Amendment) Regulations 2002 (currently in draft form).

2 The amended provisions apply to all those whose EWC was on or after 30 April 2000.

3 For a detailed account of all maternity rights see C Palmer and J Wade, *Maternity and Parental Rights* (LAG, 2001).

4 MPL Regs 1999 reg 21. This is called a composite right.

- members of the armed forces;[5]
- police officers, though they have similar rights under the Police Regulations;[6]
- share fisherwomen.[7]

18.7 Provided the appropriate notice is given, all employees are entitled to OML irrespective of the hours they work, their length of service, and whether permanent or temporary. The non-renewal, on the same terms, of a fixed-term contract that expires during maternity leave is a dismissal. Such a dismissal will bring the woman's employment to an end, although she will still be entitled to statutory maternity pay if she qualified for it prior to dismissal. Rights on dismissal are covered at para 16.35.

18.8 An employee is entitled to AML if she is entitled to OML (ie, if she gives the required notice), and where the EWC is before 6 April 2003, she has been continuously employed by the same employer for a year at the beginning (ie, on the Sunday) of the eleventh week before the EWC.[8] Continuous employment includes any week in which the employee has a contract of employment (written or oral) with her employer. Thus an employee may be on sick leave, on holiday, or on unpaid leave and still have a contract of employment.[9]

Notice requirements for ordinary and additional maternity leave

Normal notice

18.9 Where the EWC is before 6 April 2003 an employee must notify her employer at least 21 days before her OML starts or, if that is not reasonably practicable, as soon as reasonably practicable, of:

- the fact that she is pregnant; and
- the EWC; and
- the date on which she intends to start her maternity leave (provided it is not earlier than the beginning of the eleventh week

5 ERA 1996 s192, which extends rights to the armed forces, has not yet been implemented.
6 Ibid s200.
7 Ibid s199(2), though see also s199(7) for provisions relating to other mariners.
8 MPL Regs 1999 reg 5. Where the EWC is on or after 6 April 2003, the employee must have been employed for 26 weeks by the 15th week before EWC.
9 ERA 1996 s10. There are special rules when an absence from work, when there is no contract, may be treated as continuous employment.

before the EWC); the employer may request that this notice be given in writing.[10]

The various elements of the notice may be given at different times if the employee wishes.

18.10 Where the EWC is on or after 6 April 2003, the notice must be given during the fifteenth week before the EWC and if the employee wants to change the date of the start of her maternity leave she will be required to give 28 days' notice. Within 28 days of receiving the employee's notice (or revised notice) the employer must write to the employee stating the date she is due to return – on the assumption she will take her full leave.

The 'trigger rule'

18.11 If a woman is absent wholly or partly because of pregnancy from the first day after the beginning of the sixth week before the EWC, her maternity leave will be automatically triggered.[11] (Many employers in practice overlook short absences during this period with the result that women may choose to begin their leave later.) If a woman's leave is triggered by the six week (four weeks from 2003) rule, she may not be able to give her employer appropriate notice of the start of her leave. Whether she has or not she must inform her employer, as soon as reasonably practicable:

- of the fact that she is pregnant;
- of the date of her EWC; and
- that her absence is pregnancy-related or that she has given birth.[12]

The employer may ask for this notice to be in writing.[13] Sickness that is unrelated to pregnancy does not trigger maternity leave, and the woman can take sick leave in the normal way. Whether the sickness is related to pregnancy will be a question for medical opinion.

18.12 Where the EWC is on or after 6 April 2003 the trigger will occur at the beginning of the fourth week before the EWC.

Early birth

18.13 Where the woman gives birth before the date she notified her employer she intended to start her leave, and so has been unable to give

10 MPL Regs 1999 reg 4.
11 MPL Regs 1999 reg 6(1)(b).
12 Ibid reg 4(3).
13 Ibid reg 4(5).

the appropriate notice, she must inform her employer as soon as reasonably practicable of the EWC and that she has given birth. This notice must be given in writing if the employer so requires.

Medical certificate

18.14 In all cases in which it requested by the employer, the woman must provide a medical certificate signed by a doctor or registered midwife and giving the EWC.[14]

Notice required for contractual rights

18.15 Where the woman claims the benefit of more favourable contractual terms but there is no provision in the contract (or by agreement with the employer) for notice, the statutory provisions regarding notice will apply.[15]

Not reasonably practicable

18.16 It will be a question of fact whether it was reasonably practicable for the employee to give the required notice of the start of her maternity leave. Absence from work because of pregnancy complications may constitute a good reason for failure to give such notice, particularly if the woman was unaware of her obligations. If the woman has just started with a new employer she may not be able to give the full notice.[16]

Failure to comply with notice requirements

18.17 A woman is only entitled to statutory OML and AML and to the benefit of her terms and conditions during OML if she has given the required notice before going on leave,[17] or it was not reasonably practicable for her to do so. But the continuation of the woman's contract of employment during the maternity leave does not turn on her provision of notice to the employer. Her employment will continue, therefore, unless and until terminated by herself or the employer.

14 Ibid reg 4(1)(b), which provides that a woman claiming SMP must produce such a certificate.

15 *Kolfor Plant Ltd v Wright* [1982] IRLR 311, EAT.

16 28 days where the EWC is on or after 6 April 2003.

17 MPL Regs 1999 reg 4.

Termination by the employer of the woman's contract, for a reason related to her pregnancy, childbirth or maternity leave, will be automatically unfair under ERA 1996 s99 (see para 16.48). It may also be an ordinary unfair dismissal (see para 16.55)[18] and may be discriminatory contrary to the Sex Discrimination Act (SDA) 1975 (see para 16.37). If the woman is disciplined this may be an unlawful detriment contrary to ERA 1996 s47C and MPL Regulations 1999 reg 19 (see para 16.61).

Further notice provisions relating to additional maternity leave

18.18 The notice provisions for AML are exactly the same as for OML as set out above. Where the EWC is on or before 6 April 2003, once leave has begun the employer may, not earlier than 21 days before the end of a woman's OML period (ie, after 15 weeks of OML), make a written request for *written* confirmation of:

- the date of childbirth; and
- whether the woman intends to return to work at the end of her AML period.[19]

The request must be in writing and accompanied by a statement explaining how the employee determines the date on which her AML will end and warning of the consequences of failure to reply.[20] It is probably not necessary for the employer to advise the woman that she can, by giving 21 days notice, return earlier. It would, however, be good practice to do so.

18.19 The employee must provide the written confirmation within 21 days of receiving the request for information.[21] She is not obliged to give an actual date of her return, but need only state her intention to return. This notice requirement will no longer apply where the EWC is on or after 6 April 2003.

18 See *Thurisamy v Alma Enterprises Ltd*, ET 27627/94 (unreported) where a woman was dismissed because she failed to give proper notice won her claim for unfair dismissal.

19 MPL Regs 1999 reg 12(1).

20 Ibid reg 12(3).

21 Ibid reg 12(1).

Failure to comply with notice provisions for additional maternity leave

18.20 A woman's failure to respond to the employer's proper written request for information about her intention to return does not operate to bring her contract of employment to an end. The employer may, however, take 'appropriate disciplinary action' against her. In addition, she will lose her protection under ERA 1996 s47C and MPL Regulations 1999 reg 19 against being subjected to a 'detriment' (see para 16.61) and her protection under ERA 1996 s99 and MPL Regulations 1999 reg 20 from 'automatic' unfair dismissal (see para 16.48).[22] Having said this, an employer which decides to take disciplinary action must follow its disciplinary procedure (see para 32.15). If the action leads to dismissal the woman, although unable to claim automatically unfair dismissal, may still have a claim for ordinary unfair dismissal (see para 16.55) and/or discrimination contrary to the SDA 1975 (see para 16.37).

Commencement of leave

18.21 A woman cannot start her maternity leave before the start of the eleventh week before the EWC (unless the baby is born before this date). The EWC is the date specified by the MATB 1 certificate[23] or any other certificate from the midwife or doctor.

18.22 The woman can generally decide when her maternity leave starts. The start date will be either:

- the date she chooses and notifies to her employer (see para 18.9); or
- the date she gives birth; or
- where she has a pregnancy-related absence during the six weeks (four weeks where the EWC is on or after 6 April 2003) before the EWC, the beginning of this absence (see para 18.11).[24]

Any contractual provision to the effect that the woman must start her maternity leave at a specified time is overridden by the statute, which

22 Ibid reg 12(2).

23 This is the certificate issued by the woman's doctor or midwife after week 26 of pregnancy showing the date on which the baby is due. If no MAT B1 is available it is usually possible for a woman to produce other certification of the EWC.

24 MPL Regs 1999 reg 6.

allows her to choose the start date (subject to the 'trigger rule' and premature birth). Maternity leave runs continuously from the actual day it starts.[25]

Dismissal or resignation before the eleventh week before the expected week of childbirth

18.23 A woman who is dismissed or resigns before she reaches the eleventh week before the EWC will not be employed and will not have the right to maternity leave (OML or AML).[26] But dismissal for a reason related to her pregnancy will generally be automatically unfair and discriminatory (see paras 16.37 and 16.48). Furthermore, the dismissed woman may still be entitled to statutory maternity pay.[27]

Statutory rights during ordinary and additional maternity leave

18.24 Although a woman on maternity leave continues to be an employee, she has no right to receive full pay during OML or AML unless this is provided by the contract of employment or agreed with the employer. Apart from wages or salary, most rights and benefits continue during OML. The same cannot be said of AML.

Rights during ordinary maternity leave

18.25 The ERA 1996 provides for the maintenance of terms and conditions of employment (apart from remuneration) during OML.[28] Remuneration is defined as sums payable to an employee 'by way of wages or salary'.[29] It is clear that a woman is not entitled to full pay during OML. Nor is she entitled to statutory or contractual sick pay. She is, however, entitled to the maintenance of other benefits such as:

25 Ibid reg 7(1).

26 A mere statement by the employee that she does not intend to return, without specifying a date from which her resignation is to take effect, should not count as a resignation. If the employee subsequently complies with all the notice provisions, she should be entitled to return.

27 See C Palmer and J Wade, *Maternity and Parental Rights* (LAG, 2001).

28 ERA 1996 s71(4)–(6) and MPL Regs 1999 reg 9.

29 MPL Regs 1999 reg 9.

- accrued holiday leave;
- the benefit of a company car;
- mortgage subsidy;
- pension contributions paid by the employer;[30]
- other 'perks'.

18.26 Entitlement to a bonus or commission will depend on the type of bonus and commission. It may be argued that a bonus paid at Christmas or paid to all workers should be paid on the basis that, if it is paid to all workers equally, it is not part of the woman's pay or wages.[31] On the other hand, if the bonus payment is attributable to periods during which the woman has been on OML or AML and it qualifies as 'pay or wages' under MPL Regulations 1999 reg 9, she will not be entitled to it. The position is far from clear. Bonuses and commission relating to work done prior to maternity leave should be paid.[32] But any contractual bonus or commission which relates to work which would have been done during the woman's maternity leave is likely to qualify as 'pay or wages' within the Regulations and she is not, therefore, likely to be entitled to payment of it.

18.27 The contract continues during OML, as does continuity of service for both contractual and statutory rights. The position in relation to notice pay is set out at para 18.31.

Rights during additional maternity leave

18.28 During AML the position is more complex.[33] Although the contract continues,[34] the employee is entitled under the ERA 1996 only to the benefit of the employer's implied obligation to her of trust and confidence and any terms and conditions of her employment relating to:

- her contractual notice period (and, arguably, notice pay – see below);

30 ERA 1996 s71 and see Social Security Act 1989 Sch 5, para 3, which provides that the employer must continue to pay pension contributions as though the woman was working normally and irrespective of whether she receives SMP or returns to work at the end of her leave.

31 See *Gus Home Shopping Ltd v (1) Green (2) McLaughlin* [2001] IRLR 75, EAT, discussed at para 17.16.

32 See Case 333/97 *Lewen v Denda* [1999] ECR I-7243; [2000] IRLR 67.

33 ERA 1996 s73 and MPL Regs 1999 reg 17.

34 MPL Regs 1999 reg 17 does not explicitly provide that the contract continues but this is the effect of the regulation and the DTI guidance confirms this.

- compensation if she is made redundant;
- disciplinary or grievance procedures.[35]

18.29 The employee is bound by her implied obligation of good faith to the employer and by any terms and conditions of employment relating to:

- notice;
- the disclosure of confidential information;
- the acceptance of gifts or other benefits; or
- the employee's participation in any other business.[36]

18.30 In relation to other benefits the position will depend, with one exception, on the terms of the contract or agreement between the employer and employee. The exception is that entitlement to statutory holiday under the Working Time Regulations 1998[37] continues to accrue throughout AML as well as OML, although contractual holiday does not accrue during AML by virtue of the ERA 1996.[38]

Notice pay during ordinary maternity leave, ordinary maternity leave and parental leave

18.31 The ERA 1996 provides for payment of notice pay 'in respect of any period during which the employee is absent from work wholly or partly because of pregnancy or childbirth'.[39] This does not apply where the contractual notice period required from the employer is at least one week longer than the relevant statutory minimum.[40] Employees with contractual rights in excess of the legal minimum will not, therefore, benefit even from the statutory right to notice pay. Nor will they be able to pursue a right to notice pay through an equal pay claim (see para 18.33). Finally, as we saw at para 18.25 above, their contractual rights to 'pay', including notice pay, do not apply during OML or AML.

35 Ibid reg 17(1)(a).
36 Ibid reg 17(1)(b).
37 SI No 1833.
38 Though the contractual position may be more favourable.
39 ERA 1996 ss86–91.
40 Ibid s87(4).

Discrimination and equal pay during ordinary and additional maternity leave

18.32 Although the law is uncertain, there is a distinction between:

a) the less favourable treatment of a woman as a worker – in relation, for example, to appraisals, training, promotion, dismissal – where protection from discrimination continues from the beginning of her pregnancy through to the end of maternity leave (see para 16.13); and
b) the less favourable treatment of a woman in relation to pay and other contractual benefits during maternity leave, where a claim is less likely to succeed.

18.33 Claims in relation to (a), if they concern non-contractual matters, ought to be brought under the SDA 1975 (see para 16.37) and, if they concern contractual matters, under the Equal Pay Act (EqPA) 1970 (see para 18.34). Claims in respect of (b) ought, if they concern pay, to be brought under ERA 1996 s23, as an unlawful deduction of wages, as well as under the EqPA 1970 (though according to the EAT in *Alabaster v Woolwich plc and Social Security Secretary*[41] a claim cannot be made under the EqPA 1970 when a woman is on maternity leave).

Less favourable treatment of women as 'workers'

18.34 There must be no discrimination at any time, either prior to or during leave, in respect of working conditions which affect a woman in 'her capacity as a worker'. A woman claiming sex discrimination in these circumstances has automatic protection against less favourable treatment and does not need to show how a comparable man would be treated.[42] Thus, any less favourable treatment which affects a woman in the longer term, before or after her maternity leave, is unlawful discrimination.

18.35 In *Brown v Rentokil*[43] the ECJ confirmed that the Equal Treatment Directive (ETD) affords a woman protection from the beginning of her pregnancy and during the period of maternity leave granted her by national law. Less favourable treatment such as dismissal, for a reason connected with a woman's pregnancy or absence on maternity

41 [2000] IRLR 754. This case has now been referred to the ECJ by the Court of Appeal; [2002] IRLR 420, CA.

42 This degree of protection is sometimes known as 'protected status'.

43 Case 394/96 [1998] ECR I-4185; [1998] IRLR 445.

leave, constitutes sex discrimination. Although all the dismissal cases decided by the ECJ in this context have concerned discrimination on grounds of pregnancy, the same principles apply to dismissal because of absence on maternity leave.[44]

18.36 In *Gillespie*[45] the ECJ concluded that a woman should receive the benefits and protection she acquires 'in her capacity as a worker' throughout her maternity leave, despite not being entitled to full pay during that period. In *Thibault*, the ECJ held that EC law is intended 'to ensure substantive equality between men and women regarding both access to employment and working conditions'.[46] A woman denied a performance appraisal when she returned to work because she had been on maternity leave was discriminated against. Thus, protection from discrimination extends not just to dismissal but also to the 'long-term' rights of an employee. This would include access to employment and working conditions, for example, promotion, pay reviews, appraisals, dismissal and consultation in relation to redundancy.[47]

Pay and contractual benefits during maternity leave

18.37 In *Gillespie* the ECJ held that a woman on maternity leave is in a special protected position and cannot be compared with an employee at work. She cannot, therefore, claim equal pay in relation to her maternity pay. The ECJ held that, although benefits paid by an employer to a woman on maternity leave constitute 'pay', there was no requirement that women should continue to receive full pay during maternity leave. It is for the national legislation to set the amount of

44 There is a yet unresolved question as to whether this protection lasts longer than the minimum period of leave prescribed by the PWD (18 weeks in the UK). So far the ECJ has generally not made any distinction regarding the protection available during the different periods of leave available in different EU countries but in *Brown v Rentokil*, ibid, it specifically said that protection lasted until the end of the maternity leave period granted by *national* law. See also Case 179/88 *Hertz (Handels-og Kontorfunktionaerer-nes Forbund i Danmark (acting for Hertz) v Dansk Arbejdsgiverforening (acting for Aldi Marked K/S))* [1990] ECR I-3979; [1991] IRLR 31, ECJ.

45 Case 342/93 *Gillespie v Northern Health and Social Services Board* [1996] ECR I-475; [1996] IRLR 214, ECJ

46 Case 136/95 *Caisse Nationale d'Assurance Vieillesse des Travailleurs Salariés (CNAVTS) v Thibault* [1998] ECR I-2011; [1998] IRLR 399.

47 See also *Capeling v British Airways* (1999) DCLD 39; and *McGuigan v TG Baynes*, EAT 1114/97 (unreported, available on LEXIS); and *GUS Home Shopping Ltd v Green and McLaughlin* [2001] IRLR 75, EAT.

maternity pay, provided the amount is not so low as to undermine the purpose of maternity leave – the protection of women before and after giving birth.

18.38 The ECJ also held, in *Gillespie*, that a woman was entitled to have a pay rise reflected in her maternity pay (where this pay was calculated as a fraction of ordinary pay), as such pay was a benefit payable to her as a worker.[48] The courts have tended to hold that no comparison can be made, at least under the EqPA 1970, between a woman on maternity leave and a man.[49] It is difficult, therefore, to challenge the denial of contractual benefits to a woman on AML. If a claim is to be made it should be under the ERA 1996 as well as the EqPA 1970 (see *Alabaster*,[50] para 18.33).

Pay accrued or acquired prior to maternity leave

18.39 Benefits acquired or accrued *prior to* maternity leave must be preserved and, if they become payable to the rest of the workforce while the woman is on OML or AML, must be paid to her then. Such benefits include, for example, a backdated pay rise (see *Gillespie*[51]) and a bonus payment relating to the previous year (see *Lewen*[52]).

Right to return to work after maternity leave

Return after ordinary maternity leave

18.40 If a woman is only entitled to OML she does not need to give notice of her return to work unless she wants to return earlier than at the end of her OML, in which case she must give 21 days' notice of the date of her return. Failure to give notice of early return entitles the employer to postpone her return until she has given 21 days' notice. Where the EWC is on or after 6 April 2003 the notice period is likely to be extended to 28 days.

48 See *Alabaster v Woolwich plc and Social Security Secretary* [2000] IRLR 754, EAT; [2002] EWCA Civ 211, CA, now referred to the ECJ.

49 *Clark v Secretary of State for Employment* [1996] IRLR 578, CA; see also *Boyle v Equal Opportunities Commission* (Case 411/96) [1998] ECR I-6401, [1998] IRLR 717, ECJ.

50 [2000] IRLR 754, EAT; [2002] EWCA Civ 211, CA

51 The pay rise should be reflected in maternity pay (see para 18.37).

52 Case 333/97 *Lewen v Denda* [1999] ECR I-7243; [2000] IRLR 67, in which the ECJ held that a woman on parental leave should not be denied the percentage of the bonus that she had earned as a worker while she was at work.

18.41 The only situation in which a woman cannot return to work after the end of OML is where there is some statutory prohibition on working, such as the ban on working for two weeks after the birth (see para 17.55), or a health and safety risk to the woman because she has recently given birth or is breastfeeding and she had been suspended (see para 17.41).

18.42 If a woman returns to work immediately after OML she is entitled to return to exactly the same job[53] on the same terms and conditions of employment as if she had not been absent. 'Job' is defined as 'the nature of the work which [s]he is employed to do in accordance with his contract and the capacity and place in which [s]he is so employed'.[54] The only exception is if she is made redundant during her leave in which case she is automatically entitled to be offered any suitable available job (see para 16.49).[55]

18.43 Where an employee is not allowed to return at all or to her original job she will be treated as having been dismissed by the employer. If her employer does not expressly dismiss her she may be able to resign and claim constructive dismissal, though this is a difficult area and advice should be sought (see para 15.105). If the dismissal is related to the woman's pregnancy or maternity leave it will be discriminatory and automatically unfair. If the change in her job is due to her absence but is not sufficient to enable her to resign and claim constructive dismissal, she may have a detriment claim (see para 16.61).

Return after additional maternity leave

18.44 The assumption is that a woman entitled to AML will return at the end of her AML. If she wants to return earlier, she must give 21 days' notice of the date of her return (likely to increase to 28 days from April 2003). Failure to give notice of early return entitles the employer to postpone her return until she has given the required notice.

18.45 A woman returning after AML is also entitled to return to the job in which she was employed before her absence *unless* this is not 'reasonably practicable' for a reason other than redundancy.

18.46 Where it is not reasonably practicable for the woman to return to the same job – and the onus is on the employer to show this – she must be given another job which is suitable for her and appropriate

53 ERA 1996 s235.
54 Ibid s71(4)(c) and (7).
55 MPL Regs 1999 reg 10.

for her to do in the circumstances.[56] This is likely to apply where there has been a reorganisation (falling short of redundancy), in which case she must be given a similar job which has the same or better status and terms and conditions as the old job. The woman should be consulted about any changes which occur during her leave in the same way as she would be while still at work.

18.47 A refusal to permit a woman to return to her job because, for example, the employer decides to keep on her temporary replacement – or for another reason related to her pregnancy or maternity leave – is likely to be both 'automatically' unfair dismissal and discrimination contrary to the SDA 1975.

Exceptions to right to return after additional maternity leave

18.48 There are two exceptions to the right to return to the same job after AML:

- where the employee is redundant, subject to her right to be offered any suitable alternative employment;[57] and
- where it is not reasonably practicable for a reason other than redundancy to allow the woman to return to her job, she is entitled to return to another job which is suitable for her and appropriate for her to do in the circumstances.[58]

18.49 The onus is on the employer to show that it is not reasonably practicable to allow the woman to return to her old job. In addition, small employers (with five or fewer employees) are not liable for automatically unfair dismissal where it is not reasonably practicable for the employer or any successor to allow the employee to return to the same job or to offer a job which is suitable for her and appropriate in the circumstance.[59] The employer may still be liable for ordinary unfair dismissal and discriminatory dismissal (see paras 16.37 and 16.48).

Terms and conditions on return from ordinary maternity leave

18.50 The terms and conditions should be the same as though the woman returning from leave had not taken OML. Her contract is to be treated

56 MPL Regs 1999 reg 18(2) and (4). The 'exception' to the right to return in small workplaces in reg 20(6) does not remove an employer's liability for sex discrimination.

57 MPL Regs 1999 reg 10 – this exception also applies to OML.

58 Ibid reg 18(2) and (4).

59 Ibid reg 20(6).

as having continued throughout the period of leave. So, too, is her access to benefits and accrual of service-related benefits.

Terms and conditions on return from additional maternity leave

18.51 A woman should not be disadvantaged by her absence on maternity leave so that when she returns it must be:

- on terms and conditions as to remuneration that are no less favourable than those which would have applied had she not been absent;[60]
- with her seniority, pension rights and similar rights as they would have been if the period prior to her AML were continuous with her employment following her return from work; and
- otherwise on terms and conditions no less favourable than she would have received if she had not been absent after the end of her OML.

The period of AML itself does not count towards length of service for contractual rights such as pension, but does count for the purpose of statutory rights such as redundancy pay.

Failure to return at the end of maternity leave

18.52 A woman who does not return after her leave should be treated like any other employee who does not return after authorised leave. The employer should not assume that, because the woman has not returned, she is not intending to return. The employer should investigate and apply the normal disciplinary procedures. If the reason for her failure to return is that she is ill she should be able to go on sick leave, like any other sick employee, and to claim contractual sick pay (where it exists).[61] In *Rashid v Asian Community Care Services Ltd*,[62] the EAT held that a failure to return to work after maternity leave does not in itself terminate the contract of employment. It must be shown that the employee intended the failure to return to end the contract.[63]

18.53 If the woman is sick for a long time, the employer may consider

60 Ibid reg 18(5)(a)(i).

61 Note that SMP is not payable during any week during which the woman works.

62 EAT 480/99 (unreported, available on LEXIS).

63 Although this case was decided under the old law, there is no reason why it should not apply to OML and AML under the present regime.

terminating her contract but must adopt a fair procedure including consultation and a medical investigation and not be harsher than usual in applying the procedure. No account should be taken of any pregnancy-related sickness which occurred before or during her leave or of the leave itself (see para 16.13). If the employer dismisses a woman who has taken maternity leave because she is sick and does not return, this may be automatically unfair and discriminatory if the reason is related to her pregnancy or maternity leave (see paras 16.37 and 16.48). However, if the dismissal takes place after the end of maternity leave, a claim under the SDA 1975 will require that a comparison be made with how male employees are or would be treated.

Contractual and composite rights

18.54 An employee may have both a statutory right to return and a contractual right; this is known as a 'composite' right. The ERA 1996 provides that an employee who has both the right to return to work under the ERA and another right to return to work after absence because of pregnancy or childbirth (under a contract of employment or otherwise) may not exercise the two rights separately. She may however, in returning to work, take advantage of whichever right is, in any particular respect, the more favourable.[64]

New maternity and parental rights where the EWC is on or after 6 April 2003: a summary

Overview

18.55 The Employment Act 2002 and draft regulations (the Maternity and Parental Leave (Amendment) Leave Regulations 2002[65] and the Paternity and Adoption Leave Regulations 2002) provide for changes to OML, AML and the introduction of adoption leave (ordinary and additional) and paternity leave.

18.56 Many maternity rights will remain unchanged, including the right to paid time off for antenatal care, the 2-week period of compulsory

64 MPL Regs 1999 reg 21.

65 The draft Maternity and Parental Leave (Draft MPL) Regulations amend the Maternity and Parental Leave, etc, Regulations 1999. It is expected that the regulations will be finalised in the Autumn of 2002.

maternity leave, the health and safety provisions, rights during maternity leave (including right to suitable alternative work on redundancy), the right to return and protection from unfair dismissal and detriment. The following changes are based on the draft regulations (as at 22 July 2002).

18.57 The new maternity rights apply where the mother's *expected* week of childbirth (EWC) begins on or after 6 April 2003 even if the baby is born prematurely.[66]

18.58 Employees (meaning the biological father, spouse or partner of the child's mother) are entitled to two weeks' paternity leave where the EWC or birth is on or after 6 April 2003.[67]

18.59 Adoption leave and paternity leave for adopters applies where a child is either matched or placed for adoption on or after 6 April 2003.[68]

Maternity leave

Ordinary maternity leave (OML)

18.60 OML is to be increased to 26 weeks.[69] It can still start at any time from the beginning of the 11th week before the EWC *unless* the employee has a pregnancy-related absence (including birth) in the *four weeks* (not six weeks as previously) prior to the EWC in which case she will immediately be triggered onto her leave.[70]

Additional maternity leave (AML)

18.61 Employees, entitled to OML, who have 26 weeks' service by the notification week (ie, the 15th week immediately before the EWC) will qualify for AML.[71] This is the same service qualification as for statutory maternity pay. They will no longer have to be employed for 1 year by the 11th week before EWC. AML will begin when OML ends and run for 26 weeks so that an employee will be entitled to a total of 52 weeks' maternity leave.[72]

66 Draft MPL Regs reg 2(1). The rate of maternity/paternity pay will not go up until 6 April 2003 where the baby is premature.
67 Draft Paternity and Adoption Leave (Draft PAL) Regulations reg 3(1).
68 Ibid reg 3(2).
69 MPL Regs 1999 reg 12D as amended by Draft MPL Regs.
70 Ibid reg 12C as amended.
71 Ibid reg 12B as amended.
72 Ibid reg 12D(4) as amended.

New notice provisions for maternity leave

18.62 Pregnancy, the expected week of childbirth and the planned date of the start of maternity leave must be notified to the employer in the notification week, or if this is not reasonably practicable, as soon as is reasonably practicable.[73] This is much earlier than previously. The employer may request the notification in writing. The employee can vary the start of her leave provided she gives notice 28 days notice (before the date originally notified or new start date whichever is earlier) or if this is not reasonably practicable as soon as reasonably practicable.[74]

18.63 After the employee's notice, the employer must, within 28 days, write to the employee stating her expected date of return if she takes her full leave.[75]

18.64 Where the employee is triggered on to maternity leave, so that the date for starting leave changes unexpectedly, the normal notice requirement does not apply but she must still notify her employer as soon as is reasonably practicable that her absence is related to her pregnancy.[76]

18.65 The provision whereby an employer could write to the employee after childbirth requesting confirmation of an intention to return is to be repealed.

Early return from maternity leave

18.66 As with the present provisions, there appears to be an assumption that an employee who is entitled only to OML will return the day after the end of 26 weeks and an employee entitled to AML will return the day after the end of the 52 weeks.[77] An employee who intends to return earlier must give 28 days' notice of her return (instead of 21 days' notice).[78] If she fails to give the notice the employer may postpone her return until she has given appropriate notice, though not beyond the end of her maternity leave.[79]

73 MPL Regs 1999 reg 12A(1) as amended by Draft MPL Regs.

74 Ibid reg 12A(2) as amended.

75 Ibid reg 12A(4) as amended.

76 Ibid reg 12A(6) as amended.

77 Ibid reg 12(G)(1) as amended. It is not clear whether a woman, who is entitled to AML, can return at the end of OML without giving 28 days notice, see MPL Regs 1999 reg 12A(5) as amended by Draft MPL Regs.

78 MPL Regs 1999 reg 12G as amended by Draft MPL Regs.

79 Ibid reg 12G(2)–(4) as amended.

Statutory maternity pay

18.67 For those who satisfy the service and earnings qualifying conditions, statutory maternity pay will run for 26 weeks during the whole of the OML period. It will be paid at 90% of average pay for the first 6 weeks and than at the rate of £100 or 90% of pay whichever is the lower for the remaining 20 weeks. The details are outside the scope of this book.

Adoption leave and pay

18.68 Since 1999 there has been a right for adoptive parents to take 13 weeks' unpaid parental leave. From April 2003 one of newly adoptive parents, who has been employed for 26 weeks by the date he or she has been notified of being matched with a child for adoption,[80] will be entitled to 26 weeks' ordinary adoption leave and 26 weeks' additional adoption leave, a total of 52 weeks' leave.[81] If the placement ends during the adoption leave period, the adopter will be able to stay on leave for up to 8 weeks (of the remaining leave) after the end of the placement.[82]

18.69 Either adopter can take the leave but it cannot be split between them. The other adopter or the partner of the adopter can take paternity leave.

18.70 For those who qualify, adoption pay will be paid for 26 weeks during the whole of the ordinary adoption leave period, at a flat rate of £100 or 90% of pay whichever is the lower. The details are outside the scope of this book.

18.71 The leave can start:

- from the date of the child's placement or, if the employee is working that day, the following day; or
- from a fixed date up to 14 days before the expected date of placement, but not later than the date of placement.[83]

Notice provisions

18.72 Adopters must inform their employers of their intention to take adoption leave, date due for placement and start of leave, within 7 days of being notified that they have been matched for adoption (or, if this is

80 Draft PAL Regs reg 12(2).
81 Ibid regs 13(1) and 18(1).
82 Ibid reg 16.
83 Ibid reg 13(2).

not reasonably practicable, as soon as is reasonably practicable).[84] The employee may vary the start of leave by giving 28 days notice or as soon as reasonably practicable.[85] The employer must, within 28 days of notification, write to the employee setting out the date the employee is due to return to work.[86] If the employee wants to return to work before the end of the leave, he or she must give 28 days notice (as with maternity leave).

18.73 The employer may request evidence (being a document issued by the adoption agency) stating:

a) the name and address of the agency;
b) the name and address of the employee;
c) the date on which the employee was notified that he or she had been matched with the child; and
d) the date of placement or the date on which the agency expects to place the child with the employee.[87]

18.74 The provisions covering the adopter's return to work and rights during leave are materially the same as for ordinary and additional maternity leave.[88] Where an employee is made redundant during adoption leave he or she will be entitled to any suitable alternative employment which exists.[89]

18.75 The adopter will be entitled £100 per week (or 90% of earnings whichever is the less) for 26 weeks provided their earnings average at least £75 (the Lower Earnings Limit for national insurance).

Paternity leave[90]

18.76 Where the baby is born on or after 6 April 2003, or the EWC begins on or after that date, fathers (and partners of the mother), will be entitled to take either one week or two consecutive weeks' paternity leave.[91] Similarly, where the child has been matched for or placed for adoption on or after 6 April 2003, an adoptive parent (of either sex) not taking adoption leave, will be entitled to paternity leave.[92] The qualifying conditions are:

84 Draft PAL Regs reg 14.
85 Ibid reg 14(3).
86 Ibid reg 14(5).
87 Ibid reg 12(1) and (3).
88 Ibid regs 15 and 17.
89 Ibid reg 22. This is identical to the provisions relating to maternity leave.
90 Draft PAL Regs reg 4 (birth) and reg 7 (adoption).
91 Ibid regs 3(1) and 5(1). Odd days may not be taken.
92 Ibid regs 3(2) and 8(1).

a) the employee must have been employed for 26 weeks by the mother's notification week (or in the case of adoption 26 week ending with the week in which the child's adopter is notified of being matched with the child);
b) the employee must have or expect to have responsibility for the upbringing of the child; and
c) the employee must be the 'father' of the child. A 'father' is the biological or adoptive parent (not taking adoptive leave) or the spouse or partner of the child's mother or adopter. A 'partner' can include same sex partners who live with the mother 'in an enduring family relationship'.[93]

Notice provisions: paternity leave

18.77 In respect of a birth, notice must be given in or before the notification week (the 15th week before the EWC).[94] For an adopter, notice must be given no more than 7 days after the adopter was notified of adoption.[95] The date given for the start of leave may be varied on 28 days notice.[96] If it is not reasonably practicable for the employee to give this notice, it must be given as soon as is reasonably practicable.

18.78 The notice to the employer is of:

- the EWC or date on which the child is expected to be placed with the adopter;
- the length of period the employee wants to take; and
- the start of the leave.[97]

18.79 In addition, employees must, if requested, provide evidence in a document which contains:

- the name of the employee;
- the EWC or date of birth or date on which the child is expected to be placed with the adopter and, if the placement has already occurred, the date of the placement,
- the length of the period of leave to be taken;
- the start date of the leave;
- for adopters, the date on which the adopter was notified that he or she had been matched with the child.[98]

93 Draft PAL Regs regs 2(1), 4(2) and 7(2).
94 Ibid reg 6.
95 Ibid reg 9.
96 Ibid regs 6(3) and 9(3).
97 Ibid regs 6(1) and 9(1).
98 Ibid regs 4(1)(6), 4(6)(7), 7(1)(b) and (5)(6).

18.80 The leave may start from the date of the child's birth or first day of EWC (or placement for adoption) or from a fixed period or fixed date after the baby is expected (or placement expected).[99] The leave must be taken within 56 days of the birth or first day of EWC (or placement).[100]

18.81 The parent or adopter will also be entitled to paternity pay of £100 (or 90% of his average pay whichever is the lower) provided his or her earnings average at least £75 (the Lower Earnings Limit for national insurance).

18.82 Employees are entitled to the benefit of their normal terms and conditions of employment during paternity leave except for remuneration and are entitled to return to the same job. They are treated in the same way as women on ordinary maternity leave.

Employment Protection

18.83 It will be automatic unfair dismissal under Employment Rights Act 1996 s99 or unlawful detriment (section 47C) if the only or principal reason for the dismissal/detriment is that the employee took or sought to take adoption leave or paternity leave. The existing protection relating to maternity leave, parental leave and time off for dependants still applies. Thus, for example, if billing targets are not reduced for a parent taking leave, or promotion or a pay rise is denied, this is likely to be a detriment and may also be sex discrimination.

99 Draft PAL Regs regs 5 and 8.

100 Ibid reg 5(1) (birth) and reg 8(1) (adoption).

CHAPTER 19

Parental leave

Key points

19.1
- Employees, including adopters, with one year's service can take up to 13 weeks' unpaid parental leave for each child under five – for parents of disabled children the permitted leave is 18 weeks.
- Parental leave must be taken:
  - before the child is five; or
  - within five years of the child being placed for adoption; or
  - if the child is entitled to disability living allowance, before the child is 18.
- A default scheme sets out the rules where there is no workforce or collective agreement between employer and employees.
- It is unlawful to subject an employee to a detriment or dismiss him or her for taking parental leave.

Background and statutory framework

19.2 The Parental Leave Directive[1] (PLD) introduced the right to parental leave (PL) and to leave for workers with dependants. The directive became applicable to the UK only when the incoming Labour government signed the Social Charter in 1997, with a deadline of December 1999 for implementation in the UK. This chapter summarises the main provisions. To date there have been no reported decisions on PL.

19.3 The PLD was implemented by the Employment Relations Act 1999[2] which introduced amendments to the Employment Rights Act (ERA) 1996, and by the Maternity and Parental Leave etc Regulations (MPL Regulations) 1999.[3] The TUC challenged the fact that the right to PL initially applied only in relation to children born after 15 December 1999. This has now been rectified.

19.4 The statutory right is to unpaid PL. Such leave can be taken at any time prior to the child's fifth birthday including, in the case of the mother, as an extension of ordinary or additional maternity leave (OML or AML).

1 Council Directive 96/34.

2 Employment Relations Act 1999 ss76–80 and Sch 2.

3 SI No 3312, regs 13–22; Employment Relations Act 1999 Schs 1 and 2. Advisory publications on parental and dependants leave are available from www.dti.gov.uk/er/individual.htm.

19.5 There are three parts to the PL scheme:

- the basic legal minimum provisions – amount of leave, definition of parent, and age of child in respect of whom leave may be taken;
- any workforce or collective agreement between employer and employee;
- the default provisions which apply if there is no workforce or collective agreement.

Each of these parts will be dealt with in turn.

Coverage of the parental leave provisions

19.6 Only employees with one year's service, at the time the leave is taken, are entitled to PL. The right is available both to permanent and temporary employees, irrespective of their hours of work. The exceptions are set out in para 16.9.

Legal minimum entitlements

19.7 The legal minimum entitlement to PL is as follows:

- The employee must have or expect to have responsibility for the child. Mothers automatically have parental responsibility, as do fathers who are married to the mother, who have parental responsibility, or who are registered on the birth certificate.[4] Others can acquire parental responsibility through a legal agreement with the mother or by a court order. Adoptive parents have parental responsibility. The parents of a child do not have to be living with the child in order to qualify for PL.
- The employee must have one year's continuous employment with the employer by the time he or she starts the PL. If the employee changes employer he or she has to wait a further year to requalify for leave.[5]
- The leave must be taken to care for the child. Note that, if the default provisions apply, leave can be taken in periods of no less than one week.
- The maximum leave is 13 weeks per child unless the child is disabled, in which case the total period of leave available increased to

4 MPL Regs 1999 reg 13(2).

5 Ibid reg 13(1)(a).

18 weeks on 10 January 2002. If an employee moves to a new employer he or she remains entitled only to the balance of the PL period not taken with the previous employer and may, as stated above, begin to take this remaining leave only after a year's qualifying service.[6]

- The child must be under five years old during the period of PL unless:
  - the child has been adopted, in which case PL can be taken for up to five years after the placement or the date of the child's eighteenth birthday, whichever is earlier;[7]
  - the child is in receipt of disability living allowance, in which case PL can be taken up to the date of the child's eighteenth birthday;
  - the employer has postponed PL which the employee sought to take before the child's fifth birthday (see para 19.24);
  - the provisions set out immediately below apply.

19.8 As mentioned above, entitlement to PL originally applied only in relation to children born on or after 15 December 1999. Following legal challenge by the TUC and a reference by the domestic courts to the European Court of Justice (ECJ), the MPL Regulations 1999 were amended to extend entitlement to PL (subject to satisfaction of the qualifying period) to parents of all children who were under five on 15 December 1999. Parents of children born or placed for adoption between 15 December 1994 and 14 December 1999 will have three years and one week to take PL from the date (10 January 2002) the amending Regulations came into force.[8]

Terms and conditions during parental leave

19.9 Although the contract continues during PL, most contractual terms do not continue unless there is agreement that they will continue. The provisions are the same as those governing AML (see para 18.28). Entitlement to paid annual holiday under the Working Time Regulations 1998[9] accrues during PL in the same way as it does during AML. Other contractual holiday entitlement does not accrue. The employer

6 The calculation of a week is set out in MPL Regs 1999 reg 14.

7 Ibid reg 15(c).

8 Maternity and Parental Leave (Amendment) Regulations 2001 SI No 4010 – see EOR 98.

9 SI No 1833.

is not obliged to pay pension contributions during PL unless the leave is paid.[10]

19.10 For the purposes of statutory employment protection, PL counts as continuous service. In relation to contractual rights such as seniority, pensions, etc, the period of PL does not count and the period immediately prior to it is treated as continuous with the period after leave.[11]

19.11 Although the MPL Regulations 1999 do not require employers to pay a bonus during PL, failure to pay a bonus to a woman may be indirect discrimination contrary to article 141 of the EC Treaty (this is because women are much more likely to take PL).[12] In *Lewen v Denda*[13] the condition for payment of a bonus was that the worker was in active employment at the time the bonus was awarded. The ECJ held that failure to pay a bonus to a woman on PL could amount to indirect sex discrimination. But on the facts of the case it did not, because the bonus was paid to encourage workers' hard work in the future, as opposed to rewarding them for past work. It appears from the decision in *Lewen* that the reason for which the bonus was given (encouragement of future productivity) was sufficient to justify any indirect discrimination. If, on the other hand, the bonus had related to work done in the previous year, the indirect discrimination involved in refusing it to women on PL would not have been justified. The purpose of the bonus and the period to which it related were crucial to its legality.

Right to return after parental leave

Parental leave of four weeks or less except when taken immediately after additional maternity leave

19.12 An employee is entitled to return to the job in which he or she was employed before the leave. This also applies where parental leave of four weeks or less is taken immediately after OML. Thus, the position is the same as a woman returning from OML (see para 18.40).

10 Social Security Act 1989 Sch 5 provides that paid family leave should be treated as if the employee is working normally and receives the remuneration actually paid during that period.

11 MPL Regs 1999 reg 18(5)(b).

12 Note that the new definition of indirect discrimination imposed by the Sex Discrimination (Indirect Discrimination and Burden of Proof) Regulations 2001 SI No 2660 should make it easier to prove indirect sex discrimination (see para 7.10).

13 Case 333/97 [1999] ECR I-7243; [2000] IRLR 67.

Parental leave of more then four weeks

19.13 The right to return is the same as after AML (see para 18.44). The employee is entitled to return to the same job or, if this is not reasonably practicable, to a job which is suitable for that employee and appropriate for him or her to do.[14] If an employee is concerned about his or her job on return from leave, he or she may want to limit the leave to four weeks at any one time.[15]

Parental leave of no more than four weeks taken immediately after additional maternity leave

19.14 Where a woman takes PL of less than four weeks immediately after AML, she is entitled to return to the job in which she was employed prior to her AML unless:

- it would not have been reasonably practicable for her to return to that job if she had returned at the end of her AML; *and*
- it is still not reasonably practicable at the end of her PL.

If these provisions apply she is entitled to return to a suitable alternative appropriate job.[16]

19.15 The right to return after PL is the same as that which applies in relation to AML. It is a right to return on the same terms and conditions relating to pay, with preserved seniority, pension and other rights, and otherwise on terms and conditions not less favourable than those that would have applied had the employee not been absent. PL has the same effect on continuity for the purposes of contractual rights, the period prior to leave being treated as continuous with the period after leave and the leave itself being ignored (see para 18.51). In relation to statutory rights the period of PL, like that of AML, itself counts towards continuous service.

Collective and workplace agreements

19.16 Employers and employees are free to negotiate the details of PL but to be binding the agreement must be either:

14 MPL Regs 1999 reg 18.

15 Note that under the default scheme, which applies in the absence of a collective or workplace agreement, employees are only entitled to take four weeks leave per child in any one year (see below).

16 MPL Regs 1999 reg 18(3).

- a collective agreement, negotiated between the employer and independent trade union; or
- a workforce agreement between the employer and employees where the agreement:
  - is in writing;
  - lasts for a specified period not exceeding five years;
  - applies to all relevant members of the workforce, or of a group within the workforce;
  - is signed by representatives of the workforce;
  - has been provided, with guidance, by the employer to all employees so they can understand it.

19.17 The election of representatives must satisfy a number of conditions. These are set out in the MPL Regulations 1999.[17] The default provisions will apply to any employee whose contract of employment does not include a provision that gives entitlement to PL and incorporates or operates by reference to all or part of a collective or workforce agreement.[18]

The default provisions

19.18 In the absence of a binding collective or workforce agreement, the default provisions apply. These set out evidence and notice requirements, the length of leave that can be taken at any one time, and postponement of leave.

Evidence of parental responsibility, etc

19.19 The employer may require evidence of the employee's responsibility for the child, the child's date of birth (or date of placement if adopted), and the child's entitlement to disability living allowance. This may include the birth certificate, parental responsibility order (if there is one), or adoption papers.

Notice requirements

19.20 The employee must give notice, 21 days before the beginning of the leave, of the dates on which the leave is to begin and end. Where the

17 MPL Regs 1999 Sch 1. These provisions are very similar to those relating to working time workforce agreements.

18 Ibid reg 16.

father is to take leave from the date of the child's birth the notice (which must also be given 21 days in advance) must instead specify the expected week of childbirth and the proposed duration of leave. PL can then start on the day the baby is born, even if born early or late.

19.21 Where the child is to be adopted and the leave is to be taken from the date of the child's placement, the notice (also 21 days) must specify the week in which the placement is expected to occur and the proposed duration of the leave. PL may then start on the date of actual placement, whenever this occurs. The notice period is likely to increase to 28 days from 6 April 2003 unless the child is disabled, in which case it will remain at 21 days.

Period of leave

19.22 PL must be taken a week at a time or in multiples of a week. It is not possible to take a day or two at a time, unless the child is in receipt of disability living allowance.[19]

19.23 An employee is not entitled to take more than four weeks' leave in respect of any child during a particular year.[20] A year runs from the date on which the employee first became entitled to take PL in respect of the child.

Postponement of leave

19.24 Save in the case of fathers taking leave at the time of the birth, and parents at the time of placement for adoption, employers may postpone PL where they consider that the operation of the business would be unduly disrupted if the employee took leave during the period.[21] In order to postpone leave, the employer must:

- Within seven days of the employee's notice to the employer, give the employee notice in writing of the postponement, stating the reason and giving the dates when the leave can be taken. These may include a period after the child's fifth birthday.
- Allow the employee to take leave of the same length no later than six months after the leave was due to commence. The employer must consult the employee about the date to which the leave has been postponed.[22]

19 MPL Regs 1999 Sch 2, para 7 does not specify the minimum amount of time that may be taken where the child receives disability living allowance.

20 Ibid Sch 2, para 7.

21 Ibid Sch 2, para 6.

22 Ibid Sch 2, para 6(c)(ii).

If the employer unreasonably postpones the leave, the employee can complain to an employment tribunal (ET), which must balance the needs of the employer and the business against the needs of the employee.

Individual parental leave agreements

19.25 The default provisions act as a legal minimum but there is nothing to stop the employer and employee reaching agreement to improve upon these default provisions.[23] By contrast with collective or workforce agreements, which may contain better or worse provisions than the default provisions, individual agreements cannot be less favourable to the employee than the default provisions.

Rights and remedies

19.26 An employee can, within three months of the event, make a complaint to an ET that the employer:

- unreasonably postponed a period of PL; or
- prevented or attempted to prevent the employee from taking PL.[24]

If the claim succeeds the ET must make a declaration and may award such compensation as is just and equitable, having regard to the employer's behaviour and the loss suffered by the employee.[25]

Dismissal and detriment

19.27 It is unlawful to treat an employee less favourably or to dismiss him or her because:

- he or she took or sought to take PL;
- he or she refused to sign a workforce agreement; or
- he or she carried out (or proposed to carry out) any activities as a workforce representative or candidate in an election to be a representative.[26]

23 MPL Regs 1999 reg 21 and Sch 2, para 7.

24 ERA 1996 s80(1).

25 Ibid s80(4).

26 Ibid s99; MPL Regs 1999 regs 19 and 20.

An employee who is dismissed for exercising the right to PL may also have a claim under ERA 1996 s104 (dismissal for asserting a statutory right – see para 16.59).

Parental leave and sex discrimination

19.28 Where a woman is treated less favourably than a man, or vice versa, in relation to PL, the worker may have a claim for direct sex discrimination. A woman may, in addition, be able to claim indirect sex discrimination if employees who take PL are treated less favourably than those who do not. For example, if employees on PL are denied a Christmas bonus, whereas employees on other unpaid leave receive one, this practice may impact disproportionately on women who are more likely to take PL then men (see *Lewen v Denda*,[27] para 18.39).

27 Case 333/97 [1999] ECR I-7243; [2000] IRLR 67.

CHAPTER 20

Dependants leave

Key points

20.1
- An employee can take unpaid time off to care or arrange care for a dependant where:
  - the dependant is ill, injured, assaulted, gives birth or dies; or
  - arrangements for the care of a dependant break down; or
  - there is an unexpected incident involving a child at school.
- A dependant is a spouse, child, parent, or person living in the same household as the employee (other than as an employee, tenant, or lodger).
- The employee is entitled to 'a reasonable amount of time off'.
- An employee who takes time off is protected against dismissal and detriment.

Background and statutory framework

20.2 The Parental Leave Directive[1] (PLD) provided for the first time a right under EC law to unpaid dependants leave (DL). This right is to reasonable time off to deal with certain unexpected or sudden emergencies and to make any longer term arrangements. It has been transposed into domestic law by Employment Rights Act (ERA) 1996 ss57A and 57B. The provisions entitle employees to time off in relation to dependants other than children, elderly parents and mothers giving birth. These broader rights are outside the scope of this book.

Who is entitled to dependants leave?

20.3 Only employees are entitled to DL. The right is available to all employees, male and female, irrespective of their hours of work or length of service and regardless of whether they are employed indefinitely or on temporary contracts. A limited number of employees are excluded from ERA 1996 rights, including rights to DL. These exclusions are discussed at para 16.9 above.

1 Council Directive 96/34/EC.

What events are covered by the right?

20.4 An employee is entitled to take a reasonable amount of time off during working hours in order to take action which is necessary:

- to provide assistance on an occasion when a dependant falls ill, gives birth or is injured or assaulted;
- to make arrangements for the provision of care for a dependant who is ill or injured;
- in consequence of the death of a dependant;
- because of the unexpected disruption or termination of arrangements for the care of a dependant; and/or
- to deal with an incident involving a child of the employee that occurs unexpectedly in a period during which an educational establishment which the child attends is responsible for him or her.

Time off for dependants' illness, giving birth, injury or assault

20.5 The time off to which employees are entitled is to provide assistance when a dependant falls ill, gives birth or is injured or assaulted.[2] This applies where a baby or child is ill or has been injured. The DTI's guidance, *Time off for dependants – detailed guidance for employers and employees*, states that the right to time off may also apply in relation to a deterioration of an existing condition.[3]

20.6 Where necessary, an employee can also take time off to help a dependant when she is having a baby. This does not include taking time off after the birth to care for the child, though the employee may be entitled to parental leave (see chapter 19). From 2003, employees will be entitled to paternity leave (see para 18.76).

Time off to make arrangements for the care of an ill or injured dependant

20.7 This is to enable a parent to make longer-term arrangements for the care of a dependant, for example by employing a temporary carer or taking a sick child to stay with relatives.[4] There is likely to be an

2 ERA 1996 s57A(1)(b).

3 URN 99/1186, available at www.dti.gov.uk/er/individual/dependants.pdf.

4 Ibid.

overlap between the rights discussed here and in para 20.5, although the latter is intended to cover the initial period of illness and this the making of longer-term care arrangements. If a child is likely to be ill for a substantial period, the parent is entitled to time off to make arrangements for care, provided the child is well enough to be left with a carer. It would be reasonable for the parent to stay with a child who is very ill but thereafter to make alternative arrangements for any subsequent period.

20.8 It is not clear how much time off will be regarded as 'reasonable' but the PLD states that the entitlement arises in cases of 'force majeur', which suggests that on-going pre-planned care such as a hospital appointment would probably not be permitted as DL. The government's view is that such time off is not currently an entitlement under the ERA 1996, though the DTI's consultation document, *Work & Parents: Competitiveness and Choice,* suggested that:

> One option would be to include routine hospital appointments within the right to emergency leave. This is unlikely to increase the level of absence from the workplace significantly and, therefore, should have little impact on employers. But it would benefit parents with disabled or sick children.[5]

There is nothing in the legislation that requires a medical certificate to show that the child is ill. However, an employer may want a doctor's certificate or letter about the length of the illness in order to establish that it is still necessary to allow the time off.[6]

Time off in relation to the death of a dependant[7]

20.9 The DTI guidance states that time off to make funeral arrangements and attending the funeral would be covered by the ERA 1996. The DTI guidance says that if the funeral is overseas, the employer and employee will need to agree a length of absence that is reasonable in the circumstances.

5 Cm 5005, 2000, para 4.32 (www.dti.gov.uk/er/review.htm). It does not appear that this will be changed though the regulations were in draft at the time of writing and may be subject to change.

6 The DTI guidance states that employers who think that an employee is abusing the right to time off should deal with the situation according to their normal disciplinary procedures, which would include asking for a doctor's certificate or letter.

7 ERA 1996 s57A(1)(c).

Time off for the unexpected disruption or termination of a dependant's care[8]

20.10 The DTI guidance says that time off can be taken where the normal carer of the dependant is unexpectedly absent, for example if the childminder fails to turn up or a nursery is unexpectedly closed. This should also cover a situation where the other parent, who is normally the carer, is ill or suddenly leaves the family.

Time off to deal with an unexpected incident at school[9]

20.11 This only covers a child or adopted child. The DTI guidance says that an employee can take time off to deal with a serious incident involving his or her child during school hours – if, for example, the child has been involved in a fight, is distressed, or is being suspended from school.

Who is a dependant?[10]

20.12 In all cases a dependant is a spouse, a child, a parent, a person living in the same household as the employee, otherwise than as his or her employee, tenant, lodger or boarder.[11] It covers:

- unmarried partners, including same-sex partners;
- children, including those such as stepchildren who are not the employee's children but who live in the same house, whatever their age.

20.13 In addition, for the purposes of paras 20.7 or 20.9 above (sickness or injury of dependant) a 'dependant' also includes 'any person who reasonably relies on the employee':

- for assistance when the person falls ill, is injured or assaulted; or
- to make arrangements for the provision of care in the event of illness or injury.

20.14 For the purposes of para 20.10 (disruption of care arrangements) 'dependant' includes a person who reasonably relies on the employee to make arrangements for the provision of care.

8 ERA 1996 s57A(1)(d).
9 Ibid s57A(1)(e).
10 Ibid s57A(3)–(6).
11 Ibid s57A(3).

How much time off is allowed?

20.15 An employee is allowed a 'reasonable amount of time during the employee's working hours in order to take action which is necessary'.[12] Account may be taken of:

- who else is available to help;
- the amount of time off required;
- the closeness of the relationship between the employee and the dependant;
- any other relevant factors.

The employer should take account of the employee's individual circumstances. It will be a question of fact and what is 'reasonable' in every situation.

20.16 The DTI guidance states that there may be times when both parents should be able to take time off work at the same time. This might be, for example, where the child is having an operation, has had an accident or is very ill. The guidance also states that, in most cases, one or two days should be sufficient to deal with the problem, though this will depend on individual circumstances.

Notification duties

20.17 The employee must tell the employer the reason for and expected length of his or her absence as soon as reasonably practicable.[13] There is no requirement to inform the employer in advance but, if the employee is at work, he or she should generally be able to tell the employer before leaving. If this is not reasonably practicable (because, for example, the child is ill at night and has to go to hospital), the employee must inform the employer as soon as reasonably practicable of the reason for and expected length of absence. This notice need not be in writing.

20.18 An employee who fails to give the employer prompt and appropriate notice has no entitlement to DL, and the employer may refuse requested leave and/or treat leave taken by the employee as unauthorised. Having said this, an employer who refuses leave or penalises an

12 ERA 1996 s57A(1).

13 Ibid s57A(2) confirms that, if an employee is unable to inform the employer about the need for absence until he or she has already returned to work, and the employee is back at work before being able to do so, then the length of absence will already be known.

employee because of his or her view that inadequate notice was given will breach the ERA 1996 if an employment tribunal (ET) decides that he or she was mistaken as to the reasonableness of the notice given by the employee. An employee can complain to an ET that he or she has been unreasonably refused time off, or has been subjected to an unlawful detriment in connection with DL. Ultimately, the tribunal will be the judge of the question whether reasonable notice was given.[14]

Reasonable refusal?

20.19 It may be reasonable to refuse time off if the employee's spouse or partner is not working and is available to care for the child or other dependant. However, it will depend on the circumstances. So, for example, it may be unreasonable to refuse leave if, for example, the spouse or partner had a job interview, or a breastfed child needed his or her mother because he or she was ill.

Protection from dismissal, detriment and discrimination in connection with dependants leave

20.20 Employees are protected from being penalised or dismissed because they have taken, or have sought to take, time off in accordance with ERA 1996 ss57A and 57B. They may also challenge unreasonable refusals of time off work. There are three possible claims in connection with DL:

- A complaint of unreasonable refusal of time off work.[15]
- A complaint of unlawful subjection to a detriment in connection with a request for time off work.[16] An example might be if the employee was told that she could not take unpaid time off but had to take her holiday leave instead.
- A complaint of automatically unfair dismissal in connection with taking or requesting time off work.[17] The provisions are the same as those applying in relation to parental leave (see para 19.27).

14 ERA 1996 s57B.

15 Ibid.

16 Maternity and Parental Leave etc Regs 1999 SI No 3312, reg 19.

17 ERA 1996 s104.

Discrimination

20.21 Where a woman is treated less favourably than man (or a man less favourably than a woman) in connection with DL, she (or he) may claim direct sex discrimination. A woman may, in addition, be able to claim indirect sex discrimination if employees who take such leave are treated less favourably than those who do not (if, for example, the employer requirement prohibits employees from taking time off to care for sick children). In order to escape a finding of unlawful discrimination the employer would have to show that the requirement or practice is justified (see chapter 7).

Complaint and remedies

20.22 A complaint must be made within three months from the date when the refusal, detriment or dismissal occurred or, if this is not practicable, within such further period as is reasonable (see chapter 32). Where the employee complains that the employer has unreasonably refused them time off the tribunal can: [18]

- make a declaration that the complaint is well-founded;
- award compensation which is 'just and equitable' having regard to the employer's fault in refusing to allow time off; and any loss sustained by the employee.

Remedies for other claims are set out in chapter 33.

18 ERA 1996 s57B.

CHAPTER 21

Rights to child-friendly working hours and protection from less favourable treatment

continued

Key points

21.1
- A woman may have the right to work part-time or other child-friendly hours after her baby is born.
- Unlawful indirect sex discrimination may be established where a woman can show that:
  - an employer has applied to her a provision, criterion or practice,
  - which is or would be to the detriment of a considerably larger proportion of women than of men, and
  - which is to her detriment, and
  - which the employer cannot show to be justifiable.
- A refusal to permit a man to work child-friendly hours, when a woman would be allowed to, will be direct discrimination.
- The less favourable treatment of a part-time worker than of a full-time worker may be indirect sex or marital discrimination.
- The less favourable treatment of a part-time worker than of a full-time worker may also breach the Part-time Workers (Prevention of Less Favourable Treatment) Regulations (PTW Regulations) 2000,[1] provided that the workers perform similar work under the same types of contract.
- Full-time workers who become part-time are afforded new protection under the PTW Regulations.
- The employer is, however, always permitted to justify a difference in treatment between part-time and full-time workers on objective grounds.

Background and statutory framework

21.2 Many women returning from maternity leave want to adjust or reduce their hours to enable them to combine work and family responsibilities. Women may find childcare impossible to reconcile with long working hours, or with working hours that are inflexible or that require flexibility to suit the employer, rather than the worker. Given that the responsibility of childcare is, at present, disproportionately shouldered by women, an employer's unjustified refusal to allow a change or reduction in hours may be indirect sex discrimination. And given that married workers are more likely to have responsibility for

1 SI No 1551.

children than are single workers, such an unjustified refusal may also amount to indirect discrimination on grounds of marriage.

21.3 The prohibition of unjustified indirect discrimination by the Sex Discrimination Act (SDA) 1975 has the effect that a woman should be able to vary her hours of work on her return from maternity leave (or, for example, when children start school), without being forced into a different job. Only if her particular job cannot be done on child-friendly working hours may a woman have to try to negotiate a change in job to accommodate working hours that are suitable to her needs.

21.4 A woman may have a claim of indirect discrimination on grounds of sex or marriage if she is treated less favourably because she is working part-time or other 'child-friendly' hours. In addition, the PTW Regulations 2000 provide that an employer must not treat part-time workers (male or female) less favourably than full-time workers unless this can be 'objectively justified'. These provisions came into force on 1 July 2000.

21.5 This chapter looks briefly at:

- how the indirect sex discrimination provisions can be used to secure child-friendly working hours; and
- how the prohibition on unjustified indirect discrimination (on grounds of sex and marriage) and the PTW Regulations 2000 may be used to challenge the less favourable treatment of part-time workers.

Chapter 7 deals with the main principles of indirect sex and marital discrimination including the relevant cases; chapters 22–27 with equal pay and less favourable treatment of part-timers in relation to contractual terms. From 6 April 2003 employees (male and female) will have a right to request a change in their working patterns and the employer will be required to follow a procedure to consider the request. These draft provisions are summarised at para 21.102 onwards.

Access to child-friendly working hours

What are child-friendly working hours?

21.6 Child-friendly hours cover a range of working hours that enable a woman to combine work and childcare. These might include:

- part-time working and job-sharing;
- flexible hours to suit childcare arrangements;
- term-time working;

- working from home;
- career breaks; and
- fixed hours not subject to change by the employer at short notice.

The main legal provisions

21.7 The definition of indirect discrimination is set out at para 7.10. Its application to sex discrimination in employment is covered at para 7.7.[2] Other relevant provisions are:

- Equal Opportunities Commission (EOC) code of practice;
- EC Recommendation on Childcare;
- Human Rights Act (HRA) 1998;
- contract of employment.

EOC code of practice

21.8 Employers and tribunals must take account of the EOC Code of Practice for the elimination of discrimination on the grounds of sex and marriage and the promotion of equality of opportunity in employment.[3] The code of practice states that:

> There are other forms of action which could assist both employer and employee by helping to provide continuity of employment to working parents, many of whom will have valuable experience or skills. Employers may wish to consider with their employees whether certain jobs can be carried out on a part-time or flexi-time basis.

EC Recommendation on Childcare

21.9 The 1992 EC Recommendation on Childcare is intended to provide a work environment that takes into account 'the needs of all working parents with responsibility for the care and upbringing of children'.[4] The guidance to the Recommendation suggests that:

- 'Hours can be reduced by part-time work, by (temporarily) reduced working hours and by jobshare ... It is not common yet for either option to be available at professional and managerial levels, although there is, in practice, little reason why this should be so';
- 'Hours can be staggered by shift work or flexitime. These options can include a very wide range of possibilities – term-time working,

2 SDA 1975 s6.
3 Available from www.eoc.org.uk.
4 92/241/EEC [1992] OJ L123/16.

weekly shifts, three- or four-day weeks, weekly/monthly/annual balancing of hours'.[5]

Although the Recommendation is not binding, it is intended 'as a tool, to be used both separately and in partnership, by government at all levels, social partners, and practitioners, to help them translate policy into effective practice'. In *Grimaldi v Fonds des Maladies Professionelles*[6] the European Court of Justice (ECJ) ruled that domestic courts are bound to take recommendations into account in order to decide disputes.

Human Rights Act 1998

21.10 A requirement to work excessively long (or antisocial) hours may deprive an employee of his or her right to respect for private and family life under article 8 of the European Convention on Human Rights. Where men and women are treated differently in this context, there may be a breach of article 8 read with article 14. For the convention rights and their implementation in domestic law by the HRA 1998 see chapter 9.

The contract of employment

21.11 Some contracts provide that the employer will try to accommodate requests to work part-time and lay down a procedure for employees to follow. In *Taylor v Secretary of State for Scotland*[7] the House of Lords found that an equal opportunities policy which had been negotiated with the trade union formed part of employees' individual contracts of employment, despite its aspirational character. Failure to follow such a policy may breach an employment contract.

The definition of indirect sex discrimination

21.12 The Sex Discrimination (Indirect Discrimination and Burden of Proof) Regulations (BP Regulations) 2001[8] introduced a new definition of indirect sex and marital discrimination in employment cases. The

5 Guidance on implementing the 1992 Council Recommendation on childcare (92/241/EEC).

6 Case 32/88 [1989] ECR 4407; [1990] IRLR 400.

7 [2000] 3 All ER 90; [2000] IRLR 502, although their Lordships there ruled that 'on its true construction, the equal opportunities policy had neither removed the employer's right to terminate the contract when staff reached the minimum retirement age, nor its discretion regarding the retention of staff beyond that age'.

8 SI No 2660. This amended SDA 1975 s1(2)(b).

original definition (which still applies to sex discrimination outside the employment context and to race discrimination) required a woman to show that:

- a 'requirement or condition' was applied to her which was or which would have been applied equally to a man, but with which
- a considerably smaller proportion of women than men could comply, and which
- was to her detriment because she could not comply with it.

Once these factors were established by an applicant, a finding of unlawful indirect discrimination would follow unless the employer could show that the application of the requirement or condition was justifiable.

21.13 The Burden of Proof Directive[9] was implemented in the UK by the BP Regulations 2001. Where they apply, they provide that unlawful sex indirect discrimination will be established where a woman shows that:

- a 'provision, criterion or practice' has been applied to her which has been or would be applied equally to a man, but
- which would be to the detriment of a considerably larger proportion of women than of men, and
- which is to her detriment.

As was previously the case, the establishment of these factors by the applicant will result in a finding of unlawful indirect sex discrimination unless the employer can show that the application of the requirement or condition was justifiable irrespective of sex.

21.14 The burden of proof has also changed in employment-related cases concerning discrimination on grounds of sex or married status. Once the complainant proves facts from which an employment tribunal (ET) 'could ... conclude in the absence of an adequate explanation that the respondent has committed an act of discrimination against the complainant,' the burden moves to the employer to show that he or she did not discriminate. The tribunal *must* uphold the complaint where the employer cannot show that he or she did not discriminate.

21.15 Below is a brief summary of the differences between the old and new definitions of indirect discrimination, and a fuller explanation of the impact of the changes made by the BP Regulations 2001. All the cases discussed in this book are based on the old definition. It should be borne in mind that a claim which has failed in the past because of

9 Council Directive 97/80/EC.

the old, restrictive definition of indirect sex discrimination, may succeed under the new definition. For a detailed explanation of indirect sex discrimination see chapter 7.

Old and new definitions of indirect sex discrimination

The first step

21.16 The SDA 1975 originally required the applicant to show that a 'requirement or condition' was applied to her which was or which would have been applied equally to a man. Such a requirement or condition could include obligations:

- to work full-time;
- to work overtime;
- to work antisocial hours;
- to be office-based all week;[10] or
- to do rotating shifts.[11]

21.17 The new definition of indirect discrimination requires that the applicant identify a 'provision, criterion or practice'. This is a very wide definition and, besides covering all the situations above and any other contractual requirements, is likely to apply to any workplace practice. It is still advisable for a woman not to take any action until it is clear that her employer has refused her request for child-friendly hours or refuses to make a decision. It may otherwise be argued that the provision, criterion or practice has not been applied to the woman.[12]

Disparate impact

21.18 The original SDA 1975 definition of indirect discrimination required that the applicant establish that 'a considerably smaller proportion' of women than of men could comply with the requirement or

10 In *Lockwood v Crawley Warren Group Ltd* (2001) DCLD 47, the EAT held that the employer applied a requirement or conditions when it refused a new mother's request to work at home. The EAT held that a request to work from home at one's expense is conceptually similar to a request to work part-time.

11 See *Hale and Clunie v Wiltshire Healthcare NHS Trust* (1999) DCLD 39, in which the selection for redundancy of nurses who could not work rotating shifts was held to be indirect discrimination on grounds of marriage. See also *Chief Constable of Avon and Somerset Constabulary v Chew*, EAT 503/00, 28 September 2001 (unreported, available on LEXIS).

12 Under the old definition no 'requirement or condition' would be proved unless the employer had refused a request for a change in hours or refused to make a decision.

condition imposed by the discriminator. The new definition of indirect discrimination contains a similar provision, although it is no longer necessary to show that women 'cannot comply' with the requirement, only that it is to the detriment of a considerably larger proportion of women than men. The correct approach to indirect discrimination is considered in chapter 7.

21.19 There is no rule as to what amounts to 'considerably larger' – the factors to be considered are set out at para 21.17. Disparate detrimental impact might be shown by:

- 'Common knowledge' that women are less likely to work child-unfriendly hours than men and so they would suffer a detriment were they required to do so. Statistics show that over 80 per cent of part-time workers are women, and that women work part-time because of childcare responsibilities.[13]
- A demonstration that, within the workplace, a considerably smaller proportion of women work child-unfriendly hours. This information can be obtained through the questionnaire procedure (see para 23.13) or by putting written questions to the employer (see para 32.118).[14]
- Evidence from a labour market statistician or sociologist on working patterns of men and women.

21.20 In *Chief Constable of Avon and Somerset Constabulary v Chew*[15] the EAT held that tribunals could have regard to the following:

- the make-up and overall numbers of the workforce under consideration;
- the point that no man was disadvantaged by the practice or policy at issue;
- the effect of a change in numbers of men and women, for example, when the numbers of women were small, a reduction could have a dramatic effect on the proportion who were disadvantaged;
- the history of, or relevant to, the relevant workforce; and
- the inherent or inherently likely effect of the condition or requirement.

13 See *London Underground v Edwards* [1995] IRLR 355. Statistics are available from the EOC and Labour Force Surveys.

14 Usually the pool will be men and women doing similar work and it would not generally be appropriate to compare a secretary with a managing director. In *London Underground v Edwards (No 2)* [1998] IRLR 364, for example, the comparison was between male and female train drivers to whom the new (antisocial) rostering arrangements applied.

15 EAT 503/00, 28 September 2001 (unreported, available on LEXIS).

21.21 The changes to the burden of proof in sex discrimination may have the effect that, once a woman provides some information showing that a considerably larger proportion of women than men are likely to suffer a detriment by working full-time, the burden of proof will shift to the employer to disprove disproportionate adverse effect.

Detriment

21.22 Under the old definition the applicant had to establish that she had suffered a detriment as a result of her inability to comply with the requirement or condition imposed by the discriminator. The applicant no longer has to show that she 'cannot comply' with the disputed 'provision, criterion or practice'. This is a significant improvement. Under the old definition employers were able to argue, for example, that women could work long hours if they obtained appropriate childcare. If a woman expressed a 'preference' for particular hours of work, this might be taken to show that she 'could' comply with other required hours but chose not to do so. These problems should no longer exist.[16]

21.23 A woman will suffer a detriment in any case in which she has been put at a disadvantage[17] (see para 15.70). This would include, for example:

- being forced to resign, a situation which may also to amount to a constructive dismissal;
- being forced to work the hours required by the employer – in *Home Office v Holmes*[18] the Employment Appeal Tribunal (EAT) accepted that this resulted in 'excessive demands on [the applicant's] time and energy';
- being forced into a lower paid job in order to work part-time; and
- not being able to see her child as much as she wishes.

Justification

21.24 The final element of indirect discrimination has not changed. Under the new provisions, as under the old, the burden is on the employer to prove justification in order to avoid a finding based on the three

16 Evidence about childcare should no longer be necessary. It will also be easier for a woman to argue for child-friendly working hours even if she has been working child-unfriendly hours. The fact that she has been able to work long hours so can comply with them, is no longer relevant.

17 See *Garry v Ealing LBC* [2001] IRLR 681, CA (see para 15.85).

18 [1984] IRLR 299.

factors (set out above) established by the applicant. The test of justification is set out in the *Bilka-Kaufhaus* case:

- Does the disparately impacting provision, criterion or practice condition correspond to a real need on the part of the employer?
- Is it appropriate to achieve that aim?
- Is it necessary to achieve that aim?[19]

21.25 The tribunal must carry out a critical evaluation of whether the employer's reasons demonstrate a real need – for example, for the hours of work demanded of the worker. If there is such a need, the tribunal must then consider whether the need is sufficient to outweigh the impact of the requirement both on the worker herself and on women generally.[20] The greater the impact of the demand (for example, to work long hours) in terms of the number of women adversely affected by it, and/or the seriousness of its impact on any individual complainant, the harder it will be for the employer to justify.[21]

21.26 The Court of Appeal held, in *Whiffen v Hesley Hall Ltd*,[22] that the employer must show that a disparately impacting requirement is '*necessary* to meet the employer's *needs*.' The ECJ has held that generalised assertions, such as that 'job sharers have less experience than full-timers' were not sufficient to provide justification for indirect sex discrimination.[23]

21.27 Ultimately, the question of justification is mainly a factual one, though the legal test must be followed. An employee who wants to change her hours of work should consider carefully how the job can be done on child-friendly hours, and try to answer all the employer's concerns about how it would work. In senior jobs, particularly, it may be helpful if the employee who wishes to work part-time can avoid being out of the office on two consecutive days, and is willing to be contacted in cases of emergency. Note that:

19 Case 170/94 *Bilka-Kaufhaus GmbH v Weber von Hartz* [1986] ECR I-1607; [1986] IRLR 317.

20 *Allonby v Accrington and Rossendale College* [2001] IRLR 364, CA. See also *Bilka-Kaufhaus*, ibid.

21 *London Underground v Edwards (No 2)* [1998] IRLR 364, though see the decision in *Jones v Manchester University* [1993] IRLR 218, CA on the limits of the latter.

22 [2001] IRLR 468, CA. For an application of the test in practice see *Hale and Clunie v Wiltshire Healthcare NHS Trust* (1999) DCLD 39.

23 Case 243/95 *Hill and Stapleton v Revenue Commissioners* [1998] ECR I-3739; [1998] IRLR 466.

- A blanket policy against job-sharing or part-time work will be difficult to justify because no consideration will have been given to whether any particular job could be done on different hours.
- There is no intrinsic reason why supervisory-level jobs cannot be done on a job-sharing basis.
- The possibility of increased costs do not necessarily constitute justification for a refusal to permit part-time or other 'flexible' forms of working. In *Home Office v Holmes*,[24] the Home Office argued that its costs would be increased by employing two part-timers, rather than one full-timer. The EAT preferred the applicant's evidence that the civil service was losing valuable trained personnel when women left to start families and that efficiency had increased when part-timers were introduced in some departments.[25]
- An assumption that the introduction of part-time working or job-sharing will result in the duplication of work will not be sufficient justification for refusing such forms of work.
- Ensuring continuity of service or production is a common argument for opposing job-sharing. It has been recognised by some tribunals, however, that this problem is often more imagined than real.
- Failure by the employer to follow their own policy may be relevant. In *Amos v IPC Magazines*[26] the ET said it would be a 'strange and inconsistent outcome to accept that justification had been established when there had been such a number of significant failures to follow the respondent's own maternity policy'.
- The fact that a worker has already been working different hours without difficulty is likely to be a factor.[27]
- The fact that permitting part-time or flexible working in one case may set a precedent in others will not be a sufficient justification for its refusal unless the employer could show that, for example, the proportion of employees working such hours made it very difficult to arrange meetings, and/or that a disproportionate burden was being placed on full-time workers.

24 [1984] IRLR 299.

25 See Case 243/95 *Hill and Stapleton v Revenue Commissioners* [1998] ECR I-3739; [1998] IRLR 466.

26 ET 2301499/00, 4 April 2001 (unreported).

27 See *Rothwell t/a DC's Chuckwagon and Pizza Pie*, ET 2902130/1999 (unreported).

A practical solution may be to agree to a trial period. In *Southall v London Chamber of Commerce and Industry*[28] the ET rejected the applicant's argument that the imposition of a three-month trial period either had a disparate impact or was unjustified.

Supporting a claim for part-time/ flexible working

21.28 The employer should be required to provide good and substantiated reasons why it is not possible to allow a woman to work part-time or to perform her job on a job-share or other 'flexible' basis. The employee can ask for this information in the questionnaire (see para 32.13). It is also useful to obtain the following information:

- General information about the advantages of part-time work and job-sharing. In some cases a representative from a charity such as New Ways to Work has given very helpful evidence.
- Evidence of other similar jobs that have been done on a job-share, part-time or other flexible basis.
- Evidence of how the job can be done on a part-time, job-share or other flexible basis.
- Whether there are other ways in which the work can be effectively carried out. If there is too much work for a part-time worker, for example, a job share should be considered.

Options for women refused 'child-friendly' hours

21.29 In *British Telecommunications plc v Roberts*[29] the applicants, who worked full-time, took maternity leave at the same time. Both women wanted to return to their posts but on a job-sharing basis. They were offered the option of either returning full-time or working part-time (which involved unsocial hours plus Saturday working). Neither applicant wanted to lose her job so one opted for part-time working under protest and the other returned to work full-time, also under protest. Both brought claims for direct discrimination. On appeal, the EAT referred the cases back to the ET to consider the claims of indirect discrimination, having overruled the ET's findings of direct discrimination.

21.30 The applicants in the *BT v Roberts* case could have resigned and claimed constructive dismissal in which case the ET would have had

28 ET 2204702/00, 14 June 2001 (unreported).
29 [1996] IRLR 601.

to decide whether the refusal to allow them to work part-time or to job-share was a sufficiently serious breach of contract to amount to a dismissal.[30] If the requirement to work full-time had been regarded as justified, the applicants would have been left with neither jobs nor remedies. It is not advisable for a woman to stay away from work if her employer refuses to change her hours as she could be disciplined or dismissed for unauthorised absence.

The rights of men to 'child-friendly' working hours

21.31 Men who are refused child-friendly working hours will be unable to establish indirect sex discrimination. Since women are primarily responsible for childcare, a man will not be able to show that a requirement to work full-time has a disproportionate impact on men. But direct discrimination will occur if a woman would be permitted to work child-friendly hours and a man in similar circumstances is not.

21.32 In *Walkingshaw v John Martin Group*[31] a male vehicle technician was told that he could not work reduced hours in order to care for his son because it was too complicated. The ET found that, if he had been a woman, his request would have been examined closely and would, on the balance of probabilities, have been granted. It was not fatal to the claim that there was no part-time female employee in the applicant's department and he could compare his treatment with that of a female employee in a different department.

Remedies

21.33 Tribunals may, of course, award compensation for sex discrimination. They may also make recommendations which could include, for example, a recommendation that a particular applicant be allowed to work part-time or to job-share.

30 See *Ward v Gruner and Jahr*, ET 3201305/99 (unreported) in which an ET found that, although the applicant retained the same job title after her return from maternity leave, her tasks and responsibilities had been substantially taken away from her and her job status was significantly downgraded. The ET held that this was less favourable treatment which was a breach of her contract and entitled her to resign without notice and claim unfair dismissal and sex discrimination. Note that dismissal includes constructive dismissal – SDA 1975 s82(1A)(b).

31 ET S/401126/00 (unreported).

The rights of part-time workers

Introduction to the Part-time Workers Regulations 2000

21.34 The PTW Regulations 2000 give part-time workers, male and female, rights to the same terms and conditions (on a pro rata basis where appropriate) as full-time workers who are employed on the same type of contract and who do broadly similar work.[32] In addition, a full-time worker who transfers to part-time work should retain no less favourable terms and conditions than before.

21.35 PTW Regulations reg 5(1) provides that:

> A part-time worker has the right not to be treated by his employer less favourably than the employer treats a comparable full-time worker –
> (a) as regards the terms of his contract; or
> (b) by being subjected to any other detriment by any act, or deliberate failure to act, of his employer.

This prohibition on discrimination applies only if (reg 5(2)):

> (a) the treatment is on the ground that the worker is a part-time worker, and
> (b) the treatment is not justified on objective grounds.

21.36 In determining whether a part-time worker has been treated less favourably than a comparable full-time worker, reg 5(3) provides that the pro rata principle shall be applied unless it is inappropriate.

Comparing the models of protection

21.37 Even though the provisions under the PTW Regulations 2000, the Equal Pay Act (EqPA) 1970 and the SDA 1975 are very different, an applicant will often have a claim under either the EqPA 1970 or the SDA 1975 (depending on whether the alleged discrimination concerns contractual terms or non-contractual matters) and, in addition, a claim under the PTW Regulations 2000 (which cover both). There are many differences between these three pieces of legislation. In particular, a claim for equal treatment of full-time and part-time workers under the EqPA 1970 and SDA 1975 requires that all the elements of indirect discrimination are satisfied (see chapter 7). Under the PTW Regulations 2000, by contrast, the question is whether a part-time worker has been treated less favourably than a full-time comparator and, if this has happened, whether the discrimination can be justified

32 In force 1 July 2000.

by the employer.[33] Further, the BP Regulations 2001 apply only in relation to sex discrimination under the SDA 1975, although it is likely that the courts will apply the same definition of indirect discrimination under the EqPA 1970.[34]

21.38 In some situations the PTW Regulations 2000 will provide better protection. In others, a claim is more likely to succeed under the discrimination legislation. The table below sets out the main points of comparison between the SDA 1975, the EqPA 1970 and the PTW Regulations 2000.

PTW Regulations 2000	EqPA 1970	SDA 1975
Apply to contractual and non-contractual discrimination where an actual (narrowly defined) comparator exists	Only applies to pay and contractual terms where there a comparator exists	Applies to non-contractual terms and requires only a hypothetical comparator
Apply to men and women workers, including the self-employed, contract workers and apprentices	Applies to men and women workers, but indirect discrimination provisions protect only women in this context	Applies to men and women workers, but indirect discrimination provisions protect only women in this context
Comparator can be same-sex, but must have a similar type of contract to the applicant	Comparator must be opposite sex but need not have same type of contract as the applicant	Comparator must be opposite sex but need not have same type of contract as the applicant
Comparator must be engaged in the same or broadly similar work for the same employer	Comparator must be doing like work, work rated as equivalent, or work of equal value, for the same or an associated employer	Comparator, real or hypothetical, must be a man in similar circumstances, not necessarily one doing the same or similar work. Comparison is usually with workers in the same employment.[35]

continued

33 So there is no need to show disproportionate impact.

34 The EqPA 1970 does not contain any definition of indirect sex discrimination but it is accepted, mainly because of EC law, that indirect discrimination in pay is prohibited.

35 Though the labour market situation will often be relevant.

PTW Regulations 2000	**EqPA 1970**	**SDA 1975**
Employer may justify a difference in treatment between a part-time and a full-time worker on objective grounds	Employer may rely on material factor defence, similar in practice to the objective justification test	Employer may justify indirect sex discrimination on objective grounds
Three-month time limit with just and equitable extensions	Six-month time limit with no power to extend	Three-month time limit with just and equitable extension
Worker can request written statement giving reasons for less favourable treatment	No power to request written statement stating different in pay. May use questionnaire procedure	Applicant can serve a sex discrimination questionnaire
Power for ET to order: – declaration – recommendation – compensation (limited)	The ET used only to be able to award two years' back pay but the ECJ has held this to be a breach of EC law and this limit is now wrong (see *Preston*,[36] para 21.00 below)	No cap on compensation which can include injury to feelings

The coverage of the Part-time Workers Regulations 2000[37]

21.39 The coverage of the PTW Regulations 2000 is not restricted to employees (past or present). They apply, rather, to:

- employees who work or worked under a contract of employment, written or oral;
- trainees and apprentices;[38] and
- individuals who work or have worked under a contract, express or implied, under which they undertake personally to undertake any work or services for another. This would include, for example, self-employed and contract workers, but not those working under

36 *Preston v Wolverhampton Healthcare NHS Trust (No 2)* [2001] 2 AC 455; [2001] IRLR 237, which followed the ECJ decision in Case 78/98 *Preston v Wolverhampton Healthcare NHS Trust (No 1)* [2000] ECR I-3201; [2000] IRLR 506.

37 For exclusions under the SDA 1975 and EqPA 1970 see chapter 11.

38 For definitions see PTW Regs 2000 reg 1(1).

contracts where the individual is a profession or business providing services to clients or customers.[39]

In addition, the PTW Regulations 2000 apply to:

- Crown employees and workers, who are protected in the same way as other employees and workers.[40]
- Those in the armed forces, except in relation to service as a member of the reserve forces in so far as that service consists in undertaking certain training obligations. Complaints by members of the armed forces must first be made to an officer under the service redress procedures and a complaint cannot be made if the redress application is withdrawn.[41]
- House of Lords staff employed under a contract with the Corporate Officer of the House of Lords.[42]
- House of Commons staff who have been appointed by the House of Commons Commission or who are members of the Speaker's personal staff.[43]
- The police, including those holding the office of constable or an appointment as a police cadet.[44]

Holders of judicial offices are not covered where they are paid on a daily fee-paid basis.[45]

21.40 No qualifying period for protection applies under the PTW Regulations 2000.[46] Nor does the upper age limit on unfair dismissal protection apply in connection with them.[47]

'Full-time' and 'part-time' workers

21.41 The PTW Regulations 2000 embrace the 'pro rata principle', which provides that part-time workers should enjoy equivalent benefits in connection with each hour worked as comparable full-time workers. 'Weekly hours' refers to the hours a worker is contractually required to work each week, ignoring any absences or overtime. If he or she

39 PTW Regs 2000 reg 1(2)(b).
40 Ibid reg 12.
41 Ibid reg 13.
42 Ibid reg 14.
43 Ibid reg 15.
44 Ibid reg 16.
45 Ibid reg 17.
46 ERA 1996 s108(3)(i).
47 Ibid s109(2)(i).

works fluctuating hours, it is the weekly average of such hours. The distinction between a full-time and a part-time worker depends on the 'custom and practice' of the employer in relation to workers employed by the employer under the same type of contract as the applicant.[48] A full-time worker is one who is paid by reference to the time he or she works and is 'identifiable as a full-time worker'. A part-time worker is one who is paid by reference to the time he or she works and is not identifiable as a full-time worker.

The relevant comparator

21.42 A part-time worker can only compare herself or himself with a full-time worker:

- with a similar contract; and
- doing broadly similar work; and
- at the same establishment or, if there is no full-time worker with a similar contract engaged in similar work at the same establishment, at a different establishment;[49] and
- working for the same employer.

21.43 There is no concept of associated employers under the PTW Regulations 2000 as there is under the SDA 1975 and EqPA 1970. Nor can the part-time worker use a hypothetical comparator under the PTW Regulations 2000 as she may under the SDA 1975.

Working under 'similar' contracts

21.44 The comparison, for the purpose of determining whether there has been less favourable treatment, is between workers with similar contracts. It is not possible, for example, to compare a permanent employee with one on a fixed-term contract. The different categories of worker are as follows:

- permanent employees (who are not apprentices);
- employees on a fixed-term contract (who are not apprentices);
- employees who are employed under contracts of apprenticeship;
- workers who are not employees and do not have fixed-term contracts;
- workers who are not employees and who do have fixed-term contracts;

48 PTW Regs 2000 reg 2(1) and (2).
49 Ibid reg 2(4).

- any other description of worker that it is reasonable for the employer to treat differently from other workers on the ground that they have a different type of contract.[50]

21.45 Draft regulations have been published which propose to allow individual part-timers to compare themselves with a full-time colleague irrespective of whether either's contract is permanent or fixed-term. The proposals also state that whether a particular worker is contracted to work for a time-limited or for an indefinite period may, depending on the facts of the case, be a relevant factor in determining whether less favourable treatment of a part-timer is acceptable.[51]

Broadly similar work

21.46 The full-time worker with whom the part-timer can compare herself or himself must be 'engaged in the same or broadly similar work [as the part-timer] having regard, where relevant, to whether they have a similar level of qualification, skills and experience'. This is similar, but not identical, to the 'like work' comparison under the EqPA 1970 (see chapter 23).[52]

21.47 Under the regulations, the question whether workers are doing broadly similar work takes into account levels of qualification, skill and experience only 'where relevant'. Thus, if a full-time comparator has more skill and experience than the applicant, but does not use them in his or her job, they should not be taken into account.

21.48 Despite the differences between the tests under the PTW Regulations 2000 and the EqPA 1970, cases decided under the EqPA 1970 are likely to be relevant in deciding whether workers are doing similar work for the purpose of the PTW Regulations 2000.

Workers who transfer from full-time to part-time work

21.49 In a case in which a full-time worker transfers to part-time work and is then treated less favourably, the PTW Regulations 2000 do not require another actual comparator. Rather, the comparator is the part-time worker when he or she was engaged in full-time work. This provision applies when:

50 PTW Regs 2000 reg 2(3).

51 See www.dti.gov.uk/er/fixed/ptime.htm. See also EDR 103, March 2002.

52 Under the EqPA 1970 a comparison can be made with another employee doing work rated as equivalent under a job evaluation scheme and/or an employee doing work of equal value – see further para 22.16.

- the worker was previously a full-time worker;
- the worker's contract is terminated or varied;
- he or she continues to work under a new or varied contract, whether of the same type or not; and
- he or she is required or agrees to work fewer hours.

21.50 Regulation 3 does not require that the work done before and after the transition to part-time status was the same as or equivalent to that done after. The job could, in theory, be entirely different. Having said this, the regulations only prohibit less favourable treatment after a transfer to part-time work when such treatment is on the ground that the worker is part-time, and is not justifiable.[53]

Workers returning part-time after absence

21.51 A worker who changes from full-time to part-time work after an absence of less than 12 months is not required to compare herself or himself with another worker doing similar work on a similar contract.[54] Provided that the following factors apply, the worker should retain the same pay and benefits (pro rata) as he or she had as a full-time worker:

- he or she must have been a full-time worker immediately before the absence (whether the absence followed a termination of the worker's contract or not);
- he or she must return to work for the same employer within a period of less than 12 months from the start of the absence;
- he or she must return to the same job or to a job at the same level, whether under different or varied contract, irrespective of whether it is the same type of contract;
- he or she must be required to work fewer weekly hours than he or she was doing immediately before the period of absence.[55]

This provision (reg 4) will cover the case of a woman returning part-time after an extended period of maternity-related leave. What is important to note is that where the transition to part-time work occurs

53 PTW Regs 2000 reg 3.

54 Note that the PTW Regs 2000 give no right to return to work part-time after maternity leave but the guidance encourages employers to consider this.

55 Ibid reg 4 assumes that the comparison is with a worker with the same contract as the applicant prior to her/his absence. In other words the comparison is with the worker's previous full-time contract.

after a break in employment, the requirement for an actual comparator is disapplied only in a case in which the applicant returns to the same or an equivalent job.

'Less favourable' treatment

21.52 Less favourable treatment occurs when a part-time worker is denied the same pay, benefits and other treatment (pro-rated where appropriate) to that enjoyed by full-timers. A part-time worker has the right, under the PTW Regulations 2000, not to be treated less favourably than a comparable full-time worker on the ground that he or she is a part-time worker, unless the employer can show that the discrimination is objectively justified. This right applies:

- in relation to the terms of his or her contract; and
- in relation to any other detriment to which the part-time worker is subjected by any act, or deliberate failure to act, of the employer.[56] Although no specific mention is made of dismissal, the compliance guidance[57] states that the criteria used to select jobs for redundancy should be objectively justified and that part-time workers must not be treated less favourably than comparable full-time workers. This should also apply to any other type of dismissal.

There are notes to the regulations and compliance guidance, which, although not legally binding, give some indication of how the regulations should be interpreted.

The application to cases of less favourable treatment of the Part-time Workers Regulations 2000, the Equal Pay Act 1970 and the Sex Discrimination Act 1975

21.53 In order to challenge discrimination under the PTW Regulations 2000, a part-time worker must find an appropriate comparator and show that the less favourable treatment complained of is by reason that he or she is a part-time worker, the onus then passing to the employer to establish that the discrimination is objectively justified. If

56 PTW Regs 2000 reg 5(1).

57 'Notes on how to comply with the regulations', available at www.dti.gov.uk/er/notes.pdf.

the EqPA 1970 or the SDA 1975 is relied upon to challenge discrimination against a part-time worker, the worker must show that she has been subjected to indirect discrimination on grounds of sex or married status before the employer is required to establish objective justification.[58] The differences between the EqPA 1970 and the SDA 1975 are set out at paras 11.29 and 11.32. The most significant of these is that the EqPA 1970 covers contractual terms and the SDA 1975 non-contractual provisions.

21.54 In the following paragraphs we consider the respective application of the PTW Regulations 2000 and the SDA 1975 and EqPA 1970 to specific types of discrimination against part-time workers. It is important to bear in mind that the PTW Regulations 2000 regulate the less favourable treatment of part-time workers only where such treatment is *by reason of* their working part-time. The SDA 1975 and EqPA 1970, on the other hand, regulate discrimination against part-time workers only to the extent that such discrimination amounts to indirect discrimination on grounds of sex or marital status. Whether discrimination against part-time workers is challenged under the PTW Regulations 2000 or under the EqPA 1970 or the SDA 1975, employers will escape a finding against them if they can establish that the discrimination was objectively justifiable.

Basic pay

21.55 The PTW Regulations 2000 provide that part-time workers must not receive a lower basic rate of pay than comparable full-timers by reason of their working part-time. The prohibition on less favourable treatment does not apply where the reason for the less favourable treatment is not the difference in status between part-time and full-time workers – where, for example, a part-time worker is paid a lower hourly rate than a full-timer because his or her performance has been rated less highly by a non-discriminatory performance-related pay scheme.

21.56 Under the EqPA 1970 and article 141 of the EC Treaty, an employer must justify a difference in pay between part-time and full-time workers only if it amounts to indirect discrimination on grounds of sex or marriage (see para 25.49).[59] The EqPA 1970 is not concerned with 'pay' as such, rather with discrimination in contractual terms. 'Pay' is

58 Or, in the case of a male part-time worker, that he has been subjected to direct sex discrimination (see para 21.31).

59 The woman (or man) must, of course, be doing like work, work rated as equivalent or work of equal value with a comparable man (or woman).

very broadly defined under article 141 to cover not only wages and salaries but also, among other things, productivity and performance-related pay, contractual pensions, redundancy pay and payments for time off for union duties (see para 22.27).[60] To the extent that 'pay' within article 141 does not come within the EqPA 1970, because, for example, it is not contractual, discrimination in connection with it may be challenged under the SDA 1975.[61] Account must also be taken of the EOC code of practice on equal pay.

Increments based on length of service

21.57 The PTW Regulations 2000 do not expressly deal with increments based on length of service,[62] but the service of a part-time worker should be treated as equivalent to that of a full-time worker unless it is objectively justified to do otherwise (see para 21.35).

21.58 In *Hill and Stapleton*[63] the ECJ ruled that article 141 was breached by a practice by which two years' service in a job-sharing capacity were treated as equivalent to a single year of full-time service for the purpose of calculating increments based on length of service. The practice was shown to have a disparate impact on women and the ECJ held that an employer cannot justify discrimination arising from a job-sharing scheme solely on the ground that avoidance of such discrimination would involve increased costs. The ECJ also held that generalised assertions, such as 'job sharers have less experience than full-timers', were not sufficient to justify indirect discrimination.

Overtime payments

21.59 A part-time employee is only entitled to receive overtime rates of pay under the PTW Regulations 2000 if a comparable full-time worker would receive overtime rates for the hours worked.[64] Thus, where

60 See Case 96/80 *Jenkins v Kingsgate (Clothing Productions) Ltd* [1981] ECR 911; [1981] IRLR 228, ECJ and *(No 2)* [1981] IRLR 388, in which the EAT held that the employer must show that the difference in pay between full-time and part-time workers is reasonably necessary in order to obtain some result (other than cheap labour) which the employer wishes to achieve, for economic or other reasons.

61 See, eg, Case 12/81 *Garland v British Rail Engineering Ltd* [1982] ECR 359; [1982] IRLR 257.

62 This is not necessary as the PTW Regs 2000 cover 'terms' of the contract.

63 Case 243/95 *Hill and Stapleton v Revenue Commissioners* [1998] ECR I-3739; [1998] IRLR 466.

64 PTW Regs 2000 reg 5(4).

overtime rates are paid to full-time workers who exceed their normal hours of 35 per week, a part-time worker who normally works 21 hours per week will not be entitled to payment at the higher rate until he or she works more than 35 hours in a week.

21.60 According to the ECJ in *Stadt Lengerich v Helmig*, it is lawful to provide for the payment of overtime for part-time workers only for hours worked in excess of the normal working hours for full-time employees.[65] Thus part-time workers were not entitled to overtime payments until they had exceeded the normal hours of full-timers.

Shift allowances and unsocial hours payments

21.61 Where workers are entitled to antisocial hours payments, shift allowances and weekend payments, the compliance guidance issued under the PTW Regulations 2000 points out that these should be paid on the same basis to part-time and full-time workers. Failure to pay shift allowances and unsocial hours payments to part-time workers is also likely to be a breach of the EqPA 1970 and article 141, provided indirect sex discrimination can be proved (see para chapter 7). If the payments are non-contractual (ie, discretionary) the claim would properly be brought under the SDA 1975.

Bonuses

21.62 Part-time workers should be entitled to be paid any bonus on a pro rata bonus, unless its refusal can be objectively justified by the employer. The compliance guidance issued under the PTW Regulations 2000 states that the same principle of equality applies to enhanced rates of pay (such as bonuses) as to basic pay.

21.63 In the *Krüger* case[66] the ECJ held that the exclusion of part-time workers from the scope of a collective agreement that provided for the grant of a special annual bonus amounted to indirect discrimination contrary to article 141 where it affected a considerably higher percentage of women than men. The employers argued that such workers did not pay social security contributions and that this was in accord with German government policy, upheld by the ECJ in the *Nolte* and

65 Cases 34, 50 and 78/93 [1994] ECR I-5727; [1995] IRLR 216.

66 Case 281/97 *Krüger v Kreiskrankenhaus Ebersberg* [1999] ECR I-5127; [1999] IRLR 808.

Megner cases,[67] to meet a demand for part-time work. The ECJ was not persuaded that this justified the policy, saying that the margin of discretion given to member states is not to be accorded to employers. The court held that it was not a question of national legislation or a basic principle of the social security system, 'but of the exclusion of persons in minor employment from the benefit of a collective agreement which provides for the grant of a special annual bonus, the result of this being that, in respect of pay, those persons are treated differently from those governed by that collective agreement'.[68] As in the case of discretionary shift allowances, discrimination in relation to non-contractual bonuses ought to be challenged under the SDA 1975. If the position is unclear it is advisable to claim under both EqPA 1970 and SDA 1975; Article 141 and PTW Regulations 2000.

Profit sharing, share options schemes

21.64 Under the PTW Regulations 2000 the benefits of profit sharing and share option schemes should be available, on a pro rata basis, to part-time workers. The same principles should apply under the EqPA 1970, although there have been no reported cases on profit sharing or share options schemes.

Contractual sick and maternity pay

21.65 A part-time worker should receive equivalent sick and maternity benefits to those enjoyed by comparable full-time workers unless the employer can justify discrimination between them. It is difficult to anticipate when such discrimination would be justified. The guidance issued under the PTW Regulations 2000 points out that the pro rata principle applies to:

- the rate of sick or maternity pay;
- the length of any service required to qualify for the benefits;[69] and
- the length of time for which the payment is received.

67 Respectively, Case 317/93 *Nolte v Landesversicherungsanstalt Hannover* [1995] ECR I-4625; [1996] IRLR 225 and Case 444/93 *Megner v Innungskrankenkasse Theinland-Pfalz Nolte* [1995] ECR I-4741; [1996] IRLR 236.

68 The ECJ distinguished two previous cases, *Nolte* and *Megner*, ibid, on the grounds that they concerned social insurance schemes which fell within the broad margin of discretion of member states.

69 See Case 243/95 *Hill and Stapleton v Revenue Commissioners* [1998] ECR I-3739; [1998] IRLR 466.

21.66 Discrimination against part-time workers in respect of sick pay is likely to breach article 141 and the EqPA 1970.[70] It is hard to see, however, how discrimination between part-time and full-time workers in connection with maternity benefits could amount to sex discrimination for the purposes of the EqPA 1970, article 141 or (in the case of non-contractual benefits), the SDA 1975 (see para 18.32 above).

Occupational pensions

21.67 The guidance to the PTW Regulations 2000 suggests that employers cannot deny access to occupational pensions to part-time workers (male and female), unless discrimination against part-timers is justified on objective grounds. Where a successful claim is made under the regulations, however, it may be backdated for no more than two years from the date of the complaint. The government proposes to remove the two-year limit in response to the House of Lords' decision in *Preston v Wolverhampton Healthcare Trust*.[71] This will affect the compensation payable by employers where they discriminate unlawfully against part-timers in respect of pension provision.[72]

21.68 It is likely also to be a breach of the EqPA 1970 and article 141 to exclude part-timers from a pension scheme.[73] A two-year limit on backdating imposed by the EqPA 1970 was held, in *Preston*, to contravene article 141 (see para 10.79).

Health insurance, subsidised mortgages, staff discounts

21.69 The PTW Regulations 2000 provide that benefits such as these should be provided on a pro rata basis to part-time workers where possible. The compliance guidance states that where a benefit, such as health insurance, cannot be applied pro rata, this is not of itself an objective justification for denying it to part-time workers.

21.70 The same principles apply under the EqPA 1970 as under the PTW

70 Case 171/88 *Rinner-Kuhn v FWW Spezial-Gebaudereinigung GmbH* [1989] ECR I-2743; [1989] IRLR 493, ECJ.

71 *Preston v Wolverhampton Healthcare NHS Trust (No 2)* [2001] 2 AC 455; [2001] IRLR 237.

72 See www.dti.gov.uk/er/fixed/ptime.htm – the consultation on the draft regulations ended on 15 April 2002.

73 Case 170/94 *Bilka-Kaufhaus GmbH v Weber von Hartz* [1986] ECR I-1607; [1986] IRLR 317; Case 57/93 *Vroege v NCIV Instituut voor Volkshuisvesting BV* [1994] ECR I-4541; [1994] IRLR 651, ECJ.

Regulations 2000, assuming indirect sex discrimination is established. As before, if the offending provisions are non-contractual the claim should be made under the SDA 1975.

Company cars

21.71 It may be argued, under the PTW Regulations 2000, that a part-time worker ought to be provided with a company car if a full-time worker doing similar work would receive one. Employers may, however, be able to argue that the provision of cars to part-timers would be unduly expensive, given the increased number of workers involved. One option would be for the employer to provide a pro rata car allowance to part-time workers, or for part-time workers to share a car.

21.72 The same principles apply under the EqPA 1970 as under the PTW Regulations 2000, assuming indirect sex discrimination is established. As before, if the offending provisions are non-contractual the claim should be made under the SDA 1975.

Holidays, other leave, career breaks

21.73 The guidance to the PTW Regulations 2000 states that part-time workers, like their full-time colleagues, are entitled to minimum statutory annual leave, maternity leave and parental leave. Where enhanced by contractual conditions, part-time workers should receive pro rata holiday entitlement and other leave (including parental and maternity leave and career breaks).

21.74 The same principles apply under the EqPA 1970 as under the PTW Regulations 2000, assuming indirect sex discrimination is established. As before, if the offending provisions are non-contractual the claim should be made under the SDA 1975.

Training

21.75 The compliance guidance to the PTW Regulations 2000 states that employers should not exclude staff from training simply because they work part-time. The compliance guidance suggests that training will need to be structured wherever possible to be at the most convenient times for the majority of staff including part-timers.

21.76 Assuming indirect sex discrimination is established, refusal to pay a part-time worker for the hours spent on a training course which exceed his or her normal contractual hours would also breach article

141 and the EqPA 1970 or SDA 1975.[74] Refusal of training to a worker because he or she works part-time may also breach the SDA 1975.

Promotion

21.77 The compliance guidance to the PTW Regulations 2000 points out that:

> ... if individual companies and the economy as a whole are to reap the full benefit of the flexibility part-time work can offer, then more types of job and levels of management must be opened to part-time workers ... Part-time workers should also be given equal opportunity to seek promotion.

The guidance states that 'previous or current part-time status should not of itself constitute a barrier to promotion to a post, whether the post is full-time or part-time'.

21.78 A claim for failure to promote must be brought under the SDA 1975 and will, of course, turn on proof of indirect sex or marital discrimination. In *Gold v Tower Hamlets LBC*[75] an ET ruled that a solicitor had been discriminated against when she was not promoted because she was job-sharing.

21.79 Where promotion is based on length of service and part-time workers are deemed to accrue service at a slower rate, this may also amount to unlawful sex discrimination. In the *Gerster* case the applicant, a part-timer, worked half normal full-time hours.[76] She applied for promotion, access to which was based on merit and length of service. The employer refused to treat her part-time employment as equivalent to full-time service, crediting her (in accordance with the normal practice) with two-thirds of her actual service. As a result she was denied promotion. The ECJ ruled that the Equal Treatment Directive[77] (ETD) was breached by a practice whereby part-time employees accrued service more slowly, and so took longer to achieve promotion, than full-timers where this disproportionately disadvantaged women and was not justified. In order to establish that such discrimination was justified, an employer would need to show that there

74 Case 360/90 *Arbeiterwohlfahrt der Stadt Berli eV v Botel* [1992] ECR I-03589; [1992] IRLR 423, ECJ.

75 Case 05608/91/LN/C.

76 Case 1/95 *Gerster v Freistaat Bayern* [1997] ECR I-5253; [1997] IRLR 700, and Case 243/95 *Hill and Stapleton v Revenue Commissioners* [1998] ECR I-3739; [1998] IRLR 466.

77 Council Directive 76/207/EC.

was a link between length of service (in the sense of hours worked) and the acquisition of a certain level of knowledge or experience necessary for the job.

Dismissal for redundancy

21.80 Part-timers should be treated no less favourably than their full-time equivalents in relation to redundancy. Selecting part-timers for redundancy before full-timers is likely to breach the PTW Regulations 2000. The compliance guidance states that the criteria used to select workers for redundancy should be objectively justified, and that part-time workers must not be treated less favourably than comparable full-time workers.

21.81 Assuming indirect sex discrimination is established, the adoption of part-time working as a criterion for redundancy selection is likely to be unjustified and therefore unlawful under the SDA 1975.[78] In *Allonby v Accrington and Rossendale College*[79] the employers terminated the contracts of part-time hourly-paid staff and offered them work as subcontractors on lower pay. The Court of Appeal accepted that a requirement had been imposed on workers that, in order to continue to be employed by the college, they had to be employed full-time. It went on to hold that, if the proportion of women able to comply with this requirement was considerably smaller than the proportion of men who could comply with it, and if the employer could not justify its adoption, unlawful indirect discrimination would be established. The test for justification is set out at para 21.24 above.

21.82 The exclusion of part-timers from access to a severance payment on redundancy or other termination of employment is likely to amount to unlawful indirect sex discrimination.[80] However, the House of Lords ruled, in *Barry v Midland Bank plc*,[81] that a redundancy scheme whereby redundancy pay was based on earnings (in the case of the applicant, part-time earnings) at the time of redundancy, rather than on her previous full-time earnings, was not unlawful because it was justifiable and not discriminatory (see para 7.58).

78 *Clarke v Eley Kynock Ltd* [1982] IRLR 382. The EAT also said that a dismissal which is indirectly discriminatory is also likely to be unfair.

79 *Allonby v Accrington and Rossendale College* [2001] IRLR 364, CA.

80 Case 33/89 *Kowalska v Freie und Hansestadt Hamburg* [1990] ECR I-2591; [1990] IRLR 447 ECJ.

81 *Barry v Midland Bank plc* [1999] 1 WLR 1465; [1999] IRLR 581.

Other benefits contingent on length of service

21.83 The PTW Regulations 2000 make no express mention of benefits contingent upon length of service. But the principles applicable under the regulations are likely to be the same as those established under the EqPA 1970, the SDA 1975 and EC law.

21.84 In *Nimz*[82] the ECJ held that an agreement whereby the entire length of service of full-time workers was taken into account for reclassification to a higher salary grade, but only half the service of part-timers, was a breach of article 141 where this had a disproportionate adverse effect on women. It was not justifiable. The ECJ held that, although seniority goes hand in hand with experience which, in principle, should allow the employee to carry out his/her tasks better, the objectivity of such a criterion depended on all the circumstances of each case.

21.85 In *Kording v Senator fun Fionanzen*[83] German legislation provided that the length (in years) of professional experience required for exemption from a qualifying examination was increased in the case of part-time workers. The ECJ held that this would breach the ETD if substantially fewer men than women worked part-time, unless it was justified by objective factors unrelated to any discrimination. Such justification would be supplied if it were established that the extra hours worked made a significant difference to the competence of the worker. Similar principles applied in *Gerster* and in *Hill and Stapleton* (see para 21.87).

Part-time Worker Regulations continued

Objective justification under the Part-time Worker Regulations

21.86 The test for justification under the PTW Regulations 2000 is very similar to that for the objective justification of indirect sex discrimination. But it is likely that, in order to avoid a finding that discrimination against part-time workers breaches the regulations, the employer will have to show that the less favourable treatment was:

82 Case 184/89 *Nimz v Freie und Hansestadt Hamburg* [1991] ECR I-297; [1991] IRLR 222.

83 Case 1/95 [1997] ECR I-5253; [1997] IRLR 710.

- in pursuit of a legitimate objective – for example, a genuine business objective;
- necessary to achieve that objective; and
- an appropriate way to achieve the objective.[84]

21.87 In *Hill and Stapleton*,[85] which involved a challenge under article 141, the ECJ held that an employer had not justified a practice whereby job-sharers' length of service was treated as half that of a full-timer in a situation where a job-sharer could acquire the same experience as a full-timer. The fact that the avoidance of discrimination would involve increased costs did not justify the indirect sex discrimination involved. Nor was it justified by the fact that there was an established practice of crediting only actual service or that the practice was said to establish a reward system which maintained staff motivation, commitment and morale. Similarly, in *Jørgensen*[86] (a claim brought under the ETD) the ECJ remarked that permitting budgetary considerations to justify indirect discrimination would have the effect that the application of the principle of equal treatment might vary according to the state of the public finances of the particular member state. This is the more true in relation to private sector employers in relation to whom, further, the ECJ does not apply the same margin of appreciation as is accorded to member states. It would be surprising if the ECJ adopted a different test for the PWD than it has under article 141, although it is entitled to do so.

The right to a written statement of reasons for less favourable treatment

21.88 A worker who believes that she has been treated less favourably than a full-time worker can ask the employer for a written statement giving particulars of the reasons for the treatment,[87] and in a dismissal case, written reasons for the dismissal. The employer must provide her with a statement within 21 days of the request.

84 PTW Regs 2000 reg 5(2)(b) and see Case 170/94 *Bilka-Kaufhaus GmbH v Weber von Hartz* [1986] ECR I-1607; [1986] IRLR 317.

85 Case 243/95 *Hill and Stapleton v Revenue Commissioners* [1998] ECR I-3739; [1998] IRLR 466.

86 Case 226/98 *Jørgensen v Foreningen Af Speciallæger & Sygesikringens Forhandlingsudvalg* [2000] ECR I-02447; [2000] IRLR 726.

87 PTW Regs 2000 reg 6. Reg 6(4) provides that this does not apply where the treatment in question consists of the dismissal of an employee, and the employee is entitled to a written statement of reasons for dismissal under ERA 1996 s92.

21.89 The written reasons are admissible as evidence in any proceedings under the PTW Regulations 2000. If an employer deliberately and without reasonable excuse fails to provide a statement, or provides one which is evasive or equivocal, an ET may draw any inference which it considers just and equitable to draw. This might include an inference that the part-time worker has been treated less favourably because he or she was working part-time.[88]

21.90 These provisions are similar to the questionnaire procedure that applies under the SDA 1975 and EqPA 1970, except that the only information which may be required under the regulations relates to the reason for the less favourable treatment alleged.

Unfair dismissal and the right not to be subjected to a detriment

21.91 It is automatically unfair to dismiss a worker if the reason, or principal reason, for the dismissal is that the worker has:

- brought proceedings against the employer under the PTW Regulations 2000; or
- requested a written statement of reasons under the regulations; or
- given evidence or information in connection with proceedings brought under the PTW Regulations 2000 by any worker; or
- otherwise done anything under the Regulations in relation to the employer or any other person; or
- alleged that the employer had infringed the PTW Regulations 2000, provided the allegation is made in good faith, even if it is not true; or
- refused or proposed to refuse to forego a right under the PTW Regulations 2000.[89]

21.92 Workers also have the right not to be subjected to any detriment by any act, or deliberate failure to act, by their employers in connection with one of the grounds specified above. It is sufficient to establish unlawful detriment or automatically unfair dismissal that the employer believes or suspects that the worker has done or intends to do any of the things mentioned in at the list above provided the allegation is made in good faith, even if it is not true.

88 PTW Regs 2000 reg 6(2) and (3). Note this is the same as the questionnaire procedure discussed at para 32.23.

89 Ibid reg 7, and see also ERA 1996 s105(7E) which applies where the principal reason a worker is selected for redundancy is her or his part-time status.

Employers' liability

21.93 As under the SDA 1975, any less favourable treatment by another worker is treated as being the responsibility of the employer irrespective of whether the employer knew or approved of the action. An employer is also liable for acts of an agent done with the employer's authority. Liability is discussed in detail in chapter 31. The employer will not be liable if he or she took such steps as were reasonably practicable to prevent the worker from:

- doing that act; or
- doing, in the course of the worker's employment, acts of that description.[90]

Procedure under the Part-time Worker Regulations

21.94 A worker must bring a claim within three months of the date of the less favourable treatment or detriment. See para 32.53 for the rules applicable in respect of 'continuing acts' of discrimination and discriminatory policies. If the act complained of is part of a series of similar acts or failures, the time limit runs from the last act of the series. Those in the armed forces have six months in which to bring a claim though, as in other cases, they must bring an internal complaint in the first instance (see para 11.62).[91] A tribunal may hear a claim brought out of time when it is just and equitable to do so.[92]

21.95 If a complaint relates to a term of the contract, the less favourable treatment takes place each day during which the contract subsists, and so is treated as continuing for as long as the contract continues.[93] This does not apply where the worker changes from being a full-time worker to a part-time worker, whether or not after a break. In this situation the claim must be brought within three months from the first day on which the applicant worked under the new or varied contract or the first day on which the applicant returned to work.[94]

21.96 A deliberate failure to act is treated as done on the day it was decided on. In the absence of evidence to the contrary this will be when the person:

- does an act inconsistent with doing the act not done; or
- would no longer be expected to do the act not done.

90 PTW Regs 2000 reg 11.
91 Ibid regs 8(2) and 13.
92 Ibid reg 8(3).
93 Ibid reg 8(4)(a).
94 Ibid reg 8(4)(b).

Remedies

21.97 If a tribunal upholds a complaint it may make such of the following orders as it considers 'just and equitable':

- a declaration as to the rights of the employer and worker;
- an order that the employer pay compensation;
- a recommendation that the employer take, within a specified period, reasonable action, in the circumstances of the case, to obviate or reduce the adverse effect on the worker of any less favourable treatment.[95]

21.98 If the complaint relates to access to membership of an occupational pension scheme or to an individual's treatment under the rules of such a scheme, none of the above remedies may apply to a period earlier than two years before the date on which the complaint was presented.[96] This limitation is almost certainly inconsistent with EC law (see the discussion of *Preston*[97] at para 10.79). It is proposed to remove the two-year time limit and this is likely to happen by the end of 2002.

21.99 The amount of compensation awardable is such as the tribunal considers 'just and equitable' in all the circumstances having regard to the infringement and any loss attributable to the infringement, having regard to the pro rata principle except where it is inappropriate to do so.[98]

21.100 Losses which may be compensated under the PTW Regulations 2000 include:

- any expenses reasonably incurred by the complainant in consequence of the infringement; and
- loss of any benefit which he or she might reasonably be expected to have had but for the infringement.[99]

21.101 No compensation is payable for injury to feelings.[100] Compensation may be reduced where either:

- the complainant fails to mitigate her or his loss; or

95 PTW Regs 2000 reg 8(7).
96 Ibid reg 8(8).
97 *Preston v Wolverhampton Healthcare NHS Trust (No 2)* [2001] 2 AC 455; [2001] IRLR 237.
98 PTW Regs 2000 reg 8(9).
99 Ibid reg 8(10).
100 Ibid reg 8(11).

- the treatment by the employer was to an extent caused or contributed to by the complainant's action.[101]

If the employer fails, without reasonable justification, to comply with a recommendation made by an ET the tribunal may, if it thinks it just and equitable to do so, increase the amount of compensation required to be paid or, if no compensation was ordered, make an order for compensation.[102]

The right to request flexible working

21.102 This new right to request a change of working patterns, which comes into force in April 2003, will apply only to employees not to workers (unlike the Sex Discrimination Act (SDA) 1975, which prohibits indirect sex and marital discrimination). It applies to men and women (unlike the SDA 1975 which generally only enables women to make a claim for indirect discrimination). However, its major failing is that the legislation does not give tribunals the power to question the commercial validity of the employer's decision. By contrast, under the SDA 1975 a tribunal can award compensation where an employer cannot justify a refusal to allow flexible hours and it can make recommendation that the employer grant the employee's request.

21.103 The following is a summary of the proposals, based on the Employment Act 2002 which amends ERA 1996 and draft regulations.

Conditions of entitlement

21.104 The following conditions must be met in order to qualify for entitlement.

a) The employee must have been continuously employed for at least 26 weeks at the date of application and not be an agency worker, nor a member of the armed forces;[103]
b) The employee must be:
   (i) the mother, father, adopter, guardian or foster parent of the child; or

101 Ibid reg 8(12) and (13).

102 Ibid reg 8(14).

103 Flexible Working (Eligibility, Complaints and Remedies) Regulations 2002 reg 3(1)(a). ERA 1996 s80F(8).

(ii) married to one of the above and living with the child; or
(iii) the partner of a person within (i) above;[104] and

c) the employee must have or expect to have responsibility for the upbringing of the child under 6 years old or a disabled child under the age of 18;[105] and
d) the employee must not have made another application to work flexibly under this procedure during the previous 12 months.

21.105 The proposed procedure for requesting Flexible Working is that:

- Employees may request a new working pattern at any time from the birth of their child up to 14 days before their child's 6th birthday, or, if disabled, 18th birthday. This must be for the care of their child.[106]
- The proposal may relate to the hours worked, times at which the hours are worked, place of work (including working at home), any other aspect of her/his terms and conditions of employment as may be specified by regulations.[107]
- An application must be in writing (whether be in manuscript, typed or sent by e-mail) must state whether (and, if so, when) a previous application has been made and be signed and dated.[108] The application must:
  - state that it is such an application;
  - specify the change applied for and the date on which it is proposed the change should become effective;
  - explain what effect, if any, the employee thinks making the change would have on the employer and how, in his or her opinion, any such effect might be dealt with; and
  - explain the relationship between the employee and the child and how the change will enable the employee to care for the child.[109]
- The employer shall only refuse the applicant on one of a number of specified grounds. These are additional costs, detrimental effect on ability to meet customer demand, inability to re-organise work

104 FW (Eligibility) Regs 2002 reg 3(1)(b). Partner means a person (whether of a different or the same sex) who lives with the child and the mother, father, adopter or foster parent in an enduring family relationship, but is not a blood relative.

105 Ibid reg 3(1)(c).

106 ERA 1996 s80F(3).

107 RA 1996 s80F(1)(a).

108 FW (Eligibility) Regs 2002 reg 4; there may be a prescribed form.

109 ERA 1996 s80F(2).

among existing staff, inability to recruit additional staff, detrimental impact on quality or performance, insufficiency of work during periods the employee proposes to work, planned structural changes and any other grounds specified by regulations.[110]

- If the employer agrees to the proposed variation it should notify the employee within 28 days of the application, stating the agreed contract variation and the date from which the variation is to take effect.[111]
- In the absence of agreement (as above) there should be a meeting within 28 days to consider the request. If the individual who would consider the application is on holiday or sick leave at the time the application is received, the time limit will be extended to 28 days after the date on which the individual returns.[112]
- The employer should write to the employee within 14 days of the date of the meeting, either accepting the request and giving a start date, confirming a compromise or rejecting the request and giving a sufficient explanation of the business reasons for doing so and setting out the appeals procedure.[113]
- The employee may appeal within 14 days after the date of the notice of the decision. A notice of appeal must be in writing and set out the grounds of appeal and be signed and dated by the employee. There may be a prescribed form which must be used.[114]
- Within 14 days of being informed in writing that the employee wishes to appeal the employer should arrange an appeal meeting, unless the employer has notified the employee in writing of its decision to uphold the appeal, specifying the contract variation agreed to and the date it is to take effect.[115]
- An employer shall notify the employee, in writing, of his or her decision on an appeal within 14 days after the date of the appeal meeting. The decision must be signed and dated. Where the employer upholds the appeal the agreed contract variation must be specified and a start date. If the appeal is dismissed, the employer must set out the grounds on which the dismissal is based.[116]

110 ERA 1996 s80G (1)(b).
111 Flexible Working (Procedural Requirements) Regulations 2002 reg 3(2).
112 FW (Procedural) Regs 2002 reg 13.
113 Ibid regs 4 and 5.
114 Ibid regs 6 and 7.
115 Ibid reg 8.
116 Ibid regs 9 and 10.

Provisions relating to time limits

21.106 There are detailed rules for deciding when an application is made and when the employer takes the appropriate steps.[117] Thus, unless the contrary is proved, if the application is sent by post it is assumed to arrive in the ordinary course of the post, if by fax it is deemed to arrive the same day, provided this is before 4 pm. There is provision for the parties to agree to an extension of any of the time limits. The agreement must be recorded in writing by the employer, specify the time limit concerned and the date on which the extension is to end, and be sent to the employee, in writing, signed and dated.[118]

Right to be accompanied

21.107 The employee has a right to be accompanied, by a trade union employee or official or another employee, at the initial meeting and the appeal. The companion cannot answer questions for the employee but can confer with the employee and address the meeting. If the chosen companion is not available the employer must grant an employee's request for a postponement provided it is reasonable and not more than five days later.[119]

Complaint to Employment Tribunal

21.108 Under the Employment Rights Act 1996 as amended, the employee can make a complaint that the employer:

- failed to deal with the application under the prescribed procedure;
- refused the application on a ground other than one prescribed;
- rejected the application on incorrect facts.[120]

21.109 A complaint cannot be made to an ET unless the employer has notified the employee of a decision to reject the application on appeal or commits a breach of the procedure.

21.110 The time limit for bringing a claim is three months from the date the employee is notified of the decision on appeal or breach of the procedure. An extension of time may be given if it was not reasonably

117 FW (Eligibility) Regs 2002 reg 5.
118 FW (Procedural) Regs 2002 reg 12.
119 Reg 14 Procedural regs
120 ERA 1996 s80H(1)–(4).

practicable for the complaint to be presented before the end of three months.[121]

21.111 Where the complaint is upheld the ET:

- must make a declaration to that effect;
- may make an order for reconsideration of the application; and
- make an award of compensation to be paid to the employee. This will be subject to a maximum number of weeks' pay (to be decided).[122]

21.112 The draft regulations provide that the employee can complain to an ET of the following procedural breaches:

- failure to hold a meeting to discuss the employee's application or failure to hold an appeal meeting;
- failure to give notice to an employee of its decision about the employee's application or decision on appeal;
- failure to provide an employee with a right of appeal.[123]

The above apply even if the application has not been rejected or disposed of by agreement or withdrawn.

21.113 In addition, a complaint can be made in relation to:

- a refusal to allow the employee the right to be accompanied by an appropriate person; or
- a refusal to allow an appropriate postponement; or
- a threat to refuse in either situation.[124]

A complaint must be brought within 3 months.

21.114 Thus, no compensation is payable if the employer properly follows the procedure but still refuses the request, even where there are no objective reasons for such a refusal. Most parents should claim under both the new procedure and the indirect discrimination provisions of the Sex Discrimination Act 1975.

Protection from detriment and dismissal

21.115 ERA 1996 as amended ss47D and 104C provide that an employee has the right not to be subjected to any detriment by any act, or deliberate failure to act, by his employer done on the grounds that the employee:

121 ERA 1996 s80H(5).

122 Ibid s80I.

123 FW (Eligibility) Regs 2002 reg 6(a)–(c).

124 Draft FW (Procedural) Regs 2002 reg 15.

- made or proposed to make an application for flexible working;
- exercised or proposed to exercise a right to follow the procedure requesting flexible working;
- brought proceedings against the employer; or
- alleged the existence of any circumstance which would constitute a ground for bringing such proceedings.

CHAPTER 22

Overview of equal pay

continued

Key points

22.1 • The Equal Pay Act (EqPA) 1970 and article 141 of the EC Treaty regulate pay-related sex discrimination.

- No special statutory provisions deal with race or disability discrimination in pay, which must be challenged under the Race Relations Act (RRA) 1976 and the Disability Discrimination Act (DDA) 1995 respectively.
- The EqPA 1970 regulates discrimination not only in relation to (contractual) 'pay', but also in relation to all other contractual terms including (but not limited to) wages, bonuses, shift payments, overtime, service pay, mortgages, etc.
- The EqPA 1970's protections extend to 'workers' very broadly defined and with relatively few exceptions.
- Article 141 can be relied on to challenge sex discrimination in relation to 'pay', very broadly defined to include sick pay, maternity pay and occupational pensions and other statutory benefits, travel concessions and any other consideration arising from the employment, whether it is contractual or not.
- To the extent that the EqPA 1970 is ineffective to challenge sex-related pay discrimination (where, for example, there is no 'comparator' in the same employment which is required by the Act), it may be that article 141 can be relied upon in the employment tribunals to remedy the deficiency.
- A woman can claim equal pay and contractual terms under the EqPA 1970 with a man:
  - who is employed by the same or an associated employer;
  - who works in the same establishment or one in which similar terms and conditions apply; and
  - who is engaged in:
    - like work;
    - work rated as equivalent under a job evaluation scheme; or
    - work of equal value to hers.
- The EqPA 1970 can be used to challenge both direct and indirect discrimination in pay.
- The EqPA 1970 permits challenge in relation to any individual contractual term.
- It is for the applicant to choose her comparator(s) who need not be 'representative' of other male workers. Where, however, a male comparator is atypical the employer may be successful in

defending the claim on the basis that the difference in pay is not sex-based.
- It may be possible to find out about potential comparators' pay by using the questionnaire procedure or the provisions which entitle recognised trade union representatives to information. EqPA 1970 s7A provides a right to issue a questionnaire.[1]
- The Employment Act 2002 also provides that equal pay claimants raise a grievance under the employers' grievance procedure or statutory grievance procedure before making an application to the employment tribunal (ET).[1a]

Background and statutory framework

22.2 Although it is over 25 years since the implementation of the EqPA 1970, the average hourly pay of women in full time work is still only 82 per cent that of men. For part-time women workers the gender-pay gap is 41 per cent, such women only earning on average 59 per cent of the male hourly rate.[2] Equal Opportunities Commission (EOC) research demonstrates that the gender pay gap increases as women grow older. Whereas a woman in her early twenties earns, on average, 91 per cent of the hourly rate of a man of similar age, this proportion falls to 87 per cent for women in their thirties, 75 per cent for women in their forties and 72 per cent for women in their fifties.[2a]

22.3 The overall pay gap between men and women is wide in most European countries. The UK gender pay gap is the fourth worst in Europe, only Germany, Portugal and Austria having larger wage differtentials.[3] Horizontal and vertical segregation remain a dominant feature of the structure of female employment, with significant implications for women's pay.

22.4 Article 141 of the EC Treaty (formerly article 119 of the Treaty of Rome) has direct effect in the UK and may be relied upon by women claiming equal pay before an employment tribunal (ET) in the sense that, if the EqPA 1970 is less advantageous in any respect than article

1 Employment Act 2002 s42 inserts a new EqPA 1970 s7A. Regulations will provide for a form of questionnaire.

1a Employment Act 2002 s32.

2 New Earnings Survey, 2000, Office of National Statistics.

2a D Grimshaw and J Rubery, *The Gender Pay Gap: a Research Review* (2001).

3 Gender pay equity in Europe: a comparative study; available from www.eurofound.eu.int.

141, the applicant can rely directly on article 141 and the ET must disapply the less generous provision of the domestic legislation (see para 10.67).

22.5 Ever since the EqPA 1970 was passed its users have complained of its complexity and of the length of time of proceedings taken under it. Significant equal pay cases often involve large number of claimants – 15,000 in the *Enderby* (speech therapists) litigation, for example.[4] There are often a number of appeals in such cases and, as in the speech therapists' case, one or more issues of EC law may be referred to the European Court of Justice (ECJ), resulting in further delay. Where the applicants succeed, the cost to the employer far outweighs any discrimination case under the SDA 1975, which usually only involve only a single applicant. This encourages employers to delay cases as much as possible and to appeal at all stages.

22.6 The procedures laid down by the EqPA 1970 involve a number of stages. Too often, tribunals do not strictly timetable the progress of cases and there are long delays between stages. The excessive delays can mean that, in the big cases, many women bringing claims have retired or left by the time their case has concluded.

22.7 The complexity of the equal pay law is partly due to the ECJ's case-law in connection with article 141. This is binding on ETs, but it may be difficult to reconcile with the narrow drafting of the EqPA 1970 (see para 22.9). Although most pay discrimination is systemic – arising from discrimination in pay arrangements and job segregation, rather than from the terms of individuals' employment contracts – the EqPA 1970 focuses on the contract of each individual woman making a claim and on the contract(s) of her named comparator(s). The Act does not easily lend itself to claims arising from discrimination in pay structures or collective agreements. Furthermore, ETs have no power to apply the decision in one or more cases to other cases where the women are doing the same job as the original applicant. Each woman has to claim individually and, unless cases settle, tribunals must determine each individually.

22.8 In February 2001, an Equal Pay Task Force set up by the EOC called for changes to the EqPA 1970 to speed up cases taken under the Act. It also recommended that equal pay cases were heard by ET chairmen and wing members with greater expertise in the area than

4 Case 127/92 *Enderby v Frenchay Health Authority* [1993] ECR I-5535; [1993] IRLR 591. The judgment of the ECJ was on the preliminary point as to whether there was a material factor defence. It was assumed that the jobs were of equal value. There was subsequent litigation on the equal value issue and on compensation.

is currently often the case; that an expert be involved in assisting an ET throughout an equal pay case and that tribunals be given the power to extend the remedy in a successful equal pay case to other employees doing the same job as the applicant. Perhaps most importantly, the Task Force recommended the imposition of a statutory duty on employers to carry out pay reviews. These reviews would be designed to identify gender pay gaps in the workforce, and their results would be published so as to enable employees and their unions or other representatives to work with employers to eradicate pay discrimination. In the absence of positive moves to close the gender pay gap, the findings of an employer's pay review could be evidence of sex discrimination in equal pay cases. The government has not adopted the proposals for compulsory pay reviews but supports voluntary reviews. The EOC has produced an equal pay review kit on their website[4a] which provides guidance to carrying out reviews. It is also revising its 1997 code of practice which will be in force from April 2003. The Employment Act 2002 extends the questionnaire procedure to equal pay claims. It also proposes the implication of a contractual grievance procedure into all contracts of employment. It also implies that the initial steps of this procedure would have to be followed by anyone wishing to make an equal pay claim prior to any tribunal application (see further chapter 32).

Outline of the Equal Pay Act 1970 and article 141 EC

22.9 Although both women and men can claim equal pay it is assumed here that equal pay applicants are women, since women suffer the overwhelming bulk of sex-related pay discrimination and comprise the overwhelming majority of applicants under the EqPA 1970.

22.10 The EqPA 1970 covers pay and other contractual terms, provided that the applicant can identify a 'comparable man' whose terms are, in any respect, better than hers.[5] If the complaint relates to non-contractual pay or benefits, such as a discretionary bonus or pension, it must be made under the SDA 1975. A claim under the EqPA 1970 cannot succeed unless the woman can identify a man in the same employment who is engaged in comparable work (see para 22.16).

4a www.eoc.org.uk.

5 See *Hayward* v *Cammell Laird* [1988] 1 AC 894; [1988] IRLR 257, HL, discussed at para 22.31.

22.11 These rigid distinctions imposed by the EqPA 1970 do not apply under EC law. Article 141 EC, in this respect, provides that:

> 1. Each Member State shall ensure that the principle of equal pay for male and female workers for equal work or work of equal value is applied.
> 2. For the purpose of this Article, 'pay' means the ordinary basic or minimum wage or salary and any other consideration, whether in cash or in kind, which the worker receives directly or indirectly, in respect of his employment, from his employer. Equal pay without discrimination based on sex means:
> (a) that pay for the same work at piece rates shall be calculated on the basis of the same unit of measurement;
> (b) that pay for work at time rates shall be the same for the same job.

Article 141 requires equality in 'pay', which is very widely defined to cover contractual and non-contractual matters. EC law may provide a remedy where there is none under the EqPA 1970, and it is advisable accordingly to bring a claim under article 141 and the Equal Pay Directive[6] (EPD), as well as the EqPA 1970. Article 141 can be relied on in tribunals as well as courts (see para 10.68), though it must be pleaded in conjunction with domestic law. The European Commission has adopted a Memorandum on Equal Pay for Work of Equal Value[7] and a Code of Practice on the implementation of equal pay for work of equal value for women and men.[8] For the effect of the memorandum and code of practice see para 10.11.

Coverage of the Equal Pay Act 1970

22.12 The EqPA 1970 applies only where the applicant and her comparator(s) are employed at an establishment in Great Britain.[9] Where it does apply it requires equal treatment for women (and men) in pay and other contractual terms. The SDA 1975's provisions prohibiting victimisation apply in connection with complaints under the EqPA 1970 as well as those under the SDA 1975 (see further chapter 4). Parties cannot contract out of the EqPA 1970, and any agreement by an employee not to bring a claim is void unless it is part of a settlement

6 Council Directive 75/117/EEC.
7 COM (94)6.
8 COM (96)336.
9 EqPA 1970 ss1(1), (6) and (12).

made with the assistance of ACAS or a compromise agreement (see para 32.112).[10]

22.13 The EqPA 1970 protects those working under contracts of service (ie, employees). It also applies to those working under contracts of apprenticeship and contracts personally to execute any work or labour (which includes at least some freelancers[11]). The coverage of the EqPA 1970 is, in this respect, the same as that of the SDA 1975 (and the RRA 1976 – see para 11.28). It applies to full-time and to part-time workers, whether permanent or temporary and irrespective of age and length of service. In addition, the EqPA 1970 applies to:

- Crown and government department employees;
- members of the armed forces, although such workers must first complain to an officer under the service redress procedures before making a claim to an ET;[12]
- House of Lords staff employed under a contract with the Corporate Officer of the House of Lords;[13]
- House of Commons staff who have been appointed by the House of Commons Commission or who are members of the Speaker's personal staff.[14]

22.14 Most trainees will fall within the extended definition of 'employment' under the EqPA 1970 (read with article 141 and the EPD – see para 10.32). This will mean that allegations of discrimination in trainees' pay or other contractual terms will be dealt with in the same way as discrimination in pay of other employees. If, in any particular case, a trainee is not employed under a contract within the extended definition, the SDA 1975 would in any event prohibit discrimination in the terms on which the person was offered training, and would also prohibit the discriminatory subjection of the trainee to any 'detriment'

10 Ibid s6(1)(a) provides that an equality clause does not operate in relation to terms affected by laws regulating the employment of women or affording special treatment to women in connection with pregnancy and childbirth. Most protective legislation was repealed by SDA 1986 s7 or by the Employment Act 1989, so that the exception for provisions affected by laws regulating women's employment is unlikely now to apply. Note that statutes passed prior to the SDA, which impose a requirement to do a discriminatory act, are of no effect (see para 11.105).

11 EqPA 1970 s1(6).

12 Ibid s7A. Note the time limit is extended to nine months from the end of employment – ibid s7A(8).

13 Ibid s1(10A).

14 Ibid s1(10B).

under that Act. The practical consequence is that such trainees are generally protected from sex-related pay discrimination.[15]

22.15 The EqPA 1970 does not apply to those holding statutory office.[16] It does not apply, therefore, to the police. Article 141, however, applies to 'workers'. The category of 'workers' under article 141 was considered by Northern Ireland's Court of Appeal in *Perceval-Price v Department of Economic Development*,[17] a claim for access to a pension scheme which was brought by two women 'chairmen' of ETs. As office holders, the women were excluded from the provisions of the Equal Pay Act (Northern Ireland) Act 1970 (which is materially identical to the EqPA 1970). Their claim to be 'workers' for the purposes of article 141 was accepted by the court, which ruled that the term had to be interpreted broadly and in a purposive fashion so as to include within the definition all people who are engaged in a relationship which is broadly that of employment rather than being self-employed or independent contractors. Office-holders may, accordingly, rely on the direct effect of article 141 to bring claims as 'workers'.

The 'equality clause'

22.16 The EqPA 1970 provides that a woman's contract shall contain an 'equality clause' in any case in which she and a man in the 'same employment' (see para 22.35) are employed on:

- like work;
- work rated as equivalent under a job evaluation scheme; or
- work of equal value.

The 'equality clause' has the effect that, if any term of the applicant's contract (whether it is concerned with pay or not) is less favourable than a term of a similar kind in her 'comparator's' contract, the woman's contractual term shall be changed so that it is no less favourable than his.[18] In addition, if the woman's contract does not include a term corresponding to a term in the comparator's contract which is of benefit to him, her contract shall be amended to include such a term. The availablity of back-dated pay awards is discussed at para 27.55.

15 Also, by virtue of the RRA 1976, from race-related pay discrimination.
16 EqPA 1970 s1(8)(a).
17 [2000] IRLR 380.
18 EqPA 1970 s1(2).

The 'material factor' defence

22.17 The equality clause does not operate if the employer proves that the difference in pay between the applicant and her comparator is genuinely due to a material factor which is not the difference of sex. The 'GMF' defence is further discussed in chapter 25.[19]

Indirect discrimination in pay

22.18 Unlike the SDA 1975, the EqPA 1970 does not define direct or indirect discrimination. But if a comparator's more favourable term is the result of direct sex discrimination or of unjustified indirect sex discrimination, any attempt by the employer to defend the claim using the GMF defence should fail as the reason for the difference in pay will be the difference of sex. If, for example, women account for a higher proportion of part-time than of full-time workers within a workforce, and part-time workers have less favourable contractual terms than full-time workers engaged in work of equal value, an employer will have to justify the less favourable treatment of part-timers (see para 7.116) in order to avoid an adverse finding under the EqPA 1970.

22.19 In the *Bilka Kaufhaus* case the issue was whether excluding predominantly female part-time workers from an occupational pension scheme was a breach of article 141.[20] The ECJ found that:

- article 141 was infringed by the exclusion of part-time workers from an employer's occupational pension scheme, where that exclusion affected a far greater number of women than men, unless the employer showed that the exclusion was based on objectively justified factors unrelated to any discrimination on grounds of sex;
- an employer could justify the exclusion of part-time workers, irrespective of their sex, from its occupational pension scheme on the ground that it sought to employ as few part-time workers as possible, if it was found that the means chosen for achieving that objective corresponded to a real need on the part of the undertaking, were appropriate with a view to achieving the objective in question, and were necessary to that end.

19 Ibid s1(3).

20 Case 170/84 *Bilka Kaufhaus GmbH v Weber von Hartz* [1986] ECR 1607; [1986] IRLR 317, ECJ.

21 See note 1 above. See also appendix B for precedent questionnaire.

For further examples of indirect discrimination in pay see paras 25.24–25.25 and 25.32.

Proving pay discrimination

22.20 The burden is on the applicant to show that she is doing like work, equivalent work or work of equal value with her comparator. The burden is on the employer to prove that there is a material factor defence if this is relied upon (see para 25.11).

22.21 EqPA 1970 s7A[21] provides for a questionnaire procedure in equal pay claims. Although the employer is not obliged to reply to a questionnaire, failure to do so may lead to the ET making an inference (see para 32.23). See also para 22.49 for the right of recognised trade unions in this context to information.

Victimisation in connection with the Equal Pay Act 1970

22.22 Women who are victimised for involvement in an equal pay claim can make a complaint under the SDA 1975 (see chapter 4).

Equal 'pay'

'Pay' under the Equal Pay Act 1970

22.23 Despite its title, the EqPA 1970 regulates discrimination in all contractual terms whether they are strictly concerned with pay or not. Most contracts deal not only with basic 'wages' but also with bonuses, shift payments, overtime time, length-of-service increments, sick pay and holiday pay and other money paid (see chapter 26 for how pay systems discriminate against women). The EqPA 1970 also regulates other contractual terms such as those governing entitlement to holidays, sick leave, health insurance and travel concessions.

22.24 State pensions are not covered by the EqPA 1970. Equal treatment in occupational pensions is covered by the equal treatment rule in the Pensions Act 1995, which adapts the provisions of the EqPA 1970 for pensions claims. Occupational pensions are 'pay' for the purpose of article 141. They are considered in detail in chapter 27. Maternity pay is 'pay' under article 141 but neither it nor the EqPA 1970 requires that men are given paternity rights equivalent to the maternity rights which are provided for women. For 'equal pay' in the context of maternity leave see further para 18.33.

'Discretionary' pay and other terms

22.25 If a disputed payment is discretionary (this could be the case in relation to a bonus), any claim must be made under the SDA 1975 rather than the EqPA 1970 (see para 11.30). But whether a payment is discretionary or not, it is 'pay' for the purposes of article 141 which, as explained above, has direct effect in the ETs. The claim should be brought under the SDA 1975 and article 141.

22.26 In *Benveniste v University of Southampton*[22] the applicant challenged her appointment as a lecturer at a lower salary than other lecturers already in post. The employers decided to appoint her at the lower point because of severe financial constraints operating at the date of her appointment. When these passed she was given some additional increments but remained on a lower salary than her comparator, a man of the same age and qualifications. Dr Benveniste brought an equal pay claim in response to which the employer argued that there was no term in her contract which was less favourable than in the contracts of her comparators – the level at which she was appointed was not the subject of any contractual term, but was at the discretion of the university. The Court of Appeal held that there was indeed a term in her contract – namely the term as to her salary – which was less favourable to her than the similar terms in the contracts of the comparators. She won her equal pay claim.

Article 141 and the definition of 'pay'

22.27 Article 141 defines pay as 'the ordinary basic or minimum wage or salary or any other consideration, whether in cash or in kind, which the worker receives, directly or indirectly, in respect of his employment from his employer'. The key question is whether the benefit is received because of the employment relationship. Pay includes 'all emoluments in cash or kind paid or payable, on condition they are paid, even indirectly, by the employer, as a result of the worker's employment'. This is a very wide definition and has been interpreted broadly to include all payments including bonuses, maternity pay, payments on dismissal and pensions. For further discussion of this see chapter 10.

22.28 As explained above (para 22.25), if a woman seeks to claim the benefit of a gratuity (or other non-contractual benefit), she must bring

22 [1989] IRLR 122.

her claim under the SDA 1975 (read, if necessary, with EC law), rather than under the EqPA 1970.

22.29 Payments made as part of the state social security system and not arising from the employment relationship – such as state pensions – are not pay. Neither are payments made under schemes which are governed by legislation, which lack any element of agreement between employer and employee, and which are compulsorily applicable to general categories of workers.[23] Such schemes are likely to come within the Equal Treatment Social Security Directive (SSD), which is further considered in chapter 27.

22.30 The question whether the benefit is 'pay' for the purposes of article 141 does not depend on whether the payment or benefit derives from legislation on the one hand, or from a collective agreement or the individual's contract of employment on the other.

The principle of equal pay applies to each identifiable term

22.31 In *Hayward v Cammell Laird Shipbuilders Ltd*[24] the House of Lords ruled that each contractual term must be compared separately with the equivalent provision of the comparator's contract. If, for example, a man's contract contains a term that he is to be provided with the use of a car and the woman's contract does not, her contract is to be treated as less favourable than his in that respect. It was wrong, said their Lordships (overruling both the Court of Appeal and the Employment Appeal Tribunal (EAT)), to consider the contract as a whole and to determine whether the woman's contract was less favourable taking account of all the different terms.[24a]

22.32 If then, as in *Hayward*, a woman is paid a lower basic rate than her comparator but receives more generous sick pay and meal breaks, she will be entitled (unless the employer establishes a GMF) to an increase in her basic rate of pay, the comparator then being free to bring a claim for the same sick pay and meal breaks as the woman. This interpretation is supported by the decision in *Barber v Guardian Royal Exchange Assurance Group*[25] in which the ECJ held that equal pay

23 Case 262/88 *Barber v Guardian Royal Exchange Assurance Group* [1990] ECR I–1889; [1990] IRLR 240.

24 [1988] 1 AC 894; [1988] IRLR 257, HL.

24a The ECJ came to a similar view in *Jorgensen v Foreningen* Case 226/98 [2000] IRLR 726.

25 Case C-262/88 [1990] ECR I–1889; [1990] IRLR 240.

must be ensured in respect of 'each element of remuneration and not only on the basis of a comprehensive assessment of the consideration paid to workers'.

Equal pay comparators

22.33 The EqPA 1970 requires there to be an actual comparator of the opposite sex working 'in the same employment' (see para 22.35) at the same time as the applicant. A comparison cannot be made with a person of the same sex even where the person is a transsexual[26] (but see para 5.22).

22.34 Article 141 is wider in two respects. In the first place, the comparison can be made with a predecessor or successor (see paras 22.45 and 22.47). Secondly, the definition of 'associated employer' is wider (see para 22.36).[27]

'Working in the same employment'

22.35 The EqPA 1970 requires that the comparator must be working:

- for the *same* employer or an *associated* employer; and
- at the same establishment as the applicant, or at an establishment in Great Britain in which 'common' terms and conditions apply with the establishment in which the applicant works. If the employees are working at the same establishment, that is sufficient; the question of whether there are common terms and conditions does not arise.[28]

'Associated employers'

22.36 Employers are treated as 'associated' for the purposes of the EqPA 1970 if either:

- one is a company of which the other has direct or indirect control; or
- both are companies of which a third person has control.

26 EqPA 1970 s1(1).

27 However in Case 249/96 *Grant v South West Trains* [1998] ECR I-621; IRLR 206, the ECJ held that art 141 did not cover discrimination on grounds of sexual orientation.

28 *Lawson v Britfish Ltd* [1988] IRLR 53, EAT.

22.37 In *Scullard v Knowles and Southern Regional Council for Education and Training*[29] the applicant was employed as a further education unit manager by an independent voluntary association of local education authorities which was attached to a regional advisory council. The unit was supported and funded by the Department for Education and Employment (DfEE). The applicant argued that she should be able to compare herself, for the purposes of an equal pay claim, with men working for other regional advisory councils. Her claim was dismissed by an ET because the 'councils' were not 'companies' and so did not fall within the EqPA 1970's definition of associated employers. The EAT held that the test under article 141 was whether the applicant and her comparators are employed 'in the same establishment or service', pointing out that no distinction had been drawn by the ECJ in *Defrenne (No 2)*[30] between work carried out 'in the same establishment or service' of limited companies, on the one hand, and other employers, on the other. The EAT suggested that relevant factors in determining whether employees were 'in the same establishment or service' under article 141 were:

- whether the regional advisory councils were directly or indirectly controlled by a third party, eg, the DfEE;
- the extent and nature of control exercised by the third party;
- whether common terms and conditions of employment were observed in the regional advisory councils for the relevant class of employees.[30a]

22.38 In *Ratcliffe v North Yorkshire CC*,[31] women who were employed by a council direct service organisation as catering assistants preparing school meals and as school cleaners, brought successful equal value cases comparing their work with other local government employees. During the course of that litigation, the provision of catering and cleaning services in the schools was put out to competitive tender. The education authority was divided into areas. Tenders were accepted from outside contractors in respect of some areas and some of the former staff were re-employed by the contractors.

22.39 Women employed by external contractors were on lower rates of pay than council employees. They brought further equal pay claims relying on article 141 to compare themselves with current male

29 [1996] IRLR 344.

30 Case 43/75 *Defrenne v Sabenna (No 2)* [1976] ECR 455.

30a See also *Hasley v Fair Employment Agency* [1989] IRLR 106, NICA.

31 [1995] 3 All ER 597; [1995] IRLR 439, HL.

employees of the council whose work had (prior to contracting-out) been rated as of equal value to their own under the local government job evaluation study.

22.40 An ET dismissed the complaint because it held that the council did not control the women's wages. In *Lawrence v Regent Office Care*[31a] the Court of Appeal referred to the ECJ the question whether employees who were now employed by private contractors, including former employees of a county council, were entitled to bring an equal pay claim relying on article 141 to compare themselves with current employees of the council whose work had been rated as of equal value to their own. The Court of Appeal took the view that this was a novel and difficult question.[32] In *South Ayrshire Council v Morton*,[32a] primary school headteachers (75% women) claimed equal pay with secondary school headteachers (75% men). Ms Morton named as her comparator a male headteacher employed by a different education authority. The Court of Session held that article 141 allowed her to rely on her comparator even though there was a different employer. The rates of pay were set by the Scottish Joint Negotiating Committee (SJNC), under the general control of the secretary of state and the education authority were obliged to implement the SJNC settlement. The court held that that constituted a national collective agreement as contemplated in *Defrenne (No 2)*.[33]

22.41 Shortly afterwards, the Court of Appeal referred to the ECJ a number of questions arising from the claim of a part-time further education lecturer, Debra Allonby.[34] She, together with all other part-time lecturers employed by a further education college (for which she had worked for 12 years), had been made redundant. The part-time workers, who were predominantly female, were informed that they would only be employed by the college in the future as agency workers registered with Education Lecturing Services. As an agency worker, Ms Allonby lost benefits such as sick pay and holidays, access to the pension scheme, and statutory protection from dismissal to which she had previously been entitled. She also lost any hope of a career.

31a [2000] IRLR 608.

32 The Advocate General's Opinion (14 March 2002) found that article 141 did not have direct effect in the circumstances of the case, stating that there was direct effect only where the regulation of terms and conditions had a common source. The ECJ judgment is awaited.

32a [2002] IRLR 256.

33 Case 43/75 *Defrenne v Sabenna (No 2)* [1976] ECR 455.

34 *Allonby v Accrington and Rossendale College* [2001] IRLR 364.

She brought an equal pay claim against Education Lecturing Services, seeking to compare herself with a male lecturer still employed by the college. She also claimed access to the teachers pension scheme (see para 27.23). The issue referred to the ECJ was whether, on the facts of the case, article 141 allowed a comparison between Ms Allonby and a lecturer employed by the college. The case is yet to be heard.

'Common terms and conditions'

22.42 When a woman and her comparator are not working at the same establishment, common terms and conditions must apply, either generally or for employees of the relevant classes in the two establishments, in order to permit a claim under the EqPA 1970.

22.43 In *Leverton v Clywd CC*[35] a nursery nurse compared herself with a clerical worker also employed by the county council but working at a different site. The employees were covered by the same collective agreement. The EAT and the Court of Appeal held that, because the comparator worked different hours and had different holidays to the applicant, the two were not 'in the same employment'. The House of Lords disagreed, holding that the comparison was between the terms and conditions of employment observed at the establishment at which the woman is employed and the establishment at which the men are employed, and applicable either generally or to a particular class or classes of employees to which both the woman and the men belong. Their Lordships pointed out that it was inevitable that contractual terms and conditions would vary greatly between individuals, despite there being common terms and conditions observed generally in the establishments. It was sufficient, for the purposes of an EqPA 1970 claim, that the terms and conditions were established by the same collective agreement.

22.44 In *British Coal Corporation v Smith*,[36] over 1,000 canteen workers and cleaners working for British Coal (at 47 different establishments) claimed equal pay with 150 comparators also employed by British Coal (at 14 different establishments). The House of Lords held that 'common terms and conditions' referred to terms and conditions which are substantially comparable on a broad basis, rather than requiring 'the same' terms and conditions subject only to minor differences. In this case the terms and conditions prevailing at all the establishments at issue were governed by national agreements,

35 [1989] AC 706; [1989] IRLR 28.

36 [1996] 3 All ER 97, [1996] IRLR 404, HL.

though there were local variations relating to an incentive bonus and to concessionary coal. There may, then, still be common terms and conditions between establishments even though there are local variations of a national scheme.[37]

Comparison with predecessor or hypothetical man

22.45 In *Macarthys Ltd v Smith*[38] the ECJ held that, for the purposes of article 141, a woman could compare herself with her male predecessor. Ms Smith also argued that, even if there had never been a man doing like work with her, she could still claim to be paid the rate which a (hypothetical) man would have been paid. But the ECJ ruled that, under article 141, a woman cannot claim the salary to which she would be entitled were she a man, in the absence of any man who was currently performing, or had previously performed, similar work. The reason given was that:

> In cases of actual discrimination falling within the scope of direct application of Article [141], comparisons are confined to parallels which may be drawn on the basis of concrete appraisals of the work actually performed by employees of different sex within the same establishment or service. It does not apply to indirect and disguised discrimination, the identification of which implies comparative studies of entire branches of industry and therefore, requires, as a prerequisite, the elaboration by the Community and national legislative bodies of criteria of assessment.

22.46 In the *Allonby* pension claim (para 27.25 above) the ECJ is being asked to rule whether, in the context of a statutory scheme covering a whole occupational group, a woman must have a comparator in the same employment. There are many cases where statutory provisions have been found to discriminate contrary to article 141 without any comparator being identified.[39] This subject is covered in more detail in chapter 10.

37 See *Thomas v National Coal Board* [1987] IRLR 451, EAT. And in *Ratcliffe v North Yorkshire CC* [1995] 3 All ER 597; [1995] IRLR 439, women employed by a direct services organisation set up to submit an in-house tender for council catering services were able to compare themselves with other council employees provided there were common terms and conditions at their different establishments.

38 Case 126/79 [1980] ECR 1275; [1980] IRLR 210.

39 Eg, Case 171/88 *Rinner-Kühn v FWW Spezial-Gebaüdereingung GmbH* [1989] ECR 2743; [1989] IRLR 493, ECJ (statutory sick pay scheme) and Case C-167/97 *R v Employment Secretary ex p Seymour Smith* [1999] ECR I-0623; [1999] IRLR 253, ECJ.

Comparison with successor

22.47 In *Diocese of Hallam Trustees v Connaughton*[40] the applicant's successor, a man, was appointed at a considerably higher salary than she had enjoyed. The EAT held that she was entitled to rely on article 141 to claim equal pay with him. The EAT stated that the scope of article 141 includes complaints based upon the use of an immediate successor as a notional contemporaneous comparator.

Identification of the comparator

22.48 It is for the woman, not the tribunal, to choose her male comparator. In some workforces – particularly large or non-unionised ones – it may be difficult for a woman to find a man with whom to compare herself, because of lack of information about other employees' pay and terms and conditions. The applicant in *Leverton*, a nursery nurse, was unable to find a male comparator in her workplace. She produced evidence, from the respondent council and the union, that the pay of nursery assistants compared unfavourably with that of clerical staff in local government. The ET granted her request for discovery of the job descriptions of the men in clerical jobs, recognising the difficulty of obtaining information in large organisations. The employer appealed but the EAT upheld the ET decision stating that, as the nurse had produced evidence of a prima facie case, she was entitled to the information[41] (see also para 32.119 for provisions relating to discovery).

22.49 The Employment Act 2002 permits the use of the questionnaire procedure in relation to EqPA 1970 cases (see para 22.8). Furthermore, employers have a duty to disclose to a recognised trade union:

> ... information (a) without which the trade union representatives would be to a material extent impeded in carrying on ... collective bargaining with him, and (b) which it would be in accordance with good industrial relations practice that he should disclose to them for the purposes of collective bargaining.[42]

The Disclosure of Information code of practice requires disclosure of information such as earnings and hours analysed according to sex and giving, where appropriate, distributions and make-up of pay, showing any additions to basic rate of salary and to the numbers

40 [1996] IRLR 505.

41 *Leverton v Clwyd CC* [1985] IRLR 197, EAT.

42 Trade Union and Labour Relations (Consolidation) Act (TULRCA) 1992 s181.

analysed according to sex.[43] Employers are exempt from disclosure where the compiling of information would involve a disproportionate amount of work or expenditure compared to the value of the information in the conduct of collective bargaining. A reference may be made to the Central Arbitration Committee if the employer refuses to comply with this obligation and the Committee may order disclosure.[44]

22.50 The Equal Pay Task Force has recommended that employers be required to provide the identity of comparable male employees to avoid any difficulty.

22.51 The EPD provides that member states shall take measures necessary to ensure that the principle of equal pay is applied and shall see that effective means are available to ensure that this principle is observed.[45] Failure to provide an adequate means of discovery to enable women to gain access to information about possible comparators may be in breach of this duty.

A representative man?

22.52 In *Thomas*[46] the EAT rejected the employer's argument that the male comparator should be representative of the men performing like work and that he should not be an anomalous man. As the EAT pointed out, the statute refers to 'a man', not 'a representative man'. However, if the man is not typical because, for example, he has protected pay, the employer may have a GMF defence (see para 25.11).

Where there has been a job evaluation scheme

22.53 If there has been an analytical and non-discriminatory job evaluation scheme which has rated the woman's work as less valuable than the man's, a claim by the woman for equal pay with a higher rated man will generally fail. But a higher rated man could be a valid comparator where the difference in rating is marginal, so that the woman and the man are in the same pay band (see paras 23.26 and 24.47).

43 *ACAS Code of Practice 2: Disclosure of Information to trade unions for collective bargaining purposes* (1997).

44 TULRCA 1992 s183.

45 EPD art 6.

46 *Thomas v National Coal Board* [1987] IRLR 451, EAT.

Comparison with more than one man

22.54 There is no reason why a woman should not compare herself with more than one man. In *Hayward*[47] a canteen cook claimed equal value with three male employees – a painter, a joiner and a thermal insulation engineer. It will generally be in the woman's interest to compare herself with several employees as this will increase her chance of being awarded equal pay with at least one of them. Some caution should be exercised however – in *Leverton* Lord Bridge warned applicants against casting their net over too wide a range of comparators.

Race discrimination in pay

22.55 Pay discrimination is frequently regarded as a problem related to sex. But rates of pay are frequently tainted by race discrimination. A report published by the TUC in 2002[47a] showed that Pakistani and Bangladeshi male workers were earning £150 less per week than white counterparts, Caribbean men £115, Indian men £5 less. Most ethnic minority women earned more than their white counterparts mainly because they worked longer hours. The TUC called for the use of pay reviews to monitor the pay of black workers.

22.56 A worker claiming that he or she is paid less, or has less favourable contractual terms and conditions, than a worker of a different race will have to establish direct or indirect discrimination under the RRA 1976. In other words, he or she will have to prove either that he or she would have been treated more favourably 'but for' his or her race; or that he or she has suffered a detriment because of his or her inability to comply with a requirement or condition imposed by the employer which, although it applied or would have applied equally to people of a different racial group, was such that people of the applicant's racial group were less likely to be able to comply with it than were others.[48] The definition of indirect discrimination has not been affected by the Burden of Proof Regulations (BP Regulations) 2001[49] (see para 7.10), and continues to suffer from the shortcomings identified in chapter 7. And direct discrimination remains difficult to prove, not least

47 *Hayward* v *Cammell Laird* [1988] 1 AC 894; [1988] IRLR 257, HL.

47a Black and under paid, available on the TUC website at www.tuc.org.uk.

48 And which the employer has not objectively justified – see para 7.116.

49 Sex Discrimination (Indirect Discrimination and Burden of Proof) Regulations 2001 SI No 2660.

because of the non-application of the BP Regulations 2001 to race discrimination. But, by contrast with the position under the EqPA 1970, a worker who wishes to claim race discrimination in pay does not have to identify an actual comparator, much less one engaged in like work, work rated as equivalent or work of equal value. It will be sufficient if it can be proved that the worker would have received higher pay had he or she been of a different racial group.

22.57 There have been a number of challenges to racially discriminatory pay practices. In *Campbell v Datum Engineering Co Ltd*,[50] for example, the African-Caribbean applicant (the only ethnic minority employee of a staff of 60) brought a claim under the RRA 1976 when he discovered that he was paid a lower hourly rate than at least one other person who was doing the same work. In the absence of a satisfactory explanation from the employer, an ET found that the discrimination was on racial grounds, and he was awarded compensation including an amount for injury to feelings.

22.58 *Sougrin v Haringey Health Authority*[51] arose out of a challenge by three nurses against grading decisions made by their employer. Two of the nurses (Ms Sougrin and Mrs Macdonald) were black, the other white. The employer allowed the white nurse's appeal on the basis that she was acting up into a higher grade for more than 15 per cent of her time. The appeals by the black nurses failed. An ET upheld Mrs Macdonald's claim of race discrimination, finding that the grading system (which provided for automatic regrading if a nurse were 'acting up' to the next grade for at least 15 per cent of the time), indirectly discriminated against her. Mrs Macdonald secured a financial settlement of her claim.[52]

22.59 The difficulties with bringing such pay-related challenges under the RRA 1976 lie in getting evidence of other employees' pay, and in proving that the differences challenged are due to race discrimination. The position would be improved if the principles of transparency set out in the *Danfoss* case[53] (see para 25.46) were applied in race discrimination cases. This would ensure that, where similar and/or equally valuable jobs are performed by groups of workers in which

50 (1995) DCLD 24.

51 [1991] IRLR 447, EAT.

52 Ms Sougrin's claim failed because it was out of time (see para 32.42) – this decision was upheld at [1992] IRLR 416, CA. See also *Wakeman v Quick Corporation* [1999] IRLR 424, discussed at para 3.42.

53 Case 109/88 *Handels-og Kontorfunktionaerernes Forbund I Danmark v Dansk Arbejdsgiverforening (acting for Danfoss)* [1989] ECR 3199; [1989] IRLR 532.

different racial groups predominate and are paid differently, the employer would be required to explain the pay system and why the difference in pay is not due to race. *Danfoss* does not currently apply outside the sex discrimination sphere. See para 10.84 for discussion of the Race Directive,[54] to be implemented into domestic legislation in 2003, which will improve the situation.

54 Council Directive 2000/78/EC.

CHAPTER 23

'Like work' and 'work rated as equivalent'

continued

Key points

23.1

- A woman may claim equal pay (and other contractual terms) with a comparator who is engaged in work:
  - which is 'like' hers, or
  - which has been rated as equivalent under an appropriate job evaluation scheme (JES), or
  - which is of equal value to hers (see further chapter 24).
- Jobs will be regarded as 'like' if:
  - they are same or broadly similar work, and
  - if any differences between them are not 'of practical importance in relation to terms and conditions of employment'.
- In assessing whether jobs are 'like':
  - trivial differences between jobs should be ignored;
  - the frequency with which different tasks are actually performed is important;
  - the time at which work is done is not generally relevant; and
  - the practical reality, rather than the contractual position, is decisive.
- Since the implementation of the equal value claim (see chapter 24), few 'like work' cases have been litigated.
- Jobs will be regarded as having been 'rated as equivalent' if they have been assigned equal (or comparable) value by a non-discriminatory, analytical JES.
- Such a scheme can also block an equal pay claim in relation to a job which has been rated as of higher value than an applicant's.
- Once an appropriate JES has assigned comparable value to a man's and a woman's job, the woman should receive the same pay and terms and conditions of employment unless the employer can establish that a genuine material factor defence applies (see further chapter 25).
- If the applicant's job has been rated as equivalent to that of a man's under a completed JES, she will be able to bring a 'work rated as equivalent' claim even if the scheme is not actually implemented.

Background and statutory framework

23.2 Under the Equal Pay Act (EqPA) 1970 a woman can claim that she is engaged in:

a) like work;
b) work rated as equivalent under a JES; or
c) work of equal value to that done by her comparator.

This chapter looks at the first two types of equal pay claims.[1] It should be noted, however, that it is best to make an equal value claim in the alternative to a claim of like work or work rated as equivalent. If a claim of type (a) or (b) fails, an employment tribunal (ET) can go on to consider the equal value claim.

Like work

23.3 It is for the applicant to show that she is doing like work. The EqPA 1970 provides that a woman is to be regarded as employed on like work with a man if:

- they are engaged in work of the same or a broadly similar nature; and
- there are no differences 'of practical importance in relation to terms and conditions of employment' in the tasks they perform.[2]

These stages must be considered separately, though it is often difficult to distinguish them in practice.[3]

Broadly similar work

23.4 It is a question of fact whether jobs are broadly similar. The type of work, and the skill and knowledge required to do it, must be considered in broad terms. It is the nature of the work which is important, and trivial differences which are not of practical importance in relation to the terms and conditions of employment should be disregarded. In *Capper Pass Ltd v JB Lawton*,[4] for example, the applicant cooked between 10 and 20 lunches for managers and directors and

1 EqPA 1970 s1(2)(a) and (b).
2 Ibid s1(4).
3 *Capper Pass Ltd v Lawton* [1976] IRLR 366, EAT.
4 Ibid.

worked a 40-hour week. Her comparator cooked 350 meals a day and worked a 45-hour week. Their work was held to be broadly similar.

The timing of work

23.5 Differences in the time at which the jobs are done does not justify a difference in their basic rates of pay. In *Dugdale v Kraft Foods Ltd*,[5] the Employment Appeal Tribunal (EAT) held that the comparators (who did the same work as the applicants, but at night) should be compensated by the payment of a night shift premium, rather than a difference in basic hourly rate. The same principle applies to overtime and Sunday work,[6] though any differences of practical importance such as added responsibility (if, for example, the comparator works alone and unsupervised at night) may defeat a 'like work' claim.[7]

The frequency of tasks

23.6 In *Coomes v Shields*[8] the Court of Appeal ruled that ETs should take into account the things actually done by workers and the frequency with which they are done in assessing 'like work' claims, rather than paying too much attention to their strict contractual obligations. In that case the applicant, who worked in a betting shop, was paid a lower hourly rate than a man doing the same work. The employer argued that the man had an additional security role which justified the higher pay. There had been no trouble in the shop during the time it was operated by the employers. The applicant was awarded equal pay.

Responsibility

23.7 In *Eaton Ltd v Nuttall*[9] the EAT held that the degree of responsibility involved in carrying out a job may be decisive if it puts the comparator into a different grade than the applicant. An obligation to supervise or to control may also be relevant if it is exercised in practice, as in *Waddington v Leicester Council for Voluntary Services*.[10]

5 [1976] IRLR 368, EAT.
6 *Electrolux Ltd v Hutchinson* [1976] IRLR 410, EAT, and *National Coal Board v Sherwin* [1978] IRLR 22, EAT.
7 *Thomas v National Coal Board* [1987] IRLR 451, EAT.
8 *E Coomes (Holdings) Ltd v Shields* [1978] IRLR 263.
9 [1977] IRLR 71.
10 [1977] IRLR 32, EAT. See further para 23.9.

Work done in practice

23.8 In *Maidment v Cooper*[11] the EAT ruled that the applicant and her comparator were not employed on like work in a case in which, although a large part of their jobs were the same, some of the comparator's duties were significantly different to those of the applicant. The applicant's work mainly involved packing duties, although she also did some clerical work. The man similarly worked mainly as a packer, but also did storeman's duties. The EAT went on to rule that no issue arose under the EqPA 1970 from the fact that the discrepancy in remuneration between the woman and her comparator was not commensurate with the difference in the work that each did. Such a disproportionate difference in pay may, however, breach article 141.

Extra responsibilities and lower pay

23.9 In *Waddington* the EAT ruled that a woman who was supervising a man who was paid more than she for performing otherwise similar work was not engaged in 'like work' with him. The decision pre-dated the introduction of the equal value claim (see further chapter 24). It was, in any event, wrong. In *Murphy v Bord Telecom Eireann*[12] the ECJ ruled that article 141 must be interpreted as covering the case where the applicant is doing work of higher value than that of the comparator. According to that court, to find otherwise would render the principle of equal pay ineffective since an employer could circumvent it by assigning additional duties to women while paying them lower wages than men.

Conclusion – establishing 'like work'

23.10 It is often difficult to judge whether a woman and her comparator are engaged in like work, and the outcome will depend on the facts in each case. Detailed evidence of the work actually done will need to be provided to the ET. It is useful to have a timetable of an average week showing the tasks done by applicant and comparator and the time spent on each task. Any documents, such as job descriptions, which establish the duties of the job should be in the tribunal bundle. It is important to remember that the applicant will need to call evidence

11 [1968] IRLR 462.
12 Case 157/86 [1988] ECR 673; [1988] IRLR 267.

which establishes not only what she does but also, in the same way, precisely what the male comparator does.

23.11 Women who fail in a like work claim may be able to establish that their work is of equal value to that of their comparator(s). Equal value claims are considered further in chapter 25.

Work rated as equivalent under a job evaluation scheme

Introduction

23.12 If the woman's work and that of her comparator(s) has been evaluated under the same JES, her equal pay claim may be affected in one of two ways. In the first place, if the scheme has evaluated her job as equivalent to that of one or more of her comparators, she may bring her claim under EqPA 1970 s1(5). If, on the other hand, her comparator's work has been rated as more valuable than hers under a JES, this can be relied upon by an employer to defeat her claim.[13] This second aspect of the JES is dealt with in chapter 24, which deals with equal value claims.

23.13 There is at present no obligation on an employer to carry out a JES. But job evaluation is an essential tool in securing pay equality. Without it, it is impossible to ascertain whether and to what extent sex segregation in the workforce has resulted in or perpetuated unequal pay.

'Job evaluation'

23.14 Job evaluation is concerned with assessing the value of different jobs and putting the jobs in a hierarchy of value. This is bound to be in part at least a subjective process. The term 'felt fair' ranking system is often used to indicate that the end result of a ranking process is not scientific, but that it reflects the value that those in the organisation give to the jobs concerned.

23.15 As women's jobs have been historically undervalued, it is important that any JES builds into the factor headings and the weight given to various factors, safeguards against the undervaluation of 'female' as distinct from 'male' job characteristics. Although it is not legally required, it is good practice for job evaluation to be carried out with

13 EqPA 1970 s2A(2).

the involvement of a joint committee of employers and union or worker representatives. Those carrying out the evaluation should be trained – in particular, in recognising the historic under-valuation of women's work.[14] As one job evaluation expert has pointed out:

> ... the whole process of job evaluation is inherently judgmental and, insofar as the judgments are made predominantly by men on the basis of existing relativities, inevitably extremely suspect.[15]

Job evaluation schemes are concerned with measuring the value of *jobs*, not of the workers performing them. Job content alone is measured, factors such as length of service and productivity being irrelevant. It is assumed that the job is being done properly, and experience and qualifications are relevant to the evaluation of the job only in so far as they are required for it.[16]

What is a valid job evaluation scheme?

23.16 Not every JES will count under the EqPA 1970 for the purpose either of founding or defeating a claim. EqPA 1970 s1(5), which defines in what circumstances a woman is to be regarded as employed on work rated as equivalent, requires that the JES be 'analytical'. An analytical JES describes each job under various factor headings which reflect the mental and physical demands of the job on the employee. Examples would be responsibility, strength, stamina, dexterity, decision-making, knowledge, and working conditions. In contrast, other forms of JES may rank whole jobs in order of 'value' or 'worth' without breaking the jobs down according to the particular demands made by them of workers.

23.17 EqPA 1970 s1(5) provides that a woman is to be regarded as employed on work rated as equivalent with that of her comparator:

- if her job and his have been given an equal value, in terms of the demands made on a worker under various headings (for instance, effort, skill, decision) by a job evaluation study (which must have been undertaken with a view to evaluating the jobs to be done by all or any of the employees); or

14 See para 23.40 on ways of avoiding sex bias.

15 D Wainwright, 'Why equal value is dynamic for pay structure', *Personnel Management*, October 1983. The same is true to today.

16 But see *Evesham v North Hertfordshire Health Authority and Health Secretary* [2000] IRLR 257, CA, in which an independent expert, in deciding that the applicant's job was of equal value to that of her comparator, had taken into account her greater length of service and experience.

- if their jobs would have been given equal value but for the fact that they were evaluated under a system setting different values for men and women on the same demands under any heading.

Introduction to job evaluation techniques

23.18 When an analytical job evaluation is first carried out, the normal procedure involves the selection of 'benchmark' jobs, each of which represents a group of the same or similar jobs. Each 'benchmark' job is evaluated by being awarded a mark in relation to each of the selected factors and the marks totalled. That stage will be carried out by a joint committee of management and trade unions or management alone. It is important that trade unions are involved and that there is good gender mix on the committee if the evaluation is to be fair and avoid sex bias. At some stage in large schemes it is likely that the various factors will be weighted to produce a 'felt fair' ranking order. When the committee is satisfied that the weighting of the factors produces an acceptable hierarchy of benchmark jobs, other jobs are evaluated to produce a final ranking order.

23.19 JES results are often produced by feeding the marks for each job that has been evaluated into a computer which applies any weighting and produces the final mark. Jobs which have not been evaluated to produce the final ranking order are unlikely to be individually evaluated unless their position in the ranking order is disputed. They will be slotted into the hierarchy on the basis of an assessment of which of the evaluated jobs they approximate to.

23.20 Once the ranking order has been established the list of jobs will be broken down into pay grades (which may themselves be broken down into pay bands). Pay grades are often the subject of negotiations with the trade unions and are not a matter for decision by the JES committee. They, together with other aspects of job evaluation schemes, are further discussed below.

Bringing a 'work rated as equivalent' claim

23.21 This part of the chapter looks first at a straightforward equal pay claim in which a JES has been implemented, before considering more difficult issues which may arise in connection with job evaluation schemes.

23.22 If the applicant's job and that of her comparator(s) have been rated as equivalent under the same JES, and the JES has been implemented, an equality clause will operate so as to entitle her to equally favourable contractual terms unless the employer proves the genuine material factor (GMF) defence (see chapter 25).[17] The employer may seek to defend the disparity in pay or contractual terms by showing that it is due to a non-sex-based material factor – for example, a London allowance where the man but not the woman is employed in London.[18]

23.23 A material factor defence should not succeed if the matter relied upon by the employer is an aspect of the job which has been taken into account in the JES. For example, if the JES takes into account environmental factors, which include hot dusty working conditions, the employer should not be able to justify an environmental allowance paid to the male comparator on the grounds that his working conditions are worse than those of the applicant.[19]

Evidence required for a 'work rated as equivalent' claim.

23.24 If the applicant's job and that of her comparator have been rated equally in a JES, the employer is likely to concede that their jobs are rated as equivalent and to defend the claim by pleading the GMF defence. If it is not clear, from the grounds of resistance, whether the employer is disputing that the work is rated as equivalent, the applicant should serve a request for further particulars of the defence to clarify the position.[20] If the employer does accept that the jobs are rated as equivalent, no detailed evidence or expert witness will be required on the JES, unless the employer seeks to put forward as a GMF an aspect of the job already taken into account by the job evaluation.

23.25 If, however, the employer argues that the woman's job, or that of her comparator, has not been evaluated by the JES, proof of the evaluation will be needed. The employer should be asked to supply the necessary documents on the JES.[21] Unless the applicant is supported by her trade union and it is able to supply a witness with sufficient knowledge of the JES, it may be necessary to have an expert witness on job evaluation.

17 EqPA 1970 s1(2)(b) and (5).

18 Ibid s1(3) – see further chapter 25.

19 Though see *McGregor* v *GMBATU* [1987] ICR 505, EAT.

20 See para 32.117 on the procedure for obtaining further particulars of the defence.

21 See para 32.119 on discovery.

'Equivalent' work

23.26 In *Springboard Sunderland Trust v Robson*[22] the EAT held that in order to decide whether two jobs were rated as equivalent, it is necessary to look at the JES in its entirety. If the JES grade/pay bands had been established in advance, it was necessary to consider the allocation of jobs to particular pay grades or scales at the end of the job evaluation process. Although, in *Robson*, the applicant and her comparator had been awarded different points (he had 428; she had 410), their work was to be regarded as rated as equivalent because the JES provided that all employees who had between 410 and 449 points should be placed in the same salary grade. She was therefore entitled to equal pay with that of her comparator.

23.27 The EAT did not decide in *Robson* whether the applicant would have succeeded if the job evaluation had not yet been implemented, but the marks were so close that it was probable that any implementation would result in the applicant being in the same pay grade as her comparator. In such a case, however, the applicant's claim should succeed.[23]

Out of date job evaluation schemes

23.28 The relevant date on which the respective value of jobs must be determined is the date of the application to the tribunal. The issue for the tribunal is whether, on that date, the jobs of the woman and her comparator(s) had been evaluated. If the JES was carried out prior to that date, and the jobs involved have changed significantly since, the employer may rely on these changes to argue that the work of the woman and her comparator should no longer be rated as equivalent. It is for tribunal to decide whether the changes are sufficiently significant to invalidate the evaluation of the jobs for the purpose of the equal pay claim. If they are, evidence of the evaluation may still be introduced in an equal value claim.[24]

22 [1992] IRLR 261.

23 See also Equal Pay Directive (EPD) art 6 which requires member states to see that effective means are available to ensure that the principle of equal pay is observed. It is strongly arguable that denying a woman equal pay because of an insignificant lower ranking would be a breach of art 6.

24 See chapter 24.

Not yet implemented job evaluation schemes

23.29 Once the JES has been carried out and a woman's job evaluated as being equivalent in value to that done by a man, the man and woman should receive the same pay and terms and conditions of employment unless there is a difference between them which would amount to a material factor defence (see chapter 25). In *O'Brien v Sim-Chem Ltd*[25] the House of Lords considered the implications for equal pay of a JES which had been completed but whose implementation had been delayed when the government, with whom the employers contracted, announced a pay policy which was, in the employer's view, inconsistent with the implementation of the scheme. The House of Lords ruled that the JES took effect, for the purposes of the EqPA 1970, as soon as it had been completed – not when it was put into operation by the adoption of a new grading structure.[26]

'Benchmark' and 'non-benchmark' jobs

23.30 It is very unusual for a JES to evaluate all jobs in a workplace. The question therefore arises whether a 'work rated as equivalent' claim can be brought in relation to non-benchmark jobs (which have not themselves been evaluated under each of the headings adopted by the JES). This question is likely to be of particular importance in a case in which the JES has not yet been implemented, and only a sample of benchmark jobs have been evaluated. If only those in benchmark jobs were able to claim equal pay in reliance on the JES, the majority of women would be barred from a claim of this sort even if their jobs were almost identical to the benchmark jobs.

23.31 No decision, as yet, has directly decided this point, although some guidance can be drawn from the decision of the Court of Appeal in *Bromley v Quick Ltd*.[27] There the issue was whether the employer could use the JES as a defence to an equal value claim (see further para 24.16). Woolf LJ (as he then was) took the view that the employer could rely on a JES to defeat the claims, not just of women in benchmark jobs, but also of those employed in other jobs provided that there was no material difference between these and the benchmark jobs. If this is correct, it should equally apply to circumstances in

25 [1980] 1 WLR 734; [1980] IRLR 151.

26 That is, carried out and its evaluations and resulting pay grades accepted.

27 [1988] IRLR 249.

which an applicant whose individual job has not been evaluated is relying on the evaluation of a similar benchmark job.[28]

23.32 If a tribunal accepts that non-benchmark jobs may be 'rated as equivalent', it may be necessary for the applicant at the tribunal to be assisted by an expert witness who could give evidence as to the similarities for the purpose of JES of the jobs concerned.

Discriminatory job evaluation schemes

23.33 EqPA 1970 s1(5) provides that a woman's job will be rated as equivalent to that of her comparator if they have been accorded equal value by an appropriate JES *or if they would have been given an equal value but for the evaluation being made on a system setting different values for men and women on the same demand under any heading*. This proviso appears to apply only in relation to directly discriminatory schemes, and there are no reported instances in which a 'work rated as equivalent' claim has succeeded on these grounds. If, however, a JES rates the jobs of an applicant and her comparator as unequal, she may still succeed in an equal value (as distinct from a 'work rated as equivalent') claim if she can show that the JES was directly or indirectly discriminatory, or that it was non-analytical (see *Eaton v Nuttall*,[29] below).

Job evaluation scheme techniques

23.34 As explained above, the main distinction in types of JES is between 'analytical' and 'non-analytical' schemes. A JES must be 'analytical' in order to 'count' for the purposes of the EqPA 1970 (ie, to found a 'work rated as equivalent' claim or to defend an equal value claim). What this means is that the jobs of each worker covered by the study must have been valued in terms of the demand made on the worker under various headings.

23.35 The different types of analytical and non-analytical JES were explained in an appendix to the EAT's decision in *Eaton Ltd v Nuttall*.[30]

28 Lord Dillon and Lord Neill took the view that for EqPA 1970 s2A(2) to be satisfied it was not enough that representative benchmark jobs had been evaluated, in addition the job of the woman and her comparator had to be evaluated under headings. Section 2A(2) does not apply to work rated as equivalent claims and the slightly broader wording of s1(5) may support Lord Woolf's view. As suggested above, the requirement of effective remedy in art 6 EPD would also be supportive.

29 [1977] IRLR 71 – see further para 23.35.

30 Ibid.

Non-analytical job evaluation schemes

23.36 The main types of non-analytical job evaluation schemes consist of:

- *Job ranking*: these schemes involve consideration and hierarchical ranking of 'whole' jobs which are ordered on a 'felt fair' basis and then grouped into grades for the purposes of fixing pay levels. The 'felt fair' basis of ordering frequently entails maintaining the status quo by undervaluing traditionally undervalued 'female' jobs. This JES technique makes no attempt to analyse why one order of jobs is thought to be fairer than another.
- *Paired comparison*: these schemes involve the 'whole job' comparison of each job with each other job covered by the scheme. Points of 0, 1 or 2 are awarded in respect of each comparison of each job according to whether its overall importance is judged to be less than, equal to or more than its immediate comparator. Points awarded for each job are then totalled and a ranking order produced. Like job ranking, 'paired comparison' schemes make no attempt to analyse why one job is more important than another. They tend, therefore, to perpetuate traditional views about the relative value of 'male' and 'female' jobs.
- *Job classification*: this system is similar to job ranking save that it adopts the reverse order. A broad grading structure is established first, and individual jobs fitted into it. Jobs considered typical of each grade are selected as 'benchmarks' and other jobs compared with these benchmarks and placed in their appropriate grade. Such schemes may well be discriminatory, as work done by men and skills mainly held by men are likely to find a place near the top of the grading structure, while women's work is downgraded to the bottom.

Analytical schemes

23.37 The main types of analytical job evaluation schemes consist of:

- *Points assessment*: this system, the most common in use, breaks down each job into a number of factors, eg, skills, responsibility, physical and mental requirements and working conditions. Each of these factors may be analysed further. Points are awarded for each factor according to a predetermined scale, and the total points decide a job's place in the ranking order. Usually the factors are weighted so that, for example, more or less weight may be given to hard physical conditions or to a high degree of skill. This method provides scope for a complete re-evaluation of the worth of different jobs. It is likely to be effective only if taken into account and the weightings given are not discriminatory (see paras 23.38–23.40).

- *Factor comparison*: this system employs the same principles as points assessment but uses only a limited number of factors, such as skill, responsibility and working conditions. A number of 'key' jobs are selected because their wage rates are generally agreed to be 'fair'. The proportion of the total wage attributable to each factor is then decided (sometimes by a computer programme), and a scale produced showing that part of the pay of each key job which is attributable to each factor. The other jobs are then compared with this scale, factor by factor, so that a rate is finally obtained for each factor of each job and the total pay for each job is reached by adding together the rates for its individual factors. The danger with this system is that it tends to perpetuate the historical undervaluation of 'female' job characteristics.

An example of a discriminatory JES[31]

23.38

Factors[32]	**Maintenance fitter**	**Company nurse**
Skill:		
– Experience in job,	10	1
– Training	5	7
Responsibility:		
– For money,	0	0
– For equipment and machinery,	8	3
– For safety,	3	6
– For work done by others	3	0
Effort:		
– Lifting requirements,	4	2
– Strength required,	7	2
– Sustained physical effort	5	1
Conditions:		
– physical environment,	6	0
– working position,	6	0
– hazards	7	0
TOTAL	64	22

31 Taken from the EOC's *Job Evaluation Schemes free of sex bias* (1994, revised edn).

32 Each factor is scored on a scale from 1 to 10. For simplicity, no weighting has been applied.

This set of factors is discriminatory because it covers many aspects of the male job but very few which relate to the female job. Furthermore, some of the characteristics which relate to the male job overlap. 'Strength required', for example, duplicates to some extent 'sustained physical effort', with the result that a high score on one will often be associated with a high score on the other. The same is true of 'lifting requirement' and 'strength required'. Note that the difference in scores on the factor 'experience in job' completely outweighs the more significant difference in the factor 'training'.

23.39 Awarding a score of 0 to a nurse in relation to hazards must be inaccurate as it is inconceivable that she is not working with some hazards such as infectious diseases, or sharp instruments.

Avoiding bias in job evaluation schemes

23.40 An analytical JES which is free of sex bias will reduce the impact of sex discrimination on pay. It will also serve as a watertight defence for an employer faced with an equal value claim from a woman whose job has been rated as less valuable than that of her chosen comparator (see para 24.16). Account should be taken of the Equal Opportunities Commission's (EOC) Code of Practice on Equal Pay which came into force on 26 March 1997.[32a] It is therefore in the interests of all parties for any JES to be non-discriminatory. The EOC has drawn up guidance on how to avoid sex bias in job evaluation schemes, and the Court of Appeal in *Bromley v Quick*[33] approved the use of the EOC's booklet on the need to avoid bias. The main points made by that booklet are as follows:

- A commitment to a fair job evaluation may require a change in traditional assumptions about the value attributed to work predominantly carried out by women. For example, it is a commonly held belief that women are 'natural' carers, with the effect that caring for others is not seen as a rewardable skill. Jobs such as nursing and caring for the elderly or disabled require many skills and should be rewarded on this basis.
- Women should be fairly represented on all JES committees and discussions. Lack of participation by women in the carrying out of a JES may mean that the study is incomplete and open to challenge.

32a A revised edition will be available from April 2003 from www.eoc.org.uk.
33 [1988] IRLR 249.

- Everyone involved in the JES – in particular the chairs of JES committees – should be given training on how sex bias in job evaluation can arise.
- Regular progress reports should be given to all employees so they can raise concerns about any possible sex bias in the conduct of a JES.
- Minutes and records should be kept in connection with the carrying-out of any JES in case there is a subsequent complaint of discrimination.
- Guidance and training should be given to those writing job descriptions with a comprehensive list of elements to be included. Both job-holders and their managers should be involved in this process.
- The long tradition of using different titles for the jobs of women and men who are doing essentially the same work has frequently denoted a status difference ('supervisor' and 'manager'; 'secretary' and 'administrator' or 'personal assistant'; 'operator' and 'technician'; 'cook' and 'chef'). It should not be allowed to obscure the relative value of jobs.
- 'Male' jobs which have become deskilled through technological change may still be regarded as skilled, even though the work is similar to 'female' jobs which are classified as unskilled.
- The identification of factors and sub-factors involved in jobs is crucial. Factors associated with work done by women, such as manual dexterity and concentration, must not be left out, and length of service should be included only to the extent that it is necessary for the job.
- Factors are often weighted according to how important they are to the work of the organisation; one factor may be given 10 per cent, another 1 per cent. Care should be taken to ensure that the factors on which the male jobs scored highly are not given unjustifiably high weights. Extreme weights should not be given to factors which are exclusively found in jobs performed predominantly by one sex.
- Schemes often use benchmark jobs which are seen as typical of a grade or group of jobs. A representative sample of female jobs should be included to ensure that the JES takes account of job elements which are peculiar to predominantly female jobs.

CHAPTER 24

Work of equal value

Key points

24.1
- The equal pay for work of equal value provisions allow women to claim equal pay with a man or men doing different jobs which are of 'equal value' to those done by the claimants.
- A claim could equally be made by a man in relation to a woman or women doing different, equally valuable but more highly paid work. In practice, such claims are never made.
- The burden of proof is on the equal value claimant, although the employment tribunal (ET) usually appoints an independent expert to report whether the claimant's job is of equal value to (or greater value than) that or those of her comparator(s).
- A job evaluation scheme (JES) that has rated the claimant's job as less valuable than that of her comparator(s) will block an equal value claim if it is analytical and non-discriminatory.
- The relative value of jobs for the purposes of an equal value claim is determined by evaluating the demands made by their jobs on the claimant and her comparator(s). This is usually done by an independent expert.
- There is a complex procedure for equal value claims which will involve different hearings (including a directions and preliminary hearing) as well as, in most cases, the appointment of an independent expert.
- An independent expert may choose the method by which the claimant's job and that of her comparator are evaluated, provided that it is analytical and non-discriminatory. The expert's report may be excluded if it does not comply with the rules or is unsatisfactory. The parties may each call an expert.

Background and statutory provisions

24.2 Equal Pay Act (EqPA) 1970 s1(1) provides that a woman is entitled to equal treatment under the terms of her contract with a man 'in the same employment' (see para 22.36):

> (a) where the woman is employed on like work with [the] man ...
> (b) where the woman is employed on work rated as equivalent with that of [the] man ...
> (c) where a woman is employed on work which, not being work in relation to which paragraph (a) or (b) above applies, is, in terms of

> the demands made on her (for instance under such headings as effort, skill and decision), of equal value to that of [the] man ...

The right to equal treatment operates by means of the insertion into the woman's employment contract of an 'equality clause' (see para 22.16), and does not apply where the employer makes out the genuine material factor (GMF) defence (see further chapter 25 and below). 'Like work' and 'work rated as equivalent' are dealt with in chapter 23. Here we consider in detail the procedures applicable to claims for equal pay for work of equal value.

24.3 The equal value provisions of the EqPA 1970 allow a woman to claim the same pay as a man in the same employment when she is doing work which is of at least the same value as his, even though their jobs may be entirely different. The value of work is measured in terms of the demands it makes on the worker (see s1(1)(c) above), and a woman's job may be as valuable as one done by a man whose title sounds more important and whose pay is much greater than hers. Women laundry workers have compared themselves with storemen and forklift truck drivers, women assembly operators with storemen and warehousemen, clerical administrative workers with warehouse operatives, a female technical author with a male software engineer and female speech therapists with male psychologists and pharmacists.[1]

24.4 Under UK law the burden of proof is on the applicant to show that the work is of equal value. But in most cases the ET will appoint an independent expert (IE) to investigate the jobs done by the claimant (or claimants) and her (or their) comparator(s). IEs' conclusions, although sometimes challenged by employers, are normally accepted by tribunals.

24.5 If a woman's work is the same as or broadly similar to a man's, or if it has already been rated as equivalent to a man's by a job evaluation scheme (JES), a claim should be made under EqPA 1970 s1(1)(a) and (b) (above and chapter 23) as well as under s1(1)(c). In such a case the tribunal will deal with the s1(1)(a) and (b) claims first.

24.6 The EqPA 1970 only allows an equal value claim to be determined if the woman is not employed on like work or work rated as equivalent to that of her chosen comparator.[2] This makes sense as the procedure under s1(1)(a) and (b) is simpler and quicker than that applicable to

1 The Equal Opportunities Review (EOR) does a periodic equal value update which summarises the type of jobs which have been compared. Most recently, see (1999) 88 EOR. The EOR is published by Industrial Relations Service and available at www.eordirect.com.

2 EqPA 1970 s1(2)(c).

s1(1)(c) claims. But the fact that a woman is employed on like work or work rated as equivalent with one man does not prevent her claiming she is employed on work of equal value to that of another man. In *Pickstone v Freemans plc*[3] female warehouse operatives claimed that their jobs were of equal value to that of a male warehouse checker. The employers argued that an equal value claim could only be made if there were no men doing like work or work rated as equivalent to that done by the claimant(s), and that the women's claims were blocked by the existence of male warehouse operative who was paid the same as them. The House of Lords ruled that the existence of the man doing the same work as the claimants was irrelevant to their equal value claim, pointing out that accepting the employer's argument would permit employers to evade equal work provisions by employing a token man on the same work as a group of women who were deliberately paid less than a group of men employed on work of equal value.[4] If, on the other hand, a comparator was doing like work with a claimant who named him in an equal value claim, the claim should be dealt with as a like work claim under Sex Discrimination Act (SDA) 1975 s1(1)(a) and the delays and expense associated with appointing an IE avoided.

Multiple applications

24.7 Some equal value claims are brought by very large numbers of claimants, usually with the support of their trade union(s). In those cases it is usual for there to be standard grounds of application for all the claimants or for various groups of claimants. The President of the ETs may be consulted by the claimants' representatives about having all the cases heard by a single tribunal, in which case the claims are normally consolidated and sample cases often chosen to be heard first. There is no formal procedure whereby the results of such sample cases will be binding in respect of the other cases, but where the facts relating to the cases are very similar it is normally anticipated that the major issues of dispute will be determined once the sample cases are heard.

24.8 In *Ashmore v British Coal Corporation* the Court of Appeal upheld an ET decision to strike out the applicant's equal pay claim.[5] The ET

3 [1988] 1 AC 66; [1988] IRLR 357.

4 See also Case 400/93 *Specialarbejderforbundet I Danmark v Dansk Industri acting for Royal Copenhagen A/s* [1995] ECR I-1275; [1995] IRLR 648, ECJ.

5 [1990] IRLR 283.

had previously dismissed sample claims by Ms Ashmore's fellow canteen workers on the basis that the employer had a GMF defence in that the comparator, Mr Dugdale, worked at night and alone. Mrs Ashmore's attempt to litigate her claim on the basis that she, like Mr Dugdale, worked at night and alone was struck out as an abuse of process, the ET holding that the employer's GMF defence was bound to defeat her claim. Although the sample cases were not formally test cases the Court of Appeal held that, where sample cases have been chosen so that the tribunal can investigate all the relevant evidence as fully as possible, and findings have been made on that evidence, it is contrary to the interests of justice and public policy to allow those same issues to be litigated again, unless there is fresh evidence which justifies reopening the issue. The correct test for determining whether fresh evidence is of such a kind that the court should permit a claim which would otherwise be an abuse of process is that it 'should entirely change the aspect of the case'.

Procedure for equal value claims

24.9 Equal value claims typically involve a number of stages, and the procedure laid down in the EqPA 1970 and the related rules of procedure (Equal Value Rules) are complicated.[6] The main stages – completion of the IT1 and IT3, referral to ACAS, requests for further and better particulars, discovery and written answers – are the same as for other equal pay and discrimination claims (see further chapter 32), EqPA 1970 s7A provides for a questionnaire procedure as in sex discrimination claims to equal pay claims (see further para 22.49). But the Equal Value Rules include steps additional to those which apply to other cases. The precise procedure and sequence of hearings may vary in different cases, but the usual steps are set out below.

The directions hearing

24.10 A directions hearing is generally held in equal value cases. In it, the ET may consider:

- if a like work or work rated as equivalent claim is also made, disposing of this claim first;

6 ETs (Equal Value) Complementary Rules of Procedure (Sch 3 to the ETs (Constitution and Rules of Procedures) Regulations (ET Regs) 2001 SI No 1171).

- the identification of comparators;
- whether further particulars are required from either party;
- if the employer is contending that there are no reasonable grounds for determining that the work is of equal value under EqPA 1970 s2A (see para 24.16), fixing a preliminary hearing to deal with that matter;
- if the employer is relying on the GMF defence (see chapter 25), whether that defence should be dealt with before or after the issue of equal value is determined;
- if a number of equal pay claims are made by claimants in the same employment, consolidating the cases so that they will be heard together. Such an order may be made if:
  - there is a common question of law or fact in some or all of the originating applications; or
  - the relief claimed arises out of or is in respect of the same facts; or
  - for any other reason it is desirable to make an order (Employment Tribunal Rules[7] r20).

As with other cases an order may also be made for discovery and/or written answers.

The preliminary hearing

24.11 Equal value claims progress from directions hearing to preliminary hearing at which the tribunal is likely to deal with:

- The question whether an independent expert is to be appointed.
- Any GMF defence raised by the employer, if it has been decided at the direction hearing that such a defence should be heard before equal value is determined.
- Any contention by the employer that there are no reasonable grounds for determining that the work is of equal value. It may be argued that the claim is hopeless, or that the claimant's job has been rated as less valuable than that of her comparator(s) by a valid JES (see below).
- Any issue relating to the entitlement of the claimant to bring the proceedings, such as whether she has identified a comparator 'in the same employment' or whether her claim is in time, namely within six months of the end of the employment –EqPA 1970 s2(4).

7 ET Rules of Procedure (ET Regs 2001 Sch 1).

24.12 Tribunals sometimes choose to determine the equal value issue without having appointed an IE. If they do so they must adjourn after the preliminary hearing in order to allow the parties the chance to appoint and receive reports from their own experts. It is unusual for tribunals to determine the question of value (save in 'hopeless cases' – see para 24.24) without the report of an IE, and this step would only generally be taken in a case in which there are few applicants and the issues appear to be comparatively simple.[8] It is difficult to envisage situations in which a tribunal would have the expertise and time to carry out the non-discriminatory, analytical evaluation of the two or more jobs being compared that is required to decide properly whether the jobs are of equal value. This might change if tribunals were to be assisted by an expert assessor as recommended by the Equal Pay Task Force – see further paras 22.8 and 26.50.

24.13 In some cases, one or more of the parties have their own job evaluation experts, and a tribunal can decide the question of value by hearing both experts and preferring one to the other. But if only one party has an expert, the absence of an IE would leave the other (almost invariably the claimant) at a distinct disadvantage. The Employment Tribunal (Constitution and Rules of Procedure) Regulations (ET Regulations) 2001[9] now provide that their overriding objective is to enable tribunals to deal with cases justly and that includes ensuring that the parties are on an equal footing.[10] It could be argued that, for a tribunal to determine the issue of value in circumstances in which only one party (the employer) had access to expert evidence would be contrary to that overriding objective.[11]

The material factor defence

24.14 The material factor or GMF defence may be raised by the employer at the preliminary hearing,[12] or in the event that the claimant's job is eventually determined as being of at least equal value to that of her chosen comparator. The purpose of hearing the defence at the preliminary stage is that, if it succeeds, the application is dismissed

8 See (1999) 88 EOR for details.

9 SI No 1171.

10 ET Regs 2001 reg 10.

11 Though we shall see below that the power of a tribunal to determine that the jobs of the claimant(s) and any comparator(s) are of equal value benefits claimants by preventing the dismissal as 'hopeless' of claims without the claimant at least being given an opportunity to put evidence to support her claim before the tribunal.

12 ET Rules of Procedure r11(2E), as amended by the Equal Value Rules.

and the tribunal spared the time and expense of commissioning an IE's report. If a GMF defence put forward by an employer is not heard at this stage it will be dealt with in the event that a finding of equal value is made.

24.15 If a GMF defence is unrelated to the duties of the jobs in question (as in the case of a market forces defence based on the need to attract and retain those in the comparator's job), it may be sensible to hear it at the preliminary stage. But if the defence raises issues related to the duties of the posts to be compared (such as particular skill requirements or responsibilities associated with the comparator's job), dealing with it at this stage will result in the tribunal having to hear evidence relating to these matters twice. In those circumstances it is better to determine equal value first, so that the tribunal makes findings as to the duties of the jobs with the benefit of the expert's or experts' report(s). The GMF defence is considered in greater detail in chapter 25.

'No reasonable grounds': impact of an existing job evaluation scheme

24.16 EqPA 1970 s2A provides that:

> (1) Where ... a dispute arises as to whether any work is of equal value as mentioned in section 1(2)(c) above the tribunal may either –
> (a) proceed to determine that question; or
> (b) unless it is satisfied that there are no reasonable grounds for determining that the work is of equal value as so mentioned, require a member of the panel of independent experts to prepare a report with respect to that question;
> and, if it requires the preparation of a report under paragraph (b) of this subsection, it shall not determine that question unless it has received the report.
> (2) Without prejudice to the generality of ... subsection (1) above, there shall be taken, for the purposes of [that subsection], to be no reasonable grounds for determining that the work of a woman is of equal value as mentioned in section 1(2)(c) above if –
> (a) that work and the work of the man in question have been given different values on a study such as is mentioned in section 1(5) above[13]; and

13 For instance, 'a study undertaken with a view to evaluating [under 'various headings (for instance effort, skill, decision)'] the jobs to be done by all or any of the employees in an undertaking or group of undertakings', such a study not being one which sets 'different values for men and women on the same demand under any heading'.

(b) there are no reasonable grounds for determining that the evaluation contained in the study was (within the meaning of subsection (3) below[[14]]) made on a system which discriminates on grounds of sex.

In 2000 the government proposed the repeal of the 'no reasonable grounds' defence.[15] But as yet no legislation has ensued.

24.17 It was explained at para 22.16 that a woman is entitled to equal pay with a man whose job has been rated as equivalent to hers by a JES, unless the differential is justified by a 'material factor not the difference of sex' (the GMF defence). If, on the other hand, a JES has rated the woman's job as less valuable than that of her comparator, and the scheme was analytical and non-discriminatory, she will be precluded by EqPA 1970 s2A(2) from making an equal value claim.[16]

24.18 In *McAuley v Eastern Health and Social Services Board*,[17] Northern Ireland's Court of Appeal ruled that a JES could only be used as a defence to an equal value claim if it was carried out in the undertaking or groups of undertakings for which the complainant worked. The court there rejected the argument that a JES carried out for and applied to health boards in Great Britain could block a claim brought by women working for a Northern Irish health board.

24.19 An analytical and non-discriminatory JES which rates the claimant's job as less valuable than that of her comparator will block an equal value claim whenever the scheme is begun, provided that it is completed before the final hearing, though a scheme initiated after a claim has been made will block the claim only if it evaluated the jobs done on the date the proceedings were issued.[18]

24.20 We saw in chapter 23 that a non-analytical JES which has rated an applicant's job as equivalent to that of her comparator will not found an equal pay claim under EqPA 1970 s1(1)(b). In *Bromley v Quick*[19] the

14 EqPA 1970 s2A(3) provides that: 'An evaluation contained in a study such as is mentioned in section 1(5) above is made on a system which discriminates on grounds of sex where a difference, or coincidence, between values set by that system on different demands under the same or different headings is not justifiable irrespective of the sex of the person on whom those demands are made'.

15 DfEE, 'Towards Equal Pay for Women', available at http://www.dfes.gov.uk/consultations/archive/archive1.cfm?CONID=6.

16 Ibid. It is arguable that EqPA 1970 s2A is in breach of art 2 of the Equal Pay Directive (Council Directive 75/117/EEC), which requires member states to enable all employees who consider themselves wronged by failure to apply the principle of equal pay to pursue their claims by judicial process (see further para 10.33).

17 [1991] IRLR 467.

18 See *Dibro Limited v Hore* [1990] IRLR 129, EAT.

19 [1988] IRLR 249.

Court of Appeal ruled that an equal pay claim would not be blocked where a non-analytical scheme (such as one using job-ranking, paired comparisons or job classification) had rated the claimant's job as less valuable than that of her comparator. According to the court, an employer seeking to have an equal value claim dismissed because there has been a JES must show that the scheme satisfies the requirements of EqPA 1970 s1(5) (which demands that the study evaluates jobs in terms of the demand made on the worker under various headings such as effort, skill, decision, etc).

24.21 In *Bromley* the issue was that, although benchmark jobs had been evaluated on a factor demand basis (see para 23.30 as to benchmark jobs), the jobs of the claimants and their comparators had been slotted into the ranking order of jobs produced from the benchmark jobs on a 'whole job' basis. No written job descriptions had been produced for these jobs. Even though the claimants had appealed the evaluation of their jobs, with the effect that their jobs had been evaluated at that stage in terms of demands made under selected factors, there had been no appeal by the comparators whose jobs had never, accordingly, been subject to analytical evaluation. Woolf LJ, who alone dealt with this issue, indicated that it might have been sufficient to defeat the women's claims that only one of their jobs had been evaluated, if the jobs done by the others was not materially different (though it would be open to an employee to contend that her job was different).

24.22 We have seen above that a JES must be analytical in nature if its unequal rating of a claimant's job and that of her comparator is to block an equal value claim. Just as the 'no reasonable grounds' cannot be founded on a non-analytical scheme, nor can it be founded on a JES which discriminates on grounds of sex – ie 'where a difference, or coincidence between values set by that system on different demands under the same or different headings is not justifiable irrespective of the sex of the person on whom those demands are made'.[20] If a scheme awards different points to men and women for the same level of effort under any particular factor it will discriminate on grounds of sex.[21] If it awards more points in respect of demands (such as physi-

20 EqPA 1970 s2A(3).

21 In Case 237/85 *Rummler v Dato-Druck* [1986] ECR 2101; [1987] IRLR 32 the applicant argued that she should have been placed in a higher pay grade because the work was, for her as a woman, heavy physical work. The same work did not require so much effort from a man. The ECJ held that it would be discriminatory to use values which represent the average capabilities of employees of one sex. This would discriminate against men and would be unlawful. Thus, women cannot be awarded more points because physical work is more effort for women than men.

cal effort) which are more common in jobs held by men than to demands (such as mental concentration) which are traditionally found in women's jobs, it is also likely to be discriminatory. In *Rummler v Dato-Druck GmBH*[22] a JES awarded points in respect of 'heavy work', which favoured men. The ECJ ruled that, in order to avoid sex discrimination, the JES should also take account of criteria in respect of which female employees may show particular aptitude. There are a number of job-related factors likely to favour men; giving weight to them might be discriminatory unless equal weight is given to factors which are likely to be important in jobs done by women (see para 23.33).

24.23 Article 1(2) of the Equal Pay Directive[23] (EPD) provides that a job classification system 'must be based on the same criterion for men and women and so drawn up so as to exclude any discrimination on the grounds of sex'. In *Bromley v Quick*, Dillon LJ pointed out (obiter) that:

> As there are no universally accepted external criteria available for measuring how much of a factor or quality is involved in a particular job or for measuring what relative weights ought to be attached to different factors or qualities involved, to differing extent, in various jobs, every attempt at job evaluation will inevitably at some stages involve value judgments which are inherently to some extent subjective ... Where there are such objective elements, care has to be taken to see that sex discrimination is not, inadvertently let in.

It is for the employer to show that the JES is not discriminatory. This will involve explanations of the factors taken into account by it and of how the scheme works.[24]

'Hopeless' cases

24.24 When EqPA 1970 s2A was introduced, a government spokesman explained that only 'hopeless' cases would be dismissed on the basis that there were 'no reasonable grounds' for saying the work was of equal value.[25] An ET must consider whether a case is 'hopeless' before considering whether to refer it to an IE.[26] The hopelessness of a case must be judged on the basis of all the evidence at the preliminary

22 Case 237/85 *Rummler v Dato-Druck* [1986] ECR 2101; [1987] IRLR 32.

23 Council Directive 75/11/EEC.

24 *Bromley v Quick* [1988] IRLR 249.

25 HL Debates col 924, 5 December 1983.

26 *Sheffield City Council v Siberry* [1989] ICR 208.

hearing. In *Donnehy v Sealink UK Ltd*,[27] for example, the claimant had presented a 'home made' IT1 which failed to identify any comparator or basis for alleging pay discrimination. By the time of the preliminary hearing she had commissioned an expert to prepare a report and give evidence on her behalf. The ET dismissed her claim on the grounds she had failed to make out a prima facie case at the time her claim was submitted. The EAT disagreed, ruling that all the relevant evidence should be considered at the preliminary hearing and the question looked at in the round to answer the question 'was there no reasonable basis for the claim?'.[28]

Determining value without the appointment of an independent expert

24.25 Until 1996 the EqPA 1970 s2A(1) provided that tribunals could not determine that a claimant and her comparator were engaged in work of equal value without first receiving the report of an IE. Tribunals could dismiss an equal value claim at the preliminary stage, without appointing an IE, on the basis that there were 'no reasonable grounds' for determining that the jobs were of equal value. In 1996 the EqPA 1970 was amended to allow the tribunal to determine that a claimant and her comparator are engaged in work of equal value without reference to an IE.[29] The amended s2A is at 24.16 above. ET Rules r10A, as amended by the Equal Value Rules, provides that:

(1) In any case involving an equal value claim where a dispute arises as to whether work is of equal value to other work in terms of the demands made on the person employed on the work (for instance under such headings as effort, skill and decision) (in this rule, hereinafter referred to as "the question") the tribunal shall, except in cases where it is satisfied that there are no reasonable grounds for determining the question in the affirmative, determine whether to require an expert to prepare a report with respect to the question.
(2) Before determining under paragraph (1) whether to require an expert to prepare a report the tribunal shall give the parties an opportunity to make representations to the tribunal as to whether an expert should be so required.
(3) Where the tribunal has determined not to require an expert to prepare a report it may nevertheless, at any time during its consideration of the question, require an expert to prepare a report,

27 [1987] IRLR 120.

28 Ibid.

29 EqPA 1970 s2A was amended by the Sex Discrimination and Equal Pay (Miscellaneous Amendments) Regulations 1996 SI No 438, as of 31 July 1996.

but shall not do so unless it has given the parties a further opportunity to make representations to the tribunal as to whether an expert should be so required.

24.26 In *Wood v William Ball Ltd*[30] the EAT ruled that a tribunal had to give the parties the opportunity to obtain their own expert evidence before dismissing an equal value claim on the basis that it had no reasonable prospect of success under EqPA 1970 s2A(2). Even if a tribunal is of the view, at the preliminary hearing, that the equal value claim is hopeless, it must nevertheless adjourn the hearing to give the claimant the chance to obtain her own expert evidence.[31] Thus, at the preliminary hearing, the tribunal must decide whether an expert's report is to be obtained by the tribunal itself or by the parties. If the report is to be obtained by the parties, the tribunal will have to determine the case on the basis of the evidence presented to it.[32] The mere fact that a claimant fails to persuade a tribunal to appoint an IE does not preclude an eventual ruling in her favour on the strength of expert evidence produced by the parties themselves. Nor does it preclude a later decision by the tribunal to appoint an IE itself (ET Rules r10A(3), above).

Appointment of an independent expert

24.27 If an IE is not appointed the tribunal must, as was mentioned above, adjourn to permit the parties to produce evidence on the equal value issue. If the tribunal does decide to commission an IE's report it will select an expert from an ACAS panel of experts, most of whom carry out their duties on a part-time basis.[33] The tribunal will then issue an instruction to the expert to prepare a report and will generally draw up a timetable, including the date by which the parties should send their representations to the expert. Some tribunals will hold a separate directions hearing once they have decided to appoint an IE, to which

30 [1999] IRLR 773.

31 The issue in *Wood* concerned an allegedly 'hopeless' case rather than one in which the 'no reasonable grounds' defence was based on a pre-existing JES. In the latter case one would expect the relevant evidence as to the JES and the issues to be brought before the ET at the preliminary hearing, an adjournment for that purpose not being necessary.

32 Note the point in para 24.13 as to the overriding objective of the ET Rules of Procedure.

33 People are appointed to the panel for a period of two years, but their appointments are renewable.

the expert is invited and at which a timetable is agreed with him or her.

24.28 The tribunal's instruction to the IE must be in writing and must set out:

- the address of the place where the claimant works or worked;
- the question whether the work of the applicant and her comparator is of equal value;
- the identity of the comparator or comparators;
- the date by which the IE is required to send his or her report to the tribunal; and
- the dates by which the IE must send progress reports to the tribunal.[34]

The instruction issued to the independent expert must also require that the expert shall:

- take account of all relevant information and representations;
- before drawing up his or her report, produce and send to the parties a written summary of the information and representations and invite comments from them;
- prepare a report which shall reproduce a summary and contain an account of any representations, and any conclusion (with reasons) as to whether the work is of equal value; and
- take no account of the difference of sex and act fairly.[35]

24.29 Having issued instructions to an IE the tribunal will then adjourn the hearing, pending receipt of the expert's report.[36] These reports may take months and the procedure by which the tribunal monitors the expert's progress by way of progress reports is intended to reduce delays. If the IE states that he or she is unable to keep to the ET's timetable the tribunal may give written notice either:

- that the IE is required to send the report by the required date; or
- that a later date is substituted; or
- that the IE be replaced by another. This step may be taken, however, only where it is 'in the interests of justice'. In most cases it would be likely to cause further delay.

34 ET Rules of Procedure r10A(4) as amended by the Equal Value Rules. This information must also be sent to the parties, together with instructions that a party which unreasonably delays the preparation of the IE's report may have an award of costs made against them, which may include the costs of the IEs and may be struck out.

35 Ibid r10A(4).

36 Ibid r10A(6).

Powers of the independent expert

24.30 In addition to the rules regarding discovery, inspection and the calling of witnesses which are available in respect of all tribunal hearings, the ET may, on the application of the IE, require anyone with relevant information or documents to provide them.[37] An ACAS officer cannot be required to provide such information. Nor can a person who would have good grounds for refusing to comply with the requirement were it made in connection with a tribunal hearing.[38] An application can be made by the person concerned to vary or set aside the tribunal's requirement.[39]

24.31 It may be essential for the IE to see employees at work, but the tribunal has no power to order an employer to allow the expert access to the workplace in order to obtain the information necessary to his or her report. In practice, however, employers normally do allow IEs access. It may be easier for the employer to allow such access than itself to produce detailed specifications of the jobs done by the claimant(s) and her (or their) comparator(s).

Independent expert practice

24.32 It is for the IE to decide how to evaluate the jobs of the claimant(s) and her (or their) comparator(s). Experts must, however, proceed analytically by looking at the demands made on by jobs under headings such as effort, skill, and decision-making.[40] But IEs are not undertaking complete job evaluation schemes, being concerned only with comparing two or more jobs. They usually devise their own methods of evaluation, using the minimum number of factors which will allow an examination of the principal demands of the jobs in question. Factors – and sometimes sub-factors – appropriate to the jobs of the claimant(s) and any comparator(s) are identified, and some points or other marking system devised. Express weighting is occasionally used (see para 23.34 for discussion of job evaluation methodology).

24.33 IEs will normally draw up a job description based on interviews with the job-holders and their supervisors and observation of their work. In some cases, experts have not drawn up job descriptions but have relied on those prepared by the parties. This can lead to

37 ET Rules of Procedure r5A.
38 Ibid r4(5A).
39 Ibid r4(5C).
40 Ibid r10A(1).

difficulties if the job descriptions relied upon turn out to be less than satisfactory, or if they are challenged by one of the parties. Unless the parties have agreed job descriptions for the jobs of both the claimant(s) and any comparator(s), such descriptions being in a standard format or being consistent with the IE's own observation of the jobs, it is preferable that the expert puts forward his or her own job descriptions.

24.34 The factors and sub-factors chosen by IEs will depend on the demands made by the jobs being evaluated. In the 1998 speech therapist test cases the nine IEs involved, who adopted a common approach and methodology at the request of the ET, used the following six factors and 14 sub-factors in comparing the value of the jobs done by the claimants and by their comparators (clinical psychologists and hospital pharmacists):[41]

- Knowledge:
  - knowledge base;
  - development;
  - experience.
- Responsibilities:
  - responsibility for patients/clients in the provision of a service;
  - managing work for self and others;
  - plant/equipment/resources;
  - training, mentoring.
- Mental demands:
  - concentration/accuracy;
  - stress/pressure.
- Physical demands and environment:
  - physical effort;
  - working conditions;
  - hazards.
- Decision-making/initiative:
  - complexity/analysis,
  - freedom to act;
- Relationships.

These factors and sub-factors were regarded as appropriate to the evaluation of the particular jobs being compared – there professions

41 *Worsforld v Southampton District Health Authority and Employment Secretary*, see (1999) 88 EOR. Preliminary questions concerning the GMF had come before the EAT in *Enderby v Frenchay Health Authority* [1991] IRLR 44 (see also the decision of the ECJ in Case 127/92 *Enderby*[1993] ECR I-5535; [1993] IRLR 591).

allied to medicine. Different factors will, of course, be appropriate in evaluating clerical jobs, production jobs, etc. When very different jobs are being compared it is vital that the factors relied upon by the evaluators capture the significant aspects of both.

24.35 Having obtained all the necessary information, including that supplied by the parties, and having received the representations of the parties, the IE prepares a written summary and invites the parties to make representations upon it.[42] The final report must take these representations into account.

The independent expert's report

24.36 The usual format of the IE's report is as follows:

- The details of the claimant's job (or claimants' jobs) and that (or those) of her comparator(s) are set out in the form of lists of tasks performed with factual details about what is involved (such as lifting weights of 20 kilos for about 10 metres). Language which involves value judgments, such as 'lifts light weights and carries them a short distance' does not provide the information that will enable accuracy and consistency of facts to be checked, nor will it allow the ET to assess the evaluation of the task. Similarly, a description which states 'requires a very high degree of prolonged concentration' should be avoided in favour of 'needs to concentrate to the exclusion of all other matters during about four daily sessions of 50 minutes'.
- A work analysis section collects and lists the material relevant to each factor of evaluation (for example, concentration or physical effort).
- A section (often with appendices) explains the method of evaluation used, defines the factors (and any sub-factors and levels within the factors) and sets out the scoring system.
- An assessment or evaluation section compares the relevant jobs factor by factor.
- A concluding section sets out the IE's opinion on whether the claimant's job (or claimants' jobs) are of equal value to that (those) of her (their) comparator(s) and includes a brief resume of the reasons behind the conclusion.

24.37 The expert's report must contain a summary of the representations made by the parties, the IE's conclusion as to whether the jobs

42 ET Rules of Procedure r10A(5).

compared are of equal value and the reasons for the conclusion.[43] The expert's completed report is sent to the ET which sends a copy to each party.[44]

24.38 The tribunal may require the IE to provide a written explanation on any matter in the report, or to give further consideration to the question of equal value, and to provide his/her conclusion in writing.[45] If the tribunal does this, notice must be given to both parties. This requirement broadly follows the same procedure as the original report (ie, the form of the instructions to the IE and the provisions in relation to delay are similar). The IE's reply must then be sent to the parties which can make representations. This can all be done by correspondence.

The 'equal value' hearing

24.39 Once the IE's report is received by the tribunal a hearing date may be fixed not earlier than 14 days from the time that the report was sent to the parties.[46] If either party wants the IE to attend, the tribunal must order his or her attendance. The tribunal may also ask the IE to attend of its own accord.[47]

Admitting the independent expert's report

24.40 The IE's report will be admitted at the resumed hearing provided it is not excluded by the tribunal on the grounds that:

- the expert has not complied with the rules relating to the summary representations and the report; or
- the report could not reasonably have reached the conclusion it did; or
- for some reason (other than the ET's disagreement with the IE's conclusions) the report is unsatisfactory.[48]

24.41 The tribunal must take account of the IE's oral and written evidence and the parties may give evidence and call and question witnesses

43 ET Rules of Procedure r10A(5)(c).
44 Ibid r10A(16).
45 Ibid r10A(20)–(21).
46 Ibid r10A(16).
47 Ibid r11(2A).
48 Ibid r8A(17) and (18).

(including the IE and the parties' experts).[49] If the parties wish to dispute any facts contained in the IE's report they should do so at this stage. The Equal Value Rules state that, once the IE's report has been admitted, no party to a case may give evidence, or question any witness, on any matter of fact upon which a conclusion in the report is based, unless it is relevant to a GMF defence or unless the IE came to no conclusion as to whether the jobs were of equal value because of failure by the parties to provide relevant information.[50]

24.42 If a tribunal decides not to admit an IE's report it is required to issue a fresh requirement for an expert's report to be prepared.[51] Most reports are admitted.[52] In *Aldridge v British Telecommunications plc*[53] the EAT expressed the view that, because of the inevitable delay if a fresh report was ordered, tribunals should encourage all the necessary evidence to be given at the admission stage. They should admit experts' reports and thereafter, if necessary, hear any further expert evidence before reaching a decision. If a tribunal considers an IE's report to be unsatisfactory it could give it little weight, and may prefer the evidence of an expert witness called by either side. Although the facts upon which an IE's conclusions are based may not be challenged once his or her report is admitted, the tribunal may consider other evidence, including that given subsequent to the admission stage, in reaching its conclusions.

24.43 In *Tennants Textile Colours Ltd v Todd*[54] the Court of Appeal held that the ET had erred in concluding that, once the IE's report had been admitted in evidence, the findings of fact contained in it were binding on the parties. This seems a surprising in view of the Equal Value Rules. However, the main ruling was that either party could make submissions to contradict the IE's conclusions and that, although the IE's report must obviously carry considerable weight as the Equal Value Rules gave it a status of unusual authority and importance, it was still open to the tribunal to reject the IE's report. This is plainly right. In some cases rather than rejecting the report the ET has carried out its own analysis and adjusted the IE's scores.[55]

49 ET Rules of Procedure r10A(19).

50 Ibid r11(2C)–(2D).

51 Ibid r10A(18).

52 See (1999) 88 EOR, which reported that expert reports had been admitted in all but four of the cases reviewed,.

53 [1990] IRLR 10.

54 [1989] IRLR 3.

55 *Worsforld v Southampton District Health Authority and Employment Secretary*, see (1999) 88 EOR.

The independent expert's report at the hearing

24.44 Once the independent expert's report has been admitted the equal value hearing proceeds in the same way as other ET claims. The only difference is that the IE is likely to be called to give evidence. Although factual matters in the report cannot usually be disputed at this stage, the IE's conclusion and analysis of the facts can be challenged – see *Tennants Textile v Todd* above. It will be important to look very carefully at the method of evaluation used by the IE. Should it be discriminatory, the report should be rejected.[56] Provided that notice has been given to the tribunal and other parties, any party can call an expert each who may be cross-examined and re-examined in the normal way.[57]

The parties' experts

24.45 Each party may, on giving notice to the tribunal, call its own expert witness to:

- challenge the JES at the initial stage;
- give expert evidence at any stage.

In addition, each party may use an expert to:

- Draw up job descriptions;
- Make submissions to the IE on the issue of equal value;
- Provide assistance in cross-examining the IE and/or other parties' experts.[58]

24.46 The tribunal has no power to require that an applicant be interviewed by her employer's expert witness, or that an applicant's expert witness have access to her comparators. But in practice the parties should be advised to co-operate. In addition, questions may be put to the employer by the applicant's representative if information is required as to the comparator. In order to obtain information under the normal procedure provided for by the ET Rules, see chapter 32. The tribunal's powers in this respect were reviewed in *Lloyds Bank PLC v Fox*.[59]

56 ET Rules of Procedure r10A(6)(d).

57 Ibid r11(2B).

58 The issue of experts' reports is usually dealt with at the directions hearing and experts' reports will be exchanged prior to the hearing. Late introduction of such a report may lead to an adjournment and a possible costs order.

59 [1989] IRLR 103, EAT.

Work of 'equal value'

24.47 A tribunal may be faced with a situation in which an IE has found that there is a marginal difference in the scores of the applicant and the comparator (or, if the tribunal has conducted its own job evaluation, it may have accepted a report from a party's expert which came to the same conclusion). The question then arises what is meant by equal value. In *Springboard Sunderland Trust v Robson*[60] the EAT upheld a tribunal's decision that the claimant's job had been rated as equivalent to that of her comparator for the purposes of a claim under EqPA 1970 s1(1)(b) (see para 23.26). The scores of the claimant and her comparator were 410 and 428 points respectively, but when the points were converted to grades the claimant and her comparator would have been in the same grade. A similar broad approach has been taken by a number of tribunals in determining equal value claims.[61]

24.48 If the claimant succeeds in her equal value claim the tribunal then has to award an equality clause with the effect that 'any term of the woman's contract' which is less favourable to the woman 'than a term of a similar kind in the contract under which that man is employed' is modified so as not to be less favourable (EqPA 1970 s1(2)(c)). In *Evesham v North Hertfordshire Health Authority and Health Secretary*,[62] the Court of Appeal found that the claimant was entitled to be placed at the same point on an incremental pay scale as her comparator even though she had six years of service as against his one year. Part of the reason for this decision was that, when the IE found her job was of equal value to that of the comparator, he had taken her greater length of service and experience into account. In addition, the claimant is entitled to arrears of remuneration. Although the EqPA 1970 limits this to two years, as a result of a ruling of the ECJ, this limit has been held to be unlawful and the appropriate period is six years (see para 33.12).

60 [1992] IRLR 262.
61 (1999) 88 EOR.
62 [2000] IRLR 257.

CHAPTER 25

The material factor defence

Key points

25.1
- An equal pay claim will be defeated if an employer establishes that the difference in pay is genuinely due to a material factor which is not the difference of sex.
- If the factor relied upon by the employer is tainted by sex, the material factor defence will not succeed.
- If the difference in pay arises from indirect discrimination, the employer must objectively justify it in order to avoid an unfavourable finding under the Equal Pay Act (EqPA) 1970 read with article 141 of the EC Treaty.
- In order to establish such objective justification the employer must show:
  - the factual basis for the difference;
  - that the factor is significant and relevant in that it explained the difference in pay, existed at the date the wages were fixed, still exists and is genuinely the reason for the pay differential, rather than an ex post facto justification of it;
  - (if reliance on the factor disproportionately disadvantages women), that reliance upon the factor is objectively justifiable.
- Among the material factor defences put forward by employers have been:
  - geography;
  - red circling;
  - flexibility;
  - merit or good performance;
  - productivity;
  - training;
  - skills, experience or qualifications;
  - length of service;
  - 'market forces';
  - differences in contractual terms.

Background and statutory provisions

25.2 This chapter considers the employer's defence to an equal pay claim. Under the EqPA 1970, whether the claim is in respect of 'like work', 'work rated as equivalent' or 'work of equal value'. EqPA 1970 s1(3) provides that:

> An equality clause [see para 22.16] shall not operate in relation to a variation between the woman's contract and the man's contract if the employer proves that the variation is genuinely due to a material factor which is not the difference of sex.

25.3 The function of the genuine material factor (GMF) defence is to prevent the claim succeeding where the difference in pay is nothing to do with the fact that the applicant is a woman and the comparator is a man. The EqPA 1970 is not a fair wages act. It is concerned only with sex-related pay discrimination. A difference in pay may be unfair but, unless it involves sex discrimination, any attempt to challenge it under the EqPA 1970 is unlikely to succeed.

25.4 What the employer had to prove to satisfy the defence was a matter of uncertainty for many years. The main dispute was whether the employer had to justify a pay differential between the applicant and her comparator in all circumstances, or only if the difference in pay was in some way discriminatory. In *Tyldesley v TML Plastics Ltd*[1] a man was paid more because it was believed that he understood and was committed to the concept of 'total quality management'. The Employment Appeal Tribunal (EAT) held that this could found a GMF defence, provided it was not tainted by gender discrimination. The issue in this case was whether the employer had to objectively justify paying the man more for the reasons given. It was not the applicant's case that the pay practice was discriminatory in that it had a disproportionate effect on women in the workforce. In those circumstances, the EAT found the employment tribunal (ET) had erred in ruling that the employer had to objectively justify the higher pay. It would have still been open to the ET to reject the employer's explanation, or to find that the system was discriminatory.[2]

25.5 *Tyldesley* was approved by the House of Lords in *Glasgow City Council v Marshall*[3] in which Lord Nicholls, for their Lordships, declared:

> The scheme of the [EqPA 1970] is that a rebuttable presumption of sex discrimination arises once the gender-based comparison shows that a woman, doing like work or work rated as equivalent or work of equal value to that of a man, is being paid or treated less favourably than the man. The variation between her contract and the man's contract is presumed to be due to the difference of sex. The burden

1 [1996] IRLR 395.

2 See also *Yorkshire Blood Transfusion Service v Plaskitt* [1994] IRLR 395, discussed at para 25.12 below.

3 [2000] 1 WLR 333; [2000] IRLR 272. See also *Strathclyde Regional Council v Wallace* [1998] 1 WLR 259; [1998] IRLR 146, HL.

> passes to the employer to show that the explanation for the variation is not tainted with sex. In order to discharge this burden the employer must satisfy the tribunal on several matters. First, that the proffered explanation, or reason, is genuine, and not a sham or pretence. Second, that the less favourable treatment is due to this reason. The factor relied upon must be the cause of the disparity. In this regard, and in this sense, the factor must be a 'material' factor, that is, a significant and relevant factor. The factor must be 'material' in a causative sense, rather than in a justificatory sense. Third, that the reason is not 'the difference of sex', which is apt to embrace any form of sex discrimination, whether direct or indirect. Fourth, that the factor relied upon is or, in a case within section 1(2)(c) [EqPA 1970], may be a 'material' difference, that is, a significant and relevant difference, between the woman's case and the man's case.

It follows that an employer who proves the absence of sex discrimination, direct or indirect, is under no obligation to prove a 'good' reason for any pay disparity. If there is any evidence of sex discrimination, such as evidence that the factor producing the disputed pay difference has a disparately adverse impact on women, the employer will be called upon to satisfy the tribunal that the difference in pay is objectively justifiable. But an employer who proves the absence of sex discrimination is not obliged to justify the pay disparity.

25.6 That, at any rate, is the position under the EqPA 1970 read in isolation. But in *Brunhofer v Bank der Osterrichischen Postparkasse,*[4] in which a single woman claimed equal pay with a man placed in the same skill category under a collective agreement, the European Court of Justice (ECJ) ruled that it was for the employer to justify different pay for work of equal value on the basis of objective factors unrelated to any discrimination based on sex.

25.7 It is questionable, after *Brunhofer*, whether an explanation such as that made by the employer in *Tyldesley* would suffice to permit a pay difference under article 141. However, the facts in *Brunhofer* appear to have involved an allegation of direct discrimination. The approach of the House of Lords in *Marshall* may be reconciled with this ruling if the latter is confined to cases where it is conceded that there is no sex discrimination. The ECJ stated, in *Brunhofer*, that 'the differences in treatment prohibited by Article [141] are exclusively those based on the difference in sex of the employees concerned'.[5] If, as in *Marshall*, the absence of sex discrimination is conceded, it would follow from *Brunhofer* that the pay difference would not have to be justified.

4 Case 381/91 [2001] ECR I-4961; [2001] IRLR 571, para 66.
5 Ibid, para 40.

'Material factor' and 'material difference' compared

25.8 EqPA 1970 s1(3) provides that, in the case of a like work or 'work rated as equivalent' claim, the GMF put forward by the employer, if it is to succeed, 'must be a material difference between the woman's case and the man's'. In an 'equal value' claim, on the other hand, the GMF 'may be such a material difference'. In either case the burden of proof is on the employer to show that the GMF defence applies.

25.9 Until the House of Lords decision in *Rainey v Greater Glasgow Health Board*,[6] the 'material difference' defence (ie, that applicable to 'like work' and 'work rated as equivalent' claims) was limited to characteristics personal to the worker, such as length of service, superior skill or qualifications and red circling. No extrinsic factors (such as market forces) would suffice.[7] The Equal Pay (Amendment) Regulations 1983,[8] which introduced 'equal value' claims, deliberately extended the defence in equal value claims so as to include 'material factors' of wider scope than 'material differences', as previously interpreted. But in *Rainey*, a like work case, the House of Lords cast doubt on whether there was any distinction between a 'material difference' and a 'material factor'. The House of Lords overruled the decision in *Clay Cross*[9] in which the Court of Appeal had adopted a restrictive approach to 'material differences'. Lord Keith, for their Lordships, relied on the decision of the ECJ in *Bilka-Kaufhaus GmbH v Weber von Hertz*[10] (see para 7.117):

> The decision of the European Court on Article [141] must be accepted as authoritative ... There is now no reason to construe section 1(3) [EqPA 1970] as conferring greater rights on a worker in this context than does article [141] of the Treaty. It follows that a relevant difference for purposes of section 1(3) may relate to circumstances other than the personal qualifications or merits of the male and female workers who are the subject of comparison.

25.10 The House of Lords held, in *Rainey*, that a 'material difference' connected with economic factors affecting the efficient conduct of the employer's business or other activity may well be relevant to the GMF

6 [1987] AC 224; [1987] IRLR 26.

7 This because of the decision in *Clay Cross (Quarry Services) Ltd v Fletcher* [1979] ICR 1, CA, discussed below. The House of Lords in *Rainey* overruled the decision in *Clay Cross* on the intrinsic/extrinsic distinction.

8 SI No 1794.

9 *Clay Cross (Quarry Services) Ltd v Fletcher* [1979] ICR 1, CA.

10 Case 170/84 [1986] ECR 1607; [1986] IRLR 317, ECJ.

defence. Their Lordships had there to consider a pay difference between male and female prosthetists (artificial limb-fitters). The employer had decided to offer a limb-fitting service previously provided only by the private sector. It recruited the applicant at an appropriate NHS rate of pay, but had to offer better terms and conditions to attract those previously employed in the private sector. Without 'poaching' private sector staff the employer would not have been able to offer the service. Of those recruited from the private sector, all were male. Nevertheless the House of Lords accepted that the employer had made out the defence (see further para 25.36).

Requirements for the material factor defence

25.11 In order successfully to plead a GMF an employer must prove:

- the factual basis upon which the employer relies to establish the material factor;
- that the material factor existed and was known to the employer at the date when the wages were fixed and/or like work, etc, commenced (whichever was later) and thereafter up to the date of the equal pay hearing;[11]
- that this material factor is causally relevant so it truly explains and was responsible for the difference between the woman's rate of pay (or bonus, car allowance or any other contractual term) and that of her comparator(s);[12]
- that the factual basis on which the employer relies to establish the material factor is not itself founded upon or tainted by direct sex discrimination;[13]
- if the factor relied upon is indirectly discriminatory on grounds of sex, that reliance upon it is nevertheless justified.[14]

11 *Beneviste v University of Southampton* [1989] IRLR 123, CA. See also Case 381/91 *Brunhofer v Bank der Osterrichischen Postparkasse* [2001] ECR I-4961; [2001] IRLR 571 in which the ECJ held that a difference in pay awarded on appointment could not be justified by factors which only became known only after the employees took up their duties.

12 See *Glasgow City Council v Marshall* [2000] 1 WLR 333; [2000] IRLR 272.

13 However, see para 25.17 and *Ratcliffe v North Yorkshire CC* [1995] 3 All ER 597; [1995] IRLR 439, in which the House of Lords threw doubt on the difference between direct and indirect discrimination when applying EqPA 1970 s1(3) – see para 25.36.

14 Case 170/84 *Bilka-Kaufhaus GmbH v Weber von Hertz* [1986] ECR 1607; [1986] IRLR 317, ECJ.

If the material factor accounts for only part of the variation in pay, the defence is only partly made out and the applicant is entitled to an increase to the extent to which the defence is not made out.[15]

Stages in determining whether a material factor defence succeeds

25.12 There is no defined list of factors which may be pleaded under the GMF defence. The employer may raise any reason for the difference in pay if it satisfies the points at para 25.11. The burden on the employer is considerably greater if the factor is one which puts women at a disadvantage (ie, is *indirectly* discriminatory), as in such cases the employer must objectively justify its role in determining pay.[16]

25.13 But if no discrimination is involved, the defence succeeds provided the employer can provide an explanation for the difference which is accepted as true, which operated when the salaries were fixed and which continued to explain the pay differential at the time of the equal pay claim. Even if the difference in pay is the result of a careless mistake it will suffice if it is the genuine explanation.[17]

Examples of possible material factor defences

25.14 The following are some examples of material factors raised by employers. They are, however, only examples, and in each case the explanation of the employer has to be examined to see if it passes the tests set out above.

Geographical differences

25.15 An employer is likely to pay employees working in London more than employees working elsewhere. There may also be differentials based on geographical location between places outside London on a cost of living or shortage of labour basis. Such distinctions are unlikely to be

15 Case 127/92 *Enderby v Frenchay Health Authority* [1993] ECR I –5535; [1993] IRLR 591, ECJ, see para 25.40.

16 See para 25.48 for what constitutes discrimination and what is required for the employer to justify a material factor.

17 *Yorkshire Blood Transfusion Service v Plaskitt* [1994] IRLR 395 (approved *Strathclyde Regional Council v Wallace* [1998] 1 WLR 259; [1998] IRLR 146, HL, the careless mistake was placing the comparator in the wrong grade under Whitley Council Rules).

tainted by sex. Further, even if mainly men work in one location and women in another, the employer is likely to be able to justify 'London weighting' or similar practices.

Red circling

25.16 This is a method by which the pay and benefits of a particular worker are protected. It commonly happens if there has been a reorganisation which involves downgrading some posts. The individuals in the posts at the time may have their pay personally protected, possibly on a stand-still basis, while new entrants will go onto the new lower rate. This might be indirectly discriminatory if the post has been historically occupied by men but new entrants include a significant proportion of women. If this is the case, the employer will be required to justify the red circle. Considerations might include the reason for the post being occupied historically by men, for how long the pay advantage for those protected was to last, and whether the red circle was part of a collective agreement that in other parts of the workforce had advantaged women. Personal pay protection may also be provided when an individual is downgraded due to health reasons. Unless such a policy was being operated in a discriminatory fashion, no justification would be necessary.

25.17 If the reason for the original salary protection was tainted by discrimination, the GMF defence should fail. So salary protection for 'male' jobs is unlikely to be held to be justified as its origin is likely to be discriminatory job segregation. This is so even if the origin of the salary protection precedes the EqPA 1970. In *Snoxell and Davies* v *Vauxhall Motors Ltd*,[18] for example, the applicants were employed as inspectors doing the same work as male inspectors who were on a higher rate of pay. When Vauxhall regraded the work in 1970, before the EqPA 1970 was in force, the 'male' rate was 'equalised' downwards to a 'unisex' rate but those men already employed as inspectors had their salaries 'red-circled' at the original 'male' rate. Ms Snoxell and Davies successfully claimed equal pay with the men on the protected rate, the EAT holding that:

> An employer can never establish in terms of s1(3) that the variation between the woman's contract and the man's contract was genuinely due to a material difference (other than the difference of sex) between her case and his when it can be seen that past discrimination has contributed to the variation. To allow such an answer would be

18 [1977] IRLR 123, EAT.

contrary to the spirit and intent of the Equal Pay Act. Though the original discrimination may have occurred before the effective date of the Act, and accordingly was not then unlawful, it cannot have been the intention of the legislation to permit the perpetuation of the effects of earlier discrimination.

Higher productivity

25.18 There are many different forms of productivity or payment by results payment systems. Discrimination may arise if the 'female' jobs are either excluded from access to such payments or have a less favourable payment system than 'male' jobs. If the employer relies on the comparator's higher productivity, it will be necessary to examine the method of measurement to ensure it is not discriminatory. The employer must prove that the man is more productive. If it is not clear how productivity is measured, and there is evidence that women generally score lower, the scheme is likely to be discriminatory (see immediately below).

Merit and commission payments

25.19 Elements of pay may be determined by an assessment of the quality of work, usually in clerical or administrative jobs. For example, in the civil service and related agencies, merit payments are associated with marks achieved in annual performance appraisals. The same considerations arise as for productivity payments. It is for the employer to show that the system is non-discriminatory if women as a group do less well than men. In the *Danfoss* case the ECJ held that where statistics (relating to a significant number of workers) showed that women employed on the same work as men earned, on average, less for the quality of their work, the higher payments to men could not be justified by the employer. According to the court it was inconceivable that the work carried out by female workers would be generally of a lower quality than that of men.[19]

25.20 Commission payments are particularly common in the sales sector. Again, if men generally earn more than women, an employer will have to prove that the system is non-discriminatory in design and fairly operated if it is to pass muster under the EqPA 1970.

19 Case 109/88 *Handels-og Kontorfunktionaerernes Forbund I Danmark v Dansk Arbejdsgiverforening (acting for Danfoss)* [1989] ECR 3199; [1989] IRLR 532. See Case 400/93 *Specialarbejderforbundet I Danmark (Applicants) v Dansk Industri, acting for Royal Copenhagen A/S* [1995] ECR I-1275; [1995] IRLR 647 for the limited application of this principle in the context of piecework.

Training

25.21 The employer may justify the use of the criterion of vocational or other training to determine pay, but only where it is demonstrated that such training is of importance for the performance of the specific duties entrusted to the worker.[20] Note that there should also be equal access to training (see para 15.3).

Responsibility

25.22 In some cases, extra responsibility has been held to amount to a GMF defence.[21] This does not appear correct, as it is a demand of the job which should have been taken into account in measuring whether the work of the applicant and comparator was 'like', 'equivalent', or of equal value. However, if sex discrimination was absent and the tribunal found that differences in responsibility were the reason for the disparity – whether or not a good reason – the GMF defence may succeed (see para 25.4).

Skill, qualifications and working conditions.

25.23 Skill and qualifications and working conditions have been given as examples of factors which might constitute a material difference between the work of an applicant and her comparator.[22] The same points can be made in this context as in the case of responsibility, above.

20 *Danfoss*, ibid.

21 *McGregor v General Municipal Boilermakers and Allied Trade Union* [1987] ICR 505, EAT; *Edmonds v Computer Services (South West) Ltd* [1977] IRLR 359. In the latter the EAT distinguished between paying the man more because of the present exercise of responsibility and paying him more because, in view of his age and experience, he had the potential to exercise responsibility. It held that in the first situation, the exercise of responsibility was something that is done as part of the work and so was to be taken into account when deciding whether the work was like work. However, the potential to exercise responsibility could be a material factor justifying higher pay. Such an approach would appear to leave the door open to vague justification for higher pay unrelated to actual duties. It is to be hoped that it would not be repeated today.

22 *Shields v E Coomes (Holdings) Ltd* [1978] IRLR 263, CA; *Clay Cross (Quarry Services) Ltd v Fletcher* [1979] ICR 1, CA; *McGregor*, ibid; and *Davies v McCartneys* [1989] IRLR 439, EAT (though in the last of these cases the jobs were considered on the facts not to be of equal value).

Experience and length of service

25.24 Service increments and long service benefits may discriminate against women who, on average, are likely to have shorter service than men because of breaks in their working lives caused by child-birth and dependant care responsibilities. There are also areas of employment which have only had significant numbers of women comparatively recently, so that a payment system which rewards long service will be indirectly discriminatory if it is not justified.

25.25 In *Nimz v Freie und Hansestadt Hamburg*[23] the payment system placed full-time employees in a higher grade after six years but part-time employees doing less than three-quarters of the hours only after 12 years. The ECJ held that this practice required justification in a case in which 90 per cent of part-time workers, but only 55 per cent of full-timers, were women. Although the ECJ had previously accepted (in the *Danfoss* case) that seniority is related to experience which, in general, improves performance, in *Nimz* the court required the employer to prove that seniority was associated with actual improvement in the work performed which 'depends on all the circumstances in a particular case and, in particular on the nature of the relationship between the nature of the work performed and the experience gained from the performance of that work upon completion of a certain number of working hours'.[24] Where the employer is unable to do so the GMF defence should fail.

25.26 In *Crossley v ACAS*[25] the applicant complained of a payment structure which, prior to 1992, had been based on annual increments. After that date, annual increments were replaced by merit payments but (predominantly male) workers with long service retained a higher pay grade. Mrs Crossley earned between £3,000 and £4,000 less than her male comparators and would never catch up under the present payment system. The ET found that the pay system was unlawful discrimination under article 141, applying *Nimz*, and rejected the asserted GMF defence that the payment system rewarded service and was necessary for retention of staff.

23 Case 184/89 [1991] ECR I-297; [1991] IRLR 222, ECJ. Compare Case 109/88 *Handels-og Kontorfunktionaerernes Forbund I Danmark v Dansk Arbejdsgiverforening (acting for Danfoss)* [1989] ECR 3199; [1989] IRLR 532, in which the ECJ held that seniority goes together with experience and need not be justified. *Nimz* is the later authority and is to be preferred. *Nimz* is also consistent with Case 1/95 *Gerster v Freiestaat Bayern* [1997] ECR I- 5253; [1998] IRLR 699, ECJ.

24 For further comment on this see para 26.30.

25 (2000) 44 DCLD.

Statutory provisions

25.27 In *R v Secretary of State for Social Services ex p Clarke*,[26] speech therapists in the NHS claimed that they were doing work of equal value with clinical psychologists and pharmacists. The employers argued, as a preliminary issue, that health authorities were required by statute to pay their employees according to the salary scales agreed by the Whitley Council. These scales were approved by the Secretary of State for Social Services and were enacted by way of statutory instrument. The High Court held that this did not satisfy the GMF defence. It is now well established that the direct effect of article 141 takes precedence over domestic statute and that any domestic statute must be disapplied if necessary to give way to an applicant's entitlement to equal pay.[27]

'Balancing' terms

25.28 Where a woman receives lower pay than her comparator but is entitled to other more advantageous terms, the employer may argue that the fact that she is compensated for lower pay is a material factor defence. In *Hayward v Cammell Laird Shipbuilders Ltd* the House of Lords established the principle that the right to equal 'pay' for comparable work applied in respect of each element of pay.[28] Whether the existence of contractual terms which were *more* favourable to the applicant than to her comparator could balance contractual terms which were *less* favourable to her than to him was not determined, the employers not having pleaded the GMF defence. But Lord Mackay stated (obiter) that an employer seeking to rely upon more advantageous terms as a defence to an equal pay claim would have to show, at least, that the less favourable term in the woman's contract was due to other more favourable terms.

25.29 In *Leverton v Clwyd CC*[29] the House of Lords held that the difference in working hours and length of holidays between the applicant's contract and her comparator's did constitute a GMF defence. Their Lordships ruled that:

> ... where a woman's and a man's regular annual working hours ... can be translated into a notional hourly rate which yields no

26 [1988] IRLR 22, DC.

27 See chapter 10.

28 [1988] AC 894; [1988] IRLR 257.

29 [1989] AC 706; [1989] IRLR 28.

> significant difference, it is a legitimate – if not necessary – inference that the difference in their annual salaries is both due to and justified by the difference in the hours they work annually and has nothing to do with the difference in sex.

Careful calculations ought to be done, however, to ensure that there is true parity between the applicant and her comparator.

25.30 The approach of the UK courts to the GMF is consistent with that of the ECJ to article 141. In *Barber v Guardian Royal Exchange Assurance Group*[30] the ECJ ruled that equal pay must be ensured in respect of 'each element of remuneration and not only on the basis of a comprehensive assessment of the consideration paid to workers'. This approach was seen as essential because genuine transparency, permitting effective review, is assured only if the principle of equal pay applies to each of the elements of remuneration granted to men and women. And in the *Jämställdhetsombudsmannen v Örebro Läns Landsting* case[31] the same court held that, in determining if women were paid less than their comparators, the basic salary had to be compared and an inconvenient hours supplement paid to the applicant midwives and not to the comparator technicians should not be taken into account. The ECJ accepted, however, that if unequal pay was established such as to give rise to a prima facie case of indirect sex discrimination requiring justification by the employer, midwives' shorter working hours might constitute an objective reason unrelated to any discrimination on grounds of sex justifying the difference in pay.

25.31 The difficulties in assessing the value of such benefits as sick pay, longer holidays and fringe benefits, in order to determine whether they fully compensate for lower pay are enormous. Employees will generally have different views about which are the most valuable terms and if women are denied the choice of having the most favourable 'package' this may, in itself, be discrimination. If this is to be a defence, the employer should have to show that the difference in pay is directly attributable to the other more favourable contractual term (see para 25.13).

30 Case 262/88 [1990] ECR 1889; [1990] IRLR 240.

31 Case 236/98 [2001] ECR I- 02189; [2000] IRLR 421.

Discrimination between part-timers and full-timers

25.32 In most areas of employment a greater proportion (usually about 80 per cent) of part-time workers are women. Discrimination against part-timers will, therefore, generally have a disproportionately disadvantageous impact on women. Such discrimination, if connected with 'pay', will breach article 141 unless the employer can justify it for reasons unrelated to any discrimination on grounds of sex (see para 22.18). For this reason, the part-time/full-time distinction will only rarely amount to a valid GMF. See para 26.47 and chapter 21 for discrimination against part-time workers under the Part Time Workers Regulations.

Market forces as a material factor defence

25.33 'Market forces' is a term used to cover a variety of circumstances. The employer may say that a higher rate has to be offered to recruit for the job in question because that is the market rate. A variation on the theme is the claim that, unless the higher rate is paid, it will not be possible to retain employees in post. However, if the market discriminates in that jobs traditionally occupied by women are paid less than 'male' jobs of equal value, that discrimination is imported into the employment in question if market forces are relied upon.

25.34 In *Ratcliffe v North Yorkshire CC*[32] the ET rejected a 'market forces' argument put forward by the employer on the grounds that it was discriminatory. The three applicant dinner ladies, whose pay had been reduced in connection with compulsory competitive tendering, claimed equal pay with male employees whose jobs had been rated as of equal value. The ET found that the employers had failed to establish a GMF defence, a decision upheld by the House of Lords. The employers perceived a need to reduce the pay of dinner ladies in order to be able to compete in the open market against private contractors. According to the ET this factor, while it may have been 'material', was due to the difference of sex. The labour market for catering staff was almost exclusively female, whereas the council employees employed on work of equivalent value were mostly men. The ET ruled that the pay disparity arose from:

> ... the general perception in the United Kingdom, and certainly in North Yorkshire, that a woman should stay at home to look after

32 [1995] 3 All ER 597; [1995] IRLR 439, HL.

> the children and if she wants to work it must fit in with that domestic duty and a lack of facilities to enable her, easily, to do otherwise.

The employers had reduced the women's wages because, in order to obtain contracts, they had to compete with commercial caterers who paid women employees less than the local government rate. Nevertheless, the House of Lords found that the ET was entitled to find that this was not a material difference *other than* the difference of sex. The fact was that the employers re-engaged the women at rates of pay less than those received by men engaged on work which had been rated as equivalent. The women could not have found other suitable work, and were obliged to take the wages offered if they were to continue with this work. To reduce the women's wages below that of their male comparators was the very kind of discrimination in relation to pay which the EqPA 1970 sought to remove.

Examples of 'market forces' material factor defences

25.35 In many circumstances, upholding a material factor defence will tend to undermine the principle of equal pay for work of equal value because of gender segregation and discrimination in the labour market. Thus, what is perceived as 'women's work' (for example, caring, welfare and secretarial tasks) is undervalued and underpaid while 'men's work' (for example, labouring, portering, forestry) is more appropriately rewarded. The fact that most employers underpay 'women's work' is a form of discrimination which ought not to provide a defence. Nonetheless, there have been many cases in which 'market forces' GMFs have been put forward by employers.

25.36 In *Rainey v Greater Glasgow Health Board*[33] the House of Lords held that a difference connected with economic factors affecting the efficient carrying on of the employer's business may found a GMF defence. The House of Lords found that:

- As a matter of fact, prosthetists who entered employment from private practice had to be paid more than an existing female prosthetist or the NHS prosthetic service would never have been set up. It was, therefore, necessary to pay the comparator (and all those others recruited from the private sector, rather than 'directly' by the employer) more than the standard NHS rate.
- It was simply a coincidence that all those recruited from private practice were men, there being no evidence of discrimination.

33 [1987] AC 224; [1987] IRLR 26, HL.

- There were sound, objectively justified, administrative reasons for placing male and female prosthetists (save for those recruited on higher salaries from the private sector) on to the Whitley Council scale. From an administrative point of view it would have been anomalous and inconvenient if prosthetists alone were subject to a different salary scale and negotiating machinery than other NHS employees.
- There was no evidence of discrimination in the Whitley Council scales.

The potentially discriminatory nature of the 'market forces' GMF in *Rainey* was not recognised by the House of Lords in light of its conclusion that the exclusively male composition of the prosthetists recruited from the private sector, and the contrast between this and the composition of those 'directly' recruited into the NHS, was nothing more than a coincidence.

25.37 The fact that the women agreed to lower wages, in order to keep their jobs, will not amount to a GMF defence if there is any taint of discrimination.[34] As Lord Denning declared in *Clay Cross (Quarry Services) Ltd v Fletcher*:[35]

> An employer cannot avoid his obligations under the EqPA 1970 by saying 'I paid him more because he asked for more', or 'I paid her less because she was willing to come for less'. If any such excuse was permitted the Act would be a dead letter.

Retention payments

25.38 Rainey and Clay Cross concerned market forces in relation to job applicants. But these forces can also operate by pressurising employers to increase the wages of existing workers in order to retain staff. Where such a practice impacts disadvantageously upon women (because the upward pressure acts predominantly in relation to 'male' jobs of comparable value to 'female' jobs), the employer will have to justify the resulting pay differentials. This will require proof of the need to reduce labour turnover, and proof that such turnover is higher in the work group which includes the comparator than in the applicant's group. If the employer argues that higher pay has in the past

34 In the absence of discrimination it would appear to be open to the ET which found this was the genuine reason – applying *Glasgow City Council v Marshall* [2000] 1 WLR 333; [2000] IRLR 272, to accept it as a GMF defence.

35 [1979] ICR 1, CA.

reduced labour turnover, an analysis of both the figures showing the reductions and the reasons given as to why the reductions occurred will be important. In addition, the employer must show that the same treatment is given to women and men where the market pressures are the same.

Different pay systems

25.39 Where different unions represent the various groups in the workforce, separate collective bargaining processes may operate. Where different bargaining structures have resulted in unequal pay between equally valuable 'male' and 'female' jobs, employers have attempted to justify the differentials by reference to the pay-setting process.[36]

25.40 In *Enderby v Frenchay Health Authority*[37] the ECJ considered a pay difference which arose between equally valuable jobs as a result of the different collective bargaining structures applicable thereto. The court held that the fact that the respective rates of pay of two equally valuable jobs – one of which was carried out almost exclusively by women and the other mainly by men – were reached by separate collective bargaining processes was not sufficient objective justification even where, as here, there was no evidence of discrimination in either collective bargaining process. To hold otherwise would, according to the ECJ, permit the principle of equal pay to be circumvented (see further para 25.14).

25.41 In *British Road Services Ltd v Loughran*[38] Northern Ireland's Court of Appeal held that separate pay structures based on different collective agreements did not amount to a GMF defence if the applicants are a member of a class of which a 'significant' number are female. The ECJ's reference, in *Enderby*, to an 'almost exclusively' female job was, according to the court, merely a reference to the facts of the case and did not intend to impose the principle that, unless the

36 This was done successfully, for example, in *Reed Packaging Ltd v Boozer* [1988] IRLR 833, which should no longer be considered good law (see discussion of *Enderby*).

37 Case 127/92 [1993] ECR I-5535; [1993] IRLR 593, ECJ.

38 [1997] IRLR 92, NICA. And in *British Coal Corporation v Smith* [1996] IRLR 404, the House of Lords held that the simple existence of separate pay structures is not a defence. The question is whether there are objective criteria justifying the difference in benefits (or pay) received by the applicants and their comparators, which were not tainted by sex discrimination.

disadvantaged group could be described as being 'almost exclusively' female, a presumption of discrimination could not arise.

25.42 Despite *Enderby* and *Loughran*, however, it appears that the collective bargaining process may be a relevant factor in justifying pay differentials. In the *Royal Copenhagen* case[39] the ECJ ruled that the national court may take account of the fact that pay was determined by collective bargaining or by negotiation at local level in assessing whether differences between the average pay of two groups of workers are due to objective factors unrelated to any discrimination on grounds of sex.

General rules applying to material factor defences

The material factor must be genuine

25.43 As explained above, any difference between the salaries or terms and conditions of the applicant and her comparator must be 'genuinely due to' and 'caused by' the material factor at issue if the GMF defence is to succeed. In many cases the employer is unable to bring evidence that the material factor relied upon is in fact the reason for the difference in pay. In *Ryder v Warwickshire CC*,[40] for example, the applicants (caterers, cleaners and caretakers) challenged the payment of bonuses to their comparators (gardeners and roadworkers) but not to them. The employers asserted that the bonus was paid as an incentive to and in reward for increased productivity. The ET rejected the productivity justification as a 'sham', no evidence having been produced which truly linked the bonus scheme to improvements in productivity:

> Looking at matters in the round, we find that the real reason for paying the bonuses now is that they have been paid for many years and the first respondent dare not take them away for fear of industrial unrest. Nor do they feel able to equalise the pay of the female applicants because they cannot identify the resources to do so.

Where the employer argues that differences in pay are due to a number of material factors (such as different hours of work or rotas, flexibility, red circling and collective bargaining) the employer must show that *each factor* is genuine and is the cause of a difference in pay.

39 Case 400/93 *Specialarbejderforbundet I Danmark (Applicants) v Dansk Industri, acting for Royal Copenhagen A/S* [1995] ECR I-1275; [1995] IRLR 647.

40 ET 1301481/97 (unreported).

25.44 In *Enderby* the ECJ was asked what should happen if the employer could only justify part of the difference of pay between speech therapists and pharmacists on the basis it needed to pay more to pharmacists in order to recruit. Having accepted that the state of the employment market could constitute an objectively justified economic ground for a difference in pay the ECJ continued:

> If the national court is able to determine precisely what proportion of the increase in pay is attributable to market forces, it must necessarily accept that the pay differential is objectively justified to the extent of that proportion. If that is not the case, it is for the national court to assess whether the role of market forces in determining the rate of pay was sufficiently significant to provide objective justification for part or all of the difference. Therefore, it must determine, if necessary by applying the principle of proportionality, whether and to what extent the shortage of candidates for a job and the need to attract them by higher pay constitutes an objectively justified economic ground for the difference in pay between the jobs in question.

So in the appropriate case the tribunal must find that part of the difference in pay is justified and part is not. The applicant will then succeed in relation to that part of the difference which is not justified.

The material factor must be current

25.45 The employer cannot rely on a material factor which no longer exists. The applicant in *Beneviste v University of Southampton*[41] was appointed to a lower point on a salary scale than men doing like work. The employer said that this was due to financial constraints. This reason ceased to operate as a GMF once these financial constraints had disappeared.

The pay system must be transparent

25.46 When a pay system is not transparent the burden of proof may shift to the employer to show that pay practices are not discriminatory once a female worker establishes, by comparison with a relatively large number of employees, that the average pay of female workers is lower than that of male workers in the same grade. In the *Danfoss* case[42] the employers paid the same basic minimum pay to workers in the same

41 [1989] IRLR 123,CA.

42 Case 109/88 *Handels-og Kontorfunktionaerernes Forbund I Danmark v Dansk Arbejdsgiverforening (acting for Danfoss)* [1989] ECR 3199; [1989] IRLR 532.

pay grade. Grading was determined by job classification. But additional payments were made to individuals within a grade on the basis of employees' 'flexibility'. This resulted in consistently higher pay for men and there was no way of working out how their pay rates were reached. The ECJ held that where, in such circumstances, there was a lack of transparency, the burden was on the employer to show an absence of discrimination. The workers would otherwise be deprived of any effective means of achieving equal pay.

25.47 Performance-related pay schemes which result in consistently higher pay for men may be discriminatory. In *Danfoss* the ECJ held that criteria relating to the quality of work which systematically discriminated against women were automatically unfair as, the ECJ pointed out, it was inconceivable that women's work would be of a consistently lower quality than men's. However, quality needs to be distinguished from quantity of work. In the *Royal Copenhagen* case[43] the ECJ held that sex discrimination was not established on the basis that a piecework pay scheme resulted in lower average wages for a predominantly female group of workers than for a predominantly male group of workers carrying out work of equal value. If it was not possible to identify the factors which determined the rates or units of measurement used to calculate pay, however, the burden would shift to the employer to explain how the pay was calculated.

The material factor defence and direct and indirect discrimination

25.48 In the *Ratcliffe* case[44] Lord Slynn declared, for the House of Lords, that tribunals and courts determining EqPA 1970 cases should not be concerned with the Sex Discrimination Act (SDA) 1975's distinction between so-called 'direct' and 'indirect' discrimination. As the discrimination in *Ratcliffe* was direct, these remarks were obiter.

25.49 In *Strathclyde Regional Council v Wallace,*[45] a case in which the applicants conceded that there was no discrimination, Lord Browne-Wilkinson expressed the further obiter view that Lord Slynn's remarks in *Ratcliffe* should not be taken too far, and that ECJ rulings on pay dis-

43 Case 400/93 *Specialarbejderforbundet I Danmark (Applicants) v Dansk Industri, acting for Royal Copenhagen A/S* [1995] ECR I-1275; [1995] IRLR 647.

44 [1998] 1 WLR 259; [1998] IRLR 146, HL. See para 25.34 for the facts.

45 [1998] IRLR 26, HL.

crimination were to be respected. He pointed out that the article 141 cases did not draw the same firm legal demarcation between direct and indirect discrimination as does the SDA 1975. Lord Browne-Wilkinson then suggested that an employer could justify both direct and indirect discrimination in pay. This is almost certainly wrong, given that the GMF defence requires a material factor which is *not the difference of sex*. Nor has there ever been a case in which the ECJ has accepted that direct sex discrimination in pay could be justified.

25.50 Having said this, it is hard to argue with Lord Browne-Wilkinson's remark that the distinction between 'direct' discrimination and 'indirect' discrimination may not always be clear. This is particularly apparent in cases where there is job segregation. Men and women may be segregated because of direct discrimination, and a pay practice may have disparate impact on a predominantly female group and therefore be indirectly discriminatory.

25.51 In the *Enderby* case[46] it was accepted by both sides that there was no deliberate intention to treat women less favourably, but the applicants argued that the salaries of speech therapists were artificially depressed because of the speech therapists' profession's predominantly female composition. It was found that the fact that lower paid workers (speech therapists) were almost exclusively female was not a 'statistical freak', but was due to the fact that the nature of the work (which allows employees to work part-time) made it particularly attractive to women, while the low pay made it especially unattractive to men. The ECJ held that, where significant statistics disclose an appreciable difference in pay between two jobs of equal value, one of which is carried out almost exclusively by women and the other predominantly by men, article 141 requires the employer to show that the difference is based on objectively justified factors unrelated to any discrimination on the ground of sex.

25.52 The existence of sex-segregated groups of workers (doing work of equal value), where the group of women is paid less than the group of men, can be said *either* to raise a presumption of discrimination (which is rebuttable by evidence to the contrary) *or* to have a disproportionate adverse impact on women. In either case, the employer must prove that the difference in pay (in respect of jobs assumed to be of equal value) can be justified on grounds other than sex.

25.53 Where there are separate groups of workers, segregated by sex, any comparison must be between all the relevant workers in a similar

46 Case 127/92 *Enderby v Frenchay Health Authority* [1993] ECR I-5535; [1993] IRLR 593, ECJ.

situation. In the *Royal Copenhagen* case[47] there were two main groups, turners and painters. Both groups were subdivided. The painters were divided into two groups, one consisting mainly of women which was the lowest-paid group (group B) and the other consisting wholly of women which was the highest-paid group (group C). The lowest-paid women compared their pay to a predominantly male subgroup of higher-paid turners (group A). Thus, one group of women was paid less than the mainly male group and the other group of women was paid more. The ECJ held that, where a comparison is made between two groups which are segregated by sex, the groups compared must encompass all the workers who, taking into account a set of factors such as the nature of the work, the training requirements and the working conditions, can be considered to be in a comparable situation. The groups cannot be formed in an arbitrary manner so that one comprises mainly women and the other mainly men. They must cover a relatively large number of workers to ensure the differences are not due to purely fortuitous or short-term factors or to differences in the individual output of the workers.

25.54 The degree of job segregation must be significant to give rise to an inference of sex discrimination in pay. When *Enderby* went back to the ET the respondents challenged the assertion that clinical psychologists were predominantly male. The statistics showed men predominating in eight out of ten years, ranging from 68 to 54 per cent of the total profession. The ET was impressed with the persistency and consistency of the figures which showed that, throughout the period, men predominated and there was therefore a prima facie case of sex discrimination.

25.55 In *Loughran v British Road Services Ltd*[48] the ET accepted that a prima facie case of discrimination had been shown as the applicants were in a group (of clerical workers) which was 75 per cent female and their comparators were in a group (of warehouse workers) which was 100 per cent male. The Northern Ireland Court of Appeal stated that:

> ... the relevance of a number of females in the group is an indicator of its being traditionally a less well paid group on account of its being composed mainly of women. Logically, a group comprised of 75% females and 25% males has the capacity to provide such an indication.

47 Case 400/93 *Specialarbejderforbundet I Danmark (Applicants) v Dansk Industri, acting for Royal Copenhagen A/S* [1995] ECR I-1275; [1995] IRLR 647.

48 [1997] IRLR 92, NICA.

Thus, evidence that there is job segregation to any significant extent should be sufficient to raise a presumption of direct discrimination or disproportionate adverse impact.[49] In *Loughran* the defence that there were separate bargaining structures was rejected as it was tainted by discrimination.

49 See chapter 7 on indirect discrimination and chapter 10 on indirect discrimination.

CHAPTER 26

Collective agreements and discriminatory pay systems

continued

Key points

26.1
- The Equal Pay Act (EqPA) 1970 requires that collectively agreed terms which are incorporated from collective agreements into employees' contracts of employment must be free from discrimination.
- Whether or not collectively agreed terms are incorporated into individuals' contracts of employment, Sex Discrimination Act (SDA) 1975 s77 and SDA 1986 s6 provide that such terms are void and unenforceable if they discriminate (directly or indirectly) on grounds of sex.
- Also rendered void and unenforceable by the SDAs are discriminatory terms imposed by:
  - employers;
  - workers' organisations;
  - employers' organisations;
  - professional or trade organisations;
  - any body which can confer an authorisation or qualification that is needed for a profession or trade.
- Article 141 of the EC Treaty requires that a discriminatory term, contractual or otherwise, must be applied to the benefit of those excluded in the past, though terms may be levelled-down for the future.
- Many elements of pay systems are discriminatory. The following, in particular, should be carefully examined for discrimination:
  - overtime provisions;
  - shift pay;
  - service increments;
  - bonus schemes and productivity pay;
  - flexibility and mobility payments;
  - attendance payments;
  - differential treatment of part-time workers.

Background and statutory provisions

26.2 This chapter considers sex discrimination in pay systems, collective agreements and rules of undertakings; and how such discrimination may be challenged. Race discrimination in this context is much less regulated, those provisions dealing with 'collective' sex discrimination resulting, for the most part, from the UK's membership of the EC which did not, until very recently, regulate race discrimination as such.[1] To the extent that race discrimination legislation has had any impact in this context it has been as a result of the application of the ordinary provisions of the Race Relations Act (RRA) 1976, rather than any directed specifically at 'collective' forms of discrimination. This is considered further at para 26.21.

26.3 Discrimination in pay systems, collective agreements and the rules of 'undertakings' (see further para 26.8 below) is regulated in the first instance by SDA 1986 s6 which provides that the following are void in so far as they discriminate (directly or indirectly) on grounds of sex:

(1) (a) any term of a collective agreement, including an agreement which was not intended, or is presumed not to have been intended, to be a legally enforceable contract;
(b) any rule made by an employer for application to all or any of the persons who are employed by him or who apply to be, or are, considered by him for employment;
(c) any rule made by an organisation, authority or body to which subsection (2) below applies for application to all or any of its members or prospective members or to all or any of the persons on whom it has conferred authorisations or qualifications or who are seeking the authorisations or qualifications which it has power to confer.

26.4 The provisions of the SDA 1986, like those of the SDA 1975, must be interpreted consistently, so far as this is possible, with the relevant provisions of EC law. The EC provision most applicable in the present context is article 4 of the Equal Treatment Directive[2] (ETD) which provides that:

> Member States shall take all necessary measures to ensure that ... any provisions contrary to the principle of equal treatment which are included in collective agreements, individual contracts of employment, internal rules of undertakings or in rules governing the independent occupations and professions shall be, or may be declared, null and void or may be amended.

26.5 The EqPA 1970, as it was originally enacted, permitted the modification of directly discriminatory terms in collective agreements and

1 As distinct from discrimination on grounds of (EC) nationality – see further chapter 10.

2 Council Directive 76/207/EEC.

in pay structures (s3). And SDA 1975 s77 provided discriminatory *contractual* terms were void. But indirectly discriminatory terms of collective agreements were, unless legally binding,[3] outside the scope of the legal provisions. Furthermore, no attempt was made to regulate discrimination in connection with the rules of undertakings.

26.6 The European Commission took enforcement action against the UK on the grounds that it was in breach of article 4 ETD,[4] and the SDA 1986 resulted. No enforcement mechanism was provided in respect of this provision until 1993, when the Trade Union Reform and Employment Rights Act provided a right to appeal to an employment tribunal (ET) for a declaration that the offending provision is void.[5]

Sex discrimination in collective agreements and rules of undertakings

Collective agreements

26.7 Collective agreements are negotiated between employers and trade unions (which act on behalf of their members). This book is concerned only with those agreements relating to employees' contracts of employment on matters such as pay, hours of work, holidays, and other working conditions. The SDA 1975 and the SDA 1986 now regulate discrimination in both binding and non-binding collective agreements.

Rules of 'undertakings'

26.8 'Undertakings' include employers; organisations of workers and of employers; organisations 'whose members carry on a particular profession or trade for the purposes of which the organization exists'; and authorities and bodies 'which can confer an authorisation or qualification which is needed for, or facilitates, engagement in a particular profession or trade'.[6] This definition would include, for example, the General Medical Council, the Law Society and other similar bodies (see further chapter 12).

3 Which is and was then very rarely the case.
4 Case 165/82 *European Commission v UK* [1983] ECR 3431; [1984] IRLR 28.
5 SDA 1986 s4A.
6 Ibid s6. Compare SDA 1975 s13 and RRA 1976 s12 which prohibit discrimination by qualifying bodies.

What agreements and rules are covered?

26.9 The SDA 1986 regulates discrimination in terms and rules made by a wide range of organisations.[7] It covers the following:

- any term of a collective agreement, whether or not intended to be a legally enforceable contract;
- any rule made by an employer relating to employees or potential employees;
- any rule applied by an undertaking to its members or prospective members or to people on whom it has conferred authorisations or qualifications (or on those seeking the same).

Who is protected?

26.10 SDA 1986 s6 protects not only existing employees and members of undertakings, but also job applicants and those who are seeking membership of undertakings.

Void terms

26.11 The effect of the SDA 1986 is, as mentioned above, that discriminatory contractual terms contained in binding and non-binding collective agreements and rules of employers and other bodies (as set out above) are void or may be declared void by an ET. Employees (and prospective employees) may challenge such terms whether or not they are party to any contract that exists.

26.12 An individual who may be affected in future by a discriminatory term or rule in the future, may challenge the term or rule.[8] This is likely to be of assistance in relation to terms which are indirectly discriminatory,[9] or which place pregnant women at a particular disadvantage, for example:

- a term excluding pregnant women from a sick pay scheme, which could be challenged by a woman who either is, or may in the future become, pregnant;

7 SDA 1986 s6.

8 Whether an employee or someone actively seeking to become an employee.

9 SDA 1986 s6(4A). See *Meade-Hill v British Council* [1995] IRLR 476, in which a mobility clause was successfully challenged by a woman to whom it might have been applied in future.

- a redundancy scheme which may be indirectly discriminatory – for example, by providing that part-time workers are to be made redundant before full-time workers. Such a scheme could be challenged under SDA 1986 s6 even before a redundancy situation arose.

The tribunal only has power to declare a term void, and may not amend it (see below). But a woman may have other remedies in addition to a claim under SDA 1986 s6. These are considered below.

26.13 The SDA 1986 preserves any rights which the woman may have under the contract, despite the voiding of the discriminatory term. It also preserves the rights of the men to the extent that they are no more favourable than the women's rights.[10] If, for example, an employer provides training for men but not women, and the agreement is part of the employee's contract, she can claim the benefit of the training. If only men are given training and the agreement is not part of the employee's contract, the term is void so that neither the man nor the woman can claim the right to the training – at least under UK law.

26.14 A different situation would arise if training was available for both men and women but, for example, part-time workers had to pay a contribution to its cost. If this provision was part of the part-timers' contracts and was found to be discriminatory, the employer would not be able to rely on it to recover the cost of training from the part-timers against whom the term discriminates (ie, those women unable to comply with the requirement to work full-time). (The women could also rely on the EqPA 1970 to claim the benefit of an equality clause – see para 26.18.) Furthermore, because the SDA 1986 protects any rights the employee might otherwise have under the contract, these part-time women workers, like full-time workers, would be entitled to the training without being required to pay. Part-time female workers who are able to comply with the requirement to work full-time would not benefit from SDA 1986 s6,[11] but any part-time men who are unable to comply would be entitled to the same treatment as female part-timers in the same position.

26.15 If a collectively agreed term is incorporated into a woman's contract of employment she can, as a party to the agreement, apply to the county court for an order that the unenforceable term be removed

10 SDA 1986 s6(5).

11 Ibid s6(4).

or modified. Such order may include provisions relating to a period before the making of the order.[12]

Consistency of the Sex Discrimination Act 1986 with EC law

26.16 In *Kowalska v Freie und Hansestadt Hamburg*[13] the ECJ held that a term in a collective agreement which provided that only full-time workers would receive redundancy pay was indirectly discriminatory where 'a considerably smaller percentage of men than of women work part time, unless the employer shows that the provision is justified by objective factors unrelated to any discrimination on grounds of sex'. The ECJ ruled that an individual could rely on article 141 to challenge a discriminatory provision in a collective agreement. It further ruled that the disadvantaged group was entitled to the more favourable treatment given to the advantaged group:

> ... where there is discrimination in a provision of a collective agreement, the members of the group which is disadvantaged because of that discrimination must be treated in the same way and have the same system applied to them as applied to other workers, in proportion to their working hours.

This approach was confirmed in *Nimz v Freie und Hansestadt Hamburg*[14] in which the ECJ held that, if a provision in a collective agreement was indirectly discriminatory contrary to article 141, those disadvantaged by the provision should be treated no less favourably than their comparators.

26.17 The approach of the ECJ has important implications for UK law. Any provisions of a collective agreement (binding or not) which favour men must be extended to women, rather than merely treated as void. It is clear from this that, in so far as collective terms relate to

12 SDA 1975 ss77(5) and (6). The procedure is complex and, given that the remedy is merely a declaration of voidness, it is not surprising that there have been exceedingly few applications under s77 although see *Meade-Hill v British Council* [1995] IRLR 476. That case was brought in the county court as it preceded the 1993 Trade Union Reform and Employment Rights Act amendment to permit applications to be brought under s77 in the ET.

13 Case 33/89 [1990] ECR I-2591; [1990] IRLR 447.

14 Case 184/89 [1991] ECR I-297; [1991] IRLR 222 – see para 26.30 for further discussion. However, in pension cases the ECJ has ruled that, although in respect of past discrimination the disadvantaged group must be given the more favourable treatment, in respect of future benefits levelling-down is permitted, see chapter 7.

'pay' (for the broad definition of this under article 141 see chapter 10), applicants may rely on article 141.

Situations in which the Equal Pay Act 1970 applies

26.18 As the EqPA 1970 applies to contractual terms, it will apply to any term of a collective agreement which is incorporated into the employee's contract of employment.[15] There are three ways in which the terms of a collective agreement may become part of employees' contracts of employment:

- if an employee's contract of employment states that the terms of the collective agreement are to be treated as part of the contract;
- if an employee's contract impliedly incorporates the terms of the collective agreement. If, as a matter of long practice, contractually agreed terms are applied to employees' contracts, a term may be implied into individuals' contracts to the effect that this incorporation will occur;
- if the union acts as an agent for employees. This is rarely successfully argued.[16]

Only those terms which are suitable for incorporation will form part of individual employees' contracts of employment. Terms will not be appropriate for incorporation only if they are primarily concerned with individual and substantive, rather than collective and procedural, matters.[17]

26.19 In most cases in which unions negotiate pay, hours of work and other matters affecting individual workers; collectively agreed terms which deal with those matters will be incorporated into employees' contract of employment. The EqPA 1970 gives employees the right not to be paid less, or to receive other less favourable terms, than others doing 'like work', 'work rated as equivalent' or work of equal value (see para 22.16). These rights can be enforced by making a complaint to an ET.

26.20 Collectively agreed terms which are not incorporated into contracts of employment do not give employees the right of challenge,

15 EqPA 1970 s1.

16 While agency may be established on the facts in some cases, it will not account for the incorporation of collectively agreed terms into non-members' contracts of employment.

17 See *NCB v NUM* [1986] IRLR 439, HC; *Alexander v Standard Telephones & Cables Plc* [1991] IRLR 286, HC.

the EqPA 1970 applying only to contractual terms. However, if such terms relate to 'pay' within the meaning of article 141[18] a claim may be made under the SDA 1975 interpreted in accordance with article 141.

Race discrimination in collective agreements

26.21 RRA 1976 s72 provides that contractual terms which contravene the Act's prohibition on discrimination are void or, as against another party to the contract, unenforceable. This differs from SDA 1975 s77, read with SDA 1986 s6, in that it applies only to contractual terms and not, therefore, to collectively agreed terms which, until incorporated into contracts of employment, are not legally binding. Assuming the term has been incorporated, the victim of discrimination can rely on the term to the extent that it provides a benefit, but the employer cannot enforce any discriminatory aspect of it.

26.22 A person who has an interest in a contract which contains an unenforceable term can apply to a designated county court for an order to remove or modify the unenforceable term. There is an exception for compromise agreements.

Sex discrimination in pay systems

26.23 The Equal Opportunities Commission (EOC) Code of Practice on Equal Pay (1997) recognises that:

> Sex discrimination in pay now occurs primarily because women and men tend to do different jobs or to have different work patterns. As a result it is easy to undervalue the demands of work performed by one sex compared with the demands associated with jobs typically done by the other.[19]

This section looks at how pay systems tend to discriminate against women and at ways of challenging the discrimination.

18 See para 10.28.

19 Available at www.eoc.org.uk/cseng/legislation/code_of_practice_equal_pay.asp. A revised code will be in force from April 2003.

Job segregation and pay discrimination

26.24 Both the European Commission and the EOC confirm that, although the difference between women's and men's incomes is due to a number of factors, one of its main causes is the segregation of men's and women's jobs. Segregation is both:

- **Vertical**: Men and women are concentrated in different types of jobs, with typically male jobs being given a higher value and more pay than women's jobs. The different valuation of 'male' and 'female' jobs is often historical and is based on traditional values ascribed to 'male' and 'female' work. These often discriminatory assumptions may be reflected in current grading schemes; and
- **Horizontal**: It is common for men to be in the majority at managerial level and women to occupy lower graded jobs.

26.25 There are areas of employment (such as local authorities) in which pay for jobs predominantly occupied by men includes elements in addition to basic pay – bonuses, overtime and on-call allowances, productivity incentives, etc – which are not typically offered in respect of jobs of equivalent grades occupied predominantly by women. Separate collective agreements for different (and sex-segregated) occupational groups may allow salary structures to reflect the differential negotiating power of men and women. Some occupations are even more segregated as there is a disproportionate concentration of ethnic minority women in lower status, lower paid jobs.

Discrimination in the allocation of overtime, shift payments, bonuses, etc

26.26 Even when women are paid the same basic hourly rate of pay as men, men's basic wages are often topped up by other payments, such as overtime, shift pay, service increments, bonuses and productivity pay, attendance payments, flexibility and mobility payments. Each element of the contract should be analysed for sex and race discrimination. In addition, part-time workers should receive the same payments as full-time workers, calculated on a pro-rata basis.[20]

20 See chapter 21.

Overtime

26.27 Many women cannot work overtime because of family responsibilities. Part-time workers may not receive overtime payments unless they exceed the standard weekly hours for the undertaking even though, on any one day, they may work longer than their contractual hours or the standard daily hours. In *Stadt Lengerich v Helmig*[22] the ECJ held that article 141 was not breached where overtime supplements were only paid for hours worked in excess of the normal full-time working hours Thus, part-time workers were not entitled to overtime supplements when they exceeded *their* normal working hours. The ECJ took the view that no discrimination had occurred because the overall pay of full-timers and part-timers was the same for the same number of hours worked.

Shift pay

26.28 The fact that a man and woman work at different times should not defeat an equal pay claim in respect of basic pay, though a premium may be payable for antisocial hours. In *NCB v Sherwin and Spruce*[23] the EAT held that, if a man and a woman do the same work, the mere fact that they do it at different times should not affect their basic rates of pay. The EAT disaggregated the antisocial element of the men's pay and compared the basic rates.

26.29 Premiums are commonly paid for working antisocial hours – generally before 6 am and after 10 pm. Even though shift work may not be available to women (this itself may be discriminatory), it would be hard to argue that workers should not be paid extra for working such hours. However, women frequently do split duties (working, for example, from 6 am to 10 am and then from 7 pm to midnight). This is particularly common in the predominantly female health service and in hotels in which there are many women workers. Shift payments should be paid on an equal basis to jobs that are done predominantly by men and those done by women.

22 Case 399/92 [1994] ECR I-5727; [1995] IRLR 216.

23 [1978] IRLR 122, EAT. However, in *Thomas v NCB* [1987] IRLR 451, a case involving the same comparator, the EAT upheld a tribunal's decision that the fact that the comparator worked exclusively on nights constituted an additional responsibility such as to be a difference of practical importance for the purposes of EqPA 1970 s1(4). This decision would appear to arise from the additional responsibility, not the time of work. See further chapter 25.

Seniority and service-related payments

26.30 The usual justification for service-related payments is that they reduce job turnover. Recruiting new employees involves a lengthy and costly advertising and interviewing process, as well as training costs for new staff. Service payments and benefits are also made in recognition of the employees' increased experience. The *Nimz* case[24] concerned a challenge to a practice whereby full-time workers were automatically entitled to promotion after six years, part-timers having to wait for 12 years. The ECJ held that the practice breached article 141, unless its disproportionate impact on women could be objectively justified. This would require that the employer proves that seniority actually goes hand-in-hand with an improvement in the work performed which 'depends on all the circumstances in a particular case and, in particular on the nature of the relationship between the nature of the work performed and the experience gained from the performance of that work upon completion of a certain number of working hours'.[25]

26.31 If payments are made in respect of seniority, the following conditions will minimise the risk of discrimination:

- part-time workers should be eligible for incremental seniority payments after the same period as full-timers;
- any period of employment should count as part of the qualifying period, as should both ordinary and additional maternity leave (see chapter 18);
- service payments should begin as early as possible, preferably after one year's service. If the justification for increments is an increase in efficiency this is a cumulative process and starts shortly after the beginning of service;
- it is important that incremental scales are similar for all employees, irrespective of grade.

26.32 Sometimes, employees in lower grades have to wait much longer to reach the top of their scale. Some employers impose bars so that progression depends on management discretion. There is evidence that

24 Case 184/89 *Nimz v Freie und Hansestadt Hamburg* [1991] ECR I-297; [1991] IRLR 222.

25 This approach marked a change from the decision in Case 109/88 *Handels-og Kontorfunktionaerernes Forbund I Danmark v Dansk Arbejdsgiverforening (acting for Danfoss)* [1989] ECR 3199; [1989] IRLR 532, decided only a year before, in which the ECJ had ruled that an employer did 'not have to provide special justification for recourse to the criterion of length of service, for it goes hand in hand with experience, which generally enables the employee to perform his duties later'. This should no longer be regarded as good law.

more women and black workers are adversely affected by such bars which, accordingly, need to be closely monitored to ensure that they continue to operate only if objectively justified.

Bonus schemes and productivity pay

26.33 There are many different types of productivity-related pay.[26] The most significant are:

- each worker is paid according to the work he or she has done (this is piece-work);
- a bonus is awarded if more than the allocated work is carried out in the time allowed;
- a flat-rate payment is made to certain workers, often in exchange for the workers agreeing a new system of working;
- a bonus is given to a group of workers to be shared between them.

26.34 Much women's work (such as cleaning and catering) is suitable for payment of bonuses because it is possible to assess the productivity of those doing it. Typically, however, such work has not attracted bonuses. Other jobs, such as those in nursing and home-help, may not be appropriate for bonus payments. But if, within a single undertaking such as a local authority, there are predominantly male jobs which are of equal value to predominantly female jobs, the wages for such jobs should be the same. Bonus schemes should not be a way of maintaining the differentials between men's and women's wages.

26.35 In order to establish a material factor defence based on the alleged higher productivity of the male group (see para 25.18), an employer must show how and on what basis the payments are made and that the criteria are non-discriminatory (or, if indirectly discriminatory, nevertheless objectively justified). It is unlikely that there would be a real difference in productivity between male workers and female workers, since such a difference would only arise if the women worked less hard than the men. Not to offer the women the opportunity to earn equal wages to those of men doing work of equal value is discriminatory. In the absence of a bonus scheme it is likely that the women's productivity has not been measured and, if this is so, the employer will have real difficulty in proving the women's productivity is lower than that of the men.

26 See chapter 25 for such payments and the material factor defence.

Flexibility and mobility payments

26.36 Employers sometimes pay an extra sum to employees whose job requires them to be flexible in what work they do, at what times and where. Women tend to be more tied to set hours which revolve round dependant care responsibilities. In the *Danfoss* case[27] the ECJ held that, where the flexibility of the worker is used as a criterion for pay increments and this works systematically to the disadvantage of female workers, the employer may justify the use of the criterion only by demonstrating that such adaptability is important and relevant for the performance of the specific duties of the worker. The same reasoning applies to the reward of mobility (see para 7.40[28]).

Attendance payments

26.37 Payments are sometimes made for good attendance. Women may have had to take time off to look after sick children and dependants and may consequently not be eligible for these payments. There is now a statutory right to time off in these circumstances which should assist. If women receive, on average, lower attendance payments than men, employers will have to establish objective justification.

Paid leave for training

26.38 Where a part-time woman worker attends a work-related training course which extends beyond her normal working hours, she should be paid for the full period attended.[29] In *Arbeiterwohlfahrt der Stadt Berlin eV v Bötel*[30] the applicant attended a training course as a member of the staff committee. National legislation provided that members of the staff committee had to be released from work without a reduction in salary, if this was necessary to perform their duties. The applicant was paid only in respect of her normal hours, rather than for all of the hours she spent on the training course. The ECJ ruled that, the majority of part-timers affected being women, the legislative provisions were indirectly discriminatory and contrary to article 141 unless objectively justified. The court further pointed out that, if part-time

27 Case 109/88 *Handels-og Kontorfunktionaerernes Forbund I Danmark v Dansk Arbejdsgiverforening (acting for Danfoss)* [1989] ECR 3199; [1989] IRLR 532.

28 See discussion of *Meade-Hill v British Council* [1995] IRLR 476.

29 And, in order to avoid direct discrimination, part-time men will have to receive equal terms.

30 Case 360/90 [1992] ECR I-3589; [1992] IRLR 432.

workers were not paid equally, it would dissuade them from acting as members of a staff committee, making the adequate representation of (predominantly female) part-timers all the more difficult.

26.39 A different decision was reached in *Manor Bakeries Ltd v Nazir*,[31] in which the EAT held that an employer did not discriminate against a part-time employee who was paid only for her normal (part-time) working hours in respect of her full-time attendance at an annual trade union conference. Such attendance was not, in the EAT's view, 'work'. The decision in *Nazir* is inconsistent with *Bötel* and should not be followed. The payment was provided for in the collective agreement and was made as a result of the employment relationship. It was, therefore, 'pay' for the purposes of article 141.

Part-time workers

26.40 In 2000 there were over seven million part-time workers in the UK – about a quarter of the workforce.[32] Women account for 86 per cent of part-time workers, and 40 per cent of all women workers, but only 4 per cent of men, work part-time. Many part-time jobs are junior and low-paid, and atypical workers, including part-timers, face significant barriers in obtaining training and promotion.

26.41 Discrimination against part-time workers has been common. They have often been denied access to benefits such as sick pay, housing loans, occupational pensions, overtime, bonuses, service increments and severance payments, etc. See also para 15.152 for discrimination in severance payments. Until 1995, employment protection legislation operated qualifying thresholds which excluded many part-time workers. The rule was that an employee had to be regularly employed for at least 16 hours a week for that week fully to count towards continuous service.[33] That rule was successfully challenged by the EOC as a breach of article 141.[34]

26.42 A number of ECJ decisions have established that discrimination against part-time workers amounts to unlawful indirect sex

31 [1996] IRLR 604.

32 Labour Force Survey, June–August 2000.

33 Until 1995, those who worked between eight and 16 hours a week had to work for five years, rather than the then two in the case of full-time workers, to qualify for full statutory protection while those who worked under eight hours a week could never earn such protection.

34 *R v Employment Secretary ex parte EOC* [1995] 1 AC 1; [1994] IRLR 176.

discrimination.[35] Many collective agreements have been amended to give part-time employees equal treatment in respect of sick pay, holidays and pensions. But pockets of discrimination remain. In addition, the use of agency and 'self-employed' workers to replace part-time employees has increased and may permit employers to avoid the obligation of equal treatment.[36]

26.43 Where pressure for a shorter working week leads to a reduction in hours for full-time workers but not for part-timers, the hourly rate for such full-time workers may be increased so that their pay remains the same while the pay of part-time workers is unaffected. Such discrimination may well be indirectly discriminatory.

Challenging discrimination under the Sex Discrimination Act 1975 and the Equal Pay Act 1970

26.44 The broad principle is that part-time workers should have the same pay and other benefits, on a pro rata basis, as full-timers. It may be difficult to enforce this principle if a claim is brought under the EqPA 1970. First, the woman must find a comparator engaged in 'like work', 'work rated as equivalent' or work of equal value and working, broadly, in the same establishment for the same associated employer.[37] Many female part-timers work only with other women.

26.45 If a claim is not contractual, it must be made under the SDA 1975 rather than the EqPA 1970. The effect of this, broadly speaking, is that the applicant does not have to show an actual comparator. Rather, the SDA 1975 requires that the circumstances of the woman and any actual or hypothetical man must be the same (see para 3.14).

26.46 There is no choice about whether to bring a claim under the EqPA 1970 or the SDA 1975, which are mutually exclusive (see paras 11.29 and 11.32). But both Acts must be interpreted consistently with article 141 when a claim concerns 'pay' under the very broad definition adopted by that provision.[38] Article 141 applies whether the matter at issue is contractual or non-contractual. It is uncertain to what extent

35 Case 170/84 *Bilka Kaufhaus GmbH v Weber von Hartz* [1986] ECR 1607, [1986] IRLR 317, ECJ; Case 33/89 *Kowalska v Freie und Hansestadt Hamburg* [1990] ECR I-2591, [1990] IRLR 447; Case 171/88 *Rinner-Kühn* [1989] ECR 2743, [1989] IRLR 493, ECJ.

36 See discussion of *Allonby v Accrington and Rossendale College* [2001] IRLR 364, CA below.

37 See chapter 22.

38 See chapter 10.

the direct effect of article 141 permits a claim in a case (brought under the EqPA 1970) in which there is no actual comparator in the same employment doing equal work, but where discrimination can be proved by way of statistics. It may be that, at least in some circumstances, a claim can succeed where part-timers are treated less favourably, provided that disparate impact can be shown and the justification defence not made out. This issue has been referred to the ECJ in the case of *Allonby* (see further chapters 10 and 15).[39]

Part-time Workers Regulations

26.47 The Part Time Workers (Prevention of Less Favourable Treatment) Regulations 2000,[40] which came into force in July 2000, implement the Part-time Work Directive.[41] The Regulations provide part-time workers with some protection against discrimination, but they apply only where the part-time worker can identify a suitable full-time 'comparator' (very narrowly defined) and can establish that the discrimination was solely because the applicant worked part-time. Even in such cases discrimination can be objectively justified. The Regulations are discussed in detail in chapter 21.

Conclusion

26.48 Article 6 of the Equal Pay Directive[42] provides that member states must see that effective means are available to ensure that the principle of equal pay is applied. They have an obligation to introduce into their national legal systems such measures as are necessary to enable all employees who consider themselves wronged by a failure to apply the principle of equal pay to pursue their claims by judicial process.

26.49 In *European Commission v UK*[43] the ECJ ruled that 'in the final count, individuals should have the possibility of succeeding in the argument that the two jobs in question are of equal value'. Yet because legal aid is unavailable for ET cases, because equal pay procedures are so complex, and because applicants are not generally able to afford independent expert witnesses, many, unless supported

39 *Allonby v Accrington and Rossendale College* [2001] IRLR 364, CA.

40 SI No 1551.

41 Council Directive 97/81/EC.

42 Council Directive 75/117/EEC.

43 Case 61/82 [1982] IRLR 2601; [1982] IRLR 332.

by trade unions or the EOC, are deprived of their rights. In *Aldridge v British Telecommunications plc*[44] the EAT condemned equal pay procedures as scandalous and stated that they amounted to a 'denial of justice to women seeking remedy through the judicial process'. The *Enderby* litigation is now in its seventeenth year, and only recently have most of the cases been settled or heard.[45]

26.50 In *Emmott v Minister for Social Welfare*[46] the ECJ ruled that member states are required to ensure the full application of directives in a sufficiently clear and precise manner so that, where directives are intended to create rights for individuals, the latter can ascertain the full extent of those rights and, where necessary, rely on them before the national courts. This obligation has not been fulfilled in relation to pay discrimination. In February 2001, the UK government published proposals for speeding up and simplifying equal pay cases.[47] At around the same time the Equal Pay Task Force set up by the EOC reported with more wide-ranging proposals.[48] The proposals have yet to be implemented save for the introduction of a questionnaire procedure for the applicant to obtain information from the employer in the Employment Act 2002 (see chapter 32).

44 [1990] IRLR 19, EAT. See also *British Coal Corporation v Smith* [1989] AC 706; [1989] IRLR 28 in which Lord Slynn stated that the time taken to complete equal pay cases defeated an essential purpose of the legislation.

45 Case 127/92 *Enderby v Frenchay Health Authority* [1993] ECR I-5535; [1993] IRLR 593, ECJ.

46 Case 208/90 [1991] I-ECR 4269; [1991] IRLR 387.

47 DfEE (now Department for Work and Pensions), *Towards Equal Pay for Women* (2001).

48 *Just Pay*, the report of the Equal Pay Task Force to the EOC (2001).

CHAPTER 27

Discrimination in occupational pension schemes

continued

Key points

27.1

- Payments under occupational pension schemes constitute 'pay' under article 141 of the EC Treaty and the Equal Pay Act (EqPA) 1970;
- Article 141 applies to most aspects of occupational pension schemes, including (but not limited to):
  - access to an occupational pension scheme;
  - pensionable ages;
  - contributions made by the employer and employee;
  - transitional provisions;
  - survivors' benefits.
- Article 141 applies in the context of pensions, as in other aspects of 'pay', to indirect as well as direct sex discrimination, subject to objective justification by the employer.
- Article 141 does not apply to:
  - the statutory social security scheme;
  - the use of actuarial factors in funded defined-benefit schemes;
  - additional voluntary contributions.
- Article 141 applies in the context of pensions, as in other aspects of 'pay', to indirect as well as direct sex discrimination, subject to objective justification by the employer.
- The obligations to ensure equal treatment for members and survivors do not apply to benefits in respect of service before 17 May 1990, save in respect of:
  - the right to join a scheme (which may date back to 1976);
  - where a right to join is retroactive, the benefits which accrued during the intervening period; and
  - provided in both cases that worker pays his/her contributions for that period.
- Contributions to schemes must be the same for men and women, unless the exception for actuarial factors applies.
- Article 141 is implemented in domestic legislation by the Pensions Act 1995 and associated regulations.
- The domestic legislation largely reflects the pension-related case-law under article 141.
- It expressly permits inequality in relation:
  - to bridging pensions designed to equalise the overall payments to men and women when the statutory scheme (the age of entitlement to which varies as between men and women) is taken into account;

- to variations in pensions paid by contracted-out final salary schemes, where the variation is due to different indexation factors between men and women which are attributable to the state earnings-related pension scheme; and
- in specified circumstances, to variations in pensionable benefits attributable to actuarial factors.

Background and statutory framework

27.2 Traditionally, men and women in the UK have retired at different ages; 65 for men and 60 for women. Occupational pension schemes were generally based on the different retirement age and some excluded married women. The Sex Discrimination Act (SDA) 1975 and EqPA 1970, as they were originally enacted, contained provisions exempting retirement and pension from the prohibitions on sex discrimination. But developments in EC law have had a significant impact on domestic law. Sex discrimination in relation to age retirement and occupational pension schemes is now unlawful, and married women must be treated the same as married men (and vice versa). With a few exceptions, sex discrimination is prohibited both in relation to access to occupational schemes and the benefits provided by them.

27.3 The development of EC case law has also led to the passage of the Pensions Act (PA) 1995 and the Occupational Pension Schemes (Equal Treatment) Regulations (OPS Regulations) 1995,[1] both of which largely reflect in statutory form the decisions of the European Court of Justice (ECJ). But the sweeping prohibitions on sex discrimination in the context of pensions turn in significant part on the categorisation of *occupational* (but not state) pensions as 'pay' within the meaning of article 141. UK state pension provisions still apply a different retirement age in the case of men and women, and the Sex Discrimination (Social Security) Directive (SSD)[2] continues to allow different treatment for men and women in relation to access to a state pension, contributions periods and the consequences for other benefits.[3] The state pension provisions are to be gradually equalised by 2020.

1 SI No 3185.
2 Council Directive 79/7/EEC.
3 See Case 9/91 *R v Social Security Secretary ex p EOC* [1992] ECR I-4297; [1992] IRLR 376, ECJ.

27.4 The Sex Discrimination (Occupational Social Security) Directive (OSSD)[4] which was amended from 1 July 1997,[5] implements existing ECJ case-law on equal treatment of men and women in occupational social security schemes.

27.5 The Race Relations Act (RRA) 1976 contains no special provisions dealing with pensions although any race discrimination in pensions, whether direct or indirect, is likely to be unlawful under that Act (see para 15.39)[6]. For disability discrimination in pensions, see chapter 15 and, in particular, para 15.47.

27.6 This chapter looks first at the equal pay cases and how they affect occupational pensions (including access, contributions and benefits), then at the statutory provisions in the PA 1995 and the OPS Regulations 1995. Finally, it summarises the provisions of the OSSD.

Terminology

27.7 It is important to grasp the differences between the various types of pension provision in order to understand the implications for them of the equality legislation. The main types of pension scheme are:

- the statutory social security pension scheme;
- the State Earnings-Related Pension Scheme (SERPS);
- personal pension schemes;
- occupational pension schemes.

Statutory social security pension scheme

27.8 The state pension scheme is governed by social security legislation which has been consolidated in the Social Security Contributions and Benefits Act 1992 and the Social Security Administration Act 1992. Entitlement to a statutory pension depends on having paid the

4 Council Directive 86/378/EEC, as amended by Council Directive 96/97/EEC. This has been implemented in the UK by the PA 1995 and the OPS Regs 1995.

5 By Directive 96/97/EEC, which was intended to bring the OSSD into line with decisions of the ECJ in cases including Case 262/88 *Barber v GRE Assurance* [1990] ECR I-1889, [1990] IRLR 240, ECJ; Case 110/91 *Moroni v Firma Collo GmbH* [1993] ECR I-6591, [1994] IRLR 130, ECJ; Case 170/84 *Bilka Kaufhaus GmbH v Weber von Hartz* [1986] ECR 1607, [1986] IRLR 317, ECJ; Case 128/93 *Fisscher v Voorhuis Hengelo BV* [1994] ECR I-4583, [1994] IRLR 662, ECJ, all discussed below.

6 RRA 1976 ss1 and 4(2) prohibit discrimination in benefits, facilities or services while s4(2)(b) covers any other detriment. See *Barclays Bank plc v Kapur* [1991] ICR 208.

relevant national insurance contributions on earnings above the lower earnings limit, and upon having reached pensionable age. Whether someone qualifies for the state pension is a matter entirely distinct from the relationship between that person and his or her employer. State pension payments are not considered 'pay' for the purposes of article 141 and, as a matter of EC law, they are governed by the SSD.[7] Both this and the state scheme pension scheme generally are outside the scope of this book.

State earnings-related pension scheme

27.9 SERPS is an earnings-related pension based on the average earnings of the employee. It was replaced by the second state pension from 6 April 2002 by the Child Support, Pensions and Social Security Act 2000. As a result there will be no accruals of SERPS' rights after 6 April 2002 although existing rights are protected.. An occupational pension scheme which provides benefits which are at least equivalent (or can be deemed to be equivalent) to those provided by SERPS can contract out of SERPS. The employer and employee pay a lower social security contribution, and the employee's rights to a SERPS pension are rebated or, in respect of employment after 5 April 1997, completely extinguished.

Personal pension schemes

27.10 These schemes are not connected to the employment relationship. They were taken out historically by the self-employed, but more recently also by employees. Employers may contribute to personal pensions (in a 'Group Personal Pension Scheme'), in which case the contributions and pensions would qualify as an 'employer-provided benefit'. The government introduced the stakeholder pension in the Welfare Reform and Pensions Act 1999, a new form of regulated personal pension. Although employers are not required to make contributions to such schemes they are under a number of obligations to designate a scheme for their employees, to allow access to the scheme and to provide a payroll facility for the deductions of contributions. Personal pensions are outside the scope of this book.

7 This directive covers certain social security benefits (non-means-tested benefits) but it contains a number of exclusions relating to the equalisation of state pensions.

Occupational pension schemes

27.11 Occupational pension schemes may be governed by the contract of employment, by legislative provisions, and by trust law. The important factor is that the pension is paid as a result of the employment relationship. Only employees and office-holders (such as directors) are eligible to join occupational pension schemes. There are different types of occupational scheme:

- **Final salary scheme or defined-benefit schemes**: the pension payments made by such schemes are based on the salary of the employee at the time of retirement, or the average salary earned over the final few years of employment. A fraction of the salary (usually 1/60th of final salary for each year of pensionable service) is payable to the member on retirement, the employer's contributions being calculated in order to cover the costs of providing the pension.
- **Money purchase scheme or defined contributions schemes**: these schemes are financed by the investment of contributions made by employer and employee, the final pension payments usually being determined by the annuity which can be purchased with the money accumulated over the years of contribution. The sums involved have to be within Inland Revenue limits.
- **A combination of final salary and money purchase** is sometimes adopted. Like final salary schemes such schemes may be either:
  - **contributory** (the usual form of scheme), in which the employee contributes a percentage of salary (usually about 5 per cent of pensionable earnings); or
  - **non-contributory**, in which case only the employer contributes.

Statutory public sector pension schemes

27.12 Uncertainty prevailed in ECJ case-law as to whether public sector pension schemes governed by statute were within the scope of article 141 until the decision of that court in *Bestuur van het Algemeen Burgerlijk Pensionfunds v Beune*.[8] The ECJ there held that pensions paid under a statutory civil service scheme were 'pay' within article 141. The court ruled that the only possible decisive criterion for whether a pension was 'pay' is whether the pension is paid to the worker as a result of the employment relationship between the employee and his/her former employer. If the pension paid by the public employer concerns only a

8 Case 7/93 [1994] ECR I-4471, ECJ.

particular category of workers, if it is directly related to the period of service, and if its amount is calculated by reference to the employee's salary, it is comparable to a private occupational pension scheme.[9]

Miscellaneous aspects of 'pensions'

Retirement lump sums

27.13 At retirement, the individual may normally be able to choose to 'commute' pension rights so that a one-off, tax-free lump sum is payable in addition to a reduced pension.

Actuarial factors

27.14 Actuarial factors are those linked to demographic assumptions, such as the life expectancies of men and women. As women live on average seven years longer than men, their pensions are more expensive than those of men and may require the employer to pay higher contributions. If, in a money purchase scheme, the same contributions are made by the employer towards men's and women's pensions, the man is likely to receive a larger regular pension.

Contracted-in and contracted-out schemes

27.15 A pension scheme may be contracted in to the statutory scheme, or contracted out of it. In a contracted-in scheme, members are part of the statutory state scheme and build up rights to the basic state pension and to SERPS. A contracted-out scheme is a substitute for SERPS and reduced contributions are paid to the national scheme.

Additional voluntary contributions

27.16 Additional voluntary contributions (AVCs) are voluntary payments made by employees in order to secure additional benefits. They are separately identified from the main pension fund.

Bridging pensions

27.17 Bridging pensions bridge the gap which arises between the occupational pension and state pension because women are entitled to

9 In *Griffin v London Pension Fund Authority* [1993] IRLR 248, the EAT held that a local government pension scheme which was determined exclusively by statutory provisions was outside article 141. This decision must be regarded as wrongly decided in the light of *Beune*, ibid.

receive their state pension at 60, while men must wait until they are 65. Pension schemes which pay pensions from age 60 sometimes provide additional payments to men aged between 60 and 65 to compensate them for the fact they are not yet entitled to a state pension.

The impact of EC law: an overview

27.18 Payments under occupational pension schemes constitute 'pay' for the purposes of article 141 and the EqPA 1970. If a pension scheme trust deed contains provisions which are contrary to the principle of equal treatment under article 141, the trustees and employers must take all steps to amend the provisions.

The scope of article 141 EC

27.19 European law has had a major influence on pensions. Article 141 applies to public and private sector employees, to contracts between private individuals and to all collective agreements which regulate paid employment. It applies to all types of scheme which arise out of the employer/employee relationship (see para 10.28).[10]

27.20 Article 141 will override any conflicting provisions of national law (see chapter 10). There is a huge body of case-law on the application of article 141 to pensions. One of the domestic limitations on the operation of the equality principle in the pensions context is that a claim for equal treatment in pensions must be made under the PA 1995. Like the EqPA 1970, the PA 1995 requires that the applicant identify an appropriate comparator (narrowly defined as discussed in chapters 22–24). Remedies available under the PA 1995 are restricted both by time limits and by restrictions on the backdating of claims (see para 27.57). There have been a number of challenges to these restrictions in domestic law. These are considered below. The law in this area is complex and the following is a summary of the main points.

'Pay' under article 141 EC

27.21 The prohibition on sex discrimination imposed by article 141 applies to 'pay' which includes:

10 Case 7/93 *Bestuur van het Algemeen Burgerlijk Pensionfunds v Beune* [1994] ECR I-4471, ECJ.

a) pension schemes which arise from the employment relationship, whether they are contracted-in or contracted-out of the statutory scheme;[11]
b) schemes which are made compulsory by law, whether the reason for their compulsory nature is due to social policy or to considerations relating to competition in a particular economic sector, provided they are part of the employment relationship;[12]
c) schemes which supplement or complement the state scheme;[13]
d) contributory and non-contributory schemes;[14]
e) final salary and money purchase schemes;[15]
f) access to occupational pension schemes;[16]
g) pensionable ages applicable to schemes such as those at (a)–(e) above;[17]
h) employer contributions to pension schemes;[18]
i) benefits paid under relevant pension schemes including those paid to survivors;[19]
j) transitional provisions aimed at reducing discrimination over a period;[20]

11 Case 262/88 *Barber v GRE Assurance* [1990] ECR I-1889; [1990] IRLR 240, ECJ.

12 Case 435/93 *Dietz v Stichting Thuiszorg Rotterdam* [1996] ECR I-5223; [1996] IRLR 693. In the UK, pension schemes cannot be compulsory.

13 Case 262/88 *Barber v GRE Assurance* [1990] ECR I-1889; [1990] IRLR 240, ECJ and Case 110/91 *Moroni v Firma Collo GmbH* [1993] ECR I-6591, [1994] IRLR 130, ECJ. Under German law, if a worker claimed a state pension before normal retirement age he or she could claim early payment of the company pension. The ECJ held in *Moroni* that the direct and close interdependence of the statutory and occupational schemes could not have the consequence of excluding the occupational pension scheme from article 141. The court also ruled that the provisions of the SSD could not limit the scope of article 141.

14 Case 200/91 *Coloroll Pension Trustees Ltd v Russell* [1993] ECR I-4879; [1994] IRLR 586, ECJ.

15 Ibid.

16 Case 57/93 *Vroege v NCIV Instituut voor Volkshuisvesting BV* [1994] ECR I-4541; [1994] IRLR 651, ECJ, and Case 128/93 *Fisscher v Voorhuis Hengelo BV* [1994] ECR I-4583; [1994] IRLR 662, ECJ.

17 Case 262/88 *Barber v GRE Assurance* [1990] ECR I-1889; [1990] IRLR 240, ECJ.

18 Case 69/80 *Worringham and Humphreys v Lloyds Bank* [1981] ECR 767; [1981] IRLR 178, ECJ.

19 Case 109/91 *Ten Oever v Stichting Bedrijfspensioenfonds voor het Glazenwassers-en Schoonmaakbedrijf* [1993] ECR I-4879; [1993] IRLR 601, ECJ.

20 Case 28/93 *Van Den Akker v Stichting Shell Pensioenfonds* [1994] ECR I-4527; [1994] IRLR 616, ECJ, and Case 408/92 *Smith v Avdel Systems Ltd* [1994] ECR I-4435; [1994] IRLR 602, ECJ.

k) indirect discrimination in pensions, such as the less favourable treatment of part-time workers, where this is not objectively justified.[21]

Note that article 141 applies to each element of remuneration. It is no defence to say that an employee who is not entitled to a pension at the same age as his or her comparator will receive a higher terminal payment than the comparator. Each benefit must be equal (see para 22.31).

27.22 Article 141 does *not* apply to the following aspects of pensions:

- the statutory social security scheme which is governed by legislation and does not involve any agreement within the trade or undertaking;
- the use of actuarial factors in final salary schemes;[22]
- inequalities in the amounts of lump sums, transfer values and reduced pensions on taking early retirement, which depend on arrangements chosen for funding the scheme[23] (see para 27.46);
- AVCs[24] – when a member of a pension scheme has the option of making additional contributions, these contributions being administered by the scheme, additional benefits flowing from these contributions are not 'pay' under article 141 (see para 27.50);
- Bridging pensions (see para 27.51).

Comparator-less cases

27.23 In *Coloroll Pension Trustees Ltd v Russell* the ECJ ruled that article 141 did not generally apply to schemes which have at all times had members of only one sex, given that there would be no available comparator.[25] In *Allonby v Accrington and Rossendale College*,[26] the Court of Appeal has referred to the ECJ the question whether the female applicant needed a comparator in the same employment in order to claim access to the Teachers Superannuation Scheme to which she, as a self-employed agency worker, was denied access in accordance with the scheme's rules.

21 Case 170/84 *Bilka Kaufhaus GmbH v Weber von Hartz* [1986] ECR 1607; [1986] IRLR 317, ECJ.

22 Case 200/91 *Coloroll Pension Trustees Ltd v Russell* [1993] ECR I-4879; [1994] IRLR 586, ECJ.

23 Case 152/91 *Neath v Hugh Steeper Ltd* [1994] ECR I-6935; [1994] IRLR 91, ECJ, and see *Coloroll*, ibid.

24 *Coloroll*, ibid.

25 Ibid.

26 [2001] IRLR 364.

27.24 The scheme applies to all teachers employed in an educational establishment. It is a statutory scheme managed by the Secretary of State. The issue for the ECJ will be whether, if the exclusion of self-employed teachers can be shown to be indirectly discriminatory in that a significantly higher proportion of self-employed teachers than employed teachers are women, a claim under article 141 requires that the applicant identifies a comparator in the same employment. To require Ms Allonby to do so would be fatal to her claim, as all teachers under contract to the agency concerned are self-employed and are denied access to the pension scheme.

27.25 Before the Court of Appeal Ms Allonby relied upon *Defrenne (No 2)*,[27] in which the ECJ ruled that article 141 had direct effect in certain circumstances including forms of 'direct' discrimination 'in particular those which have their origin in legislative provision or in collective labour agreements and which may be detected on the basis of a purely legal analysis of the situation'. The reference to 'direct' in this context appears to refer to forms of discrimination which may be identified without any further domestic measures, and is to be contrasted with 'disguised', rather than 'indirect', discrimination. The discrimination of which Ms Allonby complained was indirect in that it was her case that self-employed teachers who were excluded from the scheme had a higher proportion of women than employed teachers. However, it was not disguised as the exclusion of self-employed teachers was plain from the regulations.

Claims by men

27.26 If a pension provision is not applied, for example, in the case of part-time women workers (because it would indirectly discriminate against them), its enforcement against a part-time man would constitute direct sex discrimination. His comparators would be the women who have succeeded in the indirect discrimination claim.

27.27 In *Preston v Wolverhampton Healthcare NHS Trust*[28] the House of Lords upheld the Court of Appeal in refusing to strike out a claim by a male part-timer despite the fact that there were no women part-timers in his pension scheme with whom he could compare himself. The applicant argued that the exclusion of temporary and part-time workers was indirectly discriminatory against women and that, if part-time women workers would have been entitled to pension

27 Case 149/77 *Defrenne v Sabena (No 2)* [1978] ECR 1365.

28 [1998] IRLR 197.

benefits, he should also be so entitled. The Court of Appeal held that, if a man were not able to institute proceedings unless and until a female employee was admitted to a scheme in the future, he would be prejudiced in his claims for equal pay. A female part-time employee might not be admitted until the conclusion of all the proceedings. The woman would be able to get backdated benefits but the man, if not allowed to institute proceedings, would have no remedy for the same period.

Retroactivity

27.28 The obligation to ensure equal treatment, in relation to benefits for members and for survivors, does not apply to benefits in respect of service before 17 May 1990.[29] In *Barber*[30] the ECJ held that member states and others involved in the provision of pensions had been entitled, prior to the date of the decision, to consider that article 141 did not apply to occupational pensions. This assumption had been reasonable in light of exceptions contained in the Social Security Directives[31] and, if the *Barber* judgment were to be applied retrospectively, the ECJ accepted that its financial implications would cause serious difficulties for pension schemes. In its subsequent decision in *Ten Oever*[32] the ECJ held that all new pensions paid after 17 May 1990 must not be based on discriminatory provisions after that date. The limitation on the effect of the *Barber* judgment was incorporated in the Maastricht Treaty Barber Protocol and now forms part of article 141.[33] Where the benefits payable under a pension scheme are not linked to length of actual service – as in the case, for example, of a lump-sum payment made if the member dies during employment, article 141 applies if the death occurred on or after 17 May 1990.

29 Unless the employee had already issued proceedings or made an equivalent claim – see *Howard v Ministry of Defence* [1995] ICR 1074, EAT, in which asserting a claim by correspondence was held to be insufficient.

30 Case 262/88 *Barber v GRE Assurance* [1990] ECR I-1889; [1990] IRLR 240, ECJ.

31 SSD art 7(1) and OSSD art 9(a).

32 Case 109/91 *Ten Oever v Stichting Bedrijfspensioenfonds voor het Glazenwassers-en Schoonmaakbedrijf* [1993] ECR I-4879; [1993] IRLR 601, ECJ.

33 Protocol 2, which came into force on 1 November 1993, provides that: '[f]or the purposes of Article [141] of this Treaty, benefits under occupational social security schemes shall not be considered as remuneration if and in so far as they are attributable to periods of employment prior to 17th May 1990, except in the case of workers or those claiming under them who have before that date initiated legal proceedings or introduced an equivalent claim under the applicable national law'.

27.29 The limit on retroactive effect does not apply to the right to join the scheme (see *Fisscher*[34]), or to the right to payment of a retirement pension where the worker was excluded from membership of the scheme in breach of article 141. In *Dietz v Stichting Thuiszorg Rotterdam*[35] the ECJ considered the position of a woman who had been employed for seven hours a week until she reached the age of 61 when she took voluntary early retirement. She was excluded from the compulsory occupational pension scheme, which only applied to workers who worked more hours than she did. Ms Dietz claimed she was entitled under article 141 to a pension based on her periods of employment after 8 April 1976 (the date of the *Defrenne (No 2)*[36] judgment in which the ECJ ruled for the first time that article 141 had direct effect). The ECJ held that she was entitled to join the scheme (as from 1976), and was also entitled to payment of a retirement pension. As the court pointed out, membership of a pension scheme would be of no interest to employees if it did not confer entitlement to the benefits provided.

27.30 Where a worker is able to claim retroactively the right to join an occupational pension scheme and to claim the benefits, he or she must still pay the contributions relating to the period of membership concerned.[37] Enforcing such claims (to join and to receive the benefits) has now been made easier because the time limits and the limitation on claiming arrears in the PA 1995 and EqPA 1970 have been set aside (see para 27.57).

'Levelling down'

27.31 EC law does not permit inequality to be eradicated by retrospective 'levelling down'.[38] Employees who have been disadvantaged must be given the same rights as other employees in relation to service before the discrimination was removed (although, in cases to which the *Barber* restriction applies, only as from 17 May 1990). Treatment must be equalised upwards in respect of the period where there was discrim-

34 Case 128/93 *Fisscher v Voorhuis Hengelo BV* [1994] ECR I-4583; [1994] IRLR 662, ECJ.

35 Case 435/93 *Dietz v Stichting Thuiszorg Rotterdam* [1996] ECR I-5223; [1996] IRLR 693.

36 Case 149/77 *Defrenne v Sabena (No 2)* [1978] ECR 1365.

37 Case 128/93 *Fisscher v Voorhuis Hengelo BV* [1994] ECR I-4583, [1994] IRLR 662, ECJ and Case C-435/93 *Dietz v Stichting Thuiszorg Rotterdam* [1996] ECR I-5223; [1996] IRLR 693.

38 Case C-200/91 *Coloroll Pension Trustees Ltd v Russell* [1993] ECR I-4879; [1994] IRLR 586, ECJ and the PA 1995, see para 27.60.

ination. But once the discrimination has been removed, the employer can reduce the advantages previously enjoyed by employees, provided male and female employees are treated equally.[39] This is subject, however, to the provisions in the trust deed and trust law which may prevent trustees altering a scheme if it would reduce women's future benefits. If this is the case, no levelling-down would be permitted.[40] In addition, if pension entitlement is part of the contract of employment it is doubtful whether the employer can make a unilateral variation disadvantageous to the employee.

The practical impact of article 141

Access to occupational pension schemes

27.32 There must be no discrimination, direct or indirect, in access to a pension scheme. The exclusion of women (or categories of women, such as married women) will breach article 141.[41] Any less favourable treatment of part-time workers, where this is indirectly discriminatory and cannot be objectively justified, will also be unlawful.[42]

27.33 In *Fisscher*[43] the applicant was employed between January 1978 and April 1992. Until January 1991 she was excluded from the pension scheme because she was a married woman. When she was permitted to join the scheme on 1 January 1991 she was allowed to backdate her membership for a period of three years. She claimed to be entitled to membership with effect from 1976 – the date of the *Defrenne (No 2)* decision.[44] Similarly, in *Vroege*[45] the applicant was excluded from the pension scheme because the rules allowed only men and unmarried women working at least 80 per cent of the normal full working day to be members. Mrs Vroege never worked more than 80 per cent of the working day. The rules were changed in 1991 but she was not allowed

39 Case 408/92 *Smith v Avdel Systems Ltd* [1994] ECR I-4435; [1994] IRLR 602, ECJ.

40 See *Lloyds Bank Pension Trust Corporation v Lloyds Bank plc* [1996] PLR 263, Ch D.

41 Case 128/93 *Fisscher v Voorhuis Hengelo BV* [1994] ECR I-4583, [1994] IRLR 662, ECJ.

42 See Case 170/84 *Bilka Kaufhaus GmbH v Weber von Hartz* [1986] ECR 1607, [1986] IRLR 317, ECJ and Case 57/93 *Vroege v NCIV Instituut voor Volkshuisvesting BV* [1994] ECR I-4541; [1994] IRLR 651, ECJ.

43 Case 128/93 *Fisscher v Voorhuis Hengelo BV* [1994] ECR I-4583, [1994] IRLR 662, ECJ.

44 Para 27.25 above.

45 Case C-57/93 *Vroege v NCIV Instituut voor Volkshuisvesting BV* [1994] ECR I-4541; [1994] IRLR 651, ECJ.

to purchase years of membership in respect of her service prior to 1991.

27.34 In both *Fisschler* and *Vroege* the ECJ held that the *Barber* limitation on claiming retroactive benefits did not apply to the right to join an occupational pension scheme. Unlike *Barber*[46] (where employers acted in good faith and there would be a risk of serious difficulties if a limitation were not applied), it had been clear since the decision in *Bilka Kaufhaus*[47] that there should be equal access to pension schemes. As *Bilka Kaufhaus* did not limit its effect in time, the applicants could backdate their membership to the date of the *Defrenne (No 2)* decision and receive benefits relating to this period. This is subject to the successful applicants paying retrospective contributions,[48] and to national rules on time limits (see paras 27.82 and 27.57).

Differential pension ages

27.35 Equal pension benefits under occupational pension schemes must be paid to men and women at the same age. In *Barber* the ECJ held that benefits under a private, contracted-out, occupational pension scheme constitute 'pay' under article 141. Mr Barber was a member of a such a scheme in which the normal pensionable age was three years earlier than the relevant statutory pensionable age (62 for men and 57 for women). In the event of redundancy, men who had reached 55 and woman who had reached 50 were entitled to an immediate pension as well as a payment equal to the statutory redundancy payment.

27.36 Mr Barber was made redundant when he was 52, so he was not granted an immediate pension. He complained that, if he had been a woman, he would have received an immediate pension. The ECJ ruled that benefits paid by an employer to a worker in connection with the latter's compulsory redundancy were 'pay' for the purposes of article 141 whether they are paid under a contract of employment, by virtue of legislative provisions, or on a voluntary basis. Article 141 was, accordingly, breached by the imposition of an age condition

46 Case 262/88 *Barber v GRE Assurance* [1990] ECR I-1889; [1990] IRLR 240, ECJ.

47 Case 170/84 *Bilka Kaufhaus GmbH v Weber von Hartz* [1986] ECR 1607, [1986] IRLR 317, ECJ.

48 Case 128/93 *Fisscher v Voorhuis Hengelo BV* [1994] ECR I-4583, [1994] IRLR 662, ECJ and Case 435/93 *Dietz v Stichting Thuiszorg Rotterdam* [1996] ECR I-5223; [1996] IRLR 693.

which differed according to sex in respect of pensions paid under a contracted-out scheme, even if the difference between the pensionable age for men and that for women was based (as it was in *Barber*) on the national statutory state pension scheme. The same principles apply to contracted-in occupational pension schemes (see the *Moroni* case[49]).

Each element of payment must be equal

27.37 The ECJ also held in *Barber* that the principle of equal pay applied to each element of remuneration, not to the total consideration paid to workers (see para 27.21).

Different contributions by employers for men and women

27.38 In *Worringham and Humphreys v Lloyds Bank,*[50] male and female clerical staff joined different occupational pension schemes. Women under 25 did not have to contribute, and they received nothing if they left the bank before they were 25. Men under 25 were obliged to pay a contribution but the employer made up the difference so that the net pay of men and women was the same. Men leaving the bank before they were 25 received their contributions back. The employer's contributions for the men meant that their gross pay was higher than women's, with implications for salary-related benefits. The ECJ held that the employer's contributions should be treated as pay and should be equal for men and women.

Survivors' pensions

27.39 A survivor's pension provided for by an occupational pension scheme is 'pay' for the purposes of article 141. As the ECJ pointed out in *Coloroll,*[51] the benefit derives from the survivor's spouse's membership of the scheme and the pension is vested in the survivor by reason of the employment relationship between the employee and member.

49 Case 110/91 *Moroni v Firma Collo GmbH* [1993] ECR I-6591, [1994] IRLR 130, ECJ.

50 Case 69/80 *Worringham and Humphreys v Lloyds Bank* [1981] ECR 767; [1981] IRLR 178, ECJ.

51 Case 200/91 *Coloroll Pension Trustees Ltd v Russell* [1993] ECR I-4879; [1994] IRLR 586, ECJ.

27.40 In *Razzouk and Beydoun v European Commission*[52] the ECJ held that restricting the payment of contractual survivors' pensions to widows was discriminatory. Mr Razzouk's wife had worked for the EC. When she died, Mr Razzouk was refused a pension. Survivors' pensions were granted automatically to widows, but provided only to widowers who were permanently incapacitated and unable to work. The ECJ awarded Mr Razzouk a pension with interest. The decision was not reached under article 141, rather on the basis of staff regulations governing the treatment of community officials. The fact that the court ruled that the regulations' discrimination against male surviving spouses was contrary to 'a fundamental right' is, nevertheless, instructive as to its likely approach in a case brought under article 141.

Transfer of rights from one scheme to another

27.41 Where there is a transfer between pension schemes, for example, on a change of job, the second scheme must increase benefits to eliminate any effect of previous discrimination.[53] If there is insufficient funding so to do, the scheme should do everything possible to ensure that there is equality. It may need to make a claim against the first scheme for the necessary additional sums. The members of the scheme should receive a pension calculated in accordance with the principle of equal treatment. This is also limited to service subsequent to 17 May 1990.

Transitional provisions

27.42 An employer which raises the pensionable age for women to that which applies to men cannot take steps to limit the consequences of this change for women. Any such transitional arrangements would discriminate against men. In *Van den Akker v Stickting Shell Pensioenfonds*[54] the pension scheme had a normal pensionable age of 60 for men and 55 for women. The age was equalised at 60 in 1985 but, under transitional arrangements, existing women members were given the option of maintaining the pensionable age of 55. After *Barber*

52 Cases 75 and 112/82 [1984] ECR 1509, ECJ.

53 Case 200/91 *Coloroll Pension Trustees Ltd v Russell* [1993] ECR I-4879; [1994] IRLR 586, ECJ.

54 Case 28/93 *Van Den Akker v Stichting Shell Pensioenfonds* [1994] ECR I-4527; [1994] IRLR 616, ECJ.

the pension fund abolished, with effect from 1 June 1991, the option for women to maintain a pensionable age of 55. The applicants, who had elected to maintain this age, challenged the pension fund's argument that this was necessary as a result of the *Barber* decision. The ECJ held that equality could be achieved by equalising at the age of 60, even though this reduced the advantage previously enjoyed by women. Once equalisation had occurred, the employer could not treat women more favourably in respect of post-*Barber* service, even if the more favourable treatment arose from an election made by women before the *Barber* judgment. However, between 17 May 1990 and 1 June 1991 (when equalisation was implemented), pension rights for men and women had to be calculated on the basis of the lower retirement age of 55 (see para 27.35).

Less favourable treatment of part-time workers/members

27.43 Direct and indirect discrimination in relation to pensions is unlawful. In *Bilka-Kaufhaus* and in *Vroege* the ECJ held that the exclusion of part-time workers from pension schemes is contrary to article 141 if a higher proportion of part-time workers than of full-time workers are women, unless the employer can objectively justify the discriminatory treatment.

Exclusion of low-grade workers from pension schemes

27.44 Under German social security law, individuals working fewer than 15 hours per week whose income does not exceed one-seventh of the average monthly salary are called 'minor' workers. They are not covered by the statutory old-age insurance scheme and do not pay statutory contributions. In *Nolte*[55] and in *Megner,*[56] cleaners who worked no more than ten hours per week and who were categorised as 'minor' for the purposes of German law claimed that their exclusion from the statutory state insurance schemes breached article 141. The ECJ ruled that people in minor employment are part of the 'working population' within the meaning of the SSD. The court went on to rule, however, that the exclusion of such workers from the statutory state scheme

55 Case 317/93 *Nolte v Landesversicherungsanstalt Hanover* [1995] ECR I-4625; [1996] IRLR 225.

56 Case 444/93 *Megner & Scheffel v Innungskrankenkasse Vorderpfalz* [1995] ECR I-4625; [1996] IRLR 236.

was justifiable (see para 7.126). The claim was brought under the SSD, as distinct from article 141. It is important to note that the ECJ permits member states a wider margin of discretion in relation to matters of social policy than is permitted in the context of article 141.

Length of service requirements

27.45 Length of service requirements may discriminate indirectly against women (see para 25.24). An employer may be able to justify such a requirement if the setting-up costs of pension schemes are high, and if it would be impractical to provide a pension for an employee who was not going to stay for very long. One solution, which is sometimes adopted, is to allow access after a year of service and to backdate entitlement to the start of employment.

Exceptions to the equal treatment principle

Actuarial factors outside article 141

27.46 In a final salary (or defined benefit) occupational pension scheme, actuarial assumptions about the life expectancy of men and women are used to assess the level of contributions that are necessary to fund the scheme. Since women live, on average, longer than men, employers must make higher contributions for female members than male members in order to achieve equal annual retirement pensions. The inequality in contributions by employers can affect the respective entitlements of men and women to lump sum payments and can effect transfer values, both of which are often based on the amount of contributions that have been paid in respect of that member.

27.47 In *Neath v Hugh Steaper Ltd*[57] the ECJ held that, in respect of final salary occupational pension schemes, the employer's commitment to its employees concerns the payment of a periodic pension. As this is based on final salary, the employer must make sufficient contributions to meet this commitment. Although the periodic pension is 'pay' under article 141, the funding arrangements chosen to secure the pension are not. Thus, where an employer pays higher contributions for women because of their longer life expectancy, these contributions do not offend article 141 even though this may mean, as it did in *Neath*, that the lump sums and transfer values applicable to male em-

57 Case 152/91 *Neath v Hugh Steeper Ltd* [1994] ECR I-6935; [1994] IRLR 91, ECJ.

ployees are lower than those to which female employees are entitled. No breach of article 141 occurs, because the inequality is based on actuarial factors taken into account in funding arrangements.

27.48 The principles outlined immediately above also apply where a reversionary pension is payable to a dependant in return for the surrender of part of the annual pension, and where a reduced pension is paid when the employee opts for early retirement. Funding arrangements based on actuarial factors are outside article 141 (at least for defined benefit schemes) and so is any inequality in the amounts of those benefits arising from the use of actuarial factors in the funding of the scheme.

27.49 The ECJ's ruling on actuarial factors was related to final salary occupational pension schemes which fall outside article 141 and capital benefits or substitute benefits arising out of such funding arrangements (which are based on actuarial factors). In money purchase schemes, equal contribution will, in the absence of unisex annuity rates, result in lower pensions for women. There is a direct correlation between the amount invested on behalf of each member and the amount of the resulting pension payable to that member. In these circumstances it is likely that such contributions would be held to be pay under article 141.

Additional voluntary contributions

27.50 In *Coloroll*[58] the ECJ ruled that the principle of equal treatment applies to all pension benefits paid by a scheme. This is so whether they are paid for by employers' contributions or by a combination of employers' and employees' contributions. Once such contributions are paid into the scheme, they are managed as a single fund out of which benefits are paid. But the ECJ distinguished AVCs paid by employees to secure additional benefits such as an additional fixed pension or additional lump sums. Such additional benefits are calculated separately, solely on the basis of the value of the contributions paid, and are credited to a distinct fund. Under the Social Security Act 1986, all UK pension schemes are obliged to offer arrangements to enable members to secure additional benefits on a money purchase basis. Where the scheme does no more than provide the necessary arrangements to manage the additional sums, article 141 does not apply.

58 Case 200/91 *Coloroll Pension Trustees Ltd v Russell* [1993] ECR I-4879; [1994] IRLR 586, ECJ.

Bridging pensions

27.51 Article 141 is not breached by the payment to a man of a higher pension designed to compensate him for not receiving the state retirement pension which would be paid to a woman (see para 27.66).

Enforcing pension equality

27.52 Employee members of pension schemes can enforce the EqPA 1970 or article 141 against their employers or the trustees of the scheme, whether they work for the private or public sector.

27.53 When a member has died, leaving a spouse or other person entitled to the benefit of the pension, the survivor can enforce the provisions of article 141. Since the pension scheme is a trust, the survivor does not have to be a party to the employment contract to enforce his or her rights and can bring a claim for breach of trust as a beneficiary. As the ECJ pointed out in *Coloroll*, article 141 would be deprived of all its effectiveness as far as survivors' pensions were concerned if the survivor were to be denied the possibility of enforcing the provision.

27.54 In *Coloroll* the ECJ ruled that the direct effect of article 141 can be relied on against the employer *and* the trustees or administrators of an occupational scheme. Thus the trustees are bound by the principle of equal treatment when carrying out their duties. If there is a conflicting provision in the trust deed, the trustees must do all they can to eliminate the discrimination, including seeking a declaration from the court.

Remedies

27.55 If a woman (or man) has been treated less favourably in relation to pension arrangements, the employer and trustee is obliged to remedy this by, for example, paying additional sums into the scheme or paying out of surplus funds or the fund's assets. This applies even if no claim has been made against the employer. The national court is under an obligation to order such measures. If funds are insufficient, the ECJ has held that the problem must be resolved on the basis of national law in the light of the principle of equal pay. Presumably, the resolution will depend on the facts of the case but the end result should be that men and women receive equal benefits.

27.56 In *Preston*[59] the applicants argued that they should be able to receive compensation for the loss of benefits under the pension scheme. The Court of Appeal held that the only remedy was a declaration as to their rights of access to the scheme. The court stated that the majority of applicants were not yet entitled to benefits under the scheme. The benefits flowed from the rights of access and contributions.

Time limits

27.57 In *Preston*, 22 TUC co-ordinated test cases were brought by nearly 60,000 part-time workers who complained that their exclusion from occupational pension schemes breached article 141. The schemes in question had been amended between 1986 and 1995 so as to allow part-time workers to join. The applicants' claims were for the right to retrospective membership for periods of employment prior to the amendments. The cases came before the tribunal on preliminary points concerning the application to their claims of:

- the time limit in EqPA 1970 s2(4), which provided that claims must be brought within six months of the end of employment;
- EqPA 1970 s2(5) as amended by Occupational Pension Schemes (Equal Access to Membership) Regulations (OPS(EAM) Regulations) 1976,[60] reg 12, which limited arrears of remuneration or damages to the period of two years prior to the date of the claim.

The tribunal, the EAT and the CA found that both section 2(4) and section 2(5) EqPA applied. The House of Lords referred to the ECJ the question whether these limits were compatible with EC law. In particular, the House of Lords asked whether they complied with the principle of EC law that national procedural rules for a breach of Community law must be no less favourable than those which apply to similar claims of a domestic nature. Many of the applicants had been employed on short-term contracts sometimes with intervals between contracts. The House of Lords, furthermore, asked whether a time limit that required the claim to be brought within six months of the end of any contract rather than just the last contract was compatible with EC law. The ECJ ruled that:

59 *Preston v Wolverhampton Healthcare NHS Trust* [1997] IRLR 233, CA. Although the Court of Appeal judgment was overturned on time limits (see para 27.57) the judgment stands on this point.

60 SI No 142, which apply the two-year limitation in EqPA 1970 s2(5) to actions for access to pension schemes.

- the six-month time limit for bringing claims was not necessarily contrary to EC law, it being for the national courts to decide if that limitation period was less favourable than other similar actions in domestic law;
- the limitation on calculation of service for the purposes of compensation to the two-year period prior to the date of the claim was in breach of EC law;
- the requirement that the claim had to be brought within six months of each contract where there had been a stable relationship resulting from a series of short-term contracts concluded at regular intervals in respect of the same employment to which the same pension scheme applied, was in breach of EC law.

The case then returned to the House of Lords to apply the ECJ's ruling to the applicants' appeals. The House of Lords ruled that:[61]

- The employers could not rely on EqPA 1970 s2(5) and OPS(EAM) Regulations 1976 reg 12 to defeat a claim for periods of pensionable service prior to two years before the date of the claim to be taken into account.
- The employee must pay contributions owing in respect of the period for which membership was claimed retrospectively.
- The rule that pensionable service is to be calculated only by reference to service after a date falling no earlier than two years prior to the date of the claim was precluded by Community law, in that it made it excessively difficult or impossible in practice for individuals relying on Community law to exercise their rights, since it prevented the entire record of service completed by those concerned from being taken into account for the purposes of calculating pension benefits.
- Future pension benefits, therefore, had to be calculated by reference to full and part-time periods of service subsequent to 8 April 1976.[62]
- The suitable comparator claim by reference to which it could be determined whether the EqPA 1970 s2(4) limitation was less favourable was, in a case concerning access to membership of a pension scheme, a claim for breach of contract.

61 *Preston v Wolverhampton Healthcare NHS Trust (No 2)* [2001] 2 AC 455; [2001] IRLR 237, HL.

62 The date of the ECJ decision in Case 149/77 *Defrenne v Sabena (No 2)* [1978] ECR 1365.

- The six-month time limit on claims in EqPA 1970 s2(4) was not less favourable than the six-year time limit for bringing a claim for breach of contract so the provision did not breach the principle of equivalence. The time limit of six years runs from each complete cause of action and there would be a separate cause of action every time an obligation to make a periodic pension payment to the trustees was breached. In contrast, a claim brought within six months of the termination of employment under the EqPA 1970 can go back to the beginning of employment or 8 April 1976, whichever is the later. Moreover, an equal pay claimant can wait until the employment is over, thus avoiding the possibility of friction with the employer if proceedings to protect her position were brought within the period of employment, as would be necessary in a breach of contract case since the six-year limitation runs from the accrual of a completed cause of action. The lower costs involved in an ET claim, the shorter time scale if proceedings finish there, and the informality of the proceedings were also relevant.
- Where there are intermittent contracts of service without a stable employment relationship, the period of six months under EqPA 1970 s2(4) runs from the end of each contract of service. This does not violate Community rules as to effectiveness and equivalence.
- However, where such contracts are concluded at regular intervals in respect of the same employment in a stable employment relationship, the six-month period runs from the end of the last contract forming part of that relationship. The question as to which of the applicants could satisfy that condition would be referred back to the ET.

27.58 The effect of the House of Lords ruling is that the six-month time limit for bringing claims applies to pension claims. In any claim for equal pay or equal pensions, if the applicant has been employed on a series of a contracts within a stable employment relationship, the time limit runs from the end of the last contract. If this is not the situation – if, for example, there were intervals between contracts and periods of other employment – the time limit applies to each contract relied upon. The limitation of two years on calculation of service for the purpose of compensation or pension entitlement does not apply and service may be calculated back to 8 April 1976 if there had been a stable employment relationship for that period of time and the claim had been brought in time.

Statutory provisions relating to equal treatment in pension schemes

27.59 Following the *Barber* case the government introduced legislation to bring UK law in line with EC law. The relevant parts of the Pensions Act (PA) 1995, which came into force on 1 January 1996, broadly follow the ECJ's rulings though, as the equal treatment provisions in PA 1995 mirror those of the EqPA 1970, claims can only be made where there is a comparator of the other sex in the same employment (see para 22.33).[63]

Pensions Act 1995 and the Occupational Pension Scheme (Equal Treatment) Regulations 1995

27.60 The PA 1995's equal treatment provisions are supplemented by the OPS Regulations 1995, most of which amend the EqPA 1970's exceptions and remedies. The Regulations came into force on 1 January 1996 and, for the most part, apply only apply to pensionable service on or after 17 May 1990 (but see para 27.28).[64]

The equal treatment rule

27.61 Occupational pension schemes are to be treated as containing an 'equal treatment rule'. This is a rule which relates to:

- access to membership of the pension scheme; and
- how members of the scheme are treated, for example, in relation to benefits and contributions.

The 'equal treatment rule' requires that there must be equal access to the pension scheme and equal treatment of existing members. Both direct and indirect sex discrimination are prohibited. Where occupational pension terms differ according to the person's family or marital status, the comparison is between a man and a woman with the same

63 Some of the provisions were previously in force. The OPS(EAM) Regs 1976, as amended by the OPS(EAM) Amendment Regs 1995 SI No 1215, made direct and indirect sex discrimination in access to occupational pension schemes unlawful. The new Act also covers benefits, thus implementing the *Barber* decision. It effectively replaces Social Security Act 1989 Sch 5, most of which was not brought into force.

64 PA 1995 s62.

family or marital status.[65] Terms for the benefit of dependants of members are also covered.[66]

27.62 The PA 1995 operates in a very similar way to the EqPA 1970 and it is specifically provided that the 'equal treatment rule' is to be construed as one with EqPA 1970 s1 (see chapters 22–24).[67]

When does the equal treatment rule apply?

27.63 The requirement in the PA 1995 of equal treatment applies when a woman is employed:

- on 'like work' with a man in the same employment (see para 23.3);
- on 'work rated as equivalent' to that done by a man in the same employment (see para 23.12); or
- on work which is of 'equal value' to that done by a man in the same employment (see chapter 24).

If, in these circumstances, the woman's access to the scheme or its treatment of her as a member is less favourable than that of her comparator, the scheme's terms must be modified so as to be no less favourable.[68] The PA 1995 applies equally to men and women.

27.64 The PA 1995, like the EqPA 1970, imposes a rebuttable assumption that discrimination has occurred in a case in which a woman establishes that she has been treated less favourably than a man engaged in like work, work rated as equivalent or work of equal value. The respondent – in this case the trustees or managers of the scheme[69] – must prove (by means of the material factor defence – see further chapter 25) that the reason for the unequal pay/pension is not tainted by discrimination in order to defend a claim.

27.65 The PA 1995 also provides that trustees and managers may not exercise their discretionary powers in a discriminatory way.[70] The effect of the equal treatment rule is that the term providing the discretion is treated as modified so as not to allow the discretion to be exercised in a way which is discriminatory on grounds of sex.

65 PA 1995 s63(2).
66 Ibid s63(1).
67 Ibid s63(4).
68 Ibid s63(3).
69 Ibid s63(4).
70 Ibid s62(5).

Exceptions to equal treatment

27.66 Employers are not required to treat comparable male and female workers equally with respect to pensions where:

- The GMF defence applies – in brief, the equal treatment rule does not apply if the difference in treatment between the woman and her comparator is genuinely due to a material factor which:
  - is not the difference of sex; and
  - is a material difference between the woman's case and the man's.[71]

  It is for the trustees or managers of the occupational pension scheme to prove the material factor defence; or
- The treatment concerns the *terms* on which members are treated, as distinct from *access* to pension schemes, and the pensionable service predates 17 May 1990; or[72]
- The variation in pay is due to actuarial factors which fall within a prescribed class or description and differ for men and women in relation to:
  - the calculation of employers' contributions; or
  - the determination of benefits (ie, payment or other benefit made to or in respect of a member).

  Different actuarial factors cover differences in the average life expectancy of men where the aim is to provide equal periodical pension benefits for men and women. The exception under consideration covers:[73]
  - lump sum payments consisting of a commuted periodical pension or part of such a pension;
  - periodical pensions granted in exchange for a lump sum payment;
  - money purchase benefits within Pension Schemes Act (PSA) 1993 s181(1);
  - transfer credits and any rights allowed to a member by reference to a transfer from a personal pension scheme;
  - transfer payments including a cash equivalent under PSA 1993 s94;
  - periodical pensions payable in respect of a member who opts to take such benefits before normal pension age or in respect of a

71 PA 1995 s62(4).

72 Ibid s63(6).

73 Ibid s64(3) and OPS Regs 1995 reg 15.

  member who defers taking such benefits until after normal pension age;
  - benefits payable to another person in exchange for part of a member's benefits and the part of the member's benefits given up for that purpose;
  - benefits provided in respect of a member's voluntary contributions under PSA 1993 s111; or
- The pension is a *bridging pension* designed to equalise the overall payments to men and women of equal age when differential state pensionable ages are taken into account.[74] This exception was established by the ECJ in *Birds Eye Walls Ltd v Roberts*.[75] It applies where a man:
  - has not reached state pensionable age but would have done so if he were a woman;
  - is in receipt of an occupational pension; and
  - receives an additional amount of pension (not exceeding the amount of Category A retirement pension) which is no more than a woman with the same earnings would receive from the state scheme.

  In such circumstances a man may be paid an additional amount so that he is receiving the same total amount as a woman who is entitled, in addition to her occupational pension, to a state retirement pension.[76] This still applies, even if the woman does not actually receive the state pension because she has not paid her national insurance contributions.

27.67 The principle in *Roberts* also applies where an occupational scheme is a contracted-out final salary scheme under which the member receives more than he or she would have done if he or she had been of the other sex, but that extra amount does not exceed the SERPS top-up. Thus, the occupational pension may differ between a man and woman to take account of the difference between the top-up from SERPS he or she actually receives and the amount he or she would receive if he or she were of the opposite sex.[77] This is intended to cover the situation where there are differences in the rate of occupational

74 PA 1995 s64(2).

75 Case 132/92 [1993] ECR I-5579; [1991] IRLR 29. Note that in Case 7/93 *Bestuur van het Algemeen Burgerlijk Pensionfunds v Beune* [1994] ECR I-4471, the ECJ did not accept that a difference in the state pension justified inequality in an occupational pension.

76 OPS Regs 1995 reg 13.

77 Ibid reg 14.

pensions on account of part of the inflation-proofing of the guaranteed minimum pension element which is paid as part of SERPS.[78]

27.68 The PA 1995 enables further regulations to be made which may permit further variables or amend or repeal the exceptions relating to bridging pensions and actuarial factors or permit further variations.[79]

Consistency of the exceptions to equal treatment permitted by domestic law and article 141

27.69 It is arguable that the actuarial exceptions in the OPS Regulations 1995 are much wider than permitted by European law and could therefore be challenged under article 141. Thus, if, the decision in *Neath*[80] is limited to final salary schemes where the funding arrangements are unequal (because of the different life expectancy of men and women) so, arguably, should these exceptions be (see para 27.47).

Indirect discrimination in pensions

27.70 If a woman is denied access to a pension scheme because she is working part-time, national legislation allows her to challenge her exclusion only if she can identify a man doing like work, work rated as equivalent or work of equal value who has access to the scheme. The onus will then shift to the employer to show that the difference in treatment between the applicant and her comparator is due to a GMF which is not discriminatory (ie, neither directly nor indirectly and unjustifiably discriminatory).

27.71 The SDA 1975 model, which does not require an actual comparator, is more consistent with the approach taken by the ECJ in the *Bilka-Kaufhaus,*[81] *Vroege*[82] and *Royal Copenhagen*[83] cases than that adopted by the EqPA 1970. The appropriate test under EC law may well be whether the exclusion affects a disproportionate number of members of one sex, rather than whether an actual comparator can be identified. So, for example, the ECJ ruled in the *Vroege* case that,

78 See the Memorandum by the Department of Social Security to the Select Committee on the Scrutiny of Delegated Powers; House of Lords Paper 25 (Session 1994–95) (HMSO, January 1995), para 65.

79 PA 1995 s64(4).

80 Case 152/91 *Neath v Hugh Steeper Ltd* [1994] ECR I-6935; [1994] IRLR 91, ECJ.

81 Case 170/84 *Bilka Kaufhaus GmbH v Weber von Hartz* [1986] ECR 1607, [1986] IRLR 317, ECJ

82 Case 57/93 *Vroege v NCIV Instituut voor Volkshuisvesting BV* [1994] ECR I-4541; [1994] IRLR 651, ECJ

where a practice had a significant adverse impact on a particular gender, a prima facie case of discrimination contrary to article 141 was established (see also para 27.23).

27.72 The applicant in *Allonby*[84] complained that she was excluded from the Teachers Superannuation Scheme, which required members to be employed under a contract of service. Allonby was a self-employed agency worker. She, in common with all the (disproportionately female) part-time lecturers formerly employed by Accrington and Rossendale College, had been made redundant and her services subsequently contracted back by the college through Education Lecturing Services (ELS), an agency.

27.73 Ms Allonby argued that the exclusion of self-employed teachers from the Teachers Superannuation Scheme was indirectly discriminatory. She had no comparator in the 'same employment', all ELS lecturers being self-employed and, therefore, excluded from the scheme. The Court of Appeal referred to the ECJ a question as to whether article 141 had direct effect so as to entitle Ms Allonby to claim access to the statutory occupational pension scheme for teachers (the terms of which confine membership to teachers employed under a contract of employment). Such a claim would involve Allonby either comparing herself with a male lecturer employed by the college, or showing statistically that a considerably smaller proportion of female than of male teachers who were otherwise eligible to join the scheme could comply with the requirement of being employed under a contract of employment and establishing that the employment requirement was not objectively justified. The outcome of the reference in *Allonby* will clarify in what circumstances article 141 applies without the need for a comparator in the same employment.

Transfer of undertakings

27.74 Occupational pension schemes are specifically excluded from the general rule that all the transferor's liabilities shall be transferred to the transferee where the Transfer of Undertakings Regulations apply.[85] This exclusion does not, however, apply to any provision of an occupational scheme which does not relate to benefits for old age,

83 Case 400/93 [1995] ECR 1275; [1995] IRLR 648.

84 *Allonby v Accrington and Rossendale College* [2001] IRLR 364.

85 Transfer of Undertakings (Protection of Employment) Regulations (TUPE Regs) 1981 SI No 1794).

invalidity or survivors.[86] So, although there is no obligation for the transferee to maintain a previous pension, rights which have accrued at the time of transfer are protected.[87] There is a parallel exception in the Acquired Rights Directive.[88] But the EAT ruled in *DJM International Ltd v Nicholas*[89] that a subsisting allegation of sex discrimination will be transferred, and it must be assumed that this would also apply to an existing equal pay claim, including one made under the PA 1995.

Enforcement of the domestic statutory provisions

27.75 Trustees or managers are given power to make appropriate alterations to a scheme by way of resolution in order to comply with the equal treatment rule. This applies if they do not otherwise have the power or if the procedure is unduly complex or protracted or involves the obtaining of consents which cannot be obtained (or cannot be obtained without delay).[90]

27.76 The same provisions apply to disputes and enforcement as apply under the EqPA 1970 (see chapter 26).[91] The applicant will be the member (or prospective member) of the scheme. The respondents will be the trustees or managers of the scheme.[92] But in tribunal proceedings the employer shall, for the purposes of the rules governing procedure, be treated as a party and be entitled to appear and be heard.[93]

27.77 Claims must be must be made within six months of the woman being employed in relevant employment to which the scheme relates.[94] In *Preston*[95] the House of Lords ruled that the six-month time limit applied. If there had been a series of contracts but a stable employ-

86 TUPE Regs 1981 reg 7(2), added by Trade Union Reform and Employment Rights Act 1993 s33(5).
87 TUPE Regs 1981 reg 6.
88 Council Directive 77/187/EEC art 3(3).
89 *DJM International Ltd v Nicholas* [1996] IRLR 76.
90 PA 1995 s65. Section 65(2) provides that alterations may be backdated.
91 EqPA 1970 s2 and PA 1995 s63(4).
92 PA 1995 s64(3)(b). The references in the EqPA 1970 to employers and employees are to be treated as references to trustees or managers (on the one hand) and members or prospective members (on the other).
93 OPS Regs 1995 reg 4; EqPA 1970 s2(5A).
94 PA 1995 s63(4)(c).
95 See para 27.57.

ment relationship, time ran from the end of the employment relationship. If that was not the situation and there had been a series of non-continuous employment contracts, time ran from the end of each contract. The PA 1995 provides that arrears of pay can be awarded only in respect of the two years prior to the issue of proceedings. In *Preston*, however, the House of Lords ruled that the two-year rule could not be applied where access to the pension scheme had been denied in breach of article 141 EC.[96]

27.78 Different remedies apply to pension scheme members and pensioners. The aim is to put the disadvantaged member or pensioner in the position he or she would have been in had the principle of equal treatment applied. Thus, compensation will be awardable only to pensioners rather than to existing members (who would not yet be entitled to a pension).

27.79 The same principles apply whether the claim is for a breach of the equal treatment rule imposed by the OPS Regulations 1995, or for breach of a contractual equality clause which relates to membership of or rights under a scheme.[97]

Equal treatment in access to membership

27.80 Where there has been a breach of an equality clause or of the 'equal treatment' rule in relation to the terms on which a person becomes a member of a pension scheme, the court or tribunal may declare that an employee is entitled to be admitted to the scheme as from a specified date. OPS Regulations 1995 reg 5, which limited the date of retrospective admission to no earlier than two years prior to the date the proceedings were instituted, was held to be contrary to article 141 in *Magorrian*[98] and *Preston*.[99]

27.81 If the date an ET deems the successful applicant to be admitted to membership of the pension scheme pre-dates its decision, the tribunal may require the employer to provide such resources as are

96 Ibid.

97 OPS Regs 1995 regs 5 and 10.

98 Case 246/96 *Magorrian and Cunningham v Eastern Health and Social Services Board* [1997] ECR I-7153; [1998] IRLR 86, ECJ. The court held that periods of service completed by part-time workers who have suffered indirect discrimination based on sex must be taken into account as from 8 April 1976 (the date of the judgment in *Defrenne (No 2)*, for the purposes of calculating the additional benefits to which they are entitled.

99 Case 78/98 [2000] IRLR 506; [2000] ECR I-03201.

necessary to make up for the loss in respect of the employee's accrued rights without the employee paying any further contribution.[100]

Equal treatment for existing members[101]

27.82 Where there has been a breach of the equality clause or of the equal treatment rule in respect of the terms on which members of a scheme are treated, the court or tribunal may declare that a member has a right to equal treatment in respect of a specified period, provided that is not prior to 17 May 1990 (the date of the *Barber* decision). The employer must provide the resources to ensure that the member has the same accrued rights for the period as other members within the two-year limit without the employee paying any further contribution. It is clear from the decisions in *Magorrian* and *Preston* that the two-year limit is a breach of article 141. But the ECJ has ruled that those whose membership of pension schemes is back-dated by virtue of an article 141 claim must pay the contributions due from the (back-dated) date of their admission to the scheme.[102]

27.83 A member who is not a pensioner member is not entitled to any payment by way of arrears of benefits or damages for breach of the equal treatment rule.[103]

Claim by pensioner member[104]

27.84 Where there has been a breach of the equality clause or the equal treatment rule relating to the terms of a scheme, a pensioner member can claim damages or any other financial award. The employer must, once again, provide the resources.[105]

100 OPS Regs 1995 reg 5(7A).

101 Ibid regs 6 and 11.

102 See Case 128/93 *Fisscher v Voorhuis Hengelo BV* [1994] ECR I-4583, [1994] IRLR 662, ECJ and Case 57/93 *Vroege v NCIV Instituut voor Volkshuisvesting BV* [1994] ECR I-4541; [1994] IRLR 651, ECJ. In contrast, OPS Regs 1995 reg 7 provides that the employer must pay the contributions. This apparent contradiction has not been resolved by any amendment of the regulations.

103 OPS Regs 1995 reg 3.

104 Ibid regs 7 and 12.

105 Ibid.

Other beneficiaries under the scheme

27.85 There are no provisions in the PA 1995 for other beneficiaries, such as survivors, to make a claim, though OPS Regulations 1995 reg 1 defines a pensioner member as a person entitled to the present payment of pension or other benefits derived through a member. The PA 1995 should be interpreted to allow a beneficiary to make a claim. It may be wise, however, also to make a claim under the ordinary provisions of the EqPA 1970 and article 141.

The Pensions Ombudsman

27.86 The Pensions Ombudsman has power to investigate and determine complaints made by a member (or his/her survivor) about maladministration by the trustees or managers of an occupational or personal pension scheme.[106]

106 Pensions Schemes Act 1993 ss145–152.

CHAPTER 28

Harassment

continued

Key points

28.1
- Harassment is not defined in terms by the Sex Discrimination Act (SDA) 1975, the Race Relations Act (RRA) 1976 or the Disability Discrimination Act (DDA) 1995.
- Harassment may be unlawful under the SDA 1975, the RRA 1976 or the DDA 1995 if it amounts to less favourable treatment and a detriment.
- Harassment may be defined as unwanted conduct of a racial, sexual or disability-related nature, or other conduct based on sex, race or disability affecting the dignity of women and men. This can include unwelcome physical, verbal or non-verbal conduct.
- In determining whether particular conduct amounts to 'harassment' sufficient to establish 'detriment' under the discrimination provisions:
  - all the acts complained of should be looked at together rather than regarded piecemeal;
  - a one-off act, if sufficiently serious, might itself constitute actionable harassment;
  - a largely subjective test is applied, so that the first question is whether the complainant considered the treatment complained of offensive. But in all cases, for harassment to be established, the treatment complained of must be objectively capable of amounting to harassment.
- Intention and motive are largely irrelevant in determining whether particular conduct amounts to harassment.
- Where the harassment is sex, race or disability-specific there is no need to compare the treatment afforded the complainant with the treatment which was or would have been afforded a person of a different sex, race or status.
- Harassment on grounds of sexual orientation was not unlawful under the SDA 1975 if it occurred prior to the implementation of the Human Rights Act (HRA) 1998 on 2 October 2000. Such harassment may be unlawful under the SDA 1975 if it occurs after that date.
- Harassment may give rise to other causes of action outside the SDA 1975, the RRA 1976 or the DDA 1995.

Background and statutory provisions

28.2 This chapter deals principally with harassment, both inside and outside the workplace, on a 'prohibited ground' (ie, sex, race, married status, gender reassignment or disability). Harassment on these or other grounds may amount to a criminal assault, may breach the Protection from Harassment Act (PHA) 1997 and may give rise to a personal injury claim (see para 28.59). It may also infringe the HRA 1998 if it is done by a 'public authority'[1] and may amount to a civil wrong (a 'tort'). This is dealt with below.

28.3 Most reported cases of harassment arise out of treatment at work. But the same principles apply to harassment outside the workplace. Harassment can take many forms. These include:

- leering, ridicule, embarrassing remarks or jokes, unwelcome comments about dress or appearance, deliberate abuse or insults;
- hostile action intended to isolate the victim, giving too much or too little work, unjustifiable criticism; and
- repeated and/or unwanted physical contact, demands for sexual favours and physical assaults.[2]

28.4 'Harassment' is not specifically defined or proscribed by the SDA 1975, the RRA 1976 or the DDA 1995. However, where it constitutes less favourable treatment on the grounds of sex, race or is related to disability and it occurs in circumstances covered by the SDA 1975, RRA 1976 or DDA 1995 (for example, employment, goods and services, housing, etc) it will be unlawful direct discrimination.[3]

The prevalence and effects of harassment

28.5 Sexual and racial harassment and harassment for a reason relating to disability remain common both inside and outside the workplace. Twelve million workers in Europe consider themselves to be victims

1 See chapter 9.

2 See, eg, the Report of the Employment and Social Affairs Committee of the European Commission, 'Harassment at the Workplace' (July 2001, doc ref 2001/2339 (INI)).

3 For more on direct race and sex discrimination, see chapter 3 and for disability discrimination, see chapter 6.

of harassment,[4] and a recent TUC survey showed that over a quarter of women questioned had experienced sexual harassment.[5]

28.6 Harassment can and often does have a very debilitating effect on its victims. The Employment and Social Affairs Committee of the European Commission recently reported that:

> The effects of harassment on the health are devastating. The victim suffers stress, nervous tension, headaches/migraines and depression, and develops psychosomatic illnesses such as stomach ulcers, colitis, thyroid problems, insomnia, high blood pressure and skin diseases. In most cases victims of harassment take long-term sick leave or even resign from their jobs. In addition, harassment has significant effects on the productivity and economic performance of the firm or public-service department concerned because of the absenteeism it generates and the costs and benefits that have to be paid as a result of sickness or redundancy. The cost of harassment to businesses and society is therefore very high.[6]

28.7 A recent study by a European Health and Safety Agency identified bullying in the workplace as one of the new occupational 'risk' factors with a psychological dimension.[7] When proved, it is usually treated very seriously indeed by courts and employment tribunals (ETs). Most of the very high awards of compensation in discrimination cases arise out of complaints of harassment. For example, in *Yeboah v Hackney LBC*[8] an award of £380,000 was made to a senior black African employee who suffered a prolonged campaign of harassment. And in *HM Prison Service v Salmon*[9] an award of £76,344.88 was made to a woman prison officer whose sexual harassment resulted eventually in depressive illness.

4 'Second European Survey on Working Conditions in the European Union', European Foundation for the Improvement of Living and Working Conditions, (Office for Official Publications of the European Communities, 1997).

5 'No excuse – no harassment at work' (TUC Women's Conference Survey Report, 1999).

6 'Harassment at the Workplace', n2 above.

7 'The State of Occupational Safety and Health in the European Union' (European Agency for Health and Safety at Work, 2000) cited in 'Harassment at the Workplace', n2 above.

8 ET 56617/94, 1998 (unreported) – the sum was ordered to be paid by consent.

9 [2001] IRLR 425. See further para 28.59 below and see chapter 33 on remedies generally.

Harassment on multiple grounds

28.8 In the workplace at least, women are most at risk of harassment.[10] But harassment inside and outside the workplace can and often does occur on more than one ground.[11] Black women, for example, often suffer multiple disadvantage as do lesbians and disabled people from ethnic minority groups.[12] When harassment occurs in connection with more than one protected ground, proceedings should be brought under more than one of the discrimination Acts. So, for example, a black woman sexually harassed by a white supervisor might bring proceedings under the SDA 1975 and the RRA 1976.[13]

Defining harassment

28.9 As stated above, harassment is not defined by the SDA 1975, RRA 1976 or DDA 1995. However, guidance as to the meaning of harassment can be obtained from a number of sources.

European Commission's Code of Practice

28.10 The European Commission's Code of Practice on protecting the dignity of women and men at work[14] defines sexual harassment as:

> Unwanted conduct of a sexual nature, or other conduct based on sex affecting the dignity of women and men at work. This can include unwelcome physical, verbal or non-verbal conduct.

28.11 A range of behaviour may be considered to constitute sexual harassment. Conduct will be unacceptable if:

- it is unwanted, unreasonable and offensive to the recipient;
- a person's rejection of or submission to such conduct is used explicitly or implicitly as a basis for a decision which affects that

10 'Harassment at the Workplace', note 2 above.
11 See, eg, Code of Practice in rented housing (CRE, 1991).
12 See Code of Practice on protecting the dignity of women and men at work, annexed to the European Commission's Recommendation on the Protection of Dignity of Women and Men at Work: 91/131/EEC. See also 'No excuse – no harassment at work', n5 above, and 'Harassment at the Workplace', note 2 above.
13 For an example of a black male complaining of sexual harassment see *Acharee v Chubb Guarding Services Ltd t/a Chubb Security Personnel* (2000) DCLD 43.
14 See note 12 above.

person's access to vocational training or to employment, continued employment, promotion, salary or any other employment decisions; and/or
- it creates an intimidating, hostile or humiliating working environment for the recipient.

28.12 The European Commission's code of practice makes it clear that the essential characteristic of sexual harassment is that it is unwanted by the recipient, and that it is for each individual to determine what behaviour is acceptable to him or her and what he or she regards as offensive. Sexual attention becomes sexual harassment if it is persisted in once it has been made clear that it is regarded by the recipient as offensive, although a single incident may constitute sexual harassment if sufficiently serious. It is the unwanted nature of the conduct which distinguishes sexual harassment from friendly behaviour which is welcome and mutual.[15]

28.13 In 'Racial Harassment at Work: What Employers Can Do About It' the Commission for Racial Equality (CRE) states that the European Commission's definition of sexual harassment 'can usefully be extended to racial harassment'.[16]

Harassment in the workplace

28.14 The European Commission's definition of harassment[16a] is wide enough to cover abuse; sexist, racist or disability-related 'jokes' and conduct which is explicitly sexist, racist or related to disability (gesticulating; depicting sexist, racist or offensive disability-related materials and slogans; distributing sexist, racist or offensive disability-related publications and so on). It is also wide enough to cover much more petty acts of harassment which, taken together, have a

15 In *Wadman v Carpenter Ferrer Partnership* [1993] IRLR 374 the EAT held specifically that the code provided useful guidance to ETs hearing sexual harassment cases. Although Council recommendations have no binding effect, national tribunals and courts should use them as an aid to construction when hearing cases within the scope of the recommendation. In Case 32/88 *Grimaldi v Fonds Des Maladies Professionelles* [1989] ECR 4407; [1990] IRLR 400 the ECJ held that the recommendation could not be considered as 'lacking in legal effect'. It held that domestic courts are bound to take recommendations into consideration in order to decide disputes submitted to them, in particular where they are capable of clarifying the interpretation of other provisions of national or EC law.

16 CRE, 1995, p9. See also the EOC, 'Good Practice Guide for Employers: Dealing with Sexual Harassment' (2001) pp1–2 (available at www.eoc.org.uk).

16a With appropriate modification to cover race and disability.

cumulative effect so as to cause disadvantage to workers in the workplace, for example:

- not passing on messages;
- hiding or moving work;
- ostracising;
- allocating menial tasks;
- allocating too much work.

Further guidance is provided in 'Racial Harassment at Work: What Employers Can Do About It'. This guidance relates to racial harassment but can be adapted to deal with harassment on other grounds. It states:

> Racial harassment may be deliberate and conscious. But it can also be unintentional; 'I meant no offence', or 'it was just a joke' is a common, sometimes genuine protest when someone has been oblivious to another person's feelings or sensitivities ... Unlawful discrimination as defined by the Race Relations Act need not be conscious, and as a Tribunal once remarked, 'it certainly does not need to be motivated; the great majority of people believe they have no prejudices'. Whilst the intention of the perpetrator may provide an explanation for the harassment, it can never be an excuse.
>
> The [employment tribunals] have consistently ruled that there can be 'no degree of acceptability' for racist banter and abuse in the workplace. The context is irrelevant and any use of it is an expression of racial prejudice ...
>
> The most important rule for employers faced with complaints of racial harassment is that the perception and interpretation of the person who feels harassed must be central to the consideration of any complaint of harassment.[17]

28.15 The European Commission's code of practice and the CRE guidance are both directed at employment-related harassment. But the definition of harassment adopted by both documents can be applied to other types of harassment. Furthermore, the CRE's 1991 Code of Practice in Rented Housing: For the Elimination of Racial Discrimination and the Promotion of Equal Opportunities describes racial harassment thus (paragraph 5.2):

> Racial harassment includes not only physical attacks on persons and damage to property, but also verbal abuse and any other form

17 The Code of Practice for the elimination of discrimination in the field of employment against disabled persons or persons who have had a disability (issued by the Secretary of State in 1996) deals with harassment at paras 6.22 and 6.23 and makes it clear that harassment will almost always amount to a 'detriment'.

> of behaviour which deprives people of peaceful enjoyment of their homes on grounds of racial origin.

The Race and Employment Directives

28.16 The Race Directive[18] (RD) and the Employment Directive[19] (ED) both define harassment in terms, and deem it to be discrimination for the purposes of the directives. The dates by which the new provisions must be implemented are given at paras 10.84 and 10.93 above. In the meantime, the definitions of harassment under the directives are a useful aid to interpretation of the domestic legislation.

28.17 Article 2(3) RD states that:

> Harassment shall be deemed to be discrimination … when an unwanted conduct related to racial or ethnic origin takes place with the purpose or effect of violating the dignity of a person and of creating an intimidating, hostile, degrading, humiliating or offensive environment.

Article 2(3) ED states that:

> Harassment shall be deemed to be a form of discrimination … when unwanted conduct related to any of the grounds referred to in Article 1 [namely, religion or belief, disability, age or sexual orientation] takes place with the purpose or effect of violating the dignity of the person and of creating an intimidating, hostile, degrading, humiliating or offensive environment.

Harassment outside the workplace

28.18 Outside the workplace, as well as inside it, both serious and less serious acts of harassment will fall within the definition above. Examples of harassment outside the workplace might include:

- racial, sexual and disability-related abuse;
- graffiti and verbal abuse on housing estates;
- assaults by the police;
- repeated knocking on doors;
- repeated demands that a person produce driving documents to the police;
- requirements for the repeated submission of completed application forms in respect of the provision of services.

18 Council Directive 2000/43/EC.

19 Council Directive 2000/78/EC.

Unlawful harassment

28.19 Harassment, as defined above, will amount to less favourable treatment.[20] Where the harassment is on the grounds of sex, gender reassignment, marital status, race or is related to disability and occurs in circumstances prohibited by Parts II or III of the SDA 1975, RRA 1976 or DDA 1995, then it will be unlawful.[21]

28.20 Parts II and III of the SDA 1975, RRA 1976 and DDA 1995 make 'less favourable treatment' – including harassment – unlawful:

- in all cases in which it occurs in the employment field and amounts to a 'detriment';[22]
- in the case of racial and sexual harassment only,[23] if it occurs in the field of education and amounts to a 'detriment'[24] (for example, harassment in the playground or classroom);
- in the case of race, sex and disability-related discrimination, if it occurs in relation to the management of premises and amounts to a 'detriment'[25] (for example, harassment on housing estates);
- in the case of race and sex[26] discrimination, if there is a refusal to provide goods, facilities or services or where they are not provided 'in the like manner'[27] or, in the case of disability discrimination, where there is less favourable treatment in the standard of service provided (for example, harassment in cafes and bars).[28]

In practice there is a good deal of overlap, in the context of harassment, between 'less favourable treatment' and 'detriment'. Thus a

20 Less favourable treatment means no more than 'disadvantage': *Jeremiah v Ministry of Defence* [1979] IRLR 436. It is difficult to conceive of any harassment, as defined above, which would not amount to a disadvantage. As with proving direct discrimination, it is not necessary to show intention or motive to harass.

21 Parts II and III of the SDA 1975, RRA 1976 and DDA 1995 are dealt with in chapters 29 and 30.

22 SDA 1975 s6(2)(b), RRA 1976 s4(2)(c) and DDA 1995 s4(2)(d).

23 But not disability-related discrimination because the DDA 1995 does not deal with discrimination in the field of education in the same way as the SDA 1975 and RRA 1976: see chapter 30. Discrimination in relation to marital status and gender reassignment is prohibited only in the employment and related fields: SDA 1975 ss2(A) and 3.

24 SDA 1975 s22 and RRA 1976 s17 in the field of education.

25 SDA 1975 s30, RRA 1976 s21 and DDA 1995 s22 in relation to the disposal and management of premises.

26 Marital discrimination and discrimination on the ground of gender reassignment is not made unlawful outside the employment and related fields.

27 SDA 1975 s29 and RRA 1976 s20.

28 DDA 1995 s19.

person who is harassed to the extent that it amounts to less favourable treatment is very likely to establish that such harassment amounts to a detriment,[29] to service in a different manner or to sub-standard service.[30]

Proving harassment

28.21 In determining whether harassment amounts to less favourable treatment and whether it amounts to a detriment, to service in a different manner or to sub-standard service, regard should be had to the following principles.

The need to consider acts of harassment together

28.22 When looking at acts of harassment, particularly which by themselves appear petty, it is important to look at the whole picture because the overall picture is often more serious than first seems from looking at its component parts.[31] A court or tribunal should not be invited to make findings in respect of each alleged incident of harassment separately, but should be urged to consider all the acts *together* in determining whether or not they might properly be regarded as harassment. In *Driskel v Peninsular Business Services Ltd*[32] the applicant complained of sexual harassment when her manager subjected her to sexual banter and comments over a period of about three months. On the day before she was due to have an interview with him for promotion, he recommended to her that she should 'wear a short skirt and see-through blouse showing plenty of cleavage if she wanted to be successful'. Her subsequent complaint of sexual harassment was rejected by her employers who refused to move her manager. As a result, Mrs Driskel refused to return to her old job and was dismissed. She complained of sex discrimination, arguing that she had been subject to sexual harassment by her manager and that this caused her dismissal. The ET accepted Mrs Driskel's account of the earlier

29 For the purposes of SDA 1975 ss6(2)(b), 22 and 30; RRA 1976 ss4(2)(c), 17 and 21; DDA 1995 ss4 and 22.

30 For the purposes of SDA 1975 s29, RRA 1976 s20 and DDA 1995 s19.

31 The same approach is taken to determining whether or not the treatment complained of is on grounds of sex, race or related to disability: see *Anya v Oxford University* [2001] IRLR 377 and chapter 4.

32 [2000] IRLR 151.

incidents in which comments had been made with a sexual connotation, but concluded that she had not objected at the time and that her manager could not have known that she found them offensive. The ET accepted that the comments made immediately before the promotion interview had been made, but found that the remarks were intended as flippant, that they could not reasonably have been taken seriously, and that they were not in fact taken seriously by Mrs Driskel. The ET therefore rejected Mrs Driskel's sex discrimination claim. The EAT allowed her appeal, giving guidance on the proper approach to a complaint of harassment.

28.23 According to the EAT in *Driskel*, the ET should approach harassment-as-discrimination claims as follows:

- 'The Tribunal hears the evidence and finds the facts ... [I]t is desirable not to include in this exercise judgments as to the discriminatory significance, if any, of individual incidents – judgment thus far should be limited to the finding of all facts that are prima facie relevant. If ad hoc assessments "discrimination or no" are made the result is a fragmented and discursive judgment; more importantly, there is the potential ... for ignoring the impact of the totality of successive incidents, individually trivial.'
- 'The Tribunal then makes a judgment as to whether the facts as found disclose apparent treatment of the female applicant by the respondents as employers in one or more of the respects identified in [SDA 1975] section 6(2)(a) and (b) that was less favourable than their treatment, actual or potential, of the male employee.'
- 'The Tribunal further considers any explanation put forward on behalf of the respondent employers. In the light of any such explanation is the discrimination so far potentially identified real or illusory?'[34]

In *Driskel* the EAT concluded that, had the ET found all the facts before making a judgment as to whether or not each of the acts complained of amounted to unlawful discrimination, it would have put each of the incidents in context and would have found that the harassment amounted to 'discrimination of a high order'.[35] The EAT went on to make two further important points:

- First, the absence of a contemporaneous complaint regarding any incident of sexual harassment does not necessarily negate a finding that the incident complained of was 'unwanted'. In con-

34 [2000] IRLR 151 para 12.
35 Ibid para14.

sidering the relevance of any failure to complain, an ET or court must consider the circumstances. In Mrs Driskel's case any 'instinct to complain must ... be inhibited by the fact that she wanted the promotion that would come from the approval of [the harasser]'.[36]

- Secondly, *intention is largely irrelevant.* In Mrs Driskel's case, the EAT commented that the ET's finding that the remark regarding Mrs Driskel attending the interview in sexually provocative dress 'was flippant and was not meant to be taken seriously' missed the point. The EAT concluded that it was irrelevant that the harasser did not actually expect Mrs Driskel to attend the interview in sexually provocative dress; 'what is relevant is that by this remark (flippant or not) he was undermining her dignity as a woman'.[37]

28.24 Mrs Driskel's case followed the case of *Reed and Bull Information Systems Ltd v Stedman*,[38] in which similar observations were made. In that case the applicant complained of a course of conduct by Mr Reed. The ET found that no single incident was serious enough to constitute sexual harassment, but found that there had been a series of events with a pervading sexual innuendo and sexist stance. It upheld Ms Stedman's complaint of sex discrimination. The EAT rejected an appeal against that decision and gave the following guidance:

> Sexual harassment is a short term for describing a type of detriment ... The question in each case is whether the alleged victim has been subjected to a detriment and, second, was it on the ground of sex. Motive and intention of the alleged discriminator is not an essential ingredient, as in any other direct discrimination case, although it will often be a relevant factor to take into account. Lack of intent is not a defence ...
>
> The essential characteristic of sexual harassment is that it is words or conduct which are unwelcome to the recipient and it is for the recipient to decide for themselves what is acceptable to them and what they regard as offensive ... Because it is for each individual to determine what they find unwelcome or offensive, there may be cases where there is a gap between what a Tribunal will regard as acceptable and what the individual in question was prepared to tolerate ... It is particularly important in cases of alleged sexual harassment that the fact-finding Tribunal should not carve up the

36 Ibid.
37 Ibid.
38 [1999] IRLR 299.

case into a series of specific incidents and try and measure the harm or detriment in relation to each. As it has been put in an USA Federal Appeal Court decision (Eighth Circuit):[40]

> 'Under the totality of the circumstances analysis, the District Court [the fact-finding Tribunal] should not carve the work environment into a series of incidents and then measure the harm occurring in each episode. Instead the trier of fact must keep in mind that "each successive episode has its predecessors, that the impact of the separate incidents may accumulate, and that the work environment created may exceed the sum of the individual episodes".'

Thus, for example, as here, a blatant act of a sexual nature, such as the deliberate looking up of the victim's skirt whilst she was sitting down, may well make other incidents, such as asking to be shown personal photographs which the victim was looking at at work, take on a different colour and significance. Once unwelcome sexual interest has been shown by a man in a female employee, she may well feel bothered about his attentions which, in a different context, would appear quite unobjectionable.[41]

Thus, observations, remarks or other treatment which may appear trivial when looked at alone may evidence sexual or racial harassment or disability-related harassment when they are seen as part of their overall context.

28.28 These cases were cases of sexual harassment in employment but the same principles apply in relation to racial and disability-related harassment inside and outside the employment-related field.

One-off acts

28.29 It can be seen from the above that the concept of harassment suggests a course of conduct or a number of incidents which together undermine the victim's dignity. However, a one-off act may, if sufficiently serious, amount to 'harassment' and to a detriment for the purposes of the SDA 1975, RRA 1976 or DDA 1995.

28.30 In *Insitu Cleaning Co Ltd v Heads*[42] the EAT upheld a tribunal finding that the applicant had been unlawfully discriminated against when a manager, the son of one of the directors of the company for whom she worked, said to her in a meeting 'Hiya, big tits'. The EAT

40 *USA v Gail Knapp* 955 F 2d 564 (1992).

41 [1999] IRLR 299, paras 25–29.

42 [1995] IRLR 4.

concluded that the ET was entitled to conclude that the one incident itself was sufficiently serious to amount to sexual harassment and, accordingly, to a detriment under the SDA 1975. The EAT held that the question whether any act of harassment amounted to a detriment was largely a matter of fact for the tribunal, and that whether a single act of verbal sexual harassment was sufficient to found a complaint was also a question of fact and degree:

> It seems to be the argument that because the code refers to 'unwanted conduct' it cannot be said that a single act can ever amount to harassment because until done and rejected it cannot be said that the conduct is 'unwanted'. We regard this argument as specious. If it were correct it would mean that a man was always entitled to argue that every act of harassment was different from the first and that he was testing to see if it was unwanted: in other words it would amount to a licence for harassment ... The word 'unwanted' is essentially the same as 'unwelcome' or 'uninvited'. No-one, other than a person used to indulging in loutish behaviour, could think that the remark made in this case was other than obviously unwanted.[43]

Thus, even a single act of harassment which affects the dignity of the victim may constitute a detriment and amount to unlawful treatment.

Subjective and objective tests for 'harassment'

28.31 As can be seen from the above,[44] in determining whether or not any treatment complained of amounts to harassment a very subjective test is applied. The question whether the treatment amounts to harassment very much depends on the victim's assessment of it. But the test is not wholly subjective. For treatment to amount to discrimination and to become unlawful it must be *less favourable* treatment.[45] It is for the tribunal hearing the case to determine upon 'an objective assessment ... of all the facts',[46] whether the treatment can be said to be 'disadvantageous' to the applicant.[47]

43 Ibid paras 8–11.

44 The guidance in *Reed and Bull Information Systems Ltd v Stedman* [1999] IRLR 299, and the Commission code of practice, note 12 above.

45 And 'unreasonable' – Commission Code of Practice, ibid para 2.

46 *Driskel v Peninsular Business Services Ltd* [2000] IRLR 151, para.12.

47 *Driskel*, ibid, and thus to a detriment for the purposes of the Acts or, objectively assessed, to treatment which is not in the like manner as is normal or is sub-standard in the particular circumstances.

28.32 The case of *Smith v Vodafone UK Ltd*[48] illustrates this point. Ms Smith complained of sex discrimination after a male colleague said 'you've got some lovely melons there' when he came across her sitting at her desk with a punnet of melon slices in front of her. A tribunal found as a matter of fact that the co-worker had been referring to the melons, rather than to Ms Smith's breasts, and that, on realising the double meaning of his remark, he immediately became embarrassed and apologised to her. The applicant laughed with her colleagues but later complained of sex discrimination, contending that the remark referred to her breasts and that she was offended by it. The ET concluded, as a matter of fact and degree, that the remark did not amount to sexual harassment of Ms Smith. The EAT dismissed her appeal. It concluded that the facts disclosed 'hypersensitivity' on Ms Smith's part and that the double meaning of the expression 'melons' did not affect her dignity at work when it was used to refer to the actual melons and was not directed at her breasts.[49] The EAT agreed with the ET that the *Insitu* case was distinguishable because 'big tits' was obviously offensive and demeaning and incapable of bearing any innocent explanation.[50]

28.33 Thus even where conduct is subjectively perceived as harassment, it must objectively be capable of being so for it to become unlawful.

'Provocation' and consent

28.34 In harassment cases, treatment will only be unlawful where it is unwanted – it cannot otherwise be said to be 'detrimental'. This means that issues of provocation and consent sometimes arise. In practice these issues only ever arise in *sexual* harassment cases.

28.35 In *Steele v Optika Ltd*[51] the applicant complained of sexual harassment when her male colleague, who was also a friend, organised a male strippergram as a birthday present for her. The strippergram had handcuffed Ms Steele and undressed to a g-string. He then placed her over his shoulder and took off his g-string so that her face was close to his naked groin. This was watched by her colleagues. Ms Steele apparently enjoyed and co-operated with the show, and afterwards kissed the strippergram. Some time later she complained of sexual harassment. The ET dismissed her complaint on the ground

48 EAT 0054/01, 2001 (unreported).
49 Ibid paras 22 and 23.
50 Ibid para 24.
51 (1997) DCLD 31.

that the show was not unacceptable to or unwanted by Ms Steele. The ET found that she had 'entered into the spirit' of the strippergram with 'evident enjoyment' and, when asked at the time whether the incident had caused her embarrassment, said 'not at all ... I only wish I could have spent longer with him'. The ET was apparently also influenced by the fact that Ms Steele was 'an active and willing participant in sexually explicit banter' with the colleague who organised the strippergram, and in other sexually-related conduct in finding that the incident had caused her no detriment.

28.36 It is clear from the decision in *Steele* that the conduct of a complainant may be relevant in determining whether she has suffered a detriment. In *Snowball v Gardener Merchant*,[52] too, the EAT upheld an ET decision permitting the admission of evidence relating to the claimant's sexual behaviour. The EAT accepted that the disputed evidence was relevant to the applicant's credibility, because she denied allegations that she talked freely to colleagues about her attitude to sexual matters. Similarly, in *Wileman v Minilec Engineering Ltd*[53] the EAT concluded that the ET had been entitled to take account of the fact that a claimant wore scanty and 'provocative' clothing at work as one element in deciding whether any treatment she suffered amounted to a detriment. The EAT appeared to accept that, even where the conduct was unwanted, the damage caused may be less serious in a complainant who engaged in similar (but consensual) conduct herself and that compensation might be lower than in other cases. In our view this is wrong. Wearing short skirts cannot be a licence to harass. Furthermore:

- Simply because a complainant accepts or welcomes comments by one person does not mean they cannot be unwanted, offensive and unlawful when made to her by another person.[54]
- The fact that a woman *submits* to conduct which she finds offensive does not mean that it is not unwanted. Where a woman submits to or tolerates such harassment because she is concerned about her working (or other) conditions, such treatment is still unwanted. The European Commission's code of practice on harassment makes this clear.[55]

52 [1987] IRLR 397.

53 [1988] IRLR 143.

54 *Wileman*, ibid.

55 See Recommendation 91/131/EEC, art 1 and, in particular, Commission code of practice, art 2, note 12 above.

- Because of the potential relevance of previous sexual conduct, respondents sometimes wish to cross-examine women intrusively about their private lives; provocation and consent. This can be very unpleasant indeed. Respondents who adopt this course should be warned, by letter and at any hearing, that, in the event that the claim succeeds, aggravated and exemplary damages[56] will be sought in respect of that conduct.

Complaints

28.37 The fact that a complainant does not complain of harassment does not mean that he or she cannot prove that it was unwanted, detrimental and unlawful. Many people do not complain of harassment or do so only after a long delay.

28.38 The Equal Opportunities Commission (EOC) recently reported that, in a review of sexual harassment cases decided by the ETs in the period 1998 to 2001, most women had initially not reported the sexual harassment for fear of losing their jobs.[57] Similar anxieties might be reflected in other areas (for example, fear of being evicted from one's home for complaining of sexual harassment by a landlord). But it is advisable to complain of harassment if possible:

- first, if the complaint is dealt with inadequately, this will be good evidence to rebut any defence by the harasser's employers that they took such steps as were reasonably practicable to prevent the harassment;[58]
- second, it will provide a good explanation for any delay in instituting proceedings and thus will be grounds for extending the time limit if it has already expired.[59]

28.39 Where no contemporaneous complaint has been made, it is helpful to provide an explanation for this (for example, that the person to whom the complaint would be made was the harasser himself; fear of what might follow, etc). This will help rebut any suggestion that the absence of a complaint was because the allegation was recently fabricated.

56 See chapter 33.
57 EOC, 'Sexual harassment at work' (2001).
58 SDA 1975 s41(3), RRA 1976 s32(3) and DDA 1995 s58(5), and see chapter 31.
59 See, eg, *Aniagwu v Hackney LBC* [1999] IRLR 303 and chapter 32.

Harassment on one of the prohibited grounds

28.40 As stated above, 'harassment' must constitute less favourable treatment *and* a detriment (or, in certain contexts, amount to treatment in a different manner to that which is normally provided[60] or sub-standard service[60a]), for it to be unlawful under the SDA 1975, RRA 1976 or DDA 1995. Furthermore, of course, the harassment must be:

- on the ground of the complainant's sex;[61] or
- on racial grounds;[62] or
- related to a disabled person's disability;[63] or
- (in the case of discrimination in the employment and related fields only), on grounds of gender reassignment[64] or marital status.[65]

28.41 In the context of harassment complaints, there are two types of cases:

- those cases where the treatment complained of is sex-, race- or disability-specific, when it is not necessary to identify a real or hypothetical comparator; and
- those cases which are *not* sex-, race- or disability-specific when it is necessary to identify a real or hypothetical comparator.

Sex, race and disability-specific harassment

28.42 Where the treatment complained of is sex-,[66] race- or disability-specific, as is often the case with harassment, then it is *because* of the complainant's sex, race or disability and therefore must be on those grounds. This removes the need for comparisons.

28.43 One of the leading cases in which this principle was established is *Porcelli v Strathclyde Regional Council.*[67] In *Porcelli* the complainant was sexually harassed by two of her male co-workers. The respondents argued that the treatment did not amount to sex discrimination because the harassment resulted from the co-workers' dislike of the complainant, rather than from her sex. According to the respondents,

60 SDA 1975 s29 and RRA 1976 s20.

60a DDA 1995 s19.

61 SDA 1975 s1(1)(a).

62 RRA 1976 s1(1)(a).

63 DDA 1995 ss5, 19 and 24.

64 SDA 1975 s2A as inserted by Sex Discrimination (Gender Reassignment) Regulations 1999 SI No 1102, reg 2(1).

65 SDA 1975 s3.

66 By which, for the purposes of this part, is included gender reassignment and marital status.

67 [1986] IRLR 177.

the men would have treated an equally disliked male co-worker as badly as they treated the applicant. But the Scottish Court of Sessions rejected the respondents' appeal against a finding of unlawful sex discrimination and held as follows:

> Although [the ET] were satisfied that [the harassers] would have treated a male colleague whom they disliked as much as they disliked the applicant just as unpleasantly, they appear to have accepted that the campaign against the applicant included the treatment which I have labelled 'sexual harassment' – a weapon which would not have been employed in a comparable campaign against such a man. Such treatment was treatment of the applicant because she was a woman, regardless of the motive behind it ...

28.44 Where sex, race or disability is used as a 'weapon' to harass a complainant, then it is not necessary for a court or tribunal to ask itself whether a person of a different sex, racial group or disability status would have been treated in the same way in comparable circumstances. Such treatment is treatment 'on grounds of' sex or race and it is also clearly treatment 'related to' disability.[68] A further illustration can be seen in the case of *Burton and Rhule v De Vere Hotels Ltd*.[69] In this case the applicants were subjected to explicit racial abuse from Bernard Manning, an 'entertainer'. In allowing their appeal against an ET's rejection of their RRA 1976 complaint the EAT held, amongst other things, that the tribunal had erred in asking itself whether it could be said that the treatment was on racial grounds. Smith J stated for the EAT that:

> In our view the Tribunal did impose upon the employees a burden additional to that imposed by the RRA 1976, namely the burden of showing that the employers subjected the employee to the detriment of racial harassment on racial grounds. In effect, they required the employees to show that the employers were themselves affected by racial bias or animus. That is not necessary ...[70]

28.45 A woman who is subject to sex-specific abuse (eg, 'big tits'[71]), or to remarks or conduct with obvious sexual connotations (eg, having her

68 And see *BT v Williams* [1997] IRLR 669 in which *Porcelli* was followed and in which it was held that, where the conduct complained of constitutes sexual harassment and is in itself gender-specific, there is no necessity to look for a male comparator. Compare however the decision of the Court of Appeal in *Smith v Gardner Merchant Ltd* [1998] IRLR 510 in which the court disapproved of the approach taken in *Williams*.

69 [1996] IRLR 596.

70 Ibid at 598.

71 *Insitu Cleaning Ltd v Heads* [1995] IRLR 4.

skirt looked up by a colleague[72]) will not have to point to a comparator (real or hypothetical) to demonstrate that the treatment amounts to sex discrimination. In *Insitu Cleaning Ltd v Heads*[73] the employers argued that the remark 'big tits' was not sex-related, in that a similar remark could have been made to a man (for example, in relation to a balding head or a beard). This defence was resoundingly rejected by the EAT as 'absurd': 'a remark by a man about a woman's breasts cannot sensibly be equated with a remark by a woman about a bald head or a beard. One is sexual the other is not.'

28.46 Other examples of sexually or racially specific treatment include:

- exposure of a penis by a male sales manager to a female sales representative;[74]
- the subjection of a German employee to Nazi salutes over a period of time;[75]
- questioning of a junior employee as to whether she knew what a '69' was;[76]
- calling a person a 'goddamn Yank', a 'thick Paddy', 'typical Irish' and a 'Black cunt'.[77]

Similarly, harassment based on stereotyping ('women like to be complimented', 'black men like to think they have long penises') constitutes discrimination on the grounds of sex or race (or, as the case may be, discrimination related to disability) without the need for any comparison.[78]

28.47 In the case of sexual harassment it should be remembered that it does not matter that the *motive* for the harassment is not 'sexually related'. One might sexually harass a woman by, for example, calling her a 'slag'.[79] The fact is that this term could hardly be regarded as amounting to a sexual overture does not make it any the less sexual harassment.[80]

72 *Reed and Bull Information Systems Ltd v Stedman* [1999] IRLR 299.

73 [1995] IRLR 4.

74 *Bloomfield v Quadrant Stationery* (1998) DCLD 38.

75 '... aimed at him and which occurred, ... because he was German' – *Rupertinger v Delphi Packard Electrical Systems Ltd* (1998) DCLD 36.

76 *McCusker v McDonald* (1997) DCLD 31.

77 *Ruzio v Tescos Stores and Lea* (1995) DCLD 24; *McCauley v Auto Alloys Foundry Ltd and Taylor* (1994) DCLD 21 and *Bellifantie v British Rail* (1994) DCLD 21.

78 *Hurley v Mustoe* [1981] ICR 490; *Ealing LBC v Garry* [2001] IRLR 681. For a similar case see *Yeboah v Crofton and Hackney LBC* [2002] IRLR 634.

79 *Young v McLeod and John McLeod & Co* (1995) DCLD 25.

80 *Porcelli v Strathclyde Regional Council* [1986] IRLR 177, para 9.

Overheard abuse

28.48 Harassment need not be directed at the complainant personally. If it is sex-, race- or disability-specific, abuse might still be unlawful if it is overheard. There is earlier authority to the contrary effect. In *De Souza v Automobile Association*,[81] for example, the Court of Appeal upheld a finding that overheard racial abuse, where it was not intended that it would be overheard (though it was referring to the complainant), could not be said to have 'subject[ed] her to any ... detriment'. But it is unlikely that the same decision would be made on those facts now. This is because there is a growing awareness of the indignity caused by racial abuse in the workplace to black workers – the absence of a direct reference to the complainant, or an intention that the abuse be heard by the complainant, is unlikely to prevent overheard derogatory comments being regarded as actionable discrimination. This is so particularly in the light of recent authorities indicating that motive and intention are unnecessary ingredients in direct discrimination.[82] So, for example, in *Chin v Post Office*[83] an ethnic minority employee witnessed the name-calling ('black bastard', 'Zulu warrior' and 'tribes Mandela') to which a black fellow-employee was frequently subject. Though the remarks were not addressed to the complainant, a tribunal upheld his complaint that the harassment and abuse of his fellow worker caused and constituted a detriment to him (the complainant). This case highlights the importance of acknowledging that sexist, racist and disability-related abuse undermines the dignity of all women, black and ethnic minority and disabled people.[84]

Treatment which is comparatively less favourable

28.49 If harassing treatment is *not* sex-, race- or disability-specific, a finding of discrimination requires a comparison to be made between the treatment accorded the applicant and that which was or would have been accorded to someone of a different relevant group (whether sexual, racial, disability status, etc). The same principles apply as they do in any direct discrimination case.[85] Thus the person who complains of such harassment must establish that he or she was less

81 [1986] IRLR 103.

82 See chapter 3.

83 (1997) DCLD 31.

84 Compare *Stewart v Cleveland Guest (Engineering) Ltd* [1994] IRLR 440.

85 See chapters 3 and 6.

favourably treated than the harasser treated or would have treated a person:

- of a different sex, marital status or racial group; or
- who did not intend to undergo or who had not undergone (or was not undergoing) gender reassignment; or
- to whom the reason for any disability related treatment did not apply.[85a]

28.50 Examples of gender, race and disability *neutral* cases (where a comparison is needed) include:

- refusing overtime, issuing disciplinary warnings, ostracising;[86]
- calling a person a 'dumb bastard' (in a case other than that involving a DDA 1995 claim by a person to whose disability this remark could reasonably be seen as directed);[87]
- abusing a person in non-sex-, race- or disability-specific terms.

The complainant must compare his or her treatment with that which was or would have been meted out to a person of a different sex, race or disability status. This is so even where one of the background causes is sex-, race- or disability-*specific*, if the operative cause of the less favourable treatment was sex-, race- or disability-*neutral*. Thus the application of a race-neutral disciplinary rule ('no fighting') to an Asian worker who became embroiled in a fight with a co-worker after being racially abused, was not treatment which was race-specific.[88]

Nude pictures

28.51 As can be seen from the above, if the treatment is sex-, race- or disability-specific it is discriminatory without the need for a comparator:

> ... if a form of unfavourable treatment is meted out to a woman [or a black person or a person from an ethnic minority or disabled person] to which a man [or a white person or non-disabled person] would not be vulnerable, she [or he] has been discriminated against.[89]

Some limits are placed upon the extent of this principle by the EAT's decision in *Stewart v Cleveland Guest (Engineering) Ltd*,[90] in which it upheld an ET ruling that the display of calendars and other pictures of

85a See *Clark v Novacold* [1999] IRLR 318.

86 *Armitage, Marsden and HM Prison Service v Johnson* [1997] IRLR 162.

87 *Smith v Bowater Labels Ltd* (1995) DCLD 23.

88 *Sidhu v Aerospace Composite Technology Ltd* [2000] IRLR 602.

89 *Porcelli v Strathclyde Regional Council* [1986] IRLR 177, para 7.

90 [1994] IRLR 440.

nude and partially nude women, by her male co-workers, did not amount to sex discrimination against Ms Stewart. This was so notwithstanding that, as the tribunal had found, she was genuinely and reasonably offended by the pictures and indeed complained about them and that, accordingly, she was subjected to a 'detriment' for the purposes of SDA 1975 s6(2)(b). The ET ruled against her on the basis that a 'hypothetical' male might have been equally offended by the display and the pictures were not 'aimed at women or a woman'. The appeal at the EAT was heard by three men, and the decision probably suffers for that. The EAT ruled that the ET was entitled to reach the conclusion that the display of such pictures was gender 'neutral' because a man might have found them equally offensive.

28.52 In our view the EAT's decision in *Cleveland Guest* was plainly wrong. It ignores that which underpins sexual and other forms of harassment and what makes such harassment uniquely offensive – a lack of respect for the dignity of a person *as* a woman, *as* a black person or *as* a disabled person. The nude pictures genuinely and reasonably undermined Ms Stewart's dignity *as a woman* in the workplace. Though such pictures may have offended men, they plainly would not have undermined their dignity *as men.* In the words of M Rubenstein:[91]

> It is well documented that pin-ups of nude women can poison the working environment of female employees and be highly offensive to a woman who seeks to deal with her fellow employees with dignity. The thesis of this case, that whether a woman has a legal right to object or whether she must endure the humiliation of working in such an environment is dependent upon whether a hypothetical man might also object, is preposterous ... A woman is harassed by a pin up of nude women because she is a woman. A man, actual or hypothetical, may object to pin-ups of nude women, but it will not be on the grounds of his sex. Women are 'vulnerable' to pin-ups in a way in which men are not.

28.53 In *Cleveland Guest* Mummery J (now LJ) stated that the case turned on it own facts; that in each case the question whether treatment amounts to sex discrimination is a question of fact; and that the EAT was not deciding that it would *never* be an act of sex discrimination to display pin-ups in the workplace.[92] Given those remarks, and the

91 [1994] IRLR 438, 'Highlights'. Rubenstein drafted the European Commission's Code of Practice on harassment, note 12 above.

92 [1994] IRLR 440, para 31.

extent to which the case has been criticised, it probably can be safely assumed that it would not now be followed.

'Sex' discrimination and harassment connected with sexual orientation

28.54 A recent decision of the Court of Appeal limits the extent to which gender-specific abuse will found a complaint of sex discrimination by itself (ie, without the need for a comparator). In *Pearce v Governors of Mayfield School*[93] the applicant, a school teacher, suffered horrendous homophobic abuse by pupils over a prolonged period of time. The abuse was gender-specific, because it related to her as a woman and as a lesbian. The abuse included words and expressions such as 'lesbian shit', 'lezzie', 'lemon', and 'dyke'. In one particular incident, pupils persistently called out the word 'pussy' and made comments about the smell of fish and cat food. At the end of that particular day, Ms Pearce found an opened tin of cat food and half its contents in her coat pocket.

28.55 The abuse Ms Pearce suffered was certainly related to and caused by her sexual orientation. But it was also plainly gender-specific. The Court of Appeal, nevertheless, upheld the decisions of the ET and the EAT in concluding that the abuse did not constitute sex discrimination. The Court of Appeal decided that, because the abuse was motivated by Ms Pearce's sexual orientation, the proper comparator was a male homosexual who, the ET found, would have been subjected to similar abuse (albeit in the form of different words). Accordingly, there was no less favourable treatment on the ground of sex.[94]

28.56 The decision in *Pearce* should be regarded as wrong. A male homosexual subject to gender specific abuse (for example, verbal taunts of 'poofter') should also have a remedy for that gender specific abuse. The fact that a pupil might subject a lesbian teacher and a gay male teacher to *gender-specific* homophobic abuse does not mean neither are discriminated against on grounds of sex. Rather, it means that they are *both* discriminated against on grounds of sex. This case is due to be heard by the House of Lords in February 2003. It can be noted that the decision in *Pearce* may well have been different if the harassment had occurred after the coming into force of the HRA 1998 (see chapter 9).

93 [2001] IRLR 669.

94 Compare the recognition by the Court of Appeal in *Smith v Gardner Merchant* [1998] IRLR 510, that harassment could be on grounds of sex *as well as* sexual orientation.

Liability and remedies

28.57 Liability and remedies are dealt with in chapters 31 and 33. There are, however, a number of points that are worth noting here.

28.58 Liability is commonly an issue in harassment cases:

- A harasser's employer will often argue that the harassment was done outside the course of employment and thus they cannot be liable for it.[95] If this happens advisers should note the very wide meaning given to 'course of employment' in the SDA 1975, RRA 1976 and DDA 1995 – see in particular *Jones v Tower Boot Co Ltd*,[96] discussed in chapter 31.
- A harasser's employer will often argue that, even if the harassment was done during the course of the harasser's employment, the employer nevertheless took such steps as were reasonably practicable to prevent the harasser doing it or doing it during the course of his employment.[97] If this happens advisers must focus on the steps an employer took *before* the harassment occurred and on whether any relevant policies were effectively implemented.[98] The various codes of practice (below) are crucial in determining whether all reasonably practicable steps were in fact taken.

28.59 Remedies are also often controversial in harassment cases. This is because of the real harm that harassment frequently causes to its victims.[99]

- When a person loses his or her job (by resigning or otherwise) or home because of harassment, losses flowing from that (loss of wages; costs of a move, etc) can be claimed as compensation.[100]
- When injury to health has been caused by the harassment, a claim for compensation for personal injury can be made in proceedings under the SDA 1975, RRA 1976 or DDA 1995 in the ET or in the county court (depending on whether it is an employment-related claim or not). Indeed, if injury to health has been caused by harassment and a claim in discrimination has been instituted, the

95 SDA 1975 s41(1), RRA 1976 s32(1) and DDA 1995 s58(1). See chapter 31.

96 [1997] IRLR 168.

97 SDA 1975 s41(3), RRA 1976 s32(3) and DDA 1995 s58(5).

98 *Caniffe v West Riding of Yorkshire Council* [2000] IRLR 555 and see para 31.14 onwards.

99 See para 33.6 onwards.

100 Ibid.

claim for compensation for personal injury must be made in those proceedings.[101]

- In appropriate cases an award of aggravated damages[102] and, now, exemplary damages may also be made.[103]

Harassment and the codes of practice

28.60 The EOC, CRE and the National Disability Council (now replaced by the Disability Rights Commission) have issued codes of practice and guidance relating to various aspects of the SDA 1975, RRA 1976 and DDA 1995. The codes and guidance contain advice on steps which an employer or other body might take to avoid discrimination. Some of these codes have statutory force, and some are issued pursuant to the Commissions' general powers. In all cases they are likely to be influential. These codes are very important in the context of harassment cases.

28.61 First, the codes and guidance might be used to assist in the identification of unlawful harassment – see, for example, the CRE's 'Racial Harassment at Work: What Employers Can Do About It',[104] the CRE's Code of Practice in rented housing,[105] and the EOC's 'Good Practice Guide for Employers: Dealing with Sexual Harassment'.[106] Second, the codes and guidance might be used to identify the steps which an employer should take before it can make out the defence that it has taken such steps as were reasonably practicable to prevent the harasser from doing the harassment or doing it during the course of his employment.

28.62 In the context of harassment cases at work, the EOC recommends that employers should:[107]

- develop a clear policy for preventing and tackling sexual harassment;

101 *Sherriff v Klyne Tugs (Lowestoft) Ltd* [1999] IRLR 481. See also para 32.38.

102 *Armitage, Marsden and HM Prison Service v Johnson* [1997] IRLR 162. See para 33.34.

103 *Kuddus v Chief Constable of Leicestershire* [2001] UKHL 29. See para 33.38.

104 CRE, 1995, p9.

105 CRE, 1991, para 5.2.

106 EOC, 2001, pp1 and 2.

107 'Good Practice Guide for Employers: Dealing with Sexual Harassment' (EOC, 2001). See also 'Code of Practice: Equal Opportunity policies, Procedure and Practices in Employment' (EOC, 1985).

- make sure that everyone is aware of and understands the policy;
- treat sexual harassment as a health and safety issue;
- lead by example – make managers and supervisors responsible;
- monitor policy implementation;
- adopt a complaints and investigations procedure for dealing formally and informally with sexual harassment; and
- adopt a disciplinary and appeals procedure that conforms to ACAS guidelines.

28.63 The CRE recommends that employers should:[108]

- adopt a policy on racial harassment;
- properly communicate the policy to all employees;
- provide training on the policy and procedures to be followed where a person wishes to complain;
- make clear how complaints of racial harassment will be dealt with;
- provide for an informal and formal investigation and complaints procedure;
- monitor, review and evaluate the policy and complaints of racial harassment; and
- make clear to contractors, customers and clients that harassment (towards its employees) will not be tolerated.

28.64 In the specific context of education provision the CRE recommends that:[109]

- schools monitor pupil attendance and take steps to address issues, including harassment, which adversely affect attendance;
- schools should take account of any complaints of alleged racial harassment against a pupil when dealing with disruptive behaviour by him or her;
- a 'whole school' approach should be taken to tackling racial discrimination –all staff should be given responsibility for implementing the school's racial harassment policies;
- clear procedures should be put in place for dealing with racial harassment promptly, firmly and consistently;
- immediate action should be taken to remove racist graffiti;
- all staff should be trained to deal with racial harassment; and

108 'Racial Harassment at Work: What Employers Can Do About It'. See also the CRE's Code of Practice for the elimination of racial discrimination and the promotion of equality of opportunity in employment (1984), available at www.cre.gov.uk.

109 'Learning for All, Standards for Racial Equality in Schools' (CRE, 2000).

- a sensitive and structured system of support should be put in place for victims of racial harassment.

28.65 The CRE suggests, in the context of owner-occupied housing, that those involved in sales, financing and providing related services in respect of such homes can help to combat the 'growing and serious' problem of racial harassment by:[110]

- in the case of lending institutions, treating seriously any reports of racial harassment and treating sympathetically people in such positions; and
- in the case of local authorities, developing appropriate strategies so that an effective advisory/support service can be offered to victims of racial harassment.

28.66 In relation to rented housing the CRE recommends that:[111]

- larger landlords set up effective support systems for victims of harassment;
- efficient arrangements should be made to rehouse victims where this is their wish, where investigations confirm the existence of racial harassment and where other housing stock is available to the landlord;
- attempts should be made to identify the perpetrators of the harassment and appropriate steps taken;
- local authorities should develop a strategy for assisting victims of racial harassment where they are not local authority tenants;
- tenants and prospective tenants should be advised that racial harassment will not be tolerated and that action will be taken when incidents occur;
- larger landlords should develop an effective and regular system of liaison with other agencies including tenants' associations to develop a common strategy for tackling harassment; and
- policies and procedures on racial harassment should contain clear guidance to staff on their responsibilities and possible courses of action.

110 Code of Practice in non-rented (owner occupied) housing (CRE, 1992) paras 4.7–4.8.

111 Code of Practice in rented housing, paras 5.1–5.3.

Protection from Harassment Act 1997 and other causes of action

28.67 A detailed examination of other causes of action available in cases of harassment is outside the scope of this work. However, advisers should be aware that, in some cases, victims may have a remedy in other torts (civil wrongs). This may be useful where:

- the harassment is on grounds other than those protected by the SDA 1975, RRA 1976 or DDA 1995 (for example, on grounds of sexual orientation);
- the time limit for bringing proceedings under the SDA 1975, RRA 1976 or DDA 1995 has expired and an extension has been refused; or
- the circumstances in which the harassment has occurred fall outside the SDA 1975, RRA 1976 or DDA 1995.

28.68 The most significant and relevant torts are:[112]

- assault and battery;
- private nuisance;[113]
- the common law tort of harassment in respect of which injunctive relief is available;[114]
- harassment under the PHA 1997.

Furthermore, where the harasser is a public authority or is employed by a public authority, the harassment may breach HRA 1998 s6 as

112 But see also: false word or verbal threats at common law (*Wilkinson v Downton* [1897] 2 QB 57, *Janvier v Sweeney* [1919] 2 KB 316); Housing Act 1988 s27 (harassment and unlawful eviction); Protection for Eviction Act 1977 s3 (unlawful eviction); Public Order Act 1986 ss4, 4A and 5; Telecommunications Act 1984 s43(1)(a) (as amended by Criminal Justice and Public Order Act 1994 s92); and Malicious Communications Act 1988 s1. Advisers should also note the new wider meaning of vicarious liability at common law following the decision in *Lister v Hesley Hall Ltd* [2002] 1 AC 215; [2001] IRLR 472, HL (see further para 31.7) which makes it easier to hold an employer of the harasser liable for common law torts such as assault.

113 *Malone v Laskey* [1907] 2 KB 141.

114 *Khorasandjian v Bush* [1993] QB 727 and see *Burris v Azadani* [1995] 1 WLR 1372 in which Lord Bingham MR reviewed the law of harassment in the context of the courts' power to grant interlocutory injunctive relief and concluded that the jurisdiction derived from Supreme Court Act 1981 s37(1) and County Courts Act 1984 s38 was not limited to restraining conduct which is in itself tortious or otherwise unlawful but extends to the protection of 'the legitimate interests of those who have invoked [the courts'] jurisdiction' (at 1377).

contravening articles 8 and 14 of the European Convention on Human Rights (further discussed in chapter 9).

28.69 The PHA 1997 creates a new statutory tort of harassment.[115] Section 1 provides that:

> (1) A person must not pursue a course of conduct –
> (a) which amounts to harassment of another, and
> (b) which he knows or ought to know amounts to harassment of the other.
> (2) For the purposes of this section, the person whose course of conduct is in question ought to know that it amounts to harassment of another if a reasonable person in possession of the same information would think the course of conduct amounted to harassment of the other.

There is no precise definition of harassment within the terms of the PHA 1997 but s7 provides that '[r]eferences to harassing a person include alarming the person or causing the person distress'. A 'course of conduct' must involve conduct on at least two occasions[116] (s7(3)), and 'conduct' includes speech (s7(4)). 'Harassment' for the purposes of the PHA 1997 might consist of words alone, so long as they were repeated on more than one occasion.[117] Whether a person ought to have known that his course of conduct amounts to harassment is an objective test, that is, whether a reasonable person in possession of the same information would think the conduct amounts to harassment.

28.70 Where there is an actual or apprehended breach of PHA 1997 s1 the victim may bring proceedings under s3 of the Act and, in such proceedings, damages might be awarded and injunctive relief granted (s3(1) and (2)).

28.71 PHA 1997 s1(1) does not apply to a course of conduct:

> if the person who pursues it shows –
> (a) that it was pursued for the purpose of preventing or detecting crime,
> (b) that it was pursued under any enactment or rule of law or to comply with any condition or requirement imposed by any person under any enactment, or

115 The Act also creates a criminal offence of harassment which is outside the scope of this work. Cases in the criminal sphere may however be relevant to civil claims because the Act adopts the same definition of harassment for the purposes of the civil and criminal jurisdiction.

116 Compare under the SDA 1975, RRA 1976 or DDA 1995: *Insitu Cleaning v Heads* [1995] IRLR 4.

117 Such words are therefore actionable without proof of damage. Compare the common law where words alone, not constituting an assault by themselves, are actionable only on proof of damage: *Janvier v Sweeney* [1919] 2 KB 316.

(c) that in the particular circumstances the pursuit of the course of conduct was reasonable.

The Court of Appeal has recently indicated that the repeated publication of stories calculated to incite racial hatred against a black woman was capable of amounting to harassment under the PHA 1997.[118] This harassment would not have been actionable under the RRA 1976 because there is no provision in the RRA 1976 covering harassment in these circumstances. For this reason, the PHA 1997 may have some residual usefulness in discrimination cases. Section 2 of the Act also creates a criminal offence of harassment.

118 *Thomas v News Group Newspapers Ltd* [2002] EMLR 4.

CHAPTER 29

Race and sex discrimination outside the employment field

continued

Key points

29.1 • Sex Discrimination Act (SDA) 1975 Pt III and the Race Relations Act (RRA) 1976 Pt III create a number of unlawful acts outside the employment field, making some instances of sex and race discrimination unlawful in connection with:
  - education;
  - the provision of goods, facilities and services;
  - the disposal and management of premises and the granting of licences and tenancies;
  - barristers and pupil barristers.
- The RRA 1976 prohibits some acts of race discrimination which otherwise fall outside the Act but which are committed by a public authority carrying out any of its functions. The SDA 1975 contains no equivalent provision.
- The RRA 1976 regulates discrimination by private members' clubs. The SDA 1975 contains no equivalent provision though some discrimination by such clubs will be unlawful on the basis that it breaches other provisions of that Act.
- The RRA 1976 also regulates certain discrimination by charities. The SDA 1975 contains no equivalent provision.
- The SDA 1975 and the RRA 1976 contain very many exceptions to their prohibitions on discrimination outside the employment field.

Background and statutory provisions

29.2 This chapter considers the application of the SDA 1975 and the RRA 1976 to discrimination outside the employment field. Disability discrimination outside the employment field is dealt with in chapter 30.

29.3 SDA 1975 Pt III and RRA 1976 Pt III create a number of unlawful acts outside the employment field. In summary, SDA 1975 Pt III makes it unlawful to discriminate:

- in the provision of education and related services;
- in the provision of goods, facilities and services;
- in the disposal and management of premises; and
- in relation to barristers (see further para 11.65).

RRA 1976 Pt III has wider scope. In addition to replicating the unlawful acts in SDA 1975 Pt III as set out above, RRA 1976 Pt III makes it unlawful for planning authorities and public authorities more generally to racially discriminate. It also makes it unlawful for private members clubs to racially discriminate.

29.4 The most significant difference between the scope of SDA 1975 Pt III and RRA 1976 Pt III is that discrimination by public authorities is not unlawful under the SDA 1975 unless the discrimination falls within the scope of one of the other unlawful acts.[1] The provision outlawing discrimination by public authorities in the RRA 1976 was inserted by the Race Relations Amendment Act (RRAA) 2000, following the Stephen Lawrence Inquiry Report which recommended that:

> the full force of the Race Relations legislation should apply to all police officers, and the chief officers of police should be made vicariously liable for the acts and omissions of their officers relevant to that legislation.[2]

This recommendation proved necessary because the courts had narrowly interpreted the goods, facilities and services provisions of the SDA 1975 and the RRA 1976 (see para 29.90) so that most public functions – including those of police officers – fell outside their scope. Furthermore, because of the special position of police officers, chief officers of police were not vicariously liable as employers for the discriminatory actions of their officers.[3] These lacunae have been filled by the RRA 1976 but remain in the SDA 1975. There are no current plans, as far as we are aware, to introduce legislation outlawing sex discrimination by public authorities or to make chief constables liable under the SDA 1975 for sex discrimination by their police officers.[4]

29.5 There is very little reported case-law under SDA 1975 Pt III and RRA 1976 Pt III by comparison with Pts II of the Acts, which apply to discrimination related to employment. This is probably due to a lack of awareness of the provisions outlawing discrimination outside the employment field, coupled with the costs of litigating such cases (the

1 That is, under the employment, education, goods, services and facilities or housing provisions.

2 Sir William Macpherson of Cluny, *The Stephen Lawrence Inquiry* (Cm 4262-I, 1999) Recommendation 11, available at www.archive.official-documents.co.uk/document/cm42/4262/4262.htm.

3 Unless it was possible to argue that the chief officer had done some act directly him or herself, which is usually difficult to establish.

4 See chapter 31 for the circumstances in which a chief constable will be liable for the discriminatory acts of his or her police officers in the employment field.

general rule in the county court is that the loser pays the costs of the successful party) and the typically small awards of compensation made.

29.6 Despite this, the Stephen Lawrence inquiry and the public debates which followed it generated an increased awareness of the rights existing under SDA 1975 Pt III and RRA 1976 Pt III. Further, there is a growing awareness about the real hurt that discrimination can cause and awards of compensation in the employment tribunals (ETs) are increasing. This is likely to find reflection in the awards made by the county courts. Many advisers now recognise that the courts are likely to award larger sums. Recently, a successful claim of race discrimination against a planning authority resulted in an agreed award of £750,000, as well as an award of very substantial costs against the respondent (see further para 29.50 below).[5] While this was an unusual case (and the only successful case of race discrimination in the planning field of which we are aware), it illustrates the fact that very significant awards are achievable in the county court just as they are in the ETs.

29.7 The potential claims which might arise from a particular act of discrimination often overlap. For example, racial harassment on a local authority housing estate may give rise to claims under RRA 1976 ss19B, 20 and 21, which deal respectively with public authorities, services and facilities and housing.[6] Advisers should therefore be alert to all possible claims.

29.8 RRA 1976 Pt IV contains provisions which make void certain discriminatory provisions in charitable instruments. No similar provision is made in the SDA 1975.

'Discrimination'

29.9 'Discrimination' has the same meaning in SDA 1975 Pt III and RRA 1976 Pt III as in Pts II, with one important exception. Indirect sex discrimination is defined differently for the purposes of the employment-related provisions of the SDA 1975, on the one hand (these include s35A, which deals with discrimination against barristers and is found

5 *Davis v Bath and North-East Somerset DC*, Case 9324149, Bristol County Court, 2001 (unreported).

6 Though it should be noted that RRA 1976 s19B does not apply to acts which are made unlawful by other provisions of the RRA 1976. Thus, while it might be prudent to bring proceedings under other provisions if there is doubt about whether or not the act complained of falls within the scope of s19B, if it is found to fall within any other provision of the Act s19B will not apply.

in SDA 1975 Pt III,[7] and any other provision of Pt III so far as it applies to vocational training[8]), and the non-employment related provisions of the SDA 1975 and all provisions of the RRA 1976, on the other. The different meanings given to indirect sex discrimination are described fully in chapter 7. (It should also be noted that discrimination against married people and discrimination on grounds of gender reassignment does not contravene SDA 1975 Pt III, except those provisions which broadly relate to employment.[9])

29.10 The burden of proof applicable to discrimination claims also differs between the employment-related provisions of the SDA 1975, on the one hand, and the non-employment-related provisions of the SDA 1975 and all provisions of the RRA 1976, on the other. Here, again, 'employment-related' is broadly defined to include those provisions of SDA 1975 Pt III mentioned above.[10] Except in employment-related sex discrimination claims the burden of proof remains with the claimant on a balance of probabilities. Guidance about the proper approach to discharging the burden of proof can be found in chapters 3 and 7. The same principles apply to claims under Pts III of the Acts.

29.11 Given their close connection with Pts II of the Acts the provisions dealing with barristers and with vocational training are dealt with in chapters 11 and 12.

Education

Introduction

29.12 The importance of equality and integration in education cannot be overstated. Inequality in the provision of education affects life chances and feeds into 'the familiar cycle of cumulative disadvantage' identified by the White Paper which preceded the RRA 1976.[11] Thus:

> The formal education system directly impacts upon the lives of almost the whole of the population. It is, at least potentially, a life-

7 Or advocates in Scotland: s35B.

8 This is because of the Sex Discrimination (Indirect Discrimination and Burden of Proof) Regulations (BP Regs) 2001 SI No 2660.

9 In which case only *direct* discrimination on grounds of gender-reassignment is regulated – see SDA 1975 ss2A, 35A and 35B.

10 SDA 1975 s66A, introduced by BP Regs 2001 reg 6.

11 *Race Discrimination* (1975, Cmnd 6234) para 7.

> long means to individual achievement, personal growth and the expansion of economic opportunity.[12]

29.13 Widespread complaints of unfair treatment in the education system by minority communities,[13] coupled with hard evidence that certain minority groups suffer real and significant disadvantage in the education system, indicate that the education system is not free of discrimination. Bangladeshi, black and Pakistani pupils achieve less than other pupils at all stages of compulsory education.[14] Black Caribbean children have equal, if not higher, ability than white children on entrance to schools but do least well at school. In 1998, 29 per cent of Pakistani and black pupils and 33 per cent of Bangladeshi pupils achieved five or more GCSEs at Grades A to C compared with 47 per cent of all white pupils and 54 per cent of Indian pupils. African-Caribbean pupils were over four to six times more likely to be excluded than white pupils and many of those excluded were of higher than average ability, although the schools saw them as under-achieving.[15]

29.14 There is recent evidence that girls excluded from school are an 'under estimated minority'; their exclusion often informal or for fixed periods and sometimes self-imposed.[16]

29.15 The Cantle report, which followed the disturbances in Oldham, Bradford and elsewhere in the spring and summer of 2001, was particularly struck by the depth of polarisation in towns and cities:

> The extent to which these physical divisions were compounded by so many other aspects of our daily lives, was very evident. Separate educational arrangements, community and voluntary bodies, employment, places of worship, language, social and cultural networks, means that many communities operate on the basis of a series of parallel lives. These lives often do not seem to touch at any point, let alone overlap and promote any meaningful interchanges ... There is little wonder that ignorance about each other's communities can easily grow into fear; especially where this is exploited by

12 P Weller, A Feldman and K Purdam, *Religious Discrimination in England and Wales* (2001) Home Office Research Study 220, p36.

13 *Religious Discrimination in England and Wales* pp 37 onwards.

14 'Disadvantage and Discrimination in Britain Today – The Facts' (CRE, 2001), available at www.cre.gov.uk.

15 Ibid.

16 National Children's Bureau ,'Not a Problem? Girls and School Exclusion', reported in (2002) *Guardian* 9 January.

> extremist groups determined to undermine community harmony and foster divisions.[17]

The report notes in particular that '[i]n terms of community cohesion ... a significant problem is posed by existing and future mono-cultural schools, which can add significantly to the separation of communities described above'. The report recommends that schools should not limit their intake to one culture or ethnicity and should take steps to make themselves 'attractive to other cultures and ethnicities from a wider area'.[18] It makes other recommendations to address the problems of mono-cultural schools, the tendency towards eurocentric curricular and pervasive Christian worship.[19]

29.16 The Cantle report noted that most people the researchers spoke to felt that more faith schools would add to the lack of contact and understanding between communities and that 'we need to break that down'.[20] It also notes the paradoxical recognition that, as Christian faith-based schools were already supported, 'fairness demanded that the same facility should be available to the Muslim and other communities'.[21] It seems inevitable that an increase in faith-based schools will in turn increase social division and intolerance. However the Education Act 2002 (in line with the White Paper, *Schools – Achieving Success*) encourages the provision of education through faith-based schools notwithstanding that the link between equality, respect for diversity and a lack of polarisation in education and community cohesion is clearly made in the Cantle report.

29.17 As to sex equality, girls are still too frequently victims of discriminatory stereotyping in education. The European Council Recommendation on the balanced participation of women and men in the decision-making process recommended, as late as 1996, that member states 'alert those involved in education and training at all levels, including those responsible for teaching materials', to the importance of 'a realistic and complete image of the roles and abilities of women and men in society, free of prejudice and discriminatory stereotypes'.[22]

17 'Community Cohesion: A Report of the Independent Review Team chaired by Ted Cantle' (Home Office, 2001), paras 2.1 and 2.3, available at www.homeoffice.gov.uk ('Cantle report').

18 Ibid paras 5.8.6 and 5.8.7.

19 Ibid para 5.8.13.

20 Ibid para 5.8.8.

21 Ibid.

22 Council Recommendation on the balanced participation of women and men in the decision making process (96/694/EC), art 2.

29.18 The EOC states that, notwithstanding the introduction of the national curriculum, decisions on optional subjects remains 'strongly influenced by gender'.[23] In particular choices on vocational subjects 'generally reflect the traditional pattern of the labour market'.[24] 'In this way certain pathways through employment are immediately closed down'[25] and existing patterns of pay disadvantage are replicated. Gender differences permeate all levels of the education system so that gender stereotyping is as prevalent at degree level as at other levels.[26]

29.19 Boys, too, suffer specific disadvantage in the education system. They generally perform less well than girls in most subjects, and four times as many boys as girls were excluded from schools in England in 1996.[27]

29.20 There are compelling grounds for strong and effective legislation against discrimination in the education field. But although SDA 1975 Pt III and RRA 1976 Pt III contain measures against discrimination, there has been very little individual litigation under those provisions. The Commission for Racial Equality (CRE) has conducted a number of formal investigations into inequalities in the education sphere,[28] but there are very few reported cases under the education provisions of the Acts.[29]

Race and sex discrimination

29.21 SDA 1975 Pt III and RRA 1976 Pt III both outlaw discrimination in education. SDA 1975 s22 makes it unlawful for a person specified in relation to an educational establishment specified ('the responsible body') to discriminate against a woman or a man:

(a) in the terms on which it offers to admit her to the establishment as a pupil, or
(b) by refusing or deliberately omitting to accept an application for her admission to the establishment as a pupil, or

23 'Women and Men in Britain: Sex Stereotyping: from School to Work' (EOC, 2001) available at www.eoc.org.uk.

24 'Women and Men in Britain'.

25 Ibid.

26 Ibid and EOC, 'Research Findings: Gender and Differential Achievement in Education and Training: A Research Review' (1998) also available at www.eoc.org.uk.

27 Ibid.

28 See www.cre.gov.uk/pupls/cat_fi.html.

29 For examples of some cases taken up by the CRE, see: 'Lessons of the Law: A casebook of racial discrimination in education' (CRE, 1991).

(c) where she is a pupil of the establishment –
   i) in the way it affords her access to any benefits, facilities or services, or by refusing or deliberately omitting to afford her access to them, or
   ii) by excluding her from the establishment or subjecting her to any other detriment.

RRA 1976 s17 is in materially identical terms.

Educational establishments and responsible bodies

29.22 The educational establishments caught by SDA 1975 s22 and RRA 1976 s17 are specified in column 1 of the sections. They include all schools and other educational establishments maintained by local educational authorities; private schools; special schools; universities and other further and higher education institutions.

29.23 In respect of each educational establishment set out under column 1, the responsible body is identified in column 2 of the relevant section. This is the body against which any proceedings should be issued where a complaint is made under SDA 1975 s22 or RRA 1976 s17. In the case of schools and other educational establishments maintained by a local education authority the responsible body is the local education authority or the governing body (depending on the discriminatory act complained of and which function it relates to).

29.24 Governing bodies now have significant responsibilities for educational provision in their institutions. These responsibilities include admissions and exclusions, resource allocation and the implementation of the national curriculum. Where a discrimination claim relates to the exercise of any of these functions, it should be made against the governing body. In respect of other educational institutions, proceedings should be issued against the governing body which is the responsible body in each case.[30]

Pupils

29.25 SDA 1975 s22A and RRA 1976 s17A provide that 'pupil' includes, for the purposes of the sections, 'any person who receives education at a school or institution' to which those sections apply (for example, pupils in schools; students in universities, etc).

30 In the case of Scotland, the responsible body may be the managers of the educational establishment or the Board of Management, depending on the institution concerned.

Admissions

29.26 It is unlawful to discriminate in the terms on which an educational establishment offers to admit a pupil or by refusing or deliberately omitting to accept an application for admission.

29.27 It would therefore be unlawful for an educational establishment to impose racial quotas for example. Thus the suggestion made in the Cantle report that, in an effort to avoid mono-cultural schools, faith-based schools in particular should be required to limit admissions from particular groups, would be unlawful without a change in legislation.[31] At present the education provisions contain no scope for lawful positive action.

29.28 More common than directly discriminatory admission criteria are those which have the effect of excluding pupils from particular racial groups. Such criteria will be unlawful if they are unjustifiable. Examples include:

- a criterion that depends on an applicant's siblings already being in the school when the school is already predominantly comprised of one racial group;
- a criterion that depends upon residence in a particular geographical area, where most of the residents of that area are of one racial group;
- entry criteria that depend upon the assessment of ability, aptitude, attainment, intelligence or character where those assessments are culturally biased.[32]

Examples of direct discrimination in respect of admissions to educational establishments might include the following:

- a refusal to admit children of foreign nationality in the UK on racial grounds;[33]
- a requirement, applied on racial grounds, that parents produce passports or other documentary evidence as proof of a child's entitlement to education in a maintained school;[34]
- a requirement that ethnic minority students have better qualifications than others in order to gain admission to a school.[35]

31 Cantle report, para 5.8.11.

32 Code of Practice for the elimination of discrimination in education (CRE, 1992), para 33.

33 See DES Circular 11/88 Annex B, cited at para 26 of the Code of Practice for the elimination of racial discrimination in education (CRE, 1989).

34 Ibid.

35 See, eg, 'Medical School Admissions: Report of a Formal Investigation into St George's Hospital Medical School' (CRE, 1988).

29.29 The CRE has issued a non-statutory code of practice for the elimination of discrimination in education which gives some guidance on the circumstances in which discrimination at the admission stage might occur.[36] In particular it notes that 'if admissions were determined by catchment areas that disproportionately excluded pupils from particular racial groups, this would be unlawful, unless it could be justified (for example, on nearness to the school)'.[37] Furthermore, it advises that 'generally, the placement of English as a second language (ESL) pupils in separate centres and their removal from mainstream schooling cannot be justified and constitutes indirect discrimination'.[38]

Uniforms

29.30 It might be indirectly racially discriminatory and unlawful, if not justified, to require a pupil to wear a particular uniform for admission into a school. In *Mandla v Dowell-Lee*[39] the House of Lords held that a requirement that a school uniform cap be worn as a condition of entry into a school amounted to indirect race discrimination, because turban-wearing Sikh boys could not in practice comply with the requirement. In that case the requirement to wear a school cap was held not to be justifiable and thus the condition was unlawful having regard to the terms of RRA 1976 s17. Similarly, a rule that girls wear skirts and/or do not wear headgear could have the effect of excluding a considerably higher proportion of Muslim girls (who may chose to wear trousers and the hijab), thus constituting indirect discrimination against certain racial groups.[40]

29.31 Case-law at the moment indicates that different uniform requirements as between boys and girls is unlikely to constitute discrimination. This is because the courts have held that the imposition of different dress codes on men and women is unlikely to amount to the

36 CRE, 1989 and 1992. A similar code has been issued for Scotland (Code of Practice for the Elimination of Racial Discrimination in Education – Scotland, 1989). Further recommendations can be found in 'Learning for All: Standards for Racial quality in Schools' (CRE, 2000), available at www.cre.org.uk.

37 Para 31.

38 Para 32. The CRE has undertaken a formal investigation into this practice (see 'Teaching English as a second language: Report of a formal investigation in Calderdale LEA' (CRE, 1996)), to which the code of practice refers.

39 [1983] 2 AC 548; [1983] IRLR 209. The House of Lords held in this important case that Sikhs constituted an ethnic group for the purposes of the RRA 1976.

40 'Equality and School Uniforms' (EOC, 2000) para 30, available at www.eoc.org.uk.

less favourable treatment of either sex. This issue is discussed at para 3.33. The Equal Opportunities Commission (EOC) has, however, issued a briefing on school uniforms in which it states that 'out of date stereotypes should not dictate appropriate dress for girls and boys' and gives advice about how to deal with differential dress codes (for example, 'no trousers' rules for girls).[41]

Educational benefits, facilities and services

29.32 The SDA 1975 and the RRA 1976 make it unlawful for an educational establishment to discriminate in the way it affords a pupil access to any benefits, facilities or services or by refusing or deliberately omitting to afford them access to them.[42] Any discrimination in the provision of any benefits related to the provision of education will, therefore, be unlawful. Examples might include:

- allocating work experience placements in accordance with racial or gender stereotypes;
- determining applications for grants, bursaries or scholarships on the grounds of race or sex or by the application of indirectly discriminatory criteria;
- the charging of higher fees for overseas students by private schools or other educational institutions.[43]

Discrimination in respect of other services connected with education might be unlawful under the SDA 1975 and the RRA 1976, for example in the statementing of special educational needs. A failure to provide a pupil with a statement of special educational needs or indeed the provision of such a statement on the grounds of race or sex or upon indirectly discriminatory criteria would be unlawful.

Exceptions

29.33 SDA 1975 s26 provides an exception from s22 (unlawful discrimination in relation to educational establishments) and s25 (general statutory duty,[44] see below) in respect of single-sex establishments. Single-sex establishments are establishments which admit pupils of one sex only or which admit pupils of the opposite sex only excep-

41 'Equality and School Uniforms' (EOC, 2000) para 30.
42 SDA 1975 s22(c) and RRA 1976 s17(c).
43 The charging of higher fees will only be lawful where it is done under statutory or ministerial authority – RRA 1976 ss41 and 42. See code of practice, paras 53–58.

tionally or in comparatively small numbers to particular courses of instruction or teaching classes.[45] A similar exception is made in respect of schools which permit only one sex to board but which are otherwise not single-sex establishments.[46]

29.34 Where a school is a 'single-sex establishment', notwithstanding that it takes pupils of the opposite sex in comparatively small numbers for particular courses of instruction or teaching classes, the fact that pupils of one sex are confined to particular courses of instruction or teaching classes does not amount to an unlawful act within SDA 1975 s22(c)(i) and does not contravene the duty in s25.[47] Provision is made for single-sex establishments which are becoming co-educational, which may maintain discriminatory admissions during a transitional period.[48]

29.35 The unlawful acts created in the employment field and the general statutory duties do not apply to any further or higher education course in physical education.[49]

Detriment and harassment

29.36 SDA 1975 s22(c)(ii) and RRA 1976 s17(c)(ii) respectively make it unlawful for an educational establishment to discriminate by subjecting a pupil to a 'detriment'. This would certainly cover harassment on the grounds of sex or race by teachers and other pupils. Harassment, including in the field of education, is dealt with fully in chapter 28.

29.37 Other discriminatory treatment that might constitute a detriment[50] would include:

- refusing to enter pupil for a particular examination;
- encouraging pupils to take subjects or allocating pupils to subjects based on gender or racial stereotyping;
- compiling assessments, reports, pupil profiles or records of achievement in a discriminatory way; and
- allocating pupils to teaching groups (sets or streams) in a discriminatory way.

44 And SDA 1975 s25A.
45 Ibid s26(1).
46 Ibid s26(2).
47 Or ibid s25A.
48 Ibid s27.
49 Ibid s28.
50 There may be an overlap between SDA 1975 s22(c)(i) and (ii) and RRA 1976 s17(c)(i) and (ii).

Schools exclusions

29.38 SDA 1975 s22(c)(ii) and RRA 1976 s17(c)(ii) provide that it is unlawful for an educational establishment to discriminate by excluding a pupil. Such an exclusion might be temporary or permanent. As stated above, there is significant evidence of discrimination in exclusions. Most of the evidence points to the disproportionately high level of exclusions of black boys. However, there is evidence too that girls are an 'under estimated minority' in exclusions.[51] Advisers should always check to see whether a claim might be made in both sex and race discrimination in appropriate cases.

29.39 The CRE has issued 'Exclusion from School and Racial Equality: A Good Practice Guide' which recommends, among other things, that schools:[52]

- introduce a behaviour policy which should include a disciplinary framework which ensures that exclusion, with the disruption, stigma and financial loss it brings, remains a last resort;
- involve pupils in drawing up a code of conduct setting out the system of rewards for good behaviour and sanctions against unacceptable behaviour which will be used at school;
- draw up 'home-school contracts';
- introduce a pastoral care policy which includes measures to provide pupils with a sense of well-being and of belonging to the school community;
- identify special educational needs and always consider whether disciplinary problems stem from unrecognised special needs;
- introduce an equal opportunities policy;
- provide appropriate training for staff;
- monitor disciplinary incidents and exclusions by reference to the ethnic origins of the pupils concerned and analyse the data concerned to identify any patterns which might indicate that the school's policies or practices should be changed.

The Good Practice Guide has no statutory force but it is likely that a court would treat seriously a failure to comply with any relevant recommendations contained within it. It might usefully be adapted for sex discrimination cases.

51 National Children's Bureau ,'Not a Problem? Girls and School Exclusion', reported in (2002) *Guardian* 9 January.

52 CRE, 1997.

Bringing proceedings

29.40 As stated above, proceedings under SDA 1975 ss22 and 23 and RRA 1976 ss17 and 18 must be brought against the 'responsible body'. Proceedings are brought in the county court.[53]

29.41 The time limit for bringing proceedings is different as between the SDA 1975 and the RRA 1976 (following amendments to the RRA 1976 introduced by the RRAA 2000). The time limit for bringing proceedings under the education provisions of the SDA 1975 is eight months.[53a] The time limit for bringing proceedings under the RRA 1976 is six months.[54] In respect of a claim under the SDA 1975's education provisions (ss22 and 23), proceedings may not be instituted unless the claimant has given notice of her claim to the Secretary of State and either the Secretary of State has by notice informed the claimant that he does not require further time to consider the matter, or the period of two months has elapsed since the notification was given.[55] The object behind this provision was to permit the Secretary of State to make observations on (and presumably in appropriate cases to remedy) any claim of discrimination before it was litigated. However the practice has become no more than a formality and in the usual case the Secretary of State does not respond at all, or responds with a mere acknowledgement of the notice. The RRAA 2000 amended the RRA 1976 to repeal the requirement that a claimant wait for the Secretary of State to request further time or for the period of two months to elapse before issuing proceedings and excluded from the requirement altogether claims against certain institutions.[56] Save in the case of proceedings against such institutions the RRA 1976 now requires a claimant to give notice to the Secretary of State before instituting proceedings, but does not require him or her to delay instituting them thereafter.[57]

Other unlawful acts

29.42 SDA 1975 s23 and RRA 1976 s18 provide that it is unlawful for a local education authority,[58] in carrying out any of its functions which fall

53 Ibid s66 and RRA 1976 s57. See further chapter 32.
53a Ibid s76(2).
54 RRA 1976 s68(2).
55 RRA 1976 s66(5).
56 RRA 1976 s57(5) and (5A).
57 Ibid s57(5).
58 In Scotland as well as England and Wales: SDA 1975 s23(1) and RRA 1976 s18(1) and (2).

outside ss22 and 17 respectively, to do any act which constitutes sex or racial discrimination.[59] *R v Birmingham City Council ex p EOC*[60] involved a challenge under SDA 1975 s23 to the provision by the council of selective education. The council made provision for 600 children to enter voluntary-aided grammar schools. As a result of the policies of the schools, 390 places were allocated to boys while only 210 were allocated to girls. The effect was that a girl with a borderline test result had a substantially smaller chance of obtaining education at a selective school than a boy. The House of Lords made a declaration that the council was in breach of s23.

29.43 SDA 1975 s23A and RRA 1976 s18A make it unlawful for the Learning Skills Council for England, the National Council for Education and Training for Wales, and the Higher Education Funding Council for England or Wales, to do any act which constitutes sex or race discrimination in carrying out their functions under the Education Acts and the Learning and Skills Act 2000. Sections 23B and 18B of the Acts make similar provision in relation to Scotland.

29.44 SDA 1975 s23D and RRA 1976 s18D make it unlawful for the Teacher Training Agency to do any act which constitutes sex or race discrimination in carrying out its functions under the Education Act 1994.

29.45 SDA 1975 s25 imposes a general statutory duty upon local education authorities (LEAs), education authorities in Scotland and certain of the responsible bodies for educational institutions including schools maintained by LEAs. This duty is 'to secure that facilities for education provided by it, and any ancillary benefits or services, are provided without sex discrimination'.[61] Breach of this duty does not give rise to any claim in compensation by an individual, individuals being restricted to bringing claims in the county court under SDA 1975 ss22 and 23.[62]

29.46 RRA 1976 s71, as amended by the RRAA 2000, provides that every body specified by Sch 1A to the Act 'shall in carrying out its functions, have due regard to the need to eliminate unlawful racial

59 This would appear to exclude victimisation. For the meaning of 'sex discrimination' and 'race discrimination' see SDA 1975 s5 and RRA 1976 s3.

60 [1989] AC 1155; [1989] IRLR 173.

61 See note 53 above. A similar duty is imposed upon certain institutions concerned with post-16 education and training by SDA 1975 s25A.

62 *R v Birmingham ex p EOC* [1989] AC 1155; [1989] IRLR 173, para 17 (per Lord Griffiths) and SDA 1975 s25(4). And see SDA 1975 s25(2) for the powers of the Secretary of State in relation to the performance of the duty in England and Wales (s25(3) and (5) for Scotland).

discrimination and to promote equality of opportunity and good relations between persons of different racial groups'. Schedule 1A[63] includes, among others, local authorities and the governing bodies of schools maintained by LEAs.[64] The RRAA 2000 has also amended the RRA 1976 to introduce new and broad statutory duties upon specified bodies.[65]

29.47 By an order introduced under the RRA 1976, obligations are imposed upon specified bodies concerned with education (for example, certain Funding Councils) to produce Race Equality Schemes by 31 May 2002. There is no such obligation on LEAs or the governing bodies of schools maintained by LEAs and the like. However, LEAs and schools maintained by LEAs, among others, are obliged to prepare written statements of policies for promoting race equality and to undertake impact assessments ethnic monitoring.[66]

29.48 Other provisions which may be relevant to cases in the education field, are SDA 1975 s29 and RRA 1976 s20, which prohibit discrimination in the provision of goods, facilities and services, SDA 1975 s30 and RRA 1976 s21 which prohibit discrimination in the management of premises, and RRA 1976 s19B which prohibits discrimination by public authorities in relation to ancillary benefits and other matters falling outside RRA 1976 s17.[67]

Planning

Race Relations Act 1976

29.49 The RRA 1976 (but not the SDA 1975) makes specific provision in relation to discrimination by planning authorities. Section 19A of the Act makes it 'unlawful for a planning authority to discriminate against a person in carrying out their planning functions'. This provision was inserted by the Housing and Planning Act 1986.[68] All authorities in England, Wales and Scotland are covered,[69] as are all

63 As amended by the RRA 1976 (General Statutory Duty) Order 2001 SI No 3457.

64 Boards of management in Scotland.

65 RRA 1976 s71 and Sch 1A as amended by RRA 1976 (General Statutory Duty) Order 2001.

66 RRA 1976 (Statutory Duties) Order 2001 SI No 3458.

67 RRA 1976 s19B does not apply if the act is made unlawful by another provision of the RRA 1976: s19B(6). SDA 1975 ss78–79 make provision for discriminatory educational charitable instruments and SDA 1975 s34 makes wider provision.

68 Section 55.

69 RRA 1976 s19A(2).

planning functions under the Town and Country Planning Act 1990[70] and related planning statutes.[71]

29.50 There has been, as far as we are aware, only one successful case brought under the planning provisions. This is the case of *Davis v Bath and North East Somerset DC*[72] in which the county court found that the claimant had been subjected to direct race discrimination when the council's planning officers repeatedly obstructed his applications for planning permission in relation to the development of a site. The council paid into court the sum of £750,000 which was awarded to the claimant with costs.

29.51 The CRE has issued some guidance on discrimination in the planning field. This guidance is included in the report of the Wirral Town Planning Institute (CRE Working Party) produced before the amendment to the Act bringing planning authorities specifically within its scope.[73] The report recommends, among other things, that local authorities should:

- ensure that they and all their staff are aware of the content of and their legal position under the RRA 1976;
- continually re-assess their policies and practice to see if discrimination is occurring;
- ensure that valid information is collected on racial groups in order to inform their assessment of their policies and practice to see if discrimination is occurring;
- monitor the impact of their policies on racial minorities.

The report further advises that town planners should be aware of the diverse characteristics of racial groups in their area and of how existing policies of land use and development control may fail to reflect this diversity. This guidance has no statutory force but it is likely that a court would treat seriously a failure to comply with any relevant recommendations contained within it.

29.52 Any planning functions falling outside RRA 1976 s19A might fall within ss19B[74] or 20 of the Act. If in doubt, proceedings should be brought under all of these provisions.

70 And the Town and Country Planning (Scotland) Act 1997.

71 RRA 1976 s19A(3).

72 Case 9324149, Bristol County Court, 2001 (unreported).

73 CRE, 1984.

74 RRA 1976 s19B(6) provides that s19B will not apply if the act complained of is made unlawful by another provision.

Bringing proceedings

29.53 Proceedings in relation to planning complaints, like other Pt III claims, are brought in the county court.

Public authorities

Introduction

29.54 The Stephen Lawrence inquiry report defined 'institutional racism' as:

> ... the collective failure of an organisation to provide an appropriate and professional service to people because of their colour, culture or ethnic origin. It can be seen or detected in processes, attitudes and behaviour which amount to discrimination through unwitting prejudice, ignorance, thoughtlessness, and racist stereotyping which disadvantage minority ethnic people.[75]

The inquiry found institutional racism in the investigation of Stephen Lawrence's death and in the treatment of his family and of Duwayne Brooks (Stephen's friend and witness to his murder). Furthermore, the inquiry team cautioned that:

> ... [their] conclusions as to the Police Services should not lead to complacency in other institutions and organisations. Collective failure is apparent in many of them, including the Criminal Justice system. It is incumbent upon every institution to examine their policies and the outcome of their policies and practices to guard against disadvantaging any section of our communities.[76]

29.55 The impetus for change to the RRA 1976 to enable legal challenge to such racism became irresistible and the RRAA 2000 followed. It inserted into the RRA 1976 a new s19B which makes it 'unlawful for a public authority in carrying out any functions of the authority to do any act which constitutes discrimination'. Much of such discrimination had been placed beyond the scope of the anti-discrimination legislation by narrow judicial interpretation of its provisions (particularly those concerned with discrimination in the provision of goods, facilities and services).[77]

29.56 The SDA 1975 contains no provision equivalent to RRA 1976 s19B.

75 Sir William Macpherson of Cluny, *The Stephen Lawrence Inquiry* (Cm 4262-I, 1999), para 6.34.

76 Ibid para 46.27.

77 See para 29.90 below.

'Public authority'

29.57 'Public authority', for the purposes of RRA 1976 s19B, includes any person 'certain of whose functions are functions of a public nature'.[78] In relation to a particular act, however, a person is not a public authority by virtue only of the fact that certain of its functions are functions of a public nature if the nature of the particular act under challenge is private. This means, for example, that a private company providing security services to a prison might be a public authority for the purposes of the RRA 1976 because certain of its functions are functions of a public nature. It might be liable under RRA 1976 s19B if it were to carry out any such function in a discriminatory way. But in respect of those parts of its functions which are of a private nature (for example, selecting employees, opening bank accounts, purchasing stationery, etc), it would not be a public authority for the purposes of s19B.

29.58 Certain bodies are excluded from the meaning of 'public authority' for the purpose of s19B. These are:

- either House of Parliament;
- a person exercising functions in connection with proceedings in Parliament;
- the security services
- the secret intelligence service;
- government communications headquarters;
- any unit or part of a unit of any of the naval, military or air forces of the Crown which is for the time being required by the Secretary of State to assist the government communications headquarters in carrying out its functions.

Examples of public functions

29.59 RRA 1976 s19B is very wide indeed. It does not limit (subject to what is said below under exceptions) the meaning of 'any functions'. The sort of functions which might for the first time be caught by the RRA 1976 include the following:

- the functions of the police relating to stop and search, arrests, criminal investigations, and the detention of suspects;
- the regulatory and law enforcement powers of bodies such as Customs and Excise, local authority officers, tax inspectors,

78 RRA 1976 s19B(2).

trading standards officers and the Health and Safety Executive including in the collection of taxes, the investigation of frauds and the inspection of residential care homes;
- the allocation of prisoners in prisons and the imposition of prison discipline;
- the preparation of pre-sentence reports by the Probation Service;
- certain core functions of the Immigration and Nationality Directorate of Home Office and the functions of private bodies performing immigration functions such as running immigration detention centres;[79]
- the granting of licences by licensing authorities such as those for street trading, gaming and liquor; and
- certain determinations by mental health authorities.[80]

The police

29.60 By far the most significant impact of the RRAA 2000 and the insertion of RRA 1976 s19B is likely to be in relation to the police. As stated above, the amendments to the RRA 1976 have the effect that it is now possible to bring proceedings in race discrimination against the police in respect of those acts done by them and falling within the exercise of their discretion as constables (for example, arrest, detention and charging).

29.61 The CRE and the Association of Chief Police Officers have issued a joint practical guide to policing and racial equality: 'Policing and Racial Equality: a Practical Guide to the ACPO Strategy Policy document, setting the standards for policing: meeting community expectation'.[81] This provides guidance on securing racial equality and service delivery. It does not have any statutory force but it is likely that a court would treat seriously a failure to comply with any relevant recommendations contained within it. It recommends, among other things, that:

- unit commanders and department heads ensure that the identification of community needs and priorities take full account of the ethnic composition of the area;
- unit commanders and department heads ensure the satisfactory implementation of non-discriminatory practices and procedures;

79 Though see the exemptions below.

80 See 'Strengthening the Race Relations Act' (CRE, 2000), available at www.cre.org.uk and www.homeoffice.gov.uk/raceact/outracdi.htm.

81 CRE, 1993.

- unit commanders and department heads ensure that the agreed ethnic monitoring records are kept and regularly evaluated;
- individual officers are fully aware of their central professional responsibility to carry out all their duties in a fair and non-discriminatory way;
- ethnic monitoring is incorporated at the earliest relevant stage of criminal procedures and, in particular, custody officers record their perception of the ethnic origin of the arrested person on the custody record;
- ethnic monitoring procedures are used in areas in which police behaviour may be modified as a result (these include stop and search, the searching of premises, arrests, etc).

Vicarious liability for police officers

29.62 Until the RRA 1976 was amended by the RRAA 2000, a chief constable was not liable under the RRA 1976 for the actions of his or her individual officers. This is because of the unusual position of police officers who are 'employees', but hold the common law office of constable. The RRA 1976 made provision for an employer to be liable for the discriminatory acts of its employees, but did not make provision for chief constables to be liable for the actions of their constables.[83] Thus, any claimant wishing to bring proceedings under the RRA 1976 against the police had to do so against the individual officer concerned.[84] Identification of the constable concerned might be problematic, and a remedy against an individual constable difficult to enforce.

29.63 New RRA 1976 s76A provides that the holding of the office of constable as a member of the police force or as a special constable is to be treated as employment by the chief officer of police. Furthermore, anything done by a person holding such an office in the performance, or purported performance, of his functions shall be treated as done in the course of that employment for the purposes of RRA 1976 s32 (which imposes vicarious liability on employers for the discrimin-

83 There was limited provision for liability to arise under the employment provisions as against a chief officer of police: see chapter 31.

84 And there was limited opportunity to bring proceedings under the unamended RRA 1976 as against a constable outside the employment field. RRA 1976 s20 would provide the only route so to do and its scope has been narrowly prescribed by the courts, see below.

atory acts of their employees).[85] A defence is available to an employer in such circumstances by virtue of RRA 1976 s32(3) (see further chapter 31), but it is unlikely to be made out unless the chief constable has complied with the CRE/ACPO guidance described above.

29.64 The amendments to the RRA 1976 mean that a claimant bringing proceedings under s19B (or indeed any other provision of the RRA 1976) can now bring those proceedings against the relevant chief constable as well as the individual police officer concerned. Section 76A applies only in respect of discriminatory acts occurring after the coming into force of the relevant provisions of the RRAA 2000, namely 2 April 2001. In respect of acts occurring before that date, the individual officers only will be liable. This lacuna remains in the SDA 1975 to which the RRAA 2000 does not apply.[86]

Exceptions to Race Relations Act 1976 s19B

Introduction

29.65 It will not be surprising to readers familiar with the development of the law of race discrimination to discover that there are wide – and discriminatory – exemptions from the scope of RRA 1976 s19B.

Judicial acts

29.66 RRA 1976 s19C provides for exceptions from s19B in respect of judicial and legislative acts.

Racist immigration laws

29.67 RRA 1976 s19C further provides that s19B does not apply 'to any act of, or relating to, imposing a requirement, or giving an express authorisation ... in relation to the carrying out of immigration and nationality functions' of a kind mentioned in s19D(3).

29.68 RRA 1976 s19D provides, in particular, that '[s]ection 19B does not make it unlawful for a relevant person to discriminate against another person on grounds of nationality or ethnic or national origins in carrying out immigration and nationality functions'. A 'relevant person', for these purposes, is a minister of the Crown acting personally or any other person acting in accordance with a relevant

85 Provision is also made for treating the holding of such office as employment for the purposes of the employment provisions in RRA 1976 Pt II, see para 31.34. For full discussion of vicarious liability see chapter 31.

86 *Chief Constable of Bedfordshire Police* v *Liversedge* [2002] IRLR 15.

authorisation.[87] A 'relevant authorisation' is defined by RRA 1976 s19D(3) as 'a requirement imposed or express authorisation given with respect to a particular case or class of case, by a Minister of the Crown acting personally or with respect to a particular class of case by...[specified enactments[88]] or by any instrument made under or by virtue of any of those enactments'. 'Immigration and nationality functions' are the functions which may be exercised under the main immigration statutes.[89]

29.69 Thus, RRA 1976 s19D permits the relevant minister to discriminate on grounds of nationality or ethnic or national origins (but not colour or race), and provides that any other person may also do so as long as he or she is acting in accordance with a relevant authorisation. This obviously permits widespread discrimination in the exercising of immigration functions, subject only to the making of a relevant authorisation. Two such authorisations have been issued.[90] The first allows discrimination against certain nationalities and the second against various ethnic and national groups – namely Kurds, Roma, Albanians, Tamils, Pontic Greeks (Greeks from the Black Sea region), Somalis, Afghans and ethnic Chinese with travel documents issued by Malaysia or Japan.

29.70 The apparent rationale behind the authorisations is that these groups are deemed more likely to be bogus asylum seekers or illegal immigrants. The authorisations are currently being challenged as unlawful by a judicial review application supported by Liberty, a human rights organisation.[91] In the meantime, on 11 June 2002 the Home Office announced to Parliament that the second authorisation was revoked.[92] They are arguably unlawful because of their breadth, and because of the fact that certain of the groups they identify might be racial groups by reference to colour and race, rather than only nationality, ethnic or national origins. As mentioned above, s19D only permits discrimination on the latter three grounds in relation to immigration. It might well also be inconsistent with the European Convention

87 RRA 1976 s19D(2).
88 The main immigration statutes, ibid s19D(5).
89 Ibid s19D(4) and (5).
90 Race Relations (Immigration and Asylum) Authorisation 2001 made on 27 March 2001, permitting discrimination of the grounds of nationality in certain circumstances and Race Relations (Immigration and Asylum) (No 2) Authorisation 2001 made on 23 April 2001, permitting discrimination against certain ethnic and national groups.
91 See (2002) *Guardian* 2 January.
92 Though it will still apply in respect of decisions before that date.

rights scheduled to the Human Rights Act (HRA) 1998 (see further chapter 9).

29.71 It should be noted that the authorisations and the s19D exemption have been subjected to particular criticism because parliament has, in any case, already made provision for exempting from the scope of the RRA 1976 large parts of the regulatory provisions governing immigration. RRA 1976 ss41 and 42 provide that the RRA 1976 will not render any act unlawful if it is done:

- in pursuance of any enactment or order in council;
- in pursuance of any instrument made under any enactment by a minister;
- in order to comply with any condition or requirement imposed by a minister by virtue of any enactment;
- if it is an act of discrimination against another on the basis of that other's nationality or place of ordinary residence or the length of time for which he or she has been present or resident in or outside the UK or an area within the UK, if that it is done:
  a) in pursuance of any arrangements made by or with the approval of or for the time being approved by a minister, or
  b) in order to comply with any condition imposed by a minister;
- for the purpose of safeguarding national security if the doing of that act was justified by that purpose.

These provisions are considered in chapter 11. In the present context their extent is such that, even leaving aside s19B, any act done in pursuance of the Immigration Rules is excluded from scrutiny under the RRA 1976, and most other regulatory provisions governing immigration are also outside the scope of that Act.

29.72 RRA 1976 s19E, as amended by the RRAA 2000, requires that a monitor be appointed by the Secretary of State to oversee the exceptions provided by ss19C and D in relation to immigration and nationality cases. The monitor, who is not to be a member of the Secretary of State's staff, is to monitor 'the likely effect on the operation of the exception in section 19D of any relevant authorisation relating to the carrying out of immigration and nationality functions which has been given by a minister acting personally and the operation of that exception in relation to acts which have been done by a person acting in accordance with such an authorisation.[93] He or she is obliged to make an annual report on the discharge of his or her functions.[94] As far as we are aware, no monitor has yet been appointed and, in that respect,

93 RRA 1976 s19E(1) and (3).
94 s19E(4).

the Secretary of State is in breach of his obligations under the RRA 1976 as amended.

Criminal prosecutions

29.73 By RRA 1976 s19F of the amended RAA 1976, s19B does not apply to a decision *not* to institute criminal proceedings, to any act done for the purposes of enabling such a decision to be made, to a decision not to continue criminal proceedings, to any act done for the purposes of enabling that decision to be made, or to any act done for the purposes of securing that proceedings are not continued.

29.74 The s19F exception does not extend to a decision *to* institute criminal proceedings or to continue them, or to any act done for the purposes of enabling such decisions to be made. The effect of the exception is that, were the police to decline to charge or the Crown Prosecution Service to decline to prosecute a person suspected of a racially motivated crime, that decision and any acts related to it may not be the subject of challenge under s19B. But a decision to charge or to prosecute a person in circumstances in which a person of a different racial group has not been charged or prosecuted will lend itself to challenge under RRA 1976 s19B. A decision, for example, to charge a black man for assault in circumstances in which he says he was defending himself against an attack by a white assailant or group of white assailants will be open to challenge under s19B, if, for example, the white assailant or assailants were not the subject of charge or prosecution. This is because the black suspect will be complaining not of a decision not to prosecute the white assailant or assailants but rather a decision to charge and prosecute him. This will fall within the scope of s19B and outside the scope of the exception in s19E.

29.75 There is still, nevertheless, concern about the breadth of the exception in s19F. The expression 'any act done' for the purpose of enabling a decision to prosecute or to discontinue proceedings would seem, on its face, to permit discriminatory acts done by the police at very early stages of an investigation. However, the purpose of the exception appears to be to ensure that the role of the courts in determining guilt remains sacrosanct.[95]

Other exceptions

29.76 Other exemptions, which apply more generally to unlawful acts created outside the employment field, are dealt with below.

95 See, eg, Lord Bassan, HL Debates col 180, 14 December 1999.

Bringing proceedings

29.77 RRA 1976 s57 provides that proceedings under RRA 1976 s19B are to be taken in the county court.

29.78 Provisions apply in particular to claims under s19B. Where a claim is made under s19B in respect of an act done by a person carrying out public investigator functions or functions as a public prosecutor, the county court may only make an award of damages or a declaration,[96] and has no power to grant any other remedy[97] unless the court is satisfied that the remedy concerned would not prejudice a criminal investigation, a decision to institute criminal proceedings or any criminal proceedings. By RRA 1976 s57(4C) and (4D) a court is obliged to grant a stay[98] of any proceedings under s57 on the application of a party, where the grounds of the application are that the proceedings would cause prejudice to particular criminal proceedings, a criminal investigation, or a decision to institute criminal proceedings, unless the court is satisfied that the continuance of the proceedings would not result in the prejudice alleged.

29.79 In respect of claims arising under s19B out of alleged acts of discrimination committed by an immigration authority under the main immigration statutes or an appeal to an immigration appellate body in respect of the same, proceedings may not be brought in the county court under RRA 1976 s57(1) if the question whether the act was unlawful by virtue of s19B was, or could have been raised in proceedings on an appeal under the Special Immigration Appeals Commission Act 1997 or the Immigration and Asylum Act 1999, or it has been decided in such proceedings that the act was not unlawful. The object of this exception is to ensure that all complaints of racial discrimination in relation to immigration decisions are dealt with by the immigration appellate authorities as part of the 'one stop' immigration appeals procedure established by the Immigration and Asylum Act 1999.

29.80 Those cases with a national security element must be subject to appeal to the Special Immigration Appeals Commission (under the Special Immigration Appeals Commission Act 1997). RRA 1976 s57A(3) provides that, where it has been decided in the relevant immigration proceedings that an act to which the claim relates was unlawful by virtue of s19B, a claim might be brought under s57(1) (ie,

96 Or in Scotland, a declarator.

97 RRA 1976 s57(4A).

98 Or sist in Scotland.

in the county court), and that court will treat that act as an act which is unlawful by virtue of s19B for the purposes of the proceedings before it. This will not, however, affect the validity of any decision made by the immigration authority concerned.[99] Judicial review proceedings are, however, available to challenge immigration decisions in the normal way.

29.81 RRA 1976 s65(7) provides that the questionnaire procedure does not apply in relation to any proceedings before the immigration appellate authorities.[100] Furthermore, a court is not entitled to draw an adverse inference from a failure to respond to the questionnaire procedure when, at the doing of any relevant act, the respondent was carrying out functions as a public investigator or public prosecutor, and reasonably believed that a reply or a different reply would be likely to prejudice any criminal investigation, any decision to institute criminal proceedings, or any criminal proceedings, or would reveal the reasons behind a decision not to institute, or a decision not to continue, criminal proceedings.[101]

Goods, facilities and services

Introduction

29.82 SDA 1975 s29 and RRA 1976 s20 make it unlawful, in certain circumstances, for a person to discriminate in the provision of goods, facilities and services.

29.83 SDA 1975 s29 provides that:

(1) It is unlawful for any person concerned with the provision (for payment or not) of goods, facilities or services to the public or a section of the public to discriminate against a woman who seeks to obtain or use those goods, facilities or services –
   (a) by refusing or deliberately omitting to provide her with any of them, or
   (b) by refusing or deliberately omitting to provide her with goods, facilities or services of the like quality, in the like manner and on the like terms as are normal in his case in relation to male members of the public or (where she belongs to a section of the public) to male members of that section.

RRA 1976 s20 is in materially the same terms.

99 RRA 1976 s57A(4).
100 Ibid s65(7).
101 Ibid s65(4A) and (B).

'Goods, facilities and services'

29.84 'Goods' are not defined by either the SDA 1975 or the RRA 1976. As far as we are aware, there has been no contentious litigation around the meaning of this word and it should be and is given its ordinary meaning.

29.85 SDA 1975 s29(2) and RRA 1976 s20(2) provide a non-exhaustive list of examples of facilities and services for the purposes of ss29(1) and 20(1) of the Acts. The examples are as follows:

- access to and use of any place which members of the public are permitted to enter;
- accommodation in a hotel, boarding house or other similar establishment;
- facilities by way of banking or insurance or for grants, loans, credits or finance;
- facilities for education;
- facilities for entertainment, recreation or refreshments;
- facilities for transport or travel;
- the services of any profession or trade, or any local or other public authority.

It can be seen at once that there is on the face of it an overlap between the 'goods, facilities and services' provisions of the SDA 1975 and the RRA 1976 and other provisions, in particular:

- SDA 1975 ss22–23 and RRA 1976 ss17 and 18 (education);
- RRA 1976 s19B (public authorities);
- SDA 1975 s30 and RRA 1976 s21 (premises).

It will often be the case that proceedings will be issued under more than one of the provisions of the SDA 1975 and the RRA 1976 in proceedings in the county court.[102]

29.86 The words 'facilities' and 'services' are given very wide meaning and are certainly wide enough to cover discrimination by pubs and (non-membership) clubs[103] and services provided by a doctor, nursery, bank or other financial institution.

102 It should be noted that RRA 1976 s19B does not apply to acts which are made unlawful by other provisions of the RRA 1976, so while it might be prudent to bring proceedings under other provisions if there is doubt about whether or not the act complained of falls within the scope of s19B, if it is found to be so s19B will not apply. (See, eg, RRA 1976 s23 for other limitations.)

103 See para 29.119 below for clubs.

29.87 In *Gill v El Vino Co Ltd*[104] a well-known wine bar in London was found to have discriminated against the women plaintiffs contrary to SDA 1975 s29 when its staff refused to serve them at the bar but required them to sit at tables if they wished to drink in the wine bar.

29.88 In *James v Eastleigh BC*[105] the House of Lords overturned a decision of the county court and Court of Appeal and it held that concessionary entrance charges offered to women over the age of 60 and men over the age of 65 (the discrimination reflecting state pensionable ages) were unlawful discrimination under SDA 1975 s29:

> The words 'goods, facilities or services' are not defined in the Act. They must be given their ordinary and natural meaning. 'Goods' are any movable property, including merchandise or wares. 'Facilities' include any opportunity for obtaining some benefit or for doing something. 'Services' refer to any conduct tending to the welfare or advantage of other people, especially conduct which supplies their needs. Each of these expressions is deliberately vague and general; taken together, they cover a very wide range of human activity.[106]

29.89 The EOC has issued a series of useful briefings on sex equality in the provision of 'goods, facilities and services'. They are available on the EOC website[107] and include:

- 'Sex Equality and Finance' (2001) which gives examples of the circumstances in which differential treatment in relation to the provision of financial services and facilities will be unlawful. These include the refusal of a mortgage to a woman because she is pregnant; the refusal to put a woman's name first when opening a joint account; the offer of windfall payments and voting rights to the first-named account holders of joint accounts; the refusal of a loan to a woman because she works part-time, etc.
- 'Sex Equality in Pubs and Night Clubs' (2000) which gives some illustrations of the circumstances in which differential treatment by pubs and night clubs will be unlawful. These include the offer of free admission to women only, or the offer of free or reduced-price drinks to women, and a refusal to serve women drinks in pint glasses.
- 'Sex Equality and Services' (2000) which gives some illustrations of the circumstances in which differential treatment in the pro-

104 [1983] 1 All ER 398; [1983] IRLR 206.

105 [1990] 2 AC 751; [1990] IRLR 288.

106 A Lester and G Bindman, *Race and Law* (Penguin, 1972) p260.

107 www.eoc.org.uk.

vision of services will be unlawful. These include the provision of reserved prime car parking spaces for women only (for reasons of safety).[108]

Facilities and services provided by public authorities

29.90 Although the words 'facilities and services' have (given their ordinary and natural meaning) wide reach, the courts have narrowed the scope of SDA 1975 s29 and RRA 1976 s20 by a series of decisions in cases arising in the public sector. SDA 1975 s29(2)(g) and RRA 1976 s20(2)(g) provide that 'facilities' and 'services' include 'the services of any ... local or other public authority'. But the courts have given a narrow meaning to those expressions.

29.91 In *R v Immigration Appeal Tribunal ex p Kassam*[109] the Court of Appeal dismissed an appeal against a decision of the High Court refusing an application for judicial review against decisions of the Secretary of State and the Immigration Appeal Tribunal ordering the deportation of the applicant in circumstances alleged to be discriminatory. The court concluded that, when giving leave to enter or remain in the UK in the exercise of powers under the Immigration Act 1971 or rules made thereunder, the Secretary of State was not 'any person concerned with the provision ... of ... facilities ... to the public' for the purposes of SDA 1975 s29. The court reasoned that, read in their 'natural and ordinary meaning', the words in s29 were not aimed at the Secretary of State when he was exercising powers concerned with giving leave to enter or remain under the Immigration Act 1971:

> The word 'facilities' in that section is flanked on one side by the word 'goods' and on the other 'services'. This suggests to my mind that the word 'facilities' is not to be given a wholly unrestricted meaning but must be limited or confined to facilities that are akin to goods or services ... When the Secretary of State allows an immigrant to enter and stay in this country, he is granting a permission, he is not providing a facility.[110]

29.92 In *R v Entry Clearance Officer ex p Amin*[111] the House of Lords was concerned with the special voucher scheme under which certain Commonwealth citizens could apply to settle in the UK, so long as

108 See also 'Good Practice Guide: Service Delivery', available at www.eoc.org.uk/cseng/advice/ service_delivery.asp.

109 [1980] 1 WLR 1037.

110 Ibid, per Stevenson LJ at 1044.

111 [1983] 2 AC 818.

they were the head of a household. Ms Amin complained that this indirectly discriminated against women and, in judicial review proceedings, relied upon SDA 1975 s29. The House of Lords, Lord Fraser giving the leading judgment, rejected the complaint under s29 on the grounds that the SDA 1975's express coverage of acts done on or behalf of the Crown[112] extended only to acts of a similar kind to those which might be done by a private person.[113] Thus the special voucher scheme was outside the scope of s20, as were any decisions involving the exercise of executive discretion.

29.93 The courts have not always been consistent in the approach they have taken to public authority functions and the exercising of executive discretion. In *Savjani v Inland Revenue Commissioners*[114] the Court of Appeal distinguished *Kassam* in determining the question whether the Inland Revenue was concerned with the provision of services under RRA 1976 s20. The Court of Appeal concluded that the Inland Revenue did indeed provide such a service by the provision, dissemination and implementation of regulations which enabled the taxpayer to know that he was entitled to a deduction or a repayment of tax and which might entitle him to know how to satisfy the Inspector or the Board if he was so entitled and which would enable him to obtain the actual deduction or repayment which Parliament said he was to have.[115] And in *Alexander v Home Office*[116] a prisoner succeeded in a claim under s20 regarding the allocation of work to him. No point was taken, at least at the Court of Appeal, that his claim fell outside s20.[117]

29.94 More recently, in *Farah v Metropolitan Police Commissioner*,[118] a Somali refugee complained that she had been attacked in London by white youths who had set a dog on her and caused injury to her. When she summoned the police they arrested her on no good ground, rather than taking action against the white youths. Ms Farah had then

112 SDA 1975 s85 and see RRA 1976 s75.

113 [1983] 2 AC 818 at 834–835 in particular. The House of Lords also held that SDA 1975 s29 was concerned with the direct provision of facilities and services, not the mere grant of permission to use facilities. This seems particularly strange and unjustified by the wording of the SDA 1975 and RRA 1976 and is unlikely to be followed. See further indirect access to benefits, SDA 1975 s50 and RRA 1976 s40.

114 [1981] QB 458.

115 Ibid, per Templeman LJ at 467.

116 [1988] 1 WLR 968.

117 The Court of Appeal increased the award of compensation for injury to feelings from £50 to £500.

118 [1998] QB 65.

been charged with various criminal offences, including causing unnecessary suffering to a dog, but when she had appeared to answer the summons no evidence was offered against her. She was acquitted and commenced proceedings under RRA 1976 s20 contending (among other things) that the police officers had deliberately omitted to provide her with services she sought or services on the like terms to those normally provided by the officers to other members of the public and that criminal proceedings had been brought against her on racial grounds. The police applied to strike out her complaints of race discrimination on the ground that they did not disclose complaints justiciable under s20. The Court of Appeal concluded that those parts of a police officer's duties involving the provision of assistance to or the protection of members of the public amounted to services to the public for the purposes of s20.[119] In *Farah* the Court of Appeal was not concerned with whether or not the pursuing, arresting and charging of alleged criminals amounted to the provision of a service for the purposes of s20:[120]

> What is said is that the service sought by the plaintiff was that of protection and that she did not, because of her race, obtain the protection that others would have been afforded. It seems to me that that is no less the provision of a service than is the giving of directions or other information to a member of the public who seeks them.[121]

The Court of Appeal was particularly influenced by the words of Lord Fraser in *Amin* but nevertheless concluded that certain aspects of police officers' activities fell within the Act:

> Lord Fraser ... drew a distinction between acts done on behalf of the Crown which are of a kind similar to acts that might be done by a private person and acts done by a person holding statutory office in the course of formulating or carrying out government policy, the latter being quite different in kind from any act that would ever be done by a private person. The assertion in the pleading is that officers failed to react to the plaintiff's emergency telephone call, to investigate her account at the scene, and to afford her protection – all on account of her colour.
>
> These acts (or services) which the plaintiff sought from the police were, to my mind, acts which might have been done by a private

119 Prior to the amendments introduced by the RRAA 2000, however, vicarious liability did not attach to the Police Commissioner – or indeed any chief constable – for the discriminatory acts of his officers: see chapter 31.

120 [1998] QB 65 at 78.

121 Ibid.

person. The second category envisaged by Lord Fraser covers those acts which a private person would never do, and would normally only ever be performed by the police, eg gaining forcible entry into a suspected drugs warehouse. Here the officers would be carrying out government policy to which the Act would not apply. Moreover, they would be performing duties in order to prevent and detect crime and exercising their powers to enable them to perform those duties.[122]

29.95 The Court of Appeal recently went further in *Brooks v Metropolitan Police Commissioner*,[123] a case arising out of the murder of the claimant's best friend, Stephen Lawrence, in a racist attack. Mr Brooks complained that various police officers had discriminated against him contrary to RRA 1976 s20. The numerous allegations of discrimination fell into two broad categories, namely (1) allegations of failing to protect, assist and support him and (2) allegations of failing to investigate the crime with appropriate competence and vigour.[124] The judge at first instance struck out parts of Mr Brooks' claim, in particular those parts which related to the investigation of the crime. The Court of Appeal allowed Mr Brooks' appeal and permitted the complaints made regarding the investigation of the crime to proceed on the grounds that they were capable of falling within the scope of s20. This followed a concession by counsel for the police officers that 'it would be "technically possible" for an individual police officer to be asked to provide investigatory services by a member of the public, and to respond in a way which would fall foul of section 20(1)(a) or (b)'.[125]

29.96 Furthermore, and significantly, the Court of Appeal accepted in *Brooks* that an express request for services did not need to be made before s20 (and therefore SDA 1975 s29) could become engaged. It is possible for a person to 'seek services' for the purposes of RRA 1976 s20 and SDA 1975 s29 even without having made his or her needs known to each person concerned with the provision of those services, and it was therefore open for Mr Brooks to say that 'at least by implication, he sought not only protection, assistance and support, but also investigatory services'.[126]

122 [1998] QB 65 at 85, per Otton LJ.

123 [2002] EWCA Civ 407.

124 Ibid para 817.

125 Ibid para 36.

126 Ibid para 39. This is likely to be a particularly important ruling in the public services sphere where commonly a service or facility will not be expressly requested (eg, an ambulance or police officer to stop at the site of an accident) but would be expected.

29.97 Thus SDA 1975 s29 and RRA 1976 s20 have been given a fairly wide meaning, particularly when the complaint is outside the immigration field. This is important because it means a wide range of complaints against public authorities might fall within the scope of s29 and s20 and, more particularly, because a complaint cannot be made under the new RRA 1976 s19B where the act about which the complaint is made is made unlawful by virtue of any other provision of the RRA 1976.[127] Many of the acts which fall within the scope of s20, having regard to the Court of Appeal's judgments in *Farah*, *Brooks* and *Savjani*, would appear to fall more comfortably now within s19B. However, given that the courts have ruled that certain functions of public authorities do fall within the scope of s20, any race discrimination claim against a public authority in respect of the performance of any of its functions should be brought under s19B and s20 to ensure that the claim does not fail for having been brought under the wrong section.

Sex- and race-specific facilities and services

29.98 SDA 1975 s29(3) provides that:

> For the avoidance of doubt it is hereby declared that where a particular skill is commonly exercised in a different way for men and for women it does not contravene subsection (1) for a person who does not normally exercise it for women to insist on exercising it for a woman only in accordance with his normal practice or, if he reasonably considers it impracticable to do that in her case, to refuse or deliberately omit to exercise it.

29.99 Therefore, a barber providing hairdressing and shaving facilities for men could lawfully refuse to offer the same for women. Though there is no comparable provision in the RRA 1976, given that s29(3) is 'for the avoidance of doubt' it can properly be assumed that parliament intended that service providers would not be required to alter the goods, facilities or services they offer where they are aimed at the tastes or needs of a particular racial group so as to make them attractive to all racial groups. Thus a café specialising in jerk chicken and rice and peas would not be required by the RRA 1976 to offer sausage, egg and chips as well.

29.100 However the SDA 1975 and the RRA 1976 do prohibit discrimination in the provision of such goods, facilities and services as are offered by the provider and, to avoid indirect discrimination, it may

127 RRA 1976 s19B(6)(a).

on occasions be necessary for the conditions upon which such goods, facilities or services are offered to be altered. Thus a service offered only to people living in one geographical area, where the effect of the geographical restriction is to exclude certain racial groups, might be indirectly discriminatory and, if unjustified, unlawful. Similarly a condition for the making of a loan on a house that the house had a front garden might indirectly discriminate against Asians where a considerably smaller proportion of Asians had houses with front gardens.[128]

'Section of the public'

29.101 For a claim to succeed under SDA 1975 s29 or RRA 1976 s20, the claimant must show that the alleged discriminator is a person 'concerned with the provision (for payment or not) of goods, facilities or services to the *public or a section of the public*' (emphasis added). The SDA 1975 and the RRA 1976 are not therefore concerned with purely private or one-off arrangements.

29.102 In *Dockers Labour Club & Institute Limited v Race Relations Board*,[129] the Board sought a declaration that the Dockers Labour Club, which operated a colour bar such that only white people were admitted into its club, was acting unlawfully. The House of Lords followed one of its earlier decisions[130] by holding that the club did not provide facilities or services to the public, or a section of it. The club elected its members adopting a genuine process of selection, and was thus not accessible to the public or a section of it but properly operated within the private sphere. The House of Lords also held that the same principle applied where clubs, operating under reciprocal arrangements with other clubs, offered hospitality or temporary membership to members of the other club. Even in such circumstances, so long as *each* club exercised 'a rigorous choice in electing their members', there would be no discrimination within the meaning of RRA 1976 s20 (or SDA 1975 s29) because the clubs would truly be operating within the private sphere.

29.103 The effect of the decision in the *Dockers Labour Club* case, which was reached under the RRA 1976's predecessor (the RRA 1968), has

128 'Mortgage allocation in Rochdale', CRE formal investigation report (1985).

129 [1976] AC 285. The board was the predecessor of the CRE and the claim was brought under RRA 1968 s2(1) which was in similar terms to SDA 1975 s29 and RRA 1976 s20.

130 *Race Relations Board v Charter* [1973] AC 868.

been limited by changes introduced by the later Act. Discrimination by private members clubs is now made expressly unlawful under the RRA 1976.[131] But the SDA 1975 contains no equivalent provision. Sexually discriminatory membership policies by clubs are not made unlawful by the SDA 1975 and male-only private clubs remain a feature of British life.

29.104 Prisoners have been held to constitute a section of the public.[132] Children in the care of a local authority have also been held to constitute a section of the public to whom foster parents provided services or facilities,[133] though foster arrangements have now been taken outside the scope of the RRA 1976.[134]

Exceptions

29.105 There are, perhaps unsurprisingly, wide exceptions to the 'goods, facilities and services' provisions in the SDA 1975 and RRA 1976. These are dealt with below under 'other exceptions' because of their general application.

Bringing proceedings

29.106 SDA 1975 s66 and RRA 1976 s57 provide that proceedings under SDA 1975 s29 and RRA 1976 s20 are to be taken in the county court.

29.107 As stated above, given that the courts have ruled that certain functions of public authorities do fall within the scope of RRA 1976 s20, any claim of discrimination under the RRA 1976 against a public authority in respect of the performance of any of its functions should be brought under ss19B and 20 to ensure that the claim does not fail for having been brought under the wrong section. Similarly, certain claims might fall within the scope of SDA 1975 s30 and RRA 1976 s21 ('premises', see below) and again proceedings should therefore be issued under both sections.

131 Subject to some exceptions: RRA 1976 s25, see below.

132 *Alexander v Home Office* [1988] 1 WLR 968, though apparently this point was not taken, at least on appeal.

133 *Applin v Race Relations Board* [1975] AC 259.

134 RRA 1976 s23(2).

Premises and housing

Introduction

29.108 SDA 1975 s30 and RRA 1976 s21 make it unlawful for a person to discriminate in relation to premises and housing. SDA 1975 s30 provides that:

> (1) It is unlawful for a person, in relation to premises in Great Britain of which he has power to dispose, to discriminate against a woman –
> (a) in the terms on which he offers her those premises, or
> (b) by refusing her application for those premises, or
> (c) in his treatment of her in relation to any list of persons in need of premises of that description.
> (2) It is unlawful for a person, in relation to premises managed by him, to discriminate against a woman occupying the premises –
> (a) in the way affords her access to any benefits or facilities, or by refusing or deliberately omitting to afford her access to them, or
> (b) by evicting her, or subjecting her to any other detriment.

RRA 1976 s21 is in materially identical terms.

29.109 There is no doubt that, particularly in so far as race is concerned, discrimination in housing remains a serious problem.[135] Such discrimination has a long history and, no doubt mindful of that, parliament conferred power on the CRE to issue codes of practice on the elimination of discrimination in the field of housing and the promotion of equality of opportunity in the field of housing between people of different racial groups.[136] The CRE has issued two codes of practice:

- Code of Practice in rented housing, for the elimination of racial discrimination and the promotion of equal opportunities (1991);
- Code of Practice in non-rented (owner-occupied) housing, for the elimination of racial discrimination and the promotion of equal opportunities (1992).

Both codes have been subject to parliamentary approval pursuant to the negative resolution procedure provided for by the RRA 1976.[137] Though a failure on the part of a person to observe any provision of the codes is not itself unlawful, in any proceedings under the RRA

135 See V Karn and D Phillips, 'Race and Ethnicity in Housing, a Diversity of Experience', in T Blackstone et al (eds), *Race Relations in Britain, a Developing Agenda* (1998) p128.

136 RRA 1976 s47(1)(c) and (d).

137 Ibid s47(4) and (5).

1976 the codes are admissible in evidence and 'if any provision of such Code appears to the ... Court ... to be relevant to any question arising in the proceedings it shall be taken into account in determining that question'.[138] The EOC has no equivalent power under the SDA 1975 to issue a code of practice in relation to premises.[139] However, in appropriate cases the CRE codes may be used by analogy.[140] Both codes of practice give guidance on how discrimination might be avoided and are a useful tool in pursuing any claims of race discrimination.

Disposal of premises

29.110 As can be seen from the above, it is unlawful for a person to discriminate in the disposal of any premises over which he or she has power of disposal. This applies to rented premises as it does to owner-occupied premises, and there is no limitation under the SDA 1975 or RRA 1976 as to the meaning of the term 'premises'. Thus commercial as well as domestic premises are covered. Furthermore, the wide expressions used in SDA 1975 s30(1) and RRA 1976 s21(1) make it clear that discrimination in respect of *any* arrangements to dispose of premises will be caught by those provisions. Thus the granting of tenancies and licences are plainly covered, as is the sale of premises.

29.111 The codes of practice give examples of the sort of discrimination that will be caught by RRA 1976 s21 (and by analogy SDA 1975 s30). These include:

- the imposition by a local authority of a lengthy residence qualification for accommodation with which people of one racial group are less able to comply than others;
- the operation of a rule whereby the sons and daughters of current tenants are given rehousing priority (where they are not entitled to the same by law or under the terms of their tenancy agreements), where this serves to advantage one or more racial groups over others;
- the operation of a system which depends only on word-of-mouth

138 RRA 1976 s47(10).

139 The EOC has provided a useful briefing: 'Sex Equality and Accommodation' (2001).

140 And harassment in connection with sexual orientation is unfortunately not uncommon on housing estates and might yet be declared unlawful under the SDA 1975, having regard to the HRA 1998 – see further chapter 8.

recommendations from existing tenants, where this serves to advantage one or more racial groups over others;[141]

- the operation by an estate agent of a policy of not providing information on properties in 'Asian areas' to white people because of a perception that they would not be interested in such properties thus discriminating against Asian vendors who have placed their properties with the estate agent.[142]

29.112 Furthermore, SDA 1975 s31 and RRA 1976 s24 provide that, where the licence or consent of the landlord or any other person is required for the disposal to a person of premises comprised in a tenancy, it is unlawful for the landlord or other person to discriminate by withholding the licence or consent for disposal of the premises to him or her, as the case may be.[143] The exemptions that apply in relation to the disposal of premises apply equally to the granting of a licence or consent.[144]

Management of premises

29.113 As can be seen from the above, SDA 1975 s30(2) and RRA 1976 s21(2) make it unlawful for a person, in relation to premises managed by him or her, to discriminate against a person occupying those premises. These provisions are very wide. The 'detriment' provision is certainly wide enough to cover harassment on the grounds of sex or race by landlords and other tenants. Harassment, including in the field of housing, is dealt with fully in chapter 28.

29.114 Other discriminatory treatment that might be unlawful under ss30(2) and 21(2) would include:

- giving preferential treatment to white tenants by redecorating their flats and not those of similar minority tenants, when the properties are in a similar condition;

141 See the Code of Practice in rented housing, paras 4.2 onwards, for these and other examples.

142 See Code of Practice in non-rented housing, paras 3.2 onwards, for this and other examples – though query whether this would truly fall under RRA 1976 s21 rather than s20 (facilities and services) unless the estate agent was acting as agent for a discriminator or knowingly aiding the commission of a discriminatory act (RRA 1976 ss32 and 33, see chapter 32).

143 SDA 1975 s31(1) and RRA 1976 s24(1). 'Tenancy' is defined, in the normal way, by ss31(3) and (24)(iv) – these provisions apply to tenancies created before the passing of the SDA 1975 and RRA 1976 as well as to others (SDA 1975 s31(4) and RRA 1976 s24(5)).

144 SDA 1975 s31(2) and RRA 1976 s24(2).

- responding more quickly and efficiently to requests for repair from one racial group than another; and
- encouraging and providing facilities to tenants associations on certain estates only where most residents are from one particular racial group compared to other estates where they are represented in smaller numbers.[145]

Exceptions

29.115 SDA 1975 s30 and RRA 1976 s21 do not apply to the provision of accommodation in 'small' premises, or the disposal of such premises, if the person providing the accommodation or disposing of the premises (or a near relative) resides and intends to continue to reside in the premises and accommodation in the premises is shared by that person with other people residing on the premises who are not members of the household.[146] Premises are 'small' for the purposes of these provisions where:

- they comprise residential accommodation for one or more households in addition to the accommodation occupied by the person providing the accommodation or seeking to dispose of the premises (or a near relative); and
- there is not normally residential accommodation for more than two such households; and
- only the person providing the accommodation or seeking to dispose of the premises and any member of his household reside in the accommodation occupied by him; *or*
- there is not normally residential accommodation on the premises for more than six people in addition to the person providing the accommodation or seeking to dispose of the premises (or a near relative).[147]

29.116 SDA 1975 s30(1) and RRA 1976 s21(1) do not apply to a person who owns an estate or interest in the premises and wholly occupies them, unless he or she uses the services of an estate agent for the purposes of the disposal of the premises, or publishes or causes to be published an advertisement in connection with the disposal.[148]

145 See Code of Practice in Rented Housing, paras 4.29 onwards, for these and other examples.

146 SDA 1975 s32 and RRA 1976 s22.

147 SDA 1975 s32(2) and RRA 1976 s22(2).

148 SDA 1975 s30(3) and RRA 1976 s21(3).

Thus an owner-occupier seeking to sell his or her premises privately, without intending to advertise or to use the services of an agent, is free to choose to whom he or she wishes to sell.

29.117 SDA 1975 s31(1) and RRA 1976 s24(1) do not apply in the same circumstances in which ss30(1) and 21(1) do not apply (above). The exceptions apply equally to claims of discrimination in connection with premises brought under SDA 1975 s29 and RRA 1976 s20 (the 'goods, facilities and services' provisions).[149]

Bringing proceedings

29.118 SDA 1975 s66 and RRA 1976 s57 provide that proceedings under SDA 1975 ss30 and 31 and RRA 1976 ss21 and 24 are to be taken in the county court. Since, as we saw above, certain claims relating to premises might fall within the scope of SDA 1975 s29 and RRA 1976 s20 (the 'goods, facilities and services' provisions), proceedings in relation to premises should also be issued under these provisions.

Race discrimination by private clubs

Introduction

29.119 RRA 1976 s25 prohibits race discrimination by private members clubs. Section 25(1) provides that the prohibition applies to 'any association of persons (however described, whether corporate or unincorporate, and whether or not its activities are carried on for profit) if (a) it has 25 or more members; and (b) permission to membership is regulated by its constitution and is so conducted that the members do not constitute a section of the public within the meaning of section 20(1)'. Section 25(1)(c) also excludes from the operation of the provision those bodies such as trade unions and employers' organisations to which RRA 1976 s11 applies (see further chapter 12). Section 25(2) and (3) provides that:

> (2) It is unlawful for an association to which this section applies, in the case of a person who is not a member of the association, to discriminate against him –
>
> (a) in the terms on which it is prepared to admit him to membership; or
>
> (b) by refusing or deliberately omitting to accept his application for membership.

149 SDA 1975 s32 and RRA 1976 s22.

(3) It is unlawful for an association to which this section applies, in the case of a person who is a member or associate of the association, to discriminate against him –
- (a) in the way it affords him access to any benefits, facilities or services, or by refusing or deliberately omitting to afford him access to them; or
- (b) in the case of a member, by depriving him of membership, or varying the terms on which he is a member; or
- (c) in the case of an associate, by depriving him of his rights as an associate, or varying those rights; or
- (d) in either case by subjecting him to any other detriment.

29.120 RRA 1976 s25(4) defines 'member' and 'associate of an association' for the purposes of s25. A member is a person who belongs to the association 'by virtue of his admission to any sort of membership provided for by the constitution'. A person is an associate if, not being a member of the association, 'he has under its constitution some or all of the rights enjoyed by the members'.

29.121 RRA 1976 s25 contains a wide prohibition against discrimination by clubs. This has the effect of circumventing the decision of the House of Lords in the *Dockers Labour Club* case.[150] Discrimination by clubs whose membership and admission is truly regulated by a constitution will be unlawful under s25 though it is not unlawful under s20 which will, however, apply to clubs whose membership is not truly so regulated.

29.122 The SDA 1975 contains no equivalent of RRA 1976 s25 with the effect that sex discrimination by private members clubs is not unlawful.[151] As is the case under the RRA 1976, discrimination by a club which is not in reality a private members club is likely to fall within the scope of the goods and services provisions (SDA 1975 s29). But a club which genuinely selects its members on personal grounds (rather than, for example, accepting anyone who will pay a fee) falls outside the scope of the SDA 1975.[152]

Bringing proceedings

29.123 RRA 1976 s57 provides that proceedings under RRA 1976 s25 must be taken in the county court. Given that certain claims might fall

150 [1976] AC 285.

151 Thus, eg, the Garrick Club is able to operate a male-only membership policy, enjoyed by, eg, the Lord Chancellor.

152 The EOC has issued a useful briefing on sex equality and private members clubs: 'Sex Equality and Private Members Clubs' (2001).

within the scope of s20 rather than s25, race discrimination claims should be issued under both ss20 and 25.

Exceptions

29.124 RRA 1976 s25 applies only to clubs with 25 or more members and does not apply to trade unions and employers' organisations (whose regulation under the Acts is considered in chapter 12).[153]

Charities

29.125 RRA 1976 s34 has the effect of making any provision in a charitable instrument void in so far as it provides for the conferring of benefits on people of a class defined by reference to colour. This provision applies whenever the instrument took or takes effect. Where such provision is made, s34 provides that the instrument is to be read as if it provided for the conferring of such benefits on people of the class which results if the restriction by reference to colour is removed or, where the original class is defined by reference to colour only, on people generally.[154]

Other exceptions

Introduction

29.126 The SDA 1975 and RRA 1976 provide numerous exceptions from the unlawful acts created outside the employment field.[155] Some of those exceptions apply to the unlawful acts created by both the SDA 1975 and the RRA 1976, others are peculiar to one or other of those statutes.

29.127 It is important to note that, while a person who facilitates access to benefits, facilities or services provided by any other person (the 'actual provider') may be liable (together with the actual provider) in respect of any discrimination in the provision of those benefits,

153 RRA 1976 s25(1).

154 Ibid s34(1) RRA 1976. A broad exemption operates in relation to the other unlawful acts created by the RRA 1976 and those created by the SDA 1975, see below.

155 The exemptions which apply in the employment field are dealt with in chapter 13.

facilities or services, he or she is also entitled to rely on any exception created by the relevant Act which applies to the actual provider.[156]

29.128 The exceptions which apply to both sex and race discrimination will be dealt with first, followed by those exemptions which are peculiar to the SDA 1975 or RRA 1976.

General exceptions

29.129 SDA 1975 s35(3) and RRA 1976 s23(1) make it clear that the provisions concerned with discrimination in relation to goods, services and facilities, housing and premises do not apply to any acts of discrimination which are rendered unlawful by the employment or education provisions. Thus, for example, a pupil who wishes to complain about the facilities offered to him or her by a school must complain under the education provisions rather than under RRA 1976 s20 or SDA 1975 s29.

Territorial limits

29.130 The unlawful acts created by the SDA 1975 and dealt with in this chapter do not apply to goods, facilities or services outside Great Britain[157] except:

- SDA 1975 s29(1) (prohibition on discrimination in the provision of goods, services or facilities) applies to the provision of facilities for travel outside Great Britain where the refusal or omission occurs in Great Britain or on a ship, aircraft or hovercraft as described in subsection (3)[158] (namely to any ship registered at a port of registry in Great Britain and any aircraft or hovercraft registered in the UK and operated by a person who has his principal place of business, or is ordinarily resident in Great Britain and any ship, aircraft or hovercraft belonging to or possessed by Her Majesty in right of the government of the UK, even if the ship, aircraft or hovercraft is outside Great Britain);[159]
- SDA 1975 ss22, 23 and 25 (prohibition on discrimination in education) apply where they relate to travel on a ship registered to a port of registry in Great Britain, and benefits, facilities or services provided on a ship so registered.[160]

156 SDA 1975 s50 and RRA 1976 s40.
157 SDA 1975 s36.
158 Ibid s36(2).
159 Ibid s36(3) and notice that the same provision is not made by the RRA 1976.
160 SDA 1975 s36(5).

29.131 The unlawful acts created by the RRA 1976 and dealt with by this chapter do not apply in respect of benefits, facilities or services outside Great Britain[161] except:

- RRA 1976 s20 (prohibition on discrimination in the provision of goods, services or facilities) applies to the provision of facilities for travel outside Great Britain where the refusal or omission occurs in Great Britain or on a ship, aircraft or hovercraft within subsection 4[162] (namely to any ship registered at a port of registry in Great Britain and any aircraft or hovercraft registered in the UK and operated by a person who has his principal place of business, or is ordinarily resident, in Great Britain, even if the ship, aircraft or hovercraft is outside Great Britain);[163]
- RRA 1976 s19B (prohibition on discrimination by public authorities) applies in relation to granting entry clearance (within the meaning of the Immigration Act 1971), applies in relation to acts done outside the UK, as well as those done within Great Britain.[164]

Furthermore, SDA 1975 s29(1) and RRA 1976 s20(1) do not apply to facilities by way of banking or insurance or for grants, loans, credit or finance where the facilities are for a purpose to be carried out, or in connection with risks wholly or mainly arising, outside Great Britain.[165]

29.132 The provisions dealing with the territorial limitations under the SDA 1975 and RRA 1976 both contain a general proviso that such sections do not render unlawful an act done in or over a country outside the UK, or in or over that country's territorial waters, for the purpose of complying with the laws of that country.[166] The other unlawful acts dealt with by this chapter make it clear on their face that they extend only to England, Wales and Scotland.[167]

Charities

29.133 SDA 1975 s43 provides a general exemption to the unlawful acts created in both the employment and the non-employment field in respect of provisions contained in charitable instruments which

161 RRA 1976 s27(1).
162 Ibid s27(1)–(3).
163 Ibid s27(4).
164 Ibid s27(1A).
165 SDA 1975 s36(1)(b) and RRA 1976 s27(2)(b).
166 SDA 1975 s36(4) and RRA 1976 s27(5).
167 And see SDA 1975 s87 and RRA 1976 s80.

confer benefits on persons of one sex only (disregarding any benefits to people of the opposite sex which are exceptional or are relatively insignificant).[168]

29.134 RRA 1976 s34 exempts from the employment and non-employment prohibitions on discrimination charitable instruments which provide for the conferring of benefits on people of a class which is defined by reference to racial group other than by reference to colour. As mentioned above, charitable instruments which contain provisions conferring benefits on people of a class defined by reference to colour have the effect for all purposes as if provided for conferring the like benefits on people of the class which results if the restriction by reference to colour is disregarded or, where the original class is defined by reference to colour only, on people generally.

Sport and competitions

29.135 SDA 1975 s44 exempts from both the employment and the non-employment provisions discrimination related to the participation of a person as a competitor in events involving any sport, game or other activity of a competitive nature where the physical strengths, stamina or physique of the average woman puts her at a disadvantage to the average man where the activities are confined to competitors of one sex. This is a broad exemption and one which the EOC has recommended should be changed – particularly for young people because, though girls are unlikely to be at a physical disadvantage to boys pre-puberty, case-law has established that this exception applies to children as well as adults.[169] RRA 1976 s39 exempts from both the employment and the non-employment provisions discrimination on the basis of nationality, place of birth or length of residence in a particular area or place in selecting one or more people to represent a country, place or area, or any related association, in any sport or game or in pursuance of the rules of any competition so far as they relate to eligibility to compete in any sport or game.[170]

168 SDA 1975 ss78 and 79 provide a means by which charitable instruments in the educational field might be altered in England and Wales and in Scotland respectively.

169 'Sex Equality in Sport' (2000, EOC).

170 See *GLC v Farrar* [1980] ICR 266 and *British Judo Association v Petty* [1981] ICR 660.

Discriminatory training

29.136 SDA 1975 s48 and RRA 1976 s38 exempt certain discriminatory training provided by employers. This is dealt with in chapters 5 and 11. SDA 1975 s48 and RRA 1976 s38 make it clear that such discrimination cannot be challenged under the education and goods, facilities and services provisions.[171]

Statutory authority and national security

29.137 SDA 1975 s52 and the RRA 1976 s42 exempt any acts done for the purposes of safeguarding national security, although the exemption applies under the RRA 1976 only if the doing of the act was justified by that purpose.[172] The special procedures established by the RRA 1976 in this context are outside the scope of this book.

29.138 SDA 1975 s51A provides that none of the non-employment provisions (except in so far as they apply to vocational training) renders unlawful any act done by a person if it was necessary for that person to do it in order to comply with the requirement of an existing statutory provision within the meaning of s51. 'Existing statutory provision' (as defined by s51(3)) means any provision of an Act passed before the SDA 1975 or an instrument approved or made by or under an Act passed before the SDA 1975 (including one approved or made after the passing of the SDA 1975) and any Act passed after the SDA 1975 which re-enacts with or without modification a provision of an Act passed before the SDA 1975, in so far as the re-enacted provision is concerned.

29.139 RRA 1976 s41 provides that neither the non-employment nor the employment provisions of the Act render unlawful any acts of discrimination done in pursuance of any enactment or order in council; in pursuance of any instrument made under any enactment by a minister of the Crown; or in order to comply with any condition or requirement imposed by a minister of the Crown (whether before or after the passing of the RRA 1976) by virtue of any enactment. In so far as s41 applies to enactments, orders in council or instruments these include enactments, orders in council and instruments passed or made after the passing of the RRA 1976.

29.140 In *Hampson v Department of Education and Science*[173] the House of Lords considered the effect of RRA 1976 s41(1) on a claim by a teacher

171 SDA 1975 ss22 and 29 and RRA 1976 ss17 and 20.

172 As amended by RRAA 2000 s7.

173 [1990] IRLR 302.

from Hong Kong seeking approval of her teaching qualification to enable her to teach in a state school in Britain which was the subject of refusal by the Education Secretary. It was conceded by the defendants that the action constituted indirect discrimination in that a requirement (a three-year course as opposed to the two-year course undertaken by the claimant) was imposed with which a smaller proportion of the applicant's racial group could comply. But they contended that the action was taken in pursuance of an instrument made under an enactment (the Education Act 1980) by a minister of the Crown. The House of Lords concluded that s41 did not apply so as to exempt from the RRA 1976 acts done pursuant to a discretion as to the decision made. In this case the Secretary of State was under a duty to make a decision under the instrument as to whether to withhold approval or not but was not obliged by statute to withhold approval to the claimant. The House of Lords concluded that the words 'in pursuance of any instrument' are confined to acts done in the *necessary* performance of an express obligation contained in the instrument under consideration and do not include acts done in the exercise of a power or discretion conferred by the instrument.[174]

29.141 RRA 1976 s41(2) exempts acts done under statutory authority in relation to nationality or place of ordinary residence or the length of time a person has been present or resident in or outside the UK not merely where the act has been undertaken pursuant to existing legislation or statutory instrument, but also in pursuance of arrangements made with the approval of, or for the time being approved by, a minister of the Crown or in order to comply with any condition imposed by a minister of the Crown.[175] Thus departmental circulars and ministerial pronouncements are excluded from the ambit of the RRA 1976 and, as is intended, immigration control is largely removed from the unlawful acts created by the RRA 1976.[176]

Sex Discrimination Act exemptions

29.142 The SDA 1975 creates a number of specific exemptions related to the unlawful acts outside the employment field, sometimes with the plain object of positively advantaging women who would otherwise be disadvantaged by existing discrimination. However this is not

174 See further chapter 11.
175 RRA 1976 s41(2).
176 Though see now the amendments introduced by the RRAA 2000 and, in particular, ss19B, 19D and 19E.

always so and some of the exemptions have been subject to particular criticisms as having entrenched stereotypical ideas about women.

Political parties

29.143 SDA 1975 s33 provides that nothing in s29(1) (which prohibits discrimination in the provision of goods, facilities and services) is to be interpreted as affecting any special provision for persons of one sex only in the constitution, organisation or administration of a political party, or any act done in pursuance of such a provision.[177] A 'political party' for the purposes of s33 is one which has as its main object, or one of its main objects, the promotion of parliamentary candidatures for the UK Parliament or is an affiliate of, or has as an affiliate, or has similar formal links with, such an organisation.[178] This provision has allowed women's sections to operate lawfully within the Labour party for many years. The RRA 1976 contains no comparable provision.[179]

Voluntary bodies

29.144 SDA 1975 s34 contains an exemption from s29(1) (goods, facilities and services) and s30 (premises and housing) in relation to discrimination by voluntary bodies. 'Voluntary bodies' are bodies whose activities are carried out otherwise than for profit and which are not set up by any enactment. The exemption permits voluntary bodies to restrict their membership to people of one sex; and to provide benefits, facilities or services to members where the membership is restricted to membership of one sex even though membership of the body is open to the public or to a section of the public. Furthermore, any provision constituting the main object of a voluntary body which provides for the conferring of benefits on people of one sex only is not made unlawful by SDA 1975 ss29 or 30.

177 SDA 1975 s33(2) and (3).

178 Ibid s33(1).

179 Though RRA 1976 s35 might cover such arrangements – see below. Furthermore, it can be noted that following enactment of the Sex Discrimination (Election Candidates) Act 2002 the arrangements made for selecting candidates for election for the purpose of reducing inequality in the numbers of men and women elected, as candidates of the party, to be members of the body concerned are not affected by the employment and non-employment provisions of the SDA 1975 which do not render unlawful anything done in accordance with such arrangements (SDA 1975 s42A as amended).

Insurance

29.145 By SDA 1975 s45 the treatment of a person in relation to an annuity, life assurance policy, accident insurance policy, or similar matter involving the assessment of risk is exempt from the unlawful acts created both in the employment and non-employment fields where the treatment was affected by reference to actuarial or other data from a source on which it was reasonable to rely and was reasonable having regard to the data and any other relevant factors. This exemption, as with all exemptions, should be read narrowly and is limited to the types of policies defined. It does not apply, for example, to credit arrangements or to occupational pensions, in respect of which men and women must be treated equally.[180] The EOC has recommended that the government repeal this exception[181] and has remarked that most insurance companies use sex-based actuarial factors to determine cost of insurance coverage, resulting in different charges as between men and women for similar insurance. The EOC believes that the introduction of unisex actuarial factors would not raise insurmountable technical problems (and in the USA the adoption of such factors did not produce any major problems).[182] But the exemption remains in place. The provision is particularly undesirable given that liability turns in part upon a determination of what is 'reasonable', which makes it difficult to predict the outcome of any litigation. It is not made clear who ultimately decides what is 'reasonable'. If it is a county court judge who is unlikely to have any great deal of experience in sex discrimination it does not engender much confidence.

Sex-specific facilities and services and communal accommodation

29.146 SDA 1975 s46 exempts from the unlawful acts created by the SDA 1975 sex discrimination in the admission of people to communal accommodation if the accommodation is managed in a way which, given the exigencies of the situation, comes as near as may be to fair and equitable treatment of men and women.[183] 'Communal accommodation' is defined by s46(1) and (2) as:

180 'Sex Equality and Insurance' (2001, EOC).
181 Ibid.
182 Ibid.
183 SDA 1975 s46(3).

(a) Residential accommodation including dormitories and other shared sleeping accommodation that, for reasons of privacy or decency, should be used exclusively by either men or women (but which may include some shared sleeping accommodation for men, and some for women, or some ordinary sleeping accommodation);

(b) Residential accommodation all or part of which should be used by men only, or by women only, because of the nature of the sanitary facilities serving the accommodation.

29.147 What is 'fair and equitable' is to be determined having regard to a number of factors, namely:

- whether and how far it is reasonable to expect that the accommodation should be altered or extended or that further alternative accommodation should be provided;
- the frequency of the demand or need for use of the accommodation by men as compared with women.[184]

29.148 Furthermore, sex discrimination in the provision of any benefit, facility or service is not unlawful if the benefit, facility or service cannot properly and effectively be provided except for those using communal accommodation and, in the relevant circumstances, the woman (or, as the case may be, the man) could lawfully be refused the use of the accommodation by virtue of the communal accommodation exemption.[185]

29.149 SDA 1975 s35 provides that a person who provides facilities or services restricted to men does not contravene the goods, facilities and services provision (SDA 1975 s29(1)) if:

- the place is, or is part of, a hospital, resettlement unit provided under Supplementary Benefits Act 1976 Sch 5 or other establishment for people requiring special care, supervision or attention; or
- the place is (permanently or for the time being) occupied or used for the purposes of an organised religion, and the facilities or service are restricted to men so as to comply with the doctrines of that religion or avoid offending the religious susceptibilities of a significant number of its followers;
- the facilities or services are provided for or are likely to be used by

184 Ibid s46(4).

185 Ibid s46(5). Section 46(7) provides that the general duty in SDA 1975 s25 does not apply to sex discrimination falling within the exemptions relating to communal accommodation. There is further provision made in relation to discrimination falling within the employment provisions and dealt with in chapter 11.

two or more people at the same time and, the facilities or services are such, or those people are such, that male users are likely to suffer serious embarrassment at the presence of a woman, or the facilities or services are such that a user is likely to be in a state of undress and a male user might reasonably object to the presence of a female user; or

- the services or facilities are such that physical contact between the user and any other person is likely, and that other person might reasonably object if the user were a woman.

Thus, sex specific sauna facilities and changing rooms would be lawful as would, probably, self-defence classes which involve close physical contact between participants.[186]

Race Relations Act exemptions

29.150 The RRA 1976, like the SDA 1975, creates a number of specific exemptions related to the unlawful acts outside the employment field, again sometimes with the object of overcoming disadvantage to racial minorities.

Special needs of racial groups in regard to education, training or welfare

29.151 RRA 1976 s35 exempts from the employment and non-employment provisions of the RRA 1976 any act done in affording people of a particular racial group access to facilities or services to meet the special needs of people of that group in regard to their education, training or welfare, or any ancillary benefits. 'Special' is not defined for the purposes of this provision but it appears to mean something other than exclusive. Thus, a need which is present in all communities but present to a greater degree among one racial group would seem sufficient to satisfy this section, for example, language and health needs.

Fostering

29.152 RRA 1976 s23(2) exempts from s20 (the prohibition on discrimination in the provision of goods, facilities and services) fostering arrangements (for payment or otherwise) of children, elderly people or people requiring a special degree of care and attention.[187]

186 'Sex Equality and Services' (2000, EOC).
187 RRA 1976 s23(2).

CHAPTER 30

Disability discrimination outside the employment field

continued

Key points

30.1

- The main focus of the Disability Discrimination Act (DDA) 1995 at the time of its implementation was on employment-related discrimination and the other parts of the Act were considerably less well known and the rights granted by them less utilised.
- As the rolling programme of implementation brings into force the non-employment provisions of the DDA 1995, and as these provisions gain recognition, so the rights they provide will gain in importance and become better known and, it is hoped, respected.
- Those provisions of the DDA 1995 which provide rights in respect of goods, services and facilities will be fully implemented by October 2004. A new and comprehensive statutory Code of Practice was published in May 2002 to enable service providers to prepare for their legal obligations under these provisions.
- The goods and services provisions in the DDA 1995prohibit less favourable treatment for a reason related to the disabled person's disability and impose on service providers a duty to make reasonable adjustment (defined somewhat differently from that found in the employment-related provisions of the Act) to the needs of the disabled. They also prohibit victimisation in connection with complaints about goods and services.
- The DDA1995 provides protection from disability discrimination in relation to premises. Leaseholders also have powers to require their landlords to consent to adjustments to be made to their premises in certain circumstances.
- In the field of education, substantive individual rights against disability discrimination come into force in September 2002. These provide protection from 'discrimination' which is defined to include victimisation; unjustified less favourable treatment for a reason which relates to a disabled person's disability; and unjustified failure to comply with a duty to make reasonable adjustment in relation to admission arrangements, education and associated services and student services and exclusions.
- In the transport field, the rights provided by the DDA 1995 are not yet fully in force. Regulations concerning accessibility are in force in the railway industry and for coaches and buses. Taxi regulations are anticipated shortly and taxi drivers are under an obligation, enforceable by prosecution, to assist and facilitate disabled people and their guide dogs.

Background and statutory provisions

30.2 Like the sex and race discrimination legislation, the Disability Discrimination Act (DDA) 1995 regulates discrimination beyond the field of employment. By contrast with the implementation of the earlier legislation, however, that of the DDA 1995 has been gradual and not all of its provisions have yet to come into force. The prohibition of disability discrimination outside the field of employment is principally contained in the DDA 1995 itself, though the Special Educational Needs and Disability Act (SENDA) 2001, which has significantly augmented the relevant provisions of the DDA 1995, is also important. Some parts came into force in September 2002.

30.3 The non-employment provisions of the DDA 1995, like those concerned with employment, are augmented by a number of useful and important statutory codes of practice which, although not statements of the law, are admissible in proceedings and the provisions of which courts and tribunals must take into account where relevant.[1] The three main codes considered in this chapter are the Disability Discrimination Act code of practice: rights of access – goods, facilities, services and premises (which is referred to as the Part III code of practice, because it deals with the duties imposed by Part III of the DDA 1995); the DDA 1995 Part IV code of practice for schools; and the DDA 1995 Part IV code of practice for providers of post-16 education and related services (the post-16 education code of practice).[1a] These last two codes deal with Part IV of the DDA 1995 as amended by SENDA 2001.

30.4 This chapter will deal with the legal protection from disability discrimination other than in the employment field – that is – in the provision of goods, services and facilities (DDA 1995 Part III); in housing and property-related issues (DDA 1995 Part III); in education (DDA 1995 Part IV as amended by SENDA 2001); and in transport (DDA 1995 Part V). The employment-related provisions of the DDA 1995 are dealt with in parts I and II of this book.

30.5 The coverage of the non-employment provisions of the DDA 1995 is not as extensive as the comparable provisions of the sex and race discrimination legislation, most notably in the field of transport and education. In addition the government has adopted a staged programme of implementation of the non-employment rights in the

1 DDA 1995 s51.

1a Both codes of practice are avilable at www.drc.org.uk.

DDA 1995 which is, even now, only partially complete. The policy reason given by the government for the gradual phasing-in of the DDA 1995 is that it provides a sufficient lead-in time to enable advance preparation for the new rights – the Equal Pay Act 1970 had a five year time lag from enactment to commencement date.

30.6 A constant theme in the disability discrimination legislation, which distinguishes it from the sex and race discrimination legislation, is the asymmetrical nature of the rights. The DDA 1995 confers rights on disabled people rather than a right to equal treatment regardless of disability. It goes beyond a formal approach to equality. As with the employment provisions, whether or not a person is 'disabled' within the meaning of the DDA 1995 is a crucial issue. The non-employment provisions of the DDA 1995 use the same definition of disability as the employment provisions and there should be no difference in approach to the meaning of disability between that established by the Employment Appeals Tribunal (EAT) under the Act's employment-related provisions (see para 2.47) and that adopted by courts dealing with its other provisions.

30.7 The rights set out in this chapter are mainly adjudicated in the county or High Court rather than the employment tribunal. School education cases are heard by the Special Educational Needs and Disability Tribunal (SENDIST) which has specialist expertise in educational matters. There have been remarkably few cases to date on the non-employment provisions of the DDA 1995[2] and the Disability Rights Commission (DRC) favours the extension of the jurisdiction of the ETs to hear all DDA 1995 Part III cases, given their expertise in other areas of the DDA 1995.

30.8 Procedural issues are dealt with in chapter 32 but it is important to note that the DRC provides a free conciliation service for DDA 1995 Part III complaints in England Scotland and Wales.[3] Free conciliation

2 Between December 1996 and February 2001 53 cases were initiated under DDA 1995 Part III compared with 8,908 under the Part II employment-related provisions of the Act: S Leverton, *Monitoring the DDA 1995 (Phase 2)*, in-house report 91, Department for Work and Pensions.

3 This under powers contained in DDA 1995 s28 as amended by Disability Rights Commission Act 1999 s10. Prior to the enactment of the DRCA 1999 (and the creation of the DRC and disbanding of the National Disability Council on 25 April 2000), conciliation services were provided by the Disability Access Rights Advisory Service (DARAS). 'Conciliation' is defined as advice and assistance provided by a conciliator to the parties to a dispute with a view to promoting its settlement otherwise than through the courts (DDA 1995 s28(8) as substituted by DRCA 1999).

will also be available for DDA 1995 Part IV conciliation cases from September 2002 to coincide with the implementation of some of the education provisions.[3a] In the two year period to 19 April 2002, the DRC conciliation service dealt with 190 cases and achieved a 60% settlement rate.[4]

'Discrimination'

30.9 The DDA 1995 makes discrimination against disabled people unlawful in certain areas such as in the provision of goods, services and facilities, and in relation to premises. Crucial to understanding the scope and coverage of the DDA 1995 is a grasp not only of the spheres of activity it covers, but also of the meaning of 'discrimination' it employs. The non employment-related provisions of the Act, like its employment-related provisions, regulate three forms of disability discrimination: unjustified less favourable treatment of disabled people for a reason relating to their disability; unjustified failure to provide a reasonable adjustment for a disabled person; and victimisation (this last whether the person victimised is disabled or not).

30.10 Behind the similarities, there are significant differences in the detail of the duty to make reasonable adjustment and in the test for justification both between the employment-related provisions of the DDA 1995 on the one hand and the non-employment-related provisions on the other, and also between the different types of non-employment-related provisions. The different definitions are set out below. The definition of victimisation is constant throughout the DDA 1995 (see chapter 4), although at present it applies only in relation to DDA 1995 Part III and, from September 2002 to DDA 1995 Part IV, and not to the transport provisions in DDA 1995 Part V.

3a Under powers conferred by DDA 1995 s31B (amended pursuant to SENDA 2001 s37).

4 DRC press release 19 April 2002, available at www.drc.org.uk.

Goods, facilities and services

Introduction

30.11 The extent to which disabled people are included in society and are able to enjoy the opportunities and have access to the facilities available to the general public on equal terms depend, to a large extent, on the legislative prohibition of disability discrimination. DDA 1995 Part III (sections 19–21) sets out the law relating to disability discrimination in relation to goods, facilities and services.

30.12 The DDA 1995 makes it unlawful for a service provider (including a provider of goods or facilities) to discriminate against a disabled person:

- by refusing to provide (or by deliberately not providing) any service which it provides (or is prepared to provide) to members of the public;
- in the standard or manner of service it provides to the disabled person; or
- in the terms on which it provides the service to the disabled person.

It is also unlawful for a service provider to fail to comply with a duty of reasonable adjustment in circumstances in which the effect of that failure is to make it impossible or unreasonably difficult for the disabled person to make use of any such service.[5]

30.13 A revised statutory code of practice, the Part III code of practice, has been in force since 27 May 2002. Issued by the DRC, it runs to some 175 pages and provides many practical examples and advice on how to comply with DDA 1995 Part III. The new Part III code of practice replaces the original Part III code which was issued in 1996 and revised in 1999. It anticipates the duties to make reasonable adjustment to physical features which will be implemented in October 2004 (see para 30.40). The length of the Part III code of practice may seem daunting but it is extremely clear and well set out and, unlike many other statutory codes of practice, includes an index which makes it much less impenetrable.

30.14 Since December 1996 it has been unlawful for service providers unjustifiably to treat disabled people less favourably for a reason related to their disability. Since October 1999 service providers have had to make reasonable adjustments, short of physical alterations to premises, for disabled people in their service delivery. Such

5 DDA 1995 s19(1) and (2).

adjustments might include, for example, the provision of extra help or changes to the way in which a service is provided. A duty to make reasonable adjustment in relation to physical features of premises will come into force on 1 October 2004. It will require the removal, adaptation or alteration of physical features, if the physical features make it impossible or unreasonably difficult for disabled people to make use of a service.

30.15 Education and transport are, at present, explicitly excluded from DDA 1995 Part III[6] and are considered at paras 30.105–30.168 below. But the education exemption will be removed on 1 September 2002 when SENDA 2001 begins to be implemented.[7] The effect of this will be that the goods and services provisions will cover any provider of education previously exempted from DDA 1995 Part III and not covered by the definition of education in Part IV of the Act (see further para 30.132 onwards below).

'Goods, facilities and services'

30.16 Section 19 of the Disability Discrimination Act 1995 provides that it is unlawful for a provider of 'services' (which includes goods and facilities) to discriminate against a disabled person in certain circumstances.[8] A person is a provider of services if he or she is concerned with the provision of services to the public or a section of the public in the UK.[9] The DDA 1995 contains no definition of 'service' 'facility' or 'goods' but does include (DDA 1995 s19(3)) a non-exhaustive list of examples:

- (a) access to and use of any place which members of the public are permitted to enter;
- (b) access to and use of means of communication;
- (c) access to and use of information services;
- (d) accommodation in a hotel, boarding house or other similar establishment;
- (e) facilities by way of banking or insurance or for grants, loans, credit or finance;
- (f) facilities for entertainment, recreation or refreshment;
- (g) facilities provided by employment agencies
- (h) the services of any profession or trade, or any local or other public authority.

6 DDA 1995 s19(5)(a) and (b) respectively.

7 SENDA 2001 repeals DDA 1995 s19(5)(a), (5)(ab) and (6).

8 DDA 1995 s19(2)(a).

9 DDA 1995 s19(2)(a).

30.17 The Part III code of practice adds to this list of examples.[10] The parliamentary intention was 'to provide a universal, all-embracing right of non-discrimination against disabled people . . . applicable to all providers of goods, facilities and services to the general public'.[11] What 'to the public' means is considered at para 30.22 below. It is irrelevant whether a service is provided free or for payment.[12] The protection from discrimination covers both children and adults and the capacity in which the disabled person receives the service is likely to be immaterial. It is also to be borne in mind that it is the provision of the service that is affected by DDA 1995 Part III, and not the nature of the service or the type of establishment. So for example, although DDA 1995 Part III expressly excludes transport from its prohibitions on discrimination in the provision of goods, services and provisions, an airline company's online booking facility available to the public via its website would be a 'service' for the purposes of DDA 1995 Part III just as the flight itself would be if Part III did not specifically exempt the latter. Equally, DDA 1995 Part III applies to an invitation by a television company to members of the public to participate in a game show by telephoning its national call centre.[13]

30.18 It is important to be clear about what the service is and about the identity of its provider. If, for example, a bank provides a cash machine facility inside a supermarket the bank will be the provider of the banking service and is likely to be responsible for any duties that may arise under the DDA 1995 in respect of the cash machine, although the facility is located on the supermarket's premises. The supermarket is, however, likely to be responsible for ensuring that the cash machine is physically accessible to disabled customers using its premises.[14]

30.19 The small employer exemption in the DDA 1995 (see chapter 13) has no counterpart in the Act's non employment-related provisions. We have already noted the transport and education exclusions but their extent is limited. The education exemption does not extend to non-educational services provided by any school or college or university such as, for example, a parent-teacher association (PTA) fundraising event or a university conference not aimed wholly or mainly at students.

30.20 The extent of the education exemption has already been tested in

10 See, for example, para 2.14 of the code of practice
11 HC Debate Standing Committee E, 16 February 1995, cols 290–291.
12 DDA 1995 s19(2)(c).
13 Part III code of practice, para 2.17.
14 Part III code of practice, para 2.30.

the courts. In *White v Clitheroe Grammar School*[15] the claimant challenged the refusal of the defendant school to allow him to participate in both a school exchange trip to Germany and a watersports holiday in France. On a preliminary point the county court found that 'education which is ... provided at ... the school' (exempted from DDA 1995 Part III by section 19(5) of the Act) did not have to be physically provided at the school buildings but that it included systematic instruction provided as part of the services of the school. Accordingly as the German trip emphasised the learning of the German language in a contextual situation and was a substitute for attendance at school, it was exempted from the services provisions of the DDA 1995 even though it was voluntary and depended on parental financial contribution. The French trip, on the other hand, was essentially a holiday (albeit with useful instruction) and therefore fell outside the education exemption. It was, accordingly, covered by DDA 1995 Part III.

30.21 The transport exemption applies to 'any service so far as it consists of the use of any means of transport'.[16] The Part III code of practice points out that transport providers are not wholly exempt from DDA 1995 Part III, as the illustration of an airline internet booking service above (see para 30.18) illustrates. Another example is of a wheelchair user who has no claim under the DDA 1995 if a ferry she wishes to travel on is not accessible. If, however, she is refused service in the buffet bar of the ferry terminal because of her disability, she is likely to have a DDA 1995 Part III claim. The DDA 1995 as it impacts on transport is set out at para 30.105 onwards below and a detailed examination of the scope of the transport exclusions at para 30.107.

'Section of the public'

30.22 A service must be available to the public or a section of the public to come within DDA 1995 Part III.[17] The DDA 1995 does not define who is a member of the public. Manufacturers and designers are not covered unless they supply goods or services direct to the public.[18] Some public bodies will provide a service which may be covered by the DDA 1995 in certain situations, but not in others. For example, the police will provide a service under the DDA 1995 when giving

15 Preston County Court (District Judge Ashton) 11 December 2001, Case No.BB002640.

16 DDA 1995 s19(5)(c).

17 DDA 1995 s19(2)(c).

18 Part III code of practice, paras 2.40 and 2.42.

advice and information about crime prevention, but are unlikely to be providing a service when arresting someone.[19]

30.23 Disability Discrimination Act s19(3)(a) provides, as an example of a 'service' covered by Part III of the Act, access to and the use of any place which members of the public are permitted to enter. A particularly thorny issue relates to the common parts of a multi-occupancy building. The Part III code of practice points out that the DDA 1995 does not expressly state whether or not the landlord is a service provider under the DDA 1995 in respect of the common parts.[20] The Part III code of practice speculates that if members of the public are permitted to enter the premises, the landlord is likely to be a service provider. It lists some factors likely to be relevant for a court in considering whether members of the public are permitted to enter.[21] These include whether tenants provide services actually in, rather than from, the building, and security and screening arrangements. Also relevant may be whether the landlord provides services such as lifts and security. The Part III code of practice advises landlords of premises with more than one occupier to anticipate that they may have responsibilities to make the common parts accessible to disabled people.[22]

30.24 Private members' clubs are not covered by DDA 1995 Part III because they do not provide services to the public, save in relation to any such services as they do provide. So, for example, the refusal by a private golf club to admit a disabled golfer to membership is not prohibited by the DDA 1995. If, however, the golf club hires out its facilities for a wedding reception, the 1995 Act applies to this service. And if the club allows non-members to use the course, a refusal to allow a disabled golfer to play is likely to be subject to the Act.[23]

Unlawful discrimination

30.25 Section 19 of the Disability Discrimination Act 1995 provides that discrimination against disabled people will be unlawful under Part III of the Act where it consists of:

- a refusal to provide, or a deliberate failure to provide, to the disabled

19 Part III code of practice, para 2.14, and see *R v Entry Clearance Officer Bombay ex p Amin* [1983] AC 81 discussed at para 29.92.

20 Part III code of practice, para 2.20.

21 Part III code of practice, para 2.25.

22 Part III code of practice, para 2.27.

23 Part III code of practice, para 2.38.

person any service which the service provider[24] provides, or is prepared to provide, to members of the public;

- a failure to comply with any duty imposed on the service provider[25] by DDA 1995 s21 (see para 30.34 below) in circumstances in which the effect of that failure is to make it impossible or unreasonably difficult for the disabled person to make use of any such service;
- discrimination in the standard of service which the service provider[26] provides to the disabled person or the manner in which such service is provided; or
- discrimination in the terms on which the service provider[27] provides a service to the disabled person.[28]

30.26 The scope of the prohibition on discrimination in the provision of goods, facilities and services provisions is wide. The Part III code of practice (paras 3.17–3.22 of the code) provides helpful examples. Failure to provide a service would include, for example, a situation in which bar staff pretended not to see a disabled person who was trying to be served at the bar.[29] Unlawful discrimination in the standard of service provided would include rudeness to, or the harassment of, a disabled customer or, for example, an instruction by the manager of a fast food outlet that a person with a severe facial disfigurement sit at a table out of sight of other customers. Discrimination in the terms of service provided would include requiring a disabled person to pay a larger deposit for a holiday booking than would be required from a non-disabled person.

Less favourable treatment

30.27 'Discrimination' includes, for the purposes of the goods and services provisions of the employment-related provisions of the DDA 1995, three forms of treatment:

- unjustified less favourable treatment of a disabled person;
- unjustified failure to make a reasonable adjustment to the needs of a disabled person; and

24 Including – DDA 1995 s19(2) – a provider of goods or facilities.
25 Ibid.
26 Ibid.
27 Ibid.
28 DDA 1995 s19(1).
29 Example provided at para 3.17 of the Part III code of practice.

- victimisation in connection with the DDA 1995 of a person whether disabled or not.

30.28 The less favourable treatment and victimisation provisions came into force on 2 December 1996. The definition of less favourable treatment in the goods, facilities and services provisions in DDA 1995 Part III is identically worded to the employment definition (see para 6.7 above). A provider of services discriminates against a disabled person if, for a reason which relates to the disabled person's disability, he or she treats the disabled person less favourably than he or she treats or would treat others to whom that reason does not apply,[30] unless he or she can show that the treatment in question is justified.[31] The justification defence which applies to discrimination in the provision of goods, facilities and services is narrower (see para 30.52 below) than that which applies in the context of employment.

30.29 The fact that the prohibition on less favourable treatment is identically worded between the employment-related provisions of the DDA 1995 on the one hand and its goods and services provisions on the other would suggest that the test is the same and that the employment-related case law such as the decision of the Court of Appeal in *Clark v TDG Ltd t/a Novacold*[32] will apply to the goods and services provisions. The Part III code of practice assumes that this is the case.[33] Interestingly, however, the Court of Appeal took a narrower view in *R v Powys CC ex p Hambridge (No 2)*,[34] a case relating to the charging structure of home care services levied by a local authority. It is thought, however, that this case is limited to its particular facts and is unlikely to be followed. Significantly, the Part III code of practice, which was revised after the *Powys* case, makes no reference to it. And recently, in *White v Clitheroe Grammar School*[35] (see para 30.20 above), Ashton DJ adopted the reasoning in *Clark* in a very comprehensive and considered judgment.

30.30 The question whether an employer needs to know of a disabled person's disability in order to have treated him or her less favourably exercised the courts under the employment provisions in the

30 DDA 1995 s20(1)(a).

31 DDA 1995 s20 (1)(b).

32 [1999] IRLR 318, fully discussed at para 6.7.

33 See, for example, Part III code of practice, paras 3.3–3.10.

34 [2000] TLR 196; (2000) 3 CCLR 231.

35 Preston County Court (District Judge Ashton) 29 April 2002, Case No BB002640. This was the full merits hearing of the case following the preliminary hearing on the scope of the education exemption.

early case law, the eventual conclusion being that knowledge was immaterial.[36] The Part III code of practice assumes that the same test applies under the goods and services provisions as under those concerned with employment – an assumption which must logically be correct given the identical wording of the subsections. The Part III code provides an example in which a pub employee orders a customer who is lying prone on a bench seat to leave the premises, assuming that she has had too much to drink. The customer is, however, lying down as a result of a disability, rather than because of her consumption of alcohol. The refusal by the pub employee to provide the disabled customer with further service is 'for a reason which relates to the disabled person's disability' and will be unlawful unless the service provider is able to show that the treatment in question is justified within the DDA 1995.[37]

30.31 The code of practice recommends that service employers instruct their staff accordingly, and provides a list of steps which service providers should consider taking to ensure compliance with their duties.[38] Employers will be vicariously liable for discrimination by their employees in the course of their employment unless they have taken such steps as are reasonably practicable to prevent the acts or omissions occurring.[39] The vicarious liability provisions are the same as those which apply in relation to the employment-related provisions of the DDA 1995 (see para 31.2).

30.32 There have been several county court cases under DDA 1995 Part III. *Caulfield v Sole Mio*[40] and *Sheldon v Taj Restaurant*[41] both concerned restaurants' refusals to serve disabled diners. Both restaurants were wheelchair accessible. Ms Sheldon was awarded £1,000 compensation after she was instructed to leave the restaurant because her electric wheelchair was, according to its manager, obstructing him and his staff. Mr Caulfield, was awarded £400 compensation after he was refused access to a restaurant on the basis that it was fully booked, his dining companion having been told that there was a table available.

30.33 Less favourable treatment will amount to discrimination unless the service provider can show the treatment to be justified – see para 30.52 below.

36 See para 6.12 above.
37 See Part III code of practice, para 3.11 and para 30.52 below.
38 See Part III code of practice, para 3.16.
39 DDA 1995 s58.
40 Edinburgh Sheriff's Court, Case No A 579/01 (4 December 2001) – unreported.
41 Brentford County Court, C/N BF 103152 (29 November 2001) – unreported.

Duty to make reasonable adjustment

30.34 The second form of discrimination against disabled people consists of an unjustified failure to make reasonable adjustments to meet their needs. This is potentially the most far reaching of the new rights and is not yet fully in force, its implementation having been delayed to enable service providers to prepare for their new obligations. The Part III code of practice describes the duty, which requires service providers to take positive steps to make their services accessible to disabled people, as the cornerstone of the DDA 1995. Here we look at what the duty consists of and, at para 30.52, we set out the justification defence. The reasonable duty of adjustment duty which applies under DDA 1995 Part III is not the same as the duty imposed by DDA 1995 Part II in the employment context.

30.35 Disability Discrimination Act 1995 s21 sets out what the Part III duty to adjust consists of. DDA 1995 s20(3) and (4) details the justification test applicable to the provision of goods, services and facilities and DDA 1995 s19(1)(b) the circumstances in which a failure to comply with the duty will be unlawful – for instance, where a service provider fails to comply with the duty to adjust and where the effect of that failure is to make it impossible or unreasonably difficult for the disabled person to make use of such service. Once again the Part III code of practice is invaluable to understanding the complex provisions of the DDA 1995 and contains numerous helpful examples.[42]

30.36 Broadly, the service provider's duty is to take reasonable steps to make adjustments to enable disabled people to make use of a service where it would be impossible or unreasonably difficult for them to do so without the adjustment. The duty is therefore a general duty owed to disabled people at large, but its breach is only actionable by an individual disadvantaged disabled person. The duty to make reasonable adjustments falls into three main areas which are being introduced in stages. They are described in the Part III code of practice as a series of duties as they are not mutually exclusive.[43]

30.37 The first obligation imposed on service providers is a duty to take reasonable steps to change a practice, policy or procedure which makes it impossible or unreasonably difficult for disabled people to make use of the services provided by the service provider to other members of the public.[44] This provision came into force in October

42 See Part III code of practice, chapters 4 and 5 in particular.

43 Part III code of practice, para 4.6.

44 DDA 1995 s21(1).

1999. Examples of what it might require would include waiving a policy such as a restaurant dress code of a collar and tie which is unreasonably difficult or impossible for a would-be diner suffering from severe psoriasis (a skin complaint).[45] In *White v Clitheroe Grammar School*[46] (para 30.20 above) the policy at issue was a headmaster's stance of supporting the decision of a teacher supervising a school water sports trip not to permit a disabled pupil to participate in it. The court held that this policy could make it unreasonably difficult for a disabled student to join a school trip because it created the potential for discrimination by the teacher which would then be routinely supported by the headmaster.

30.38 The second obligation on service providers consists of a duty to take such steps as it is reasonable, in all the circumstances of the case, for the service provider to have to take in order to provide an auxiliary aid or service if it would enable or facilitate the disabled person's use of the service.[47] The statute suggests that this information might have to be provided on audio tape or through a sign language interpreter as well as through the standard channels. Other examples are given by the Part III code of practice (see paras 5.10–5.16 of the code). The duty to adjust has been in force since October 1999 except that service providers are not required to do anything which would involve a permanent alteration to the physical fabric of premises when providing an auxiliary aid until the physical features adjustment provisions of the DDA 1995 come into force in October 2004.[48]

30.39 The claimant in *Baggley v Kingston upon Hull CC*,[49] a wheelchair user, was unable fully to enjoy a Mel C concert as there was no viewing platform for wheelchair users. The District Judge in the small claims court decided that the concert venue was not in breach of its DDA 1995 s21(4) duties and that it had not therefore committed an act of unlawful discrimination contrary to DDA 1995 s19(1)(b). It was the respondents case that providing a viewing platform, although capable of amounting to the provision of an auxiliary aid or service, was not a reasonable step in all circumstances of the case to have to take. The county court upheld the small claims' court decision.

45 Part III code of practice, para 5.5.

46 Preston County Court (District Judge Aston) 29 April 2002, Case No BB002640 (see note 35 and para 30.20 above).

47 DDA 1995 s21(4).

48 Disability Discrimination (Services and Premises) Regulations 1999 SI No 1191) (DD Regs 1999).

49 Hull County Court, 8 March 2002, Case No KH 101929 – unreported.

30.40 The third obligation on service providers relates to the physical features of their premises. DDA 1995 s21(2) provides that:

> where a physical feature (for example, one arising from the design or construction of a building or the approach or access to premises) makes it impossible or unreasonably difficult for disabled persons to make use of a service, it is the duty of the service provider to take such steps as it is reasonable, in all the circumstances of the case, for it to have to take in order to:
> (a) remove the feature;
> (b) alter it so that it no longer has that effect;
> (c) provide a reasonable means of avoiding the feature; or
> (d) provide a reasonable alternative method of making the service in question available to disabled persons.

30.41 The obligation to provide a reasonable alternative method (DDA 1995 s21(2)(d)) came into force in October 1999, but the remaining provisions do not come into force until 1 October 2004. The DDA 1995 does not, of course, prohibit compliance in advance of its implementation and, because of the long lead-in period, little leeway is likely to be given after implementation on the grounds that the rights provided thereby are new.

30.42 Clearly, of the four options listed at DDA 1995 s21(2)(a)–(d), the removal of the offending feature will be the best option for the disabled person concerned and provide for the most inclusive approach. At the other end of the scale, the least satisfactory method for the disabled person is likely to be for the service to be provided by an alternative method. For example, it would be preferable to a wheelchair user to be able to sit next to her friends in the cinema than to be placed somewhere out of the way apart from her friends. Also, it would be preferable to a wheelchair user to access a museum through its front door, any obstructive steps having been removed, rather than by a back entrance past the dustbins. The DDA 1995 is, however, silent as to whether one method is to be preferred as an adjustment over another, and the duty to adjust appears to be satisfied whichever method is chosen provided that it is effective in making it not unreasonably difficult or impossible for the disabled person to access the service.

30.43 Much may depend on defining the service. In the cinema example, if the service is described as simply watching the film, the space at the back away from her friends would appear to amount to a reasonable adjustment to the needs of the wheelchair user. If, however, the service were to be described as watching the film in the company of friends in a collective atmosphere (as opposed to on a video at home for example), it may be possible to argue that sitting with one's friends and sharing popcorn during a film is part of the service which would not be met by sitting apart. As the Part III code of practice states, the focus of the DDA 1995 is on results. Where there is a physical barrier, the service provider's aim should be to make its services accessible to disabled people.[50] The approach which will be taken by the courts to the physical features provisions of the DDA 1995 will become apparent after their implementation in October 2004.

30.44 The scope of the term 'physical features' is wide and its precise delineation is set out in the Disability Discrimination (Services and Premises) Regulations 1999 (DD Regs 1999).[51] Temporary as well as permanent features are covered and physical features include features arising from the design or construction of a building occupied by a service provider; any feature on the premises including any approach to, exit from or access to such a building; fixtures, fittings, furniture and furnishings, equipment or materials in or on the premises, and any other physical element or quality of land comprised in the premises. It also includes fixtures, fittings, furnishings, furniture, equipment or materials brought onto the premises by or on behalf of the service provider to do with providing services to the public.

30.45 The duty associated with the physical features of premises is owed by service providers to 'disabled people' at large – it is not a duty that is weighed up in relation to each individual disabled person who wants to access a service provider's services.[52] Accordingly, the duty applies regardless of whether the service provider or its staff know that a particular member of the public is disabled, or whether the service provider currently has disabled customers.[53] It is an objective test which is not limited to any particular disability and it will be important for service providers to think beyond the wheelchair stereotype of disability in considering the ways in which their service may be impossible or unreasonably difficult for disabled people to access.

30.46 The Part III code of practice sets out some general principles to be applied in considering reasonable adjustments, and provides examples of reasonable steps a service provider might have to take to make its services accessible to disabled people. It stresses the importance of training staff and anticipating the requirements of disabled

50 Part III code of practice, para 5.36.

51 Reg 3.

52 Part III code of practice, para 4.13.

53 Para.4.15, Part III code of practice.

customers. The duty is a continuing and evolving one, compliance with which should be regularly reviewed.

30.47 The DDA 1995 provides no definition of what is meant by 'reasonable steps' and its scope for regulations to be drawn up[54] has not yet been fully utilised. The Disability Discrimination (Providers of Services) (Adjustment of Premises) Regulations 2001,[54a] provides some guidance in the context for building alterations (see para 30.89 below). Once again the Part III code of practice offers assistance in listing some of the factors to be taken into account. It suggests that the duty to make adjustments will vary according to the type of service being provided, the size and nature of the service provider and the resources available to it, and with the effect of the disability on the individual disabled person. The factors to be taken into account in determining what steps ought reasonably to be taken might include (para 4.22 of the code) the effectiveness of the step in overcoming the difficulty in accessing the service faced by the disabled person; the extent to which it is practicable for the service provider to take the steps; the financial and other costs of making the adjustment; the extent of any disruption which taking the steps would cause; the extent of the service provider's financial and other resources; the amount of resources already spent on making adjustments; and the availability of financial or other assistance. DDA 1995 s20(7) provides that a service provider is not required to take any steps which would cause him or her to incur expenditure beyond a prescribed maximum which has yet to be established.

30.48 The DDA 1995 does not require a service provider to take any steps which would fundamentally alter the nature of the service in question or the nature of his or her trade, profession or business.[55] So, for example, a nightclub with low level lighting will not be required to adjust the lighting to accommodate customers who are partially sighted if this would fundamentally change the atmosphere or ambience of the club.[56]

30.49 The DDA 1995 does not allow a service provider to pass on the additional costs of compliance with the reasonable adjustment duty to disabled customers alone.[57]

30.50 We have seen that it is unlawful for a service provider unjustifiably

54 DDA 1995 s21(5)(a) and (b).

54a SI No 3253.

55 DDA 1995 s21(6).

56 Part III code of practice, para 4.28.

57 DDA 1995 s20(5) and Part III code of practice, paras 4.30 and 4.31.

to fail to comply with a duty to make reasonable adjustments if the effect of that failure is to make it impossible or unreasonably difficult to make use of the service.[58] The DDA 1995 does not define what is meant by unreasonably difficult, but the Part III code of practice sets out the matters to be taken into account in determining this issue. These include whether the time, inconvenience, effort, discomfort or loss of dignity entailed in using the service would be considered unreasonable by other people if they had to endure similar difficulties.[59] Once again, the definition of what the service comprises will be relevant in delineating the scope of the duty and the more expansive and detailed the service, the more likely the duty to adjust will arise.

30.51 The claimant in *Roper v Singing Hills Golf Club Ltd*,[60] who had multiple sclerosis, challenged the refusal of his local golf club (which was open to the public) to permit his use of a motorised golf cart on the grounds that to do so would lead to irreparable damage to the turf. In particular, it had been suggested by the golf club that the turf had only recently been laid and that, until it had a chance to settle, there was no prospect of the claimant being allowed the use of the motorised cart. This is apparently a common predicament facing disabled golfers. The county court decided that the golf course should make a reasonable adjustment to allow Mr Roper to use his golf buggy on the course in dry weather conditions. The implication of the ruling is that the golf course will also have to change its 'no buggy' policy to allow other disabled people to enjoy the same level of provision.

Justification

30.52 Less favourable treatment and breach of a reasonable adjustment duty each constitute discrimination if the service provider cannot show that the treatment in question is justified.[61] The justification test is the same for both forms of discrimination and is two-fold. It is unlike the test in the employment provisions of the DDA 1995, being narrower in scope, and it may therefore be harder for service providers than employers to justify disability discrimination. Discrimination is only justified under the goods and services provisions if, in the opinion of the service provider, one of five specified statutory

58 DDA 1995 s19(1)(b).
59 Part III code of practice, para 4.33.
60 Haywards Heath County Court, 26 April 2001, Case No HH 000855 – unreported.
61 DDA 1995 s20(1)(a) and (2)(b).

conditions is satisfied *and* it is reasonable, in all the circumstances of the case for the service provider to hold that opinion.[62]

30.53 The test for justification is part objective and part subjective, focusing both on the service provider's belief as to whether a statutory condition is satisfied (subjective) and on the reasonableness of that belief (objective). The Part III code of practice explains that a service provider should take into account all the circumstances including any information which is available; any advice which it would be reasonable to seek; and the opinion of the disabled person; as well as any reasonable adjustments that could be made. The lawfulness of the alleged discriminatory act or omission will be judged at the time it was done and not with the benefit of hindsight.[63]

30.54 The first statutory condition in accordance with which disability-related discrimination may be justified is where the treatment is necessary in order not to endanger the health or safety of any person including the disabled person him or herself.[64] This is likely to be the most frequently relied-on justification. The Part III code of practice warns against a spurious reliance on health and safety and urges that the service provider must have a reasonable belief and must not rely on generalised and stereotypical assumptions about disabled people (such as the view that a wheelchair user is an automatic hazard in a fire). It is for the management of the establishment concerned, with advice from the licensing authority or local fire officer, to make any special provision needed for a wheelchair user of premises in the event of a fire.[65]

30.55 The second statutory condition in accordance with which disability-related discrimination may be justified is where the disabled person is incapable of entering into an enforceable agreement, or of giving informed consent, and where for that reason the discriminatory treatment is reasonable in that case.[66] The Part III code of practice warns that it would not likely be justifiable, for example, for a jeweller to refuse to sell a pair of earrings to a person with a learning disability on the grounds that the disabled person did not understand the nature of the transaction, if her order was clear and she was able to pay for the earrings.[67] Nor will this condition be satisfied where another person

62 DDA 1995 s20(3).
63 Part III code of practice, paras 7.8–7.10.
64 DDA 1995 s20(4)(a).
65 Part III code of practice, para 7.2.
66 DDA 1995 s20(4)(b).
67 Part III code of practice, para 7.15.

is acting for the disabled person under an enduring power of attorney or under functions under Mental Health Act 1983 Part VII or where, in Scotland, a curator bonis, tutor or judicial factor has been appointed in relation to the disabled person.[68]

30.56 The claimant in *Dexter v Npower*[69] had a neurological condition which caused her to shake. Notwithstanding her full mental capacity NPower, through its agents, refused to accept her signature to a contract for supply of gas and electricity without countersignature from a neighbour. There was no objective justification for the requirement, the supplier's insistence apparently being motivated by the mistaken belief that someone with Mrs Dexter's condition lacked mental capacity to make contractual arrangements. Mrs Dexter won her case, the justification defence having failed, and was awarded £850.

30.57 The third statutory condition in accordance with which disability-related discrimination may be justified applies to cases in which the discrimination takes the form of a refusal or deliberate failure to provide a service to a disabled person which the service provider provides or is prepared to provide, to a member of the public.[70] The justification defence is available if the treatment is necessary because the service provider would otherwise be unable to provide the service to members of the public.[71] So for example, a tour guide might lawfully refuse to take a person with a severe mobility impairment on a tour of old city walls because of a well-founded belief that the extra help that person would require from the guide would prevent the party from completing the tour.[72] But such a refusal will only be justified if other people using the service would be effectively *prevented* from doing so, rather than merely delayed or inconvenienced. So, for example, requiring a disabled customer whose speech impairment makes it difficult to explain the service they want to go to the back of the queue while other customers are served is unlikely to be justified.[73]

30.58 The fourth statutory condition in accordance with which disability-related discrimination may be justified is where a service provider provides an inferior service (service of a lower standard, in a worse manner or on worse terms) in circumstances in which this is necessary to enable the service provider to provide the service to the

68 DDA 1995 s20(7), DD Regs 1999 reg 8 and Part III code of practice, para 7.16.
69 Swindon County Court, 23 April 2001, Case No SN005348 – unreported.
70 Discrimination made unlawful by DDA 1995 s19(1)(a).
71 DDA 1995 s20(4)(c).
72 Part III code of practice, para 7.18.
73 Part III code of practice, para 7.19.

disabled person or to other members of the public.[74] An example would be where a hotel restricts a wheelchair user's choice of bedrooms to those with level access to the lift, these bedrooms being noisier or having more restricted views than others. If the disabled person would otherwise be unable to use the hotel, the restriction is necessary and the level of service justified.[75] The service provider should, however, consider whether a reasonable adjustment could be made before it relies on this justification and cannot justify the treatment simply because of other people's preferences or prejudices.[76]

30.59 The fifth statutory condition in accordance with which disability-related discrimination may be justified is where a service provider charges a disabled person more for some services than it charges to other people.[77] The Part III code of practice explains that this may apply where the service is individually tailored to the requirements of the disabled customer,[78] but justification on this ground cannot apply where the extra costs result from the provision of a reasonable adjustment.[79] If, for example, a pedicurist charges clients a flat rate for certain foot treatments which generally take 30 minutes, it is likely that she will be able to justify charging a disabled person whose treatment takes twice as long, more than the usual rate where the extra cost reflects the additional time needed to provide the service.[80] If, however, a wine merchant's shop is inaccessible to mobility-impaired disabled people, and the merchant arranges home delivery as a reasonable adjustment for such customers, it will not be entitled to charge them for home delivery even though it makes such a charge to other customers.[81]

30.60 The five conditions set out above are exhaustive – unless the alleged discriminator reasonably believes that one of them applies, discriminatory treatment is incapable of justification.

30.61 One of the few cases heard in the UK under DDA 1995 Part III is *Rose v Bouchet*,[82] a Scottish case which concerned the identically-worded test for justification as it applies to discrimination in relation

74 DDA 1995 s20(4)(d).
75 Part III code of practice, para 7.21.
76 Part III code of practice, para 7.22.
77 DDA 1995 s20(4)(e).
78 Part III code of practice, para 7.24.
79 DDA 19945 s20(5) and see para 30.49 above.
80 Part III code of practice, para 7.24.
81 Part III code of practice, para 4.31.
82 [1999] IRLR 463.

to premises (see para 30.75 below). The defender had refused to let a flat to the claimant who was blind and had an assistance dog, because the access to the flat was reached from the street by five steps which had no handrail. There was a drop of approximately two and a half feet to ground level on one side and a smaller drop on the other. The claimant explained his disability on the telephone to the defender whose immediate response was that he considered access to the flat dangerous for a blind person. The defender then consulted his wife while the claimant waited on the telephone. She agreed and so the respondent told Mr Rose that the flat would not be safe for him and so Mr Bouchet was unwilling to let it to him.

30.62 The Sheriff Principal held that it was sufficient to meet the subjective part of the test that Mr Bouchet believed there to be a danger to the claimant. Had this stated belief been a fabrication or concoction the subjective aspect of the justification test would not have been made out. More controversially, the Sheriff Principal upheld the Sheriff court's judgment that there was no obligation on the facts of this case for Mr Bouchet, to have obtained more information before finalising his opinion. This case is likely to turn on its facts, which were that Mr Rose had become angry on the telephone and raised his voice. This, the Sheriff Principal considered, absolved the defender from making further enquiry of the claimant as to whether there was a health and safety risk. Strictly speaking a judgment from the Sheriff Principal is of persuasive authority only in England and Wales. But as the relevant provisions in the DDA 1995 at issue in *Rose* apply throughout the UK the decision is likely to be extremely persuasive. The *Rose v Bouchet* case is controversial and both the current and revised 1999 codes of practice on right of access to goods, facilities, services and premises, now specify that the view of the disabled person should be taken into account in order for the alleged discriminator's belief in the justification to be reasonable.

30.63 More recently the court in *White v Clitheroe Grammar School*[83] adopted a rigorous approach to justification in finding that the refusal to allow a child on a school water sports trip had not been justified on health and safety grounds. The school had not properly investigated the safety of the proposed trip for the claimant, who had insulin-dependent diabetes and who on a previous school trip had had a hypoglycaemic attack which the school believed was because he had failed to manage his condition properly. The school chose instead to

83 Preston County Court (District Judge Ashton) 29 April 2002, Case No BB002640 (see note 35 and para 30.20 above).

rely on the individual teacher supervising the trip to make the decision. The school did not, the court ruled, have reasonable grounds for its stated belief either in the pupil's alleged irresponsibility or in the risk to his health and safety. The court ruled that 'If the opinion was to be reasonably held any underlying assumptions would have to be checked ... [there would need to be] ... a reasoned assessment of the implications of any increased risk'. In that case neither the pupil, his parents nor his doctors had been consulted by the school nor had further inquiries been made of the company running the trip. There was no serious attempt at a risk assessment taking into account the nature of the holiday and the medical realities.

30.64 The policy under consideration in the *White* case was that the teacher would make the decision and the school would support this decision. It was a policy which could make it unreasonably difficult for a disabled student to join a school trip because it created the potential for discrimination by the teacher which would then be routinely supported by the headmaster. The court held that this did not amount to justification under the DDA 1995 which requires a reasonably held opinion that discrimination is necessary in order not to endanger the health or safety of the disabled person or others. Delegation to staff without setting the criteria for their decision-making and requiring them to act fairly cannot avoid liability under the Act.

30.65 *White* provides a rigorous analysis of the justification provisions and examination of the reasons put forward by the respondent. By doing so, it demonstrates that *Rose v Bouchet*[84] turns on its own particular facts – namely, Mr Rose's angry outburst.

30.66 Generally, though, there have been remarkably few cases under the goods and services provisions of the DDA 1995 to date and so, *White* apart, there is as yet no reliable body of case law to inform the statutory provisions. In addition until the reasonable adjustment duty in relation to physical features comes into force in October 2004 it will not be clear how effective the goods, facilities and services provisions overall will be in enabling access to disabled people to the everyday services that others take for granted.

Insurance, guarantees and deposits

30.67 The treatment of a disabled person in relation to insurance, guarantees and deposits, would ordinarily fall within the goods, facilities and services provisions of the DDA 1995. However, the Act anticipates

84 [1999] IRLR 463.

(section 20(6)–(8)) that regulations may make special provision in this area, and may exempt some types of discrimination from the scope of the DDA 1995. The DD Regs 1999 do indeed modify the impact of the DDA 1995 on discrimination by way of less favourable treatment in relation to insurance, guarantees and deposits. These special rules have no impact on the duty of service providers to make reasonable adjustments.

30.68 The DD Regs 1999, which apply to insurance policies entered into, renewed or reviewed after 2 December 1996, provide that less favourable treatment for a reason related to the disabled person's disability will be justified when it is based on information such as actuarial or statistical data or a medical report, provided that three conditions are satisfied. First, the information must be relevant to the assessment of the risk to be insured. Second, the information must be from a reliable source. Third, the less favourable treatment must be reasonable having regard to the information relied on and other relevant factors.[85] These special rules apply only to the provision of insurance services by an insurer.

30.69 Not all insurance-related discrimination will be exempted by the DD Regs 1999. If, for example, a person with a diagnosis of manic depression is required to pay twice the normal premium for motor insurance, the insurer relying on actuarial data relating to the risks posed by a person during a manic episode, the fact that the applicant produces credible evidence that he has been stable on medication for some years and has an unblemished driving record will mean that the three conditions set out above are unlikely to be fulfilled by the insurer.[86] Insurers should not adopt blanket policies unless they can meet the three conditions.

30.70 In relation to guarantees,[87] the special rules set out in the DD Regs 1999 deal with situations in which a disabled person's disability results in higher than average wear and tear to goods or services supplied, and where it would not therefore be reasonable to expect service providers to honour a guarantee.[88] Less favourable treatment is deemed by the DD Regs 1999 to be justified where:[89]

85 DD Regs 1999, reg 2.

86 Part III code of practice, para 8.

87 A guarantee includes any document (however described) by which a service provider undertakes that the purchase price of goods, facilities services provided will be refunded if they are not of satisfactory quality; or services in the form of goods provided will be replaced or repaired if not of satisfactory quality. It does not matter whether the guarantee is legally enforceable –DD Regs 1999, reg 5(2).

88 DD Regs 1999, reg 5(2).

89 DD Regs 1999, reg 5.

- the service provider has provided a guarantee;
- damage has occurred for a reason which relates to the disabled person's disability;
- the service provider has refused to provide a replacement, repair or refund under the guarantee;
- the refusal is because the damage is above the level at which the guarantee would normally be honoured; and
- the refusal is reasonable in all the circumstances of the case.

30.71 The special rules about deposits deal with the question of whether a service provider can refuse to return a deposit in full if damage has occurred to the goods or facilities because of the customer's disability or a reason related to it.[90] Again, if (and only if) the service provider meets all the statutory conditions, its refusal to refund in full will be deemed justified. The conditions are that:

- the refusal is because the damage is above the level at which the service provider would normally refund the deposit in full; and
- the refusal is reasonable in all the circumstances of the case.

Chapter 8 of the Part III code of practice provides commentary and examples of the operation of the special rules.

Victimisation

30.72 The victimisation provisions (see chapter 4) apply to the goods, facilities and service provisions just as they do to employment cases.[91] It is irrelevant whether the person victimised is disabled or not. The question is whether he or she has performed a protected act.[92] An example of an act of victimisation in the goods and services context would be if the non-disabled dining partner of a disabled person is asked to leave a restaurant or is shouted at by a member of staff because he or she has complained of discrimination in the standard of service provided to his or her disabled dining companion. Only the disabled diner would be able to bring a complaint relating to less favourable treatment or a failure by the restaurant to make a reasonable adjustment. But the companion is entitled to complain of victimisation, to which no justification defence applies, under the DDA 1995.

90 DD Regs 1999 reg 6(2).
91 DDA 1995 s55.
92 As explained at para 4.20.

Enforcement

30.73 A claim under DDA 1995 Part II must be brought in the county court in England, Wales or Northern Ireland and in Scotland in the Sheriff court. Chapter 32 considers procedure in detail. Compensation is the usual remedy but injunctions (in Scotland interdicts) are also available in appropriate circumstances. Declarations can also be very important in goods, facilities and services cases. In addition, the Disability Rights Commission (DRC) has established an independent conciliation service to assist promotion of settlement of disputes.[93]

Terms of agreement

30.74 Any term in an agreement is void and unenforceable if its effect is to require someone to do something which would be unlawful under DDA 1995 Part III. This provision applies to services, facilities and goods as well as to premises (see para 30.75 onwards), and it applies to contractual clauses or terms which would exclude or limit the operation of DDA 1995 Part III or prevent someone making claim under Part III DDA 1995. The only exception is an agreement to settle or compromise a claim brought under the Act.[94]

Selling, letting or managing premises

Introduction

30.75 Disability Discrimination Act 1995 Part III contains provisions making it unlawful for landlords and other persons to discriminate against disabled people in relation to the sale, letting or management of premises.[95] The victimisation provisions also apply. The provisions came in to force in December 1996. There is no duty to make reasonable adjustments to premises which are sold, let or managed in order to meet the needs of disabled people but, if the person managing or disposing of the premises is also a service provider, s/he will be covered by the goods, facilities and service provisions considered above (and see para 30.75 onwards below). In addition, special provisions apply to employers, trade organisations and service providers occupying

93 DDA 1995 s28 and sch3 para 6(2), as amended by the DRCA 1999.
94 DDA 1995 s26.
95 DDA 1995 ss22–24.

premises under a lease as against their own landlords in order to enable them to comply with their own reasonable adjustment duties as employers, trade organisations and service providers. These are dealt with at paras 30.91–30.101. Once again, the Part III code of practice is of great assistance – in particular its chapter 9.

Unlawful discrimination

30.76 Section 22(1) of the Disability Discrimination Act 1995 makes it unlawful for a person with power to dispose of premises to discriminate against a disabled person in any of three ways:

(a) in the terms on which he or she offers to dispose of the premises to the disabled person;
(b) by refusing to dispose of a property to a disabled person; or
(c) in his or her treatment of a person on a housing or accommodation waiting list.

30.77 'Disposal' includes the selling or letting of premises, granting a right to occupy premises, assigning a tenancy and sub-letting,[96] but the provisions of the DDA 1995 do not automatically apply to private occupiers disposing of premises by private agreement or transaction. DDA 1995 s22(1) applies to the disposal of premises or an interest therein by an owner-occupier only if (DDA 1995 s22(2)) he or she uses an estate agent or advertises the property.[97] 'Advertisement' is widely defined, however, to include every form of advertisement or notice, whether to the public or not.

30.78 It is also unlawful for a person or a business that manages premises to discriminate against a disabled occupier in any of three ways:

- in the way in which he or she permits the disabled person to make use of any benefits or facilities;
- by refusing (or deliberately omitting) to permit the disabled person to make use of any benefits or facilities; or
- by evicting the disabled person, or subjecting him or her to any other detriment.[98]

30.79 Finally, DDA 1995 s22(4) makes it unlawful for any person whose licence or consent is required for the disposal of any leased or sub-let

96 DDA 1995 s22(6).
97 DDA 1995 s22(6) defines an estate agent as a person who, by way of profession or trade, provides services for the purpose of finding premises for persons seeking to acquire them or assisting in the disposal of premises.
98 DDA 1995 s22(3).

premises to discriminate against a disabled person by withholding such licence or consent.

30.80 Disability Discrimination Act 1995 s22(1) provides a limited exemption in relation to small dwellings. Broadly, multi-occupancy residential buildings in which accommodation (other than access or storage space) is shared by two or three separate households, or by the main occupier and up to six other individuals, are excluded from the application of DDA 1995 s22. The exemption does not apply to non-residential property and the person with the power to dispose of the premises must live there and be sharing the accommodation on the premises with other people who are not members of his or her household.[99] But if, for example, the owner of a four bedroom house has converted two bedrooms into bed-sit accommodation for two people, and he continues to live in the house with his family, the house satisfies the DDA 1995 definition of small premises and would be exempt from its premises provisions.[100]

'Discrimination' and 'justification'

30.81 We have seen above the circumstances under which discrimination will breach the DDA 1995. We have also seen how the definition of discrimination within the context of the DDA 1995 is not constant and varies according to the field of activity being protected. In the context of the premises provisions, only unjustified less favourable treatment constitutes discrimination and neither a person with power to dispose of premises nor the manager of premises owes a duty to disabled people to make reasonable adjustments.[101]

30.82 Disability Discrimination Act 1995 s24 provides that a person discriminates against a disabled person if, for a reason related to the disabled person's disability, he or she treats him less favourably than he or she treats or would treat others to whom that reason does not or would not apply, and he or she cannot show that the treatment in question is justified.[102] The definition of 'less favourable treatment' in this context is identical to that which applies in the employment context and in relation to goods, facilities and services (see paras 6.7 and

99 DDA 1995 s23(2)(a) and (b).

100 Part III code of practice, para 9.21.

101 Although see paras 30.91–30.101 for the obligations of landlords to service providers, employers and trade organisations to assist them to discharge their reasonable adjustment duties.

102 DDA 1995 s24(1)(a) and (b).

30.27 onwards). Readers are referred to para 6.7 onwards for a detailed analysis.

30.83 Like other forms of discrimination regulated by the DDA 1995, discrimination in relation to premises can be justified. We have seen already that the justification defence under the employment provisions is potentially far reaching whereas, in the goods, facilities and services provisions, justification is only made out if the alleged discriminator reasonably believes that one of five statutory conditions is met. The test for justification which applies in the context of premises very closely mirrors that applicable to the goods and services provisions of the DDA 1995 and will only be met if certain statutory criteria are met. Discriminatory treatment in relation to premises will only be justified if the alleged discriminator actually and reasonably believes that one of four statutory conditions is met.[103] This, like the test which applies in relation to goods, facilities and services, is both a subjective and objective test and knowledge of the disabled person's disability would seem to be irrelevant.

30.84 The four statutory conditions are very similar to the goods and services conditions. The first is where the treatment is necessary in order not to endanger the health or safety of any person (which may include the disabled person).[104] The second is that the disabled person is incapable of entering into an enforceable agreement or of giving an informed consent, and for that reason the treatment is reasonable in that case.[105] The third applies in cases where a person managing premises has treated a disabled occupier less favourably in the way in which the disabled person is allowed to make use of any benefits or facilities. Such discrimination will be justified where the discriminator reasonably believes it to be necessary to enable the disabled person or the occupiers of other premises forming part of the building to make use of the benefit or facility.[106] The fourth condition applies where the manager of premises refuses or deliberately fails to permit the disabled person to make use of any benefits or services, because he or she reasonably believes that this is necessary to permit occupiers of other premises forming part of the building to make use of the benefit or facility.[107]

103 DDA 1995 s24(2).
104 DDA 1995 s24(3)(a).
105 DDA 1995 s24(3)(b).
106 DDA 1995 s24(3)(c).
107 DDA 1995 s24(3)(d).

30.85 The four conditions are exhaustive – unless the alleged discriminator reasonably believes that one of the four conditions apply, the less favourable treatment is incapable of justification.

30.86 The leading case to date on justification under DDA 1995 Part III is *White v Clitheroe Grammar School*,[108] *Rose v Bouchet*[109] also being relevant here as it deals explicitly with the premises provisions. The cases are discussed at paras 30.61–30.66 above.

Deposits

30.87 The DD Regs 1999 make special provision for the situation where a person with power to dispose of premises asks a tenant to provide a deposit. The rule is broadly similar to the special provision in relation to deposits and goods, services and facilities (see para 30.67). Less favourable treatment of a disabled person in respect of a deposit will be justified under DD Regs 1999 reg 7 if and only if:

(a) the landlord (or other person with power to dispose of premises) grants a disabled person the right to occupy premises (whether under a formal tenancy agreement or otherwise);
(b) the disabled person is required to provide a deposit which is refundable at the end of the occupation if the premises and contents are undamaged;
(c) the landlord refuses to refund some or all of the deposit because the premises or contents have been damaged for a reason which relates to the disabled person's disability, and the damages are above the level at which the landlord would normally refund the deposit in full; and
(d) it is reasonable in all the circumstances for the landlord to refuse to refund the deposit in full.

30.88 Disability Discrimination Regulations 1999 reg 7 does not justify a landlord charging a disabled person a higher deposit than he or she would charge to other people, or asking the disabled person for a deposit when other people would not be expected to provide one.

108 Preston County Court (Ashton DJ) 29 April 2002, Case No BB002640.
109 [1999] IRLR 463.

Leases, building regulations and reasonable adjustments

Introduction

30.89 We have seen that employers, trade organisations and service providers may be under a duty to make reasonable adjustments (see chapters 12 and 13 and para 30.34 above). We have also seen that the adjustment required may include alteration to premises and physical features (although in the case of service providers only after 1 October 2004). There is however, no comparable duty to make adjustments to premises in respect of the disposal or management of premises (para 30.75 above).

30.90 Where an employer or trade organisation (or, after 1 October 2004, a service provider) is an owner of their premises it will have the power and right to make reasonable adjustments to its own buildings to meet its statutory duty. Where, however, an employer or trade organisation is a tenant it may not, depending on the provisions of its lease, have the power to make adjustments and it may therefore be difficult for it to discharge its duties to make reasonable adjustments. By making alterations to the building the employer might breach covenants in its lease – by not making them it may breach its duty to adjust. The DDA 1995 therefore makes special provision where an employer, trade organisation or service provider (the 'occupier') occupies premises under a lease. These provisions, which are intended to fill any lacunae in the provisions made by occupiers and their landlords, are principally set out in DDA 1995 s16 in respect of employers and trade organisations and in DDA 1995 s27 and Sch 4 in respect of service providers. They are supplemented by the Disability Discrimination (Employment) Regulations 1996 (DD(E) Regulations 1996),[110] the Disability Discrimination (Providers of Services) (Adjustment of Premises) Regulations 2001 (the 2001 Regulations),[111] and the Disability Discrimination (Sub-leases and Sub-tenancies) Regulations 1996 (the 1996 Regulations).[112] Part III code of practice, paras 6.26–6.49 are also relevant.

110 SI No 1455.
111 SI No 3253.
112 SI No 1333.

Leases

30.91 The provisions of the DDA 1995 apply where:

- an occupier – be it a trade organisation or service provider (from 2004) or further or higher education institution (from 2005) or employer (in force since 1996) – occupies premises under a lease;
- the terms of the lease prevent the occupier from making an alteration to premises; and
- the alteration is one which the occupier proposes to make to comply with the reasonable adjustment duty.[113]

30.92 A 'lease' is defined to include a tenancy, sub-lease or sub-tenancy and an agreement for a lease, tenancy, sub-tenancy or sub-lease.[114] The DDA 1995 overrides the terms of the lease so as to entitle the occupier to make the alteration with the written consent of the immediate landlord ('lessor'), provided the occupier has first written to the lessor asking for consent to make the alteration. The lessor cannot unreasonably withhold consent but may attach reasonable conditions to it.[115] If the terms of the lease impose conditions which apply if the occupier alters the premises or entitle the lessor to impose conditions when consenting to the occupier's altering of the premises, the provisions also apply as the occupier is treated as not being entitled to make the alteration.[116]

30.93 If the occupier fails to seek the written consent of the lessor to make the adjustment (where consent is required) the occupier will not be able to rely on the restriction in the lease in seeking to justify the failure to make a reasonable adjustment.[117]

30.94 The lessor may him or herself be a tenant of a superior landlord and may hold a lease which includes terms preventing alterations to the premises or attaching conditions to any alteration and therefore may not be in a position to consent to the occupiers request to do the alterations. Provisions apply for the occupier's landlord to apply to his or her superior landlord in writing for consent to the alteration and for the consent not to be unreasonably withheld.[118]

30.95 The mechanics of seeking the lessor's consent are outside the

113 DDA 1995 ss16(1) and 27(1).

114 DDA 1995 ss16(3) and 27(3). Further definitions are provided by the 1996 Regs.

115 DDA 1995 ss16(2) and 27(2).

116 DDA 1995 ss16(4) and 27(4).

117 DDA 1995 Sch 4 Pt I, para 1 and Sch 4 Pt II, para 5.

118 1996 Regs.

scope of this publication but are set out in the 1996 Regulations (in force since December 1996) in respect of employers and the 2001 Regulations (in force from 2004) in relation to trade organisations and service providers and for further and higher education institutions from September 2005.[118a] The code of practice on rights of access to goods, facilities, services and premises (in particular see chapter 6) also provides detailed guidance. In the education context, chapter 7 of the Part IV code of practice for providers of post-16 education and related services is also helpful.

30.96 It is deemed not reasonable for an employer or trade organisation to take a step that would otherwise amount to a reasonable adjustment under DDA 1995 s6 if a number of conditions are satisfied:

- the step must be contrary to the terms of any lease under which the employer occupies the premises;
- the employer must have applied to the lessor in writing to take the step and indicated in writing that it proposed to take the step, subject to the lessor's consent, in order to comply with its reasonable adjustment duty;
- the lessor must have withheld that consent;
- the occupier must have informed the disabled person that it applied for the consent of the lessor and that the lessor has withheld it.[119]

30.97 The circumstances are narrow and require written verification. A lessor may be joined (in Scotland, sisted) to tribunal proceedings either by the claimant or the employer where a question arises about the alteration of premises occupied under a lease, in order to determine whether the lessor had unreasonably refused consent or imposed unreasonable conditions on it.[120] A tribunal has power to declare whether consent has been unreasonably withheld or unreasonable conditions attached to it, and power to order that compensation be paid by the lessor to the applicant and to order the lessor to make the adjustments concerned.

30.98 The position will be broadly similar in relation to physical adjustments required to be made by providers of services from October 2004. In addition to the right to join the lessor to the proceedings, however, there will be a right to apply to the county or Sheriff court for a declaration and order in relation to a lessor's refusal to consent or

118a DDA 1995 s28W (amended by SENDA 2001 s31) is scheduled to come into force in September 2005.

119 DD(E) Regs 1996 reg 14.

120 DDA 1995 Sch 4 para 2.

imposition of conditions to consent for the premises to be altered in response to a written request.[121] This reflects the difference in reasonable adjustment duty between the employment and goods and services provisions, and the fact that the duty to adjust to accommodate service users is owed at large.

Statutory and other obligations

30.99 An employer (or, when the provisions come into force, a service provider or trade organisation) may be subject to binding obligations, other than to their landlord, in relation to adjustments to be made to their physical premises. These might include a requirement for listed building consent, planning permission or for compliance with fire regulations which amount to statutory obligations. Mortgage restrictions or restrictive covenants may also apply.

30.100 It will still be necessary for an employer (and, after October 2004, a service provider or trade organisation) to obtain any statutory consent necessary to make adjustments to its physical premises. The Part III code of practice recommends that service providers plan for and anticipate the need to obtain consent to make a particular adjustment. The Part III code states that, where consent has been refused, there is likely to be a means of appeal. Whether or not the service provider's duty to take such steps as is reasonable includes pursuing an appeal will depend on the circumstances of the case.[122] The employer, etc, will be unlikely to escape liability if it merely assumes that consent would not be forthcoming – consent or approval to the necessary works must actually be sought.

30.101 Regulation 10 of the DD(E) Regs 1996 provides that it is always reasonable for an employer or landlord to take steps to obtain the consent of another person (such as a mortgagor) to make the alteration where required, but that it is never reasonable to make the alteration before the consent is obtained. In seeking to obtain consent an employer or landlord may (but will not necessarily) need to go to a court or tribunal: whether this is necessary to comply with the DDA 1995 will depend on all the circumstances of the case.

121 DDA 1995 Sch 4 para 6.
122 Part III code of practice, paras.6.29 and 6.30.

Building regulations

30.102 Building regulations in force set out requirements for reasonable provision to be made for disabled people to gain access to and use new buildings, and apply to new buildings, to new ground floor extensions, and to some other new extensions to public buildings and places of employment.[123] Their detail is outside the scope of this publication, but we consider here the interplay between them and the duties imposed by the DDA 1995 to make reasonable adjustments.

30.103 Under the employment provisions of the DDA 1995, if certain conditions are met to do with building regulations an employer will not be required to make particular adjustments to its building. The conditions are that the building[124] must have been constructed in accordance with Part M of the Building Regulations (Access and facilities for disabled people) in England and Wales (in Scotland, with Part T of the Technical Standards regarding access for disabled people);[125] that the building must have met the requirements of Part M or T at the time the building work was carried out; and that the building must continue to meet substantially those requirements as they were then (Part M has been in force since 1985, but its coverage and scope has changed over the years). In other words, provided that a building met the current building regulations at the time of its construction, and provided that it would still comply with those regulations, an employer will not be required to make an adjustment that would go beyond the regulations as they applied at the time of construction.

30.104 Similar provisions will apply in relation to the premises of service providers from October 2004 and chapter 6 of the Part III code of practice provides a helpful explanation of the regulatory framework in building construction and the DDA 1995. The link with building regulations for goods, facilities and services is different than for employment. Approval Document M which applies to the goods, facilities and services provisions is much more detailed than part M (applicable in the employment field) and the exemptions under Approval Document M applies only for 10 years, whereas in the employment context the exemption is infinite.

123 Currently Building Regulations 2000 SI No 2531.

124 'Building' is defined by DD(E) Regs 1996 reg 2 as an erection or structure of any kind.

125 DD(E) Regs 1996.

Transport

Introduction

30.105 The Disability Rights Commission (DRC) has stated of public transport and the needs of disabled people that:

> The vast majority of disabled people experience significant levels of social exclusion because the design and operation of Britain's transport system has failed to deliver an appropriate and accessible service. Disabled people do not generally travel through choice, and make only those journeys that they consider essential. Prolonged negative experience causes disabled people to continually re-evaluate what is an essential journey and contributes to shrinking journey patterns and social isolation.
>
> Most disabled people have had poor experiences of public transport, an exposure to unequal levels of risk and much of which has led to personal injury. This has caused a dramatic reduction in their confidence in using public transport again. Difficult journeys constitute the majority rather than the minority of disabled people's transport experience. The historic failure of the industry to meet their requirements in either access or operational terms has created a network from which they are largely excluded.[126]

30.106 Despite this, the prohibitions made by the DDA 1995 on discrimination in relation to the provision of services do not apply to any service so far as it consists of the use of any means of transport.[127] Provisions relating to land based transport vehicles are set out in DDA 1995 Part V (ss32–49) and provide a very different regime which is based largely on criminal liability and is not yet fully in force. The DDA 1995 does not create a general right of access to transport.

30.107 Before considering each of the various categories of means of transport it is worth noting the scope of the exclusion of transport from DDA 1995 Part III. There have been two known cases on the meaning of the term 'the use of any means of transport'. While it is clear that it precludes a challenge under DDA 1995 Part III in relation to the accessibility of, for example a tram or a bus, ancillary services and facilities and all the infrastructure related to the means of transport which do not themselves involve the use of the mode of transport itself are outside the transport exclusion and covered by DDA 1995

126 DRC response to the Cabinet Office Consultation on Transport and Social Exclusion, November 2001 is available from www.drc.org.uk.

127 DDA 1995 s19(5)(b).

Part III.[127a] In *McMurty v Virgin Trains*,[127b] at a preliminary hearing on the transport exclusion, the judge held that assistance at a station for a visually impaired passenger and his dog was not covered by the transport exemption. So, for example, a café on a railway platform clearly falls within the service provisions but the on-train buffet car does not. Transport infrastructure such as bus or tram stops, stations and termini fall within the DDA 1995 Part III service provisions as do airport facilities. Timetables, ticketing arrangements, booking facilities and waiting areas for example would also be covered by DDA 1995 Part III. In *Rimmer v British Airways plc*,[128] the claimant asked for a seat at the bulkhead of the aeroplane to provide her with extra leg-room to relieve the pain of her arthritis. British Airways refused and Ms Rimmer cancelled her booking. She then issued proceedings under DDA 1995 Part III, arguing that British Airways had failed to take adequate steps to change their policy, practice or procedure in the allocation of seats to accommodate her special requirements making it impossible to make use of the airline service. British Airways sought to rely on the transport exclusion. The judge held that 'the use of any means of transport' includes the allocation of seats and drew a distinction between a failure by an airline to make access to the booking facilities available to a disabled person (which would be outside the transport exclusion and therefore covered by DDA 1995 Part III) and a failure by an airline to take account of special requests when a disabled person books a service. The latter circumstance, it was held, clearly related to the use of the transport and therefore fell within the exception.

30.108 It therefore appears that the transport exclusion in DDA 1995 Part III is being interpreted narrowly and a presumption being applied that – unless a transport provider can show it comes within the exclusion – the prohibition on discrimination in the provision of facilities and services will apply.

30.109 The structure of DDA 1995 Part V is to confer regulation making power on the Secretary of State for Transport to enact accessibility standards to enable disabled passengers to get on and off and to be carried in reasonable safety and comfort on trains, public service vehicles (PSVs– ie, buses and coaches) and taxis. Regulations are

127a Code of practice paras 2.8 and 2.21.
127b Newcastle upon Tyne County Court, NE 140154 (unreported).
128 Great Grimsby County Court, GG 100921, 26 September 2001 (unreported).
128a This provision is in force only in England, Wales and Northern Ireland, and not yet in Scotland.

in place for trains and PSVs, but not yet for taxis. The DDA 1995 provides no regulation-making powers in relation to other forms of transport. The DDA 1995 imposes two statutory duties on taxi drivers towards disabled passengers (see para 30.123), of which only one is presently in force.[128a] No civil liability is incurred, or will be incurred once the regulations are in place and in force, for any breach of DDA 1995 Part V. The enforcement mechanism applicable to DDA 1995 Part V consists of a licensing or certification system backed up by criminal sanctions.

30.110 The forms of transport not specifically addressed by the regulatory framework of DDA 1995 Part V include aircraft and maritime transport, vehicle breakdown recovery services, car rental, private hire and minicabs.[129] However as explained above, the goods and services provisions of DDA 1995 Part III will apply to, for example a ferry operator or airline or minicab booking system and any other service other than the actual use of the means of transport itself.

30.111 Other initiatives relating to disability and transport are outside the scope of this publication. These include the orange/blue badge car parking permit scheme; reduced bus fare schemes operated by local authorities; voluntary measures taken by licensing authorities concerning, for example, the wheelchair accessibility of taxis; and measures such as local bye-laws benefiting disabled transport users which are dependent on the political will of local councils. Here, however, we will only be considering that statutory framework at present and in the imminent future.

Trains and trams

30.112 Sections 47 and 48 of the Disability Discrimination Act 1995 enable rail vehicle accessibility regulations to be made, after appropriate consultation, for the purpose of ensuring that it is possible for disabled people to get on and off regulated rail vehicles in safety and without unreasonable difficulty; to be carried in such vehicles; and, in the case

129 There is an exception to the generality of the private hire/minicab exclusion. Regulations may be made to require hire cars at some airports and other transport facilities (meaning ports, airports, railway stations or bus stations) to be accessible to disabled people where there is a franchise agreement in operation (DDA 1995 s33). A private member's bill is currently before parliament which will, if enacted, include private taxis in the DDA 1995 transport provision.

of disabled wheelchair users, to do so whilst remaining in their wheelchairs.[130]

30.113 The Rail Vehicle Accessibility Regulations 1998 (RVA Regs 1998) were introduced pursuant to these sections.[131] They came into force in November 1998 and were amended from 31 December 2001 by the Rail Vehicle Accessibility (Amendment) Regulations 2000.[132] The Disability Rights Commission describes these Regulations as:

> ... comparatively innovative and radical regulations that formally acknowledge the design requirements of disabled people, and make meeting those requirements mandatory. Mandatory requirements provide compelling motivation for those implementing them, particularly when breaching these requirements is a criminal and not a civil offence.[133]

30.114 The RVA Regs 1998 only apply to 'regulated rail vehicles', that is, any rail vehicles to which the regulations are expressed to apply.[134] They apply to passenger-carrying vehicles used on railways, tramways, monorail systems or magnetic levitation systems and systems which are track-based with side guidance which were first brought into use, on or after 1 January 1999. They apply, therefore, only to new rolling stock, although the Strategic Rail Authority is also requiring compliance with the accessibility standards at the refurbishment stage within its code of practice – Train and Station Services for Disabled Passengers.

30.115 The accessibility standards set out in the RVA Regs 1998 are very detailed and technical and are outside the scope of this book. Suffice it to say they appear comprehensive, covering exterior and interior aspects of a rail vehicle and such things as catering services, audible and visual announcements inside and outside the rail vehicle toilets, and sleeping compartments.[135] Regulated rail vehicles must continue to meet the standards imposed by the RVA Regs 1998 all the time that the vehicle runs in passenger service which therefore have implications for rail vehicle maintenance and inspection.

30.116 It is a criminal offence for an 'operator' (a person having management of the rail vehicle) to use a regulated rail vehicle for carriage

130 DDA 1995 s46(1).

131 SI No 2456.

132 SI No 3215.

133 Paragraph 15.1 of the DRC response to the Cabinet Office Consultation on Transport and Social Exclusion, note 126 above.

134 DDA 1995 s46(6).

135 RVA Regs 1998 regs 4–24.

which does not conform with any appropriate provision of the RVA Regs 1998. A person uses a rail vehicle for carriage if that rail vehicle is used for the carriage of members of the public for hire or reward at separate fares (these provisions do not, therefore, cover trains which have been privately hired or commissioned, for example, for a school trip).[136] Breach of the RVA Regs 1998 is punishable in the magistrates court with a fine not exceeding level 4 on the standard scale.[137]

30.117 The Rail Vehicle (Exemption Applications) Regulations 1998[138] (1998 Regs) provide for exemptions to be made from the RVA Regs 1998. The application for an exemption order must be in writing and must provide details not only of the specific requirement(s) from which exemption is sought, but also of the reasons why exemption is sought; the effect of the exemption on disabled people; any measures which could be taken to enable disabled people to use the rail vehicle if the exemption were to be granted; and the period of time sought for the exemption. The Secretary of State must consult the Disabled Persons Transport Advisory Committee (DPTAC) before granting an exemption order.

30.118 If a disabled person encounters difficulty in using a rail vehicle we recommend that he or she writes to the rail operator, the Department of Transport Local Government and the Regions (DTLR) and the DPTAC, as well as the DRC. Their details appear in the list of useful addresses in appendix A at the end of this book. It may also be useful to inform the Strategic Rail Authority.

Buses and coaches (public service vehicles)

30.119 The Public Service Vehicles Accessibility Regulations 2000 (PSV Regs 2000) have been in force since 30 August 2000.[139] A PSV is a vehicle adapted to carry more than eight passengers and meeting the definition set out in the Public Passenger Vehicles Act 1981. Broadly, the PSV Regs 2000 cover buses and coaches and contain a list of exempt PSVs such as ambulances and prison vans.[140] The PSV Regs 2000, like the RVA Regs 1998, apply only to new vehicles. They are being gradually implemented depending on the type of vehicle concerned – whether it is a single or double-decker, for example, and the

136 DDA 1995 s46(10).
137 DDA 1995 s46(3)–(4).
138 SI No 2457, made under DDA 1995 s47.
139 SI No 1970.
140 PSV Regs 2000 reg 4.

tonnage of the vehicle. The PVA Regulations are to be fully implemented by 2020. They are divided into those which apply to the provision of wheelchair accessible spaces and those which apply to general accessibility issues such as colour, operability of bell pushes, slip resistance of flooring and so on. This reflects the comparative difficulties of redesigning different features of the bus. All new buses must meet all PSV Regs 2000 regulations.

30.120 The purpose of the PSV Regs 2000, like that of the RVA Regs 1998, is to ensure that it is possible for disabled people to get on and off regulated PSVs in safety and without unreasonable difficulty (and, in the case of disabled people in wheelchairs, that they can do so do so while remaining in their wheelchairs); and to be carried in safety and reasonable comfort.[141]

30.121 The PSV Regs 2000 make it a criminal offence not to have either an accessibility certificate or a type vehicle approval certificate and conformity certificate.[142] The former certificate demonstrates that a vehicle examiner has issued an accessibility certificate in respect of a particular vehicle. The latter certificate confirms that a particular vehicle is covered by a type vehicle approval certificate which is intended to obviate the need for individual inspection where the vehicle conforms to the type vehicle.[143] The PSV Regs 2000 provide a review and appeal mechanism against a refusal of an application for the approval of a vehicle.[144]

30.122 It is suggested that disabled people who have encountered difficulties in using a PSV raise the matter with the bus company or coach operator, the licensing authority, the DTLR and DPTAC as well as contacting the DRC.

Taxis

30.123 At present the only relevant DDA 1995 provision in force is section 37 which imposes duties on the driver of a taxi which has been hired either by a disabled person who is accompanied by his guide or hearing dog, or by a person who wishes such a disabled person to

141 DDA 1995 s40.

142 Liability is on the PSV operator. Jurisdiction is in the magistrates court which may impose a penalty of up to a maximum of level 4 on the standard scale (DDA 1995 s41(3)).

143 DDA 1995 ss41 and 42 and PSV Regs 2000 regs 6–17.

144 DDA 1995 s44 and PSV Regs 2000 reg 19.

accompany him or her in the taxi.[145] These duties are to carry the passenger and his or her dog, to allow the dog to remain with the passenger, and not to make an additional charge for doing so.[146] Section 37 has been in force since April 2001 in England and Wales and is expected to come into force in Scotland and Northern Ireland by the end of 2002. A taxi driver who fails to comply with this duty is liable to prosecution in the Magistrates Court and a fine not exceeding level 3.

30.124 The taxi licensing authority has power to issue a certificate of exemption on medical grounds from the DDA 1995 s37 obligations to taxi drivers if it is satisfied this is appropriate having regard, inter alia, to the physical characteristics of the taxi.[147] The certificate must be exhibited on the taxi. The exemption certificate will relate to a specified taxi or type of taxi and be for a period of time specified in the certificate. Refusal to issue a certificate of exemption may be appealed to the magistrates court.[148]

30.125 Section 36 of the Disability Discrimination Act 1995, which is not yet in force, will impose further duties on taxi drivers where the taxi has been hired by a disabled person who is a wheelchair user (the passenger), or by a person who wishes such a disabled person to accompany him or her in the taxi. These duties are to take the passenger and the wheelchair in the taxi whether the passenger is sitting in either the wheelchair or a passenger seat; not to charge extra for doing so; and to take such steps as are necessary to ensure that the passenger is carried in the taxi in safety and reasonable comfort.[149] DDA 1995 s36 will also require drivers to give such assistance as may be reasonably required to enable disabled passengers to get in and out of their taxi (whether they remain in their wheelchairs or not) and to load and unload disabled passengers' luggage (including, if the passenger does not wish to remain in his or her wheelchair, that wheelchair).[150]

30.126 The taxi licensing authority will be able to exempt taxi drivers from the duties to be imposed by DDA 1995 s36 if satisfied that it is

145 Taxi is defined as one licensed under the Town Police Clauses Act 1847, the Metropolitan Public Carriage Act 1869 or the Local Government (Miscellaneous Provisions) Act 1976 (or, in Northern Ireland, the Road Traffic (Northern Ireland) Order 1981). Broadly it means a taxi which can ply for hire, as distinct from a minicab which must be pre-booked.

146 DDA 1995 s37(3).

147 DDA 1995 s37(5)–(8).

148 DDA 1995 s38.

149 DDA 1995 s36(3).

150 DDA 1995 s36(3)(e).

appropriate to do so on medical grounds or on the ground that a driver's physical condition makes it impossible or unreasonably difficult for him or her to comply with the duties.[151] The certificate of exemption will be for a specific duration and must be displayed in the taxi. Breach of the DDA 1995 s36 duty will be a criminal offence punishable in the magistrates court with a fine up to a maximum of level 3 on the standard scale.[152]

30.127 The DDA 1995 s36 duty will not come into force until taxi accessibility regulations have been drafted and implemented. Sections 32–35 of the Disability Discrimination Act 1995 enable the Secretary of State to make regulations for the purpose of securing that it is possible for disabled people get in and out of taxis safely and to be carried in taxis in reasonable comfort and safety and, in the case of disabled wheelchair users, to do so whilst remaining in their wheelchairs. These regulations, yet to be passed, will be referred to generally as the Taxi Accessibility Regulations[153] (TA Regs). Some licensing authorities have already introduced accessibility requirements as a condition of granting a taxi licence. This is a voluntary measure (voluntary, that is, for the licensing authority rather than taxi owner or operator) and not yet required by the DDA 1995. The Secretary of State will be able to make exemption regulations having regard to circumstances prevailing in the licensing area if the TA Regs would result in an unacceptable reduction in the number of taxis. Except in very limited circumstances a taxi licensing authority will not be able to grant a taxi licence (a licence to ply for hire) unless the vehicle conforms to the TA Regs.[154]

30.128 The taxi is the most used form of public transport for disabled people – it would clearly be counter-productive if the effect of the introduction of regulations were to strangle the taxi trade. However the DRC's verdict on the lack of progress in the promulgation of taxi accessibility regulations is forthright:

> Taxis are critical to disabled people's independent travel patterns, largely because they are unable to access other modes of transport. Apart from the additional expense in using taxis rather than the cheaper modes of transport, disabled people are still experiencing discrimination while using taxis. The parameters for the design of the vehicle under the DDA 1995 are not yet determined; the formal

151 DDA 1995 s36(7).
152 DDA 1995 s36(5).
153 DDA 1995 s32(1).
154 DDA 1995 s34.

consultation on the accessibility regulations has still not yet been circulated. Discrimination from drivers refusing to take either the disabled person or their assistance dog is still commonplace despite the introduction of DDA 1995 s37.[155]

30.129 The position in Northern Ireland and Scotland is a little different. Equivalent provision can be made in Scotland by amendments to the Civic Government (Scotland) Act 1982 and similar provision may be made in Northern Ireland subject to modifications in DDA 1995 Sch 8, parags 16–23. No taxi provisions are yet in force in Scotland and Northern Ireland.

Travel by air and boat

30.130 Aviation and shipping transport are both excluded from DDA 1995 Part III insofar as they amount to the use of a means of transport. Nor are they covered by the regulation-making powers set out in DDA 1995 Part V.

Education

Introduction

30.131 The importance of educational opportunities has long been acknowledged as crucial in the battle for equality. Clearly the attainment of qualifications and access to education assists individuals in competing equally in the labour market and in accessing better paid and more secure employment. As the government has acknowledged:

> [Education] is vital to the creation of a fully inclusive society, a society in which all members see themselves as valued for the contribution they make. We owe all children – whatever their particular needs and circumstances – the opportunity to develop their full potential, to contribute economically, and to play a full part as active citizens.[156]

30.132 Despite this, the DDA 1995, unlike the sex and race discrimination legislation, originally excluded the provision of education from its

155 Para 7.9 of the DRC response to the Cabinet Office Consultation on Transport and Social Exclusion, note 126 above.

156 David Blunkett, Secretary of State for Education and Employment, in 'Meeting Special Educational Needs: A Programme of Action' (DfEE www.dfee.gov.uk/senap/index.htm).

goods and services provisions.[157] Instead of conferring individual rights to protection from disability discrimination the DDA 1995, on enactment, merely required the governing bodies of maintained mainstream schools, further and higher education institutions and Local Education Authorities (LEAs) to publish information annually about their admission arrangements for disabled pupils and students and adult education and their facilities for disabled students.

30.133 The Special Education Needs and Disability Act 2001 (SENDA 2001) changes the position substantially by removing the exemption of education from the goods and services provisions of the DDA 1995 and by amending the current DDA 1995 Part IV to introduce duties not to discriminate in education.

30.134 There is a rolling programme of implementation of the SENDA 2001 provisions. The less favourable treatment provisions and some of the reasonable adjustment provisions will come into force on 1 September 2002; a duty to make adjustments involving the provision of auxiliary aids and services on 1 September 2003; and a duty to make adjustments to physical features of premises on 1 September 2005.

30.135 The new statutory rights are accompanied by two new statutory codes of practice issued by the Disability Rights Commission (DRC) – the DDA 1995 Part IV post-16 education code of practice and the DDA 1995 Part IV code of practice for schools.[158] As is the case with other statutory codes their relevant provisions, although not legally binding, may be taken into account by tribunals and courts.

Scope of the education provisions

30.136 Until 1 September 2002 'education' (including private as well as state education, higher and further as well as primary and secondary education) was excluded from DDA Part III.[159] The exemption in the DDA 1995 covered 'education which is funded, or secured, by a relevant body ... or is at any other establishment which is a school'. The list of relevant bodies and the statutory definition of schools together provided comprehensive coverage of educational institutions covered by the exemption. Schools, colleges and educational establishments are not exempt from the employment provisions of the DDA 1995 in their capacity as employers.

30.137 The exemption in the DDA 1995 did not cover non-educational

157 DDA 1995 s19(5)(a).

158 Available from www.drc.org.uk.

159 DDA 1995 s19(5)(a) and (6).

facilities and services which an educational institution happens to provide – such as allowing the public to use the swimming pool, or hosting a PTA event. But the DD Regs 1999 extended the education exemption to cover youth and community services provided by LEAs and voluntary organisations such as the Woodcraft Folk, to research facilities and to assessments (eg, public exams).[160]

30.138 From 1 September 2002 the education exemption contained in DDA 1995 Part III is repealed and schools, colleges and higher education institutions are under new duties, by virtue of an amended DDA 1995 Part IV, not to discriminate against disabled students. The coverage of the amended DDA 1995 Part IV is not coterminous with the education exemption of DDA 1995 Part II. Private universities and colleges, for example, are not covered by the amended DDA 1995 Part IV.[161] Since the DDA 1995 Part III education exemption is repealed in its entirety from 1 September 2002 it means that institutions not covered by the amended DDA 1995 Part IV will be caught by the goods and services provisions, all things being equal.

30.139 This book will consider the law as at 1 September 2002. Northern Ireland is not covered by the SENDA 2001 amendments to the DDA 1995, responsibility for equal opportunity as well as educational matters having been devolved to the Northern Ireland assembly.

Schools

Special educational needs

30.140 Part I of the Special Educational Needs and Disability Act 2001 (SENDA 2001) amends the Education Act 1996 to strengthen the rights of children in England and Wales with special educational needs (SEN) to be educated in mainstream schools where parents want this and the interests of children can be protected. It seeks to foster the increased inclusion of such children and safeguard the efficient education of all pupils. SENDA 2001 requires Local Education Authorities (LEAs) to make arrangements for services to provide parents of children with SEN with advice and information, and a means of resolving disputes with schools and LEAs. The provisions are designed to dovetail with existing duties under the existing SEN framework. The detail of the changes to the existing legislation for children with SEN is outside the scope of this publication. A child

160 DD Regs 1999 reg 9.

161 These are fully discussed in chapter 3 of the post-16 education code of practice.

with SEN is not necessarily disabled as defined for the purposes of the DDA 1995. Nor does a disabled child necessarily have SEN. Different provisions apply in Scotland and Northern Ireland.

Disability discrimination duties

30.141 A new DDA 1995 s28A prohibits all schools from discriminating against disabled children in their admission arrangements, in the education and associated services provided by the school, and in relation to exclusions from the school. The term education and associated services is broad. The code of practice for schools illustrates the breadth of the term describing it as covering all aspects of school life and lists 22 examples, such interaction with peers, access to school clubs and activities, school discipline and sanctions, the serving of school meals, breaks and lunchtimes, as well as the more obvious examples of the curriculum, teaching and learning.[162] Disabled pupils and prospective pupils are covered by the legislation.[163] 'Disability' has the meaning set out in DDA 1995 s1 as detailed at para 2.47 onwards above.

30.142 Discrimination in the context of school education is defined by DDA 1995 s28B to cover unjustified less favourable treatment and a failure to make reasonable adjustments which is to the disabled person's detriment. The definition of 'less favourable treatment' is the same as that which applies in the employment context (see para 6.7 onwards) but, by contrast with the position there, a responsible body will not be taken to have treated a disabled pupil less favourably if it did not know, and could not reasonably have been expected to know, that the pupil was disabled.[164]

30.143 The definition of 'justification' which applies in the education context is also similar to that which applies in relation to employment – less favourable treatment of a person is justified only if the reason for it is both material to the circumstances of the particular case and substantial.[165] Less favourable treatment of a person will also be justified if it is the result of a permitted form of selection.[166] Permitted forms of selection vary depending on the type of school and on whether it is

162 DDA 1995 Pt IV code of practice for schools para 4.23.

163 By SENDA 2001 s11. A pupil is defined in education legislation – Education (Scotland) Act 1980 s135(1) and Education Act 1996 s3(1).

164 DDA 1995 s28B(4) as amended by SENDA 2001 s12.

165 DDA 1995 s28B(7) as amended by SENDA 2001 – see para 6.38 above.

166 DDA 1995 s28B(6) as amended by SENDA 2001.

in England, Wales or Scotland.[167] A school which selects its intake on the basis of academic ability is likely to be able to justify its refusal to admit an 11 year old with learning difficulties who fails its admission test.[168] By contrast, an independent school which selects its pupils on the basis of the common entrance examination is unlikely to be able to justify its rejection of a pupil who has learning and behavioural difficulties but who has passed that examination.[169]

30.144 The duty to make reasonable adjustments is set out in DDA 1995 s28C which provides that a school's 'responsible body' must take such steps as it is reasonable for it to have to take to ensure that:

(a) in relation to the arrangements it makes for determining the admission of pupils to the school, disabled persons are not placed at a substantial disadvantage in comparison with persons who are not disabled; and
(b) in relation to education and associated services provided for, or offered to, pupils at the school by it, disabled pupils are not placed at a substantial disadvantage in comparison with pupils who are not disabled.

30.145 The responsible body is not, however, required to:

- remove or alter a physical feature (for example, one arising from the design or construction of the school premises or the location of resources); or
- provide auxiliary aids or services to disabled pupils.

This differs from the duty on further and higher education institutions where there will be no such exemption when the reasonable adjustment provisions are fully in force. The relevant minister is empowered to make regulations as to reasonableness.

30.146 In general, in England and Wales the governing body is the 'responsible body' in a maintained school; the LEA for a pupil referral unit or maintained nursery; and the proprietor[170] of an independent school or special school which is not maintained by an LEA. In

167 The code of practice on school admissions (1999) for England, the Welsh Office code of practice on school admissions (April 1999). In Scotland, Scottish Ministerial approval is required for selection of pupils and all schools (whether publicly funded or not) are subject to the Race Relations Act 1976 and the Sex Discrimination Act 1975.

168 Code of practice for schools para 5.23A.

169 Code of practice for schools para 5.23B.

170 The Education Act 1996 states that the proprietor is the person or group of people responsible for the management of the school, which would include the trustees, the governing body, the private owner or the management group of the school.

Scotland the education authority will be the responsible body for a school managed by an education authority; the proprietor in the case of an independent school; the board of management for a self-governing school, and the managers of the school in the case of a grant-aided school.

30.147 Although the duty to make reasonable adjustments in the context of education mirrors the general approach of DDA 1995 s6 in the employment context (see para 6.15 onwards above) the duty is owed, like the duty in relation to the provision of goods and services, to pupils at large. It is therefore described by the education codes of practice as an anticipatory duty in.[171] Having said this, it is necessary for a disabled pupil to show that the failure to comply with the duty has been to his or her detriment[172] and a breach of any such duty is not actionable per se.[173] Although the duty to adjust is an anticipatory one, the consequences of this are diluted because a responsible body will not be regarded as discriminating against a person contrary to the DDA 1995 by failing to make a reasonable adjustment if it shows that, at the time in question, it did not know and could not reasonably be expected to know that the person was disabled and that its failure to take the step was attributable to that lack of knowledge.[174]

30.148 In deciding whether it is reasonable for a responsible body to take a particular step in order to comply with the duty to make reasonable adjustment, it must have regard to the statutory code of practice (the code of practice for schools). Like the other codes of practice issued under the DDA 1995 this code is thorough and helpful and explains the provisions by making extensive use of practical examples.

30.149 DDA 1995 s28C introduces the concept of a confidentiality request which impacts on the duty to make reasonable adjustment. A confidentiality request is a request which asks for the nature, or the existence, of a disabled person's disability to be treated as confidential and which is either made by that person's parent, or by a disabled person who is reasonably believed by the responsible body to have sufficient understanding of the nature of the request and its effects.[175] Where a confidentiality request has been made of which the responsible body is aware, whether the adjustment could be made whilst

171 Code of practice for schools para 6.12; post-16 education code of practice para 5.5.

172 DDA 1995 s28B(2)(a) as amended by SENDA 2001 s12.

173 DDA 1995 s28C(8) as amended.

174 DDA 1995 s28B(3) as amended.

175 DDA 1995 s28C(7) as amended.

preserving confidentiality must be taken into account in considering the reasonableness of the adjustment in question.

30.150 As with the employment provisions, a failure to make a reasonable adjustment will not amount to discrimination if the failure to comply with the duty is justified.[176] Justification has the same definition as where the alleged discrimination consists of less favourable treatment (see para 30.143).

30.151 There is an interplay between the duty to make reasonable adjustment and the prohibition of unjustifiable less favourable treatment in the education context, just as there is in employment (see para 6.49 above). If a responsible body is under a reasonable adjustment duty, but fails without justification to comply with that duty and treats a disabled person less favourably, the less favourable treatment cannot be justified unless it would have been justified even had the responsible body complied with that duty to adjust.[177] This is more fully explained at para 6.49 above.

Planning duties

30.152 In line with government policy towards inclusion, new sections 28D and 28E of the Disability Discrimination Act 1995 (DDA 1995), introduced as amendments by Special Educational Needs and Disability Act 2001 (SENDA 2001), set out strengthened requirements on LEAs and schools in England and Wales to draw up accessibility strategies and accessibility plans respectively in order to improve access to education at schools over time. They must address planned improvements in access to the curriculum; physical improvements to increase access to education and associated services; and improvements in the provision of information in a range of formats for disabled pupils.

30.153 The Scottish Executive has brought forward draft legislation to introduce a duty on all those responsible for schools to prepare accessibility strategies to address improvements in access to the curriculum; improvement to the physical environment to increase access to education and associated services; and improvements in the provision of information to disabled pupils.[178]

Residual duties of education authorities

30.154 SENDA 2001 amends the DDA 1995 by inserting new sections 28F and 28G which make it unlawful for an LEA in England and Wales, or

176 DDA 1995 s28B(2) as amended.
177 DDA 1995 s28B(8) as amended.
178 Education (Disability Strategies and Pupils' Records)(Scotland) Bill.

an education authority in Scotland, to discriminate against a disabled pupil or prospective pupil in the discharge of its functions under the various Acts relating to education.[179] These are intended to cover the general education-related functions of authorities which affect pupils or prospective pupils generally. As we have seen, an LEA or Scottish education authority will be under the amended DDA 1995 Part IV duties where it is the responsible body for a school. When considering which anti-discrimination duties applies to its schools functions, an authority should first look at whether the duties under DDA 1995 s28A, set out above, apply. If they do not, then the duties under DDA 1995 ss28F and 28G, which are referred to as 'residual duties', may apply. The types of function covered by the residual duties are likely to include the education authority's policy and arrangements on school admissions and exclusions and the deployment of the authority's non-delegated budget, policies on early years provision, sports and cultural activities. 'Discrimination' in the context of the residual duties is materially identical to DDA 1995 s28B and the reasonable adjustment duty is materially identical to DDA 1995 s28C.

Enforcement

30.155 Enforcement of the new duties under DDA 1995 ss28A–G is through the renamed and suitably empowered Special Educational Needs and Disability Tribunal (SENDIST)[180] in England and Wales and, in Scotland, in the Sheriff court.[181] Financial compensation is not available as a remedy but SENDIST has wide powers to award any remedy it thinks appropriate other than compensation.[182] The Disability Rights Commission (DRC) has set up an independent conciliation service for disputes arising out of the education provisions to promote settlements of disputes without recourse to the courts.

30.156 A new section 28K is added to the DDA 1995 by SENDA 2001 s20 which provides for a right of redress for claims of disability discrimination in admissions decisions, against a maintained school or City Academy, to be made through admission appeals panels – the bodies set up to consider admission appeals. Provision is also made for a right of redress for claims of disability discrimination in permanent exclusion decisions against a maintained school or City Academy[183]

179 Education Act 1996; Education (Scotland) Act 1980; Standards in Scotland's Schools, etc, Act 2000.

180 DDA 1995 ss28H–J as amended.

181 DDA 1995 s28N as amended.

182 DDA 1995 s28I(3) and (4) as amended.

183 DDA 1995 s28L as amended.

to be made through exclusion appeals panels – the bodies set up to consider appeals against permanent exclusions.

30.157 The victimisation provisions of the DDA 1995 are also extended to include DDA 1995 Part IV by SENDA 2001 with effect from 1 September 2002.[184]

Further and higher education institutions

Disability discrimination duties

30.158 As with school education, the DDA 1995 has been amended with effect from 1 September 2002 to make disability discrimination unlawful in the higher education (HE) and further education (FE) sectors although the full extent of the reasonable adjustment duty will not be in force until September 2005. The term used is 'education institution' which, in England and Wales, means an institution within either the higher or further education sector[185] or designated in an order made by the Secretary of State. While the term may include private institutions, at present wholly privately-funded post-16 providers and providers of work based training will not be covered by DDA 1995 Part IV but will come within the goods, facilities and services provisions of DDA Part III. In Scotland, too, the provisions will apply, broadly to publicly funded FE and HE institutions.[186]

30.159 The post-16 education code of practice is extremely helpful in covering the complexity and detail of the new provisions.

30.160 DDA 1995 Part IV as amended makes it unlawful for the body responsible for an educational establishment to discriminate against a disabled person (DDA 1995 s28R(1)):

(a) in the arrangements it makes for determining admissions to the institution;
(b) in the terms on which it offers to admit him or her to the institution; or
(c) by refusing or deliberately omitting to accept an application for his or her admission to the institution.

30.161 It will also be unlawful to discriminate against a disabled student in the student services provided or offered, or in excluding the student

184 SENDA 2001 s38(7) which extends DDA 1995 s55.
185 As defined in the Further and Higher Education Act 1992 (see DDA 1995 s28R(8) as amended).
186 The detailed scope is set out in DDA 1995 s28R(7) as amended.

temporarily or permanently from the institution.[187] Once again, the code of practice explains the full range of the term 'student services' with a list of examples including independent learning opportunities, such as e-learning, job references, learning equipment, financial advice, accommodation services, and campus or college shops – as well as the more obvious examples of teaching, learning, day and evening adult education courses.[187a]

30.162 The responsible body is generally the governing body of the educational institution. DDA 1995 Sch 4B sets out a comprehensive table of the bodies responsible for education institutions in England, Scotland and Wales.

30.163 The victimisation provisions are also extended to educational institutions and provide protection against victimisation whether the person victimised is disabled or not (see chapter 4 for the meaning of victimisation).[188]

30.164 The meaning of 'discrimination' in the context of education institutions is almost identical to that which applies in relation to schools in its definition of less favourable treatment(see para 30.141 above) and is set out in the new DDA 1995 s28S. However, the reasonable adjustment duty is wider than that for schools. The provision of auxiliary aids and the alteration or removal of physical features will be included in the reasonable adjustment duty for further and higher education institutions, whilst they are specifically excluded from the reasonable adjustment for schools.[188a] However, the duty of reasonable adjustment in force from September 2002 is only insofar as this does not involve physical alterations or the provision of broadly auxiliary aids and services. In September 2003 the duty will be extended to make reasonable adjustments other than those requiring the removal or alteration of physical features, with the physical features aspect of the duty coming into force in September 2005. Another difference is that two additional grounds of justification are provided in relation to discrimination by FE and HE institutions while the additional ground which applies to schools (that relating to 'permitted form of selection') does not apply to such institutions. Instead, less favourable treatment and/or a failure to comply with a duty to make reasonable adjustment will be justified if it is necessary in order to maintain (a)

187 DDA 1995 s28R(1)–(3) as amended. Student services are any service that an institution provides or offers to provide wholly or mainly for students attending or undertaking courses – DDA 1995 s28R(2) and (11).

187a Post-16 education code of practice para 3.14.

188 DDA 1995 ss26, 28R(4) and 55 DDA as amended.

188a DDA 1995 s28T(2) (as amended by SENDA 2001 s28).

academic standards; or (b) standards of any other prescribed kind. There is scope for the minister to prescribe standards to be maintained that would justify less favourable treatment. The DDA 1995 also allows for future regulations to list any standards, treatments or circumstances that may also provide reasons to justify less favourable treatment. There are similar provisions for schools concerning confidentiality requests.

30.165 An example of the academic standards justification is provided in the Post 16 Education code of practice as follows: a severely dyslexic student applies to take a course in journalism. She does not have the literacy necessary to complete the course because of her dyslexia. The college rejects her, using the justification of her academic standards. This is likely to be lawful.[189] By contrast, a policy of rejecting all dyslexic journalism applicants without considering the applicant's level of dyslexia or ability, or the range of possible adjustments is unlikely to be lawful.[190] In other respects the meaning of discrimination is identical in HE and FE as it is in the schools context.

Enforcement, remedies and procedure

30.166 Enforcement of the new provisions will be through the county court (in Scotland the Sheriff court). Financial compensation, including compensation for injury to feelings, may be awarded and declarations are also available.[191] The DRC is setting up an independent conciliation service for disputes arising out of the education provisions to promote settlements of disputes without recourse to the courts.[191a]

30.167 The provisions in DDA 1995 Parts II and III which give rights to leaseholders to seek permission from their landlord or superior landlord to make alterations in order to comply with their duties not to discriminate against disabled people (see paras 30.91–30.98) apply also to educational institutions which lease premises.[192]

Planning and information duties

30.168 Under the DDA 1995, as it was implemented in 1996, there were obligations on LEAs in relation to further education to give information about facilities for disabled people[193] and the Learning and Skills Council in England and the national Council for Education and

189 Post-16 education code of practice, example 4.27A.
190 Post-16 education code of practice, example 4.27B.
191 DDA 1995 s28V as amended.
191a Using its powers under DDA 1995 s31B (as amended by SENDA 2001 s37).
192 DDA 1995 s28W as amended.
193 Education Act 1996 s528.

Training in Wales could require institutions in the FE sector to give such information as a condition of grant.[194] They could also impose conditions on FE institutions relating to their provision for disabled pupils. The Higher Education Funding Councils had to require institutions in the HE sector to give such information as a condition of grant.[195] SENDA 2001 withdraws these duties and powers with effect from 1 September 2002.[196]

Statutory authority or national security

30.169 Like the SDA 1975 and the RRA 1976, the DDA 1995 does not make unlawful discriminatory acts which are done for the purposes of safeguarding national security or in pursuance of a statutory authority.[197] The DDA 1995 provisions are discussed at para 13.42, the similar provisions of the SDA 1975 and RRA 1976 at para 29.137 above. DDA 1995 s59 applies across all parts of the Act.

Terms of agreements

30.170 Both Part III and, from 1 September 2002, Part IV of the Disability Discrimination Act 1995 have anti-avoidance provisions to prevent contracting-out of DDA 1995 obligations. Broadly, any term in a contract or other agreement is void (and therefore unenforceable) if its effect is to require someone to do something which would be unlawful under the DDA 1995, exclude or limit the operation of the DDA 1995, or prevent someone making a claim. The only exception is an agreement to settle or compromise a claim brought under the DDA 1995.[198]

194 Learning and Skills Act 2000 ss6 and 35.
195 Further and Higher Education Act 1992 s65.
196 SENDA 2001 s34.
197 DDA 1995 s59.
198 For schools see DDA 1995 s28P as amended; for post-16 education see DDA 1995 s28X and, in relation to goods and services and premises see DDA 1995 s26.

CHAPTER 31

Liability for discrimination

Key points

31.1
- An employer is liable for any unlawful acts of discrimination done by its workers during the course of their employment.
- The test for determining whether an act has been done during the course of employment for the purposes of the Sex Discrimination Act (SDA) 1975, Race Relations Act (RRA) 1976 or Disability Discrimination Act (DDA) 1995 is a very broad one.
- A worker for whose acts an employer is found liable will also be personally liable if named in the originating application or claim form.
- An employer will have a defence to a claim of vicarious liability if it took such steps as were reasonably practicable to prevent the worker doing the discriminatory act, or from doing it in the course of his or her employment.
- A person might also be liable for the discriminatory acts of others where the discriminatory act in question was sufficiently under his or her control that he or she might have prevented it or reduced the extent of it.
- A person who knowingly aids a person to discriminate unlawfully is liable for that unlawful act of discrimination.
- Chief officers of police are liable for acts of race (but not sex or disability) discrimination carried out by their officers after 2 April 2001.
- A principal will be liable for those acts of his or her agents which are within the express or implied authority of the agent.
- Where a principal is liable for a discriminatory act done by its agent, the agent may also be liable.

Background and statutory provisions

31.2 SDA 1975 s41(1) provides that:

> Anything done by a person in the course of his employment shall be treated for the purposes of this Act as done by his employer as well as by him, whether or not it was done with the employer's knowledge or approval.

RRA 1976 s32(1) and DDA 1995 s58(1) are in materially similar terms.[1] They have the effect of making employers liable for those discriminatory acts of their workers which are done in the course of their employment, whether or not they are done with the employer's knowledge or approval.[2] Importantly, it is plain from the SDA 1975, RRA 1976 and DDA 1995 that employers may be liable for the acts of *all* their workers, rather than only those of managerial staff.[3]

31.3 An employer will have a defence to a claim based on vicarious liability arising under SDA 1975 s41(1), RRA 1976 s32(1) and DDA 1995 s58(1) (usually described as 'vicarious liability') where it can prove that it took such steps as were reasonably practicable to prevent the worker from doing the discriminatory act or from doing, in the course of his or her employment, acts of that description.[4] This is dealt with below.

In the course of employment

31.4 An employer will only be liable for discriminatory acts done by its employees (inclusing workers) *in the course of their employment.* In *Jones v Tower Boot Co Ltd*[5] the Court of Appeal gave a wide meaning to the expression 'course of employment'. There the applicant, a 16-year-old boy, was subjected to horrific physical and verbal racial abuse. This included employees burning his arm with a hot screwdriver, whipping him on the legs with a welt, throwing bolts at him, and trying to put his arm in a lasting machine. The Employment Appeal Tribunal (EAT) adopted the test of vicarious liability which at that time applied at common law – namely whether the employees concerned were acting in a way which was authorised by the employer or in a way which was a mode, although an improper mode, of acting in an authorised way. The EAT concluded (by a majority) that the employer was not liable because the acts could not be described as an improper mode of performing authorised tasks. The Court of Appeal robustly rejected this test together with the implicit assumption that

1 Save that RRA 1976 s32(1) in terms provides that it does not apply in respect of offences under the RRA 1976.

2 'Employee' is given a very wide meaning to include workers – SDA 1975 s82, RRA 1976 s78 and DDA 1995 s68(1).

3 *De Souza v Automobile Association* [1986] IRLR 103.

4 SDA 1975 s41(3), RRA 1976 s32(3) and DDA 1995 s58(5).

5 [1997] ICR 254, CA. *Irving v Post Office* [1981] IRLR 289, CA, must now be wrong. See the comments in *Waters v Metropolitan Police Commissioner* [1997] IRLR 589, CA.

the more heinous the acts of harassment, the less likely the employer would be liable under the discrimination legislation.

31.5 The Court of Appeal held in *Jones v Tower Boot* that the 'course of employment' test in the RRA 1976 (and therefore the SDA 1975 and DDA 1995) was not the same as the test for vicarious liability at common law. The purpose of the vicarious liability provisions in the discrimination legislation was, according to the court:

> To deter racial and sexual harassment in the workplace through a widening of the net of responsibility beyond the guilty employees themselves by making all employers additionally liable for such harassment, and then supplying them with the reasonable steps defence under s.32(3) [RRA 1976[6]] which will exonerate the conscientious employer who has used his best endeavour to prevent such harassment, and will encourage all employers who have not yet undertaken such endeavour to take the steps necessary to make the same defence available in their own workplace.[7]

The effect of the decision in *Jones v Tower Boot* is to make employers liable as a matter of course for discrimination occurring in the work place (and in certain circumstances outside it), subject only to the employer making out the statutory defence.

31.6 The fact that an employer expressly prohibits an employee from carrying out the act complained of does not take the act outside the 'course of employment', although it may assist the employer in making out the statutory defence (see below).

31.7 It can be noted that the House of Lords in *Lister v Helsey Hall*[8] has now brought the common law test of vicarious liability closer to the *Tower Boot* definition. There the warden of a boarder's house in a school sexually abused a number of pupils who brought a county court action some years later. On appeal the House of Lords held that the respondent school was vicariously liable for the warden's actions, ruling that the correct approach is to concentrate on the relative closeness of the connection between the nature of the employment and the employee's wrongdoing, and to ask whether it would be fair and just to hold the employer vicariously liable. The House of Lords concluded that the fact that the warden's actions were an abuse of his position did not sever the connection with his employment. This means that in cases in which more than one cause of action is relied upon (particularly outside the employment field, where discrimination claims

6 SDA 1975 s41(3) and DDA 1995 s58(5).
7 [1997] ICR 254, para.38.
8 [2002] 1 AC 215; [2001] IRLR 472.

will usually be pursued alongside other complaints), questions of vicarious liability which arise under statute and at common law are likely to be determined on similar principles.

Discrimination outside working hours

31.8 SDA 1975 s41(1), RRA 1976 s32(1) and DDA 1995 s58(1) recognise that discrimination may occur as between employees in circumstances such that an employer is not liable for it. The 'in the course of employment' requirement draws the line between those incidents for which an employer might be liable and those for which it will not. But that line is sometimes difficult to discern.

31.9 Discrimination may occur in a rest break; just before going home, or outside the workplace altogether, and in some such cases such discrimination might be found to have been 'in the course of employment' so as to make the employer liable for it. There are, as the Court of Appeal recognised in *Jones v Tower Boot*, an infinite variety of circumstances and in each case it will be a question of fact for each court or tribunal to resolve, having regard to the broad test set down in that case. A court or tribunal might find an employer liable for acts of discrimination notwithstanding that they were done outside working hours and outside the workplace altogether. Each case will, however, turn very much on its own facts.

31.10 In *Sidhu v Aerospace Composite Technology*[9] the applicant was subjected to racial abuse by a fellow employee during a family day out at a theme park. The day out had been organised by the employer and participants were told to report any problems to a senior manager who was also there. The Court of Appeal upheld the employment tribunal's (ET) decision that the harassment did not fall within the course of the harasser's employment, although it recognised that another ET could properly have reached the opposite conclusion.

31.11 The Court of Appeal in *Sidhu* did not consider its decision to be incompatible with *Chief Constable of the Lincolnshire Police v Stubbs*,[10] in which a woman police officer had been subjected to sexual harassment by a male officer during a drink in a pub after her shift. The EAT in that case found that the harassment did fall within the course of employment.

9 [2000] IRLR 602.
10 [1999] IRLR 81.

Workers' liability

31.12 A worker who discriminates 'in the course of his employment' such that his employer is liable for it (or would be but for the statutory defence described below) is personally liable under the SDA 1975, RRA 1976 or DDA 1995 for that discrimination in whichever field it occurs (for example, whether it relates to employment, education, housing, etc). This is because the perpetrator is deemed to 'aid' his or her employer's vicarious liability for his or her actions.[11] This applies even where the employer makes out the statutory defence (see para 31.14 below), in which case the guilty employee will find himself solely liable.[11a] Thus in any case where an employer might make out such defence, a complainant should consider bringing proceedings against the employee as well as the employer.[12]

31.13 If the acts of discrimination complained of are not done in the course of employment the employee will not be liable under the SDA 1975, RRA 1976 or DDA 1995 and nor will any liability attach to the employer.[13]

The employer's defence

31.14 By SDA 1975 s41(3):

> In proceedings brought under this Act against any person in respect of an act alleged to have been done by an employee of his it shall be a defence for that person to prove that he took such steps as were reasonably practicable to prevent the employee from doing that act, or from doing in the course of his employment acts of that description.

RRA 1976 s32(3) and DDA 1995 s58(5) are in the same terms.

11 An employer is vicariously liable for an employer's act of discrimination by virtue of SDA 1975 s41(1), RRA 1976 s32(1) and DDA 1995 s58(1). The employee who perpetrated the act of discrimination is deemed to have aided his/her employer's vicarious liability by SDA 1975 s42(2), RRA 1976 s33(2) and DDA 1995 s57(2). Liability for knowingly aiding unlawful acts of discrimination arises under SDA 1975 s42(1), RRA 1976 s33(1) and DDA 1995 s57(1).

11a *Yeboah v Crofton* [2002] IRLR 634.

12 Where liability is joint, the court or ET will apportion compensation between the employer and individual discriminator. Thus in *Armitage, Marsden and HM Prison Service v Johnson* [1997] IRLR 162, £500 was awarded against each of the individual respondents as well as £27,500 against the Prison Service – see further chapter 33.

13 There may be other liability for harassment (see para 31.23).

31.15 This defence is available only to a claim of vicarious liability against an employer – it is not available to the employee who is said to have done the discriminatory act.

31.16 The defence depends upon an employer establishing that it took such steps *before* the relevant discriminatory act occurred.[14] In *Canniffe v East Riding of Yorkshire Council*[15] the EAT concluded that the proper approach to determining whether the defence is made out is, first, to identify whether the respondents took any steps at all to prevent the employee from doing the act or acts complained of in the course of his employment; and, second (having identified what steps, if any, the employer took), to consider whether there were any further steps the employer could have taken which were reasonably practicable. Whether the taking of any such steps would have been successful in preventing the acts of discrimination in question is not determinative. An employer will not be exculpated if it has not taken reasonably practicable steps simply because, if it had done, so they would not have prevented the discrimination from occurring. In this regard, the EAT recognised that, if it were otherwise, the more serious the act of discrimination, the more likely that the employer would escape liability.

31.17 The question whether an employer has adopted an equal opportunities policy and otherwise followed the recommendations in any relevant codes of practice issued by the Equal Opportunities Commission (EOC), Commission for Racial Equality (CRE) or Disability Rights Commission (DRC) will be very significant in determining whether they have made out the statutory defence. The size of the employer will also be a relevant consideration, so that the larger the employer the greater the expectation that it will properly implement and observe an equal opportunities policy.[16]

31.18 In *Balgobin and Francis v Tower Hamlets LBC*,[17] an alleged harasser was suspended pending the outcome of an inquiry after a complaint by two women. The inquiry was inconclusive and the harasser was returned to work. The majority of the EAT held that the employers had made out the statutory defence in circumstances where there was proper and adequate staff supervision and the employer had made known its equal opportunities policy. The EAT found that 'it was very difficult to see what steps in practical terms the employers could

14 See, eg, *Martins v Marks & Spencer plc* [1998] IRLR 326, CA.
15 [2000] IRLR 555.
16 See *A v Civil Aviations Authority* (1996) DCLD 27.
17 [1987] IRLR 401.

reasonably have taken to prevent that which had occurred from occurring'.

31.19 If it were the case that an employer had only to establish that there was in place a system for supervising staff and an equal opportunities policy, in order to successfully make out the statutory defence, it would be all too easy to avoid liability and the policy behind the discrimination legislation would be undermined. There are many other steps that could be taken to avoid discriminatory harassment. As was pointed out by the applicant in *Balgobin*, these might include the provision of training for all staff, clear guidelines for dealing with harassment, the categorisation of harassment as gross misconduct, and so on. It is likely that, in the light of the strong policy statements made by the Court of Appeal in *Jones v Tower Boot* about the prevention of discrimination; the EC Commission's Recommendation and Code of Practice on the protection of the dignity of men and women at work;[18] and the formulation of the two-stage test in *Canniffe*, that the decision in *Balgobin* would not be followed now.

31.20 In other ET cases, employers have not avoided liability so easily. In *Earlam v VMP Ltd and Andrews*,[19] for example, the tribunal stated that, bearing in mind the European code of practice, a large company should take the following steps to avoid harassment:

- issue a policy statement about harassment, defining it and stating that it will not be permitted or condoned;
- establish a complaints procedure, specifying to whom complaints should be made and setting out the consequences for perpetrators;
- provide training; and
- ensure that managers and supervisors are aware of the factors which contribute to a working environment free of sexual harassment.

Formal complaints

31.21 As SDA 1975 s41(1), RRA 1976 s32(1) and DDA 1995 s58(1) make plain, it is not necessary for a complaint to be made before an employer can be found liable for a discriminatory act carried out by one of its employees. Liability does not depend upon knowledge. But it may be helpful, whether or not it is intended to initiate proceedings, to make a complaint. A complaint may have the effect of causing the

18 92/131/EEC, see chapter 28.

19 (1995) DCLD 25. See also *Hurtley v Halfords & Leach*, *Wilson v J Sainsbury plc* and *Dias v Avon CC*, all reported in DCLD 25.

discrimination to cease and, in any case, will provide contemporaneous evidence of the problem. Furthermore, a failure to investigate a complaint once made might itself lead to further grounds of complaint.

31.22 In *Bracebridge Engineering v Darby*[20] the applicant reported sexual harassment to her manager. The EAT found that the manager's investigation of the complaint was not an in-depth inquiry, and that she was too easily persuaded that there was insufficient evidence to substantiate the claims. The manager should have known that the allegation could have led to the harassers' suspension, and in any event she should have carried out a full investigation. The applicant was therefore entitled to take the view that her allegations were being brushed aside, and was justified in terminating her contract of employment. The EAT ruled that it must be asked whether the 'term whereby the mutual obligation, trust, confidence and support and the obligation not to undermine the confidence of the female staff had been breached. In a case of this nature where sexual discrimination and investigation are concerned it is an extremely important one for the female staff'.[21]

Liability for acts of third parties

31.23 An employer may be liable for the discriminatory acts of third parties, that is people who are not the employer's employees or workers. In *Burton and Rhule v De Vere Hotels*[22] the EAT held that an employer had subjected its employees to racial harassment when a third party (an 'entertainer' at the employer's hotel)[23] racially and sexually harassed them. In reaching this conclusion, the EAT held that an employer might be held to have subjected an employee to the detriment of racial harassment if the event in question was sufficiently under the control of the employer that it could, by the application of good employment practice, have prevented the harassment or reduced the extent of it.[24]

31.24 There are many illustrations of the application of the principle in *Burton and Rhule*. Each case very much turns on its own facts, but the critical issue in each case in which the employer was found to have

20 [1990] IRLR 3.
21 Ibid at 6.
22 [1996] IRLR 596.
23 For whose actions the employer would not be *vicariously* liable under the Acts.
24 See chapter 28.

had control over the events in question was whether it took proper steps to prevent or reduce the harassment. In *Thompson v Black Country Housing Association Ltd*,[25] for example, an ET found that the respondent (a care home for people with learning disabilities) had done everything that could have been reasonably expected to curb the racist abuse of a care worker by a resident of the home. The ET ruled that, in the particular circumstances of the case, it would have been impossible to eradicate the effects of the resident's racism other than by expelling her from the home. The respondent had discussed the possibility of so doing with the applicant who had rejected it. Instead, the respondent had issued the resident with a warning that she would be expelled from the home if she persisted in her racist behaviour. In those particular circumstances, the ET concluded that the employers were not liable for the racial harassment perpetrated upon the applicant by the resident.

31.25 In *Bennett v Essex County Council*,[26] however, the EAT allowed an appeal against a finding by an ET that a school was not liable for the racial harassment of a black teacher by pupils, since the school did not take all reasonable steps to prevent the harassment. The EAT concluded that the ET's decision otherwise was irrational. Similarly in *Bhimji v Wigan and Leigh College*,[27] the respondent was held liable for the racist and sexist abuse perpetrated by students upon a female Asian lecturer in circumstances where, as the ET found, the abuse was sufficiently under the control of the college such that by the application of good educational practice it could have prevented it or reduced the extent of it.

31.26 In *Pearce v Governing Body of Mayfield School*,[28] however, while Hale LJ concluded that the ET was entitled to find that a school was liable for the harassment perpetrated upon a school teacher by the pupils on the basis of the principle in *Burton and Rhule*, Judge and Henry LJJ concluded otherwise.

31.27 In *Ado-Jingwa v Connex South Eastern Ltd*[29] a railway conductor complained of racial abuse by passengers. The ET found that the respondent was not liable since it had taken sufficient steps to minimise the risk to staff from customers, such as displaying posters advising the travelling public that it would not tolerate ill-treatment

25 (1999) DCLD 39.
26 (2000) DCLD 42.
27 (2001) DCLD 48.
28 [2001] IRLR 669, para 40 (Hale LJ), paras 60–62 (Judge LJ) and 88 (Henry LJ).
29 (2001) DCLD 48.

against its staff, providing incident report forms to staff, introducing CCTV and giving conductors mobile phones to call for assistance if required. In *Motcho v Greene King Retail Services Ltd*,[30] however, an ET decided that the respondent was liable for racist abuse of a chef by regular customers in the pub in which he worked. The landlord of the pub had also subjected the applicant to racial abuse, and had done so in front of the customers in such a way as to encourage their abuse. The customers were well-known to the landlord, who had the power to bar customers and to 'set the tone'.

31.28 As to the steps a service provider might take to prevent harassment within its control, it can be noted that, in one case in which a boy had been refused a job as a waiter because the respondent restaurant's customers purportedly preferred to be served by waitresses, the ET recommended that the respondent publish on its menus a statement to its customers to the effect that it was an equal opportunities employer.[31]

31.29 *Burton and Rhule* and the cases cited above show the extent to which a person falling within the scope of one of the unlawful acts within the SDA 1975, RRA 1976 or DDA 1995 may be liable for discrimination which occurs in circumstances over which they have some control. These cases relate to the employment field, but the principle applies equally outside the employment field to, for example, harassment cases in schools and on housing estates.

Liability of others aiding discrimination

31.30 By SDA 1975 s42(1) and RRA 1976 s33(1):

> A person who knowingly aids another person to do an act made unlawful by this Act shall be treated for the purposes of this Act as himself doing an unlawful act of the like description.

DDA 1995 s57(1) is in materially similar terms. Thus a person who knowingly aids another to do an unlawfully discriminatory act will be liable for that act.

31.31 A person aids another if he or she helps or assists, or co-operates or collaborates with him or her (*Anyanwu v South Bank Students' Union and South Bank University*[32]). To amount to 'aid', it is not necessary for the person's help to be substantial or productive, so

30 (2001) DCLD 49.

31 *Anthony v Marlows Ltd t/a Marlows Restaurant* (2001) DCLD 49.

32 [2001] 1 WLR 638; [2001] IRLR 305, para 33, per Lord Steyn.

long as it is not so insignificant as to be negligible.[33] The aid must be knowingly given and thus a general attitude of helpfulness and co-operation will not be enough. An aider must know that the person he or she is aiding is treating another person less favourably on grounds of race, sex or disability, or that he or she is about to do so or is thinking of doing so (*Hallam v Avery*[34]). In most cases there will be little doubt that aid was given 'knowingly' if it is found to have been given at all.[35]

31.32 'Aiding' cases in which the aider is not an employee are quite rare, but they might include, for example, a harasser who is not an employee. No proceedings were issued against the 'entertainer' in *Burton v Rhule* (see para 31.23). But he could properly have been joined as a respondent with the employer who was found liable for his actions.

31.33 A person who aids a discriminator is not liable if, in so doing, he or she was acting in reliance on the discriminator's statement that the act was not unlawful and it was reasonable for him to rely on that statement.[36] Such a case would be very unusual – we have not come across a single one.

Vicarious liability of chief constables

31.34 Before 2 April 2001 a chief constable could not be vicariously liable for any act of discrimination perpetrated by his or her police officers. Vicarious liability can, as we saw above, arise in respect of acts done by 'workers' as well as 'employees'. But, prior to that date, the discrimination Acts did not extend vicarious liability to those responsible for office-holders such as police officers.[37] Liability in sex and race discrimination arose against a chief constable or police authority, in the employment context, only where the act complained of was done by the chief constable him or herself or by the police authority itself.[38] No liability at all arose (or arises) under the DDA 1995 which does not contain any provisions dealing with discrimination by the police.

33 [2001] IRLR 305, para 5, per Lord Bingham.
34 [2001] 1 WLR 655; [2001] IRLR 312, HL.
35 Ibid para 11.
36 SDA 1975 s42(3), RRA 1976 s33(3) and DDA 1995 s57(3).
37 *Farah v Metropolitan Police Commissioner* [1998] QB 65. This case arose under the RRA 1976 but the principle applies equally to the SDA 1975 and DDA 1995.
38 SDA 1975 s17 and RRA 1976 s16. *Chief Constable of Cumbria v McGlennon* [2002] EAT 10/01 (unreported).

31.35 Since the passing of the Race Relations (Amendment) Act (RRAA) 2000, the holding of the position of police constable is to be treated as 'employment' for the purposes of the RRA 1976, so that vicarious liability may arise as against a chief constable for acts of race discrimination carried out by police officers.[39] No such amendment has been made to the SDA 1975 or the RRA 1976, so neither chief constables nor police authorities may be held vicariously liable under the SDA 1975, or liable at all (see para 31.34) under the DDA 1995.

31.36 In *Chief Constable of Bedfordshire Police v Liversidge*[40] the EAT allowed an appeal against an ET's refusal to strike out a claim of race discrimination against the Chief Constable which arose out of the treatment of one officer by another prior to the implementation of the RRAA 2000. The EAT concluded that the ET was wrong to hold that the Chief Constable might be vicariously liable for the discriminatory acts of his officers done before 2 April 2001 (the RRAA 2000's implementation date). The amendment of the RRA 1976 by the RRAA 2000 did not have retrospective effect and, accordingly, no vicarious liability arose. The Court of Appeal has recently upheld the decision of the EAT.[40a]

31.37 In proceedings in race discrimination in respect of discrimination which occurred before 2 April 2001, therefore, as in proceedings under the SDA 1975 and DDA 1995 whenever the act complained of occurred, no claim of employment-related discrimination may be pursued in relation to the treatment by one police officer of another. This is the case both in relation to claims against the officer him or herself and in relation to claims against the chief constable or police authority which turn on vicarious liability. Nevertheless it may be possible to bring claims of discrimination against a chief constable and police authorities arising out of discrimination by fellow officers where they can be said to be *directly* liable for it (see: the principle in *Burton and Rhule* above).

31.38 The position is the same in relation to non-employment discrimination, except that a police officer may be individually liable under the SDA 1975, RRA 1976 or DDA 1995 for discrimination in the performance of his or her duties where the acts in relation to which discrimination occurred fall within the scope of the 'facilities and services' provisions of the Acts (see chapters 29 and 30).[41] A police

39 RRA 1976 s76A (inserted by RRAA 2000). RRA 1976 s16 was repealed by the RRAA 2000.

40 [2002] IRLR 15.

40a *Liversidge v Chief Constable of Bedfordshire Police* [2002] IRLR 651.

41 *Farah v Metropolitan Police Commissioner* [1998] QB 65.

officer might, for example, be providing facilities or services for the purposes of the Acts when providing assistance to members of the public. He or she will be personally liable under the relevant Act if he or she discriminates in providing those services, though the chief constable will not be vicariously liable unless the discrimination is on grounds of race and takes place after 2 April 2001.

31.39 It should be noted that a chief constable is vicariously liable for the actions of his or her officers in respect of torts (civil wrongs) other than those arising under the discrimination legislation.[42] Such torts include, for example, negligence, false imprisonment and assault. It is often the case, particularly in race discrimination complaints against the police, that other causes of action (or complaints of other torts) arise out of the same facts. In such cases the chief constable should be joined along with the individual officers responsible for the doing of the discriminatory act.

31.40 The RRAA 2000's amendments apply only to the RRA 1976. But it is arguable that liability may attach to a chief constable for employment-related sex discrimination under the Equal Treatment Directive[43] (ETD) with which, if possible, the SDA 1975 should be read consistently. The ETD requires member states (article 16) to introduce 'such measures as are necessary to enable all persons who consider themselves wronged by a failure to apply to them the principle of equal treatment ... to pursue their claims by judicial process'. Community law requires that such measures must be 'equivalent' to those available in comparable cases and must be 'effective'.[44] The principle of equal treatment means (articles 1 and 2) that 'there shall be no discrimination whatsoever ... as regards working conditions'. Where a police officer suffers from discrimination in working conditions (by, for example, harassment from another officer), he or she should have access to the usual judicial protections afforded in comparable cases. This requirement would appear to be breached if a woman police officer does not have access to a claim against her employer – the chief constable or police authority. Accordingly, it is at least arguable that the SDA 1975 should be read in a way which gives a police constable a right to make such a claim.

42 Police Act 1964 s48(1).

43 Council Directive 76/207/EEC.

44 Case 326/99*Levez v Jennings (Harlow Pools) Ltd (No 2)* [1998] ECR I-7835; [1999] IRLR 36; Case C-246/96 *Magorrian and Cunningham v Eastern Health and Social Services Board* [1997] ECR I-7153; [1998] IRLR 86 and Case 33/76 *Rewe v Landwirtschaftskammer Saarland* [1976] ECR 1989.

Liability of principals

31.41 SDA 1975 s41(2), RRA 1976 s32(2) and DDA 1995 s58(2) make principals liable for the discriminatory acts of their agents.[45] The relationship of principal and agent arises where one person – the principal – consents to another person – the agent – acting on his or her behalf. Where an agent has authority (either express or implied, and whether given before or after the event) to act for the principal, both the principal and the agent will be liable for the discriminatory acts of the agent.[46]

31.42 In *Lana v Positive Action Training in Housing (London) Ltd*[47] the applicant was placed by the respondent as a trainee with another company, WM. Very soon after she announced that she was pregnant, WM informed the respondent that it wished to dispense with her services. The respondent terminated its training contract with the applicant on the basis that it did not have any work to offer her. The EAT allowed an appeal against a finding that Ms Lana had not been discriminated against by Positive Action Training, holding that WM was the agent of the respondent and that, accordingly, the respondent was liable for any discriminatory acts done by it.

31.43 The EAT in *Lana* concluded that liability did not arise only where authority had been given to do a discriminatory act (which will rarely if ever be authorised) but also where authority had been given to do an act which was capable of being done in a discriminatory manner, as well as in a lawful manner. The agents in this case had authority to terminate the placement and, if they did so in a discriminatory way, Positive Action Training was liable under SDA 1975 s41(2).

Codes of practice

31.44 In order to avoid liability for discrimination, whether vicarious or direct under the principle in *Burton and Rhule*, employers and principals should follow and adopt the CRE Code of Practice for the elimination of racial discrimination and the promotion of equality of opportunity in employment (1983), the EOC Code of Practice on sex discrimination; equal opportunities policies, procedures and practices

45 DDA 1995 s58(2) is somewhat differently worded but this does not seem significant in practice.

46 SDA 1975 ss41(2) and 42, RRA 1976 ss32(2) and 33, DDA 1995 ss58(2) and 57.

47 [2001] IRLR 501.

in employment (1985), the Guidance on matters to be taken into account in determining questions relating to the definition of disability and the code of practice for the elimination of discrimination in the field of employment against disabled persons or persons who have a disability (1996) issued under the DDA 1995, the Code of Practice on the protection of the dignity of men and women at work issued by the European Commission[48] and the other relevant EOC, CRE and DRC guidance.[49]

48 Commission Recommendation 92/131/EEC and code of practice.

49 For example Racial Harassment at Work; what employers can do about it (CRE, 1995). See further chapter 28.

CHAPTER 32

Procedure

continued

continued

Key points

32.1 • Discrimination claims must be brought in the employment tribunal if they arise under Part II of the Sex Discrimination Act 1975, the Race Relations Act 1976 or the Disability Discrimination Act 1995. Most other claims (including a number of claims which concern 'employment' broadly defined, but which arise other than under Parts II of the relevant Act), must be brought in the county court. In suitable cases actions might also proceed by way of judicial review in the High Court;

- Tribunal cases must be brought within three months of the discrimination alleged (ie, no later than three months less one day after the act complained of). The time limit is six months less one day in cases brought under the Equal Pay Act 1970 and, in county court cases, is generally six months (eight months in education cases brought under the Sex Discrimination Act and up to nine months in race cases in which an application has been made to the Commission for Racial Equality for assistance);
- In cases brought under Disability Discrimination Act (DDA) 1995 Parts III and IV which have been referred to the Disability Rights Commission (DRC) for conciliation within the six-month period, time is extended by a further two months;
- In all discrimination cases except those arising from the Equal Pay Act 1970, courts and tribunals may extend the time limit where it is 'just and equitable' to do so;
- The Employment Act 2002 proposes that an employee complaining of discrimination will, in most cases, first have to follow the initial step of a new statutory grievance procedure which will be implied into the contract of employment. This will entail submitting a written grievance to the employer and giving the employer 28 days to reply before bringing a tribunal claim;
- A Part II claim is made by lodging an IT1 with the tribunal. This will be sent to the employer who has 21 days to lodge its response (the IT3). Most claims other than under Part II of the relevant Act are made by completing a claim form which the county court issues. The claim form must either be accompanied or followed within 14 days of its service by the Particulars of Claim;
- All tribunal claims are sent by the tribunal to a conciliation officer at ACAS;
- Claims of disability discrimination against schools and Local

Education Authorities in England and Wales are commenced in the Special Educational Needs Disability Tribunal. The time limit is six months from the act of discrimination complained of with a discretion to extend where it is just and equitable to do so. If the dispute has been referred to the Disability Rights Commission for conciliation within the six month period, the time for bringing a claim is extended by a further two months.

- A questionnaire can be served on the employer in discrimination cases whether they are concerned with employment or not. The questionnaire may be served within three months of the alleged discrimination or within 21 days of lodging the IT1. The time limit for the service of questionnaires in county court cases is six months unless the alleged discriminator is an educational authority in cases of sex and race discrimination, in which case the limit is eight months. In county court cases the questionnaire may only be served after proceedings have been started with the leave of the court and within the period specified by the court.
- Further information can be obtained in discrimination cases through:
  - A request for further and better particulars
  - Written questions
  - Disclosure of documents;
- Directions hearings are often held in discrimination cases to plan for the main hearing;
- A restricted reporting order can be made by an employment tribunal to prevent publication of proceedings, but only where there are allegations of sexual misconduct or in Disability Discrimination Act 1995 cases in which there is evidence of a personal nature;
- Costs can only be awarded by tribunals where a party has acted vexatiously, abusively, disruptively or otherwise unreasonably, or the bringing or conducting of the proceedings by a party has been misconceived. The costs regime in the county court differs, losing parties generally being liable for the successful side's costs.
- Claimants (and respondents) may appeal from a tribunal to the EAT within 42 days of the date on which extended reasons were sent to him or her. Appeals from the county court go, with permission, to the Court of Appeal.

Background and statutory framework

32.2 The procedures applicable to discrimination claims differ between those claims brought under Part II of the Sex Discrimination Act 1975 (SDA 1975), the Race Relations Act 1976 (RRA 1976) or the Disability Discrimination Act 1995 (DDA 1995), on the one hand, and those brought under other Parts of those Acts (generally Part III, though also Parts V in the case both of the RRA 1976 and SDA 1975 and Parts IV and V in the case of the DDA 1995). Part II claims are brought in the employment tribunal (ET) while other claims are brought in the county court and, in the case of school education cases under the DDA 1995 in England and Wales, the Special Educational Needs and Disability Tribunal (SENDIST). As noted above, judicial review may also be used, in a suitable case, to challenge a practice, policy or decision of a public authority on the grounds that it is unlawful under one of the Acts. Judicial review is not generally granted, however, when an alternative remedy exists.

32.3 The division between Parts II and the other provisions of the Acts *generally* corresponds to the division between the regulation of discrimination related to employment, on the one hand, and other forms of discrimination, on the other. Having said this, a number of claims which arise under the other Parts of the Acts relate to 'employment' in the widest sense – for instance, discrimination affecting barristers and discrimination in vocational training. Claims in respect of such discrimination go, with other non-Part II claims, to the county court. But, in cases of sex and race discrimination as we shall see below, they are covered by the enhanced EC provisions applicable to sex discrimination. Thus, for example, where a barrister claims in the county court to have been the victim of discrimination on grounds of sex, or direct discrimination on grounds of gender reassignment, the burden of proof will be that applicable to employment-related sex discrimination claims (see para 3.85).

32.4 This chapter contains a summary of the practice and procedure in tribunals and courts for the rights set out in the table below.[1] References to the ET Rules are, unless otherwise stated, to the Employment Tribunals Rules of Procedure, scheduled to the Employment Tribunals (Constitution and Rules of Procedure) Regulations 2001.[2]

1 This book does not cover employment law other than discrimination and maternity and parental rights.

2 2001 SI No 1171. These supercede the Employment Tribunals (Constitution and Procedure) Regulations 1993.

References to the CPRs are to the Civil Procedure Rules which are applicable to litigation in the county court.

Overriding objective of the rules of procedure

32.5 The overriding objective of the ET Rules, and of the CPRs, is to enable tribunals and courts to deal with cases justly. Dealing with a case justly includes, so far as practicable:

- Ensuring that the parties are on an equal footing;
- Saving expense;
- Dealing with the case in ways which are proportionate to the complexity of the issues; and
- Ensuring that it is dealt with expeditiously and fairly.[3]

There are special rules for equal value claims under the Equal Pay Act 1970 (EqPA 1970). These are detailed in chapter 24.

32.6 The bulk of the chapter is concerned with litigation in the tribunals, county court litigation being considered at para 32.173 below. As is made clear there, however, there is much overlap between the rules applicable in the tribunals and in the county court and paras 32.173–32.210 make frequent reference back to the paragraphs which deal with litigation in the tribunals.

Litigating in the employment tribunals – an introduction

32.7 A worker should first consider what he or she wants from legal proceedings and how far he or she is prepared to take any legal action. A worker who wants to keep his or her job, and to maintain a good working relationship with the employer, should think very carefully before taking proceedings or even instructing a lawyer to act. The best first source of advice is likely to be a trade union. Legal action will almost inevitably lead to deterioration in the employment relationship and many people find the strain of working with tribunal proceedings pending intolerable. Although the discrimination Acts provide protection from victimisation, this is generally inadequate compensation for the loss of a job. A priority for many workers is a good reference, but an ET cannot order an employer to write a reference in terms that

3 2001 SI No 1171 reg 10.

are acceptable to the worker. This will only be achieved by negotiation or mediation and is often linked to a compromise agreement.

32.8 When litigation is being considered it is important that all potential legal actions and the remedies to which they give rise are considered. In addition to the protection afforded by the EqPA 1970, the SDA 1975, the RRA 1976 and the DDA 1995, there are an increasing number of maternity and family rights with different remedies, which are also set out in the table below. Details of the remedies available are set out in chapter 33.

The right	Statute	Qualifying period	Time limit for bringing claim	Remedy	Misc. points to note
Sex, marital & gender reassignment discrimination (dismissal, detriment, demotion, promotion, victimisation, etc).	SDA 1975 as amended.	None.	Within 3 months starting with the date of the act complained about.**	See chapter 33. Declaration. Recommendation. Compensation. Injury to feelings. Personal injury.	Applies to workers including employees and the self-employed. Questionnaire procedure available.
Complaint that contract term or collective agreement is void.	SDA 1986 s6(4A).	None.	6 months.	Declaration that the term is void.	
Complaint that contract, rule or collective agreement is void.	SDA 1975 s77.	None.	None.	Declaration that the term is void.	

** The ET may extend time if just and equitable to do so (see para 32.44).

Race discrimination (dismissal, detriment, demotion, promotion, victimisation etc).	RRA 1976 as amended.	None.	Within 3 months starting with the date of the act complained about.**	Declaration, recommendation, compensation including injury to feelings and personal injury.	Applies to workers including employees and the self-employed. Questionnaire procedure available.
Disability discrimination (dismissal, detriment, demotion, promotion etc).	DDA 1995.	None.	Within 3 months starting with the date of the act complained about.**	Declaration, recom-mendation, compensation including injury to feelings and personal injury.	Applies to workers including employees and the self-employed. Questionnaire procedure available.
Equal pay.	EqPA 1970, Article 141 EC	None.	Within 6 months of termination of contract with no extension possible.		Applies to workers including employees and the self-employed. Questionnaire procedure will be available, probably from April 2003.

continued

The right	Statute	Qualifying period	Time limit for bringing claim	Remedy	Misc. points to note
Preliminary complaint by EOC/CRE.	SDA 1975 s73(1). RRA 1976 s64(1).	N/A.	6 months starting with date of act complained of.	– Finding of discrimination. – Order declaring the rights of the party. – Recommendation	Applies to workers including employees and the self-employed.
Application by EOC or CRE in connection with discriminatory advertising and/or pressure to discriminate.	SDA 1975 s72(2)(a). RRA 1976 s63(2)(a).	N/A.	6 months starting with date of act complained of.	– Finding of discrimination. – Order declaring the rights of the party. – Recommendation	Applies to workers including employees and the self-employed.
Ordinary unfair dismissal.	Employment Rights Act 1996 (ERA 1996) ss94–98.	One year.	Within 3 months.*	Compensation for loss of earnings.	Only applies to employees.
Wrongful dismissal (ETl claims only).	Employment Tribunals Extension of Jurisdiction (England and Wales) Order 1994 SI No 1623.	None.	Within 3 months of effective date of termination.	Notice pay.	Only applies to employees.

* The ET may extend time if it was not reasonably practicable to bring claim within 3 months.

** The ET may extend time if just and equitable to do so (see para 32.44).

Rights linked to maternity

The right	Statute	Qualifying period	Time limit for bringing claim	Remedy	Misc. points to note
Paid time off for ante-natal care.	ERA 1996 ss55–57.	None.	Within 3 months.*	Declaration, compensation for loss of pay.	Only applies to employees.
Automatically unfair dismissal.	ERA 1996 s99 reg 20, Maternity & Parental Leave Regulations 1999 (MPL Regs 1999).	None.	Within 3 months.*	Compensation for loss of earnings.	Only applies to employees.
18 weeks Ordinary Maternity Leave.**	ERA 1996 s71.	None.	N/A.	See chapter 16.	
29 weeks Additional Maternity Leave.**	ERA 1996 s73.	1 year at beginning of 11th week before EWC.***	N/A.	See chapter 16.	
Parental leave.	ERA 1996 s80(1) and MPL Regs 1999.	One year.	Within 3 months.*	Declaration, compensation.	Only applies to employees. Leave is unpaid..

* The ET may extend time if it was not reasonably practicable to bring claim within 3 months.

** 26 weeks from April 2003.

*** 26 weeks by the end of 15 weeks before the EWC from April 2003.

continued

Rights linked to maternity, *continued*

The right	Statute	Qualifying period	Time limit for bringing claim	Remedy	Misc. points to note
Emergency leave for dependants.	ERA 1996 s57A.	None.	Within 3 months.*	Declaration, compensation.	Only applies to employees. Leave is unpaid
Protection from detriment in connection with maternity and parental leave, etc.	ERA 1996 s47C, and MPL Regs 1999, reg 19.	None.	Within 3 months.*	Declaration, compensation.	Applies only to employees.
Dismissal for Health & Safety reasons/ assertions of statutory right.	ERA 1996 s104.	None.	Within 3 months.*	Compensation.	Applies only to employees.
Right to alternative work before maternity suspension.	ERA 1996 s67.	None.	Within 3 months starting with 1st day of suspension.		
Right to be paid during maternity suspension.	ERA 1996 s68.	None.	Within 3 months starting with day claim is made.		

Written reasons if dismissed when pregnant or on leave.	ERA 1996 s92(4).	None.	Within 3 months.*	Declaration, 2 weeks' pay.	Applies only to employees. Applies if the employee does not request a statement.
Less favourable treatment of part-time workers.	Part-time Work Regulations.	None.	Within 3 months.*	Declaration, recommendation, compensation.	Workers but comparison is with those on similar contract doing similar work.
Health and safety on grounds of pregnancy.	Health and Safety at Work Act 1974 (prosecution); ERA 1996 ss67–68.	None.	Employment Tribunal claim: within 3 months.*		Employees only, although all workers have basic protection.

* The ET may extend time if it was not reasonably practicable to bring claim within 3 months.

From April 2003 the following rights will also apply (see chapters 18 and 21 for details)

The right	Statute	Qualifying period	Time limit for bringing claim	Remedy	Misc. points to note
2 weeks' paid paternity leave for birth and adopted children.	Employment Act 2002 and Paternity and Adoption Leave Regulations (draft).	26 weeks by the end of the 15th week before the EWC/ placement for adoption.	Within 3 months.	Declaration Compensation Recommendation.	Employees only.
26 weeks' ordinary adoption leave.	Employment Act 2002 and Paternity and Adoption Leave Regulations (draft).	26 weeks by the end of the 15th week before the EWC/ placement for adoption.	Within 3 months.	Declaration Compensation Recommendation.	Employees only.
26 weeks' additional adoption leave.	Employment Act 2002 and Paternity and Adoption Leave Regulations (draft).	26 weeks by the end of the 15th week before the EWC/ placement for adoption.	Within 3 months.	Declaration Compensation Recommendation.	Employees only.
To request flexible working.	Employment Act 2002 and draft Flexible Working (Eligibility, Complaints and Remedies) Regulations and draft Flexible Working (Procedural Requirements) Regulations.	26 weeks' continuous service with the same employer.	Within 3 months.	Declaration Compensation Recommendation.	Employees only.

European law

32.9 Account should be taken of EC law in advising claimants. At present this is relevant largely in connection with sex-related cases, although this will change in July 2003 (see further paras 10.84 and 10.93). The main relevant provisions prior to that date are:

- The Equal Treatment Directive (ETD);[4]
- Article 141 and the Equal Pay Directive (EqPD);[5]
- The Pregnant Workers Directive;[6]
- The Parental Leave Directive;[7]
- The Part-time Workers Directive;[8]
- The Burden of Proof Directive.[9]

32.10 It is clear from the table above that the UK anti-discrimination legislation protects job applicants and workers as well as employees. This is wider than the ERA 1996 which, in most situations, only protects employees.[10] The Part-time Workers (Prevention of Less Favourable Treatment) Regulations (the PTW Regulations) also protect workers as well as employees. EC law goes further and protects ex-workers who have been victimised as a result of carrying out a 'protected act', such as bringing tribunal proceedings. Although EC law only applies, at present, in relation to sex discrimination, it is to be extended to cover other forms of discrimination (such as race, religion, sexual orientation and disability discrimination). The same principles will apply in relation to these grounds of discrimination as apply at present in relation to sex. The details of who is protected by the anti-discrimination legislation are set out in chapters 11 and 13.

32.11 EC directives can only be directly relied on in claims against public bodies or employers carrying out functions of the State (ie, where they are emanations of the State). In relation to private employers, tribunals and courts must try to interpret UK law in line with EC Law. Article 141 of the EC Treaty, by contrast, is directly applicable and is enforceable in UK courts and tribunals against all employers (see chapter 10). In all cases a claim under EC law must be linked to

4 Council Directive 76/207/EEC.
5 Council Directive 75/117/EEC.
6 Council Directive 92/85/EEC.
7 Council Directive 96/34/EEC, as amended by Directive 97/75/EEC.
8 Council Directive97/81/EC.
9 Council Directive 97/80/EC.
10 Exceptions include unlawful deductions of wages.

UK legislation and domestic procedures, and the relevant domestic remedies will apply (see chapter 10).

32.12 Tribunals must also take into account the provisions of the Human Rights Act 1998 (HRA 1998), which partially incorporates the European Convention of Human Rights into UK law.[11] The relevant provisions are summarised in chapter 9.

An introduction to employment tribunals

32.13 ETs have no powers other than those given to them by statute (for example the SDA, RRA, DDA, the Employment Rights Act 1996 (ERA 1996) or the European Communities Act 1972. Tribunal decisions are persuasive but not binding on other tribunals.

32.14 Tribunal procedure is meant to be informal and accessible to litigants in person. For example, there are no strict rules of evidence and the tribunal has a wide power to regulate its own procedure.[12] Despite the intended informality, tribunal procedure is becoming increasingly technical, particularly where the parties are represented. Some tribunal Chairmen are quite interventionist in that they will explain the law and procedure. Others are not and expect the parties to present their case unaided. There is no requirement that the panel in a discrimination case includes members with specialist knowledge of race, sex or disability discrimination, though the Regional Chair will attempt to have a member with specialist knowledge if possible.[13]

Steps to consider before bringing a claim

Negotiate first

32.15 In some cases a worker will want to try to reach agreement with the employer. This is particularly important where, for example, a worker

11 The HRA 1998 came into force on 2 October 2000.

12 Rule 11 provides that the Tribunal shall seek to avoid formality and shall not be bound by any enactment relating to the admissibility of evidence. It shall make such inquiries of persons appearing before it and witnesses as it considers appropriate, and shall conduct the hearing in such manner as it considers most appropriate for clarification of the issues before it and generally to the just handling of the proceedings.

13 See *Habib v Elkington & Co Ltd* [1981] IRLR 344 in which the EAT held that it may, as a matter of fairness, be appropriate for the Tribunal to contain a member with the relevant knowledge, but that the choice was a matter for the relevant authorities.

is trying to negotiate child friendly working hours. If the worker can deal with the employer's arguments about why her or his proposed hours are unworkable, he or she may be able to reach a compromise. Even if this is not possible, the worker will be in a better position to argue that the employer's refusal is not justified. It is also sometimes possible, at this stage, to obtain information as to why the complainant has been treated less favourably.

32.16 A worker should consider taking out a grievance prior to beginning legal action where a grievance procedure exists (see further below), although there is, at the date of writing, no obligation on the worker to do so. At present the time limits continue to run and are not put on hold by taking out a grievance (see further para 32.42).

The Employment Act 2002: introduction of a statutory grievance procedure

32.17 Section 30 of the Employment Act 2002 introduces a statutory grievance procedure as an implied term of all contracts of employment which will be binding on employers and employees. The proposal is that employees will be barred from bringing any claim (including a discrimination claim under the SDA, the RRA 1976, the DDA 1995 and the EqPA 1970), unless they have followed the first step in the statutory grievance procedure. This involves submitting a written grievance to the employer and giving the employer 28 days to respond. The time limit for lodging tribunal proceedings will be extended to allow the employee to send the letter to the employer and for the employer to reply. Thus, the grievance should be put in within four months of the event giving rise to the grievance (although the time limit will be shorter than four months by a few days: depending on the length of the calendar month in question). An ET may refuse to hear a claim brought by an employee who has resigned because he or she has been discriminated against unless he or she has first raised a grievance. An exception may, however, be permitted for claims relating to bullying, violence and harassment. Regulations detailing the procedure will be published in Autumn 2002.

32.18 If either the employer or employee fails to follow the statutory grievance procedure any compensation awarded can be varied by between 10 and 50 per cent. Time limits for bringing a claim in the tribunal will be extended to allow time for the grievance to be decided. The details will be contained in regulations which have not been published at the time of writing.

Appeal procedures

32.19. Compensation for unfair dismissal may be reduced if there is an appeal procedure of which the employee has been given written details and has failed to use. Compensation may be increased if the employer provides an appeal procedure but prevents an employee from appealing against the dismissal under it.[14] The maximum by which compensation can be increased or decreased is two weeks' pay. This does not apply in discrimination cases, though it is advisable, where practicable, to appeal discriminatory dismissals.

The Employment Act 2002: introduction of a statutory disciplinary procedure

32.20 The Employment Act also incorporates statutory dismissal and disciplinary procedures into employees' contracts of employment. These will set out minimum standards which may be improved upon by the contract. If the employer fails to comply with the procedure, the employee will be treated as having been unfairly dismissed.

Written statement of reasons for dismissal

32.21 An employer is obliged to provide a written statement of reasons for dismissal where an employee is dismissed either during her pregnancy or maternity leave. This applies whether or not she requests such as statement and irrespective of length of service.[15] An employee (as distinct from a worker) who is dismissed in other circumstances may request such a statement, provided that he or she has been employed for at least one year ending with the effective date of termination.[16] A written statement is admissible in evidence.[17] The Employment Act 2002 strengthens employees' rights in connection with a written statement including the introduction of compensation of up to 2 weeks' pay where the claim has been lodged in conjunction with another matter: it is not a freestanding right to compensation.

Written statement of reasons for differential treatment of part-time workers

32.22 A part-time worker who is not given pro rata rights with a comparable full-time worker may ask for a written statement of reasons. The

14 ERA 1996 s127A, which came into force on 1 January 1999.
15 ERA 1996 s92(4).
16 ERA 1996 s92 (1)–(3).
17 ERA 1996 s92(5).

employer must reply within 21 days and the statement is admissible in proceedings (see para 32.148).

Questionnaire procedure

32.23 Questionnaires are very helpful in most discrimination claims. They enable information to be elicited before tribunal proceedings have been started which is an exception to the general rule. In cases under the SDA, RRA 1976 and DDA 1995 (but not the ERA 1996) the complainant can ask the respondent any question relevant to the discrimination. The questions may include questions relating to matters of evidence.[18] Standard forms are provided under each Act but the questions need to be tailored to each case.[19] The purpose of this is to help a complainant decide if she or he should start proceedings and to assist the presentation of the claim in the most effective way. A reply to the questionnaire should be requested within (say) 21 days, and the employer should be advised as to the consequences of a failure to reply (see below).

32.24 The Employment Act 2002 extends the questionnaire procedure to claims under the Equal Pay Act 1970 from April 2002.[20] (It is arguable in any event that the EqPA 1970, as a schedule to the SDA, is already covered by the SDA's questionnaire procedure.)

Time limits for serving questionnaires

32.25 A questionnaire may be served on the employer at any time up to three months from the act of discrimination or, if served after proceedings have been commenced, within 21 days of their commencement. Otherwise the permission of the tribunal is required.[21]

32.26 If the time limits for tribunal claims permit, it is advisable to serve a questionnaire before bringing a claim. This is particularly useful

18 SDA 1975 s74(1), RRA 1976 s65(1) and DDA 1995 s56.

19 Sex Discrimination (Questions and Replies) Order 1975 (1975 SI No 2048); Race Relations (Questions and Replies) Order 1977 (1997 SI No 842) and the Disability Discrimination (Questions and Replies) Order 1996 (1996 SI No 2793). See Tamara Lewis, *SDA and RRA Questionnaires: How to use the questionnaire procedure* (Central London Law Centre 1996). The form is available from DfEE publications on 0845 6022260.

20 EqPA 1970 s7B as amended by Employment Act 2002 s42.

21 See *Williams v Greater London Citizens Advice Bureaux Service* [1985] ICR 545, in which the EAT refused an extension of time on the basis that there had been no satisfactory explanation for the delay.

when the grounds for the discrimination claim are not clear. It is possible, with leave of the tribunal, to serve another questionnaire if, after receiving a reply to the first, further questions need to be asked. The EAT has approved this, saying it is a 'sensible and necessary part of the procedure'.[22]

Replies to the questionnaire

32.27 The questions in and replies to the statutory questionnaires are admissible in evidence.[23] If the employer deliberately and without reasonable excuse fails to reply within a reasonable period, or is evasive or equivocal, the court or tribunal may draw any inference from that fact that it thinks just and equitable, including an inference that the employer has discriminated unlawfully.[24] If the employer refuses to reply to a question in the questionnaire, it may be possible to ask questions again in a request for written answers. Some tribunals are reluctant to allow claimants to have what is regarded as a 'second go', but this approach is wrong; there being nothing in the ET Rules to suggest that written questions cannot be asked if a questionnaire has been served.[25] There is no predetermined time limit for replying to a questionnaire under the SDA 1975, RRA 1976 and DDA 1995, but the government intends to introduce a time limit of 8 weeks for completion of an EqPA 1970 questionnaire by an employer.[25a]

What questions?

32.28 Any questions can be asked in the statutory questionnaire. However, if too many questions or irrelevant questions are asked the respondent may refuse to reply on the grounds that they are oppressive; and the tribunal may refuse to draw an inference from this refusal. The questions which should be asked depend on the nature of the case. It is helpful to ask questions about the reasons why the employer treated the complainant in the discriminatory way alleged; how others in similar circumstances were treated; the breakdown of workers by sex, race and disability; and the employer's equal opportunities policies (if any).

22 *Carrington v Helix Lighting Ltd* [1990] IRLR 6, EAT.
23 SDA s74(2)(a), RRA 1976 s65(2)(a) and DDA 1995 s56(3)(a).
24 SDA s74(2)(b), RRA 1976 s65(2)(b) and DDA 1995 s56(3)(b).
25 SDA 1975 s74(5) provides that it is without prejudice to any other rules regulating interlocutory and preliminary matters in the tribunal.
25a In regulations yet to be made by the secretary of state at the time of writing.

32.29 In a discriminatory dismissal claim it would be useful to ask about:

- The reasons why the complainant was dismissed, who made the decision and when;
- If the dismissal was allegedly for conduct or performance reasons, details of the reasons;
- Details of other workers dismissed in similar circumstances; and
- What procedure should have been followed and whether it was followed.

32.30 In an indirect discrimination case, it might be useful to ask for:

- Statistical information about, for example, the numbers of women and men who work part-time; and
- A breakdown of employees by race, sex, according to position and grade within the organisation;

32.31 In a disability claim, questions might be asked about:

- What adjustments were considered and/or made by the employer;
- Any equal opportunities policy and how it has been implemented (including training); and
- The employer's reason for the treatment.

It is also worth requesting copies of relevant documents, though these may also be sought on discovery (see para 32.119). A sample questionnaire is in appendix B.

32.32 The tribunal should take account of any inconsistencies between answers given in the questionnaire and the grounds of resistance in the employer's answer to the claim and/or the oral evidence before it.[26]

Contemporaneous notes

32.33 Workers should make a contemporaneous note of all relevant matters as they happen, or as soon after they happened as possible, including meetings and conversations with the employer. These can later be used to substantiate the worker's case.[27]

26 See *Hinks v Riva Systems and another* EAT 501/96, in which the EAT criticised the ET for failing to take account of such inconsistencies.

27 The originals must be kept and these can be referred to at the hearing. The notes must not subsequently be changed in any way and will have to be disclosed to the respondent prior to the hearing.

Letter before action

32.34 Before issuing proceedings it is usually advisable, if there is time before the expiry of the time limit, for the worker or her/his representative to write a letter to the employer setting out the broad nature of the claim. It is important that the information contained in the letter is accurate in every respect, as the respondent may use it at the hearing to highlight inconsistencies in the case.

32.35 If re-employment or reinstatement is sought, the employer should be informed as soon as possible so as to try to reduce the chance of a replacement worker being employed.

Duty to mitigate

32.36 In recruitment and dismissal cases a claimant should take steps to find alternative employment. Evidence of such steps will be required, so it is important to keep a record of job applications, interviews, visits to the job centre and any other measures taken to find work. The costs of taking such steps are recoverable (provided that relevant evidence is made available to the tribunal – see para 32.148).

Bringing a tribunal claim

Initial steps

32.37 Bringing an ET claim generally involves the following sequence of events:

- The service of a questionnaire in discrimination cases (either before or after the IT1 is lodged) (see above);
- The lodging of an IT1 within 3 months of the alleged discrimination;
- The lodging by the employer of an IT3 within 21 days of its receipt of the IT1;
- Applications for Further and Better Particulars;
- The issue of written questions (not always necessary);
- An application for Discovery of documents;
- The obtaining of medical evidence to support a disability discrimination claim and/or personal injury claim and/or injury to feelings, which is sometimes necessary to include claimant's medical records;

- Directions hearing (sometimes);
- Preparation for main hearing, to include:
- Drafting witness statements (6 copies);[27a]
- Request for witness orders (if necessary);
- Compiling index bundle of documents for tribunal (6 copies);
- The hearing.

Estoppel

32.38 There is a general rule, subject to some exceptions, that once an issue has been decided by a court or tribunal it cannot be re-litigated subsequently (except by way of an appeal). Further, all issues capable of being raised should be raised in the proceedings. These rules (*estoppel* rules) can give rise to problems where, for example:

- A claimant withdraws a claim and issues further similar proceedings in the same tribunal or court or a different one;[28] and
- Where is a claim for personal injury and discrimination, a decision has to be taken as to whether it is better to bring proceedings in the ET, county court or High Court.[29]

32.39 A number of decisions were reviewed in *Rothschild Asset Management Ltd v Ako*, a case in which the claimant's employment had transferred from one employer to another.[30] The claimant withdrew proceedings (for unfair dismissal and race discrimination) against the transferor employer and then lodged a further claim against both the transferor and the transferee. The difficulty for Ms Ako was that, where an IT1 claim is withdrawn it is dismissed *by an ET decision*. The CA however ruled that her case had not been the subject of a decision capable of giving rise to an estoppel, distinguishing the procedure in the ETs and other courts. The CA upheld the EAT's decision to allow the second application to proceed.[31] The CA ruled that an ET should

27a A copy for each of the three tribunal members, a copy for the witness table, and a copy each for yourself and your opponent.

28 As, for example, in *Lennon v Birmingham City Council* [2001] IRLR 826, in which a discrimination claim for harassment and stress-related illness was withdrawn in the ET (and dismissed) and the claimant's claim for breach of contract and negligence was struck out in the ordinary courts. This case was distinguished in *Ako*, see note 30, below.

29 It is now clear that a personal injury claim can be made in the ET in a discrimination case – *Sheriff v Klyne Tugs (Lowestoft) Ltd* [1999] IRLR 481.

30 [2002] IRLR 348, CA.

31 The distinction was based on the different rules for discontinuance and dismissal in the higher courts.

examine the factual matrix to decide whether the claimant had genuinely intended to abandon the claim. In this case it was clear Ms Ako had not, having simply withdrawn to permit fresh proceedings against both employers to be brought.[32]

32.40 It is usually advisable for all claims to be brought in one court or tribunal. If, during the course of an unfair dismissal claim, it becomes clear that the reason for the dismissal is discrimination, it is preferable to request an amendment, rather than start new proceedings which may not be allowed.[33] If an amendment is refused, it may or may not be possible to bring a further claim. It is for this reason it is usually preferable to bring forward all claims at the same time.[34] If the name of the respondent or detailed nature of the claim is unclear at the outset, the claim can be argued in the alternative with an amendment being made as soon as possible,[35] once the position has been clarified. If a claim is withdrawn with the intention of re-issuing proceedings and recommencing, this should be made clear.[36]

Claims by executors of deceased claimants

32.41 In *Harris v Lewisham & Guy's Mental NHS Trust*[37] the CA held that a complaint brought under the discrimination statutes survives the death of the complainant. A similar decision was reached by the EAT in Scotland in *James Murray & Co (Cupar) Ltd & Anor v The Executors of the late Gary Soutar*.[38]

32 The CA, having reviewed all the authorities, distinguished *Barber v Staffordshire Country Council* [1996] ICR 379 and *Lennon v Birmingham City Council* [2001] IRLR 826. The CA also rued that an ET, on being notified of the withdrawal of a claim, should ask the claimant for a statement of the circumstances of the decision to withdraw before deciding whether to make an order dismissing the proceedings. See also *Sajid v Sussex Muslim Society* [2002] IRLR 113.

33 See *Divine-Bortey v Brent London Borough Council* [1998] ICR 886, CA.

34 See *Air Canada and another v Basra* [2000] IRLR 683, in which a claim for race discrimination was followed by a claim, in a second tribunal, for race victimisation and sex discrimination after the first tribunal had refused an amendment to include these claims.

35 Clearly, it is not advisable to argue weak cases and account needs to be taken of the danger of costs being incurred (see para 32.164).

36 See *Sajid v Sussex Muslim Society* [2002] IRLR 113.

37 [2000] IRLR 320.

38 EOR 104, April 2002 p25.

Time limits for bringing a tribunal claim

32.42 Different time limits apply to claims brought under the various Acts. So, too, do different tests for making applications outside the relevant time limits.

Employment discrimination claims other than under the Equal Pay Act 1970

32.43 A discrimination claim must be lodged with the ET *within* three months (ie, no later than three months less one day) of the act of discrimination complained of. Thus if the discrimination occurs on 4 January the claim must be lodged with the tribunal by midnight on 3 April of the same year. Under the SDA 1975 and RRA 1976, the time limit is six months for members of the armed forces who have to use an internal procedure first (see para 11.64).[39] Complaints brought by the commissions (relating to discriminatory advertisements or instructions to discriminate) must be brought within six months.[40]

32.44 The SDA 1975, RRA 1976 and DDA 1995 provide that an ET 'shall not consider a complaint ... unless it is presented to the tribunal before the end of the period of three months beginning when the act complained of was done'.[41] The application of this apparently simple rule is not always easy, and the following should be borne in mind:

- Where there is an express dismissal by the employer, time usually runs from the termination of employment;
- Where there is a constructive dismissal, time may run from the date of the discrimination (amounting to a fundamental breach of contract) by the employer which led to the worker's resignation;
- A distinction must be made between a continuing course of discrimination and one act with continuing consequences;
- A deliberate omission is treated as done when the employer 'decided upon it';
- If a complainant is outside the three-month time limit, the tribunal may extend time where it is 'just and equitable' to do so.

39 SDA 1975 s85(9A) and RRA 1976 s75(8). The DDA 1995 contains no parallel provisions, as s64(7) of the Act excludes the armed forces from its employment protection provisions.

40 SDA 1975 s76(4) and RRA 1976 s68(4) respectively.

41 SDA 1975 s76(1), RRA 1976 s86(1) and DDA 1995 Sch 3, para 3(1).

Dismissals by the employer

32.45 If the claim relates to a discriminatory dismissal the time limit runs from the termination of the employment contract, not when notice was given or when the act of discrimination leading to the dismissal took place.[41a] In *Yaseen v Strathclyde Regional Council and another*,[42] for example, the claimant was dismissed after a series of allegedly discriminatory reports spanning a two-year period. The last of these reports was five months before the claimant's complaint to the Tribunal. The EAT accepted that the time within which a claim had to be brought ran from the termination of the claimant's contract. The claimant was entitled, said the EAT, to wait for confirmation of his dismissal before deciding to act.[43]

32.46 In *British Gas Services Ltd v McCaull*,[44] too, the EAT ruled that time does not run in respect of a discriminatory dismissal until the notice of dismissal expires and the employment ceases. The EAT said that, in dismissal cases, individuals suffer detriment as a result of discrimination when they find themselves out of work.

Appeal against dismissal

32.47 If there is an appeal against dismissal the claimant must show that her or his employment continued pending the appeal if time is not to run until the dismissal of that appeal. Further, since the courts have restricted the application of the discrimination legislation to 'person[s] employed', claimants cannot challenge discrimination in the conduct of post-dismissal appeals.[45] At present a worker can challenge post-employment discrimination only when it amounts to victimisation under the SDA.[46]

41a *Gloucester Working Men's Club and Institute v James* [1986] ICR 603, EAT.

42 6/1990, EAT, unreported.

43 In *Lupetti v Wrens Old House Ltd* [1984] 348 IRLR the EAT held that the discrimination occurs when the notice expires, not when it is given.

44 [2001] IRLR 60, Keene J at para 25. See also *Gloucester Working Men's Club & Institute v James and another* [1986] ICR 603, EAT and *Lupetti*, above, note 43.

45 *Adekeye v Post Office* [1993] IRLR 324; *Nagarajan v Agnew* [1994] IRLR 61. See also para 11.44. Although the ECJ ruled in *Coote v Granada Hospitality Ltd* (Case 185/97) [1998] ECR I-5199, [1998] IRLR 656 that post-employment victimisation breached the SDA, this has been construed very narrowly by the domestic courts to apply only in relation to post-employment victimisation under the SDA rather than to any other post-employment victimisation under that Act or the RRA 1976 – see para 11.45.

46 Such a claim having been accepted by the EAT in *Coote v Granada Hospitality Ltd (No 2)* [1999] IRLR 452. See further para 11.46.

32.48 In an ordinary unfair dismissal claim the time limit runs from the effective date of termination, although a claim may be brought after notice has been given but before the effective date of termination.[47] There are no parallel provisions under the discrimination legislation.

Constructive dismissal

32.49 The SDA was amended in 1986 so that the term 'dismissal' includes constructive dismissal.[48] Neither the RRA 1976 nor the DDA 1995 refer to constructive dismissal. In *Derby Specialist Fabrication Ltd v Burton*,[49] however, the EAT held that the reference to 'dismissal' in RRA 1976 s4(2)(c) should be taken to include constructive dismissal. In such a case the time limit for presenting a complaint runs from the date of the claimant's resignation.[50]

32.50 A different decision was reached in a claim brought under the DDA 1995. In *Metropolitan Police Commissioner v Harley*[51] the EAT, without reference to *Derby*, held that 'dismissal' under the DDA 1995 did not include constructive dismissal. The time limit for challenge to the discriminatory act upon which the claimant had tried to found a constructive dismissal, accordingly, ran from the date of that act rather than the date of the claimant's resulting resignation. This decision is not necessarily limited to DDA 1995 cases, the EAT also having ruled that, even if it was wrong and 'dismissal' under the DDA 1995 included constructive dismissal, the 'act complained of' for the purposes of the time limit was the alleged repudiatory breach by the employer. The EAT based this ruling on the CA's decision in *Cast v Croydon College*, in which it was held that, in respect of a non-continuing or 'one-off' repudiatory breach relied on for a constructive dismissal, the 'act complained of' was the employer's breach.[52]

32.51 There are therefore at least two irreconcilable decisions. *Harley* is arguably wrong, particularly as it means that there are different rules for ordinary constructive dismissal and discriminatory constructive

47 ERA 1996 s111(3), which states that a tribunal shall consider a complaint presented after notice is given but before the effective date of termination. There are no parallel provisions under the SDA, RRA 1976 and DDA 1995.

48 SDA s81(1A).

49 [2001] IRLR 69.

50 It was also held that there was continuing discrimination that lasted until his resignation.

51 [2001] IRLR 263.

52 [1998] IRLR 318. A different decision was reached in *Reed v Stedman* [1997] IRLR 299, in which the EAT ruled that the last act of discrimination was the complainant's resignation.

dismissals. There may, however, be a distinction between the SDA 1975 on the one hand, and the RRA 1976 and the DDA 1995 on the other. In any event, to avoid the danger of being out of time complainants should, if possible, lodge a claim within three months of the employer's conduct that led to their resignation and 'constructive dismissal'.

32.52 If, for example, a woman returns to work after maternity leave and finds that her job responsibilities have been taken away from her and she resigns some weeks or months later, it is safer to lodge the complaint for discrimination within three months of her return from work, even if she is still at work. If she then resigns and works her notice period, she may need to lodge a further claim for dismissal after the contract has terminated.

Continuing discrimination

32.53 Generally, time runs from the act of discrimination. However, where there is 'continuing discrimination', time will run from the end of any continuing policy or practice of discrimination which could, in some circumstances, be later than the date of any final 'act' towards the applicant. In discrimination cases there is often more than one act of discrimination. Each act will be discrimination but it may also be a continuing course of conduct (see *Anya*[53]).[54]

32.54 The RRA 1976 s68(7)(b), SDA 1975 s76(6)(b) and DDA 1995 Sch 3, para 3(3)(b) provide that:

(a) where the inclusion of a term in a contract renders the making of the contract an unlawful act, that act shall be treated as extending throughout the duration of the contract;
(b) an act extending over a period shall be treated as done at the end of that period; and
(c) a deliberate omission shall be treated as done when the person in question decided upon it.

53 [2001] IRLR 377, CA. See also *Wade v West Yorkshire Police* EAT/899/96 and EAT/900/96, in which the EAT held that the tribunal should look at the allegations of harassment jointly and deal with the contention that the conduct complained of was all part of a piece. Some apparently trivial incidents may appear in a different light if they are seen as a pattern of behaviour.

54 But see also *Bayless v Hounslow LBC* (21 March 2002, as yet unreported) in which the CA held that an ET had been entitled to find that the acts of discrimination did not extend into the three-month period. The most recent acts complained of did not constitute discrimination so were not part of the continuing course of discrimination.

32.55 In relation to (a), time does not run until the end of the contract or when the term is varied to remove the discrimination.

32.56 In relation to (b) the distinction between continuing discrimination and one act of discrimination with continuing consequences is often difficult to make. There will be an act extending over a period where the employer has a discriminatory regime, rule, or practice in accordance with which decisions are taken from time to time. In such a case time begins to run from the end of the policy or of the applicant's employment.

32.57 In *Barclays Bank plc v Kapur and other*[55] the HL held that the effect of an allegedly racially discriminatory pension scheme (which distinguished employees whose previous service was in Africa, rather than in Europe) continued throughout the claimants' employment. The HL held that to maintain a continuing regime which adversely affects an employee is an act which continues so long as it is maintained. As their Lordships pointed out, to require an employee to work on less favourable terms as to pension is as much a continuing act as to require him or her to work for lower wages. It was an act extending over a period, rather than a deliberate (one-off) omission. The claim therefore had to be brought within three months of the date of termination of employment, not three months from the decision not to credit the employees' service in Africa.

32.58 Where there is no such regime, rule, practice or principle, an act that affects an employee will not be treated as continuing even though the effect of the act continues over a period. Thus, in contrast to the *Barclays Bank* case, the CA ruled in *Sougrin v Haringey Health Authority*[56] that a decision not to regrade an employee (in the absence of a discriminatory policy relating to regrading) was a one-off decision with continuing consequences. Time, therefore, ran from the decision itself.

32.59 In *Owusu v London Fire and Civil Defence Authority*[57] the EAT ruled that a succession of specific instances was capable of indicating the existence of a practice amounting to a continuing act extending over a period. There the continuing act consisted of a practice which excluded the claimant from being regarded or allowed opportunities to 'act up'. The EAT held that 'the continuing consequences do not make it a continuing act. On the other hand, an act does extend over a period of time if it takes the form of some policy, rule or practice, in accordance

55 [1991] IRLR 136.
56 [1992] IRLR 416.
57 [1995] IRLR 574.

with which decisions are taken from time to time'.[58] Mummery J also stated that, whether the disputed decisions in fact amount to a practice as opposed to a series of one-off decisions, depended on the evidence. In *Owusu* the EAT did not accept that a failure to promote the claimant (as opposed to the failure to regrade) was a continuing act but specific instances with continuing consequences.

32.60 In *Cast v Croydon College*[59] the CA also held that a series of refusals to allow the claimant to work part-time (or to job-share) amounted to a discriminatory policy and therefore to a continuing act extending over a period. There could, the CA held, be a 'policy' for the purposes of establishing continuing discrimination even if it was not of a formal nature, or expressed in writing, and even though it was confined to a particular post as it was in this case (see below).

32.61 The distinction between a continuing act and a one-off act with continuing consequences may not be clear until the evidence has been heard. It is therefore not good practice to have a preliminary hearing to decide if the claim is in time. It is better to hear all the evidence and the tribunal can then decide both time limits and liability.

Repeated refusal of a right or benefit in the absence of a discriminatory practice

32.62 In *Cast v Croydon College* (where the issue was the refusal to allow the claimant to jobshare) the CA held that, where there are repeated requests to work different hours, the three months runs from the date the last request was refused, provided that it was reconsidered. If the employer does not reconsider the request, but merely refers back to and confirms the earlier decision, this will not be a fresh act of discrimination.

32.63 Where there is no employment relationship, for example, where the discrimination is in respect of an application for a job, the existence of a continuing practice may not be sufficient for time to keep running. The complaint must be made within three months of the discrimination. However, where there is a series of acts of discrimination, the time limit may run from the last act.[60]

58 Ibid para 21.

59 [1998] IRLR 318.

60 In *Tyagi v BBC World Service* [2001] IRLR 465 the BBC employed the claimant until July 1997. In April 1997 his application for a post as producer was rejected. In July 1998 he made a claim to the tribunal claiming that the selection process

32.64 In *GMC v Rovensksa*[61] a doctor applied to the General Medical Council (GMC) for registration as a doctor in the UK. The GMC required her to pass or obtain exemption from a language test. She attempted to obtain an exemption on four occasions but failed, the last rejection being dated 2 December 1991. Her solicitor then wrote pointing out her qualifications and enclosing a reference. The CA accepted that the letter was a fresh application for exemption from the test, rather than simply a solicitor's letter. The GMC's reply (on 10 January 1992) was negative. Dr Rovenska lodged her claim on 31 March 1992. The CA held that, if its regime was indirectly discriminatory, the GMC would have committed a fresh act of unlawful discrimination each time it refused to allow the claimant limited registration without taking the test. Thus, the most recent letter on her behalf, which advanced a new argument based on the claimant's qualifications, was a further application and time ran from the date of the GMC's response to the letter in which the application was refused.[62]

Omissions

32.65 The RRA 1976 s68(7)(c), SDA 1975 s76(6) and DDA 1995 Sch 3, para 3(3) & (4) provide that:

> a deliberate omission shall be treated as done when the person in question decided upon it

and that

> in the absence of evidence establishing the contrary a person shall be taken .... to decide upon an omission when he does an act inconsistent with doing the omitted act or, if he has done no such inconsistent act, when the period expires within which he might reasonably have been expected to do the omitted act if it was to be done.

for the post was racially discriminatory. A tribunal held that the complaint was out of time. The CA held that, where the claimant is not an employee, he or she cannot complain of a policy of 'continuing discrimination' extending over a period. What is being complained of is the particular employment. See also *Amies v Inner London Education Authority* [1977] ICR 308 EAT.

61 [1997] IRLR 367.

62 This was followed by *Lewane v Department for Education and Employment*, EAT 1447/96, unreported.

32.66 A decision not to confer a benefit on a worker is treated as being done when the employer makes the decision not to confer that benefit. But in the absence of evidence to the contrary, there is an assumption that a person decides on the discriminatory omission when he or she does an act inconsistent with the omitted act. If no inconsistent act occurs, the decision not to confer the benefit etc. will be taken to have been made at the date on which the employer might reasonably have been expected to have conferred the benefit.

32.67 In *Swithland Motors plc v Clarke and others* [63] four male employees claimed sex discrimination when they were not offered alternative work after having been made redundant when their employers became some time insolvent. The decision not to offer them employment was made before they were told, as no offers could be made until after the transfer of the undertaking took place following the insolvency. Their complaints were lodged more than three months after the decision was taken but less than three months after they were told of the decision. The EAT held that 'decided' meant 'decided at a time and in circumstances when [the person taking the decision] is in a position to implement that decision'. Thus time ran from the time the new employers were in a position to offer the new employment and did not do so, ie after the transfer.

Some practical examples

Discriminatory contractual provisions or rules

32.68 In *Calder v James Finlay Corporation Ltd*[64] a refusal to give the claimant a mortgage subsidy because she was a woman was held to be continuing discrimination.

Failure to implement remedial measures relating to racial abuse

32.69 In *Littlewoods Organisation plc v Traynor*[65] the claimant's first claim, based on racially abusive remarks, was held to be out of time. He then brought a further claim that his employers' alleged failure to institute remedial measures following his initial complaint was capable of being a continuing act of discrimination. The EAT held that this claim was in time.

63 1994 ICR 231.
64 [1989] IRLR 55.

Refusal of child-friendly working hours as indirect sex discrimination

32.70 Negotiations over child friendly working hours give rise to particular practical difficulties, though claims of discrimination arising from them are subject to the normal rules. Time runs from either of the following:

- Where there is a single refusal to allow child-friendly hours, the date of that refusal; or
- The date of the last refusal, where there have been several requests, each of which was considered by the employer and refused. Note that if there are only repeated requests and refusals without further consideration by the employer, time will run from the date of the first refusal; or
- Where there is a policy (written or by custom) of not allowing child-friendly hours, whether in relation to the workforce, a section of the workforce or the individual job, the date the policy ceased or the claimant's contract terminated.[66]

The statutory right to request flexible working contained in the Employment Act 2002 will come into force some time in 2003. A complaint that the employer has rejected the request or breached the procedures must be lodged with the tribunal within 3 months of the date on which the employee is notified of the employer's decision on the appeal or of the date on which the breach of the regulation was committed.[66a]

Refusal to accept a grievance

32.71 Where the alleged discrimination consists of a refusal by the employer to accept a grievance, time begins to run from the date on which the decision was communicated to the claimant rather than the date when the decision was made.[67] In *Rhys-Harper v Relaxion Group plc*,[68] however, the complaint related to the employers' failure to carry out a proper investigation into allegations of sexual harassment which were only made after the dismissal. The EAT and CA held that,

65 [1993] IRLR 154 .

66 *Cast v Croydon College*, note 48, above.

66a Employment Act 2002 s47 introducing new ERA 1996 s80H(5)(a) and (b) and the Flexible Working (Procedural Requirements) Regulations (draft).

67 *Aniagwu v London Borough of Hackney* [1999] IRLR 303, EAT.

68 [2001] IRLR 360.

because the woman was no longer employed at the time the grievance was brought, she could not challenge the alleged discrimination.[69]

Internal appeal following dismissal

32.72 An act complained of can include discrimination in relation to an appeal against dismissal but only if this took place during the worker's employment. If the appeal takes place after the end of the employment, the worker is no longer 'employed' and so is not protected by the legislation.[70]

The Employment Act 2002

32.73 The regulations which the government proposes to draw up under the Employment Act 2002 concerning the utilisation of the statutory internal grievance procedure had not been drafted at the time of writing. The government has stated, however, that time limits will be extended to allow for the completion of a statutory grievance procedure and it is likely to be for a further period of 3 months.

Equal pay

32.74 An equal pay claim must be brought within six months of the employee leaving the employment.[71]

32.75 Where there are intermittent contracts of service without a stable employment relationship, the period of six months runs from the end of each contract of service. However, where contracts are concluded at regular intervals in respect of the same employment and there is a stable employment relationship, the six-month period runs from the end of the last contract. Whether there is a stable employment relationship will be a question of fact.[72]

Time limits under EC law

32.76 There are no specific time limits for claims brought relying on EC law. The ECJ has held that time limits are for the member states to decide provided that:

69 The CA rejected the argument that this situation was analogous to post-employment victimisation which is prohibited by EC law (see *Coote*, note 41, above)

70 *Adeke (No 2)*, note 41, above.

71 EqPA 1970 s2(4).

72 *Preston v Wolverhampton Healthcare NHS Trust* [2001] 2 AC 455, [2001] IRLR 237.

- Such conditions are not less favourable than those relating to similar actions under national law; and
- The conditions are not such as to make it virtually impossible to exercise EC rights.[73]

Rights under EC law are not freestanding and must be brought in conjunction with the relevant domestic legislation whose time limits will apply.[74]

Human Rights Act 1998

32.77 A claim under the HRA 1998 must be made within one year of the act complained of unless (as is the case if the claim is brought by way of judicial review) stricter time limits apply. Claims directly under the HRA 1998 cannot be brought in the employment tribunal but the ET must interpret relevant legislation in a way that is compatible with the HRA 1998, in so far as that is possible.

The Employment Rights Act 1996

32.78 For all claims under the ERA 1996, the Maternity and Parental Leave Regulations 1999 and the PTW Regulations 2000 (including claims in respect of unfair dismissal and in connection with time-off rights and claims in respect of written reasons and unlawful deduction of wages) the time limit for bringing a claim is three months less one day. When the Employment Act 2002 provisions come into force, claims under the right to request flexible working provisions,[75] claims in respect of paternity leave[75a] and adoption leave[75b] will also be 3 months less a day.

73 *Emmott v Minister for Social Welfare* (Case 208/90) [1991] ECR I-4269, [1991] IRLR 387 ECJ; see also *Rewe-Zentralfinanz eG Landwirtschalfskammer fur das Saarland* (Case 39/73) [1976] 2 ECR 1989 and *Fisscher v Voorhuis Hengelo BV* (Case 128/93) [1994] ECR I-4583, [1994] IRLR 662, ECJ.

74 *Biggs v Somerset County Council* [1996] IRLR 203, CA.

75 ERA 1996 ss80F–H (as amended by Employment Act 2002 s47).

75a ERA 1996 s80A (as amended by Employment Act 2002 s1) and Social Security Contributions and Benefits Act 1992 ss171ZA–K (as amended by Employment Act 2002 s1).

75b ERA 1996 ss75A–D and Social Security Contributions and Benefits Act 1992 ss171L–T (both amended by Employment Act 2002 s3).

Unfair dismissal claims

32.79 In unfair dismissal cases, the three months run from the effective date of termination.[76] Where a woman is dismissed while on maternity leave, the dismissal will bring her contract to an end.[77]

'Detriment' claims[78]

32.80 A claim (under ERA 1996 s47C or D) that an employee has been subjected to a detriment for a reason relating to her pregnancy, childbirth, maternity, time off for maternity, paternity, adoption or dependants leave or a request to work flexibly must be made to an ET within three months:

a) Beginning with the date of the act or failure to act to which the complaint relates or,
b) Where that act or failure is part of a series of similar acts or failures, the last of them, or
c) Within such further period as the tribunal considers reasonable in a case where it is satisfied that it was not reasonably practicable for the complaint to be presented before the end of the three months.[79]

32.81 Where an act extends over a period, the 'date of the act' is the date of the last day of that period, and a deliberate failure to act shall be treated as done when it was decided on (see further para 32.65 above). For example, if a training programme runs over a period of a year and an employee is not offered any training because she wants to take Additional Maternity Leave (AML) and/or family leave, the time limit would probably run from the end of the year by which stage it will be clear that the woman is not going to be offered any training. On the other hand, if a woman is not promoted because she is on AML, time will run from the date of the decision not to promote her. This may be extended if promotion could be achieved at any time, rather than only when a particular vacancy arose.

Redundancy

32.82 An application for a redundancy payment must be made within six months of the redundancy.[80] Where the claim is for discrimination

76 ERA 1996 s97.
77 MPL Regulations reg7(5).
78 ERA 1996 s47C.
79 ERA 1996 s48.
80 ERA 1996 s164.

contrary to the SDA 1975, RRA 1976 or DDA 1995 in connection with a redundancy, the three-month limit applies. An application for notice pay in the event of redundancy must also be brought within three months.

Unlawful deduction of wages

32.83 This claim (formerly under the Wages Act 1986) must be made within three months of the last deduction of wages.[81]

Breach of contract

32.84 A six-year time limit applies to claims of breach of contract in the county court. Proceedings may be brought in an ET where there is a claim for breach of contract is outstanding or arises at the termination of employment, but the time limit for bringing such a claim is three months less one day from the effective date of termination.[82]

Out of time claims

32.85 An application may be made to lodge a claim outside the time limit. The test is different under the ERA, on the one hand, and the SDA, RRA 1976 and DDA 1995 on the other.

The Employment Rights Act 1996

32.86 Under the ERA 1996 the ET has power to extend time to such further period as the tribunal considers reasonable in a case where it is satisfied that it was 'not reasonably practicable for a complaint to be presented' within the three months (see below). This test is a fairly strict one.

32.87 Examples where time has been extended include those where the claimant has had a physical or mental illness and has no adviser acting for her; and postal delays which were more severe than those which should have been predicted. Ignorance of rights or mistaken belief as to essential matters may or may not be sufficient.[83] In one

81 ERA 1996 s23(3).

82 Employment Tribunals (Extension of Jurisdiction) (England and Wales) Order 1994 reg 7 (1994 SI No 1623).

83 Ignorance of rights was not enough to extend the time limit in *Biggs v Somerset County Council* [1996] IRLR 203, CA. *Cf Glenlake Computers Ltd v Hands* (EAT 434/99), where the employee was confused about his rights arising on a transfer situation and was allowed to proceed with his claim out of time.

case a young pregnant woman was allowed to claim out of time after she was incorrectly advised by a CAB.[84] But whether or not it was reasonably practicable to bring a claim in time is a question of fact and it is difficult to generalize about tribunal decisions in this area except to say that the longer the delay the less likely an ET is to grant an extension.

32.88 Once a tribunal has found that it was not reasonably practicable for the complaint to be presented in time, it must then decide whether the claim was brought within a further reasonable period.

The Sex Discrimination Act 1975, Race Relations Act 1976 and Disability Discrimination Act 1995

Note that there is no power to extend the (six month) time limit under the EqPA.[85]

32.89 A court or tribunal may consider any out of time complaint under the SDA, RRA 1976 or DDA 1995 if 'in all the circumstances of the case, it considers that it is just and equitable to do so'.[86] This form of words gives tribunals more flexibility to allow out of time claims than under the ERA 1996 (above). There is a wide discretion to do what is just and equitable and a tribunal can take into account anything it considers relevant.[87]

32.90 The discretion to grant an extension of time is as wide as that given to the civil courts by section 33 of the Limitation Act 1980 to decide whether to extend time in personal injury actions.[88] The tribunal must consider the prejudice which each party would suffer as a result of the grant or refusal of an extension and have regard to all the circumstances, in particular:

- The length of and reasons for the delay;
- The extent to which the cogency of the evidence is likely to be affected by the delay;
- The extent to which the respondent had co-operated with any requests for information;
- How quickly the claimant acted once he or she knew of the facts giving rise to the claim;

84 *Cheshire v Intasave Travel and Shipping Ltd*, S/2642/89.
85 The challenge to the time limit in the EqPA 1970 under Article 141 failed in *Preston*, note 67 above.
86 SDA 1975 s76(5), RRA 1976 s68(6) and DDA 1995 Sch 3 para 3(2) respectively.
87 See *Hutchison v Westward Television* [1977] IRLR 69.
88 *British Coal Corporation v Keeble* [1997] IRLR 336, EAT; *Mills and Crown Prosecution Service v Marshall* [1998] IRLR 494.

- The steps take by the claimant to obtain appropriate professional advice once he or she knew of the possibility of taking action.

32.91 An extension of three years was allowed in *Mills and another v Marshall*[89] in which the claimant presented a claim for discrimination three years after the ECJ's decision, in *P v S & Cornwall*, that discrimination against transsexuals was unlawful.[89a] The EAT held that the words 'just and equitable' 'could not be wider or more general', and stated that the ET had to balance all the factors including, importantly and perhaps crucially, whether it was possible to have a fair trial notwithstanding the delay. The discretion to extend time, according to the EAT, is unfettered and the ET may take account of the date from which the complainant could reasonably have become aware of her right to present a worthwhile claim.

32.92 In *BCC v Keeble*[90] the EAT held that it was 'just and equitable' to extend the time limit because the reason for the delay was the claimant's 'wholly understandable' mistaken understanding of the law. The EAT pointed out that the discretion under the SDA 1975 was very much wider than under the ERA 1996.[91]

32.93 Factors that will be taken into account include those set out above and, in addition:

- The reason for and extent of the delay;[92]
- The health of the claimant; this might include, for example, a difficult birth or subsequent postnatal illness;
- The merits of the case;[93]
- Any other relevant circumstance.

89 [1998] IRLR 494.

89a [1996] IRLR 347.

90 [1997] IRLR 336, EAT.

91 See also *Hawkins v Ball and Barclays Bank plc* [1996] IRLR 258, in which *Biggs* was distinguished because it was an unfair dismissal claim governed by the 'reasonably practicable' test.

92 See *Osajie v London Borough of Camden* EAT 317/96, in which the tribunal allowed the claimant's claim to proceed out of time as the employer's had delayed in responding to her efforts to obtain further information from them before deciding whether to pursue a race discrimination claim. The EAT stated that the claimant was entitled to seek information before deciding whether to make a claim, and that the respondents should have dealt with the complaints timeously.

93 But if the merits are considered the parties should be invited to make submissions – see *Lupetti v Wrens Old House Ltd* 1984 [ICR] 348, EAT.

Effect of grievance procedure

32.94 In *Aniagwu v London Borough of Hackney*[94] the claim related to the refusal of a loan and the following of a grievance procedure. The EAT held that it was just and equitable to hear a race discrimination complaint brought outside the requisite three-month time limit where the reason was an attempt to seek redress through a grievance procedure. EAT expressed the view that, unless there was some particular feature about the case or the respondents could demonstrate some particular prejudice, every tribunal would inevitably conclude that it is a responsible and proper attitude for someone first to redress a grievance through the employer's internal grievance procedure.

32.95 *Aniagwu* can no longer be relied upon in this respect, following *Robinson v Post Office*[95] in which the EAT upheld an ET's decision (in a DDA 1995 case) that it was not just and equitable to extend the time limit when the claimant made an out of time claim after pursuing an internal appeal. The EAT held that there was no principle that, wherever there was an unexhausted internal procedure, awaiting its outcome was necessarily an acceptable reason for delay in lodging a claim. It was a factor to be considered amongst others. In *Apelogun-Gabriels v Lambeth LBC*[96] the Court of Appeal upheld the *Robinson* approach (but see changes proposed by the Employment Act 2002).

32.96 As long as the claimant believes he or she had a good reason for missing the time limit, there is generally nothing to lose by making the claim.

The IT1 (tribunal claim) and how it is processed

32.97 All tribunal claims must be lodged:

- With the office of employment tribunals specified on the IT1 form for the postal district concerned; or
- (in Northern Ireland), with the Office of the Employment Tribunals or the Fair Employment Tribunal.

Claims for breach of contract must be brought in the county court except when they are outstanding or arise on termination of employ-

94 [1999] IRLR 303, EAT. However, where the complaint is that the grievance procedure is racially discriminatory, time will not usually run until the result is known. In *Aniagwu* the claim was made three months after the date of the decision, so was one day late.

95 [2000] IRLR 804, EAT.

96 [2002] IRLR 116, CA.

ment, while some claims in respect of maternity pay are brought other than at an ET). A tribunal claim is brought by lodging a Notice of Application (IT1) at the tribunal local to the employer's place of work. An application can be faxed. IT1s are available from the local job centre or advice agency. The claim must arrive at the tribunal by the expiry of the relevant time limit (discussed above).

32.98 The following information must be given on the application:

- The name and address of the claimant,
- The name and address of the respondent, and
- The grounds for the claim.

In *Dodd v British Telecom plc*[97] the EAT ruled that the other information requested by the IT1 form was directory rather than mandatory. The written application need contain only sufficient information to identify who is making it, against whom, and what sort of complaint it is. It is possible to make a claim by letter provided it contains the information listed above, though it is better to use the standard IT1 form.

Content of application

32.99 The main incidents on which the claimant will rely should be set out, including acts of discrimination which occurred outside the time limit, which may be taken into account.[98] A sample IT1 is in appendix B.

32.100 It is important to set out all the relevant facts and the nature of the claims (including those under EC law and the HRA) but it is not necessary to quote from the statute. A subsequent amendment to add a further claim, is more likely to be allowed if the facts set out in the IT1 support it. One word of warning: if a claimant claims for breach of contract (even if the claim is not set out clearly as being so) the employer can counterclaim against the claimant for breach of contract. Thus, if there is a claim for statutory notice pay or holiday pay, and there is a danger of any counterclaim, it is advisable to claim *only* by way of a claim for unlawful deduction of wages, so that it cannot be treated as a claim for breach of contract.[99]

97 [1980] IRLR 16, EAT.

98 See *Eke v Commissioners of Customers and Excise* [1981] IRLR 334, EAT.

99 A claim by an employer can only be made in specified circumstances, one of which is that the employee has brought a breach of contract claim at the end of his or her employment see Article 4 of the Employment Tribunals Extension of Jurisdiction Order 1994.

32.101 In *Housing Corporation v Bryant*[100] the claimant made no reference to victimisation in her IT1, claiming only unfair dismissal and sex discrimination. In order to prove victimisation she would have had to show that she had been dismissed because of her allegation of sexual harassment. She did not say this in her application and her request to amend was refused because there was no link between her victimisation claim and the grounds of her original claim. The EAT held that it was an entirely new claim brought out of time. It is therefore advisable, not only to state the fact giving rise to the claim, but also to make it clear whether the claim is for direct discrimination, indirect discrimination and/or victimisation. These can be argued in the alternative which is the safest option if the position is not clear.

32.102 Sometimes the strength of any part of a claim will only become apparent after documents have been disclosed or the replies to the questionnaire received and it may be necessary to provide further particulars of the claim and may expose the claimant to a costs order against them if the application was misconceived. A claim can also be withdrawn (whether it forms the whole or part of an application) if it becomes clear that it has no chance of success. However, no claim should be made unless it is genuine. A very weak claim is likely to undermine the strength of the stronger claims. If possible it is advisable (in discrimination claims) to serve a questionnaire early as the replies may reveal whether or not there has been discrimination.

32.103 In a DDA 1995 claim in which both less favourable treatment and a failure to make a reasonable adjustment is alleged it is strongly recommended that the application refers to both. There is as yet no appellate case law considering whether an IT1 which refers to 'disability discrimination' would enable an applicant to argue both forms of action at a hearing. But it is doubtful whether this would be permitted where an employer is given no indication that both claims are being advanced.

'Piggy-backing' EC law claims

32.104 Where a claim is made relying directly on EC law it is crucial to 'piggy back' the EC claim on the relevant UK statute, as there is no free-standing right to rely on EC law.[101] As EC law does not mirror UK law, more than one statute might be appropriate. Until recently it was accepted by most tribunals and courts that the 'way in' for equal pay

100 [1999] ICR 123, CA.

101 See *Biggs*, note 69, above.

claims under Article 141 was the EqPA 1970. But in *Alabaster v The Woolwich plc and the Secretary of State for Social Security*[102] the EAT held that a claim which involved pregnancy or maternity discrimination could not be made with reliance on the EqPA 1970. An EqPA 1970 case necessarily involves a comparison between two workers of a different sex, whereas it is not possible to compare a pregnant woman with a man. According to the EAT, the only claim that could be made was for an unlawful deduction of wages under ERA 1996. The case has been referred to the ECJ by the CA.[103]

Vicarious liability and related issues

32.105 The SDA s41(1), RRA 1976 s32(1) and DDA 1995 s58(1) provide that an employer is liable for discrimination by one employee towards another which takes place in the course of the discriminating employee's 'course of employment', irrespective of whether the discrimination was done with the employer's knowledge or approval.[104] 'In the course of employment' is to be interpreted very broadly. In *Jones v Tower Boot Co Ltd*[105] (a race discrimination claim) the CA held that employers are liable for all acts of racial and sexual harassment committed by their employees, which take place during their employment, unless the employer can establish the defence set out in SDA s41(3), RRA 1976 s32(3) and DDA 1995 s58(5). The defence permits an employer to escape liability where it can prove that it 'took such steps as were reasonably practicable to prevent the employee from doing that act, or from doing in the course of his employment acts of that description'.[106]

32.106 An employee who discriminates 'in the course of his employment' will be personally liable under the SDA 1975, RRA 1976 or DDA 1995 provided that the employer would have been liable by virtue of SDA s41(1), RRA 1976 s32(1) and DDA 1995 s58(1), *even where the employer successfully pleads the defence* established by SDA s41(3), RRA 1976 s32(3) or DDA 1995 s58(5). If the employee is to be made liable he or she must be named on the IT1. If he or she is found liable he or she

102 [2000] IRLR 754. The claim related to statutory maternity pay and the backdating of a pay rise after the qualifying period.

103 [2002] IRLR 420, CA.

104 SDA 1975 s41.

105 [1997] IRLR 168.

106 This is taken from the SDA 1975 and RRA 1976. The DDA 1995 formulation is identical in substance if not in form.

may be ordered to pay compensation. This commonly happens in harassment claims. Liability is covered in detail in chapter 31. The employer should always be named. If there is any doubt about the identity of the employer, it is advisable to name all the alternatives.

32.107 Dismissal by a school with a delegated budget is deemed to be a dismissal by the governing body, though any compensation will be payable by the local education authority.[107]

Transfer cases

32.108 Where an undertaking has been transferred where the Transfer of Undertakings (Protection of Employment) (TUPE) Regulations 1981 apply and employees have their employment transferred, any rights accrued under the former employer may only be enforced against the new employer.[108] Thus, the transferee should be named as a respondent. As it is not always clear if and when there has been a transfer it may be safer to include the old employer as well. The claim can be withdrawn against the transferor once the position has been clarified.

Combined cases

32.109 If two separate claims arise out of the common questions of law or fact it is advisable to ask that they be combined and heard at the same time.[109] This commonly happens in discrimination claims where a claim follows one incident of discrimination, and is followed in turn by more incidents, or by the resignation of the employee who then claims constructive dismissal and further discrimination and/or unfair dismissal. In discrimination cases it is very important that all related acts of discrimination are heard by the same tribunal.

Test cases

32.110 There are no rules regarding test cases but the EAT has held that the hearing of test cases is within the tribunal's general power to regulate its own procedure.[110] Test cases are particularly useful in equal pay

107 Article 6(3), Education (Modification of Enactments Relating to Employment) Order 1989 (1989 SI No 901).

108 This also applies in discrimination claims see *DJM International Ltd v Nicholas* [1996] IRLR 76.

109 ET Rules rule 20.

110 See *Bristol Channel Ship Repairers Ltd v O'Keefe and others* [1978] ICR 691.

cases in which a large number of claimants in one grade claim equal pay with one or more comparators (see also para 24.7). In *Ashmore v British Coal Corporation*,[111] which involved 1,500 like work claims, the Tribunal ordered that the bulk of claims should be stayed pending the outcome of representative sample cases. The sample cases were dismissed and Ms Ashmore, who tried to have her claim reactivated, had it struck out on the basis that it was vexatious and an abuse of process. The CA held it was contrary to the interests of justice and public policy to allow the same issues to be litigated again, unless there was fresh evidence.[112]

ACAS and settlement

32.111 All claims are sent to ACAS which has a duty to conciliate. Any discussions with ACAS are privileged and may not be used in evidence in the tribunal. If ACAS negotiates an agreement between the parties, the ACAS officer will draw up a COT3 which will be a binding agreement. In Northern Ireland the claims are sent to the Labour Relations Agency (LRA).

Compromise agreements

32.112 If the parties agree a settlement without ACAS (or, in Northern Ireland, the LRA), the agreement will *only* be valid if:

- It is in writing;
- It relates to the specific complaint;
- The employee has received independent legal advice from a qualified lawyer or independent adviser who is insured to give such advice;
- The agreement identifies the adviser; and
- It states that the conditions regulating compromise agreements are satisfied.[113]

A letter signed by an claimant to the effect that he or she will not bring proceedings is ineffective and will not prevent a claim being brought.

32.113 There are many advantages in settling including avoidance of the risk of losing, saving of costs, and the limited remedies a tribunal can order. However, agreements need to be drafted carefully to ensure

111 [1990] IRLR 283, [1990] ICR 485.

112 A different decision was reached in *DES v Taylor* [1992] IRLR 308 in which the parties had not been part of the first case.

113 ERA1996 s203, SDA s77, RRA 1976 s72 and DDA 1995 s9.

that they are not too wide. It is common to exclude pensions rights and personal injury claims (in so far as they are not part of the discrimination claim) from any settlement.

The employer's response: the IT3

32.114 The tribunal will send a copy of the IT1 to the employer who then has 21 days to submit its response (the IT3) to the tribunal, though this time limit is often extended.[114]

32.115 The IT3, also called the 'notice of appearance' should set out:

- The respondent's full name and address;
- Whether or not the respondent intends to resist the application; and
- If the respondent does intend to resist, sufficient particulars to show the grounds of resistance.[115]

Stages before the tribunal hearing

Amendment

32.116 Either before or at the hearing the tribunal can allow amendments which may either change the basis of the claim (from, say, unfair dismissal to discrimination) or add an additional claim (such as of discrimination) or even add an additional party. A new claim, at least where the facts are not set out in the original, will be subject to the rules on time limits. An amendment is likely to be allowed only if the facts set out in the claim would also give rise to a claim of discrimination. The test is whether hardship or injustice would be caused to either party by granting or withholding permission to amend.[116] In some cases – where the text of the IT1 clearly shows, for example, sex discrimination as well as an unfair dismissal claim – the tribunal may decide that it unnecessary to amend the IT1 even though the only cause of action actually stated is unfair dismissal.[117]

114 ET Rules rule 3 provides that the employer must indicate the grounds on which the claim is resisted.

115 ET Rules rule 3(1).

116 *Cocking v Sandhurts (Stationers) Ltd* [1974] ICR 650, NIRC.

117 See *Selkent Bus Co Ltd v Moore* [1996] ICR 836 and *Housing Corporation v Bryant* [1999] ICR 123. The test is whether there is a causative link between the various causes of action.

Further particulars of IT1 and IT3

32.117 Either party can ask for further details of the grounds on which a party relies and of any facts and contentions in the ET1 or ET3 that are relevant. This should first be done by letter to the other side asking for a reply within (say) 14 days. If answers are not forthcoming the tribunal may, on application, order the provision of further particulars.[118] A tribunal may also, of its own accord, ask for further details of either party's case, though not for details of evidence to be given at the hearing (this distinction is not always easy to draw).

Written answers

32.118 A tribunal may also make an order, either at the request of a party or of its own motion, that written answers be given to specific questions.[119] These are similar to interrogatories in the High Court or county court. Voluntary answers should first be sought and, if these are refused, an application can be made to the tribunal for an order. Some tribunals are reluctant to allow written questions which are the same or similar to questions in the questionnaire. This is arguably wrong, as the procedures are quite separate. Written answers can be ordered by the tribunal, whereas there is no compulsion on an employer to reply to the questionnaire.

Discovery

32.119 Documentation can be crucial to a discrimination case which is often proved by inferences of discrimination rather than by direct evidence.

Criteria for discovery

32.120 The main criteria is that the documents are relevant to an issue in the case. The CA set out important criteria for deciding on order for discovery in discrimination cases in *West Midlands Passenger Transport Executive v Singh.*[120] These are:

- The evidence need not decisively prove that the respondent had discriminated: the question is whether it may tend to prove the case;

118 ET Rules rule 4(3).
119 ET Rules rule 4(3).
120 [1988] IRLR 186, CA.

- Statistical evidence may show a discernible pattern of less favourable treatment and may give rise to an inference of discrimination;
- Evidence is often accepted from employers that they have a policy of non-discrimination. If this goes to prove they do not discriminate then the converse is true;
- The suitability of candidates can rarely be measured objectively. A high failure of members of a particular group may indicate a discriminatory attitude involving stereotyped assumptions.

The most common reasons for refusing to supply documents are that they are confidential, protected by the Data Protection Act 1998, irrelevant, or covered by public interest immunity or by legal professional privilege.

Confidentiality

32.121 In *Science Research Council v Nassé* the HL laid down the following guidelines to deal with claims of confidentiality arising in the context of discrimination claims:[121]

- Employers usually have the information necessary to prove discrimination;
- No principle of public interest immunity protects documents which the employer considers confidential, such as those relating to other employees and commercially (or otherwise) sensitive documents;
- Confidentiality alone does not make documents immune from discovery, although a tribunal might have regard to the fact that the documents are confidential and that to order disclosure would involve a breach of confidence;
- Relevance alone, though necessary, does not provide an automatic test for ordering discovery;
- The ultimate test is whether discovery is necessary for disposing fairly of the proceedings, or for saving costs;
- In order to decide whether discovery is necessary, notwithstanding confidentiality, the tribunal should inspect the documents and consider whether justice can be done by adopting special measures, such as 'covering up', substituting anonymous references for specific names.

121 [1979] 3 WLR 762, [1979] IRLR 465.

In *Knight v Department of Social Security*[122] the EAT reiterated that confidentiality was not in itself a basis for refusing disclosure and overrode a tribunal decision to sit by itself, with the claimant, to consider the documents. The EAT held that it was inappropriate to hold that documents were relevant but to refuse to provide them to the claimant.

Public interest immunity

32.122 This arises where disclosure would be injurious to the public interest. This may cover a 'class' of documents irrespective of the contents or 'contents' where only specified parts of documents are protected from disclosure. In *Halford v Sharples*[123] the following principles were established:

- All relevant documents are subject to disclosure, unless their exclusion can be justified on a recognised ground. The duty to justify exclusion is a heavy one;
- Documents can be excluded on public interest grounds. In balancing the competing needs, relevant factors include the importance of the documents to the litigation, the extent of the injustice caused by their non-disclosure and the importance of the litigation to the parties and to the public.
- The courts have a power to inspect and order disclosure, but the power to inspect should be used with extreme care.

Legal professional privilege

32.123 Communication between lawyers and their clients with a view to the litigation in hand is privileged. This does not apply to non-lawyers, such as personnel advisers.[124]

Procedure for discovery

32.124 If the claimant is aware that the employer has particular documents he or she should make a specific request for these as well as a request for all other relevant documents. It is preferable to ask for a list of all relevant documents, as well as copies of them, to avoid any dispute

122 [2002] IRLR 249; the documents consisted of the claimant's original test papers, those completed by the 32 successful candidates, the test questions and the application forms of the other candidates.

123 [1992] ICR 583, CA.

124 *New Victoria Hospital v Ryan* [1993] IRLR 202, EAT.

over whether a document has been disclosed. There is no duty on the parties to disclose documents unless the tribunal has made an order for discovery.[125]

32.125 If a party refuses to disclose all relevant documents an application should be made to the tribunal for a discovery order. The test to be applied in deciding whether disclosure or production of the documents should be ordered is whether they are material and relevant to the issues in the proceedings. The tribunal will not allow a fishing expedition – where a claimant looks for documents to back up a claim that has not otherwise been substantiated.[126] The tribunal can refuse to order discovery if it is not necessary either for disposing fairly of the matter or for saving costs.[127]

32.126 Relevant documents will depend on the circumstances but examples include:

- The claimant's personnel file;
- The employer's equal opportunities policies, if any;
- In recruitment or promotion cases, criteria used for shortlisting and selection, application forms of other candidates, interview notes, notes of any discussion by the interview panel, breakdown of candidates by race, sex or disability;
- In dismissal cases, notes of any disciplinary interviews, disciplinary and/or redundancy procedures, criteria for redundancy (if applicable);

32.127 In indirect discrimination cases, which are based on statistical evidence, useful information may be obtained from:

- Censuses and surveys (population census, Labour Force Survey; New Earnings Survey; annual census of employment);
- Publications (such as *Labour Market Trends*, the *Equal Opportunities Review, Social Trends*);
- Organisations such as the EOC, CRE, DRC, Labour Research Department, Central Office of Information, TUC, and universities' research departments.

125 ET Rules rule 4(5)(b). Lawyers are under a duty not to put forward misleading information.

126 *Ministry of Defence v Meredith* [1995] IRLR 539, EAT.

127 The power to make the order under rule 4(5)(b) of the ET Rules is the same as for a county court.

Agreed bundle of documents and chronology

32.128 Usually there is an agreed bundle of documents for the hearing. Tribunals prefer to have one bundle with a contents page and page numbers. This should be paginated with the tribunal documents (such as IT1, IT3, questionnaires and further and better particulars) at the beginning, followed by documents in chronological order. A chronology is also very useful.

32.129 It is usually the claimant's responsibility to prepare the bundle, though sometimes the respondent will agree to do so. Four copies are required (one for each panel member and one for the witness), though it is advisable to produce six (one for the claimant and one for the respondent).

Power to strike out

32.130 The tribunal has power to strike out the whole or part of the IT1 or IT3 if a party does not comply with a tribunal order.[128] In practice this is rarely done.

Witnesses and experts

32.131 Both parties can call witnesses and the tribunal can order a witness to attend and produce relevant documents. An application for a witness order is made by letter to the secretary of the tribunals with an explanation as to why the evidence is relevant and necessary and reasons why the witness may not otherwise be prepared to attend (because, for example they work for the respondent).[129]

32.132 It is not advisable to call a witness unless they are willing to give evidence. A hostile witness is likely to be damaging to the party calling them.

32.133 Tribunals may order the parties to prepare written statements and exchange them before the hearing.[130] The witness statement may be read aloud by the witness at the hearing, although some tribunals will prefer for the members to read witness statements themselves. Representatives may be permitted to ask additional questions on points which are not referred to in the statement. A well-written statement can make all the difference to the chances of success. It

128 ET Rules rule 4(8)(b).

129 ET Rules rule 4(5). The tribunal may also order the witness to produce relevant documents.

130 ET Rules rule 4(3).

should start with a brief explanation of the background, then set out the relevant facts in chronological order, stating, where appropriate why the claimant thinks he or she has been discriminated against and, if appropriate, examples of how others have been treated more favourably.

Medical evidence in DDA 1995 cases

32.134 Medical evidence can be useful in DDA 1995 cases in establishing whether an applicant is disabled. Such evidence will most usually be required to establish whether an individual has a mental impairment within the meaning of the DDA 1995[131] and where it is disputed that an individual has a physical impairment.[132] If the applicant is on medication the doctor could usefully discuss the effect of the treatment to assist the court or tribunal in its task of ignoring the effects of treatment in assessing the effect of the impairment on a person's normal day-to-day activities.[133] Beyond that, medical evidence is not usually relevant in determining whether an impairment has a substantial effect on the person's normal day to day activities: the applicant's own evidence and that of his or her family and friends as to what he or she cannot do, or can only do with difficulty, is likely to be more cogent.[134] It is possible that medical evidence could be required as to whether a condition is likely to be long term and in establishing the prognosis of progressive conditions.

32.135 Where there is a dispute about medical evidence, tribunals encourage the appointment of an agreed expert and an organized process of exchange of medical evidence which is not agreed.[135]

32.136 Directions hearings are particularly important in DDA 1995 cases in which the applicant's disability is a matter of dispute and where it is unclear whether a claim relates to less favourable treatment, a failure to make reasonable adjustments, or both.

Directions hearings

32.137 If it considers it appropriate a tribunal may give directions about any matter in relation to the proceedings. Directions may be given at a

131 See, for example *Morgan v Staffordshire University* [2002] IRLR 190.
132 See, for example *College of Ripon & York St. John v Hobbs* [2002] IRLR 85.
133 As it is required to do – see para 2.64.
134 *Vicary v British Telecommunications plc* [1999] IRLR 680.
135 *De Keyser v Wilson* [2001] IRLR 324.

hearing or by letter. Common directions relate to clarification of the issues, discovery, further and better particulars, and estimated length of the hearing and date. A directions hearing can be a useful way of planning the hearing and, if the tribunal does not list for a directions hearing, either party can ask the tribunal for a hearing. Some tribunals issue automatic directions, sometimes with the notice of hearing which set out procedure for exchange of witness statements and bundles. Note that strictly speaking 'exchange' means just that. Neither party should have the advantage of reading the other's statements before preparing their own.[136]

Pre-hearing review

32.138 A tribunal has a discretion, either on the application of a party or of its own motion, to hold a pre-hearing review to determine whether the application or arguments of either party have any chance of success. If the ET thinks there are no reasonable prospects of success, it may require a deposit of up to £500 from a party as a condition of continuing.[137]

Preliminary hearings

32.139 There may be a preliminary hearing to hear any issue relating to the entitlement of a party to bring or contest proceedings (eg, whether the claimant is an employee or has satisfied the one-year qualifying period to bring an ordinary unfair dismissal claim).[138]

Adjournments, extension of time

32.140 The tribunal has power to grant an extension of time[139] or adjourn a hearing. For example, an adjournment may be granted if the claimant is ill, about to give birth or has recently given birth, where a witness is

136 See *Martins v Marks and Spencer plc* [1999] IRLR 349 and *Goodwin v Patent Office* [1999] IRLR 4, EAT where the EAT and CA respectively said it would be good practice to hold a directions hearing in discrimination claims.

137 ET Rules rule 7(4).

138 Rule 6 of the ET Rules provides that notice must be sent to the parties giving them an opportunity to submit representations in writing and to advance oral argument before the tribunal.

139 ET Rules rule 17.

ill, or where there are proceedings pending in the High Court or county court.[140]

Equal value cases

32.141 There are special rules for equal value cases and these are covered in chapter 24.

The tribunal hearing

32.142 This will be in public. At least 14 days' notice of the hearing date must be given. Some tribunals will split the remedies hearing from the main hearing of the case but parties should be prepared to give evidence of loss, injury to feelings, etc on the day of the main hearing as most tribunals will expect to deal with both issues in the allocated time. It is useful to prepare a schedule of loss.

Burden of proof

32.143 The tribunal will decide the case on a balance of probabilities. The burden of proof is important for the order of proceedings. The party who has to prove any particular issue will usually start. The burden of proof in employment cases differs as between the SDA 1975, on the one hand, and the RRA 1976 and DDA 1995, on the other (see paras 3.54 and 3.85).

32.144 Where an employee has one year's service, she can claim ordinary unfair dismissal. First he or she must prove she has been dismissed. This is normally in dispute only in constructive dismissal cases, in which the employer may claim that the employee voluntarily resigned. The employee will then start, as he or she will need to prove that she has been dismissed.

32.145 Once it has been established that there has been a dismissal, the tribunal must find if the reason for dismissal was a potentially 'fair' reason such as misconduct or redundancy (see chapter 15).[141] If the employer cannot show a fair reason for the dismissal the dismissal will be unfair (see para 15.103). If the dismissal was for a potentially fair reason, the ET must then decide if the dismissal was fair and reasonable in the circumstances.

140 The tribunal has power to adjourn and to order costs when a party has sought an adjournment – ET Rules rule 14(4).

141 ERA 1996 s98(1) and (2).

32.146 Where an employee has less than one year's service, he or she must establish that the reason for the dismissal is an automatically unfair one if he or she is to be able to challenge it at all. The principles are similar to those for establishing discrimination. If it is established that the dismissal was for an automatically unfair reason the employer has no defence to an unfair dismissal claim.[142]

32.147 In discrimination cases the burden is on the claimant so that she will usually go first although in sex discrimination cases the burden may be reversed where the claimant's case strong, in which case the tribunal may ask the respondent to go first. Where the claim is for both an unfair dismissal and discrimination the claimant will usually open but there are no clear rules and the tribunal will decide if the parties do not agree. The tribunal has a very wide discretion as to how the proceedings are conducted. There is a duty on tribunals to 'make such inquiries of persons appearing before it and witnesses as it considers appropriate'.[142a]

Evidence

32.148 The main evidence is often given through the witnesses reading out their statements. Hearsay evidence is often allowed in tribunals, though is not as valuable as first hand evidence. In discrimination cases, events which took place both before and after the discrimination may be used in evidence 'if logically probative of a relevant fact'.[143]

32.149 If a witness cannot come to the tribunal but submits a written statement the tribunal will decide how much importance to give to the statement, taking into account the fact that the witness cannot be cross-examined. Such statements are less valuable than live evidence.

32.150 The detail of the hearing is beyond the scope of this book. Usually, however, the order is as follows:

a) The party who opens may make a brief opening statement though some tribunals will not want to hear an opening but just to have the issues clarified. After this, the first witness will be called, asked to read his or her statement and questioned;
b) Each witness will be questioned (cross-examined) by the other side and the tribunal will ask questions if it wants;

142 Even if an employee fails to establish an automatically unfair dismissal, he or she may, if he or she has a year's qualifying service, succeed in an ordinary unfair dismissal claim.

142a ET Rules rule 11(1).

143 *Chattopadhyay v Headmaster of Holloway School* [1981] IRLR 487, EAT.

c) There may then be re-examination, which consists of further questions which have arise out of the cross-examination;
d) The same procedure will take place in relation to each witness;
e) When all the opening party's witnesses have given evidence, the same process applies to the other side;
f) Finally, both parties have a right to make a closing speech. Normally, the party who started, addresses the tribunal last, but the tribunal will decide this.

If either party intends to refer to cases, these should be copied for the other side and tribunal or, at the least, they should be given the names and references.

Allegations of discrimination against the tribunal

32.151 In *Bennett v London Borough of Southwark* the claimant's lay representative, having been refused an adjournment, said to the Tribunal 'If I was a white barrister I would not be treated in this way', and 'If I were an Oxford-educated white barrister with a plummy voice I would not be put in this position'.[144] The Tribunal felt it could not continue with the hearing. A different Tribunal then struck out the claim because of the scandalous conduct of the proceedings.

32.152 The CA held that the first Tribunal should not have withdrawn, but should have had a short adjournment or ignored the allegation. The Tribunal should at least have pointed out the possible consequences of the representative's statement and invited him to withdraw it. Even if it was not withdrawn, the CA stated that a tribunal should be very cautious about adopting a course which involves the waste of significant costs and time. The CA held that the first Tribunal was wrong to withdraw and the second Tribunal wrong to strike out the claim for scandalous conduct of proceedings. The case was remitted to a fresh Tribunal. Sedley LJ stated, for the Court, that: 'If a situation were ever to arise in which it could responsibly and relevantly be said that a tribunal or court was treating black and white advocates differently, there would be no impropriety in a measured submission to that effect.'[145] In this case, however, there was no basis for such a claim and the representative's behaviour was criticised.[146]

144 [2002] IRLR 407.

145 See *Laher v London Borough of Hammersmith & Fulham*, EAT 215/91 (unreported), in which a chairman was held to have displayed bias by asking an applicant of Asian origin but British nationality if he spoke English and where he came from.

32.153 It is advisable for an employee bringing a claim to watch another tribunal case to get an idea of what it is like.

Restricted reporting orders

32.154 The ET Rules enable a party to apply for restricted reporting of his or her case in two circumstances:

- Where there are allegations of sexual misconduct;
- Where, under the DDA, evidence of a personal nature is likely to be heard by the tribunal.[147]

A restricted reporting order (RRO) is one that prohibits the publication in Great Britain of identifying matter in a written publication available to the public or its inclusion in a relevant programme for reception in Great Britain.[148]

32.155 Sexual misconduct is defined as 'the commission of a sexual offence, sexual harassment or other adverse conduct (of whatever nature) related to sex, and conduct is related to sex whether the relationship with sex lies in the character of the conduct or in its having reference to the sex or sexual orientation of the person at whom the conduct is directed.'[149]

32.156 Under the DDA, 'evidence of a personal nature' means any evidence of a medical, or other intimate, nature which might reasonably be assumed to be likely to cause significant embarrassment to the complainant if reported.[150] Only the complainant and not the respondent, can apply for an order, but the tribunal can also make an order of its own motion.

32.157 The application for an RRO can be made by a party, or the tribunal of its own volition, at any time before the decision is made. The parties must be given an opportunity to present their oral arguments at a hearing. Where there is an RRO the following applies:

- The tribunal must specify the parties who may not be identified;
- The order remains in force until the decision is promulgated, unless it is revoked before then; and

146 In *Tchoula v Netto Foodstores Ltd* (EAT 1378/96), the EAT set out general guidance for tribunals when dealing with discrimination claims.

147 ET Rules rule 16(1) and (2).

148 Employment Tribunals Act 1996 s11(6).

149 Ibid.

150 ETA 1996 s12(6).

- A notice must be displayed on the notice board of the tribunal and on the door of the tribunal room stating which proceedings cannot be reported.[151]

The fact that the parties agree an RRO is not sufficient. The tribunal must be satisfied that it is in the public interest that the press should be deprived of the right to communicate information.[152]

32.158 In *Chief Constable of the West Yorkshire Police v A*[153] a woman who had undergone gender reassignment was turned down for a police post on grounds that she was still legally male and so could not conduct searches of female suspects. The ET made a RRO on the basis that the case involved 'sexual misconduct'. The EAT disagreed, pointing out that: 'If all that was required for 'sexual misconduct' was that it was conduct which was 'adverse' by way of having reference to the sex or sexual orientation of the person to whom it was directed, every case of sex discrimination would be a case of 'sexual misconduct'. The term 'sexual misconduct', according to the EAT, required conduct to which some 'moral obloquy' was attached.

Equal Treatment Directive remedy

32.159 The EAT went on to rule, in *Chief Constable of the West Yorkshire Police v A*, that it had a jurisdiction, derived from the Equal Treatment Directive, to make an RRO in respect of an appeal against a tribunal's decision.[154] Without a RRO, said the EAT, the claimant would have been deterred from seeking a remedy and the EC principle of effectiveness required that the claimant should not be subject to procedural rules which rendered virtually impossible or excessively difficult the exercise of rights under EC law. Thus an RRO was ordered protecting the claimant, in perpetual terms, from identification as the individual concerned in the appeal against the tribunal decision. There is no reason why the same principles should not apply in ETs in cases in which they cannot rely on the RRO powers granted by the ET Rules. At present, of course, these EC principles apply only in sex discrimination cases.[155]

151 ET Rules rule 16(5)(c).

152 *X v Z Ltd* [1998] ICR 43 at 45–46.

153 [2000] IRLR 465.

154 Note that the respondent was an emanation of the State so bound by the Directive, unlike a private employer.

155 The ET rules, in the alternative, that they could rely on the ETD and there was no appeal against this part of the decision.

RRO only applies to person making allegation or person affected by it

32.160 In *Associated Newspapers Ltd v London (North) IT*[156] the High Court held that the power to make a restricted reporting order only exists in respect of a person making the allegation of sexual misconduct or a person 'affected by' such an allegation, including a witness. It did not apply to a local authority or the Chief Executive of the authority, neither of whom were witnesses who gave any direct evidence about the alleged sexual misconduct. The Court ruled that an RRO should be of no wider scope than is necessary to achieve the purposes of the legislation – to enable complaints of sexual harassment to be brought and witnesses to give evidence about incidents without being deterred by fear of intimate sexual details about them being publicised.

32.161 The restriction on reporting only lasts until the ET's decision has been promulgated. There are conflicting decisions as to whether relates to the liability hearing or any remedies hearing.[157]

32.162 The EAT does not have statutory power to make a restricted reporting order in an appeal against a decision on a question of liability.[158] The only proceedings in which the EAT has statutory power to make an RRO are appeals from the tribunal's grant or refusal of an order. Although the EAT has inherent power to make interlocutory orders, including a RRO, this is unlikely to be used apart from in exceptional cases.[159]

32.163 Where there has been a sexual offence, the tribunal must omit or delete from the Register, or any decision, document or record of the proceedings, which is available to the public, any identifying matter which is likely to lead members of the public to identify any person affected by or making such an allegation.[160] Breach of these provisions is an offence.[161]

156 [1998] IRLR 569.

157 In *Chessington World of Adventures v Reed ex p News Group Newspapers* [1998] IRLR 56, the EAT held that the RRO lasts until the end of the liability hearing only, while in *Chief Constable of West Yorkshire v A* the EAT held that it continued until the remedies decision had been made.

158 *Chessington*, ibid. This was cited in the subsequent case of *A*, the more recent authority. However, the press were represented in the *Reed* case, which may have made a difference.

159 Again, see *Chessington*, ibid.

160 ET Rules rule 15(6).

161 ETA 1996 ss11(2) and 12(3).

Tribunal costs

32.164 Costs can awarded by the ETs where there has been:

- Unreasonable conduct,
- Failure to agree or reply to a request for reinstatement,
- A request for an adjourment,
- A pre-hearing review which ordered a deposit.

Unreasonable conduct

32.165 The power is to award costs where a party has 'in bringing the proceedings, or a party or a party's representative has in conducting the proceedings, acted vexatiously, abusively, disruptively or otherwise unreasonably or the bringing or conducting of the proceedings by a party has been misconceived'.[162] This is substantially wider than the old rules as costs can now be awarded where a claim is misconceived.[163] 'Misconceived' cases include those which have no reasonable prospect of success,[164] and tribunals have a duty to consider making a costs order. It is likely that tribunals will make more costs orders – for example, in cases in which parties withdraw claims or defences near to the date of the hearing, fail to comply with directions or do not appear at the hearing. The CA recently held that, where the applicant had brought a sex and race discrimination claim against the respondent purely as part of a determined vendetta, the fact that the tribunal had not investigated whether she had the means to pay her employers' costs before making a costs order was 'not relevant'.[165] In response to the harsh impact of the judgment in *Kovacs* the Employment Act 2002 contains powers to enable tribunals to take a party's means into account in assessing costs. At the time of writing these powers had not bee exercised nor regulations drafted to that effect.

162 ET Rules rule 14(1).

163 See *Marler Ltd v Robertson* [1974] ICR 72, National Industrial Relations Court; *Stein v Associated Dairies Ltd* [1982] IRLR 447, EAT.

164 Employment Tribunals (Constitution and Rules of Procedure) Regulations 2001 reg 2(2), (note 2 above).

165 *Kovacs v Queen Mary & Westfield College & Royal Hospitals NHS Trust* [2002] IRLR 414, CA.

Failure to agree reinstatement or re-engagement

32.166 Costs must be awarded if a claimant has said that he or she wants reinstatement or re-engagement, and has told the respondent at least seven days before the hearing, but the proceedings have to be postponed because the respondent has failed to provide reasonable evidence as to the availability of the job from which the claimant was dismissed.[166]

Postponement

32.167 Costs may be awarded where there is an application for an adjournment even in the absence of unreasonable behaviour.[167] Costs are either limited to £10,000 or must be taxed. The previous limit was £500.

The tribunal decision

32.168 The tribunal's decision can be a majority one. It may be given at the end of a hearing or at a later date. Written reasons must be given in extended form in discrimination cases; in other cases the decision may be given in summary form. The decision will then be registered and is open to inspection.

Review of decisions

32.169 A tribunal has power to review its decision on specified grounds.[168]

Enforcement

32.170 Enforcement of compensation orders is in the county court.[169]

166 ET Rules rule 14(5).
167 ET Rules rule 14(4).
168 Employment Tribunal Regulations 1993, Sch 1 reg 11
169 A tribunal may be able to hear a claim for breach of the agreement under its contractual jurisdiction but only where the claim arises or is outstanding on the termination of the employment; see *Rock-It Cargo Ltd v Green* [1997] IRLR 581, EAT. Agreements made some time after termination must be enforced in the county court.

Appealing a tribunal decision

32.171 An unsuccessful claimant may appeal to the EAT on a point of law. The appeal must be made within 42 days from the date on which extended written reasons were sent to the appellant, rather than the date of deemed service.[170] Extended reasons are always given in sex discrimination cases but in unfair dismissal cases most tribunals issue only summary reasons and a claimant who wants extended reasons must request them either at the hearing or afterwards by writing to the tribunal within 21 days of the date the summary reasons decision is sent to the parties.

32.172 The EAT will decide, usually at a preliminary hearing, whether the appeal has any prospects of success. If not, it will not be allowed to proceed. An appeal to the EAT can be made at the same time as an application for review.[171] The detail of reviews and appeals is outside the scope of this book. The EAT's decisions are binding on ETs and county courts. Further appeals are available, with permission, to the CA and HL. A tribunal or court can refer a question about the interpretation of European law to the ECJ (see para 10.17).

County court claims

32.173 Claims under Parts III of the SDA 1975, the RRA 1976 and the DDA 1995 must generally be brought in the county court, whether they concern employment-related discrimination (ie, discrimination against barristers or in connection with vocational training), or other forms of discrimination covered by the Acts (see further chapter 29).[172] Only those county courts which have been designated by the Lord Chancellor to hear race discrimination claims may do so. In addition, the High Court has power to make a declaration in proceedings in which it is alleged that there has been unlawful discrimination.[173]

32.174 The DDA's education provisions are a little different – as of 1 September 2002, the school education provisions are dealt with in the

170 ET Rules rule 3. See *Hammersmith and Fulham LBC v Ladejobi* [1999] ICR 673, EAT.

171 ET Rules rule 11.

172 Claims under other Parts of the Acts (Parts V of the SDA 1975 and RRA 1976 and Part VI of the DDA 1995 – which deals with further and higher education) are also brought in the county court.

173 Ealing London Borough Council v Race Relations Board [1972] AC 342, HL.

Special Educational Needs and Disability Tribunal (SENDIST) in England and Wales. The transport provisions in DDA 1995 Part V do not confer individually enforceable rights but impose criminal liability which is prosecuted in the magistrates court.

32.175 Claims must generally be brought before the end of the period of six months beginning when the act complained of was done.[174] If the claim is one of discrimination under the RRA 1976 or the SDA 1975 by an educational establishment, or discrimination by a local education authority in respect of its functions under the Education Acts, the claimant must give notice of the claim to the Secretary of State before starting proceedings in the county court. Proceedings under the SDA 1975 may not be commenced until *either* the Secretary of State has given notice to the claimant that no further time is required to consider the matter, *or* the period of two months has elapsed since the date of the notice.[175] The RR(A)A amended the RRA 1976 to remove the requirement that claimants delay proceedings after giving notice to the Secretary of State. The time limit for proceedings under the RRA 1976 is set at six months in education cases, while in those SDA 1975 cases in which notice to the Secretary of State is required the time limit for bringing proceedings is extended by two months.[176] Where an application for assistance is made to the CRE the six-month time limit is extended by two months (this being the period within which the CRE must reach a decision), unless the CRE extend the time for reaching its decision by a month in which case the time limit for commencing proceedings is nine months.[177]

32.176 The Disability Rights Commission (DRC) has set up a free conciliation service under its powers under the Disability Rights Commission Act 1999. If a dispute is referred to the DRC conciliation service before the end of the six-month limitation period, the period within which civil proceedings must be commenced is extended by a further two months.[178]

Overlap with employment tribunal provisions

32.177 The provisions discussed at para 32.85 above in connection with continuing discrimination, omissions and the extension of time limits

174 SDA 1975 ss57 and 76(2)(a), RRA 1976 s68 and DDA 1995 Sch 3, para 6.
175 SDA 1975 s57(5) and RRA 1976 s66(5).
176 SDA 1975 s76(2)(b) and RRA 1976 s68(2)(b).
177 RRA 1976 ss66(3), (4) and 68(3).
178 DDA 1995 Sch 3 para 6(2) as amended.

apply in claims under Parts III of the SDA, RRA 1976 and DDA 1995 as well as in employment-related Part II cases. In applying time limits the guidance in respect are continuing discrimination and admissions in paragraph 6.3 and 6.4 applies in non-discrimination cases. Many other aspects of the procedure applicable in the county court are the same as those discussed above in connection with ETs (see, for example, the discussion of questionnaires at para 32.23 and the taking of contemporaneous notes). The CPRs incorporate the same overriding objective – that courts deal with cases justly – which is now also found in the ET Rules (see para 32.5).

Assessors

32.178 In race and sex discrimination claims in the county (in Scotland, the Sheriff) court, the judge may be assisted by two assessors appointed from a list of persons maintained by the Secretary of State who have special knowledge and experience of problems connected with the type of claim in question.[179]

32.179 The CPRs provide that assessors shall assist the court in dealing with the case, and shall take such part in the proceedings as the court may direct. In particular, the court may direct the assessor to prepare a report for it on any matter at issue in the proceedings, and may direct the assessor to attend the whole or any part of the trial to advise the court on any such matter. If the assessor prepares a report for the court before the trial has begun the court will send a copy to each of the parties who may use it at trial. The remuneration to be paid to the assessor for his or her services shall be determined by the court and shall form part of the costs of the proceedings. The court may order any party to deposit a specified sum in respect of the assessor's fees in the court office and, where it does so, the assessor will not be asked to act until the sum has been deposited.[180]

32.180 At least 21 days before appointing an assessor, the court must notify each party in writing of the name of the proposed assessor, of the matter in respect of which the assistance of the assessor will be sought, and of assessor's qualifications to give that assistance. Any party may take objection to a person who has been proposed for appointment as an assessor, such objection to be filed in writing with the Court within seven days of the receipt of the notification of the

179 SDA 1975 s66(6) and RRA 1976 s67(4).
180 CPR rule 35.15.

appointment of the assessor. Objections will be taken into account by the court in deciding whether or not to make the appointment.

32.181 Copies of any report prepared by the assessor must be sent to each of the parties, but assessors neither give oral evidence nor are they open to cross-examination or questioning.[181]

Steps before action

32.182 The CPRs contain certain pre-action protocols which outline steps that the parties should take to seek information and to provide information to each other about a prospective legal claim. The pre-action protocol for personal injury claims will apply in discrimination claims which include a claim for damages for psychiatric or other personal injury. In cases not covered by any approved protocol the court will expect the parties to act reasonably in exchanging information and documents relevant to the claim and in generally trying to avoid starting legal proceedings. In all cases, therefore, a potential claimant should send a letter to the other side setting out the broad nature of the contemplated claim before starting proceedings. Any document which substantiates the claim might be provided at this stage with the aim of encouraging the other party to enter into discussions on settlement. Consideration should also be given to alternative forms of dispute resolution such as arbitration or mediation.

32.183 The full details of the personal injury protocol are outside the scope of this book. It is particularly directed to road traffic, tripping and slipping and accident at work cases which include an element of personal injury of a value less than £15,000, but those pursuing other personal injury claims are expected to follow the spirit of the protocol which includes a letter of claim setting out a clear summary of the facts on which the claim is based, together with an indication of the nature of any injuries suffered and any financial loss incurred. The defendant is expected to reply within 21 days. Where insurers are involved that should be identified. If the defendant denies liability he should enclose, with the letter of reply, any documents in his possession which are material to the issues between the parties and which would be likely to be ordered to be disclosed by the court by way of an application for pre-action disclosure or disclosure during proceedings. The claimant should send to the defendant as soon as is practicable a Schedule of Special Damages (that is, an itemised claim for

181 Practice Direction 35, para 6.

monetary loss) with supporting documents, particularly where the defendant has admitted liability.

32.184 When a claim is made under the SDA 1975, RRA 1976 or DDA 1995 the claimant must give notice to the relevant commission and file a copy of the notice with the court.

Launching a county court claim

The claim form

32.185 To start a claim a claimant must complete a claim form and request that the court issues it. The claim form must be headed with the title of the proceedings which should state the claim number, the relevant court, and the full name and status (ie, claimant or defendant) of each party. The nature of the claim must be stated precisely and the remedy sought must be specified. If money is claimed, the form must state that the claimant expects to recover:

- Not more than £5,000; or
- More than £5,000 but not more than £15,000; or
- More than £15,000.

Alternatively, the claimant may state that he or she cannot say how much he or she expects to recover.

32.186 If damages for personal injury are sought the claim form must state whether the claimant expects to recover more than, or not more than, £1 000 general damages for pain, suffering and loss of amenity (CPR rule 16.2 and 3).

The Particulars of Claim

32.187 The Particulars of Claim, which set out the details of the claim, may either be contained in the claim form or be served on the defendant within 14 days of the service of the claim form. The claim form must be served on the defendant within four months of its date of issue, unless it is served out of the jurisdiction in which case the time limit is six months. An application may be made to the court to extend the time for service. When Particulars of Claim are served on a defendant they must be accompanied by a form for defending the claim, a form for admitting the claim, and a form for acknowledging service. A claimant must use Practice Form N1 or Practice Form N208. The claim form and, if they are not included in the claim form, the Particulars of Claim, must be verified by a statement of truth. The form of the statement of truth is as follows: 'I believe [or 'The Claimant believes'] that the facts stated in this claim form [or 'these Particulars of Claim] are true.'

32.188 The Particulars of Claim must include a concise statement of the facts on which the claimant relies (CPR, rule 16.4(1)(a)). They must state any claim for aggravated, exemplary or provisional damages, with the grounds for that claim (CPR, rule 16.4(1)(c) and (d)). If the claimant seeks interest, the Particulars of Claim must state whether he or she does so under a contract, under an Act (and if so which), or on some other basis (and, if so what). If the interest is being claimed under the RRA 1976, SDA 1975 or DDA 1995 the Particulars of Claim should so state. In a claim for a specified sum of money the Particulars must also state the percentage rate, the date from which interest is claimed, the date (no later than the date of issue) to which it is claimed, the amount so calculated and the daily rate claimed thereafter (CPR, rule 16.4(2)(b)).

32.189 In personal injury claims the Particulars of Claim must contain the claimant's date of birth and brief details of his injuries. A Schedule of Special Damages (if claimed) must be attached. A medical report must also be attached if medical evidence is relied upon and, if provisional damages are claimed, the relevant details must be given (Practice Direction 16, para 4). In a Disability Discrimination Act 1995 case it may advisable to lodge a medical report addressing the issue of the disability where this is likely to be in dispute.

32.190 Particulars of Claim may, but do not have to, refer to the points of law relied upon, give names of witnesses, and attach supporting documents (including any experts' reports).[183] Court fees are payable on a sliding scale according to the value of the claim.

The defendant's response

32.191 Once the claim has been served the defendant must respond to the claim by an Acknowledgment of Service if he or she is unable to file a Defence in time, or wishes to dispute the court's jurisdiction. Otherwise the defendant must file a Defence within 14 days after service of the Particulars of Claim, unless the claim form is served outside England and Wales when special rules apply. If a defendant does not respond in one of these matters judgment in default of defence may be requested or applied for.

32.192 A defence must state which allegations in the Particulars of Claim are:

183 Practice Direction 16, para.16.3.

- Admitted;
- Denied; and/or
- Neither admitted, nor denied, but are required to be proved (CPR, rule 16.5(1)).

32.193 Reasons for denial of an allegation must be given together with the defendant's version of events, if this differs from the version given in the Particulars of Claim (CPR, rule 16.5(2)). Allegations not specifically dealt with in the Defence are deemed to be admitted unless:

- The Defence sets out the nature of the defendant's case in relation to that issue; or
- The allegation relates to an amount of money and the amount is not expressly admitted.

32.194 Where the claim is for personal injury the claimant must attach a medical report in respect of his alleged injuries. The defendant in the Defence should state whether he or she agrees, disputes, or neither agrees nor disputes but has no knowledge of the matters contained in the medical report. Where he or she disputes any part of the medical report, the defendant must provide reasons for so doing. Where the defendant has obtained a medical report on which he or she intends to rely the report must be attached to his or her Defence (Practice Direction 16, para 14(1)).

Management tracks

32.195 Once a case is defended the court will send the parties an 'allocation questionnaire' which must be replied to and which gives information to enable the court to decide to which track to allocate the case. Cases are allocated to one of three 'management tracks' depending on their nature, value and complexity. The three tracks are:

- The small claims track;
- The fast track; and
- The multi-track.

32.196 The small claims track is the normal track for most claims with a financial value not exceeding £5,000. The fast track is the normal track for most claims between £5,000 and £15,000, and the multi-track is the normal track for any claim for which the others are not normal – ie, generally for claims in excess of £15,000. The value of the claims is not the only factor which is taken into account in allocating claims however. The fast track, for example, is the only normal track for a claim between £5,000 and £15,000 where the trial is likely to last for no more than one day. It may well be therefore that a discrimination claim with a small financial value would be a multi-track case because of its complexity and the length of the trial.

32.197 Many discrimination cases will be allocated to the multi-track procedure because of the length of time of the trial and the complexity of the issues involved. Once the case has been allocated, case management directions may be given without a hearing to create a timetable for the steps to be taken before trial. Instead or as well as giving directions, the court may fix a case management conference or a pre-trial review. Directions deal with disclosure of documents and service of witness statements and expert evidence, and may regulate the amendment of statements of case and the provision of further information. Normal directions would include the filing or service of any further information needed to clarify a party's case, standard disclosure, simultaneous exchange of witness statements, the instruction of a single joint expert (if an expert such as a medical expert is required) or simultaneous exchange of experts' reports. In a case involving more than one expert the court will usually order discussion between experts and a statement on the matters they have, and those they have not, agreed.

32.198 The court will fix a case management conference if it appears that it cannot properly give directions on its own initiative and no agreed directions have been filed which it can approve. At a case management conference the parties must ensure that all relevant documents (including witness statements and experts' reports) are available to the judge and that all the parties know what directions each seeks. It may be useful therefore to revert to the para 32.183 protocol in order to encourage the defendant to set out its case fully at an early stage, and to provide relevant documents.

Disclosure of documents

32.199 The standard disclosure rules require a party to disclose documents on which it relies to prove its case. If a party fails to disclose such documents it will be unable to rely upon them in court without the court's permission. Parties are required to disclose not only those documents which support their case, but those which adversely affect their own case and those which support the other party's case. If a court just orders disclosure without identifying any particular documents to be disclosed, the standard disclosure rules apply (see para 32.183 above).

32.200 A party is required to make a reasonable search for documents which it must disclose. Each party makes a list of documents identifying each document, and serves it on the other party. Each party must disclose documents which are or have been in the party's control. The list should include such documents with a statement as to what has happened to them. The list of documents must include a disclosure statement setting out the extent of the search made and certifying that the party understands the duty to disclose and that, to the best of his or her knowledge, he or she has complied with it. There is a prescribed form for this purpose (N265).

32.201 The principles in respect of the criteria for discovery, confidentiality, public interest immunity and legal professional privilege are set out above at para 32.119. They apply in the present context as well as in the ETs.

Bundles

32.202 Before the trial the claimant normally has the responsibility for preparing a bundle of documents, a chronology, and (possibly) a brief case summary setting out the issues of fact which are agreed or in dispute, and the evidence needed to decide them. The case summary should not exceed 500 words in length. If the claimant is unrepresented and the defendant is represented the court may order the defendant to undertake this work at the case management conference (see further para 32.198).

Witnesses

32.203 Both parties may call witnesses in the county court as they may in the ET. In addition, a party may apply to the court for a witness summons. A witness summons should be applied for more than seven days before the date of trial. The court will serve the summons on the witness unless the party wishes to do so, in which case the court should be so notified. The party issuing the summons must deposit with the court a sum sufficient to pay for the witnesses' expenses in travelling to the court and returning to his or her home or place of work, and a sum in respect of the period during which earnings or benefits will lost, or such lesser sum as it may be proved a witness will lose as a result of his attendance at court due to the witness summons. The witness summons is in form N20.[184]

184 CPR Rule 34 and Practice Direction 34.

The trial

32.204 The trial will normally take place at a civil trial centre. The trial dates will normally be fixed a long way in advance for a multi-track case, though if the case is allocated to the fast track it may be arranged at short notice. The judge will generally have read the papers in the trial bundle in advance, and may not wish to hear an opening address from the parties.[185] The general rule is that, if a party has served a witness statement and wishes to rely at trial on the evidence of the witness, he or she must call the witness to give oral evidence unless the court orders otherwise or the party puts the statement in as hearsay evidence.[186]

32.205 Where a witness is called to give oral evidence his or her witness statement should stand as his evidence in chief unless the court orders otherwise. This means that the witness will not read his statement but, having identified it, will normally be cross-examined. A witness may only amplify his witness statement before cross-examination with the permission of the court and in relation to new matters which have arisen since the witness statement was served on the other party. If a witness statement has not been served within the time specified by the court the witness may not be called to give oral evidence unless the court gives permission.

32.206 The application of the burden of proof (para 32.142 above) and the order to be adopted at the trial (para 32.150 above) applies in the county court as in the ETs. If either party intends to refer to cases, the whole of the case concerned should be provided to the judge and to the other side. In a case of any complexity it is helpful to provide a written Skeleton Argument setting out in outline the factual issues and the points of law on which the party relies upon to support their case.

Costs and public funding

32.207 Public funding is available for proceedings in the county court. By contrast with the position in tribunal cases the unsuccessful party will normally have to pay the costs of proceedings in the county court. Costs may be assessed by the judge at the end of the hearing or, if the

185 Practice Direction 29, para.10.

186 CPR rule 32.5. The details of hearsay evidence are outside the scope of this book. Any party intending to allow hearsay evidence must when he serves a witness statement inform the other parties that the witness is not being called to give oral evidence and give the reason why the witness will not be called.

judge so orders, by a detailed assessment of a bill of costs. Detailed assessment of costs will not commence until the conclusion of the proceedings The detailed rules on costs are outside the scope of this work.

32.208 When the court orders (whether by summary assessment or detailed assessment) that the costs of a litigant in person are to be paid by any other person, those costs must not exceed (except in the case of disbursements) two thirds of the amount which would have been allowed if the litigant in person had been represented by a legal representative. Costs allowed to the litigant in person may consist of:

- Such costs as would have been allowed if the work had been done or disbursements made by a legal representative on the litigant in person's behalf;
- The payments reasonably made by the claimant for legal services relating to the conduct of proceedings; and
- The cost of obtaining expert assistance in connection with assessing the claim for costs.

The litigant in person is allowed to recover any reasonable disbursements in full. It is for the litigant to prove financial loss, which usually means loss of earnings. He or she must produce to the court written evidence to support the claim, and must serve a copy of that evidence on any party against whom costs are sought at least 24 hours before the hearing at which the question of loss may be decided (Practice Direction 48, paragraph 1.7). Special rules on costs apply in cases in which an offer to settle and a payment into court have been made. These are contained in rule 36 of the CPRs, and not covered in this work.

Appeals

32.209 Appeals from the county court may go, with the leave of the court, to the Court of Appeal. If the trial court refuses leave, an application for leave to appeal may be made directly to the CA. Appeal from the CA is to the HL.

CHAPTER 33

Remedies and enforcement

Key points

33.1
- This chapter deals with the remedies that may be awarded following a finding of unlawful discrimination, equal pay and enforcement action which might be taken by the Equal Opportunities Commission (EOC), Commission for Racial Equality (CRE) and Disability Rights Commission (DRC).
- Employment tribunals may declare that a claimant who succeeds in an equal pay claim is entitled to an equality clause requiring her employer to give no less favourable terms and conditions than her comparator and arrears of remuneration of up to six years.
- Employment tribunals (ETs) and the county courts have wide powers to order compensation following a finding of unlawful discrimination. Such compensation may cover:
  - injury to feelings;
  - personal injury, and
  - aggravated damages.
- In appropriate cases an ET and county court may award exemplary damages.
- An ET and county court may make an award of interest in respect of losses which are the subject of an award of compensation.
- In addition to awarding compensation ETs may make declarations and recommendations, and county courts may make declarations and grant injunctions.
- The EOC, CRE and DRC have power to assist individual complainants and to litigate in their own names.
- The EOC and the CRE have exclusive power to bring proceedings in respect of certain unlawful acts.
- The EOC, CRE and DRC may conduct formal investigations and issue enforceable non-discrimination notices.
- The CRE has power to enforce compliance with the new specific statutory duties introduced by the Race Relations (Amendment) Act (RRAA) 2000.

Remedies: background and statutory provisions

33.2 The remedies which may be awarded following a finding of unlawful discrimination under the Sex Discrimination Act (SDA) 1975, the

Race Relations Act (RRA) 1976 and the Disability Discrimination Act (DDA) 1995 are provided for by the Acts themselves.

33.3 By SDA 1975 s65 and RRA 1976 s56, where an ET finds a complaint of discrimination made out it:

> shall make such of the following as it considers just and equitable –
> (a) An order declaring the rights of the complainant and the respondent in relation to the Act to which the complaint relates;
> (b) An order requiring the respondent to pay to the complainant compensation of an amount corresponding to any damages he could have been ordered by a county court or by a sheriff court to pay to the complainant if the complaint had fallen to be dealt with under [the provisions relating to claims brought in the county court[1]];
> (c) A recommendation that the respondent take within a specified period action appearing to the Tribunal to be practicable for the purpose of obviating or reducing the adverse effect on the complainant of any acts of discrimination to which the complaint relates.

DDA 1995 s8(2) is in materially the same terms, although the power to make recommendations appears on its face to be somewhat wider.[2]

33.4 Where a county court (in Scotland a sheriff court) finds that a complaint of unlawful discrimination is well-founded it may make any award by way of remedy that the High Court or the Court of Session (in Scotland) could make in proceedings in tort or (in Scotland) for breach of statutory duty (SDA 1975 s66(2), RRA 1976 s57(2) and DDA 1995 s25(5)).

33.5 Remedies for breach of an equality clause inserted by the Equal Pay Act (EqPA) 1970 are dealt with below.

Equal pay

Equality clause

33.6 If an equal pay claim is successful the employment tribunal will declare that the claimant is entitled to an equality clause. An equality clause has the effect of amending her contract so that she is entitled to not less favourable terms and conditions than those of her comparator. If she has terms in her contract which are of a similar kind to

1 SDA 1975 s66, RRA 1976 s57 and DDA 1995 s8(3).
2 See below.

his (eg, sick pay) but are less favourable, her contract is treated as modified so that the term is not less favourable. If he has a term in his contract, (eg, for the use of a company car), which she does not have, then her contract is modified to provide for such a clause. It is of course for the claimant in making her claim to identify such clauses and make plain what it is she is claiming.

Remuneration

33.7 The tribunal may also award arrears of remuneration. EqPA 1970 s2(5) limits such awards for a period not earlier than two years prior to the date on which the claim was received by the tribunal. However, in *Levez v T H Jennings (Harlow Pools)*,[2a] the ECJ ruled that the two year backstop in EqPA 1970 on equal pay awards could not be relied upon if the delay in bringing the claim was attributable to the fact that the employer deliberately misrepresented to the employee the level of remuneration received by the male comparators. When this case was remitted to the UK, the EAT ruled that the prohibition on the two-year limit was of general application.[3] The EAT there held that the six year limit in the Limitation Act 1980 applied to all claims under the EqPA 1970.

33.8 In *Evesham v North Hertfordshire Health Authority*,[3a] the Court of Appeal held that a speech therapist was only entitled to be placed on the same point on the incremental scale as her comparator although she had five years' experience and had received three annual increments while her comparator was in his first year of service and had no annual increments. The Court said that in deciding that her work was of equal value to that of her comparator, the independent expert had taken into account their respective experience and so she was not entitled to be placed higher up the scale than he was. If her claim had been based on a job evaluation study which did not take experience into account in evaluating jobs then the result might have been different.

Pensions

33.9 For remedies on pension claims, see paras 27.55 and 27.75 to 27.86.

2a (Case 326/96) [1998] ECR I-7835; [1999] IRLR 36.
3 [1999] IRLR 764.
3a [2000] IRLR 257.

Compensation

Introduction

33.10 By far the most important remedy in practice in a discrimination case is compensation (or 'damages' as such an award is commonly known in civil proceedings).

33.11 ETs and county courts have powers to award compensation corresponding to any award which could have been ordered by a county court (in Scotland, a sheriff court) in any claim in tort.[4] Awards of compensation are unlimited in both the county courts and the ETs,[4a] and average awards are growing.[5] The average award in race and disability cases in 2000 was just over £13,000, that in sex discrimination cases £9,500 – an increase from 1999 of 39 per cent in race cases and 31 per cent in sex and disability cases.[6] While average awards are fairly low, some can be very high. In *Bower v Schroder Securities Ltd*,[7] for example, an ET awarded a female city equities analyst £1.4 million after a finding of sex discrimination.

The measure of compensation

33.12 The SDA 1975, RRA 1976 and DDA 1995 provide that an ET has power to make such order as it considers 'just and equitable'.[8] ETs do not have a general discretion as to the amount to award in compensation. Once an ET has decided that it is 'just and equitable' to make an order for compensation it must do so having regard to the normal principles applicable in respect of civil wrongs more generally.[9] Thus the conduct of a complainant is rarely relevant to the amount of compensation that might be ordered.[10]

4 Or (in Scotland) in reparation for breach of statutory duty, ie in any other civil wrong: SDA 1975 ss66(1), (2) and 65(1)(b); RRA 1976 ss57(1), (2) and 56(1)(b); DDA 1995 ss8(2)(b), (3), 25(1) and (5).

4a Sex Discrimination and Equal Pay (Remedies) Regulations 1993 SI No 2978 and the Race Relations (Remedies) Act 1994, which removed the caps on compensation in sex and race discrimination cases.

5 At least in the ETs where such analysis has been undertaken: EOR 100 (2001), p 12.

6 Ibid.

7 (2001) DCLD 48 and EOR 102 (2002).

8 SDA 1975 s65(1), RRA 1976 s56(1) and DDA 1995 s8(2).

9 *Hurley v Mustoe (No 2)* [1983] ICR 422.

10 See 'mitigation' at para 33.44 below for the circumstances in which the conduct of the complainant might be relevant.

33.13 The correct measure of damages in the ET and the county court is tortious (that which applies to other civil wrongs) rather than contractual.[11] A complainant is entitled to compensation in respect of all losses caused by the discriminatory act. This is important because, in respect of claims of discrimination arising out of contractual relationships (employment and tenancies), a complainant is entitled not merely to compensation reflecting the obligations under the contract but rather, so far as is possible, to be put in the same position she would have been in if the discriminatory act not been committed. So, for example, an employee whose contract of employment is terminable on notice will be entitled to claim compensation for all losses flowing from a discriminatory termination (based on how long she would otherwise have been employed by her employer) rather than for the notice period only.[12]

33.14 A complainant may claim compensation for any pecuniary loss attributable to the unlawful discrimination.[13] As stated above, the question in all cases is whether losses were caused by the discrimination: 'as best as money can do it, the [complainant] must be put into the position she would have been in but for the unlawful conduct of [the discriminator]'.[14] The court or tribunal will have regard to a number of general matters:

- Because compensation compensates a complainant for (net) losses only, a complainant must give credit for any savings made in consequence of an unlawful discriminatory act. Thus, if as a result of a discriminatory act a woman loses her job, she is entitled to claim her net loss of pay. In determining her net loss of pay she will have to discount from the total loss any sums saved by way of child care costs and any other costs saved by reason of unemployment. Otherwise she would be in a better position than she would have been had the discriminatory act not occurred.
- In determining the complainant's losses, the discriminator must take the victim as he or she finds her. This is sometimes referred to as the 'eggshell skull principle'. If a victim is particularly sensitive or particularly susceptible to hurt of one sort or another, then so long as the loss or hurt is caused by the discrimination the extent of it is immaterial – the discriminator will be liable for it

11 *Ministry of Defence v Cannock* [1994] IRLR 509, EAT. See also *Ministry of Defence v Wheeler* [1998] IRLR 23, CA.

12 As she would be entitled to claim in contract.

13 *Coleman v Skyrail Oceanic Ltd* [1981] IRLR 398, CA.

14 *Ministry of Defence v Cannock* [1994] IRLR 509 at 517 per Morrison J.

all.[15] This is particularly important in harassment cases where some complainants might be particularly vulnerable and less able to cope with the discrimination and might therefore react particularly severely.

- A complainant is obliged to take reasonable steps to keep losses flowing from a discriminatory act to a minimum – this is known as the 'duty to mitigate' and is dealt with at para 33.44 below.

Heads of damage

33.15 Compensation is usually awarded under the following heads:

- **past loss**, for example, loss of earnings and benefits, cost of moving house, school or obtaining alternative services up to the date of the hearing, less any earnings received or financial savings made;[16]
- **future losses** including loss of earnings and benefits, additional accommodation costs, etc;
- **injury to feelings**;
- **personal injury**;
- **aggravated damages**; and[17]
- **exemplary damages**.

Past loss

33.16 Compensation in respect of past financial losses (special damages) is usually fairly straightforward. A complainant should simply calculate the loss of wages and the expenses attributable to finding other work or accommodation as the case may be.[18] Loss is calculated by reference to the general principle that a complainant is entitled to be put in the same position, or as nearly as possible, as he would have been in, had he not suffered the unlawful act complained of. Therefore, as stated, loss of earnings is recoverable net of tax and national insurance.[19]

15 Subject to mitigation, see para 33.44 below.

16 Again subject to mitigation.

17 These last four 'heads' are commonly known as 'general damages'. Interest is awardable on special and general damages: see below.

18 Though if a claim is made for the increased costs of purchasing a more expensive home, credit must be given for the increased value of the capital acquired at the end of any mortgage term.

19 *British Transport Commission v Gourley* [1956] AC 185; *Cooper v Firth Brown Ltd* [1963] 1 WLR 418.

33.17 Difficulties may arise where there is some element of uncertainty about the losses, for example, about the sums that an employee might have earned. In such cases the court or tribunal must take account of that uncertainty. This is done not by the making of a finding of fact on the balance of probabilities (by asking whether it is more likely than not that the complainant would have got job x), but rather by the assessment of a 'chance' (by asking what the chances are that, had the complainant not been dismissed, she would have got job x). This assessment must be made having regard to the complainant's own circumstances. If a tribunal concludes that a complainant had a 75 per cent chance of being promoted to a particular post but for the discrimination found proved it will award compensation amounting to 75 per cent of the whole loss attributable to the failure to be promoted.[20] Where there are a number of uncertain related future events the assessment is cumulative. If, for example, a tribunal concludes that there was a 90 per cent chance of obtaining promotion 1 and then a 50 per cent chance of obtaining promotion 2 and the loss between the current post and the notional promotion 1 is £10,000, the complainant will be entitled to recover 90 per cent of that loss, ie, £9,000. If the loss between notional promotion 1 and notional promotion 2 is £10,000, the loss attributable to the discrimination is 50 per cent of the 90 per cent, ie, £4,500.[21]

Future loss

General

33.18 Future losses are frequently the most complex to determine, particularly where the unlawful act results in continuing losses over a long future period. Commonly (though not exclusively) this occurs where the unlawful discriminatory act has caused a personal injury that prevents a person working for a long period and perhaps the rest of a working life.

33.19 Where there is certainty about short-term future losses there will be no difficulty. As with past loss claims, they should simply be totalled up. There are, however, a number of particular problems associated with continuing future losses:

- The problem of 'accelerated receipt'. This refers to the fact that, by converting continuing future losses into an award of compensation, the complainant receives much sooner the sums of money

20 *Ministry of Defence v Cannock* [1994] IRLR 509, EAT.
21 *Ministry of Defence v Wheeler* [1998] IRLR 23, CA.

that she would otherwise have received later on (for example, a claim for compensation in respect of wage losses for ten years will result in a complainant receiving a lump sum now in respect of wages she would not otherwise have received for ten years). This means the complainant has the benefit of the investment value of a lump sum which she would not otherwise have had.

- The risk of mortality. We all run a risk of early death. By awarding compensation in respect of future losses the complainant avoids the risk that she would not have received those monies anyway because she might have died before the sums would have been earned.
- The problem of certainty. It is usually impossible to be certain about what would have happened in the future, particularly the long term future.

33.20 Account must be taken of these matters because otherwise the complainant might be put in a better position than if the discriminatory act had not occurred. The usual way to calculate compensation for long-term future losses is by adopting the multiplier/multiplicand approach to assessment. This takes account of the risks described above arising out of uncertainty and mortality rates. It is done as follows:

- A lump sum is calculated to represent the current value (that is at the date of calculation) of losses which will accrue in the future (earnings, expenses, etc). The annual net loss will represent the figure known as the 'multiplicand'.
- The multiplicand is calculated in much the same basis as past loss. It will, therefore, include the annual earnings lost in consequence of the unlawful act as well as any other losses which must be annualised for the purposes determining the multiplicand.
- A 'multiplier' is then applied to the multiplicand. The multiplier is determined by reference to the number of years in respect of which the losses can be expected to continue. However the multiplier is reduced from a figure representing the full number of years in respect of which the loss is expected to continue, to take into account contingencies including mortality. The appropriate multiplier, having regard to the extent of the injury, may be gleaned from the Ogden Tables.[22] The appropriate discount rate is

22 The Joint Working Party of Actuaries and Lawyers, chaired by Michael Ogden (HMSO, 1984) approved in *Wells v Wells* [1999] 1 AC 345 and reprinted in Kemp and Kemp, *The Quantum of Damages* Vol 1.

2.5 per cent.[23] The Ogden Tables make provision for mortality. However, further discount must be made to have regard to other contingencies. Guidance on the appropriate discount can be found in the Ogden Tables but will depend on the industry in which the complainant was employed (and security of employment); the risk of illness in the complainant's particular case in any event (which might be very material in a case of psychiatric injury); and other contingencies. The Ogden Tables give credit for accelerated receipt.

- Where the assessment of the future losses depends upon uncertainties (for example, the question whether a person would have been promoted and, if so, when), this must be built into the multiplicand (by reducing it to take account of chance) or the multiplier as above.[24]

In complex cases expert reports may be required on the assessment of future losses (for example, employment consultants on employment prospects, estate agents on property values or rents, forensic accountants etc).

Pensions

33.21 Where future pension losses are likely to be small – because an injury is temporary in nature and any break in pensionable employment is short term – a tribunal may make an award in respect of pension losses based on the loss of the employer's pension contribution.[25] In other cases, pension losses may be calculated *either*:

- by determining the cost to the complainant of purchasing the pensionable benefits – equivalent to the lost benefits – in the market place. This is determined by obtaining estimates from insurance companies; *or*
- by determining the present net value of the complainant's loss and applying an appropriate multiplier using the Ogden Tables. The resultant figure must be discounted to take account of other contingencies: *Auty v National Coal Board*.[26]

In the case of a reduced lump sum, the difference in value should be calculated at today's values and then a discount applied for acceler-

23 Damages Act 1996 s1, since June 2001.

24 There is little science about these matters! The object is to reach the fairest assessment of an unknown sum as is possible.

25 Ogden Tables, paras 6–121.

26 [1985] 1 WLR 784.

ated receipt (with a discount rate of 2.5 per cent). A further discount should be applied for other contingencies: *Auty*.

Disadvantage on the labour market

33.22 A complainant who does not suffer an immediate loss of earnings, or who suffers a reduced loss of earnings but is vulnerable in the future to a loss of earnings because of injury caused by the unlawful act, may claim compensation for 'disadvantage in the labour market'.[27] Essentially this compensates a complainant for loss of earning capacity. To support a claim under this head a complainant will need to show that his or her prospects for the future are affected by the illness or other disadvantage he or she suffered in consequence of the unlawful act. This is particularly important where the respondent responsible for the unlawful act continues to employ the complainant but where there is a risk that that employment will cease in the future. A complainant who might find him or herself in the labour market and more vulnerable than he or she otherwise would have been but for the unlawful act is entitled to be compensated for that. There is no science about the way in which a sum under this head will be calculated, but it is usual to assess it by reference to the annual loss a complainant might expect to suffer.[28]

Injury to feelings

33.23 A court or tribunal may make an award of compensation in respect of the 'injury to feelings' suffered by a complainant following a finding of unlawful discrimination.[29] Awards of compensation for injury to feelings are increasing. The average award in respect of injury to feelings made by ETs in the year 2000 was £7,216 in race discrimination; £3,737 in sex discrimination and £5,802 in disability cases – an increase in all race and disability cases from the year before.[30]

33.24 General guidance on awards of injury to feelings can be found in the case of *Armitage, Marsden and HM Prison Service v Johnson*:[31]

27 *Moeliker v A Reyrolle & Co Ltd* [1997] 1 WLR 132 and see *Smith v Manchester Corporation* [1974] 17 KIR 1 (or 'handicap in the labour market' as it is commonly described).

28 Illustrations of awards under this head might be found in Kemp and Kemp, Vol 2.

29 SDA 1975 s66(4), RRA 1976 s57(4) and DDA 1995 ss8(4) and 25(2).

30 EOR 100 (2001), p12. A small decrease was noted in sex discrimination cases.

31 [1997] IRLR 162.

(1) Awards for injuries to feelings are compensatory. They should be just to both parties. They should compensate fully without punishing the tortfeasor. Feelings of indignation at the tortfeasor's conduct should not be allowed to inflate the award.
(2) Awards should not be too low, as that would diminish respect for the policy of the anti-discrimination legislation. Society has condemned discrimination and awards must ensure that it is seen to be wrong. On the other hand, awards should be restrained, as excessive awards could ... be seen as the way to untaxed riches.
(3) Awards should bear some broad general similarity to the range of awards in personal injury cases. We do not think this should be done by reference to any particular type of personal injury award; rather to the whole range of such awards.
(4) In exercising their discretion in assessing a sum, Tribunals should remind themselves of the value in everyday life of the sum they have in mind. This may be done by reference to purchasing power or by reference to earnings.
(5) Finally, Tribunals should bear in mind Lord Bingham's reference [in *John v MGN*[32]] to the need for public respect for the level of awards made.

An award of compensation for injury to feelings does not automatically flow from a finding of unlawful discrimination. Injury to feelings, like other loss and damage, must be proved.[33]

33.25 In appropriate cases an award for injury to feelings may include a sum for loss of enjoyable or congenial employment: *Ministry of Defence v Cannock*.[34] There would seem to be no reason why an award of compensation for injury to feelings might not reflect the hurt caused by damage to reputation in appropriate cases: for example, *Yeboah v Hackney LBC and Crofton*.[35] There is some authority which indicates that, where it is appropriate to make an award of injury to feelings, it would not be proper to make an award of less than £750.[36] Illustrations of awards for injury to feelings can be found in the *EOR Discrimination Case Law Digest* and include the following:[36a]

- *Mustafa v Ancon Clark Ltd*:[37] award of £135,166.24 against an employer, including compensation of £21,500 for injury to feelings

32 [1996] 3 WLR 593.

33 *Coleman v Skyrail Oceanic Ltd* [1981] IRLR 398, CA.

34 [1994] IRLR 509, EAT.

35 ET 56617/94, 1998 (unreported).

36 *Doshoki v Draeger Ltd* [2002] IRLR 340 and *Sharifi v Strathclyde Regional Council* [1992] IRLR 259; *Deane v Ealing LBC* [1993] IRLR 209, in which £500 was held to be the bottom of the range.

36a See also *ICTS (UK) Ltd v Tchoula* [2000] IRLR 643.

37 ET 2800894/96, 1999 (unreported).

and general damages associated with psychiatric injury, and £1,795.89 against an individual.

- *Whitehead v Isle of Wight NHS Trust*:[38] award of £35,000 for injury to feelings against employer and £2,500 for injury to feelings against an individual for sexual harassment.
- *Bamieh v Crown Prosecution Service*:[39] award of £30,000 for injury to feelings including aggravated damages to an Asian barrister who was unlawfully discriminated against on grounds of race and victimised and whose employer 'wished to rub her face in the dirt'.
- *HM Prison v Salmon*:[40] award of £21,000 for injury to feelings to a female prison officer subjected to sexual harassment by her work colleagues.
- *Fasipe v London Fire and Civil Defence Authority*:[41] award of £25,000 for injury to feelings (including aggravated damages) in respect of a finding of race discrimination and victimisation.

In comparing awards regard should be had to the change in the value of money. Increases should be accounted for by reference to the impact of inflation. An inflation table can be found in Kemp and Kemp, *The Quantum of Damages* Vol 2. Where an award of compensation for injury to feelings is made in respect of discrimination it is appropriate to make a global award.[41a]

Compensation for personal injury

Introduction

33.26 It is plain, on a proper reading of the statutory provisions, that a court or tribunal might make an award of compensation in respect of personal injury under the SDA 1975, RRA 1976 and DDA 1995. The Court of Appeal confirmed in *Sheriff v Klyne Tugs (Lowestoft) Ltd*[42] that this was the case.

33.27 Advisers need to be particularly cautious about exploring with complainants whether they might have a personal injury because the Court of Appeal made it clear in *Sheriff* that, in accordance with the normal principles, a complainant has a duty to bring forward all his complaints in one tribunal. A complainant who suffers from a per-

38 (2000) DCLD 42.

39 (2000) DCLD 44.

40 (2001) DCLD 48, upheld by the EAT at [2001] IRLR 425.

41 (2001) DCLD 49.

41a *ICTS (UK) Ltd v Tchoula* [2000] IRLR 643.

42 [1999] IRLR 481.

sonal injury in consequence of unlawful discrimination must ensure that the personal injury claim is made the subject of any discrimination proceedings or he or she risk losing the right to litigate the issue. As stated above, the normal tortious principles apply to discrimination complaints. A complainant must show that his injury has been caused by the unlawful act of discrimination.

33.28 Most commonly, discrimination-related personal injury claims either arise out of assaults or comprise claims of psychiatric injury. In cases of injury caused by assault (bruising, abrasions and so on) issues of causation are unlikely to be problematic.[43] Where a complainant claims compensation for psychiatric injury in consequence of unlawful discrimination, causation is usually more complex. This is in part because psychiatrists are undecided or not in agreement about the specific causes of psychiatric illness. But in a claim for compensation a complainant need only demonstrate, upon reliable psychiatric evidence, that the unlawful discrimination caused or materially contributed to the psychiatric injury.[44] This is important because ordinarily a psychiatrist will suggest that there is more than one cause for the onset of psychiatric injury.

33.29 Where a claim for personal injury is made, medical evidence will be required. In the case of psychiatric injury a report from a consultant psychiatrist will be needed and, almost invariably,[45] the psychiatrist will be required to attend the court or tribunal to give evidence.

33.30 Financial losses flowing from a personal injury caused by unlawful discrimination may be claimed in the usual way. These may include, in addition to the usual claims, compensation for:

- cost of care;
- cost of DIY and other maintenance previously undertaken by the complainant;
- cost of medical care;
- costs attributable to receiving medical care (taxis, etc);
- cost of private medical care in appropriate cases.

Pain, suffering and loss of amenity

33.31 An award of compensation will usually may be made for the *pain, suffering and loss of amenity* consequent upon personal injury. Such

43 For an illustration of where a complainant was the subject of racially discriminatory assaults in the course of his employment, see *Jones v Tower Boot Co Ltd* [1997] IRLR 168.

44 See *Winfield and Jolowicz on Tort* (15th edn) pp199 onwards.

45 Save, perhaps, where the report is very full and is agreed.

awards can be substantial. Claims in respect of pain, suffering and loss of amenity, like other compensation claims, must be proved.

33.32 Guidance on the appropriate level of awards for pain, suffering and loss of amenity can be found in the Judicial Studies Board's *Guidelines for the Assessment of General Damages in Personal Injury Cases*. These indicate the range of awards appropriate to cases in which particular damage has been suffered and indicate the factors which will be taken into account in determining the size of an award in a particular case. Commentaries on personal injury cases to which a complainant's case might be compared can be found in Kemp and Kemp, Vol 2. In having regard to any comparable cases, account should be taken of the impact of inflation and sums increased accordingly. An inflation table can be found in Kemp and Kemp, Vol 2.

Interest

33.33 Interest on awards of damages for pain, suffering and loss of amenity in personal injury cases heard in the county court are usually assessed at the rate of 2 per cent flat per annum from the date of presentation of the claim to the date of computation. ET claims are governed by a separate statutory scheme[46] regulating the interest applicable to compensation in discrimination cases including pain, suffering and loss of amenity – see para 33.40 below.

Tax

33.34 Income and Corporation Tax Act 1988 ss148 and 188 provide that no tax is payable on an award of damages for personal injury.

Aggravated damages

33.35 As a matter of principle an award of aggravated damages might be made in a case of race or sex discrimination: *Armitage, Marsden and HM Prison Service v Johnson*.[47] An award of compensation for aggravated damages might be made where 'the [complainant's] ... sense of injury resulting from the wrongful ... act is justifiably heightened by the manner in which or motive for which the Defendant did it'.[48] This

46 Employment Tribunals (Interest on Awards in Discrimination Cases) Regulations (ET (Interest) Regs) 1996 SI No 2803.

47 Note 31 above.

48 *Broome v Cassell* [1972] AC 1027 at 1124 *per* Lord Diplock.

may include conduct after the discrimination has occurred up until the hearing.[49]

33.36 Northern Ireland's Court of Appeal took the view in *McConnell v Police Authority for Northern Ireland*[50] that aggravated damages should not be an extra sum over and above compensation for injury to feelings. Instead, any element of aggravation ought to be taken into account in determining the extent of the injury to feelings. In practice, the element of aggravated damages is often separately determined.

33.37 Awards for aggravated damages have been made in the following cases by way of illustration:

- *Armitage v Johnson:*[51] an award of aggravated damages was upheld by the Employment Appeal Tribunal (EAT) in respect of the manner in which the complainant's complaints of race discrimination were investigated by the prison (£7,500).
- *Sharif v Yorkshire Envelope Company Ltd:*[52] an award of aggravated damages was made to take account of, among other things, the manner in which the case was conducted against the complainants, including branding one of the complainants 'a trouble-maker' and subjecting him to 'a character assassination' (£10,500 for four workers).
- *Poontah v Brittania & Project Design Limited and Lewis:*[53] an award of aggravated damages of £3,000 was made to an engineer subject to 'appalling' race discrimination whereby he was 'humiliated, intimidated and degraded'.

An apology may operate by way of mitigation to a claim for aggravated damages – see *Armitage v Johnson.*[54]

Exemplary damages

33.38 Exemplary damages are unlike compensatory damages because they do not operate to *compensate* a victim for loss or hurt but rather to

49 *Armitage v Johnson*, note 31 above; *Zaiwalla & Co and another v Walia* [2002] BLD 280823254, and see *Hussain v Resourcing Solution (Edinburgh) Ltd and Matsell* (2000) DCLD 44 for an example of where an award of aggravated damages was higher than the award for the act of discrimination itself.

50 [1997] IRLR 625.

51 [1997] IRLR 162.

52 (1998) DCLD 37.

53 (2001) DCLD 47.

54 For guidance in a comparable jurisdiction see *Thompson v Metropolitan Police Commissioner* [1998] QB 498.

punish the wrongdoer. Until recently such damages were not available in discrimination cases,[55] the law having developed in such a way as to permit them only in respect of a limited number of causes of action (or types of claims). The House of Lords has, however, now held that such damages are not restricted to certain causes of action and are available in any case in which the criteria for awarding exemplary damages are met.[56] The criteria for awarding exemplary damages are that:

- the conduct complained of constitutes oppressive, arbitrary or unconstitutional actions by servants of the government (this is obviously relevant in cases against the police and other public servants); or
- the defendant's conduct is calculated to make a profit for himself that may exceed the compensation payable to the complainant (this will be less common in discrimination cases but may arise in unusual circumstances, for example, refusing to dismiss an harasser who earns a company large sums because the cost of compensating his victims is less than the cost of dispensing with the services of the harasser); or
- the awarding of exemplary damages is expressly authorised by statute (the SDA 1975, RRA 1976 and DDA 1995 do not expressly authorise the awarding of exemplary damages so this is unlikely to be significant in discrimination cases).

33.39 In all cases exemplary damages may only be awarded if the compensation otherwise available is inadequate to punish the wrongdoer. Exemplary damages should be considered in all serious cases of discrimination, particularly where the actual loss is limited and so compensation is likely to be small. There is little guidance as to the appropriate level of any award of exemplary damages. In *Thompson and Hsu v Metropolitan Police Commissioner*[57] however the Court of Appeal indicated, in the context of civil claims against the police for false imprisonment, that exemplary damages are unlikely to be less than £5,000 (or the case is probably not one which justifies an award of exemplary damages at all) while the figure of £50,000 should be regarded as the absolute maximum. These figures should be adjusted to take account of inflation.

55 *Broome v Cassell* [1972] AC 1027; *Deane v Ealing LBC* [1993] IRLR 209.

56 *Kuddus (AP) v Chief Constable of Leicestershire Constabulary* [2001] UKHL 29.

57 [1998] QB 498.

Interest

33.40 In discrimination cases a court or tribunal has power to award interest on losses up until the hearing.[58] Interest compensates a complainant for loss of use of the money that he is eventually awarded in compensation. It therefore only attaches to compensation in respect of losses which accrue before the hearing. This is important to bear in mind when looking at aggravated damages awarded in respect of conduct at the hearing and compensation for future losses in particular.

33.41 The Employment Tribunals (Interest on Awards in Discrimination Cases) Regulations 1996 (ET (Interest) Regulations) provide that interest may be awarded by an ET in respect of compensation for injury to feelings for the period beginning when the act complained of was done and ending on 'the day of calculation' which, in practice, is the date of the remedies hearing in the ET.[59] Interest is to be awarded at the rate prescribed for the special investment account (prior to 1 August 1999 8 per cent, thereafter and until 1 February 2002 7 per cent and since then 6 per cent). In respect of compensation for other losses occurring before the date of calculation, interest is awarded for the period beginning on the mid-point date (the date half way between the date of the act complained of and the day of the calculation which, as stated above, is generally the date of the remedies hearing). This practice takes account of the fact that, where there is a continuing loss, not all of the loss arises on the date on which the act occurred. Again, interest is awarded at the special investment account rates.

33.42 The ET (Interest) Regulations 1996 provide in terms that interest must not be awarded 'for a loss or matter which ... occur[s] after the day of calculation'.[60] An ET may award interest in respect of a different period than that prescribed by the Regulations or for such different periods in respect of various sums where it considers that in the circumstances serious injustice would be otherwise caused (reg 6(3)). An ET must give reasons if it fails to give an award of interest as prescribed by the ET (Interest) Regulations 1996, or awards interest in respect of a period other than that prescribed.

58 ET (Interest) Regs 1999 and County Courts Act (CCA) 1984 s69. Interest will also accrue on an award of compensation made by a tribunal or court at 8% for as long as it remains unpaid: Employment Tribunals (Interest) Order 1990 SI No 479 and CCA 1984 s74.

59 The ET (Interest) Regs 1996 revoked the Sex Discrimination and Equal Pay (Remedies) Regulations 1993 SI No 2798 and the Race Relations (Interest on Awards) Regulations 1994 SI No 1748.

60 ET (Interest) Regs 1996 reg 5.

33.43 Interest in the county court is regulated by County Courts Act 1984 s69. In a discrimination case, interest on financial losses is likely to be calculated on the same basis as in the ETs. It is unclear what rate would be adopted in respect of an award for injury to feelings. Interest in respect of compensation for pain, suffering and loss of amenity in personal injury cases heard in the county courts is usually assessed at the rate of 2 per cent flat per annum from the date of issuing the claim to the date of computation. A similar rate might be adopted in respect of injury to feelings, but there is no authority on this point.

Mitigation

33.44 Complainants are under a duty to 'mitigate' their losses. This means that a complainant must take reasonable steps to keep his or her losses to a minimum (by, for example, finding alternative employment after a dismissal, or accommodation after a disputed eviction).[61] Whether a complainant has properly mitigated is a question of fact in each case. The burden of proving a failure to mitigate is on the defendant alleging it, who must provide evidence. A vague submission of failure to mitigate unsupported by any evidence is unlikely to succeed.

33.45 The extent of a complainant's duty to mitigate is to 'act reasonably in order to mitigate his loss', not to do everything *possible*.[62] Where a complainant has not acted reasonably a tribunal or court will deduct from any award of compensation a sum equivalent to that which would have been saved had he or she properly mitigated. Complications may sometimes arise where the court needs to assess the chance of a particular loss occurring, coupled with the effect of a failure to mitigate. Where a complainant has failed to mitigate, a court or tribunal should give the defendant credit for the sums the complainant would have saved had he or she acted reasonably. Where a reduction has to be made for the possibility of a chance *and* a deduction in respect of a failure to mitigate the proper approach is to deduct the figures discounted for a failure to mitigate from the total loss, and then to apply a percentage discount to reflect the chance that the loss might have occurred in any event: *Ministry of Defence v Wheeler*.[63]

61 *Fougére v Phoenix Motor Co Ltd* [1996] ICR 495.

62 *AG Bracey Ltd v Iles* [1973] IRLR 210.

63 [1998] IRLR 23, CA.

Tax

33.46 Some compensation is taxable. The rules relating to taxation are very complex and outside the scope of this book. As a very general guide, compensation in respect of lost money which would have been taxable in the hands of a complainant is taxable.[63a] If any sum in compensation will be taxable in the hands of the complainant, it should be 'grossed' up to take account of any tax that will need to be paid upon it.

Exemptions

Indirect discrimination

33.47 SDA 1975 ss65(1A), (1B) and 66(3) and RRA 1976 s57(3) limit the circumstances in which compensation might be ordered following a finding of indirect discrimination.

33.48 In non-employment sex discrimination cases, and in both employment and non-employment race discrimination cases, an award of compensation in respect of indirect discrimination will not be made where the discriminator proves that the requirement or condition in question was not applied with the intention of treating the claimant unfavourably on the ground of his sex or racial group as the case may be.

33.49 In cases of indirect sex discrimination in the employment field, no award of compensation will be made if the employer proves that the provision, criterion or practice in question was not applied with the intention of treating the complainant unfavourably on the ground of her sex or marital status as the case may be, unless (1) the ET makes a declaration as to the rights of the parties and any recommendation as if it had no power to make an award of compensation, and (2) at that point considers that it is just and equitable to make an order for compensation as well. The SDA 1975 originally contained the same limitation on compensation for indirect discrimination as the RRA 1976. But following a number of ET decisions holding that the SDA 1975 did not comply with the Equal Treatment Directive[64] and the EAT's decision in *McMillan v Edinburgh Voluntary Organisations Council*[65] that the SDA 1975's 'unambiguous' provisions could not be

63a Though the first £30,000 of any sum in compensation paid in connection with the termination of a person's employment is not subject to tax: Income and Corporation Taxes Act 1988 s148.

64 76/207/EC.

65 EAT/1995/536 (unreported).

interpreted so as to permit an award in respect of unintentional discrimination, the Sex Discrimination and Equal Pay (Miscellaneous Amendments) Regulations 1996 were passed.[66] It is generally believed that the amending regulations were motivated by the government's fear that it would otherwise be subject to legal action under the *Francovich* principle.[67]

33.50 It will be an unusual case in which a declaration and a recommendation will be sufficient to remedy a wrong done by way of indirect sex discrimination. It will only be in those cases where those remedies alone are sufficient that the ET will be entitled to decline to make an award of compensation.[68]

33.51 In determining 'intentionality' for the purposes of making an award of compensation in an indirect discrimination case, the EAT held in *London Underground v Edwards*[69] that an intention to apply the requirement or condition under challenge, together with knowledge of its impact on the complainant as a member of the particular group disadvantaged, is sufficient to establish intentionality. And in *Walker Ltd v Hussain*[70] the EAT rejected an appeal against an award of compensation made to a number of Muslims who were disciplined for taking time off during Eid. Mummery J ruled that:

> As a matter of ordinary English, 'intention' in this context signifies the state of mind of a person who, at the time when he does the relevant act (i.e. the application of the requirement or condition resulting in indirect discrimination),
> (a) Wants to bring about the state of affairs which constitutes the prohibited result of unfavourable treatment on racial grounds; and
> (b) Knows that that prohibited result will follow from his acts ...
> Depending on the circumstances, the Tribunal may infer that a person wants to produce certain consequences from the fact that he acted knowing what those consequences would be ...

Intention might, accordingly, be *inferred* from knowledge of the consequences which in most cases is not difficult to establish.

66 SI No 438.
67 *Francovich* is discussed in chapter 10.
68 It is difficult to see what SDA 1975 s65(1A) adds, given that the ET has a discretion based on what is 'just and equitable' to select the order it wishes to make in any case.
69 [1995] IRLR 355.
70 [1996] IRLR 1.

Prosecutions, etc

33.52 By RRA 1976 s57(4a):

> As respects an act which is done, or by virtue of section 32 or 33 is treated as done, by a person in carrying out public investigative functions or functions as a public prosecutor and which is unlawful by virtue of Section 19(B), no remedy other than –
> (a) damages, or
> (b) A declaration or, in Scotland, a declarator;
> shall be obtainable unless the court is satisfied that the remedy concerned would not prejudice a criminal investigation, a decision to institute criminal proceedings or any criminal proceedings.

'Criminal investigation' is defined by RRA 1976 s57(4B).[71] This means that, while generally speaking any remedy might be awarded in respect of a discrimination complaint in the county court as might be awarded in relation to any other tort, an injunction will not be ordered in respect of an act done by a person carrying out public investigator functions or functions as a public prosecutor unless the court is satisfied that the remedy concerned would not prejudice a criminal investigation, a decision to institute criminal proceedings or any criminal proceedings.

Declarations

33.53 ETs and county courts have power to make 'declarations'. A declaration is a statement declaring the rights of the complainant and respondent. This will simply reflect the findings in the decision of the ET or the judgment of the court.

71 '(a) Any investigation which a person in carrying out functions to which Section 19B applies has a duty to conduct with a view to it being ascertained whether a person should be charged with, or in Scotland prosecuted for, an offence, or whether a person charged with or prosecuted for an offence is guilty of it; (b) Any investigation which is concerned by a person in carrying out functions to which Section 19B applies and which in the circumstances may lead to a decision by that person to institute criminal proceedings which the person has power to conduct; or (c) Any investigation which is conducted by a person in carrying out functions to which Section 19B applies and which in the circumstances may lead to a decision by that person to make a report to the Procurator Fiscal for the purpose of enabling him to determine whether criminal proceedings should be instituted; and "public investigator functions" means functions of conducting criminal investigations or charging offenders; and in this sub-section "offence" includes any offence under the Army Act 1955, the Air Force Act 1955, or the Naval Discipline Act 1957 (and "offender") shall be construed accordingly).'

Recommendations

Introduction

33.54 As stated above, the SDA 1975, RRA 1976 and DDA 1995 all permit an ET (but not a county court) to make a recommendation upon a finding of unlawful discrimination. The recommendations they may make are limited by the terms of the provisions themselves.

33.55 SDA 1975 s65(1) and RRA 1976 s 56(1) permit an ET to make a recommendation 'that the respondent take within a specified period action appearing to the tribunal to be practicable for the purpose of obviating or reducing the adverse effect on the complainant of any act of discrimination to which the complaint relates'.

33.56 DDA 1995 s8(2)(c) contains a similar provision though the power appears slightly wider ('that the respondent take within a specified period action appearing to the tribunal to be reasonable, in all the circumstances of the case, for the purpose of obviating or reducing the adverse effect on the complainant of *any matter* [emphasis added] to which the complaint relates').

33.57 Where an ET makes a recommendation and 'without reasonable justification' the respondent fails to comply with it, then 'if they think it just and equitable to do so' the ET may increase the amount of any compensatory award or, if an order of compensation was not made, may make such an order.[72]

Limitations

33.58 The power to make recommendations in the SDA 1975 and RRA 1976 has three principal limitations:

- An ET may only make a recommendation for the purpose of obviating or reducing the adverse effect on the complainant of the discriminatory act. There is no power to make a recommendation generally to prevent further discriminatory acts. The ET's role is limited to mitigating the effect on the complainant of the particular discriminatory act.
- In *British Gas v Sharma*[73] the EAT held that an ET had erred in making a recommendation under the RRA 1976 that the employers promote the complainant to the next suitable vacancy. The EAT concluded that the ET did not have the power to make such a

72 SDA 1975 s65(3), RRA 1976 s56(4) and DDA 1995 s8(5).

73 [1991] IRLR 101.

recommendation because the RRA 1976 does not allow positive discrimination. According to the EAT, to promote the complainant without considering other applicants who might have superior qualifications for the vacancy could amount to direct discrimination against those other applicants on the grounds of race. In so holding the EAT relied on the decision of the Court of Appeal in *Noone v North West Regional Thames RHA (No 2)*.[74]

- The ET must in all cases fix the period within which the recommendation must be complied.[75]

33.59 As stated above, s8(2)(c) contains a similar, though apparently slightly wider, power to make recommendations to that contained in the SDA 1975 and RRA 1976. While a recommendation under the DDA 1995 must be directed at obviating or reducing adverse effects as against the complainant, the adverse effects need only be *related* to the complaint made, not necessarily consequent upon it. This might permit an ET to recommend a change to a policy or rule even if the policy or rule was not itself the subject of complaint. To take an example – if a disabled person complained of disciplinary action taken against him due to absence related to his disability and the employers unsuccessfully contended that he was treated equally under an absence policy,[76] an ET may recommend that the written warning be expunged (as it could do under the SDA 1975 and RRA 1976) and that the policy be varied (which it almost certainly could not unless the complaint was about the policy itself). Otherwise the power in the DDA 1995 suffers from the same deficiencies as those in the SDA 1975 and RRA 1976.

Injunctions

33.60 The county courts (but not the tribunals) have power to grant injunctions – binding and enforceable orders that a person refrain from doing a particular thing (for example, refrain from harassment), or that a person do a particular thing (provide a child with a place at a school).[77]

33.61 The rules that relate to injunctions are complex and outside the

74 [1988] IRLR 530.

75 The recommendation in *Sharma* was defective for this reason also. See also *Fasuyi v Greenwich LBC* (2001) DCLD 47.

76 As in *Clarke v Novacold* [1999] ICR 951.

77 See Civil Procedure Rules Pt 25.

scope of this book. They can however be a very useful remedy, particularly in cases of on going discrimination, and should always be borne in mind.

33.62 In the USA injunctions have been an important device in tackling structural discrimination and there is an argument, particularly where 'human rights' are engaged, that such orders may be required to effect a proper remedy in certain cases.[78]

Enforcement: statutory commissions

Introduction

33.63 SDA 1975 s53, RRA 1976 s43 and Disability Rights Commission Act (DRCA) 1999 s1 establish the EOC, the CRE and the DRC. These statutory commissions together have the express statutory functions of working towards the elimination of sex, race and disability discrimination; promoting equality of opportunity; and keeping under review the workings of the SDA 1975, EqPA 1970, RRA 1976 and DDA 1995. The DRC has the additional express statutory duty of taking such steps as it considers appropriate with a view to encouraging good practice in the treatment of disabled persons.[79] The commissions have a range of powers to assist them in carrying out those functions.[80] In addition they have power to issue codes of practice (and, in the case of the DRC, codes of guidance) in respect of certain matters.[81]

33.64 The commissions have specific powers to 'assist' individual complainants (by the provision of legal assistance)[82] but may also litigate in their own names.

78 Clayton and Tomlinson, *The Law of Human Rights,* (OUP, 2000), paras 21.152 onwards.

79 SDA 1975 s53(1), RRA 1976 s43(1) and DRCA 1999 s2.

80 SDA 1975 s54 (research and education), s55 (review of discriminatory provisions in health and safety legislation), ss54–61 (formal investigations), s67 (the issuing of non-discrimination notices) and Sch 3 (general powers to assist them in the conduct of their business); RRA 1976 s44 (assistance to organisations), s45 (research and education), ss48–52 (formal investigations), s58 (issuing of non-discrimination notices) and Sch 1 (general powers permitting them to carry on their business); DRCA 1999 s3 (formal investigations), s4 (non-discrimination notices), Schs 1 and 2 (general powers permitting them to carry on business) and Sch 3 (formal investigations).

81 SDA 1975 s56A, RRA 1976 ss47(1) and 71C; DDA 1995 ss3 and 53A; and see DRCA 1999 s9 for the effect of consultation on codes of practice undertaken by the National Disability Council.

82 SDA 1975 s75, RRA 1976 s66 and DRCA 1999 s7.

Proceedings brought by the commissions

33.65 The commissions may litigate in their own names as 'interveners' in proceedings already commenced between other parties, but rarely do so.[83] Furthermore, their general powers extend to permitting them to bring proceedings in their own right (see, for example, *R v Employment Secretary ex p EOC*[84]). The EOC and CRE also have express and exclusive power to bring proceedings in certain circumstances, namely, in respect of:

- discriminatory practices;[85]
- discriminatory advertisements;[86]
- instructions to discriminate;[87] and
- 'pressure' or inducements or attempted inducements to discriminate.[88]

Formal investigations

33.66 The commissions have important powers to conduct 'formal investigations' for any purpose connected with the carrying out of their duties.[89] They must carry out such investigations if required to do so by the Secretary of State.

33.67 The powers of formal investigation were hoped to provide the main thrust behind the new anti-discrimination legislation, but the impact of 'emasculating' judicial decision-making has limited the scope and effectiveness of these powers.[90] In summary, however, the commissions have power to carry out 'general' or 'named' investigations[91] and, if upon such an investigation they conclude that a person has committed or is committing a discriminatory act, they may serve a 'non-discrimination notice'. Such notices are

83 Though the court's permission would be required for the same – see, eg, *Anyanwu v South Bank Student's Union* [2001] IRLR 305.

84 [1994] IRLR 176.

85 SDA 1975 s37 and RRA 1976 s28.

86 SDA 1975 s38 and RRA 1976 s29.

87 SDA 1975 s39 and RRA 1976 s30.

88 SDA 1975 s40 and RRA 1976 s31.

89 SDA 1975 s57(1), RRA 1976 s48(1) and DRCA 1999 s3(1) and (2).

90 'Unnatural Justice for discriminators' (1984) 47 MLR 334 at 334–335. See A McColgan, *Discrimination Law, Text, Cases and Materials* (Hart, 2000), pp 293 onwards for a discussion of the same.

91 SDA 1975 ss57–60, RRA 1976 ss48–64 and DRCA 1999 ss3–6 and Sch 3. Note that the powers of the DRCA 1999 are somewhat different.

enforceable by injunction in the county court. Details of formal investigations conducted by the commissions may be found on their websites.[92]

New enforceable duties: the Race Relations (Amendment) Act 2000

33.68 The RRAA 2000 has introduced into the RRA 1976 new general and specific statutory duties enforceable by the CRE. The general statutory duty imposed upon all bodies specified in RRA 1976 Sch 1A requires that those bodies 'have due regard to the need (a) to eliminate unlawful racial discrimination and (b) to promote equality of opportunity and good relations between persons of different racial groups'.[93] Further, the Secretary of State has power to impose specific statutory duties upon certain specified bodies (and he has done so by the Race Relations Act 1976 (Statutory Duties) Order 2001[94]) for the purposes 'of ensuring the better performance' of the general statutory duties.[95]

33.69 Where the CRE is satisfied that a body has failed to comply with any specific statutory duty it may serve a 'compliance notice' which is itself enforceable through the county court.[96]

92 www.eoc.org.uk; www.cre.gov.uk and www.drc-gb.org.

93 RRA 1976 s71(1). Note that Sch 1A has been amended to include additional bodies by the Race Relations Act 1976 (General Statutory Duty) Order 2001 SI No 3457. See also the code of practice, and the Race Relations Act 1976 (General Statutory Duty: Code of Practice) Order 2002, which appointed 31 May 2002 as the day on which the code of practice containing the CRE's guidance in relation to the performance of the duties under RRA 1976 s71(1) and (2) came into effect.

94 Imposing an obligation on specified bodies to publish race equality schemes by 31 May 2002.

95 RRA 1976 s71(2).

96 RRA 1976 ss71D and 71E.

CHAPTER 34

Financial help and legal advice

Key points

34.1
- Public funding is available in the county court, High Court, Court of Appeal and House of Lords.
- Public funding is not available for representation in tribunals.
- Limited public funding is available on a means-tested basis for advice and assistance in relation to bringing an ET claim.
- Public funding is available for hearings in the Employment Appeal Tribunal (EAT), the Court of Appeal, the House of Lords and the European Court of Justice (ECJ) if financial and merits tests are satisfied. The ECJ can itself award limited legal aid if no other form of legal aid is available.
- Unions often provide legal help for their members.
- Law centres, citizens advice bureaux and other advice agencies may provide legal help and/or representation.
- The Equal Opportunities Commission (EOC), Commission for Racial Equality (CRE) and Disability Rights Commission (DRC) give help and assistance with sex and race discrimination cases and may provide representation in cases that fall within their current priorities.
- Legal costs insurance can provide cover for the legal costs of taking a discrimination case.
- Contingency fees arrangements (agreement that a fee is paid only if the case is won) may also be available.

Introduction

34.2 This chapter looks briefly at ways of paying for the costs of bringing a claim for discrimination.

Public funding

34.3 Public funding by the Legal Services Commission (LSC) – previously legal aid – is available for claims in the county court and High Court but is subject to a means and merits test, the details of which are outside the scope of this book. Rarely, it is available even where the means and merits test is not met where there is sufficient public interest. Public funding does not cover representation at the employment tribunal (ET).[1] The Lord Chancellor has made specific discretionary provisions for public funding in employment discrimination cases where this is necessary for there to be a fair trial under ECHR article 6. However, legal advice and assistance with the preparation of employment cases may be available for those on a low income and with little capital. The equivalent of two hours' advice is available in the first instance but extensions may be obtained. There is no limit to the number of extensions, the only test being whether the grant of an extension is reasonable. The LSC has, however, stated that it considers that the average ET discrimination case should take no longer than four hours to prepare and that, where there are complex legal issues or substantial documentation, this could be extended by a further three to six hours. Only solicitors with a franchise can do publicly funded work, so complainants who may be eligible should check if the solicitors can do publicly funded work.[2]

34.4 Public funding is available (for those who come within the income and capital limits) for appeal to the EAT or to the higher courts, provided that the case has sufficient merit. It is also available for claims in the county court and higher courts. The details are outside the scope of this book.

34.5 Generally, any money recovered as a result of the case goes to repay the LSC up to the amount spent on legal costs. This is known as the statutory charge, and applies to most public funding. It does not, however, apply to ET or EAT awards.[3] The details are outside the scope of this book.

Unions

34.6 Unions sometimes provide legal help for complainants. Even if local branch officers or stewards are not familiar with discrimination law, national officers – particularly equalities officers – and legal departments should be able to help. If the local officer is unwilling to help, a full-time officer or national equalities officer may advise.

1 It is available in some cases in Scotland.

2 The position is different in Scotland where some public funding is available.

3 Previously a tribunal applicant would have had to repay the solicitor's fees out of compensation recovered. This statutory charge has now been abolished for employment-related claims under the Legal Help scheme.

Other agencies

34.7 A local law centre, citizens advice bureau or other advice agency in the area may offer legal advice and/or representation in relation to ET claims. In addition, the Free Representation Unit and the Bar Pro Bono Unit may be approached for assistance with representation. The Free Representation Unit is an organisation of trainee and junior barristers who represent claimants. It takes referrals from citizens advice bureaux, law centres and solicitor members. The Bar Pro Bono Unit is an organisation of practising barristers which will also take referrals from solicitors and law centres and occasionally individuals. Both organisations provide free representation in employment cases.

34.8 A number of additional organisations provide assistance in specific areas of discrimination law. For names and addresses of these see Appendix 1.

Equal Opportunities Commission, Commission for Racial Equality and Disability Rights Commission

34.9 The EOC can give advice or financial assistance in relation to claims brought under the Sex Discrimination Act (SDA) 1975 and the Equal Pay Act (EqPA) 1970; the CRE in relation to claims brought under the Race Relations Act (RRA) 1976; and the DRC in relation to claims brought under the Disability Discrimination Act 1995. Assistance may include:

- advice;
- the negotiation of a settlement;
- arrangements for assistance by a solicitor or barrister;
- arrangements for representation by any person (for example, a trade union officer);
- any other form of assistance the commissions consider appropriate.[4]

34.10 The CRE must consider and decide on any written application within two months of receiving it unless it gives notice that it intends to extend the period to three months.[5] This does not extend the three-month time limit within which a claim must be brought (see para 32.42), although it does extend the six-month time limit for

4 SDA 1975 s75(2), RRA 1976 s66(2) and Disability Rights Commission Act 1999 s7(3).

5 RRA 1976 s66(4).

non-employment cases. The EOC and DRC are under no equivalent obligation.

Criteria for awarding assistance

34.11 The SDA 1975, RRA 1976 and Disability Rights Commission Act 1999 enable the commissions to grant assistance if they think fit to do so:[6]

- on the ground that the case raises the question of principle; or
- on the ground that it is unreasonable, having regard to the complexity of the case, or to the applicant's position in relation to the respondent or another person involved, or to any other matter, to expect the applicant to deal with the case unaided; or
- by reason of any other special consideration.

The commissions will also consider whether the case falls within one of their current priorities. Only a small proportion of cases are supported by the commissions.

34.12 The EOC, CRE and DRC will usually advise about the drafting of questionnaires and IT1s until a decision is made by the relevant legal committee about whether or not the commission will give assistance. The commissions also advise on agencies and solicitors who handle discrimination cases. Any costs or expenses recovered by the applicant must be repaid to the commissions. Costs are not usually paid out of compensation, though the commissions do have power to recover costs.[7]

Legal costs insurance

34.13 Many people are not aware that they have legal costs insurance, which often covers the costs of proceedings (including lawyers' fees). All applicants should check whether they have such cover under their:

- mortgage;
- house insurance;
- contents insurance; or
- other policies.

6 SDA 1975 s75(1), RRA 1976 s66(1) and Disability Rights Commission Act 1999 s7(2).

7 SDA 1975 s75(3), RRA 1976 s66(5) and Disability Rights Commission Act 1999 s8.

Some policies include legal costs insurance free of charge. Others require a small additional premium of about £20 per year. Usually the insurance cover is limited to a maximum (for example, £25,000 or £50,000). There is also often a waiting period, which means that the insurance policy must have been taken out well before any claim occurs. Many policies cover employment matters, including discrimination. However, some exclude claims under the EqPA 1970.

34.14 It is also worth checking if a credit card gives any cover. Barclaycard, for example, provides unlimited free access to a legal helpline which is staffed by experienced employment lawyers.

34.15 It is important to note that applicants have a right to choose their solicitor, subject to a limit on their charges. Such a right should be expressly recognised in the policy.[8]

34.16 With discrimination as common as it is, a cynic might consider that any woman or black worker should take out such insurance! There are also some companies which provide legal insurance after a claim has arisen.

Contingency fees – no win, no fee

34.17 Contingency fees arrangements are agreements whereby an applicant who does not win his or her case will not have to pay the solicitor's legal fees. If the applicant does win, the solicitor's legal fees will come out of any compensation awarded. The downside, from the applicant's point of view, is that the solicitor is likely to charge a significant increase on normal fees in order to compensate for the risk that no fees will be recovered in unsuccessful cases. The solicitor may also take a percentage of the compensation.

34.18 There are different types of agreement for contingency fees and these are beyond the scope of this book. The Law Society may be able to give advice to solicitors prepared to do work on this basis. Generally, solicitors are likely to do a case on a contingency fee basis if it is a good case with a strong chance of recovering substantial compensation. However, applicants should make sure that they are not liable to

8 Insurance Companies (Legal Expenses Insurance) Regulations 1990 SI No 1159, reg 6 provides that 'where, under a legal expenses insurance contract, recourse is had to a lawyer ... to defend represent or serve the interests of the insured in any enquiry or proceedings, the insured shall be free to choose that lawyer'. Infringement of this regulation is an offence under the Insurance Companies Act 1982.

pay a substantial amount of compensation to a solicitor who has done very little work.

Instructing a solicitor

34.19 It is worth shopping around for a solicitor who is experienced in discrimination and whose hourly rate is reasonable, and it is worth travelling to find the right person. Local advice agencies may be able to help and the commissions should have a list of experienced solicitors.[9]

34.20 It is important to find out the hourly rate and there are often standard rates for all letters (for example, 12 minutes) and telephone calls (six minutes). Costs in a discrimination claim can be very high and applicants should ask for an estimate.[10] Solicitors should provide financial information as and when requested as most keep computerised time records, so that the number of hours spent on a case can be assessed easily. In order to save costs it is sensible to type a summary of the facts, in chronological order and to provide relevant documents (including the contract of employment and correspondence about the dispute in question).

9 Solicitors on the panels approved by the commissions are a good place to start. The Maternity Alliance also has a list of solicitors who specialise in discrimination.

10 A four to five-day discrimination claim can cost up to £20,000 including preparation, disbursements and counsel. Cases often settle and cost much less but this is unpredictable.

APPENDICES

APPENDIX A

Useful resources

Statutory Commissions

Voluntary organisations that provide advice, representation, or information about advice agencies

Organisations that provide representation only

Organisations that provide research

Tribunals

Other

STATUTORY COMMISSIONS

Commission for Racial Equality (CRE)
St Dunstan's House
201–211 Borough High Street
London SE1 1GZ

Tel: 020 7939 0000
Fax: 020 7939 0001
e-mail: info@cre.gov.uk
web: www.cre.gov.uk

Disability Rights Commission (DRC)
Freepost MID 02164
Stratford-upon-Avon CV37 9BR

Tel: 08457 622 633
Fax: 08457 778 878
Textphone: 08457 622 644
e-mail: enquiry@drc-gb.org
web: www.drc-gb.org

Equal Opportunities Commission (EOC)
Arndale House
Arndale Centre
Manchester M4 3EQ

Tel: 0845 601 5901
Fax: 0161 838 1733
e-mail: info@eoc.org.uk
web: www.eoc.org.uk

Equality Commission Northern Ireland
Equality House
7–9 Shaftesbury Avenue
Belfast BT2 7DP

Tel: 028 90 500600
Fax: 028 90 248687
Textphone: 028 90 500589
e-mail: information@equlityni.org
web: www.equalityni.org

VOLUNTARY ORGANISATIONS THAT PROVIDE ADVICE, REPRESENTATION, OR INFORMATION ABOUT ADVICE AGENCIES

National Association of Citizens Advice Bureaux (NACAB)
Myddleton House
115–123 Pentonville Road
London N1 9LZ

Tel:	020 7833 2181
Fax:	020 7833 4371
web:	www.nacab.org.uk

Disability Alliance
Universal House
88–94 Wentworth Street
London E1 7SA

Tel:	020 7247 8776 (voice and minicom)
Fax:	020 7247 8765
web:	www.disabilityalliance.org.uk

Disability Law Service Free Legal Advice
39–45 Cavell Street
London E1 2BP

Tel:	020 7791 9800
Fax:	020 7791 9802
Minicom:	020 7791 9801
e-mail:	advice@dls.org.uk

Discrimination Law Association (DLA)
PO Box 36054
London SW16 1WF

Tel:	020 8769 2020
Fax:	020 7769 3030
e-mail:	info@discrimination-law.org.uk

Federation of Information and Advice Centres (FIAC)
4 Deans Court
St Paul's Churchyard
London EC4V 5AA

Tel:	020 7489 1800 (national)
	020 7489 7920 (London)
Fax:	020 7489 1804 (national)
	020 7489 7924 (London)
e-mail:	national@fiac.org.uk
	london@fiac.org.uk
web:	www.fiac.org.uk

Law Centres Federation (LCF)
Duchess House
18–19 Warren Street
London W1T 5LR

Tel:	020 7387 8570
Fax:	020 7387 8368
e-mail:	info@lawcentres.org.uk
web:	www.lawcentres.org.uk

Lesbian and Gay Employment Rights (LAGER)
Unit 1G Leroy House
436 Essex Road
London N1 3QP

Tel:	020 7704 6066 (gay men's helpline)
	020 7704 8066 (lesbian helpline)
	020 7704 2205 (administration and general enquiries)
Fax:	020 7704 6067
e-mail:	lager@dircon.co.uk
web:	www.lager.dircon.co.uk

Liberty
21 Tabard Street
London SE1 4LA

Tel: 020 7403 3888
020 7378 8659 (advice to public)
0808 808 4546 (advice to lawyers and advisers)

Fax:	020 7407 5354
e-mail:	info@liberty-human-rights.org.uk
web:	www.liberty-human-rights.org.uk

Maternity Alliance
45 Beech Street
London EC2P 2LX

Tel:	020 7588 8583 (office)
	020 7588 8582 (information line)
Fax:	020 7588 8584
e-mail:	info@maternityalliance.org.uk
web:	www.maternityalliance.org.uk

Parents at Work
45 Beech Street
London EC2Y 8AD

Tel:	020 7628 3565
Fax:	020 7628 3591
e-mail:	info@parentsatwork.org.uk
web:	www.parentsatwork.org.uk

Rights of Women
52–54 Featherstone Street
London EC1Y 8RT

Tel:	020 7251 6575 (administration)
	020 7251 6577
	(advice line Tues–Thurs 2–4pm and 7–9pm, Fri 12–2pm)
Fax:	020 7490 5377
e-mail:	info@row.org.uk
web:	www.rightsofwomen.org.uk (forthcoming December 2002)

Stonewall
46–48 Grosvenor Gardens
London SW1W 0EB

Tel:	020 7881 9440
Fax:	020 7881 9444
e-mail:	info@stonewall.org.uk
web:	www.stonewall.org.uk

ORGANISATIONS THAT PROVIDE REPRESENTATION ONLY

Bar Pro Bono Unit
7 Gray's Inn Square
London WC1R 5AZ

Tel: 020 7831 9711
Fax: 020 7831 9733
e-mail: enquiries@barprobonounit.f9.co.uk
web: www.barprobonounit.org.uk

Free Representation Unit
Fourth Floor
Peer House
8–14 Verulam Street
London WC1X 8LZ

Tel: 020 7831 0692
Fax: 020 7831 2398
web: www.fru.org.uk

Referrals can only be made through law centres, Citizen's Advice Bureaux and other referral agencies.

ORGANISATIONS THAT PROVIDE RESEARCH

Central Office of Information
COI Communication
Hercules House
Hercules Road
London SE1 7DU

Tel: 020 7928 2345
Fax: 020 7928 5037
web: www.coi.gov.uk

Department of Trade and Industry (Employment Relations)
DTI Enquiry Unit
1 Victoria Street
LondonSW1H 0ET

Tel: 020 7215 5000
Minicom: 020 7215 6740
e-mail: enquiries@dti.gsi.gov.uk
web: www.dti.gov.uk (general)
www.dti.gov.uk/er (employment relations)

Labour Research Department
78 Blackfriars Road
London SE1 8HF

Tel:	020 7928 3469
Fax:	020 7928 0621
e-mail:	info@lrd.org.uk
web:	www.lrd.org.uk

New Ways to Work
26 Shacklewell Lane
London E8 2EZ

Tel:	020 7503 3283
	020 7503 3578 (helpline)
Fax:	020 7503 2386
e-mail:	information@new-ways.co.uk
web:	www.new-ways.co.uk

Office of National Statistics
The Library
Office of National Statistics
Cardiff Road
Newport NP10 8XG

Tel:	0845 601 3034
Minicom:	01633 812399
Fax:	01633 652747
e-mail:	info@statistics.gov.uk
web:	www. statistics.gov.uk

Runnymede Trust
Suite 106
The London Fruit and Wool Exchange
Brushfield Street
London E1 6EP

Tel:	020 7377 9222
Fax:	020 7377 6622
e-mail:	info@runnymedetrust.org
web:	www.runnymedetrust.org

TRIBUNALS

Employment Tribunal Service
Central Office
Central Office of the Employment Tribunal
19–29 Woburn Place
London WC1H OLU

Tel:	020 7273 8575
Fax:	020 7273 8686
web:	www.employmenttribunals.gov.uk (for access to published information about how to apply to a tribunal, addresses of tribunals)

Employment Appeal Tribunal
Central Office
Audit House
58 Victoria Embankment
London EC4Y 0DS

Tel:	020 7273 1041
Fax:	020 7273 1045
web:	www.employmentappeals.gov.uk

Special Educational Needs and Disability Tribunal (SENDIST)
7th Floor Windsor House
50 Victoria Street
London SW1H 0NW

Tel:	01325 392555 (special educational needs helpline)
	020 7925 5750 (discrimination helpline)
Fax:	020 7925 6926 (general)
e-mail:	tribunalqueries@sendist.gsi.gov.uk
web:	www.sentribunal.gov.uk

OTHER

British and Irish Legal Information Institute
web: www.bailii.org

Disabled Person Transport Advisory Committee (DPTAC)
Zone 1/14
Great Minster House
76 Marsham Street
London SW1P 4DR

Tel: 020 7944 8011
Textphone: 020 7944 3277
Fax: 020 7944 6998
e-mail: dptac@dft.gsi.gov.uk
web: www.dptac.gov.uk

ENQUIRE (National Advice Service for Special Educational Needs in Scotland)
Children in Scotland
5 Shandwick Place
Edinburgh EH2 4RG

Tel: 0131 222 2400
Textphone: 0131 222 2439
Typetalk: 0800 959598
Fax: 0131 228 9852
e-mail: enquire.seninfo@childreninscotland.org.uk
web: www.childreninscotland.org.uk

1990 Trust
Suite 12 Winchester House
9 Cranmer Road
Kennington Park
London SW9 6EJ

Tel: 020 7582 1990
Fax: 0870 127 7657
e-mail: blink1990:blink.org.uk
web: www.blink.org.uk

APPENDIX B

Precedents – employment

IT1 – APPLICATION TO AN EMPLOYMENT TRIBUNAL

Application to an Employment Tribunal

- If you fax this form you do not need to send one in the post.
- This form has to be photocopied. Please use CAPITALS and black ink (if possible).
- Where there are tick boxes, please tick the one that applies.

For office use

Received at ET

Case number

Code

Initials

1 Please give the type of complaint you want the tribunal to decide (for example, unfair dismissal, equal pay). A full list is available from the tribunal office. If you have more than one complaint list them all.

2 Please give your details

Mr ☐ Mrs ☐ Miss ☐ Ms ☐ Other ______

First names

Surname

Date of birth

Address

Postcode

Phone number

Daytime phone number

Please give an address to which we should send documents if different from above

Postcode

3 If a representative is acting for you please give details
(all correspondence will be sent to your representative)

Name

Address

Postcode

Phone | Fax

Reference

4 Please give the dates of your employment

From ______ to ______

5 Please give the name and address of the employer, other organisation or person against whom this complaint is being brought

Name

Address

Postcode

Phone number

Please give the place where you worked or applied to work if different from above

Address

Postcode

6 Please say what job you did for the employer (or what job you applied for). If this does not apply, please say what your connection was with the employer

IT1(E/W)

7 Please give the number of normal basic hours worked each week

Hours per week

9 If your complaint is not about dismissal, please give the date when the matter you are complaining about took place

8 Please give your earning details

Basic wage or salary

£ : per

Average take home pay

£ : per

Other bonuses or benefits

£ : per

10 Unfair dismissal applicants only

Please indicate what you are seeking at this stage, if you win your case

☐ Reinstatement: to carry on working in your old job as before (an order for reinstatement normally includes an award of compensation for loss of earnings).

☐ Re-engagement: to start another job or new contract with your old employer (an order for re-engagement normally includes an award of compensation for loss of earnings).

☐ Compensation only: to get an award of money

11 Please give details of your complaint

If there is not enough space for your answer, please continue on a separate sheet and attach it to this form.

12 Please sign and date this form, then send it to the appropriate address on the back cover of this booklet, (see postcode list on pages 13-16).

Signed

Date

IT1(E/W)

MATERNITY RIGHTS DETAILS OF COMPLAINT – IT1 BOX 11

1. The respondent is a substantial company, with 50 stores in the UK, employing some 5,000 staff.
2. The applicant commenced working for the respondent on 20 March 1998 as Head of Personnel. She was promoted to Director of Human Resources in August 2000 and became a Board Member.
3. In February 2002 the applicant told the Chief Executive, Ms Smith, that she was pregnant. The applicant said her doctor had advised her to avoid working long hours and travelling for approximately two months. Despite this, the respondent took no steps to reduce the applicant's work and she continued working long hours.
4. At the applicant's appraisal, in April 2002, Ms Smith told the applicant that there were problems with the applicant's performance and she needed to improve her people management skills. This was the first time the applicant's performance had been criticised.
5. In May 2002 the applicant was told that, as a result of the company restructuring, she would no longer be on the Company Board, her title would be changed to Head of Human Resources and instead of reporting to the Chief Executive, she would report to Mr Walker, the Finance Director.
6. On 6 June 2002 the applicant was signed off sick by her doctor for two weeks and advised to avoid stress for the remainder of her pregnancy.
7. The applicant started her maternity leave on 8 July 2002. Her baby was born on 15 August 2002.
8. On 16 October 2002 the applicant met with Ms Smith to discuss her return to work. The applicant said that she would have to leave work at 5.30pm most days. She also asked Ms Smith if she could work four days a week or if full-time working at least one day from home every week. Ms Smith said she would consider it.
9. At the meeting on 16 October, Ms Smith told the applicant that the company had recently appointed a new Director, Mr Wright, who had taken over responsibility for Personnel to whom the applicant would be reporting on her return from leave. The applicant asked why she had not been considered for the position and was told that she did not have the relevant experience since, after the takeover, the company had grown substantially over the previous three months.
10. On 18 October 2002, Ms Smith wrote to the applicant confirming that Mr Wright would become Director of Personnel and would take over some of the applicant's responsibilities. Ms Smith also stated that the applicant could not work at home one day a week, nor work part-time as the company was not set up for this.
11. On 21 November 2002 Ms Smith wrote to the applicant stating that her position was redundant and the only position available was Personnel Officer, but her salary would remain the same.
12. On 28 November 2002, the applicant wrote to the respondent stating that the alternative position was not suitable as it did not have the same status.
13. The discrimination suffered by the applicant as a result of the applicant's

pregnancy and absence on maternity leave extended over a period for the purposes of Sex Discrimination Act 1975 s76(6); the respondent:

a. failed to carry out a health and safety assessment or take steps to safeguard the health and safety of the applicant and her baby;
b. placed unreasonable work demands on the applicant when she was pregnant;
c. unjustifiably criticised the applicant's work;
d. removed the applicant from the Board of Directors which was effectively a demotion;
e. failed to consult with the applicant about the re-organisation when she was on maternity leave;
f. failed to consider the applicant for promotion to Director of Personnel, when she was on maternity leave;
g. failed to consult the applicant about her redundancy;
h. selected the applicant for redundancy because of her absence on maternity leave and/or because she requested part-time work or partial working from home.

14. Further, the applicant was dismissed by reason of redundancy and the reason or principal reason for the dismissal was the applicant's pregnancy and/or impending maternity leave. Further, the respondent failed to offer the applicant suitable alternative work. The dismissal was therefore unfair (under Employment Rights Act 1996 s99).
15. Further, the dismissal was an unfair under Employment Rights Act 1996 s98 in that:
    a. the respondent made the applicant redundant because she was on maternity leave;
    b. the respondent did not properly consult the applicant because of her absence on maternity leave;
    c. the respondent did not consider or offer the applicant suitable alternative employment.
16. Further, the refusal to allow the applicant to leave work at 5.30pm and to work at home one day a week is indirect sex/marital discrimination.
17. The applicant claims:
    a. a declaration that she has suffered sex discrimination;
    b. compensation for sex discrimination, including injury to feelings, aggravated and exemplary damages and interest;
    c. a recommendation;
    d. a declaration that she has been unfairly dismissed and reinstatement/re-engagement/compensation.

SAMPLE SDA 1975 QUESTIONNAIRE

Please note that these are sample questions and each questionnaire must be adapted to the circumstances of each case. Copies of relevant documents should also be requested.

1. Is it accepted that in March 2002 the applicant told the Chief Executive that she was pregnant and she has been advised by her doctor to avoid working long hours?
2. If not, what communication do you say took place between the applicant and the Chief Executive?
3. Please state:
   a. what action the respondent took to protect the health of the applicant and her baby and, in particular, to ensure that she did not continue to work long hours;
   b. whether a health and safety assessment was carried out on the work of the applicant and, if so, when, by whom and what steps were recommended to be taken. If no assessment was carried out, why not.
4. Please provide details of the alleged problems with the applicant's performance, stating:
   a. when the problems first arose;
   b. each allegation of poor performance, including dates;
   c. whether the alleged poor performance was raised with the applicant and, if so, when and by whom; if not, why not.
5. Please provide details of the restructuring which led to the appointment of the new Director stating:
   a. when the first discussion about restructuring took place and between whom;
   b. when the decision was taken, by whom and who was consulted;
   c. all reasons for the restructuring;
   d. whether any changes were made to the status or job title of any other employees and, if so, please provide details of the employees and the changes made.
6. When was the new Director appointed? Please state:
   a. date of appointment;
   b. whether the position was advertised and, if so, where and when;
   c. why it was decided to appoint a Director;
   d. qualifications and experience of the new Director;
   e. why the applicant was not consulted about the position or if you say she was consulted give full details;
   f. whether the applicant was considered for the position and, if not, why not. If so, please state why she was considered unsuitable.
7. Why was the applicant removed from the Company Board? Please state:
   a. when the decision was made and by whom;
   b. who was consulted and when;
   c. all reasons why the applicant was removed from the Board.

8. Please state why some of the applicant's responsibilities were to be removed from her when she returned from maternity leave.
9. Please state:
   a. what consideration was given if any, and by whom, to the applicant's request to work from home one day a week;
   b. all reasons why the respondent formed the view that the applicant could not work from home one day a week;
   c. whether any other employee works at home and, if so, state the number, gender, grade, department ,job title, period of time this arrangement existed or commenced and reason for it.
10. Please state:
    a. what consideration was given, and by whom, to the applicant's request to work part-time;
    b. all reasons why the applicant could not work part-time;
    c. the number of full-time and part-time workers employed by the respondents, stating:
       – whether male or female;
       – whether married;
       – grade, department and job title.
11. How many women have taken maternity leave over the previous five years? Please state:
    a. how many women did not return, grade and job title of the women and reasons for their not returning;
    b. whether any women returned to a different job or different responsibilities, if so the numbers and dates concerned and reasons for the change in job or responsibilities, identifying the changes concerned and giving the reasons.

EQUAL PAY ACT 1970 DETAILS OF COMPLAINT – IT1 BOX 11

1. I am a woman employed by the respondents at their establishment at [place] as a [job title].
2. I am employed on:
   [like work with AB[1] , a male [job title] in the same employment] or
   [work rated under a job evaluation study [specify[2]] as equivalent with that of AB, a male sales assistant in the same employment] or
   [work of equal value to that of AB, a male clerk in the same employment].[3]
3. The term of my contract relating to pay is [or has become] less favourable than that in AB's contract in that my hourly rate of pay is £10 whereas AB's hourly rate is £12. We are both entitled to an annual bonus but I understand that his bonus is more than mine. Further, my contract does not contain a term corresponding to a term in AB's contract whereby he is entitled to an additional weeks sick pay after 5 years service. (Add any other contractual terms which are claimed.)
4. (If it is claimed that the employer operates a discriminatory pay system that should be stated, for example that the bonus payments are made to the comparators jobs which are done by a predominantly male group while the applicant's job which is done by a predominantly female group does not receive bonus).
5. Accordingly, my claim is for:
   a. a declaration that the term of my contract relating to pay shall be treated as modified so as to be not less favourable than that contained in AB's contract;
   b. a declaration that my contract shall be treated as including the term in AB's contract relating to sick pay;
   c. arrears of remuneration for the period from [date[4]] to the date of the hearing at the rate of £30 per week.

1 More than one comparator may be named and in all but the most obvious claims it is better to name 2 or 3 as it increases the chances that the work will be found to be like work, equivalent or of equal value to one of them.

2 Include the name of the job evaluation study if known such as 'JES' or when it was carried out and by whom (eg, the name of the consultants).

3 It is possible to claim like work, work rated as equivalent or work of equal value in the alternative. If any or all may apply this is the best course of action.

4 The EqPA 1970 restricts the claim for arrears to a period of two years prior the date the claim was made. However, this has been found to be contrary to EC law and the maximum period is now six years prior to the date of claim.

SAMPLE EQUAL PAY ACT 1970 QUESTIONNAIRE

The nature of the claim may be set out in the claim to the tribunal but specific questions should then be added such as:

1. Do you agree that the applicant is employed on like work with AB?
2. If not please specify each difference you rely upon.
3. Do you agree that the applicant is employed on work rated as equivalent to AB?
4. If not, why not?
5. Do you agree that AB's job and the applicant's job were job evaluated (add any details such as name of job evaluation study and when the jobs were evaluated)?
6. Do you agree that the result of that study was that the applicant's job was ranked as equal or higher than AB's.
7. If not state the marks or ranking that you say the applicant's job and AB's job were awarded.
8. If you contest that the applicant's job is like work and/or work of equal value to that of AB do you agree that it is of equal value.
9. If not, specify in terms of the demands of the applicant's job why you say it is not of equal value to that of AB.
10. Do you agree that the applicant's pay is £10 per hour and AB's pay is £12 per hour?
11. If not, state the hourly rates for both the applicant and AB.
12. Please state what bonus AB has received over the last 6 years.
13. What reason do you give for the applicant's lower hourly rate?
14. If, as the applicant believe, the bonus received by AB has been higher than the applicant's bonus, what reason do you give for AB's higher bonus.
15. Do you say that the variations in hourly pay and bonus in the applicant's contract and AB's contract are due to material factors which are not related to the difference in sex?
16. If so, what do you say that material factor is?
17. In what way is it the cause of the difference in hourly pay and bonus?[1]

1 Depending on the circumstances it may be necessary to ask further questions either initially or when the answers have been received to show discrimination or clarify the employers defence , for example if it is a case where part-time workers are receiving lower pay of less favourable benefits, questions may be needed as to numbers and gender of part-time and full time workers .

DDA 1995 DETAILS OF COMPLAINT – IT1 BOX 11

1. I am disabled. I have a physical/mental impairment, [insert name of impairment and in the case of a mental impairment state how it is a clinically well-recognised illness [eg, by reference to WHO-ICD see para 2.56]. It has a substantial and long-term effect on my ability to carry out normal day-to-day activities. The effect of any impairment has lasted for at least 12 months/is likely to last for at least 12 months/is likely to last for the rest of my life. In particular [here list the capacities affected (see para 2.63) and give examples of what cannot be done or only done with difficulty] or would do if the effect of treatment was ignored [set out the medication or treatment, if applicable, that is to be disregarded in assessing disability (see para 2.83)]. [Deal also with any special features – eg, progressive conditions, past disability, severe disfigurements.]
2. I consider that I have been subjected to disability discrimination. For a reason which relates to my disability, I have been treated less favourably by the respondent than he treats or would treat others to whom that reason does not apply. The less favourable treatment included the following:
   a. [here set out each incident of less favourable treatment. For example, I was not appointed to the post of secretary/I was dismissed following my sickness absence]
3. The reason for my treatment related to my disability in that [set out the details, eg, I was successful at interview for the post of secretary but failed the medical examination/my sickness absence was related to my disability].
4. The respondent is under a duty of reasonable adjustment which they have failed to comply with in my case. The arrangements made by or on behalf of the respondent/physical features of premises occupied by them placed me at a substantial disadvantage in comparison with people who are not disabled. [Set out the details – eg, the medical examination and the requirements of the medical report as a precondition of an offer of employment/ the sickness absence policy/ lack of wheelchair access to the building where I worked].
5. The respondent knew or ought reasonably to have known of my disability and the disadvantage I faced because [set out details – eg, I informed them of my disability in the application form/it is self-evident from my wheelchair/I informed occupational health].
6. The respondent failed to take reasonable steps to prevent the arrangements/physical features having that effect. [You do not have to list what the employer could have done (they are for the employer to identify), but it helps if you can – it is best expressed as a non-exhaustive list or as examples and can be open and non-specific as well as providing concrete proposals. For example, the respondents could have made adjustments to their premises/allowed me to alter my working hours/workplace/transferred me to a light duties post or other vacancy/removed the heavy lifting part of my job/adapted my computer].
7. [In dismissal cases there may also be an unfair dismissal claim if the applicant qualifies for the right, see para 15.96 above.]
8. And I claim:
   (a) a declaration that I have suffered disability discrimination;

(b) compensation for disability discrimination, including injury to feelings, aggravated and exemplary damages and interest;
(c) a recommendation;
[(d) in unfair dismissal claims: reinstatement/re-engagement/compensation and a declaration that I have been unfairly dismissed.]

SPECIMEN LETTER OF INSTRUCTION TO DOCTOR IN A CASE UNDER DDA 1995

Dear [insert name of doctor]

Re [full name of patient, address and their date of birth]

I act for the above named in connection with proceedings for disability discrimination against her former employer/name of the respondent. Whether my client is disabled is in issue in the case and I would be grateful if you could prepare a medical report to address the following points:

1. Please identify my client's mental illness by reference to the WHO-ICD or other well recognised classification of diseases, or if the condition is not contained in a classification of diseases please explain in detail how the condition is recognised by a respected body of medical opinion.[1]
2. Please set out the diagnostic guidelines in the classification that contains my client's illness or enclose a copy of the relevant medical records.
3. Please explain the presence or absence of the symptoms in the diagnostic guidelines in my client's case that lead you to diagnose her/him as having that condition and set out why you consider that the symptoms are attributable to that condition.

   [The following paragraphs may be needed in cases of physical as well as mental impairment.]

   a. If my client is being treated for her/his condition, please describe the treatment (eg, name and dosage of medication, counselling, psychotherapy, etc) and describe the effect of the treatment. If the effect of treatment were to be disregarded how much would my client's ability to carry out normal day to day activities be affected? Please describe the effect of the condition, if it were untreated, on any of the following capacities – mobility; manual dexterity; physical co-ordination; continence; ability to lift, carry or otherwise move everyday objects; speech hearing or eyesight; memory or ability to concentrate learn or understand; perception of the risk of physical danger.
   b. If my client's condition is progressive, please outline the likely progression in his/her case and whether, and if so to what extent, my client's ability to carry out normal day to day activities is likely to be affected in the future. Please describe the likely future effect of the condition on any of the following capacities – mobility; manual dexterity; physical co-ordination; continence; ability to lift, carry or otherwise move everyday objects; speech hearing or eyesight; memory or ability to concentrate learn or understand; perception of the risk of physical danger.
4. How long is my client's condition likely to last?
5. Is my client's condition likely to recur?

1 There is, technically, a fourth possible route to establishing a mental impairment within the DDA 1995 with proof by substantial and specific medical evidence of a mental impairment which neither results from, nor consists of a mental illness. It is unlikely to arise in practice, but if it does, the doctor should be asked to address this.

I enclose my client's form of consent to a medical examination and for the preparation of your report.[2] I agree to be responsible for your reasonable fees/please let me know what your fees will be and agree these with me before your examination. Please send the appointment directly to my client and let me know when it will take place. I must have the report by ____________, please let me know if this is will not be possible.

[In County Court proceedings the report will need to contain the form of words specified in the CPR and you should remind the doctor of these].

Yours etc.

2 Ensure your client signs a form of consent enabling the doctor to examine her/him and have access to relevant medical records. If your client has been treated by several people – eg, GP, therapists, and one or more hospitals, you will need a form of consent for each doctor/institution to be provided to the doctor preparing the report.

APPENDIX C

Precedents – non-employment

PARTICULARS OF CLAIM – RACE RELATIONS ACT 1976 – SCHOOLS

IN THE   COUNTY COURT   Claim No.
BETWEEN:

AB
(BY HIS LITIGATION FRIEND AND MOTHER MRS B)
claimant

And

(1) THE GOVERNORS OF THE ANY TOWN MIDDLE SCHOOL
(2) A TEACHER
defendants

PARTICULARS OF CLAIM

1. The claimant is Black and is of mixed racial origins (African-Caribbean/White).
2. The claimant's date of birth is ....
3. At all material times the claimant was a pupil at the Any Town Middle School ('the school').
4. For the purposes of the matters set out below, the first defendant is the responsible body, within the meaning of section 17 of the Race Relations Act 1976, for the school. The first defendant was at material times the claimant's form teacher and was at all material times employed by the school.
5. On ________ at or about ______ the claimant was playing in the playground in the school when he was physically attacked by a child called X ('the incident'). The second defendant witnessed the incident and admonished the claimant. On the same day the second defendant prepared a written report stating that the claimant had been responsible for an incident of violent behaviour and submitted the report to the head teacher. The second defendant made no such report about the conduct of X.
6. On __________ the head teacher excluded the claimant from the school for a period of three days in consequence of the report made by the second defendant and referred to above. X was not so excluded and no action was taken against him in respect of the incident.
7. By reason of the facts and matters aforesaid the first and second defendants have discriminated against the claimant on racial grounds contrary to section 1(1)(a) read with section 17 and sections 32 and 33 of the Race Relations Act 1976.

Particulars of Race Discrimination

The claimant repeats the matters set out under paragraphs 5 and 6 above. The first, and second defendants have failed to provide any adequate explanation for the aforesaid difference in treatment and the claimant avers that the reason for the treatment was his racial origin.

[any other particulars]

8. By reason of the facts and matters aforesaid the claimant has suffered injury to his feelings, distress, anxiety and educational disadvantage.

Particulars

[set out particulars of injury, distress etc]

9. Further the aforesaid treatment of the claimant was a gross affront to his personal dignity and integrity for which aggravated damages should be awarded. In addition to the facts and matters set out above the claimant will rely on the fact that the defendants have failed to apologise for the treatment afforded him.
10. Further the aforesaid actions of the first defendant were arbitrary, oppressive and unconstitutional and the claimant claims exemplary damages.
11. The claimant has applied to the Commission for Racial Equality for assistance pursuant to section 66 of the Race Relations Act 1976. By a letter dated __________the Commission for Racial Equality have extended the time for institution of proceedings by reason of section 66(4) of the Race Relations Act 1976.
12. Further the claimant claims interest pursuant to section 69 of the County Courts Act 1984 on such sums as are found to be due to the claimant at such rate and for such period as the Court thinks fit.

AND THE CLAIMANT CLAIMS:

1. A declaration that the defendants have discriminated against him contrary to section 17 of the Race Relations Act 1976;
2. Damages, including aggravated and exemplary damages; and
3. Interest as aforesaid pursuant to section 69 of the County Courts Act 1984.

STATEMENT OF TRUTH, etc.

PARTICULARS OF CLAIM – RACE RELATIONS ACT 1976 – PRISONS

IN THE COUNTY COURT   Claim No.

BETWEEN:

YZ

claimant

and

THE HOME OFFICE

defendants

PARTICULARS OF CLAIM

1. The claimant was at all material times and from ________ until ________ a prisoner: From ________ until ________ at HM Prison Softime and from ______ to ______ at HMP Hardtime.
2. The defendant is and was at all material times responsible for prisons and the aforesaid prisons in particular. The defendant provides facilities and services to a section of the public, namely prisoners, within the meaning of section 20 of the Race Relations Act 1976.
3. Further and/or alternatively the defendant manages premises for the purposes of section 21 of the Race Relations Act 1976, namely the aforesaid prisons.
4. HM Prison Softime is an open prison and the regime involves less incarceration than at a closed prison.
5. The claimant was categorised a Category D prisoner prior to his transfer to HMP Softime and enjoyed a number of privileges including [......state privileges.........].
6. On ________ the claimant overheard [two prison officers, state names] make racially abusive remarks [describe] to a prisoner called Y whose racial origins are [state]. The claimant was shocked and distressed by the incident.
7. The aforesaid racial abuse constituted less favourable treatment of the claimant and/or the said Y and was unlawful by reason of section 20(1)(b) and/or section 21(2)(c) read with sections 32 and 33 of the Race Relations Act 1976.
8. The claimant complained about the racially abusive remarks in a letter dated ____ to [name], the Governor of HMP Softime.
9. On ________ the claimant was transferred to HM Prison Hardtime.
10. The claimant did not enjoy the same privileges at HM Prison Hardtime as he had enjoyed at HMP Softime [particularise].
11. The claimant was moved because he had made the complaint described at paragraph 8 above.
12. By reason of the facts and matters aforesaid the claimant has been unlawfully victimised within the meaning of section 20(1)(b) and/or section 21(2)(c) read with section 2(1)(c) and/or (d) and section 32 of the Race Relations Act 1976.

Particulars of Victimisation under sections 20 and 21 of the Race Relations Act 1976

The claimant will rely upon the fact that the defendant treated him less favourably when it,

a. transferred the claimant from HMP Softime to HMP Hardtime;

b. removed or caused to be removed the privileges described in paragraph 10 above;

c. subjected him otherwise to the treatment described at paragraphs 9 and 10 above;

by reason that he had done something by reference to the Race Relations Act 1976 in relation to the defendant or any other person and/or alleged that the defendant or another person had committed an act which would amount to a contravention of the Race Relations Act 1976, by reporting the incident of racial abuse as set out at paragraph 8 above.

The aforesaid treatment amounted to a refusal or deliberate omission to provide the claimant with facilities or services or a refusal or deliberate omission to provide the claimant with facilities or services in the like manner as are normal in relation to other prisoners.

Further the aforesaid treatment amounted to a detriment.

13. Further and/or alternatively by reason of the facts and matters set out above the defendant victimised the claimant contrary to section 2 of the Race Relations Act 1976 read together with section 19B of the Race Relations Act 1976.

Particulars of Victimisation under section 19b of the Race Relations Act 1976

The claimant repeats the matters set out under paragraph 12 above.

14. By reason of the matters aforesaid the claimant suffered loss of privileges, inconvenience, distress, anxiety, embarrassment, injury to his feelings and humiliation.

Particulars

[include particulars]

15. Further the aforesaid treatment of the claimant was a gross affront to his personal dignity and integrity for which aggravated damages should be awarded. In addition the claimant will rely in support of his claim for aggravated damages upon:

a. the failure of the defendant to apologise to him for the aforesaid treatment;

b. the failure by the defendant to respond to the Questionnaire served pursuant to section 65 of the Race Relations Act 1976;

c. the persistence of the treatment notwithstanding the claimant's complaints made on............

16. Further the aforesaid treatment was arbitrary, oppressive and unconstitutional and the claimant claims exemplary damages.

17. Further the claimant claims interest pursuant to section 69 of the County Courts Act 1984 on the amount found to be due at such rate and for such periods as the Court may think fit.

AND the claimant claims:

(1) A Declaration that the claimant has been discriminated against contrary to sections 2, 19B, 20 and 21 of the Race Relations Act 1976.

(2) Damages including aggravated and exemplary damages.

(3) Interest pursuant to section 69 of the County Courts Act 1984 as aforesaid.

STATEMENT OF TRUTH, etc

SDA 1975 s74(1)(A) QUESTIONNAIRE OF PERSON AGGRIEVED

1. To .... [name of person to be questioned]
   of .... [address]

(i) We .... and .... of .... consider that you may have discriminated against us contrary to the Sex Discrimination Act 1975.

(ii) We are homosexual and we lived together as a couple and as joint tenants of .... between ....and........... These premises were let to us by .... City Council ('the Council') pursuant to a tenancy agreement under which the Council covenanted to provide us with quiet enjoyment of the premises. Further, they covenanted to,
[add material terms]

(iii) We believe that all other tenants of the Council and in particular those who occupied residences neighbouring ours had tenancy agreements in the same terms.

(iv) From .... we suffered harassment from our neighbours who were also tenants of the Council. This harassment only ended when we moved home in .... The harassment was persistent, very distressing and homophobic in character. We suffered from abuse, noise nuisance and physical intimidation [particularise harassment]

(v) We reported the harassment to the Council on numerous occasions
[particularise complaints]

(vi) We believe that the Council failed to take adequate action to support and protect us and failed to take prompt action against the perpetrators of the harassment. We believe that there is no explanation for this apart from the fact of our sexuality and the fact that we have made repeated complaints of sexuality based harassment to the Council. Further, we believe that the incidents of harassment were sufficiently under the control of the Council that they could by the application of good practice have prevented the harassment or reduced the extent of it and accordingly the Council is liable for those events.

(vii) We believe that the Council has discriminated against us on the ground of our sexuality and that treatment amounts to discrimination on the ground of our sex within the meaning of section 1 of the Sex Discrimination Act 1975 and is unlawful under section 30 of the Sex Discrimination Act 1975.

2. Do you agree that the statement in paragraph 1 above is an accurate description of what happened? If not, in what respect do you disagree or what is your version of what happened?
3. Do you accept that your treatment of us was unlawful discrimination by you against us? If not:
   a. why not,
   b. for what reason did we receive the treatment accorded to us, and
   c. how far did considerations of sexual orientation and sex affect your treatment of us?

4. Please answer the following further questions:
   a. Please:
      – provide a copy of our tenancy agreement with you (and any variations notified to us) in respect of our tenancy at ....; and
      – state whether all tenants of yours were subject to the same terms.
   b. Please state in respect of every incident of harassment identified above whether you accept that you were made aware of the said incident and, if so:
      – when you say you became aware of the said incident; and
      – when you say you became aware of the identity of the perpetrators of the said incident; and
      – what, if any, action you took in respect of the said incident; and
      – if no action was taken by you, please state why, providing full particulars of the explanation in each case.
   c. Please state in respect of each complaint referred to above;
      – whether you accept that the complaint was made;
      – the identity of the person to whom the complaint was made;
      – the sexual orientation (if known) and sex of the person to whom complaint was made;
      – whether the person to whom complaint was made had received training in the investigation of complaints of homophobic and/or sexual harassment and, if so, please provide full particulars of the same;
      – what action was taken in respect of each of the said complaints including but not limited to:
        • whether action was taken under section 130 of the Highways Act 1980;
        • whether action was taken pursuant to your powers under section 222 of the Local Government Act 1972;
        • whether any action was taken against the tenants of yours identified as responsible for the harassment by you as landlord pursuant to the terms of the tenancy agreements between you and the said tenants and your statutory powers;
        • whether action was taken under the Crime and Disorder Act 1998 in relation to anti-social behaviour orders, and
      – in each case where such action was not taken, please state why, providing full particulars of the explanation in each case.
5. Please state whether you have in place a policy on homophobic harassment and/or sexual harassment and if so:
   a. please state the date upon which the policy first came into force and provide copies of each policy in place since ....;
   b. please state, in respect of each incident and complaint referred to above, how the policy was applied in our case;
   c. in respect of each occasion on which you have had cause to take action under any or each of your said policies in the 5 year period preceding ....; please:
      – identify the occasion;
      – state the nature of the harassment;

- state the nature of the action taken under the policy; and
- identify the sexual orientation (if known) and sex of the victim of the harassment concerned and, where known, the sexual orientation and sex of any perpetrators.

6. Please state whether you have in place a policy for the exercising of your powers under section 222 of the Local Government Act 1972 and, if so:
   a. please state the date upon which the policy came into force and provide copies of each policy in place since ......;
   b. please state in respect of each incident and complaint referred to above how that policy was applied in our case;
   c. in respect of each occasion on which you have had cause to take action under section 222 of the Local Government Act 1972 in the 5 year period preceding ......; please:
      - identify each such occasion;
      - state the nature of the incident in respect of which action was taken;
      - state the nature of the action taken;
      - identify the sexual orientation (if known) and sex of the person against whom any such action was taken and, where relevant, the sexual orientation and sex of any victim whose interests were being promoted or protected by such action.
7. Please state whether you have a policy in respect of the taking of possession proceedings against those of your tenants responsible for the harassment of others (whether those others are your tenants or not) and as against tenants with whom such harassers reside or visit and if so; please:
   a. state the date upon which such policy came into force and provide copies of each such policy in place since ....;
   b. state in respect of each incident and complaint referred to above how that policy was applied in our case;
   c. in respect of each occasion in which you have had cause to take action under each such policy in the 5 year period preceding ......; please:
      - identify each said occasion;
      - state the nature of the harassment;
      - state the nature of the action taken;
      - identify the sexual orientation (if known) and sex of the tenant and/or other harasser and of the victim.

   Please state in each case whether possession proceedings were instigated and in each case whether possession was obtained.
8. Please state whether you have any conditions or terms in the tenancy agreements between you and tenants of yours identified as responsible for the harassment described above relating to harassment and, if so, please state:
   a. when such conditions were first put in place;
   b. whether action has been taken against any tenants under such conditions in respect of any of the incidents or complaints set out above and if so; in respect of each occasion:
      - identify the occasion;

- state the nature of the action taken;
- identify the sexual orientation (if known) and sex of the tenant and/or other harasser;
- state in each case whether possession proceedings were instigated and in each case whether possession was obtained.

c. in respect of each occasion upon which possession proceedings have been instigated relying on such conditions in the 5 year period preceding .... as against any tenants; identify in respect of each case:
- the sexual orientation (if known) and sex of the tenant concerned;
- the sexual orientation (if known) and sex of the victim;
- the nature of the harassment;
- whether the proceedings resulted in a possession order.

9. Please state whether you have in place a policy for supporting victims of homophobic and sexual harassment. If so, please:
   a. identify the date upon which the policy first came into force;
   b. provide copies of each of the policies in place since ....;
   c. in respect of each incident and complaint identified above, please state how the policy was applied in our case.
10. In respect of each incident and complaint set out above, please state what steps were taken by you to identify the perpetrators of the harassment.
11. Please state whether you monitor incidents of homophobic and sexual harassment and, if so, please provide details of each incident, by reference to the sexual orientation and sex of the perpetrator, where known, and the victim, in the 5 year period preceding ....
12. Please state whether you have in place a strategy for exercising your powers under section 222 of the Local Government Act 1972 and, if so, please state:
   a. on what date the strategy first was formulated and, in respect of each strategy developed since .... please provide a copy of the same;
   b. please state how such strategy was applied in respect of each of the incidents and complaints set out above.
13. Please state whether you have in place any regular system of liaison with other agencies regarding homophobic and sexual harassment and if so please describe the same during the period .... to date.
14. Please state whether you monitor the effectiveness of your policies and procedures in relation to homophobic and sexual harassment and, if so, please provide details of those monitoring systems and any reports produced in consequence during the period .... to date.
15. Please state whether you have in place an equal opportunities policy and/or an anti-discrimination policy in relation to service delivery and housing management. If so:
   a. please state the first date upon which such policy/policies came into force and provide copies of each such policy since ......;
   b. please state in respect of each incident and complaint set out above, how the policy/policies was/were applied in our case.
16. Please state whether you have in place a procedure for investigating complaints of discrimination. If so:

a. please state the first date upon which such policy came into force and provide copies of each such policy since ....;
b. please state in respect of each incident and complaint set out above, how the policy was applied in our case.

Our address for any reply you may wish to give to the questions raised above is ...

(Signatures of. ....)
(Date)

NB – By virtue of section 74 of the Sex Discrimination Act 1975 this questionnaire and any reply are (subject to the provisions of the section) admissible in proceedings under the Act and a court or tribunal may draw and such inference as is just and equitable from a failure without reasonable excuse to reply within a reasonable period, or from an evasive or equivocal reply, including an inference that the person questioned has discriminated unlawfully.

APPENDIX D

Northern Ireland – comparison of legislation

Sex Discrimination Act 1975 – Sex Discrimination (Northern Ireland) Order 1976

Race Relations Act 1976 – Race Relations (Northern Ireland) Order 1997

SEX DISCRIMINATION ACT 1975: SEX DISCRIMINATION (NORTHERN IRELAND) ORDER 1976

This table shows which section of the SDA 1975 corresponds with which rule of the SDO 1976

Section/rule title	SDA 1975	SDO 1976
Sex discrimination against women	1	3
Sex discrimination against men	2	4
Sex discrimination against married people	3	5
Gender reassignment discrimination	2A	4A
Victimisation	4	6
Discrimination against applicants and employees	6	8
Discrimination by employers	6–10	8–13
Genuine occupational qualifications	7	10
Discrimination against contract workers	9	12
Partnerships	11	14
Trade Unions, etc	12	15
Qualifying bodies	13	16
Provision of vocational training	14	17
Employment Agencies	15	18
Police	17	19
Prison Officers	18	20
Ministers of Religion etc	19	21
Midwives	20	22
Discriminatory practices	37	38
Discriminatory advertisements	38	39
Instructions to discriminate	39	40
Pressure to discriminate	40	41
Liability of employers and principals	41	42
Aiding unlawful acts	42	43
General exceptions	43–52A	44–53
EOC/Equality Commission	53–61	54–61
Enforcement	62–76	62–76
Jurisdiction of Employment Tribunals	63	63
Remedies	65	65
Assistance from Commission	75	75
Limitation period	76	76

RACE RELATIONS ACT 1976 – RACE RELATIONS (NORTHERN IRELAND) ORDER 1997

This table shows which section of the RRA 1976 corresponds with which rule of RRO 1997

Section/rule title	RRA 1997	RRO 1997
Racial discrimination	1	3
Victimisation	2	4
Meaning of 'racial grounds', etc	3	5
Discrimination against applicants and employees	4	6
Discrimination in employment field	4–16	6–17
Genuine occupational qualifications	5	8
Discrimination against contract workers	7	9
Partnerships	10	12
Trade Unions etc	11	13
Qualifying bodies	12	14
Provision of vocational training	13	15
Employment Agencies	14	16
Police	16	17
Charities	34	34
Discriminatory practices	28	28
Discriminatory advertisements	29	29
Instructions to discriminate	30	30
Pressure to discriminate	31	31
Liability of employers and principals	32	32
Aiding unlawful acts	33	33
General exceptions	35–42	35–41
CRE/Equality Commission	43–52	42–50
Enforcement	53–69	51–66
Jurisdiction of Employment Tribunals	54	52
Remedies	56	53
Assistance from Commission	66	64
Limitation period	68	65

Index